PRINCIPLES OF

MARKETING

FOURTH CANADIAN EDITION

———

PHILIP KOTLER
NORTHWESTERN UNIVERSITY

GARY ARMSTRONG
UNIVERSITY OF NORTH CAROLINA

PEGGY H. CUNNINGHAM
QUEEN'S UNIVERSITY

PRENTICE HALL CANADA INC.
SCARBOROUGH, ONTARIO

Canadian Cataloguing in Publication Data

Kotler, Phillip
   Principles of marketing

4th Canadian ed.
Canadian 3rd edition by Philip Kotler, Gary Armstrong,
Peggy H. Cunningham and Robert Warren.
Includes index
ISBN 0-13-679267-7

1. Marketing. 2. Marketing – Management. I. Armstrong, Gary.
II. Cunningham, Margaret H. III. Title

HF5415.K636 1999   658.8   C98-930495-7

Prentice-Hall, Inc., Upper Saddle River, New Jersey
Prentice-Hall International (UK) Limited, London
Prentice-Hall of Australia, Pty. Limited, Sydney
Prentice-Hall Hispanoamericana, S.A., Mexico City
Prentice-Hall of India Private Limited, New Delhi
Prentice-Hall of Japan, Inc., Tokyo
Simon & Schuster Southeast Asia Private Limited, Singapore
Editora Prentice-Hall do Brasil, Ltda., Rio de Janeiro

ISBN 0-13-679267-7

Publisher: Patrick Ferrier
Acquisitions Editor: Mike Ryan
Senior Marketing Manager: Ann Byford
Senior Developmental Editor: Lesley Mann
Copy Editor: Dianne Broad
Production Editor: Mary Ann McCutcheon, Kelly Dickson
Production Coordinator: Jane Schell
Photo Research: Hilary Forrest
Cover Design: Gary Beelik
Cover Image: Wes Thompson, First Light
Interior Design: Kyle Gell Art & Design
Page Layout: Kyle Gell Art & Design

Original English Language edition published by
Prentice Hall, Inc., Upper Saddle River, New Jersey
Copyright © 1999

2 3 4 5   CP   03 02 01 00 99

Printed and bound in Canada

Every reasonable effort has been made to obtain permissions for all articles and data used in this edition. If errors or omissions have occurred, they will be corrected in future editions provided written notification has been received by the publisher.

Visit the Prentice Hall Canada Web site! Send us your comments, browse our catalogues, and more at **www.phcanada.com**. Or reach us through e-mail at **phcinfo_pubcanada@prenhall.com**.

Philip Kotler is S. C. Johnson & Son Distinguished Professor of International Marketing at the Kellogg Graduate School of Management, Northwestern University. He received his master's degree at the University of Chicago and his Ph.D. at M.I.T., both in economics. Dr. Kotler is author of *Marketing Management: Analysis, Planning, Implementation, and Control* (Prentice Hall), now in its ninth edition and the most widely used marketing textbook in graduate schools of business. He has authored several other successful books and he has written over 90 articles for leading journals. He is the only three-time winner of the coveted Alpha Kappa Psi award for the best annual article in the *Journal of Marketing*. Dr. Kotler has been awarded numerous major honours. In 1989, he received the Charles Coolidge Parlin Award, which each year honours an outstanding leader in the field of marketing. Dr. Kotler has served as chairman of the College on Marketing of the Institute of Management Sciences (TIMS) and a director of the American Marketing Association. He has consulted with many major U.S. and foreign companies on marketing strategy.

Gary Armstrong is Professor and Chair of Marketing in the Kenan-Flagler Business School at the University of North Carolina at Chapel Hill. He holds undergraduate and master's degrees in business from Wayne State University in Detroit, and he received his Ph.D. in marketing from Northwestern University. Dr. Armstrong has contributed numerous articles to leading business journals. As a consultant and researcher, he has worked with many companies on marketing research, sales management, and marketing strategy. But Professor Armstrong's first love is teaching. He has been very active in the teaching and administration of North Carolina's undergraduate business program. His recent administrative posts include Associate Director of the Undergraduate Business Program, Director of the Business Honours Program, and others. He works closely with business student groups and has received several campuswide and Business School teaching awards. He is the only repeat recipient of the school's highly regarded Award for Excellence in Undergraduate Teaching, which he won for the third time in 1993.

Peggy Cunningham is Associate Professor of Marketing at Queen's University School of Business. She received her undergraduate degree from Queen's University, completed her MBA at the University of Calgary, and earned her Ph.D. in marketing from Texas A&M University. Dr. Cunningham worked in industry for ten years before becoming an academic which has allowed her to bring the perspective of the practitioner to the study of marketing. She conducts research in the fields of marketing ethics, strategic alliances, and cause-related marketing. She is a devoted teacher who tries to inspire her students to fully realize their full and unique potential. In recognition of these efforts, she has received several teaching and service awards including the Frank Knox award for teaching excellence, a campus-wide award granted by undergraduate students. She is also an active member of the American Marketing Association.

BRIEF TABLE OF CONTENTS

CONTENTS

9 NEW-PRODUCT DEVELOPMENT
AND LIFE-CYCLE STRATEGIES *310*

10 PRICING CONSIDERATIONS
AND APPROACHES *340*

13 RETAILING AND WHOLESALING   *430*

16 PERSONAL SELLING AND SALES MANAGEMENT   534

17 DIRECT AND ONLINE MARKETING   564

PART IV MANAGING MARKETING

18 COMPETITIVE STRATEGIES:

Philip Kotler and Gary Armstrong are among the best-known names in marketing and have long been recognized for their expertise and unique perspectives about the field. When I was first asked to adapt their text for the Canadian marketplace, I was pleased to take on this challenge, because the product was so strong to start with. However, I also realized that there are distinct challenges to marketing in Canada that had to be considered in our discussion. These challenges include regional and language differences, multiculturalism, population dispersion, different regulatory policies and philosophies, the small domestic marketplace and resulting mandate for global sales, a highly concentrated retail environment, and unique cultural and ethical norms and values that distinguish Canadian business from its American counterparts. In addition, many Canadian firms are operating units of large, multinational firms; thus, marketing in Canada often necessitates integrating Canadian strategies with the global programs of the parent firm.

Despite these differences, considerable common ground can be found in the practice of visionary marketing. Marketing is the business function that identifies customer needs and wants, determines which target markets the organization can serve best, and designs appropriate products, services, and programs to serve these markets. However, marketing is much more than just an isolated business function—it is a philosophy that guides the entire organization. The goal of marketing is to create customer satisfaction profitably by building value-laden relationships with important customers. The marketing department cannot accomplish this goal by itself. It must team up closely with other departments in the company and partner with other organizations throughout its entire value-delivery system to provide superior value to customers. Thus, marketing calls upon everyone in the organization to "think customer" and to do all they can to help create and deliver superior customer value and satisfaction. As Professor Stephen Burnett of Northwestern puts it, "In a truly great marketing organization, you can't tell who's in the marketing department. Everyone in the organization has to make decisions based on the impact on the consumer."

Many people see marketing only as advertising or selling. But real marketing does not involve the art of selling what you make so much as knowing *what* to make! Organizations gain market leadership by understanding consumer needs and finding solutions that delight customers through superior value, quality, and service. If customer value and satisfaction are absent, no amount of advertising or selling can compensate.

Marketing is all around us, and we all need to know something about it. Marketing is used not only by manufacturing and service companies, wholesalers, and retailers, but also by all kinds of individuals and organizations. Lawyers, accountants, and doctors use marketing to manage demand for their services. So do hospitals, museums, and performing arts groups. No politician can get the needed votes, and no resort the needed tourists, without developing and carrying out marketing plans. *Principles of Marketing* is designed to help students learn about and apply the basic concepts and practices of modern marketing as they are used in a wide variety of settings: in product and service firms, consumer and business markets, profit and non-profit organizations, domestic and global companies, and small and large businesses.

People throughout these organizations need to know how to define and segment a market and how to position themselves strongly by developing need-satisfying products and services for chosen target segments. They must know how to price their offerings to make them attractive and affordable and how to choose and manage intermediaries to make their products available to customers. And they need to know how to advertise and promote products so customers will know about and want them. Clearly, marketers need a broad range of skills in order to sense, serve, and satisfy consumer needs.

Students also need to know marketing in their roles as consumers and citizens. Someone is always trying to sell us something, so we need to recognize the methods they use. And when students enter the job market, they must do "marketing research" to find the best opportunities and the best ways to "market themselves" to prospective employers. Many will start their careers with marketing jobs in sales forces, in retailing, in advertising, in research, or in one of a dozen other marketing areas.

APPROACH AND OBJECTIVES

Principles of Marketing takes a *practical, managerial* approach to marketing. It provides a rich depth of practical examples and applications, showing the major decisions that marketing managers face in their efforts to balance the organization's objectives and resources against needs and opportunities in the marketplace. Each chapter opens with a major example describing an actual company situation. Boxed Marketing Highlights, profiles of actual marketing practitioners, short examples, colour illustrations, video cases, and company cases highlight high-interest ideas, stories, and marketing strategies that bring the subject to life.

Principles of Marketing tells the stories that reveal the drama of modern marketing: how global firms and small entrepreneurial upstarts alike have thrived by understanding their customers, building relationships with them, and creating superior value. You'll read about the global marketing machine behind Nike, and the evolution of Cirque du Soleil, the small Montreal performance troupe that has taken the world by storm. You'll learn the story of Canadian Tire's continued success in the face of aggressive competitors from the United States, uncover the strategies of Canada's pharmaceutical firms working in a highly regulated and changing environment, and witness the ongoing wars between Canada's two large breweries. You'll understand why Canadians across the country should be proud of their business and marketing acumen when you read of the exploits of Bombardier's success in the cut-throat aerospace market, of Intrawest's efforts to be the host to vacationers the world over, and the insights of master merchandiser Harry Rosen that helped him build a retailing empire. We've worked to make *Principles of Marketing* a leading-edge provider of information about today's marketing practices. We show how organizations of all types have wrestled with questions of how best to use technology to serve both domestic and global consumers. We stress the importance of ethics and social responsibility throughout the text.

Ultimately, *Principles of Marketing* gives marketing students a comprehensive and innovative managerial and practical introduction to marketing. Its style and extensive use of examples and illustrations make the book straightforward, easy to read, and enjoyable.

NEW IN THE FOURTH CANADIAN EDITION

The fourth Canadian edition of *Principles of Marketing* offers important improvements in organization, content, and style. New major themes we've developed include:

◆ *Marketing and technology*—technology is affecting marketing as never before. As EDS chairman Les Alberthal noted in a 1997 speech, technology-enabled marketing is bringing significant changes in our ability to understand and serve customers. Marketers must not only understand the new challenges of marketing high technology, but they must also learn to market with technology. Technology has affected every aspect of marketing practice, from conducting research projects to designing the marketing communications mix. The management of databases and the direct marketing practices that this enables is one of the fastest-growing areas of marketing. The Internet is an important facet of marketing with technology since it exposes local markets to global competition.

◆ *Integration of product and services marketing*—there are few pure products or services. Marketers must understand that it is often the combination of product and service offerings that leads to competitive advantage. High-quality products must be accompanied by equally high-quality support services. Moreover, the service sector is the fastest-growing sector of the Canadian economy. It is driving Canada's domestic and international market growth.

◆ *Integrated marketing communications*—we've focused on integrating all elements of the communications mix from direct marketing to public relations.

A carefully revised and updated Chapter 1 introduces and integrates these and other major marketing themes to set the stage at the beginning of the course. An innovative Chapter 18 on building customer relationships through value, satisfaction, and quality returns the student to these important concepts as a means of tying marketing together at the end of the course. And we've woven the topics on product and service marketing into a comprehensive Chapter 8 that is positioned at the centre of the text.

Some of the latest developments in marketing are reflected in a completely new Chapter 17, which provides a detailed discussion of direct and online marketing. Examples throughout the text emphasize how the Internet has affected all aspects of marketing. We describe, for example, how it can be utilized in tasks as varied as gathering research information or managing the sales force. Our "Spotlight on the Internet" (pp. xxvi-xxvii) documents the extensive integration of World Wide Web material throughout the text.

To encourage students to learn about and explore Internet technology, we have included Weblinks (Internet addresses of companies and organizations) in the margins of the text. Students can go online with Weblinks to discover first-hand how companies are using this technology. Our Companion Website at **www.prenticehall.ca/kotler** will provide regular updates to these Internet resources, as well as access to marketing news groups, NetSearch modules using key words from the text, and our online Study Guide.

www.prenticehall.ca/kotler

The fourth Canadian edition contains many other important changes:

◆ The objectives at the beginning of each chapter have been revised so that they are succinct and clear, and the end-of-chapter summaries are now keyed to these objectives.

◆ Many new chapter-opening cases and Marketing Highlights have been added, reflecting the "best practices" of firms on the forefront of Canadian and international business.

◆ We have condensed material from earlier editions so that we could add leading-edge topics such as marketing with technology (Internet marketing, kiosk marketing, and so on) and direct marketing.

◆ More practitioner profiles, entitled Marketers Speak Out, show students how the lessons of marketing are put to use by real-life marketers.

◆ A number of new chapter-ending company cases and CBC video cases have been added.

◆ Comprehensive cases have been moved to Appendix 1 for easier reference.

◆ The tables, figures, examples, and references throughout the text have been thoroughly updated with information from such sources as Statistics Canada, *Canadian Business, Strategy: The Canadian Marketing Report, Marketing* magazine, and the business press.

◆ We provide the most current Canadian statistics and issues, from Michael Adams' psychographic groups (based on his book *Sex in the Snow*) to data on current trends in Canadian retailing.

CONTINUING THEMES

Every chapter reflects the current marketing emphasis on delivering customer value and satisfaction, and on building customer relationships. Revisions in the fourth edition continue to emphasize a number of major marketing themes, including:

◆ *Relationship marketing*—keeping customers and capturing customer lifetime value by building value-laden customer relationships.

◆ *Internet and direct marketing*—how to use direct marketing programs and the Internet for strategic advantage, and the challenges of integrating them into the marketing mix (featured in an all-new chapter).

◆ *Services marketing*—marketing strategies that service firms need to employ for ongoing success in the fastest-growing sector of the economy.

◆ *Marketing in the Canadian environment*—the features that make Canada both challenging and exciting, including a focus on regionalism, the growth of ethnic markets, and the threats posed by foreign competition.

◆ *Delivering superior customer value, satisfaction, and quality*—market-centred strategy and "taking care of the customer."

◆ *Global marketing*—chapter-by-chapter integrated coverage, plus a full chapter focusing on international marketing considerations and the quality management programs of ISO 9000 and 14000.

◆ *Marketing ethics, environmentalism, and social responsibility*—chapter-by-chapter integrated coverage, plus a full chapter on marketing ethics and social responsibility.

◆ *Total marketing quality*—the importance of customer-driven total quality as a means of delivering total customer satisfaction.

◆ *Value-delivery systems*—how cross-functional teamwork within companies and cross-company, supply-chain partnerships create effective customer value-delivery systems.

LEARNING AIDS

Many aids are provided within this book to help students learn about marketing. The main ones are

◆ *Chapter-opening objectives.* Each chapter begins with learning objectives that preview the flow of concepts in the chapter.

◆ *Chapter-ending summaries of objectives.* At the end of each chapter, summaries are linked to chapter objectives to reinforce main points and concepts.

◆ *Chapter-opening examples.* Each chapter starts with a dramatic marketing story that introduces the chapter material and arouses student interest.

◆ *Full-colour figures, photographs, advertisements, and illustrations.* Throughout each chapter, key concepts and applications are illustrated with strong, full-colour visual materials.

◆ *Marketing Highlights.* Additional examples and important information are presented in Marketing Highlight exhibits throughout the text.

◆ *Marketers Speak Out.* Interviews with marketing professionals are interspersed throughout the text, highlighting real-life marketing experiences.

◆ *Review questions and exercises.* Each chapter contains a set of discussion questions covering the main chapter points. "Applying the concepts" exercises build individual and group process and leadership skills.

◆ *Key terms.* Key terms are highlighted within the text, defined in page margins, and listed at the end of each chapter with page references. In the subject index, the page on which each key term is defined is printed in bold.

◆ *Company cases.* Company cases for class or written discussion are provided at the end of each chapter and four comprehensive cases are included in an appendix. These cases challenge students to apply marketing principles to real companies in real situations.

◆ CBC *Video cases.* Twenty written video cases are provided at key points in the text, supported by exciting videos from CBC news programs. These videos and cases help to bring key marketing concepts and issues to life in the classroom.

◆ *Appendixes.* Four appendices (Comprehensive Cases, Measuring and Forecasting Demand, Marketing Arithmetic, and Careers in Marketing) provide additional, practical information for students.

◆ *Indexes.* Company/Brand/Name and Subject indexes reference all information and examples in the book. Pages on which Weblink addresses appear are printed in bold in the Company/Brand/Name Index. Pages on which key terms are defined are printed in bold in the Subject Index.

◆ *Weblinks.* Exciting and useful Internet sites are discussed throughout the text and are easily identifiable by the Weblinks icon.

SUPPLEMENTS

A successful marketing course requires more than a well-written book. Today's classroom requires a dedicated teacher and a fully integrated teaching system. *Principles of Marketing* is supported by an extensively revised and expanded system of supplemental learning and teaching aids:

FOR THE INSTRUCTOR

◆ *Instructor's Resource Manual with CBC Video Guide (ISBN 0-13-973603-4).* This comprehensive guide includes a chapter summary for a quick overview, a list of key teaching objectives, and answers to all end-of-chapter discussion and case questions. A highly detailed lecture outline cuts preparation time by thoroughly integrating the video material and cases. In addition, the manual summarizes each video and provides answers to the video case discussion questions.

◆ *Test Item File (ISBN 0-13-973595-X).* The test item file contains over 2200 multiple-choice, true/false, and essay questions. Correct answers, including suggested essay answers, and difficulty levels are provided for all questions. The proportion of application-type questions has been increased to 60 percent for the fourth edition.

◆ WIN *PH Custom Test (ISBN 0-13-973611-5).* This powerful computerized testing package uses a state-of-the-art software program which provides fast, simple, and error-free test generation. Entire tests can be previewed on-screen before printing. PH Custom Test can print multiple variations of the same test, scrambling the order of questions and multiple-choice answers.

◆ *Colour Transparencies.* Expanded and improved for the fourth edition, this package of full-colour transparencies highlights key concepts for presentation. Each transparency is accompanied by a full page of teaching notes that includes relevant page references and discussion points from each chapter, as well as additional material from supplementary sources. (Please contact your Prentice Hall sales representative for details.)

◆ *Transparency Resource Package (ISBN 0-13-973637-9).* With up to 20 slides per chapter in Powerpoint 4.0, this disk allows you to present transparencies

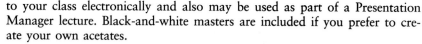

to your class electronically and also may be used as part of a Presentation Manager lecture. Black-and-white masters are included if you prefer to create your own acetates.

www.tv.cbc.ca/venture

♦ *PH/CBC Video Library.* Prentice Hall Canada and the CBC have worked together to bring you 20 segments from such notable CBC programs as *Venture, Market Place, The National Magazine,* and *Undercurrents.* Designed specifically to complement the text, this case collection is an excellent tool for bringing students into contact with the world outside the classroom. These programs have extremely high production quality, present substantial content, and have been chosen to relate directly to chapter content. (Please contact your Prentice Hall sales representative for details. These videos are subject to availability and terms negotiated upon adoption of the text.)

♦ *Marketing Casebook (ISBN 0-13-973652-2).* To supplement courses that put particular emphasis on case analysis, this casebook has been prepared. Cases included are generally longer and more detailed than end-of-chapter Company Cases but usually not as extensive as Comprehensive Cases.

www.prenticehall.ca/kotler

♦ *Companion Web Site.* The fourth edition's Companion Web Site includes an online study guide with multiple choice and true/false questions, an online marketing plan, Internet destinations and research tools to CBC video cases, and more. See **www.prenticehall.ca/kotler**.

FOR THE STUDENT

♦ *Study Guide (ISBN 0-13-973660-3).* The Study Guide includes chapter overviews, objectives, key terms and definitions, and detailed outlines for note-taking and review. Short Essay questions centre on a case that is designed to illustrate and apply topics in marketing. Each case in the section either is a synopsis of a recent article in marketing or has been drawn from the author's experiences in the field. To reinforce students' understanding of the chapter material, the guide includes a section of multiple-choice and true/false questions. Suggested answers for all short essay, multiple choice and true/false questions are provided for students' self-checking. Additional sections include a marketing research paper, a project outline, and a special careers appendix.

■ ACKNOWLEDGMENTS

No book is the work only of its authors. We owe much to the pioneers of marketing who first identified its major issues and developed its concepts and techniques. Our thanks also go to our colleagues at the School of Business, Queen's University, the University of Manitoba, J. L. Kellogg Graduate School of Management, Northwestern University, at the Kenan-Flagler Business School, University of North Carolina at Chapel Hill, for ideas and suggestions. Preparation of the Canadian edition was greatly facilitated by Gary Armstrong, who kindly provided electronic files for the manuscript of the U.S. eighth edition. We also thank Auleen Carson of Wilfrid Laurier University, who wrote the new CBC video cases, and all of the enthusiastic marketing professionals who granted interviews for the Canadian third and fourth editions, including:

Alexandra Acs-Lowen, Kraft Canada
Valerie Bell, H.J. Heinz of Canada
Lindsey Davis, Kraft Canada
Sandra Hawken, Leo Burnett
Mike Henanan, Loyalty Management Group
Nick Jones, Communiqué
J.J. Lee, H.J. Heinz of Canada

Jeff Norton, Procter & Gamble Canada
Bruce Pope, Molson
Jim Shenkman, Brunico Communication Inc.
Rob Shields, Loyalty Management Group
Arthur Soler, Cadbury Chocolate
Jay Whiteside
Susan Young, Imperial Oil

We owe a debt of gratitude to all the professors and instructors who provided suggestions on how to improve the text. Reviewers who gave thoughtful and detailed responses include:

Deborah L. Andrus, University of Calgary
May Aung, University of Guelph
Patricia Badeen, Algonquin College
Wes Balderson, University of Lethbridge
J. Neil Beattie, Sheridan College
Brad Berry, Mohawk College
Auleen Carson, Wilfrid Laurier University
J. Brad Davis, Wilfrid Laurier University
Jim Deakin, Sheridan College
Kerry Jarvis, Seneca College
Robert Jershy, St. Clair College
Ashwin Joshi, Saint Mary's University
Stephen Lee, Algonquin College
Shelley M. Rinehart, University of New Brunswick—Saint John
Louise Ripley, York University
Terry Seawright, McMaster University
Donald Shiner, Mount Saint Vincent University
Malcolm Smith, University of Manitoba
Shirley Taylor, Queen's University

We also owe a great deal to the people at Prentice Hall Canada who helped develop this book. Our sincere thanks for the support of the editorial team: Mary Ann McCutcheon, Production Editor, for her enthusiastic and attentive monitoring of a very complex project; Dianne Broad for her superb copyediting; Kyle Gell, designer, who was asked to make a fine design better, and did; hard-working Lesley Mann, Senior Developmental Editor; Mike Ryan, Acquisitions Editor; and Pat Ferrier, Publisher. Without their support, hard work, and insightful suggestions, we never could have made the tight deadlines associated with this project. Special thanks also to Ann Byford, Senior Marketing Manager, and the Prentice Hall sales team, especially Cathleen Sullivan, who never called without having something new and exciting to discuss.

Finally, we owe many thanks to our students, who make good teaching possible, and to our families—for their constant support and encouragement. To them, we dedicate this book.

Peggy Cunningham

Philip Kotler   Gary Armstrong

The Prentice Hall Canada

companion Website...

Your Internet companion to the most exciting, state-of-the-art educational tools on the Web!

The Prentice Hall Canada Companion Website is easy to navigate and is organized to correspond to the chapters in this textbook. The Companion Website is comprised of four distinct, functional features:

1) **Customized Online Resources**

2) **Online Study Guide**

3) **Reference Material**

4) **Communication**

Explore the four areas in this Companion Website. Students and distance learners will discover resources for indepth study, research and communication, empowering them in their quest for greater knowledge and maximizing their potential for success in the course.

A NEW WAY TO DELIVER EDUCATIONAL CONTENT

1) Customized Online Resources

Our Companion Websites provide instructors and students with a range of options to access, view, and exchange content.

- **Mailing lists** enable *instructors* and *students* to receive customized promotional literature.

- **Syllabus Builder** allows *instructors* to construct an online syllabus linked to specific modules in the Companion Website.

- **Preferences** enable *students* to customize the sending of results to various recipients, and also to customize how the material is sent, e.g., as html, text, or as an attachment.

- **Help** includes an evaluation of the user's system and a tune-up area that makes updating browsers and plug-ins easier. This new feature will enhance the user's experience with Companion Websites.

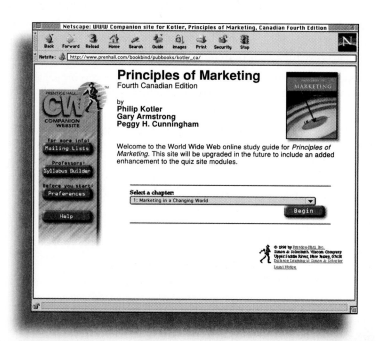

www.prenticehall.ca/

2) Online Study Guide

Interactive Study Guide modules form the core of the student learning experience in the Companion Website. These modules are categorized according to their functionality:

- True-False
- Fill-in-the-Blank
- Multiple Choice
- Essay questions

All of these modules provide students with the ability to send answers to our grader and receive instant feedback on their progress through our Results Reporter. (The only exception is Essay questions, where suggested answers are displayed.) References back to the textbook ensure that students take advantage of all resources available to enhance their learning experience.

3) Reference Material

Reference material broadens text coverage with up-to-date resources for learning. **Web Destinations** provides a directory of Web sites relevant to the subject matter in each chapter. **NetNews (Internet Newsgroups)** are a fundamental source of information about a discipline, containing a wealth of brief, opinionated postings. **NetSearch** simplifies key term search using 5 Internet search engines.

4) Communication

Companion Websites contain the communication tools necessary to deliver courses in a **Distance Learning** environment. **Message Board** allows users to post messages and check back periodically for responses. **Live Chat** allows users to discuss course topics in real time, and enables professors to host online classes.

Communication facilities of Companion Websites provide a key element for distributed learning environments. There are two types of communication facilities currently in use in Companion Websites:

- **Message Board** – this module takes advantage of browser technology providing the users of each Companion Website with a national newsgroup to post and reply to relevant course topics.

- **Live Chat** – enables instructor-led group activities in real time. Using our chat client, instructors can display Website content while students participate in the discussion.

Companion Websites are currently available for:
- Starke: Contemporary Management in Canada
- Evans: Marketing Essentials
- Horngren: Cost Accounting
- Horngren: Introduction to Financial Accounting

Note: CW '99 content will vary slightly from site to site depending on discipline requirements.

The Companion Website for the new edition will be:

www.prenticehall.ca/kotler

PRENTICE HALL CANADA

1870 Birchmount Road
Scarborough, Ontario M1P 2J7

To order:
Call: 1-800-567-3800
Fax: 1-800-263-7733

For samples:
Call: 1-800-850-5813
Fax: (416) 299-2539
E-mail: phcinfo_pubcanada@prenhall.com

SPOTLIGHT ON THE INTERNET

The third Canadian edition of *Principles of Marketing* was one of the first marketing textbooks in North America to give serious attention to the Internet and its impact on contemporary marketing. The fourth edition offers even more Internet content, with the inclusion of an exciting new chapter on Direct and Online Marketing, and additional Weblinks directing students to some of the most innovative sites online. We can attest first hand to the power of the Internet as a research tool that gives access to the most current information available. We used it extensively in writing the fourth edition.

In addition to the new chapter, information on how the Internet is being used to support all facets of marketing practice has been integrated into the chapters. This includes the Internet as a marketing research tool, the Internet in new product development, and the importance of the Internet in international marketing. You'll find analysis, issues, examples, and questions about the Net in every chapter:

Chapter 1:

◆ "Internet" defined (p. 22)

◆ new section on the Information Technology Boom contains a special subsection on the Internet. Three examples discuss innovative approaches to Internet marketing, ranging in scale from Toyota to a small retail chain that specializes in penguin-related products (pp. 22–23).

◆ Internet boom included among the major 21st century challenges covered by Learning Objective 4 (p. 29)

Chapter 2:

◆ how Canadian Tire uses its Internet site to tailor its product offerings to consumers' needs (p. 39)

◆ new Practitioner Profile of Jim Shenkman (Brunico Communication Inc.) discusses entrepreneurial strategies for the future, including Internet development) (pp. 60–61)

Chapter 3:

◆ new Marketing Highlight 3-1 on the World Village Project web site (p. 82)

◆ using the Internet to reach the gay market (p. 90)

◆ new Discussing the Issues question 2 requires students to explore the Statistics Canada Internet site (p. 104)

Chapter 4:

◆ updated chapter opening case on Canadian beer wars explains how Molson and Labatt use the Internet to build customer relationships (p. 113)

◆ intelligence-gathering resources on the World Wide Web are described in the section entitled Surfing the Internet and Online Databases in Marketing Highlight 4-1 (p. 119)

◆ the section on Gathering Secondary Information includes detailed discussions of Commercial Data Sources, Online Databases and Internet Data Sources, and Advantages and Disadvantages of Secondary Data (pp. 124-127)

◆ Table 4-2, "Sources of Secondary Data," includes a detailed description of Internet Data Sources (p. 126)

◆ "online databases" defined (p. 126)

◆ the section on Planning Primary Data Collection includes using the Internet for electronic focus groups (p. 132)

◆ new Marketing Highlight 4-4, "Marketing Research on the Internet" (p. 133)

◆ Marketing Highlight 4-5 includes a brief description of the Internet Advertising and Marketing Bureau of Canada (p. 151)

Chapter 5

◆ chapter-long consumer profile shows how Jennifer Wong uses the Internet to research a purchase (p. 161)

◆ a demographic and behavioural profile of Internet users is provided in a new subsection on Cultural Factors (pp. 160-1)

◆ SRI's lifestyle classification system (VALS) for Internet users is described; a Weblink directs readers to an online questionnaire that allows them to find out what classification they fall within (p. 167)

◆ new Practitioner Profile of Lindsey Davis, Kraft Canada, discusses legal and ethical issues in developing Internet marketing of products directed at children (p. 179)

Chapter 6

◆ new Marketing Highlight 6-3, "Business-to-Business Buying and the Internet"(p. 213)

◆ section on Government Markets includes new paragraph on Canadian Business Service Centre (Internet service about federal and provincial business assistance programs) (p. 215)

◆ new Applying the Concepts question 3 includes an Internet exercise using the Industry Canada web site (p. 217)

Chapter 7:

◆ Marketing Highlight 7-2, "Socially Responsible Market Targeting," notes criticism that Internet marketing ignores the poorer members of society who don't own computers (p. 243)

◆ how Cadbury Canada used their Internet site as part of an integrated communications program to support the launch of their new candy bar, Time Out (p. 245)

Chapter 8

◆ examples illustrate how service companies provide consumers with greater access of information by using the Internet (p. 295)

Chapter 9:

◆ new Marketing Highlight 9-2 discusses Internet potential for Virtual Reality Test Marketing (p. 324)

◆ new CBC Video Case "Profiting from the "Net" profiles the young entrepreneur who started Interlog, the Internet service provider company (p. 339)

Chapter 10:

◆ Internet strategies of Canadian Airlines and Air Canada (p. 363–64)

Chapter 11:

◆ new Marketing Highlight 11-1 discusses Internet sites developed by Canadian automakers to combat CarMax Auto superstores (p. 373)

Chapter 12:

◆ new Marketing Highlight 12-1 includes discussion of Goodyear's award-winning Internet site (p. 401)

◆ Applying the Concepts question 2 asks students to evaluate web sites of mail-order retailers in terms of the degree to which they support or conflict with authorized dealers (p. 425)

Chapter 13:

◆ new Marketing Highlight 13-3, "Retailing Goes Online," includes descriptions and web sites for companies marketing music, books, flowers, apparel, and food on the Internet (p. 451–52)

◆ question 3 in CBC Video Case, "Cashing in on the Book Boom," asks students to analyse the impact that new Canadian superstores like Chapters and Indigo books will have on Internet booksellers like Amazon.com

Chapter 15:

◆ discussion of coupons expanded to include Internet coupon sites (p. 517)

◆ effective use of Internet in public relations, both for information and crisis-management purposes (p. 524)

Chapter 16:

◆ section on Supervising Salespeople includes new paragraph on impact of the Internet (p. 550)

Chapter 17:

◆ all-new chapter focuses on Direct and Online Marketing; Weblinks throughout provide Internet addresses of companies and organizations discussed

◆ Chapter Objective 4 focuses on impact of Internet on electronic commerce; Objective 5 asks students to identify benefits of online marketing (pp. 595–96)

◆ Key Terms include corporate web site, electronic commerce, Internet, marketing web site, online ads, online marketing, and webcasting (p. 595)

◆ opening case on Dell Computer Corporation discusses how this direct marketing pioneer is using the Internet to cut costs and offer more services and information to buyers, resulting in online sales of more than $3 million per day (pp. 566–67)

◆ data on Canadian Internet use (p. 569)

◆ new Marketing Highlight 17-1 describes how Fingerhut's web site customizes interactions with customers (p. 572)

◆ new developments in direct marketing include increasing use of e-mail (p. 574) and Internet catalogues from retailers such as Tilley Endurables and L.L. Bean (p. 576)

◆ new section on Window on the Future: Online Marketing and Direct Commerce includes headings discussing Rapid Growth of Online Marketing; Who Uses the Net?; The Benefits of Online Marketing; Online Marketing Channels; and The Promise and Challenges of Online Marketing (pp. 578-90)

◆ new Practitioner Interview with Nick Jones, New Media Evangelist at Communiqué, discusses developments and challenges in Internet marketing (pp. 579–80)

◆ new Marketing Highlight 17-2 describes how Pillsbury uses its Internet site to develop customer relations without engaging in direct selling (p. 585)

◆ discussion of privacy issues in direct marketing includes a description of Microsoft's controversial use of a "Registration Wizard" when Windows 95 was launched (p. 593)

◆ Discussing the Issues questions 1, 4, 6, and 7 focus on e-mail and Internet marketing applications (pp. 595–96)

◆ Applying the Concepts questions require students to evaluate and analyse web sites

◆ Company Case features Internet bookseller Amazon.com

◆ CBC Video Case focuses on "Virtual Banking at ING Direct" and the impact of new banking technologies on the Canadian marketplace; question 3 requires students to evaluate the differences between the web sites for ING and the Citizens Bank of Canada (p. 601)

Chapter 18:

◆ new opening case includes discussion of Internet developments at Intel, including virtual Web communities, online payment systems, and 3-D online chat rooms (pp. 631-633)

Chapter 19

◆ description of how the NBA uses its Internet site to reach a global audience beyond North America (p. 644)

◆ new Marketing Highlight 19-1 discusses the global impact of the Internet (p. 649-50)

◆ Applying the Concepts question 1 requires students to use Internet resources to compile information on an emerging economy in which they will market a software product (p. 671)

Chapter 20:

◆ discussion of the Imagine program for corporate philanthropy includes web site of firms and non-profit organizations involved (p. 677)

◆ the section on Enlightened Marketing discusses the Waste Tracker system developed by Walsh Integrated Environmental Systems (Montreal) and shows how the company is using the Internet to crack the market for effective waste management (pp. 695–96)

Company/Brand/Name Index

◆ Do you need to find an Internet address? Check the organization's entry in our Company/Brand/Name Index—the page on which a Weblink appears is printed in bold. Updated web site addresses are provided in the "Destinations" section of our Companion Website at **www.prenticehall.ca/kotler.**

*Principles of
Marketing*

C H A P T E R 1

MARKETING IN A
CHANGING WORLD

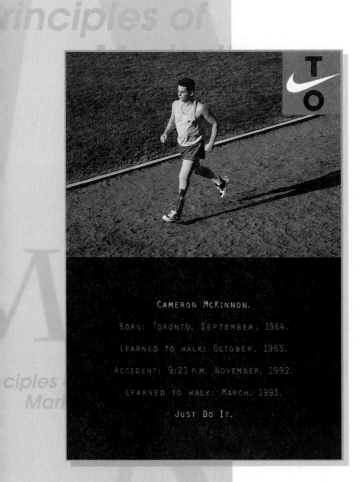

CAMERON MCKINNON.

BORN: TORONTO, SEPTEMBER, 1964.

LEARNED TO WALK: OCTOBER, 1965.

ACCIDENT: 9:21 P.M. NOVEMBER, 1992.

LEARNED TO WALK: MARCH, 1993.

JUST DO IT.

The Nike "swoosh"—it's everywhere! Just for fun, try counting the swooshes whenever you pick up the sports section of the newspaper, look around your classroom, watch a pick-up basketball game, or tune into a televised tennis match. Nike has built the ubiquitous swoosh (which represents the wing of Nike, the Greek goddess of victory) into one of the best-known brand symbols on the planet. In fact, the symbol is so well known that the company routinely runs ads without even mentioning the Nike name. You may be surprised to find that your Nike shoes, or your Nike hat or T-shirt, carry no brand identification other than the swoosh.

The power of the brand and its logo speak loudly to Nike's superb marketing skills. The company's now-proven strategy of building superior products around popular athletes has forever changed the face of sports marketing. Nike does more than just spend hundreds of millions of dollars on celebrity endorsements and attention-getting ads. Nike's success is also due to its ability to build relationships—between Nike, its athletes, its channel members, and its customers. These relationships began by providing serious athletes, who were frustrated by the lack of innovation in athletic equipment, with technically superior running and basketball shoes.

Today, Nike markets a way of life, a sports culture, a "Just Do It!" attitude. Nike's success has endured because it cares about its customers' lives, not just about their bodies. It doesn't just promote sales, it promotes *sports* and the many benefits of sports participation for both women and men. As the company notes on its web page: "Nike has always known the truth—it's not so much the shoes but where they take you." When you lace up your Nike running shoes, you link yourself, in at least some small way, to a genuine passion for sport, a maverick disregard for convention, hard work, and serious sport performance.

OBJECTIVES

When you finish this chapter, you should be able to

1. Define marketing and discuss its core concepts.

2. Discuss marketing management and examine how marketers manage demand and build profitable customer relationships.

3. Compare the five marketing management philosophies.

4. Analyse the major challenges facing marketers heading into the next century.

Nike
info.nike.com/

Although Nike's global success is unquestionable, one has to ask how Nike has accomplished this. What does the company do, in a country such as Canada, for example, where sports like basketball aren't central to the national sports culture? Does Nike market its products the same way in every country, or does it respond to local conditions? Is it sufficient to replace American sports heroes such as Michael Jordan with Canadian athletes?

While there have been many similarities in Nike's marketing strategy in Canada and the United States, there have also been marked differences. Nike believed that the key to building the Canadian market for their products was to encourage grassroots participation in target sports—in other words, to help build some sports from the ground up. Nike knew from its U.S. experiences that support of playground basketball helped to make it the brand of choice among the sport's fan base of casual and serious enthusiasts. Therefore, as part of its Canadian effort, Nike partnered with Basketball Canada and NBA Canada to target young fans.

In addition to creating excitement about basketball centred on Canada's two new professional teams—the Raptors and the Vancouver Grizzlies—the partners created a new marketing foundation called Future Hoops. Their initial project is to promote the men's and women's national teams competing at the World Championships in 1998 and at the 2000 Summer Olympics in Sydney, Australia. Future Hoops also sponsors youth basketball camps, clinics, and community leagues that provide opportunities for underprivileged youths to play the game and attend professional events. Nike provides financial and marketing support for the program, while NBA Canada promotes Future Hoops through signage at Raptors and Grizzlies games, and public service announcements during telecasts. "It's a good marriage," explains Ken Allen, national sports marketing manager with Nike Canada. "We will be able to contribute to the development of the game at the grassroots level, and that will keep both the sport and the business healthy."

Building on another successful U.S. strategy, Nike introduced a $1.5-million national charitable program called Nike PLAY Canada. Olympic rower Silken Laumann is the honorary chairperson. Nike PLAY Canada is designed to get youths off the streets by helping to provide and fund safe athletic facilities, equipment, and events in Canadian communities. In the United States, the acronym PLAY stands for "Participate in the Lives of America's Youth"; in Canada, it has been changed to "All Youth."

Promoting the sport of basketball wasn't sufficient to build relationships with Canadians, however. In Canada, winter sports reign and hockey is king. Thus, in 1995, Nike purchased the Canadian firm, Canstar, the maker of Bauer, Lange, Daoust, Micron, and Mega skates as well as two brands of protective equipment, Cooper and Flak. Nike intends to drop all of these individual brand names to follow a dual branding strategy. It will build a "superbrand" under the Bauer name, and another line under the Nike name. The two brands will be used in both Canada and the United States. Having two brands is important. Hockey players are a brand-loyal group and, in Canada, Nike doesn't have the reputation in hockey equipment of Bauer, which currently has 60 percent of the Canadian market. In the United States, however, where hockey is in its infancy, Nike's reputation for high-performance equipment will appeal to new players. Over 2.5 million Americans currently play hockey and 3.2 million play roller hockey. Both markets are growing rapidly.

Development of relationships with National Hockey League players will promote the brand. Nike currently outfits six NHL teams, including the Toronto Maple Leafs. (Its chief Canadian rival, CCM, outfits 10 teams.) Recognizing the soaring popularity of women's hockey, Nike didn't stop there. Nike Canada has signed sponsorship deals with five members of the Canadian National Women's team.

To further develop its presence in the hockey market, Nike Canada began one more social marketing initiative through a multimillion-dollar sponsorship deal with the Canadian Hockey Association. Nike's objectives are to promote the sport and to help children across Canada develop hockey skills. As part of its strategy of using grassroots initiatives to build relationships, Nike will donate 5000 coaching manuals to Atom (ages 10–11) and Pee Wee (ages 12–13) amateur hockey organizations across Canada. The company has designed an achievement program that will award players with certificates as they progress through 10 skills-development camps. In return for this support, Nike's logo will appear on manuals, materials, jerseys, and venue sites.

Will Canadian hockey equipment manufacturer, CCM, surrender to the onslaught of Nike easily? Don't bet your hockey skates. The CCM brand name is both well known and respected. It still holds a 40 percent share of the market. Marketers at CCM recently hit the road, visiting retailers and distributors to re-establish relationships and assure them that CCM intends to be around for the long haul. The company is also investing heavily in research and development, with the goals of being the provider of the best hockey equipment in the world, and appealing to sophisticated Canadian hockey equipment buyers. CCM believes that it has some breathing space in its fight against Nike. Since hockey players are notoriously conservative, CCM believes that "the key here is that tastes change very slowly . . . It's a very loyal market, very loyal to the brand. So CCM has time," says CCM President, Gerald Wasserman.[1]

Nike's Canadian strategy didn't stop with its entry into the hockey market, however. When Canadian snowboarder Ross Rebagliati won gold at the 1998 Nagano Winter Olympics, he and his fellow team members were wearing clothing marked with Nike's universal swoosh.

Nike has also launched a made-in-Canada advertising campaign to support its marketing efforts. Bill Redford, director of marketing for Nike Canada, stressed the importance of a uniquely Canadian campaign. "In the past, we almost tried to be all things to all people, but now we're focusing . . . We want to create an identity in major cities and feature that city so people know it's not a U.S. campaign." Beginning with the Toronto market, Nike celebrates local heroes who embody the spirit of "Just Do It." The ads feature eight everyday local Torontonians who have exceptional goals—people such as Ed Bacon, a 63-year-old marathon runner who competed in the 1997 Shoppers Drug Mart Toronto Marathon, although he started to run only in 1996 and trained for just six months. Even though Bacon finished last, he completed the race nonetheless. All of the advertising is punctuated with a variation of the swoosh logo. The swoosh is bracketed vertically by the letters "TO." Redford stresses that Nike "is not selling product. We're selling Nike as a good company, and we want to create a tie between the consumer in Toronto and Nike." Nike's efforts have certainly paid off handsomely. Nike is currently tied with Nissan as Canada's most-liked TV advertiser.

Taking care of customers and making key sports a central part of their lives has paid off handsomely for Nike. Over the past decade, Nike's revenues have grown at an incredible annual rate of 21 percent. Last year alone, total revenues increased by 36 percent. While Nike can be said to dominate the world marketplace with its 27 percent share of the international market, the company also realizes that continued growth must come from overseas markets, not the mature North American marketplace.

To dominate globally, Nike must dominate soccer, the world's most popular sport but one that Nike has almost totally ignored until now. The company hopes to become the world's number-one supplier of soccer footwear, apparel, and equipment for World Cup 2002. Elbowing its way to the top by 2002 won't be easy. World soccer has long been dominated by Germany's Adidas, which is the number-two player in the world sporting-goods market. Adidas is betting that it can beat the cocky Nike in the same way that its spokesperson, Canada's

Donovan Bailey (the Canadian sprinter who owns the 100-metre world record) beat Nike's celebrity American runner, Michael Johnson. The race between these two global sports marketing giants will be interesting to watch.

Many factors contribute to making a business successful. However, today's successful companies at all levels have one thing in common—like Nike, they are strongly customer-focused and heavily committed to marketing. These companies share an absolute dedication to understanding and satisfying the needs of customers in well-defined target markets. They motivate everyone in the organization to produce superior value for their customers, leading to high levels of customer satisfaction.

WHAT IS MARKETING?

Marketing, more than any other business function, deals with customers. Creating customer value and satisfaction are at the very heart of modern marketing thinking and practice. Although we will explore more detailed definitions of marketing later in this chapter, perhaps the simplest definition is this one: Marketing is the delivery of customer satisfaction at a profit. The goal of marketing is to attract new customers by promising superior value, and to keep current customers by delivering satisfaction.

Wal-Mart has become the world's largest retailer by delivering on its promise "We sell for less—always." Mountain Equipment Co-op is Canada's largest outdoor recreational equipment co-operative due to its focus on providing its more than 700 000 members with the lowest reasonable prices, high-quality, environmentally responsible products, and informative, helpful service.[2] And Coca-Cola, long the world's leading soft drink, delivers on the simple but enduring promise, "Always Coca-Cola"—always thirst-quenching, always good with food, always cool, always a part of your life. These and other highly successful companies know that if they take care of their customers, market share and profits will follow.

Some people believe that only large business organizations operating in highly developed economies use marketing, but sound marketing is critical to the success of every organization—whether large or small, for-profit or non-profit, domestic or global. Large for-profit firms such as Coca-Cola, Bell, IBM, Nortel, Zellers, and Marriott use marketing. But so do non-profit organizations such as universities, hospitals, museums, symphonies, and even churches. Moreover, marketing is practised throughout the world. Most countries in North and South America, Western Europe, and the Far East have well-developed marketing systems. Even in Eastern Europe and the former Soviet republics, where marketing has long had a bad name, dramatic political and social changes have created new opportunities. Business and government leaders in most of these nations are eager to learn everything they can about modern marketing practices.

You already know a lot about marketing—it's all around you. You see the results of marketing in the abundance of products that line the store shelves in your nearby shopping mall. You see marketing in the advertisements that fill your TV screen, magazines, and mailbox. At home, at school, where you work, where you play—you are exposed to marketing in almost everything you do. Yet, there is much more to marketing than meets the consumer's casual eye. Behind it all is a massive network of people and activities competing for your attention and purchasing dollars.

This book will give you a more complete and formal introduction to the basic concepts and practices of today's marketing. In this chapter, we begin by defining marketing and its core concepts, describing the major philosophies of marketing thinking and practice, and discussing some of the major new challenges that marketers now face.

TABLE 1-1 *Three Functions Required in All Organizations and Sample Decisions Made by People Working in These Functional Areas*

Organization	Marketing	Operations	Finance/Accounting
Nike	Develop relationships with new distributors. Manage distributor incentive program. Prepare sales forecast for new product launch. Work with operations on production schedules. Determine prices for new product line. Work with advertising agency on new promotional materials.	Oversee building of new offshore plant. Improve efficiency of basketball-shoe line. Work with marketing to develop production schedules for new product line. Develop specifications for suppliers of materials for new product line.	Develop financing package for new plant. Review supplier payment program to determine if changes required for new supplier. Prepare budgets, and proforma cash flow statements for new product line. Develop repurchase plan stock buyback.

MARKETING DEFINED

Many people think of marketing only as selling and advertising. And no wonder—every day we are bombarded with television commercials, newspaper ads, direct mail, and sales calls. However, selling and advertising are only the tip of the marketing iceberg. Table 1-1 shows that marketing is one of three key core functions that are central to all organizations. Marketers act as the customers' voice within the firm and marketers are responsible for many more decisions than just advertising or sales. They analyse industries to identify emerging trends. They determine which national and international markets to enter or exit. They conduct research to understand consumer behaviour and use this information to divide markets into the groups that the firm can best serve with its products and services. They design integrated marketing mixes—products, prices, channels of distribution, and promotion programs. No matter what the decision, however, marketers always focus on *satisfying customer needs*.

The above paragraph describes what marketers *do*. But what does the term marketing *mean*? We define **marketing** as a social and managerial process by which individuals and groups obtain what they need and want through creating and exchanging products and value with others. To explain this definition, we examine the following important terms: *needs, wants, and demands; products; value, satisfaction, and quality; exchange, transactions, and relationships;* and *markets*. Figure 1-1 shows that these core marketing concepts are linked, with each concept building on the one before it.

Marketing
A social and managerial process by which individuals and groups obtain what they need and want through creating and exchanging products and value with others.

NEEDS, WANTS, AND DEMANDS

The most basic concept underlying marketing is that of human needs. Human **needs** are states of felt deprivation. Humans have many complex needs. These include basic *physical* needs for food, clothing, warmth, and safety; *social* needs for belonging and affection; and *individual* needs for knowledge and self-expression. These needs are not invented by marketers; they are a basic part of the human composition.

Needs
States of felt deprivation.

Wants are the form taken by human needs as they are shaped by culture and individual personality. A hungry person in Canada may want a hamburger, french fries, and a pop. A hungry person in Bali may want mangoes, suckling pig, and beans. Wants are described in terms of objects that will satisfy needs.

Wants
The form taken by human needs as they are shaped by culture and individual personality.

People have almost unlimited wants but limited resources. Thus, they want to choose products that provide the most value and satisfaction for their money.

FIGURE 1-1   *Core marketing concepts*

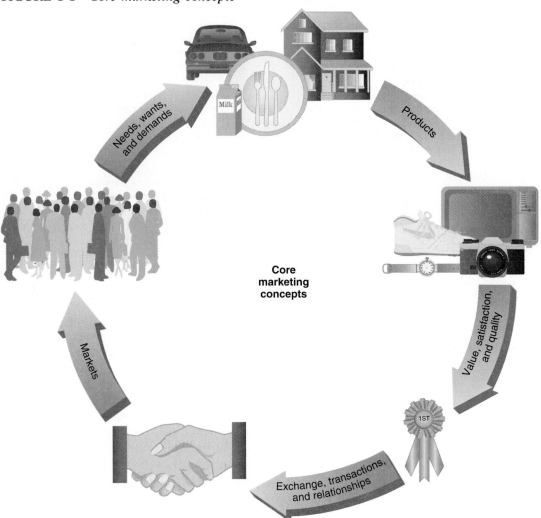

Demands
Human wants that are
backed by buying power.

When backed by buying power, wants become **demands.** Consumers view products as bundles of benefits and choose products that give them the best bundle for their money. Thus, one consumer in the market for a car will buy a Honda Civic since it satisfies the need for reliable transportation and fuel economy and it is within his or her limited budget. Another will purchase a Mercedes-Benz since he or she values and can afford its comfort, luxury, and status.

Outstanding marketing companies go to great lengths to learn about and understand their customers' needs, wants, and demands. They conduct consumer research, focus groups, and customer clinics. They analyse customer complaint, inquiry, warranty, and service data. They train salespeople to watch for unfulfilled customer needs. They observe customers using their own and competing products, and interview them in depth about their likes and dislikes.[3] Understanding customer needs, wants, and demands in detail provides important input for designing marketing strategies (see Marketing Highlight 1-1).

In these outstanding companies, people at all levels—including top management—stay close to customers in an ongoing effort to understand their needs and wants. For example, top executives from Wal-Mart spend two days each week visiting stores and mingling with customers. At Marriott International Inc., chairman of the board and president Bill Marriott personally reads 10 percent of the

UNDERSTANDING CONSUMER NEEDS AND WANTS

No one knows better than Mom, right? But does she know how much underwear you own? Jockey International does. Or the number of ice cubes you put in a glass? Coca-Cola knows that one. Or which pretzels you usually eat first—the broken ones or the whole ones? Try asking Frito-Lay. Big companies know the whats, wheres, hows, and whens of their consumers' needs, wants, and demands. They figure out all sorts of things about us that we don't even know ourselves. To marketers, this isn't trivial pursuit—knowing all about customer needs is the cornerstone of effective marketing. Most companies research us in detail and amass mountains of facts.

Coca-Cola knows that we put 3.2 ice cubes in a glass, see 69 of its commercials every year, and prefer cans out of vending machines to be at a temperature of 2°C. Did you know that 38 percent of North Americans would rather have a tooth pulled than take their car to a dealership for repairs? For every 10 000 Canadians in 1992, there were 8.13 automated teller machines, while there were only 5.26 for every 10 000 Americans and 3.36 for every 10 000 Germans, according to the Canadian Bankers Association. An Angus Reid poll of Canadian men found that 86 percent believed women spent more time in the bathroom, and that this extra time equalled four minutes. Lever

Brothers Co. uncovered the fact that 79 percent of women said they didn't trust their husbands to do the laundry. A group called Tidy Britain did a 10-year survey that uncovered that 33 percent of the litter that washed up on Britain's shores originated in Canada. When male readers were surveyed by the Quebec business monthly, *Affaires Plus*, 77.6 percent said their families were their top priority, but only 6.8 percent would make a sacrifice in their career to improve their family life. If you send a husband and a wife to the store separately to buy beer, there is a 90 percent chance they will return with different brands.

Nothing about our behaviour is sacred. Procter & Gamble once conducted a study to find out whether most of us fold or crumple our toilet paper; another study showed that 68 percent of consumers prefer their toilet paper to unwind over the spool rather than under. Abbott Laboratories figured out that one in four of us has "problem" dandruff, and Kimberly Clark, which makes Kleenex, has calculated that the average person blows his or her nose 256 times a year.

People aren't easy to figure out, however. A few years ago, Campbell Soup gave up trying to learn our opinions about the ideal-sized meatball after a series of tests showed that we prefer one so big it wouldn't fit in the can.

Of all businesses, however, the prize for research thoroughness may go to toothpaste makers. Among other things, they know that our favourite toothbrush colour is blue and that only 37 percent of us are using one that's more than six months old. About 47 percent of us put water on our brush before we apply the paste, 15 percent put water on after the paste, 24 percent do both, and 14 percent don't wet the brush at all.

Thus, most big marketing companies have answers to all the what, where, when, and how questions about their consumer demand. Seemingly trivial facts add up quickly and provide important input for designing marketing strategies. But to influence demand, marketers need the answer to one more question: Beyond knowing the whats and wherefores of demand, they need to know the *whys*—what *causes* us to want the things we buy? That's a much harder question to answer.

Sources: John Koten, "You Aren't Paranoid If You Feel Someone Eyes You Constantly," *Wall Street Journal,* March 29, 1985, pp. 1, 22; "Offbeat Marketing," *Sales & Marketing Management,* January 1990, p. 35; and Warren Clements, "Spectrum: Statistical Lore for Everyday Living," *Report on Business*, July 1993, p. 160; July 1994, p. 164; February 1995, p. 92; January 1995, p. 112, January 1996, p. 116.

Patriot Computer Corporation
www.patriot.com/

Product
Anything that can be offered to a market for attention, acquisition, use, or consumption that might satisfy a want or need. It includes physical objects, services, persons, places, organizations, and ideas.

8000 letters and two percent of the 750 000 guest comment cards submitted by customers each year. And at Markham, Ontario-based Patriot Computer Corporation, quality, service, and competitive pricing have made the company the leading Canadian-owned computer manufacturer. Every Patriot executive and worker is devoted to creating high-quality products. The company's customer research has shown that building consistent quality into their computers is the key to success and customer satisfaction. Higher quality means fewer returns, fewer computers that are "dead on arrival," and fewer service calls. This strategy has propelled Patriot from a company consisting of its three founders and a secretary to one employing over 250 people.[4] All in all, understanding customer needs, wants, and demands in detail provides important input for designing marketing strategies.

PRODUCTS AND SERVICES

People satisfy their needs and wants with products and services. A **product** is anything that can be offered to a market to satisfy a need or want. The concept of

Patriot is the leading Canadian-owned computer manufacturer and employs 250 people.

Purolator
www.purolator.com

Canada Post
www.mailposte.ca

Products do not have to be physical objects. In this ad, the "product" is tennis. "Imagine six hours of classes, one after another, interrupted only by a couple of fish sticks . . . Introduce your kids to tennis."

product is not limited to physical objects—anything capable of satisfying a need can be called a product. In addition to tangible goods, products also include **services**, which are activities or benefits offered for sale that are essentially intangible and do not result in the ownership of anything. Examples include banking, airline, and home repair services. Thus, broadly defined, products include entities such as *persons, places, organizations, activities,* and *ideas.* Consumers decide which entertainers to watch on television, which places to visit on vacation, which organizations to support through contributions, and which ideas to adopt. To the consumer, these are all products.

Many sellers make the mistake of focusing more on the physical products they offer than on the benefits produced by these products. They see themselves as selling a product rather than providing a solution to a need. A manufacturer of drill bits may think that the customer needs a drill bit, but what the customer *really* needs is a hole. These sellers may suffer from "marketing myopia."[5] They are so taken with their products that they focus only on existing wants and lose sight of underlying customer needs. They forget that a physical product is only a tool to solve a consumer problem. These sellers have trouble if a new product comes along that serves the need better or less expensively. The customer with the same *need* will *want* the new product.

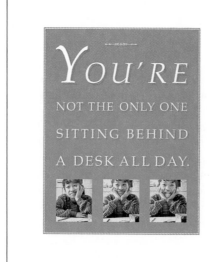

YOU'RE
NOT THE ONLY ONE
SITTING BEHIND
A DESK ALL DAY.

VALUE, SATISFACTION, AND QUALITY

Customer value
The difference between the values the customer gains from owning and using a product and the costs of obtaining the product.

Customer satisfaction
The extent to which a product's perceived performance matches a buyer's expectations.

Total quality management (TQM)
Programs designed to constantly improve the quality of products, services, and marketing processes.

Bell Advantage has focused its marketing efforts on those customers who define quality as highly reliable service under all circumstances.

Consumers usually face a broad array of products and services that might satisfy a given need. How do they choose among these many products and services? Consumers make buying choices based on their perceptions of the value that various products and services deliver.

Customer value is the difference between the values the customer gains from owning and using a product and the costs of obtaining the product. For example, Purolator customers gain a number of benefits. The most obvious are fast and reliable package delivery. However, when using Purolator, customers also may receive some status and image values. Using Purolator usually makes both the package sender and the receiver feel more important. When deciding whether to send a package via Purolator, customers will weigh these and other values against the money, effort, and psychic costs of using the service. Moreover, they will compare the value of using Purolator against the value of using other shippers—UPS, Federal Express, Canada Post—and select the one that gives them the greatest delivered value.

Customers often do not judge product values and costs accurately or objectively. They act on *perceived* value. For example, does Purolator really provide faster, more reliable delivery? If so, is this better service worth the higher prices that Purolator charges? Canada Post argues that its express service is comparable, and its prices are much lower. However, judging by the increasing number of people using courier services and fax machines, many consumers doubt these claims. The challenge faced by Canada Post, therefore, is to change these customer value perceptions.

Customer satisfaction depends on a product's perceived performance in delivering value relative to a buyer's expectations. If the product's performance falls short of the customer's expectations, the buyer is dissatisfied. If performance matches expectations, the buyer is satisfied. If performance exceeds expectations, the buyer is delighted. Outstanding marketing companies go out of their way to keep their customers satisfied. Satisfied customers make repeat purchases, and they tell others about their good experiences with the product. The key is to match customer expectations with company performance. Smart companies aim to *delight* customers by promising only what they can deliver, then delivering *more* than they promise.

Customer satisfaction is closely linked to quality. In recent years, many companies have adopted **total quality management (TQM)** programs, designed to constantly improve the quality of their products, services, and marketing processes. Quality has a direct impact on product performance, and hence on customer satisfaction.

In the narrowest sense, quality can be defined as "freedom from defects." But most customer-centred companies go beyond this narrow definition of quality. Instead, they define quality in terms of customer satisfaction. Bell Advantage realized that quality of phone service is defined in terms of reliability—under even the most extraordinary circumstances. Recent advertisements for their Advantage service state that even in the case of a disaster such as a fire, Bell will re-route calls to a business in only five minutes. Motorola, a company that pioneered total quality efforts in the United States, believes that "Quality has to do something for the customer. . . . Our definition of a

Thanks to the fire department, no lives were lost.
Thanks to *Advantage 800*™ service, no business was lost.

The reliability of our *Advantage 800* service is unquestioned. But even though over 99.99% of all calls through our long distance network get delivered to their destinations, that doesn't do you much good if the destination – your business – has suffered through a fire or natural disaster or even just a breakdown of your office network.

Have all your calls re-routed in only 5 minutes. That's why, for a one-time setup fee, *Advantage 800* service offers the option of having all the calls into your 800 number re-routed to another, pre-arranged number within 5 minutes of your calling us. That number can be another office, another business, or even your home.

See what we can do for your business. Five minute call re-routing is only one of the things that distinguish *Advantage 800* from any other 800 service. We can offer you numerous other ways to increase efficiency and profitability, and they're all as close as a phone call. Just call 1-800-889-6542, and an *Advantage* rep will give you all the details.

Bell *Advantage 800* service. Everything in business should be this reliable.

Bell ADVANTAGE

1-800-889-6542

defect is 'if the customer doesn't like it, it's a defect.'"[6] These customer-focused definitions suggest that a company has achieved total quality only when its products or services meet or exceed customer expectations. Thus, the fundamental aim of today's *total quality* movement has become *total customer satisfaction*. We will examine customer satisfaction, value, and quality more fully in Chapter 18.

EXCHANGE, TRANSACTIONS, AND RELATIONSHIPS

Exchange
The act of obtaining a desired object from someone by offering something in return.

Transaction
A trade between two parties that involves at least two things of value, agreed-upon conditions, a time of agreement, and a place of agreement.

Relationship marketing
The process of creating, maintaining, and enhancing strong, value-laden relationships with customers and other stakeholders.

Marketing occurs when people decide to satisfy needs and wants through exchange. **Exchange** is the act of obtaining a desired object from someone by offering something in return. Exchange is only one of many ways people can obtain a desired object. For example, hungry people can find food by hunting, fishing, or gathering fruit. They could beg for food or take food from someone else. Or they could offer money, another good, or a service in return for food.

As a means of satisfying needs, exchange has much in its favour. People do not have to prey on others or depend on donations. Nor must they possess the skills to produce every necessity for themselves. They can concentrate on making things they are good at making and trade them for needed items made by others. Thus, exchange allows a society to produce much more than it would with any alternative system.

Whereas exchange is the core concept of marketing, a transaction is marketing's unit of measurement. A **transaction** consists of a trade of values between two parties. In a transaction, we must be able to say that one party gives X to another party and gets Y in return. For example, you pay Sears $350 for a television set. This is a classic *monetary transaction*, but not all transactions involve money. In a *barter transaction*, you might trade your old refrigerator in return for a neighbour's second-hand television set.

In the broadest sense, the marketer tries to bring about a response to some offer. The response may be more than simply "buying" or "trading" goods and services. A political candidate, for instance, wants a response called "votes," a church wants "membership," and a social-action group wants "idea acceptance." Marketing consists of actions taken to obtain a desired response from a target audience toward some product, service, idea, or other object.

Rather than focusing on single, one-time transactions with multiple consumers, more and more firms are working to develop long-term relationships with key customers. By delivering the products, services, and prices that most closely match selected customer needs, companies foster long-term customer loyalty. In other words, customers become committed to a company or its brands and repeatedly transact with the same marketer or purchase the same brand of product or service. Repeated transactions are only part of the relationship, however. Forward-thinking marketers encourage their customers to become actively involved in company decisions. The business is viewed as a partnership between a firm and its customers in which both parties derive mutual benefit.[7] This is what is known as relationship marketing. Marketers who retain customers and form a relationship with them get to know customer needs better. They can tailor their products and structure the

Relationship marketing: To get to know customers better, Ford invites them to brainstorming sessions.

systems within their firms so that customer needs are even more precisely met. In this way, relationship marketers strengthen the company/customer bond.

Building relationships with customers is important but it is only one facet of relationship marketing. Ultimately, a company wants to build a unique company asset called a marketing network. A *marketing network* consists of the company and all of its supporting stakeholders: customers, employees, suppliers, distributors, retailers, advertising agencies, and others with whom it has built mutually profitable business relationships. Increasingly, competition is not between companies but rather between whole networks, with the prize going to the company that has built the better network. The operating principle is simple: Build a good network of relationships with key stakeholders, and profits will follow.[8]

MARKETS

Market
The set of all actual and potential buyers of a product or service.

The concept of exchange leads to the concept of a market. A **market** is the set of actual and potential buyers of a product. These buyers share a particular need or want that can be satisfied through exchange. Thus, the size of a market depends on the number of people who exhibit the need, have resources to engage in exchange, and are willing to offer these resources in exchange for what they want.

Originally the term *market* stood for the place where buyers and sellers gathered to exchange their goods, such as a village square. Economists use the term *market* to refer to a collection of buyers and sellers who transact in a particular product class, as in the housing market or the grain market. Marketers, however, see the sellers as constituting an industry and the buyers as constituting a market. The relationship between the *industry* and the *market* is shown in Figure 1-2. Sellers and the buyers are connected by four flows. The sellers send products, services, and communications to the market; in return, they receive money and information. The inner loop shows an exchange of money for goods; the outer loop shows an exchange of information.

FIGURE 1-2 *A simple marketing system*

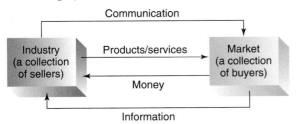

Modern economies operate on the principle of division of labour, where each person specializes in producing something, receives payment, and buys needed things with this money. Thus, modern economies abound in markets. Producers go to resource markets (raw-material markets, labour markets, money markets), buy resources, turn them into goods and services, and sell them to intermediaries, who sell them to consumers. The consumers sell their labour, for which they receive income to pay for the goods and services they buy. The government is another market that plays several roles. It buys goods from resource, producer, and intermediary markets; it pays them; it taxes these markets (including consumer markets); and it returns needed public services. Thus, each nation's economy and the whole world's economy consist of complex interacting sets of markets that are linked through exchange processes.

Marketers are keenly interested in markets. Their goal is to understand the needs and wants of specific markets and to select the markets that they can serve best. In turn, they can develop products and services that will create value and satisfaction for customers in these markets, resulting in sales and profits for the company.

MARKETING

The concept of markets finally brings us full circle to the concept of marketing. Marketing means managing markets to bring about exchanges for the purpose of satisfying human needs and wants. Thus, we return to our definition of marketing

FIGURE 1-3 *Main actors and forces in a modern marketing system*

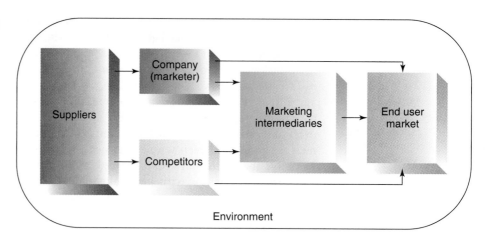

as a process by which individuals and groups obtain what they need and want by creating and exchanging products and value with others.

Exchange processes involve work. Sellers must search for buyers, identify their needs, design good products and services, set prices for them, promote them, and store and deliver them. Activities such as product development, research, communication, distribution, pricing, and service are core marketing activities. Although we normally think of marketing as being carried on by sellers, buyers also carry on marketing activities. Consumers do "marketing" when they search for the goods they need at prices they can afford. Company purchasing agents do "marketing" when they track down sellers and bargain for good terms.

Figure 1-3 shows the main elements in a modern marketing system. In the usual situation, marketing involves serving a market of end users in the face of competitors. The company and the competitors send their respective products and messages directly to consumers or through marketing intermediaries to the end users. All of the actors in the system are affected by major environmental forces (demographic, economic, physical, technological, political/legal, social/cultural).

Each party in the system adds value for the next level. Thus, a company's success depends not only on its own actions, but also on how well the entire value chain serves the needs of final consumers. Zellers cannot fulfil its promise "The lowest price is the law!" unless its suppliers provide merchandise at low costs. And Ford cannot deliver high quality to car buyers unless its dealers provide outstanding service.

MARKETING MANAGEMENT

Marketing management
The analysis, planning, implementation, and control of programs designed to create, build, and maintain beneficial exchanges with target buyers for the purpose of achieving organizational objectives.

We define **marketing management** as the analysis, planning, implementation, and control of programs designed to create, build, and maintain beneficial exchanges with target buyers for the purpose of achieving organizational objectives. Thus, marketing management involves managing demand, which in turn involves managing customer relationships.

DEMAND MANAGEMENT

Most people think of marketing management as finding enough customers for the company's current output, but this is too limited a view. The organization has a desired level of demand for its products. At any point in time, there may be no demand, adequate demand, irregular demand, or too much demand, and marketing management must find ways to deal with these different demand states. Marketing management is concerned not only with finding and increasing demand, but also with changing or even reducing it.

For example, Banff National Park is badly overcrowded in the summer. And power companies, such as Ontario Hydro, sometimes have trouble meeting demand during peak usage periods. In these and other cases of excess demand, the needed marketing task, called **demarketing**, is to reduce demand temporarily or permanently.[9] The aim of demarketing is not to destroy demand, but only to reduce or shift it. Thus, marketing management seeks to affect the level, timing, and nature of demand in a way that helps the organization achieve its objectives. Simply put, marketing management is *demand management*.

Demarketing
Marketing to reduce demand temporarily or permanently— the aim is not to destroy demand, but only to reduce or shift it.

BUILDING PROFITABLE CUSTOMER RELATIONSHIPS

Managing demand means understanding and working with customers. A company's demand comes from two groups: new customers and repeat customers. Traditional marketing theory and practice have focused on attracting new customers and making the sale. Today, however, the emphasis is shifting. Beyond designing strategies to *attract* new customers and create *transactions* with them, companies now are striving to *retain* current customers and build lasting customer *relationships*.

Why the new emphasis on keeping customers? In the past, companies facing an expanding economy and rapidly growing markets could practise the "leaky-bucket" approach to marketing. Growing markets meant a plentiful supply of new customers. Companies could keep filling the marketing bucket with new customers without worrying about losing old customers through the holes in the bottom of the bucket. However, companies today are facing some new marketing realities. Changing demographics, a slow-growth economy, more sophisticated competitors, and overcapacity in many industries—all of these factors mean that there are fewer new customers to go around. Many companies now are fighting for shares of flat or fading markets. Thus, the costs of attracting new customers are rising. In fact, it costs five times as much to attract a new customer as it does to keep an existing customer satisfied.[10]

Companies are also realizing that losing a customer means more than losing a single sale—it means losing the entire stream of purchases that the customer would make over a lifetime of business. For example, the *customer lifetime value* of a Taco Bell customer exceeds $16 000.[11] For General Motors or Ford, the customer lifetime value of a customer might well exceed $470 000. Thus, working to retain customers makes good economic sense. A company can lose money on a specific transaction, but still benefit greatly from a long-term relationship.

Attracting new customers remains an important marketing management task. However, the focus today is shifting toward retaining current customers and building profitable, long-term relationships with them. The key to customer retention is superior customer value and satisfaction. With this in mind, many companies are going to extremes to keep their customers satisfied. (See Marketing Highlight 1-2.)

MARKETING MANAGEMENT PHILOSOPHIES

The role that marketing plays within a company varies according to the overall strategy and philosophy of each firm. While some firms place a primary emphasis on tailoring their products and services to meet customers' needs, others focus on improving production efficiency of existing products. Some firms have mixed management philosophies, which can result in conflicts about the roles of the

CUSTOMER RELATIONSHIPS: KEEPING CUSTOMERS SATISFIED

Some companies go to extremes to coddle their customers. Consider the following examples:

◆ Although Speedy Muffler King Inc., a Toronto-based worldwide company, changes its advertisements depending on the country in which the outlet is located, it never changes its business philosophy, "Treat customers with respect, fix their cars fast, and do it properly." To build customer trust and demystify car repair, Speedy technicians carefully explain what needs fixing and what doesn't. Customers are welcome to watch the work being done. And so that individual owner-managers can effectively monitor both service demands and customer relationships, Speedy restricts its outlets to eight service bays, whereas competitors may have 20 or more. These practices have resulted in 90 percent of Speedy's customers being very satisfied with the service.

◆ Ted Abbott, president of James Ross Limited, a small manufacturing firm located in Brockville, Ontario that sells equipment to paper mills, personally calls customers if they have any complaints about his firm's products or services. He believes that customers want immediate and fair solutions if they experience problems. He notes that customers are frequently surprised that he is personally concerned about their complaints. This concern with customer satisfaction has helped this small firm take on a much larger global competitor both in Canada and worldwide.

◆ A frustrated homeowner faces a difficult and potentially costly home plumbing repair. He visits the nearby Home Depot store, prowls the aisles, and picks up an armful of parts and supplies— $67 worth in all—that he thinks he'll need to do the job. However, before he gets to the checkout counter, a salesperson heads him off and, after some coaxing, finally convinces him that there's a simpler solution to his repair problem. The cost: $5.99 and a lot less trouble.

From a dollars-and-cents point of view, these examples sound like a crazy way to do business. How can you make money by giving away your products, or talking your customers into paying less? Yet studies show that going to such extremes to keep customers happy—though costly—goes hand in hand with good financial performance. Satisfied customers come back again and again. Thus, in today's highly competitive marketplace, companies can well afford to lose money on one transaction if it helps to cement a profitable long-term customer relationship.

Keeping customers satisfied involves more than simply opening a complaint department, smiling a lot, and being nice. Companies that do the best job of taking care of customers set high customer service standards and often make seemingly outlandish efforts to achieve them. At these companies, exceptional value and service are more than a set of policies or actions—they are a company-wide attitude, an important part of the overall company culture. Concern for the consumer becomes a matter of pride for everyone in the company. Four

Seasons Hotels, long known for its outstanding service, tells its employees the story of Ron Dyment, a porter in Toronto who forgot to load a departing guest's briefcase in his taxi. Dymont called the guest, a lawyer in Washington, DC, and learned that he desperately needed the briefcase for a meeting the following morning. Without first asking for management approval, Dyment hopped on a plane and returned the briefcase. The company named Dyment Employee of the Year. Similarly, the Nordstrom department store chain thrives on stories about its service heroics, such as employees dropping off orders at customers' homes or warming up cars while customers spend a little more time shopping. There's even a story about a customer who got a refund on a tire— Nordstrom doesn't carry tires, but it prides itself on a no-questions-asked return policy!

There's no simple formula for taking care of customers, but neither is it a mystery. According to the president of L. L. Bean, "A lot of people have fancy things to say about customer service . . . but it's just a day-in, day-out, ongoing, never-ending, unremitting, persevering, compassionate type of activity." For the companies that do it well, it's also very rewarding.

Sources: Bill Kelley, "Five Companies That Do It Right—And Make It Pay," *Sales & Marketing Management,* April 1988, pp. 57–64; Timothy Pritchard, "Exhaustive Management," *Globe and Mail,* June 1994, pp. B1, B5; Richard S. Teitelbaum, "Keeping Promises," *Fortune,* special issue on "The Tough New Consumer," Autumn/Winter 1993, pp. 32–33; and Patricia Sellers, "Companies That Serve You Best," *Fortune,* May 31, 1993, pp. 74–88; www.speedy.com

different functional areas (marketing, production, research and development, and so on) within the firm.

There are five alternative concepts under which organizations conduct their marketing activities: the *production, product, selling, marketing,* and *societal marketing* concepts.

Production concept
The philosophy that consumers will favour products that are available and highly affordable and that management should therefore focus on improving production and distribution efficiency.

THE PRODUCTION CONCEPT

The **production concept** holds that consumers will favour products that are available and highly affordable. Therefore, management should focus on improving production and distribution efficiency. This concept is one of the oldest philosophies that guides sellers.

The production concept is still a useful philosophy in two situations. The first occurs when the demand for a product exceeds the supply. Here, management should look for ways to increase production. The second situation occurs when the product's cost is too high and improved productivity is needed to bring it down. To its dismay, Ottawa's Corel Corporation found that a production orientation doesn't automatically lead to success. Instead, production capabilities must match increased demand. In 1996, Corel acquired WordPerfect as a means of entering the office suite and word processing markets. The company believed that it could use the efficient, low-cost production technologies it had learned with the production of its initial product, CorelDRAW!, to bring down prices in the office suites market and take away market share from its giant rival, Microsoft, in the retail and corporate markets in Canada and the United States. Corel announced its strategy with a huge advertising blitz. Although many customers found the offer attractive, Corel's strategy failed when its production capabilities could not meet the new levels of demand. Many orders were shipped late, alienating both customers and distributors.[12]

Corel Corporation
www.corel.com/

THE PRODUCT CONCEPT

Product concept
The philosophy that consumers will favour products that offer the most quality, performance, and innovative features.

Some managers define their business by the products they sell, rather than by the problem that the customer uses the product to solve. The **product concept** holds that consumers will favour products that offer the most quality, performance, and innovative features. Thus, an organization should devote energy to making continuous product improvements. Many high-tech firms have fallen into this trap, believing that if they can build a better mousetrap, the world will beat a path to their door.[13] But they are often rudely shocked. Buyers may well be looking for a better solution to a mouse problem, but not necessarily for a better mousetrap. The solution might be a chemical spray, an exterminating service, or something that works better than a mousetrap. Furthermore, a better mousetrap will not sell unless the manufacturer designs, packages, and prices it attractively; places it in convenient distribution channels; brings it to the attention of people who need it; and convinces buyers that it is a better product.

The product concept also can lead to "marketing myopia." For instance, railway management once thought that users wanted *trains* rather than *transportation* and overlooked the growing challenge of airlines, buses, trucks, and cars. Many universities have assumed that high school graduates want a liberal arts education and have thus overlooked the increasing challenge of vocational colleges.

THE SELLING CONCEPT

Selling concept
The idea that consumers will not buy enough of the organization's products unless the organization undertakes a large-scale selling and promotion effort.

Many organizations follow the **selling concept**, which holds that consumers will not buy enough of the organization's products unless it undertakes a large-scale selling and promotion effort. The concept is typically practised with *unsought goods*—those that buyers do not normally think of buying, such as encyclopedias or insurance. These industries must be good at tracking down prospects and selling them on product benefits.

Most firms practise the selling concept when they have overcapacity. Their aim is to sell what they make rather than make what the market wants. Thus, marketing based on hard selling carries high risks. It focuses on creating sales transactions rather than on building long-term, profitable relationships with customers. It assumes that customers who are coaxed into buying the product will like it. Or, if they don't like it, they will possibly forget their disappointment and buy it again later. These are usually poor assumptions to make about buyers. Most studies show that dissatisfied customers do not buy again. Worse yet, while the average satisfied customer tells three others about good experiences, the average dissatisfied customer tells 10 others his or her bad experiences.[14]

THE MARKETING CONCEPT

Marketing concept
The marketing management philosophy that holds that achieving organizational goals depends on determining the needs and wants of target markets and delivering the desired satisfactions more effectively and efficiently than competitors do.

The **marketing concept** holds that achieving organizational goals depends on determining the needs and wants of target markets and delivering the desired satisfactions more effectively and efficiently than competitors do. The marketing concept has been stated in colourful ways such as "We make it happen for you" (Marriott); "Reliability is our service" (CanPar); "To fly, to serve" (British Airways), and "We're not satisfied until you are" (GE). J.C. Penney's motto also summarizes the marketing concept: "To do all in our power to pack the customer's dollar full of value, quality, and satisfaction."

The selling concept and the marketing concept are sometimes confused. Figure 1-4 compares the two concepts. The selling concept takes an *inside-out* perspective. It starts with the factory, focuses on the company's existing products, and calls for heavy selling and promotion to obtain profitable sales. It focuses heavily on customer conquest—getting short-term sales with little concern about who buys or why. In contrast, the marketing concept takes an *outside-in* perspective. It starts with a well-defined market, focuses on customer needs, co-ordinates all the marketing activities affecting customers, and makes profits by creating long-term customer relationships based on customer value and satisfaction. Under the marketing concept, companies produce what consumers want, thereby satisfying consumers and making profits.[15]

FIGURE 1-4 *The selling and marketing concepts contrasted*

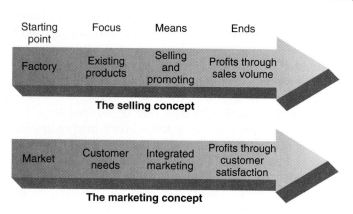

Many successful and well-known companies have adopted the marketing concept. Procter & Gamble, Disney, Corel, Bombardier, and Mountain Equipment Co-Op follow it faithfully. L.L. Bean, the highly successful catalogue retailer of clothing and outdoor sporting equipment, was founded on the marketing concept. In 1912, in his first circulars, L.L. Bean included the following notice: "I do not consider a sale complete until goods are worn out and the customer still is satisfied. We will thank anyone to return goods that are not perfectly satisfactory. . . . Above all things we wish to avoid having a dissatisfied customer."

Today, L.L. Bean dedicates itself to giving "perfect satisfaction in every way." For example, it recently revised its catalogues to make it easier for Canadian customers to place their orders. To inspire its employees to practise the marketing concept, L.L. Bean displays posters around its offices that proclaim the following:

> What is a customer? A customer is the most important person ever in this company—in person or by mail. A customer is not dependent on us, we are dependent on him [or her]. A customer is not an interruption of our work, he [or she] is the purpose of it. We are not doing a favor by serving him [or her], he [or she] is doing us a favor by giving us the opportunity to do so. A customer is not someone to argue or match wits with—nobody ever won an argument with a customer. A customer is a person who brings us his [or her] wants—it is our job to handle them profitably to him [or her] and to ourselves.

In contrast, many companies claim to practise the marketing concept, but do not. They have the *forms* of marketing, such as a marketing vice-president, product managers, marketing plans, and marketing research, but this does not mean that they are *market-focused* and *customer-driven* companies. The question is whether they are finely tuned to changing customer needs and competitor strategies. Formerly great companies—General Motors, IBM, Sears, Zenith—all lost substantial market share because they failed to adjust their marketing strategies to the changing marketplace.

Societal marketing concept
The idea that the organization should determine the needs, wants, and interests of target markets and deliver the desired satisfactions more effectively and efficiently than competitors in a way that maintains or improves the consumer's and society's well-being.

Johnson & Johnson
www.johnsonandjohnson.
com/home.html

Johnson & Johnson's concern for society is summarized in its credo and in the company's actions over the years. Says one J&J executive, "It's just plain good business."

Several years of hard work are needed to turn a sales-oriented company into a marketing-oriented company. The goal is to build customer satisfaction into the very fabric of the firm. Customer satisfaction is no longer a fad. As one marketing analyst notes: "It's becoming a way of life in corporate America . . . as embedded into corporate cultures as information technology and strategic planning."[16]

THE SOCIETAL MARKETING CONCEPT

The **societal marketing concept** holds that the organization should determine the needs, wants, and interests of target markets. It should then deliver superior value to customers in a way that maintains or improves the consumer's *and the society's* well-being. The societal marketing concept is the newest of the five marketing management philosophies. Companies embracing this concept include such firms as the Upper Canada Brewing Company, which has saved $20 000 per year by following the "3Rs" philosophy of Reduce, Recycle, and Reuse. The Royal Bank spearheads the "Imagine" campaign, a social marketing effort designed to encourage Canadian corporations to donate one percent of their pre-tax profits to charitable and social causes.

The societal marketing concept questions whether the pure marketing concept is adequate in an age of environmental problems, resource shortages, rapid population growth, worldwide economic problems, and neglected social services. It asks if the firm that senses, serves, and satisfies individual wants is always doing what's best for consumers and society in the long run. According to the societal marketing concept, the pure marketing concept overlooks possible conflicts between consumer *short-run wants* and consumer *long-run welfare*.

Our Credo

We believe our first responsibility is to the doctors, nurses and patients, to mothers and fathers and all others who use our products and services. In meeting their needs everything we do must be of high quality. We must constantly strive to reduce our costs in order to maintain reasonable prices. Customers' orders must be serviced promptly and accurately. Our suppliers and distributors must have an opportunity to make a fair profit.

We are responsible to our employees, the men and women who work with us throughout the world. Everyone must be considered as an individual. We must respect their dignity and recognize their merit. They must have a sense of security in their jobs. Compensation must be fair and adequate, and working conditions clean, orderly and safe. We must be mindful of ways to help our employees fulfill their family responsibilities. Employees must feel free to make suggestions and complaints. There must be equal opportunity for employment, development and advancement for those qualified. We must provide competent management, and their actions must be just and ethical.

We are responsible to the communities in which we live and work and to the world community as well. We must be good citizens — support good works and charities and bear our fair share of taxes. We must encourage civic improvements and better health and education. We must maintain in good order the property we are privileged to use, protecting the environment and natural resources.

Our final responsibility is to our stockholders. Business must make a sound profit. We must experiment with new ideas. Research must be carried on, innovative programs developed and mistakes paid for. New equipment must be purchased, new facilities provided and new products launched. Reserves must be created to provide for adverse times. When we operate according to these principles, the stockholders should realize a fair return.

Johnson & Johnson

Consider the fast-food industry. Most people view today's giant fast-food chains as offering tasty and convenient food at reasonable prices. Yet many consumer and environmental groups have voiced concerns. Critics point out that hamburgers, fried chicken, french fries, and most other fast foods sold are high in fat and salt. The convenient packaging leads to waste and pollution. Thus, in satisfying consumer wants, the highly successful fast-food chains may be harming consumer health and causing environmental problems.

Such concerns and conflicts led to the societal marketing concept. As Figure 1-5 shows, the societal marketing concept calls upon marketers to balance three considerations in setting their marketing policies: company profits, consumer wants, and society's interests. Originally, most companies based their marketing decisions largely on short-run company profit. Eventually, they began to recognize the long-run importance of satisfying consumer wants, and the marketing concept emerged. Now many companies are beginning to consider society's interests when making their marketing decisions.

One such company is Johnson & Johnson, rated recently in a *Fortune* magazine poll as America's most admired company for community and environmental responsibility. J&J's concern for societal interests is summarized in a company document called "Our Credo," which stresses honesty, integrity, and putting people before profits.[17]

FIGURE 1-5 *Three considerations underlying the societal marketing concept*

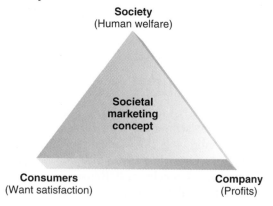

Society
(Human welfare)

Societal
marketing
concept

Consumers
(Want satisfaction)

Company
(Profits)

The company backs its commitment with actions. Consider the tragic tampering case in which eight people died from swallowing cyanide-laced capsules of Tylenol, a Johnson & Johnson brand. Although J&J believed that the pills had been altered in only a few stores, not in the factory, it quickly recalled all of its product. The recall cost the company $240 million in earnings. In the long run, however, the company's swift recall of Tylenol strengthened consumer confidence and loyalty, and Tylenol remains the leading brand of pain reliever in the United States. In this and other cases, J&J management has found that doing what's right benefits both consumers and the company. Imperial Oil is another company that firmly believes in "doing well by doing good." The firm has been one of Canada's leading corporate donors for over 80 years. It recently developed the Esso Kids Program, whereby the company supports over 200 activities, ranging from promoting childhood safety and injury prevention, to helping teenage parents raise their children, to funding post-secondary education, to supporting children's sporting activities such as swimming and hockey. Consumers have responded strongly to Imperial's efforts and the firm believes that giving consumers additional reasons to buy Esso products will help to build customer loyalty and relationships in an industry characterized by heavy brand-switching.[18]

MARKETING CHALLENGES INTO THE NEXT CENTURY

Marketing operates within a dynamic global environment. Every decade calls upon marketing managers to develop fresh new ideas about their marketing objectives and practices. Rapid changes can quickly outdate yesterday's winning strategies. As management thought-leader Peter Drucker once observed, a company's winning formula for the last decade will probably be its undoing in the next decade.

What are the marketing challenges as we head into the twenty-first century? Today's companies are wrestling with changing customer values and orientations, economic stagnation, environmental decline, increased global competition, and a host of other economic, political, and social problems. However, these problems

Queen's University International Study Centre
castle.isc.queensu.ca/ isc/welcome.html

"How do you market a castle?" Queen's University International Study Centre is using marketing to create awareness of its programs.

Religious orders such as Sisters of Charity are using marketing to overcome outdated stereotypes.

also provide marketing opportunities. We now look more deeply into several key trends and forces that are changing the marketing landscape and challenging marketing strategy: growth of non-profit marketing, rapid globalization, the changing world economy, and the call for more socially responsible actions.

GROWTH OF NON-PROFIT MARKETING

In the past, marketing has been most widely applied in the business sector. In recent years, however, marketing also has become a major component in the strategies of many non-profit organizations, such as universities, hospitals, museums, symphonies, and even churches. Consider the following examples:[19]

> In 1993, Alfred Bader made a generous donation to Queen's University: Herstmonceux Castle, which is located in Hailsham, East Sussex, England. The university faced the challenge of how to successfully market the international programs offered at the castle to students across Canada. The marketing team gathered data about which segments of students to target, and what types of promotional materials raise the greatest awareness of the programs. Queen's solution was to enter into a relationship with other universities and to open the programs to their students. Queen's initiated the Canadian University Study Abroad program with four partners: the University of British Columbia, University of Toronto, University of Western Ontario, and Dalhousie University.

Religious orders seeking to recruit priests and nuns believe that they are suffering from old stereotypes: A help wanted ad based on these sterotypes would read:

"Help Wanted: Stern, silent, joyless young people with strong knees to work in a dying profession. Must be chaste, sober, compliant and willing to make a commitment for life . . . Remuneration: Vow of poverty.[20]

To counteract these images, Les Rédemptoristes, a Catholic order from Quebec, developed an advertising campaign to demonstrate to its young target audience the dynamic and interesting possibilities of taking on the challenges of a religious life. The campaign ran a series of ads in college and university newspapers followed by the development of a web page (www.cssr.net). The second phase included an outdoor advertising campaign that placed ads on Montreal and Quebec city buses. The program was successful beyond the order's wildest dreams, generating more than 200 serious responses per year.[21]

Other non-profit marketing efforts involve partnerships between for-profit corporations and not-for-profit organizations. Some non-profits receive royalties, licensing fees, or increased donations in return for the use of their names and symbols. Corporations use the non-profits' brand marks to increase recognition of their products or the perceived value of their products. For example, the Heart and Stroke Foundation of Canada receives fees or support from a number of corporate sponsors including Becel margarine. The Children's Miracle Network (CMN), a non-profit organization that funds programs in Canadian children's hospitals, allows Heinz Canada to place the CMN logo on baby food jars and cereal boxes. Heinz calls this program Labels for Life. Parents are asked to save the labels and return them to any one of the 11 children's hospitals associated with the CMN.

Children's Miracle Network
www.cmncan.ca/

Heinz then donates 10 cents for every label submitted. In 1997 alone, 200 000 parents from across Canada sent in three million labels. The program has raised over $1 million to date for children's hospitals.

Even government agencies have shown an increased interest in marketing. Various government agencies are now designing *social marketing campaigns*. Health Canada has partnered with a number of private firms and agencies to discourage smoking, excessive drinking, and drug use. CBC Radio and the Toronto Transportation Corporation (TTC) have partnered with the National Gallery of Canada and the Ontario Gallery of Art to promote the *OH! Canada Project*, which showcases paintings by the Group of Seven. The continued growth of non-profit and public-sector marketing presents new and exciting challenges for marketing managers.

THE INFORMATION TECHNOLOGY BOOM

The explosive growth in computer, telecommunications, and information technology has had a major impact on the way companies bring value to their customers. The technology boom has created exciting new ways to learn about and track customers, create products and services tailored to meet customer needs, distribute products more efficiently and effectively, and communicate with customers in large groups or one-to-one. For example, through videoconferencing, marketing researchers at a company's headquarters in Calgary can monitor focus groups in Halifax or Paris without ever stepping on to a plane. With only a few clicks of a mouse button, a direct marketer can tap into online data services to learn anything from what car you drive to what you read to what flavour of ice cream you prefer.

Every 20 years since 1900, the amount of computer power that can be bought for one dollar has increased a thousand-fold. That's a million-fold increase in just the last 35 years.[23] Using today's vastly more powerful computers, marketers create detailed databases and use them to target individual customers with offers designed to meet their specific needs and buying patterns. With a new wave of communication and advertising tools—ranging from cellular phones, fax machines, and CD-ROMs to interactive TV and video kiosks at airports and shopping malls—marketers can focus on selected customers with carefully targeted messages. Through electronic commerce, customers can design, order, and pay for products and services—all without ever leaving home. From virtual-reality displays that test new products to online virtual stores that sell them, the boom in computer, telecommunication, and information technology is affecting every aspect of marketing.

The Internet

Internet
A vast and burgeoning global web of computer networks, with no central management or ownership.

Perhaps the most dramatic new technology surrounds the development of the Information Superhighway and its backbone, the Internet. The **Internet** is a vast and burgeoning global web of computer networks, with no central management or ownership. The Internet links computer users of all types around the world. Anyone with a PC and modem—or TV and set-top "Web box"—and the right software can browse the Internet to obtain or share information on almost any subject. They can interact with other users.[24] Companies are using the Internet to link employees in remote offices, distribute sales information more quickly, build closer relationships with customers and suppliers, and sell and distribute their products more efficiently and effectively.

Internet usage surged in the 1990s with the development of the user-friendly World Wide Web. More than 50 million people surf the Internet each month, up from just one million people in late 1994. There may be as many as four to six million web sites worldwide, and these numbers are growing explosively.[25] The advent of the World Wide Web has given companies access to millions of new customers at a fraction of the cost of print and television advertising. Companies of all types are now attempting to snare new customers in the Web. For example:

Next Stop South Pole
www2.bway.net/South
penguin/html-web_store.cgi

Carmakers such as Toyota (www.toyota.com) use the Internet to develop relationships with owners, as well as to sell cars. Toyota's site offers product information, dealer services and locations, leasing information, and much more. For example, visitors to the site can view any of seven lifestyle magazines—*alt.Terrain, A Man's Life, Women's Web Weekly, Sportzine, Living Arts, Living Home,* and *Car Culture*—designed to appeal to Toyota's well-educated, above-average-income target audience.

The Ty web site (www.ty.com) builds relationships with children who collect Beanie Babies by offering extra information, including the "birth date" of the 50-plus toys, highlights on special Beanie Babies each month, promotion of newly developed Beanie Babies, and even an honour-role section that includes a child's photo and grades. Is it effective? In less than a year, based on the counter on the site, ty.com received over 266 million visitors.

The very small retail chain Next Stop South Pole (NSSP) sells only penguin-related products—T-shirts, plush toys, porcelain reproductions, books, and others. A search for "penguins" on the Web yields Pete & Barb's Penguin Page ("the best source for information about penguins"), which contains a link to the NSSP Web site. The web site contains pages from the store's direct-mail catalogue and a link to its e-mail mailbox, where visitors can request the full printed catalogue. The Internet gives NSSP access to consumers around the world at very little cost.[26]

It seems that almost every business—from garage-based start-ups to established giants such as IBM, GE, and Canadian Airlines—is setting up shop on the Internet. All are racing to explore and exploit the Web's possibilities for marketing, shopping, and browsing for information. However, for all its potential, the Internet does have drawbacks. It's yet to be seen how many of the millions of Web surfers will become actual buyers. Although the value of a web site is difficult to measure, the reality is that few companies have made any money from their Internet efforts. And the Web poses security problems. Companies that link their internal computer networks to the outside world expose their systems to possible attacks by vandals. Similarly, consumers are wary about sending credit-card account numbers or other confidential information that may be intercepted in cyberspace and misused. Finally, using the Web can be costly. For companies to maximize the Internet, they must invest heavily in leased telephone lines, powerful computers and other technologies, and Internet specialists.

However, given the lightning speed at which Internet technology and applications are developing, it's unlikely that these drawbacks will deter the millions of businesses and consumers who are logging onto the Net each day. "Marketers aren't going to have a choice about being on Internet," says Midori Chan, vice president of creative services at Interse, which helped put Windham Hill Records and Digital Equipment Corp. on the Internet. "To not be on the Internet ... is going to be like not having a phone."[27] We will examine these online marketing developments more fully in Chapter 17.

RAPID GLOBALIZATION

The world economy has undergone radical change during the past two decades. Geographical and cultural distances have shrunk with the advent of jet planes, fax machines, global computer and telephone hookups, world television satellite broadcasts, and other technical advances. This has allowed companies to greatly expand their geographical market coverage, purchasing, and manufacturing. The result is a vastly more complex marketing environment, for both companies and consumers.

Today, almost every company, large or small, is touched in some way by global competition—from the neighbourhood florist that buys its flowers from Mexican nurseries, to the small Vancouver clothing retailer that sources its merchandise in Asia, to the Canadian electronics manufacturer competing in its home markets with giant Japanese rivals, to the large North American consumer goods producer introducing new products into emerging markets abroad.

Canadian firms have been challenged at home by the skilful marketing of European and Asian multinationals. Companies such as Toyota, Siemens, Nestlé, Sony, and Samsung often have outperformed their North American competitors. Similarly, Canadian companies in a wide range of industries have found new opportunities abroad. Labatt, Imperial Oil, Alcan, Bombardier, and dozens of other companies have developed truly global operations, making and selling their products worldwide. As a result of the efforts of such firms, Canada is now one of the world's leading exporters. It ranks seventh in the world in terms of export sales, which translates into $145 billion annually. Furthermore, Canadian export trade is forecast to increase as a result of the signing of the North American Free Trade Agreement (NAFTA), which formalized rules of trade among the United States, Canada, and Mexico. The United States, with its population of 270 million, is still Canada's primary trading partner. With the devaluation of the Canadian dollar, our exports to the United States have been burgeoning; however, trade with Mexico (with a population of 92 million) has stagnated due to Mexico's recent economic crisis and the devaluation of the peso. Marketing Highlight 1-3 provides an example of a company taking advantage of international marketing opportunities.

Today, companies are not only trying to sell more of their locally produced goods in international markets, they also are buying more components and supplies abroad. For example, Alfred Sung, a Canadian top fashion designer, may choose cloth woven from Australian wool with printed designs from Italy. He will design a dress and fax the drawing to a Hong Kong agent, who will place the order with a mainland China factory. Finished dresses will be airfreighted to New York and Montreal, where they will be redistributed to department and specialty stores.

Marketers used to believe that "country of origin" had a significant influence on the image that consumers formed of certain goods. For example, Canadian consumers in the early 1970s thought that automobiles originating in Japan were of low quality. Today, many goods and services are "hybrids," with design, material purchasing, manufacturing, and marketing occurring in several countries. Thus such "country-of-origin" assessments cannot be applied. Consider, for example, the recent film, *The Santa Clause*, starring Tim Allen. The movie was filmed in Oakville, Ontario, a small town just outside Toronto. Both Canadians and Americans worked on the production. The film was cut and edited in Hollywood, and then marketed worldwide.

Thus, managers in countries around the world are asking: Just what is global marketing? How does it differ from domestic marketing? How do global competitors and forces affect our business? To what extent should we "go global"? Many companies are forming strategic alliances with foreign companies, even competitors, who serve as suppliers or marketing partners. The past few years have produced some surprising alliances between competitors such as Ford and Mazda, General Electric and Matsushita, and AT&T and Unitel. Winning companies in the next century may well be those that have built the best global networks.[28]

THE CHANGING WORLD ECONOMY

A large part of the world has grown poorer during the past few decades. A sluggish world economy has resulted in more difficult times for both consumers and marketers. Around the world, people's needs are greater than ever, but in many areas, people lack the means to pay for needed goods. Markets, after all, consist of people with needs *and* purchasing power. In many cases, the latter is currently lacking. In North America, although wages have risen, real buying power has declined, especially for the less skilled members of the workforce. Many households

GOING GLOBAL: COCA-COLA DOMINATES

The Coca-Cola Company is certainly no stranger to global marketing. Long the world's leading soft-drink maker, the company now sells its brands in more than 200 countries. In fact, in recent years, as U.S. business continues to grow, Coca-Cola has revved up every aspect of its global marketing. The result: world leadership in the soft-drink business.

The great "global cola wars" between Coca-Cola and rival Pepsi have become decidedly one-sided. Coca-Cola now outsells Pepsi three to one overseas, and Coca-Cola boast four of the world's five leading soft-drink brands: Coca-Cola, Diet Coke, Sprite, and Fanta. Coca-Cola has handed Pepsi a number of crushing international soft-drink sales. During the same period, Coca-Cola has reported strong growth in Latin America and grew a stunning 29 percent in China, 17 percent in India, and 16 percent in the Philippines.

Pepsi is now retrenching its efforts abroad by focusing on emerging markets—China, India, and Indonesia—where Coke is growing but ample opportunities for growth still exist. Together, these three emerging markets boast 2.4 billion people, nearly half the world's total population. With their young populations, exploding incomes, and underdeveloped soft-drink demand, they represent prime potential for Coca-Cola and Pepsi. For example, China's 1.2 billion consumers drink an average of only five servings of soft drinks per year, compared with 343 in North America, creating heady opportunities for growth. And Indonesia, with 200 million people, nearly all of them Muslims forbidden to consume alcohol, is what former Coca-Cola Chairman and CEO Roberto Goizueta calls a "soft-drink paradise."

But even in these emerging markets, Pepsi will find the going rough in the face of Coca-Cola's international marketing savvy and heavy investment. For instance, by the turn of the century, Coca-Cola will have spent almost $2.8 billion building state-of-the-art Asian bottling plants and distribution systems. And Coca-Cola possesses proven marketing prowess. It carefully tailors

its ads and other marketing efforts for each local market. For example, its Chinese New Year television ad featured a dragon in a holiday parade, adorned from head to tail with red Coke cans. The spot concluded: "For many centuries, the colour red has been the colour for good luck and prosperity. Who are we to argue with ancient wisdom?" In India,

Coca-Cola's popularity is growing in China but it does not yet dominate Pepsi.

Coca-Cola aggressively cultivates a local image. It claimed official sponsorship for World Cup Cricket, a favourite national sport, and used Indian cricket fans rather than actors to promote Coke products. Coca-Cola markets effectively to both retailers and imbibers. Observes one Coke watcher, "The company hosts massive gatherings of up to 15 000 retailers to showcase everything from the latest coolers and refrigerators, which Coke has for loan, to advertising displays. And its salespeople go house-to-house in their

quest for new customers. In New Delhi alone, workers handed out more than 100 000 free bottles of Coke and Fanta last year."

Nothing better illustrates Coca-Cola's surging global power than the explosive growth of Sprite. Sprite's advertising uniformly targets the world's young people with the tagline: "Image is nothing. Thirst is everything. Obey your thirst." The campaign taps into the rebellious side of teenagers, and into their need to form individual identities. According to Sprite's director of brand marketing, "The meaning of [Sprite] and what we stand for is exactly the same globally. Teens tell us it's incredibly relevant in nearly every market we go into." However, as always, Coca-Cola tailors its message to local consumers. In China, for example, the campaign has a softer edge. "You can't be irreverent in China, because it's not acceptable in that society. It's all about being relevant [to the specific audience]," notes the marketer. As a result of such smart targeting and powerful positioning, Sprite's worldwide sales have surged 35 percent in the past three years, making it the world's number-four soft-drink brand.

Coca-Cola's success as a global power has made it one of the most enduringly profitable companies in history. How profitable has Coca-Cola been over the decades? Incredibly, a single share of Coca-Cola stock purchased for $56 in 1919 would be worth $6 785 800 today. As of December 31, 1997, the one share purchased at $40 in 1919 would be worth $6 581 189.

Sources: Quotations from Mark L. Clifford and Nicole Harris, "Coke Pours into Asia," *Business Week*, October 28, 1996, pp. 72–77; and Mark Gleason, "Sprite is Riding Global Ad Effort to No. 4 Status," *Advertising Age*, November 18, 1996, p. 30. Also see Lori Bongiorno, "Fiddling with the Formula at Pepsi," *Business Week*, October 14, 1996, p. 42; and Patricia Sellers, "Why Pepsi Needs to Become More Like Coke," *Fortune*, March 3, 1997, pp. 26–27; www.coca-cola.com; www.pepsi.com

Today's forward-thinking companies are responding to the ethics and environmental movements. Here, the Upper Canada Brewing Company advertises its commitment to waste reduction—demonstrating not only its environmental concerns but also the fact that these actions are economical.

have managed to maintain their buying power only because both spouses work. However, many workers have lost their jobs as manufacturers have "downsized" to cut costs.

Current economic conditions create both problems and opportunities for marketers. Some companies are facing declining demand and see few opportunities for growth. Others, however, are developing new solutions to changing consumer problems. Many are finding ways to offer consumers "more for less." Wal-Mart rose to market leadership on two principles, emblazoned on every Wal-Mart store: "Satisfaction Guaranteed" and "We Sell for Less—Always." Consumers enter a Wal-Mart store, are welcomed by a friendly greeter, and find a huge assortment of good-quality merchandise at everyday low prices. The same principle explains the explosive growth of factory outlet malls and discount chains—these days, customers want value. This even applies to luxury products: Toyota introduced its successful Lexus luxury automobile with the headline "Perhaps the First Time in History that Trading a $72 000 Car for a $36 000 Car Could Be Considered Trading Up."

THE CALL FOR MORE ETHICS AND SOCIAL RESPONSIBILITY

Another factor in today's marketing environment is the increased call for companies to take responsibility for the social and environmental impact of their actions. Corporate ethics has become a hot topic in almost every business arena, from the corporate boardroom to the business school classroom. And few companies can ignore the renewed and very demanding environmental movement.

The ethics and environmental movements will place even stricter demands on companies in the future. Consider recent environmental developments. After the fall of communism, the West was shocked to find out about the massive environmental negligence of the former Eastern Bloc governments. In many Eastern European countries, the air is fouled, the water is polluted, and the soil is poisoned by chemical dumping. In 1992, representatives from more than 100 countries attended the Earth Summit in Rio de Janeiro to consider how to handle such problems as the destruction of rain forests, global warming, endangered species, and other environmental threats. Clearly, in the future companies will be held to an increasingly higher standard of environmental responsibility in their marketing and manufacturing activities.

THE NEW MARKETING LANDSCAPE

The past decade taught business firms everywhere a humbling lesson. Domestic companies learned that they can no longer ignore global markets and competitors. Successful firms in mature industries learned that they cannot overlook emerging markets, technologies, and management approaches. Companies of every sort learned that they cannot remain inwardly focused, ignoring the needs of customers and their environment. A number of Canadian companies, particularly in the retail sector, undervalued marketing, and are struggling or have gone bankrupt. Firms such as Eaton's, Woodwards, Dylex, and Massey-Ferguson failed to understand their evolving marketplace, and changing customer needs and value perceptions.

JEFF NORTON, ASSISTANT BRAND MANAGER, PROCTER & GAMBLE CANADA

Jeff Norton works for Procter & Gamble Canada (P&G), a company that employs more than 4000 Canadians and operates four Canadian manufacturing facilities. P&G markets a vast array of consumer packaged goods that are known around the world for their high quality. The firm is also renowned as a founder of modern marketing practice. The company's insights about marketing have been on the leading edge of the discipline throughout its history. Although everyone at P&G focuses on building the Canadian business, employees also search for ways to apply their insights of the Canadian marketplace to marketing products around the world.

While he was exploring various job opportunities, Jeff discovered that P&G was the most rigorous of all the marketing companies. He was impressed by P&G's approach of challenging assumptions and demanding that employees support their recommendations with strong analysis. Jeff spent four months working for the company as a summer intern, working on real projects with the Bounce team.

When Jeff began his full-time career with P&G, he appreciated the fact that P&G offered a highly intensive training program for new employees, known as "brand college." During two intense weeks of interactive course sessions, P&G's new employees are taken through all phases of product marketing—from idea assessment to getting a product into consumers' hands through great advertising. Now, as a full-time assistant brand manager, Jeff has worked for P&G for four months. Jeff's job is typical of what you might be doing if you decide to become a marketer and to work for a packaged goods company.

Unlike many people who enter marketing, Jeff is somewhat unique in that he didn't start his education by entering a business program. Instead he started as a film student because he was interested in media and wanted a broad arts education. By his

second year, however, he was looking for a place where he could apply his general knowledge. He switched into business school, though it wasn't until his course work in third year that he discovered that marketing was the one area in business where practitioners had to bring together all elements— from strategy development to implementation. Marketers not only use their information-gathering and analysis skills, but they must always watch the financial and cost implications of a plan. They must be creative in identifying new ways of advertising products and services. They must link their understanding of consumers with their

Jeff Norton

ability to design products and services designed to make buyers' lives easier. Jeff firmly believes that a key success factor for companies is their ability to focus on the end user.

As an assistant product manager, Jeff's days are filled with thinking about the executional details associated with marketing plans. Even with a product such as fabric softener, Jeff and his colleagues at P&G believe their decisions are making someone's life easier and better. The job can be somewhat overwhelming at times, however. Jeff works in the laundry and

cleaning products division, and each brand is a big business in and of itself.

Jeff is pleased that he doesn't have to work alone. He appreciates other employees' willingness to help him if necessary, and the ongoing, on-the-job training that P&G offers. About three times each month, Jeff participates in a specialized course or seminar on some aspect of marketing.

Jeff's daily tasks are twofold. He does creative work that is focused on promotion-oriented decisions associated with marketing Bounce. In brainstorming sessions, people on the team ask if there is a different place mentally or physically that they should have the product. This is quite a challenge since fabric softeners are low-involvement products.

The second part of Jeff's responsibilities involves performing data analysis. He reviews vast amounts of data to try to identify hidden nuggets of information that can be leveraged into a big idea to help market the brand. Jeff soon realized the big difference between the case studies he did at university and his work in the "real world." In a case study, all the information is laid out for you. At work, Jeff must write his own case—deciding what information is important, and what should be ignored. Next, he must execute the solution, implementing what he thinks will be the best alternative to solve a problem.

No matter what he is doing, Jeff tries to step back and think about how the detailed-oriented work that fills his days relates to the big picture and to P&G's strategy. He focuses on where the brand fits in the category and into the overall business of the company. He reminds himself that nothing he does is in isolation from the overall objectives of P&G. "You can never just think that this is just a small product in global organization and that what you do doesn't really matter," Jeff stresses. It makes the ordinary, everyday things he does in his job seem more meaningful.

As we move into the next century, companies will have to become customer-oriented and market-driven in all that they do. It's not enough to be product- or technology-driven—too many companies still design their products without customer input, only to find them rejected in the marketplace. It's not enough to be good at winning new customers—too many companies forget about customers after the sale, only to lose their future business. Not surprisingly, we are now seeing a flood of books with titles such as *The Customer Driven Company, Customer Intimacy, Customers for Life, Turning Lost Customers into Gold, Customer Bonding, Sustaining Knock Your Socks Off Service,* and *The Loyalty Effect.*[29] These books emphasize that the key to success on the rapidly changing marketing landscape will be a strong focus on the marketplace and a total marketing commitment to providing value to customers.

Summary of Chapter Objectives

Today's successful companies share a strong focus on and a heavy commitment to marketing. Modern marketing seeks to attract new customers by promising superior value, and to keep current customers by delivering satisfaction. Sound marketing is critical to the success of all organizations, whether large or small, for-profit or non-profit, domestic or global.

Many people view marketing as only selling or advertising. But marketing combines many activities—marketing research, product development, distribution, pricing, advertising, personal selling, and others—designed to sense, serve, and satisfy customer needs while meeting the organization's goals. Marketing operates within a dynamic global environment. Rapid changes can quickly make yesterday's winning strategies obsolete. In the next century, marketers will face many new challenges and opportunities. To be successful, companies will have to be strongly market focused.

1. **Define marketing and discuss its core concepts.**

   Marketing is a social and managerial process by which individuals and groups obtain what they need and want through creating and exchanging products and values with others. The core concepts of marketing are *needs, wants, and demands; products and services; value, satisfaction, and quality; exchange, transactions, and relationships*; and *markets. Wants* are the form assumed by human needs when shaped by culture and individual personality. When backed by buying power, wants become *demands*. People satisfy their needs, wants, and demands with products

and services. A *product* is anything that can be offered to a market to satisfy a need, want, or demand. Products also include *services* and other entities such as *persons, places, organizations, activities,* and *ideas.*

In deciding which products and services to buy, consumers rely on their perception of relative value. *Customer value* is the difference between the values the customer gains from owning and using a product, and the costs of obtaining and using the product. *Customer satisfaction* depends on a product's perceived performance in delivering value relative to a buyer's expectations. Customer satisfaction is closely linked to *quality*, leading many companies to adopt *total quality management (TQM)* practices. Marketing occurs when people satisfy their needs, wants, and demands through exchange. Beyond creating short-term exchanges, marketers need to build long-term relationships with valued customers, distributors, dealers, and suppliers.

2. **Define marketing management and examine how marketers manage demand and build profitable customer relationships.**

   Marketing management is the analysis, planning, implementation, and control of programs designed to create, build, and maintain beneficial exchanges with target buyers for the purpose of achieving organizational objectives. It involves more than simply finding enough customers for the company's current output. At times, marketing is also concerned with changing or even reducing demand. Managing demand means understanding and working with customers. Beyond designing strategies to *attract* new customers and create *transactions* with them, today's companies are focusing on *retaining* current customers and building lasting *relationships* through offering superior customer value and satisfaction.

3. **Compare the five marketing management philosophies.**

Organizations can be guided by five different philosophies. The role that marketing plays within the firm will vary depending on the corporate philosophy. The *production concept* holds that consumers favour products that are available and highly affordable; management's task is to improve production efficiency and bring down prices. The *product concept* holds that consumers favour products that offer the most quality, performance, and innovative features; thus, little promotional effort is required. The *selling concept* holds that consumers will not buy enough of the organization's products unless it undertakes a large-scale selling

and promotion effort. The *marketing concept* holds that achieving organizational goals depends on determining the needs and wants of target markets and delivering the desired satisfactions more effectively and efficiently than competitors do. The *societal marketing* concept holds that the company should determine the needs, wants, and interests of target markets. Generating customer satisfaction *and* long-run societal well-being are the keys to achieving both the company's goals and its responsibilities.

4. **Analyse the major challenges facing marketers heading into the next century.**

As they head into the next century, companies are wrestling with changing customer values and orientations, a sluggish world economy, the growth of non-profit marketing; the information technology boom, including the Internet; rapid globalization, including increased global competition; a call for greater ethical and social responsibility, and a host of other economic, political, and social challenges.

Key Terms

Customer value *(p. 11)*
Customer satisfaction *(p. 11)*
Demands *(p. 8)*
Demarketing *(p. 15)*
Exchange *(p. 12)*
Internet *(p. 22)*
Market *(p. 13)*

Marketing *(p. 7)*
Marketing concept *(p. 18)*
Marketing management *(p. 14)*
Needs *(p. 7)*
Product *(p. 9)*
Product concept *(p. 17)*
Production concept *(p. 16)*

Relationship marketing *(p. 12)*
Selling concept *(p. 17)*
Societal marketing concept *(p. 19)*
Total quality management *(p. 11)*
Transaction *(p. 12)*
Wants *(p. 7)*

Discussing the Issues

1. Discuss why *you* should study marketing.

2. Nike was used as the opening example for this chapter. Nike's strategy can be described as "core value marketing." Firms that use this strategy attempt to form relationships with customers based on a sharing of their core values. The firm aligns its values with those of its key customers. What values has Nike tapped? What values must the company tap in the future? Why is this type of strategy so powerful? What

other Canadian firms use this strategy? Use the web sites developed by these companies to support your response.

3. Historian Arnold Toynbee and economist John Kenneth Galbraith have argued that the desires stimulated by marketing efforts are not genuine: "A man who is hungry need never be told of his need for food." Decide whether this is a valid criticism of marketing. Explain why or why not.

4. Many people dislike or fear certain products and would not "demand" them at any price. Can you suggest ways that a health-care marketer might manage the *negative* demand for such products as colon cancer screenings?

5. Identify the single biggest difference between the marketing concept and the production, product, and selling concepts. Discuss which concepts are easiest to apply in the short run. Predict which concept you believe can offer the best long-term success.

6. Some people, such as economist Milton Friedman, don't believe that corporations should allocate funds to solve social problems. Instead, he believes this is the mandate of elected governments. According to Friedman, corporations' only responsibilities are to maximize the wealth of the firm's stockholders while respecting the law. The societal marketing concept, however, takes a different view of corporate responsibility. Debate the pros and cons of each argument. What do you think is the social responsibility of Canadian corporations? Are these responsibilities the same when corporations market globally?

Applying the Concepts

1. Go to McDonald's and order a burger. Note the questions you are asked, and observe how special orders are handled. Next, go to Wendy's, Harvey's, or a local pizza restaurant and order a burger or a pizza. Note the questions you are asked here, and observe whether special orders are handled the same way as they are at McDonald's.

   ◆ Did you observe any significant differences in how orders are handled?
   ◆ Consider the differences you saw. Do you think the restaurants have different marketing management philosophies? Which is closest to the marketing concept? Is one closer to the selling or production concept?
   ◆ What are the advantages of closely following the marketing concept? Are there any disadvantages?

2. Visit your local mall. Find the directory sign. List five major categories of stores, such as department stores, shoe, book, and women's clothing shops, and restaurants. List the competing stores in each category, and walk past them and quickly observe their merchandise and style. Look at the public spaces of the mall, and note how they are decorated. Watch the shoppers in the mall.

   ◆ Are the competing stores really unique, or could one substitute for another?
   ◆ Did the shoppers efficiently buy items from a shopping list, as in a grocery store, or did they take a different approach?
   ◆ Four basic goals for the marketing system have been suggested: maximizing consumption, consumer satisfaction, choice, or quality of life. Discuss whether you think the mall serves some of these goals better than others.

References

1. Quotations from Linda Himelstein, "The Swoosh Heard 'Round the World," *Business Week*, May 12, 1997, p. 76; and Jeff Jensen, "Marketer of the Year," *Advertising Age*, December 16, 1996, pp. 1, 16. Also see Himelstein, "The Soul of a New Nike," *Business Week*, June 17, 1996, p. 70; Gary Hamel, "Killer Strategies that Make Shareholders Rich," *Fortune*, June 23, 1997, pp. 70–83; John Wyatt, "Is It Time to Jump on Nike?" *Fortune*, May 26, 1997, pp. 185–186, and Nike's World Wide Web page at www.nike.com. David Chilton, "Canstar Adopts Nike Approach with Planned Bauer Superbrand," *Strategy, The Canadian Marketing Report*, November 27, 1995, p. 1; Kathleen Deslauriers, "Dominance by Brand: Nike in the Running in the Greater Toronto Area," *Strategy, The Canadian Marketing Report*, April 28, 1997, p. 16; Alan Freeman, "Adidas Gaining on Its Rivals," *Globe and Mail*, September 26, 1997, p. B7; John Heinzl, "Logos an Olympic Event," *Globe and Mail*, October 20, 1997, p. B6; Ken Allen's quotation from Meriiam Mesbah, "Special Report: Sponsorship and Event Marketing: NBA and Nike to

Net Young Fans Through Future Hoops," *Strategy, The Canadian Marketing Report*, March 3, 1997, p. 22; Gerald Wasserman's quotation from Luis Millan, "Ice Follies," *Canadian Business*, June 1997, p. 132; Lara Mills, "Women Get in the Game," *Marketing*, April 7, 1997, pp. 12–13; Bill Redford's quotation from Pattie Summerfield, "Nike Attacks Canada," *Strategy, The Canadian Marketing Report*, July 10, 1995, p. 1; Erica Zloic, "Nike Gets Into Social Marketing," *Strategy, The Canadian Marketing Report*, October 27, 1997, p. 2.

2. Mountain Equipment Co-Op, *Membership Information Booklet*, pp. 1–2.

3. See P. Ranganath Nayak, Albert C. Chen, and James F. Reider, "Listening to Customers," *Prism*, Arthur D. Little, Inc., Second Quarter, 1993, pp. 43–57.

4. "Company Growth Attributed to Quality Standards," *Advertising Supplement to the Globe and Mail*, December 16, 1997, p. 5.

5. See Theodore Levitt's classic article, "Marketing Myopia," *Harvard Business Review*, July–August 1960, pp. 45–56.

6. Lois Therrien, "Motorola and NEC: Going for Glory," *Business Week*, special issue on quality, 1991, pp. 60–61.

7. Jagdish N. Sheth and Atul Parvatiyar, "Relationship Marketing in Consumer Markets: Antecedents and Consequences," *Journal of the Academy of Marketing Science*, 23 (4), 1995, pp. 255–271.

8. See James C. Anderson, Hakan Hakansson, and Jan Johanson, "Dyadic Business Relationships Within a Business Network Context," *Journal of Marketing*, October 15, 1994, pp. 1–15.

9. For more discussion on demand states, see Philip Kotler, *Marketing Management: Analysis, Planning, Implementation, and Control* (Englewood Cliffs, NJ: Prentice Hall, 1994), pp. 14–15.

10. See Joan C. Szabo, "Service=Survival," *Nation's Business*, March 1989, pp. 16–24; and Kevin J. Clancy and Robert S. Shulman, "Breaking the Mold," *Sales & Marketing Management*, January 1994, pp. 82–84.

11. Patricia Sellers, "Companies That Serve You Best," pp. 74–88.

12. Patrick Brethour, "Corel Launches Attack on Corporate Market," *Globe and Mail*, September 24, 1996, p. B4; Carolyn Leitch, "Corel Warns Loss May Hit $4-million," *Globe and Mail*, September 26, 1996, pp. B1, B6.

13. Ralph Waldo Emerson offered this advice: "If a man . . . makes a better mousetrap . . . the world will beat a path to his door." Several companies, however, have built better mousetraps and failed. One was a laser mousetrap costing $1,500. Contrary to popular assumptions, people do not automatically learn about new products, believe product claims, or willingly pay higher prices.

14. Barry Farber and Joyce Wycoff, "Customer Service: Evolution and Revolution," *Sales & Marketing Management*, May 1991, p. 47.

15. See Don E. Schultz, "Traditional Marketers Have Become Obsolete," *Marketing News*, June 6, 1994, p. 11.

16. Howard Schlossberg, "Customer Satisfaction: Not a Fad, but a Way of Life," *Marketing News*, June 10, 1991, p. 18. Also see Bernard J. Jaworski and Ajay K. Kohli, "Market Orientation: Antecedents and Consequences," *Journal of Marketing*, July 1993, pp. 53–70.

17. See "Leaders of the Most Admired," *Fortune*, January 29, 1990, pp. 40–54.

18. Speech by Barbara J. Hedjuk, President, Imperial Oil Charitable Foundation, Social Marketing for Business Conference, Toronto, November 9, 1995.

19. For other examples, and for a good review of non-profit marketing, see Philip Kotler and Alan R. Andreasen, *Strategic Marketing for Nonprofit Organizations* (Englewood Cliffs, NJ: Prentice Hall, 1991).

20. Andre Picard, "Modern Tactics for an Ancient Cause," *Globe and Mail*, November 12, 1997, p. A2.

21. Andre Picard, "Modern Tactics for an Ancient Cause," p. A2.

22. Heinz Canada's web page (http://heinzbaby.com), Recent press releases, "Heinz Ups Support of Children's Hospitals," June 2, 1997.

23. Don Peppers and Martha Rogers, *The One-to-One Future* (New York: Doubleday, 1993), p. 315.

24. For more on the basics of using the Internet, see Raymond D. Frost and Judy Strauss, *The Internet: A New Marketing Tool* (Upper Saddle River, NJ: Prentice Hall, 1997).

25. Brad Edmondson, "The Wired Bunch," *American Demographics*, June 1997, pp. 10–15; and Amy Cortese, "A Census in Cyberspace," *Business Week*, May 5, 1997, p. 84. For the most recent statistics, check the results of an ongoing survey of Internet usage conducted by CommerceNet and Nielsen Media Research, www.commerce.net/nielsen/.

26. Pete & Barbara's Penguin Pages is located at http://ourworld.compuserve.com/homepages/Peter_and_Barbara_Barham/.

27. Peter H. Lewis, "Getting Down to Business on the Net," *The New York Times*, June 19, 1994, 3, 1:2. Also see John Deighton, "The Future of Interactive," *Harvard Business Review*, November–December 1996, pp. 151–162; Debora Spar and Jeffrey Bussgang, "The Net," *Harvard Business Review*, May–June 1996, pp. 125–133; and Andy Reinhardt, "Zooming Down the I-Way," *Business Week*, April 7, 1997, pp. 76–87.

28. For more on strategic alliances, see Jordan D. Lewis, *Partnerships for Profit: Structuring and Managing Strategic Alliances* (New York: The Free Press, 1990); Peter Lorange and Johan Roos, *Strategic Alliances: Formation, Implementation, and Evolution* (Cambridge, MA: Blackwell Publishers, 1992); and Frederick E. Webster, Jr., "The Changing Role of Marketing in the Corporation," *Journal of Marketing*, October 1992, pp. 1–17.

29. Richard C. Whitely, *The Customer Driven Company* (Reading, MA: Addison-Wesley, 1991); Robert L. De-

sanick, *Keep the Customer* (Boston: Houghton Mifflin Co., 1990); Charles Sewell, *Customers for Life: How to Turn the One-Time Buyer into a Lifetime Customer* (New York: Pocket Books, 1990); William H. Davidow and Bro Uttal, *Total Customer Service: The Ulti-* *mate Weapon* (New York: Harper & Row, 1989); and Karl Albrecht, *The Only Thing that Matters: Bringing the Customer into the Center of Your Business* (New York: Harper Business, 1992).

Company Case 1

MADE-IT: WORKING TOWARD UNIVERSITY

How would you feel about starting a business with your mother? How would your mother feel about starting a business with you? The Ewing Marion Kauffman Foundation hopes the idea sounds appealing to many mothers and daughters. The Kauffman Foundation sponsors programs to support entrepreneurs and has developed a program called Mother and Daughter Entrepreneurs-In Teams (MADE-IT). The program's goal is to encourage mothers and their high-school-aged daughters to start a business that will provide the financial support for the daughter to attend university.

THE GIBSONS

Mary Gibson, a counsellor at Clarke Junior High School, saw an advertisement in her local newspaper seeking applications for the MADE-IT program. Mary showed the ad to her 13-year-old daughter Megan.

Megan knew that she would love to work with her mother. She also realized that she could save her earnings to pay for university. The only question was when the two would have time to start their own business. Megan was very involved in her school and her community. Mary also kept a busy schedule with her job, family, and community activities. They decided to think it over.

The night before the application was due, they had still not decided to apply. Finally, the pair decided to at least give it a try and see what might happen. They worked diligently on the application, individually writing essays explaining why they would like to work together and what they would like to achieve through the MADE-IT program. They finally completed their application at 1:00 a.m. on the day it was due.

A few weeks later, MADE-IT notified the Gibsons that their application had reached the next stage in the screening process—the interview. Following the interview, program managers invited Mary and Megan to participate in the program. In May 1997, they learned that they would attend the June training institute held at Drake University. By the time they arrived at the university, they would be expected to have developed a good idea as to what type of business they planned to start.

THE PLAN

Later that month, Mary picked up some information on a company called Creative Memories®. To learn more about the opportunities available to them. Mary and Megan attended one of the company's workshops two weeks later. There they learned that the company had about 34 000 consultants. As Creative Memories consultants, Mary and Megan would hold classes in their home for approximately six to 10 students at a time. They would teach their clients how to preserve photographs and memorabilia, and the importance of preserving their photographs properly. The representatives provide clients with photo-safe albums, supplies, and education in a variety of ways—home classes, ongoing monthly workshops, one-on-one meetings, and presentations to clubs and organizations. To become a consultant, one must purchase a $250 starter kit that contains the basic supplies to start the business. Representatives work at their own pace and earn profit from workshop participant fees and product sales. While attending the Creative Memories workshop, Megan began a Gibson family scrapbook, and they both agreed that becoming representatives for Creative Memories was a viable possibility.

Once Mary and Megan arrived at Drake University for the MADE-IT training program and were settled into their dorm room, they and the other mother-daughter pairs formed into small groups. Each group's assignment was to discuss each team's business idea, so that the team could return to the large group with its final business proposal. Mary and Megan discussed the Creative Memories idea with their group and decided that it would be the basis for their home-based business. While attending the program, Mary and Megan also learned how to write a business plan and how to conduct market research. They attended seminars and heard presentations from an accountant, attorney, tax specialist, and other speakers. In addition to the training, MADE-IT offers participants two years of support from expert entrepreneurs in order to help the teams work through the problems that arise in starting a new business.

GETTING DOWN TO BUSINESS

Armed with the knowledge provided by Creative Memories training and the MADE-IT institute, Mary and Megan got to work.

The Gibsons believed that there was a vast target market for Creative Memories classes and products. Creative Memories makes many styles of albums available to highlight specific family occasions, such as wedding albums, baby albums, and albums specifically designed for children. Mary and Megan believed that local families would readily accept the photo preservation concept, but it was a small region, with a population of only about 4600 people. Mary and Megan felt it would not take long to saturate their initial target market—families with children up to age 14. Therefore, they believed it would be necessary to explore more niche markets.

Essentially, the Creative Memories representative's product is the knowledge and tools to preserve family or personal photographs and memorabilia in a safe manner so they will last for generations. Over the years, many family photographs deteriorate prematurely due to incorrect preservation practices. All of Creative Memories' products are acid-free, lignin-free, and guaranteed photo-safe. Creative Memories is the first photo preservation company in the world to participate in the Approved Preservation Practices® program, established by Wilhelm Imaging Research, Inc. Creative Memories' participation in the program guarantees that its programs, practices, and products meet rigid standards for photograph preservation.

The first step in the selling process is to find people to participate in an initial home class in which the customer learns the importance of proper preservation, cropping, layout techniques, and mounting methods, and how to develop a journal. At the initial class, the representatives typically assist the customers in beginning their album by completing the first album page. The $15 fee covers all the materials necessary to complete the first page.

The consultants then encourage customers to purchase an album and the necessary materials to continue working on it. Customers can purchase other supplies in addition to the album itself: mounting supplies, templates, scissors for decorative edging, mounting paper, stickers, die-cut shapes, and photo labelling pencils. To create an attractive album, a customer would need to spend approximately $75 to $95. Customers do not have to order all supplies at the initial class. They can contact consultants at any time to replenish or order

new supplies. After the initial class, the customer can set up monthly workshop times in which Creative Memories representatives will work with them or their friends and family members in completing their album and also provide other tools and construction aids that a person would not normally buy. At the workshops, customers can also buy single pieces of paper, for example, rather than an entire pack.

The Gibsons were planning one to two initial home classes per week and were hoping to hold one to two second-time workshops per month. Each workshop lasts for approximately 2.5 hours.

For the most part, Mary and Megan will depend on word-of-mouth to promote their business. They have received much local media attention through their participation in the MADE-IT program. They also displayed their products and a completed album of their own family history at a county fair booth and received 62 leads for possible workshop participants.

Mary and Megan were also considering the option of expanding their business into the neighbouring city located approximately 45 minutes from their hometown. While the population is much larger, 126 000 people, going to the city would create problems in terms of travel time and communications. However, it is possible for them to recruit other consultants in other areas. If they do this, they must provide the education and support for the new consultants, and, in return, they would earn a small percentage of the sales that those consultants make. Rather than focusing on selling supplies and holding training classes, it is also possible to focus entirely on recruiting other consultants. People who take this route pass through three levels of management—first becoming a unit manager, then a director, and finally a senior director.

The Gibsons report that starting their own business is, to say the least, tough. They have gotten off to a slow start and are having trouble finding the time to spend on the business. Mary has been contacting potential clients by phone, which she must do at certain times of the day. She is having trouble finding the right time to catch people at home and to fit the calls into her own schedule. Finding the time to schedule workshops has also been difficult. The Gibsons wonder if they have overlooked anything in their planning. They know that starting any business is not easy and that there are many things to think about. However, they hope that by working together, they can make it.

QUESTIONS:

1. What consumer needs and wants are the Gibsons attempting to satisfy? Is there a demand for their product? What societal forces may be affecting this demand?

2. How will Mary and Megan create value for their customers?

3. What exchanges are involved in the relationship between the Gibsons and their customers and between the Gibsons and Creative Memories?

4. What management philosophy do the Gibsons appear to be following? If they approached you for advice, what recommendations would you make to the Gibsons as they start their business? What things have they forgotten or what improvements could they make in their marketing plans?

5. Would the Creative Memories business concept work in the international market? Why or why not?

Source: This case was modified by Peggy Cunningham from an original case written by Kristen Cashman, Undergraduate Research Fellow, Bryan School of Business and Economics, University of North Carolina at Greensboro. Mary and Megan Gibson, the Kaufmann Foundation, and Creative Memories® assisted in the development of this case.

Video Case 1

THE RACE TO MARKET

There is always more than one way to market a product, as the case of two entrepreneurs in Guelph, Ontario, shows. The men launched almost identical products in completely different ways. Each man hoped to be successful in marketing bike trailers: six-kilogram, covered wagons that attached to bikes and could be used as a cart or a stroller. Although the two men, who were also neighbours, had originally planned to be partners in developing and marketing the product, differing marketing management philosophies meant that they could not work together. Instead they became competitors.

WIKE was the idea of Bob Bell, an engineer who believed there was a market for a cheaper version of existing bike trailers. He began developing the product in his basement with the assistance of one other person. He hoped for a slow and steady development and marketing process. He was convinced that he could perfect the design of the product so that it could be made inexpensively and therefore sold cheaper than other trailers. The North American market for this product is about 140 000 units per year, at an average price of $500. Bob wanted to sell the product for half that price.

Central to Bob's plan was extensive product development, which included hiring the local bike club to put the trailer through product testing. He would use the community of Guelph as a test market while product development was taking place and, after perfecting the product, sell the rights to WIKE to another company, which could sell it nationally.

The WIKE was launched at the Guelph farmers' market. Bob posted a special introductory price of $177.25 and had local musicians sing his product jingle. Although he almost sold out that day, Bob also realized that he needed to further revise the product to be suitable for carrying kids. Although he had resisted the idea of carting kids in the stroller for safety reasons, Bob realized that this was a key consideration for customers. Almost everyone at the farmers' market had asked him about this feature.

Michael (Mick) Sharpe marketed his bike trailer, The Wonder Wagon, in a completely different way. From a product development standpoint, he realized early that carrying kids would be key to the success of the product. Consequently he developed and added a five-point harness to be used for transporting kids. Mick also believed that the product should be sold nationally right away. He took out a bank loan, rented a manufacturing facility, and hired five employees to ensure that he could handle orders on a national level.

Mick's goal was to sell 2500 Wonder Wagons a year. Rather than sell directly to the ultimate consumer, he focused on recruiting retailers to stock the Wonder Wagon. As a former sales manager, Mick used sales presentations to get as many dealers interested in the product as possible. Since Mick also planned to sell the product for half the price of existing bike trailers, he believed that many retailers would be interested in the larger profit margins offered by the Wonder Wagon. As further incentive to stock the product, he offered to split the cost of advertising with the retailer. Mick particularly targeted national retailers as potential dealers, believing that they offered one of the best ways to reach large groups of customers. Recognizing that a key geographic market for his product is the west coast of Canada, where people can cycle year round, Mick supplemented his marketing efforts in that region by becoming a corporate sponsor for the Vancouver charitable biking event, Ride for Life.

Each entrepreneur saw results from his approach. As a result of Bob's product development and marketing efforts, he sells all the WIKEs he can make and has already met with one interested buyer for national rights. Mick's various marketing efforts have also paid off. Two national retailers as well as several independent retailers have agreed to stock the Wonder Wagon.

QUESTIONS

1. Which marketing management philosophy is each entrepreneur following?

2. Which entrepreneur do you think will be successful in the long run? Why?

3. Do you think the success of each philosophy followed would be different if the product was being developed and marketed by a large company instead of a small one?

Source: This case was prepared by Auleen Carson and is based on "Buggy Wars," *Venture* (June 26, 1994).

CHAPTER 2

STRATEGIC PLANNING AND THE MARKETING PROCESS

As international competitors attack our markets from abroad, strategic planning is becoming more important than ever. No company knows this better than Canadian Tire, one of Canada's oldest retailers. Two brothers, John and A. J. Billes, founded the company in a Toronto garage in 1922. These visionary siblings recognized the potential of the "after market" as automobile sales took off. They were pioneers in developing a chain of dealers using modern franchise concepts, believing that owners would be more effective operators than hired managers. Canadian Tire "money" is as well known to Canadian consumers as the loonie.

Despite generations of consistent profitability and innovation, the firm seemed to lose its bearings in the 1980s. It bled resources into a poorly conceived U.S. market-entry strategy rather than updating its Canadian infrastructure. People thought it forgot the importance of customer service and reliable products. One analyst noted, "Over the years, Canadian Tire Corporation Limited had managed to get indifference down to an art."[1] Customers could rarely find store personnel, let alone ask them for assistance. It is no wonder that business analysts were forecasting the extinction of this dinosaur of Canadian retailing when Home Depot, the U.S. giant do-it-yourself home improvement chain known for its obsession with customer service, entered the Canadian marketplace in 1994.

How did Canadian Tire respond to the significant threat posed by such U.S. paragons of marketing as Wal-Mart and Home Depot? It embraced a multi-pronged strategy based on three key initiatives: improving efficiency and cutting costs so that it could lower prices to meet those of retailers such as Home Depot; adding value through improved product mixes, convenient stores, and new products and services that meet emerging customer needs; and building better relationships with suppliers, store owners, and customers.

Canadian Tire
www.canadiantire.com/

When you finish this chapter, you should be able to

1. Explain company-wide strategic planning and its four steps.

2. Discuss how to design business portfolios and growth strategies.

3. Explain functional planning strategies and assess marketing's role in strategic planning.

4. Describe the marketing process and the forces that influence it.

5. List the marketing management functions, including the elements of a marketing plan.

Rather than trying to be everything to everyone, Canadian Tire instead focused on three strategic product/market areas—automotive, sports and leisure goods, and home products—in which it believed the company had a significant competitive advantage over its would-be competitors. While Canadian Tire had already established a strong reputation among Canadian consumers in auto parts, it lacked breadth in the areas of home entertainment, pet products, and decorating items. Adding and strengthening these lines was important if Canadian Tire was to retain its target customer base of 18- to 40-year-olds. The expanded product lines have also made the stores more desirable as family shopping experiences. Improved inventory tracking systems have allowed Canadian Tire to rationalize its product lines, dropping slow-moving items and replacing them with those in demand by local customers.

However, simply expanding product lines would have been counterproductive if the retailer was unable to successfully display its merchandise. Thus, store expansion and refurbishing was another key ingredient in Canadian Tire's strategy. Today, following a billion-dollar spending spree, many of the company's 424 stores have been totally remodelled while others have been relocated. The upgraded stores have wider aisles and a broader merchandise mix. Store design has been standardized so that customers can shop in a Canadian Tire store with the same sense of familiarity whether they are in Calgary, Alberta, or London, Ontario.

The new stores come in two formats: a 28 000-square-foot version and a 53 000-square-foot model, built according to market size, retail base in the market, and availability of desirable locations. In the new stores, easy-to-read store maps, colour-coded displays, and aisle markers direct customers to products. Shelf-talkers—signs placed directly above products—provide both verbal information and diagrams of the products to facilitate customer search. Wide aisles make cart navigation easy while avoiding the sense of crowding and clutter so common in the old stores. Advanced lighting systems add to the clean and modern atmosphere. The new store formats are not only appealing to customers, but they also provide service providers with the tools to serve customers better, including touch-screen computers to help staff locate products, and buzzers to help customers indicate their need for assistance. The renewal strategy has been so successful that sales have risen by 45 to 50 percent.

In an effort to further improve service and target key, profitable customers, new specialty stores are also being developed. For example, the PartsSource is a new specialty store designed for professional installers and die-hard, car fix-it-your-selvers who would not typically visit a Canadian Tire store. Canadian Tire is also testing an automotive "store-within-a-store" concept. At test locations, a separate entrance is provided directly to auto parts so that customers don't have to wander through general merchandise before they reach the parts they need. Stores are also offering a "lend-a-tool" program. Customers can borrow expensive, specialized tools that allow them to instal replacement auto parts.

The final prong in Canadian Tire's strategy of renewal is its focus on relationships and the revamping of the corporate culture. Key relationships include those with its independent store owners, suppliers, and customers. Although somewhat corny, new corporate slogans such as "Customers Rule" and "Customers for Life" have marked this transformation. Canadian Tire doesn't focus on the individual transaction; instead it stresses keeping customers for life. Yet, how does a company find out more about its customers, and what they want and value now and in the future? How does it do this when those customers are harried shoppers who rush in and out of stores, lacking the time to shop—let alone the time to talk to researchers or to fill out lengthy questionnaires. In other words, how does a company implement a strategy of customer intimacy?

One can find the answers by understanding how technology is changing marketing strategy. Canadian Tire is a leader in database marketing initiatives and the customer loyalty programs it has developed using this knowledge base. Canadian Tire's "money" was the first ground-breaking loyalty program. It brought customers back to the stores so they could spend these premiums. But Sandy McTire (the icon on every Canadian Tire dollar) had one big problem. When customers used their Canadian Tire bucks, they yielded no information about the customer. However, new premiums offered through Canadian Tire's own credit card, or the newly launched Canadian Tire Options MasterCard, are another story. When customers use these cards at a computerized cash register, they leave a data trail that helps Canadian Tire to know them better and serve them better. Eight million Canadian consumers currently carry these cards and Canadian Tire exploits this vast information resource to its advantage.

Credit cards are a major convenience for customers and of great importance to Canadian Tire since over half of all purchases made in their stores are on credit. Not only did the cards help the company learn more about customers, but they also helped the company win the fight against non-traditional competitors—the bank cards. The new Canadian Tire credit cards award customers with points for every dollar they spend in Canadian Tire stores. These points can be redeemed to earn savings on merchandise instantly, right at the cash register. As one Canadian Tire representative noted, simplicity is the key to a successful loyalty program: "The easier the program is to understand, the more tangible the rewards, the more effective it's going to be."[2] Mining the database that the credit-card usage generates allows Canadian Tire to identify key customer segments and design specific strategies to build their loyalty to the company. It allows the firm to better understand who their best customers are, what goods and services they purchase most frequently, and what promotions and special offers they respond to.

Canadian Tire has more than 4.5 million names in its database. Insights provided by analysis of this core resource helps Canadian Tire to better allocate the $25 to $30 million it spends annually on marketing. The information is so rich that Canadian Tire knows which customers are members of its auto club, which people use credit cards, and which cards they use. They can track what types of products people buy and which stores they buy them from. This knowledge allows Canadian Tire to target their products and services with precision, eliminating wastage or avoiding bothering people with offers of products or services that would not interest them. Although Canadian Tire could generate additional revenues by selling the information from this core resource, it refuses to do so. As Tom Gauld, president of the division that manages the database notes, "When customers do business with Canadian Tire, they do business on an element of trust with the company. I think the selling or sharing of lists breaks that trust."[3]

To further support its customers and card users, Canadian Tire now has a call centre staffed by 700 people in Welland, Ontario. Gauld stresses that it is the most fundamental part of their marketing program. The call centre is the heart of two-way communication with customers. It puts customers in touch instantaneously with people who can answer their questions and solve their problems while also providing Canadian Tire with insight about their needs, wants, and values. The call centre also acts as the hub of Canadian Tire's auto club and roadside assistance program, which now rivals that of the Canadian Automobile Association. It allows the firm to offer extended warranties of many of the household products it sells. It can provide customers with other value-added services such as insurance and travel services. The strategy is powerful. "If we can present the right offer to the right customer at the right time, we have more sales and more relationships with that customer," explains Gauld.[4] Another aspect of Canadian Tire's strategy of tailoring its offerings to precisely meet its customers' needs can be found on the company's web site. By using this interactive site, customers can request information on sales, promotions, and product specials tailored specifically to meet their needs.

The relationship-building efforts directed at customers were parallelled with others designed to improve relations between head office and its 390 independent store owners, as well as relationships with its suppliers. The compensation system has been altered so that buyers are rewarded on meaningful retailing criteria—how well items purchased for the stores sell. Customer service policies, including a no-hassle return policy, have been revamped. Restocking teams have been hired to work during the hours that stores are closed so that floor personnel can focus on customer service rather than shelf maintenance. Training programs to improve customer sensitivity and product knowledge have been instituted.

Has the strategy been successful? Evidence of success exists on a number of fronts. In 1996, Canadian Tire won Hardware Merchandising's and Quincaillerie Materiaux's Outstanding Retailer Award. More importantly, profits increased by 25 percent between 1992 and 1994. This trend has continued and in 1997 profits are still growing at a rate in excess of 12 percent. Customer spending per visit, which is a key indicator of retail success, has increased from approximately $21 per visit to $30 per visit. The firm's stock price has been steadily increasing since market analysts like the strategies Canadian Tire has been following, and believe that they will enable the firm to generate profits over the long term. The new strategies combined with the fact that Canadian Tire kept an iron grip on prime locations, has dampened the success of Home Depot, whose launch into Canada has not been as successful as many people had forecast.

Dramatic strategic and marketing planning actions have transformed Canadian Tire into a vigorous and profitable company—one better matched to its changing market opportunities. All companies must look ahead and develop long-term strategies to meet the changing conditions in their industries. Each company must identify the game plan that makes the most sense given its specific situation, opportunities, objectives, and resources. The hard task of selecting an overall company strategy for long-run survival and growth is called *strategic planning*.

In this chapter, we look first at the organization's overall strategic planning. Next, we discuss marketing's role in the organization as it is defined by the overall strategic plan. Finally, we explain the marketing management process—the process that marketers undertake to carry out their role in the organization.

STRATEGIC PLANNING

Many companies operate without formal plans. Some managers are so busy they have no time for planning, think that only large corporations need formal planning, or argue that the marketplace changes too quickly for a plan to be useful—that it would end up collecting dust.

Yet formal planning can yield many benefits for all types of companies, large and small, new and mature. It encourages management to think ahead systematically. It forces the company to sharpen its objectives and policies, leads to better coordination of company efforts, and provides clearer performance standards for control. The argument that planning is less useful in a fast-changing environment makes little sense. In fact, the opposite is true: Sound planning helps the company to anticipate and respond quickly to environmental changes, and to better prepare for sudden developments.

Companies usually prepare annual plans, long-range plans, and strategic plans. The *annual plan* is a short-term marketing plan that describes the current marketing situation, the company objectives, the marketing strategy for the year, the action program, budgets, and controls. Without a clear set of objectives, how could a marketing manager integrate the advertising, pricing, product, and distribution programs? The *long-range plan* describes the major factors and forces affecting the organization during the next several years. It includes the long-term objectives, the major marketing strategies that will be used to attain them, and the resources required. This long-range plan is reviewed and updated each year so that the company always has a current long-range plan.

Whereas the company's annual and long-range plans deal with current businesses and how to keep them going, the strategic plan involves adapting the firm to take advantage of opportunities in its constantly changing environment. We define **strategic planning** as the process of developing and maintaining a strategic fit between the organization's goals and capabilities and its changing marketing opportunities.

Strategic planning sets the stage for the rest of the planning in the firm. It relies on defining a clear company mission, setting supporting company objectives, designing a sound business portfolio, and coordinating functional strategies (see Figure 2-1). At the corporate level, the company first defines its overall purpose and mission. This mission then is turned into detailed supporting objectives that guide the whole company. Next, headquarters decides what portfolio of businesses and products is best for the company and how much support to give each one. In turn, each business and product unit must develop detailed marketing and other departmental plans that support the company-wide plan. Thus, marketing planning occurs at the business-unit, product, and market levels. It supports company strategic planning with more detailed planning for specific marketing opportunities.[5]

Strategic planning
The process of developing and maintaining a strategic fit between the organization's goals and capabilities and its changing marketing opportunities.

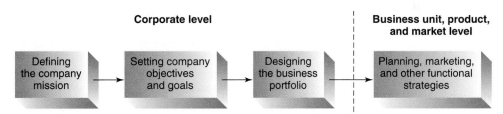

FIGURE 2-1 *Steps in strategic planning*

DEFINING THE COMPANY MISSION

An organization exists to accomplish something. At first, it has a clear purpose or mission, but over time its mission may become unclear as the organization grows and adds new products and markets, or faces new conditions in the environment. When management senses that the organization is drifting, it must renew its search for purpose. It is time to ask: What is our business? Who is the customer? What do consumers value? What will our business be? What should our business be? These simple-sounding questions are among the most difficult the company will ever have to answer. Successful companies continuously raise these questions and answer them carefully and completely.

Mission statement
A statement of the organization's purpose—what it wants to accomplish in the larger environment.

Many organizations develop formal mission statements that answer these questions. A **mission statement** is a statement of the organization's purpose—what it wants to accomplish in the larger environment. A clear mission statement acts as an "invisible hand" that guides people in the organization so that they can work independently and yet collectively toward overall organizational goals. It helps employees understand the values of the firm and acts as a guide to instil ethical organizational as well as marketing behaviour. The public is increasingly demanding that companies adopt socially responsible behaviour. The ability of some firms, such as Loblaw, The Body Shop, and McDonald's, to align ethical values with corporate missions has led them to be regarded with increased goodwill by many consumers.

Traditionally, companies have defined their businesses in product terms ("We manufacture furniture"), or in technological terms ("We are a chemical-processing firm"). But mission statements should be *market-oriented*. Market definitions of a business are better than product or technological definitions. Products and technologies eventually become outdated, but basic market needs may last forever. A market-oriented mission statement defines the business in terms of satisfying basic customer needs. Thus, Cantel is in the communications business, not the telephone business. 3M does more than just make adhesives, scientific equipment, and health-care products. It solves people's problems by putting innovation to work for them. Table 2-1 provides several other examples of product-oriented versus market-oriented business definitions.

3M Company
www.mmm.com/

TABLE 2-1 *Market-Oriented Business Definitions*

Company	Product-Oriented Definition	Market-Oriented Definition
M.A.C Cosmetics	We make cosmetics	We sell lifestyle and self-expression; tolerance of diversity, and a platform for the outrageous
Disney	We run theme parks and make films	We provide fantasies and entertainment
Zellers	We run discount stores	We offer products and services that deliver superior value to Canadians
Xerox	We make copying, fax, and other office machines	We make businesses more productive by helping them scan, store, retrieve, revise, distribute, print, and publish documents
Canadian Tire	We sell tools and home improvement items	We provide advice and solutions that transform ham-handed people into Mr. and Ms. Fixits

Management should avoid making its mission too narrow or too broad. A pencil manufacturer that says it is in the communication equipment business is stating its mission too broadly. Missions should be *realistic*—Singapore Airlines would be deluding itself if it adopted the mission to become the world's largest airline. Missions should also be *specific*. Many mission statements are written for public relations purposes and lack specific, workable guidelines. The statement "We want to become the leading company in this industry by producing the highest-quality products with the best service at the lowest prices" sounds good, but it is full of generalities and contradictions. Celestial Seasonings' mission statement is very specific: "Our mission is to grow and dominate the specialty tea market by exceeding consumer expectations with: The best-tasting, 100 percent natural hot and iced teas, packaged with Celestial art and philosophy, creating the most valued tea experience. . . .[6]

Missions should fit the *market environment*. The organization should base its mission on its *distinctive competencies*. McDonald's could probably enter the solar energy business, but that would not take advantage of its core competence—providing low-cost food and fast service to large groups of customers.

Finally, mission statements should be *motivating*. A company's mission should not be stated as making more sales or profits—profits are only a reward for undertaking a useful activity. A company's employees need to feel that their work is significant and that it contributes to people's lives. Andyne Computing Limited, one of Canada's most successful software companies, captures its aspirations for the future in its mission statement. "Our mission is to be a world leader in providing information access and decision support for informed business decisions."[7] Microsoft's mission goal has been IAYF—"information at your fingertips"—to put information at the fingertips of every person.[8]

One recent study found that "visionary companies" set a purpose beyond making money. For example, Walt Disney Company's aim is "making people happy." But even though "profits" may not be part of these companies' mission statements, they are the inevitable result. The study showed the 18 visionary companies outperformed other companies in the stock market by a ratio of more than six to one over the period from 1926 to 1990.[9]

SETTING COMPANY OBJECTIVES AND GOALS

The company's mission needs to be turned into detailed supporting objectives for each level of management. Each manager should have objectives and be responsible for reaching them. For example, Monsanto operates in many businesses, including agriculture, pharmaceuticals, and food products. The company defines its mission as one of helping to feed the world's exploding population while also sustaining the environment. This mission leads to a hierarchy of objectives, including business objectives and marketing objectives. Monsanto's overall objective is to create environmentally better products and get them to market faster at lower costs. For its part, the agricultural division's objective is to increase agricultural productivity and reduce chemical pollution by researching new pest- and disease-resistant crops that produce high yields without chemical spraying. But research is expensive and requires improved profits to plough back into research programs. So improving profits becomes another major business objective. Profits can be improved by increasing sales or reducing costs. Sales can be increased by improving the company's share of the domestic market, by entering new foreign markets, or both. These goals then become the company's current marketing objectives.

Marketing strategies must be developed to support these marketing objectives. To increase its market share, Monsanto may increase its product's availability and promotion. To enter new foreign markets, the company may cut prices and target large firms abroad. These are its broad marketing strategies. Each broad marketing strategy must then be defined in greater detail. For example, increasing the product's promotion may require more salespeople and more advertising; if so, both requirements will have to be spelled out. In this way, the firm's mission is translated into a set of objectives for the current period. The objectives should be as specific as possible. The objective to "increase our market share" is not as useful as the objective to "increase our market share to 15 percent by the end of the second year."

Company mission: 3M states its mission not as making office products, but as creating innovations that "make your work—make your life—simpler, more efficient, more productive."

DESIGNING THE BUSINESS PORTFOLIO

Business portfolio
The collection of businesses and products that comprise the company.

Guided by the company's mission statement and objectives, management now must plan its **business portfolio**—the collection of businesses and products that comprise the company. The best business portfolio is the one that best fits the company's strengths and weaknesses to opportunities in the environment. The company must (1) analyse its *current* business portfolio and decide which businesses should receive more, less, or no investment, and (2) develop growth strategies for adding *new* products or businesses to the portfolio.

ANALYSING THE CURRENT BUSINESS PORTFOLIO

Portfolio analysis
A tool by which management identifies and evaluates the various businesses that make up the company.

The major activity in strategic planning is business **portfolio analysis**, whereby management evaluates the businesses that make up the company. The company will want to put strong resources into its more profitable businesses and phase down or drop its weaker ones. For example, in recent years, John Labatt Ltd. has strengthened its portfolio by selling off its less attractive businesses, including food products (Ault Foods, Catelli-Primo Ltd., Johanna Dairies, and Everfresh Juice Co.) as well as its profitable Sports Network, to invest more heavily in products and technologies for its brewing business. Such tactics provided Labatt with the resources to develop its ice beer. The company benefited in two ways from this product launch: it was able to license the technology in foreign markets such as the United States, Europe, Japan, and Mexico, while also improving its market position in Canada.

Strategic business unit (SBU)
A unit of the company that has a separate mission and objectives and that can be planned independently from other company businesses. An SBU can be a company division, a product line within a division, or sometimes a single product or brand.

Management's first step is to identify the key businesses making up the company. These can be called the strategic business units. A **strategic business unit** (SBU) is a unit of the company that has a separate mission and objectives and that can be planned independently from other company businesses. An SBU can be a company division, a product line within a division, or sometimes a single product or brand.

The next step in business portfolio analysis calls for management to assess the attractiveness of its various SBUs and decide how much support each deserves. In some companies, this is done informally. Management examines the company's collection of businesses or products and decides how much each SBU should contribute and receive. Other companies use formal portfolio-planning methods.

The purpose of strategic planning is to identify ways in which the company can best use its strengths to take advantage of attractive opportunities in the environment. So most standard portfolio-analysis methods evaluate SBUs on two important dimensions—the attractiveness of the SBU's market or industry and the strength of the SBU's position in that market or industry. The best-known portfolio-planning methods were developed by the Boston Consulting Group, a leading management consulting firm, and by General Electric.

Growth-share matrix
A portfolio-planning method that evaluates a company's strategic business units (SBUs) in terms of their market growth rate and relative market share. SBUs are classified as stars, cash cows, question marks, or dogs.

The Boston Consulting Group Approach

Using the Boston Consulting Group (BCG) approach, a company classifies all its SBUs according to the **growth-share matrix** shown in Figure 2-2. On the vertical axis, *market growth rate* provides a measure of market attractiveness. On the horizontal axis, *relative market share* serves as a measure of company strength in the market. By dividing the growth-share matrix as indicated, four types of SBUs can be distinguished:

Stars
High-growth, high-share businesses or products that often require heavy investment to finance their rapid growth.

◆ **Stars.** Stars are high-growth, high-share businesses or products. They often need heavy investment to finance their rapid growth. Eventually their growth will slow down, and they will turn into cash cows.

Cash cows
Low-growth, high-share businesses or products; established and successful units that generate cash that the company uses to pay its bills and support other business units that need investment.

◆ **Cash cows.** Cash cows are low-growth, high-share businesses or products. These established and successful SBUs need less investment to hold their market

FIGURE 2-2 *The BCG growth-share matrix*

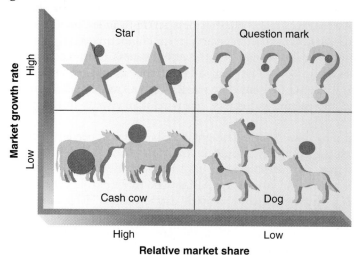

Question marks
Low-share business units in high-growth markets that require a lot of cash in order to hold their share or become stars.

Dogs
Low-growth, low-share businesses and products that may generate enough cash to maintain themselves but do not promise to be large sources of cash.

FIGURE 2-3 *General Electric's strategic business-planning grid*

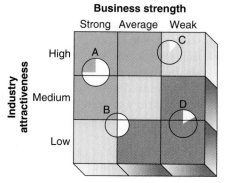

share. Thus, they produce a lot of cash that the company uses to pay its bills and to support other SBUs that need investment.

◆ **Question marks.** Question marks are low-share business units in high-growth markets. They require a lot of cash to hold their share, let alone increase it. Management has to think hard about which question marks it should try to build into stars and which should be phased out.

◆ **Dogs.** Dogs are low-growth, low-share businesses and products. They may generate enough cash to maintain themselves, but do not promise to be large sources of cash.

The 10 circles in the growth-share matrix represent a company's 10 current SBUs. The company has two stars, two cash cows, three question marks, and three dogs. The areas of the circles are proportional to the SBU's dollar sales. This company is in fair shape, although not in good shape. It wants to invest in the more promising question marks to make them stars, and to maintain the stars so that they will become cash cows as their markets mature. Fortunately, it has two good-sized cash cows whose income helps finance the company's question marks, stars, and dogs. The company should take decisive action concerning its dogs and its question marks. The picture would be worse if the company had no stars, if it had too many dogs, or if it had only one weak cash cow.

Once it has classified its SBUs, the company must determine what role each will play in the future. One of four strategies can be pursued for each SBU. The company can invest more in the business unit to *build* its share. Or it can invest just enough to *hold* the SBU's share at the current level. It can *harvest* the SBU, milking its short-term cash flow regardless of the long-term effect. Finally, the company can *divest* the SBU by selling it or phasing it out and using the resources elsewhere.

As time passes, SBUs change their positions in the growth-share matrix. Each SBU has a life cycle. Many SBUs start out as question marks and move into the star category if they succeed. They later become cash cows as market growth falls, then finally die off or turn into dogs toward the end of their life cycle. The company needs to add new products and units continuously so that some will become stars and, eventually, cash cows that will help finance other SBUs.

The General Electric Approach

General Electric introduced a comprehensive portfolio planning tool called a *strategic business-planning grid* (see Figure 2-3). Like the BCG approach, it uses a matrix with two dimensions—one representing industry attractiveness (the vertical axis) and one representing company strength in the industry (the horizontal axis). The best businesses are those located in highly attractive industries where the company has high business strength.

The GE approach considers many factors besides market growth rate as part of industry attractiveness. It uses an industry attractiveness index composed of market size, market growth rate, industry profit margin, amount of competition, seasonality and cyclicality of demand, and industry cost structure. Each factor is rated and combined in an index of industry attractiveness. For our purposes, an industry's attractiveness will be described as high, medium, or low. For example, Kraft has identified numerous highly attractive industries—natural foods, specialty frozen foods, physical fitness products, and others. It has withdrawn from less attractive industries such as bulk oils and cardboard packaging.

For *business strength,* the GE approach again uses an index rather than a simple measure of relative market share. The business strength index includes factors such as the company's relative market share, price competitiveness, product quality, customer and market knowledge, sales effectiveness, and geographic advantages. These factors are rated and combined in an index of business strength, which can be described as strong, average, or weak. Thus, Kraft has substantial business strength in food and related industries, but is relatively weak in the home appliances industry.

The grid is divided into three zones. The green cells at the upper left include the strong SBUs in which the company should invest and grow. The yellow diagonal cells contain SBUs that are medium in overall attractiveness. The company should maintain its level of investment in these SBUs. The three purple cells at the lower right indicate SBUs that are low in overall attractiveness. The company should seriously consider harvesting or divesting these SBUs.

The circles represent four company SBUs; the areas of the circles are proportional to the relative sizes of the industries in which these SBUs compete. The pie slices within the circles represent each SBU's market share. Thus, circle A represents a company SBU with a 75 percent market share in a good-sized, highly attractive industry in which the company has strong business strength. Circle B represents an SBU that has a 50 percent market share, but the industry is not very attractive. Circles C and D represent two other company SBUs in industries where the company has small market shares and not much business strength. Altogether, the company should build A, maintain B, and make some hard decisions on what to do with C and D.

Management also would plot the projected positions of the SBUs with and without changes in strategies. By comparing current and projected business grids, management can identify the major strategic issues and opportunities it faces.

Problems with Matrix Approaches

The BCG, GE, and other formal methods revolutionized strategic planning. However, such approaches have limitations. They can be difficult, time-consuming, and costly to implement. Management may find it difficult to define SBUs and measure market share and growth. In addition, these approaches focus on classifying *current* businesses but provide little advice for *future* planning. Management must still rely on its own judgment to set the business objectives for each SBU, to determine what resources each will be given, and to identify which new businesses should be added.

Formal planning approaches can also lead the company to place too much emphasis on market-share growth or growth through entry into attractive new markets. Using these approaches, many companies plunged into unrelated and new high-growth businesses that they did not know how to manage—with very bad results. At the same time, these companies often were too quick to abandon, sell, or milk to death their healthy mature businesses. As a result, many companies that diversified too broadly in the past now are narrowing their focus and getting back to the basics of serving one or a few industries that they know best.

Despite these and other problems, and although many companies have dropped formal matrix methods in favour of more customized approaches that are better suited to their situations, most companies remain firmly committed to strategic planning. Roughly 75 percent of the Fortune 500 companies practise some form of portfolio planning.[10]

Such analysis is no cure-all for finding the best strategy. But it can help management to understand the company's overall situation, to see how each business or product contributes, to assign resources to its businesses, and to orient the company for future success. When used properly, strategic planning is just one important aspect of overall strategic management—a way of thinking about how to manage a business.[11]

DEVELOPING GROWTH STRATEGIES

Product/market expansion grid
A portfolio-planning tool for identifying company growth opportunities through market penetration, market development, product development, or diversification.

Beyond evaluating current businesses, designing the business portfolio involves finding businesses and products the company should consider in the future. One useful device for identifying growth opportunities is the **product/market expansion grid**,[12] shown in Figure 2-4. We apply it here to Levi Strauss & Co., the clothing manufacturer whose traditional lines include 501 blues and newer lines such as Dockers.

First, Levi Strauss management might consider whether the company's major brands can achieve deeper **market penetration**—making more sales to present customers without changing products in any way. For example, to increase its jeans sales, Levi Strauss might cut prices, increase advertising, get its products into more stores, or obtain better store displays and point-of-purchase merchandising from its retailers. Basically, Levi Strauss management would like to increase usage by current customers and attract customers of other clothing brands to Levi's.

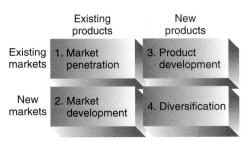

FIGURE 2-4 *Market opportunity identification through the product/ market expansion grid*

Second, Levi Strauss management might consider possibilities for **market development**—identifying and developing new markets for its current products. For instance, managers could review new *demographic markets*—children, senior consumers, women, ethnic groups— to determine whether any new groups could be encouraged to buy Levi Strauss products for the first time. For example, Levi Strauss recently launched new advertising campaigns to boost its jeans sales to women. Managers also could review new *geographical markets*. During the past few years, Levi Strauss has substantially increased its marketing efforts and sales to Western Europe, Asia, and Latin America. It is now targeting newly opened markets in Eastern Europe, Russia, India, and China.

Market penetration
A strategy for company growth by increasing sales of current products to current market segments without changing the product in any way.

Market development
A strategy for company growth by identifying and developing new market segments for current company products.

Product development
A strategy for company growth by offering modified or new products to current market segments.

Diversification
A strategy for company growth by starting up or acquiring businesses outside the company's current products and markets.

Third, management could consider **product development**—offering modified or new products to current markets. Current Levi Strauss products could be offered in new styles, sizes, and colours. Or Levi Strauss could offer new lines and launch new brands of casual clothing to appeal to its current customers. This occurred when Levi Strauss introduced its Dockers line, which now accounts for more than $1.39 billion in annual sales.

Fourth, Levi Strauss might consider **diversification**. It could start up or buy businesses outside of its current products and markets. For example, the company could move into industries such as men's fashions, recreational and exercise apparel, or other related businesses. Some companies try to identify the most attractive emerging industries. They feel that half the secret of success is to enter attractive industries instead of trying to be efficient in unattractive ones. However, a company that diversifies too broadly into unfamiliar products or industries can lose its market focus. For example, prior to 1984 Levi Strauss diversified hastily into a jumbled array of businesses, including skiwear, men's suits and hats, and other specialty apparel. In 1985, however, new management sold these unrelated businesses, refocused the company on its core business of jeans, and designed a solid growth strategy featuring closely related new products and bolder efforts to develop international markets. These actions resulted in a dramatic turnaround in the company's sales and profits.

PLANNING FUNCTIONAL STRATEGIES

The company's strategic plan establishes what kinds of businesses the company will be in and its objectives for each. Then, within each business unit more detailed planning must take place. The major functional departments in each unit—marketing, finance, accounting, purchasing, manufacturing, human resources, and others—must work together to accomplish strategic objectives.

Marketing's Role in Strategic Planning

There is much overlap between overall company strategy and marketing strategy. Marketing looks at consumer needs and the company's ability to satisfy them; these same factors guide the company mission and objectives.

Marketing plays a key role in the company's strategic planning in several ways. First, marketing provides a guiding *philosophy*—the marketing concept—which suggests company strategy should revolve around serving the needs of important consumer groups. Second, marketing provides *inputs* to strategic planners by helping to identify attractive market opportunities and by assessing the firm's potential to take advantage of them. Finally, within individual business units, marketing designs *strategies* for reaching the unit's objectives.

Within each business unit, marketing management must determine the best way to help achieve strategic objectives. Some marketing managers will find that their objective is not necessarily to build sales. Rather, it may be to hold existing sales with a smaller marketing budget, or it actually may be to reduce demand. Thus, marketing management must manage demand to the level stipulated by head-office strategic planners. Marketing helps to assess each business unit's potential, but once the unit's objective is set, marketing's task is to carry it out profitably.

Marketing and the Other Business Functions

Marketers play an important role in delivering customer value and satisfaction. However, marketing cannot do this alone. Because consumer value and satisfaction are affected by the performance of other functions, *all* departments must work together to deliver superior value and satisfaction. Marketing plays an integral role to help ensure that all departments work together toward this goal.

Conflict Between Departments

Each business function has a different view of which publics and activities are most important. Operations focuses on suppliers and production; finance is concerned with stockholders and sound investment; marketing emphasizes consumers and products, pricing, promotion, and distribution. Ideally, all functions should work in harmony to produce value for consumers. But in practice, departmental relations are full of conflicts and misunderstandings. The marketing department takes the consumer's perspective. But when marketing tries to develop customer satisfaction, it often causes other departments to do a poorer job *in their terms*. Marketing department actions can increase purchasing costs, disrupt production schedules, increase inventories, and create budget headaches. Thus, the other departments may resist bending their efforts to the will of the marketing department.

Yet marketers must get all departments to "think consumer" and to place the consumer at the centre of company activity. Customer satisfaction requires a total company effort to deliver superior value to target customers.

> Creating value for buyers is much more than a "marketing function"; rather, [it's] analogous to a symphony orchestra in which the contribution of each subgroup is tailored and integrated by a conductor—with a synergistic effect. A seller must draw upon and integrate effectively . . . its entire human and other capital resources. . . . [Creating superior value for buyers] is the proper focus of the entire business and not merely of a single department in it.[13]

The Du Pont "Adopt a Customer" program recognizes the importance of having people in all of its functions who are "close to the customer." Through this program, people working in Du Pont's plants maintain a direct relationship with customers. For example, operators from Du Pont's nylon-spinning mills visit customers' factories where Du Pont nylon is transformed into swimsuits and other garments, talking to the operators about quality and other problems they encounter with the nylon. Then the Du Pont operators represent their customers on the factory floor. If quality or delivery problems arise, the operators are more likely to see their adopted customers' perspective and to make decisions that will keep customers happy.[14]

Thus, marketing management can best gain support for its goal of consumer satisfaction by working to understand the company's other departments. Marketing managers must work closely with managers of other functions to develop a system of functional plans under which various departments can work together to accomplish the company's overall strategic objectives.

STRATEGIC PLANNING AND SMALL BUSINESS

Many discussions of strategic planning focus on large corporations with many divisions and products. However, small businesses also can benefit greatly from sound strategic planning. Whereas most small ventures start out with extensive business and marketing plans used to attract potential investors, strategic planning often falls by the wayside once the business gets going. Entrepreneurs and presidents of small companies are more likely to spend their time "putting out fires" than planning. But what does a small firm do when it finds that it has taken on too much debt, when its growth is exceeding production capacity, or when it's losing market share to a competitor with lower prices? Strategic planning can help small business managers to anticipate such situations and determine how to prevent or handle them. Marketing Highlight 2-1 provides examples of how small companies used very simple strategic-planning tools to chart their course.

Clearly, strategic planning is crucial to a small company's future. Thom Wellington, president of Wellington Environmental Consulting and Construction, Inc., says that it's important to do strategic planning at a site away from the office. An off-site location offers psychologically neutral ground where employees can be "much more candid," and it removes entrepreneurs from the scene of the fires they spend so much time stamping out.[15]

THE MARKETING PROCESS

The strategic plan defines the company's overall mission and objectives. Within each business unit, marketing plays a role in helping to accomplish the overall strategic objectives. Marketing's role and activities in the organization are shown in Figure 2-5, which summarizes the entire **marketing process** and the forces influencing company marketing strategy.

Marketing process
The process of (1) analysing marketing opportunities; (2) selecting target markets; (3) developing the marketing mix; and (4) managing the marketing effort.

Target consumers stand in the centre. The company identifies the total market, divides it into smaller segments, selects the most promising segments, and focuses on serving and satisfying these segments. It designs a marketing mix composed of factors under its control—product, price, place, and promotion. To find the best marketing mix and put it into action, the company engages in marketing analysis, planning, implementation, and control. Through these activities, the company watches and adapts to the marketing environment. We will now look briefly at each element in the marketing process. In later chapters, we will discuss each element in more depth.

TARGET CONSUMERS

To succeed in today's competitive marketplace, companies must be customer-centred—winning customers from competitors by delivering greater value. But before

MARKETING HIGHLIGHT 2 - 1

SMALL BUSINESS GROWTH

Small businesses are responsible for much of the growth in the Canadian business sector. In recognition of this trend, the Canadian government has begun to focus more on helping entrepreneurs. *A Guide for Canadian Small Business* can be found on the Internet (www.rc.gc.ca). As a recent article on Canada's best-managed private companies noted, strategic planning is as important for small, private firms as it is for their much larger rivals. "We found that the winning companies all have a clear vision and a strategic direction . . . they were always focused. They recognize that they have a competitive advantage and are exploiting it." Two other factors—communicating corporate vision and enhancing employee morale—added to their success. The strategies of many small Canadian businesses are illustrated in the video cases that follow each chapter. Some of the examples provided below were selected from those who won awards in 1996 as some of Canada's Best-Managed Private Companies.

Sabian Ltd., Meductic, New Brunswick

Business: Musical Cymbals

Employees: 100

Annual Sales: $20 million

Forty percent of the cymbals sold around the world come from this small company located in New Brunswick. Its big-name clients include Big Sugar, Phil Collins, Elton John, Eric Clapton, and the Red Hot Chili Peppers. In fact, watch Big Sugar's video for the song, Diggin' a Hole, and you can see the Sabian brand name on the drummer's cymbal. The firm is highly focused and makes six different series of cymbals, which are exported to more than 95 countries. Knowing the market and the customer for this specialized product is at the heart of the company's strategy. The company must be highly customer focused since, according to company president Bill Jildjian, "Each musician decides which product is best suited to expressing him- or herself. In that respect it's more of a collaboration than a business deal."

Source: "Banging the Drum in New Brunswick," *The Financial Post*, December 14, 1996, p. 42.

Cirque du Soleil, Montreal, Quebec

Business: Entertainment

Employees: 1250

Annual Sales: $150 million

Through a series of evolving five-year plans, Cirque du Soleil (www.cirquedu-soleil.com) transformed itself from a small group of young street performers founded in 1984 into a world-renowned entertainment company.

It began by doing 44 shows per year viewed by 30 000 spectators, to holding 1390 performances seen by audiences in excess of 15 million.

The first years focused on issues of survival. Since there was no circus tradition in Canada, it had to build demand for its services from the ground up. Certainly few Canadians thought of the circus as artistic so the group had to carefully position the company in the minds of Canadians. Then, Cirque du Soleil began to develop five-year plans in 1989, only five years after its inception. The first plan outlined strategies for market expansion into Europe, Japan, and the United States. The second plan focused on the development of permanent venues for the circus such as the

ones now in place in Las Vegas and Disney World.

Source: "Balancing Act Finds Its Place in the Sun," *The Financial Post*, December 14, 1996, p.14; www.cirquedusoleil.com

Mascoll Beauty Supply Ltd., Toronto, Ontario

Business: Beauty Products for African-Canadians

Employees: 25

Annual Sales: Unknown

Beverley Mascoll established her business with $700, an idea, industry experience, and the trunk of her car. Beginning her firm with one product line—a hair relaxer she packaged at her kitchen table—she has developed her company into one that now sells over 3000 items. From the earliest days, she understood the power of niche marketing based on personal service. She offered a unique benefit in Canada. No other company was marketing beauty products designed specifically for individuals of African descent. Yet, Mascoll knew that black women spend six times more on hair care and cosmetics than do Caucasian women. Furthermore, they don't scrimp on these products even when times are bad. Consequently, she discovered a recession-proof business. She also found a market where she could ride a growth wave. When she started her business, fewer than 50 000 people of African descent lived in Canada, but since then that number has grown tenfold. Mascoll also understood that few beauticians knew how to treat "black hair." Thus, part of her strategy was to train her customers. She brought the hottest styles to Canada and invited people to their demonstrations, thereby creating demand for her products. Today, Mascoll is not only successful, but also dedicated to giving back to her community. She has worked with Dalhousie University in Halifax to establish the first black history professorship chair in Canada and recently founded the Beverley Mascoll Community Foundation, a philanthropic organization that offers scholarships to deserving students, supports community work, and funds a summer camp for sick children.

Source: Margaret Cannon, "Looking Good, Doing Good," *Report on Business*, December 1996, pp. 99–104.

IKE Inc., St. Catharines, Ontario

Business: Software Entrepreneur

Annual Sales: Less than $1 million

Derek Patriquin and David Roach, founders of IKE (the acronym for Interactive Knowledge-based Enterprises or "I Know Everything") describe their five years as software entrepreneurs as a "trip through hell." Yet, with three products under their belt, they are among the only 10 percent of software firms that survive to market their first product. Three problems overwhelm most software start-up companies: cash, a saturated industry dominated by big-name players, and a product instead of a market focus. IKE still relies on "love money," cash raised from family and friends, to fund its business. And substantial funding is necessary. One industry analyst stresses that without a budget of at least a million dollars, most firms don't have a chance. Such a large budget is essential because Canadian firms must gain acceptance in both the U.S. and Canadian markets.

Entry barriers into this market are substantial. Big-name firms, such as Microsoft, Electronic Arts, Broderbund, and SoftKey, dominate the industry. Unless firms can successful license their product with one of these giants, it is almost impossible to get retail distribution. The big-name firms that license and then publish other's software are viewed as the talent scouts of the industry. Without the logo of one of these companies, retailers are reluctant to take a chance distributing an unknown product. The final flaw in the strategy of many software entrepreneurs is their lack of market orientation. They fall in love with their product and believe that if it's good enough, the world will beat a path to their door. "The failure to do market research before ploughing tens of thousands of dollars into development is perhaps the most common blunder that trips up software start-ups." Derek Patriquin and David Roach have learned a lot about marketing, distribution, and business management since 1992 when they conceived their company in a St. Catharines pub. Rapid changes in technology can change an industry overnight and this hope keeps dreams of riches dancing in the heads of these two entrepreneurs.

Source: Joanna Pachner, "We've Been Through Hell," *The Financial Post* magazine, October 1997, pp. 50–57, quotation from p. 54.

Smart Technologies Inc., Calgary, Alberta

Business: Interactive Whiteboards

Employees: 100

Annual Sales: $10 million

If your university is upgrading its classrooms to meet the needs of the electronic age, you will see Smart Technologies' products becoming part of the classroom setting. Interactive electronic whiteboards allow users in classrooms or boardrooms to access and display information from the Internet, run video and CD-ROM presentations, or demonstrate spreadsheets in real time. They allow multiple sites to work from the same information display. In New Brunswick, students at 90 different remote sites can participate in lectures. Nova Corporation of Alberta uses the technology to train its employees at 12 different locations. Smart Technologies had great strategic insight about how a new market would evolve. With the costs of corporate travel rising rapidly, management believed that more and more meetings would be conducted without people flying to different locations to meet in person. Another of the keys of the firm's strategy is forming partnerships with key firms such as Intel and PictureTel Corporation, which have about half the global market for video-conferencing systems.

Source: "Magic Moment in Vegas," *The Financial Post*, December 14, 1996, p. 46; smartdna.com

Silent Witness Enterprises Ltd., Surrey, British Columbia

Business: Security Cameras

Employees: 25

Annual Sales: $1.9 million

The founders of Silent Witness didn't start their business with a new product; instead, they developed a better product—one that is smaller, cheaper, more versatile, and more durable than rival infrared cameras. The veracity of this claim is witnessed by its ability to take on much larger rivals such as Sony and Panasonic, and receive coverage of its exploits in the Wall Street Journal. The ability to design

such a good product was based on the fact that the founding partners knew their market. Bob Galbraith was chief coroner of British Columbia and a former member of the RCMP, and Rob Bakshi was a computer consultant to the coroner's office. The company sells 95 percent of its products to American customers. They captured fifty percent of the market for vandalism-plagued school buses. It has leveraged this success onto a line of surveillance systems for public transit buses, and through a distributor, now sells cameras for general use in U.S. schools, businesses, and "smart homes." However, winning in the United States isn't enough for this firm. They have plans to begin marketing in Europe, South America, and Asia.

Source: Deborah Jones, "Candid Cameras," *Report on Business*, April 1996, pp. 109–112.

The following steps summarize the process by which the small firms described above create their strategic plan, from which a number of department and individual employee plans follow. The process hinges on an assessment of the company, its place in the market, and its goals.

1. Identify the major elements of the business environment in which the organization has operated over the previous few years.

2. Describe the mission of the organization in terms of its nature and function for the next two years.

3. Explain the internal and external forces that will affect the mission of the organization.

4. Identify the basic driving force that will direct the organization in the future.

5. Develop a set of long-term objectives that will identify what the organization will become in the future.

6. Outline a general plan of action which defines the logistical, financial, and personnel factors needed to integrate the long-term objectives into the total organization.

Source: Leslie Brokaw, "The Secrets of Great Planning," *Inc.*, October 1992, p. 152; and Philip Kotler, *Marketing Management: Analysis, Planning, Implementation, and Control*, 9th ed. (Upper Saddle River, NJ: Prentice Hall, 1997), Chapter 3.

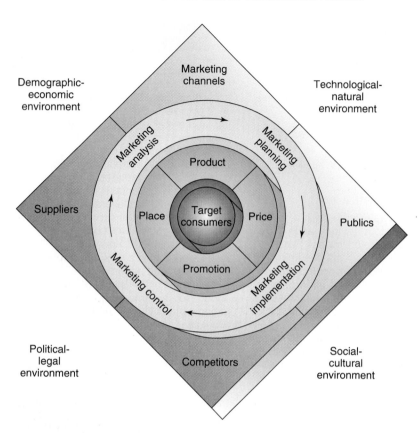

FIGURE 2-5 *Factors influencing company marketing strategy*

it can satisfy consumers, a company must first understand their needs and wants. Thus, sound marketing requires a careful analysis of consumers.

Terry Ortt, who became president of Canada's Journey's End Corp. in 1992, understood the need for this type of information. Although conventional wisdom was that Journey's End customers were mainly businesspeople on two-day trips, after digging through 10 million guest registration cards, Ortt discovered that this was a myth. Instead of businesspeople, 45 percent of his guests were from rural areas. Understanding the value of this information, Ortt developed a sophisticated database to track guests' needs and wants from the time they request wake-up calls to what they eat for breakfast. The power of a database lies in its ability to track actual customers' behaviour versus their intentions or what they say they do. This information will allow the firm to provide the unique services demanded by individual guests, reward them for repeat visits and multiple night stays, and allow them to target promotional information on specials to each guest by name.[16]

Companies know that they cannot satisfy all consumers in a given market—at least not all consumers in the same way. There are too many different kinds of consumers with too many different kinds of needs. And some companies are in a better position to serve certain segments of the market. Thus, each company must divide up the total market, choose the best segments, and design strategies for profitably serving chosen segments better than its competitors do. This process involves three steps: *market segmentation, market targeting,* and *market positioning.*

Market Segmentation

The market consists of many types of customers, products, and needs, and the marketer has to determine which segments offer the best opportunity for achieving company objectives. Consumers can be grouped in various ways based on geographic, psychographic, and behavioural factors. The process of dividing a market into distinct groups of buyers with different needs, characteristics, or behaviour who might require separate products or marketing mixes is called **market segmentation.**

Market segmentation
Dividing a market into distinct groups of buyers with different needs, characteristics, or behaviour who might require separate products or marketing mixes.

Market segment
A group of consumers who respond in a similar way to a given set of marketing stimuli.

Every market has market segments, but not all ways of segmenting a market are equally useful. For example, Tylenol would gain little by distinguishing between male and female users of pain relievers if both purchase the product to relieve headaches and respond to marketing efforts in the same way. A **market segment** consists of consumers who respond in a similar way to a given set of marketing efforts. In the car market, for example, consumers who choose the biggest, most comfortable car regardless of price comprise one market segment. Another market segment would be customers who care mainly about price and operating economy. It would be difficult to make one model of car that was the first choice of every consumer. Companies are wise to focus their efforts on meeting the distinct needs of one or more market segments.

Market Targeting

Market targeting
The process of evaluating each market segment's attractiveness and selecting one or more segments to enter.

After a company has defined market segments, it can enter one or many segments of a given market. **Market targeting** involves evaluating each market segment's attractiveness and selecting one or more segments to enter. A company should target segments in which it can generate the greatest customer value and sustain it over time. A company with limited resources might decide to serve only one or a few special segments. This strategy limits sales, but can be very profitable. Or a company might choose to serve several related segments—perhaps those with different kinds of customers but with the same basic wants. Or a large company might decide to offer a complete range of products to serve all market segments.

Most companies enter a new market by serving a single segment, and if this proves successful, they add segments. Large companies eventually seek full market coverage. They want to be the "General Motors" of their industry. GM says that it makes a car for every "person, purse, and personality." The leading company normally has different products designed to meet the special needs of each segment.

Market Positioning

After a company has decided which market segments to enter, it must decide what "positions" it wants to occupy in those segments. A product's *position* is the place the product occupies relative to competitors in consumers' minds. If a product is

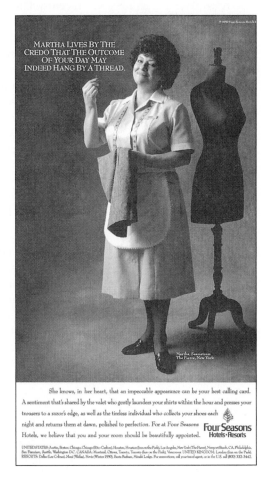

Market positioning: Comfort and Quality Inns position on value—they don't "add frills that only add to your bill." In contrast, Four Seasons Hotels positions on luxury. For those who can afford it, Four Seasons offers endless amenities—such as a seamstress, a valet, and a "tireless individual who collects your shoes each night and returns them at dawn, polished to perfection."

perceived to be exactly like another product on the market, consumers would have no reason to buy it.

Market positioning is arranging for a product to occupy a clear, distinctive, and desirable place in the minds of target consumers relative to competing products. Thus, marketers plan positions that distinguish their products from competing brands and give them the greatest strategic advantage in their target markets. For example, Buick has "the power of understatement." Saturn is "a different kind of company, different kind of car." Mazda has "a passion for the road," and Toyota consumers say "I love what you do for me." Jaguar is positioned as "a blending of art and machine," whereas Mercedes is "engineered like no other car in the world." The luxurious Bentley is "the closest a car can come to having wings." Such deceptively simple statements form the backbone of a product's marketing strategy.

Market positioning
Arranging for a product to occupy a clear, distinctive, and desirable place relative to competing products in the minds of target consumers.

In positioning its product, the company first identifies possible competitive advantages on which to build the position. For example, if the company has the capability of being the lowest cost producer in an industry, it can position its products as offering the best value to consumers relative to all other competitors. There are many other ways of creating a unique place in consumers' minds, however. Companies can position their products on the basis of superior quality, the image associated with a particular lifestyle, relative to a particular competitor (for example, 7-Up "The Uncola"), or on the basis of a unique feature or benefit. Cadbury recently launched a new chocolate bar, Time Out, using an integrated, multimedia campaign (www.cadbury.chocolate.ca/time.out). Its positioning statement for the product could have been written as follows: For *time-pressed adults* (the target market) who *need an energy boost* (statement of need), *Time Out* (the brand) is a *chocolate bar* (product category), that is a *perfect way to take a break* (key benefit or reason to buy). Unlike *rich, heavy chocolate bars* (competitive offerings), our product/service *is a light wafer snack with a chocolate wave* (statement of differentiation). Once the company has chosen a desired position, it must take strong steps to deliver and communicate that position to target consumers. The company's entire marketing program should support the chosen positioning strategy.

Cadbury
www.cadbury.chocolate.ca/

MARKETING STRATEGIES FOR COMPETITIVE ADVANTAGE

To be successful, the company must do a better job than its competitors of satisfying target consumers. Thus, marketing strategies must be geared to the needs of consumers and also to the strategies of competitors.

Designing competitive marketing strategies begins with thorough competitor analysis. The company constantly compares the value and customer satisfaction delivered by its products, prices, channels, and promotion with that of its close competitors. In this way it can discern areas of potential advantage and disadvantage. The company must formally or informally monitor the competitive environment to answer these and other important questions: Who are our competitors? What are their objectives and strategies? What are their strengths and weaknesses? And how will they react to different competitive strategies we might use?

The competitive marketing strategy a company adopts depends on its industry position. A firm that dominates a market can adopt one or more of several *market-leader* strategies. Well-known leaders include Coca-Cola (soft drinks), McDonald's (fast food), Caterpillar (large construction equipment), Kodak (photographic film), Loblaw (grocery retailing), and Boeing (aircraft). *Market challengers* are runner-up companies that aggressively attack competitors to get more market share. For example, Pepsi challenges Coke, and Compaq challenges IBM. The challenger might attack the market leader, other firms of its size, or smaller local and regional competitors. Some runner-up firms will choose to follow rather than challenge the market leader. Firms using *market-follower* strategies seek stable market shares and profits by following competitors' product offers, prices, and marketing programs. Smaller firms in a market, or even larger firms that lack established positions, often adopt *market-nicher* strategies. These firms specialize in serving market niches that major competitors overlook or ignore (see Marketing Highlight 2-2). "Nichers" avoid direct confrontations with the majors by specializing along market, customer, product, or marketing-mix lines. Through smart niching, low-share firms in an industry can be as profitable as their larger competitors. We will discuss competitive marketing strategies more fully in Chapter 18.

DEVELOPING THE MARKETING MIX

Marketing mix
The set of controllable tactical marketing tools—product, price, place, and promotion—that the firm blends to produce the response it wants in the target market.

Ford Canada
www.ford.ca/

Once the company has decided on its overall competitive marketing strategy, it is ready to begin planning the details of the marketing mix. The marketing mix is one of the major concepts in modern marketing. We define **marketing mix** as the set of controllable tactical marketing tools that the firm blends to produce the response it wants in the target market. The marketing mix consists of everything the firm can do to influence the demand for its product. The many possibilities can be collected into four groups of variables known as the "four Ps": *product, price, place,* and *promotion.*[17] Figure 2-6 shows the particular marketing tools under each P.

Product means the "goods-and-service" combination the company offers to the target market. Thus, a Ford Taurus "product" consists of nuts and bolts, spark plugs, pistons, headlights, and thousands of other parts. Ford offers several Taurus styles and dozens of optional features. The car comes fully serviced and with a comprehensive warranty that is as much a part of the product as the tailpipe.

Price is the amount of money customers have to pay to obtain the product. Ford calculates suggested retail prices that its dealers might charge for each Taurus. But Ford dealers rarely charge the full sticker price. Instead, they negotiate the price with each customer, offering discounts, trade-in allowances, and credit

FIGURE 2-6 *The four Ps of the marketing mix*

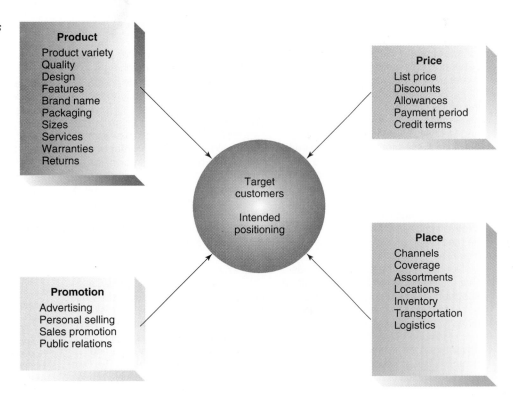

THRIVING IN A GIANT'S SHADOW

When someone says "fast-food restaurant," what's the first name that comes to mind? Chances are good that it's McDonald's, the world's largest food-service organization. Ask the same question in the Philippines, however, and the first name uttered likely will be Jollibee. In the grand scheme of global commerce, Jollibee Foods Corporation isn't exactly a household name. But in its niche—the Philippines—it's leader of the burger market.

At first glance, the rivalry between Jollibee and McDonald's looks like no contest. McDonald's has more than 21 000 outlets in 96 countries, 2735 of them in Asia alone. By comparison, Jollibee has fewer than 225 restaurants, contributing just $250 million in annual revenues. Despite these lopsided numbers, however, small Jollibee is giving giant McDonald's more than it can handle. Jollibee captures a 75 percent share of the Philippines' hamburger chain market and 55 percent of the fast-food market as a whole. And its sales are growing rapidly and profitably.

What's Jollibee's secret? Smart niching. Whereas McDonald's exports largely standardized fare to consumers around the world, Jollibee is relentlessly local—it concentrates on serving the unique tastes of Filipino consumers. Jollibee cooks up sweet, spicy burgers and serves seasoned chicken and spaghetti with sweet sauce, the way Filipinos like it.

Beyond its special understanding of the Filipino palate, Jollibee has also mastered the country's culture and lifestyle. "What happens in the normal Filipino family is that weekends are especially for children," notes a Filipino business analyst, "and parents try to ask their children where they want to eat." Jollibee lures kids with in-store play activities and a cast of captivating characters. Its hamburger-headed Champ, complete with boxing gloves, goes head-to-head with McDonald's Hamburglar. And its massive orange-jacketed bee and a blonde spaghetti-haired girl named Hetti are better known and loved in the Philippines than Ronald McDonald.

Jollibee has some additional advantages in this seemingly unfair rivalry. Although much smaller in global terms than McDonald's, Jollibee concentrates its limited resources within the Philippines, where its restaurants outnumber McDonald's by two to one. It also receives a measure of protection through government regulations that limit McDonald's and other foreign competitors. But its primary advantage comes from simply doing a better job of giving Filipino consumers what they want. Small can be beautiful, and Jollibee has shown that—through smart niching—small players can compete effectively against industry giants.

Through smart market niching, Jollibee has knocked out McDonald's.

In an effort to conquer Jollibee's niche, McDonald's is launching a comeback. The company is rapidly adding new locations and introducing its own Filipino-style dishes. However, Jollibee managers don't seem overly worried about their rival's new moves. McDonald's may have greater universal appeal, but Jollibee knows its niche. "Maybe they'll gain market share," says Jollibee's chief executive, "but I don't think anybody can beat us out because, in the final analysis, the customer is the one deciding." Notes the business analyst, "The Jollibee burger is similar to what a Filipino mother would cook at home."

Like Jollibee, many small Canadian companies have successfully used niche marketing strategies. For example, Benkris & Co., the small Calgary kitchenware company, has made national headlines after being named innovative retailer of the year. The owners, Bev and Rick Durvin, have translated an initial $24 000 investment into a one-million-dollar-a-year business. What are their keys to success in an industry characterized by fierce competition among large national retailers such as Hudson's Bay or Eaton's, and plagued by sluggish sales growth?

First, they live their mission statement rather than framing it and hanging it on the wall. Their mission is "to create an excitement for quality selection and service." While this statement may seem vague, implementing it is a very exact task. They concentrate on fulfilling their customers' needs and desires. Their intimate knowledge of customers has enabled them to tailor their assortment to the needs of local markets (each of their three stores has a unique product mix).

Next, they understand the value of a unique product mix, offering an assortment of kitchen goods ranging from Mexican glassware to exotic teas. They also understand that shopping is a highly sensual experience. Their stores are visually appealing, their displays striking, and their stores filled with the aroma of freshly ground coffee. They show products in use in the cooking classes that they run along with their retail business.

Perhaps most importantly, they never underestimate the value of good, knowledgable, personalized customer service. Not only do they spend heavily on staff training, but they also allow staff members to take products home to use so they know how their stock of kitchen appliances performs. They hire staff members based on their enthusiasm and interpersonal skills instead of on their retail experience, and they reward and compensate them generously. Finally, they have made their stores a fun place for both their staff and their customers, following the philosophy that creativity and a sense of fun can turn even bad decisions into marketing opportunities.

Sources: Quotations from Hugh Filman, "Happy Meals for McDonald's Rival," *Business Week*, July 29, 1996, p. 77; and Cris Prystay and Sanjay Kumar, "Asia Bites Back," *Asian Business*, January 1997, pp. 58–60. Also see John H. Christy and Gustavo Lombo, "Foreign Gems," *Forbes*, November 4, 1996, pp. 268–262. Ellen Roseman, "Getting It Together," *Globe and Mail*, June 20, 1994, p. B8.

terms to adjust for the current competitive situation and to bring the price into line with the buyer's perception of the car's value.

Place includes company activities that make the product available to target consumers. Ford maintains a large body of independently owned dealerships that sell the company's many different models. Ford selects its dealers carefully and supports them strongly. The dealers keep an inventory of Ford automobiles, demonstrate them to potential buyers, negotiate prices, close sales, and service the cars after the sale.

Promotion means activities that communicate the merits of the product and persuade target customers to buy it. Ford spends more than $850 million worldwide each year on advertising to tell consumers about the company and its products. Dealership salespeople assist potential buyers and persuade them that Ford offers the best car for them. Ford and its dealers offer special promotions— sales, cash rebates, low financing rates—as added purchase incentives.

An effective marketing program blends all of the marketing mix elements into a coordinated program designed to achieve the company's marketing objectives by delivering value to consumers. The marketing mix constitutes the company's tactical tool kit for establishing strong positioning in target markets.

MANAGING THE MARKETING EFFORT

The company wants to design and put into action the marketing mix that will best achieve its objectives in its target markets. Figure 2-7 shows the relationship between the four marketing management functions—*analysis, planning, implementation,* and *control.* After careful analysis of its situation, the company develops overall strategic plans. These company-wide strategic plans are then translated into marketing and other plans for each division, product, and brand. Through implementation, the company turns the plans into actions. Control consists of measuring and evaluating the results of marketing activities and taking corrective action where needed.

MARKETING ANALYSIS

Managing the marketing function begins with a complete analysis of the company's situation. The company must analyse its markets and marketing environment to identify attractive opportunities and avoid environmental threats. It must analyse company strengths and weaknesses, as well as current and possible marketing actions, to determine which opportunities it can best pursue. Marketing analysis

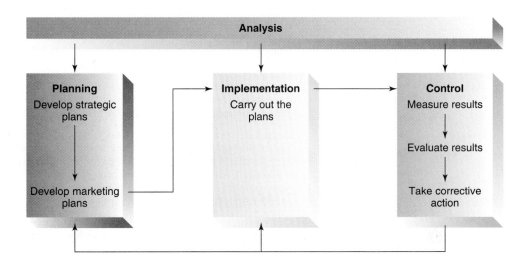

FIGURE 2-7 *The relationship between analysis, planning, implementation, and control*

feeds information and other inputs to each of the other marketing management functions. We discuss marketing analysis more fully in Chapter 4.

MARKETING PLANNING

Through strategic planning, the company decides what it wants to do with each business unit. Marketing planning involves deciding on marketing strategies that will help the company attain its overall strategic objectives. A detailed marketing plan is needed for each business, product, or brand. What does a marketing plan look like? Our discussion focuses on product or brand plans.

Table 2-2 outlines the major sections of a typical product or brand plan. The plan begins with an executive summary that quickly overviews major assessments,

TABLE 2-2 *Contents of a Marketing Plan*

Section	Purpose
Executive summary	Presents a brief summary of the main goals and recommendations of the plan for management review, helping top management to find the plan's major points quickly. A table of contents should follow the executive summary.
Current marketing situation	Describes the target market and the company's position in it, including information about the market, product performance, competition, and distribution. This section includes: • A *market description* that defines the market and major segments, then reviews customer needs and factors in the marketing environment that may affect customer purchasing. • A *product review* that shows sales, prices, and gross margins of the major products in the product line. • A review of *competition*, which identifies major competitors and assesses their market positions and strategies for product quality, pricing, distribution, and promotion. • A review of *distribution* that evaluates recent sales trends and other developments in major distribution channels.
Threats and opportunity analysis	Assesses major threats and opportunities that the product might face, helping management to anticipate important positive or negative developments that might have an impact on the firm and its strategies.
Objectives and issues	States the marketing objectives that the company would like to attain during the plan's term and discusses key issues that will affect their attainment. For example, if the goal is to achieve a 15 percent market share, this poses the key issue: How can market share be increased?
Marketing strategy	Outlines the broad marketing logic by which the business unit hopes to achieve its marketing objectives and the specifics of target markets, positioning, and marketing expenditure levels. It outlines specific strategies for each marketing mix element and explains how each responds to the threats, opportunities, and critical issues spelled out earlier in the plan.
Action programs	Spells out how marketing strategies will be turned into specific action programs that answer the following questions: *What* will be done? *When* will it be done? *Who* is responsible for doing it? And *how much* will it cost?
Budgets	Details a supporting marketing budget that is essentially a projected profit-and-loss statement. It shows expected revenues (forecasted number of units sold and the average net price) and expected costs (of production, distribution, and marketing). The difference is the projected profit. Once approved by higher management, the budget is the basis for materials buying, production scheduling, personnel planning, and marketing operations.
Controls	Outline the controls that will be used to monitor progress and allow higher management to review implementation results and spot products that are not meeting their goals.

goals, and recommendations. The main section of the plan presents a detailed analysis of the current marketing situation, and of potential threats and opportunities. It next states major objectives for the brand and outlines the specifics of a marketing strategy for achieving them. A **marketing strategy** is the marketing logic by which the company hopes to achieve its marketing objectives. It consists of specific strategies for target markets, positioning, the marketing mix, and marketing expenditure levels. In this section, the planner explains how each strategy responds to threats, opportunities, and critical issues outlined earlier in the plan. Additional sections of the marketing plan lay out an action program for implementing the marketing strategy, along with the details of a supporting *marketing budget*. The last section outlines the controls that will be used to monitor progress and take corrective action.

Marketing strategy
The marketing logic by which the business unit hopes to achieve its marketing objectives.

MARKETING IMPLEMENTATION

Planning good strategies is only a start toward successful marketing. A brilliant marketing strategy counts for little if the company fails to implement it properly. **Marketing implementation** is the process that turns marketing strategies and *plans* into marketing *actions* to accomplish strategic marketing objectives. Implementation involves day-to-day, month-to-month activities that effectively put the marketing plan to work. Whereas marketing planning addresses the *what* and *why* of marketing activities, implementation addresses the *who, where, when,* and *how.*

Marketing implementation
The process that turns marketing strategies and plans into marketing actions to accomplish strategic marketing objectives.

Many managers think that "doing things right" (implementation) is as important as, or even more important than, "doing the right things" (strategy). Yet both are critical to success. However, companies can gain competitive advantages through effective implementation. One firm can have essentially the same strategy as another, yet win in the marketplace through faster or better execution. Still, implementation is difficult—it is often easier to develop good marketing strategies than it is to execute them.

People at all levels of the marketing system must work together to implement marketing plans and strategies. At Procter & Gamble, for example, marketing implementation requires day-to-day decisions and actions by thousands of people both inside and outside the organization. Marketing managers make decisions about target segments, branding, packaging, pricing, promoting, and distributing. They work with people elsewhere in the company to get support for their products and programs. They talk with engineering about product design, with manufacturing about production and inventory levels, and with finance about funding and cash flows. They also work with outside people, such as advertising agencies to plan advertising campaigns and the media to obtain publicity support. The sales force urges retailers to advertise P&G products, provide ample shelf space, and use company displays.

Successful implementation depends on how well the company blends its people, organization structure, decision and reward systems, and company culture into a cohesive action program that supports its strategies. At all levels, the company must be staffed by people who have the needed skills, motivation, and personal characteristics. The company's formal organization structure plays an important role in implementing marketing strategy. So do its decision and reward systems. For example, if a company's compensation system rewards managers for short-run profit results, they will have little incentive to work toward long-run market-building objectives.

Finally, to be successfully implemented, the firm's marketing strategies must fit with its company culture, the system of values and beliefs shared by people in the organization—the company's collective identity and meaning. Marketing strategies that do not fit the company's culture will be difficult to implement. For example, a decision by Procter & Gamble to increase sales by reducing product

MARKETERS SPEAK OUT

JIM SHENKMAN, ENTREPRENEUR

Jim Shenkman is good at coming up with new business ideas and turning them into reality. He took a small, family-owned, freight forwarding company and helped build it into the second-largest firm of its type in Canada. The firm was sold in the early 1980s when he realized that if you lacked the resources to operate on a world scale, like Federal Express, you could no longer play in the game.

He then turned his attention to getting an FM radio licence. Although his application was unsuccessful, he realized that there was an interesting hole in the Canadian communications market—there just wasn't enough trade information for broadcasters and producers. While there were many successful U.S. publications covering different segments of this industry on a monthly, weekly, and even daily basis, most people he talked to didn't think even one publication combining all of these segments would succeed in Canada. In 1986, Jim formed Brunico Communications Inc. and, without any previous experience in publishing or production, launched *Playback*. It wasn't long before sales were 2.5 times his original, most optimistic forecast. The biweekly paper positions itself as Canada's broadcast and production journal, serving the

information needs and interests of those involved in Canadian TV broadcasting and in TV, film, and commercial production.

By 1989, with the success of *Playback* well established, Jim was getting restless again. There was a clear need for a publication that focused on strategies for marketers, rather than simply on the business

Jim Shenkman

of ad agencies and the media. Thus, *Strategy: The Canadian Marketing Report*, was launched as a second, biweekly paper. The timing, however, was unfortunate. The economy was

just heading into a long recession, resulting in cutbacks to the size and budgets of marketing departments, consolidations of companies, and a significant shift of marketing decision-making power to the United States. The new paper served a real need for marketers, however. *Strategy* survived and soon developed into the leading marketing publication in Canada.

With two successful publications under his belt, many would think that Jim would be content. Not likely! Three years ago, he started to ask, "What next?" A chance conversation with a Canadian producer gave Jim the idea for an international magazine covering a niche sector in which Canada excelled: children's television. He attended a trade show in France and confirmed that the idea was a winner. Whereas the world already had 80 or more trade publications that covered the kids' market as part of their more general sector coverage, none offered an overall perspective. Thus, in January 1996, Brunico launched *KidScreen*, about reaching children through entertainment, and the title became a world leader in less than two years. *KidScreen*'s success has proven that a leading international magazine can be published out of Canada. It also resulted in the opening of a Brunico office in Los Angeles.

quality and charging low prices would not work well. It would be resisted by P&G people at all levels who identify strongly with the company's reputation for quality. Because company culture is so hard to change, companies usually design strategies that fit their current cultures, rather than trying to change their styles and cultures to fit new strategies.

MARKETING DEPARTMENT ORGANIZATION

The company must design a marketing department that can carry out marketing analysis, planning, implementation, and control. If the company is very small, one person might do all of the marketing work—research, selling, advertising, customer service, and other activities. As the company expands, a marketing department organization emerges to plan and carry out marketing activities. In large companies, this department contains many specialists. Thus, General Mills has product managers, salespeople and sales managers, market researchers, advertising experts, and other specialists.

Modern marketing departments can be arranged in several ways. The most common form of marketing organization is the *functional organization* in which different marketing activities are headed by a functional specialist—a sales manager, advertising manager, marketing research manager, customer service manager, new-product manager. A company that sells across the country or internationally

In 1997, *RealScreen* was born. This magazine is aimed at people who produce, broadcast, and market documentary, information magazine, and lifestyle programming. *RealScreen* became a hit from its very first issue and is the only publication of its kind in the world.

What next for Jim and his company? Well, Jim has realized that the real potential value of Brunico is based not simply on the paper publications he has launched, but on the brands that these titles represent. He sees the key to greater success as continued relationship-building with his customers, catering to the information and marketing solutions they are seeking. The reputations of the publications and his organization can be leveraged into many ancillary products and services. Jim and his team are now launching innovative online services, conferences, award shows, newsletters, and directories, and are preparing to offer direct response marketing solutions.

Jim has learned a lot of lessons getting small, upstart ventures off the ground. First, he says no entrepreneur should ever underestimate the amount of financing that will be needed. There are only two times a businessperson should seek to raise funds, he believes. When your idea is just a dream; you can get people excited enough to invest. And if you survive until the business is a proven success to the world at large, you can attract investment at a reasonable price. Getting start-up capital in Canada, isn't as difficult as some people think, says Jim. If you have good ideas, the money to back them up is there. Often it is just as easy to raise a large sum of money as a small amount. And from personal experience, he says to always keep in mind the possibility of the next recession by having adequate financing and maintaining the flexibility to reduce costs quickly.

Jim has learned that being an expert in a field is not necessarily a prerequisite to success. Jim studied political science and urban studies before becoming a lawyer. He didn't know anything about the freight forwarding business, publishing, or film production when he started in these ventures. However, he is perceptive, willing to flout conventional wisdom, very organized, disciplined, and solution-oriented. He attends as many conferences and trade shows to listen, look, and meet people, and reads as many related trade publications as possible. Armed with the knowledge he acquires, he can quickly develop a business plan aimed at carving out a niche market for a product or service. He is a generalist with eyes wide open.

Ultimately, Jim aspires to be more than a successful entrepreneur. As exciting as it has been to identify good niche opportunities and offer better service and better products, he longs to be a true "agent of change." He marvels at those who have developed visions of serving markets in an entirely different manner. Examples that come to his mind include the pioneers behind Federal Express, CNN, Dell Computers, and 1-800-Flowers.

As you can see from the above paragraphs, Jim tries to follow his own advice. He's certainly been entrepreneurial and often among the first to identify trends and opportunities. Aside from new product ideas, Brunico was also one of the first in the world to use desktop publishing when the technology was just getting off the ground in the mid-1980s and among the first to offer full text searching of its Internet publications in the mid-1990s. Jim isn't sure just where the company's Internet products will take them, but he recognizes that this technology is revolutionizing the way people do business and marketing. By the time others have figured out its potential, you can bet Jim will already have moved on, always aspiring to be a visionary and, one day, a true agent of change.

Source: www.brunico.com

often uses a *geographic organization* in which its sales and marketing people are assigned to specific countries, regions, and districts. Geographic organization allows salespeople to settle into a territory, get to know their customers, and work with a minimum of travel time and cost.

Companies with many, very different products or brands often create a *product management organization*. Using this approach, a product manager develops and implements a complete strategy and marketing program for a specific product or brand. Procter & Gamble first used product management in 1929. A new company soap, Camay, was not doing well, and a young P&G executive was assigned to focus exclusively on developing and promoting this product. He was successful, and the company soon added other product managers.[18] Since then, many firms, especially in the food, soap, toiletries, and chemical industries, have set up product management organizations. Today, the product management system is firmly entrenched. However, recent dramatic changes in the marketing environment have caused many companies to rethink the role of the product manager (see Marketing Highlight 2-3).

For companies that sell one product line to many different types of markets that have different needs and preferences, a *market management organization* might be best. Many companies are organized along market lines. A market management organization is similar to the product management organization.

RETHINKING BRAND MANAGEMENT

Brand management has become a fixture in most consumer packaged-goods companies. Brand managers plan long-term brand strategy and watch over their brand's profits. Working closely with advertising agencies, they create national advertising campaigns to build market share and long-term consumer brand loyalty. The brand management system made sense in its earlier days, when the food companies were all-powerful, consumers were brand loyal, and national media could reach mass markets effectively. Recently, however, many companies have begun to question whether this system fits well with today's radically different marketing realities.

Two major environmental forces are causing companies to rethink brand management. First, consumers, markets, and marketing strategies have changed dramatically. Today's consumers face an ever-growing set of acceptable brands and are exposed to never-ending price promotions. As a result, they are becoming less brand loyal. Also, whereas brand managers have traditionally focused on long-term, national brand-building strategies targeting mass audiences,

today's marketplace realities demand shorter-term, sales-building strategies designed for local markets.

A second major force affecting brand management is the growing

Rethinking the role of the product manager: Campbell set up "brand sales managers."

power of retailers. Larger, more powerful, and better-informed retailers are now demanding more trade promotions in exchange for scarce shelf space. The increase in trade promotion spending leaves fewer dollars for

national advertising, the brand manager's primary marketing tool. Retailers also want more customized "multibrand" promotions that span many of the producer's brands and help retailers to compete better. Such promotions are beyond the scope of any single brand manager and must be designed at higher levels of the company.

These and other changes have significantly changed the way companies market their products, causing marketers to rethink the brand management system that has served them so well for many years. Although it is unlikely that brand managers will soon be extinct, many companies are now groping for alternative ways to manage their brands.

One alternative is to change the nature of the brand manager's job. For example, some companies are asking their brand managers to spend more time in the field working with salespeople, learning what is happening in stores and getting closer to the customer. Campbell Soup created "brand sales managers," a combination of product managers and salespeople charged with handling brands in the field,

Market managers are responsible for developing long-range and annual plans for the sales and profits in their markets. This system's main advantage is that the company is organized around the needs of specific customer segments.

Large companies that produce many different products flowing into many different geographic and customer markets use some *combination* of the functional, geographic, product, and market organization forms. This assures that each function, product, and market receives its share of management attention. However, it can also add costly layers of management and reduce organizational flexibility. Still, the benefits of organizational specialization usually outweigh the drawbacks.[19]

MARKETING CONTROL

Marketing control
The process of measuring and evaluating the results of marketing strategies and plans, and taking corrective action to ensure that marketing objectives are attained.

Because many surprises occur during the implementation of marketing plans, the marketing department must practise constant marketing control. **Marketing control** involves evaluating the results of marketing strategies and plans and taking corrective action to ensure that objectives are attained. It involves the four steps shown in Figure 2-8. Management first sets specific marketing goals. It then measures its performance in the marketplace and evaluates the causes of any differences between expected and actual performance. Finally, management takes corrective action to close the gaps between its goals and its performance. This may require changing the action programs or even changing the goals.

working with the trade, and designing more localized brand strategies.

As another alternative, Procter & Gamble, Colgate-Palmolive, Kraft-General Foods, RJR-Nabisco, and other companies have adopted *category management* systems. Under this system, brand managers report to a category manager who has total responsibility for an entire product line. For example, at Procter and Gamble, the brand manager for Dawn liquid dishwashing detergent reports to a manager who is responsible for Dawn, Ivory, Joy, and all other liquid detergents. The liquids manager, in turn, reports to a manager who is responsible for all of P&G's packaged soaps and detergents, including dishwashing detergents, and liquid and dry laundry detergents.

Category management offers many advantages. First, rather than focusing on specific brands, category managers shape the company's entire category offering. This results in a more complete and coordinated category offer. Perhaps the most important benefit of category management is that it links up better with new retailer "category buying" systems, in which retailers have begun making

their individual buyers responsible for working with all suppliers of a specific product category.

Some companies are combining category management with another concept: *brand teams* or *category teams.* For example, instead of having several cookie brand managers, Nabisco has three cookie category management teams—one each for adult rich cookies, nutritional cookies, and children's cookies. Headed by a category manager, each category team includes several marketing people—brand managers, a sales planning manager, and a marketing information specialist—who handle brand strategy, advertising, and sales promotion. Each team also includes specialists from finance, research and development, manufacturing, engineering, and distribution. Thus, category managers act as small businesspeople, with complete responsibility for an entire category and with a full complement of people to help them plan and implement category marketing strategies.

Thus, although brand managers are far from extinct, their jobs are changing. Such changes are much needed. The brand management

system is product-driven, not customer-driven. Brand managers focus on pushing their brands out to anyone and everyone, and they often concentrate so heavily on a single brand that they lose sight of the marketplace. Even category management focuses on products, for example, "cookies" as opposed to "Oreos." But today, more than ever, companies must start not with brands, but with the needs of the consumers and retailers that these brands serve. Colgate recently took a step in this direction. It moved from *brand management* (Colgate brand toothpaste) to *category management* (all Colgate-Palmolive toothpaste brands) to a new stage, *customer need management* (customers' oral health needs). This last stage finally gets the organization to focus on customer needs.

Sources: See Robert Dewar and Don Schultz, "The Product Manager: An Idea Whose Time Has Gone," *Marketing Communications,* May 1989, pp. 28–35; "Death of the Brand Manager," *The Economist,* April 9, 1994, pp. 67–68; and George S. Low and Ronald A. Fullerton, "Brands, Brand Management, and the Brand Manager System: A Critical-Historical Evaluation," *Journal of Marketing Research,* May 1994, pp. 173–190.

FIGURE 2-8 *The control process*

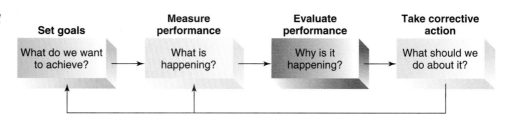

Set goals
What do we want to achieve?

Measure performance
What is happening?

Evaluate performance
Why is it happening?

Take corrective action
What should we do about it?

Operating control involves checking ongoing performance against the annual plan and taking corrective action when necessary. Its purpose is to ensure that the company achieves the sales, profits, and other goals set out in its annual plan. It also involves determining the profitability of different products, territories, markets, and channels.

Strategic control involves considering whether the company's basic strategies are well matched to its opportunities. Marketing strategies and programs can quickly become outdated, and each company should periodically reassess its overall approach to the marketplace. A major tool for such strategic control is a **marketing audit.** The marketing audit is a comprehensive, systematic, independent, and periodic examination of a company's environment, objectives, strategies, and activities to determine problem areas and opportunities. The audit provides good input for a plan of action to improve the company's marketing performance.[20]

Marketing audit
A comprehensive, systematic, independent, and periodic examination of a company's environment, objectives, strategies, and activities to determine problem areas and opportunities and to recommend a plan of action to improve the company's marketing performance.

The marketing audit covers *all* major marketing areas of a business, not just a few trouble spots. It is normally conducted by an objective and experienced outside party who is independent of the marketing department. Table 2-3 shows the kinds of questions the marketing auditor might ask. The findings may come as a surprise—and sometimes as a shock—to management. Management then decides which actions make sense and how and when to implement them.

TABLE 2-3 *Marketing Audit Questions*

MARKETING ENVIRONMENT AUDIT

The Macroenvironment

1. *Demographic.* What major demographic trends pose threats and opportunities for this company?

2. *Economic.* What developments in income, prices, savings, and credit will affect the company?

3. *Natural.* What is the outlook for costs and availability of natural resources and energy? Is the company environmentally responsible?

4. *Technology.* What technological changes are occurring? What is the company's position on technology?

5. *Political.* What current and proposed laws will affect company strategy?

6. *Cultural.* What is the public's attitude toward business and the company's products? What ethical norms and values regulate the conduct of individuals and business? What changes in consumer lifestyles might have an impact?

The Task Environment

1. *Markets.* What is happening to market size, growth, geographic distribution, and profits? What are the major market segments?

2. *Customers.* How do customers rate the company on product quality, service, and price? Do they view the company as being ethical and trustworthy? How do they rate the company in terms of its environmental policies? How do they make their buying decisions?

3. *Competitors.* Who are the major competitors? What are their strategies, market shares, and strengths and weaknesses?

4. *Channels.* What main channels does the company use to distribute products to customers? How are they performing?

5. *Suppliers.* What trends are affecting suppliers? What is the outlook for the availability of key production resources?

6. *Publics.* What key publics provide problems or opportunities? How should the company deal with these publics?

MARKETING STRATEGY AUDIT

1. *Business mission.* Is the mission clearly defined and market-oriented?

2. *Marketing objectives.* Has the company set clear objectives to guide marketing planning and performance? Do these objectives fit with company opportunities and resources?

3. *Marketing strategy.* Does the company have a sound marketing strategy for achieving its objectives? Have ethical issues associated with segmentation and the marketing of products and services been considered?

4. *Budgets.* Has the company budgeted sufficient resources to segments, products, territories, and marketing mix elements?

TABLE 2-3   *continued*

MARKETING ORGANIZATION AUDIT

1. *Formal structure.* Is there a formal mechanism for reporting ethical issues and concerns? Does the chief marketing officer have adequate authority over activities affecting customer satisfaction? Are marketing activities optimally structured along functional, product, market, and territory lines?

2. *Functional efficiency.* Do marketing and sales communicate effectively? Is the marketing staff well trained, supervised, motivated, and evaluated?

3. *Interface efficiency.* Does the marketing staff work well with manufacturing, R&D, purchasing, human resources, and other non-marketing areas?

MARKETING SYSTEMS AUDIT

1. *Marketing information system.* Is the marketing intelligence system providing accurate and timely information about marketplace developments? Are company decision-makers using marketing research effectively? Is a system in place to protect the privacy of customers' information? Is there a mechanism whereby consumers can correct errors in their personal information? Do consumers have the right to refuse to allow their information to be used for marketing purposes?

2. *Marketing planning system.* Does the company prepare annual, long-term, and strategic plans? Are they used?

3. *Marketing control system.* Are annual plan objectives being achieved? Does management periodically analyse the sales and profitability of products, markets, territories, and channels? Do they ensure that ethical standards are maintained?

4. *New-product development.* Is the company well organized to gather, generate, and screen new-product ideas? Does it carry out adequate product and market testing? Has the company succeeded with new products?

MARKETING PRODUCTIVITY AUDIT

1. *Profitability analysis.* How profitable are the company's different products, markets, territories, and channels? Should the company enter, expand, or withdraw from any business segments? What would be the consequences?

2. *Cost-effectiveness analysis.* Do any marketing activities have excessive costs? How can costs be reduced?

MARKETING FUNCTION AUDIT

1. *Products.* Has the company developed sound product-line objectives? Should some products be phased out? Should some new products be added? Would some products benefit from quality, style, or feature changes?

2. *Price.* What are the company's pricing objectives, policies, strategies, and procedures? Are the company's prices in line with customers' perceived value? Are price promotions used properly?

3. *Distribution.* What are the distribution objectives and strategies? Does the company have adequate market coverage and service? Should existing channels be changed or new ones added?

4. *Advertising, sales promotion, and publicity.* What are the company's promotion objectives? How is the budget determined? Is it sufficient? Are advertising messages and media well developed and received? Does the company have well-developed sales promotion and public relations programs?

5. *Sales force.* What are the company's sales-force objectives? Is the sales force large enough? Is it properly organized? Is it well trained, supervised, and motivated? How is the sales force rated relative to those of competitors?

THE MARKETING ENVIRONMENT

Managing the marketing function would be hard enough if the marketer had to deal only with the controllable marketing-mix variables. But the company operates in a complex marketing environment, consisting of uncontrollable forces to which the company must adapt. The environment produces both threats and opportunities. The company must carefully analyse its environment so that it can avoid the threats and take advantage of the opportunities.

The company's marketing environment includes forces close to the company that affect its ability to serve its consumers, such as other company departments, channel members, suppliers, competitors, and publics. It also includes broader demographic and economic forces, political and legal forces, technological and ecological forces, and social and cultural forces. The company must consider all of these forces when developing and positioning its offer to the target market. The marketing environment is discussed more fully in Chapter 3.

Summary of Chapter Objectives

Strategic planning sets the stage for the rest of the company planning. Marketing contributes to strategic planning, and the overall plan defines marketing's role in the company. Although formal planning offers a variety of benefits to companies, not all companies use it or use it well. Many discussions of strategic planning focus on large corporations; however, small business also can benefit greatly from sound strategic planning.

1. **Explain company-wide strategic planning and its four steps.**

   Strategic planning involves developing a strategy for long-run survival and growth. It sets the stage for the rest of the company planning and consists of four steps: defining the company's mission, setting objectives, designing a business portfolio, and developing functional plans. *Defining a clear company mission* begins with drafting a formal *mission statement*, which should be market oriented, realistic, motivating, and consistent with the market environment. The mission is then transformed into detailed *supporting goals and objectives* to guide the entire company. Based on those goals and objectives, the company headquarters designs a *business portfolio*, deciding which businesses and products should receive more or fewer resources. In turn, each business and product unit must develop detailed marketing plans in line with the company-wide plan. Comprehensive and sound marketing plans support company strategic planning by identifying specific opportunities.

2. **Discuss how to design business portfolios and develop growth strategies.**

   Guided by the company's mission statement and objectives, management plans its *business portfolio*, or the collection of businesses and products that comprise the company. To produce a business portfolio that best fits the company's strengths and weaknesses to opportunities in the environment, the company must (1) analyse its *current* business portfolio to decide which businesses should receive more, less, or no investment, and (2) develop growth strategies for adding *new* products or businesses to the portfolio. The company might use a formal portfolio-planning method such as the *BCG growth-share matrix* or the *General Electric strategic-planning grid*. But many companies are now designing more customized portfolio-planning approaches that better suit their unique situations. Beyond evaluating current *strategic units*, designing the business portfolio involves finding businesses and products that the company should consider for the future. The *product/market expansion grid* suggests four possible growth paths: market penetration, market development, product development, and diversification.

3. **Explain functional planning strategies and marketing's role in strategic planning.**

   Each of the company's *functional departments* provides inputs for strategic planning. Once strategic objectives have been identified, management within each business must prepare a set of *functional plans* that coordinates the activities of the marketing, finance, manufacturing, and other departments. A company's success depends on how well each department performs its customer-value-adding activities, and on how well the departments work together to serve the customer. Each department has a different idea about which objectives and activities are most important. The marketing department stresses the consumer's perspective, while the operations department may be more concerned with reducing production costs. In order to develop a system of plans that will best accomplish the firm's overall strategic objectives, marketing managers must work to understand other functional managers' perspectives.

Marketing plays an important role throughout the strategic planning process. It provides *inputs* to strategic planning concerning attractive market possibilities, and marketing's customer focus serves as a *guiding philosophy* for planning. Marketers design *strategies* to help meet strategic objectives, and prepare programs to carry them out profitably. Marketing also plays an integral role to help ensure that departments work together harmoniously toward the goal of delivering superior customer value and satisfaction.

4. **Describe the marketing process and the forces that influence it.**

The *marketing process* matches consumer needs with the company's capabilities and objectives. Consumers are at the centre of the marketing process. The company divides the total market into smaller segments, selecting the segments it can best serve. It then designs a *marketing mix* to differentiate its marketing offer and position this offer in selected target segments. The marketing mix consists of product, price, place, and promotion decisions.

5. **List the marketing management functions, including the elements of a marketing plan.**

To find the best mix and put it into action, the company engages in marketing analysis, marketing planning, marketing implementations, and marketing control. The main components of a *marketing plan* are the executive summary, current marketing situation, threats and opportunities, objectives and issues, marketing strategies, action programs, budgets, and controls. To plan good strategies is often easier than to carry them out. To be successful, companies must implement the strategies effectively. *Implementation* is the process that turns marketing strategies into marketing actions.

Most of the responsibility for implementation goes to the company's marketing department. Modern marketing departments are organized in a number of ways. The most common form is the *functional marketing organization*, in which marketing functions are directed by separate managers who report to the marketing vice president. The company might also use a *geographic organization* in which its sales force or other functions specialize by geographic area. The company may also use the *product management organization*, in which products are assigned to product managers who work with functional specialists to develop and achieve their plans. Another form is the *market management organization*, in which major markets are assigned to market managers who work with functional specialists.

Marketing organizations carry out marketing control. *Operating control* involves monitoring current marketing results to ensure that the annual sales and profit goals will be achieved. *Strategic control* ensures that the company's marketing objectives, strategies, and systems fit with the current forecasted marketing environment. It uses the *marketing audit* to determine marketing opportunities and problems and to recommend short-run and long-run actions to improve overall marketing performance. Through these activities, the company watches and adapts to the marketing environment.

Key Terms

Business portfolio *(p. 44)*	Diversification *(p. 47)*	Cash cows *(p. 44)*

Discussing the Issues

1. Identify some of the benefits of a "rolling" five-year plan—that is, why should managers take time to write a five-year plan that will be changed every year?

2. In a series of job interviews, you ask three recruiters to describe the missions of their companies. One says, "To make profits." Another says, "To create customers." The third says, "To fight world hunger." Analyse and discuss what these mission statements tell you about each company.

3. An electronics manufacturer obtains the semiconductors it uses in production from a company-owned subsidiary that also sells to other manufacturers. The subsidiary is smaller and less profitable than are competing producers, and its growth rate has been below the industry average during the past five years. Define which cell of the BCG growth-share matrix this strategic business unit would fall into. What should the parent company do with this SBU?

4. As companies become more customer- and marketing-oriented, many departments find that they must change their traditional way of doing things. List several examples of ways that a company's finance, accounting, and engineering departments can help the company become more marketing-oriented.

5. The General Electric strategic business-planning grid provides a broad overview that can be very helpful in strategic decision-making. Identify the types of decisions for which this grid would be helpful. Are there other types of strategic decisions where it is not useful?

6. Blockbuster Video is the market leader in home video rentals. It offers two-night rentals, large attractive stores, and a wide variety at moderately high prices. Discuss how you would use market challenger, market follower, and market nicher strategies to compete with Blockbuster.

Applying the Concepts

1. Sit down with an AM-FM radio and pencil and paper. Make a simple chart with four columns titled: *Frequency, Call Letters* (optional but helpful), *Format,* and *Notes.* Tune across the AM and FM bands from beginning to end, and make brief notes for each station with adequate reception. In the *Format* column, note the type of programming, such as student-run, public, classic rock, alternative, religious, and so forth. Under the *Notes* column, write down any station slogans you hear (such as "Your Concert Connection"), events that the station is sponsoring, and the types of advertising you hear.

   ◆ Total the number of stations you received, and add up how many stations share each format. How many different market segments do these stations appear to target?

   ◆ Are any stations positioned in an unusually clear and distinctive way? How?

   ◆ Do advertisers choose different types of stations for different types of products? Does their market segmentation make sense? Give examples.

2. Think about the shopping area near your campus. Assume that you wish to start a business here, and are looking for a promising opportunity for a restaurant, a clothing store, or a music store.

◆ Is there an opportunity to open a distinctive and promising business? Describe your target market, and how you would serve it differently than current businesses do.

◆ What sort of marketing mix would you use for your business?

References

1. Stephen Shaw, "Special Report: Card Marketing, Frequency Marketing Wins Points with Customers: Canadian Tire, Chapters Report Successful Program," *Strategy, The Canadian Marketing Report*, July 22, 1996, p. 22.

2. "Direct Response Interview: Tom Gauld, President, Canadian Tire Acceptance Limited," *Strategy, The Canadian Marketing Report*, September 14, 1997, p. SDR12.

3. John Deverell, "The Tire's Trump Cards," *The Toronto Star*, July 20, 1997, p. D6.

4. Arthur Johnson, "Don't Tread on This Tire," *Canadian Business*, October 1995, p. 11; Susanne Craig, "Canadian Tire accelerates," *The Financial Post*, December 21, 1996, p. 69; John Lorinc, "Road Warriors," *Canadian Business*, October 1995, pp. 26–43; Zena Olijnyk, "Canadian Tire Continues Strong Performance as Profit Rises 12.5%," *The Financial Post*, May 10, 1997, p. 11.

5. For a more detailed discussion of corporate and business-level strategic planning as they apply to marketing, see Philip Kotler, *Marketing Management: Analysis, Planning, Implementation, and Control*, 8th ed. (Englewood Cliffs, NJ: Prentice Hall, 1994), Chapters 3 and 4.

6. Romauld A. Stone, "Mission Statements Revisited," *SAM Advanced Management Journal*, Winter 1996, pp. 31–37.

7. Andyne Computing Limited, *1996 Annual Report*, p. 2.

8. See Bradley Johnson, "Bill Gates' Vision of Microsoft in Every Home," *Advertising Age*, December 19, 1994, pp. 14–15. For more on mission statements, see J. W. Graham and W. C. Havlick, *Mission Statements: A Guide to the Corporate and Nonprofit Sectors* (New York: Garland Publishing, 1994); P. Jones and L. Kahaner, *Say It and Live It: The 50 Corporate Mission Statements That Hit the Mark* (New York: Doubleday, 1995); and Thomas A. Stewart, "A Refreshing Change: Vision Statements That Make Sense," *Fortune*, September 30, 1996, pp. 195–196.

9. Gilbert Fuchsberg, "'Visioning' Mission Becomes Its Own Mission," *The Wall Street Journal*, January 7, 1994, pp. B1, 3.

10. Richard G. Hamermesh, "Making Planning Strategic," *Harvard Business Review*, July–August 1986, pp. 115–120. Also see Henry Mintzberg, "The Rise and Fall of Strategic Planning," *Harvard Business Review*, January–February 1994, pp. 107–114.

11. See Daniel H. Gray, "Uses and Misuses of Strategic Planning," *Harvard Business Review*, January–February 1986, pp. 89–96; and Roger A. Kerin, Vijay Mahajan, and P. Rajan Varadarajan, *Contemporary Perspectives on Strategic Planning* (Boston: Allyn & Bacon, 1990).

12. H. Igor Ansoff, "Strategies for Diversification," *Harvard Business Review*, September–October 1957, pp. 113–124.

13. John C. Narver and Stanley F. Slater, "The Effect of a Market Orientation on Business Profitability," *Journal of Marketing*, October 1990, pp. 20–35.

14. See Brian Dumaine, "Creating a New Company Culture," *Fortune*, January 15, 1990, p. 128; and Howard E. Butz, Jr., and Leonard D. Goodstein, "Measuring Customer Value: Gaining Strategic Advantage," *Organizational Dynamics*, Winter 1996, pp. 63–77.

15. Bradford McKee, "Think Ahead, Set Goals, and Get Out of the Office," *Nation's Business*, May 1993, p. 10.

16. John Southerst, "Customer Crunching," *Canadian Business*, September 1993, pp. 28–35.

17. The four *P* classification was first suggested by E. Jerome McCarthy, *Basic Marketing: A Managerial Approach* (Homewood, IL: Irwin, 1960). For more discussion of this classification scheme, see Walter van Waterschoot and Christophe Van den Bulte, "The 4P Classification of the Marketing Mix Revisited," *Journal of Marketing*, October 1992, pp. 83–93.

18. Joseph Winski, "One Brand, One Manager," *Advertising Age*, August 20, 1987, p. 86.

19. For more complete discussions of marketing organization approaches and issues, see Robert W. Ruekert, Orville C. Walker, Jr., and Kenneth J. Roering, "The Organization of Marketing Activities: A Contingency Theory of Structure and Performance," *Journal of Marketing*, Winter 1985, pp. 13–25; and Ravi S. Achrol, "Evolution of the Marketing Organization: New Forms for Turbulent Environments," *Journal of Marketing*, October 1991, pp. 77–93.

20. For details, see Kotler, *Marketing Management: Analysis, Planning, Implementation, and Control*, 8th ed., Chap. 27.

Company Case 2

TRAP-EASE: THE BIG CHEESE OF MOUSETRAPS

One April morning, Martha House, president of Trap-Ease, entered her office in Moncton, New Brunswick. She paused for a moment to contemplate the Ralph Waldo Emerson quotation that she had framed and hung near her desk.

> If a man [can] . . . make a better mousetrap than his neighbor . . . the world will make a beaten path to his door.

Perhaps, she mused, Emerson knew something that she didn't. She *had* the better mousetrap—Trap-Ease—but the world didn't seem all that excited about it.

Martha had just returned from the National Hardware Show in Toronto. Standing in the trade show display booth for long hours and answering the same questions hundreds of times had been tiring. Yet, this show had excited her. Each year, National Hardware Show officials held a contest to select the best new product introduced at the show. Of the more than 300 new products introduced at that year's show, her mousetrap had won first place. Such notoriety was not new for the Trap-Ease mousetrap. *Canadian Business* magazine had written an article about the mousetrap, and the television show *Market Place* and trade publications had featured it. Despite all of this attention, however, the expected demand for the trap had not materialized. Martha hoped that this award might stimulate increased interest and sales.

A group of investors who had obtained worldwide rights to market the innovative mousetrap had formed Trap-Ease in January. In return for marketing rights, the group agreed to pay the inventor and patent holder, a retired rancher, a royalty fee for each trap sold. The group then hired Martha to serve as president and to develop and manage the Trap-Ease organization.

The Trap-Ease, a simple yet clever device, is manufactured by a plastics firm under contract with Trap-Ease. It consists of a square, plastic tube measuring about 15 cm long and 4 cm square. The tube bends in the middle at a 30-degree angle, so that when the front part of the tube rests on a flat surface, the other end is elevated. The elevated ends holds a removable cap into which the user places bait (cheese, dog food, or some other tidbit). A hinged door is attached to the front end of the tube. When the trap is "open," this door rests on two narrow "stilts" attached to the two bottom corners of the door.

The trap works with simple efficiency. A mouse, smelling the bait, enters the tube through the open end. As it walks up the angled bottom toward the bait, its weight makes the elevated end of the trap drop downward. This elevates the open end, allowing the hinged door to swing closed, trapping the mouse. Small teeth on the ends of the stilts catch in a groove on the bottom of the trap, locking the door closed. The mouse can be disposed of live, or it can be left alone for a few hours to suffocate in the trap.

Martha believed that the trap had many advantages for the consumer when compared with traditional spring-loaded traps or poisons. It appeals to consumers who want a humane alternative to spring traps. Furthermore, with Trap-Ease, consumers can avoid the unpleasant "mess" they encounter with the violent spring-loaded traps—it creates no "clean-up" problem. Finally, the consumer can reuse the trap or simply throw it away.

Martha's early research suggested that women are the best target market for the Trap-Ease. Men, it seems, are more willing to buy and use the traditional, spring-loaded trap. The targeted women, however, do not like the traditional trap. They often stay at home and take care of their children. Thus, they want a means of dealing with the mouse problem that avoids the unpleasantness and risks that the standard trap creates in the home.

To reach this target market, Martha decided to distribute Trap-Ease through national grocery, hardware, and drug chains such as Safeway, Zellers, Canadian Tire, and Shoppers Drug Mart. She sold the trap directly to these large retailers, avoiding any wholesalers or other intermediaries.

The traps sold in packages of two, with a suggested retail price of $2.99. Although this price made the Trap-Ease about five times more expensive than smaller, standard traps, consumers appeared to offer little initial price resistance. The manufacturing cost for the Trap-Ease, including freight and packaging costs, was about 31 cents per unit. The company paid an additional 8.2 cents per unit in royalty fees. Martha priced the traps to retailers at 1.49 per unit and estimated that, after sales and volume discounts, Trap-Ease would realize net revenues from retailers of 1.29 per unit.

To promote the product, Martha had budgeted approximately $60 000 for the first year. She planned to use $50 000 of this amount for travel costs to visit trade shows and to make sales calls on retailers. She would use the remaining $10 000 for advertising. So far, however, because the mousetrap had generated so much publicity, she had not felt that she needed to do much advertising. Still, she had placed advertising in

Chatelaine and in other "home and shelter" magazines. Martha was the company's only "salesperson," but she intended to hire more salespeople soon.

Martha had initially forecasted Trap-Ease's first-year sales at 500 000 units. Through April, however, the company had sold only several thousand units. Martha wondered if most new products got off to such a slow start, or if she was doing something wrong. She had detected some problems, although none seemed overly serious. For one, there had not been enough repeat buying. For another, she had noted that many of the retailers kept their sample mousetraps on their desks as conversation pieces—she wanted the traps to be used and demonstrated. Martha wondered if consumers were also buying the traps as novelties rather than as solutions to their mouse problems.

Martha knew that the investor group believed that Trap-Ease had a "once-in-a-lifetime chance" with its innovative mousetrap. She sensed the group's impatience. She had budgeted approximately $150 000 in administrative and fixed costs for the first year (not including marketing costs). To keep the investors happy, the company needed to sell enough traps to cover those costs and make a reasonable profit.

In these first few months, Martha had learned that marketing a new product is not an easy task. For example, one national retailer had placed a large order with instructions that the order was to be delivered to the loading dock at one of its warehouses between 1:00 and 3:00 PM on a specified day. When the truck delivering the order had arrived late, the retailer had refused to accept the shipment. The retailer had told Martha it would be a year before she got another chance. Perhaps, Martha thought, she should send the retailer and other customers a copy of Emerson's famous quotation.

QUESTIONS

1. Martha and the Trap-Ease Investors believe they face a "once-in-a-lifetime" opportunity. What information do they need to evaluate this opportunity? How do you think the group would write its mission statement? How would *you* write it?

2. Has Martha identified the best target market for Trap-Ease? What other market segments might the firm target?

3. How has the company positioned the Trap-Ease relative to the chosen target market? Could it position the product in other ways?

4. Describe the current marketing mix for Trap-Ease. Do you see any problems with this mix?

5. Who is Trap-Ease's competition?

6. How would you change Trap-Ease's marketing strategy? What kinds of control procedures would you establish for this strategy?

7. Develop a budget based on the numbers in the case. Is it realistic? Would you make changes?

Video Case 2
GOING FOR BROKE:
THE *LOONEYSPOONS* LAUNCH

The *Looneyspoons* cookbook was the creation of Janet and Greta Podleski, two sisters from Ottawa, Ontario, who believed that there was a market for a low-fat cookbook that took the mystery out of cooking low-fat food. As the name implies, the book does more than simply present recipes. Cartoons and jokes appear on every page and even the recipe names, such as the Barbra Streisand-inspired "The Way We Stir," let readers know that the authors don't take themselves too seriously. However, the marketing efforts of this duo showed an incredible seriousness and dedication to their product. The book was launched into one of the most competitive book categories in the country. Since more than 2000 cookbooks are introduced in Canada a year (one every five hours), a strong marketing effort was required to get their product noticed.

Over an 18-month period, the Podleski sisters invested thousands of dollars and hours into product development for their book, typically testing five to six meals per day. Once the recipes were developed, they spent additional hours compiling the book. Both Janet and Greta had quit their jobs so, after using all of their investments and RRSPs, they maximized their credit card debt and held desperation garage sales to finance the cookbook. Although they were convinced of the market viability of their product, publishers were harder to convince. After several publishers turned them down, Greta and Janet decided they needed a partner to help them publish the book themselves. They turned to David Chilton, the well-known financial advisor and author of *The Wealthy Barber*. Chilton was initially sceptical about the concept but after speaking with the sisters at length and reviewing their marketing and book proposal, he became a one-third partner in their business, Granet Publishing.

Chilton convinced Janet and Greta that promotion was a critical factor that would lead to their success. He advised them to spend all of their available time making calls to the media to set up interviews and then to get on the road to promote the book. Chilton had spent 230 days a year on the road promoting his own book and he knew first-hand the importance of an author being visible. The Podleski sisters set up promotional visits to retailers, book signings, and national radio and TV interviews, and often Chilton's association with the book opened retailer and media doors. At times the partnership with Chilton was a double-edged sword, however. For example, in one half-hour radio interview scheduled with Janet and Chilton that was supposed to highlight

Looneyspoons, the host of the show spent more than half of the time asking Chilton financial questions and only after 16 minutes asked Janet about the cookbook.

Distribution was another major concern. Unlike most products, books that are not sold by retailers can be returned to the publisher for a full refund for up to one year. This increased the pressure on the authors to continue to promote the book even after national retailers such as Chapters and Smithbooks had placed large orders. Shipping problems also complicated the distribution process. When the Podleskis arrived in Vancouver for a press tour, they discovered that no bookstores in the area had received books. This meant that the sisters had to call every bookstore in Vancouver to inform them that the book was available but was delayed due to shipping difficulties.

Tension in the Granet Publishing partnership developed when the Podleskis were unable to schedule the number of interviews that Chilton believed was necessary in important markets such as Vancouver. Chilton also wanted to focus efforts nationally while the Podleskis were thinking more on a local level. The difficulties in resolving these tensions were made worse by the physical distance between the partners. Chilton lives in the Kitchener-Waterloo area while the Podleskis live in Ottawa. A meeting in the middle at a roadside motel cleared the air, refocused the efforts of the partnership, and allowed them to consider long-term plans such as the development of a second cookbook.

One month after the launch of *Looneyspoons*, 20 000 copies of the book were sold, due at least in part to a national radio interview on CBC where the recipes received a favourable review from Vicki Gabereau. Although this number of sales was almost as much as year one of sales of *The Wealthy Barber*, the partners, and especially Chilton, still had reservations. They ran out of books, which meant that another printing had to be done. And although several copies of the books had been sold, no money had been received from those orders yet, which meant that Chilton had to invest more money to cover the cost of the printing. On the positive side, book sales in Ottawa had reached a critical mass, which means that the books were being sold as a result of word of mouth alone. However, sales in other markets, such as Calgary, were spotty. Consequently, the Podleski sisters had to continue to try to keep *Looneyspoons* top of mind for both consumers and retailers.

QUESTIONS

1. How would you characterize the marketing planning process followed by the publishing team thus far?

2. Is a formal marketing planning process necessary or realistic in this kind of business situation?

3. What recommendations would you make for strengthening the marketing planning and implementation process for *Looneyspoons*?

4. Read the Marketers Speak Out profile of Jim Shenkman. What lessons could the sisters have learned from Jim?

Source: This case was prepared by Auleen Carson and is based on "Looneyspoons," *Venture* (December 22, 1996); www.tv.cbc.ca/venture/archives/looney_spoons_961222/.

C H A P T E R *3*

THE GLOBAL MARKETING ENVIRONMENT

If you found this booklet helpful,
please pass it along to
a friend or family member who
could also benefit from it.
Other helpful resources:

**THE SOCIETY OF
OBSTETRICIANS AND
GYNAECOLOGISTS OF
CANADA**

**LA SOCIÉTÉ
DES OBSTÉTRICIENS
ET GYNÉCOLOGUES
DU CANADA**

*Committed to informed reproductive health care for Canadians.
Pour des choix éclairés en matière de reproduction au Canada.*

*Osteoporosis
Society
of Canada*

*La Société
de l'Ostéoporose
du Canada*

*The Osteoporosis Society of Canada is committed to improving the
bone health of women in midlife and preventing post-menopausal osteoporosis.*

The Osteoporosis Society of Canada and the Society of Obstetricians
and Gynaecologists of Canada are working together to promote awareness
and understanding of menopause and osteoporosis.
For more information please call 1-800-463-6842, a toll-free women's health
information line provided for you as a free public service.

Dedicated to advancements in postmenopausal health.

ew industries are more global than the pharmaceutical industry. Sixty-four publicly traded, multinational firms that market brand-name drugs, dominate this industry. At first glance, these giant firms appear immune to outside influences. What companies could be more secure in their command of stable market shares and long-term growth and profitability prospects than drug manufacturers? Blockbuster drugs that improve quality of life, such as Prozac, or promise of a cure for AIDS, could earn a pharmaceutical firm over $500 million a year. "Ethical" drugs save lives, treat illnesses, and work miracles like never before. Demand should be growing as the population ages and health problems increase.

Yet even these mammoth companies must pay close attention to changes in their micro- and macroenvironments. For example, in Canada, the competitive and political environments have a huge impact on the future of drug marketing. Bill C-91, the bill that grants 20 years of patent protection to developers of brand-name drugs, is being reviewed. Canada's 14 privately owned generic drug makers are lobbying to have periods of patent protection shortened. The costs of developing and marketing drugs continue to escalate, international pharmaceutical firms are merging so that they can bring together the resources and market power essential to gain a significant share of world markets. The competition among these multinational giants is becoming increasingly fierce. Second, fewer new drugs are being developed and launched as the technology involved with the research process becomes more expensive and breakthrough products become more difficult to find.

Prescription drug marketing is extremely complex. "Suppose a pharmaceutical product were a bridge and you, the consumer had to walk across it. Not only would a doctor have to show you the way across, and a pharmacist open the gate, but Health Canada would be hovering nearby to ensure the bridge proprietor (i.e., the pharmaceutical company) wasn't making any claims about the product in order to entice you to cross. On the upside, though, a private or government health care plan would likely pick up the toll."[1]

OBJECTIVES

When you finish this chapter, you should be able to

1. Describe the environmental forces that affect the company's ability to serve its customers.

2. Explain how changes in the demographic and economic environments affect marketing decisions.

3. Identify the major trends in the firm's natural and technological environments.

4. Explain the key changes in the political and cultural environments.

5. Discuss how companies can react to the marketing environment.

Thus, although pharmaceutical companies often begin their marketing programs by providing information to doctors, they have learned that they must target new stakeholders and publics with their drug communications. For example, many Canadians have company-sponsored health plans that cover at least some of the costs of prescription drugs. In the face of increasing competition, firms are trying to reduce costs on many fronts, including the costs of their benefit programs. For example, when Marion Merrell Dow of Montreal launched its Nicoderm patch designed to help people stop smoking, the company recognized the need to include decision-makers for corporate benefit plans as part of the target audience. This decision required Nicoderm marketing managers to reposition the benefit claims they made about their product. Whereas their traditional audience of doctors and pharmacists valued information about the efficiency and safety of the Nicoderm patch in helping people to stop smoking, corporate decision-makers, who administer a firm's health plan, were more concerned with issues such as absenteeism costs, lost employee productivity, and the costs of long-term disability arising from smoking. Thus, the new promotional materials focused on these benefits.

Drug manufacturers must meet strict government safety guidelines on testing and marketing drugs. Heightened attention has been paid to government involvement as economic concerns have become front-page news. Provincial governments have been fighting ballooning deficits, which has given rise to concern about the escalating costs of health care. In fact, the entire Canadian health care system is in turmoil as government struggles to control costs. Rather than merely paying the bills submitted for treatments, governments are starting to demand a role in determining which drugs are prescribed and what they cost. Furthermore, governments are starting to demand that cheaper, generic versions of drugs be used wherever possible. New drugs must offer significant benefits over the versions they replace or governments will not include them in the list of medicines they cover. For example, Ontario added only 17 of the 107 new drugs that entered the market during the past two years.

The Canadian demographic landscape is also changing. Not only is the population aging and demanding more and more medical services and products, but the composition of the population is also being radically altered. It is no longer sufficient for marketers to understand only the needs of English and French consumers. Immigration from various countries has given rise to growing ethnic markets whose special needs for information in their native language must be addressed.

The demand for information is not restricted to ethnic markets. Many consumers' attitudes toward health care are changing. Whereas Canadians once relied on the medical profession to take care of their health, increasing numbers of people are becoming much more proactive about their role in personal health care. Rather than being concerned about receiving the best treatment for health problems, attention is being directed at disease prevention. Drug manufacturers must develop products and services that address this trend. Some firms, like Astra Pharma of Mississauga, Ontario, have developed a toll-free telephone service called "Sharing a Healthier Future" to address consumers' growing need for health information. The company has integrated this information service with a range of promotional tools such as newspaper ads, consumer magazine advertorials on coping with specific diseases, and television programming on health problem management. Other firms are working to directly target specific groups of consumers. For example, a manufacturer of a cholesterol-reducing agent uses low-fat cookbooks to reach its audience.

Growing knowledge has empowered consumers to demand wider access to, and distribution of, over-the-counter drugs. With access to medicines, many consumers believe they can take care of themselves more effectively and more cheaply than institutional health care providers. Thus, pharmaceutical companies can no longer just target doctors with their promotional and informational messages. They must now also include consumers, insurance companies, government decision-makers, and pharmacists.

These consumer demands have given rise to a new group of marketing intermediaries in the marketplace. Consider what has happened in Quebec as an example. The province accounts for about 25 percent of total Canadian sales of patent medicines. Over 1450 pharmacies serve the public, but new entrants are expanding these numbers. What is interesting is that these new players are not from among pharmacies' traditional competitors. Instead the new competition is coming from mass merchandisers such as Zellers and Wal-Mart. These discounters are building in-store pharmacies to take advantage of consumers' growing price sensitivity along with their growing demands for convenience and one-stop shopping. Entering the drug business is not as easy as selling toothpaste. Quebec law demands that a pharmacy must be owned by a licensed pharmacist. Thus, the mass merchandisers must convince one to set up operations within their store. However, stores such as Zellers believe that once consumers recognize the advantage of using in-store services that include not only drugs but also health maintenance equipment such as self-serve blood pressure machines, the entire nature of the market will change.[2]

As the description of pharmaceutical marketing indicates, marketers must understand and respond to a vast array of forces from both the macro- and microenvironments when they plan and execute their marketing strategies.

Marketing environment
The factors and forces outside marketing's direct control that affect marketing management's ability to develop and maintain successful transactions with its target customers.

A company's **marketing environment** consists of the factors and forces outside marketing's direct control that affect marketing management's ability to develop and maintain successful relationships with its target customers. The marketing environment offers both opportunities and threats. Successful companies know the vital importance of continually watching and adapting to the changing environment.

A company's marketers take the major responsibility for identifying significant changes in the environment. More than any other group in the company, marketers must be the trend-trackers and opportunity-seekers. Although every manager in an organization needs to observe the outside environment, marketers have two special aptitudes. They have disciplined methods—marketing intelligence and marketing research—for collecting information about the marketing environment. They also normally spend more time in the customer and competitor environment. By conducting systematic environmental scanning, marketers can revise and adapt marketing strategies to meet new challenges and opportunities in the marketplace.

Microenvironment
The forces close to the company that affect its ability to serve its customers—the company, market channel firms, customer markets, competitors, and publics.

Macroenvironment
The larger societal forces that affect the whole microenvironment—demographic, economic, natural, technological, political, and cultural forces.

The marketing environment is composed of a *microenvironment* and a *macroenvironment*. The **microenvironment** consists of the forces close to the company that affect its ability to serve its customers—the company, suppliers, marketing channel firms, customer markets, competitors, and publics. The **macroenvironment** consists of the larger societal forces that affect the whole microenvironment—demographic, economic, natural, technological, political, and cultural forces. We look first at the company's microenvironment.

THE COMPANY'S MICROENVIRONMENT

Marketing management's job is to attract and build relationships with customers by creating customer value and satisfaction. However, marketing managers cannot accomplish this task alone. Their success will depend on other actors in the company's microenvironment—other company departments, suppliers, marketing intermediaries, customers, competitors, and various publics.

THE COMPANY

In designing marketing plans, marketing management takes other company groups into account—groups such as top management, finance, research and development (R&D), purchasing, manufacturing, and accounting. All these interrelated groups

FIGURE 3-1 *The company's internal environment*

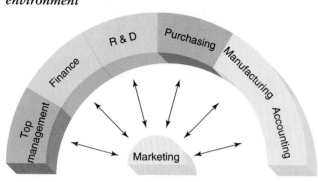

form the internal environment (see Figure 3-1). Top management sets the company's mission, objectives, broad strategies, and policies. Marketing managers must make decisions within the plans made by top management, and marketing plans must be approved by top management before they can be implemented.

Marketing managers also must work closely with other company departments. Finance is concerned with finding and using funds to carry out the marketing plan. The R&D department focuses on the problems of designing safe and attractive products. Purchasing worries about getting supplies and materials, whereas manufacturing is responsible for producing the desired quality and quantity of products. Accounting must measure revenues and costs to help marketing know how well it is achieving its objectives. Together, all of these departments have an impact on the marketing department's plans and actions. Under the marketing concept, all of these functions must "think consumer," and they should work in harmony to provide superior customer value and satisfaction.

Marketing intermediaries
Firms that help the company to promote, sell, and distribute its goods to final buyers; they include resellers, physical distribution firms, marketing-service agencies, and financial intermediaries.

SUPPLIERS

Suppliers are an important link in the company's overall customer "value delivery system." They provide the resources needed by the company to produce its goods and services. Supplier developments can seriously affect marketing. Marketing managers must be aware of supply availability—supply shortages or delays, labour strikes, and other events that can cost sales in the short run and damage customer satisfaction in the long run. Marketing managers also monitor the price trends of their key inputs. Rising supply costs may force price increases that can harm the company's sales volume.

Financial intermediaries: *Firms such as Credit Suisse offer a wide range of international financial services, from Toronto and Abu Dhabi to Barcelona and Beijing.*

MARKETING INTERMEDIARIES

Marketing intermediaries help the company to promote, sell, and distribute its goods to final buyers. They include *resellers, physical distribution firms, marketing services agencies,* and *financial intermediaries. Resellers* are distribution channel firms that help the company find customers or make sales to them. These include wholesalers and retailers who buy and resell merchandise. Selecting and working with resellers is not easy. No longer do manufacturers have many small, independent resellers from which to choose. They now face large and growing reseller organizations. These organizations frequently have enough power to dictate terms or even shut the manufacturer out of large markets.

Physical distribution firms help the company to stock and move goods from their points of origin to their destinations. Working with warehouse and transportation firms, a company must determine the best ways to store and ship goods, balancing such factors as cost, delivery, speed, and safety. *Marketing services agencies* are the marketing research firms, advertising agencies, media firms, and marketing consulting firms that help the company target and promote its products to the right markets. When the company decides to use one of these agencies, it must choose carefully because these firms vary in creativity, quality, service, and price. *Financial intermediaries* include banks, credit companies, insurance companies, and other businesses that help finance transactions or insure against the risks associated with the buying and selling of goods. Most firms and customers depend on financial intermediaries to finance their transactions.

Like suppliers, marketing intermediaries form an important component of the company's overall value delivery system. In its quest to create satisfying customer relationships, the company must do more than just optimize its own performance. It must partner effectively with suppliers and marketing intermediaries to optimize the performance of the entire system.

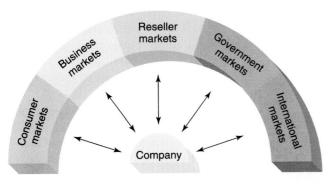

FIGURE 3-2 *Types of customer markets*

CUSTOMERS

The company needs to study its customer markets closely. Figure 3-2 shows five types of customer markets. *Consumer markets* consist of individuals and households that buy goods and services for personal consumption. *Business markets* buy goods and services for further processing or for use in their production process, whereas *reseller markets* buy goods and services to resell at a profit. *Government markets* are composed of government agencies that buy goods and services in order to produce public services or transfer the goods and services to others who need them. Finally, *international markets* consist of buyers in other countries, including consumers, producers, resellers, and governments. Each market type has special characteristics that call for careful study by the seller.

COMPETITORS

Public
Any group that has an actual or potential interest in or impact on an organization's ability to achieve its objectives.

The marketing concept states that to be successful, a company must provide greater customer value and satisfaction than its competitors. Thus, marketers must do more than simply adapt to the needs of target consumers. They also must gain strategic advantage by positioning their offerings strongly against competitors' offerings in the minds of consumers.

No single competitive marketing strategy is best for all companies. Each firm should consider its own size and industry position compared to those of its competitors. Large firms with dominant positions in an industry can use certain strategies that smaller firms cannot afford. But being large is not enough. There are winning strategies for large firms, but there are also losing ones. And small firms can develop strategies that give them better rates of return than large firms enjoy.

PUBLICS

The company's marketing environment also includes various publics. A **public** is any group that has an actual or potential interest in or impact on an organization's ability to achieve its objectives. Figure 3-3 shows seven types of publics.

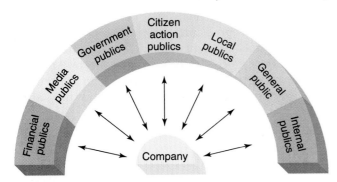

FIGURE 3-3 *Types of publics*

- ◆ *Financial publics.* Financial publics influence the company's ability to obtain funds. Banks, investment houses, and stockholders are the major financial publics.
- ◆ *Media publics.* Media publics are those that carry news, features, and editorial opinion. They include newspapers, magazines, radio and television stations, and the World Wide Web.
- ◆ *Government publics.* Management must take into account government developments. Marketers must often consult the company's lawyers on issues of product safety, truth in advertising, and other matters.

◆ *Citizen-action publics.* A company's marketing decisions may be questioned by consumer organizations, environmental groups, minority groups, and others. Its public relations department can help it stay in touch with consumer and citizen groups.

Companies market to internal publics as well as to customers: Wal-Mart Canada Inc. includes employees as models in its advertising, making them feel good about working for the company.

◆ *Local publics.* Every company has local publics, such as neighbourhood residents and community organizations. Large companies usually appoint a community-relations officer to deal with the community, attend meetings, answer questions, and contribute to worthwhile causes.

◆ *General public.* A company needs to be concerned about the general public's attitude toward its products and activities. The public's image of the company affects its buying.

◆ *Internal publics.* A company's internal publics include its workers, managers, volunteers, and the board of directors. Large companies use newsletters and other means to inform and motivate their internal publics. When employees feel good about their company, this positive attitude spills over to external publics.

A company can prepare marketing plans for these major publics as well as for its customer markets. Suppose the company wants a specific response from a particular public, such as goodwill, favourable word of mouth, or donations of time or money. The company would have to design an offer to this public that is attractive enough to produce the desired response.

THE COMPANY'S MACROENVIRONMENT

The company and all of the other actors operate in a larger macroenvironment of forces that shape opportunities and pose threats to the company. Figure 3-4 shows the six major forces in the company's macroenvironment. Marketers must track trends in the macroenvironment on both a national and international basis since business is becoming increasingly global. Since 80 percent of Canada's export trade is with the United States, keeping track of trends in the U.S. marketplace is critical.[3] The growth of the U.S. economy, which grew at a rate of 3.25 percent in 1997, has fuelled many Canadian businesses. While growth is forecast to continue, Canadian marketers must recognize that this growth may be slower than it has been previously. For example, analysts are predicting a two percent U.S. growth rate for 1998.[4] When the Hong Kong stock exchange tumbled in the fall of 1997, all North American marketers took note. Forecasts of sales that North American firms would make in Asian markets had to be revised downward. In the remaining sections of this chapter, we examine these forces and show how they affect marketing plans.

DEMOGRAPHIC ENVIRONMENT

Demography
The study of human populations in terms of size, density, location, age, sex, race, occupation, and other statistics.

Demography is the study of human populations in terms of size, density, location, age, gender, race, occupation, and other statistics. The demographic environment

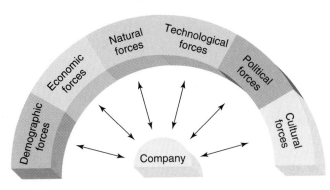

FIGURE 3-4 *Major forces in the company's macroenvironment*

is of major interest to marketers because it involves people, and people make up markets.

David Foot, an economist at the University of Toronto and author of the bestselling book, *Boom, Bust & Echo: How to Profit from the Coming Demographic Shift,* believes that demographics explains about two-thirds of everything.[5] For example, how do you explain the rapid rise in the rates charged by babysitters? Easy, says Foot, when you realize that the huge pool of boomer parents relies on a relatively small pool of baby-bust teens. He has also shown that studying demographics helps to explain the growth of some leisure markets and the decline of others. Golf has experienced a 38 percent increase in popularity over the last 25 years, pushed by its popularity among baby-boomers.

People who study demographics assume that people do certain things and purchase certain things at particular ages. For example, people in their thirties tend to have begun their families and thus are the major purchasers of baby products. While demographic information can be very useful when it comes to predicting macro trends and purchases within a product category, marketers should use the information with some caution. According to veteran Canadian pollster Allan Gregg, demographics "can be wildly simplistic."[6] Complex factors (everything from the marketing itself to an individual's values and attitudes) influence why a person buys a particular brand within a product category. Moreover, despite the best demographic predictions, people don't always follow predictable patterns. Given an aging North American population, many predicted that people would follow a healthier lifestyle and diet. But a recent report suggests that, "when it comes to food, Canadians are tired of worrying about what's good for them."[7] Unlike many Europeans, vegetarianism isn't a lifestyle choice for many Canadians. In fact, only four percent of Canadians follow this type of diet.

The world population is growing at an explosive rate. It now totals more than 5.8 billion and will reach 7.5 billion by the year 2025.[8] This population explosion has been of major concern to governments and various groups around the world for two reasons. First, the earth's finite resources can support only so many people, particularly at the living standards to which many countries aspire. The concern is that unchecked population growth and consumption may eventually result in insufficient food supply, depletion of key minerals, overcrowding, pollution, and an overall deterioration in the quality of life.

TABLE 3-1 *Key Demographic and Economic Statistics from a Sample of APEC (Asia-Pacific Economic Cooperation Conference) Countries.*

Country	Population (In millions)	Rate Population Growth	Literacy Rate	GNP Per Capita ($ billions US)	Exports ($ billions US)	Imports ($ billions US)
Australia	18.1	1.2%	99%	$ 18,720	$ 53.1	$ 61.3
Canada	29.6	1.1%	98%	$ 19,380	$ 192.2	$ 168.4
China	1299.2	1.5%	73%	$ 620	$ 148.8	$ 132.1
Indonesia	193.3	1.8%	77%	$ 980	$ 45.4	$ 40.9
Hong Kong	6.2	2.1%	90%	$ 22,990	$ 173.9	$ 196.1
Japan	125.2	0.5%	99%	$ 39,640	$ 443.1	$ 336.0
Mexico	91.8	2.2%	87%	$ 3,320	$ 79.7	$ 72.9
South Korea	44.9	0.5%	99%	$ 9,700	$ 125.1	$ 135.1
United States	263.1	0.6%	97%	$ 26,980	$ 583.9	$ 771.3

Source: Asia Pacific Foundation of Canada, APEC Secretariat, adapted from the reprint in the *Globe and Mail,* November 19, 1997, p. D4

MARKETING HIGHLIGHT 3-1

IF THE WORLD WERE A VILLAGE

Canadian author, Marshall McLuhan, created the concept of the global village in the 1960s. Today, concept is becoming reality with increasingly global communications. Think for a few minutes about the world and your place in it. If we reduced the world to a village of 1000 people who were representative of the world's population, this would be our reality:

- Our village would have 520 women and 480 men; 330 children and 60 people over age 65; 10 college graduates and 335 illiterate adults.

- We'd have 52 North Americans, 55 Russians, 84 Latin Americans, 95 Europeans, 124 Africans, and 584 Asians.

- Communication would be difficult: 165 of us would speak Mandarin, 86 English, 83 Hindu, 64 Spanish, 58 Russian, and 37 Arabic. The other half of us would speak one or more than 200 other languages.

- Among us we'd have 329 Christians, 178 Moslems, 132 Hindus, 62 Buddhists, 3 Jews, 167 non-religious, 45 atheists, and 84 others.

- About one-third of our people would have access to clean, safe drinking water. About half of our children would be immunized against infections.

- The woodlands in our village would be decreasing rapidly and wasteland would be growing. Forty percent of the village's cropland, nourished by 83 percent of

our fertilizer, would produce 72 percent of the food to feed its 270 well-fed owners. The remaining 60 percent of the land and 17 percent of the fertilizer would produce 28 percent of the food to feed the other 730 people. Five hundred people in the village would suffer from malnutrition.

- Only 200 of the 1000 people would control 75 percent of our village's wealth. Another 200 would receive only two percent of the wealth. Seventy people would own cars, one would have a computer, and that computer probably would not be connected to the Internet.

Source: Taken from The World Village Project web site, May 1997, http://www.geocities.com/Athens/Forum/1910/wvp.html

---

Second, the greatest population growth occurs in countries and communities that can least afford it. The less-developed regions of the world currently account for 76 percent of the world population and are growing at two percent per year. In contrast, the population in the more-developed regions is growing at only 0.6 percent per year. Less-developed countries often find it difficult to feed, clothe, and educate their growing populations. Moreover, the poorer families in these countries often have the most children, which reinforces the cycle of poverty.

The explosive world population growth has major implications for business. A growing population means growing human needs to satisfy. Depending on purchasing power, it may also mean growing market opportunities. For example, to curb its skyrocketing population, the Chinese government has passed regulations limiting families to one child each. As a result, Chinese children are spoiled and fussed over as never before. Known in China as "little emperors," Chinese children are being showered with everything from candy to computers as a result of what's known as the "six-pocket syndrome." As many as six adults—including parents, grandparents, great-grandparents, and aunts and auncles—may be indulging the whims of each child. This trend has encouraged toy companies such as Japan's Bandai Company (known for its Mighty Morphin Power Rangers), Denmark's Lego Group, and Mattel to enter the Chinese market.[9]

The world's large and highly diverse population poses both opportunities and challenges (see Marketing Highlight 3-1). Thus, marketers keep close track of demographic trends and developments in their markets, both at home and abroad. They track changing age and family structures, geographic population shifts, educational characteristics, and population diversity. Statistics Canada offers a wealth of information for marketers interested in demographic trends. Here, we discuss the most important demographic trends in Canada.

Statistics Canada
www.statcan.ca

Changing Age Structure of the Canadian Population

The population of Canada is expected to exceed 30 million in 1998 and may reach 40 million by the year 2016. The single most important demographic trend in Canada is the changing age structure of the population. The Canadian population is getting *older*. The median age of the Canadian population is now 35. This is the point at which half of the population is younger and half is older. Just 30 years ago, the median age was 25.[10] Two reasons explain this trend. First, there is a long-term slowdown in the birth rate, so there are fewer young people to pull down the population's average age. Second, life expectancy is increasing, so there are more older people to pull up the average age.

Baby boom
The major increase in the annual birth rate following World War II and lasting until the early 1960s. The "baby boomers," now moving into middle age, are a prime target for marketers.

During the **baby boom** that followed World War II and lasted until the early 1960s, the annual birth rate reached an all-time high. The baby boom created a huge "bulge" in age distribution—the nine million baby boomers now account for almost one-third of Canada's population. And as the baby-boom generation ages, the nation's average age increases. Because of its sheer size, many major demographic and socioeconomic changes in Canada and the United States are tied to the baby-boom generation (see Marketing Highlight 3-2).

Although there was a baby boom in both Canada and the United States, it is important for Canadian marketers to recognize that our baby boom was unique. It started later than the American version (1947 versus 1946) and lasted longer (the American boom ended in 1964; the Canadian boom continued until 1966). While the American baby boom resulted in 3.5 children per family, the Canadian boom produced four children. Furthermore, the baby boom was not a worldwide phenomenon. No developed countries, other than Australia and New Zealand, experienced the same expansion in the birth rate. In Europe, there was no baby boom, and in Japan, the birth rate declined during the baby-boom years, which explains why these countries have a higher proportion of older people in their societies.[11]

The baby boom was followed by a "birth dearth," and by the mid-1970s the birth rate had fallen sharply. This decrease was caused by smaller family sizes resulting from the desire to improve personal living standards, from the increasing number of women working outside the home, and from improved birth control. Although family sizes are expected to remain smaller, the birth rate has climbed again as the baby-boom generation moves through the childbearing years and creates a second but smaller "baby boomlet." However, following this boomlet, the birth rate will again decline as we move into the twenty-first century.[12]

Figure 3-5 on page 86 shows the changing age distribution of the Canadian population through 2041. The differing growth rates for various age groups will strongly affect marketers' targeting strategies. For example, the baby boomlet has created a large and growing "kid market." In North America, children under 17 years of age influence over $3 billion worth of purchases each year. After years of "bust," markets for children's toys and games, clothes, furniture, and food are enjoying a "boom." For instance, Sony and other electronics firms are now offering products designed for children. Many retailers are opening separate children's clothing chains, such as GapKids and Kids 'Я' Us. Such markets will continue to grow through the remainder of the century before again decreasing as the baby boomers move out of their childbearing years.[13]

To serve the large and growing "kid market," many retailers are opening separate children's chains. For example, Toys 'Я' Us opened Kids 'Я' Us.

THE BABY BOOMERS, THE GENERATION XERS, AND THE SUNSHINE GENERATION

Demographics involve people, and people make up markets. Thus, marketers track demographic trends and groups carefully. Some of today's most important demographic groups are described below.

The Baby Boomers

The postwar baby boom, which began in 1947 and ran through 1966, produced a population explosion. Since then, the baby boomers have become one of the biggest forces shaping the marketing environment. The fact that Maureen Kempston Darkes, a 47-year-old lawyer, was recently named CEO of General Motors of Canada Ltd., is important not only because she is one of the few women to attain such a position, but also because it is an indication of the power that baby boomers, in general, are now wielding in Canadian business. The boomers have presented a moving target, creating new markets as they grew through infancy to pre-adolescent, teenage, young-adult, and now middle-age years.

The baby boomers account for a third of the population but comprise 40 percent of the workforce and earn over half of all personal income. Today, the aging boomers are moving to the suburbs, settling into home ownership, and raising families. Many people who are turning 45 are reaching a milestone many find unthinkable: becoming grandparents. However, they are determined to fight the stereotypes long associated with this life cycle stage. They are more active, and look and feel younger than their predecessors did. Furthermore, they prefer not to be confronted with advertising or products that address their age or label them as being old. Thus, many products are being re-tooled to meet their needs in a more subtle way. This group is also responsible for the explosive growth of products such as seamless bifocals, large-print books, and products such as Oil of Olay that help them combat wrinkles. Since 36 percent of the people going to the movies are over the age of 40, theatres have been aggressively refurbishing. It isn't enough just to show movies that appeal to older audiences; middle-aged people demand bigger screens, more comfortable seating, and better food.

Boomers are reaching their peak earning and spending years. They constitute a lucrative market for housing, furniture and appliances, children's products, low-calorie foods and beverages, physical fitness products, high-priced cars, convenience products, and financial services.

Converse targets Generation Xers with this black and white ad for Jack Purcell sneakers. The ad is "soft sell," and makes fun of a favourite GenXer target—advertising itself.

Baby boomers cut across all walks of life. But marketers typically have paid the most attention to the small upper crust of the boomer generation—its more educated, mobile, and wealthy segments. These segments have gone by many names. In the 1980s, they were called YUPPIES (young urban professionals); YUMMIES (young upwardly mobile mommies), and DINKs (dual-income, no-kids couples). In the 1990s, however, YUPPIES and DINKs have given way to a new breed, with names such as DEWKs (dual earners with kids); MOBYs (mother older, baby younger); WOOFs (well-off older folks); or just plain GRUMPIES (just what the name suggests).

The older boomers are now in their fifties; the youngest are in their thirties. Thus, the boomers are evolving from the "youthquake generation" to the "backache generation." They're slowing up, having children, and settling down. They're experiencing the pangs of midlife and rethinking the purpose and value of their work, responsibilities, and relationships. Community and family values have become more important, and staying home with the family has become their favourite way to spend an evening.

Of significance when examining the boomer market in Canada, is the shift that sees boomers going from being net-borrowers to being net-savers. Many plan to retire early—almost one-third plan to stop working before they reach age 60. This has resulted in the recent phenomenal growth of Canadian mutual funds.

This increased wealth among boomers is also evident in the travel market. The generation who developed their wanderlust backpacking around Europe and Asia in their twenties, now has the money to go beyond standard vacations. While boomers often seek vacations with an environmental focus, or those that promise something exotic or thrilling, they also want to be coddled with a gourmet meal at the end of the day.

Even though some markets are benefiting, others are threatened as the boomers age. Once the prime consumers of Molson and Labatt beer, boomers are moving away from beer consumption, with the result that these brewers are facing flat or declining markets.

The Generation Xers

Marketers' focus has shifted in recent years to a new group—those born between 1965 and 1976. Six million strong in Canada and representing $140 billion in disposable income, this group represents an extremely important market. Author Douglas Coupland calls them "Generation X." Others call them baby busters, the Nexus generation, twentysomethings, or YIFFIES—young, individualistic, freedom-minded, few.

Many who belong to the 18 to 29 age group hate the label "Generation X." In contrast to the boomers, who were an easy group to target, defining this younger generation is not as easy. Companies that wish to market to them or recruit them as employees are turning to such firms as Toronto's D-Code Inc., a consulting company that helps companies and governments appreciate what makes 18- to 34-year-olds tick. This techno-savvy generation was raised on music, television, computers, and video games. They are satisfied, independent, and optimistic. Quality of life is more important than money to those entering the workforce; longer vacations and funky office space may be more important than the signing bonus. Lacking confidence in business, and educational and government institutions, this group tends to be highly self-reliant. Their confidence is reflected in their number-one career choice—becoming an entrepreneur. However, this generation is also more likely to be unemployed or underemployed. They are more accepting of change than are baby boomers, and they delay getting married, having children, and buying a home longer than do their predecessors. Only 21 percent of members of this generation plan to buy a home in the next two years.

Marketers must remember that this generation is a highly diverse group and resent being clustered into a single market. They are also highly critical of advertising and are extremely savvy about its underlying purpose. As Eric Blais noted in *Marketing*, this is a generation "who no longer cares what McCain has done to their fries." Growing up on a diet of Saturday-morning cartoons and advertising promises that didn't deliver, they enjoy parodying advertising slogans, revelling in producing distorted advertising slogans such as "At Speedy you're a nobody." However, Xers do share a set of influences. Increasing divorce rates and higher employment for mothers have made them the first generation of latchkey kids. Whereas the boomers created a sexual revolution, the Xers have lived in the age of AIDS.

The Xers buy lots of products, such as sweaters, boots, cosmetics, electronics, cars, fast food, beer, computers, and mountain bikes. However, their cynicism makes them savvy shoppers. Because they often did much of the family shopping when growing up, they are experienced shoppers. Their financial pressures make them value-conscious, and they like lower prices and a more functional look.

Generation Xers share new cultural concerns. They care about the environment and respond favourably to companies such as The Body Shop and Ben & Jerry's, which have proven records of environmentally and socially responsible actions.

Generation Xers will have a big impact on the workplace and marketplace of the future. They are poised to displace the lifestyles, culture, and materialistic values of the baby boomers. By the year 2010, they will have overtaken the baby boomers as a primary market for almost every product category.

The Sunshine Generation

Also labelled the echo generation (the boomer's children) and the millennial (they will start to enter maturity after the year 2000), or Generation Y (building of the Gen-X label), this generation was born between 1980 and 1995. While the oldest members are in their teens, the youngest are still toddlers. This group is attracting increased attention from marketers because of its impact on certain product categories. Children's movies earn the biggest dollar at the box office, and they are a major market for fashion and consumer goods.

This group has been immersed in technology as no generation before it. They have had information access unequalled by any preceding group. As a result, they are more aware of global issues and have a sense of themselves as part of a larger world community. This awareness has a

cost, however, They believe they have a calling to fix the problems created by the older generations—significant problems such as environmental degradation, war, crime, and poverty. The archetype of this generation is Craig Kielburger, the famous teenage Canadian activist who has developed a global campaign against child labour and founded an international youth movement, Free The Children. How this generation will evolve remains a big question. They face a world full of questions and ambiguity about their roles as individuals, spouses, parents, workers, and consumers.

Sources: Howard Schlossberg, "Aging Baby Boomers Give Marketers a lot of Changes to Consider," *Advertising Age,* April 12, 1993, p. 10; Campbell Gibson, "The Four Baby Booms," *American Demographics,* November 1993, pp. 36–40; Cyndee Miller, "Xers Know They're a Target Market, and They Hate That," *Marketing News,* December 6, 1993, pp. 2, 15; Jeff Giles, "Generalizations X," *Newsweek,* June 6, 1994, pp. 62–69; Nathan Cobb, "Agent X," *The Boston Globe,* September 28, 1994, pp. 35, 40; Nicholas Zill and John Robinson, "The Generation X Difference," *American Demographics,* April 1995, pp. 24–39. Harvey Schacter, "Power Shift," *Canadian Business,* August 1995, pp. 20–30 and Eric Blais, "Generation X: Targeting a Tough Crowd That's Not Easily Impressed," *Marketing,* June 6, 1994, pp. 13–15. Eric Beauchesne, "Generation X Not the Lost Generation: Survey," *Kingston Whig Standard,* June 15, 1997, p. 22; Christopher Harris, "Faith in Popcorn," *Globe and Mail,* May 10, 1997, p. C10; Deborah Jones, "Here Comes the Sunshine Generation," *Globe and Mail,* May 10, 1997, pp. D1, D2; Dorothy Lipovenko, "Growing Old is a Baby-booming Business," *Globe and Mail,* April 6, 1996, pp. A1, A4; Dorothy Lipovenko, "Rich Boomers Aiming to Retire Earlier than Parents, Poll Says," *Globe and Mail,* October 10, 1996, p. B10; Gayle MacDonald, "The Eyes and Ears of a Generation," *Globe and Mail,* February 4, 1997, p. B13; Leonard Zehr, "Gen-Xers Heading Home: Survey," *Globe and Mail,* February 13, 1997, p. B9; www.freethechildren.org

At the other end of the spectrum, it is projected that almost 13 percent of Canadians will be over 65 by 2001, with the percentage increasing to 25 percent by 2031. As this group grows, so will the demand for retirement communities, quieter forms of recreation, single-portion food packaging, life-care and health-care services, and leisure travel.[14]

FIGURE 3-5 *Projection for Canada, Provinces, and Territories, 1993 to 2041*

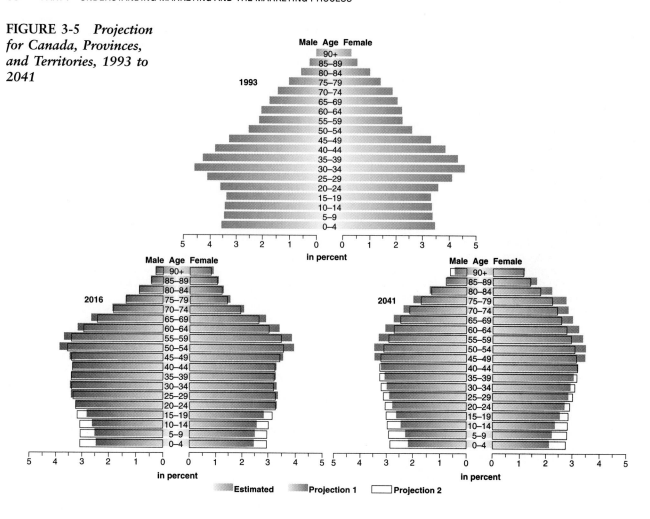

Source: Statistics Canada, Catalogue 91520 occasional, December 1994.

Seniors represent a unique marketing challenge. For example, seniors value information in advertising materials and reasoned arguments instead of claims based on sex and impulse. This group seeks convenience, quality, comfort, and security in many of their purchases. Seniors are also heavy users of some product categories. Being avid consumers of information, seniors represent a much larger market for books, newspapers, and magazines than the rest of the Canadian population. Seniors also represent almost 50 percent of the luxury car market and one-third of new home sales.

Seniors are wealthier than many stereotypes would have us believe. "Whoopies" (well-off older people), or Canadians over the age of 49, account for two-thirds of Canada's disposable income. Many seniors are debt-free, but this fact should not be taken as an indication that they are price-insensitive. Seniors are experienced, knowledgeable, value-conscious consumers. Many are active and well educated and resent being classified as "old people." Although some will have more leisure time than the rest of the population, many others plan to work beyond the traditional retirement age.

Packaging is another important issue for many seniors. While many marketers have responded to their dietary concerns by placing more details about product ingredients on labels, marketers have often forgotten that reading the fine print on packages is difficult for many older consumers. Wrestling with childproof caps is a source of constant frustration among individuals whose joints are

Maxwell House* and other brands are targeting smaller households with single-serve portions.

*Registered Trademark of Kraft Canada Inc.

inflamed by arthritis. Some over-the-counter drug producers have responded to this concern with easy-to-open containers especially designed for this market. Similarly, cleaning products are not only being made in smaller containers to meet the needs of seniors who often live alone, but they are also being made in easier-to-handle containers. Windex, for example, now comes in a bottle with an indented neck that is easier to grip.[15]

The Changing Family

The North American ideal of the two-children, two-car suburban family has lately been losing some of its lustre. People are marrying later and having fewer children. Despite the recent "baby boomlet," the number of married couples with children will continue to decline through the end of the century. In fact, couples with no children under 18 now comprise almost half of all families.[16]

Also, the number of working women has increased greatly. Currently, over 50 percent of all women over the age of 16 work outside the home or are looking for a job, and 1.1 million of these working women fall between the ages of 25 to 34—the age when many have children. Since these women are constantly short of time, the demand for convenience goods and services is growing. Marketers of tires, automobiles, insurance, travel, and financial services are increasingly directing their advertising to working women. As a result of the shift in the traditional roles and values of husbands and wives, with husbands assuming more domestic functions such as shopping and child care, more food and household appliance marketers are targeting husbands.

Finally, the number of non-family households is increasing. Many young adults leave home and move into apartments. In Canada, the average age at which females now marry is 25, while it is 28 for males. In the age bracket 30 to 34, 20 percent of men and 18 percent of women choose to remain single.[17] Non-family and single-parent households are the fastest-growing categories of households. These groups have unique needs. For example, they need smaller apartments; inexpensive and smaller appliances, furniture, and furnishings; and food that is packaged in smaller sizes.

Geographic Shifts in Population

Canadians are a mobile people with approximately one in 10, or 2.9 million Canadians, moving each year. Among the major trends are the following:

◆ *Canadian Regionalism.*[18] As Table 3-2 indicates, the rates of population change vary by region. While some regions of Canada are growing in population, others are shrinking. During the period 1991-94, the populations of Newfoundland and Saskatchewan decreased while the populations of the other provinces grew. While the total Canadian population grew by 4.41 percent during this period, British Columbia, the Yukon, and the N.W.T. grew by approximately seven percent. Alberta and Ontario also exceeded the national average in terms of population growth, but the remaining provinces fell below national growth rates.

◆ *Movement from rural to urban and suburban areas.* For more than a century, Canadians have been moving from rural to urban areas. The urban areas show a faster pace of living, more commuting, higher incomes, and greater variety of goods and services than can be found in the small towns and rural areas that dot Canada.

TABLE 3-2 *Canadian Markets*

Province	1994 Population (000)	1994 % Canada	% Change 91–94	Total HH (000)
Newfoundland	568.3	1.99	−0.04	181.0
Prince Edward Island	132.9	0.47	2.39	46.1
Nova Scotia	920.4	3.23	2.28	338.0
New Brunswick	732.2	2.57	1.15	263.5
Quebec	7183.9	25.21	4.17	2789.6
Ontario	10 603.5	37.21	5.14	3873.2
Manitoba	1102.8	3.87	1.00	415.4
Saskatchewan	982.3	3.45	−0.67	364.4
Alberta	2669.8	9.37	4.88	967.9
British Columbia	3511.9	12.32	7.00	1341.1
Yukon & NWT	91.6	0.32	7.13	28.1
Canada	28 499.6	100.00	4.14	10 608.3

Source: 1994 Canadian markets, *The Financial Post.*

◆ *Movement from the city to the suburbs.* Today's Canadian cities are often surrounded by large suburban areas. Statistics Canada calls these combinations of urban and suburban populations, Census Metropolitan Areas (CMAs). Approximately 50 percent of Canada's population lives in the top 20 CMAs. These are listed in Table 3-3 along with the estimated retail sales generated in each area. Information about CMAs is useful for marketers trying to decide

TABLE 3-3 *The Top 25 CMA Markets in Canada*

Rank	City	Population (000)	Total Retail Sales (mil $)	Per Capita Retail Sales
1	Toronto	3895.0	40 842	10 500
2	Montreal	3113.3	29 977	9600
3	Vancouver	1626.8	15 718	9700
4	Ottawa-Hull	901.5	9310	10 300
5	Edmonton	821.4	6827	8300
6	Calgary	737.3	6961	9400
7	Winnipeg	652.0	5409	8300
8	Quebec	624.8	5622	9000
9	Hamilton	610.4	5389	8800
10	London	377.3	3130	8300
11	St. Catharines/Niagara	362.1	2804	7700
12	Kitchener	358.2	3014	8400
13	Halifax	315.3	3189	10 100
14	Victoria	288.7	2443	8500
15	Windsor	261.1	2235	8600
16	Oshawa	257.6	2507	9700
17	Saskatoon	209.7	1873	8900
18	Regina	194.7	1922	9900
19	St. John's	164.4	1511	9200
20	Chicoutimi-Jonquiere	59.21	1315	8300

Source: 1992 Canadian markets, *The Financial Post.*

which geographical segments represent the most lucrative markets for their products or which areas are most critical in terms of buying media time.

A Better-Educated and More White-Collar Population

The population is becoming better educated. The rising number of educated people will increase the demand for quality products, books, magazines, and travel. It suggests a decline in television viewing because university-educated consumers watch less television than does the population at large. The workforce also is becoming more white collar. Forty percent of Canadian workers are employed in white-collar jobs (sales, clerical) and 25 percent of the workforce are classified as holding professional, managerial, and administrative positions. One-third of the workforce is in blue-collar occupations.

Increasing Diversity

Countries vary in their ethnic and racial composition. At one extreme are homogeneous countries like Japan, where almost everyone is of Japanese descent. At the other are countries such as Canada and the United States, whose populations are "salad bowls" of mixed races. Anyone who has walked the streets of Vancouver, Montreal, Calgary, or Toronto will immediately understand that visible minorities in Canada are a force to be reckoned with. The United Nations reported that Toronto is the world's most multicultural city, and the Canadian Advertising Foundation recently predicted that the combined purchasing power of ethnic markets will soon exceed $300 billion. Many ethnic markets are growing in size. For example, the Italian, German, and Chinese markets in Canada each have populations of over 400 000.

Nabisco is an example of a firm that understands the power of ethnic marketing. Its product, Magic Baking Powder, was losing share in its traditional markets, but the firm revived its lacklustre performance when it targeted Chinese and Japanese restaurants with a sampling and promotion program for its product. Unlike baking powder's traditional market of consumers, which were moving away from "scratch baking," this market valued quality baked goods. Sales in British Columbia alone increased by 14 percent as a result of this targeted sampling program.

Marketers must avoid negative stereotypes when it comes to serving ethnic markets. Statistics Canada reports that recent immigrants are harder-working and better educated than people born in Canada. Seventeen percent of immigrants hold university degrees compared with 11 percent of people born in Canada. Immigrants are also more likely to hold managerial or professional jobs, and have more stable family lives than people born in Canada.

Targeting ethnic consumers involves far more than mere tokenism, many ethnic marketing specialists warn. Merely placing a person from a visible minority in an advertisement is not sufficient evidence that you are an ethnic marketer. Communicating in the consumer's native language is often mandatory, but marketers must also face the challenge of not alienating sophisticated second-generation individuals. The TD Bank recently demonstrated the power of providing information in potential customers' native language. The bank launched a Chinese Green Info line to target potential Chinese investors. Over 300 callers per month take advantage of the service, which has generated considerable investments.

Marketers also often have to place advertisements in media directed at the particular ethnic community they wish to serve. This task is becoming easier as more publications are being targeted to specific ethnic markets. For example, Tele-Direct Publications has recently started distributing a Chinese edition of the *Yellow Pages*, and *Toronto Life* and *Maclean's* have recently launched Chinese editions. Ethnic television stations are offering programming in many cities. In terms of retailing, stores must be staffed with personnel who understand the language, customs, manners, and buying behaviour of the ethnic market.[19]

Many firms, such as Air Canada, are recognizing racial diversity in their advertising.

The diversity in the Canadian marketplace isn't restricted to ethnic markets. People's sexual orientation is another point of diversity, and there is growing tolerance of alternative lifestyles in Canada. Over 600 000 people attended Lesbian and Gay Pride events in Toronto in 1997 alone. Since homosexual consumers tend to be cosmopolitan and have high incomes, they are desirable target markets for everything from health and beauty products, to travel, fashion, entertainment, and financial services. Nonetheless, until recently, few national advertisers, with the exception of the large breweries, have created advertisements explicitly directed at this audience. One of the reasons is the lack of research on this market. Statistics Canada, for example, doesn't even ask about sexual orientation in its surveys. Another reason is the dearth of middle-of-the-road media directed at these consumers. Finally, some marketers feared that advertising in gay media or at gay events would cause a backlash from heterosexual consumers.

These things are changing. Several research firms, including Environics, a Toronto-based organization, has started gathering information on the market. A growing body of media is directed at the gay community including electronic media, such as PrideNet (http://www.pridenet.com). People who have experienced advertising to the gay community, such as Tom Blackmore, a partner in the firm Robins Blackmore, says that clients who have used creative materials that are relevant to this audience have experienced remarkable successes from their campaigns. The one mistake that marketers can make with respect to this audience is doing nothing. "It is a market that people have ignored for way too long," he explains.[20]

ECONOMIC ENVIRONMENT

Economic environment
Factors that affect consumer buying power and spending patterns.

Markets require buying power as well as people. The **economic environment** consists of factors that affect consumer purchasing power and spending patterns. Nations vary greatly in their levels and distribution of income. Some countries have *subsistence economies*—they consume most of their own agricultural and industrial output. These countries offer few market opportunities. At the other extreme are *industrial economies,* which constitute rich markets for many different kinds of goods. Marketers must pay close attention to major trends and consumer spending patterns, both across and within their world markets. Following are some of the major economic trends.

IS CANADA'S MARKETING INDUSTRY RACIST?

This question was posed to 21 marketing specialists in 1997. While most respondents denied racism in Canadian marketing, they did stress that marketers should do more to reflect Canada's multicultural reality. Rather than being overtly racist, some members of the marketing community are racist by omission, claims Suzanne Keeler of the Canadian Advertising Foundation. These people just don't include people from different backgrounds on their management teams or in their advertisements. Instead of selecting people based on their individual characteristics, they make choices based on outdated sterotypes. While many respondents noted that more and more advertisers, especially those aiming products at young people, are using people from minority populations in their ads, others, such as Deanna Dolson, advertising director of *Aboriginal Voices* magazine, claim that many advertisers haven't "opened their eyes to what native culture is."

As the importance of global marketing grows, people from different ethnic and language groups will become increasingly valuable in the roles of marketing managers, advertising creative specialists, and account executives. Today, people in charge of new product development consider the opinions of ethnic groups when developing their product concepts. Some new product categories, such as ethnic foods, depend completely on understanding ethnic target populations. B.K. Sethi, publisher of *Ethnic Food Merchandiser*, doesn't believe any marketer can afford to be racist. Liz Torlée, chairperson of the Institute of Canadian Advertising, takes a similar stance. Advertising is "an all-embracing industry, and we have to be so much in tune with consumers that we are, I hope, constantly reflecting consumers' changing attitudes."

the "how do we sell more stuff to more people in more places?" Internet solution

*1-800-426-2255. IBM is a registered trade-mark and Solutions for a small planet and CommercePoint are trade-marks of International Business Machines Corporation and are used under licence by IBM Canada Ltd. ©1997 IBM Corporation.

IBM shows people from diverse backgrounds in many of its advertisements.

Source: *Marketing*, March 3, 1997.

Changes in Income

In the 1980s, the economy entered its longest peacetime boom. Consumers fell into a consumption frenzy, fuelled by income growth, federal tax reductions, rapid increases in housing values, and a boom in borrowing. They bought and bought, seemingly without caution, amassing record levels of debt. "It was fashionable to describe yourself as 'born to shop.' When the going gets tough, it was said, the tough go shopping. In the 1980s, many ... became literally addicted to personal consumption."[21]

Free spending and high expectations were dashed by the recession in the early 1990s. Consumers have sobered up, pulled back, and adjusted to leaner times. *Value marketing* became the watchword for many marketers. They looked for ways to offer today's more financially cautious buyers greater value—just the right combination of product quality and good service at a fair price.

Today, the baby-boom generation is moving into its prime wage-earning years, and the number of small families headed by dual-career couples continues to increase. Thus, many consumers will continue to demand quality products and better service, and they will be able to pay for them.

However, the 1990s is also the decade of the "financially squeezed consumer." Some segments have increased financial burdens—repaying debts acquired during their university or college years, facing increased taxes, and saving ahead for their children's university tuition payments and retirement. These financially squeezed consumers spend more slowly and carefully. And they seek greater value in the products and services they buy.

Paradoxes of the New Economy

For decades, many analysts predicted that advances in technology would create a leisure generation—people who worked less and had more time to enjoy life. While today many people have more time on their hands, few of them would consider themselves a leisure class. With unemployment stuck at about 10 percent, many people are shut out of the workforce entirely. Twenty percent of Canadians rely on one, or multiple, part-time jobs. At the other end of the spectrum is a growing number of Canadians working more than 50 hours per week.

In the period from 1976 to 1993, the number of these "over-employed" people grew by 27 percent. Thus, while the average workweek remains at 40 hours, a growing number of people are working far less, and a growing number are working far more. This polarity in terms of hours worked is the paradox of the new economy.[22]

What are the reasons for these trends? Economic necessity is a prime culprit. In the 1950s and 1960s, a family could support itself with about 48 hours of employment. Today, family members must work 65 to 72 hours. This means increasingly that both spouses must work.[23]

Marketers must target their offerings to these two very different segments. While many who work part time will use their excess time to save money, others demand time-saving products. People at the time-pressed end of the continuum often don't even have time to eat or prepare meals. Kellogg's built an advertising campaign around this knowledge and positioned its breakfast bars as meals for people on the run. Grocery retailers are also taking notice. Since people aren't preparing meals at home the way they used to, grocers' market share is eroding. Today, about 38 percent of each food dollar is spent outside grocery stores in Canada; the average is 51 percent in the United States. Loblaw is experimenting with a strategy to win back harried consumers. The company has created *Take Me Marché* kiosks in some stores, offering ready-to-eat meals and take-home food for people who want to eat at home but don't have time to cook.[24]

Thus, marketers should pay attention to *income distribution* as well as average income. Income distribution in Canada is still very skewed. At the top are *upper-class* consumers, whose spending patterns are not affected by current economic events and who are a major market for luxury goods. There is a comfortable *middle class* that is somewhat careful about its spending but can still afford the good life some of the time. The *working class* must stick close to the basics of food, clothing, and shelter and must try hard to save. Finally, the *underclass* (persons on welfare and many retirees) must count their pennies when making even the most basic purchases.

Changing Consumer Spending Patterns

Table 3-4 shows the proportion of total expenditures made by Canadian households at different income levels for major categories of goods and services. Food, housing, and transportation use up most household income. Consumer spending patterns have changed considerably in the last 50 years. In 1947, spending on the basics (food, clothing, housing, fuel) accounted for 69 cents out of every dollar. In 1995, expenditures on these items fell to 52 cents. What expenditures account for the other 17 cents? Canadians are spending more on two categories—what Statistics Canada refers to as personal goods and services; and recreation, entertainment, education, and cultural services.[25] However, consumers at different income levels have different spending patterns. Some of these differences were noted over a century ago by Ernst Engel, who studied how people shifted their spending as their income rose. He found that as family income rises, the percentage spent on food declines, the percentage spent on housing remains constant (except for utilities such as gas, electricity, and public services, which decrease),

TABLE 3-4   *Consumer Spending at Different Income Levels*

Expenditure	INCOME LEVEL		
	Less than $10,000	30,000	$50,000 and Over
Food	21.7%	15.3%	11.8%
Housing	28.9	17.0	12.7
Utilities	5.7	3.3	2.4
Clothing	5.5	6.0	6.7
Transportation	9.5	13.8	12.9
Health Care	2.4	2.0	1.5
Entertainment	4.0	5.3	5.2
Education	0.8	0.6	1.1
Contributions	4.3	3.4	3.2
Other	2.4	2.6	2.5

Source: Statistics Canada, *Family Expenditure in Canada* 1992, Cat. No 62-555.

Engel's laws
Differences noted over a century ago by Ernst Engel in how people shift their spending across food, housing, transportation, health care, and other goods and services categories as family income rises.

and both the percentage spent on other categories and that devoted to savings increase. **Engel's laws** generally have been supported by later studies.

Changes in major economic variables such as income, cost of living, interest rates, and savings and borrowing patterns have a large impact on the marketplace. Companies watch these variables by using economic forecasting. Businesses do not have to be wiped out by an economic downturn or caught short in a boom. With adequate warning, they can take advantage of changes in the economic environment.

NATURAL ENVIRONMENT

Natural environment
Natural resources that are needed as inputs by marketers or that are affected by marketing activities.

The **natural environment** involves the natural resources that are needed as inputs by marketers or that are affected by marketing activities. Environmental concerns have grown steadily during the past two decades. Some trend analysts have labelled the 1990s as the "Earth Decade," claiming that the natural environment is the major worldwide issue facing business and the public. In many cities around the world, air and water pollution have reached dangerous levels. World concern continues to mount about the depletion of the earth's ozone layer and the resulting "greenhouse effect," a dangerous warming of the earth. And many environmentalists fear that we soon will be buried in our own trash. Marketers should be aware of the following trends in the natural environment.

Shortages of Raw Materials and Increased Pollution

Air and water may seem to be infinite resources, but air pollution chokes many of the world's cities. Smoke from fires in Indonesia polluted the air for whole nations. Water quality is already a major problem in some parts of Canada. Water shortages haunt the southern United States. Renewable resources, such as forests and food, must be used wisely.

Increased use of non-renewable resources, such as oil, coal, and various minerals, pose a serious problem. Firms making products that require these scarce resources face large cost increases, even if the materials remain available.

Industry must try to mitigate the damage it does to the quality of the natural environment. Public concern creates a large market for pollution-control solutions such as scrubbers, recycling centres, and new ways to produce and package goods that do not cause environmental damage. Concern for the natural environment has spawned the so-called *green movement*. Increasing numbers of consumers do more

Loblaw Companies Ltd.
www.loblaw.com/

business with ecologically responsible companies. They buy "environmentally friendly" products. Loblaw began its G.R.E.E.N. program in 1989. Today, it is one of the most successful environmental businesses in the world. Over 100 new products have been launched since the program's inception, while manufacturing changes have helped make dozens of other products environmentally friendly.[26]

The governments of different countries vary in their concern and efforts to promote a clean environment. For example, the German government vigorously pursues environmental quality, partly because of the strong public green movement and partly because of the ecological devastation in former East Germany. In contrast, many poor nations do little about pollution, largely because they lack the needed funds or political will.

The Canadian government passed the Environmental Protection Act in 1989. This Act established stringent pollution-control measures as well as the means for their enforcement including fines as large as $1 million if regulations are violated. Aimed at preventing environmental problems, the Act regulates the use of toxic substances, establishes emission standards, and outlines policies for handling and disposing of waste.[27] In the future, companies doing business in Canada and the United States can expect strong controls from government and pressure groups. Instead of opposing regulation, marketers should help develop solutions to the material and energy problems facing the world.

TECHNOLOGICAL ENVIRONMENT

Technological environment
Forces that create new technologies, creating new product and market opportunities.

The **technological environment** is perhaps the most dramatic force now shaping our destiny. Technology has released such wonders as antibiotics, organ transplants, and notebook computers, and such horrors as nuclear missiles, nerve gas, and the machine gun.

Every new technology replaces an older technology. Transistors hurt the vacuum-tube industry, xerography hurt the carbon-paper business, automobiles hurt the railways, and compact discs hurt phonograph records. When old industries fought or ignored new technologies, their businesses declined.

New technologies create new markets and opportunities. Marketers should watch the following trends in technology.

Fast Pace of Technological Change

Shortened product life cycles and the rapid changes in technology are the hallmarks of the late twentieth century. Many of today's common products were not available even a hundred years ago. John A. Macdonald did not know about automobiles, airplanes, or the electric light. Mackenzie King did not know about xerography, synthetic detergents, or earth satellites. And John Diefenbaker did not know about personal computers, compact disc players, or fax machines. Companies that do not keep up with technological change soon will find their products outdated. And they will miss new product and market opportunities. Marketers often face the difficult task of "envisioning" markets for products and services that didn't exist just a few years ago.

High R&D Budgets

The costs of researching and developing new, complex technologies are rapidly increasing. The United States leads the world in research and development (R&D) spending. Canada spends approximately 1.3 percent of GNP on R&D. Canada doesn't have a sterling record when it comes to R&D expenditures. Compared with other G7 countries, Canada is at the bottom of the list. The Liberal government has begun some new R&D initiatives, contributing $800 million over five years to the new Foundation for Innovation and $47 million to the establishment of Centres of Excellence to encourage private-sector/public-sector collaboration in

Marketers of new technologies engage in fierce battles to win over initial adopters. Two ads for new PCS digital communications services, one from Fido, and the other from Clearnet illustrate such a battle.

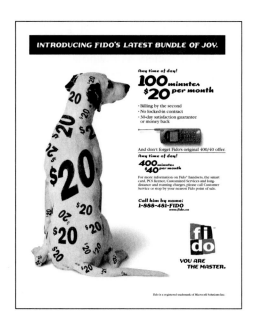

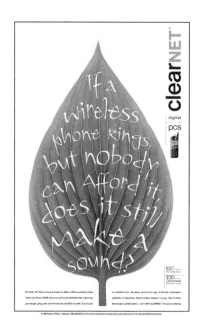

research and application development. Another $600 million has been earmarked for the Technology Partnerships Canada program, which provides interest-free loans to support R&D.[28]

The private sector has as dismal a record of R&D expenditures as does the government sector. Private-sector investment in R&D is less than half of what it is in Sweden, the United States, Japan, Germany, or France. Since many of the firms operating in Canada are branches of multinational firms, R&D is often conducted elsewhere. Some Canadian sectors take R&D investment more seriously, however. The information technology sector and telecommunications equipment industries are the powerhouses of Canadian R&D. However, a recent study suggests that much of the high-tech sector is suffering from an "innovation gap." Some of this gap is due to the fact that Canadian high-tech firms are small and thus do not have the same financial resources to invest in R&D as do their international rivals. It is important, therefore, that they focus on the worldwide niche markets that they can dominate even though they are small in size.[29] IBM Canada, Pratt & Whitney Canada (the aircraft engine manufacturer), CAE Inc. (a diversified maker of electronic products), Merck Frosst Canada (pharmaceuticals), Bell Canada, and Alcan Aluminium are among Canada's top 10 firms for R&D expenditures.[30]

Marketers need to understand the changing technological environment and the ways that new technologies can serve human needs. They need to work closely with R&D people to encourage more market-oriented research. They also must be alert to the possible negative aspects of any innovation that might harm users or arouse opposition.

POLITICAL ENVIRONMENT

Political environment
Laws, government agencies, and pressure groups that influence and limit various organizations and individuals in a given society.

Marketing decisions are strongly affected by developments in the political environment. The **political environment** consists of laws, government agencies, and pressure groups that influence and limit various organizations and individuals in a given society.

Legislation Regulating Business

Even the most liberal advocates of free-market economies agree that the system works best with at least some regulation. Well-conceived regulation can encourage competition and ensure fair markets for goods and services. Thus, governments develop *public policy* to guide commerce—sets of laws and regulations that limit business for the good of society as a whole. Almost every marketing activity is subject to a wide range of laws and regulations.

INCREASING LEGISLATION.   Legislation affecting business around the world has increased steadily over the years. Canada has many laws covering issues such as competition, fair trade practices, environmental protection, product safety, truth in advertising, packaging and labelling, pricing, and other important areas (see Table 3-5). The European Commission has been active in establishing a new framework of laws covering competitive behaviour, product standards, product liability, and commercial transactions for the 12 member nations of the European Community. Some countries have especially strong consumerism legislation. For example, Norway bans several forms of sales promotion—trading stamps, contests, premiums—as being inappropriate or unfair ways of promoting products. Thailand requires food processors selling national brands to market low-price brands also, so that low-income consumers can find economy brands on the shelves. In India, food companies must obtain special approval to launch brands that duplicate those already existing on the market, such as additional soft drinks or new brands of rice.

Understanding the public-policy implications of a particular marketing activity is not a simple matter. For example, in Canada, many laws are created at the federal, provincial, and municipal levels, and these regulations often overlap. Moreover, regulations are constantly changing—what was allowed last year may now be prohibited, and what was prohibited may now be allowed. For example, the North American Free Trade Agreement (NAFTA) replaced the Free Trade Agreement (FTA) in August 1992. It governs free trade among Canada, the United States, and Mexico. NAFTA is an historic document since it is the first trade agreement between two developed nations and a developing country.[31] It is also the

TABLE 3-5   *Major Federal Legislation Affecting Marketing*

The Competition Act

The Competition Act is a major legislative act affecting the marketing activities of companies in Canada. Specific sections and the relevant areas are

- Section 34: Pricing—Forbids a supplier to charge different prices to competitors purchasing like quantities of goods (price discrimination). Forbids price-cutting that lessens competition (predatory pricing).
- Section 36: Pricing and Advertising—Forbids advertising prices that misrepresent the "usual" selling price (misleading price advertising).
- Section 38: Pricing—Forbids suppliers to require subsequent resellers to offer products at a stipulated price (resale price maintenance).
- Section 33: Mergers—Forbids mergers by which competition is, or is likely to be, lessened to the detriment of, or against, the interests of the public.

Other selected Acts that have an impact on marketing activities:

- *National Trade Mark and True Labelling Act*—established the term "Canada-Standard" or "C.S." as a national trade mark; requires certain commodities to be properly labelled or described in advertising for the purpose of indicating material content or quality.
- *Consumer Packaging and labelling Act*—provides a set of rules to ensure that full information is disclosed by the manufacturer, packer, or distributor. Requires that all prepackaged products bear the quantity in French and English in metric as well as traditional Canadian standard units of weight, volume, or measure.
- *Motor Vehicle Safety Act*—established mandatory safety standards for motor vehicles.
- *Food and Drug Act*—prohibits the advertisement and sale of adulterated or misbranded foods, cosmetics, and drugs.

cornerstone for creating conditions that will help North American businesses compete worldwide. Access to low-cost inputs from the Mexican market helps U.S. and Canadian firms respond to offshore price competition. These firms can better match strategies of Asian competitors such as the Japanese, who have access to low-cost inputs of material and labour in countries such as China. As trade among the three countries expands, the provisions of NAFTA will continue to be updated and amended. Marketers must work hard to keep up with changes in regulations and their interpretations.

Business legislation has been enacted for various reasons. The first is to *protect companies* from each other. Although business executives may praise competition, they sometimes try to neutralize it when it threatens them. So laws are passed to define and prevent unfair competition.

The second purpose of government regulation is to *protect consumers* from unfair business practices. Some firms, if left alone, would make shoddy products, tell lies in their advertising, and deceive consumers through their packaging and pricing. Unfair business practices have been defined and are enforced by various agencies.

The third purpose of government regulation is to *protect the interests of society* against unrestrained business behaviour. Profitable business activity does not always create a better quality of life. Regulation arises to ensure that firms take responsibility for the social costs of their production or products.

New laws and their enforcement will continue or increase. Business executives must watch these developments when planning their products and marketing programs. Marketers need to know about the major laws protecting competition, consumers, and society. They need to understand these laws at the municipal, provincial, federal, and international levels.

INCREASED EMPHASIS ON ETHICS AND SOCIALLY RESPONSIBLE ACTIONS. Written regulations cannot possibly cover all potential marketing abuses, and existing laws are often difficult to enforce. However, beyond written laws and regulations, business is also governed by social codes and rules of professional ethics. Enlightened companies encourage their managers to look beyond what the regulatory system allows and to simply "do the right thing." These socially responsible firms actively seek out ways to protect the long-run interests of their consumers and the environment.

The recent rash of business scandals and increased concerns about the environment have created fresh interest in the issues of ethics and social responsibility. Almost every aspect of marketing involves such issues. Unfortunately, because these issues usually involve conflicting interests, well-meaning people can disagree honestly about the right course of action in a particular situation. Thus, many industrial and professional trade associations have suggested codes of ethics, and many companies now are developing policies and guidelines to deal with complex social responsibility issues.

Throughout the text, we present Marketing Highlight exhibits that summarize the main public-policy and social responsibility issues surrounding major marketing decisions. These exhibits discuss the legal issues that marketers should understand and the common ethical and societal concerns that marketers face. In Chapter 20, we discuss a broad range of societal marketing issues in greater depth.

CULTURAL ENVIRONMENT

Cultural environment
Institutions and other forces that affect society's basic values, perceptions, preferences, and behaviours.

The **cultural environment** is composed of institutions and other forces that affect a society's basic values, perceptions, preferences, and behaviours. People grow up in a particular society that shapes their basic beliefs and values. They absorb a world view that defines their relationships with others. The following cultural characteristics can affect marketing decision-making.

REGIONAL DIFFERENCES IN CULTURE VALUES AND PRODUCT USAGE

Canadian marketers must be sensitive to the regional differences that mark the country. Recent polls have shown that people in different parts of the nation have dramatically different values and beliefs. While it does not surprise most Canadians that Quebecers are fiercely independent, they might be surprised about the extent to which Quebecois live for today and place a high value on enjoying life. When asked the question, "We should eat, drink, and be merry, for tomorrow we may die," 71 percent of Quebec residents agreed with the statement, while people from other regions of Canada expressed agreement levels ranging from 17 to 43 percent. Quebecers are also more security-conscious than other Canadians. They put greater importance on family, and on the cultivation of friendships. Unlike the rest of Canada, they demonstrate a respect for authority. Picturing themselves as *au courant*, they stress fashion and being up to date on current events. Quebecers place less importance on earning a lot of money than do people from English Canada, and they pride themselves on being more emotional than English Canadians.

Farmers Co-operative Dairy Limited of Halifax believed Cape Breton fiddler Natalie MacMaster would have a strong appeal to Nova Scotians and featured her in a successful milk ad campaign.

Regional differences are not just limited to those between French and English Canadians. Newfoundlanders think that they are the hardest-working segment of the Canadian population, while people from British Columbia express the greatest love of reading.

These regional values often translate into different patterns of product usage. Fredericton is the capital of white-bread consumption. Montrealers eat more deep brown beans than other Canadians. Consumers in Halifax drink more Diet Coke per capita than other Canadians, and people from Manitoba and Saskatchewan have the highest per-capita consumption of Kellogg's Corn Flakes. People from Quebec consume more than half of all tomato juice sold in Canada, but Quebecers are less likely to try new products, use no-name products, or make long-distance phone calls. While marketers are often at a loss when it comes to explaining how regional values translate into different product usage patterns, marketers must still be highly sensitive to these regional differences.

Sources: Rosemary Todd, "Food for Thought," *The Globe and Mail*, March 12, 1988, p. D2; Maclean's/CTV Poll, "A National Mirror," *Maclean's*, January 3, 1994, pp. 12–15; "Portrait of the Quebec Consumer," *Marketing*, March 22, 1993, p. 14; "Quebec," advertising supplement to *Advertising Age*, November 22, 1993.

Persistence of Cultural Values

People in a given society hold many beliefs and values. Their core beliefs and values have a high degree of persistence. For example, most Canadians believe in working, getting married, giving to charity, and being honest. While such values have been described as dull, reserved, and modest, Canadians view themselves as hardworking, generous, and sophisticated. These beliefs shape more specific attitudes and behaviours found in everyday life. *Core* beliefs and values are passed from parents to children and are reinforced by schools, churches, business, and government.

Secondary beliefs and values are more open to change. Believing in marriage is a core belief; believing that people should get married early in life is a secondary belief. Marketers have some chance of changing secondary values, but little chance of changing core values. For example, family-planning marketers could argue more effectively that people should get married later than that they should not get married at all.

Shifts in Secondary Cultural Values

Although core values are fairly persistent, cultural swings do occur. Consider the impact of popular music groups, movie personalities, and other celebrities on young people's hair styling, clothing, and sexual norms. Marketers want to predict cultural shifts in order to identify new opportunities or threats. Several firms offer "futures" forecasts in this connection. For example, the Environics marketing research firm tracks regional values, such as "anti-bigness," "mysticism," "living for today," "away from possessions," and "sensuousness." Such information helps marketers cater to trends with appropriate products and communication appeals. (See Marketing Highlight 3-4 for a summary of today's cultural trends.)

The major cultural values of a society are expressed in people's views of themselves and others, as well as in their views of organizations, society, nature, and the universe.

PEOPLE'S VIEWS OF THEMSELVES.   People vary in their emphasis on serving themselves versus serving others. Some people seek personal pleasure, wanting fun, change, and escape. Others seek self-realization through religion, recreation, or the avid pursuit of careers or other life goals. People use products, brands, and services as a means of self-expression, and they buy products and services that match their views of themselves.

PEOPLE'S VIEWS OF OTHERS.   More recently, observers have noted a shift from a "me-society" to a "we-society" in which more people want to be with and serve others. Notes one trendtracker, "People want to get out, especially those 48 million people working out of their home and feeling a little cooped-up [and] all those shut-ins who feel unfulfilled by the cyberstuff that was supposed to make them feel like never leaving home."[32] Moreover, materialism, flashy spending, and self-indulgence are being replaced by more sensible spending, saving, family concerns, and helping others. The aging baby boomers are limiting their spending to products and services that improve their lives instead of boosting their images. This suggests a bright future for products and services that serve basic needs rather than those relying on glitz and hype. It also suggests a greater demand for "social support" products and services that improve direct communication between people, such as health clubs and family vacations.

PEOPLE'S VIEWS OF ORGANIZATIONS.   People vary in their attitudes toward corporations, government agencies, trade unions, universities, and other organizations. By and large, people are willing to work for major organizations, and they expect them, in turn, to carry out society's work. In recent years, there has been a decline in organizational loyalty and a growing scepticism regarding business and political organizations and institutions. People are giving a little less to their organizations and are trusting them less.

This trend suggests that organizations need to find new ways to win consumer confidence. They need to review their advertising communications to ensure that their messages are honest. They also need to review their various activities to make sure that they are perceived to be "good corporate citizens." More companies are linking themselves to worthwhile causes, measuring their images with important publics, and using public relations to build more positive images (see Marketing Highlight 3-5).

Clearly Canadian
www.clearly.ca

**Upper Canada Brewing
Company**
www.uppercanada.com/
index.html

PEOPLE'S VIEWS OF SOCIETY.   People vary in their attitudes toward their society, from patriots who defend it, to reformers who want to change it, to malcontents who want to leave it. People's orientation to their society influences their consumption patterns, levels of savings, and attitudes toward the marketplace.

The 1980s and 1990s have seen an increase in consumer patriotism. Some companies such as Zellers have responded with "made-in-Canada" themes and promotions. Others, such as Clearly Canadian or Upper Canada Brewing Company, have made national identity part of their branding strategy. Canadians do not respond to in-your-face nationalistic appeals, but love the quirky humour of Labatt Blue's television campaign built around the insights about Canada's future by two early "voyageurs," or Molson Canadian's "I am Canadian" spots.

PEOPLE'S VIEWS OF NATURE.   People vary in their attitudes toward the natural world. Some feel ruled by it, others feel in harmony with it, and still others seek

CAUSE-RELATED MARKETING: DOING WELL BY DOING GOOD

Cause-related marketing (CRM), involves the affiliation of corporate "for-profit" marketing activities with the fund-raising requirements of "not-for-profit" organizations. These programs are growing in popularity. They have acted as marketing tools to target a vast array of market segments while also addressing a wide range of social issues. For example, Molson has linked its marketing of beer to building awareness among its target audience of 18- to 24-year-olds about sexually transmitted diseases while helping to fund AIDS research. Similarly, Chanel Canada has tied its marketing of high fashion to upscale consumers with support for the Mount Sinai hospital. Beatrice Foods sponsors "The Super Cities Walk" to raise funds for multiple sclerosis. Altamira, a mutual-fund marketer, sponsors the opera as a way of attracting investment dollars from its target of business professionals.

Cause-related marketing has become one of the hottest forms of corporate giving. It lets companies "do well by doing good" by linking purchases of the company's products or services with fund-raising for worthwhile causes or charitable organizations. The term, cause-related marketing, was born in the early 1980s, when American Express offered to donate one cent to the restoration of the Statue of Liberty for each use of its credit card. American Express ended up contributing $1.7 million, but the cause-related campaign produced a 28 percent increase in card usage.

Companies now sponsor dozens of cause-related marketing campaigns each year. Many are backed by large budgets and a full complement of marketing activities. Here are recent examples:

♦ Imperial Oil teamed with the Toronto Hospital for Sick Children to sponsor a cause-related marketing campaign to reduce preventable children's injuries, which is the leading killer of children. Imperial Oil founded Safe Kids Canada and has partnered with Zellers, Janssen Pharmaceutica, Ford Motors of Canada, and Bell Canada to educate the public about potential dangers in children's everyday environments such as injuries caused by unsafe playground equipment, or the dangers of not wearing bicycle helmets. Labelling its program "strategic giving," the firm for the first time tied its philanthropic efforts to its marketing programs. Imperial decided to focus its giving on a single area where it believed it could make a difference—namely children's safety—rather than giving small sums to a wide range of charities. The program also involved Esso's franchised outlets.

Esso Kids Program
Esso

BECAUSE CANADA'S KIDS ARE CANADA'S FUTURE

Each year in Canada, the Esso Kids Program supports hundreds of charities and organizations dedicated to the health and happiness of our greatest natural resource – the young people of our country.

Programs such as our founding sponsorship of Safe Kids Canada, support of the Smart Risk Foundation for the prevention of teen accidents and the Medals of Achievement program rewarding good sportsmanship and fairplay in youth hockey, all play a part in helping young Canadians reach their goals and dreams.

Imperial Oil
Esso

Esso promoted children's safety along with its corporate logo in its Safe Kids Canada campaign.

The ads used in the campaign do not show Esso's products or services. Instead, they focus on children's safety issues such as the use of car seats. The campaign was launched during the Stanley Cup playoffs and marks a watershed in Imperial's corporate giving efforts. In May 1995, Esso dealers donated one cent for every litre of gasoline sold. In addition to the donation, dealers handed out brochures to customers about children's safety issues. The campaign has been so successful that the Ontario Community Safety Council awarded its first Safety Promotion Award to Imperial Oil for helping people think about children's in-car safety.

♦ Procter & Gamble has sponsored many cause-related marketing campaigns. For example, during the past many years, P&G has mailed out billions of coupons on behalf of the Special Olympics, helping make the event a household name. P&G supports its Special Olympics efforts with national advertising and public relations, and its salespeople work with local volunteers to encourage retailers to build point-of-purchase displays. Another example of Procter & Gamble's cause-related marketing efforts is their alignment of their Always line of feminine products to the issue of breast cancer. The company established the Always Research Grant to support promising Canadian research in the field of breast cancer. Procter & Gamble asked its employees to become involved by joining their October "Run for the Cure," and they donated the proceeds of sales of a lapel pin to the Breast Cancer Foundation.

♦ Educational issues are popular focal points for many cause-related marketing programs. Corporate funding for educational efforts is becoming increasingly important in many school districts where boards are facing shrinking budgets in the face government funding cuts. For example, the Rocky View School District near Calgary is allowing the placement of advertisements on its 160 school buses. Pepsi-Cola Canada will give Toronto schools $1.14 million in return for exclusive rights to distribute their pop and juice in schools in the city over the next three years. The money resulting from the contract will help schools to fund services such as school lunch programs. Pepsi is also providing schools with a series of videos on topics such as substance abuse and staying in schools.

Cause-related marketing has stirred some controversy. Critics are concerned that cause-related marketing might eventually undercut traditional "no-strings" corporate giving, as more and more companies grow to expect marketing benefits from their contributions. Critics also worry that cause-related marketing will cause a shift in corporate charitable support toward more visible, popular, and low-risk charities—those with more certain and substantial marketing appeal. For example, MasterCard's Choose to Make a Difference campaign raises money for six charities, each selected in part because of its popularity in a consumer poll. Finally, critics worry that cause-related marketing is more a strategy for selling than a strategy for giving, and that "cause-related" marketing is really "cause-exploitative" marketing. Thus, companies using cause-related marketing might find themselves walking a fine line between increased sales and an improved image, and charges of exploitation.

However, if handled well, cause-related marketing can greatly benefit both the company and the charitable organization. The company gains an effective marketing tool while building a more positive public image. The charitable organization gains

greater visibility and important new sources of funding. This additional funding can be substantial. In total, such campaigns now contribute some $100 million annually to the coffers of charitable organizations, and surveys show that these cause-related contributions usually add to, rather than undercut, direct company contributions. Thus, when cause marketing works, everyone wins.

Sources: See Cyndee Miller, "Drug Company Begins Its Own Children's Crusade," *Marketing News,* June 6, 1988, pp. 1, 2; "School Kids Snack for Cash," *Advertising Age,* February 2, 1990, p. 36;

Melanie Rigney and Julie Steenhuysen, "Conscience Raising," *Advertising Age,* August 26, 1991, p. 19; Nancy Arnott, "Marketing with a Passion," *Sales & Marketing Management,* January 1994, pp. 64–71; Geoffrey Smith, "Are Good Causes Good Marketing?" *Business Week,* March 21, 1994, pp. 64–65; and Craig Smith, "The New Corporate Philanthropy," *Harvard Business Review,* May–June 1994, pp. 105–116; Naomi Klein, "Only Pepsi to Be Sold in Schools," *The Globe and Mail,* January 15, 1994, p. A15; James Pollock, "Educating the Market," *Marketing,* January 19, 1995; Mark Stevenson, "What's In It for Me?" *Canadian Business,* December 1993, pp. 54–60; and Imperial Oil, "A Closer Look at SAFE KIDS Canada," January 1995; www.imperialoil.ca

Tourism is the third-largest industry in Canada. Positioning Canada as a pristine wilderness and spiritual refuge has appeal for both Canadian and international consumers.

to master it. A long-term trend has been people's growing mastery over nature through technology and the belief that nature is bountiful. More recently, however, people have recognized that nature is finite and fragile—that it can be destroyed or spoiled by human activities.

Love of nature is leading to more camping, hiking, boating, fishing, and other outdoor activities. Business has responded by offering more hiking gear, camping equipment, better insect repellents, and other products for nature enthusiasts. Tour operators are offering more tours to wilderness areas. Food producers have found growing markets for "natural" products such as natural cereal, natural ice cream, and health foods. Marketing communicators are using appealing natural backgrounds in advertising their products.

PEOPLE'S VIEWS OF THE UNIVERSE. Finally, people vary in their beliefs about the origin of the universe and their place in it. Although many Canadians practise religion, religious conviction and practice have been dropping off gradually through the years. As people lose their religious orientation, they seek goods and experiences with more immediate satisfactions. During the 1980s, people increasingly measured success in terms of career achievement, wealth, and worldly possessions. Some futurists, however, have noted an emerging renewal of interest in religion, perhaps as part of a broader search for a new inner purpose. In the 1990s, people are moving away from materialism and "dog-eat-dog" ambition to seek more permanent values and a more certain grasp of right and wrong. As one trend tracker suggests: "The Nineties will see a marked change in the way society defines success, with achievements such as a happy family life and service to one's community replacing money as the measure of one's worth."[33] She continues, "The Nineties will be a far less cynical decade than the Eighties. Yes, we will still care what things cost. But we will seek to value only those things—family, community, earth, faith—that will endure."[34]

■ RESPONDING TO THE MARKETING ENVIRONMENT

Many companies view the marketing environment as an "uncontrollable" element to which they must adapt. They passively accept the marketing environment and do not try to change it. They analyse the environmental forces and design strategies that will help the company avoid the threats and take advantage of the opportunities the environment provides.

Environmental management perspective
A management perspective in which the firm takes aggressive actions to affect the publics and forces in its marketing environment rather than simply watching and reacting to it.

Other companies take an **environmental management perspective**.[35] Rather than simply watching and reacting, these firms take aggressive actions to affect the publics and forces in their marketing environment. Such companies hire lobbyists to influence legislation affecting their industries and stage media events to gain favourable press coverage. They run "advertorials" (ads expressing editorial points of view) to shape public opinion. They press lawsuits and file complaints with regulators to keep competitors in line, and they form contractual agreements to better control their distribution channels.

Other companies find positive ways to overcome seemingly uncontrollable environmental constraints. Some forestry firms, such as Noranda, have joined the Roundtable on the Environment, a government-sponsored discussion group, to help all stakeholders affected by forestry policies better understand environmental concerns about forestry management. Cathay Pacific Airlines determined that many travellers were avoiding Hong Kong because of lengthy delays at immigration. Rather than assuming that this was a problem they could not solve, Cathay's senior staff asked the Hong Kong government how to avoid these immigration delays. After lengthy discussions, the airline agreed to make an annual grant-in-aid to the government to hire more immigration inspectors—but these reinforcements would service primarily the Cathay Pacific gates. The reduced waiting period increased customer value and thus strengthened [Cathay's competitive advantage].[36]

Marketing management cannot always affect environmental forces. In many cases, it must settle for simply watching and reacting to the environment. For example, a company would have little success trying to influence geographic population shifts, the economic environment, or major cultural values. But whenever possible, smart marketing managers will take a *proactive* rather than a *reactive* approach to the marketing environment.

Summary of Chapter Objectives

Companies must constantly watch and adapt to the *marketing environment* in order to seek opportunities and ward off threats. The marketing environment comprises all the actors and forces influencing the company's ability to transact business effectively with its target market.

1. **Describe the environmental forces that affect the company's ability to serve its customers.**

   The company's marketing environment is composed of five microenvironmental and six macroenvironmental components. The microenvironment consists of other actors close to the company that combine to form the company's value delivery system or that affect its ability to serve its customers. The first microenvironmental component is the

company's internal environment—its several departments and management levels—as it influences marketing decision making. The second component consists of the marketing channel firms that cooperate to create value—the suppliers and marketing intermediaries, including intermediaries, physical distribution firms, marketing services agencies, and financial intermediaries. The third component is made up of the five types of customer markets, including consumer, producer, reseller, government, and international markets. The fourth component consists of competitors, and the fifth comprises the seven publics with an actual or potential interest in or impact on the company's ability to meet its objectives, including the financial, media, government, citizen action, and local, general, and internal publics.

The macroenvironment consists of larger societal forces that affect the entire microenvironment. The six forces making up the company's macroenvironment include demographic, economic, natural, technological, political, and cultural forces. These forces shape opportunities and pose threats to the company.

2. **Explain how changes in the demographic and economic environments affect marketing decisions.**

Demography is the study of the characteristics of human populations. Today's demographic environment shows a changing age structure, shifting family profiles, geographic population shifts, a more-educated and more white-collar population, and increasing diversity. The economic environment consists of factors that affect buying power and patterns. The economic environment is characterized by lower real income and shifting consumer spending patterns. Today's "financially squeezed consumers" are seeking greater value—just the right combination of good quality and service at a fair price. The distribution of income also is shifting. The rich have grown richer, the middle class has shrunk, and the poor have remained poor, leading to a two-tiered market. Many companies now tailor their marketing offers to two different markets—the affluent and the less affluent.

3. **Identify the major trends in the firm's natural and technological environments.**

The natural environment shows four major trends: shortages of certain raw materials, increased costs of energy, higher pollution levels, and more government intervention in natural resource management. Environmental concerns create marketing opportunities for alert companies. The marketer should watch for four major trends in the technological environment: the rapid pace of technological change, high R&D budgets, the concentration by companies on minor product improvements, and increased government regulation. Companies that fail to keep up with technological change will miss out on new product and marketing opportunities.

4. **Explain the key changes in the political and cultural environments.**

The political environment consists of laws, agencies, and groups that influence or limit marketing actions. The political environment has undergone three changes that affect marketing worldwide—increasing legislation regulating business, strong government agency enforcement, and greater emphasis on ethics and socially responsible actions. The cultural environment is made up of institutions and forces that affect a society's values, perceptions, preferences, and behaviours. The environment shows long-term trends toward a "we-society," a return to cautious trust of institutions, increasing patriotism, greater appreciation for nature, a new spiritualism, and search for more meaningful and enduring values.

5. **Discuss how companies can react to the marketing environment.**

Companies can passively accept the marketing environment as an uncontrollable element to which they must adapt, avoiding threats and taking advantage of opportunities as they arise. Or they can take an environmental management perspective, proactively working to change the environment rather than simply reacting to it. Whenever possible, companies should try to be proactive rather than reactive.

Key Terms

Baby boom *(p. 83)*
Cultural environment *(p. 97)*
Demography *(p. 80)*
Economic environment *(p. 90)*
Engel's laws *(p. 93)*

Environmental management
  perspective *(p. 102)*
Macroenvironment *(p. 77)*
Marketing environment *(p. 77)*
Marketing intermediaries *(p. 78)*

Microenvironment *(p. 77)*
Natural environment *(p. 93)*
Political environment *(p. 95)*
Public *(p. 79)*
Technological environment *(p. 94)*

Discussing the Issues

1. McDonald's has been getting a lot of adverse press and hasn't been as successful in the late 1990s as it was in the early 1990s. What micro- and macroenvironment trends have affected McDonald's throughout the 1990s? If you were in charge of marketing at McDonald's, what plans would you make to deal with these trends?

2. Statistics Canada is beginning to post tables on its website (http://www.statcan.ca) that outline some of its findings from the 1996 census. These include tables on population projects by age group and sex, the population of Census Metropolitan Areas (CMAs), and Recent Immigrants by Last Country of Residence. Go to their web site. Print off one of these tables, analyse it, and, as a marketer, describe how this information would help you design a marketing plan for a particular target audience.

3. Canada's ethnic populations are growing quickly. By the year 2000, it is estimated that the six largest ethnic groups will encompass 2.8 million people, almost 10 percent of the current population. What are the major challenges faced by marketers attempting to serve these populations?

4. What Canadian companies have successfully used the "green revolution" as leverage to market their products or services? Why have some of these efforts caused controversy among consumers and environmental groups? Do you think corporations should continue to pursue "green marketing"? Is it a fad or a long-term trend?

5. You are the account representative working for a large Canadian advertising firm. Your chief account is Bell Canada. What trends in the Canadian marketing environment will most affect the advertising of Bell's products and services? Which ones will you advise your client to monitor most closely?

6. A major alcoholic beverage marketer is planning to introduce an "adult soft drink"—a socially acceptable substitute for stronger drinks that would be cheaper and lower in alcohol than wine coolers. What cultural and other factors might affect the success of this product?

7. Some marketing goals, such as improved quality, require strong support from an internal public—a company's own employees. But surveys show that employees increasingly distrust management, and company loyalty is eroding. How can a company market internally to help meet its goals? Identify some alternative approaches.

Applying the Concepts

1. Changes in the marketing environment mean that marketers must meet new consumer needs that may be quite different—even directly opposite—from those in the past. Ben & Jerry's became successful by making great-tasting ice cream with a huge butterfat content. They now offer lowfat frozen yogurt to appeal to soft-in-the-middle baby-boomers. You can track changes in the marketing environment by looking at how companies modify their products.

   ◆ Make a list of the products you encounter in one day that claim to be "low" or "high" in some ingredient, such as light olive oil, or high-fibre cereal.

   ◆ Take your list, and write down similar products that seem to offer the opposite characteristics.

   ◆ In each case, which product do you think came first? Do you think that this is an effective response to a changing marketing environment?

2. The political environment can have a direct impact on marketers and their plans. Changes in provincial governments such as the election in Ontario of the Harris government, in Alberta of the Klein government, or in Quebec of Lucien Bouchard, can affect the marketing environment.

   ◆ Name three industries that will probably have their marketing plans and strategies affected by political changes at the provincial level.

♦ For each of the industries that you named, list three potential strategies to help adapt to the coming changes in the political environment.

♦ Although environmental changes appear likely, are they *certain*? How should companies plan for unsettled conditions?

References

1. Lara Mills, "The New Rx for Drug Marketing," *Marketing*, September 11, 1995, p. 15

2. Gail Chiasson, "Drugs in a Big Box," *Marketing*, April 10, 1995, p. 12; Jim McElgunn, "Condition Unstable," *Marketing*, September 11, 1995, p. 16; Laura Medcalf, "Pill Pushers," *Marketing*, September 11, 1995, p. 17; "Multi-target Marketing," *Marketing*, September 11, 1995, p. 19.

3. Ian McGugan, "Cross-border Quiz," *Canadian Business*, January 1996, p. 31.

4. Brian Milner, "U.S. Growth Expected to Slow," *Globe and Mail*, November 17, 1997, pp. B1 & B2.

5. Sources: Jim McElgunn, "Foot Puts the Boot to Current 'Life-Cycle' Trends," *Marketing*, June 15, 1992, p. 1; Daniel Stoffman, "Completely Predicable People," *Report on Business*, November 1990, pp. 78–84; "Boomers Slowing Pace of Leisure," *Toronto Star*, June 20, 1993, G3.

6. Elizabeth Church, "Birth Bulge Breeds Its Own Industry," *Globe and Mail*, September 24, 1996, B12.

7. Jane Gadd, "Commitment to Healthy Diet Declines," *Globe and Mail*, November 11, 1997, p. A10.

8. Much of the global statistical data in this chapter are drawn from the *World Almanac and Book of Facts, 1993.*

9. Sally D. Goll, "Marketing: China's (Only) Children Get the Royal Treatment," *Wall Street Journal*, February 8, 1995, pp. B1, B2.

10. John Kettle, "Canada Shows Its Age," Kettle's Future, *Globe and Mail*, January 17, 1997, p. B11.

11. Daniel Stoffman, "Completely Predicable People," *Report on Business*, November 1990, pp. 78-84.

12. See Thomas Exter, "And Baby Makes 20 Million," *American Demographics*, July 1991, p. 55; Joseph Spiers, "The Baby Boomlet Is for Real," *Fortune*, February 10, 1992, pp. 101–104; Joe Schwartz, "Is the Baby Boomlet Ending?" *American Demographics*, May 1992, p. 9; and Christopher Farrell, "The Baby Boomlet May Kick in a Little Growth," *Business Week*, January 10, 1994, p. 66.

13. See Christopher Power, "Getting 'Em While They're Young," *Business Week*, September 9, 1991, pp. 94–95; James U. McNeal, "Growing Up in the Market," *American Demographics*, October 1992, pp. 46–50; Horst Stipp, "New Ways to Reach Children," *American Demographics*, August 1993, pp. 50–56; and Laura Zinn, "Teens: Here Comes the Biggest Wave Yet," *Business Week*, April 11, 1994, pp. 76–86.

14. See Diane Crispell and William H. Frey, "American Maturity," *American Demographics*, March 1993, pp. 31–42; Charles F. Longino, "Myths of an Aging America," *American Demographics*, August 1994, pp. 36–43; and Melissa Campanelli, "Selling to Seniors: A Waiting Game," *Sales & Marketing Management*, June 1994, p. 69.

15. Sources: Marina Strauss, "Seniors grasp for friendlier packaging," *Globe and Mail*, October 7, 1993, p. B4; *Today's Seniors*, October 1995, pp. 3-9; "The Countdown to the 21st Century," Vision 2000, The Royal Bank.

16. These and other statistics in this section are from "The Future of Households," *American Demographics*, December 1993, pp. 27–39; and Melissa Campanelli, "It's All in the Family," *Sales & Marketing Management*, April 1994, p. 53.

17. Dan Kerr and Bali Ram, *Focus on Canada: Population Dynamics in Canada*, Prentice Hall Inc.

18. Information in this section derived from Statistics Canada, Demography Division, Population Projections Section, "Table 24, Population of Canada by Size, Growth and Distribution for Provinces and Territories, 1993 and 2016."

19. Sources: Jim McElgunn, "Wave of New Ethnic Mmedia is Announced," *Marketing*, September 4, 1995, p. 3; Alanna Mitchell, "Study Debunks Immigrant Myths," *Globe and Mail*, July 13, 1994, p. A1–2; Isabel Vincent, "Chasing After the Ethnic Consumer," *Globe and Mail*, September 18, 1995, p. A8; "Nailing the Niche," *Marketing*, September 18, 1995, p. 20.

20. Barbara Smith, "Special Feature: Gay and Lesbian Marketing: Market Becoming More Accessible," *Strategy, The Canadian Marketing Report*, September 18, 1995, p. 35.

21. James W. Hughes, "Understanding the Squeezed Consumer," *American Demographics*, July 1991, pp. 44–50. Also see Patricia Sellers, "Winning Over the New Consumer," *Fortune*, July 29, 1991, pp. 113–125; and Brian O'Reilly, "Preparing for Leaner Times," *Fortune*, January 27, 1992, pp. 40–47.

22. Margot Bigg-Clark, "Juggling Jobs a '90s Necessity," *Globe and Mail*, July 28, 1997, pp. B1, B3; Harvey Schachter, "Slaves of the New Economy," *Canadian Business*, April 1996, pp. 86–92.

23. Nancy DeHart, "Clocking In," *Kingston Whig-Standard*, May 26, 1997, p. 15.

24. Zena Olijnyk, "Loblaw Takes a Run at Time-starved Diners," *The Financial Post*, November 11, 1997, p. 10.

25. Bruce Little, "How Canadians are Spending Their Money," *Globe and Mail*, July 15, 1996, p. A6.

26. For more discussion, see the "Environmentalism" section in Chapter 23. Also see Jacquelyn Ottman, "Environmentalism Will Be *the* Trend of the '90s," *Marketing News*, December 7, 1992, p. 13; Carl Frankel, "Blueprint for Green Marketing," *American Demographics*, April 1992, pp. 34–38; Robert Rehak, "Green Marketing Awash in Third Wave," *Advertising Age*, November 22, 1993, p. 22; and Peter Stisser, "A Deeper Shade of Green," *American Demographics*, March 1994. pp. 24–29. Patrick Carson, Julia Moulden, *Green is Gold*, Toronto: Harper Business Press, 1991, back cover.

27. Patrick Carson, Julia Moulden, *Green is Gold*, Toronto: Harper Business Press, 1991, p. 27.

28. Elizabeth Cahill, "The Liberal Record on R&D," *CAUT Bulletin ACPPU*, May 1997, p. 11.

29. Bruce Little, "Information Technology Sector Booming," *Globe and Mail*, December 6, 1996, p. B11; Mark Evans, "High-tech Sector Needs More R&D, Says Study," *The Financial Post*, August 21, 1996, p. 13.

30. "Top R&D Companies." *Report on Business*, July 1995, p. 91.

31. *North American Free Trade Agreement: An Overview and Description*, Canadian Government publication, August 1992.

32. See Cyndee Miller, "Trendspotters: 'Dark Ages' Ending; So Is Cocooning," *Marketing News*, February 3, 1997, pp. 1, 16.

33. Anne B. Fisher, "A Brewing Revolt Against the Rich," *Fortune*, December 17, 1990, pp. 89–94.

34. Anne B. Fisher, "What Consumers Want in the 1990s," *Fortune*, January 21, 1990, p. 112. Also see Joseph M. Winski, "Who We Are, How We Live, What We Think," *Advertising Age*, January 20, 1992, pp. 16–18; and John Huey, "Finding New Heros for a New Era," *Fortune*, January 25, 1993, pp. 62–69.

35. See Carl P. Zeithaml and Valerie A. Zeithaml, "Environmental Management: Revising the Marketing Perspective," *Journal of Marketing*, Spring 1984, pp. 46–53.

36. Howard E. Butz, Jr., and Leonard D. Goodstein, "Measuring Customer Value: Gaining the Strategic Advantage," *Organizational Dynamics*, Winter 1996, pp. 66-67.

Demographic Study

FIFTYSOMETHING: DON'T CALL ME OLD

"As an active mid-life generation redefines terms like 'maturity' and 'seniors,' muddled marketers are missing the selling bonanza of a decade," declares *Report on Business* reporter Kenneth Kidd. He is speaking of the "fiftysomething" age group that is doing its best to defy all the stereotypes traditionally associated with aging. If you can't help but think that people in this age group are "over the hill," remember that Paul McCartney, Raquel Welch, and Gordon Lightfoot have all had their fiftieth birthday.

In other words, if you view these people as part of a rocking-chair generation, think again! Take Marjorie, a 52-year-old professional, who is married, and has two children in university. She begins most of her days at about 5 A.M. with either a brisk rowing session across the frigid waters of Lake Ontario or a couple of miles of skating on in-line skates. She follows this workout with a 10-hour day in the office, but still finds time to sit on the board of her local chapter of the United Way. Not exactly your vision of a sedentary lifestyle!

Marjorie isn't an exception in this age group. "Fiftysomethings" are more active, better educated, and more committed to their work and communities than any generation that has gone before. It is no wonder, therefore, that they resent marketing stereotypes of being the grey-haired "geritol generation." They hate euphemisms such as the "mature" market or "the golden years." This generation is independent in its thinking, self-sufficient in terms of economic status, and interested in personal growth and revitalization, yet is also a generation that wants to give something back to society. If anything, this is a group known for "down-aging"—being 50, looking 40, and acting 30.

DEFYING CLASSIFICATION

Anyone wishing to market to this age group needs to keep some rules in mind. First, this is not a homogeneous group. People in their fifties are a diverse group whose values, needs, and health vary as much as those of you and your friends. This is a generation full of paradoxes. While some are fleeing both careers and the city for a more balanced lifestyle, others are caught up in a hectic pace rarely seen before. Corporate downsizing has forced some of the fiftysomethings to take early retirement. Finding excess time on their hands, many in this group have swollen the ranks of home-business people or have become part of a new generation of entrepreneurs. Many revel in their ability to work 30 hours a week and have time left over for leisure activities.

For other fiftysomethings, the work week has become a marathon instead of a 100-metre dash. The fiftysomethings who have retained their jobs have started to dominate both the middle and top managerial ranks of many firms. Some of their schedules are unbelievable. In just 20 years, the number of Canadians working more than 50 hours per week has increased by 27 percent. As companies have downsized, they've found that they have fewer managers to accomplish the same number of tasks. In some companies, those not working 60-hour weeks are perceived to be slacking off. Not surprisingly, these people value convenience and ease of purchasing. Shopping is viewed as a chore more often than a pleasure, and while they may hope for good service, they are often happy if they can just accomplish shopping tasks without being hassled.

The diversity of fiftysomethings may be reflected in the fact that marketers have yet been unable to develop a meaningful name for this segment of consumers. Names such as "seniors," "nearly retired," and "golden-agers" have been rejected. Despite being unable to come up with a single name for fiftysomethings, this group has been divided into four segments: venturers, organizers, worriers, and optimists.

◆ *Venturers* (23 percent of the fiftysomething market) are known for their adventurous spirit, have above-average income but more debt than others in the category since they have travelled more, and have changed jobs more frequently. They like to try new things, including new technology.

◆ *Organizers* comprise 28 percent of people in the fifty-year-old segment. These well-educated consumers have stable careers and above-average incomes. Quebecers are twice as likely to belong to this group than other Canadians.

◆ *Worriers* represent 25 percent of the category and are largely female. They are concerned about housing, health, and personal safety, and tend to avoid new technology. Their incomes are about 30 percent lower than the average in the fiftysomething group. As a result, they have travelled less.

◆ The final group are the *optimists*. Making up about 24 percent of the category, this is the best-educated group in the fiftysomething quadrant. They enjoy incomes 20 percent higher than others in this generation. They are frequently near retirement and fill the ranks of those whose personal worth exceeds $500 000.

Many people in this age group are also part of what has become known as the "sandwich generation." They have dependent generations on either side of them—dependent children on one hand, and aging, dependent parents on the other. This helps to explain why one of the predictions about marketing to this age group has never come to pass. Due to their wealth and expected amounts of growing leisure time, fiftysomethings were forecast to be the prime target for luxury travel. While they may have the money for such services, they often cannot risk leaving frail parents for long periods or abandon increasingly demanding careers. This group has been successfully targeted with "mini-vacations" that package quick but exotic getaways.

AN AFFLUENT MARKET

Despite their differences, however, fiftysomethings have some similarities that do make them interesting targets for marketers. Although the age group 50 to 65 comprises only 12 percent of the population, they account for 45 percent of the personal wealth in Canada. They comprise 1.8 million households, and have a love affair with property. The combined value of their principal residences alone equals $230 billion. And they also may own other property. Born in the period between the Great Depression and the Second World War, they have seen great financial instability, and value the security of real estate investments. This concern for financial stability also makes them one of the most debt-free generations. They often own their homes outright, and few carry outstanding credit-card balances.

Being financially conservative doesn't mean that this generation never opens its wallet. In fact, this is a time when many of these consumers are allowing themselves some of the luxuries they denied themselves during much of their lives. For the first time, they may be buying upscale automobiles rather than the conservative family sedans they drove most of their lives. This is a lesson best understood by Toyota Canada when it started marketing its Lexus automobile. Toyota wrote the book when it comes to developing a strategy to effectively market to "fiftysomethings." Realizing that only two percent of the market even knew the name "Lexus," Toyota shunned an expensive television campaign in favour of print advertisements in business magazines. The company supported this media program with a direct mailing effort based on a mailing list derived from membership lists of clubs, credit-card holders, and upper-income addresses. It used the first mailings as a base to develop ongoing correspondence with current and potential customers, stressing the value-for-money, safety, and practicality positioning of Lexus. This ability to precisely target its efforts resulted in Toyota selling 8000 cars, ranging in price from $40 000 to $67 000, in just a few months.

Unfortunately, Toyota's efforts are a rarity. Fiftysomething consumers often find themselves in a marketing no-man's land. Advertising is either aimed at younger or older audiences. Kodak, for example, stared incredulously at the results of recent research that showed that 38 percent of its customers were over 50, but that it didn't have a single ad aimed at this audience.

Even when attempts are made to communicate with fiftysomethings, they are often insulting in their nature and tone. Royal Trust got this message loud and clear when it pre-tested a retirement planning guide on the fiftysomething group. Irritated focus-group members hated the golden-age pictures, rocking chair-type images, and the "we know what's good for you" tone. They wanted a simple, straightforward message that didn't talk down to the reader.

Marketers must remember that these are experienced consumers who pride themselves on their intelligence, and want to be treated as such. They hate being patronized. They expect to be wooed with information and treated with respect and gratitude if they give an organization their business. As Kenneth Kidd so wisely noted, if corporations cannot banish their veiled seniors' pitches, they will have "fumbled the chance at unlocking the awesome wealth and spending power of people now aged 50 to 64."

QUESTIONS

1. Interview someone in the 50–59 age bracket. Ask about his or her job, lifestyle, values, and shopping habits. Ask the person if he or she falls into one of the segments described in the case.

2. Compare the profile you have drawn of this consumer with those developed by other members of your class. Do all the profiles fall within one of the four segments described in the case? Do other segments have to be added to the list?

3. Describe the factors in the macroenvironment that have affected the thinking and shopping behaviour of fiftysomething consumers.

4. Develop a list of three products that you think would appeal to each of the four segments of the fiftysomething market. Select one product from your list and describe the tactics you would use to communicate the benefits of your product to this segment of consumers.

Source: This case was written by P. Cunningham based on quotations and material taken from Kenneth Kidd, "The New Middle Age," *Report on Business*, May 1993, pp. 42–51; and other material sourced from Harvey Schachter, "Slaves of the New Economy," *Canadian Business*, April 1996, pp. 86–92.

Video Case 3

RICHARD BRANSON: GLOBAL ENTREPRENEUR

Richard Branson is an entrepreneur who is not afraid to face the challenges of the global business environment. Based in Britain, he has already had international success in such diverse businesses as entertainment, airlines, mutual funds, and cola. Branson's vision for his company is to be a "total life company" by offering whatever consumers may want in lifestyle markets. While his Virgin brand name has been launched in several different geographic markets in Europe and the United States, Branson has just recently entered the Canadian market by opening a new Virgin music store in Vancouver.

Branson's first major business success was Virgin records, whose artists included such 1980s recording stars as Phil Collins and Boy George. He then used this expertise to expand into the music retail business. The Virgin megastores cater to all types of music tastes; the New York store, for example, has 1000 listening booths and boasts the largest selection of music of any music store in the world.

Branson has a reputation for being the small competitor who challenges the establishment. He constantly surveys the business environment to identify industries with large competitors that have become complacent. Virgin is especially adept at satisfying customers by beating competitors on price, quality, or service. For example, in the airline business Branson believed that there was room for a company that put the fun back in flying. His company, Virgin Atlantic Air, changed the experience of flying to one comparable to being in a nice restaurant or club. One of his current projects is to take on Levi Stauss, which he considers to be a good company but one that charges too much for jeans. His company will try to offer the same quality as the Levi's product at a reduced price.

With annual sales of more than $4.5 billion and as Britain's largest private company, it is hard to think of Virgin as a small competitor. However, Virgin is not large in any one type of business and has no more than a 10 to 20 percent market share in any one industry. Branson has also tried to foster an entrepreneurial culture in his organization. The head office has only a small number of people who generate ideas for businesses and then pass them on to the approximately 150 companies that Branson controls. The people who manage these companies, managing directors, all have part ownership in the business and are given a lot of leeway in the management of the company. They are encouraged to be creative and are given the "freedom to make mistakes." In fact, Branson now regards his job as one of delegation and of empowering his employees to run the businesses.

Branson views his entrance into the Vancouver retail music business as only the first of many Canadian business ventures. Operating Virgin Atlantic Air in Canada may very well be his next foray into the Canadian business scene. With his ability to turn industries upside down, Canadian businesses will do well to take note of Richard Branson's Canadian plans.

QUESTIONS

1. What factors in the marketing environment will affect Branson's success with the Virgin music store in Canada?

2. Are the environmental factors identified in question one above the same as those factors that will affect the retail music stores that Branson operates in the United States and Britain?

3. How can global companies such as Branson's ensure that they have accurate tracking of the marketing environment in each country that they operate in?

Source: This case was prepared by Auleen Carson and is based on "Richard Branson," *Venture* (October 20, 1996).

CHAPTER 4

MARKETING RESEARCH AND INFORMATION SYSTEMS

The summer of 1997 witnessed some of the most heated conflicts in the Great Canadian Beer Wars[1] in recent history. Battles were waged on several fronts. The first salvo came from Molson. In a sneak attack, it ambushed Labatt's official sponsorship of the Cabot 500 celebrations in Newfoundland by marketing its Black Horse brand as the "unofficial beer of Cabot's crew." Labatt called foul since it had invested $1 million in the sponsorship, including the formulation of a lager—Cabot—brewed especially for the occasion.

In retaliation, Labatt started the next skirmish. On June 9, the company announced a $2 price cut on cases of 24 beers. The following week, Molson rallied and undercut Labatt with a $3 price reduction of its 24-packs. The next battleground involved advertising. This time, Molson fired the first shot by running its "B.C. or BS" full-page newspaper ad campaign. Molson's market research had revealed that more than 80 percent of beer drinkers believed that Labatt's Kokanee brand was made in British Columbia from glacier spring water and that this was a critical component in their purchasing decision. When Molson informed consumers that, in fact, the beer sold in Ontario was brewed in London, Ontario, Molson claims that consumers became quite upset. In fact, Molson received more than 5000 calls to the toll-free number featured in the ads.

Some industry analysts believed that Molson's ads were an indication of the company's desperation as Labatt attacked it on its home ground. Molson countered with further research, claiming that most of the people who complained about the ads were from Labatt or its ad agency. Using call-display technology that Molson uses to track calls to its customer service line, Molson established that, "We had one guy phone up from Labatt's 19 times one day using 19 different phone names, just blasting us for running the ad."[2] Labatt refused to take the fray any further. "Attacking another brewer or its brands is not our style of marketing—we'd rather let the consumer decide," countered David Kincaid, Labatt's vice-president of marketing.

OBJECTIVES

When you finish this chapter, you should be able to

1. Explain the importance of information to the company.

2. Define the marketing information system and discuss its parts.

3. Outline the four steps in the marketing research process.

4. Compare the advantages and disadvantages of various methods of collecting information.

5. Discuss the special issues some marketing researchers face, including public policy and ethics issues.

The difference in response isn't surprising given that the two firms are quite different in terms of their competitive positioning. While both brewers pursue the same core market—males age 19 to 29—they do so in very different ways. For example, at the same time that Labatt decided to move out of the concert-promotion business altogether, Molson began its "Blind Date" campaign in an attempt to link its brands with images of hipness and glamour. The contest received a lot of attention from the target market, but concert promotion isn't always smooth sailing. For example, during one of the concerts held in Vancouver, Soundgarden's lead singer announced, "Yeah, we're here because of some f...... beer company—Labatt's."[3] Labatt, in contrast, has adopted a more conservative, low-key, sports-oriented, regional strategy. In addition to avoiding public relations nightmares, an additional advantage of the Labatt program is its cost. Keeping down costs has allowed Labatt to earn about $100 million more than Molson on approximately equal volumes of beer sold.

Winning the battle for market dominance is critical. The Canadian beer market represents $11 billion in sales. Each share point is worth $10 to $16 million in incremental revenue. Canada's big two breweries—Molson and Labatt—account for 94 percent of beer sales. While Molson clings to its leadership position in the overall Canadian marketplace with a 46.8 percent share, Labatt is less than one share point behind. Labatt Blue was Canada's top brand in 1996, with 12.3 percent of the market. Molson's Canadian holds second place with 11.1 percent. Each brewer also has its regional strongholds; Labatt clearly dominates in Manitoba while Molson holds sway in Saskatchewan. Although Molson is still number one in Ontario, Labatt's strategy includes unseating its rival in that province while defending its leading position in other markets. Molson has lost share in Quebec since its brand, Canadian, doesn't sell well with the separatist crowd.

The beer market is a difficult one in which to compete. Demographics aren't on the side of these marketers. Baby boomers, once the prime target market, are now more health- and weight-conscious. Beer consumption has been dropping steadily in recent years, by 1.7 percent in 1996 alone. In 1979, when beer consumption reached its peak in Canada, the average Canadian consumed 85 litres of beer each year. Today, consumption has fallen to 65 litres per capita. For brewers, Quebec is the only bright spot on the horizon. In that province, per-capita consumption is 90.99 litres. Thus, beer marketers are fighting for share of a shrinking pie and can only gain share at the expense of their competitors. To make matters worse, competition has also increased. Whereas only 15 years ago there were just eight beer companies in Canada, today there are 60. Microbreweries now account for approximately five percent of sales.

Labatt began its challenge of Molson by attempting to build closer ties with customers. It launched a relationship-building effort, gathering the information critical to its marketing success. Using the Labatt MVP (Most Valued Patron) program, the giant brewer announced that it wanted to find a way to recognize its best customers. The program was initiated with a nationally advertised give-away program. Full-page newspaper advertisements offered interested consumers, who called a toll-free number, a free classic Labatt bottle opener in return for information on the caller's beer preferences and some demographic data including addresses. Through this multi-faceted program, Labatt built a rich database to help the company better understand its customers and market its products.

One of the rewards of membership in the Labatt program is that members receive *Beer* magazine. This publication is mailed directly to MVP members' homes, and, to reinforce the theme that members are part of a select group, Labatt stresses that the magazine is not available at newsstands. In the magazine, Labatt announces exclusive services that only MVP members can utilize. For example, the magazine describes MVP Ticketline, a toll-free number that allows patrons access to tickets for Blue Jays baseball or Argos football games. The MVP program created an interactive forum between Labatt and its customers. As *Beer* magazine proclaims, "You get a chance to tell us what you think. This whole idea of talking with our customers, not at them, is something we believe in."[4] The magazine also features a National Customer Service Number (1-800-268-BEER) and access to Labatt's web site.

Labatt Breweries
www.labatt.com

Labatt also uses an interactive computer system with the "Joel" and "Karen" characters from its advertising campaigns. Displayed as part of a two-metre-high beer can, the characters interact with people who attempt to answer beer trivia questions. Ninety percent of those using the interactive system also answer personal questions (such as providing birth dates, phone numbers, and beer preferences) that are embedded in the activity. "After all, interacting with 'Joel' is fun, and they get a money-off coupon just for playing along." Winners also quality to win T-shirts.[5]

Labatt's database is a gold mine that has allowed the firm to better understand who was attracted to its different products. It allows Labatt to receive timely information if consumers are experiencing any problems with Labatt products. The information also allows the company to target the most profitable segments of the beer drinking public and to focus their communication efforts. For example, Labatt can place its advertisements only at the sporting events most favoured by its target consumers. This information has allowed Labatt to more effectively design its radio campaigns and offer attractive purchase incentives to its consumers.

Molson Breweries On-line
www.molson.com

In addition to tracking calls to its service number, how does Molson build its customer knowledge? Like Labatt, Molson created a web site called "I Am Online." It offers bulletin boards and listings of entertainment. By monitoring the "hits" on various sections of the site, Molson will be better able to identify what makes its customers tick. The site also allows users to see what group they are part of. One area of the site allows browsers to get the profile of other users who have logged on most frequently during the previous weeks. In another section of the web page, Molson seeks feedback from visitors on the effectiveness of its ads.

In addition to its web page, Molson also uses a "Youth Posse," a team of 35 young adults who patrol the bars grabbing posters so that Molson can be on the leading edge of emerging trends. The group was formed in 1996 at the same time Molson reorganized its business into three regions: Atlantic Canada/Ontario, Quebec, and the West. Information gathered by the team is used to implement Molson's grassroots marketing efforts. For example, Molson learned from its research that consumers were more aware of the need to adopt a reasonable approach to drinking and wanted a full-flavoured, low-alcohol beer. The company launched Molson Diamond in late 1997 to meet this unmet need.

In the beer industry, the company that has the best information should win the marketing war. For this reason, the beer industry does some of the most sophisticated marketing research in the business world. Internal databases, government statistics, product codes, and scanner information from the points of sale allow beermakers to "trace sales down to almost each and every case moving off the store shelf."

But it is not enough to just have a rich database. Talented marketers must also glean insight from the information therein. Sometimes marketers hit the nail on the head. At other times, despite the best information, they miss the mark altogether. A case in point: Molson's Red Dog beer. Despite being lauded for its brilliant ad campaign, the product was withdrawn due to low sales after only six months. Similarly, Labatt Blue's two voyageurs—William and Jacques—made people feel good about Canadian icons, but failed to move beer off the shelves. Insight and interpretation of the information in the database are especially important for two reasons. First, decision-making with respect to beer is based on both emotional and rational responses, and distinct regional differences exist in the Canadian beer market. Unlike other packaged goods, where consumers make strictly rational choices based on the physical benefits of the product, beer is sold on image; blind taste tests have shown that little differentiates the taste of one brand from another. Second, beer drinkers tend to personally identify with the product—what they drink says a lot about their self-image. And self-images are often very regionally based. Campaigns that work well in Atlantic Canada are often a flop in the west. Beer marketers target their national and regional brands using values "consumers hold through life, rather than the passing fancies of youth." To date, Labatt is lauded as the stronger player in terms of regional marketing, but the beer wars may be far from over. As target consumers, you are the prize the combatants are fighting over.[6]

In order to produce superior value and satisfaction for customers, companies need information at almost every turn. As the Labatt and Molson marketing story illustrates, good products and marketing programs begin with a thorough understanding of consumer needs and wants. Companies also need an abundance of information on competitors, resellers, and other actors and forces in the marketplace.

As companies become international in scope, they need more information on larger, more distant markets. As buyers become more selective, sellers need better information about how buyers respond to different products and appeals. As sellers use more complex marketing approaches and face more competition, they need information on the effectiveness of their marketing tools. Finally, in today's more rapidly changing environments, managers need more up-to-date information to make timely decisions.

Fortunately, increasing information requirements have been met by an explosion of information technologies. The past 30 years have witnessed the emergence of small but powerful computers, fax machines, CD-ROM drives, videoconferencing, the Internet, and a host of other advances that have revolutionized information handling. Using improved information systems, companies now can provide information in great quantities. In fact, today's managers sometimes receive too much information. For example, one study found that with all the companies offering data, and with all the information now available through supermarket scanners, a packaged-goods brand manager is bombarded with one million to one *billion* new numbers each week.[7] As one analyst points out: "Running out of information is not a problem, but drowning in it is."[8]

Yet marketers frequently complain that they lack enough information of the *right* kind or have too much of the *wrong* kind. Companies have greater capacity to provide managers with information, but often have not made good use of it. Many companies are now studying their managers' information needs and designing information systems to meet those needs.

THE MARKETING INFORMATION SYSTEM

*Marketing information
system (MIS)*
People, equipment, and
procedures to gather, sort,
analyse, evaluate, and
distribute needed, timely,
and accurate information to
marketing decision-makers.

A **marketing information system (MIS)** consists of people, equipment, and procedures to gather, sort, analyse, evaluate, and distribute needed, timely, and accurate information to marketing decision-makers. Figure 4-1 shows that the MIS begins and ends with marketing managers. First, it interacts with these managers to *assess information needs*. Next, it *develops needed information* from internal company records, marketing intelligence activities, and marketing research. *Information analysis* processes the information to make it more useful. Finally, the MIS *distributes information* to managers in the right form at the right time to help them make better marketing decisions.

ASSESSING INFORMATION NEEDS

A good marketing information system balances the information managers would *like* to have against what they really *need* and what is *feasible* to offer. The company

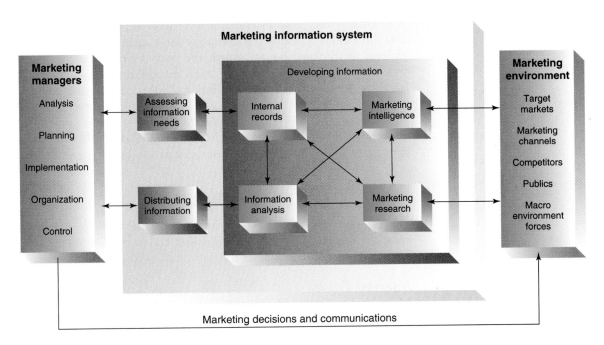

FIGURE 4-1 *The marketing information system*

begins by interviewing managers to find out what information they would like (see Table 4-1 for a useful set of questions). But managers do not always need all the information they ask for, and they may not ask for all they really need. Moreover, the MIS cannot always supply all the information managers request.

Some managers will ask for whatever information they can get without thinking carefully about what they really need. Too much information can be as harmful as too little. Other managers may omit things they ought to know, or may not know to ask for some types of information they should have. For example, managers might need to know that a competitor plans to introduce a new product during the coming year. Because they do not know about the new product, they do not think to ask about it. The MIS must watch the marketing environment in order to provide decision-makers with information they should have to make key marketing decisions.

Sometimes the company cannot provide the needed information, either because it is not available or because of MIS limitations. For example, a brand manager might want to know how competitors will change their advertising budgets next year and how these changes will affect industry market shares. The information on planned budgets probably is not available. Even if it is, the company's MIS may not be advanced enough to forecast resulting changes in market shares.

TABLE 4-1   *Questions for Assessing Marketing Information Needs*

1. What types of decisions do you make regularly?
2. What types of information do you need in order to make these decisions?
3. What types of useful information do you get regularly?
4. What types of information would you like to get that you are not getting now?
5. What types of information do you get now that you don't really need?
6. What information would you want daily? weekly? monthly? yearly?
7. What topics would you like to be kept informed about?
8. What databases would be useful to you?
9. What types of information analysis programs would you like to have?
10. What would be the four most helpful improvements that could be made in the present information system?

Finally, the costs of obtaining, processing, storing, and delivering information can mount quickly. The company must decide whether the benefits of having an item of information are worth the costs of providing it, and both value and cost are often hard to assess. By itself, information has no worth; its value comes from its *use*. In many cases, additional information will do little to change or improve a manager's decision, or the costs of the information may exceed the returns from the improved decision. Marketers should not assume that additional information will always be worth obtaining. Rather, they should weigh carefully the costs of additional information against the benefits resulting from it.

DEVELOPING INFORMATION

The information needed by marketing managers can be obtained from *internal company records, marketing intelligence,* and *marketing research.* The information analysis system then processes this information to make it more useful for managers.

Internal Data

Internal databases
Information gathered from sources within the company that can be used to evaluate marketing performance and to detect marketing problems and opportunities.

Many companies build extensive **internal databases**—computerized collections of information obtained from data sources within the company. Marketing managers can readily access and work with information in the database to identify marketing opportunities and problems, plan programs, and evaluate performance.

Information in the database can come from many sources. The accounting department prepares financial statements and keeps detailed records of sales, costs, and cash flows. Manufacturing reports on production schedules, shipments, and inventories. The sales force reports on reseller reactions and competitor activities. The marketing department maintains a database of customer demographics, psychographics, and buying behaviour. The customer service department provides information on customer satisfaction or service problems. Research studies done for one department may provide useful information for several others. Managers can use information gathered from these and other sources within the company to evaluate performance, detect problems, and create new marketing opportunities.

Here are examples of how companies use internal records information in making better marketing decisions:[9]

> *Canon Canada:* Canon Canada recently introduced a 24-hour toll-free help-line to help the company better understand the home-office market. Since customer service and repair capabilities are key features of Canon's large-business marketing efforts, this help-line is used to assess the effectiveness of these efforts for the relatively undeveloped home-office market.

Canada Trust
www.canadatrust.com

> *Canada Trust:* Canada Trust has discovered the power of interactive computer screens to tap consumers' perceptions. Using this new technology, it can access online measures of consumers' attitudes about Canada Trust's service. Customers answer a series of questions that helps individual branches measure the effectiveness of their service-quality programs. For example, customers answer questions about the speed of service, the friendliness of the staff, and the expertise of service providers. These tracking efforts have resulted in improved levels of customer satisfaction.

Ford Motor Company
www.ford.com/us/

> *Ford Motor Company.* Some firms are using the "Information Highway" to learn more about their customers. Ford Motor Company runs customer focus groups through its page on the World Wide Web. People tell Ford about their problems, preferences, and car ownership habits. In return for providing their personal information, including e-mail addresses, Ford sends customers product promotions matched to their product preferences.

> *Frito-Lay:* Frito-Lay uses its sophisticated internal information system to analyse daily sales performance. Each day, Frito-Lay's salespeople report their day's efforts via hand-held computers to Frito-Lay headquarters. Twenty-four

hours later, Frito-Lay's marketing managers have a complete report analysing the previous day's sales of Fritos, Doritos, and other brands. The system helps marketing managers make better decisions and makes the salespeople more effective. It greatly reduces the number of hours spent filling out reports, giving salespeople extra time for selling. Frito-Lay's sales are going up 10 percent to 12 percent a year without adding a single salesperson.

Internal records usually can be accessed more quickly and cheaply than other information sources, but they also present some problems. Because internal information was collected for other purposes, it may be incomplete or in the wrong form for making marketing decisions. For example, sales and cost data used by the accounting department for preparing financial statements must be adapted for use in evaluating product, sales-force, or channel performance. In addition, a large company produces great amounts of information, and keeping track of it is difficult. The database information must be well integrated and readily accessible through "user-friendly" interfaces so that managers can find it easily and use it effectively.

Marketing Intelligence

Marketing intelligence
The systematic collection and analysis of publicly available information about competitors and development in the marketing environment.

Marketing intelligence is the systematic collection and analysis of publicly available information about competitors and developments in the marketing environment. The marketing intelligence system determines what intelligence is needed, collects it by searching the environment, and delivers it to marketing managers.

Marketing intelligence can be gathered from many sources. Much intelligence can be collected from the company's own personnel—executives, engineers and scientists, purchasing agents, and the sales force. But company people are often busy and fail to pass on important information. The company must "sell" its people on their importance as intelligence-gatherers, train them to identify new developments, and urge them to report intelligence back to the company.

The company also must get suppliers, resellers, and customers to pass along important intelligence. Information on competitors can be obtained from what they say about themselves in annual reports, speeches and press releases, and advertisements. The company also can learn about competitors from what others say about them in business publications and at trade shows. Or the company can watch what competitors do—buying and analysing competitors' products, monitoring their sales, and checking for new patents (see Marketing Highlight 4-1).

Companies also buy intelligence information from outside suppliers. Using a sample of 465 stores, A.C. Nielsen of Canada gathers and sells bimonthly data on brand shares, retail prices, percentage of stores stocking an item, and percentage of stores that have run out of stock. Historically, A.C. Nielsen had a monopoly on providing data on product movements in retail chains in Canada. The federal Competition Tribunal recently ruled, however, that Nielsen's practice of signing exclusive contracts with retailers to obtain their scanner data was anti-competitive. This ruling allowed Information Resources Inc. (IRI) of Chicago to begin to compete in the Canadian market.[10]

Information Resources, Inc.
www.infores.com/

For a fee, companies can subscribe to online databases or information search services. Canadian marketers are benefiting from the increased number of research providers and the red-hot competitive climate. Giant firms such as Compusearch and Dun & Bradstreet are facing competition from smaller firms such as Syntony Marketing of Toronto or Links Database Technologies. Compusearch provides information on the consumer-spending potential for a wide variety of product categories, including home furnishings, transportation, and recreation. Not only can Compusearch reports be tailored to a specific business and trading area, but they can also incorporate a lifestyle analysis. Such a program helped Kraft Canada target high-usage neighbourhoods for its recent coffee-sampling program, which led to a dramatic increase in sales.

MARKETING HIGHLIGHT 4 - 1

INTELLIGENCE GATHERING: SNOOPING TO CONQUER

Competitive intelligence gathering has grown dramatically as more and more companies need to know what their competitors are doing. A recent survey of Fortune 500 companies found that 80 percent had some type of business intelligence strategy in place. Techniques range from quizzing the company's own employees and benchmarking competitors' products to surfing the Internet, lurking around industry trade shows, and rooting through rivals' garbage cans.

The growing use of marketing intelligence, with companies pushing to outsmart and outdo one another, raises a number of ethical issues. Although most of the above techniques are legal, and some are considered to be shrewdly competi-

however, are practices rated in the middle, such as obtaining intelligence information by searching competitors' trash, hiring away competitors' key executives or other employees, or posing as a potential customer or supplier.

Companies should take advantage of publicly available information, but they should avoid practices that might be considered illegal or unethical. With all the legitimate intelligence sources now available, a company does not have to break the law or accepted codes of ethics to get good intelligence.

Techniques that companies use to collect their own marketing intelligence fall into four major groups. Although most of these techniques are legal, do you think they are ethical?

boss, who passed the news to the intelligence unit. Using such clues as a classified ad Kodak placed seeking new people with Xerox product experience, they verified Kodak's plan—code-named Ulysses—to service Xerox copiers. . . . The warning allowed Xerox to devise a scheme to [protect its profitable service business through its] Total Satisfaction Guarantee, which allowed copier returns for any reason as long as *Xerox* did the servicing. By [the time] Kodak launched its plan, Xerox had been trumpeting its [program] for three months.

Getting Information from Recruits and Competitors' Employees

Companies can obtain intelligence through job interviews or from conversations with competitors' employees.

When holding interviews, some companies pay special attention to candidates who have worked for competitors. Job seekers are eager to impress and often have not been warned about divulging what is proprietary. Companies also send engineers to conferences and trade shows to question competitors' technical people. Often conversations start innocently—just a few fellow technicians discussing processes and problems . . . [yet competitors'] engineers and scientists often brag about surmounting technical challenges, in the process divulging sensitive information.

Companies sometimes advertise and hold interviews for jobs that don't exist in order to entice competitors' employees to spill the beans . . . Often applicants have toiled in obscurity or feel that their careers have stalled. They're dying to impress somebody.

Four other car companies have already bought one. Whatever do you suppose they want them for?

Porsche 968: The next evolution.

Collecting intelligence: Porsche notes that *"it's not unusual for car companies to check out each other's creations . . . A new Porsche gets an inordinate amount of attention."*

tive, many involve questionable ethics. In a recent survey, senior executives rated the ethics of various marketing intelligence practices. Many practices were rated as "clearly unethical," such as planting spies in competitors' facilities, bribing competitors' employees, and conducting phony job interviews. Others—such as reverse engineering, surveying competitors' customers, and reviewing competitors' patent applications, job advertisements, and financial statements—were perceived as "clearly ethical." More of a problem,

Collecting Information Internally

According to the chief of corporate intelligence for Ryder System, Inc., "Eighty percent of what you need to know can be found by talking to your own employees." Here's an example of how listening to its own people paid off for Xerox:

In early 1995, a Kodak copier salesman told a Xerox technician that he was being trained to service Xerox products. The Xerox employee told his

Getting Information from People Who Do Business with Competitors

Key customers can keep the company informed about competitors and their products:

For example, a few years ago Gillette told a large Canadian account the date on which it planned to begin selling its new Good News disposable razor in the United States. The Canadian distributor promptly called Bic and told it about the impending product launch. Bic put on a crash program and was able to start selling its razor shortly after Gillette did.

Intelligence can also be gathered by infiltrating customers' business operations:

Companies may provide their engineers free of charge to customers . . . The close, cooperative relationship that the engineers on loan cultivate with the customers' design staff often enables them to learn what new products competitors are pitching.

Getting Information from Published Materials and Public Documents

Keeping track of seemingly meaningless published information can provide competitor intelligence. For instance, the types of people sought in help-wanted ads can indicate something about a competitor's new strategies and products. Government agencies are another good source. For example:

Although it is often illegal for a company to photograph a competitor's plant from the air, there are legitimate ways to get the photos . . . Aerial photos often are on file with the U.S. Geological Survey, the Canadian Geological Survey, or Environmental Protection Agency. These are public documents, available for a nominal fee.

Zoning and tax assessment offices often have tax information on local factories and even blueprints of the facilities, showing square footage and types of machinery. This information is publicly available.

Getting Information by Observing Competitors or Analysing Physical Evidence

Companies can get to know competitors better by buying their products or examining other physical evidence.

An increasingly important form of competitive intelligence is benchmarking—taking apart competitors' products and imitating or improving on their best features. Popular since the early 1980s, benchmarking helped Xerox turn around its copying business and Ford develop the successful Taurus.

When Ford decided to build a better car back in the early 1980s, it compiled a list of some 400 features its customers said were the most important, then set about finding the car with the best of each. Then it tried to match the best of the competition. The result: the hot-selling Taurus.

Companies can also examine many other types of physical evidence. Companies have measured the rust on rails of railway sidings to their competitors' plants or have counted the tractor-trailers leaving loading bays. Some companies even rifle their competitors' garbage, which is considered abandoned property once it has left the competitors' premises. While some companies now shred technical documents, they often neglect to do this for almost-as-revealing refuse from the marketing or public relations departments.

In a recent example of garbage snatching, Avon admitted that it had hired private detectives to paw through the dumpster of rival Mary Kay Cosmetics. Although an outraged Mary Kay sued to get its garbage back, Avon claimed that it had done nothing illegal. The dumpster had been located in a public parking lot, and Avon had videotapes to prove it.

Surfing the Internet and Online Databases

The Internet provides quick and inexpensive access to a rich assortment of intelligence information. By simply checking competitors' web sites, a company can glean important details concerning rivals' products, prices, promotional campaigns, and overall marketing strategies. Using Internet search engines such as Yahoo or Infoseek, marketers can search specific competitor names, events, or trends and see what turns up. Marketers must be cautious when using Internet information, especially if they can't tell who has developed an Internet site. Some groups post false or misleading information.

There are thousands of online databases. Some are free. For example, the *Financial Post* (http://www.conoc.ca/FP/home.html) provides access to a huge stockpile of financial and other information on public companies. Industry Canada has an excellent site for business information (http://strategis.ic.gc.ca/ engdoc/main.html). Other online data sources provide information and searches for a fee. Using the Dialog or Lexus-Nexis databases, companies can conduct complex information searches in a flash from the comfort of their keyboards.

Sources: Excerpts from Steven Flax, "How to Snoop on Your Competitors," *Fortune,* May 14, 1984, pp. 29–33; Brian Dumaine, "Corporate Spies Snoop to Conquer," *Fortune,* November 7, 1988, pp. 68–76; and Jeremy Main, "How to Steal the Best Ideas Around," *Fortune,* October 19, 1992, pp. 102–106. Copyright © 1984, 1988, and 1992, Time Inc. All rights reserved. Also see Wendy Zellner and Bruce Hager, "Dumpster Raids? That's Not Very Ladylike, Avon," *Business Week,* April 1, 1991, p. 32; Benjamin Gilda, George Gordon, and Ephraim Sudit, "Identifying Gaps and Blind Spots in Competitive Intelligence," *Long Range Planning,* December 1993, pp. 107–113; and Shaker A. Zahra, "Unethical Practices in Competitive Analysis: Patterns, Causes and Effects," *Journal of Business Ethics,* 13, 1994, pp. 53–62.

Even government information providers are entering the competitive scrum. Statistics Canada has begun to aggressively market its databases and tailor them into more user-friendly formats. For example, brokers and investment firms can identify RRSP contributors in highly specific geographic regions using StatsCan information.

Research firms and agencies specializing in database compilation can provide marketers with a wealth of consumer information as well as the software tools to help them organize their internal company records. For example, Market Facts of

Canada Limited cross-references the survey data it gathers from 45 000 Canadian households.

Other firms specialize in media-related research questions. For example, iCom Information and Communications Inc. has created a hybrid information package that matches consumers' buying behaviours with their media preferences. Online databases are available in most parts of the world. For example, the *Eurobases* and *Euroscope* databases provide a wealth of information on commercial, legal, and cultural aspects of European affairs. The *Donnelly Demographics* database provides demographic data from the U.S. census plus Donnelly's own demographic projections by state, city, or zip code. Companies can use it to measure markets and develop segmentation strategies.[11] Marketers can also access information from the Canada Newswire web site.

Canada Newswire
www.newswire.ca

Some companies set up a department to collect and circulate marketing intelligence. The staff scans major publications, summarizes important news, and sends bulletins to marketing managers. The department members develop a file of intelligence information and help managers evaluate new information. These services greatly improve the quality of information available to marketing managers.[12]

Marketing Research

Managers cannot only rely on publicly available information. They often require formal studies of specific situations. For example, Toshiba may need to know how many and what kinds of people or companies will buy its new superfast laptop computer. Or Queen's University Executive Program needs to know what percentage of its target market has heard about the programs, how they heard, what they know, and how they feel. In such situations, the marketing intelligence system will not provide the detailed information needed. Managers will need marketing research.

We define **marketing research** as the systematic design, collection, analysis, and reporting of data and findings relevant to a specific marketing situation facing an organization. Every marketer needs research. Marketing researchers engage in a wide variety of activities, ranging from market potential and market share studies, to assessments of customer satisfaction and purchase behaviour, to studies of pricing, product, distribution, and promotion activities.

Marketing research
The systematic design, collection, analysis, and reporting of data and findings relevant to a specific marketing situation facing an organization.

The role of marketing researchers has changed. In earlier periods, researchers were often only consulted to evaluate existing programs. Today, companies are investing in "success insurance." They are using research to help formulate new strategies. For example, the Co-operators Insurance Company of Guelph, Ontario conducted extensive research before launching its DirectProtect home and auto insurance. Research showed the consumers valued the convenience of buying insurance over the phone, but were hesitant to do so because of the impersonal nature of the transaction. To address this concern, DirectProtect supported the service launch with a television advertising campaign showing tiny insurance salespeople coming out of phones to assure potential customers that there really was a person at the end of the line.[13]

A company can conduct marketing research in its own research department or have some or all of it done by outside firms. Whether a company uses outside firms depends on its own research skills and resources. Although most large companies have their own marketing research departments, they often use outside firms to do special research tasks or special studies. A company with no research department must buy the services of research firms.

It should be noted that while marketers strive to have as complete an understanding of consumer needs and wants as possible, they often have to make decisions with limited information. Sometimes research is just too costly, can't be completed in a timely fashion, or it cannot address all the areas of uncertainty faced by marketers. No matter how extensive their research resources, marketers still have

Research helped the Co-operators Insurance Company design its new DirectProtect home and auto insurance.

to make judgments based on their insight and experience to handle these "grey" areas.

Information Analysis

Information gathered by the company's marketing intelligence and marketing research systems often requires more analysis, and sometimes managers may need help applying the information to their marketing problems and decisions. This help may include advanced statistical analysis to learn more about both the relationships within a set of data and their statistical reliability. Such analysis allows managers to go beyond means and standard deviations in the data and to answer questions such as the following:

- What are the major variables affecting my sales and how important is each one?
- What are the best variables for segmenting my market, and how many segments exist?
- What are the best predictors of which consumers are likely to buy my brand versus my competitor's brand?
- If I raised my price 10 percent and increased my advertising expenditures 20 percent, what would happen to sales?

DISTRIBUTING INFORMATION

Marketing information has no value until managers use it to make better marketing decisions. The information gathered through marketing intelligence and marketing research must be distributed to the right marketing managers at the right time. Most companies have centralized marketing information systems that provide managers with regular performance reports, intelligence updates, and reports on the results of studies. Managers need these routine reports for making regular planning, implementation, and control decisions. But marketing managers also may need non-routine information for special situations and on-the-spot decisions. For example, a sales manager having trouble with a large customer may want a summary of the account's sales and profitability over the past year. Or a retail store manager who has run out of a best-selling product may want to know the current inventory levels in the chain's other stores. In companies with only centralized information systems, these managers must request the information from the MIS staff and wait. Often, the information arrives too late to be useful.

Developments in information technology have caused a revolution in information distribution. With recent advances in computers, software, and telecommunications, most companies are decentralizing their marketing information systems. In many companies, marketing managers have direct access to the information network through personal computers and other means. From any location, they can obtain information from internal records or outside information services, analyse the information using statistical packages and models, prepare reports on a word processor or desktop publishing system, and communicate with others in the network through electronic communications.

Such systems offer exciting prospects. They allow the managers to get the information they need directly and quickly and to tailor it to their unique needs. As more managers develop the skills needed to use such systems, and as improvements in the technology make them more economical, more and more marketing companies will use decentralized marketing information systems.

THE MARKETING RESEARCH PROCESS

The marketing research process (see Figure 4-2) consists of four steps: *defining the problem and research objectives, developing the research plan, implementing the research plan,* and *interpreting and reporting the findings.*

FIGURE 4-2 *The marketing research process*

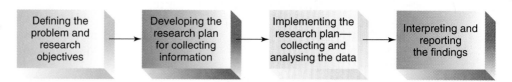

Defining the problem and research objectives → Developing the research plan for collecting information → Implementing the research plan— collecting and analysing the data → Interpreting and reporting the findings

DEFINING THE PROBLEM AND RESEARCH OBJECTIVES

The marketing manager and the researcher must work closely to define the problem carefully, and they must agree on the research objectives. The manager best understands the decision for which information is needed; the researcher best understands marketing research and how to obtain the information.

Managers must know enough about marketing research to help in planning and interpreting research results. If they know little about marketing research, they may obtain the wrong information, accept wrong conclusions, or ask for information that costs too much. Experienced marketing researchers who understand the manager's problem also should be involved at this stage. The researcher must be able to help the manager define the problem and suggest ways that research can help the manager make better decisions.

Defining the problem and research objectives is often the hardest step in the research process. The manager may know that something is wrong, without knowing the specific causes. For example, managers of a large discount retail store chain hastily decided that falling sales were caused by poor advertising, and they ordered research to test the company's advertising. When this research showed that current advertising was reaching the right people with the right message, the managers were puzzled. It turned out that the real problem was that the chain was not delivering the prices, products, and service promised in the advertising. Careful problem definition would have avoided the cost and delay of doing advertising research. In the classic New Coke case, the Coca-Cola Company defined its research problem too narrowly, with disastrous results (see Marketing Highlight 4-2).

After the problem has been defined carefully, the manager and researcher must set research objectives. A marketing research project might have one of three types of objectives. The objective of **exploratory research** is to gather preliminary information that will help define the problem and suggest hypotheses. The objective of **descriptive research** is to describe things such as the market potential for a product or the demographics and attitudes of consumers who buy the product. The objective of **causal research** is to test hypotheses about cause-and-effect relationships. For example, would a 10 percent decrease in tuition at a private school result in an enrolment increase sufficient to offset the reduced tuition? Managers often start with exploratory research and later follow with descriptive or causal research.

The statement of the problem and research objectives guides the entire research process. The manager and researcher should put the statement in writing to ensure that they agree on the purpose and expected results of the research.

Exploratory research
Marketing research to gather preliminary information that will help to better define problems and suggest hypotheses.

Descriptive research
Marketing research to better describe marketing problems, situations, or markets, such as the market potential for a product or the demographics and attitudes of consumers.

Causal research
Marketing research to test hypotheses about cause-and-effect relationships.

THE RISE AND FALL OF NEW COKE: WHAT'S THE PROBLEM?

In 1985, the Coca-Cola Company made a classic marketing blunder. After 99 successful years, it set aside its long-standing rule—"don't mess with Mother Coke"—and dropped its original formula Coke! In its place came New Coke with a sweeter, smoother taste.

At first, amid the introductory flurry of advertising and publicity, New Coke sold well. But sales soon went flat, as a stunned public reacted. Coke began receiving sacks of mail and more than 1500 phone calls each day from angry consumers. A group called "Old Cola Drinkers" staged protests, handed out T-shirts, and threatened a class-action suit unless Coca-Cola brought back the old formula. Most marketing experts predicted that New Coke would be the "Edsel of the Eighties." After only three months, the Coca-Cola Company brought back old Coke. Now called "Coke Classic," it sold side-by-side with New Coke on supermarket shelves. The company said that New Coke would remain its "flagship" brand, but consumers had a different idea. By the end of 1985, Classic was outselling New Coke in supermarkets by two to one.

Quick reaction saved the company from potential disaster. It stepped up efforts for Coke Classic and slotted New Coke into a supporting role. Coke Classic again became the company's main brand—and the country's leading soft drink. New Coke became the company's "attack brand"—its Pepsi stopper—and ads boldly compared New Coke's taste with Pepsi's. Still, New Coke managed only a two percent market share. In the spring of 1990, the company repackaged New Coke and relaunched it as a brand extension with a new name—Coke II. In 1992, after two years of test marketing in Spokane, Washington, Coca-Cola expanded Coke II distribution to several major U.S. cities. New ads proclaimed "Real Cola Taste Plus the Sweetness of Pepsi." However, with a minuscule market share of 0.3 percent, Coke II appeared destined to do little more than pester rival Pepsi.

Why was New Coke introduced in the first place? What went wrong? Many analysts blame the blunder on poor marketing research.

In the early 1980s, although Coke was still the leading soft drink, it was slowly losing market share to Pepsi. For years, Pepsi had successfully mounted the "Pepsi Challenge," a series of televised taste tests showing that consumers preferred the sweeter taste of Pepsi. By early 1985, although Coke led in the overall market, Pepsi led in share of supermarket sales by two percent. (That doesn't sound like much, but two percent of the huge soft-drink market amounts to $960 million in retail sales!) Coca-Cola had to do something to stop the loss of its market share, and the solution appeared to be a change in Coke's taste.

When Coca-Cola introduced New Coke, consumers reacted angrily—they staged protests, handed out T-shirts, and threatened class action suits to get the old formula back.

Coca-Cola began the largest new product research project in the company's history. It spent more than two years and $4 million on research before settling on a new formula. It conducted some 200 000 taste tests—30 000 on the final formula alone. In blind tests, 60 percent of consumers chose the new Coke over the old, and 52 percent chose it over Pepsi. Research showed that New Coke would be a winner and the company introduced it with confidence. So what happened?

Looking back, we can see that Coke defined its marketing research problem too narrowly. The research looked only at taste; it did not explore consumers' feelings about dropping the old Coke and replacing it with a new version. It took no account of the *intangibles*—Coke's name, history, packaging, cultural heritage, and image. However, to many people, Coke stands alongside baseball, hot dogs, and apple pie as an American institution; it represents the very fabric of America. Coke's symbolic meaning turned out to be more important to many consumers than its taste. Research addressing a broader set of issues would have detected these strong emotions.

Coke's managers also may have used poor judgment in interpreting the research and planning strategies around it. For example, they took the finding that 60 percent of consumers preferred New Coke's taste to mean that the new product would win in the marketplace, as when a political candidate wins with 60 percent of the vote. But it also meant that 40 percent still liked the original formula. By dropping the old Coke, the company trampled the taste buds of the large core of loyal Coke drinkers who didn't want a change. The company might have been wiser to leave the old Coke alone and introduce New Coke as a brand extension, as it later did successfully with Cherry Coke.

The Coca-Cola Company has one of the largest, best-managed, and most advanced marketing research operations in the United States. Good marketing research has kept the company atop the rough-and-tumble soft-drink market for decades. But marketing research is far from an exact science. Consumers are full of surprises, and figuring them out can be awfully tough. If Coca-Cola can make a large marketing research mistake, any company can.

Sources: See "Coke 'Family' Sales Fly as New Coke Stumbles," *Advertising Age,* January 17, 1986, p. 1; Jack Honomichl, "Missing Ingredients in 'New' Coke's Research," *Advertising Age,* July 22, 1985, p. 1; Patricia Winters, "Coke II Enters Markets Without Splashy Fanfare," *Advertising Age,* August 24, 1992, p. 2; Adam Shell, "Coca-Cola Keeps Fizz in Brand Name," *Public Relations Journal,* January 1994, p. VI; and Leah Richard, "Remembering New Coke," *Advertising Age,* April 17, 1995, p. 6.

DEVELOPING THE RESEARCH PLAN

The second step of the marketing research process calls for determining the information needed, developing a plan for gathering it efficiently, and presenting the plan to marketing management. The plan outlines sources of existing data and spells out the specific research approaches, contact methods, sampling plans, and instruments that researchers will use to gather new data.

Determining Specific Information Needs

Research objectives must be translated into specific information needs. For example, suppose Campbell decides to research how consumers would react to the company replacing its familiar red-and-white soup can with new bowl-shaped plastic containers that it has used successfully for some of its other products. The containers would cost more, but would allow consumers to heat the soup in a microwave oven and eat it without using dishes. This research might call for the following specific information:

◆   The demographic, economic, and lifestyle characteristics of current soup users. (Busy working couples might find the convenience of the new packaging worth the price; families with children might want to pay less and wash the pan and bowls.)

◆   Consumer-usage patterns for soup: how much soup they eat, where, and when. (The new packaging might be ideal for adults eating lunch on the go, but less convenient for parents feeding lunch to several children.)

◆   The number of microwave ovens in consumer and commercial markets. (The number of microwaves in homes and business lunchrooms will limit the demand for the new containers.)

◆   Retailer reactions to the new packaging. (Failure to get retailer support could hurt sales of the new package.)

◆   Consumer attitudes toward the new packaging. (The red-and-white Campbell soup can has become an institution—will consumers accept the new packaging?)

◆   Forecasts of sales of both new and current packages. (Will the new packaging increase Campbell's profits?)

Campbell managers will need these and many other types of information to decide whether to introduce the new packaging.

Gathering Secondary Information

Secondary data
Information that already exists somewhere, having been collected for another purpose.

Primary data
Information collected for the specific purpose at hand.

To meet the manager's information needs, the researcher can gather secondary data, primary data, or both. **Secondary data** consist of information that already exists somewhere, having been collected for another purpose. **Primary data** consist of information collected for the specific purpose at hand.

Researchers usually start by gathering secondary data. The company's internal database provides a good starting point. However, the company can also tap a wide assortment of external information sources, ranging from company, public, and university libraries to government and business publications. Table 4-2 describes a number of other important sources of secondary data, including commercial data services, online database services, and Internet data sources.

COMMERCIAL DATA SOURCES.   Companies can buy data reports from outside suppliers. For example, two firms, Nielsen Marketing research and Information Resources, Inc., sell data on brand shares, retail prices, percentages of stores stocking different brands, measures of trial and repeat purchasing, brand loyalty, and buyer demographics. These and other firms supply high-quality data to suit a wide variety of marketing information needs.

TABLE 4-2 *Sources of Secondary Data*

Internal sources

Internal sources include company profit and loss statements, balance sheets, sales figures, sales call reports, invoices, inventory records, and prior research reports.

Government publications

Statistics Canada, Demography Division, provides summary data on demographic, economic, social, and other aspects of the Canadian economy and society.

Periodicals and books

Canadian Markets, produced by the Financial Post Datagroup, provides annual demographic and retail data for over 700 Canadian urban and regional markets.

Scott's Directories lists, on an annual basis, manufacturers, their products, and their SIC codes (Standard Industrial Classification Codes), alphabetically as well as by city and region. The directory also provides the names, telephone and fax numbers of chief executives, as well as corporate information such as annual sales. Directories come in four volumes: Ontario, Quebec, Atlantic Canada, and Western Canada.

Canadian Trade Index and *Fraser's Canadian Trade Directory* provide information on manufactuers of different product categories, manufacturing equipment, and supplies.

Standard & Poor's Industry Surveys provide updated statistics and analyses of U.S. industries.

Marketing journals include the *Journal of Marketing, Journal of Marketing Research,* and *Journal of Consumer Research, Journal of the Academy of Marketing Science.*

Useful trade magazines include *Marketing, Advertising Age, Chain Store Age, Progressive Grocer, Sales & Marketing Management,* and *Stores.*

Useful general business magazines include *Canadian Business,* the *Globe and Mail's Report on Business, Business Week, Fortune, Forbes,* and *Harvard Business Review.*

Commercial Data Services

Here are just a few of the dozens of commercial research houses selling data to subscribers:

ABI Inform (1983 to present) and *Business Abstracts* (1989 to present) are examples of CD-ROM databases available in most university libraries. They contain abstracts of articles on business appearing in academic journals and the business press.

(PMB) Print Measurement Bureau (Toronto), prepares product category reports that provide information about the users of over 1000 products and services. Compares the demographic profiles of users versus non-users, and heavy versus light users on dimensions such as age, education, marital status, income, occupation, employment status, region and city, household size, residence ownership, sex, and language. Data are also matched to location where main grocery shopping occurs and are usually gathered over a two-year period.

Canadian Grocer. Produces an annual *Directory of Chains* with information of head-office locations, store locations, management names and functions, technologies used, buying policies, store sizes, private labels, and annual sales.

Card Reports. Provides annual information on different Canadian media types, the gross rating points (GRP) associated with each, and the costs of placing advertisements in the various media.

A.C. Nielsen (a division of D&B Marketing Information Services) provides supermarket scanner data on sales, market share, and retail prices (ScanTrack), data on household purchasing (Scantrack National Electronic Household Panel), data on television audiences (Nielsen National Television Index), and others.

Information Resources, Inc. provides supermarket scanner data for tracking grocery product movement (InfoScan) and single-source data collection (BehaviorScan).

The Arbitron Company provides local market radio audience and advertising expenditure information, along with a wealth of other media and ad spending data.

MMRI (Simmons Market Research Bureau) provides annual reports covering television markets, sporting goods, and proprietary drugs, giving lifestyle and geodemographic

Environics
www.environics.ca

Industry Canada
www.strategic.ic.gc.ca

U.S. Census Bureau
www.census.gov

American Demographics
www.demographics.com

Canoe
www.canoe.ca

Ecola's 24-Hour Newsstand
www.ecola.com/news

**Strategy: The Canadian
Marketing Report**
www.strategymag.com

TABLE 4-2 *continued*

data by sex, income, age, and brand preferences (selective markets and media reaching them).

Equifax Canada is the country's largest information service. It specializes in credit reports on both consumers and small businesses.

International Data

Here are only a few of the many sources providing international information:

U.S. Industrial Outlook provides projections of industrial activity by industry and includes data on production, sales, shipments, employment, etc.

United Nations publications include the *Statistical Yearbook,* a comprehensive source of international data for socioeconomic indicators; *Demographic Yearbook,* a collection of demographics data and vital statistics for 220 countries; and the *International Trade Statistics Yearbook,* which provides information on foreign trade for specific countries and commodities.

Europa Yearbook provides surveys on history, politics, population, economy, and natural resources for most countries of the world, along with information on major international organizations.

Other sources include *Political Risk Yearbook, Country Studies, OECD Economic Surveys, Economic Survey of Europe, Asian Economic Handbook,* and *International Financial Statistics.*

Internet Data Sources

A myriad of web sites can be used for market research. Both large and small companies have developed web sites as an additional means of communicating with their customers. At many company sites, you can find information about the history of the company, its products, and its financial information. At the sites for marketing research firms, you can find some interesting insights about Canadian consumers. For example, the Environics site lets users classify themselves on the 3SC Social Values Monitor. Governments also post information on the Web. For example, at the Industry Canada site, users can find a wealth of information about various sectors of the economy as well as the SIC numbers for various Canadian and U.S. industries. Marketers planning to enter the U.S. market can glean background information from the U.S. Census Bureau or from American Demographics. The U.S. government's site is designed to help small businesspeople, and can be used by both Canadian and American marketers. A number of online press services, such as Canoe exist, which marketers can search to track the effectiveness of their own and other companies' public relations efforts. Ecola's 24-Hour Newsstand allows marketers to link with the web sites of more than 2000 newspapers, journals, and computer publications. Publishers of marketing periodicals who post their material online can be a gold mine. Brunico Communications publishes *Strategy: The Canadian Marketing Report* online in addition to providing it in hard-copy format. Using keywords, marketers can search all editions for articles on a wide range of topics. Internet search engines such as Yahoo, Excite, Lycos, or Infoseek also allow marketers to locate material on special topics. Publications such as the *1997 Canadian Internet Directory* can facilitate the search for Canada's top web sites.

Online databases
A compilation of marketing information that can be accessed online.

ONLINE DATABASES AND INTERNET DATA SOURCES. Using commercial **online databases,** marketing researchers can conduct their own searches of secondary data sources. A recent survey of marketing researchers found that 81 percent use such online services for conducting research.[14] A readily available online database exists to fill almost any marketing information need. General database services such as CompuServe, Dialog, and Lexus-Nexis put an incredible wealth of information at the keyboards of marketing decision-makers. For example, a company doing business in Germany can check out CompuServe's German Company Library of financial and product information on more than 48 000 German-owned firms. A Canadian auto parts manufacturer can punch up Dun & Bradstreet Financial Profiles and Company Reports to develop biographical sketches of key General Motors,

Ford, and Chrysler executives. Just about any information a marketer might need—demographic data, today's news-wire reports, or a list of active U.S. trademarks—is available from online databases.[15]

The Internet offers a mind-boggling array of databases and other secondary information sources, many of which are free to the user. Beyond commercial web sites offering information for a fee, almost every industry association, government agency, business publication, and news medium offers free information to those tenacious enough to find their web sites. In fact, so many web sites offer data that finding the right ones can become an almost overwhelming task.

ADVANTAGES AND DISADVANTAGES OF SECONDARY DATA. Secondary data can usually be obtained more quickly and at a lower cost than primary data. For example, an Internet or online database search might provide all the information that Campbell needs on microwave-oven usage, quickly and at almost no cost. A study to collect primary information might take weeks or months to complete and cost thousands of dollars. Also, secondary sources sometimes can provide data that an individual company cannot collect on its own—information that either is not directly available or would be too expensive to collect. For example, it would be too expensive for Campbell to conduct a continuing retail store audit to find out about the market shares, prices, and displays of competitors' brands. But it can buy the InfoScan service from Information Resources, Inc.

Secondary data can also present problems. The needed information may not exist—researchers can rarely obtain all the data they need from secondary sources. For example, Campbell will not find existing information about consumer reactions to new packaging that it has not yet placed on the market. Even when data can be found, they might not be very usable. The researcher must evaluate secondary information carefully to ensure that it is *relevant* (fits research project needs), *accurate* (reliably collected and reported), *current* (up-to-date enough for current decisions), and *impartial* (objectively collected and reported).

Secondary data provide a good starting point for research and often help to define problems and research objectives. In most cases, however, the company must also collect primary data.

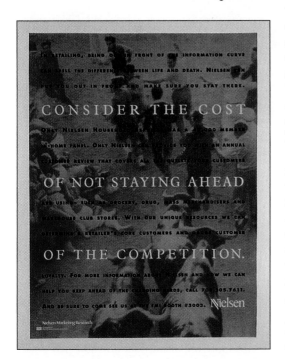

Secondary data sources: Here Nielsen Marketing Research suggests that information from its 40 000-member in-house consumer panel will give retailers a competitive edge by helping them to define their core customers and to gauge customer loyalty.

Observational research
The gathering of primary data by observing relevant people, actions, and situations.

Planning Primary Data Collection

Good decisions require good data. Just as researchers must carefully evaluate the quality of secondary information, they also must take great care when collecting primary data to assure that it will be relevant, accurate, current, and unbiased information. Table 4-3 shows that designing a plan for primary data collection calls for a number of decisions on *research approaches, contact methods, sampling plan,* and *research instruments.*

RESEARCH APPROACHES. **Observational research** is the gathering of primary data by observing relevant people, actions, and situations. For example, a maker of

TABLE 4-3 *Planning Primary Data Collection*

Research Approaches	Contact Methods	Sampling Plan	Research Instruments
Observation	Mail	Sampling unit	Questionnaire
Survey	Telephone	Sample size	Mechanical instruments
Experiment	Personal	Sampling procedure	

Mechanical observation: A.C. Nielsen attaches "people meters" to televisions in selected homes to record program viewership.

personal care products might pretest its ads by showing them to people and measuring eye movements, pulse rates, and other physical reactions. Or a bank might evaluate possible new branch locations by checking traffic patterns, neighbourhood conditions, and the location of competing branches. For example, Steelcase used observation to help design new office furniture for use by work teams.

> To learn first-hand how teams actually operate, it set up video cameras at various companies and studied the tapes, looking for motions and behaviour patterns that customers themselves might not even notice. It found that teams work best when they can do some work together and some privately. So Steelcase designed highly successful modular office units called Personal Harbor. These units are "rather like telephone booths in size and shape." They can be arranged around a common space where a team works, letting people work together but also alone when necessary. Says a Steelcase executive, "Market data wouldn't necessarily have pointed us that way. It was more important to know how people actually work."[16]

Urban Outfitters, the fast-growing specialty clothing chain, prefers observation to other types of market research. "We're not after people's statements," notes the chain's president, "we're after their actions." The company develops customer profiles by videotaping and taking photographs of customers in its stores. This helps managers determine what people are actually wearing and allows them to make quick decisions on merchandise.[17]

Several companies sell information collected through *mechanical* observation. For example, Nielsen Media Research attaches *people meters* to television sets in selected homes to record who watches which programs. It then provides summaries of the size and demographic composition of audiences for different television programs. Television networks use these ratings to judge program popularity and to set fees for advertising time. Advertisers use the ratings when selecting programs for their commercials. *Checkout scanners* in retail stores record consumer purchases in detail. Consumer products companies and retailers use scanner information to assess and improve product sales and store performance. Some marketing research firms now offer **single-source data systems** that electronically monitor both consumers' purchases and consumers' exposure to various marketing activities in an effort to better evaluate the link between the two (see Marketing Highlight 4-3).

Single-source data systems
Electronic monitoring systems that link consumers' exposure to television advertising and promotion (measured using television meters) with what they buy in stores (measured using store checkout scanners).

SINGLE-SOURCE DATA SYSTEMS: A POWERFUL WAY TO MEASURE MARKETING IMPACT

Information Resources, Inc., which operates in 26 countries, has just opened its doors in Canada. It is a leader in providing innovative information, software, and marketing software to companies engaged in the marketing, sales, and distribution of Canadians packaged goods and non-packaged goods. IRI is a major competitor to A.C. Nielsen in the United States. The company knows all there is to know about the members of its panel households—what they eat for lunch; what they put in their coffee; and what they use to wash their hair, quench their thirsts, or make up their faces. The research company electronically monitors the television programs that these people watch and tracks the brands they buy, the coupons they use, where they shop, and what newspapers and magazines they read. These households are part of IRI's BehaviorScan service, a single-source data system that links consumers' exposure to television advertising, sales promotion, and other marketing efforts with their store purchases. BehaviorScan and other single-source data systems have revolutionized the way consumer products companies measure the impact of their marketing activities.

The basics of single-source research are straightforward, and the IRI BehaviorScan system provides a good example. IRI maintains a panel of households across Canada. The company meters each home's television set to track who watches what and when, and it quizzes family members to find out what they read. It carefully records important facts about each household, such as family income, age of children, lifestyle, and product and store buying history.

IRI also employs a panel of retail stores in each of its markets. For a fee, these stores agree to carry the new products that IRI wishes to test and they allow IRI to control such factors as shelf location, stocking, point-of-purchase displays, and pricing for these products.

Each BehaviorScan household receives an identification number. When household members shop for groceries in IRI panel stores, they give their identification number to the store checkout clerk. All the information about the family's purchases—brands bought, package sizes, prices paid—is recorded by the store's electronic scanner and immediately entered by computer into the family's purchase file. The system also records any other in-store factors that might affect purchase decisions, such as special competitor price promotions or shelf displays.

Thus, IRI builds a complete record of each household's demographic and psychographic makeup, purchasing behaviour, media habits, and the conditions surrounding purchase. But IRI takes the process a step further. Through cable television, IRI controls the advertisements being sent to each household. It can beam different ads and promotions to different panel households and then use the purchasing information obtained from scanners to assess which ads had more or less impact and how various promotions affected different kinds of consumers. In short, from a single source, companies can obtain information that links their marketing efforts directly with consumer buying behaviour.

BehaviorScan and other single-source systems have their drawbacks, and some researchers are sceptical. One hitch is that such systems produce truckloads of data—more than most companies can handle. Another problem is cost: single-source data can cost marketers hundreds of thousands of dollars a year per brand. Also, because such systems are set up in only a few market areas, usually small cities, the marketer often finds it difficult to generalize from the measures and results. Finally, although single-source systems provide important information for assessing the impact of promotion and advertising, they shed little light on the effects of other key marketing actions.

Despite these drawbacks, more and more companies are relying on single-source data systems to test new products and new marketing strategies. When properly used, such systems can provide marketers with fast and detailed information about how their products are selling, who is buying them, and what factors affect purchase.

Sources: See Joanne Lipman, "Single-Source Ad Research Heralds Detailed Look at Household Habits," *Wall Street Journal,* February 16, 1988, p. 39; Joe Schwartz, "Back to the Source," *American Demographics,* January 1989, pp. 22–26; Magid H. Abraham and Leonard M. Lodish, "Getting the Most Out of Advertising and Promotion," *Harvard Business Review,* May–June 1990, pp. 50–60; and Howard Schlossberg, "IRI, Nielsen Slug It Out in 'Scanning Wars,'" *Marketing News,* September 2, 1991, pp. 1, 47.

IN A DOG EAT DOG WORLD, IT'S BETTER NOT TO BE A DOG.

Information Resources Inc. used the above ad to announce its arrival in the Canadian marketplace.

Observational research can be used to obtain information that people are unwilling or unable to provide. In some cases, observation may be the only way to obtain the needed information. In contrast, some things simply cannot be observed, such as feelings, attitudes and motives, or private behaviour. Long-term or infrequent behaviour is also difficult to observe. Because of these limitations, researchers often use observation as well as other data-collection methods.

Survey research is the approach best suited for gathering *descriptive* information. A company that wants to know about people's knowledge, attitudes, preferences, or buying behaviour often can find out by asking individuals directly.

Survey research is the most widely used method for primary data collection. The major advantage of survey research is its flexibility. It can be used to obtain many different kinds of information in many different situations. Depending on the survey design, it also may provide information more quickly and at lower cost than observational or experimental research.

Survey research
The gathering of primary data by asking people questions about their knowledge, attitudes, preferences, and buying behaviour.

However, survey research also presents some problems. Although many people believe constructing a good survey is a relatively easy matter, nothing could be further from the truth. Sometimes people are unable to answer survey questions because they cannot remember or have never thought about what they do and why. Or people may be unwilling to respond to unknown interviewers or talk about things they consider private. Respondents may answer survey questions even when they do not know the answer in order to appear smarter or more informed. Or they may try to help the interviewer by giving pleasing answers. Finally, busy people may not take the time, or they might resent the intrusion into their privacy.

Whereas observation is best suited for exploratory research and surveys for descriptive research, **experimental research** is best suited for gathering *causal* information. Experiments involve selecting matched groups of subjects, giving them different treatments, controlling unrelated factors, and checking for differences in group responses. Thus, experimental research tries to explain cause-and-effect relationships. Observation and surveys may be used to collect information in experimental research.

Experimental research
The gathering of primary data by selecting matched groups of subjects, giving them different treatments, controlling related factors, and checking for differences in group responses.

Before adding a new burger to the menu, researchers at McDonald's might use experiments to answer questions such as the following:

◆ How much will the new burger increase McDonald's sales?

◆ How will the new burger affect the sales of other menu items?

◆ Which advertising approach would have the greatest effect on sales of the burger?

◆ How would different prices affect the sales of the product?

◆ Should the new item be targeted toward adults, children, or both?

To test the effects of two different prices, McDonald's could set up the following simple experiment. It could introduce the new burger at one price in its restaurants in one city and at another price in restaurants in another city. If the cities are similar, and if all other marketing efforts for the burger are the same, then differences in sales in the two cities could be related to the price charged. More complex experiments could be designed to include other variables and other locations.

CONTACT METHODS. Information can be collected by mail, telephone, or personal interview. Table 4-4 shows the strengths and weaknesses of each contact method.

Mail questionnaires can be used to collect large amounts of information at a low cost per respondent. Respondents may give more honest answers to more personal questions on a mail questionnaire than to an unknown interviewer in person or over the phone. Also, no interviewer is involved to bias the respondent's answers. However, mail questionnaires are not very flexible—all respondents answer the same questions in a fixed order, and the researcher cannot adapt the

TABLE 4-4 *Strengths and Weaknesses of the Three Contact Methods*

	Mail	Telephone	Personal
1. Flexibility	Poor	Good	Excellent
2. Quantity of data that can be collected	Good	Fair	Excellent
3. Control of interviewer effects	Excellent	Fair	Poor
4. Control of sample	Fair	Excellent	Fair
5. Speed of data collection	Poor	Excellent	Good
6. Response rate	Poor	Good	Good
7. Cost	Good	Fair	Poor

Source: Adapted with permission of Macmillan Publishing Company from *Marketing Research: Measurement and Method*, 6th ed., by Donald S. Tull and Del I. Hawkins. Copyright © 1993 by Macmillan Publishing Company.

questionnaire based on earlier answers. Mail surveys usually take longer to complete, and the response rate—the number of people returning completed questionnaires—is often very low. Finally, the researcher often has little control over the mail questionnaire sample. Even with a good mailing list, it is hard to control *who* at the mailing address fills out the questionnaire.

Telephone interviewing is the best method for gathering information quickly, and it provides greater flexibility than mail questionnaires. Interviewers can explain difficult questions, and they can skip some questions or probe on others depending on the answers they receive. Response rates tend to be higher than with mail questionnaires, and telephone interviewing also allows greater sample control. Interviewers can ask to speak to respondents with the desired characteristics, or even by name.

However, with telephone interviewing, the cost per respondent is higher than with mail questionnaires. Also, people may not want to discuss personal questions with an interviewer. Using an interviewer also introduces interviewer bias—the way interviewers talk, how they ask questions, and other differences may affect respondents' answers. Finally, different interviewers may interpret and record responses differently, and under time pressures some interviewers might even cheat by recording answers themselves without asking respondents questions.

Personal interviewing takes two forms—individual and group interviewing. *Individual interviewing* involves talking with people in their homes or offices, on the street, or in shopping malls. Such interviewing is flexible. Trained interviewers can hold a respondent's attention for a long time and can explain difficult questions. They can guide interviews, explore issues, and probe as the situation requires. They can show subjects actual products, advertisements, or packages and observe reactions and behaviour. In most cases, personal interviews can be conducted fairly quickly. However, individual personal interviews may cost three to four times as much as telephone interviews.

Group interviewing consists of inviting six to 10 people to gather for a few hours with a trained moderator to discuss a product, service, or organization. The participants typically are paid a small sum for attending. The meeting is held in a pleasant place and refreshments are served to foster an informal setting. The moderator encourages free and easy discussion, hoping that group interactions will bring out actual feelings and thoughts. At the same time, the moderator "focusses" the discussion—hence the name **focus-group interviewing**. The comments are recorded through written notes or on videotapes that are studied later.

Focus-group interviewing Personal interviewing that consists of inviting six to 10 people to gather for a few hours with a trained interviewer to discuss a product, service, or organization. The interviewer "focuses" the group discussion on important issues.

Today, modern communications technology is changing the way that focus groups are conducted. Marketers no longer have to travel across the country. Video-conferencing links, television monitors, remote-control cameras, and digital transmission are boosting the amount of focus group research done over long-distance lines.[18]

Marketing researchers observe a focus group session.

YOUtv
www.youtv.com/

YOUtv developed a new research firm that provides interactive video booths and the ability to analyse the data gathered using them.

Focus-group interviewing has become one of the major marketing research tools for gaining insight into consumer thoughts and feelings. However, focus-group studies usually use small sample sizes to keep time and costs down, and it may be hard to generalize from the results. Because interviewers have more freedom in personal interviews, the problem of interviewer bias is greater.

Which contact method is best depends on what information the researcher wants, as well as the number and types of respondents to be contacted. Advances in computers and communications have had a large impact on methods of obtaining information. For example, most research firms now do Computer-Assisted Telephone Interviewing (CATI). Professional interviewers call respondents around the country, often using phone numbers drawn at random. When the respondent answers, the interviewer reads a set of questions from a video screen and types the respondent's answers directly into the computer. YOUtv, a young Canadian company, believed that consumers would be more open and honest in their feedback to companies if they could use video booths that they could activate themselves. But just providing firms with this technology wasn't enough, explains Ian Chamandy, co-owner of YOUtv. The company's ability to transform the raw data into meaningful information was key when Cadbury Chocolate Canada decided to use YOUtv to search for a new couple to advertise Crispy Crunch chocolate bars.[19]

Other firms are using *computer interviewing*, in which respondents sit down at a computer, read questions from a screen, and type their own answers into the computer. Electronic focus groups or electronic brainstorming is becoming a powerful and efficient way for companies to gauge customer sentiments. Twelve people are invited to a lab where a researcher poses questions. Respondents enter their responses and can read other respondents' answers on a large screen. Some companies, such as Microsoft Canada, are conducting surveys using the Internet. The company received more than 55 000 responses in just over 24 hours to a survey it conducted asking about people's relationships with computers.[20] Marketing Highlight 4-4 summarizes the advantages, drawbacks, and prospects of conducting marketing research on the Net. The Royal Bank of Canada has mastered computer-assisted interviewing without making people actually use a computer. Under a large sign that asks customers to "tell us what you think,"

MARKETING RESEARCH ON THE INTERNET

Performing marketing research on the Net is still in its infancy. But as the use of the World Wide Web and online services becomes more habit than hype for consumers, online research will become a quick, easy, and inexpensive way to tap into their opinions. The potential of the Internet as a data collection tool is evident since it is not limited by geographic boundaries, and it offers almost instant responses. People can respond to questionnaires posted on web sites in the privacy of their own homes at any time convenient to them. Currently only a small proportion of people use the Internet. However, online users tend to be better educated, more affluent, and younger than average consumers. A higher proportion are male. These are highly important consumers to companies offering products and services online. They are also some of the hardest consumers to reach when conducting a research study. Online surveys and chat sessions (or online focus groups) often prove effective in getting elusive teen, single, affluent, and well-educated audiences to participate.

"It's very solid for reaching hard-to-get segments," says Jacobson. "Doctors, lawyers, professionals—people you might have difficulty reaching because they are not interested in taking part in surveys. It's also a good medium for reaching working mothers and others who lead busy lives. They can do it in their own space and at their own convenience."

Online research isn't right for every company or product. For example, mass marketers who need to survey a representative cross-section of the population will find online research methodologies less useful. "If the target for the product or service you're testing is inconsistent with the Internet user profile, then it's not the medium to use," Jacobson points out. "Is it the right medium to test Campbell's Chunky Soup? Probably not, but if you want to test how people feel about Campbell's Web site, yes."

When appropriate, online research offers marketers two distinct advantages over traditional surveys and focus groups: speed and cost-effectiveness. Online researchers routinely field quantitative studies and fill response quotas in only a matter of days. Online focus groups require some advance scheduling, but results are virtually instantaneous. Notes an online researcher, "Online research is very fast, and time is what everybody wants now. Clients want the information yesterday."

Research on the Internet is also relatively inexpensive. Participants can dial in for a focus group from anywhere in the world, eliminating travel, lodging, and facility costs, making online chats cheaper than traditional focus groups. And for surveys, the Internet eliminates most of the postage, phone, labour, and printing costs associated with other survey approaches. Moreover, sample size has little influence on costs. "There's not a huge difference between ten and 10 000 on the Web," said Tod Johnson, head of NPD Group, a firm that conducts online research. "The cost [of research on the Web] can be anywhere from 10 percent to 80 percent less, especially when you talk about big samples."

However, using the Internet to conduct marketing research does have some drawbacks. One major problem is knowing who is in the sample. "If you can't see a person with whom you are communicating, how do you know who they really are?" asks Tom Greenbaum, president of Groups Plus. Moreover, trying to draw conclusions from a "self-selected" sample of online users, those who clicked through to a questionnaire or accidentally landed in a chat room, can be troublesome. "Using a convenient sample is a way to do research quickly, but when you're done, you kind of scratch your head and ask what it means."

To overcome such sample and response problems, NPD and many other firms that offer online services construct panels of qualified Web regulars to respond to surveys and participate in online focus groups. NPD's panel consists of 15 000 consumers recruited online and verified by telephone; Greenfield Online chooses users from its own database, then calls them periodically to verify that they are who they say they are. Another online research firm, Research Connections, recruits in advance by telephone, taking time to help new users connect to the Internet, if necessary.

Even when using qualified respondents, focus-group responses can lose something in the translation. "You're missing all of the key things that make a focus group a viable method," says Greenbaum. "You may get people online to talk to each other and play off each other, but it's very different to watch people get excited about a concept." Eye contact and body language are lost in the online world. And while researchers can offer seasoned moderators, the Internet format greatly restricts respondent expressiveness. Similarly, technology limits researchers' capability to show visual cues to research subjects. But just as it hinders the two-way assessment of visual cues, Web research can actually permit some participants the anonymity necessary to elicit an unguarded response. "There are reduced social effects online," Jacobson says. "People are much more honest in this medium."

Some researchers are wildly optimistic about the prospects for marketing research on the Internet; others are more cautious. One expert predicts that in the next few years, 50 percent of all research will be done on the Internet. "Ten years from now, national telephone surveys will be the subject of research methodology folklore," he proclaims. "That's a little too soon," cautions another expert. "But in 20 years, yes."

Sources: Portions adapted from Ian P. Murphy, "Interactive Research," *Marketing News*, January 20, 1997, pp. 1, 17. Selected quotations from "NFO Executive Sees Most Research Going to Internet," *Advertising Age*, May 19, 1997, p. 50. Also see Brad Edmondson, "The Wired Bunch," *American Demographics*, June 1997, pp. 10–15; Charlie Hamlin, "Market Research and the Wired Consumer," *Marketing News*, June 9, 1997, p. 6; and Mariam Mesbah, "Special Report: Research: Internet Research Holds Potential," *Strategy: The Canadian Marketing Report*, April 14, 1997, p. 40.

customers use a special pen to complete a questionnaire on an electronic board. The information can be downloaded directly into a database for later analysis.[21] Some U.S. researchers use Completely Automated Telephone Surveys (CATS), which employ voice-response technology to conduct interviews, but the Canadian Radio-Television and Telecommunication Commission has banned such devices in Canada.[22]

SAMPLING PLANS.   Marketing researchers usually draw conclusions about large groups of consumers by studying a small sample of the total consumer population. A **sample** is a segment of the population selected to represent the population as a whole. Ideally, the sample should be representative so that the researcher can make accurate estimates of the thoughts and behaviours of the larger population.

Designing the sample requires three decisions. First, *who* is to be surveyed (what *sampling unit*)? The answer to this question is not always obvious. For example, to study the decision-making process for a family automobile purchase, should the researcher interview the husband, wife, other family members, dealership salespeople, or all of these? The researcher must determine what information is needed and who is most likely to have it.

Second, *how many* people should be surveyed (what *sample size*)? Large samples give more reliable results than small samples. However, it is not necessary to sample the entire target market or even a large portion to get reliable results. If well chosen, samples of less than one percent of a population can often give good reliability.

Third, *how* should the people in the sample be *chosen* (what *sampling procedure*)? Table 4-5 describes different kinds of samples. Using *probability samples,* each population member has a known chance of being included in the sample, and researchers can calculate confidence limits for sampling error. But when probability sampling costs too much or takes too much time, marketing researchers often take *non-probability samples,* even though their sampling error cannot be measured. These varied ways of drawing samples have different costs and time limitations, as well as different accuracy and statistical properties. Which method is best depends on the needs of the research project.

RESEARCH INSTRUMENTS.   In collecting primary data, marketing researchers have a choice of two main research instruments—the *questionnaire* and *mechanical devices.* The *questionnaire,* by far the most common instrument, is very flexible—

TABLE 4-5   *Types of Samples*

Probability Sample	
Simple random sample	Every member of the population has a known and equal chance of selection.
Stratified random sample	The population is divided into mutually exclusive groups (such as age groups), and random samples are drawn from each group.
	The population is divided into mutually exclusive groups (such as blocks), and the researcher draws a sample of the groups to interview.
Non-Probability Sample	
Convenience sample	The researcher selects the easiest population members from which to obtain information.
Judgment sample	The researcher uses his or her judgment to select population members who are good prospects for accurate information.
	The researcher finds and interviews a prescribed number of people in each of several categories.

TABLE 4-6   *A "Questionable Questionnaire"*

Suppose that a summer camp director had prepared the following questionnaire to use in interviewing the parents of prospective campers. How would you assess each question?

1. What is your income to the nearest hundred dollars?

    People don't usually know their income to the nearest hundred dollars nor do they want to reveal their income that closely. Moreover, a researcher should never open a questionnaire with such a personal question.

2. Are you a strong or a weak supporter of overnight summer camping for your children?

    What do "strong" and "weak" mean?

3. Do your children behave themselves well at a summer camp?

    Yes ( )   No ( )

    "Behave" is a relative term. Furthermore, are "yes" and "no" the best response options for this question? Besides, will people want to answer this? Why ask the question in the first place?

4. How many camps mailed literature to you last April? this April?

    Who can remember this?

5. What are the most salient and determinant attributes in your evaluation of summer camps?

    What are "salient" and "determinant" attributes? Don't use big words on me!

6. Do you think it is right to deprive your child of the opportunity to grow into a mature person through the experience of summer camping?

    A loaded question. Given the bias, how can any parent answer "yes"?

there are many ways to ask questions. Questionnaires must be developed carefully and tested before they can be used on a large scale. A carelessly prepared questionnaire usually contains several errors (see Table 4-6).

In preparing a questionnaire, the marketing researcher must first decide what questions to ask. Questionnaires frequently leave out questions that should be answered and include questions that cannot be answered, will not be answered, or need not be answered. Each question should be checked to see that it contributes to the research objectives.

The *form* of each question is also important. *Closed-end questions* include all the possible answers, and subjects make choices among them. Part A of Table 4-7 shows the most common forms of closed-end questions as they might appear in a survey of Canadian Airline's customers. *Open-end questions* allow respondents to answer in their own words. The most common forms are shown in Part B of Table 4-7. Open-end questions often reveal more than closed-end questions because respondents are not limited in their answers. Open-end questions are especially useful in exploratory research, when the researcher is trying to determine *what* people think but not measuring *how many* people think in a certain way. Closed-end questions, on the other hand, provide answers that are easier to interpret and tabulate.

Researchers should also use care in *wording* and *ordering* questions. They should use simple, direct, unbiased wording. Questions should be arranged in a logical order. The first question should create interest if possible, and difficult or personal questions should be asked last so that respondents do not become defensive.

Although questionnaires are the most common research instrument, *mechanical instruments* also are used. We discussed two mechanical instruments—people meters and supermarket scanners—earlier in the chapter. Another group of mechanical devices measures subjects' physical responses. For example, a galvanometer measures the strength of interest or emotions aroused by a subject's exposure to different stimuli, such as an ad or picture. The galvanometer detects the minute degree of sweating that accompanies emotional arousal. The tachistoscope flashes

TABLE 4-7 *Types of Questions*

A. CLOSED-END QUESTIONS

Name	Description	Example
Dichotomous	A question offering two answer choices.	"In arranging this trip, did you personally phone Canadian?" Yes ☐ No ☐
Multiple choice	A question offering three or more answer choices.	"With whom are you travelling on this flight?" No one ☐ Children only ☐ Spouse ☐ Business associates/friends/relatives ☐ Spouse and children ☐ An organized tour group ☐
Likert scale	A statement with which the respondent shows the amount of agreement or disagreement.	"Small airlines generally give better service than large ones." Strongly disagree 1 ☐ Disagree 2 ☐ Neither agree nor disagree 3 ☐ Agree 4 ☐ Strongly agree 5 ☐
Semantic differential	A scale is inscribed between two bipolar words, and the respondent selects the point that represents the direction and intensity of his or her feelings.	*Canadian Airlines* Large __X__ : ____ : ____ : ____ : ____ : ____ : Small Experienced ____ : ____ : ____ : ____ : __X__ : ____ : Inexperienced Modern ____ : ____ : ____ : __X__ : ____ : ____ : Old-fashioned
Importance scale	A scale that rates the importance of some attribute from "not at all important" to "extremely important."	"Airline food service to me is" Extremely important 1 ____ Very important 2 ____ Somewhat important 3 ____ Not very important 4 ____ Not at all important 5 ____
Rating scale	A scale that rates some attribute from "poor" to "excellent."	"Canadian's food service is" Excellent 1 ____ Very good 2 ____ Good 3 ____ Fair 4 ____ Poor 5 ____
Intention-to-buy scale	A scale that describes the respondent's intentions to buy.	"If in-flight telephone service were available on a long flight, I would" Definitely buy 1 ____ Probably buy 2 ____ Not certain 3 ____ Probably not buy 4 ____ Definitely not buy 5 ____

B. OPEN-END QUESTIONS

Name	Description	Example
Completely unstructured	A question that respondents can answer in an almost unlimited number of ways.	"What is your opinion of Canadian Airlines?"
Word association	Words are presented, one at a time, and respondents mention the first word that comes to mind.	"What is the first word that comes to mind when you hear the following?" Airline _____ Canadian _____ Travel _____
Sentence completion	Incomplete sentences are presented, one at a time, and respondents complete the sentence.	"When I choose an airline, the most important consideration in my decision is _____
Story completion	An incomplete story is presented, and respondents are asked to complete it.	"I flew Canadian a few days ago. I noticed that the exterior and interior of the plane had very soft colours. This aroused in me the following thoughts and feelings." *Now complete the story.*
Picture completion	A picture of two characters is presented, with one making a statement. Respondents are asked to identify with the other and fill in the empty balloon.	Fill in the empty balloon.
Thematic Apperception Tests (TAT)	A picture is presented, and respondents are asked to make up a story about what they think is happening or may happen in the picture.	Make up a story about what you see.

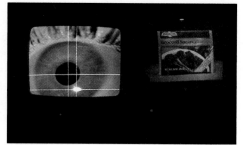

Mechanical research instruments: Eye cameras determine where eyes land and how long they linger on a given item.

an ad to a subject at an exposure range from less than one-hundredth of a second to several seconds. After each exposure, respondents describe everything they recall. Eye cameras are used to study respondents' eye movements to determine at what points their eyes focus first and how long they linger on a given item.[23]

Presenting the Research Plan

At this stage, the marketing researcher should summarize the plan in a *written proposal*. A written proposal is especially important when the research project is large and complex or when an outside firm carries it out. The proposal should cover the management problems addressed and the research objectives, the information to be obtained, the sources of secondary information or methods for collecting primary data, and the way the results will help management decision-making. The proposal also should include research costs. A written research plan or proposal assures that the marketing manager and researchers have considered all the important aspects of the research, and that they agree on why and how the research will be conducted.

IMPLEMENTING THE RESEARCH PLAN

The researcher next puts the marketing research plan into action. This involves collecting, processing, and analysing the information. Data collection can be carried out by the company's marketing research staff or by outside firms. The company keeps more control over the collection process and data quality by using its own staff. However, outside firms that specialize in data collection often can do the job more quickly and at lower cost.

The data-collection phase of the marketing research process is generally the most expensive and the most subject to error. The researcher should watch field-work closely to ensure that the plan is implemented correctly and to guard against problems with contacting respondents, with respondents who refuse to cooperate or who give biased or dishonest answers, and with interviewers who make mistakes or take shortcuts.

Researchers must process and analyse the collected data to isolate important information and findings. They need to check data from questionnaires for accuracy and completeness and code it for computer analysis. The researchers then tabulate the results and compute averages and other statistical measures.

INTERPRETING AND REPORTING THE FINDINGS

The researcher must now interpret the findings, draw conclusions, and report them to management. The researcher should not try to overwhelm managers with numbers and fancy statistical techniques. Rather, the researcher should present important findings that are useful in the major decisions faced by management.

Interpretation should not be left only to the researchers, however. They are often experts in research design and statistics, but the marketing manager knows more about the problem and the decisions that must be made. In many cases, findings can be interpreted in different ways, and discussions between researchers and managers will help identify the best interpretations. The manager will also want to check that the research project was conducted properly and that all the necessary analysis was completed. Or, after seeing the findings, the manager may have additional questions that can be answered through further sifting of the data. Finally, the manager is the one who ultimately must decide what action the research suggests. The researchers may even make the data directly available to marketing managers so that they can perform new analyses and test new relationships on their own.

Interpretation is an important phase of the marketing process. The best research is meaningless if the manager blindly accepts wrong interpretations from the researcher. Similarly, managers may have biased interpretations—they tend to accept research results that show what they expected and to reject those that they did not expect or hope for. Thus, managers and researchers must work closely when interpreting research results, and both must share responsibility for the research process and resulting decisions.[24]

OTHER MARKETING RESEARCH CONSIDERATIONS

This section discusses marketing research in two special contexts: marketing research by small businesses and non-profit organizations, and international marketing research. Finally, we look at public-policy and ethical issues in marketing research.

Marketing Research in Small Businesses and Non-Profit Organizations

Managers of small businesses and non-profit organizations often believe that marketing research can be done only by experts in large companies with big research budgets. But many of the marketing research techniques discussed in this chapter also can be used by smaller organizations in a less formal manner and at little or no expense.

Managers of small businesses and non-profit organizations can obtain good marketing information simply by *observing* things around them. For example, retailers can evaluate new locations by observing vehicle and pedestrian traffic. They can visit competing stores to check on facilities and prices. They can evaluate their customer mix by recording how many and what kinds of customers shop in the store at different times. Competitor advertising can be monitored by collecting advertisements from local media.

Managers can conduct informal *surveys* using small convenience samples. The director of an art museum can learn what patrons think about new exhibits by conducting informal "focus groups"—inviting small groups to lunch and having discussions on topics of interest. Retail salespeople can talk with customers visiting the store; hospital officials can interview patients. Restaurant managers might make random phone calls during slack hours to interview consumers about where they eat out and what they think of various restaurants in the area.

Managers also can conduct their own simple *experiments*. For example, by changing the themes in regular fund-raising mailings and watching the results, a non-profit manager can determine much about which marketing strategies work best. By varying newspaper advertisements, a store manager can learn the effects of things such as ad size and position, price coupons, and media used.

Small organizations can obtain most of the secondary data available to large businesses. In addition, many associations, local media, chambers of commerce,

J.J. Lee,
Assistant Product Manager, H.J. Heinz Company of Canada

Valerie Bell,
Group Marketing Manager, H.J. Heinz Company of Canada

J.J. Lee has only been with Heinz Canada a few months and is very excited to be working there full-time. While taking her undergraduate degree, she spent a work term with the company and gained a lot of knowledge in the product marketing field. The firm's strategic and analytical approach to marketing was very attractive to J.J., as well its history of contributing to the well-being of communities through its fundraising efforts and cause-related marketing programs. What is even more exciting is that now she is in charge of administering the cause-related marketing program between Heinz baby foods and the Children's Miracle Network (CMN). CMN is a nonprofit organization whose mission is to generate funds and awareness programs to benefit hospitalized children served by CMN associated children's hospitals and foundations. Thirteen children's hospitals are associated with CMN Canada.

At the centre of its "Save Labels, Save Lives" program is the company's promise to donate 10 cents for each Heinz baby food label or infant cereal boxtop returned by parents to their local CMN Hospital Foundation. Heinz Canada promotes the partnership extensively on their packaging, in their direct mail program, with posters and shelf talkers as well as through its web site (www.heinzbaby.com) and toll-free number. In 1997 alone, some 200 000 parents sent back three million labels. The program has run for six years and as the label on the Heinz Infant Cereal box proudly proclaims, "With the help of thousands of parents like you, we've donated over $1 000 000 to date." Each year, Heinz Canada presents a cheque to CMN during their North American-wide broadcast.

Administering the program is a rewarding but complex task. "Save Labels, Save Lives" has many facets other than the label-redemption por-

tion. J.J. must co-ordinate everything from point-of-sale materials, to determining the number of baby food labels returned by parents. She has also been involved in co-branding efforts between Heinz and LEGO, which helped to raise money for CMN's members. She has overseen the design and distribution of promotional products that were a runaway success such as the lullaby compact

J.J. Lee

disc that successfully raised awareness for the CMN program. She agonized over national radio contests that weren't as successful as anticipated. Having the main responsibility for this program within the baby food brand group certainly is challenging!

J.J. works for Valerie Bell, who has strong experience working in the packaged goods industry. Both Valerie and J.J. believe very strongly in their cause-related marketing efforts. Valerie stresses, "As a leading Canadian food processor, we will continue to invest in our people, our products and our communities." The program requires careful planning. J.J. and Valerie must carefully forecast how successful the program will be so that they can include the amount to be donated in their brand budget.

The "Save Labels, Save Lives" program is a natural extension of Heinz Canada's long-term commitment to funding medical research. Since children's hospitals and Heinz baby foods serve common target audiences, the program represents an excellent fit for all partners. It helps to positively position the brand and everyone, from the sales force to top management of the company, recognizes its strategic benefits. By helping motivate them to make the extra effort, it's a genuine morale booster for Heinz Canada employees. Consumers feel sending in labels to children's hospitals to raise funds really adds value to the products.

Heinz Canada carefully measures results to determine that the program is a true loyalty-builder among people in their target audience. Valerie and J.J. conduct ongoing research to determine whether it is a strong motivator of purchase among their target audience. They also use the bar codes on the coupons to carefully track the number of coupons and regional origins of all redeemed.

Repeatedly, Heinz research has demonstrated that if two baby foods had the same nutritional value, the association between Heinz and CMN would lead parents to purchase the Heinz product. A carefully planned, executed, researched and evaluated cause-related marketing program can be a powerful marketplace force, Valerie and J.J. believe. Moreover, it makes them feel good about themselves and their jobs. They market top-quality products while also helping Canadian children's hospitals and foundations. No wonder they come to work each morning with a smile on their faces.

Source: www.heinzbaby.com

and government agencies provide special help to small organizations. The Conference Board of Canada, federal government, and provincial governments offer dozens of free publications that give advice on topics ranging from planning advertising to ordering business signs. Local newspapers often provide information on local shoppers and their buying patterns. Many business schools will conduct marketing research for no charge as part of class projects.

In summary, secondary data collection, observation, surveys, and experiments can all be used effectively by small organizations with small budgets. Although these informal research methods are less complex and less costly, they still must be conducted carefully. Managers must think carefully about the objectives of the research, formulate questions in advance, recognize the biases introduced by smaller samples and less skilled researchers, and conduct the research systematically.

International Marketing Research

The need for information about international markets is growing as increasing numbers of companies operate on a multinational basis. Firms such as Angus Reid have begun to respond to this need. Annually, the company collects information on corporate and brand images, product usage and awareness, and values attitudes from 25 000 consumers living in 50 countries. A.C. Nielsen, the world's largest marketing research firm, has offices in more than 90 countries. "Assessment of global advertising campaigns, new product introductions, and customer satisfaction levels are key areas of concern."[25]

To meet their clients' needs, many Canadian research firms are forming partnerships and alliances with research firms throughout the world. Such partnerships allow Canadian firms to gather information in numerous markets since their partners speak the language and are familiar with the nuances of the local culture. It helps them to understand the sources of *secondary data* for that particular market and assess the reliability of that data. Millward Brown's Canadian unit, for example, achieved a global profile after conducting a 36-country brand development study for Levi Strauss. As Michael Adams, president of Toronto-based Environics, noted, "Multinational companies don't care if you're from Hamburg, Chicago or Toronto—they just want you to be able to deliver the goods."[26]

International marketing research can pose some unique challenges. For example, they may find it difficult simply to develop good samples. North American

Customs in some countries prohibit people from talking with strangers—a researcher simply may not be allowed to speak with people about brand attitudes or buying behavior.

researchers can use current telephone directories, census tract data, and several other sources of socioeconomic data to construct samples. However, such information is largely lacking in many countries.

Once the sample is drawn, the North American researcher usually can reach most respondents easily by telephone, by mail, or in person. Reaching respondents is often not as easy in other parts of the world. Researchers in Mexico cannot rely on telephone and mail data collection—most data collection is conducted door-to-door and concentrated in three or four of the largest cities. And most surveys in Mexico bypass the large segment of the population where native tribes speak languages other than Spanish. In some countries, few people have phones—there are only four phones per 1000 people in Egypt, six per 1000 in Turkey, and 32 per 1000 in Argentina. In other countries, the postal system is notoriously unreliable. In Brazil, for instance, an estimated 30 percent of the mail is never delivered. In many developing countries, poor roads and transportation systems make certain areas hard to reach, making personal interviews difficult and expensive.[27]

Differences in cultures from country to country cause additional problems for international researchers. Language is the most obvious culprit. For example, questionnaires must be prepared in one language and then translated into the languages of each country researched. Responses then must be translated back into the original language for analysis and interpretation. This adds to research costs and increases the risks of error.

Translating a questionnaire from one language to another is anything but easy. Many idioms, phrases, and statements mean different things in different cultures. For example, a Danish executive noted: "Check this out by having a different translator put back into English what you've translated from English. You'll get the shock of your life. I remember [an example in which] 'out of sight, out of mind' had become 'invisible things are insane.'"[28]

Buying roles and consumer decision processes vary greatly among countries, further complicating international marketing research. Consumers in different countries also vary in their attitudes toward marketing research. People in one country may be very willing to respond; in other countries, non-response can be a major problem. For example, customs in some Islamic countries prohibit people from talking with strangers—a researcher simply may not be allowed to speak by phone with women about brand attitudes or buying behaviour. In certain cultures, research questions often are considered too personal. For example, in many Latin American countries, people may feel embarrassed to talk with researchers about their choices of shampoo, deodorant, or other personal care products. Finally, even when respondents are *willing* to respond, they may not be *able* to because of high functional illiteracy rates.

Some of the insights and problems that arise when international marketing research is conducted and interpreted is evident when we examine American researchers' findings about Canadian consumers. The North American Free Trade Agreement has given many American firms the incentive to learn more about Canadians. Consider the validity of a recent study, conducted by the *Yankelovich Monitor*, designed to clarify the differences between American and Canadian consumers' responses to advertising.

The *Monitor* study suggests that Canadians are less homogeneous than Americans, less concerned with social conformity, and more open to pluralism. This pluralism has resulted in a lower sense of nationalism that Canadian consumers do not respond to national symbols the way Americans do. For example, the study concludes that a campaign like Chevrolet's "Heartbeat of America," would embarrass Canadians. The study suggests that Canadians are less imaginative than Americans, and have less respect for age, experience, and government. The *Monitor* study also suggests that Canadians are rational consumers who are less susceptible to emotional, image-driven advertising appeals than their American counterparts.

MARKETING HIGHLIGHT 4 - 5

PUBLIC POLICY AND ETHICS IN MARKETING RESEARCH

Most marketing research benefits both the sponsoring company and its consumers. Through marketing research, companies learn more about consumers' needs, resulting in more satisfying products and services. However, the misuse of marketing research can also harm or annoy consumers. Two major public-policy and ethics issues in marketing research are intrusions on consumer privacy and the misuse of research findings.

Intrusions on Consumer Privacy

In a report released in August 1994, the Privacy Commissioner of Canada warned about the threat to privacy presented by the use of interactive computer technology and the ability of firms to merge databases from different businesses to cross-promote products and services. Certain industries have presented special concerns. For example, while banks need to gather highly personal information to avoid credit risks and manage customers' financial assets, will this information also be used for marketing purposes?

Privacy advocates are demanding that the international Organization for Economic Co-operation and Development (OECD) rules and guidelines be followed. These rules state that customers must consent to information-gathering efforts, be informed about how their personal information will be used, and have the right to refuse to allow personal information to be used for marketing purposes. Concerns about privacy have given rise to demands for government legislation to provide Canadians with legal protection from the data-gathering efforts of businesses. Research organizations are starting to support these demands. Whereas the Canadian Direct Marketing Association long favoured self-regulation as the means to ensure ethical research and direct marketing, it has now turned to government to establish a set of basic standards: the newly formed Internet Advertising and Marketing Bureau of Canada (IAMBC) will scrutinize the practices of Internet marketers.

A 1996 study conducted by the Canadian Survey Research Council found that 73 percent of Canadians liked being surveyed. Most consumers feel positively about marketing research and believe that it serves a useful purpose. However, others strongly resent or even mistrust marketing research. A few consumers fear that researchers might use their findings to manipulate our buying. Others may have been taken in by previous "research surveys" that actually turned out to be attempts to sell them something. Most, however, simply resent the intrusion. They dislike mail or telephone surveys that are too long or too personal, or that interrupt them at inconvenient times.

Increasing consumer resentment has become a major problem for the research industry, leading to lower survey response rates in recent years. The research industry is considering several possible responses. One is to expand its "Your Opinion Counts" program to educate consumers about the benefits of marketing research and to distinguish it from telephone selling and database building. Another is to provide a toll-free number that people can call to verify that a survey is legitimate. The industry also has considered adopting broad standards, perhaps based on Europe's International Code of Marketing and Social Research Practice. This code outlines researchers' responsibilities to respondents and to the general public. For example, it says that researchers should make their names and addresses available to participants, and it bans companies from representing activities such as database compilation or sales and promotional pitches as research.

Misuse of Research Findings

Research studies can be powerful persuasion tools—companies often use study results as claims in their advertising and promotion. Today, however, many research studies appear to be little more than vehicles for pitching the sponsor's products. Few advertisers openly rig their research designs or blatantly misrepresent the findings—most abuses tend to be subtle "stretches." Consider the following examples:

A study by Chrysler contends that Americans overwhelmingly prefer Chrysler to Toyota after test driving both. However, the study included just 100 people in each of two tests. More importantly, none of the people surveyed owned a foreign car, so they appear to be favorably predisposed to U.S. cars.

A poll sponsored by the disposable diaper industry asked: "It is estimated that disposable diapers account for less than two percent of the garbage in today's landfills. In contrast, beverage containers, third-class mail, and yard waste are estimated to account for about 21 percent of the garbage in landfills. Given this, in your opinion, would it be fair to ban disposable diapers?" Not surprisingly, 84 percent said no.

Thus, subtle manipulations of the study's sample, or the choice or wording of questions, can greatly affect the conclusions reached. In other cases, so-called independent research studies actually are paid for by companies with an interest in the outcome.

Recognizing that surveys can be abused, several associations—including the Professional Marketing Research Society of Canada and the American Marketing Association—have developed codes of research ethics and standards of conduct. In the end, however, unethical or inappropriate actions cannot simply be regulated away. Each company must accept responsibility for policing the conduct and reporting of its own marketing research to protect consumers' best interests and its own.

Sources: Excerpts from Cynthia Crossen, "Studies Galore Support Products and Positions, But Are They Reliable?" *Wall Street Journal,* November 14, 1991, pp. A1, A9. Also see Betsy Spethmann, "Cautious Consumers Have Surveyers Wary," *Advertising Age,* June 10, 1991, p. 34; "MRA Study Shows Refusal Rates Are Highest at Start of Process," *Marketing News,* August 16, 1993, p. A15; Deborah McKay-Stokes, "Too Close for Comfort," *Marketing,* September 18, 1995, p. 11; James Pollock, "Information Overload," *Marketing,* October 16, 1995, pp. 12-13; Mariam Mesbah, "Special Report: Research: Internet Research Holds Potential," *Strategy: The Canadian Marketing Report*, April 14, 1997, p. 40; David Chilton, "Canadians Don't Mind Being Surveyed," *Strategy: The Canadian Marketing Report*, April 1, 1996, p. 5.

Canadians, the study notes, are practical and down to earth. They want advertising that tells them straightforward information such as, "How much does it cost?" "What will it do for me?" and "What steps do I take to buy it or use it?" Furthermore, Canadians are less materialistic than Americans, less concerned with physical enhancement, but more concerned about the environment. Canadians are sometimes paradoxes. While they hanker for the outdoors, they are also more hedonistic than their counterparts south of the border. The study concludes, "I can see a typical Canadian tramping through the bush eating Haagen-Dazs ice cream!"[29]

Public Policy and Ethics in Marketing Research

When properly used, marketing research benefits both the sponsoring company and its customers. It helps the company to make better marketing decisions, which in turn results in products and services that better meet the needs of consumers. However, when misused, marketing research also can abuse and annoy consumers. Marketing Highlight 4-5 summarizes the major public-policy and ethics issues surrounding marketing research.

Summary of Chapter Objectives

In today's complex and rapidly changing environment, marketing managers need more and better information to make effective and timely decisions. Fortunately, this greater need for information has been matched by the explosion of information technologies for supplying information. Using new technologies such as small but powerful computers, videoconferencing, the Internet, and a host of other advances, companies can now handle great quantities of information—sometimes even too much. Yet marketers often complain that they lack enough of the *right* kind of information or have an excess of the *wrong* kind. In response, many companies are now studying their managers' information needs and designing information systems to satisfy those needs.

1. **Explain the importance of information to the company.**

   Good products and marketing programs start with a thorough understanding of consumer needs and wants. Thus, the company needs sound information to produce superior value and satisfaction for customers. The company also requires information on competitors, resellers, and other actors and forces in the marketplace.

2. **Define the marketing information system and discuss its parts.**

   The *marketing information system* (MIS) consists of people, equipment, and procedures to gather, sort, analyse, evaluate, and distribute needed, timely, and accurate information to marketing decision-makers. A

well-designed information system begins and ends with the user. The MIS first *assesses information needs* by interviewing marketing managers and surveying their decision environment to determine what information is desired, needed, and feasible to obtain. Next, the MIS *develops information* from internal databases, marketing intelligence activities, and marketing research. *Internal databases* provide information on the company's own sales, costs, inventories, cash flows, and accounts receivable and payable. Such data can be obtained quickly and cheaply but often need to be adapted for marketing decisions. *Marketing intelligence* activities supply marketing executives with everyday information about developments in the external marketing environment. Intelligence can be collected from company employees, customer, suppliers, and resellers, or by monitoring published reports, conferences, advertisements, competitor actions, and other activities in the environment. *Market research* consists of collecting information relevant to a specific marketing problem faced by the company. Finally, the MIS *distributes information* gathered from these many sources to the right managers in the right form and at the right time to help them make better marketing decisions.

3. **Outline the four steps in the marketing research process.**

   The first step in the marketing research process involves *defining the problem and setting the research objectives*, which may be exploratory, descriptive, or causal. The second step consists of *developing a research plan* for collecting data from primary and secondary sources. Secondary data collection involves tapping the company's internal database plus a wide range of external information sources, including libraries, commercial data services, online database services, Internet data sources, and government and business publications. Primary data collection involves choosing a research approach (observation, survey, experiment); selecting a contact method (mail, telephone, personal, computer, the Internet); designing a sampling plan (whom to survey, how many to survey, and how to choose them); and developing research instruments (questionnaire, mechanical). The third step calls for *implementing the marketing research plan* by gathering, processing, and analysing the information. The four step consists of *interpreting and reporting the findings*. Additional information analysis helps marketing managers apply the information and provides them with sophisticated statistical procedures and models from which to develop more rigorous findings.

4. **Compare the advantages and disadvantages of various methods of collecting information.**

   Both *internal* and *external* secondary data sources often provide information more quickly and at a lower cost than primary data sources, and they can sometimes yield information that a company cannot collect by itself. However, needed data might not exist in secondary sources, and even if information can be found, it might be largely unusable. Researchers must also evaluate secondary information to ensure that it is *relevant, accurate, current*, and *impartial*. Primary research must also be evaluated for relevancy, accuracy, currency, and impartiality. Each primary data collection method has

its own advantages and disadvantages. *Observational research* can obtain information that people are unwilling or unable to provide, yet some things cannot be observed. *Survey research* is flexible and well suited for collecting *descriptive information*, but people may respond incorrectly or not at all for various reasons. *Experimental research* is best suited for collecting *causal* information but may be complex and difficult to control. Each of the various primary research contact methods—mail, telephone, personal interviews, or computer—also has its own advantages and drawbacks. For example, *mail questionnaires* can be used to collect large amounts of information cheaply but tend to be inflexible, take long to complete, have a very low response rate, and permit little control over the sample. *Focus-group interviewing* has become one of the major marketing research tools for gaining insight into consumer thoughts and feelings. However, the use of small samples may make it difficult to generalize from focus-group results. Similarly, each contact method has its advantages and disadvantages.

5. **Discuss the special issues some market researchers face, including public policy and ethics issues.**

   Some marketers face special marketing research situations, such as those conducting research in small-business, non-profit, or international situations. Marketing research can be conducted effectively by small businesses and non-profit organizations with limited budgets. International marketing researchers follow the same steps as domestic researchers but often face more and different problems. All organizations need to respond responsibly to major public policy and ethical issues surrounding marketing research, including issues of intrusions on consumer privacy and misuse of research findings.

Key Terms

Causal research *(p. 122)*

Descriptive research *(p. 122)*

Experimental research *(p. 130)*

Exploratory research *(p. 122)*

Focus-group interviewing *(p. 131)*

Internal databases *(p. 116)*

Marketing information system (MIS) *(p. 114)*

Marketing intelligence *(p. 117)*

Marketing research *(p. 120)*

Observational research *(p. 127)*

Online databass *(p. 126)*

Primary data *(p. 124)*   Single-source data systems *(p. 128)*   Survey research *(p. 130)*
Secondary data *(p. 124)*

Discussing the Issues

1. You are a research supplier, designing and conducting studies for a variety of companies. Explain the *most* important thing you can do to ensure that your clients will get their money's worth from your services.

2. Companies often test new products in plain white packages with no brand name or other marketing information. Discuss what this "blind" testing really measures. Are there any issues in applying these results to the "real" world?

3. Companies often face quickly changing environments. Analyse whether market research information can "go stale." What issues does a manager face in using these research results?

4. Design a research program that would be appropriate in the following situations, and explain why:
   a. Kellogg wants to investigate the impact of young children on their parents' decisions to buy breakfast foods.
   b. Your university bookstore wants to get some insights into how students feel about the store's merchandise, prices, and service.
   c. Swiss Chalet is considering where to locate a new outlet in a fast-growing suburb.
   d. Gillette wants to determine whether a new line of deodorant for children will be profitable.

5. Focus-group interviewing is both a widely used and widely criticized research technique in marketing. List the advantages and disadvantages of focus groups. Suggest some kinds of questions that are suitable for exploration by using focus groups.

6. You have just finished a marketing research project for Bell Canada. You tested different target segments' attitudes toward Bell's soon-to-be-launched advertising campaign. This morning you received a "Call for Research Proposals" from Sprint Canada. You are wondering how much of the knowledge you gained while doing the Bell study can be applied to the proposal for the new project. What would you recommend to the research director?

Applying the Concepts

1. "Blind" taste tests often have surprising results. Demonstrate this by conducting a product test in your classroom.
   - Purchase three comparable brands of pop such as Coca-Cola, Pepsi, and a regional favourite or store brand. Also buy three small paper cups for each student. Remove *all* identification from the bottles including labels and caps, and use paper to cover any differences in bottle design. Label the brands with neutral terms such as Brand G, Brand H, and Brand I. Pour a small sample of each into labelled cups and distribute them.
   - Ask questions and tabulate the answers: (a) What brand do you normally prefer? (b) Which sample do you prefer? (c) What brand do you think each sample is?
   - Write students' preferences on the board, then reveal which brand was which sample. Are the results what you had expected? Why or why not?

2. Run a small focus group in class to learn about the pros and cons of focus-group research.
   - Choose one class member as a moderator, and select six to eight other volunteers. Try to include at least one strong

personality and one shy member. Organize them in a circle at the front of the class.

♦ Discuss a modestly controversial issue that is of current interest to the class. Avoid issues that are very controversial or emotional. Run the group for 10 to 15 minutes.

♦ Discuss the focus group "results" with the class. Were the conclusions fair or biased? What did class members find useful about the technique, and what problems did they see?

References

1. David Menzies, "Molson Muscle," *Marketing*, August 21/28, 1997, p. 11.

2. David Menzies, "Molson Muscle," p. 11.

3. Kyle Stone, "Promotion Commotion," *Report on Business Magazine*, December 1997, p. 106.

4. Peter Boisseau, "The Suds Stud," *Canadian Business*, July 1997, p. 41.

5. Peter Boisseau, "The Suds Stud," p. 41.

6. Information on Molson and Labatt was found on their respective World Wide Web pages and in the following articles: *Beer*, Vol. 2(1), p. 5; Peter Boisseau, "The Suds Stud," *Canadian Business*, July 1997, pp. 37–43; Douglas Faulker, "Powell's Big Picture," *Marketing*, November 20, 1995, pp. 12–13; Louise Gagnon, "Aging Canadians Are Drinking Less Beer," *Marketing*, July 21, 1997, p. 4; Holly Longdale, "Molson Goes Online with "I Am" Web Site," *Strategy: The Canadian Marketing Report*, July 24, 1995, p. 8; David Menzies, "Molson Muscle," *Marketing*, August 21/28, 1997, pp. 11–13; Laura Mills, "Molson Attack Ad Leaves Labatt Unmoved," *Marketing*, August 28, 1997, p. 3; Laura Mills, "Breweries Summer Price War Ends in Tie," *Marketing*, September 29, 1997, p. 2; James Pollock, "Labatt Stronger After Buyout by Interbrew," *Marketing*, June 19, 1995, p. 3; Deborah McKay-Stokes, "Too Close for Comfort," *Digital Marketing*, a special feature of *Marketing*, September 18, 1996, pp. 11–12; Kyle Stone, "Promotion Commotion," *Report on Business Magazine*, December 1997, p. 106; Pattie Summerfield, "Molson Diamond Answers Desire for Full Taste, Lower Alcohol," *Strategy: The Canadian Marketing Report*, November 24, 1997, p. 6; and the direct mailings from the Labatt MVP program including *Beer* magazine (Labatt, Markham, Ontario), its merchandising offers, contests, and the surveys that accompanied it.

7. "Harnessing the Data Explosion," *Sales & Marketing Management*, January 1987, p. 31; and Joseph M. Winski, "Gentle Rain Turns Into Torrent," *Advertising Age*, June 3, 1991, p. 34.

8. John Neisbitt, *Megatrends: Ten New Directions Transforming Our Lives* (New York: Warner Books, 1984), p. 16. Also see Rick Tetzeli, "Surviving the Information Overload," *Fortune*, July 11, 1994, pp. 60–64.

9. See Jeffrey Rotfeder and Jim Bartimo, "How Software Is Making Food Sales a Piece of Cake," *Business Week*, July 2, 1990, pp. 54–55; and Terence P. Paré, "How to Find Out What They Want," *Fortune*, special issue on "The Tough New Consumer," Autumn/Winter 1993, pp. 39–41.

10. James Pollock, "Information Overload," *Marketing*, October 16, 1995, p. 12.

11. *Donnelly Demographics*.

12. For more on collecting competitive intelligence, see Gary B. Roush, "A Program for Sharing Corporate Intelligence," *Journal of Business Strategy*, January–February 1991, pp. 4–7; Sunil Babbar and Arun Rai, "Competitive Intelligence for International Business," *Long Range Planning*, June 1993, pp. 103–113; Benjamin Gilda, George Gordon, and Ephraim Sudit, "Identifying Gaps and Blind Spots in Competitive Intelligence," *Long Range Planning*, December 1993, pp. 107–113; and Shaker A. Zahra, "Unethical Practices in Competitive Analysis: Patterns, Causes and Effects," *Journal of Business Ethics*, 13, 1994, pp. 53–62.

13. Lesley Daw, "Success Insurance," *Marketing*, June 30, 1997, pp. 21–22.

14. "Researching Researchers," *Marketing Tools*, September 1996, pp. 35–36.

15. See Christel Beard and Betsy Wiesendanger, "The Marketer's Guide to Online Databases," *Sales & Marketing Management*, January 1993, pp. 36–41; and Susan Greco, "The Online Sleuth," *Inc.*, October 1996, pp. 88–89.

16. Justin Martin, "Ignore Your Customer," *Fortune*, May 1, 1995, pp. 121–126.

17. *Ibid.*, p. 126.

18. Rebecca Piirto Heather, "Future Focus Groups," *American Demographics*, January 1994, p. 6. Also see Norton Paley, "Getting in Focus," *Sales & Marketing Management*, March 1995, pp. 92–94; and Leslie M. Harris, "Technology, Techniques Drive Focus Group Trends," *Marketing News*, February 27, 1995, p. 8.

19. Janet McFarland, "YOUtv Captures Customer Feedback," *Globe and Mail*, November 19, 1996, p. B15.

20. Lesley Daw, "Customer Polling Takes to the Net," *Marketing*, January 27, 1997, p. 3.

21. Gail El Baroudi, "Bank Survey Is a Hit," *Globe and Mail*, October 7, 1997, p. C5.

22. Diane Crispell, "People Talk, Computers Listen," *American Demographics*, October 1989, p. 8; and Peter

J. DePaulo and Rick Weitzer, "Interactive Phones Technology Delivers Survey Data Quickly," *Marketing News,* June 6, 1994, pp. 33–34.

23. For more on mechanical measures, see Michael J. McCarthy, "Mind Probe," *Wall Street Journal,* March 22, 1991, p. B3.

24. For a discussion of the importance of the relationship between market researchers and research users, see Christine Moorman, Gerald Zaltman, and Rohit Deshpande, "Relationships Between Providers and Users of Market Research: The Dynamics of Trust Within and Between Organizations," *Journal of Marketing Research,* August 1992, pp. 314–328; Christine Moorman, Rohit Deshpande, and Gerald Zaltman, "Factors Affecting Trust in Market Research Relationships," *Journal of Marketing,* January 1993, pp. 81–101; and Arlene Farber Sirkin, "Maximizing the Client–Researcher Partnership," *Marketing News,* September 13, 1994, p. 38.

25. David Bosworth, "Special Report: Research: Canadian Market Research Going Global," *Strategy: The Canadian Marketing Report,* September 1, 1997, p. 27.

26. Bosworth, *Strategy, The Canadian Marketing Report,* p. 27.

27. Many of the examples in this section, along with others, are found in Subhash C. Jain, *International Marketing Management,* 3rd ed. (Boston: PWS-Kent Publishing Company, 1990), pp. 334–339. Also see Vern Terpstra and Ravi Sarathy, *International Marketing* (Chicago: The Dryden Press, 1991), pp. 208–213; and Jack Honomichl, "Research Cultures Are Different in Mexico, Canada," *Marketing News,* May 5, 1993, pp. 12–13.

28. Jain, *International Marketing Management,* p. 338.

29. Denis Bruce, "So What's the Difference, Eh?" *Marketing,* September 26, 1994, pp. 16-19.

Company Case 4

ENTERPRISE RENT-A-CAR: MEASURING SERVICE QUALITY

Kevin Kirkman wheeled his shiny, blue BMW coupe into his driveway, parked the car, and stepped out to check his mailbox as he did every day when he arrived home. As he flipped all the catalogues and credit-card offers, he noticed a letter from Enterprise Rent-A-Car.

THE WRECK

He wondered why Enterprise would be writing to him. Then he remembered that earlier that month, he'd been involved in a car accident. As he was driving to work one rainy morning, another car had been unable to stop on the slick pavement and had ploughed into his car as he waited at a stoplight. Thankfully, neither Kevin nor the other driver had been hurt, but both cars had sustained considerable damage. In fact, Kevin had been unable to drive his car.

Kevin had used his cellular phone to call the police; and while he waited for the officers to arrive at the accident scene, he had called his auto insurance agent. The agent had assured Kevin that his policy included coverage to pay for a rental car while he was having his car repaired. He had advised Kevin to have the car towed to a nearby auto repair shop and had given him the telephone number for the Enterprise Rent-A-Car office that served his area. The agent had noted that his company recommended using Enterprise for replacement rentals and that Kevin's policy would cover up to $25 per day of the rental fee.

Once Kevin had checked his car in at the body shop and made the necessary arrangements, he had called the Enterprise office. Within 10 minutes, an Enterprise employee had driven to the repair shop to pick him up. They had returned to the Enterprise office where Kevin had completed the paperwork to rent a Chevy Lumina. He had driven the rental car for 12 days before the repair shop had completed work on his car.

"Don't know why Enterprise would be writing me now," Kevin thought. "The insurance company paid the $25 per day, and I paid the extra because the Lumina cost a little more than that. Wonder what the problem could be?"

TRACKING CUSTOMER SATISFACTION

Once Kevin opened the envelope, he discovered that it contained a survey to determine how satisfied he was with his rental experience. The survey was accompanied by a cover letter that thanked him for using Enterprise and asked him to complete the survey so that the company could continue to improve its service. The survey itself was just one page with 13 questions (see Exhibit 1).

Enterprise executives believe that the company has become the largest rent-a-car company in the North America (in terms of revenue, number of cars in service, and number of rental locations) because of its laser-like focus on customer satisfaction, and because of its concentration on serving the home-city replacement market.

Enterprise aims to serve customers such as Kevin, who are involved in car accidents and who suddenly find themselves without a car. While the more well-known companies such as Hertz and Avis battled for business in the cut-throat airport market, Enterprise quietly built its business by cultivating insurance agents and body-shop managers as referral agents, so that when one of their clients or customers needed a replacement vehicle, the agents would recommend Enterprise. Although such replacement rentals account for about 80 percent of Enterprise's business, the company also serves the discretionary market (leisure/vacation rentals) and business market (renting cars to businesses for their short-term needs).

Throughout its history, Enterprise has followed the advice of its founder, Jack Taylor. Taylor believed that if the company took care of its customers first and its employees second, profits would follow. As a result, the company tracks customer satisfaction carefully.

About one in 20 customers will receive a letter like Kevin's. The letters are mailed to customers selected at random about seven days following completion of a rental. On average, about 30 percent of the surveyed customers will return the completed survey in the enclosed postage-paid envelope. They mail the surveys to an outside service firm, which compiles the results and provides the company with monthly reports that employees in the branches can use to review their performance.

CONTINUOUS IMPROVEMENT

Enterprise has been using the survey form for several years. However, its managers wonder how they could improve the survey. Should the survey ask additional questions? How could the company improve the response rate? Is the mail questionnaire the best way to collect customer satisfaction data? Are there any sampling issues or response biases in its system?

Kevin glanced through his living-room window at his BMW sitting in the driveway. "That's amazing," he thought, "you could never tell it had been in a wreck. The repair shop did a great job, and I'm satisfied with Enterprise also. Guess I should complete this survey to let the company know."

QUESTIONS

1. Analyse Enterprise's Service Quality Survey (Exhibit 1). What information is it trying to gather? What are its research objectives?

2. What decisions has Enterprise made with regard to primary data collection—research approach, contact methods, sampling plan, and research instruments?

3. In addition to or instead of the mail survey, what other means could Enterprise use to gather customer satisfaction and other information about its customers and competitors?

4. What recommendations would you make to Enterprise with respect to its survey process and data-collection strategy?

Source: Officials at Enterprise Rent-A-Car contributed to and supported development of this case.

EXHIBIT 4-1   *Service Quality Survey*

Please mark the box that best reflects your response to each question.

	Completely Satisfied	Somewhat Satisfied	Neither Satisfied Nor Dissatisfied	Somewhat Dissatisfied	Completely Dissatisfied
1. Overall, how satisfied were you with your recent car rental from Enterprise on January 1, 1997?	☐	☐	☐	☐	☐

2. What, if anything, could Enterprise have done better? *(Please be specific)* _____

_____

3a. Did you experience any problems during the rental process?	Yes ☐ →	3b. If you mentioned any problems to Enterprize, did they resolve them to your satisfaction?	Yes ☐
	No ☐		No ☐
			Did not mention ☐

	Excellent	Good	Fair	Poor	N/A
4. If you personally called Enterprise to reserve a vehicle, how would you rate the telephone reservation process?	☐	☐	☐	☐	☐

	Both at start and at end of rental	Just at start of rental	Just at end of rental	Neither time
5. Did you go to the Enterprise office...	☐	☐	☐	☐
6. Did an Enterprise employee give you a ride to help with your transportation needs...	☐	☐	☐	☐

7. After you arrived at the Enterprise office, how long did it take to:	Less Than 5 Minutes	5-10 Minutes	11-15 Minutes	16-20 Minutes	21-30 Minutes	More than 30 Minutes	N/A
◆ pick up your rental car?	☐	☐	☐	☐	☐	☐	☐
◆ return your rental car?	☐	☐	☐	☐	☐	☐	☐

8. How would you rate the...	Excellent	Good	Fair	Poor	N/A
◆ timeliness with which you were either picked up at the start of the rental or dropped off afterwards?	☐	☐	☐	☐	☐
◆ timeliness with which the rental car was either brought to your location and left with you or picked up from your location afterwards?	☐	☐	☐	☐	☐
◆ Enterprise employee who handled your paperwork...					
◆ at the START of the rental?	☐	☐	☐	☐	☐
◆ at the END of the rental?	☐	☐	☐	☐	☐
◆ mechanical condition of the car?	☐	☐	☐	☐	
◆ cleanliness of the car interior/exterior?	☐	☐	☐	☐	

	Yes	No	N/A
9. If you asked for a specific type or size of vehicle, was Enterprise able to meet your needs?	☐	☐	☐

	Car repairs due to accident	All other car repairs/ maintenance	Car was stolen	Business	Leisure/ Vacation	Some other reason
10. For what reason did you rent this car?	☐	☐	☐	☐	☐	☐

	Definitely will call	Probably will call	Might or might not call	Probably will not call	Definitely will not call
11. The next time you need to pick up a rental car in the city or area in which you live, how likely are you to call Enterprise?	☐	☐	☐	☐	☐

	Once - this was first time	2 times	3 - 5 times	6 - 10 times	11 or more times
12. Approximately how many times in total have you rented from Enterprise (including this rental)?	☐	☐	☐	☐	☐

	0 times	1 time	2 times	3 - 5 times	6 - 10 times	11 or more times
13. Considering all rental companies, approximately how many times within the past year have you rented a car in the city or area in which you live (including this rental)?	☐	☐	☐	☐	☐	☐

CBC 🍁 Video Case 4
TOUGH TO REACH

As the baby boomers become older and more settled in their ways, marketers are looking to the next generation to set the trends. For marketers, being the first to discover a new trend is critical. Being first allows them to enter the market before the competition and potentially capture a dominant share. In the 1980s Chrysler twice identified trends in the consumer market and took advantage of them. Early in the decade they introduced the minivan because they discovered families wanted a more versatile vehicle than the traditional station wagon. They followed this up by purchasing Jeep. This allowed Chrysler to take advantage of the growing market for sport utility vehicles.

Who will identify the trends of 1990s and how will they spot them? To date, the Generation-X market has proven to be a tough market for marketers to understand. In general, this market is very cynical when it comes to marketing and has therefore been tough to reach. Several marketing campaigns aimed at this group have failed because they were seen as insincere and heavy-handed. Interestingly, Chrysler's Neon campaign was one of the most successful in reaching this group because it was different and straightforward. One reason given for marketers not reaching this group is the campaigns are designed by someone in their mid-forties. A person from this generation does not understand the needs and behaviours of the Generation-X market.

Enter Toronto's Decode. Founded and run by a group of Toronto-based Generation-Xers, Decode seeks out the next trend and how best to reach this reach this market. Everything about the company is Generation X from the design and location of their office to the organizational structure.

Decode successfully reaches this market and is used by such large companies as Bell and Procter & Gamble to research the Generation X market.

QUESTIONS

1. Describe the different research methods Decode could use. Would you recommend one method over another? Why?
2. What types of information would Decode's clients be interested in collecting?
3. Why is Generation X so hard to reach?
4. What advantages does Decode enjoy over the competition?
5. Do you think market research will be more, or less, important to companies in the future? Why?

Source: This case was prepared by Robert Warren and is based on "Edge Marketing—Reaching Generation X," *Venture* (October 22, 1995).

Principles of
Marketing

Principles of
Marketing

inciples of
Market

ciples o
Mark

CHAPTER 5

CONSUMER MARKETS AND CONSUMER BUYER BEHAVIOUR

Few brands engender such intense loyalty as that found in the hearts of Harley-Davidson owners. "The Harley audience is granitelike," in its devotion, laments the vice president of sales for competitor Yamaha. As one quotation on their web site notes, "You don't see people tattooing Yamaha on their bodies." Each year, in early March, more than 400 000 Harley bikers rumble through the streets of Daytona Beach, Florida, to attend Harley-Davidson's Bike Week celebration. Bikers from across North America lounge on their low-slung Harleys, swap biker tales, and sport T-shirts proclaiming "I'd rather push a Harley than drive a Honda."

Riding such intense emotions, Harley-Davidson has rumbled its way to the top of the fast-growing heavyweight motorcycle market. Both the segment and Harley's sales are growing rapidly. In fact, for several consecutive years, sales have far outstripped supply, with customer waiting lists of up to three years for popular models and street prices running well above suggested list prices. "We've seen people buy a new Harley and then sell it in the parking lot for $4000 to $5000 more," says one dealer.

Harley-Davidson's marketers spend a great deal of time thinking about customers and their buying behaviour. They want to known who their customers are, what they think and how they feel, and why they buy a Harley rather than a Yamaha, or a Suzuki, or a big Honda American Classic. Why are Harley buyers so fiercely loyal? These are difficult questions—even Harley owners themselves don't know exactly what motivates their buying. But Harley management puts top priority on understanding customers and what makes them tick.

Who rides a Harley? You might be surprised. It's no longer the Hell's Angels crowd—the burly, black-leather-jacketed rebels and "biker chicks" that once comprised Harley's core clientele. New motorcycles are attracting a new breed of riders—older, more affluent, and better educated. Harley now appeals more to "Rubbies" (rich urban bikers) than to rebels. While the average Harley customer is a 43-year-old husband with a median household income of $94 000, women are an increasingly important target market. While they currently only account for 15 percent of Harley-Davidson's market, the number of female riders is growing exponentially.

When you finish this chapter, you should be able to

1. Define the consumer market and construct a simple model of consumer buyer behaviour.

2. Name the four major factors that influence consumer buyer behaviour.

3. List and understand the stages in the buyer decision process.

4. Describe the adoption and diffusion process for new products.

Female riders are in their thirties and from moderate- to high-income groups. To reach this growing audience, the Canadian division of Harley-Davidson recently commissioned female-specific advertising that built on the themes of independence, strength, and freedom, using the headline, "You never took a back seat before." The ads feature five professional Canadian women who own Harleys, including a pilot, a computer training specialists, and a bank manager. The ads ran in *Chatelaine* and *Modern Woman* magazines.[1]

Harley-Davidson
www.harley-davidson.com/

Harley-Davidson makes good bikes, and, to keep up with its shifting market, the company has upgraded its showrooms and sales approaches. But Harley customers are buying a lot more than just a quality bike and a smooth sales pitch. To gain a better understanding of customers' deeper motivations, Harley-Davidson conducted focus groups in which it invited bikers to make cut-and-paste collages of pictures that expressed their feelings about Harley-Davidsons. (Can't you just see a bunch of hard-core bikers doing this?) The company then mailed out 16 000 surveys containing a typical battery of psychological, sociological, and demographic questions, as well as subjective questions such as "Is Harley more typified by a brown bear or a lion?" The research revealed seven core customer types: adventure-loving traditionalists; sensitive pragmatists; stylish status seekers; laid-back campers; classy capitalists; cool-headed loners; and cocky misfits. However, all owners appreciated their Harleys for the same basic reasons. "It didn't matter if you were the guy who swept the floors of the factory or if you were the CEO at that factory, the attraction to Harley was very similar," explains a Harley executive. "Independence, freedom, and power were the universal Harley appeals."

These studies confirm that Harley customers are doing more than just buying motorcycles. They're making a lifestyle statement and displaying an attitude. As one analyst suggests, "Never mind that [you're] a dentist or an accountant. You [feel] wicked astride all that power." Your Harley renews your spirits and announces your independence. The classic look, the throaty sound, the very idea of a Harley—all contribute to its mystique. Owning this "North American legend" makes you a part of something bigger—a member of the Harley family. The fact that you have to wait to get a Harley makes it all that much more satisfying to have one. In fact, the company deliberately restricts its output. "Our goal is to eventually run production at a level that's always one motorcycle short of demand," says Harley-Davidson's chief executive.

Thus, understanding buyers is an essential but difficult task for Harley-Davidson—buyers are moved by a complex set of deep and subtle emotions. Buyer behaviour springs from deeply held values and attitudes, from buyers' views of the world and their place in it, from what they think of themselves and what they think of others, from common sense, and from whimsy and impulse.

Such strong emotions and motivations are captured in a recent Harley-Davidson advertisement. The ad shows a close-up of an arm, the bicep adorned with a Harley-Davidson tattoo. The headline asks, "When was the last time you felt this strongly about anything?" The ad copy outlines the problem and suggests a solution:

Wake up in the morning and life picks up where it left off. You do what has to be done. Use what it takes to get there. And what once seemed exciting has now become part of the numbing routine. It all begins to feel the same. Except when you've got a Harley-Davidson. Something strikes a nerve. The heartfelt thunder rises up, refusing to become part of the background. Suddenly things are different. Clearer. More real. As they should have been all along. The feeling is personal. For some, owning a Harley is a statement of individuality. To the uninitiated, a Harley-Davidson motorcycle is associated with a certain look, a certain sound. Anyone who owns one will tell you it's much more than that. Riding a Harley changes you from within. The effect is permanent. Maybe it's time you started feeling this strongly. Things are different on a Harley.[2]

Consumer buying behaviour
The buying behaviour of final consumers—individuals and households who buy goods and services for personal consumption.

Consumer market
All the individuals and households who buy or acquire goods and services for personal consumption.

The Harley-Davidson example shows that many different factors affect consumer buying behaviour. Buying behaviour is never simple, yet understanding it is the essential task of marketing management.

This chapter explores the dynamics of consumer behaviour and the consumer market. **Consumer buying behaviour** refers to the buying behaviour of final consumers—individuals and households who buy goods and services for personal consumption. All of these final consumers combined comprise the **consumer market.** The Canadian consumer market consists of about 29 million people who consume many billions of dollars worth of goods and services each year, making it one of the most attractive consumer markets in the world. The world consumer market consists of more than five *billion* people. At present growth rates, the world population will exceed seven billion people by 2010.[3]

Consumers around the world vary tremendously in age, income, education level, and tastes. They also buy an incredible variety of goods and services. How these diverse consumers choose among various products embraces a fascinating array of factors.

MODEL OF CONSUMER BEHAVIOUR

Consumers make many buying decisions every day. Most large companies research consumer buying decisions in great detail to answer questions about what consumers buy, where they buy, how and how much they buy, when they buy, and why they buy. The central question for marketers is: How do consumers respond to various marketing efforts the company might use? The company that really understands how consumers will respond to different product features, prices, and advertising appeals has a great advantage over its competitors. The starting point is the stimulus-response model of buyer behaviour shown in Figure 5-1. This figure shows that marketing and other stimuli enter the consumer's "black box" and produce certain responses. Marketers must determine what is in the buyer's black box.[4]

Marketing stimuli consist of the four *P*s: product, price, place, and promotion. Other stimuli include major forces and events in the buyer's environment: economic, technological, political, and cultural. All of these inputs enter the buyer's black box, where they are turned into a set of observable buyer responses: product choice, brand choice, dealer choice, purchase timing, and purchase amount.

The marketer wants to understand how the stimuli are changed into responses inside the consumer's black box, which has two parts. First, the buyer's characteristics influence how he or she perceives and reacts to the stimuli. Second, the buyer's decision process itself affects the buyer's behaviour. This chapter looks first at buyer characteristics as they affect buying behaviour, and then discusses the buyer decision process.

FIGURE 5-1 *Model of buyer behaviour*

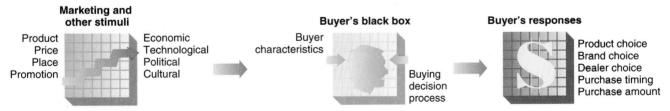

| Marketing and other stimuli | | Buyer's black box | Buyer's responses |

Product
Price
Place
Promotion

Economic
Technological
Political
Cultural

Buyer characteristics

Buying decision process

Product choice
Brand choice
Dealer choice
Purchase timing
Purchase amount

CHARACTERISTICS AFFECTING CONSUMER BEHAVIOUR

Consumer purchases are influenced strongly by cultural, social, personal, and psychological characteristics, shown in Figure 5-2. For the most part, marketers cannot control such factors, but they must take them into account. To help you understand these concepts, we will apply them to the case of a hypothetical consumer, Jennifer Wong, a 26-year-old brand manager who works for a multinational packaged-goods company in Toronto. Jennifer was born in Vancouver and her grandparents came from Hong Kong. She's been in a relationship for two years, but isn't married. She has decided that she wants to buy a vehicle but isn't sure she can afford a car. She rode a motor scooter when attending university and is now considering buying a motorcycle—maybe even a Harley.

FIGURE 5-2 *Factors influencing consumer behaviour*

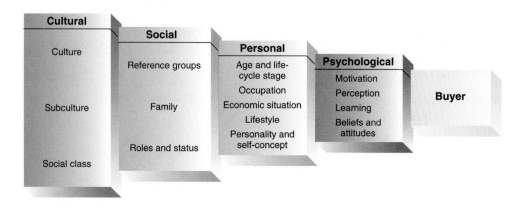

CULTURAL FACTORS

Cultural factors exert the broadest and deepest influence on consumer behaviour. The marketer needs to understand the role played by the buyer's *culture, subculture,* and *social class.*

Culture

Culture is the most basic cause of a person's wants and behaviour. Human behaviour is largely learned. Growing up in a society, a child learns basic values, perceptions, wants, and behaviours from the family and other important institutions. A recent study outlined some of the basic values shared by Canadians:

> Canada is a country that believes in freedom, dignity, respect, equality and fair treatment, and opportunity to participate. It is a country that cares for the disadvantaged at home and elsewhere, a country that prefers peaceful solutions to disputes. Canada is a country that, for all its diversity, has shared values.[5]

The study also described Canadians' commitment to community—communities of race, religion, occupation, or association. Respect for diversity has long been part of Canada's heritage. It has given birth to Canada's policies on multiculturalism, and is rooted in its policy of two official languages. Over four million Canadians now report that they can speak both English and French. Not surprisingly, Quebec has the largest number of bilingual Canadians (35 percent), but some Canadians might be surprised to learn that the most bilingual group of Canadians is Quebec's anglophones. New Brunswick is the second most bilingual province.[6]

Cultural values are constantly shifting, however. *Maclean's* magazine conducts an annual poll of Canadians' opinions on various issues. The most recent poll revealed that Canadians have lost faith in government's ability to affect society in a positive way. Increasing numbers of people believe that they will have to be self-sufficient. They expect the society of tomorrow to be a poorer, more violent place, and they are much more pragmatic about their future expectations. Canadians' main concern is jobs. Until just a few years ago, national unity was a major concern; today only nine percent of Canadians focus on this issue. In fact,

Culture
The set of basic values, perceptions, wants, and behaviours learned by a member of society from family and other important institutions.

People with professional practices are saying they don't just want a place to put their money. They want ideas. They want advice. They want solutions. Can a bank help? The answer is yes. Find out how at your nearest Bank of Montreal branch or visit us at http://www.bmo.com/

Bank of Montreal
IT *is* POSSIBLE*

* Registered trade mark of Bank of Montreal

The Bank of Montreal's campaign based on Canadians' changing values helped it break through advertising clutter and improve its corporate image.

Regal Greetings and Gifts Inc.
www.regal-greetings.com/about.htm

Subculture
A group of people with shared value systems based on common life experiences and situations.

37 percent of Canadians say they can accept Quebec becoming a separate country.[7] In a recent campaign entitled *Signs of the Times*, the Bank of Montreal picked up on these changing values. Using grainy, documentary-style, black-and-white television advertisements, the ads showed people holding handwritten signs with phrases such as "Are we going to be ok?" "Can I ever retire?" and "Will I ever be able to own my own home?" The voiceover asked, "Can a bank help?"

Canadians expect its institutions, including business, to honour its core values. Thus marketers are expected to treat customers fairly and equally. They are to market products safely and honestly. Marketers who ignore the differences among Canada's regions do so at their peril. In addressing these differences, however, marketers are expected to be inclusive in their marketing policies, and not to unfairly discriminate across segments. Marketers are required to reflect the diversity of Canadian society in their advertising. Finally, they are expected to deal with all groups of Canadians respectfully and not to promote negative stereotypes.

Every group or society has a culture, and cultural influences on buying behaviour may vary greatly among countries. Failure to adjust to these differences can result in ineffective marketing or embarrassing mistakes. For example, business representatives of a U.S. community seeking more business from Taiwan discovered this the hard way. They arrived in Taiwan bearing gifts of green baseball caps. The visitors later learned that according to Taiwan culture, a man wears green to signify that his wife has been unfaithful. The head of the community delegation later noted: "I don't know whatever happened to those green hats, but the trip gave us an understanding of the extreme differences in our cultures."[8] International marketers must understand the culture in each international market and adapt their marketing strategies accordingly.

Marketers are always trying to identify *cultural shifts* in order to discover new products that might be wanted. For example, the cultural shift toward greater concern about health and fitness has created a huge industry for exercise equipment and clothing, lower-fat and more natural foods, and health and fitness services. And the increased desire for leisure time has resulted in more demand for convenience products and services, such as microwave ovens and fast food. It also has created a huge catalogue-shopping industry. There are currently 620 different catalogue titles circulating in Canada, which account for almost $2 billion in annual sales. Sears and Regal Greetings and Gifts are the largest catalogue services, although Tilley Endurables, Harry Rosen, and The Added Touch have also been cited as noteworthy examples.[9]

Subculture

Each culture contains smaller **subcultures**, or groups of people with shared value systems based on common life experiences and situations. Subcultures include nationalities, religions, racial groups, and geographic regions. Many subcultures comprise important market segments, and marketers often design products and marketing programs tailored to their needs. Here are examples of four such important subculture groups.[10]

NATIVE CANADIANS. Native Canadians are making their voices increasingly heard both in the political arena and in the marketplace. There are 416 000 Status Indians in Canada. When Métis, non-status natives, and Inuit are added to this group, the number swells to 712 000. These Native Canadians not only have distinct cultures that have influenced their values and purchasing behaviour, but they have also profoundly influenced the rest of Canada through their art, love of nature, and concern for the environment.

CANADA'S ETHNIC CONSUMERS.   Consumers from ethnic groups represent one of the fastest-growing markets in Canada. While many Canadian businesspeople believe that marketing to these groups is only an issue in large cities such as Vancouver or Toronto, this is not the case. A recent survey by the Canadian Advertising Foundation revealed that the population of visible minorities is growing in cities across Canada. Table 5-1 shows actual populations and projections for growth by 2001.

Canadian Advertising Foundation
db.cochran.com/mnet/eng/ INDUS/ADVERT/Caf.htm

TABLE 5-1   *Visible Minorities in Urban Centres*

City	1996 Population	2001 Population
Population		
Metropolitan Toronto	1 470 000	2 110 000
Vancouver	578 000	830 000
Montreal	512 000	737 000
Edmonton	182 000	260 000
Calgary	182 000	260 000
Winnipeg	122 000	147 000
Ottawa-Hull	126 000	182 000
Halifax	40 000	57 000
Victoria	32 000	45 000
Regina	20 000	25 000

Source: Canadian Advertising Foundation.

There are a number of ethnic markets. Italian, German, and Chinese consumers comprise the three largest ethnic groups in Canada, each with a population of approximately 450 000. Portuguese, Polish, and Spanish people (with populations of 150 000 to 200 000) make up the next largest groups. These are followed by Greek, Punjabi, and Arabic Canadians, which each have populations of approximately 100 000.

Marketers must track evolving trends in various ethnic communities. Consider Chinese-Canadians, for example. In the past, most members of this ethnic group came from Hong Kong. Today they are arriving from Taiwan and mainland China. Why should marketers be concerned where Chinese immigrants come from? For language reasons, of course. While the Chinese who come from Hong Kong speak Cantonese, people from Taiwan and mainland China often speak Mandarin. Marketers must also be aware of the differences between new immigrants and those who are "integrated immigrants"—people who are second-, third-, fourth-, fifth-, and even sixth-generation Chinese-Canadians. Although marketing information often must be translated into the language of new immigrants, integrated immigrants communicate mainly in English. While Chinese-Canadians are influenced by many of the values of their adopted country, they may also share some values rooted in their ethnic history. Since they come from families who have experienced great political and social turmoil, Chinese-Canadians cling to "life-raft values": trust family, work hard, be thrifty, save, and have liquid and tangible goods. Air Canada used its knowledge of these values in a recent campaign linking Chinese-Canadians' need for security and desire to keep connected to their homeland with Air Canada's services.[11]

Not only are ethnic markets growing, but they also represent a substantial portion of the purchasing power in Canada. Ethnic markets accounted for 24 percent of the purchasing power in Canada in 1995, and are expected to grow to

人生如旅·旅程就是人生·不少如園華人來自香港。情繫港加兩地·往返兩處頻須。

楓葉航空每週八次航班·穿梭於溫哥華和香港之間·把時空緊緊連結·助您不斷縮短親情·友情及交情。

楓葉航空自一九三七年創立以來·航線由全國發展到全球一百二十餘個城市·是加國航機最旁及最多的航空公司·以服務優良和機艙設備完善善著稱。

楓葉航空·歷史悠久·信客之道經驗豐富·來往溫哥華和香港之間的航班·其 EXECUTIVE FIRST 艙座·個人空間比往年阿航空公司的商務客座更為寬敞·西服務員的波利圖·多種中·英文報刊雜誌·粵語·精美的東方及西式食譜·助您心曠神怡·高級影聲道·加上與地面無間的直撥電話·令您逍遙身處機中部感同家居。

邀遊天際情意結

楓葉航空......

楓夢情™

AIR CANADA ✈ 楓葉航空

Air Canada linked itself to the Chinese community merging two symbols: Canadian maple leaves (the airline's brand symbol) and Chinese embroidery.

over 30 percent by 2000. This translates into the purchase of $300 billion of goods and services. While some marketers hold the stereotype that immigrants purchase only low-cost goods and services, others are acutely aware that this is not the case. For example, surveys of Chinese consumers in Vancouver revealed that they intended to purchase a number of high-end products including airline tickets, home computers, televisions/stereos, mutual funds, and cellular phones.

Many ethnic groups believe that they have been neglected or misrepresented by marketers. A study conducted by the Canadian Advertising Foundation revealed that 80 percent of visible minorities believed that advertising has been targeted almost exclusively at "white" people. Yet 46 percent of this group stated that they would be more likely to buy a product if its advertising featured models from visible-minority populations.

Let's consider our hypothetical consumer. How will Jennifer Wong's cultural background influence her decision about whether to buy a motorcycle? Jennifer's parents certainly won't approve of her choice. Tied strongly to the values of thrift and conservatism, they believe that she should continue taking the subway instead of purchasing a vehicle. However, Jennifer identifies with her Canadian friends and colleagues as much as she does with her family. She views herself as a modern woman in a society that accepts women in a wide range of roles, both conventional and unconventional. She has female friends who play hockey and rugby. Women riding motorcycles is becoming a more common sight in Toronto.

MATURE CONSUMERS.   While only five percent of Canadians were aged 65 and older in 1990, this group will account for 14 percent of the population by 2000. Mature Canadians already have significant clout in the marketplace. Canadians who are currently aged 50 and older possess two-thirds of the country's disposable income, represent 25 percent of the population, and comprise one-third of the heads of households. As this group continues to age, it will dominate many market segments. The aging of the North American population has been called the most important trend of our time. It cannot be denied that the seniors market represents some exciting marketing opportunities and challenges.

Not only do mature Canadians have more discretionary income than other segments of the population, but they may also have more time to spend it. Eighty-five percent of the people in this age group are retired. Consequently, they represent a significant market for luxury and leisure products.

Too often stereotyped as feeble-minded geezers glued to their rocking chairs, seniors have long been the target of the makers of laxatives and denture products. But many marketers know that most seniors are not sick, feeble, deaf, or confused. Most are healthy and active, and they have many of the same needs and wants as younger consumers. Because seniors have more time and money, they are an ideal market for exotic travel, restaurants, financial services, and life- and health-care services. Their desire to look as young as they feel makes seniors good candidates for specially designed cosmetics and personal-care products, health foods, home physical-fitness products, and other items that combat aging. As the seniors segment grows in size and buying power, and as the stereotypes of seniors as doddering, creaky, impoverished shut-ins fade, more and more marketers are developing special strategies for this important market. For example, Sears'

"Mature Club" offers older consumers 25 percent discounts on everything from eyeglasses to lawnmowers. To appeal more to mature consumers, McDonald's employs seniors as hosts and hostesses in its restaurants and casts them in its ads.

Recognizing the special needs of mature consumers has resulted in many changes to a range of marketing practices. While manufacturers spent years developing childproof containers, they are now working to develop safe packaging that seniors can open more easily. In recent years the print on labels has become smaller to accommodate listing ingredients in both French and English. Many seniors, however, cannot read the package label even though they are highly concerned about nutritional information. Marketers are responding by developing illustrated labels that show proportions in a graphic format. They are also providing pictorial instructions about how to use the product. This has been advantageous, not only for the seniors market, but also for those new Canadians who do not read English well. Retailers, who once generated traffic in their stores with large family sizes, now feature single-serving packages that appeal to mature Canadians who may be living alone.

As is the case with ethnic markets, marketers must not fall into the trap of assuming that all seniors are alike. Seniors from different regions of Canada react to marketing appeals quite differently and have distinct product and service preferences. For example, consider the differences between the purchasing habits of consumers over the age of 55 in the rest of Canada, with seniors living in Quebec. While 90 percent of mature consumers in the rest of Canada buy no-name products, only 66 percent of Quebec's older consumers purchase no-name brands. Similarly, 51 percent of consumers in the rest of Canada buy bran-based cereals, but only 33 percent of Quebec seniors buy these products.

INTERNET USERS.   People who "surf the Net" have a culture that marketers ignore at their peril. Internet users have their own language, norms, values, and etiquette or "netiquette." Hard-sell marketing is definitely unacceptable on the Web, and marketers who violate this norm may be "flamed" or "mail bombed" by irate web users. Angry Net surfers have been known to bombard insensitive marketers with so many messages that servers and lines have been blocked, or they have posted their own "billboards" to discredit errant companies.

Over a third of Canadians who surf the Net gather information, including information on companies and services.

More than 30 million people now use the World Wide Web. Users are not the stereotypical 14-year-old "computer nerd" pounding away on a computer in the basement. Fifty percent of these users are university educated, and one-third have household incomes over $75 000. While users tend to be largely male (the ratio of males to females is 70:30) and anglophone, increasing numbers of women and francophones are starting to use the Net. Twenty-five percent of users fall in the 18 to 24 age group. Only five percent are professionals or senior managers. Two million Canadians, or eight percent of the population, use the Internet at least once a week. Internet usage also varies by city. People from Silicon Valley North—Ottawa—lead the pack. Fifteen percent of the Ottawa population use the Net. People from Toronto, Vancouver, Calgary, and Edmonton are the next most frequent users.[12] Unlike any group of consumers before them, Internet users are powerful and in control. The consumer is the one who chooses to access a web site and marketers must adjust to the idea that the Net is a means of two-way communication between a customer and a vendor, not the one-way street that media advertising represents. In other words, "They're not just listening to what the corporation wants to tell them, they're choosing the information that appeals to them." And net users value information.

Several recent articles have claimed that the Net hasn't lived up to its promise as a marketing tool. Those who make this claim base their argument on the fact that few Internet users actually make purchases over the Net. However, before marketers deny the value of the Internet, they must understand how and why people use the technology. Most people who use the Net do so for communication purposes, primarily e-mail. Another one-third use it for information and reference. Ten percent use it to access online magazines.[13] The fact that many Internet users use the technology as a source of information is important for marketers, especially those selling goods and services that require extensive information searches. Auto or real estate purchases fall into this category. Purchasers of mutual funds are renowned "information hounds" who conduct extensive comparisons among competing products.

While many consumers use the Net in the information search stage of the purchase process, its use as the final step in the transaction process has been curtailed because of several consumer concerns. People are worried about providing their credit card numbers when making an Internet purchase. Since consumers can't see or touch a product offered for sale over the Net, they fear they will have little recourse if the product they order isn't the right one, isn't delivered, or arrives broken. Consumers also have privacy concerns. They are concerned that the information they provide when making a purchase or requesting information may be sold or given to another organization without their permission. The Net allows people to purchase from companies located anywhere in the world; however, consumers may not know anything about these companies. Thus, corporate credibility and reputation are especially important for people using the Net. The Canadian Institute of Chartered Accountants (CICA) has begun a new initiative to address these consumer concerns. To build consumer trust and confidence in Internet marketers, the CICA are establishing a "seal of approval" that will appear as a logo on the web sites of companies that deliver goods and services as promised, and that respect customers' privacy.[14]

Toronto Dominion Bank
www.tdbank.ca/tdbank/
indexjava.html

The Toronto-Dominion Bank (TD Bank) is a Canadian marketer that has recently demonstrated just how well it understands the Net culture. It was recognized as one of the top 100 international business web sites, which is no small feat given the existence of over 10 000 commercial web sites. The TD Bank's web site was acknowledged for its richness of content, quality of design, and ease of use. The TD Bank viewed the Web as an effective means of providing financial information to current and potential customers.[15]

Jennifer Wong is highly computer literate. She uses a computer daily at work, carries a laptop when attending meetings outside Toronto, and has a computer in her apartment. One of the first things she did when considering a motorcycle purchase was to log onto the Internet. She learned a great deal simply by browsing the sites of producers such as Honda, Yamaha, and Harley-Davidson. She especially liked the Harley site and the annual events listed for Harley owners. She was concerned that most of these events took place in the United States, however. Using their response button, she requested information on dealers in her area and information about specific models. Jennifer also found several chat groups and posted questions to members of these groups, especially other women riders.

Social Class

Social classes
Relatively permanent and ordered divisions in a society whose members share similar values, interests, and behaviours.

Almost every society has some form of social class structure. **Social classes** are society's relatively permanent and ordered divisions whose members share similar values, interests, and behaviours. Social scientists have identified seven North American social classes (Table 5-2).

Social class is not determined by a single factor, such as income, but is measured as a combination of occupation, income, education, wealth, and other variables. In some social systems, members of different classes are reared for certain

TABLE 5-2   *Characteristics of Seven Major North American Social Classes*

Upper Uppers (Less Than 1 Percent)

Upper uppers are the social elite who live on inherited wealth and have well-known family backgrounds. They give large sums to charity, run charity balls, own more than one home, and send their children to the finest schools. They are a market for jewellery, antiques, homes, and vacations. They often buy and dress conservatively rather than showing off their wealth. While small in number, upper uppers serve as a reference group for others.

Lower Uppers (About 2 Percent)

Lower uppers have earned high income or wealth through exceptional ability in the professions or business. They usually begin in the middle class. They tend to be active in social and civic affairs and buy for themselves and their children the symbols of status, such as expensive homes, schools, swimming pools, and automobiles. They include the new rich who consume conspicuously to impress those below them. They want to be accepted in the upper-upper stratum, a status more likely to be achieved by their children than by themselves.

Upper Middles (12 Percent)

Upper middles possess neither family status nor unusual wealth. They are primarily concerned with "career." They have attained positions as professionals, independent businesspersons, and corporate managers. They believe in education and want their children to develop professional or administrative skills. They are joiners and are highly civic-minded. They are the quality market for good homes, clothes, furniture, and appliances.

Middle Class (32 Percent)

The middle class is made up of average-pay white- and blue-collar workers who live on "the better side of town" and try to "do the proper things." To keep up with the trends, they often buy products that are popular. Most are concerned with fashion, seeking the better brand names. Better living means owning a nice home in a nice neighbourhood with good schools. They believe in spending more money on worthwhile experiences for their children and aiming them toward a university education.

Working Class (38 percent)

The working class consists of those who lead a "working-class lifestyle," whatever their income, school background, or job. They depend heavily on relatives for economic and emotional support, for advice on purchases, and for assistance in times of trouble. The working class maintains sharper sex-role divisions and stereotyping.

Upper Lowers (9 percent)

Upper lowers are working (are not on welfare), although their living standard is just above poverty. They perform unskilled work for very poor pay although they strive toward a higher class. Often, upper lowers lack education. Although they fall near the poverty line financially, they manage to "present a picture of self-discipline" and "maintain some effort at cleanliness."

Lower Lowers (7 Percent)

Lower lowers are on welfare, visibly poverty stricken, and usually out of work or have "the dirtiest jobs." Often they are not interested in finding a job and are permanently dependent on public aid or charity for income. Their homes, clothes, and possessions are "dirty," "raggedy," and "broken-down."

Source: See Richard P. Coleman, "The Continuing Significance of Social Class to Marketing," *Journal of Consumer Research*, December 1983, pp. 265–280, © Journal of Consumer Research, Inc., 1983.

roles and cannot change their social positions. In Canada, however, the lines between social classes are not fixed and rigid; people can move to a higher social class or drop into a lower one. Marketers are interested in social class because people within a given social class tend to exhibit similar buying behaviour.

Social classes show distinct product and brand preferences in areas such as clothing, home furnishings, leisure activity, and automobiles. Culture, subculture, and social class are also variables that affect many purchase decisions, including whether to participate in government-run lotteries. Canadians have been avid purchasers of lottery tickets, spending more than $3 billion annually. While there is little variation in terms of whether men or women purchase the most tickets, ticket purchase rates vary by income. Fifty percent of people in low income brackets buy tickets, but over 80 percent of families in higher income brackets also dream of "winning the big one."[16] Jennifer Wong's social class may affect her motorcycle decision. As a member of the middle class, Jennifer finds herself frequently buying brand-name products that are fashionable and popular with her friends.

SOCIAL FACTORS

A consumer's behaviour also is influenced by social factors, such as the consumer's *small groups, family,* and *social roles and status.*

Groups

Group
Two or more people who interact to accomplish individual or mutual goals.

A person's behaviour is influenced by many small **groups**. Groups that have a direct influence and to which a person belongs are called *membership groups.* Some are *primary groups* with whom there is regular but informal interaction—such as family, friends, neighbours, and co-workers. Some are *secondary groups,* which are more formal and have less regular interaction. These include organizations such as religious groups, professional associations, and trade unions.

Reference groups serve as direct (face-to-face) or indirect points of comparison or reference in forming a person's attitudes or behaviour. People often are influenced by reference groups to which they do not belong. For example, an *aspirational group* is one to which the individual wishes to belong, as when a teenage hockey player hopes to play someday for the Montreal Canadiens. He identifies with this group, although there is no face-to-face contact between him and the team. Marketers try to identify the reference groups of their target markets. Reference groups expose a person to new behaviours and lifestyles, influence the person's attitudes and self-concept, and create pressures to conform that may affect the person's product and brand choices.

Opinion leaders
People within a reference group who, because of special skills, knowledge, personality, or other characteristics, exert influence on others.

Manufacturers of products and brands subject to strong group influence must determine how to reach the opinion leaders in the relevant reference groups. **Opinion leaders** are people within a reference group who, because of special skills, knowledge, personality, or other characteristics, exert influence on others. Opinion leaders are found at all levels of society, and one person may be an opinion leader in certain product areas and an opinion follower in others. Marketers try to identify opinion leaders for their products and direct marketing efforts toward them. For example, in the United States, Chrysler used opinion leaders to launch its LH-series cars—the Concorde, Dodge Intrepid, and Eagle Vision. It lent cars on weekends to 6000 community and business leaders in 25 cities. In surveys, 98 percent of the test-drivers said that they would recommend the models to friends. And it appears that they did—Chrysler sold out production the first year.[17]

The importance of group influence varies across products and brands. It tends to be strongest when the product is visible to others whom the buyer respects. Purchases of products that are bought and used privately are not much

Chrysler Corporation
www.chrysler.com/splash.cgi

affected by group influences because neither the product nor the brand will be noticed by others. If Jennifer Wong buys a motorcycle, both the product and the brand will be visible to others she respects, and her decision to buy the motorcycle and her brand choice may be influenced strongly by some of her groups, such as friends who belong to a weekend motorcycle club. Jennifer often feels left out when these friends leave for weekend road trips.

Family

Family members can strongly influence buyer behaviour. The family is the most important consumer buying organization in society, and it has been researched extensively. Marketers are interested in the roles and influence of the husband, wife, and children on the purchase of different products and services.

Husband-wife involvement varies widely by product category and by stage in the buying process. Buying roles change with evolving consumer lifestyles. In Canada and the United States, the wife traditionally has been the main purchasing agent for the family, especially in the areas of food, household products, and clothing. But with 70 percent of women holding jobs outside the home and the willingness of husbands to do more of the family's purchasing, all this is changing. For example, women now buy about 45 percent of all cars and men account for about 40 percent of food-shopping dollars.[18] Many teenagers are now responsible for doing the grocery shopping. Such roles vary widely in different countries and social classes. As always, marketers must research specific patterns in their target markets.

Such changes suggest that marketers who've typically sold their products to only women or only men are now courting the opposite sex. For example, consider the hardware business:

Swiss watch maker, TAGHeuer, appeals to consumers' desire to demonstrate their status through a product purchase.

According to the National Retail Hardware Association/Home Center Institute, women account for nearly half of all hardware-store purchases. The rise in women's tool ownership is due to more divorced women being forced to handle minor home emergencies, and more married and single women buying less expensive homes that need repairs. Home improvement retailer Builders Square identified this trend early and has capitalized on it by turning what had been an intimidating warehouse into a user-friendly retail outlet. The new Builders Square II outlets feature decorator design centres at the front of the store. To attract more women to these stores, Builders Square runs ads targeting women in *Home, House Beautiful, Woman's Day*, and *Better Homes and Gardens*. The retailer even offers bridal registries. Says a marketing director at Builders Square, "It's more meaningful to them to have a great patio set or gas grill than to have fine china."[19]

Children may also have a strong influence on family buying decisions. Chevrolet recognizes these influences in marketing its Chevy Venture minivan:

In the May issue of *Sports Illustrated for Kids*, which attracts mostly eight- to 14-year-old boys, the inside cover featured a brightly coloured two-page spread for the Chevy Venture minivan. This is General Motors' first attempt to woo [what it calls] "back-seat consumers." [GM] is sending the minivan into malls and showing previews of Disney's *Hercules* on a VCR inside. "We're kidding ourselves when we think kids aren't aware of brands," says [Venture's brand manager], adding that even she was surprised at how often parents told her that kids played a tie-breaking role in deciding which car to buy.[20]

In the case of expensive products and services, husbands and wives more often make joint decisions.[21] Although Jennifer isn't married, her boyfriend will influence her choice. He purchased a motorcycle last year and really loves it. Since he rarely lets Jennifer drive it, she really relates to the slogan on the new Harley-Davidson ads proclaiming, "You've never taken the back seat before!"

Roles and Status

A person belongs to many groups—family, clubs, organizations. The person's position in each group can be defined in terms of both role and status. A *role* consists of the activities that people are expected to perform according to the persons around them. Each role carries a *status* reflecting the general esteem given to it by society. People often choose products that show their status in society. Jennifer occupies many roles simultaneously. In her role as a daughter, she has lower status than her parents and grandparents, so she often acquiesces to their opinions with respect to family matters. In her role of a brand manager, Jennifer has high status and assumes a leadership role in her brand group. Jennifer also wants to be a leader in her social activities and often organizes group activities. Her desire to be a leader causes her to identify with leading status brands such as Harley-Davidson.

PERSONAL FACTORS

A buyer's decisions also are influenced by personal characteristics such as the buyer's *age and life-cycle stage, occupation, economic situation, lifestyle,* and *personality and self-concept.*

Age and Life-Cycle Stage

People change the goods and services they buy over their lifetimes. Tastes in food, clothes, furniture, and recreation are often age-related. Buying is also shaped by the stage of the *family life cycle*—the stages through which families might pass as they mature over time. Table 5-3 lists the stages of the family life cycle. Marketers often define their target markets in terms of life-cycle stage and develop appropriate products and marketing plans for each stage. Traditional family life-cycle stages include young singles and married couples with children. Today, however, marketers are increasingly catering to a growing number of alternative, non-traditional stages such as unmarried couples, couples marrying later in life, childless couples, single parents, extended parents (those with young adult children returning home), same-sex couples, and others.

TABLE 5-3 *Life-Cycle Stages*

Young	Middle-aged	Older
Single	Single	Older married
Single with children	Same-sex couples	Older unmarried
Married without children	Same-sex couples with children	Older with children again
Married with children	Married without children	
Divorced with children	Married with children	
	Married without dependent children	
	Divorced without children	
	Divorced with children	
	Divorced without dependent children	

Sources: Adapted from Patrick E. Murphy and William A. Staples, "A Modernized Family Life Cycle," *Journal of Consumer Research,* June 1979, p. 16; © Journal of Consumer Research, Inc., 1979. Also see Leon G. Schiffman and Leslie Lazar Kanuk, *Consumer Behavior* (Englewood Cliffs, NJ: Prentice Hall, 1994), pp. 361–370.

Occupation

A person's occupation affects the goods and services that he or she buys. Outside workers buy warm clothing and heavy boots; hospital workers wear white clothing; and workers in some service industries wear uniforms. Marketers try to identify the occupational groups that have an above-average interest in their products and services. A company can even specialize in making products needed by a given occupational group. Thus, computer software companies will design different products for brand managers, accountants, engineers, lawyers, and doctors.

Economic Situation

A person's economic situation will affect product choice. Marketers of income-sensitive goods watch trends in personal income, savings, and interest rates. If economic indicators point to a recession, marketers can take steps to redesign, reposition, and reprice their products.

Lifestyle

Lifestyle
A person's pattern of living as expressed in his or her activities, interests, and opinions.

Psychographics
The technique of measuring lifestyles and developing lifestyle classifications; it involves measuring the major AIO dimensions (activities, interests, opinions).

People coming from the same subculture, social class, and occupation may have quite different lifestyles. **Lifestyle** is a person's pattern of living as expressed in his or her **psychographics.** It involves measuring consumers' major *AIO dimensions—activities* (work, hobbies, shopping, sports, social events), *interests* (food, fashion, family, recreation), and *opinions* (about themselves, social issues, business, products). Lifestyle captures something more than the person's social class or personality; it profiles a person's whole pattern of acting and interacting in the world.

Several research firms have developed lifestyle classifications. The most widely used is the SRI *Values and Lifestyles (VALS)* typology. VALS2 classifies people according to how they spend their time and money. It divides consumers

FIGURE 5-3 *VALS2 Lifestyle Classifications*

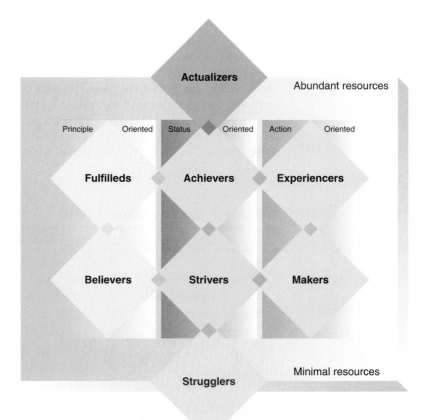

Source: Reprinted with permission of SRI International, Menlo Park, CA. VALS2 is a registered trademark of SRI International.

By using this advertisement, Sunfire targeted an audience living a specific lifestyle.

BUILT FOR DRIVERS

iVALS-Internet VALS
http://future.sri.com/
vals/iVALS.index.html

Environics 3SC Survey
www.environics.net/erg/
survey/3cs/index.shtml

into eight groups based on two major dimensions: self-orientation and resources (see Figure 5-3). *Self-orientation* groups include *principle-oriented* consumers who buy based on their views of the world; *status-oriented* buyers who base their purchases on the actions and opinions of others; and *action-oriented* buyers who are driven by their desire for activity, variety, and risk-taking. Consumers within each orientation are further classified into those with *abundant resources* and those with *minimal resources*. Consumers with either very high or very low levels of resources are classified without regard to their self-orientations (actualizers, strugglers). SRI has recently developed a new lifestyle classification system for Internet users. By logging onto their site, you can complete their questionnaire and determine which Internet user group you belong to and compare yourself to people in other categories.

These lifestyle classifications are by no means universal—they can vary significantly among countries. For example, McCann-Erickson London found the following British lifestyles: Avant Guardians (interested in change); Pontificators (traditionalists, very British); Chameleons (follow the crowd); and Sleepwalkers (contented underachievers).[22] Michael Adams, president of Environics Research Group Ltd., wrote *Sex in the Snow: Canadian Social Values at the End of the Millennium* to capture significant psychographic changes in the Canadian marketplace. He believes that psychographic changes eclipse demographic factors among Canadians. While his classification system begins with demographic factors, he divides the Canadian population along age-based lines into three groups: those over 50, baby boomers, and Generation X. Furthermore, he asserts that 12 value-based "tribes" exist within these broader groups. Table 5-4 provides descriptions of these groups.

When used carefully, the lifestyle concept can help the marketer understand changing consumer values and how they affect buying behaviour. For example, lifestyle information has helped marketers of cellular phones target consumers. While early users of the products were often corporate executives and salespeople who used their cars as their offices, later users often bought cellular phones for quite different reasons.[23] For example, while 46 percent of the Bell Mobility's customers still cite business reasons as their primary motivation for purchasing a cellular phone, 34 percent of Bell's customers now say they bought them for safety reasons. Another 19 percent of users purchased mobile phones just for convenience.

Bell Mobility
www.bellmobility.ca

TABLE 5-4 *The Social Value "Tribes" of Canada*

Groups	% Pop & Size	Motivators	Values	Exemplar
The Elders:				
Rational Traditionalists	15% 3.5 M	Financial independence, stability, and security.	Value safety, reason, tradition, and authority. Religious.	Winston Churchill
Extroverted Traditionalists	7% 1.7M	Traditional communities and institutions. Social Status.	Value tradition, duty, family, and institutions. Religious.	Jean Chrétien
Cosmopolitan Modernists	6% 1.4M	Traditional institutions. Nomadic, experience seeking.	Education, affluence, innovation, progress, self-confidence, world-perspective.	Pierre Trudeau
The Boomers:				
Disengaged Darwinists	18% 4.3M	Financial independence, stability, and security.	Self-preservation, nostalgia for the past.	Mike Harris
Autonomous Rebels	10% 2.4M	Personal autonomy, self-fulfilment, and new experiences.	Egalitarian, abhor corruption, personal fulfilment, education. Suspicion of authority and big government.	John Lennon
Anxious Communitarians	9% 2.1M	Traditional communities, big government, and social status.	Family, community, generosity, duty. Needs self-respect. Fearful.	Martha Stewart
The Gen-Xers:				
Aimless Dependents	8% 1.9M	Financial independence, stability, security. Fearful.	Desire for independence. Disengagement.	Courtney Love
Thrill-Seeking Materialists	7% 1.7M	Traditional communities, social status, experience-seeking.	Money, material possessions, recognition, living dangerously.	Calvin Klein
Autonomous Postmaterialists	6% 1.4M	Personal autonomy and self-fulfilment.	Freedom, human rights, egalitarian, quality of life.	Bart Simpson
Social Hedonists	4% .9M	Experience seeking, new communities.	Esthetics, hedonism, sexual freedom, instant gratification.	Janet Jackson
New Aquarians	4% .9M	Experience seeking, new communities.	Ecologism, hedonism.	Tori Amos

Adapted from information in: Michael Adams, "The demise of demography," *Globe and Mail*, January 8, 1997, D5; Ann Walmsley, "Canadians specific," *Report on Business*, March 1997, pp. 15-16.

Personality and Self-Concept

Each person's distinct personality influences his or her buying behaviour. **Personality** refers to the unique psychological characteristics that lead to relatively consistent and lasting responses to one's own environment. Personality is usually described in terms of traits such as self-confidence, dominance, sociability, autonomy, defensiveness, adaptability, and aggressiveness. Personality can be useful in analysing consumer behaviour for certain product or brand choices. For example, coffee makers have discovered that heavy coffee drinkers tend to be high on sociability. Thus, Maxwell House ads show people relaxing and socializing over a cup of steaming coffee.

Many marketers use a concept related to personality—a person's *self-concept* (also called *self-image*). The basic self-concept premise is that people's possessions contribute to and reflect their identities; that is, "we are what we have." Thus, to

Personality
A person's distinguishing psychological characteristics that lead to relatively consistent and lasting responses to his or her own environment.

understand consumer behaviour, the marketer must first understand the relationship between consumer self-concept and possessions. For example, the founder and chief executive of Barnes & Noble, one of North America's largest booksellers, notes that people buy books to support their self-images:

> People have the mistaken notion that the thing you do with books is read them. Wrong. . . . People buy books for what the purchase says about them—their taste, their cultivation, their trendiness. Their aim . . . is to connect themselves, or those to whom they give the books as gifts, with all the other refined owners of Edgar Allen Poe collections or sensitive owners of Virginia Woolf collections. . . . [The result is that] you can sell books as consumer products, with seductive displays, flashy posters, an emphasis on the glamour of the book, and the fashionableness of the bestseller and the trendy author.[24]

Jennifer Wong falls into Michael Adam's psychographic category of thrill-seeking materialists. Since she values material possessions, recognition, and the idea of living dangerously, owning a motorcycle instead of a traditional car, really appeals to her.

PSYCHOLOGICAL FACTORS

A person's buying choices are further influenced by four major psychological factors: *motivation, perception, learning,* and *beliefs and attitudes.*

Motivation

We know that Jennifer Wong became interested in buying a motorcycle. Why? What is she *really* seeking? What *needs* is she trying to satisfy?

A person has many needs at any given time. Some are *biological,* arising from states of tension such as hunger, thirst, or discomfort. Others are *psychological,* arising from the need for recognition, esteem, or belonging. Most of these needs will not be strong enough to motivate the person to act at any given time. A need becomes a *motive* when it is aroused to a sufficient level of intensity. A **motive** (or *drive*) is a need that is sufficiently pressing to direct the person to seek satisfaction. Psychologists have developed theories of human motivation. Two of the most popular—the theories of Sigmund Freud and Abraham Maslow—have quite different meanings for consumer analysis and marketing.

Motive (drive)
A need that is sufficiently pressing to drive the person to seek satisfaction of the need.

FREUD'S THEORY OF MOTIVATION.   Freud assumes that people are largely unconscious about the real psychological forces shaping their behaviour. He sees the person as growing up and repressing many urges. These urges are never eliminated or under perfect control; they emerge in dreams, in slips of the tongue, in neurotic and obsessive behaviour, or ultimately in psychoses.

Thus, Freud suggests that a person does not fully understand his or her motivation. Jennifer Wong, for example, may claim that her motive for buying a motorcycle is to satisfy her need for more convenient transportation. At a deeper level, however, she may be purchasing the motorcycle to impress others with her daring, and her desire to be a free spirit who doesn't follow convention.

Motivation researchers collect in-depth information from small samples of consumers to uncover the deeper motives for their product choices. They use non-directive depth interviews and various "projective techniques" to throw the ego off-guard—techniques such as word association, sentence completion, picture interpretation, and role-playing. Motivation researchers have reached some interesting and sometimes odd conclusions about what may be in the buyer's mind regarding certain purchases. For example, one classic study concluded that consumers resist prunes because they are wrinkled and remind people of sickness and old age. Despite its sometimes unusual conclusions, motivation research remains a useful tool for marketers seeking a deeper understanding of consumer behaviour (see Marketing Highlight 5-1).[25]

MARKETING HIGHLIGHT 5 - 1

"TOUCHY-FEELY" RESEARCH INTO CONSUMER MOTIVATIONS

The term motivation research refers to qualitative research designed to probe consumers' hidden, subconscious motivations. Because consumers often don't know or can't describe just why they act as they do, motivation researchers use a variety of non-directive and projective techniques to uncover underlying emotions and attitudes toward brands and buying situations. The techniques range from sentence completion, word association, and inkblot or cartoon interpretation tests, to having consumers describe typical brand users or form daydreams and fantasies about brands or buying situations. Some of these techniques verge on the bizarre. One writer offers the following tongue-in-cheek summary of a motivation research session:

Good morning, ladies and gentlemen. We've called you here today for a little consumer research. Now, lie down on the couch, toss your inhibitions out the window, and let's try a little free association. First, think about brands as if they were your *friends*. Imagine you could talk to your TV dinner. What would he say? And what would you say to him? . . . Now, think of your shampoo as an animal. Go on, don't be shy. Would it be a panda or a lion? A snake or a wooly worm? For our final exercise, let's all sit up and pull out our magic markers. Draw a picture of a typical cake-mix user. Would she wear an apron or a negligee? A business suit or a can-can dress?

Such projective techniques seem pretty goofy. But more and more, marketers are turning to these touchy-feely approaches to probe consumer psyches and develop better marketing strategies.

Many advertising agencies employ teams of psychologists, anthropologists, and other social scientists to carry out motivation research. One agency routinely conducts one-on-one, therapy-like interviews to delve into the inner workings of consumers. Another agency asks consumers to describe their favourite brands as animals or cars (say, Cadillacs versus Chevrolets) in order to assess the prestige associated with various brands.

Still another agency asks consumers to draw figures of typical brand users:

In one instance, the agency asked 50 interviewees to sketch likely buyers of two different brands of cake mixes. Consistently, the group portrayed Pillsbury customers as apron-clad, grandmotherly types, while they pictured Duncan Hines purchasers as svelte, contemporary women.

In a similar study, American Express had people sketch likely users of its gold card versus its green card. Respondents depicted gold card holders as active, broad-shouldered men; green card holders were perceived as "couch potatoes" lounging in front of television sets. Based on these results, the company positioned its gold card as a symbol of responsibility for people capable of controlling their lives and finances.

Motivation research: When asked to sketch figures of typical cake-mix users, subjects portrayed Pillsbury customers as grandmotherly types and Duncan Hines buyers as svelte and contemporary.

Some motivation research studies use more basic techniques, such as simply mingling with or watching consumers to find out what makes them tick. Saatchi & Saatchi (a British-based advertising agency) hired an anthropologist to spend time in Texas sidling up to Wrangler blue jeans wearers at rodeos and barbecues. His findings showed what the jeans company suspected: Wrangler buyers identify with cowboys. The company responded by running ads with plenty of Western touches.

In an effort to understanding the teenage consumer market better, BSB Worldwide (another ad agency) videotaped teenagers' rooms in 25 countries. It found surprising similarities across countries and cultures:

From the steamy playgrounds of Los Angeles to the stately boulevards of Singapore, kids show amazing similarities in taste, language, and attitude. . . . From the gear and posters on display, it's hard to tell whether the rooms are in Los Angeles, Mexico City, or Tokyo. Basketballs sit alongside soccer balls. Closets overflow with staples from an international, unisex uniform: baggy Levi's or Diesel jeans, NBA jackets, and rugged shoes from Timberland or Doc Martens.

Similarly, researchers at Sega of America's ad agency have learned a lot about videogame buying behaviour by hanging around with 150 kids in their bedrooms and by shopping with them in malls. Above all else, they learned, do everything fast. As a result, in Sega's most recent 15-second commercials, some images fly by so quickly that adults cannot recall seeing them, even after repeated showings. The kids, weaned on MTV, recollect them keenly.

Some marketers dismiss such motivation research as mumbo-jumbo. And these approaches do present some problems: The samples are small, and researcher interpretations of results are often highly subjective, sometimes leading to rather exotic explanations of otherwise ordinary buying behaviour. However, others believe strongly that these approaches can provide interesting nuggets of insight into the relationships between consumers and the brands they buy. To marketers who use them, motivation research techniques provide a flexible and varied means of gaining insights into deeply held and often mysterious motivations behind consumer buying behaviour.

Sources: Excerpts from Annetta Miller and Dody Tsiantar, "Psyching Out Consumers," *Newsweek,* February 27, 1989, pp. 46–47; and Shawn Tully, "Teens: The Most Global Market of All," *Fortune,* May 6, 1994, pp. 90–97. Also see Rebecca Piirto, "Words That Sell," *American Demographics,* January 1992, p. 6; and "They Understand Your Kids," *Fortune,* Special Issue, Autumn/Winter 1993, pp. 29–30.

FIGURE 5-4 *Maslow's hierarchy of needs*
Source: Adapted from *Motivation and Personality*, 2nd ed., by Abraham H. Maslow. Copyright © 1970 by Abraham H. Maslow. Reprinted by permission of Harper & Row, Publishers, Inc.

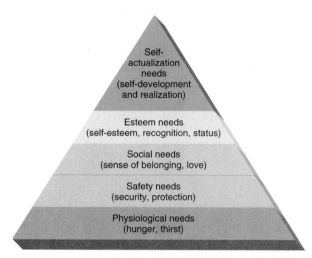

MASLOW'S THEORY OF MOTIVATION. Abraham Maslow sought to explain why people are driven by particular needs at particular times.[26] Why does one person spend much time and energy on personal safety and another on gaining the esteem of others? Maslow's answer is that human needs are arranged in a hierarchy, from the most pressing to the least pressing. Maslow's hierarchy of needs is shown in Figure 5-4. In order of importance, they are *physiological* needs, *safety* needs, *social* needs, *esteem* needs, and *self-actualization* needs. A person tries to satisfy the most important need first. When that need is satisfied, it will stop being a motivator and the person will then try to satisfy the next most important need. For example, starving people (physiological needs) will not take an interest in the latest happenings in the art world (self-actualization needs), nor in how they are perceived or esteemed by others (social or esteem needs), nor even in whether they are breathing clean air (safety needs). But as each important need is satisfied, the next most important need will come into play.

What light does Maslow's theory throw on Jennifer Wong's interest in buying a motorcycle? We can guess that Jennifer has satisfied her physiological, safety, and social needs; they do not motivate her interest in motorcycles. Her interest might come from a strong need for more esteem from others. Or it might come from a need for self-actualization—she might want to be a daring person and express herself through product ownership.

Perception

A motivated person is ready to act. How the person acts is influenced by his or her perception of the situation. Two people with the same motivation and in the same situation may act quite differently because they perceive the situation differently. When Jennifer Wong and her boyfriend visited a motorcycle dealership to look at bikes, the salesperson directed most of his comments to Jennifer's boyfriend even though Jennifer's boyfriend kept reminding him that the bike was for Jennifer. Jennifer was furious at being ignored. Even though she liked one of the bikes in the showroom, she vowed not to buy from that company.

Why do people perceive the same situation differently? All of us learn by the flow of information through our five senses: sight, hearing, smell, touch, and taste. However, each of us receives, organizes, and interprets this sensory information in an individual way. **Perception** is the process by which people select, organize, and interpret information to form a meaningful picture of the world.

People can form different perceptions of the same stimulus because of three perceptual processes: selective attention, selective distortion, and selective retention. People are exposed to a great amount of stimuli every day. For example, the average person may be exposed to more than 1500 ads in a single day. It is impossible for a person to pay attention to all these stimuli. *Selective attention*—the tendency for people to screen out most of the information to which they are exposed—means that marketers must work especially hard to attract the consumer's attention. Their message will be lost on most people who are not in the market for the product. Moreover, even people who are in the market may not notice the message unless it stands out from the surrounding sea of other ads.

Even noted stimuli do not always come across in the intended way. Each person fits incoming information into an existing mind-set. *Selective distortion* describes the tendency of people to interpret information in a way that will support what they already believe. Jennifer Wong may hear the salesperson mention some good and bad points about a competing motorcycle. Because she already has a strong leaning toward Harley, she is likely to distort those points in order to

Perception
The process by which people select, organize, and interpret information to form a meaningful picture of the world.

conclude that Harley is the better motorcycle. Selective distortion means that marketers must try to understand consumers' perspectives and how these will affect interpretations of advertising and sales information.

People will also forget much that they learn. They tend to retain information that supports their attitudes and beliefs. Because of *selective retention*, advertisers try to frame messages in ways that are consistent with people's existing beliefs. Jennifer is likely to remember good points made about the Harley and to forget good points made about competing motorcycles.

Because of selective exposure, distortion, and retention, marketers must work hard to get their messages through. This fact explains why marketers use so much drama and repetition in sending messages to their market. Interestingly, although most marketers worry about whether their offers will be perceived at all, some consumers are worried that they will be affected by marketing messages without even knowing it (see Marketing Highlight 5-2).

Learning

Learning
Changes in an individual's behaviour arising from experience.

When people act, they learn. **Learning** describes changes in an individual's behaviour arising from experience. Learning theorists say that most human behaviour is learned. Learning occurs through the interplay of *drives, stimuli, cues, responses,* and *reinforcement.*

We saw that Jennifer Wong has a drive for self-actualization. A *drive* is a strong internal stimulus that calls for action. Her drive becomes a motive when it is directed toward a particular *stimulus object,* in this case a motorcycle. Jennifer's response to the idea of buying a motorcycle is conditioned by the surrounding cues. *Cues* are minor stimuli that determine when, where, and how the person responds. Seeing motorcycles roaring along the Toronto streets, hearing about Harley's 75th anniversary special edition cycle, and receiving her boyfriend's support for buying her own motorcycle are all *cues* that can influence Jennifer's *response* to her interest in buying a motorcycle.

Suppose Jennifer buys a Harley. If she attends their weekend events, makes new friends, and just enjoys riding it around Toronto, her decision will be reinforced. If she decides to upgrade from her first bike to a more upscale model, the probability is greater that she will buy another Harley.

The practical significance of learning theory for marketers is that they can build up demand for a product by associating it with strong drives, using motivating cues, and providing positive reinforcement.

Beliefs and Attitudes

Belief
A descriptive thought that a person holds about something.

Through doing and learning, people acquire beliefs and attitudes. These, in turn, influence their buying behaviour. A **belief** is a descriptive thought that a person has about something. Jennifer Wong may believe that a Harley-Davidson is a classic bike, that it has more power than its rivals, and that it stands up well to urban driving conditions. These beliefs may be based on real knowledge, opinion, or faith, and may or may not carry an emotional charge.

Marketers are interested in the beliefs that people formulate about specific products and services, because these beliefs comprise product and brand images that affect buying behaviour. If some of the beliefs are wrong and prevent purchase, the marketer will want to launch a campaign to correct them.

Attitude
A person's consistently favourable or unfavourable evaluations, feelings, and tendencies toward an object or idea.

People have attitudes regarding religion, politics, clothes, music, food, and almost everything else. An **attitude** describes a person's relatively consistent evaluations, feelings, and tendencies toward an object or idea. Attitudes put people into a frame of mind of liking or disliking things, of moving toward or away from them. Thus, Jennifer may hold such attitudes as "Buy the best."

Attitudes are difficult to change. A person's attitudes fit into a pattern, and to change one attitude may require difficult adjustments in many others. Thus, a company should usually try to fit its products into existing attitudes rather than

SUBLIMINAL PERCEPTION—CAN CONSUMERS BE AFFECTED WITHOUT KNOWING IT?

In 1957, a researcher announced that he had flashed the phrases "Eat popcorn" and "Drink Coca-Cola" on a screen in a New Jersey movie theatre every five seconds for 1/300th of a second. He reported that although the audience did not consciously recognize these messages, viewers absorbed them subconsciously and bought 58 percent more popcorn and 18 percent more Coke. Suddenly advertising agencies and consumer-protection groups became intensely interested in subliminal perception. People voiced fears of being brain-washed, and California and Canada declared the practice illegal. Although the researcher later admitted to making up the data, and scientists failed to replicate the original results in other

executive put it, "We have enough trouble persuading consumers using a series of upfront 30-second ads—how could we do it in 1/300th of a second?"

Although advertisers may avoid outright subliminal advertising, some critics claim that television advertising uses techniques approaching the subliminal. With more and more viewers reaching for their remote controls to avoid ads by switching channels or fast-forwarding through VCR tapes, advertisers are using new tricks to grab viewer attention and to affect consumers in ways they may not be aware of. Many ad agencies employ psychologists and neurophysiologists to help develop subtle psychological advertising strategies.

used such "machine-gun editing" in recent ads—the longest shot flashed by in one and one-half seconds, the shortest in one-quarter of a second. The ads scored high in viewer recall.

Some advertisers go after our ears as well as our eyes, taking advantage of the powerful effects some sounds have on human brain waves:

> Advertisers are using sounds to take advantage of the automatic systems built into the brain that force you to stop what you're doing and refocus on the screen. . . . You can't ignore these sounds. That's why commercials are starting off with noises ranging from a baby crying (Advil) to a car horn (Hertz) to a factory whistle (Almond Joy). In seeking the right sound . . . advertisers can be downright merciless. . . . Ads for Nuprin pain reliever kick off by assaulting viewers with the whine of a dentist's drill . . . to help the viewer recall the type of pain we've all experienced. Hey, thanks.

A few experts are concerned that new high-tech advertising might even hypnotize consumers, whether knowingly or not. They suggest that several techniques—rapid scene changes, pulsating music and sounds, repetitive phrases, and flashing logos—might actually start to put some viewers under.

Some critics think that such subtle, hard-to-resist psychological techniques are unfair to consumers—that advertisers can use these techniques to bypass consumers' defences and affect them without their being aware of it. The advertisers who use these techniques, however, view them as innovative, creative approaches to advertising.

Seagram's pokes fun at subliminal advertising.

studies, the issue did not die. In 1974, Wilson Bryan Key claimed in his book *Subliminal Seduction* that consumers were still being manipulated by advertisers in print ads and television commercials.

Subliminal perception has since been studied by many psychologists and consumer researchers. None of these experts has been able to show that subliminal messages have any effect on consumer behaviour. It appears that subliminal advertising simply doesn't have the power attributed to it by its critics. Most advertisers scoff at the notion of an industry conspiracy to manipulate consumers through "invisible" messages. As one advertising agency

For example, some advertisers purposely try to confuse viewers, throw them off balance, or even make them uncomfortable:

> [They use] film footage that wouldn't pass muster with a junior-high film club. You have to stare at the screen just to figure out what's going on—and that, of course, is the idea. Take the ads for Wang computers. In these hazy, washed-out spots, people walk partially in and out of the camera frame talking in computer jargon. But the confusion grabs attention. . . . Even people who don't understand a word are riveted to the screen.

Other advertisers use the rapid-fire technique. Images flash by so quickly you can barely register them. Pontiac

Sources: Excerpts from David H. Freedman, "Why You Watch Commercials—Whether You mMean To or Not," *TV Guide,* February 20, 1988, pp. 4–7. Also see Wilson Bryan Key, *The Age of Manipulation: The Con in Confidence, The Sin in Sincere* (New York: Holt, 1989); Timothy E. Moore, "Subliminal Advertising: What You See is What You Get," *Journal of Marketing,* Spring 1982, pp. 38–47; Michael J. McCarthy, "Mind probe," *Wall Street Journal,* March 22, 1991, p. B3; and Martha Rogers and Kirk H. Smith, "Public Perceptions of Subliminal Advertising," *Journal of Advertising Research,* March/April 1993, pp. 10–17.

Honda Motor Co.
www.honda.com/

attempt to change attitudes. Of course, there are exceptions in which the great cost of trying to change attitudes may pay off. For example, in the late 1950s, Honda entered the U.S. motorcycle market facing a major decision. It could either sell its motorcycles to the small but already established motorcycle market or try to increase the size of this market by attracting new types of consumers. Increasing the size of the market would be more difficult and expensive because many people had negative attitudes toward motorcycles. They associated motorcycles with black leather jackets, switchblades, and outlaws. Despite these adverse attitudes, Honda chose the second option. It launched a major campaign to position motorcycles as good clean fun. Its theme "You meet the nicest people on a Honda" worked well, and many people adopted a new attitude toward motorcycles.[27] While the Honda advertisement may have convinced Jennifer that it is acceptable for women to ride motorcycles, it didn't create the image that Jennifer holds of herself. She liked the images in the new Harley campaign, which showed other career women with their bikes.

We can now appreciate the many forces acting on consumer behaviour. The consumer's choice results from the complex interplay of cultural, social, personal, and psychological factors. Although many of these factors cannot be influenced by the marketer, they can be useful in identifying interested buyers and in shaping products and appeals to serve consumer needs better.

Now that we have examined the influences that affect buyers, we are ready to look at how consumers make buying decisions—at consumer buying roles, types of buying decision behaviour, and the buyer decision process.

CONSUMER BUYING ROLES

The marketer needs to know what people are involved in the buying decision and what role each person plays. For many products, it is fairly easy to identify the decision-maker. For example, men typically choose their own shaving equipment and women choose their own clothes. However, consider the purchase of a family car. The oldest child might suggest buying a new car. A friend might advise the family on what kind of car to buy. The husband might choose the brand; the wife might select the price range. The husband and wife might then make the final decision jointly, and the wife might use the car more than her husband.

People might play any of several roles in a buying decision:

◆ *Initiator:* the person who first suggests or thinks of the idea of buying a particular product or service

◆ *Influencer:* a person whose views or advice influences the buying decision

◆ *Decider:* the person who ultimately makes a buying decision or any part of it—whether to buy, what to buy, how to buy, or where to buy

◆ *Buyer:* the person who makes an actual purchase

◆ *User:* the person who consumes or uses a product or service

Knowing the main buying participants and the roles they play helps the marketer fine-tune the marketing program.

TYPES OF BUYING DECISION BEHAVIOUR

Buying behaviour differs greatly for a tube of toothpaste, a tennis racket, an expensive camera, and a new car. More complex decisions usually involve more buying participants and more buyer deliberation. Figure 5-5 shows types of consumer buying behaviour based on the degree of buyer involvement and the degree of differences among brands.[28]

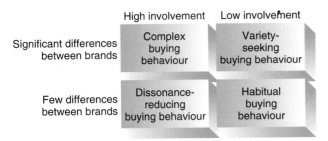

	High involvement	Low involvement
Significant differences between brands	Complex buying behaviour	Variety-seeking buying behaviour
Few differences between brands	Dissonance-reducing buying behaviour	Habitual buying behaviour

FIGURE 5-5 *Four types of buying behaviour*
Source: Adapted from Henry Assael, *Consumer Behavior and Marketing Action* (Boston: Kent Publishing Company, 1987), p. 87. Copyright © 1987 by Wadsworth, Inc. Printed by permission of Kent Publishing Company, a division of Wadsworth, Inc.

Complex buying behaviour
Consumer buying behaviour in situations characterized by high consumer involvement in a purchase and significant perceived differences among brands.

Dissonance-reducing buying behaviour
Consumer buying behaviour in situations characterized by high involvement but few perceived differences among brands.

COMPLEX BUYING BEHAVIOUR

Consumers undertake **complex buying behaviour** when they are highly involved in a purchase and perceive significant differences among brands. Consumers may be highly involved when the product is expensive, risky, purchased infrequently, and highly self-expressive. Typically, the consumer has much to learn about the product category. For example, a personal computer buyer may not know what attributes to consider. Many product features carry no real meaning: a "Pentium chip," "super VGA resolution," or "eight megs of RAM."

This buyer will pass through a learning process, first developing beliefs about the product, then attitudes, and then making a thoughtful purchase choice. Marketers of high-involvement products must understand the information-gathering and evaluation behaviour of high-involvement consumers. They need to help buyers learn about product-class attributes and their relative importance, and about what the company's brand offers on the important attributes. Marketers need to differentiate their brand's features, perhaps by describing the brand's benefits using print media with long copy. They must motivate store salespeople and the buyer's acquaintances to influence the final brand choice.

DISSONANCE-REDUCING BUYING BEHAVIOUR

Dissonance-reducing buying behaviour occurs when consumers are highly involved with an expensive, infrequent, or risky purchase, but see little difference among brands. For example, consumers buying carpeting may face a high-involvement decision because carpeting is expensive and self-expressive. Yet buyers may consider most carpet brands in a given price range to be the same. In this case, because perceived brand differences are not large, buyers may shop around to learn what is available, but buy relatively quickly. They may respond primarily to a good price or for convenience.

After the purchase, consumers might experience *postpurchase dissonance* (after-sale discomfort) when they notice certain disadvantages of the purchased carpet brand or hear favourable things about brands not purchased. To counter such dissonance, the marketer's after-sale communications should provide evidence and support to help consumers feel good about their brand choices.

HABITUAL BUYING BEHAVIOUR

Habitual buying behaviour
Consumer buying behaviour in situations characterized by low consumer involvement and few significant perceived brand differences.

Habitual buying behaviour occurs under conditions of low consumer involvement and little significant brand difference. Consider salt, for example. Consumers have little involvement in this product category—they simply go to the store and reach for a brand. If they keep reaching for the same brand, it is out of habit rather than strong brand loyalty. Consumers appear to have low involvement with most low-cost, frequently purchased products.

In such cases, consumer behaviour does not pass through the usual belief-attitude-behaviour sequence. Consumers do not search extensively for information about the brand, evaluate brand characteristics, and make weighty decisions about which brand to buy. Instead, they passively receive information as they watch television or read magazines. Ad repetition creates *brand familiarity* rather than *brand conviction*. Consumers do not form strong attitudes toward a brand; they select the brand because it is familiar. Because they are not highly involved with the product, consumers may not evaluate the choice even after purchase. Thus, the buying process involves brand beliefs formed by passive learning, followed by purchase behaviour, which may or may not be followed by evaluation.

Because buyers are not highly committed to any brands, marketers of low-involvement products with few brand differences often use price and sales promotions to stimulate product trial. In advertising for a low-involvement product, ad copy should stress only a few key points. Visual symbols and imagery are important because they can be remembered easily and associated with the brand. Ad campaigns should include high repetition of short-duration messages. Television is usually more effective than print media because it is a low-involvement medium suitable for passive learning. Advertising planning should be based on classical conditioning theory, in which buyers learn to identify a certain product by a symbol repeatedly attached to it.

Marketers can try to convert low-involvement products into higher-involvement ones by linking them to some involving issue. Procter and Gamble does this when it links Crest toothpaste to avoiding cavities. Or the product can be linked to some involving personal situation. Nestlé did this in a recent series of ads for Taster's Choice coffee, each consisting of a new soap-opera-like episode featuring the evolving romantic relationship between two neighbours. At best, these strategies can raise consumer involvement from a low to a moderate level. However, they are not likely to propel the consumer into highly involved buying behaviour.

VARIETY-SEEKING BUYING BEHAVIOUR

Variety-seeking buying behaviour
Consumer buying behaviour in situations characterized by low consumer involvement but significant perceived brand differences.

Consumers undertake **variety-seeking buying behaviour** in situations characterized by low consumer involvement, but significant perceived brand differences. In such cases, consumers often do a lot of brand-switching. For example, when buying cookies, a consumer may hold some beliefs, choose a cookie brand without much evaluation, then evaluate that brand during consumption. But the next time, the consumer might choose another brand out of boredom or simply to try something different. Brand-switching occurs for the sake of variety rather than due to dissatisfaction.

In such product categories, the marketing strategy may differ for the market leader and minor brands. The market leader will try to encourage habitual buying behaviour by dominating shelf space, keeping shelves fully stocked, and running frequent reminder advertising. Challenger firms will encourage variety seeking by offering lower prices, special deals, coupons, free samples, and advertising that presents reasons for trying something new.

THE BUYER DECISION PROCESS

We are now ready to examine the stages that buyers pass through to reach a buying decision. Figure 5-6 shows the consumer as passing through five stages: *need recognition, information search, evaluation of alternatives, purchase decision,* and *postpurchase behaviour.* Clearly, the buying process starts long before actual purchase and continues long after. Marketers need to focus on the entire buying process rather than on just the purchase decision.

FIGURE 5-6 *Buyer decision process*

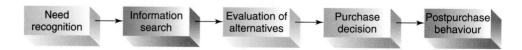

Need recognition → Information search → Evaluation of alternatives → Purchase decision → Postpurchase behaviour

The figure implies that consumers pass through all five stages with every purchase. But in more routine purchases, consumers often skip or reverse some of these stages. A woman buying her regular brand of toothpaste would recognize the need and go right to the purchase decision, skipping information search

NOW CONTAINS LESS ROWING MACHINE.

How do you make Chocolate Cake with less rowing machine? Try SPLENDA® Low-Calorie Sweetener. It's the only one created from sugar, so it's the only one that virtually cooks, bakes and tastes like sugar. In the case of this Chocolate Cake, however, with about 25% less calories. So, while we don't recommend that you quit working out, you just might find yourself spending less time rowing nowhere fast. For this or other SPLENDA® recipes please call 1-800-561-0070.

SPLENDA®. From Sugar.

Need recognition can be triggered by advertising. This Splenda outdoor ad quickly made its point to weight conscious consumers about the benefits of its product.

Need recognition
The first stage of the buyer decision process in which the consumer recognizes a problem or need.

Information search
The stage of the buyer decision process in which the consumer is aroused to search for more information; the consumer may simply have heightened attention or may go into active information search.

and evaluation. However, we use the model in Figure 5-7 because it shows all the considerations that arise when a consumer faces a new and complex purchase situation.

To illustrate this model, we will again follow Jennifer Wong and try to understand how she became interested in buying a motorcycle, and the stages she went through to make her final choice.

NEED RECOGNITION

The buying process starts with **need recognition**—with the buyer recognizing a problem or need. The buyer senses a difference between his or her *actual* state and some *desired* state. The need can be triggered by *internal stimuli* when one of the person's normal needs—hunger, thirst, sex—rises to a level high enough to become a drive. A need can also be triggered by *external stimuli*. A person passes a bakery and the sight of freshly baked bread stimulates his or her hunger. At this stage, the marketer should research consumers to determine what kinds of needs or problems arise, what brought them about, and how they led the consumer to this particular product.

Jennifer Wong might answer that she felt the need for more convenience when it came to transportation. Her office recently relocated and is no longer located near a subway station. She first considered buying a car, but soon realized that parking in downtown Toronto would pose a problem. The rising cost of gas also concerned her. Thus, her focus turned to another option—a motorcycle. By gathering such information, the marketer can identify the factors that most often trigger interest in the product and can develop marketing programs that involve these factors.

INFORMATION SEARCH

An aroused consumer may or may not search for more information. If the consumer's drive is strong and a satisfying product is near at hand, the consumer is likely to buy it. If not, the consumer may store the need in memory or undertake an **information search** related to the need.

At one level, the consumer may simply enter *heightened attention*. Here Jennifer Wong becomes more receptive to information about motorcycles. She pays attention to motorcycle ads, bikes used by friends, and conversations about motorcycles. Or Jennifer may go into *active information search,* in which she looks for reading material, surfs the Net, phones friends, and gathers information in other ways. The amount of searching she does will depend on the strength of her drive, the amount of information she starts with, the ease of obtaining more information, the value she places on additional information, and the satisfaction she gets from searching.

The consumer can obtain information from any of several sources. These include:

◆ *Personal sources:* family, friends, neighbours, acquaintances

LINDSEY DAVIS, PRODUCT ASSISTANT, KRAFT

Lindsey is a new product assistant working on children's cereals at Kraft Canada. She works on Post Cereal kids brands, including Honeycomb, Sugar Crisp, Alpha-Bits, and Fruity Pebbles. Her target audience is children between the ages of four and 13, with "gatekeeper moms" as a secondary target market to consider (as mom makes most of the purchase decisions in Canadian households).

Kraft Canada Inc. is a wholly owned subsidiary of Kraft Foods Inc. of Chicago, Illinois. Today, Kraft Canada is one of the largest consumer packaged food companies in the country. In 1996, the company posted annual revenues of $2.0 billion and sales have grown an average of 4.5 percent per year from 1991 to 1996. Kraft manufactures four of the top 10 grocery store items in Canada: Kraft Dinner Pasta Dinner, Maxwell House Instant Coffee, Kraft Thin Singles Process Cheese Slices, and Cheez Whiz Process Cheese Spread. Over the past five years, Kraft Canada has donated more than 3.6 million kilograms of food to food banks across Canada.

Lindsey works at Kraft's head office in Don Mills, Ontario, but she works closely with team members from manufacturing and sales in offices and plants across the country.

As an undergraduate student, Lindsey at first didn't consider marketing.

She wasn't sure exactly what marketers did, and coming from Victoria, British Columbia, she didn't have any role models in the field. (Corporations had lots of sales offices in her area, but few had large marketing departments.) However, she knew that she was interested in business. When she

Lindsey Davis

took her first marketing course, she realized she was especially interested in the consumer side of commerce. Unlike MIS or finance, fields that focus on technology and monetary exchanges, Lindsey found that she was drawn to marketing because it "has a personality." It offered her a

chance to draw people together from other functional areas and distant locations so that they share the same goals and understand the strategic direction of the brand.

Lindsey's first project at Kraft was developing a line extension for Alpha-Bits cereal. "I was responsible for doing everything," Lindsey says excitedly. She worked on a new package design, communicated the benefits to the sales organization, worked with the advertising agency to promote the brand extension, and helped the manufacturing plant to develop prototypes and explain product research. Since this was her first major project, Lindsey was extremely thorough in her approach. She had to clearly state her objectives for the project and keep her focus on the overall brand strategy. She had to know from the beginning what she wanted the new package to convey to consumers, and what information she wanted to jump off the shelf.

Lindsey believes that more and more packaged goods companies are realizing the value of extending key brands. Rather than constantly introducing new products, firms are beginning to concentrate on core brands and leveraging their value. Consumers already know what the brand stands for, and research to guide decisions is already in place. However, it is important to keep core

♦ *Commercial sources:* advertising, salespeople, dealers, packaging, displays
♦ *Public sources:* mass media, consumer-rating organizations
♦ *Experiential sources:* handling, examining, using the product

The relative influence of these information sources varies with the product and the buyer. Generally, the consumer receives the most information about a product from commercial sources—those controlled by the marketer. The most effective sources, however, tend to be personal. Personal sources appear to be even more important in influencing the purchase of services.[29] Commercial sources normally *inform* the buyer, but personal sources *legitimize* or *evaluate* products for the buyer. For example, doctors typically learn of new drugs from commercial sources, but turn to other doctors for evaluative information.

As more information is obtained, the consumer's awareness and knowledge of the available brands and features increase. In her information search, Jennifer Wong learned about the many camera brands available. The information also helped her drop certain brands from consideration. A company must design its marketing mix to make prospects aware of and knowledgeable about its brand. It should carefully identify consumers' sources of information and the importance

brands fresh, Lindsey stresses. Developing line extensions allows marketers to communicate new information to consumers and excite the sales force about brand innovations.

What Lindsey especially likes about her job at Kraft is the opportunity to learn by doing. "You dive right in," Lindsey says. "From the first day, you don't watch, you do!" This also means that Lindsey had to be willing to accept responsibility and make her own decisions. In fact, she has had to work for some time without direct supervision from a product manager. While this has meant that the learning curve is steep, it is also exciting to be able to gain new skills quickly. She has worked feverishly to understand the equities of her brand—learning everything from why certain colours matter in packaging to what the brand means to consumers in the target group.

Another thing about Kraft that Lindsey values is their great new training program. New hires at Kraft work on various brands for a period of one to six months and then begin a training program that they attend one or two days each week for a period of 15 weeks. They learn everything from how the budgeting system works to how the sale force is organized to the commercialization process at Kraft. Lindsey gained insights about how to motivate teams and how to develop

critical paths for project management. This training, along with the opportunity to work with a product manager who was interested in Lindsey's personal development, has helped Lindsey to acquire the skills she will need as she moves to higher levels of the organization.

Technology is posing a new set of challenges for Lindsey. Kraft sees the Internet as a "wide open sky" in terms of marketing opportunities. It is an exciting medium that allows brand managers to give their products dimension and bring brand personalities alive. However, there are a lot of copyright and legal issues to be considered especially when marketing to young children. While the Internet can be a very valuable medium for gathering information about consumers, privacy issues must be considered and consumer information must be protected from unauthorized use. Using an Internet site for national advertising is also problematic, since in Quebec, advertising to children isn't allowed. While Lindsey wants to have her brands on the leading edge of communication technology, she knows that she has to wrestle with these issues.

Finally, working with a large multinational firm can have both pluses and minuses, Lindsey believes. As part of Kraft North America, Lindsey can quickly adopt innovative ideas developed for the U.S. marketplace

and implement strategies that have a track record of success there. However, Lindsey knows that there are differences between Canadian and U.S. consumers and she has to be cognizant of these. For example, people in the children's cereals brand group in Canada have worked to keep their products wholesome. While many of the cereals are sweetened, Kraft Canada doesn't want to cross the line of making them appear more like candy. Adding marshmallows and frosting is appealing to U.S. consumers, but people at Kraft Canada constantly have to make the case that Canadian consumers value more nutritious, healthy products.

Lindsey is really happy she accepted the job at Kraft Canada. Like anyone looking for a first job, Lindsey felt some uncertainty about whether she had made the right choice. Today that uncertainty has vanished. Lindsey believes that if you are the type of person who thrives on challenge, who has the energy and drive to make things happen, who is interested in consumers and the way they think, then working for a large packaged-goods company is the right place for you. The skills Lindsey has learned as she takes on project leadership roles have broadened her horizons and are an important part of the life-long learning that will translate into all parts of her life, Lindsey believes.

of each source. Consumers should be asked how they first heard about the brand, what information they received, and what importance they placed on different information sources.

EVALUATION OF ALTERNATIVES

Alternative evaluation
The stage of the buyer decision process in which the consumer uses information to evaluate alternative brands in the choice set.

We have seen how the consumer uses information to arrive at a set of final brand choices. How does the consumer choose among the alternative brands? The marketer needs to know about **alternative evaluation**—that is, how the consumer processes information to arrive at brand choices. Unfortunately, consumers do not use a simple and single evaluation process in all buying situations. Instead, several evaluation processes are at work.

Certain basic concepts help explain consumer evaluation processes. First, we assume that each consumer views a product as a bundle of *product attributes*. For cameras, product attributes might include picture quality, ease of use, camera size, price, and other features. Consumers will vary as to which attributes they consider relevant, and they will pay the most attention to those attributes connected with their needs.

Brand image
The set of beliefs that
consumers hold about
a particular brand.

Second, the consumer will attach different *degrees of importance* to different attributes according to his or her unique needs and wants. Third, the consumer is likely to develop a set of *brand beliefs* about where each brand stands on each attribute. The set of beliefs held about a particular brand is known as the **brand image.** Based on his or her experience and the effects of selective perception, distortion, and retention, the consumer's beliefs may differ from true attributes.

Fourth, the consumer's expected *total product satisfaction* will vary with levels of different attributes. For example, Jennifer Wong may expect her satisfaction with a motorcycle to increase with better handling; to peak with a medium-weight bike as opposed to a very light or very heavy one; and to be higher for a motorcycle designed specifically for women riders. If we combine the attribute levels that give her the highest perceived satisfaction, they comprise Jennifer's ideal motorcycle. It would also be her preferred motorcycle if it were available and affordable.

Fifth, the consumer arrives at attitudes toward the different brands through some *evaluation procedure.* Consumers have been found to use one or more of several evaluation procedures, depending on the consumer and the buying decision.

We will illustrate these concepts with Jennifer Wong's motorcycle-buying situation. Suppose Jennifer has narrowed her choices to four motorcycles. And suppose that she is primarily interested in four attributes—quality, ease of handling, ergonomic design, and price. Jennifer has formed beliefs about how each brand rates on each attribute. The marketer wishes to predict which motorcycle Jennifer will buy.

Clearly, if one motorcycle rated best on all the attributes, we could predict that Jennifer would choose it. But the brands vary in appeal. Some buyers will base their buying decision on only one attribute, and their choices are easy to predict. If Jennifer wants ease of handling above everything, she will buy the motorcycle that rates highest on this attribute. But most buyers consider several attributes, each with different importance. If we knew the importance weights that Jennifer assigns to each of the four attributes, we could predict her motorcycle choice more reliably.

How consumers evaluate purchase alternatives depends on the individual consumer and the specific buying situation. In some cases, consumers use careful calculations and logical thinking. At other times, the same consumers do little or no evaluating; instead they buy on impulse and rely on intuition. Sometimes consumers make buying decisions on their own; sometimes they turn to friends, consumer guides, or salespeople for buying advice.

Marketers should study buyers to determine how they actually evaluate brand alternatives. If they know what evaluative processes go on, marketers can take steps to influence the buyer's decision. Motorcycle manufacturers that want to appeal directly to women riders can design products to appeal specifically to them. Models such as Harley's Sportster 883 Hugger are lighter in weight than some of their traditional models, with higher seats and easier handling. The company has also moved away from traditional motorcycle colours to power colours such as red. At the same time, the firm has retained traditional features such as Harley's unique engine, so "the streets never sound the same."

PURCHASE DECISION

Purchase decision
The stage of the buyer
decision process in which the
consumer actually buys the
product.

In the evaluation stage, the consumer ranks brands and forms purchase intentions. Generally, the consumer's **purchase decision** will be to buy the most preferred brand, but two factors can come between the purchase *intention* and the purchase *decision.* The first factor is the *attitudes of others.* If Jennifer's friends ride Honda motorcycles, chances of her buying a Harley will be reduced.

The second factor is *unexpected situational factors.* The consumer may form a purchase intention based on factors such as expected income, expected price, and expected product benefits. However, unexpected events may change the purchase intention. Jennifer may lose her job, some other purchase may become more urgent, or a close competitor may drop its price. Thus, preferences and even purchase intentions do not always result in actual purchase choice.

POSTPURCHASE BEHAVIOUR

Postpurchase behaviour
The stage of the buyer decision process in which consumers take further action after purchase based on their satisfaction or dissatisfaction.

The marketer's job does not end when the product is bought. After purchasing the product, the consumer will be satisfied or dissatisfied and will engage in **postpurchase behaviour** of interest to the marketer. What determines whether the buyer is satisfied or dissatisfied with a purchase? The answer lies in the relationship between the *consumer's expectations* and the product's *perceived performance*. If the product falls short of expectations, the consumer is disappointed; if it meets expectations, the consumer is satisfied; if it exceeds expectations, the consumer is delighted.

Consumers base their expectations on information they receive from sellers, friends, and other sources. If the seller exaggerates the product's performance, consumer expectations will not be met, and dissatisfaction will result. The larger the gap between expectations and performance, the greater the consumer's dissatisfaction. This suggests that sellers should make product claims that accurately represent the product's performance so that buyers are satisfied.

Cognitive dissonance
Buyer discomfort caused by postpurchase conflict.

Almost all major purchases result in **cognitive dissonance,** or discomfort caused by postpurchase conflict. After the purchase, consumers are satisfied with the benefits of the chosen brand and are glad to avoid the drawbacks of the brands not bought. However, every purchase involves compromise. Consumers feel uneasy about acquiring the drawbacks of the chosen brand and about losing the benefits of the brands not purchased. Thus, consumers feel at least some postpurchase dissonance for every purchase.[30]

Why is it so important to satisfy the customer? Such satisfaction is important because a company's sales come from two basic groups—*new customers* and *retained customers*. It usually costs more to attract new customers than to retain current ones, and the best way to retain current customers is to keep them satisfied. Satisfied customers buy a product again, talk favourably to others about the product, pay less attention to competing brands and advertising, and buy other products from the company. Many marketers go beyond merely *meeting* the expectations of customers—they aim to *delight* the customer. A delighted customer is even more likely to purchase again and to talk favourably about the product and company.

A dissatisfied consumer responds differently. Whereas, on average, a satisfied customer tells three people about a good product experience, a dissatisfied customer complains to 11 people. In fact, one study showed that 13 percent of the people who had a problem with an organization complained about the company to more than 20 people.[31] Clearly, bad word of mouth travels further and faster than good word of mouth and can quickly damage consumer attitudes about a company and its products.

Therefore, a company would be wise to measure customer satisfaction regularly. It cannot simply rely on dissatisfied customers to volunteer their complaints when they are dissatisfied. Some 96 percent of unhappy customers never tell the company about their problem. Companies should set up systems that *encourage* customers to complain (see Marketing Highlight 5-3). In this way, the company can learn how well it is doing and how it can improve. The 3M Company claims that over two-thirds of its new-product ideas come from listening to customer complaints. But listening is not enough—the company also must respond constructively to the complaints it receives.

Beyond seeking out and responding to complaints, marketers can take additional steps to reduce consumer postpurchase dissatisfaction and to help customers feel good about their purchases. For example, Toyota writes or phones new car owners with congratulations on having selected a fine car. It places ads showing

POSTPURCHASE SATISFACTION: TURNING COMPANY CRITICS INTO LOYAL CUSTOMERS

What should companies do with dissatisfied customers? Everything they can! Unhappy customers not only stop buying but also can quickly damage the company's image. Studies show that customers tell four times as many people about bad experiences as they do about good ones. In contrast, dealing effectively with complaints can actually boost customer loyalty and the company's image. According to one study, 95 percent of consumers who register complaints will do business with the company again if their complaint is resolved quickly. Moreover, customers whose complaints have been satisfactorily resolved tell an average of five

Making buyers happy: GE's Answer Centre handles customers' concerns 365 days a year, 24 hours a day.

other people about the good treatment they received. Thus, enlightened companies don't try to hide from dissatisfied customers. On the contrary, they go out of their way to encourage customers to complain, then bend over backwards to make disgruntled buyers happy again.

The first opportunity to handle complaints often comes at the point of purchase. Many retailers and other service firms teach their customer-contact people how to resolve problems and diffuse customer anger. They provide customer service representatives with liberal return and refund policies and other damage-control tools. Some companies go to extremes to see things the customer's way and to reward complaining—seemingly without regard for profit

impact. For example, Wal-Mart (Canada) accepts returns of items even when customers have obviously abused them. Such companies are not just looking for today's sale. They want a long-term relationship with customers. This generosity appears to help profits more than harm them. Such actions create tremendous buyer loyalty and goodwill, and for most retailers, customers who return items that they bought elsewhere or have already used account for less than five percent of all returns.

Many companies have also set up toll-free telephone systems to coax out and deal with consumer problems. Procter & Gamble includes a toll-free number on every consumer product it sells in the United States and Canada. P&G now receives about 800 000 mail and phone contacts about its products each year—mostly complaints, requests for information, and testimonials. This system serves as an early warning signal for product and customer problems. So far, the system has resulted in hundreds of actions and improvements ranging from tracking down batches of defective packages to putting high-altitude baking instructions on Duncan Hines brownies packages.

General Electric's Answer Centre may be North America's most extensive toll-free telephone system. It handles over three million calls a year, five percent of which are complaints. At the heart of the system is a giant

database that provides the centre's service reps with instant access to over one million answers concerning 8500 models in 120 product lines. The centre receives some unusual calls, such as when a submarine off the Connecticut coast requested help fixing a motor, or when technicians on a James Bond film couldn't get their underwater lights working. Still, according to GE, its people resolve 90 percent of complaints or inquiries on the first call, and complainers often become even more loyal customers. Although the company spends an average of $3.50 per call, it reaps two to three times that much in new sales and warranty savings.

The best way to keep customers happy is to provide good products and services in the first place. Short of that, however, a company must develop a good system for ferreting out and handling consumer problems. This is particularly important when firms market products globally and the cost of resolving customer problems increases exponentially. Such a system can be much more than a necessary evil—customer happiness usually shows up on the company's bottom line. One recent study found that dollars invested in complaint-handling and inquiry systems yield an average return of between 100 and 200 percent. Maryanne Rasmussen, vice-president of worldwide quality at American Express, offers this formula: "Better complaint handling equals higher customer satisfaction equals higher brand loyalty equals higher performance."

Sources: Quotations from Patricia Sellers, "How to Handle Consumer Gripes," *Fortune,* October 24, 1988, pp. 88–100. Also see Joyce Wycoff, "Customer Service: Evolution and Revolution," *Sales & Marketing Management,* May 1991, pp. 44–51; Frank Rose, "Now Quality Means Service Too," *Fortune,* April 22, 1991, pp. 97–108; Roland T. Rust, Bala Subramanian, and Mark Wells, "Making Complaints a Management Tool," *Marketing Management,* Fall 1992, pp. 41–45; Carl Quintanilla and Richard Gibson, " 'Do Call Us': More Companies Install 1-800 Phone Lines," *Wall Street Journal,* April 20, 1994, pp. B1, B4; and "Calming Upset Customers," *Sales & Marketing Management,* April 1994, p. 55.

satisfied owners talking about their new cars ("I love what you do for me, Toyota!"). Toyota also obtains customer suggestions for improvements and lists the location of available services.

THE BUYER DECISION PROCESS FOR NEW PRODUCTS

We have looked at the stages buyers go through in trying to satisfy a need. Buyers may pass quickly or slowly through these stages, and some of the stages may even be reversed. Much depends on the nature of the buyer, the product, and the buying situation.

New product
A good, service, or idea that is perceived by some potential customers as new.

Adoption process
The mental process through which an individual passes from first hearing about an innovation to final adoption.

We now look at how buyers approach the purchase of new products. A **new product** is a good, service, or idea that is perceived by some potential customers as new. It may have been around for a while, but our interest is in how consumers learn about products for the first time and make decisions on whether to adopt them. We define the **adoption process** as "the mental process through which an individual passes from first learning about an innovation to final adoption,"[32] and *adoption* as the decision by an individual to become a regular user of the product.

STAGES IN THE ADOPTION PROCESS

Consumers pass through five stages in the process of adopting a new product:

◆ *Awareness.* The consumer becomes aware of the new product, but lacks information about it.

◆ *Interest.* The consumer seeks information about the new product.

◆ *Evaluation.* The consumer considers whether trying the new product makes sense.

◆ *Trial.* The consumer tries the new product on a small scale to improve his or her estimate of its value.

◆ *Adoption.* The consumer decides to make full and regular use of the new product.

This model suggests that the new-product marketer should consider how to help consumers move through these stages. A manufacturer of large-screen televisions may discover that many consumers in the interest stage do not move to the trial stage because of uncertainty and the large investment. If these same consumers would be willing to use a large-screen television on a trial basis for a small fee, the manufacturer should consider offering a trial-use plan with an option to buy.

INDIVIDUAL DIFFERENCES IN INNOVATIVENESS

People differ greatly in their readiness to try new products. In each product area, there are "consumption pioneers" and early adopters. Other individuals adopt new products much later. People can be classified into the adopter categories shown in Figure 5-7. After a slow start, an increasing number of people adopt the new product. The number of adopters reaches a peak and then drops off as fewer nonadopters remain. Innovators are defined as the first 2.5 percent of the buyers to adopt a new idea (those beyond two standard deviations from mean adoption time); the early adopters are the next 13.5 percent (between one and two standard deviations); and so forth.

The five adopter groups have differing values. *Innovators* are venturesome—they try new ideas at some risk. *Early adopters* are guided by respect—they are opinion leaders in their communities and adopt new ideas early but carefully. The

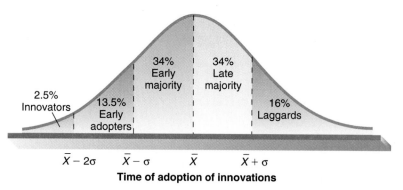

Time of adoption of innovations

FIGURE 5-7 *Adopter categorization on the basis of relative time of adoption of innovations*
Source: Redrawn from Everett M. Rogers, *Diffusion of Innovations,* 3rd ed. (New York: 1983), p. 247. Adapted with permission of Macmillan Publishing Company, Inc. Copyright © 1962, 1971, 1983 by the Free Press.

early majority are deliberate—although they rarely are leaders, they adopt new ideas before the average person. The *late majority* are sceptical—they adopt an innovation only after most people have tried it. Finally, *laggards* are tradition-bound—they are suspicious of changes and adopt the innovation only when it has become something of a tradition itself.

This adopter classification suggests that an innovating firm should research the characteristics of innovators and early adopters and should direct marketing efforts to them. In general, innovators tend to be relatively younger, better educated, and higher in income than later adopters and non-adopters. They are more receptive to unfamiliar things, rely more on their own values and judgment, and are more willing to take risks. They are less brand-loyal and more likely to take advantage of special promotions such as discounts, coupons, and samples.

INFLUENCE OF PRODUCT CHARACTERISTICS ON RATE OF ADOPTION

The characteristics of the new product affect its rate of adoption. Some products catch on almost overnight (Frisbees), whereas others take a long time to gain acceptance (personal computers). Five characteristics are especially important in influencing an innovation's rate of adoption. For example, consider the characteristics of large-screen televisions in relation to the rate of adoption:

◆ *Relative advantage:* the degree to which the innovation appears superior to existing products. The greater the perceived relative advantage of using a large-screen TV—say, in picture quality and ease of viewing—the sooner such TVs will be adopted.

◆ *Compatibility:* the degree to which the innovation fits the values and experiences of potential consumers. Large-screen TVs, for example, are highly compatible with the lifestyles found in upper-middle-class homes.

◆ *Complexity:* the degree to which the innovation is difficult to understand or use. Large-screen TVs are not very complex and will therefore take less time to penetrate homes than more complex innovations.

◆ *Divisibility:* the degree to which the innovation may be tried on a limited basis. Large-screen TVs are expensive. To the extent that people can lease them with an option to buy, their rate of adoption will increase.

◆ *Communicability:* the degree to which the results of using the innovation can be observed or described to others. Because large-screen TVs lend themselves to demonstration and description, their use will spread faster among consumers.

Other characteristics influence the rate of adoption, such as initial and ongoing costs, risk and uncertainty, and social approval. The new-product marketer must research all these factors when developing the new product and its marketing program.

CONSUMER BEHAVIOUR ACROSS INTERNATIONAL BORDERS

Understanding consumer behaviour is difficult enough for companies marketing within the borders of a single country. For companies operating in many countries,

CONSUMER-BEHAVIOUR DIFFERENCES ACROSS BORDERS: GLOBAL STANDARDIZATION OR ADAPTATION?

The marketing concept holds that marketing programs will be more effective if they are tailored to the unique needs of each targeted customer group. If this concept applies within a country, it should apply even more in international markets where demographic, economic, political, and cultural conditions vary widely. Consumers in different countries have varied needs and wants, spending power, product preferences, and shopping patterns. Because most marketers believe that these differences are hard to change, they adapt their products, prices, distribution channels, and promotion approaches to meet consumer desires in each country.

However, some global marketers are bothered by what they consider to be too much adaptation. For example, Gillette sells over 800 products in more than 200 countries. It now finds itself in a situation where it uses different brand names and formulations for the same products in different countries. For example, Gillette's Silkience shampoo is called Soyance in France, Sientel in Italy, and Silience in Germany; it uses the same formula in some cases but varies it in others. It also varies the product's advertising messages because each Gillette country manager proposes several changes that he or she thinks will increase local sales. These and similar adaptations for its hundreds of other products raise Gillette's costs and dilute its global brand power.

As a result, many companies have imposed more standardization on their products and marketing efforts. They have created so-called world brands that are marketed in much the same way worldwide. Whereas traditional marketers cater to differences between specific markets with highly adapted products, marketers who standardize globally sell more or less the same product the same way to all consumers. These marketers believe that advances in communication, transportation, and travel are turning the world into a common marketplace. They claim that people around the world want basically the same products and lifestyles. Everyone wants things that make life easier and that increase both free time and buying power. Despite what consumers say they want, all consumers want good products at lower prices.

Coca-Cola sells highly standardized products worldwide, but even Coke adapts its product and packaging somewhat to local tastes and conditions.

Thus, proponents of global standardization claim that international marketers should adapt products and marketing programs only when local wants cannot be changed or avoided. Standardization results in lower production, distribution, marketing, and management costs, and thus lets the company offer consumers higher-quality and more reliable products at lower prices. They would advise an auto company to make a world car, a shampoo company to make a world shampoo, and a farm-equipment company to make a world tractor. And, in fact, some companies have successfully marketed global products—for example, Coca-Cola, McDonald's hamburgers, Cross pens and pencils, Black & Decker tools, and Sony Walkmans. Yet, even in these cases, companies make some adaptations. Coca-Cola is less sweet or less carbonated in certain countries; McDonald's uses chili sauce instead of ketchup on its hamburgers in Mexico; and Cross pens and pencils have different advertising messages in some countries.

Moreover, the assertion that global standardization will lead to lower costs and prices, causing more goods to be snapped up by price-sensitive consumers, is debatable. Mattel Toys had sold its Barbie Doll successfully in dozens of countries without modification, but in Japan, it did not sell well. Takara, Mattel's Japanese licensee, surveyed grade 8 Japanese girls and their parents and found that they thought the doll's breasts were too big and its legs were too long. Mattel, however, was reluctant to modify the doll because this would require additional production, packaging, and advertising costs. Finally, Takara won out and Mattel made a special Japanese Barbie. Within two years, Takara had sold over two million of the modified dolls. Clearly, incremental revenues far exceeded the incremental costs.

Rather than assuming that their products can be introduced without change in other countries, companies should review possible adaptations in product features, brand name, packaging, advertising themes, prices, and other elements and determine which ones would add more revenues than costs. One study showed that companies made adaptations in one or more of these areas in 80 percent of their foreign-directed products.

So which approach is best— global standardization or adaptation? Clearly, standardization is not an all-or-nothing proposition, but rather a matter of degree. Companies are justified in looking for more standardization to help keep down costs and prices and build greater global brand power. But they must remember that although standardization saves money, competitors are always ready to offer more of what consumers in each country want, and that they might pay dearly for replacing long-run marketing thinking with short-run financial thinking. Some international marketers suggest that companies should "think globally but act locally." The corporate level gives strategic direction; local units focus on the individual consumer differences. Global marketing, yes; global standardization, not necessarily.

Sources: See Theodore Levitt, "The globalization of markets," *Harvard*

Business Review, May–June 1983, pp. 92–102; Kamran Kashani, "Beware the pitfalls of global marketing," *Harvard Business Review,* September–October 1989, pp. 91–98; Saeed Saminee and Kendall Roth, "The influence of global marketing standardization on performance," *Journal of Marketing,* April 1992, pp. 1–17; David M. Szymanski,

Sundar G. Bharadwaj, and Rajan Varadarajan, "Standardization versus adaptation of international marketing strategy: An empirical investigation," *Journal of Marketing,* October 1993, pp. 1–17; and Ashish Banerjee, "Global campaigns don't work; Multinationals do," *Advertising Age,* April 18, 1994, p. 23.

however, understanding and serving the needs of consumers can be daunting. Although consumers in different countries may have some things in common, their values, attitudes, and behaviours often vary greatly. International marketers must understand such differences and adjust their products and marketing programs accordingly.

Sometimes the differences are obvious. For example, in Canada and the United States, where most people eat cereal regularly for breakfast, Kellogg focuses its marketing on persuading consumers to select a Kellogg brand rather than a competitor's brand. In France, however, where most people prefer croissants and coffee or no breakfast at all, Kellogg advertising simply attempts to convince people that they should eat cereal for breakfast. Its packaging includes step-by-step instructions on how to prepare cereal.

Often differences across international markets are more subtle. They may result from physical differences in consumers and their environments. For example, Remington makes smaller electric shavers to fit the smaller hands of Japanese consumers; and battery-powered shavers for the British market, where few bathrooms have electrical outlets. Other differences result from varying customs. Consider the following examples:

◆ Shaking your head from side to side means "no" in most countries but "yes" in Bulgaria and Sri Lanka.

◆ In South America, Southern Europe, and many Arab countries, touching another person is a sign of warmth and friendship. In Asia, it is considered an invasion of privacy.

◆ In Norway or Malaysia, it's rude to leave something on your plate when eating; in Egypt, it's rude *not* to leave something on your plate.[33]

Failing to understand such differences in customs and behaviours among countries can mean disaster for a marketer's international products and programs.

Marketers must decide on the degree to which they will adapt their products and marketing programs to meet the unique cultures and needs of consumers in various markets. On the one hand, they want to standardize their offerings in order to simplify operations and take advantage of cost economies. On the other hand, adapting marketing efforts within each country results in products and programs that better satisfy the needs of local consumers. The question of whether to adapt or standardize the marketing mix across international markets has created a lively debate in recent years (see Marketing Highlight 5-4).

Summary of Chapter Objectives

The Canadian consumer market consists of about 29 million people who consume many billions of dollars worth of goods and services each year, making it one of the most attractive consumer markets in the world. The world consumer market consists of more than five *billion* people. Consumers around the world vary greatly in age, income, education level, and tastes. Understanding how these differences affect consumer *buying behaviour* is one of the biggest challenges marketers face.

1. **Define the consumer market and construct a simple model of consumer buyer behaviour.**

    The *consumer market* consists of all the individuals and households who buy or acquire goods and services for personal consumption. The simplest model of consumer buyer behaviour is the stimulus-response model. According to this model, marketing stimuli (the four *P*s) and other major forces (economic, technological, political, cultural) enter the consumer's "black box," and produce certain responses. Once in the "black box," these inputs produce observable buyer responses, such as product choice, brand choice, purchase timing, and purchase amount.

2. **Name the four major factors that are included in consumer buyer behaviour.**

    Consumer buyer behaviour is influenced by four key sets of buyer characteristics: cultural, social, personal, and psychological. Although many of these factors cannot be influenced by the marketer, they can be useful in identifying interested buyers and in shaping products and appeals to serve consumer needs better. *Culture* is the most basic determinant of a person's wants and behaviour. It includes the basic values, perceptions, preferences, and behaviours that a person learns from family and other important institutions. *Subcultures* are "cultures within cultures" that have distinct values and lifestyles, and can be based on anything from age to ethnicity. People with different cultural and subcultural characteristics have different product and brand preferences. As a result, marketers may want to focus their marketing programs on the special needs of certain groups.

    Social factors also influence a buyer's behaviour. A person's *reference groups*—family, friends, social organizations, professional associations—strongly affect product and brand choices. The buyer's age, life-cycle stage, occupation, economic circumstances,

lifestyle, personality, and other *personal characteristics* influence his or her buying decisions. Consumer *lifestyles*—the whole pattern of acting and interacting in the world—are also an important influence on purchase decisions. Finally, consumer buying behaviour is influenced by four major *psychological factors*—motivation, perception, learning, and beliefs and attitudes. Each of these factors provides a different perspective for understanding the workings of the buyer's black box.

3. **List and understand the stages in the buyer decision process.**

    When making a purchase, the buyer goes through a decision process consisting of *need recognition, information search, evaluation of alternatives, purchase decision,* and *postpurchase behaviour.* The marketer's job is to understand the buyer's behaviour at each stage and the influences that are operating. During *need recognition,* the consumer recognizes a problem or need that could be satisfied by a product or service in the market. Once the need is recognized, the consumer is aroused to seek more information and moves into the *information search* stage. With information in hand, the consumer proceeds to *alternative evaluation,* where the information is used to evaluate brands in the choice set. From there, the consumer makes a *purchase decision* and actually buys the product. In the final stage of the buyer decision process, *postpurchase behaviour,* the consumer takes action based on satisfaction or dissatisfaction.

4. **Describe the adoption and diffusion process for new products.**

    The product adoption process is composed of five stages: awareness, interest, evaluation, trial, and adoption. Initially, the consumer must become aware of the new product. *Awareness* leads to *interest,* and the consumer seeks information about the new product. Once information has been gathered, the consumer enters the *evaluation* stage and considers buying the new product. Next, in the *trial* stage, the consumer tries the product on a small scale to improve his or her estimate of its value. If the consumer is satisfied with the product, he or she enters the *adoption* stage, deciding to use the new product fully and regularly.

With respect to the diffusion of new products, consumers respond at different rates, depending on the consumer's characteristics and product's characteristics. Consumers may be innovators, early adopters, early majority, late majority, or laggards. *Innovators* are willing to try risky new ideas; *early adopters*—often community opinion leaders—accept new ideas early but carefully; the *early majority*—rarely leaders—decide deliberately to try new ideas, doing so before the average person does; the *late majority* try an innovation only after most people have adopted it; whereas *laggards* adopt an innovation only after it has become a tradition itself. Manufacturers try to bring their new products to the attention of potential early adopters, especially those who are opinion leaders.

Key Terms

Adoption process *(p. 183)*
Alternative evaluation *(p. 179)*
Attitude *(p. 172)*
Belief *(p. 172)*
Brand image *(p. 180)*
Cognitive dissonance *(p. 181)*
Complex buying behaviour *(p. 175)*
Consumer buying behaviour *(p. 155)*
Consumer market *(p. 155)*
Culture *(p. 156)*

Dissonance-reducing buying behaviour *(p. 175)*
Group *(p. 163)*
Habitual buying behaviour *(p. 175)*
Information search *(p. 177)*
Learning *(p. 172)*
Lifestyle *(p. 166)*
Motive (or drive) *(p. 169)*
Need recognition *(p. 177)*
New product *(p. 183)*

Opinion leaders *(p. 163)*
Perception *(p. 171)*
Personality *(p. 168)*
Postpurchase behaviour *(p. 181)*
Psychographics *(p. 166)*
Purchase decision *(p. 180)*
Social classes *(p. 161)*
Subculture *(p. 157)*
Variety-seeking buying behaviour *(p. 176)*

Discussing the Issues

1. List several factors that you could add to the model shown in Figure 5-1 to make it a more complete description of consumer behaviour.

2. In designing the advertising for a soft drink, which would you find more helpful: information about consumer demographics or consumer lifestyles? Give examples of how you would use each type of information.

3. Think about a very good or very bad experience you have had with a product. Discuss how this experience shaped your beliefs about this product. How long will these beliefs last?

4. Consumers play many different roles in the buying process: initiator, influencer, decider, buyer, and user. Describe purchases in which you've played these different roles.

5. Decide why the postpurchase behaviour stage is included in the model of the buying process. Explain what relevance this stage has for marketers.

6. For many people, changing to a healthier lifestyle would be an innovation. This might require changes in diet, exercise, smoking, and drinking. Discuss this innovation in terms of its relative advantage, compatibility, complexity, divisibility, and communicability. Is a healthy lifestyle likely to be adopted quickly by most Canadians?

Applying the Concepts

1. Different types of products can fulfil different functional and psychological needs.
   ◆ List five luxury products that are very interesting or important to you. Some possibilities might include cars, clothing, sports equipment, or cosmetics. List

five other necessities that you use that have little interest to you, such as pencils, laundry detergent, or gasoline.

♦ List the words that describe how you feel about each of the products you listed. Are there differences between the types of words you used for luxuries and necessities? What does this tell you about the different psychological needs these products fulfil?

2. Examining our own purchases can reveal ways in which buying decisions really occur.

♦ Describe the five stages of your own buyer decision process for a major purchase such as a camera, stereo, or car.

♦ Next, describe your decision process for a minor purchase such as a chocolate bar or a soft drink.

♦ Are the decision processes the same for major and minor purchases? Which steps differ, and why do they change?

References

1. Mariam Mesbah, "Harley Mag Ad Targets Women: Advertising in Chatelaine, Modern Woman," *Strategy: The Canadian Marketing Report*, April 28, 1997, p. 1.

2. Quotations from Richard A. Melcher, "Tune-Up Time for Harley," *Business Week*, April 8, 1997, pp. 90–94; Ian P. Murphy, "Aided by Research, Harley Goes Whole Hog," *Marketing News*, December 2, 1996, pp. 16, 17; and Dyan Machan, "Is the Hog Going Soft," *Forbes*, March 10, 1997, pp. 114–119. Also see "Hot Stuff," *Money*, April 1997, p. 174.

3. See Philip Cateora, *International Marketing*, 8th ed. (Homewood, IL.: Irwin, 1993), pp. 74–75.

4. Several models of the consumer buying process have been developed by marketing scholars. The most prominent models are those of John A. Howard and Jagdish N. Sheth, *The Theory of Buyer Behavior* (New York: John Wiley, 1969); Francesco M. Nicosia, *Consumer Decision Processes* (Englewood Cliffs, NJ: Prentice Hall, 1966); James F. Engel, Roger D. Blackwell, and Paul W. Miniard, *Consumer Behavior*, 5th ed. (New York: Holt, Rinehart & Winston, 1986); and James R. Bettman, *An Information Processing Theory of Consumer Choice* (Reading, MA: Addison-Wesley, 1979). For a summary, see Leon G. Schiffman and Leslie Lazar Kanuk, *Consumer Behavior*, 5th ed. (Englewood Cliffs, NJ: Prentice Hall, 1994), pp. 644–656.

5. *Shared Values: The Canadian Identity*, Ministry of Supply and Services Canada, 1991, p. 1.

6. Craig McKie and Keith Thompson, *Canadian Social Trends*, Toronto: Thompson Educational Publishing, Inc.

7. Anthony Wilson-Smith, "Future Imperfect," *Maclean's*, December 30, 1996, cover story, found on the Maclean's web site (macleans.ca/keepers/cov123096.html).

8. For this and other examples of the effects of culture in international marketing, see Philip R. Cateora, *International Marketing*, Chapter 4.

9. See Kenneth Labich, "Class in America," *Fortune*, February 4, 1994, pp. 114–126, here p. 120; *Marketing*, May 22, 1995, p. 14–15.

10. For more on marketing to native Canadians, ethnic minorities, mature consumers, or Internet surfers, see Leah Rickard, "Minorities Show Brand Loyalty," *Advertising Age*, May 9, 1994, p. 29; Thomas G. Exter, "The Largest Minority," *American Demographics*, February 1993, p. 59; Melissa Campanelli, "The Senior Market: Rewriting the Demographics and Definitions," *Sales & Marketing Management*, February 1991, pp. 63–70; Tibbett L. Speer, "Older Consumers Follow Different Rules," *American Demographics*, February 1993, pp. 21–22; Cyndee Miller, "Image of Seniors Improves in Ads," *Marketing News*, December 6, 1993, p. 8; Christopher Guly, "Getting the Message Out," *Today's Seniors*, October 1995; Jennifer Lynn, "Approaching Diversity," *Marketing*, July 30, 1995, p. 15; David Menzies, "TD Bank Opens a Branch in Cyberspace," *Marketing*, June 19, 1995, p. 11; James Pollock, "Opening Doors of Opportunity," *Marketing*, September 18, 1995; Isabel Vincent, "Chasing After the Ethnic Consumer," *Globe and Mail*, September 18, 1995; Craig McKie and Keith Thompson, *Canadian Social Trends*, Toronto: Thompson Educational Publishing, Inc; Royal Bank, "Growing Pains," *Vision 2000*, p. 3; Marina Strauss, "Seniors Grasp for Friendlier Packaging," *Globe and Mail*, October 7, 1993; Francois Vary, "Sizing Up 55-Plus," *Marketing Report on Quebec*, October 2, 1995.

11. Michael McCullough, "Staying Put," *Marketing*, September 8, 1997, p. 23; Kenneth Wong, "The Symbolic Power of Security," *Marketing*, September 8, 1997, p. 24.

12. Steve Ferley, "PMB '97 Reveals That Canadian Internet Usage Patterns Fall Along Both Language and Demographic Lines," *Digital Marketing* in *Marketing*, May 5, 1997, p. 16.

13. Steve Ferley, "PMB '97 Reveals That Canadian Internet Usage Patterns Fall Along Both Language and Demographic Lines," p. 16.

14. Randy Carr, "The Five Big Hurdles on the Road of Electronic Commerce," *Digital Marketing* in *Marketing*, May 5, 1997, p. 16; John Southerst, "Accountants Design 'Deal of Approval' for Web Trade," *Globe and Mail*, December 2, 1997, p. B15.

15. Beppi Crosariol, "The Emperor's New Web," *Report on Business*, August 1996, p. 19.

16. Craig McKie and Keith Thompson, *Canadian Social Trends*, Toronto: Thompson Educational Publishing, Inc.

17. Patricia Sellers, "The Best Way to Reach Your Buyers," *Fortune*, special issue on "The Tough New Consumer," Autumn/Winter, 1993, pp. 14–17.

18. Debra Goldman, "Spotlight Men," *Adweek*, August 13, 1990, pp. M1–M6; Dennis Rodkin, "A Manly Sport: Building Loyalty," *Advertising Age*, April 15, 1991, pp. S1, S12; Nancy Ten Kate, "Who Buys the Pants in the Family?" *American Demographics*, January 1992, p. 12; and Laura Zinn, "Real Men Buy Paper Towels, Too," *Business Week*, November 9, 1992, pp. 75–76.

19. Jeffery Zbar, "Hardware Builds Awareness Among Women," *Advertising Age*, July 11, 1994, p. 18.

20. David Leonhardt, "Hey Kids, Buy This," *Business Week*, June 30, 1997, pp. 62–67. Also see Kay M. Palan and Robert E. Wilkes, "Adolescent-Parent Interaction in Family Decisions," *Journal of Consumer Research*, September 1997, pp. 159–169.

21. For more on family decision making, see Schiffman and Kanuk, *Consumer Behavior*, Chap. 12; Michael B. Menasco and David J. Curry, "Utility and Choice: An Empirical Study of Husband/Wife Decision Making," *Journal of Consumer Research*, June 1989, pp. 87–97; Kim P. Corfman, "Perceptions of Relative Influence: Formation and Measurement," *Journal of Marketing Research*, May 1991, pp. 125–136; "The Family as a Consumer," special issue of *Psychology and Marketing*, March/April 1993; and Robert Boutilier, "Family's Strings," *American Demographics*, August 1993, pp. 44–47.

22. See "Ad Agency Finds Five Global Segments," *Marketing News*, January 8, 1990, pp. 9, 17.

23. Salem Alaton, "Look Who's Going Cellular," *Globe and Mail*, December 5, 1995, p. C1.

24. Myron Magnet, "Let's Go for Growth," *Fortune*, March 7, 1994, p. 70.

25. See Annetta Miller and Dody Tsiantar, "Psyching Out Consumers," *Newsweek*, February 27, 1989, pp.

46–47; and Rebecca Piirto, "Words that Sell," *American Demographics*, January 1992, p. 6.

26. Abraham H. Maslow, *Motivation and Personality*, 2nd ed. (New York: Harper & Row, 1970), pp. 80–106. Also see Rudy Schrocer, "Maslow's Hierarchy of Needs as a Framework for Identifying Emotional Triggers," *Marketing Review*, February 1991, pp. 26, 28.

27. See "Honda Hopes to Win New Riders by Emphasizing 'Fun' of Cycles," *Marketing News*, August 28, 1989, p. 6.

28. See Henry Assael, *Consumer Behavior and Marketing Action* (Boston: Kent Publishing, 1987), Chap. 4. An earlier classification of three types of consumer buying behavior—routine response behavior, limited problem solving, and extensive problem solving—can be found in John A. Howard and Jagdish Sheth, *The Theory of Consumer Behavior* (New York: John Wiley, 1969), pp. 27–28. Also see John A. Howard, *Consumer Behavior in Marketing Strategy* (Englewood Cliffs, NJ: Prentice Hall, 1989).

29. Keith B. Murray, "A Test of Services Marketing Theory: Consumer Information Acquisition Theory," *Journal of Marketing*, January 1991, pp. 10–25.

30. See Leon Festinger, *A Theory of Cognitive Dissonance* (Stanford, CA: Stanford University Press, 1957); and Leon G. Schiffman and Leslie Lazar Kanuk, *Consumer Behavior* (Englewood Cliffs, NJ: Prentice Hall, 1994), pp. 274–275.

31. See Karl Albrect and Ron Zemke, *Service America!* (Homewood, IL: Dow-Jones Irwin, 1985), pp. 6–7; and Frank Rose, "Now Quality Means Service Too," *Fortune*, April 22, 1991, pp. 97–108.

32. The following discussion draws heavily from Everett M. Rogers, *Diffusion of Innovations*, 3rd ed. (New York: Free Press, 1983). Also see Hubert Gatignon and Thomas S. Robertson, "A Propositional Inventory for New Diffusion Research," *Journal of Consumer Research*, March 1985, pp. 849–867.

33. For these and other examples, see William J. Stanton, Michael J. Etzel, and Bruce J. Walker, *Fundamentals of Marketing* (New York: McGraw-Hill, Inc., 1991), p. 536.

Company Case 5

THE LOONEY SCHOOL OF TENNIS

Craig Smith, President of the Looney School of Tennis, had some difficult decisions to make. The Looney School of Tennis had only been incorporated for nine months and although demand for the company product had been high, the President realized that attention was needed in several areas.

The Looney School of Tennis had two "arms" to the company: School Tennis Programs and Summer Club Management. During the school year, the Looney

School of Tennis focused on running low-cost tennis programs throughout local private and public primary and elementary schools. Although this was not the most profitable arm of the company, it was nonetheless extremely important as it served to provide a broad case of customers for the second more profitable arm of the company, Summer Club Management. While Craig was generally pleased with the level of success his company had reached in such a short period, two problem areas needed his immediate attention. First, in order to attract new primary and elementary schools, Craig had initiated a free promotion to interested schools. This involved providing a demonstration lesson to every gym class in the school, which took, on average, two full days of instruction. While this promotion had proved very successful in attracting new customers, it was also very costly and Craig was unsure if he could continue with this promotional effort. Second, Craig also had to resolve the dissatisfaction level of his tennis director, Justin Mondoux, who was unhappy with his current level of compensation.

Craig was hoping to reach some decisions and to implement "solutions" to these problem areas in time for the upcoming 1996 season.

BACKGROUND

In 1991 Craig Smith was thinking about tennis. As a competitive player and high-performance tennis coach for over 11 years, he was concerned about the overall decline in participation in the sport. In the 1970s, the tennis industry went through a dramatic growth period, but by the 1990s, the industry was hurting. The sport was simply not capturing the imagination of youngsters and this had resulted in a decline in tennis club membership and interest in competitive tennis events.

As a result of his increasing concern over this industry "recession," Craig decided to volunteer his time to local private and public schools to run children's tennis programs in order to introduce children to the sport of tennis and hopefully increase awareness and interest in the sport. This volunteer program met with overwhelming success. Feedback from both parents and the school teachers alike was excellent, and membership in local tennis clubs increased. In 1995, Craig decided to incorporate the Looney School of Tennis, an innovative grassroots company aimed at promoting the sport of tennis by offering low-cost, quality tennis lessons throughout the Ottawa-Carleton area.

THE COMPANY

The Looney School of Tennis has one product: tennis lessons. The lessons are tailored to meet the needs of various purchasers by offering lessons at various times and locations. The company emphasizes the fun aspect of the sport through grassroots school programming and by offering an innovative promotion strategy. The objective is to sell a high volume of top-quality, yet reasonably priced tennis lessons to both children and adults. Although children are the main target of Looney School lessons, adult programs are also offered in the summer club programs.

During the school year, Craig focuses his attention on running tennis programs through the private and public schools in the Ottawa-Carleton region. These programs introduce groups of approximately 20 children, at $3 per child per lesson, to the fun, athletic and positive dimensions of the sport. Lessons are held in the school gymnasium, or weather permitting in the school yard (see Appendix 1).

Once the school year is complete, the company shifts its focus toward community tennis-club management. More specifically, summer clubs, particularly those concerned with low membership levels, hire the Looney School of Tennis to completely design and oversee their summer programs. This involves the recruitment, supervision, and compensation of certified tennis professionals as well as the complete design, promotion, and implementation of all club programs, leagues, children's camps, and private lessons.

The two arms of the company are very complementary. A large percentage of children or their parents are interested in having the students continue on with the sport after being introduced to it through the school system. Parents traditionally contact the Looney School for information on tennis programs/camps offered nearby. The Looney School can then direct the children to the nearest community club managed by the company. The school programming offered by the Looney School is therefore an excellent platform to direct interest sparked by the school programs to the second focus of the company, summer club management.

The company was started with a low capital investment. Other than the computer purchased subsequent to incorporation, the yearly liability insurance fee, and the business telephone expense, the only expenses to the company are its variable costs, which consist of office supplies, photocopying, and the hourly wages paid to the instructors.

Specialized Wilson Sporting Equipment was provided under a sponsorship arrangement to the Looney School subsequent to incorporation. The equipment, such as mini-tennis racquets and tennis nets, is provided to all students for their use, free of charge, during Looney School lessons. This specialized equipment is easier for the children to handle and provides them with better control in playing the sport. This in turn results in higher success and self-confidence while taking part in the lessons.

Since the Looney School's goal is high-volume sales, the need for a large part-time staff is critical. Through his coaching activities, Craig Smith has personal contact with many high performance, provincially ranked tennis players who are interested in teaching to gain experience and to work towards their coaching certification. They are dynamic, energetic, and very good with children, and are placed in the Looney School "hierarchy" according to their age, experience, and interpersonal skills. The five levels of the hierarchy are as follows:

LOONEY TRAINEES: 15 hours of volunteer lessons

LOONEY ASSISTANTS: $6 per hour (uncertified) or $8 per hour (certified)

LOONEY PROS: $10 per hour (certified only)

TENNIS DIRECTOR: $12 per hour—Justin Mondoux

PRESIDENT: Craig Smith

Looney assistants will generally become promoted to Looney Pros after one full year. During the summer months, Looney Pros become community club head pros. This, of course, is flexible and subject to change depending on the assessment of their progress. All staff are continually trained and supervised by Craig Smith.

The satisfaction level from the schools and parents alike has been very high. Feedback has indicated that the schools are very impressed with the high quality of the lessons and particularly shocked at their low cost. In fact, the company has recently captured the interest of a local television station, CJOH TV, which has hosted two segments on the company, aired during the six o'clock news. This has directly increased school bookings and has resulted in increased awareness about the company.

The main challenge for the Looney School is to capture the interest of children, the main users of the Looney School product, who currently find the sport dull and "uncool." Fortunately for the Looney School, the massive promotional efforts launched by tennis sporting good manufacturers such as Wilson, Nike, Head, and Prince appear to be paying off as latest industry reports forecast an improvement in participation rates and racquet sales. Although the children are the principal users of the lessons, and hence the prime initiator in the decision-making process, it is critical that the Looney School be successful in reaching the schools. The Looney School must convince the Ottawa-Carleton school boards that Looney lessons will be of value to the students, parents, and teachers. School boards are looking for convenient low-cost services that provide diversity in school programming, interest in students, and satisfaction of parents. After-school programs are particularly appealing to parents who prefer to have their children participate in a healthy, low-cost, after-school activity as opposed to straight supervision.

The main problem currently facing the Looney School concerns the two-day free promotions offered to interested Ottawa-Carleton schools. As many of the schools are initially unsure of the success of running tennis programs in a gymnasium, the Looney School of Tennis decided to offer demonstrations to every gym class in the school, free of charge. This promotion appealed greatly to the schools and resulted, on average, in the booking of three schools for every 10 demonstrations provided. Most schools would book three sessions of tennis programs, with each program offering five lessons to a particular class.

Although the promotions were in great demand, unfortunately, the related expenses were high. For each demonstration the Looney School provided, a salary expense of approximately $120 (or 6 hrs x 2 days x $10/hr) was incurred, as well as a photocopying expense for flyers of approximately $35 (350 flyers x $0.10). This resulted in a total promotion expense of $155 per demo, with no guarantee of a future sale. Craig felt this situation required further attention. Before deciding whether or not it was worthwhile to change the current setup, Craig considered two options.

The first option was to request a voluntary contribution of one or two "loonies" (dollars) from the students. In this scenario, a flyer would be sent home with the children prior to the demonstration, requesting that a contribution be provided in order to defray the costs to the company. On average, 350 students attend each two-day demonstration. Craig felt that it would not be unreasonable to expect that half of the people would make some sort of contribution.

Craig decided to approach four schools, booked for upcoming demonstrations, to obtain feedback on this option. None of these schools objected to soliciting a voluntary contribution from the student. As a result, Craig decided to go ahead with a trial run on these schools to assess the reaction of the parents. Results from this trial are provided in Appendix 2.

Craig's second option was to charge each child a flat fee for the demonstration. However, he had not yet approached the schools about this option as he was unsure what their reaction would be.

The second problem that required Craig's attention was the compensation package for his tennis director, Justin Mondoux. Justin had been complaining about only working one or two hours at a time, at his hourly wage, and was looking for an improvement in his compensation package. As a result of Justin's dissatisfaction, Craig was seriously considering changing Justin's compensation from an hourly wage to a commission structure. In this scenario, Justin would be responsible for making contact and visiting with all the schools and booking/conducting all free demonstrations on his own time. In return he would receive 35 percent of the profits for each school booked for follow-on lessons. This way, the company would only be incurring a "salary expense" upon a sale. Not only would this address the concern of the costly demonstrations, but it would also serve to resolve the staffing problem previously discussed, and free up valuable time for Craig Smith, who very much needed to devote time to other areas of the business. On the other hand, Craig was concerned he would lose personal contact with the schools if he implemented this option.

Craig needed to give some serious thought to the various alternatives outlined above, prior to deciding what changes, if any, he should make and the likely effect these changes would have on the satisfaction level of his customers and staff alike.

APPENDIX 1

THE PRODUCT—SCHOOL PROGRAMMING

After School/Lunch-time Lessons: Programs are offered in packages of five lessons at $3 per lesson per child and lessons are offered either during lunch hour or as an after school program. The lessons are given in the school gym or, weather permitting, in the school yard.

End of School Tennis Fair: Toward the end of the school year, the Looney School offers to local private and public Ottawa-Carleton schools the option to book an "end of school tennis fair." This allows the children to finish their school year *"with an ace."* Children from a local primary school are bused to a nearby tennis club managed by the Looney School of Tennis. Here the children experience playing on a "real" tennis court. The fair demonstrates to the children how accessible tennis can be and how it can be played in their own neighbourhood. Children who participate in the Tennis Fair receive a certificate that he or she is a $100% tennis fanatic." The certificate also provides a phone number for more information on how to get involved in summer Looney lessons/camps at a club nearby.

APPENDIX 2

TRIAL DEMONSTRATIONS

School A
The first school that was visited is located in an upper-middle-class suburb of Ottawa, where the average home is valued at approximately $205 000 and municipal taxes average $3200. This area consists exclusively of single family homes, where approximately 80 percent of the occupants in the district own their own home. The majority of families are dual income professionals in their mid-forties. There are no public courts within a one-kilometre radius of the community.

Of the total 239 students in this school who attended the demonstrations, 177 provided a contribution, with the average contribution being $1.67. The average age of the children was 10, with only 15 percent having every played the sport previously.

School B
The second school that received a free demonstration is located in a working-class area of the city, with the average home valued at approximately $123 000 and municipal taxes running at approximately $1700. Here only approximately 40 percent of the families, which are predominantly single income families, own their own homes. The dwellings are a mixture of semi-detached and townhouses with several apartment complexes nearby. There are two public courts within a one-kilometre radius of the community.

Of the total 305 students who attended the demonstrations, 189 contributed with an average contribution of $0.41. Here the average age of the children was 12, with only eight percent having ever played the sport before.

School C
The third school that was visited is also located in a working-class district not far from the second school. The area consists mostly of garden homes, valued at approximately $112 000 and municipal taxes at $1500. Here only 35 percent of the families own their own homes. These households consisted mainly of blue-collar workers in their mid-thirties. There are no public courts within walking distance of the community.

Of the total 347 students in this school, 208 returned with an average contribution of $0.38. Here the average age of the children was 8, with 12 percent having every played the sport.

District	A Upper-middle Class	B Working Class	C Working Class	D Middle Class
Home Value	$ 205 000	$ 123 000	$ 112 000	$ 175 000
Taxes	$ 3 200	$ 1 700	$ 1 500	$ 2 500
% Homes Owned	80%	40%	35%	75%
# Public Courts	0	2	0	1
# of Students	239	305	347	198
# Contributed	177	189	208	127
Ave. Contribution	$ 1.67	$ 0.41	$ 0.38	$ 1.42
Ave. Age	10	12	8	10
% Played Before	15%	8%	12%	5%

School D

The last school visited is located in a middle-class district, with the average home valued at approximately $175 000 and municipal taxes of approximately $2500. Most families in this area are dual income young professionals, with approximately 75 percent owning their own home. There is one public court within walking distance of the community.

Of the 198 students who attended the demonstration, 127 contributed an average of $1.42. The average age of the children was 10, with only 5 percent having ever been exposed to the sport.

QUESTIONS:

1. What is Craig Smith selling?
2. What are the strengths and weaknesses of his company and its marketing plan?
3. What threats does Craig face?
4. What opportunities might he exploit?
5. Why must Craig have a thorough understanding of consumer behaviour? Why is tennis not viewed as a "cool" sport?
6. What market segments has Craig been serving? Can he present the same marketing program to each segment?
7. What alternatives can you suggest to Craig to help him solve his problems? How would you compare these alternatives?
8. What final recommendations would you make to Craig?

Source: © 1996. Faculty of Administration, University of Ottawa. This case was prepared by Andrea Gaunt under the supervision of David S. Litvack. No part of this publication may be reproduced, stored in a retrieval system, or transmitted in any form or by any means—electronic, mechanical, photocopying, recording, or otherwise—without permission of the Faculty of Administration, University of Ottawa, 136 Jean-Jacques Lussier, Ottawa, Ontario, Canada, K1N 6N5.

Video Case 5

THE CANADIAN CREDIT CRUNCH

Consumers' purchasing choices are affected by several factors, including their economic situation. Recently Canadian consumers have reorganized their purchasing patterns in an attempt to cope with large amounts of personal debt. It is estimated that the combined personal debt in Canada is equal to 92 percent of the nation's disposable income. In addition, personal bankruptcies were at an all-time high in the first half of 1996. As one analyst observed, this is the first generation in Canada that cannot expect to have a higher standard of living than their parents had.

The 1980s were a period of heavy spending in Canada. But since many consumers were spending beyond their means, most of their purchases were financed by credit cards. As a result, many consumers have not yet been able to pay off this debt, even well into the 1990s. Furthermore, several consumers have been caught in the personal debt trap of using credit card advances to pay off bills, even mortgages. Then the consumer ends up simply paying the interest on the cards every month without making payments on the amount owed. The situation is made worse if someone loses a job since it now takes longer to get another job. Faced with no job but nonetheless confident that they will eventually get one, some consumers use their credit cards to buy everything.

As a group, Canadian consumers have taken drastic action to curb their spending and pay off their debt. They seem unwilling to get into debt again. And as consumers leave their credit cards at home, retailers are feeling the crunch. Retail sales dropped off dramatically in 1995 as consumers were faced with the reality of carrying too much personal debt. But while many retailers are in trouble as a result of consumer unwillingness to spend, there are some opportunities. Consumers have revised their priorities and, therefore, their spending habits. For example, while the purchase of products has decreased, service purchases have increased. Since consumers can't afford new cars, they spend more on car servicing to maintain their old ones. If consumers don't have time to cook because they are working more hours to help pay off debt, the demand for restaurants increases. Yet another opportunity in this type of market is the professionals who counsel consumers about their debt. Credit counselling has become a significant part of many accounting practices.

QUESTIONS

1. What other factors, besides their personal financial situation, may affect consumers' willingness to spend?

2. What impact would consumer unwillingness to spend have on the Buyer Decision Process for those products and services that are purchased?

3. In addition to the businesses mentioned in the case above, can you identify other businesses that may enjoy increased sales, even when consumers are cutting back on spending?

Source: This case was prepared by Auleen Carson and is based on "Personal Debt," *Venture* (October 20, 1996).

Principles of
Marketing

Principles of
Marketi

ciples
Mark

C H A P T E R 6

BUSINESS MARKETS
AND BUSINESS
BUYER BEHAVIOUR

If anyone knows how to market to business and government clients, it is Bombardier, the company that was voted the most respected company in Canada for two consecutive years. To the chords of a 45-piece orchestra and a thousand-member choir, the company unveiled the ultimate business jet from under a giant tarpaulin bearing the image of a Canadian flag. Prime Minister Jean Chrétien and other political dignitaries were members of the invited crowd. The occasion introduced the Global Express Aircraft—known as the "Lamborghini of the sky"—to its potential purchasers, including CEOs, heads of state, and sheiks who must part with $48 million to enjoy gold-plated luxury.

Yet it has taken more than splashy product launches to compete in the global aircraft market. It has involved strategic thinking, heavy investment in new product development, and insight about what markets the company could best serve. Using some of the best business people in the world, Bombardier has carved out a niche for itself. Instead of competing in the large passenger-plane market where it would have to compete with the likes of Boeing and Airbus Industries, the company focused instead on regional and business aircraft. Before spending the millions required to develop new aircraft, Bombardier's sales force spent years studying the market. When they observed that large airlines were moving to a hub-and-spoke strategy, they forecast that an explosion of small airlines would be needed to fly passengers to the system hubs. Bombardier knew that these airlines, in both North America and Europe, would need small, efficient airplanes to fly these routes. This knowledge led them to develop their highly successful Dash 8 regional turboprop aircraft—one of the most successful regional aircrafts in the world. Bombardier also foresaw the explosive growth in international business and positioned itself to provide aircraft to CEOs who had to travel around the world to visit their far-flung operations. Recognition of this need led to the development of the Global Express Aircraft whose launch is pictured at left.

OBJECTIVES

When you finish this chapter, you should be able to

1. Define the business market and explain how business markets differ from consumer markets.

2. Identify the major factors that influence business buyer behaviour.

3. List and define the steps in the business buying-decision process.

4. Compare the institutional and government markets and explain how institutional and government buyers make their buying decisions.

Bombardier International
www.bombardier.com/

From its headquarters in Montreal, Bombardier has grown to become the third-largest aircraft manufacturer in the world. Even more impressive is that the company achieved this lofty position in just 10 years. Bombardier employs 41 000 people in plants located in nine countries and sells aircraft to corporate and government customers in 60 countries. In 1996, the company racked up $7.1 billion in sales—an impressive 20 percent increase over its revenues in 1995. Bombardier's long list of clients includes American Airlines, Delta Airlines, Deutsche Lufthansa AG, Paris-based TAG Aeronautics, Scandinavian Airlines, and a Japanese firm that wants to market Bombardier's amphibious firefighting aircraft in earthquake-prone Japan. It has added marquee aerospace companies such as Shorts, de Havilland, and Learjet to its team. The firm has entered completely new markets. It recently cracked the Eastern European market with an order worth over $590 million for 24 aircraft from a new Romanian airline. Not only will Bombardier provide modern equipment to restore Romania's air transportation system, but it will also provide a level of service unknown under planned economies.

In addition to exploring new market frontiers, the firm has launched new product initiatives. For example, Bombardier has entered into strategic alliances with several international aerospace leaders, such as Mitsubishi Heavy Industries Ltd. of Japan and BMW-Rolls Royce of Germany, to share the risks of developing and building its Global Express executive aircraft. It is partnering with Swiss-based Global Aviation Ltd. to launch an onslaught on the Chinese market.

Exploring exciting new products and new markets isn't all that is involved in marketing aircraft, however. To market its new executive aircraft, Bombardier must recognize the importance of *rational* motives and *objective* factors in buyers' decisions. Customers justify the expense of a corporate jet on utilitarian grounds, such as security, flexibility, responsiveness to customers, and efficient time use. A company buying a jet will evaluate Bombardier's Global Express aircraft on quality and performance, prices, operating costs, and service. At times, these "objective factors" may appear to be the only things that drive the buying decision. But having a superior product isn't enough to land the sale: Bombardier also must consider the more subtle *human factors* that affect the choice of a jet.

The purchase process may be initiated by the chief executive officer (CEO), a board member wishing to increase efficiency or security, the company's chief pilot, or through Bombardier's efforts, such as advertising or a sales visit. The CEO will be central in deciding whether to buy the jet, but he or she will be heavily influenced by the company's pilot, financial officer, and members of top management. The involvement of so many people in the purchase decision creates a group dynamic that Bombardier must factor into its sales planning. Who comprises the buying group? How will the parties interact? Who will dominate and who submit? What priorities do the individuals have?

Each party in the buying process has subtle roles and needs. For example, the salesperson who tries to impress both the CEO with depreciation schedules and the chief pilot with minimum runway statistics will almost certainly not sell a plane if he or she overlooks the psychological and emotional components of the buying decision. The chief pilot, as an equipment expert, often has veto power over purchase decisions and may be able to stop the purchase of a certain brand of jet by simply expressing a negative opinion about, say, the plane's bad weather capabilities. In this sense, the pilot not only influences the decision but also serves as an information "gatekeeper" by advising management on which equipment to select. The users of the jet—middle and upper management of the buying company, important customers, and others—may have at least an indirect role in choosing the equipment. Although the corporate legal staff will handle the purchase agreement and the purchasing department will acquire the jet, these parties may have little to say about whether or how the plane will be obtained and which type will be selected.

According to one salesperson, in dealing with the CEO, the biggest factor is not the plane's hefty price tag, but its image. You need the numbers for support, but if you can't find the kid inside the CEO and excite him or her with the raw beauty of the new plane, you'll never sell the equipment. If you sell the excitement, you sell the jet.

Some buying influences may come as a big surprise. Bombardier may never really know who is behind the purchase of a plane. Although many people inside the customer company can be influential, the most important influence may turn out to be someone else in the organization who has an interest in flying.

In some ways, selling corporate jets to business buyers is like selling cars and kitchen appliances to families. Bombardier asks the same questions as consumer marketers: Who are the buyers and what are their needs? How do buyers make their buying decisions and what factors influence these decisions? What marketing program will be most effective? But the answers to these questions are usually different for the business buyer. Thus, Bombardier faces many of the same challenges as consumer marketers—and some additional ones.[1]

In one way or another, most large companies sell to other organizations. Many companies, such as Alcan Aluminium, NOVA Corp., Laidlaw, 3M Canada, Northern Telecom, and countless other firms, sell *most* of their products to other businesses. Even large consumer-products companies, which make products used by final consumers, must first sell their products to other businesses. For example, Kraft Canada makes many familiar consumer products—Post cereals, KRAFT DINNER, Jell-O, Kraft peanut butter, and others. But to sell these products to consumers, Kraft Canada must first sell them to the wholesalers and retailers that serve the consumer market.

The **business market** consists of all the organizations that buy goods and services to use in the production of other products and services that are sold, rented, or supplied to others. It also includes retailing and wholesaling firms that acquire goods for the purpose of reselling or renting them to others at a profit. The **business buying process** is the decision-making process by which business buyers establish the need for purchased products and services, and identify, evaluate, and choose among alternative brands and suppliers.[2] Companies that sell to other business organizations must do their best to understand business markets and business buyer behaviour.

Kraft Canada
www.shakenbake.com/
canada/english/html

Business market
All the organizations that buy goods and services to use in the production of other products and services or for the purpose of reselling or renting them to others at a profit.

Business buying process
The decision-making process by which business buyers establish the need for purchased products and services and identify, evaluate, and choose among alternative brands and suppliers.

BUSINESS MARKETS

The business market is *huge:* Consider the buying power of just one industry, the Canadian computer equipment industry, for example. It is the eighth-largest in the world: more than 300 companies are involved in the industry, generating $5.8 billion in revenues and employing 14 000 people.[3] Add to this the thousands of other firms operating in Canada and you quickly realize that business markets involve far more dollars and items than do consumer markets. For example, consider the large number of business transactions involved in producing and selling a single set of Goodyear Tires. Various suppliers sell Goodyear the rubber, steel, equipment, and other goods that it needs to produce the tires. Goodyear then sells the finished tires to retailers, who in turn sell them to consumers. Thus, many sets of *business* purchases were made for only one set of *consumer* purchases. In addition, Goodyear sells tires as original equipment to manufacturers who instal them on new vehicles, and as replacement tires to companies that maintain their own fleets of company cars, trucks, buses, or other vehicles.

CHARACTERISTICS OF BUSINESS MARKETS

In some ways, business markets are similar to consumer markets. Both involve people who assume buying roles and make purchase decisions to satisfy needs. However, business markets differ in many ways from consumer markets.[4] The main differences, shown in Table 6-1 and discussed below, are in *market structure*

TABLE 6-1 *Characteristics of Business Markets*

Marketing Structure and Demand

- ◆ Business markets contain *fewer but larger buyers.*
- ◆ Business customers are more *geographically concentrated.*
- ◆ Business buyer demand *derives* from final consumer demand.
- ◆ Demand in many business markets is *more inelastic*—not affected as much in the short run by price changes.
- ◆ Demand in business market *fluctuates more,* and more quickly.

Nature of the Buying Unit

- ◆ Business purchases involve *more buyers.*
- ◆ Business buying involves a *more professional purchasing effort.*

Types of Decisions and the Decision Process

- ◆ Business buyers usually face more *complex buying decisions.*
- ◆ The business buying process is *more formalized.*
- ◆ In business buying, buyers and sellers work more closely together and build close long-run *relationships.*

Other Characteristics

- ◆ Business buyers often *buy directly* from producers, rather than through retailers or wholesalers.
- ◆ Business buyers often practise *reciprocity,* buying from suppliers who also buy from them.
- ◆ Business buyers more often *lease* equipment rather than buying it outright.

and demand, the *nature of the buying unit,* and the *types of decisions and the decision process* involved.

Market Structure and Demand

The business marketer typically deals with *far fewer but far larger buyers* than the consumer marketer does. For example, when Goodyear sells replacement tires to final consumers, its potential market includes the owners of the millions of cars currently in use in Canada and the United States. But Goodyear's fate in the business market depends on getting orders from one of only a few large auto makers. Even in large business markets, a few buyers typically account for most of the purchasing.

Business markets are also more *geographically concentrated.* Over 70 percent of the manufacturers in Canada are located in Ontario and Quebec, and most of these are found along the narrow corridor between Windsor and Quebec City.[5] Further, business demand is **derived demand**—it ultimately derives from the demand for consumer goods. General Motors Canada buys steel because consumers buy cars. If consumer demand for cars drops, so will the demand for steel and all the other products used to make cars. Therefore, business marketers sometimes promote their products directly to final consumers to increase business demand.

Many business markets have *inelastic demand;* that is, total demand for many business products is not affected much by price changes, especially in the short run. A drop in the price of leather will not cause shoe manufacturers to buy much more leather unless it results in lower shoe prices that, in turn, will increase consumer demand for shoes.

Finally, business markets have more *fluctuating demand.* The demand for many business goods and services tends to change more—and more quickly—than the demand for consumer goods and services does. A small percentage increase in

Derived demand
Business demand that ultimately comes from (derives from) the demand for consumer goods.

Dependable

Really, really dependable

We both pick-up and deliver. But, that's where the comparison ends!

That's because our really, really dependable air cargo services have made us the carrier of choice for many well-known, freight forwarders and national courier companies across Canada and around the world. So why not choose the air cargo service they use?

We offer air cargo services for most shipment needs; from important documents to heavy, consolidated international shipments. And, just about anything else.

Choose **Canadian Guaranteed** premium service for priority domestic and international shipments; **Canadian Express** door-to-door for next business day delivery between hundreds of communities across Canada; and **Canadian Air Freight** for economical shipments, world-wide. Even man's best friend can't beat that.

Canadian AirCargo
Really, really dependable

Need more information?
1-800-667-7000
www.cdnair.ca

While final consumers are important to Canadian Airlines, the business market is their life blood.

consumer demand can cause large increases in business demand. Sometimes a rise of only 10 percent in consumer demand can cause as much as a 200 percent rise in business demand during the next period.

Nature of the Buying Unit

Compared with consumer purchases, a business purchase usually involves *more buyers* and a *more professional purchasing effort*. Often, business buying is done by trained purchasing agents who spend their working lives learning how to buy better. The more complex the purchase, the more likely that several people will participate in the decision-making process. Buying committees composed of technical experts and top management are common in the buying of major goods. Therefore, business marketers must have well-trained salespeople to deal with well-trained buyers.

Types of Decisions and the Decision Process

Business buyers usually face *more complex* buying decisions than do consumer buyers. Purchases often involve large sums of money, complex technical and economic considerations, and interactions among many people at many levels of the buyer's organization. Because the purchases are more complex, business buyers may take longer to make their decisions. For example, the purchase of a large computer system might take many months or more than a year to complete and could involve millions of dollars, thousands of technical details, and dozens of people ranging from top management to lower-level users.

The business buying process tends to be *more formalized* than the consumer buying process. Large business purchases usually call for detailed product specifications, written purchase orders, careful supplier searches, and formal approval. The buying firm might even prepare policy manuals that outline the purchase process.

Finally, in the business buying process, buyer and seller are often much *more dependent* on each other. Consumer marketers are usually at a distance from their customers. In contrast, business marketers may roll up their sleeves and work closely with their customers during all stages of the buying process—from helping customers define problems, to finding solutions, to supporting after-sale operation. They often customize their offerings to individual customer needs. In the short run, sales go to suppliers who meet buyers' immediate product and service needs. However, business marketers also must build close *long-run* relationships with customers. In the long run, business marketers keep a customer's sales by meeting current needs *and* by working with customers to help them succeed with their own customers (see Marketing Highlight 6-1).[6]

A MODEL OF BUSINESS BUYER BEHAVIOUR

At the most basic level, marketers want to know how business buyers will respond to various marketing stimuli. Figure 6-1 shows a model of business buyer behaviour. In this model, marketing and other stimuli affect the buying organization and produce certain buyer responses. As with consumer buying, the marketing stimuli for business buying consist of the four Ps: product, price, place, and promotion. Other stimuli include major forces in the environment: economic, technological, political, cultural, and competitive. These stimuli enter the organization and are

BUSINESS MARKETERS SELL CUSTOMER SUCCESS

In the late 1980s, the Dow chemical company realigned its dozen or so widely varied plastics businesses into a single business unit called Dow Plastics. One of the first things Dow had to do was to decide how to position its new division competitively. Initial research with Dow's and competitors' customers showed that Dow

service, or lack thereof, that they received from all three suppliers. "Vendors peddled resins as a commodity," says the head of Dow Plastics' research and advertising agency. "They competed on price and delivered on time, but gave no service."

These findings led to a positioning strategy that went far

and services, but customer success. Says the agency executive, "Whether they're using Dow's plastics to make bags for Safeway or for complex aerospace applications, we have to help them succeed in their markets." This new thinking was summed up in the positioning statement: "We don't succeed unless you do."

The new positioning helped Dow Plastics to become a truly customer-oriented company. It got Dow out of selling plastics and into selling customer success. The slogan and underlying philosophy created a unifying identity for the business—one based on building relationships with customers and helping them to succeed with their own businesses. Customer problems became more than just engineering challenges. Dow's customers sell to somebody else, so the company now faced new challenges of marketing to and helping satisfy customers' customers.

As a result of its new customer-relationship orientation, Dow Plastics has now become a leader in the plastics industry. The customer-success philosophy permeates everything the business does. Whenever company people encounter a new product or market, the first question they always ask is, "How does this fit with 'We don't succeed unless you do.'?"

Dow Plastics tells customers, "We don't succeed unless you do." Building deeper customer relationships helped Dow move from number three to become a leader in its market.

Source: Portions adapted from Nancy Arnott, "Getting the Picture: The Grand Design—We Don't Succeed Unless You Do," *Sales & Marketing Management*, June 1994, pp. 74–76; www.dow.com/cgi-bin/frameup.cgi?/plastics

Plastics rated a distant third in customer preference behind industry leaders Du Pont and GE Plastics. The research also revealed, however, that customers were unhappy with the

beyond simply selling good products and delivering them on time. Dow Plastics set out to build deeper relationships with customers. The company was selling not just products

turned into buyer responses: product or service choice; supplier choice; order quantities; and delivery, service, and payment terms. To design good marketing-mix strategies, the marketer must understand what happens within the organization to turn stimuli into purchase responses.

Within the organization, buying activity consists of two major parts: the buying centre, made up of all the people involved in the buying decision, and the buying decision process. The model shows that the buying centre and the buying decision process are influenced by internal organizational, interpersonal, and individual factors as well as by external environmental factors.

BUSINESS BUYER BEHAVIOUR

The model in Figure 6-1 suggests four questions about business buyer behaviour: What buying decisions do business buyers make? Who participates in the buying

FIGURE 6-1
*A model of
business buyer
behaviour*

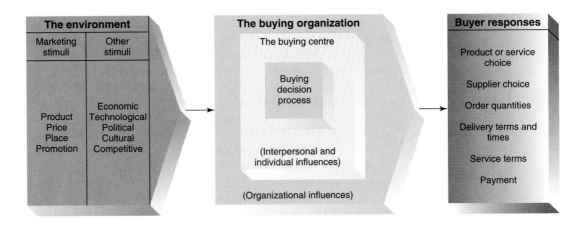

process? What are the major influences on buyers? How do business buyers make their buying decisions?

MAJOR TYPES OF BUYING SITUATIONS

There are three major types of buying situations.[7] At one extreme is the *straight rebuy*, which is a fairly routine decision. At the other extreme is the *new task*, which may call for thorough research. In the middle is the *modified rebuy*, which requires some research.

In a **straight rebuy**, the buyer reorders something without any modifications. It is usually handled on a routine basis by the purchasing department. Based on past buying satisfaction, the buyer simply chooses from the various suppliers on its list. "In" suppliers try to maintain product and service quality. They often propose automatic reordering systems so that the purchasing agent will save reordering time. "Out" suppliers try to offer something new or exploit dissatisfaction so that the buyer will consider them. They try to get their foot in the door with a small order and then enlarge their purchase share over time.

In a **modified rebuy**, the buyer wants to modify product specifications, prices, terms, or suppliers. The modified rebuy usually involves more decision participants than the straight rebuy. "In" suppliers may become nervous and feel pressured to put their best foot forward to protect an account. "Out" suppliers may view the modified rebuy situation as an opportunity to make a better offer and gain new business.

A company buying a product or service for the first time faces a **new-task** situation. In such cases, the greater the cost or risk, the larger the number of decision participants and the greater their efforts to collect information will be. The new-task situation is the marketer's greatest opportunity and challenge. The marketer not only tries to reach as many key buying influences as possible, but also provides help and information.

The buyer makes the fewest decisions in the straight rebuy and the most in the new-task decision. In the new-task situation, the buyer must decide on product specifications, suppliers, price limits, payment terms, order quantities, delivery times, and service terms. The order of these decisions varies with each situation, and different decision participants influence each choice.

Many business buyers prefer to buy a packaged solution to a problem from a single seller. Called **systems buying**, this practice began with government buying of major weapons and communication systems. Instead of buying and putting together all the components together, the government asked for bids from suppliers that would supply the components *and* assemble the package or system.

Sellers increasingly have recognized that buyers like this method and have adopted systems selling as a marketing tool.[8] Systems selling is a two-step process.

Straight rebuy
A business buying situation in which the buyer routinely reorders something without any modifications.

Modified rebuy
A business buying situation in which the buyer wants to modify product specifications, prices, terms, or suppliers.

New task
A business buying situation in which the buyer purchases a product or service for the first time.

Systems buying
Buying a packaged solution to a problem and without all the separate decisions involved.

First, the supplier sells a group of interlocking products. For example, the supplier sells not only glue, but also applicators and dryers. Second, the supplier sells a system of production, inventory control, distribution, and other services to meet the buyer's need for a smooth-running operation.

Systems selling is a key business marketing strategy for winning and holding accounts. The contract often goes to the firm that provides the most complete system meeting the customer's needs. For example, the government of Finland requested bids for a training system for Finnish air-traffic controllers. CAE Inc. of Toronto and its Germany subsidiary, CAE Electronics GmbH of Germany, developed and sold its Virtual Tower simulator. The Virtual Tower is a full-scale mock-up of an air-traffic control tower capable of simulating adverse weather conditions such as fog and snow as well as aircraft emergencies such as engine fires and crashes. The system includes radar trainers, visual display systems, and digital communication systems that transmit messages between students and simulated aircraft. CAE's ability to provide fully integrated systems has helped the company to gain over 50 percent of the world market for commercial simulation.[9] This is true systems selling.

CAE Inc.
www.cae.ca/

PARTICIPANTS IN THE BUSINESS BUYING PROCESS

Who does the buying of the trillions of dollars worth of goods and services needed by business organizations? The decision-making unit of a buying organization is called its **buying centre,** defined as all of the individuals and units that participate in the business decision-making process.[10]

The buying centre includes all members of the organization who play any of five roles in the purchase decision process.[11]

Buying centre
All the individuals and units that participate in the business buying-decision process.

Users
Members of the organization who will use the product or service; users often initiate the buying proposal and help define product specifications.

Influencers
People in an organization's buying centre who affect the buying decision; they often help define specifications and also provide information for evaluating alternatives.

Buyers
People who make the actual purchase.

Deciders
People in the organization's buying centre who have formal or informal power to select or approve the final suppliers.

Gatekeepers
People in the organization's buying centre who control the flow of information to others.

◆ **Users** are members of the organization who will use the product or service. In many cases, users initiate the buying proposal and help define product specifications.

◆ **Influencers** affect the buying decision. They often help define specifications and also provide information for evaluating alternatives. Technical personnel are particularly important influencers.

◆ **Buyers** have formal authority to select the supplier and arrange terms of purchase. Buyers may help shape product specifications, but they play their major role in selecting vendors and in negotiating. In more complex purchases, buyers might include high-level officers participating in the negotiations.

◆ **Deciders** have formal or informal power to select or approve the final suppliers. In routine buying, the buyers are often the deciders, or at least the approvers.

◆ **Gatekeepers** control the flow of information to others. For example, purchasing agents often have authority to prevent salespersons from seeing users or deciders. Other gatekeepers include technical personnel and even personal secretaries.

The buying centre is not a fixed and formally identified unit within the buying organization. It is a set of buying roles assumed by different people for different purchases. Within the organization, the size and composition of the buying centre will vary for different products and for different buying situations. For some routine purchases, one person—such as a purchasing agent—may assume all the buying-centre roles and serve as the only person involved in the buying decision. For more complex purchases, the buying centre may include 20 or 30 people from different levels and departments in the organization. According to one survey, the average number of people involved in a buying decision ranges from about three (for services and items used in day-to-day operations) to almost

Nokia portrays its products in the context of its key customers' lives.

Baxter International
www.baxter.com/

five (for such high-ticket purchases as construction work and machinery). Another survey detected a trend toward team-based buying—87 percent of surveyed purchasing executives at Fortune 1000 companies expect teams of people from different functions to be making buying decisions in the year 2000.[12]

Business marketers working in global markets may face even greater levels of buying-centre influence. A study comparing the buying decision processes in the United States, Sweden, France, and Southeast Asia found that U.S. buyers may be lone eagles compared with their counterparts in some other countries. Sweden had the highest team-buying effort while the United States had the lowest, even though the U.S. and Swedish firms had very similar demographics. In making purchasing decisions, Swedish firms depended on technical staff, both their own and suppliers', much more than the firms in other countries.[13]

A buying centre may be composed of people from more than one firm. Organizations often form alliances when developing new global products, and representatives from each organization entering the alliance may be part of the buying centre. Bombardier uses this strategy. Since the costs and risks of developing new aircraft are so high, Bombardier partners with its suppliers at the design stage. Together they determine the new plane's specifications and the components that will go into it.[14]

The buying-centre concept presents a major marketing challenge. The business marketer must learn who participates in the decision, each participant's relative influence, and what evaluation criteria each decision participant uses. For example, Baxter International, the large health-care products and services company, sells disposable surgical gowns to hospitals. It tries to identify the hospital personnel involved in this buying decision. These personnel are the vice-president of purchasing, the operating room administrator, and the surgeons. Each participant plays a different role. The vice-president of purchasing analyses whether the hospital should buy disposable gowns or reusable gowns. If analysis favours disposable gowns, then the operating room administrator compares competing products and prices and makes a choice. This administrator considers the gown's absorbency, antiseptic quality, design, and cost, and typically buys the brand that meets requirements at the lowest cost. Finally, surgeons affect the decision later by reporting their satisfaction or dissatisfaction with the brand.

The buying centre usually includes some obvious participants who are involved formally in the buying decision. It may also involve less obvious, informal participants, some of whom may actually make or strongly affect the buying decision. Sometimes, even the people in the buying centre are unaware of all the buying participants. As the Bombardier example shows, numerous stakeholders are involved in the decision. Their buying motives may vary from practical, mundane reasoning to subtle, hard-to-uncover psychological wants and fears.

MAJOR INFLUENCES ON BUSINESS BUYERS

Business buyers are subject to many influences when they make their buying decisions. Some marketers assume that the major influences are economic. They think buyers will favour the supplier who offers the lowest price, or the best product, or the most service. They concentrate on offering strong economic benefits to

FIGURE 6-2 *Major influences on business buying behaviour*

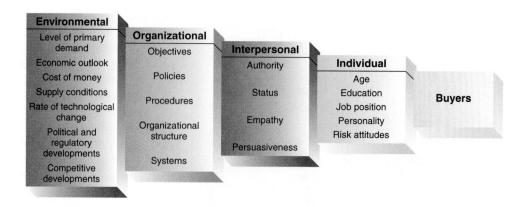

buyers. However, business buyers actually respond to both economic and personal factors. Far from being cold, calculating, and impersonal, business buyers are human and social as well. They react to both reason and emotion.

When suppliers' offers are very similar, business buyers have little basis for strictly rational choice. Because they can meet organizational goals with any supplier, buyers can allow personal factors to play a larger role in their decisions. However, when competing products differ greatly, business buyers are more accountable for their choice and tend to pay more attention to economic factors.

Figure 6-2 lists various groups of influences on business buyers—environmental, organizational, interpersonal, and individual.[15]

Environmental Factors

Business buyers are influenced heavily by factors in the current and expected *economic environment,* such as the level of primary demand, the economic outlook, and the cost of money. As economic uncertainty rises, business buyers cut back on new investments and attempt to reduce their inventories.

An increasingly important environmental factor is shortages in key materials. Many companies now are more willing to buy and hold larger inventories of scarce materials to ensure adequate supply. Business buyers also are affected by technological, political, and competitive developments in the environment. Culture and customs can strongly influence business buyer reactions to the marketer's behaviour and strategies, especially in the international marketing environment (see Marketing Highlight 6-2). The business marketer must consider these factors, determine how they will affect the buyer, and try to turn these challenges into opportunities.

Organizational Factors

Each buying organization has its own objectives, policies, procedures, structure, and systems, which the business marketer must understand. Questions such as these arise: How many people are involved in the buying decision? Who are they? What are their evaluative criteria? What are the company's policies and limits on its buyers?

Business-to-business marketers should be aware of several organizational trends in the purchasing area. The first is *upgraded purchasing.* Today's competitive pressures have led many companies to transform their old-fashioned "purchasing departments," with an emphasis on buying at the lowest cost, to "procurement departments," with a mission to seek the best value from fewer and better suppliers. The purchasing departments in many global firms are now responsible for sourcing materials and services around the world and working with strategic partners. This means that business marketers must upgrade their sales forces to match the quality of today's business buyers.

Companies are also moving toward more *centralized purchasing.* Centralized purchasing gives the company more purchasing clout, which can produce substantial savings. For the business marketer, this means dealing with fewer,

INTERNATIONAL MARKETING MANNERS: WHEN IN ROME, DO AS THE ROMANS DO

Picture this: Consolidated Amalgamation, Inc., thinks it's time that the rest of the world enjoyed the same fine products it has offered Canadian consumers for two generations. It dispatches vice-president Harry E. Slicksmile to Europe to explore the territory. Mr. Slicksmile stops first in London, where he makes short work of some bankers—he phones them. He handles Parisians with similar ease. After securing a table at La Tour d'Argent, he greets

In order to succeed in global markets North American companies must help their managers to understand the needs, customs, and cultures of international business buyers.

his luncheon guest, the director of an industrial engineering firm, with the words, "Just call me Harry, Jacques."

In Germany, Mr. Slicksmile is a powerhouse. Whisking through a lavish, state-of-the-art marketing presentation, complete with flip charts and audiovisuals, he shows 'em that this prairie boy *knows* how to make a buck. Heading on to Milan, Harry strikes up a conversation with the Japanese businessman sitting next to him on the plane. He flips his card onto his neighbour's tray and, when the two say good-bye, shakes hands warmly and clasps the man's right arm. Later, for his appointment with the owner of an Italian packaging-design firm, our hero wears his comfy corduroy sport coat, khaki pants, and deck shoes. Everybody knows Italians are zany and laid back, right?

Wrong. Six months later, Consolidated Amalgamation has nothing to show for the trip but a pile of bills. In Europe, they weren't wild about Harry.

This hypothetical case has been exaggerated for emphasis. Businesspeople are seldom such dolts. But experts say success in international business has much to do with knowing the territory and its people. By learning English and extending themselves in other ways, the world's business leaders have met North Americans more than halfway. In contrast, North Americans too often do little except assume that others will march to their music. "We want things to be just like they are at home when we travel. Fast. Convenient. Easy. So we demand that others change," says one world trade expert. "I think more business would be done if we tried harder."

Poor Harry tried, all right, but in all the wrong ways. The English do not, as a rule, make deals over the phone as much as North Americans do. It's not so much a "cultural" difference as a difference in approach. The French neither like instant familiarity—questions about family, church, or alma mater—nor refer to strangers by their first names. "That poor fellow, Jacques, probably wouldn't show anything, but he'd recoil. He'd *not* be pleased," explains an expert on French business practices. "It's considered poor taste," he continues. "Even after months of business dealings, I'd wait for him or her to make the invitation [to use first names] . . . You are always right, in Europe, to say 'Mister or 'Madam'. Calling secretaries by their first names would also be considered rude: "They have a right to be called by the surname. You'd certainly ask—and get—permission first."

Harry's flashy presentation would likely have been a flop with the Germans, who dislike overstatement and ostentatiousness. According to one German expert, however, German businesspeople have become accustomed to dealing with North Americans. Although differences in body language and customs remain, the past 20 years have softened them.

When Harry Slicksmile grabbed his new Japanese acquaintance by the arm, the executive probably considered him disrespectful and presumptuous. Harry made matters worse by tossing his business card. The Japanese revere the business card as an extension of self and as an indicator of rank. They do not *hand* it to people, they *present* it—with both hands. In addition, the Japanese are sticklers about rank. Unlike North Americans, they don't heap praise on subordinates in a room; they will praise only the highest-ranking official present.

Hapless Harry's last gaffe was assuming that Italians are like Hollywood's stereotypes of them. The flair for design and style that has characterized Italian culture for centuries is embodied in the businesspeople of Milan and Rome. They dress beautifully and admire flair, but they blanch at garishness or impropriety in others' attire.

To compete successfully in global markets, or even to deal effectively with international firms in their home markets, North American companies must help their managers to understand the needs, customs, and cultures of international business buyers. Here are additional examples of a few rules of social and business etiquette that North American managers should understand when doing business abroad.

- **France** Dress conservatively, except in the south where more casual clothes are worn. Do not refer to people by their first names—the French are formal with strangers. It should be noted that Europeans who speak French are more formal than their North American counterparts. Thus, North American should not rush to "tutoyer."

- **Germany** Be especially punctual. A businessperson invited to someone's home should present flowers, preferably unwrapped, to the hostess. Don't give red roses. These flowers are only for lovers. During introductions, greet women first and wait until they extend their hands before extending yours.

- **Italy** Whether you dress conservatively or go native in a Giorgio Armani suit, keep in mind that Italian businesspeople are style-conscious. Make appointments well in advance. Prepare for and be patient with Italian bureaucracies.

- **United Kingdom** Toasts are often given at formal dinners. If the host honours you with a toast, be prepared to reciprocate. Business entertaining is done more often at lunch than at dinner.

- **Saudi Arabia** Although men will kiss each other in greeting, they will never kiss a woman in public. A businesswoman should wait for a man to extend his hand before offering hers. If a Saudi offers refreshment, accept—it is an insult to decline it.

- **India** Although businesspeople here speak English, Canadians cannot assume that doing business will be smooth sailing. India is a conservative society marked by contrasts—a peasant culture, on one hand, and European-educated professionals on the other. Business deals take a long time to close and may be impossible without the assistance of an Indian agent to help firms understand India's impenetrable bureaucracy.

- **Japan** Don't imitate Japanese bowing customs unless you understand them thoroughly—who bows to whom, how many times, and when. It's a complicated ritual. Presenting business cards is another ritual. Carry many cards, present them with both hands so your name can be easily read, and hand them to others in order of descending rank. Expect Japanese business executives to take time making decisions and to work through all of the details before making a commitment.

Sources: Adapted from Susan Harte, "When in Rome, You Should Learn to Do What the Romans Do," *The Atlanta Journal-Constitution,* January 22, 1990, pp. D1, D6. Also see Lufthansa's *Business Travel Guide/Europe;* and Sergey Frank, "Global Negotiating," *Sales & Marketing Management,* May 1992, pp. 64–69; Brian Banks, "English too," *Canadian Business,* January 1995, pp. 20–35.

higher-level buyers. Instead of using regional sales forces to sell to a large buyer's separate plants, today's seller may use a *national account sales force.* For example, at Xerox, over 250 national account managers coordinate the efforts of an entire Xerox team—specialists, analysts, salespeople for individual products—to sell and service important national customers. National account selling demands both a high-level sales force and sophisticated marketing effort.

Business buyers are increasingly seeking *long-term contracts* with suppliers. For example, General Motors wants to buy from fewer suppliers who are willing to locate close to GM's plants and produce high-quality components. Many business marketers also offer *electronic data interchange (EDI)* systems to their customers. When using such systems, the seller links customers' computers to its own, allowing customers to order needed items instantly by entering orders directly into the computer. The orders are transmitted automatically to the supplier. Many hospitals order directly from Baxter using order-taking terminals in their stockrooms.

Finally, over the past several years, businesses around the world have adopted several innovative manufacturing concepts, such as *just-in-time production* (JIT), vendor-managed inventory systems, value analysis, total quality management, and flexible manufacturing. These practices greatly affect how business marketers sell to and service their customers. For example, just-in-time means that production materials arrive at the customer's factory exactly when needed for production, rather than being stored by the customer until used. It calls for close coordination between the production schedules of supplier and customer so that neither must carry much inventory.

Professional purchasers are tough-minded negotiators bent on improving the profitability of their firms. Dealing with them requires highly trained sales personnel.

Magna International
www.magnaint.com/

Problem recognition
The first stage of the business buying process in which someone in the company recognizes a problem or need that can be met by acquiring a good or a service.

Because JIT involves frequent delivery, many business marketers have set up locations closer to their large JIT customers. For example, Magna, the Canadian auto parts manufacturer, sets up facilities close to those of its main customers—General Motors, Ford, and Chrysler. Single sourcing is increasing rapidly under JIT—customers often award long-term contracts to only one or a few trusted suppliers. JIT also requires that the buyer and seller work closely together to speed up the order-delivery process and to reduce costs. Thus, many marketers have set up computerized electronic data interchange systems that link them to their JIT customers.[16]

Interpersonal Factors

The buying centre usually includes many participants who influence each other. The business marketer often finds it difficult to determine what kinds of *interpersonal factors* and group dynamics enter into the buying process. As one writer notes: "Managers do not wear tags that say 'decision maker' or 'unimportant person.' The powerful are often invisible, at least to vendor representatives."[17] Nor does the buying centre participant with the highest rank always have the most influence. Participants may have influence in the buying decision because they control rewards and punishments, are well liked, have special expertise, or have a special relationship with other important participants. Interpersonal factors are often very subtle. Whenever possible, business marketers must try to understand these factors and design strategies that take them into account.

Individual Factors

Each participant in the business buying decision process brings in personal motives, perceptions, and preferences. These individual factors are affected by personal characteristics such as age, income, education, professional identification, personality, and attitudes toward risk. Also, buyers have different buying styles. Some may be technical types who make in-depth analyses of competitive proposals before choosing a supplier. Other buyers may be intuitive negotiators who are adept at pitting sellers against one another for the best deal.

THE BUSINESS BUYING PROCESS

Table 6-2 lists the eight stages of the business buying process.[18] Buyers who face a new-task buying situation usually go through all stages of the buying process. Buyers making modified or straight rebuys may skip some stages. We will examine these steps for the typical new-task buying situation.

Problem Recognition

The buying process begins when someone in the company recognizes a problem or need that can be met by acquiring a specific good or service. **Problem recognition** can result from internal or external stimuli. Internally, the company may decide to launch a new product that requires new production equipment and materials. Or a machine may break down and need new parts. Perhaps a purchasing manager is unhappy with a current supplier's product quality, service, or prices. Externally, the buyer may get some new ideas at a trade show, see an ad, or receive a call from

TABLE 6-2 *Major Stages of the Business Buying Process in Relation to Major Buying Situations*

	BUYING SITUATIONS		
STAGES OF THE BUYING PROCESS	**New Task**	**Modified Rebuy**	**Straight Rebuy**
1. Problem recognition	Yes	Maybe	No
2. General need description	Yes	Maybe	No
3. Product specification	Yes	Yes	Yes
4. Supplier search	Yes	Maybe	No
5. Proposal solicitation	Yes	Maybe	No
6. Supplier selection	Yes	Maybe	No
7. Order-routine specification	Yes	Maybe	No
8. Performance review	Yes	Yes	Yes

Source: Adapted from Patrick J. Robinson, Charles W. Faris, and Yoram Wind, *Industrial Buying and Creative Marketing* (Boston: Allyn & Bacon, 1967), p. 14.

a salesperson who offers a better product or a lower price. In fact, in their advertising, business marketers often alert customers to potential problems, and then show how their products provide solutions.

General Need Description

General need description
The stage in the business buying process in which the company describes the general characteristics and quantity of a needed item.

Having recognized a need, the buyer next prepares a **general need description** that describes the characteristics and quantity of the needed item. For standard items, this process presents few problems. For complex items, however, the buyer may have to work with others—engineers, users, consultants—to define the item. The team may want to rank the importance of reliability, durability, price, and other attributes desired in the item. In this phase, the alert business marketer can help the buyers define their needs and provide information about the value of different product characteristics.

Product Specification

Product specification
The stage of the business buying process in which the buying organization decides on and specifies the best technical product characteristics for a needed item.

Value analysis
An approach to cost reduction in which components are studied carefully to determine if they can be redesigned, standardized, or made by less costly methods of production.

The buying organization then develops the item's technical **product specifications,** often with the help of a value analysis engineering team. **Value analysis** is an approach to cost reduction in which components are studied carefully to determine if they can be redesigned, standardized, or made by less costly methods of production. The team determines the best product characteristics and specifies them accordingly. Sellers, too, can use value analysis as a tool to help secure a new account. By showing buyers a better way to make an object, outside sellers can turn straight rebuy situations into new-task situations that give them a chance to obtain new business.

Many firms, such as Nortel, are becoming increasingly concerned about whether the materials they use in the design of new products are environmentally sensitive. In addition, the ability to completely recycle their products is an issue. Vendors who can offer materials to aid Nortel with this goal have considerable advantages in making sales to this firm.

Supplier Search

Supplier search
The stage of the business buying process in which the buyer tries to find the best vendors.

The buyer now conducts a **supplier search** to find the best vendors. The buyer can compile a small list of qualified suppliers by reviewing trade directories, doing a computer search, or phoning other companies for recommendations. The newer the buying task, and the more complex and costly the item, the greater the amount of time the buyer will spend searching for suppliers. The supplier's task is to get listed in major directories and build a good reputation in the marketplace. Salespeople should

As this UUNET Canada ad shows, business marketers often use advertising to alert customers to potential problems and then show how their products and services can provide solutions.

Proposal solicitation
The stage of the business buying process in which the buyer invites qualified suppliers to submit proposals.

Supplier selection
The stage of the business buying process in which the buyer reviews proposals and selects a supplier or suppliers.

watch for companies in the process of searching for suppliers and ensure that their firm is considered.

Many business buyers go to extremes in searching for and qualifying suppliers. Consider the hurdles that Xerox has set up in qualifying suppliers:

> Xerox qualifies only suppliers who meet ISO 9000 international quality standards (see Chapter 18). But to win the company's award—certification status—a supplier must first complete the Xerox Multinational Supplier Quality Survey. The survey requires the supplier to issue a quality assurance manual, adhere to continuous improvement principles, and demonstrate effective systems implementation. Once a supplier has been qualified, it must participate in Xerox's Continuous Supplier Involvement process, in which the two companies work together to create specifications for quality, cost, delivery times, and process capability. The final step toward certification requires a supplier to undergo additional quality training and evaluation. Not surprisingly, only 176 suppliers worldwide have achieved the 95 percent rating required for certification as a Xerox supplier.[19]

Proposal Solicitation

In the **proposal solicitation** stage of the business buying process, the buyer invites qualified suppliers to submit proposals. In response, some suppliers will send only a catalogue or a salesperson. However, when the item is complex or expensive, the buyer will usually require detailed written proposals or formal presentations from each potential supplier.

Business marketers must be skilled in researching, writing, and presenting proposals in response to buyer proposal solicitations. Proposals should be marketing documents, not just technical documents. Presentations should inspire confidence and should make the marketer's company stand out from the competition.

Supplier Selection

The members of the buying centre now review the proposals and select a supplier or suppliers. During **supplier selection**, the buying centre often will draw up a list of the desired supplier attributes and their relative importance. In one survey, purchasing executives listed the following attributes as most important in influencing the relationship between supplier and customer: quality products and services, on-time delivery, ethical corporate behaviour, honest communication, and competitive prices.[20] Other important factors include repair and servicing capabilities, technical aid and advice, geographic location, performance history, and reputation. The members of the buying centre will rate suppliers against these attributes and identify the best suppliers. They often use a supplier evaluation form similar to the one shown in Table 6-3. The supplier in this example rates excellent on quality, service, responsiveness, and reputation, but only fair on price and delivery. The buyer must now decide how important the two weaknesses are and compare these ratings to those of other possible suppliers. The ratings could be redone using importance weightings for the seven attributes.

Buyers may attempt to negotiate with preferred suppliers for better prices and terms before making the final selections. In the end, they may select a single supplier or a few suppliers. Many buyers prefer multiple sources of supplies to avoid being totally dependent on one supplier and to allow comparisons of prices and performance of several suppliers over time.

TABLE 6-3 *An Example of Supplier Analysis*

SUPPLIER ATTRIBUTE	RATING				
	Very poor (1)	Poor (2)	Fair (3)	Good (4)	Excellent (5)
Price competitiveness			X		
Product quality, reliability					X
Service and repair capabilities					X
On-time delivery			X		
Quality of sales representatives				X	
Overall responsiveness to customer needs					X
Overall reputation, integrity, and ethical behaviour					X
Average score = 4.29					

Order-Routine Specification

Order-routine specification
The stage of the business buying process in which the buyer writes the final order with the chosen supplier(s), listing the technical specifications, quantity needed, expected time of delivery, return policies, and warranties.

The buyer now prepares an **order-routine specification**. It includes the final order with the chosen supplier or suppliers and lists items such as technical specifications, quantity needed, expected time of delivery, return policies, and warranties. In the case of maintenance, repair, and operating items, buyers may use *blanket contracts* rather than periodic purchase orders. A blanket contract creates a long-term relationship in which the supplier promises to resupply the buyer as needed at agreed prices for a set period. The seller holds the stock and the buyer's computer automatically prints out an order to the seller when stock is needed. A blanket order eliminates the expensive process of renegotiating a purchase each time stock is required. It also allows buyers to write more, but smaller purchase orders, resulting in lower inventory levels and carrying costs.

Blanket contracting leads to more single-source buying and to buying more items from that source. This practice locks the supplier in tighter with the buyer and makes it difficult for other suppliers to break in unless the buyer becomes dissatisfied with prices or service.

Performance Review

Performance review
The stage of the business buying process in which the buyer rates its satisfaction with suppliers, deciding whether to continue, modify, or drop them.

In this stage, the buyer reviews supplier performance. The buyer may contact users and ask them to rate their satisfaction. The **performance review** may lead the buyer to continue, modify, or drop the arrangement. The seller's job is to monitor the same factors used by the buyer to ensure that the seller is giving the expected satisfaction.

We have described the stages that typically would occur in a new-task buying situation. The eight-stage model provides a simple view of the business buying decision process. The actual process is usually much more complex. In the modified rebuy or straight rebuy situation, some of these stages would be compressed or bypassed. Each organization buys in its own way, and each buying situation has unique requirements. Different buying centre participants may be involved at different stages of the process. Although certain buying-process steps usually do occur, buyers do not always follow them in the same order, and they may add other steps. Often, buyers will repeat certain stages of the process.

During the past few years, advances in technology have had a dramatic impact on the business-to-business marketing process. Increasingly, business buyers are purchasing all kinds of products and services electronically, through electronic data interchange links or on the Internet. Such high-tech purchasing gives buyers access to new suppliers, lowers purchasing costs, and hastens order processing and delivery (see Marketing Highlight 6-3). In turn, business marketers are connecting with customers online to share marketing information, sell products

BUSINESS-TO-BUSINESS BUYING AND THE INTERNET

Most of the hype over Internet commerce has focused on web sites selling books, flowers, clothes, and other retail goods. But the real Internet action has been in business goods. And that's where a lot of smart people expect it to remain. There are predictions that business-to-business Internet trade will reach $190 billion a year by the end of the decade.

As is the case with so many other things, General Electric has been in the vanguard. Since its launch last January, a web site designed and run by GE's Information Services division (GEIS) has logged $490 million worth of industrial products purchased electronically by GE divisions. This web site, coupled with its custom software, enables GE's buyers to zap out requests for bids to thousands of suppliers, who can respond over the Internet. Such electronic purchasing saves time, money, and a lot of paperwork.

Here's an example of how it works: Last month the machinery at a GE lighting factory in Cleveland broke down. GE Lighting needed custom replacement parts immediately. In the past GE would have asked for bids from just four domestic suppliers. It was just too much hassle to get the paperwork and production-line blueprints together and send them out to a long list of suppliers. But this time they posted the specifications and "requests for quotes" on GE's web site—and drew seven other bidders. The winner was a Hungarian vendor that would not even have been contacted in the days of paper purchasing forms. The Hungarian firm's replacement parts arrived quicker, and GE Lighting paid just $448 000— a 20 percent savings.

Using the Internet purchasing system, GEIS claims cost savings of 10 percent to 15 percent, thanks to more and lower bids. It also claims a five-day savings in order time, thanks to the immediacy of the Internet.

To date all orders made over GEIS' Internet purchasing systems have been by GE units. But GEIS is now offering access to its web site to outsiders. GE has jumped ahead of such companies as IBM, Microsoft, and Netscape to lead the race into business-to-business Internet commerce. The tough part of establishing such a system is just getting it started. Buyers don't want to invest in a system unless suppliers are already on board, and vice versa. "It's the classic chicken-or-the-egg problem," explains Orville Bailey, who manages GEIS' Internet project.

Here, GE's tremendous size gives it a crucial advantage. GE divisions spend more than $30 billion a year on other companies' goods and services. So when GE announced last year that it would be soliciting bids over the Internet, even the smallest, most technophobic of its suppliers listened up. Smiles Bailey, "We could build the critical mass" needed to get the Internet commerce network up and running.

Now, with its own network of industrial-goods suppliers already hooked into the system, GE is finding it easy to resell the Internet purchasing technology to other companies that want to handle their purchasing just like GE. For access to its web site, GE Information Services will charge buyers an initial fee of $98 000 and an undisclosed annual fee based on volume. Suppliers get to sign on to the system for free.

The first outside firm to sign on is Textron Automotive, a subsidiary of the $13-billion Textron, Inc. Like GE, Textron Automotive buys a lot of raw materials and components: resin, ashtrays, metal clips, and other parts used in auto dashboards and panelling. By year end, Textron Automotive hopes to place all its orders—more than $700 million a year—over the GE Information Services web site.

GEIS' Bailey expects various GE units to be buying goods at the rate of $2.8 billion a year by next year and outside firms like Textron Automotive to be doing another $4.2 billion or so. If a $188-billion market for business-to-business Internet commerce materializes by the year 2000, GE estimates that up to $70 billion of that will move over GE's Internet purchasing system. What of the much-ballyhooed retail web sites? Those sites will do an estimated $14 billion in 2000. That's one-fifth the potential volume of GE's business-goods web site alone.

Thus, the Internet promises to change dramatically the face of business buying, and hence the face of business-to-business marketing. As one expert suggests, "Internet presence is becoming as common as business cards and faxes." To stay in the game, business-to-business marketers will need a well-thought-out Internet marketing strategy to supplement their other business marketing efforts.

Sources: Portions adapted from Scott Woolley, "Double Click for Resin," *Forbes*, March 10, 1997, p. 132. Also see Kenneth Leung, "Keep This in Mind About Internet Marketing," *Marketing News*, June 23, 1997, p. 7, and Clinton Wilder, "Web-based Purchasing," *Information-week*, March 24, 1997, pp. 83–84; www.ge.com

and service, provide customer-support services, and maintain ongoing customer relationships.

INSTITUTIONAL AND GOVERNMENT MARKETS

So far, our discussion of organizational buying has focused largely on the buying behaviour of business buyers. Much of this discussion also applies to the buying practices of institutional and government organizations. However, these two non-business markets have additional characteristics and needs. Thus, in this final section, we will address the special features of institutional and government markets.

INSTITUTIONAL MARKETS

Institutional market
Schools, hospitals, nursing homes, prisons, and other institutions that provide goods and services to people in their care.

The **institutional market** consists of schools, hospitals, nursing homes, prisons, and other institutions that provide goods and services to people in their care.

Many institutional markets are characterized by low budgets and captive patrons. For example, hospital patients have little choice but to eat whatever food the hospital supplies. A hospital purchasing agent must decide on the quality of food to buy for patients. Because the food is provided as part of a total service package, the buying objective is not profit. Nor is strict cost minimization the goal—patients receiving poor-quality food will complain to others and damage the hospital's reputation. Thus, the hospital purchasing agent must search for institutional food vendors whose quality meets or exceeds a certain minimum standard and whose prices are low.

Many marketers set up separate divisions to meet the special characteristics and needs of institutional buyers. For example, Heinz produces, packages, and prices its ketchup and other products differently to better serve the requirements of hospitals, universities, and other institutional markets.

GOVERNMENT MARKETS

Government market
Governmental units—federal, provincial, and municipal—that purchase or rent goods and services for carrying out the main functions of government.

The government market offers many opportunities for companies.

The **government market** offers large opportunities for many companies. Federal, provincial, and municipal governments contain buying units. And various levels of government in countries around the world offer vast selling opportunities. Government buying and business buying are similar in many ways. But there are also differences that must be understood by companies that wish to sell products and services to governments. To succeed in the government market, sellers must locate key decision-makers, identify the factors that affect buyer behaviour, and understand the buying decision process.

The Department of Public Works and Government Services Canada helps to centralize the buying of commonly used items in the civilian section (for example, office furniture and equipment, vehicles, fuels) and in standardizing buying procedures for the other agencies. Federal military buying is carried out by the Department of National Defence.

0300 hrs.

Pouring rain.

Fog rolling in.

You sense

something

is out there.

We'll tell you

what it is.

The world's first

multi-spectral

surveillance

system

is now in full

production.

Computing Devices Canada

Government organizations typically require suppliers to submit bids, and normally they award the contract to the lowest bidder. In some cases, the government unit will make allowance for the supplier's superior quality or reputation for completing contracts on time. Governments will also buy on a negotiated contract basis, primarily in the case of complex projects involving major R&D costs and risks, and in cases where little competition exists.

Government organizations tend to favour domestic suppliers over foreign suppliers. A major complaint of multinationals operating in Europe is that each country shows favouritism toward its nationals despite superior offers made by foreign firms. The European Economic Commission is gradually removing this bias. In an effort to improve the competitiveness of Canadian businesses, products purchased by the government are evaluated for the potential to be marketed worldwide. In its infancy Bombardier was given a boost as a supplier of military vehicles. Rations developed by Magic Pan for the Canadian military are marketed to global institutions.

Like consumer and business buyers, government buyers are affected by environmental, organizational, interpersonal,

Right for the job.

- Maplehawk meets or exceeds all Canadian Search and Rescue requirements.
- Cabin size 40% larger than BLACK HAWK, the world's standard in search and rescue.
- True production aircraft. More than 2,400 Hawk family aircraft have accumulated over 4 million flight hours.
- Thousands of lives already saved by 600 SAR Hawks operating in the world's toughest terrain and climates.
- Maplehawk uses the latest cutting-edge technology, including state-of-the-art glass cockpit.
- Lowest cost to procure...$100-$300 million less than the competition.
- Lowest cost to operate...will save hundreds of millions of dollars.
- Economic benefits return 150% of contract value to Canadian taxpayers and generate thousands of jobs for Canada's workforce.
- Maplehawk fulfills future Maritime Helicopter requirements and provides additional savings through commonality.

Maplehawk. The search is over.

Team Maplehawk • Sikorsky Aircraft • CAE Aviation Ltd. • Canadian Marconi Company • GE Canada • Litton Systems Canada • Greater Halifax Partnership • Canadian Aerospace Group • Quorum Funding Corporation
Photo Courtesy of Sikorsky Aircraft and Keiler & Company

Sikorsky knows that the opinion of many stakeholders will be considered in the government's decision to purchase a new search and rescue helicopter. Therefore, it advertises the benefits of its helicopter to the Canadian public.

and individual factors. One unique aspect about government buying is that it is carefully watched by outside publics, ranging from Parliament to various private groups interested in how the government spends taxpayers' money. Because their spending decisions are subject to public review, government organizations require considerable paperwork from suppliers, who often complain about excessive paperwork, bureaucracy, regulations, decision-making delays, and frequent shifts in procurement personnel.

Most governments provide would-be suppliers with detailed guides describing how to sell to the government. The federal government issues a weekly bulletin, *Government Business Opportunities*, to alert prospective suppliers to the government's plans to purchase products or services. Both federal and provincial governments offer guides to help business firms understand their purchasing policies.[21]

Various monographs are also available to help businesses understand special issues including *Incentives in Government Contracting* by Preston McAfee (University of Toronto Press) and *Government Procurement and Canada-U.S. Trade* (Ontario Centre for International Business). Guides to the procurement policies of foreign governments are also available, including *A Report on Government Procurement in Mexico* (Townsend Trade Strategies). Various trade magazines and associations provide information on how to reach schools, hospitals, highway departments, and other government agencies. The Canada Business Service Centre is an online service established by the government to help Canadian business access information about federal and provincial government programs, and learn about opportunities for bidding on government contracts (http://info.ic.gc.cbsc/).

Many companies that sell to the government have not been marketing-oriented for a number of reasons. Total government spending is determined by elected officials rather than by any marketing effort to develop this market. Government buying has emphasized price, making suppliers invest their effort in technology to bring down costs. When the product's characteristics are specified carefully, product differentiation is not a marketing factor. Nor do advertising or personal selling matter much in winning bids on an open-bid basis.

As provincial governments downsize and move toward privatization, there are growing opportunities. Firms ranging from professional engineering firms to cleaning contractors are bidding to take over functions that government employees formerly performed. More and more companies, such as Bombardier, SNC Lavalin, Eastman Kodak, Goodyear, and Computing Devices Canada (CDC), have people who specialize in marketing to governments both nationally and internationally.

Summary of Chapter Objectives

Business markets and consumer markets are alike in some key ways. For example, both include people in buying roles who make purchase decisions to satisfy needs. But business markets also differ in many ways from consumer markets. For one thing, the business market is *enormous*, far larger than the consumer market. Within Canada alone, the business market includes more than one million organizations that annually purchase billions of dollars worth of goods and services.

1. **Define the business market and explain how business markets differ from consumer markets.**

   The *business market* consists of all organizations that buy goods and services to use in the production of other products and services or for the purpose of reselling or renting them to others at a profit. Compared to consumer markets, business markets usually have fewer, larger buyers who are more geographically concentrated. Business demand is *derived*, largely *inelastic*, and more *fluctuating*. More buyers are usually involved in the business buying decision, and business buyers are better trained and more professional than are consumer buyers. In general, business purchasing decisions are more complex, and the buying process is more formal than consumer buying.

2. **Identify the major factors that influence business buyer behaviour.**

   Business buyers make decisions that vary with the three types of buying situations: *straight rebuys, modified rebuys*, and *new tasks*. These tasks are handled by the buying centre, the decision-making unit of a buying organization, which can consist of many different persons playing many different roles. The business marketer needs to know the following: Who are the major participants? In what decisions do they exercise influence? What is their relative degree of influence? What evaluation criteria does each decision participant use? The business marketer also needs to understand the major environmental, interpersonal, and individual influences on the buying process.

3. **List and define the steps in the business buying-decision process.**

The business buying-decision process itself can be quite involved, with eight basic stages. In stage 1, *problem recognition*, someone in the company recognizes a problem or need that can be met by acquiring a product or a service. In stage 2, *general need description*, the company determines the general characteristics and quantity of the needed item. In stage 3, *product specification*, the buying organization decides on and specifies the best technical product characteristics for the needed item. In stage 4, *supplier search*, the buyer seeks the best vendors. In stage 5, *proposal solicitation*, the buyer invites qualified suppliers to submit proposals. In stage 6, *supplier selection*, the buyer reviews proposals and selects a supplier or suppliers. In stage 7, *order-routine specification*, the buyer writes the final order with the chosen supplier(s), listing the technical specifications, quantity needed, expected time of delivery, return policies, and warranties. In stage 8, *performance review*, the buyer rates its satsfaction with suppliers, deciding whether to continue, modify, or cancel the relationship.

4. **Compare the institutional and government markets and explain how institutional and government buyers make their buying decisions.**

   The *institutional market* consists of schools, hospitals, prisons, and other institutions that provide goods and services to people in their care. These markets are characerized by low budgets and captive patrons. The *government market*, which is vast, consists of government units—federal, provincial, and muncicipal—that purchase or rent goods and services for carrying out the main functions of government. Government buyers purchase products and services for defence, education, public welfare, and other public needs. Government buying practices are highly specialized and specified, with open bidding or negotiated contracts characterizing most of the buying. Government buyers operate under the watchful eye of Parliament and many private watchdog groups. Hence, they tend to require more forms and signatures, and to respond more slowly and deliberately when placing orders.

Key Terms

Business market *(p. 199)*
Business buying process *(p. 199)*
Buyers *(p. 204)*
Buying centre *(p. 204)*
Deciders *(p. 204)*
Derived demand *(p. 200)*
Gatekeepers *(p. 204)*
General need description *(p. 210)*

Government market *(p. 214)*
Influencers *(p. 204)*
Institutional market *(p. 214)*
Modified rebuy *(p. 203)*
New task *(p. 203)*
Order-routine specification *(p. 212)*
Performance review *(p. 212)*
Problem recognition *(p. 209)*

Product specification *(p. 210)*
Proposal solicitation *(p. 211)*
Straight rebuy *(p. 203)*
Supplier search *(p. 210)*
Supplier selection *(p. 211)*
Systems buying *(p. 203)*
Users *(p. 204)*
Value analysis *(p. 210)*

Discussing the Issues

1. Apple Computer paid top prices for millions of computer memory chips during an industry-wide shortage. Soon afterward, demand for memory dropped, and the chips became cheap and plentiful—leaving Apple with millions of dollars in losses. Suggest how a long-term contract might have helped in this situation.

2. Identify which of the major types of buying situations are represented by the following: (a) Chrysler's purchase of computers that go in cars and adjust engine performance to changing driving conditions, (b) Volkswagen's purchase of spark plugs for its line of vans, and (c) Honda's purchase of light bulbs for a new Acura model.

3. Explain how a marketer of office equipment could identify the buying centre for a law firm's purchase of dictation equipment for each of its partners.

4. NutraSweet and other companies have advertised products to the general public that consumers aren't able to buy. Determine how this strategy might help a company sell products to resellers.

5. Assume that you are selling a fleet of cars to be used by a company's sales force. The salespeople need larger cars, which are more profitable for you, but the fleet buyer wants to buy smaller cars. List who might be in the buying centre. Outline how you could meet the varying needs of these participants.

Applying the Concepts

1. Many companies that were formerly vertically integrated, producing their own raw materials or parts, are now using outside suppliers to produce them instead. The extreme examples of this practice, such as Dell Computer, own no production facilities and have suppliers make everything to order. This type of company has been nicknamed a "virtual corporation."

   ◆ Determine whether you think that buyers and suppliers are likely to be closer or more adversarial in this type of corporate structure.

   ◆ Name the advantages and disadvantages of this sort of supplier relationship for (a) the buyer and (b) the supplier.

2. Get a copy of a magazine aimed at final consumers (e.g., *Sports Illustrated*, *Chatelaine*) and another that is aimed at business people (e.g., *Canadian Business*, *The Financial Post Magazine*). Look at the ads in the two different types of magazines. What do the similarities and differences in the ads tell you about the similarities and differences in buying behaviour in business and consumer markets?

3. On the Canadian government web site, Strategis (http://strategis.ic.gc.ca), you will find information on different sectors of the Canadian economy (the computer industry, the engineering industry, etc.). Look at the information contained in one of these reports. Identify some of the information that would help you market goods and services to one of these sectors.

References

1. Portions adapted from Thomas V. Bonoma, "Major Sales: Who Really Does the Buying," *Harvard Business Review,* May–June 1982. Copyright © 1982 by the President and Fellows of Harvard College; all rights reserved. Quotation from John Huey, "The Absolute Best Way to Fly," *Fortune,* May 30, 1994, pp. 121–128. Also see William C Symonds and David Greising, "A Dogfight Over 950 Customers," *Business Week,* February 6, 1995, p. 66; Ann Gibbon, "Bombardier Lands 24-plane Deal, *Globe and Mail,* January 23, 1996, p. B1; Ann Gibbon, "Bombardier Profit Climbs 26% in Quarter," *Globe and Mail,* November 29, 1995, p. B6; Ann Gibbon, "Bombardier Airliner Gains New Backing," *Globe and Mail,* September 21, 1993, p. B1; Ann Gibbon, "Bombardier Sheds Dark Cloud," *Globe and Mail,* August 18, 1993, p. B1, B4.

2. This definition is adapted from Frederick E. Webster, Jr., and Yoram Wind, *Organizational Buying Behavior* (Englewood Cliffs, NJ: Prentice Hall, 1972), p. 2.

3. Industry Canada, *Sector Competitiveness Framework Series: Computer Equipment,* May 12, 1997, on web site http://strategis.ic.gr.ca.

4. For discussions of similarities and differences in consumer and business marketing, see Edward F. Fern and James R. Brown, "The Industrial/Consumer Marketing Dichotomy: A Case of Insufficient Justification," *Journal of Marketing,* Fall 1984, pp. 68–77; and Ron J. Kornakovich, "Consumer Methods Work for Business Marketing: Yes; No," *Marketing News,* November 21, 1988, pp. 4, 13–14.

5. "Canadian Markets 1988/89," *Financial Post,* Toronto, Maclean Hunter, 1989.

6. See James C. Anderson and James A. Narus, "Value–Based Segmentation, Targeting, and Relationship-Building in Business Markets," ISBM Report #12–1989, The Institute for the Study of Business Markets, Pennsylvania State University, University Park, PA, 1989; Lawrence A. Crosby, Kenneth R. Evans, and Deborah Cowles, "Relationship Quality and Services Selling: An Interpersonal Influence Perspective," *Journal of Marketing,* July 1990, pp. 68–81; Barry J. Farber and Joyce Wycoff, "Relationships: Six Steps to Success," *Sales & Marketing Management,* April 1992, pp. 50–58; and Minda Zetlin, "It's All the Same to Me," *Sales & Marketing Management,* February 1994, pp. 71–75.

7. Patrick J. Robinson, Charles W. Faris, and Yoram Wind, *Industrial Buying Behavior and Creative Marketing* (Boston: Allyn & Bacon, 1967). Also see Erin Anderson, Weyien Chu, and Barton Weitz, "Industrial Purchasing: An Empirical Exploration of the Buyclass Framework," *Journal of Marketing,* July 1987, pp. 71–86.

8. For more on systems selling, see Robert R. Reeder, Edward G. Brierty, and Betty H. Reeder, *Industrial Marketing: Analysis, Planning, and Control* (Englewood Cliffs, NJ: Prentice Hall, 1991), pp. 264–267.

9. James Bagnall, "Solo Flight: Why CAE is an Aerospace Standout," *Financial Times,* August 21, 1993, p. 3; Gail Lem, "CAE Sells Air Traffic Simulator to Finland," *Globe and Mail,* September 16, 1993, p. B5.

10. Webster and Wind, *Organizational Buying Behavior,* p. 6. For more reading on buying centres, see Bonoma, "Major Sales: Who Really Does the Buying"; and Donald W. Jackson, Jr., Janet E. Keith, and Richard K. Burdick, "Purchasing Agents' Perceptions of Industrial Buying Center Influence: A Situational Approach," *Journal of Marketing,* Fall 1984, pp. 75–83.

11. Webster and Wind, *Organizational Buying Behavior,* pp. 78–80.

12. For results of both surveys, see "I Think You Have a Great Product, But It's Not My Decision," *American Salesman,* April 1994, pp. 11–13. For more on influence strategies within buying centres, see R. Venkatesh, Ajay K. Kohli, and Gerald Zaltman, "Influence Strategies in Buying Centers," *Journal of Marketing,* October 1995, pp. 71–82.

13. Melvin R. Matson and Esmail Salshi-Sangari, "Decision Making in Purchases of Equipment and Materials: A Four-Country Comparison," *International Journal of Physical Distribution & Logistics Management,* Vol. 23, No. 8, 1993, pp. 16–30.

14. Bruce Livesey, "Ceiling Unlimited," *Report on Business,* April 1997, p. 42.

15. Webster and Wind, *Organizational Buying Behavior,* pp. 33–37.

16. See Gary L. Frazier, Robert E. Spekman, and Charles R. O'Neal, "Just-In-Time Exchange Relationships in Industrial Markets," *Journal of Marketing,* October 1988, pp. 52–57; Ernest Raia, "JIT in the '90s: Zeroing in on Leadtimes," *Purchasing,* September 26, 1991, pp. 54–57; and Sang-Lin Han, David T. Wilson, and Shirish P. Dant, "Buyer-Supplier Relationships Today," *Industrial Marketing Management,* November 1993, pp. 331–338.

17. Bonoma, "Major Sales," p. 114. Also see Ajay Kohli, "Determinants of Influence in Organizational Buying: A Contingency Approach," *Journal of Marketing,* July 1989, pp. 50–65.

18. Robinson, Faris, and Wind, *Industrial Buying Behavior,* p. 14.

19. See "Xerox Multinational Supplier Quality Survey," *Purchasing,* January 1995, p. 112.

20. See "What Buyers Really Want," *Sales & Marketing Management,* October 1989, p. 30.

21. See *Government Business Opportunities, and Selling to Government: A Guide to Government Procurement in Canada,* Supply and Services, Ottawa.

Company Case 6

BIOFOAM: Not Just Peanuts!

Like diamonds, polystyrene peanuts are forever. Every year the stash of them is growing at a rate of at least 110 million kilograms annually. Since their introduction in 1970, they have become one of the most popular forms of packaging material. They are lightweight, inexpensive, and resilient. They conform to any shape, protect superbly, resist shifting in transit, and leave no dusty residue on the goods they protect. And, of course, they are indestructible. In fact, that's the problem. Nearly every one of those peanuts used since 1970 is still with us—blowing in the wind or taking up space in a landfill. Worse yet, they will be with us for another 500 years. They're wonderful, but they're just not environmentally sound.

A small firm, Biofoam, believes that it has solved this problem. It sells peanuts made from grain sorghum that are also known as Biofoam. To make these sorghum peanuts, the company strips the grain of its nutritional value, presses it into pellets, and conveys it through a giant popper. The process creates a product that looks like tan cheese doodles, which is not surprising considering that the inventors originally started out to make a snack food. But since no one wanted to eat these tan cheese doodles, the inventors had to find other uses for them. According to Ed Alfke, Biofoam's CEO, the sorghum peanuts do as good a job as the best foam peanuts but don't cost any more. Moreover, they hold no electrostatic charge, so they won't cling to nylons or other synthetic fibres (like your carpet or clothes). Better yet, they are "absolutely, frighteningly natural," says Tom Schmiegel, a veteran of the plastics industry.

To dispose of a Biofoam peanut, you can throw it in the garbage, toss it on your front lawn; dump it in your compost bin; put it in your dog's or cat's bowl; set it out with salsa at your next party; or simply wash it down your drain. The peanut dissolves in water and has some—although limited—nutritional value. Alfke bought into the company because of its environmentally positive stance. He is convinced that green companies will profit from a global regulatory climate that's increasingly hostile to polluters. "The writing is on the wall for companies that are not environmentally friendly," he says.

Biofoam initially targeted retailers who wanted to send an environmentally friendly message to their customers, and included a Biofoam pamphlet explaining the advantages of the Biofoam peanut. The company targeted the heaviest users of Styrofoam peanuts—organizations such as the Home Shopping Network, which consumes 10 to 20 truckloads of loose fill each day at peak volume. To date, Biofoam has signed two major accounts—the Fuller Brush Company and computer reseller MicroAge.

Eventually, Biofoam will have to expand beyond environmentally sensitive firms into a broader market. To convince potential users to use Biofoam peanuts, Alfke has developed a seemingly flawless option: to be environmentally responsible without paying more or sacrificing convenience. He is willing to instal machines on the customer's premises to produce peanuts in-house—an arrangement that would give Biofoam rent-free production sites across North America. He'll even provide an employee to operate the machinery. Although this strategy might sound unusual, it has been used by other companies such as Haloid (now Xerox) to sell copies and by Tetra-Pak to sell juice boxes and milk cartons.

The in-house arrangement has benefits for both the customer and Biofoam. Users receive immediate, reliable, just-in-time delivery combined with on-site service and a five-year price guarantee with no intermediaries involved. With Biofoam on-site, users never run out of packaging, and avoid the expense of stockpiling materials. And lower production costs make Biofoam price competitive with that polystyrene. For Biofoam, the arrangement provides a rent-free network of regional manufacturing facilities and an intimacy with each customer. Because the host company will only consume about one-third of the output, Biofoam plans to sell the excess to smaller firms in the host's area.

However, this in-house production arrangement is not without disadvantages. From the host's perspective, the machinery takes up 1500 square feet of space that could be used to produce something else. Furthermore, some of the output of that 1500 square feet goes to other firms, benefiting Biofoam but doing nothing for the host. And the host has a non-employee working in its plant. In addition, the peanut-making machinery is intrusive. It consists of three machines—an extruder, a conditioning chamber, and a de-duster—joined by ducts and conveyor belts. The machines make lots of noise (like a giant air conditioner), making conversation in the vicinity impossible. The process creates a smell roughly akin to that of the inside of an old barn, and the machines produce heat, which is a potentially troubling problem. Thus, on closer inspection, the in-house arrangement is not entirely desirable. Without this arrangement, however, costs rise considerably. If it had to ship the peanuts to users, Biofoam would have to raise prices by 10 to 18 percent.

The polystyrene loose-fill industry is a dense, fragmented patchwork of diverse companies. It includes oil companies, chemicals producers, fill manufacturers, and regional distributors—all of which would suffer from Biofoam's success. The industry is much more rough-and-tumble than Alfke had expected. So far, Biofoam has a microscopic market share. The company's 1995 sales totalled only $3.6 million—not much in an industry with potential sales of $215 to $750 million a year. But the $3.6 million represented a fivefold increase over the previous year, before Alfke hit the scene. Alfke's now projects sales of $115 million by the year 2000, yielding 30 percent pre-tax profits. These projections include sales of products other than sorghum peanuts. Alfke plans to add injectible Biofoam and stiff Biofoam packaging materials. Other promising applications have been suggested, such as using Biofoam to absorb oil spills or in medicinal applications, but Alfke doesn't want to discuss those. For now, "It's important that we try to stay focused," he claims.

Can Alfke reach his ambitious goals? Many industry observers say no. Environmental claims, say these observers, don't have the same impact that they used to have. "That was something we worried about three years ago," says one purchasing agent. Even Biofoam's sales representatives are finding the market less environmentally concerned. Others, however, are more optimistic. For example, although she agrees that the newness of environmentally responsible packaging has worn off, Nancy Pfund, general partner of Hambrecht and Quist's Environmental Technology Fund, believes that many firms are still interested in environmentally friendly packaging. She notes that companies have "internalized a lot of environmental procedures without making a lot of noise about it. You also have younger people who grew up learning about the environment in school now entering the consumer market. That's a very strong trend." Such consumers will demand more responsible packaging.

Are companies that use Biofoam pleased with it? Well, some yes, some no. On the positive side is MicroAge Computer. According to Mark Iaquinto, facilities manager, MicroAge had been searching for an acceptable alternative to polystyrene. Now that it's found Biofoam, he believes that it can stop searching. On the negative side, Norbert Schneider, president of Fuller Brush Company, has concerns about the way the product crumbles in boxes filled with sharp-pointed brushes. Alfke says that Biofoam is working on a solution, but if it doesn't find one soon, Fuller Brush may change packaging suppliers.

Other firms such as Enviromold and American Excelsior have entered the market with biodegradable, water-soluble foams. Made from corn-starch-based thermoplastics, the products can be rinsed down the drain after use. They can be used in loose-fill packaging applications or be moulded in place into shaped packaging. They compare favourably with traditional packaging materials in terms of cost and performance.

Consequently, facing a stiffly competitive industry, new competitors, and a softening of environmental concerns, Biofoam faces challenges going forward. But none of this dents Alfke's enthusiasm. "I've seen a lot of deals," he claims, "and I've never, ever seen a deal as good as this one." As the successful founder and developer of Rent-A-Wreck, Alfke was a multimillionaire before age 40. After selling his interest in Rent-A-Wreck, seeking another firm to buy into, he sank millions of his own money into Biofoam. As an experienced businessman, no doubt he has seen a lot of deals. He really believes in this one, but is he right?

QUESTIONS

1. Outline Biofoam's current marketing strategy. Which elements of the marketing mix are most important for Biofoam to focus on?

2. What is the nature of demand in the loose-fill packaging industry? What factors shape that demand?

3. If you were a buyer of packaging materials, would you agree to Biofoam's offer of machines inside your plant? If not, how could Biofoam overcome your objections?

4. What environmental and organizational factors are likely to affect the loose-fill packaging industry? How will these factors affect Biofoam?

5. Is Alfke right? Is this a good deal? Would you have bought into the firm? Why or why not?

Sources: "The Latest Trends in . . . Protective Packaging," *Modern Materials Handling*, October 1996, p. P8–P12; "What the Experts Say," *Inc.*, October 1996, p. 54–55; Robert D. Leaversuch, "Water-Soluble Foams Offer Cost-effective Protection," *Modern Plastics*, April 1997, p. 32–35; David Whitford, "The Snack Food That's Packing America," *Inc.*, October 1996, pp. 51–55.

Video Case 6

INFLUENCING BUSINESS BUYING: TRADE MAGAZINES IN CANADA

The Canadian trade magazine industry is in the business of serving business. The more than 900 trade magazine titles in Canada provide information to businesspeople in all types of industries—from housewares and fashion to mining and plastics. Although many businesspeople rely on Canadian trade publications to assist them in their purchasing decisions, these magazines may be threatened by a World Trade Organization decision that will remove existing trade barriers and allow U.S. publishers to distribute their trade publications in Canada.

As businesspeople who are readers contend, trade magazines provide a comprehensive and ongoing guide to doing business in a particular industry. The publications typically include detailed information on suppliers and their products and services, identify notable trends in the industry, and discuss general business tools and how they apply to a specific industry. One reader described one trade magazine as an "index of how to get in touch with anything you need to" in a particular industry.

Unlike most consumer publications, trade magazines are usually provided to their readers free of charge. Trade magazine publishers rely almost exclusively on advertising dollars to support their publications. In total, trade magazines in Canada collect approximately $150 million in advertising every year from suppliers who hope to influence business decision making with their advertisements.

Ownership in the trade magazine industry is also different from the consumer magazine sector. While two giants, Maclean Hunter and Southam, own about 70 percent of consumer magazines, together they own only 10 percent of the trade magazines. Small publishers such as Laurie O'Halloran, publisher of *Home Style*, and Pat Maclean, who publishes *Canadian Jeweller and Style*, tend to dominate the trade magazine business. This fragmented pattern of ownership may make the demise of Canadian trade magazines even more likely in the event that U.S. competitors enter, since small publishers may not have the resources to fight the bigger competitors.

O'Halloran targets the $5-billion-per-year housewares industry with her *Home Style* magazine, which is published from her home office. While O'Halloran has some concern that large U.S. publications may try to enter her business, she is confident that they would not be able to serve the needs of the Canadian housewares industry the way she can. She cites cultural differences in the way Canadians live and buy as barriers to U.S. publishers hoping to provide a trade magazine aimed at the Canadian housewares industry. She claims that these competitors would simply not be able to provide the accurate, high-quality information that she can provide to her readers.

Not everyone shares O'Halloran's confidence, however. The Canadian government is concerned about the future of the trade magazine industry and other cultural industries affected by the World Trade Organization decision and may appeal it. Meanwhile, for now, the Canadian trade magazine industry continues to influence the purchase behaviour of businesses in a variety of business markets.

QUESTIONS

1. What characteristics of business markets make the use of trade magazines so popular among buyers in these markets?

2. How do trade magazines fit into the buying behaviour process of decision makers in business markets? What types of buying situations would lend themselves to the use of trade magazines?

3. Do you agree with O'Halloran that Canadian trade magazines, as compared to American publications, can offer something unique to Canadian business people?

Source: This case was prepared by Auleen Carson and is based on "Trade Magazines," *Venture* (February 9, 1997).

CHAPTER

7

MARKET SEGMENTATION, TARGETING, AND POSITIONING FOR COMPETITIVE ADVANTAGE

WHAT GEORGE COHON WILL BE WEARING TONIGHT.

TUESDAY, OCTOBER 28TH, 1997. GEORGE COHON, SENIOR CHAIRMAN OF McDONALD'S, WILL BE ATTENDING TONIGHT'S LAUNCH PARTY FOR HIS NEW BOOK "TO RUSSIA WITH FRIES." KITON 3-BUTTON SINGLE-BREASTED CHARCOAL GREY WITH BROWN STRIPE SUIT, LUIGI BORELLI DRESS SHIRT, BRIONI TIE, ALLEN EDMONDS BROGUE SHOES. MR. COHON'S CLOTHING SPECIALIST IS ALBERT CHOW OF TORONTO'S BLOOR STREET STORE. IN APPRECIATION FOR APPEARING HERE, A DONATION WILL BE MADE IN MR. COHON'S NAME TO RONALD McDONALD CHILDREN'S CHARITIES OF CANADA.

HARRY ROSEN
WHATEVER SUITS YOU

MONTREAL · OTTAWA · TORONTO · LONDON · WINNIPEG · CALGARY · EDMONTON · VANCOUVER · BUFFALO · 1-800-917-6736

Harry Rosen, an icon of Canadian retailing, has built his business around solving problems for his customers. And one of the main problems for men is that they are not "born shoppers." In fact, Harry Rosen has built his business around a single premise: "When it comes to clothes, most men don't have a clue." Rather than planning their purchases, they shop on impulse. Instead of developing an integrated wardrobe that works for many occasions, they typically have a mishmash of clothes that may be wrong for all occasions. Harry doesn't mince words on the subject: "Some of my private clients have a closet full of clothes, and nothing to wear."

After a short stint working for Tip Top Tailors, Harry Rosen and his brother opened their first store in Toronto in 1954 using $500 from their personal savings to launch the business. Forty-three years later, Rosen has 22 stores located in major cities across Canada as well as one in Buffalo, New York. Rosen has built his business around the cult of his personality, his willingness to move with the times, and his ability to get to know his customers. Even today, at age 66, Harry spends his Saturdays on the floor of his flagship store in Toronto. Across Canada, his stores are known for fashion, a professional sales approach, and personal service.

Harry Rosen stores don't try to meet the needs of all consumers. Instead the stores focus on the high-end niche of the menswear market. Rosen's $125 million in annual sales represent 28 percent of the sales in that market. Rosen targets businessmen and locates his stores close to the heart of the business district in each city in which he operates. He knows the importance of keeping up with the times in the fashion business. Consequently he is revamping his stores once again so that they appeal more to younger men, with whom he is currently building relationships. Rosen confesses that it took him awhile to learn to serve men who wear earrings even though he knows that they are well educated, and many are career-oriented MBAs. In the process, however, Harry knows that he must not lose touch with his older, highly profitable clientele of established business professionals.

OBJECTIVES

When you finish this chapter, you should be able to

1. Define the three steps of target margeting: market segmentation, market targeting, and market positioning.

2. List and discuss the major levels of market segmentation and bases for segmenting consumer and business markets.

3. Explain how companies identify attractive market segments and choose a market-coverage strategy.

4. Explain how companies can position their products for maximum competitive advantage in the marketplace.

Harry Rosen also understands that today's consumers differ from their predecessors in important ways. They are more sophisticated and less caught up in the pursuit of the new and novel. They are much more hard-nosed about value, and quality—rather than price—is their primary concern. This group of consumers want shopping made easier, they demand service, and they resent being treated as a homogeneous group. They want their clothes to say individual things about them. This fact has made one-to-one marketing an imperative. To accomplish this strategy, retailers such as Harry Rosen must listen to customers at every opportunity and track them on an ongoing basis.

Although Harry Rosen has always practised some form of relationship marketing, today his efforts are more high-tech. The company maintains a computerized database that records information captured at the point of sale. The system tracks the client's size, style, and manufacturer preferences. It records each item that the client has purchased. Since men often don't shop on a regular basis, sales associates use the information to notify clients when shipments from their favoured manufacturers arrive or when specials are offered on that line of clothing. Contacting clients directly leads to approximately 35 percent of Harry Rosen's sales.

Recognizing that their target market of business professionals are extremely pressed for time, the database also allows Harry Rosen's sales associates to encourage clients to make appointments to visit the store. The sales associate stands ready with pre-selected merchandise that precisely meets the client's needs. This information not only helps clients to shop more efficiently, but it also assists potential gift buyers. By checking the database, a sales associate can ensure them they are not duplicating an item that a client already has and that the gift they can purchase will complement the individual's wardrobe. The database also allows the company to precisely target its direct mailings of the company's semi-annual men's fashion magazine, *harry*, to its more than 250 000 clients.

Harry Rosen's advertising supports his highly targeted, relationship-building strategy. He advertises almost exclusively in the business section of newspapers. His ads, created for over 35 years by Reid Bell, helped the firm tell its story, acquaint customers with its stores and staff members, and build its image. In a recent speech honouring the company with the Newspaper Marketing Bureau's special award for creative excellence in Canadian daily newspaper advertising, it was noted that ads for Harry Rosen stores always assumed an intelligent consumer who enjoys provocative advertising. When Reid Bell retired in 1996, Harry Rosen turned to avant-garde agency Roche Macaulay and Partners to continue the tradition. For the first time, ads for Harry Rosen stores feature well-known Canadians such as George Cohon, senior chair of McDonald's Restaurants of Canada, dressed impeccably in a $4195 Rosen suit, shirt, and tie. The campaign is tied together with the tag line, "What so-and-so will be wearing today."

Harry Rosen's fashion savvy and ability to build lifelong relationships with customers have given the company an edge over other top-end menswear specialty stores such as Studio 67 and Holt Renfrew while also beating out department-store boutiques such as Tommy Hilfiger or Hugo Boss. Competition for men's fashion is getting tougher in Canada, however. Hollywood fashion favourite Giorgio Armani just reopened Emporio Armani in Harry's backyard. It is three times the size of the old outlet. Armani is no small competitor. Offering both women's and men's fashion, Armani has a worldwide empire of 2000 stores that generate over $2 billion in sales. Harry isn't standing still, however. He also has plans for expansion and is heading south of the border to test his mettle against retail legends such as Nordstroms and Sak's Fifth Avenue.[1]

MARKETS

Organizations that sell to consumer and business markets recognize that they cannot appeal to all buyers in those markets, or at least not to all buyers in the same

FIGURE 7-1 *Steps in market segmentation, targeting, and positioning*

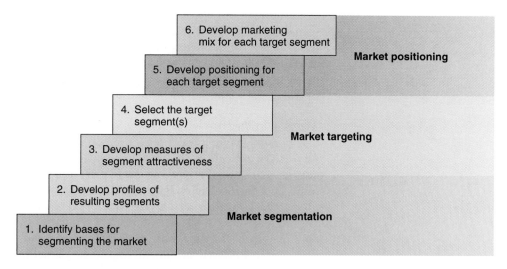

way. Buyers are too numerous, too widely scattered, and too varied in their needs and buying practices. In an era of fierce global competition, companies vary widely in their abilities to serve different segments of the market. Rather than trying to compete in an entire market, sometimes against superior competitors, each company must identify the parts of the market that it can serve best.

Today, most companies are moving away from mass marketing. Instead, they practise *target marketing*—identifying market segments, selecting one or more of them, and developing products and marketing mixes tailored to each. In this way, sellers can develop the right product for each target market and adjust their prices, distribution channels, and advertising to reach the target market efficiently. Instead of scattering their marketing efforts (the "shotgun" approach), they can focus on the buyers who have greater purchase interest (the "rifle" approach).

Figure 7-1 shows the three major steps in target marketing. The first is **market segmentation**—dividing a market into distinct groups of buyers with different needs, characteristics, or behaviour who might require separate products or marketing mixes. The company identifies different ways to segment the market and develops profiles of the resulting market segments. The second step is **market targeting**—evaluating each market segment's attractiveness and selecting one or more of the market segments to enter. The third step is **market positioning**—setting the competitive positioning for the product and creating a detailed marketing mix.

Market segmentation
Dividing a market into distinct groups of buyers with different needs, characteristics, or behaviour who might require separate products or marketing mixes.

Market targeting
The process of evaluating each market segment's attractiveness and selecting one or more segments to serve.

Market positioning
Arranging for a product to occupy a clear, distinctive, and desirable place relative to competing products in the minds of target consumers.

MARKET SEGMENTATION

Markets consist of buyers, and buyers differ in one or more ways. They may differ in their wants, resources, locations, buying attitudes, and buying practices. Through market segmentation, companies divide large, heterogeneous markets into smaller segments that can be reached more efficiently with products and services that match their unique needs. In this section, we discuss five important segmentation topics: levels of market segmentation, segmenting consumer markets, segmenting business markets, segmenting international markets, and requirements for effective segmentation.

LEVELS OF MARKET SEGMENTATION

Because buyers have unique needs and wants, each buyer is potentially a separate market. Ideally, then, a seller might design a separate marketing program for each buyer. However, although some companies attempt to serve buyers individually, many others cannot afford such a fine-grained approach and do not find complete segmentation worthwhile. Instead, they look for broader classes of buyers who differ in their product needs or buying responses. Thus, market segmentation can be carried out at many different levels. Companies can practise no segmentation (mass marketing), complete segmentation (micromarketing), or something in between (segment marketing or niche marketing).

Mass Marketing

Companies have not always practised target marketing. In fact, for most of this century, major consumer-products companies held fast to *mass marketing*—mass producing, mass distributing, and mass promoting the same product in the same way to all consumers. Henry Ford epitomized this marketing strategy when he offered the Model-T Ford to all buyers, with the reassurance that they could have the car "in any colour as long as it is black." Similarly, Coca-Cola at one time produced only one drink for the whole market, hoping it would appeal to everyone.

The traditional argument for mass marketing is that it creates the largest potential market, which leads to the lowest costs, which in turn can translate into either lower prices or higher margins. However, many factors now make mass marketing more difficult. For example, the world's mass markets have slowly splintered into a profusion of smaller segments—the baby-boomer segment here, the generation Xers there; here the Chinese market, there the French-Canadian market; here working women, there single parents; here eastern Canada, there the West. Today, marketers find it very hard to create a single product or program that appeals to all of these diverse groups. The proliferation of advertising media and distribution channels has also made it difficult to practise "one-size-fits-all" marketing:

> [Consumers] . . . have more ways to shop: at giant malls, specialty shops, and superstores; through mail-order catalogues, home shopping networks, and virtual stores on the Internet. And they are bombarded with messages pitched through a growing number of channels: broadcast and narrow-cast television, radio, online computer networks, the Internet, telephone services such as fax and telemarketing, and niche magazines and other print media.[2]

No wonder some have claimed that mass marketing is dying. Not surprisingly, many companies are retreating from mass marketing and turning to segmented marketing.

Segment Marketing

Segment marketing
Marketing that recognizes that buyers differ in their needs, perceptions, and buying behaviours.

A company that practises **segment marketing** recognizes that buyers differ in their needs, perceptions, and buying behaviours. The company tries to isolate broad segments that comprise a market and adapts its offers to more closely match the needs of one or more segments. Thus, GM has designed specific models for different income and age groups. In fact, it sells models for segments with varied *combinations* of age and income. For instance, GM designed its Buick Park Avenue for older, higher-income consumers. Marriott markets to a variety of segments—business travellers, families, and others—with packages adapted to their varying needs.

Segment marketing offers several benefits over mass marketing. The company can market more efficiently, targeting its products or services, channels, and communications programs toward only consumers that it can serve best. The company can also market more effectively by fine-tuning its products, prices, and programs to the needs of carefully defined segments. And the company may face fewer competitors if fewer firms are focusing on a particular market segment.

Niche Marketing

Niche marketing
Marketing that focuses on subgroups within the large identifiable groups in a market.

Market segments are normally large identifiable groups within a market—for example, luxury car buyers, performance car buyers, utility car buyers, and economy car buyers. **Niche marketing** focuses on subgroups within these segments. A *niche* is a more narrowly defined group, usually identified by dividing a segment into subsegments or by defining a group with a distinctive set of traits who may seek a special combination of benefits. For example, the utility vehicles segment might include light-duty pick-up trucks and sport utility vehicles (SUVs). And the SUV sub-segment might be further divided into standard SUV (as served by Ford and Chevrolet) and luxury SUV (as served by Lexus) niches.

Whereas segments are fairly large and typically attract several competitors, niches are smaller and usually attract only one or a few competitors. Niche marketers presumably understand their niches' needs so well that their customers willingly pay a price premium. For example, Ferrari receives a high price for its cars because its loyal buyers feel that no other automobile comes close to offering the product-service-membership benefits that Ferrari does.

Niching offers smaller companies an opportunity to compete by focusing their limited resources on serving niches that may be unimportant to or overlooked by larger competitors. For example, T&T Supermarkets, a small Vancouver-area grocery retailer, has been growing rapidly by catering to the burgeoning Asian market that comprises 25 percent of the Lower Mainland population.[3] However, large companies also practise niche marketing. For example, American Express offers not only its traditional green cards but also gold cards, corporate cards, and even platinum cards aimed at a niche consisting of the top-spending one percent of its 36 million cardholders.[4] And Nike not only makes athletic gear for basketball, running, and soccer, but also for smaller niches such as biking, rugby, and street hockey.

In many markets today, niches are the norm. As an advertising agency executive observed: "There will be no market for products that everybody likes a little, only for products that somebody likes a lot."[5] Other experts assert that companies will have to "niche or be niched."[6] We expand upon niche marketing later in this chapter and in Chapter 18.

Micromarketing

Segment and niche marketers tailor their offers and marketing programs to meet the needs of various market segments. At the same time, however, they do not customize their offers to individual customers. Thus, segment marketing and niche marketing fall between the extremes of mass marketing and micromarketing. **Micromarketing** is the practice of tailoring products and marketing programs to suit the tastes of specific individuals or locations. Micromarketing includes *local marketing* and *individual marketing*.

Local Marketing. Local marketing involves tailoring brands and promotions to the needs and wants of local customer groups—cities, neighbourhoods, and even specific stores. Thus, retailers such as Sears and Wal-Mart routinely customize each store's merchandise and promotions to match its specific clientele and neighbourhood demographics. Kraft helps supermarket chains identify the specific cheese assortments and shelf positioning that will optimize cheese sales in low-income, middle-income, and high-income stores, and ethnic communities.

Local marketing has some drawbacks. It can drive up manufacturing and marketing costs by reducing economies of scale. It can also create logistical problems as companies try to meet the varied requirements of different regional and local markets. And a brand's overall image might be diluted if the product and message vary in different locations. Still, as companies face increasingly fragmented markets, and as new supporting technologies develop, the advantages of local marketing often outweigh the drawbacks. Local marketing helps a company to market more effectively in the face of pronounced regional and local differences in community demographics and lifestyles. It also meets the needs of the company's "first-line customers"—retailers—who prefer more fine-tuned product assortments for their neighbourhoods.

Individual Marketing. In the extreme, micromarketing becomes **individual marketing**—tailoring products and marketing programs to the needs and preferences of

Micromarketing
The practice of tailoring products and marketing programs to suit the tastes of specific individuals or locations.

Local marketing
The practice of tailoring brands and promotions to the needs and wants of local customer groups.

Individual marketing
The practice of tailoring products and marketing programs to the needs and preferences of individual customers.

individual customers. Individual marketing has also been labelled "markets-of-one marketing," "customized marketing," and "one-to-one marketing" (see Marketing Highlight 7-1).[7] The prevalence of mass marketing has obscured the fact that for centuries consumers were served as individuals: The tailor custom-made the suit, the cobbler designed shoes for the individual, the cabinet maker crafted furniture to order. Today, however, new technologies are permitting many companies to return to customized marketing. More powerful computers, detailed databases, robotic production, and immediate and interactive communication media such as e-mail, fax, and the Internet—all have combined to foster "mass customization."[8] *Mass customization* is the ability to prepare on a mass basis individually designed products and communications to meet each customer's requirements.

Consumer marketers are now providing custom-made products in areas ranging from hotel stays and furniture to clothing and bicycles. For example, Suited for Sun, a swimwear manufacturer, uses a computer/camera system in retail stores to design custom-tailored swimsuits for women. The customer puts on an "off-the-rack" garment, and the system's digital camera captures her image on the computer screen. The store clerk applies a stylus to the screen to create a garment with perfect fit. The customer can select from more than 150 patterns and styles, which are re-imaged over her body on the computer screen until she finds the one that she likes best. The system then transmits the measurements to the factory, and the one-of-a-kind bathing suit is mailed to the delighted customer within days.

Another example is the National Industrial Bicycle Company in Japan (the Panasonic brand in North America), which uses flexible manufacturing to turn out large numbers of bikes specially fitted to the needs of individual buyers. Customers visit their local bike shop where the shopkeeper measures them on a special frame and faxes the specifications to the factory. At the factory, the measurements are punched into a computer, which creates blueprints in three minutes that would take a draftsperson 60 times that long to create. The computer then guides robots and workers through the production process. The factory is ready to produce any of 18 million variations on 18 bicycle models in 199 colour patterns and about as many sizes as there are people. The price is steep—between $545 and $3200—but within two weeks the buyer is riding a custom-made, one-of-a-kind machine.

Business-to-business marketers are also finding new ways to customize their offerings. For example, Motorola salespeople now use a hand-held computer to custom-design pagers following a business customer's wishes. The design data are transmitted to the Motorola factory, and production starts within 17 minutes. The customized pagers are ready for shipment within two hours.

The move toward individual marketing mirrors the trend in consumer *self-marketing*. Increasingly, customers are taking more responsibility for determining which products and brands to buy. Consider two purchasing agents with two different purchasing styles. The first sees several salespeople, each trying to persuade the agent to buy his or her product. The second sees no salespeople but rather logs onto the Internet; searches for information on and evaluations of available products; interacts electronically with various suppliers, users, and product analysts; and then identifies the best offer. The second purchasing agent has taken more responsibility for the buying process, and the marketer has had less influence over her buying decision.

As the trend toward more interactive dialogue and less advertising monologue continues, self-marketing will grow in importance. As more buyers look up consumer reports, join Internet product-discussion forums, and place orders via phone or online, marketers will have to influence the buying process in new ways. They will need to involve customers more in all phases of the product-development and buying process, increasing opportunities for buyers to practise self-marketing.

According to the chief designer for Mazda, "Customers will want to express their individuality with the products they buy." The opportunities offered by these

MARKETS OF ONE: CUSTOMIZING THE MARKETING OFFER

Several technologies have converged in recent years to allow companies in a wide range of industries to treat large numbers of customers as unique "markets of one." Advances in computer-design, database, interactive-communication, and manufacturing technologies have given birth to "mass customization," the process through which firms interact one-to-one with masses of customers to design products and services tailor-made to individual needs. Companies such as Harry Rosen have excelled using this strategy. Here are some other examples:

Check into any Ritz-Carlton hotel around the world, and you'll be amazed at how well the hotel's employees manage to anticipate your slightest need. Without ever asking, they seem to know that you want a non-smoking room with a king-size bed, a non-allergenic pillow, and breakfast with decaffeinated coffee. How does the Ritz-Carlton work this magic? Starting with a fervent dedication to satisfying the unique needs of each of its thousands of guests, the hotel uses a system that combines information technology and flexible operations to customize the hotel experience. At the heart of the system is a huge customer database, which contains information about guests gathered through the observations of hotel employees. Each day, hotel staffers—from those at the front desk to those in maintenance and housekeeping—discretely record the unique habits, likes, and dislikes of each guest. These observations are then transferred to a corporatewide "guest history database." Every morning, a "guest historian" at each hotel reviews the files of all new arrivals who have previously stayed at a Ritz-Carlton and prepares a list of suggested extra touches that might delight each guest. Guests have responded strongly to such markets-of-one service. Since inaugurating the guest-history system in 1992, the Ritz-Carlton has boosted guest retention by 23 percent. An amazing 95 percent of departing guests report that their stay has been a truly memorable experience.

The North American Life Assurance Co. of Toronto decided that targeted micromarketing campaigns were so important that the company formed a separate subsidiary, FNA Financial Inc., to develop the research base to identify niche markets. One of its most recent successes has occurred in their targeting of women executives and professionals living in the Toronto area. By combining information obtained from Statistics Canada, Revenue Canada, and Canada Post Corporation, with their own focus group research, FNA determined that the best prospects for North American Life's services in this niche were women aged 30 to 44, from two-income families, who were financially secure, with established careers. This group was particularly interested in long-term investment products and educational savings plans for their children. They hated "hard-sell" approaches and distrusted commissioned salespeople. Armed with their findings, FNA was able to target neighbourhoods where these women lived. Their mailings generated a 12 percent response, which is impressive given that average response rates range between four and eight percent. Furthermore, the campaign was highly cost-effective. Whereas a telemarketing campaign was projected to cost $104 for every appointment generated, this program cost only $68.

At Andersen Windows, customers now help design their own windows, whether they're complex, lofty Gothic windows or centimetres-high miniatures. Andersen uses an interactive, computerized catalogue system called Windows of Knowledge. An industry analyst describes the system: "Using this tool, a salesperson can help customers [select from 50 000 possible window components] and add, change, and strip away features until they've designed a window they're pleased with. It's akin to playing with building blocks. The computer automatically checks the window specs for structural soundness and then generates a price quote. . . . The retailer's computer transmits each order to [the factory] where it's assigned a unique 'licence plate number,' which can be tracked . . . using barcode technology from the assembly line through to the warehouse." Such "batch-of-one" manufacturing has greatly increased the customer's product selection while also reducing errors. Last year Andersen offered a whopping 188 000 different products, yet fewer than one in 200 truckloads contained an order problem. Moreover, by making almost everything to order, Andersen has greatly reduced its inventory requirements. Distributors are delighted with the Windows of Knowledge system. Says one retailer, "It's a terrific tool. It does things that would drive me crazy when I used to have to do them by hand." But the real winners are Andersen's homeowners and contractors who get just the windows they want with a minimum of hassle. All this has made Andersen a real markets-of-one advocate. Sums up one executive, "We're on a journey toward purer and purer mass customization."

The Canadian Imperial Bank of Commerce uses its sophisticated database to improve customer retention. The database contains up to 150 pieces of information on each CIBC client. By looking at specific variables, the bank can differentiate between clients who intend to remain with the bank and those who are likely to switch to another provider. The bank develops individual scores for each customer based on behavioural information such as whether he or she pays credit-card bills on time and whether he or she transfers funds to buy registered retirement savings plans with another institution. When a client is identified as a person who is likely to switch to another bank, he or she becomes the target of a new communications campaign that involves direct-mail pieces, a personal call from a bank representative, a newsletter about the benefits of one of the CIBC financial services they use, and offers of special rates on loans and mortgages.

Sources: Gordon Arnaut, "Getting to Know You; Getting to Know All About You," *Globe and Mail,* February 15, 1994, p. B27; Maurice Simms, "How One Insurance Firm Found a Niche," *Globe and Mail,* February 15, 1994, p. B27; Barbara Smith, "Treating Customers as Individuals," *Strategy: The Canadian Marketing Report,* August 24, 1992, pp. 12, 16, 18; www.cibc.com/index.html

technologies promise to turn marketing from "a broadcast medium to a dialogue medium" where the customer participates actively in the design of the product and offer.[9] We will examine the trends toward one-to-one marketing and self-marketing further in Chapter 17.

BASES FOR SEGMENTING CONSUMER MARKETS

There is no single way to segment a market. A marketer has to try different segmentation variables, alone and in combination, to find the best way to view the market structure. Table 7-1 outlines the major variables that might be used in segmenting consumer markets. Here we look at the major *geographic, demographic, psychographic,* and *behavioural variables.*

Geographic Segmentation

Geographic segmentation calls for dividing the market into different geographical units such as nations, regions, provinces, counties, cities, or neighbourhoods. A company may decide to operate in one or a few geographical areas, or to operate in all areas but pay attention to geographical differences in needs and wants.

Many companies today are "regionalizing" their marketing programs—localizing their products, advertising, promotion, and sales efforts to fit the needs of individual regions, cities, and even neighbourhoods. For example, Absolut, the makers of vodka, recently launched a regional advertising campaign, aimed at East Coast consumers.[10]

Demographic Segmentation

Demographic segmentation consists of dividing the market into groups based on variables such as age, gender, family size, family life cycle, income, occupation, education, religion, race, and nationality. Demographic factors are the most popular bases for segmenting customer groups. One reason is that consumer needs, wants, and usage rates often vary closely with demographic variables. Another is that demographic variables are easier to measure than most other types of variables. Even when market segments are first defined using other bases, such as personality or behaviour, their demographic characteristics must be known in order to assess the size of the target market and to reach it efficiently.

Geographic segmentation
Dividing a market into different geographical units such as nations, provinces, regions, counties, cities, or neighbourhoods.

Demographic segmentation
Dividing the market into groups based on demographic variables such as age, sex, family size, family life cycle, income, occupation, education, religion, race, and nationality.

Marketers at Absolut Vodka realize Canadians have strong regional ties. This first regional ad used by Absolut appeared in Atlantic Progress, *an East Coast business magazine.*

TABLE 7-1 *Major Segmentation Variables for Consumer Markets*

VARIABLE	TYPICAL BREAKDOWNS
Geographic	
Region	Maritimes, Quebec, Ontario, Prairies, British Columbia, Northern Territories
City size	Under 5000; 5000–20 000; 20 000–50 000; 50 000–100 000; 100 000–250 000; 250 000–500 000; 500 000–1 000 000; 1 000 000–4 000 000; 4 000 000 and over
Density	Urban, suburban, rural
Climate	Northern, Southern, Coastal, Prairie, Mountain
Demographic	
Age	Under 6, 6–11, 12–19, 20–34, 35–49, 50–64, 65+
Gender	Male, female
Family size	1–2, 3–4, 5+
Family life cycle	Young, single; young, married, no children; young, married, youngest child under 6; young married, youngest child 6 or over; older, married, with children; older, married, no children under 18; older, single; same-sex partners; unmarried partners, no children; unmarried partners, with children; other
Income	Under $10 000; $10 000–$15 000; $15 000–$20 000; $20 000–$30 000; $30 000–$50 000; $50 000–$75 000; $75 000 and over
Occupation	Professional and technical; managers, officials, and proprietors; clerical, sales; craftspeople, foremen; operatives; farmers; retired; students; homemakers; unemployed
Education	Grade school or less; some high school; high school graduate; college; some university; university graduate; post-graduate
Religion	Catholic, Protestant, Jewish, Muslim, other
Ethnic origin	African-Canadian, Asian, British, French, German, Scandinavian, Italian, Latin American, Native Canadian Middle Eastern, Japanese
Psychographic	
Social class	Lower lowers, upper lowers, working class, middle class, upper middles, lower uppers, upper uppers
Lifestyle	Achievers, believers, strivers
Personality	Compulsive, gregarious, authoritarian, ambitious
Behavioural	
Purchase occasion	Regular occasion, special occasion
Benefits sought	Quality, service, economy
User status	Non-user, ex-user, potential user, first-time user, regular user
Usage rate	Light user, medium user, heavy user
Loyalty status	None, medium, strong, absolute
Readiness state	Unaware, aware, informed, interested, desirous, intending to buy
Attitude toward product	Enthusiastic, positive, indifferent, negative, hostile

Age and life-cycle segmentation
Dividing a market into different age and life-cycle groups.

AGE AND LIFE-CYCLE STAGE. Consumer needs and wants change with age. Some companies use **age and life-cycle segmentation,** offering different products or using different marketing approaches for different age and life-cycle groups. One

Demographic segmentation: Johnson & Johnson targets children with Band-Aid Sesame Street Bandages; Big Bird and Cookie Monster "help turn little people's tears into great big smiles." Toyota is marketing to women who "aren't only working hard, they're playing hard."

of the largest challenges for today's marketers has been trying to determine what makes the youth market—those aged 18 to 25—tick. As Edward Caffyn of MacLaren McCann in Toronto notes, "We've labelled them, prodded them, followed them, partied with them."[11] A number of recent studies show a few reasons why. First, many young adults just don't like advertisers, don't want to be sold to, and don't want to be related to. Second, they defy the generalizations that marketers tend to make. Rather than falling into a well-defined, age-based segment, young adults are extremely diverse, and celebrate their differences rather than their similarities. Even though they disdain advertising, they enjoy watching ads, and advertising is often a topic of conversation. But since an ad intrudes on their viewing, it must provide something to compensate for the interruption. It must amuse and entertain. It can't make the mistake of telling them what is cool or implying that if you use the advertised product, you will be cool. The youth market is too savvy and cynical to accept that kind of pitch. Young adults want ads that tell them about the company and the product, and then leave it up to the viewer to decide whether they like you and your products. Ads that work share this common trait. Diesel Jeans creates a quirky world of its own; Molson Canadian's "I am" campaign lays out the essence of a brand and asks the viewer to accept it or not; and Calvin Klein ads deal with people more than they do with clothes and imply, "Be who you gotta be and everything will be cool."[12]

Marketers must be careful to guard against stereotypes when using age and life-cycle segmentation. Although you might find some 70-year-olds in wheelchairs, you will find others on tennis courts. Similarly, whereas some 40-year-old couples are sending their children off to university, others are just beginning new families. Thus, age is often a poor predictor of a person's life cycle, health, work or family status, needs, and buying power.

Gender segmentation
Dividing a market into different groups based on sex.

GENDER.   Gender segmentation has long been used in clothing, cosmetics, and magazines. For example, although early deodorants were used by both sexes, many producers are now featuring brands for one sex only. Procter & Gamble was among the first with Secret, a brand specially formulated for a woman's chemistry, packaged and advertised to reinforce the female image.

Today, many marketers use gender-based segmentation. The automobile industry knows women buy nearly half of all new cars sold and influence 80 percent of all new-car purchasing decisions. Thus, women have become a valued target market for the auto companies. "Selling to women should be no different than selling to men," notes one analyst. "But there are subtleties that make a difference."[13] Women have different frames and greater safety concerns. To address these issues, automakers are designing cars with hoods and trunks that are easier to open, seats that are easier to adjust, and seat belts that fit women better. They've also increased their safety focus, emphasizing features such as air bags and remote door locks.

In advertising, more and more car manufacturers are targeting women directly. In contrast to the car advertising of past decades, these ads portray women as competent and knowledgeable consumers who are interested in what a car is all about, not just the colour. For example, Saturn was one of the first companies to recognize how poorly women are often treated when they attempt to buy a car. Their famous "vanity mirror" ad, in which an aggressive male salesman asks a young female customer if she wants to see the vanity mirror, illustrated how women are often treated in car dealerships. Saturn used the ad to reinforce its positioning as a "different kind of company" while stressing that it was a "woman-friendly" place to buy a car.

Gender is also important when it comes to understanding consumer behaviour at the grocery checkout counter. Men comprise 37 percent of Canada's principal grocery shoppers. These men are younger than your average grocery shopper, ranging in age from 25 to 34. They are also more likely to be professionals, business owners, or senior managers who live in Quebec or British Columbia. The factors that drive male grocery shoppers differ from those that concern women. Men are not as likely to clip coupons or buy no-name products. They seem to care little about products with environmental claims. They are less concerned about nutrition than their female counterparts, showing lower preferences for reduced-calorie or "light" products. Finally, men want convenience and are willing to pay higher prices for it.[14]

Income segmentation
Dividing a market into different income groups.

INCOME.   **Income segmentation** has long been used by the marketers of products and services such as automobiles, boats, clothing, cosmetics, and travel. Many companies target affluent consumers with luxury goods and convenience services. Stores such as Neiman-Marcus, which mail their Christmas catalogues to wealthy Canadian consumers, pitch everything from expensive jewellery, fine fashions, and exotic furs to glazed Australian apricots priced at $20 a pound.

Neiman Marcus
www.neimanmarcus.com/

At the other end of the spectrum are those with restricted income. Marketers must be aware that many low-income people are quite different from traditional stereotypes. Instead of being poorly educated, many fall into "the young and the jobless" class. The unemployment rate for people aged 15 to 24 is approximately 16 percent. Many of those who are employed can only find part-time work; others who have university educations are trying to repay the loans that allowed them to pursue a degree. They are often forced to return home and live with their parents. These living arrangements free them from the burden of paying rent and buying groceries, which allows them to make more eclectic purchases with their limited income, often on entertainment-related products and services such as music, movies, and video games, as well as clothing.[15]

Psychographic Segmentation

Psychographic segmentation
Dividing a market into different groups based on social class, lifestyle, or personality characteristics.

Psychographic segmentation divides buyers into different groups based on social class, lifestyle, or personality characteristics. People in the same demographic group can have very different psychographic makeups.

SOCIAL CLASS.   In Chapter 5, we described social classes and showed that social class has a strong effect on preferences in cars, clothes, home furnishings, leisure activities, reading habits, and retailers. Many companies design products or services for specific social classes, building in features that appeal to these classes.

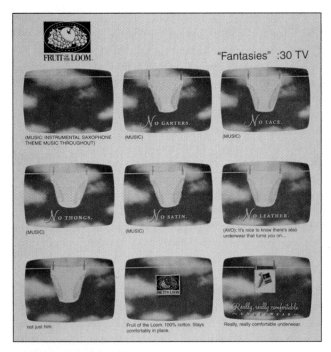

The award-winning Fruit of the Loom campaign illustrates effective gender-based segmentation.

LIFESTYLE.   As discussed in Chapter 5, people's interest in various goods is affected by their lifestyles, and the goods they buy express those lifestyles. Marketers are increasingly segmenting their markets by consumer lifestyles. Golf is one of the fastest-growing sports and is becoming an important part of many Canadians' lifestyles. Not only do they play golf, but they also watch it on television, surf the Net to track their favourite players, and spend hours in golf stores looking for the latest fashions and equipment. Specialty magazines, such as *Canada's Golf Course Ranking Magazine*, have emerged to serve marketers wishing to tap into this lucrative market.

PERSONALITY.   Marketers also have used personality variables to segment markets, giving their products personalities that correspond to consumer personalities. Successful market segmentation strategies based on personality have been used for products such as cosmetics, cigarettes, insurance, and liquor.[16]

Nokia differentiated itself by creating cellular phones in a wide range of colours that allowed people to express themselves through a functional product. Lillian Tepera, Nokia's marketing manager, says cellular phones are like watches: "They're there to serve a purpose, but people want something more than a grey or black rectangular box. People are looking for an expression of who they are, not just something to call their stockbroker with."[17]

Behavioural Segmentation

Behavioural segmentation
Dividing a market into groups based on consumer knowledge, attitude, use, or response to a product.

Occasion segmentation
Dividing the market into groups according to occasions when buyers get the idea to buy, actually make their purchase, or use the purchased item.

Behavioural segmentation divides buyers into groups based on their knowledge, attitudes, uses, or responses to a product. Many marketers believe that behaviour variables are the best starting point for building market segments.

OCCASIONS.   Buyers can be grouped according to occasions when they get the idea to buy, actually make their purchase, or use the purchased item. **Occasion segmentation** can help firms build up product usage. For example, orange juice most often is consumed at breakfast, but orange growers have promoted drinking orange juice as a cool and refreshing drink at other times of the day. In contrast, Coca-Cola's "Coke in the Morning" advertising campaign attempts to increase

Occasion segmentation: Kodak has developed special versions of its single-use camera for about any picture-taking occasion, from underwater photography to taking baby pictures.

TABLE 7-2 *Benefit Segmentation of the Toothpaste Market*

Benefit Segments	Demographics	Behaviour	Psychographics	Favoured Brands
Economy (low price)	Men	Heavy users	High autonomy, value oriented	Brands on sale
Medicinal (decay prevention)	Large families	Heavy users	Hypochondriacal, conservative	Crest
Cosmetic (bright teeth)	Teens, young adults	Smokers	High sociability, active	Aqua-Fresh, Ultra Brite
Taste (good tasting)	Children	Spearmint lovers	High self-involvement, hedonistic	Colgate, Aim

Source: Adapted from Russell J. Haley, "Benefit Segmentation: A Decision-Oriented Research Tool," *Journal of Marketing,* July 1968, pp. 30–35. Also see Haley, "Benefit Segmentation: Backwards and Forwards," *Journal of Advertising Research,* February–March 1984, pp. 19–25; and Haley, "Benefit Segmentation—20 Years Later," *Journal of Consumer Marketing,* Vol. 1, 1984, pp. 5–14.

Eastman Kodak Company
www.kodak.com/

Benefit segmentation
Dividing the market into groups according to the different benefits that consumers seek from the product.

Coke consumption by promoting the beverage as an early-morning pick-me-up. Some holidays, such as Mother's Day and Father's Day, were originally promoted partly to increase the sale of candy, flowers, cards, and other gifts. The Curtis Candy Company promoted the "trick-or-treat" custom at Halloween to encourage every home to have candy ready for eager little callers knocking at the door.

Kodak uses occasion segmentation in designing and marketing its single-use cameras. The customer simply snaps off the roll of pictures and returns the film, camera and all, to be processed. By mixing lenses, film speeds, and accessories, Kodak has developed special versions of the camera for about any picture-taking occasion, from underwater photography to taking baby pictures.

BENEFITS SOUGHT. A powerful form of segmentation is to group buyers according to the different *benefits* that they seek from the product. **Benefit segmentation** requires finding the major benefits people look for in the product class, the kinds of people who look for each benefit, and the major brands that deliver each benefit. One of the best examples of benefit segmentation was conducted in the toothpaste market (see Table 7-2). Research found four benefit segments: economic, medicinal, cosmetic, and taste. Each benefit group had special demographic, behavioural, and psychographic characteristics. For example, the people seeking to prevent decay tended to have large families, were heavy toothpaste users, and were conservative. Each segment also favoured certain brands. Most current brands appeal to one of these segments. For example, Crest toothpaste stresses protection and appeals to the family segment, whereas Aim looks and tastes good and appeals to children.

Companies can use benefit segmentation to clarify the benefit segment to which they are appealing, its characteristics, and the major competing brands. They also can search for new benefits and launch brands that deliver them.

USER STATUS. Markets can be segmented into groups of non-users, ex-users, potential users, first-time users, and regular users of a product. Potential users and regular users may require different kinds of marketing appeals. For example, one study found that blood donors are motivated by need—understanding the need for blood and blood products within the community, and with the potential of their own need for blood in the future. Blood donors were also found to be very receptive to being telerecruited to make additional blood donations; most target markets are not receptive to telerecruiters. This suggests that social agencies should use different marketing approaches for keeping current donors and attracting new ones. A company's market position will also influence its focus. Market share leaders will focus on attracting potential users, whereas smaller firms will focus on attracting current users away from the market leader.

FIGURE 7-2 *Heavy and light users of common consumer products in the U.S.*

Source: See Victor J. Cook and William A. Mindak, "A Search for Constants: The 'Heavy User' Revisited!" *Journal of Consumer Marketing*, Vol. 1, No. 4 (Spring 1984), p. 80.

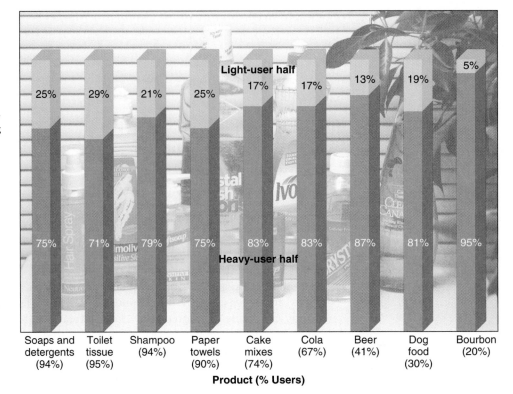

USAGE RATE. Markets also can be segmented into light-, medium-, and heavy-user groups. Heavy users are often a small percentage of the market, but account for a high percentage of total buying. Figure 7-2 shows usage rates for some popular consumer products. Product users were divided into two halves, a light-user half and a heavy-user half, according to their buying rates for the specific products. Using beer as an example, the figure shows that 41 percent of the households studied buy beer. However, the heavy-user half accounted for 87 percent of the beer consumed—almost seven times as much as the light-user half. Clearly, a beer company would prefer to attract one heavy user to its brand rather than several light users. Thus, most beer companies target the heavy beer drinker, with advertising focussed at young males.

LOYALTY STATUS. A market can also be segmented by consumer loyalty. Consumers can be loyal to brands (Tide), stores (the Bay), and companies (Ford). Buyers can be divided into groups according to their degree of loyalty. Some consumers are completely loyal—they buy one brand all the time. Others are somewhat loyal—they are loyal to two or three brands of a given product or favour one brand while sometimes buying others. Still other buyers show no loyalty to any brand. They either want something different each time they buy or they buy whatever is on sale.

A company can learn a lot by analysing loyalty patterns in its market. It should start by studying its own loyal customers. Colgate finds that its loyal buyers are more middle class, have larger families, and are more health-conscious. These characteristics identify the target market for Colgate. By studying its less loyal buyers, the company can identify which brands are most competitive with its own. If many Colgate buyers also buy Crest, Colgate can attempt to improve its positioning against Crest, possibly by using direct-comparison advertising. By looking at customers who are shifting away from its brand, the company can learn about its marketing weaknesses. As for non-loyals, the company may attract them by putting its brand on sale.

Companies need to be careful when using brand loyalty in their segmentation strategies. What appear to be brand-loyal purchase patterns might reflect little more than *habit, indifference,* a *low price,* or *unavailability* of other brands. Thus, frequent or regular purchasing may not be the same as brand loyalty—marketers must examine the motivations behind observed purchase patterns.

Using Multiple Segmentation Bases

Marketers rarely limit their segmentation analysis to only one or a few variables. Rather, they are increasingly using multiple segmentation bases in an effort to identify smaller, better defined target groups. Thus, a bank may not only identify a group of wealthy retired adults, but within that group distinguish several segments depending on their current income, assets, savings and risk preferences, and lifestyles. In other cases, companies may begin by using one segmentation base, then expand by using other bases.

One of the most promising developments in multivariable segmentation is "geodemographic" segmentation. Canadian firms marketing goods and services to the United States can link U.S. census data with lifestyle patterns to better refine their estimates of market potential down to ZIP code levels, neighbourhoods, and even blocks.

Canadian marketers know it is often essential to combine income with information on regional differences. A recent study by the Print Measurement Bureau revealed that regional differences still act as powerful determinants of Canadians' behaviour and choices. When one looks at the narrow segment of affluent consumers, one finds not only that the concentration of this group varies by region, but also by buying and lifestyle habits. Affluent consumers—people with incomes over $75 000—comprise 14 percent of the Canadian population. However, the highest concentration of affluent consumers is in Vancouver (23 percent). Affluent consumers living in Quebec have significantly different preferences when compared to the same group living in other provinces. For example, high-income French Canadians read more magazines and live in more moderately priced housing than do affluent consumers in the rest of Canada. They shop at specialty clothing stores more often and spend more on clothing and cosmetics. They are also more likely to bike, golf, swim, or ski than other affluent Canadians, who prefer to jog, garden, or visit health clubs. Although Quebec's affluent consumers don't travel as much as other high-income Canadians, they prefer Latin American destinations when they do travel. Geodemographic segmentation provides a powerful tool for refining demand estimates, selecting target markets, and shaping promotion messages.

Steelcase segments its markets based on the industries its customers operate in—in this case, B.C. Tel.

SEGMENTING BUSINESS MARKETS

Consumer and business marketers use many of the same variables to segment their markets. Business buyers can be segmented geographically or by benefits sought, user status, usage rate, and loyalty status. Yet, business marketers also use some additional variables. As Table 7-3 shows, these include business customer *demographics* (industry, company size); *operating characteristics; purchasing approaches; situational factors;* and *personal characteristics.*[18]

The table lists major questions that business marketers should ask in determining which customers they want to serve. By pursuing segments instead of the whole market, companies have a much better opportunity to deliver value to consumers and to receive maximum rewards for close attention to consumer needs. Thus, Hewlett Packard's Computer Systems Division targets specific industries that promise the best growth prospects,

TABLE 7-3   *Major Segmentation Variables for Business Markets*

Demographics

Industry: Which industries that buy this product should we focus on?

Company size: What size companies should we focus on?

Location: What geographical areas should we focus on?

Operating Variables

Technology: What customer technologies should we focus on?

User/nonuser status: Should we focus on heavy, medium, or light users or non-users?

Customer capabilities: Should we focus on customers needing many services or few services?

Purchasing Approaches

Purchasing function organization: Should we focus on companies with highly centralized or decentralized purchasing organizations?

Power structure: Should we focus on companies that are engineering dominated, financially dominated, or marketing dominated?

Nature of existing relationships: Should we focus on companies with which we already have strong relationships or simply go after the most desirable companies?

General purchase policies: Should we focus on companies that prefer leasing? Service contracts? Systems purchases? Sealed bidding?

Purchasing criteria: Should we focus on companies that are seeking quality? Service? Price?

Situational Factors

Urgency: Should we focus on companies that need quick delivery or service?

Specific application: Should we focus on certain applications of our product rather than all applications?

Size of order: Should we focus on large or small orders?

Personal Characteristics

Buyer-seller similarity: Should we focus on companies whose people and values are similar to ours?

Attitudes toward risk: Should we focus on risk-taking or risk-avoiding customers?

Loyalty: Should we focus on companies that show high loyalty to their suppliers?

Source: Adapted from Thomas V. Bonoma and Benson P. Shapiro, *Segmenting the Industrial Market* (Lexington, MA: Lexington Books, 1983). Also see John Berrigan and Carl Finkbeiner, *Segmentation Marketing: New Methods for Capturing Business* (New York: Harper-Business, 1992).

such as telecommunications and financial services. Its "red team" sales force specializes in developing and serving major customers these targeted industries.[19]

Within the chosen industry, a company can further segment by *customer size* or *geographic location*. The company might set up separate systems for dealing with large multiple-location customers, and small customers. A number of firms are targeting an emerging market: small Canadian home businesses. More than three million Canadians own their own businesses and 16.2 percent of Canadian households report that a family member either operates a home business or works from home. At 26 percent, Alberta has the largest proportion of households with home businesses, followed by Manitoba/Saskatchewan with 21 percent. Home businesses represent a growing market for office equipment. Most home businesses need computers, printers, modems, and fax machines. More than 30 percent of home businesses spend $500 to $1000 per year on office supplies.[20]

Within a given target industry and customer size, the company can segment by *purchase approaches and criteria*. For example, government, university, and industrial laboratories typically differ in their purchase criteria for scientific instruments. Government labs need low prices (because they have difficulty in getting funds to buy instruments) and service contracts (because they can easily get money to maintain instruments). University labs want equipment that needs little regular service because they don't have service people on their payrolls. Industrial labs need highly reliable equipment because they cannot afford downtime.

Table 7-3 focuses on business buyer *characteristics*. However, as in consumer segmentation, many marketers believe that *buying behaviour* and *benefits* provide the best basis for segmenting business markets. For example, a recent study of the customers of Signode Corporation's industrial packaging division revealed four segments, each seeking a different mix of price and service benefits:

◆ *Programmed buyers.* These buyers view Signode's products as not very important to their operations. They buy the products as a routine purchase, usually pay full price, and accept below-average service. Clearly, this is a highly profitable segment for Signode.

◆ *Relationship buyers.* These buyers regard Signode's packaging products as moderately important and are knowledgeable about competitors' offerings. They prefer to buy from Signode as long as its price is reasonably competitive. They receive a small discount and a modest amount of service. This segment is Signode's second most profitable.

◆ *Transaction buyers.* These buyers view Signode's products as very important to their operations. They are price- and service-sensitive. They receive about a 10 percent discount and above-average service. They are knowledgeable about competitors' offerings and are ready to switch for a better price, even if it means losing some service.

◆ *Bargain hunters.* These buyers view Signode's products as very important and demand the deepest discount and the highest service. They know the alternative suppliers, bargain hard, and are ready to switch at the slightest dissatisfaction. Signode needs these buyers for volume purposes, but they are not very profitable.[21]

This segmentation scheme has helped Signode to do a better job of designing marketing strategies that take into account each segment's unique reactions to varying levels of price and service.[22]

SEGMENTING INTERNATIONAL MARKETS

Few companies have either the resources or the will to operate in all, or even most, countries. Although some large companies, such as Coca-Cola or Sony, sell products in as many as 200 countries, most international firms focus on a smaller set. Operating in many countries presents new challenges. The different countries of the world, even those that are close together, can vary dramatically in their economic, cultural, and political composition. Thus, just as they do within their domestic markets, international firms need to group their world markets into segments with distinct buying needs and behaviours.

Companies can segment international markets using one or a combination of several variables. They can segment by *geographic location,* grouping countries by regions such as Western Europe, the Pacific Rim, the Middle East, or Africa. In fact, countries in many regions already have organized geographically into market groups or "free trade zones," such as the European Union, the European Free Trade Association, and the North American Free Trade Association. These associations reduce trade barriers between member countries, creating larger and more homogeneous markets.

Geographic segmentation assumes that nations close to one another will have many common traits and behaviours. Although this is often the case, there are many exceptions. For example, although the United States and Canada have much in common, overlooking differences between the two countries can be dangerous.

Furthermore, both differ culturally and economically from Mexico. Even within a region, consumers can differ widely. For example, many marketers think that all Central and South American countries with their 400 million inhabitants, are the same. However, the Dominican Republic is no more like Brazil than Italy is like Sweden. Many Latin Americans don't speak Spanish, including 140 million Portuguese-speaking Brazilians and the millions in other countries who speak a variety of Indian dialects.[23]

World markets can be segmented on the basis of *economic factors*. For example, countries might be grouped by population income levels or by their overall level of economic development. Some countries, such as the so-called Group of Seven—the United States, Britain, France, Germany, Japan, Canada, and Italy—have established, highly industrialized economies. Other countries have newly industrialized or developing economies (Singapore, Taiwan, Korea, Brazil, Mexico). Still others are less developed (China, India). A company's economic structure shapes its population's product and service needs and, therefore, the marketing opportunities it offers.

Countries can be segmented by *political and legal factors* such as the type and stability of government, receptivity to foreign firms, monetary regulations, and the amount of bureaucracy. Such factors can play a crucial role in a company's choice of which countries to enter and how. *Cultural factors* also can be used, grouping markets according to common languages, religions, values and attitudes, customs, and behavioural patterns.

Segmenting international markets on the basis of geographic, economic, political, cultural, and other factors assumes that segments should consist of clusters of countries. However, many companies use a different approach, called **intermarket segmentation**. Using this approach, they form segments of consumers who have similar needs and buying behaviour even though they are located in different countries. For example, Mercedes-Benz targets the world's well-to-do, regardless of their country. And PepsiCo uses ads filled with kids, sports, and rock music to target the world's teenagers. A recent study of more than 6500 teenagers from 25 countries showed that teens around the world live surprisingly parallel lives. As one expert notes, "From Rio to Rochester, teens can be found enmeshed in much the same regimen: ... drinking Coke, ... dining on Big Macs, surfin' the 'Net on their Macintosh computers.... And then there's the international teen uniform: baggy Levi's or Diesel jeans, T-shirt, Nikes or Doc Martens, and leather jacket."[24]

Similarly, an agricultural chemicals manufacturer might focus on small farmers in a variety of developing countries:

> These [small farmers], whether from Pakistan or Indonesia or Kenya or Mexico, appear to represent common needs and behaviour patterns. Most of them till the land using bullock carts and have very little cash to buy agricultural inputs. They lack the education ... to appreciate fully the value of using fertilizer and depend on government help for such things as seeds, pesticides, and fertilizer. They acquire farming needs from local suppliers and count on word-of-mouth to learn and accept new things and ideas. Thus, even though these farmers are in different countries continents apart, and even though they speak different languages and have different cultural backgrounds, they may represent a homogeneous market segment.[25]

Intermarket segmentation
Forming segments of consumers who have similar needs and buying behaviour even though they are located in different countries.

REQUIREMENTS FOR EFFECTIVE SEGMENTATION

Clearly, there are many ways to segment a market, but not all segmentations are effective. For example, buyers of table salt could be divided into blond and brunette customers. But hair colour obviously does not affect the purchase of salt. Furthermore, if all salt buyers bought the same amount of salt each month, believed all salt is the same, and wanted to pay the same price, the company would not benefit from segmenting this market.

Intermarket separation: Teens show surprising similarity no matter where in the world they live. For instance, this young woman could live almost anywhere. Thus, many companies target teenagers with worldwide marketing campaigns.

To be useful, market segments must have the following characteristics:

◆ *Measurability.* The size, purchasing power, and profiles of the segments can be measured. Certain segmentation variables are difficult to measure. For example, there are four million left-handed people in Canada—which is 15 percent of the population. Yet few products are targeted toward this left-handed segment. The major problem may be that the segment is hard to identify and measure. There are no data on the demographics of lefties, and Statistics Canada does not keep track of left-handedness in its surveys. Private data companies keep reams of statistics on other demographic segments, but not on left-handers.[26]

◆ *Accessibility.* The market segments can be effectively reached and served. Suppose a food company finds that heavy users of its brands are new Canadians. Unless there are media in the language spoken by these individuals, they will be difficult to reach.

◆ *Substantiality.* The market segments are large or profitable enough to serve. A segment should be the largest possible homogeneous group worth pursuing with a tailored marketing program. It would not pay, for example, for an automobile manufacturer to develop cars for persons whose height is less than four feet.

◆ *Actionability.* Effective programs can be designed for attracting and serving the segments. For example, although one small airline identified seven market segments, its staff was too small to develop separate marketing programs for each segment.

MARKET TARGETING

Marketing segmentation reveals the firm's market-segment opportunities. The firm now must evaluate the various segments and decide how many and which ones to target. We now look at how companies evaluate and select target segments.

Evaluating Market Segments

In evaluating different market segments, a firm must look at three factors: segment size and growth, segment structural attractiveness, and company objectives and resources.

Segment Size and Growth

The company must first collect and analyse data on current segment sales, growth rates, and expected profitability for various segments. It will be interested in segments that have the right size and growth characteristics. But "right size and growth" is a relative matter. Some companies will want to target segments with large current sales, a high growth rate, and a high profit margin. However, the largest, fastest-growing segments are not always the most attractive ones for every company. Smaller companies may find that they lack the skills and resources needed to serve the larger segments, or that these segments have too many competitors vying for market share. Such companies may select segments that are smaller and less attractive, in an absolute sense, but that are potentially more profitable for them.

Segment Structural Attractiveness

A segment might have desirable size and growth and still not offer attractive profits. The company must examine several major structural factors that affect long-run segment attractiveness.[27] For example, a segment is less attractive if it already contains many strong and aggressive *competitors*. The existence of many actual or potential *substitute products* may limit prices and the profits that can be earned in a segment. The relative *power of buyers* also affects segment attractiveness. If the buyers in a segment possess strong bargaining power relative to sellers, they will try to force prices down, demand more quality or services, and set competitors against one another, all at the expense of seller profitability. Finally, a segment may be less attractive if it contains *powerful suppliers* who can control prices or reduce the quality or quantity of ordered goods and services. Suppliers tend to be powerful when they are large and concentrated, when few substitutes exist, or when the supplied product is an important input.

Company Objectives and Resources

Even if a segment has the right size and growth and is structurally attractive, the company must consider its own objectives and resources in relation to that segment. Some attractive segments could be dismissed quickly because they do not mesh with the company's long-run objectives. Although such segments might be tempting in themselves, they might divert the company's attention and energies away from its main goals. Or they might be a poor choice from an environmental, political, or social-responsibility viewpoint. For example, in recent years, several companies and industries have been criticized for unfairly targeting vulnerable segments—children, the aged, low-income earners, and others—with questionable products or tactics (see Marketing Highlight 7-2).

If a segment fits the company's objectives, the company then must decide whether it possesses the skills and resources needed to succeed in that segment. If the company lacks the strengths needed to compete successfully in a segment and cannot readily obtain them, it should not enter the segment. Even if the company possesses the *required* strengths, it needs to employ skills and resources *superior* to those of the competition in order to really win in a market segment. The company should enter segments only where it can offer superior value and gain advantages over competitors.

SELECTING MARKET SEGMENTS

Target market
A set of buyers sharing common needs or characteristics that the company decides to serve.

Undifferentiated marketing
A market-coverage strategy in which a firm decides to ignore market segment differences and pursue the whole market with one offer.

After evaluating different segments, the company must now decide which and how many segments to serve. This is the problem of *target-market selection*. A **target market** consists of a set of buyers who share common needs or characteristics that the company decides to serve. Figure 7-3 shows that the firm can adopt one of three market-coverage strategies: *undifferentiated marketing, differentiated marketing,* and *concentrated marketing.*

Undifferentiated Marketing

Using an **undifferentiated marketing** strategy, a firm might decide to ignore market segment differences and pursue the whole market with one offer. The offer will

SOCIALLY RESPONSIBLE MARKET TARGETING

Market segmentation and targeting form the core of modern marketing strategy. Smart targeting helps companies to be more efficient and effective by focussing on the segments that they can satisfy best. Targeting also benefits consumers—companies reach specific groups of consumers with offers carefully tailored to satisfy their needs. However, market targeting sometimes generates controversy and concern. Issues usually involve the targeting of vulnerable or disadvantaged consumers with controversial or potentially harmful products.

For example, over the years the cereal industry has been heavily criticized for its marketing efforts directed toward children. Critics worry that sophisticated advertising, in which high-powered appeals are presented through the mouths of lovable animated characters, will overwhelm children's defences. They claim that toys and other premiums offered with cereals will distract children and make them want a particular cereal for the wrong reasons. All of this, critics fear, will entice children to gobble too much sugared cereal or to eat poorly balanced breakfasts. The marketers of toys and other children's products have been similarly battered, often with justification. Some critics have even called for a complete ban on advertising to children. Children cannot understand the selling intent of the advertiser, critics reason, so any advertising targeted toward children is inherently unfair.

For these reasons, in 1980 the Quebec government banned all advertising to children under age 13. The other provinces follow the Code of Advertising to Children developed by a partnership between the Canadian Association of Broadcasters and the Advertising Standards Council. The code includes the stipulation that advertisements cannot directly urge children to pressure their parents to buy products. If products, such as cereals, use premiums as part of their promotion program, then the advertising must give at least as much time to the product description as it does to the premium. The code forbids the use of well-known puppets, persons, or characters (including cartoon characters) as product endorsers. While the code has improved children's advertising on those

television and radio stations licensed by the Canadian Radio-television and Telecommunications Commission (CRTC), it has not stopped the spillover advertising from the United States— 75 percent of the advertisements seen

"Money Can Not Buy Health, But I'd Settle For A Diamond Studded Rocking Chair."
-Dorothy Parker-

▲ Altamira RRSPs
Call now: 1-800-263-7396 ext.24

More and more financial firms are recognizing the special needs of women as they target their products.

by Canadian children originate in the United States. While many of these ads are adapted to meet Canadian standards, others shown on American cable channels do not adhere to Canadian standards. For example, voice-overs are often added to children's commercials run in Canada giving information such as "batteries not included" or "some assembly required" since this is a Canadian, not an American, requirement.

Cigarette, beer, and fast-food marketers also have generated much controversy in recent years by their attempts to target vulnerable segments. For example, McDonald's and other chains have drawn criticism for pitching their high-fat, salt-laden fare to low-income consumers who are much more likely to be heavy consumers. R. J. Reynolds took heavy flak in 1990 when it announced plans to market Uptown, a menthol cigarette targeted toward low-income blacks. It quickly dropped the brand in the face of a loud public outcry and heavy pressure from African-American leaders.

Labatt Breweries of Canada was criticized for marketing its new ice beer

to young male consumers. While young males have traditionally been the main target of many brands of beer, Labatt drew criticism because of the product's higher alcohol levels, especially in the brand extension, Maximum Ice.

Women have long been concerned that they pay more for certain products and services than their male counterparts. For example, women are starting to protest when they are charged more than men for dry cleaning the same type of clothing. They object to paying three to four times more than men for a haircut. Research that sent white males, African Americans, and women to bargain for new cars at 100 dealerships revealed that white men were offered better deals when they purchased cars than were women or ethnic consumers.

While some marketers are criticized for the segments they target and for the marketing programs directed at those segments, other firms are reproached for not targeting certain groups of consumers. For example, many critics charge that the poor, who are four times less likely to buy or own a computer, have been totally left off the Information Highway. Many firms have also been reluctant to target the gay or lesbian markets. Hiram Walker is one of the first mainstream marketers to specifically target lesbian women. Their ads for Tuaca liqueur clearly suggest that the female characters are more interested in cultivating relationships with other women, using a headline from the personal ads, "Cool girl seeks sociable silent type to share 'la dolce vita'."

Not all attempts to target children, minorities, or other special segments draw such criticism. In fact, most provide benefits to targeted consumers. For example, recent statistics reveal that women now comprise 42 percent of Canada's 4.5 million RRSP contributors. While many financial institutions believe that you should reach women with your general marketing efforts, others, such as Trimark Investment Management and Altamira, are running programs with women as their specific target. Altamira broke through the rush of RRSP advertising by using pithy quotations from notable women. These firms note that women want information, not sales pitches. Furthermore, they value financial information presented at convenient times that fit into the busy schedules inherent in two-income families, such as lunch-time financial seminars. They want advice presented in a friendly, easy-to-understand format. Whereas many male customers will not admit when they do not know something, women will ask questions about financial matters but do not want to be made to feel stupid for asking.

Colgate-Palmolive's Colgate Junior toothpaste is another product targeted in a socially responsible manner. It has special features designed to get children to brush longer and more often—it's less foamy, has a milder taste, and contains sparkles, and it comes out of the tube in a star-shaped column. Other

examples include cosmetics companies that have responded to the special needs of minority segments by adding products specifically designed for black, Hispanic, or Asian women. For example, M.A.C Cosmetics offers a wide range of colours that appeal to various ethnic groups.

Thus, in market targeting, the issue is not really *who* is targeted but rather *how* and for *what*. Controversies arise when marketers attempt to profit at the expense of targeted segments—when they unfairly target vulnerable segments or target them with questionable products or tactics. Socially responsible marketing calls for segmentation and targeting that serve not just the interests of the company, but also the interests of those targeted.

Sources: Excerpts from "PowerMaster," *Fortune,* January 13, 1992, p. 82. Also see

"Selling Sin to Blacks," *Fortune,* October 21, 1991, p. 100; Dorothy J. Gaiter, "Black-Owned Firms are Catching an Afrocentric Wave," *Wall Street Journal,* January 8, 1992, p. B2; Cyndee Miller, "Cosmetics Firms Finally Discover the Ethnic Market," *Marketing News,* August 30, 1993, p. 2; and Michael Wilke, "Toy Companies Take Up Diversity Banner," *Advertising Age,* February 27, 1995, pp. 1, 8. Bruce Little, "Poor Left Behind in Computer Revolution," *Globe and Mail,* January 15, 1996, p. B11; Jim McElgunn, "Money, Marketing and Gender," *Marketing,* January 30, 1995, pp. 11–13; Cyndee Miller, "The Ultimate Taboo," *Marketing News,* Vol 29, (17), pp. 1, 18; Marina Strauss, "Labatt Targeted Youth, Consultant Says," *Globe and Mail,* July 21, 1995, B3; Keith J. Tuckwell, *Canadian Marketing in Action,* 3d ed., Scarborough: Prentice-Hall Canada Inc., 1996, p. 27; Chris Cobb, "Toying with Children's Minds," *The Kingston Whig-Standard*, December 18, 1993, p. 2; "Are Auto Dealers Biased? *Business Week,* August 14, 1995, p. 26.

FIGURE 7-3 *Three alternative market-coverage strategies*

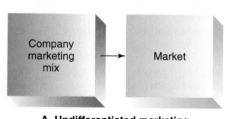

A. Undifferentiated marketing

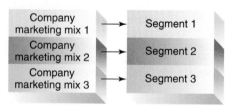

B. Differentiated marketing

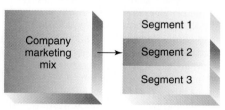

C. Concentrated marketing

focus on what is *common* in the needs of consumers rather than on what is *different*. The company designs a product and a marketing program that appeal to the largest number of buyers. It relies on mass distribution and mass advertising, and it aims to give the product a superior image in people's minds. An example of undifferentiated marketing is the Hershey Company's marketing some years ago of only one chocolate bar for everyone.

Undifferentiated marketing provides cost economies. The narrow product line keeps down production, inventory, and transportation costs. The undifferentiated advertising program keeps down advertising costs. The absence of segment marketing research and planning lowers the costs of marketing research and product management.

Most modern marketers, however, have strong doubts about this strategy. Difficulties arise in developing a product or brand that will satisfy all consumers. Firms using undifferentiated marketing typically develop an offer aimed at the largest segments in the market. When several firms do this, heavy competition develops in the largest segments, and less satisfaction results in the smaller ones. The final result is that the larger segments may be less profitable because they attract heavy competition. Recognition of this problem has led firms to be more interested in smaller market segments.

Differentiated Marketing

Using a **differentiated marketing** strategy, a firm decides to target several market segments and designs separate offers for each. General Motors tries to produce a car for every "purse, purpose, and personality." Nike offers athletic shoes for a dozen or more different sports. And Weston Foods appeals to the needs of different shopper segments with its No Frills discount stores, Loblaw's SuperCentres, and Price Club Warehouse stores. Cadbury Chocolate Canada changed the way chocolate bars were marketed by targeting its Mr.

Cadbury Canada, makers of Mr. Big and Time Out chocolate bars, uses a differentiated marketing strategy creating distinct marketing mixes for different market segments.

Big candy bars at teenagers, its Crispy Crunch bars at young adults, and its most recent offering, Time Out, to harried businesspeople. Cadbury identified a segment of the market that no other candy manufacturer was serving. The company's research showed that many of today's businesspeople are time-starved jugglers who try to balance work and family responsibilities. Calling its efforts "the biggest confectionary launch of the decade," Cadbury used a multi-faced campaign to launch the product. Cartoon-like ads were placed in the business pages of morning papers, in-store displays were set up, and a large selection of its web page (http://www.cadbury.chocolate.ca/timeout) was devoted to the new chocolate bar. Cadbury held an online contest asking participants to provide captions for their cartoons.[28] By offering product and marketing variations, these companies hope for higher sales and a stronger position within each market segment. They hope that a stronger position in several segments will strengthen consumers' overall identification of the company with the product category. They also hope for more loyal purchasing, because the firm's offer better matches each segment's desires.

Differentiated marketing typically creates more total sales than does undifferentiated marketing, and a growing number of firms have adopted this strategy. Procter & Gamble gets a higher total market share with 11 brands of laundry detergent than it could with only one. But differentiated marketing also increases the costs of doing business. Modifying a product to meet different market-segment needs usually involves extra research and development, engineering, or special tooling costs. A firm usually finds it more expensive to produce, say, 10 units of 10 different products than 100 units of one product. Developing separate marketing plans for the separate segments requires extra marketing research, forecasting, sales analysis, promotion planning, and channel management. And trying to reach different market segments with different advertising increases promotion costs. Thus, the company must weigh increased sales against increased costs when deciding on a differentiated marketing strategy.

Differentiated marketing
A market-coverage strategy in which a firm decides to target several market segments and designs separate offers for each.

Concentrated marketing
A market-coverage strategy in which a firm goes after a large share of one or a few submarkets.

Gennum Corporation
www.gennum.com/

Concentrated Marketing

A third market-coverage strategy, **concentrated marketing,** is especially appealing when company resources are limited. Instead of pursuing a small share of a large market, the firm pursues a large share of one or a few submarkets. For example, Oshkosh Truck is the world's largest producer of airport rescue trucks and front-loading concrete mixers. Recycled Paper Products concentrates on the market for alternative greeting cards. And Clearly Canadian concentrates on a narrow segment of the soft-drink market.

Concentrated marketing provides an excellent way for small new businesses to get a foothold against larger, more resourceful competitors. No firm knows this better than Gennum, an integrated chip manufacturer located in Burlington, Ontario. The firm has built a formidable presence in niche markets ignored by its large multinational rivals. "The global market for integrated circuits is worth about $63 billion, which makes Gennum, with revenues of about $23 million . . . seem like a microdot on a microchip."[29] This marketing-driven company began unobtrusively by supplying the world market with integrated circuits for hearing aids. Its technologies have had a substantial influence on the miniaturization of hearing aids around the world. Ninety percent of the company's revenues come from its export markets and it has been surprisingly successful in selling chips to the Japanese, who are renowned as masters of the art. It took patience to develop its Japanese market. The firm spent 15 years to truly understand the human dimension of business and the emphasis on trust and loyalty that is critical in the Japanese marketplace.

Through concentrated marketing, the firm achieves a strong market position in the segments (or niches) it serves because of its greater knowledge of the segments' needs and the special reputation it acquires. It also enjoys many operating economies because of specialization in production, distribution, and promotion. If the segment is well chosen, the firm can earn a high rate of return on its investment.

At the same time, concentrated marketing involves higher than normal risks. The particular market segment can turn sour. Or larger competitors may decide to enter the same segment. For example, while many niche marketers such as Jill McDonough, a 27-year-old Calgary entrepreneur, who founded Schwartzie's Bagel Noshery, have been highly successful, they always fear that this success will attract big players, like Tim Horton Donuts, into their marketplace. If small niche players like Jill do not have the marketing resources to compete, they are often forced to sell out to their larger competitors. For these reasons, many companies prefer to diversify in several market segments.

Rapid advances in computer and communications technology are allowing many large mass marketers to act more like concentrated marketers. Using detailed customer databases, these marketers segment their mass markets into small groups of like-minded buyers. For example, using home-delivery information, Pizza Hut has developed a database containing electronic profiles of the pizza-eating habits of some nine million North American customers. It uses this database to develop carefully targeted promotions.[30]

Choosing a Market-Coverage Strategy

Many factors need to be considered when choosing a market-coverage strategy. Which strategy is best depends on *company resources.* When the firm's resources are limited, concentrated marketing makes the most sense. The best strategy also depends on the degree of *product variability.* Undifferentiated marketing is more suited for uniform products such as grapefruit or steel. Products that can vary in design, such as cameras and cars, are more suited to differentiation or concentration. The *product's stage in the life cycle* also must be considered. When a firm introduces a new product, it is practical to launch only one version, and undifferentiated marketing or concentrated marketing makes the most sense. In the mature stage of the product life cycle, however, differentiated marketing begins to make more sense. Another factor is *market variability*. If most buyers have the same tastes, buy the same amounts, and react the same way to marketing efforts, undifferentiated marketing is appropriate. Finally, *competitors' marketing strategies* are important. When competitors use segmentation, undifferentiated marketing can be suicidal. Conversely, when competitors use undifferentiated marketing, a firm can gain an advantage by using differentiated or concentrated marketing.

POSITIONING FOR COMPETITIVE ADVANTAGE

Product position
The way the product is defined by consumers on important attributes—the place the product occupies in consumers' minds relative to competing products.

Volvo
www.volvo.com/index_3.html

Positioning: When you think of automobile safety, what brand comes to mind? Volvo has positioned itself powerfully on safety.

Once a company has decided which segments of the market it will enter, it must decide what "positions" it wants to occupy in those segments. A **product's position** is the way the product is *defined by consumers* on important attributes—the place the product occupies in consumers' minds relative to competing products. Thus, Tide is positioned as a powerful, all-purpose family detergent; Solo is positioned as a liquid detergent with fabric softener; Cheer is positioned as the detergent for all temperatures. In the automobile market, Toyota Tercel and Subaru are positioned on economy, Mercedes and Cadillac on luxury, and Porsche and BMW on performance. Volvo positions powerfully on safety.

Consumers are overloaded with information about products and services. They cannot re-evaluate products every time they make a buying decision. To simplify the buying process, consumers organize products into categories—they "position" products, services, and companies in their minds. A product's position is the complex set of perceptions, impressions, and feelings that consumers hold for the product compared with competing products. Consumers position products with or without the help of marketers. But marketers do not want to leave their products' positions to chance. They must *plan* positions that will give their products the greatest advantage in selected target markets, and they must design marketing mixes to create these planned positions.

POSITIONING STRATEGIES

Marketers can follow several positioning strategies. They can position their products on specific *product attributes*—Honda Civic advertises its low price; BMW promotes performance. Products can be positioned on the needs they fill or the *benefits* they offer—Crest reduces cavities; Aim tastes good. Or products can be positioned according to *usage occasions*—in the summer, Gatorade can be positioned as a beverage for replacing athletes' body fluids; in the winter, it can be positioned as the drink to use when the doctor recommends plenty of liquids. Another approach is to position the product for certain classes of *users*—Johnson & Johnson improved the market share for its baby shampoo from three percent to 14 percent by repositioning the product as one for adults who wash their hair frequently and need a gentle shampoo.

A product can also be positioned directly *against a competitor*. For example, in its ads, VISA compares itself directly with American Express, saying, "You'd better take your VISA card, because they don't take American Express." Labatt Blue Light distinguishes itself from other light beers with the slogan, "Tastes like a beer, not water." In its famous "We're number two, so we try harder" campaign, Avis successfully positioned itself against the larger Hertz. A product may also be positioned *away from competitors*—for many years, 7Up has positioned itself as the "Un-cola," the fresh and thirst-quenching alternative to Coke and Pepsi.

Finally, the product can be positioned for different *product classes*. For example, some margarines are positioned against butter, others against cooking oils. Camay hand soap is positioned with bath oils rather than with soap. Marketers often use a *combination* of these positioning strategies. Arm & Hammer baking soda has been positioned as a deodorizer for refrigerators and garbage disposals (product class *and* usage situation).

CHOOSING AND IMPLEMENTING A POSITIONING STRATEGY

Some firms find it easy to choose their positioning strategy. For example, a firm well known for quality in certain segments will go for this position in a new segment if there are enough buyers seeking quality. But in many cases, two or more firms will go after the same position. Then, each will have to find other ways to set itself apart, such as promising "high quality for a lower cost" or "high quality with more technical service." Each firm must differentiate its offer by building a unique bundle of competitive advantages that appeal to a substantial group within the segment.

The positioning task consists of three steps: identifying a set of possible competitive advantages on which to build a position, selecting the right competitive advantages, and effectively communicating and delivering the chosen position to the market.

Identifying Possible Competitive Advantages

Consumers typically choose products and services that give them the greatest value. Thus, the key to winning and keeping customers is to understand their needs and buying processes better than competitors do and to deliver more value. To the extent that a company can position itself as providing superior value to selected target markets, either by offering lower prices than competitors do or by providing more benefits to justify higher prices, it gains **competitive advantage.** But solid positions cannot be built on empty promises. If a company positions its product as *offering* the best quality and service, it must then *deliver* the promised quality and service. Thus, positioning begins with actually *differentiating* the company's marketing offer so it will give consumers more value than competitors' offers do.

Competitive advantage
An advantage over competitors gained by offering consumers greater value, either through lower prices or by providing more benefits that justify higher prices.

Not every company will find many opportunities for differentiating its offer and gaining competitive advantage. Some companies find many minor advantages that are easily copied by competitors and are, therefore, highly perishable. The solution for these companies is to keep identifying new potential advantages and to introduce them one by one to keep competitors off balance. These companies do not expect to gain a single major permanent advantage. Instead, they hope to gain many minor ones that can be introduced to win market share over a period of time.

In what specific ways can a company differentiate its offer from those of competitors? A company or market offer can be differentiated along the lines of *product, services, personnel,* or *image.*

PRODUCT DIFFERENTIATION. Differentiation of physical products takes place along a continuum. At one extreme there are highly standardized products that allow little variation: chicken, steel, aspirin. Yet even here, meaningful differentiation is possible. For example, Scott Paper and P&G have successfully differentiated paper towels—creating demand for higher quality products.

At the other extreme are products that are highly differentiated, such as automobiles, commercial buildings, and furniture. Here the company faces an abundance

There are few small packages we can't deliver.

SkyPak is a global courier service that's available through your nearest postal outlet or by calling your Canada Post sales representative. It's an established network with distribution to over 200 countries. Sending a SkyPak is simple – envelopes are available at your nearest postal outlet or by calling 1 800 661-3434. Best of all, SkyPak is prepaid, to help control your courier costs. Send what you need when you need it – delivery guaranteed.

Simply SkyPak it.

Available through MAIL POSTE

For information, call **1 800 661-3434**

Canada Post positions its international service in terms of the benefits of ease of use, cost control, and number of countries served.

of design parameters. It can offer a variety of standard or optional *features* not provided by competitors. Thus, Volvo provides new and better safety features; Air Canada's new fleet of Airbus 340 jets offers passengers wider seating. Companies also can differentiate their products on *performance*. Whirlpool designs its dishwasher to run more quietly; Procter & Gamble formulates Liquid Tide to get clothes cleaner. *Style* and *design* also can be important differentiating factors. Thus, many car buyers pay a premium for Jaguar automobiles because of their extraordinary look, even though Jaguar has sometimes had a poor reliability record. Similarly, companies can differentiate their products on such attributes as *consistency, durability, reliability,* or *repairability.*

SERVICES DIFFERENTIATION. In addition to differentiating its physical product, the firm also can differentiate the services that accompany the product. Some companies gain competitive advantage through speedy, convenient, or careful *delivery*. Deluxe, a U.S. cheque supply company, has built an impressive reputation for shipping out replacement cheques one day after receiving an order—without being late once in 12 years. And Royal Bank has opened drive-through branches to provide location convenience along with Saturday, and weekday-evening hours.

Installation also can differentiate one company from another. IBM, for example, is known for its quality installation service. It delivers all pieces of purchased equipment to the site at one time rather than sending individual components to wait for others to arrive. And when asked to move IBM equipment and install it in another location, IBM often moves competitors' equipment as well. Companies can further distinguish themselves through their *repair* services. Many an automobile buyer will gladly pay a little more and travel a little farther to buy a car from a dealer that provides top-notch repair service.

Some companies differentiate their offers by providing *customer training* service. Thus, General Electric not only sells and installs expensive X-ray equipment in hospitals, but also trains the hospital employees who will use this equipment. Other companies offer free or paid *consulting services*—data, information systems, and advising services that buyers need. For example, McKesson Corporation, a major drug wholesaler, consults with its 12 000 independent pharmacists to help them set up accounting, inventory, and computer ordering systems. By helping its customers compete better, McKesson gains greater customer loyalty and sales.

Companies can find many other ways to add value through differentiated services. In fact, they can choose from a virtually unlimited number of specific services and benefits through which to differentiate themselves from the competition. Milliken & Company provides one of the best examples of a company that has gained competitive advantage through superior service. Milliken sells shop towels to industrial launderers who rent them to factories. These towels are physically similar to competitors' towels, yet Milliken charges a higher price and enjoys the leading market share. How can it charge more for what is essentially a commodity? The answer is that Milliken continuously "decommoditizes" this product through continuous service enhancements. Milliken trains its customers' salespeople, supplies them with prospect leads and sales promotional material, and lends its own salespeople to work on Customer Action Teams. It provides computer order entry and freight optimization systems, conducts marketing research for customers, and

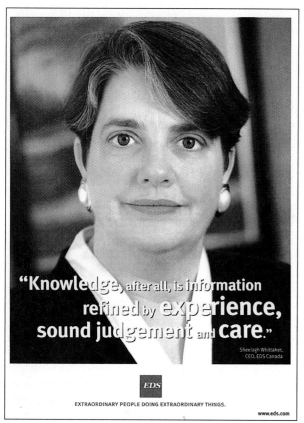

"Knowledge, after all, is information refined by experience, sound judgement and care."

Sheelagh Whittaker,
CEO, EDS Canada

EDS

EXTRAORDINARY PEOPLE DOING EXTRAORDINARY THINGS.

www.eds.com

EDS's employees are the extraordinary factor that differentiates the firm from its competitors.

sponsors quality improvement workshops. Launderers are more than willing to buy Milliken shop towels and pay a price premium because the extra services improve their profitability.[31]

PERSONNEL DIFFERENTIATION. Companies can gain a strong competitive advantage through hiring and training better people than their competitors do. Toronto's Four Seasons Hotel is famous for the service it provides to the business travellers it has targeted since the early 1970s. For years it has set the standard for business travellers by offering state-of-the art amenities. But it is not just the hotel facilities that bring in repeat customers; it is the hotel's world-class service. For example, when a Chicago-based executive was stranded without his luggage due to a flight cancellation, the hotel sent a toiletries kit to his room so he could freshen up while hotel staff went out to purchase shirts and underwear for him. And Four Seasons employees consider it all in a day's work to fly to New York to return luggage or business papers left behind by distracted business travellers. The hotel concierge, Nancy Shulman, does everything in her power to make guests feel welcome and comfortable, including renting a chartered plane to get a first-time father home for a premature delivery or sodding a balcony to make a guest's dog feel more at home.[32]

Personnel differentiation requires that a company select its people carefully and train them well. This is especially important for companies such as consulting firms, which market knowledge-based services that they tailor to their customers' needs. EDS, a company that works to solve companies' information-handling and processing problems, knows the importance of getting the best young talent available. Each year, the company holds an international case competition in Plano, Texas. Teams of students from universities around the world are invited to compete. Teams from McGill University, the University of Ottawa, and Queen's University have participated in the competition. Senior executives from EDS judge the competition and observe the teams in action. The winners are awarded $1000 scholarships and all students who perform well are recruited and may receive employment offers with the company.

IMAGE DIFFERENTIATION. Even when competing offers look the same, buyers may perceive a difference based on company or brand images. Thus, companies work to establish *images* that differentiate them from competitors. A company or brand image should convey the product's distinctive benefits and positioning. Developing a strong and distinctive image calls for creativity and hard work. A company cannot implant an image in the public's mind overnight using only a few advertisements. If "Motorola" means "quality," this image must be supported by everything the company says and does.

Symbols can provide strong company or brand recognition and image differentiation. Companies design signs and logos that provide instant recognition. They associate themselves with objects or characters that symbolize quality or other attributes, such as the McDonald's golden arches, the Prudential rock, or the Pillsbury doughboy. The company might build a brand around some famous person, as Nike did with its Air Jordan basketball shoes. Some companies even become associated with colours, such as IBM (blue) or Campbell (red and white).

The chosen symbols must be communicated through advertising that conveys the company or brand's personality. The ads attempt to establish a storyline, a mood, a performance level—something distinctive about the company or brand. The atmosphere of the physical space in which the organization produces or delivers its products and services can be another powerful image generator. Hyatt hotels have become known for their atrium lobbies and Swiss Chalet restaurants for their chalet-look. Thus, a bank that wants to distinguish itself as the "friendly bank" must choose the right building and interior design, layout, colours, materials, and furnishings to reflect these qualities.

A company also can create an image through the types of events it sponsors. For example, Imperial Oil and IBM have identified themselves closely with cultural events, such as symphony performances and art exhibits. Other organizations support popular causes. For example, Heinz gives money to hospitals and Quaker gives food to the homeless.

Selecting the Right Competitive Advantages

Suppose a company is fortunate enough to discover several potential competitive advantages. It now must choose the ones on which it will build its positioning strategy. It must decide *how many* differences to promote and *which ones*.

HOW MANY DIFFERENCES TO PROMOTE?   Many marketers think that companies should aggressively promote only one benefit to the target market. Ad man Rosser Reeves, for example, said a company should develop a *unique selling proposition* (USP) for each brand and stick to it. Each brand should choose an attribute and tout itself as "number one" on that attribute. Buyers tend to remember "number one" better, especially in an overcommunicated society. Thus, Crest toothpaste consistently promotes its anti-cavity protection, and Volvo promotes safety. What are some of the "number one" positions to promote? The major ones are "best quality," "best service," "lowest price," "best value," and "most advanced technology." A company that hammers away at one of these positions and consistently delivers on it probably will become best known and remembered for it.

Other marketers think that companies should position themselves on more than one differentiating factor. This may be necessary if two or more firms are claiming to be best on the same attribute. Steelcase, an office furniture systems company, differentiates itself from competitors on two benefits: best on-time delivery and best installation support.

Today, in a time when the mass market is fragmenting into many small segments, companies are trying to broaden their positioning strategies to appeal to more segments. For example, Lever Brothers introduced the first "3-in-1" bar soap—Lever 2000—offering cleansing, deodorizing, *and* moisturizing benefits. Clearly, many buyers want all three benefits, and the challenge was to convince them that one brand can deliver all three. Judging from Lever 2000's outstanding success, Lever Brothers easily met the challenge.

However, as companies increase the number of claims for their brands, they risk disbelief and a loss of clear positioning. In general, a company needs to avoid three major positioning errors. The first is *underpositioning*—failing to ever really position the company at all. Some companies discover that buyers have only a vague idea of the company or that they do not really know anything special about it. The second error is *overpositioning*—giving buyers too narrow a picture of the company. Thus, a consumer might think that the Steuben glass company makes only fine art glass costing $1400 and up, when in fact it makes affordable fine glass starting at around $70. Finally, companies must avoid *confused positioning*—leaving buyers with a confused image of a company. For example, Burger King has struggled without success for years to establish a profitable and consistent position. Since 1986, it has fielded six advertising campaigns, with themes ranging from "Herb the nerd doesn't eat here," and "This is a Burger King town," to "The right food for the

right times," to "Sometimes you've got to break the rules" and "BK Tee Vee." This barrage of positioning statements has left consumers confused and Burger King with poor sales and profits.[33]

WHICH DIFFERENCES TO PROMOTE? Not all brand differences are meaningful or worthwhile. Not every difference makes a good differentiator. Each difference has the potential to create company costs as well as customer benefits. Therefore, the company must carefully select the ways in which it will distinguish itself from competitors. A difference is worth establishing to the extent that it satisfies the following criteria:

◆ *Important:* The difference delivers a highly valued benefit to target buyers.

◆ *Distinctive:* Competitors do not offer the difference, or the company can offer it in a more distinctive way.

◆ *Superior:* The difference is superior to other ways that customers might obtain the same benefit.

◆ *Communicable:* The difference is communicable and visible to buyers.

◆ *Preemptive:* Competitors cannot easily copy the difference.

◆ *Affordable:* Buyers can afford to pay for the difference.

◆ *Profitable:* The company can introduce the difference profitably.

Many companies have introduced differentiations that failed one or more of these tests. The Westin Stamford hotel in Singapore advertises that it is the world's tallest hotel, a distinction that is not important to many tourists—in fact, it turns many off. Polaroid's Polarvision, which produced instantly developed home movies, bombed too. Although Polarvision was distinctive and even preemptive, it was inferior to another way of capturing motion, namely, camcorders. Thus, choosing competitive advantages on which to position a product or service can be difficult, yet such choices may be crucial to success (see Marketing Highlight 7-3).

Some competitive advantages may be quickly ruled out because they are too slight, too costly to develop, or too inconsistent with the company's profile. Suppose that a company is designing its positioning strategy and has narrowed its list of possible competitive advantages to four. The company needs a framework for selecting the one advantage that makes the most sense to develop. Table 7-4 shows a systematic way to evaluate several potential competitive advantages and choose the right one.

In the table, the company compares its standing on four attributes—technology, cost, quality, and service—to the standing of its major competitor. Let's assume that both companies stand at 8 on technology (1 = low score, 10 = high score), which means they both have good technology. The company questions whether it can gain much by improving its technology further, especially given the high cost of new technology. The competitor has a better standing on cost (8

TABLE 7-4 *Finding Competitive Advantage*

Competitive Advantage	Company Standing (1–10)	Competitor Standing (1–10)	Importance of Improving Standing (H-M-L)	Affordability and Speed (H-M-L)	Competitor's Ability to Improve Standing (H-M-L)	Recommended Action
Technology	8	8	L	L	M	Hold
Cost	6	8	H	M	M	Watch
Quality	8	6	L	L	H	Watch
Service	4	3	H	H	L	Invest

SCHOTT: POSITIONING FOR SUCCESS

Schott, the German manufacturer of glass for industrial and consumer products, had a problem deciding how to position its innovative product, Ceran, in the North American market. The product, a glass-ceramic material made to cover the cooking surface of electric ranges, seemed to have everything going for it. It was completely non-porous (and thus stain-resistant), easy to clean, and long-lasting. Best of all, when one burner was lit, the heat didn't spread; it stayed confined to the circle directly above the burner. And after 10 years, cooktops made of Ceran still looked and performed like new.

Schott anticipated some difficulty igniting demand for Ceran. First it would have to win over North American range manufacturers, which would then have to promote Ceran to middle markets—dealers, designers, architects, and builders. These middle-market customers would, in turn, need to influence final consumers. Thus, Schott's North American subsidiary set out to sell Ceran aggressively to its target of 14 North American appliance manufacturers. The subsidiary positioned Ceran on its impressive technical and engineering attributes—showing cross-sections of stoves and using plenty of high-tech talk—then waited optimistically for the orders to roll in. The appliance companies listened politely to the rep's pitch, ordered sample quantities—25 or so of each available colour—and then . . . nothing. Absolutely nothing.

Research by Schott's advertising agency revealed two problems. First, Schott had failed to position Ceran at all among the manufacturers' customers. The material was still virtually unknown, not only among final consumers but also among dealers, designers, architects, and builders. Second, the company was attempting to position the product on the wrong benefits. When selecting a rangetop to buy, customers seemed to care less about the sophisticated engineering that went into it and more about its

appearance and cleanability. Their biggest questions were, "How does it look?" and "How easy is it to use?"

Based on these findings, Schott repositioned Ceran, shifting emphasis toward the material's inherent beauty and design versatility. And it launched an extensive promotion campaign to communicate the new position to

featuring Ceran that was picked up by 150 local TV stations nationwide. To reinforce a weak link in the selling chain—appliance salespeople who were poorly equipped to answer customer questions about Ceran—the agency created a video that the salespeople could show customers on the televisions in their own appliance stores.

Now properly positioned on their inherent beauty and design versatility, Schott's Ceran cooktops are selling very well.

middle-market and final buyers. Advertising to designers and remodelers revolved around lines like "Formalwear for your kitchen," which presented the black rangetop as streamlined and elegant as a tuxedo. As a follow-up, to persuade designers and remodellers to add Ceran to their palette of materials, Schott positioned Ceran as "More than a rangetop, a means of expression." To reinforce this beauty and design positioning, ads featured visuals, including a geometric grid of a rangetop with one glowing red burner.

In addition to advertising, Schott's agency launched a massive public relations effort that resulted in substantial coverage in home design and remodelling publications. It also produced a video news release

The now properly and strongly positioned Ceran is selling well. All 14 North American appliance makers are buying production quantities of Ceran and using them in their rangetops. All offer not one, but several smooth-top models. Schott is the only smooth-top supplier in North America, and smooth-tops now account for more than 15 percent of the electric stove market. And at a recent Kitchen & Bath Show, 69 percent of all range models on display were smooth-tops. To keep up with increasing demand, Schott has built a U.S. plant just to produce Ceran for the North American market.

Source: Adapted from Nancy Arnott, "Heating Up Sales: Formalware for your Kitchen," *Sales & Marketing Management*, June 1994, pp. 77–78.

instead of 6), and this can hurt the company if the market gets more price-sensitive. The company offers higher quality than its competitor (8 instead of 6). Finally, both companies offer below-average service (4 and 3).

At first glance, it appears that the company should go after cost or service to improve its market appeal relative to the competitor. However, it must consider other factors. First, how important are improvements in each of these attributes to the target customers? The fourth column shows that cost and service improvements would both be highly important to customers. Next, can the company afford to make the improvements? If so, how fast can it complete them? The fifth column shows that the company could improve service quickly and affordably. But if the firm decided to do this, would the competitor be able to improve its service also? The sixth column shows that the competitor's ability to improve service is low, perhaps because the competitor does not believe in service or is strapped for funds. The final column then shows the appropriate actions to take on each attribute. It makes the most sense for the company to invest in improving its service. Service is important to customers; the company can afford to improve its service and can do it fast, and the competitor probably will not be able to catch up.

Communicating and Delivering the Chosen Position

Once it has chosen a position, the company must take strong steps to deliver and communicate the desired position to target consumers. All the company's marketing-mix efforts must support the positioning strategy. Positioning the company calls for concrete action, not just talk. If the company decides to build a position on better quality and service, it must first *deliver* that position. Designing the marketing mix—product, price, place, and promotion—essentially involves working out the tactical details of the positioning strategy. Thus, a firm that seizes on a "high-quality position" knows that it must produce high-quality products, charge a high price, distribute through high-quality dealers, and advertise in high-quality media. It must hire and train more service people, find retailers who have a good reputation for service, and develop sales and advertising messages that broadcast its superior service. This is the only way to build a consistent and believable high-quality, high-service position.

Companies often find it easier to develop a good positioning strategy than to implement it. Establishing a position or changing one usually takes a long time. For example, Ottawa Transit recently faced the task of repositioning its bus service. The first step in implementation was in place. It had a totally new product, its Transitway system—a series of roadways dedicated solely to express buses. However, its real challenge lay in creating a new image for the service. Not only did Ottawa Transit have to convince its riders that this wasn't a regular bus line, but it also had to completely redesign its image with its own employees, including its drivers, as well as other important stakeholder groups such as the media. It began with an outdoor campaign to develop its new identity of buses as a system of rapid transit instead of cumbersome, slow, inconvenient vehicles. It sent information kits on the service to households in Ottawa. It circulated new maps of the system, designed to look more like subway routes than bus lines to reinforce the image of speed and convenience. Television and radio ads were run to further disseminate the new image. It remains to be seen if consumers quickly grasp the concept.[34] In contrast, positions that have taken years to build can quickly be lost. Once a company has built the desired position, it must take care to maintain the position through consistent performance and communication. It must closely monitor and adapt the position over time to match changes in consumer needs and competitors' strategies. However, the company should avoid abrupt changes that might confuse consumers. Instead, a product's position should evolve gradually as it adapts to the ever-changing marketing environment.

Summary of Chapter Objectives

Organizations that sell to consumer and business markets recognize that they cannot appeal to all buyers in those markets, or at least not to all buyers in the same way. Buyers are too numerous, too widely scattered, and too varied in their needs and buying practices. Therefore, most companies today are moving away from mass marketing. Instead, they practise *target marketing*—identifying market segments, selecting one or more of them, and developing products and marketing mixes tailored to each. In this way, sellers can develop the right product for each target market and adjust their prices, distribution channels, and advertising to reach the target market efficiently.

1. **Define the three steps of target marketing: market segmentation, market targeting, and market positioning.**

   The three steps of target marketing are market segmentation, market targeting, and market positioning. *Market segmentation* is the act of dividing a market into distinct groups of buyers with different needs, characteristics, or behaviour who might require separate products or marketing mixes. Once the groups have been identified, *market targeting* evaluates each market segment's attractiveness and suggests one or more segments to enter. *Market positioning* consists of setting the competitive positioning for the product and creating a detailed marketing plan.

2. **List and discuss the major levels of market segmentation and bases for segmenting consumer and business markets.**

   Market segmentation can be carried out at many different levels, including no segmentation (mass marketing), complete segmentation (micromarketing), or something in between (segment marketing or niche marketing). *Mass marketing* involves mass producing, mass distributing, and mass promoting about the same product in about the same way to all consumers. Using *segmented marketing*, the company tries to isolate broad segments that make up a market and adapts its offers to more closely match the needs of one or more segments. *Niche marketing* focuses on more narrowly defined subgroups within these segments, groups with distinctive sets of traits that

may seek a special combination of benefits. *Micromarketing* is the practice of tailoring products and marketing programs to suit the tastes of specific individuals and locations. Micromarketing includes *local marketing* and *individual marketing*.

There is no single way to segment a market. Therefore, the marketer tries different variables to see which give the best segmentation opportunities. For consumer marketing, the major segmentation variables are geographic, demographic, psychographic, and behavioural. In *geographic segmentation*, the market is divided into different geographical units such as nations, provinces, regions, counties, cities, or neighbourhoods. In *demographic segmentation*, the market is divided into groups based on demographic variables, including age, sex, family size, family life cycle, income, occupation, education, religion, race, and nationality. In *psychographic segmentation*, the market is divided into different groups based on social class, lifestyle, or personality characteristics. In *behavioural segmentation*, the market is divided into groups based on consumers' knowledge, attitudes, uses, or responses to a product.

Business marketers use many of the same variables to segment their markets. But business markets also can be segmented by business consumer *demographics* (industry, company size), *operating characteristics*, *purchasing approaches*, and *personal characteristics*. The effectiveness of segmentation analysis depends on finding segments that are *measurable, accessible, substantial,* and *actionable*.

3. **Explain how companies identify attractive market segments and choose a market-coverage strategy.**

   To target the best market segments, the company first evaluates each segment's size and growth characteristics, structural attractiveness, and compatibility with company resources and objectives. It then chooses one of three market-coverage strategies. The seller can ignore segment differences (*undifferentiated marketing*), develop different market offers for several segments (*differentiated marketing*), or go after one or a few market segments (*concentrated marketing*). Much depends on company resources, product variability, product life-cycle stage, and competitive marketing strategies.

4. **Explain how companies can position their products for maximum competitive advantage in the marketplace.**

   Once a company has decided which segments to enter, it must decide on its *market positioning* strategy—on which positions to occupy in its chosen segments. It can posi-

tion its products on specific *product attributes*, according to *usage occasion*, for certain *classes of users*, or by *product class*. It can position either against or away from competitors. The positioning tasks consists of three steps: identifying a set of possible competitive advantages upon which to build a position, selecting the right competitive advantages, and effectively communicating and delivering the chosen position to the market.

Key Terms

Age and life-cycle segmentation (p. 231)
Behavioural segmentation (p. 234)
Benefit segmentation (p. 235)
Competitive advantage (p. 248)
Concentrated marketing (p. 246)
Demographic segmentation (p. 230)
Differentiated marketing (p. 245)
Gender segmentation (p. 232)

Geographic segmentation (p. 230)
Income segmentation (p. 233)
Individual marketing (p. 227)
Intermarket segmentation (p. 240)
Local marketing (p. 227)
Market positioning (p. 225)
Market segmentation (p. 225)
Market targeting (p. 225)
Micromarketing (p. 227)

Niche marketing (p. 226)
Occasion segmentation (p. 234)
Product position (p. 247)
Psychographic segmentation (p. 233)
Segment marketing (p. 226)
Target market (p. 242)
Undifferentiated marketing (p. 242)

Discussing the Issues

1. Describe how the Ford Motor Company has moved from mass marketing to product-variety marketing to target marketing. Select some other examples of companies whose marketing approaches have evolved over time.

2. Outline what variables are used in segmenting the market for beer. Give examples.

3. Visible minorities are now viewed as an attractive, distinct market segment. Can you market the same way to a Filipino seamstress in Montreal, a Chinese doctor in Thunder Bay, and a Hong Kong businesswoman in Vancouver? Compare the similarities and differences that you see. What does this imply about market segments?

4. Some industrial suppliers like IBM Canada achieve above-average profits by offering

service, selection, and reliability at a premium price. Suggest ways that these suppliers can segment the market to find customers who are willing to pay more for these benefits.

5. Think about your classmates in this course. Can you segment them into different groups with specific nicknames? Explain the major segmentation variable you used. Could you effectively market products to these segments? Why do you think marketers have had such difficulty reaching you, the youth market?

6. Describe the roles that product attributes and perceptions of attributes play in positioning a product. Can an attribute held by several competing brands be used in a successful positioning strategy?

Applying the Concepts

1. By looking at advertising, and at products themselves, we can often see how marketers

are attempting to position their products, and what target market they hope to reach.

(a) Define the positionings of and the target markets for Coca-Cola, Pepsi-Cola, Mountain Dew, Dr. Pepper, and 7Up. (b) Define the positionings of and target markets for McDonald's, Burger King, Wendy's, and a regional restaurant chain in your area. (c) Do you think the soft drinks and restaurants have distinctive positionings and target markets? Are some more clearly defined than others?

2. It is possible to market people as well as products or services. When marketing a person, we can *position* that individual for a particular target market. Describe briefly how you would position yourself for the following target markets: (a) for a potential employer, (b) for a potential boyfriend or girlfriend, (c) for your mother or father. Would you position yourself in different ways for these different target markets? How do the positionings differ? *Why do the positionings differ?*

References

1. Showwei Chu, "The Customer is Always Wrong," *Canadian Business*, November 28, 1997, pp. 35–37; Leanne Delap, "Armani's Worldwide Concerns," *Globe and Mail*, November 22, 1997, p. C29; David Olive, "A Brown Study," *Report on Business Magazine*, November 1997, p. 12; Laura Pratt, "Special Report: Reaching the New Consumer: Understanding Changing Expectations," *Strategy: The Canadian Marketing Report*, November 11, 1996, p. 38; Barbara Smith, "Treating Consumers as Individuals," *Strategy: The Canadian Marketing Report*, August 24, 1992, pp. 12, 16, 18; "Special Feature: Excellence in Retailing Awards," *Strategy: The Canadian Marketing Report*, June 24, 1996, p. 21.

2. Regis McKenna, "Real-Time Marketing," *Harvard Business Review*, July–August 1995, p. 87.

3. Eve Lazarus, "Supermarket Chain Caters to Asian Shoppers," *Marketing*, February 24, 1997, p. 2.

4. Edward Baig, "Platinum Cards: Move Over AmEx," *Business Week*, August 19, 1996, p. 84.

5. Laurel Cutler, quoted in "Stars of the 1980s Cast Their Light," *Fortune*, July 3, 1989, p. 76.

6. Robert E. Linneman and John L. Stanton, Jr., *Making Niche Marketing Work: How to Grow Bigger by Acting Smaller* (New York: McGraw-Hill, Inc., 1991).

7. See Don Peppers and Martha Rogers, *The One-to-One Future: Building Relationships One Customer at a Time* (New York: Currency/Doubleday, 1993).

8. See B. Joseph Pine II, *Mass Customization* (Boston: Harvard Business School Press, 1993); B. Joseph Pine II, Don Peppers, and Martha Rogers, "Do You Want to Keep Your Customers Forever?" *Harvard Business Review*, March–April 1995, pp. 103–114; Christopher W. Hart, "Made to Order," *Marketing Management*, Summer 1996, pp. 11–22; and James H. Gilmore and B. Joseph Pine II, "The Four Faces of Customization," *Harvard Business Review*, January–February 1997, pp. 91–101.

9. McKenna, "Real-Time Marketing," p. 87.

10. "Absolut East," *Marketing*, September 18, 1995, p. 2.

11. Edward Caffyn, "Just Try to Sell Me," *Marketing*, August 4, 1997, pp. 13–14.

12. Gregory Skinner, "Youth Marketing: Calvin's the Dude Who Rocks the Nation," *Strategy: The Canadian Marketing Report*, January 20, 1997, p. 13.

13. "Automakers Learn Better Roads to Women's Market," *Marketing News*, October 12, 1992, p. 2. Also see Betsy Sharkey, "The Many Faces of Eve," *Adweek*, June 25, 1990, pp. 44–49; Tim Triplett, "Automakers Recognizing Value of Women's Market," *Marketing News*, April 11, 1994, pp. 1, 2; and Leah Rickard, "Subaru, GMC Top Push to Win Over Women," *Advertising Age*, April 3, 1995, p. 524.

14. Raymond Serafin, "I Am Woman, Hear Me Roar . . . In My Car," *Advertising Age*, November 7, 1994, pp. 1, 8.

15. Deborah Read, "The Young and the Jobless," *Report on Business*, April 1996, pp. 117–118.

16. For a detailed discussion of personality and buyer behavior, see Leon G. Schiffman and Leslie Lazar Kanuk, *Consumer Behavior*, 5th ed. (Englewood Cliffs, NJ: Prentice Hall, 1994), Chap. 5.

17. Bobbi Bulmer, "Nokia Aims 'Fashionable' Phones at Women," *Marketing*, September 22, 1997, p. 3.

18. See Thomas V. Bonoma and Benson P. Shapiro, *Segmenting the Industrial Market* (Lexington, MA.: Lexington Books, 1983). For examples of segmenting business markets, see Kate Bertrand, "Market Segmentation: Divide and Conquer," *Business Marketing*, October 1989, pp. 48–54.

19. Daniel S. Levine, "Justice Served," *Sales & Marketing Management*, May 1995, pp. 63–61.

20. "Survey of the Canadian Home Business and Telecommuter Market," *Globe and Mail*, June 10, 1997, p. C2.

21. V. Kasturi Rangan, Rowland T. Moriarty, and Gordon S. Swartz, "Segmenting Customers in Mature Industrial Markets," *Journal of Marketing*, October 1992, pp. 72–82.

22. For another interesting approach to segmenting the business market, see John Berrigan and Carl Finkbeiner, *Segmentation Marketing: New Methods for Capturing Business* (New York: Harper-Business, 1992).

23. Marlene L. Rossman, "Understanding Five Nations of Latin America," *Marketing News*, October 11, 1985, p. 10; as quoted in Subhash C. Jain, *International Marketing Management*, 3rd ed. (Boston: PWS-Kent Publishing Company, 1990), p. 366.

24. Cyndee Miller, "Teens Seens as the First Truly Global Consumer," *Advertising Age*, March 27, 1995, p. 9.

25. Jain, *International Marketing*, pp. 370–371.

26. See Joe Schwartz, "Southpaw Strategy," *American Demographics*, June 1988, p. 61; and "Few Companies Tailor Products for Lefties," *Wall Street Journal*, August 2, 1989, p. 2.

27. See Michael Porter, *Competitive Advantage* (New York: Free Press, 1985), pp. 4–8 and pp. 234–236.

28. Lara Mills, "Cadbury Tells Adults to Take a Time-Out," *Marketing*, June 2, 1997, p. 3.

29. "Raking in the Chips," *Report on Business*, April 1992, pp. 39–40.

30. Christopher Power, "How to Get Closer to Your Customers," *Business Week*, special issue on economies of scale, 1993, pp. 42–45.

31. See Tom Peters, *Thriving on Chaos* (New York: Alfred A. Knopf, Inc., 1987), pp. 56–57.

312. Anne Dimon, "The Concierge Can Turn Out to be Your Friend in Need, *Globe and Mail Report on Business Travel*, Feb. 13, 1996, C9; Jeremy Ferguson, "Where Rescue Operations are Routine," *Globe and Mail Report on Business Travel*, Feb 13, 1996, C9.

33. Mark Landler and Gail DeGeorge, "Tempers Are Sizzling Over Burger King's New Ads," *Business Week*, February 12, 1990, p. 33; Gail DeGeorge, "Turning Up the Gas at Burger King," *Business Week*, November 15, 1993, pp. 62–67; and Martha T. Moore, "Whopper of a Plan," *USA Today*, April 26, 1994, pp. 1, 2.

34. Sean Eckford, "Ottawa Transit Effort Reworks Image of the Bus," *Marketing*, October 16, 1995, p. 3.

Company Case 7

POWERADE AND ALL SPORT: MUSCLING IN ON THE SPORTS-DRINK MARKET

In many ways, the sports-drink category mirrors the fitness-minded individuals that it targets. As any fitness instructor will tell you, a good workout should be followed by a cooldown. After Gatorade hit the market in 1968, the sports-drink category experienced double-digit growth. However, by 1996, growth had cooled down to 7.6 percent. Despite this, however, current sports-drink sales in North America total almost $2 billion and per-capita consumption equals almost eight litres.

Gatorade pioneered the sports-drink category and has dominated the market. Its primary competition has been mostly small, regional brands, such as 10-K from Suntory, that could rack up only small market shares. In the early 1990s, competition increased when Coca-Cola entered the market with PowerAde and PepsiCo entered with All Sport. However, although PowerAde and All Sport have made inroads, Gatorade still holds a commanding market share. Gatorade's sales lead its nearest rival's by more than $1.4 billion.

Gatorade was developed at the University of Florida in the early 1960s as a means of preventing dehydration during physical exertion and was popularized when the Florida football team used it. Stokely Van Camp, processor of canned vegetables, acquired the brand in May 1967. It positioned Gatorade as a sports drink and health food product based on its value in replacing electrolytes lost due to colds, flu, diarrhea, and vomiting. Sales grew rapidly as Stokely developed a strong position for Gatorade in the institutional team sales market. Then, in 1983, Quaker Oats purchased Stokely and expanded the sports-drink category by increasing Gatorade's distribution and promotion. Between 1983 and 1990, sales of Gatorade grew at a compound annual growth rate of 28 percent.

Sports drinks, or isotonic beverages, replace fluids and minerals lost during physical activity. Research shows that an isotonic drink's effectiveness depends on several factors. The drink should provide enough carbohydrates (glucose and sucrose working in combination) to supply working muscles, yet not too much to slow fluid absorption. It should contain the proper levels of electrolytes, particularly sodium, to enhance fluid absorption. Finally, research suggests that most people prefer a non-carbonated, slightly sweet drink when they are hot and sweaty. Taste is important because it encourages the person to consume enough drink to be effective in rehydration. A 500-millilitre serving of Gatorade contains few vitamins, no fat or protein, 60 calories, 15 grams of carbohydrates, 110 milligrams of sodium, and 25 milligrams of potassium. Gatorade's calories are about one-half the level contained in fruit drinks and non-diet soft drinks.

In 1985, the Japanese giant Suntory entered the market with 10K. Its positioning was based on the use of salt-free spring water. 10K contained 100 percent of the recommended daily allowance of vitamin C. It also had all natural flavours, fructose, 60 calories per serving, no caffeine, and one-half of the sodium of other products. Like Gatorade, Suntory focused on grocery stores as distribution outlets and targeted sports teams. Facing only limited competition, 10K increased market share in the late 1980s, primarily in the southern United States. Since the entry of Coca-Cola and PepsiCo, however, 10K's share of market has dropped to less than two percent.

Coca-Cola's PowerAde has 33 percent more carbohydrates for energy than Gatorade. It is lighter, and has less salt flavour. Coca-Cola claims that PowerAde goes down easier. When Coca-Cola entered the market, it had 1.5 million points-of-sale, including one million vending machines, compared to Gatorade's 200 000 points of sale. Coca-Cola began television and radio advertising, and it paid to make PowerAde the official drink of the 1992 Summer Olympics in Spain and the official drink of the 1996 Summer Olympics in Atlanta.

Coca-Cola has positioned PowerAde as a vital part of any athlete's "equipment." Rather than focusing only on sports stars, PowerAde targets all athletes—professionals, amateurs, and any individuals interested in fitness. By introducing packaging changes such as the 1.5-litre Powerflo PET bottle, Coca-Cola hopes to make its product a piece of equipment that better meets the user's needs. The Powerflo bottle features squeezable sides, quick-flow, a push-pull valve, and Olympic theme graphics. Coca-Cola's advertising agency, McCann-Erickson, created a series of ads whose broad theme was the determination to overcome obstacles. As the official drink of the steamy games in Atlanta, Coca-Cola ensured that plenty of PowerAde was flowing. Atlanta police officers packed PowerAde, compliments of Coca-Cola. The Salvation Army was equipped with 1.5 million free servings of PowerAde, and 1.7 million bottles of PowerAde were on hand for the athletes during competition.

In mid-1997, Coca-Cola announced that it had signed agreements to make PowerAde the official sports drink of the National Hockey League and the Womens' National Basketball Association. It is especially important for sports-drink marketers to sign sports-related marketing agreements—fans often want to drink what their sports heroes drink. For example, Coca-Cola's goal is to associate PowerAde with hockey and thus tempt the hundreds of thousands of hockey fans to drink its products. As the company's vice-president of marketing, Steve Koonin, says "We're buying more than frozen arenas . . . we're buying a mindset of hockey." Similarly, Coca-Cola plans to reach female sports fans by sponsoring women's basketball.

The NHL deal is especially significant in that the NHL's previous arrangement had been with Gatorade. "Clearly, we would have liked to have continued this relationship," says Patti Jo Sinopoli, a Gatorade spokesperson. "But Coke was willing to put a lot more money and support behind it, and we didn't feel it was appropriate for us to allow the NHL to take a higher priority than the relationships Gatorade has across so many other sports." Although the NHL deal cost only $43 million, it indicates Coca-Cola's serious approach in attacking this market. Sports drinks are the only non-alcoholic beverage market not dominated by Coca-Cola or PepsiCo. It appears that Coca-Cola is using a "circle the opposition" strategy in attacking Gatorade and its strong ties to football and professional basketball. Rather than buying its way into those major sports, Coca-Cola is obtaining sponsorships in a number of smaller sports.

PepsiCo initially entered the market with All Sport, a lightly carbonated drink that came in four flavours. Like Coca-Cola, Pepsi has approximately one million points of sale and daily contact with 250 000 retailers. Unfortunately, many athletes had the same reaction to the product as semi-pro tennis player, Paul Fortunato. "Who wants a carbonated sports drink? The last thing I need in the middle of a big point is to deal with burping," he says. After hearing such complaints, PepsiCo relaunched All Sport in mid-1996 with new neon packaging, new flavours of Cherry Slam and Blue Ice, a new ad campaign, an extra dose of "energy-packing" vitamin B, and much less carbonation. PepsiCo believes that, with its new formulation, it has found the ideal taste. The most important change is the reduction of carbonation. According to a PepsiCo spokesperson, "You probably won't even be able to tell it's there."

PepsiCo is positioning All Sport as the body quencher. Its ad campaign—sporting the slogan "The game will never be the same"—touts All Sport as a more "evolved" drink than the more traditional Gatorade. Spots show athletes drinking All Sport in the future. One ad shows well-known athletes such as Jerry Rice and Steve Young drinking All Sport during the half time of "Global Bowl LVXIII."

Meanwhile Gatorade has not been idle. It has launched new flavours, packaging changes such as the two-litre "big-grip" bottle and four packs, and beefed up advertising with memorable and popular Michael Jordan advertisements. Gatorade is positioned as the beverage for "active thirsts."

With all these marketing efforts, have competitors made a dent in Gatorade's domination of the market? Not significantly. By mid-1997, Gatorade's share of market had slipped only slightly to 78.9 percent while PowerAde's had risen by 0.9 percent to 10.2 percent, and Pepsi's All Sport had stabilized at 8.1 percent. Although

Gatorade might be tempted to dismiss these competitor gains as minor, it should note that PowerAde and All Sport are now beginning to eat into Gatorade's share. Previously the two challengers had taken sales mostly from small manufacturers and 10K. By 1997, however, those opportunities were exhausted, and competitors were beginning to take share directly from Gatorade. This could signal future problems for the Quaker brand.

Coca-Cola and PepsiCo have deep pockets, and Quaker Oats will be hard pressed to spend as much as either major competitor to protect its market share. However, because Gatorade is its major brand, Quaker they may be more willing to fight the encroachment of rivals. From Coca-Cola and PepsiCo's perspectives, sports-drink sales are still relatively small and market share gains are exceedingly costly. If Gatorade can develop creative campaigns in the future, itmay be able to stave off the challenges of PowerAde and All Sport.

As the battle for global markets heats up, however, Coca-Cola has a major advantage with its large share of the international soft-drink market and its extensive international marketing expertise. Even PepsiCo, with its switch to blue Pepsi, is picking up share internationally. According to one industry analyst, "International sports franchises and other potential partners are more likely to want to team up with a 'primo beverage player' with several brands than with a company with one brand." With satellite transmissions, fans in England and Japan are watching football and baseball and North Americans now have access to soccer and cricket. This creates the potential for international sports markets and creates international celebrity status for sports heros. While Gatorade is strongly associated with football and basketball, the sport with the greatest worldwide following is soccer. If Coca-Cola or PepsiCo could grab a major soccer sponsorship, or even a baseball sponsorship (another international sport), they would gain a significant lead in the international market.

In response to the international competitive threats posed by Coca-Cola and PepsiCo, Quaker Oats has reorganized. It has formed a separate division to market Gatorade worldwide. In addition, Gatorade is pursuing partnerships with other companies to expand worldwide distribution. But Gatorade is a new brand and an unknown firm outside North America. In addition, along with Coca-Cola and PepsiCo products, it will face other sports drink competitors in the international market, such as Lucozade (distributed by SmithKline Beecham in the U.K.).

QUESTIONS

1. What major variables have all three companies used to segment the sports drink market?

2. What kinds of market coverage strategies have the three firms used?

3. Compare the positionings of the three sports drinks. How well do their respective marketing efforts support the chosen positionings?

4. What are the competitive advantages and disadvantages of each of the firms?

5. Evaluate Gatorade's strategy for the international market. How might Gatorade be marketed successfully internationally?

Sources: "PepsiCo is Back in the Sports Drink Game," *Wall Street Journal*, March 8, 1996; "PowerAde Bottle Stands Tall for Olympic Competition," Packaging Digest, May 1996, p. 4; Angela Dawson, "PowerAde Commercials Dramatize Athletes' struggle to prevail," *Adweek*, March 31, 1997, p. 5; Nikhil Deogun, "Coca-Cola Powerade Takes on Gatorade as it Becomes NHL Official Sports Drink," *Wall Street Journal*, June 2, 1997, p. B5; Jeff Jensen, "WNBA, NHL Will Help Build Coke Brands," *Advertising Age*, June 9, 1997; Gerry Khermouch, "You Too Can Market a Sports Drink," *Brandweek*, October 30, 1995, p. 38; Kimberly Lowe, "In C-Stores, Sports Drinks Fuel the Beverage Category," *National Petroleum News*, August 1996, pp. 42–44; and Eric Sfiligoj, "Gym Dandy," *Beverage World*, March 1997, pp. 57–58.

Video Case 7

CREATING BREAD

Would you pay $6 for a loaf of bread? Manoucher Etmanen has built a $5-million-a-year business by appealing to people who will. Although most of the 900 million loaves of bread consumed by Canadians each year cost a fraction of the price that Etmanen charges, he has successfully identified a niche market of consumers who enjoy good food and are willing and able to pay high prices to get it. His Manoucher brand of bread is selling well in Canada and he is now entering the European market with his product.

Etmanen developed Manoucher bread after arriving in Canada from Iran in the late 1970s. His recipes have all been developed in secret and use the finest ingredients. He spares no expense in his choice of ingredients, knowing that discriminating consumers will be able to detect compromises in quality. The consumers who buy Manoucher bread are knowledgeable about food. They like exotic products and are also health conscious. Since gourmet food is now an attractive multi-million-dollar industry in Canada, competitiveness in this market is fierce. For Etmanen, this means that in addition to producing a high-quality product, his recipes must be protected to maintain a competitive advantage based on taste. With no patent protection for his product, Etmanen does not take security lightly—the chemist for Manoucher bread is also the head of security.

Etmanen is also careful about his choice of distribution channels. His products are typically sold in exclusive, gourmet food stores such as the David Wood stores in Toronto. These stores cater to the gourmet food consumer whom Etmanen targets. He takes a personal interest in the packaging for his product, too. He strives not only for attractive packaging that is consistent with the wholesome, but also the high-end, image that he wants his products to project.

The latest additions to the Manoucher bread line are consistent with the company's positioning in the gourmet food industry. Mediterranean Sunset bread is a new herb bread in the tradition of his previous products. But he is also starting to distribute a specialty product through gourmet food catalogues. Each loaf sold through the catalogues will be packed in a handmade wooden box. Etmanen will sell each loaf packaged this way for $32. Even more exclusive is his new Limited Edition Bread, which will be personally made by Etmanen and will cost consumers $50.

Another current project for Etmanen is the export of his product to Europe, a move that he considers will be the key to the future growth of his business. He has started by freezing his bread and sending it to Britain to be sold for $20 a loaf in such select outlets as Harrods, Selfridges, and Harvey Nichols. Despite the good reputation of the retailers stocking his product in Britain, Etmanen has personally visited these retailers to ensure that his product is being sold in a manner consistent with the Manoucher brand positioning. Etmanen believes that the real key to food selling is sampling and consequently he has spent time in the British retail outlets providing bread samples for potential customers. Etmanen plans to eventually build a bakery in Britain that will allow him to serve Britain and the rest of the European market with fresh Manoucher bread.

QUESTIONS

1. How would you describe Manoucher's competitive advantage?

2. How does Manoucher communicate its positioning in the gourmet-food segment?

3. Is the gourmet-food segment an attractive one in the long run? What are the future challenges that Etmanen will have to face if he continues to cater to this segment of consumers in Canada and Europe?

Source: This case was revised and updated by Auleen Carson from the case prepared by Deborah Andrus, and is based on "Breadman," *Venture* (March 6, 1994).

PART III

DEVELOPING
THE MARKET MIX

C H A P T E R

8

PRODUCT AND
SERVICES STRATEGIES

Two mountains. Two N64 Halfpipes. Two N64 Terrain Parks. No sheep.   Mountain info: 1-800-766-0449.   Accommodation: 1-800-944-7853.   www.whistler-blackcomb.com

Adventure, adrenaline, achievement—three powerful words used on the cover of Intrawest's 1997 annual report that exemplify the experience of both employees and guests at Intrawest resorts. Their employees are not just highly motivated, they are also passionate about their work. They have a sense of excitement and commitment that is so visible, it is a tangible asset to the company. This excitement is transferred to every guest. Intrawest's employees have mastered the art of integrating their product and service.[1]

Intrawest, headquartered in Vancouver, is North America's leading developer and operator of mountain resorts. The company owns and operates magnificent, award-winning ski areas: Whistler, Blackcomb, and Panorama in British Columbia; Tremblant and Mont Ste. Marie in Quebec; Stratton in Vermont; Copper in Colorado; Mammoth in California; and Snowshoe in West Virginia. In 1997, Intrawest hosted 5.2 million skiers and snowboarders at its resorts. The company builds, markets, and sells resort accommodation and real estate, mainly condominiums, at the base of each hill. But its success has as much to do with the company's focus on the customer and the experiences it creates as it does with the physical facilities. According to company officials, "What drives the mountain resort business is the quality of the experience our guests and owners come away with."[2]

However, some people, including demographer David Foot, don't believe that investing in active sports facilities is a wise decision as the population ages. Statistics seem to support Foot's analysis. The number of skiers and snowboarders in Canada has declined from a high of 21.5 million ski visits to 16 million. So why is Intrawest investing in more ski hills? The company cites two reasons for its decision. First, Intrawest knows that there is a growing vacation industry in which people come to mountain resorts not only to ski but also to participate in various activities throughout the summer and winter. Second, Intrawest believes

When you finish this chapter, you should be able to

1. Define *product* and the major classifications of products and services.

2. Describe the roles of product and service branding, packaging, labelling, and product support services.

3. Explain the decisions that companies make when developing product lines and mixes.

4. Identify the four characteristics that affect the marketing of a service.

5. Discuss the additional marketing considerations that services require.

This graphic shows how the various parts of Intrawest's business strategy are linked.

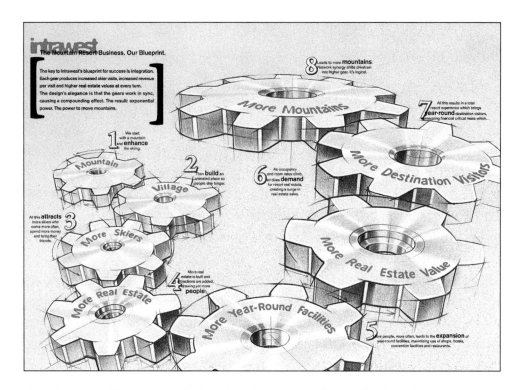

that demographics are on their side. Their research reveals that the average age of a person purchasing a recreational property is 50. These purchasers have sufficient disposable income to afford this type of luxury item. Since the leading edge of the baby-boom group is just entering this age group, Intrawest believes that it is well positioned to take advantage of a growth market. The company also believes that this group wants recreational activities where they can bring along younger family members so they can all enjoy an activity such as skiing. Developing a love of mountains and outdoor sports in the young represents a future marketing opportunity for Intrawest.

Selling a recreational property isn't the end goal for Intrawest, however. The company stresses that selling a mountain home or renting a time share is just the beginning, not the end of its task. It is the long-term stream of revenue received from people returning again and again to its resorts that makes the company profitable over the long term. Rather than relying on skiing alone, Intrawest is investing money in its properties: it is building mountain-top theatres, water parks, children's play areas, entertainment centres, and outdoor educational facilities. In other words, it is creating year-round recreational experiences that appeal to people from around the world who are interested in "destination" vacations.

Thus, Intrawest's strategic edge lies in its ability to integrate three sectors of the leisure industry: resort operations (skiing, golfing, hiking, mountain biking, retail, food and beverage), resort real estate development, and its vacation club (or timeshare) business. Intrawest also has a network of operations from which the company achieves economies of scale: they market together, purchase together, and learn from each other.

Marketing is an important part of the company's strategy. It is investing to build equity in the brand name, Intrawest. It wants the name to be synonymous worldwide with unique resort experiences in breathtaking places. Building brand equity is a costly exercise, so developing an effective and efficient marketing program is important. To accomplish its goals, Intrawest has turned to database marketing. It began to build its database with lists of season passholders. It added the names of resort visitors, leads from consumer shows, and replies generated from cards in its advertisements. Intrawest enters lifestyle information into its database so that it can develop profiles of people who will generate the most long-term value for the firm. It can then target its marketing efforts directly at these individuals.

While Intrawest markets its products and services primarily to baby boomers, it also understands the importance of other age groups. In the next millennium, the company will target Generation 2000—people aged 18 to 35—who comprise the largest single segment of customers for mountain resorts. These people are high-frequency guests who have more flexibility in choosing the time for their vacation than do people with school-age children. Intrawest also recognizes the importance of teenagers, who significantly influence the choice of family vacations. Teenagers have also driven the interest in extreme sports and represent an important group of buyers for sports gear. To appeal to these groups, Intrawest uses humour in its breakthrough advertising directed at its target audience of affluent North American, European, and Japanese consumers. Its ads also include the company's toll-free telephone number and its web site address.

Understanding the company's target market is important. Intrawest not only competes for these customers with other mountain resorts in Canada, the United States, Europe, and Japan, but also for market share with all other leisure companies, from cruise ships to amusement parks. For this reason, Intrawest wants to offer such a variety of vacation choices within the Intrawest network that guests will return again and again.

Intrawest
www.intrawest.com/

Is Intrawest's strategy working? The proof of success is in the company's bottom line. In the 1996 to 1997 period alone, profits surged 54 percent to $27.1 million. Having the strategic vision to integrate product and service strategies can be a powerful and profitable endeavour![3]

Clearly, Intrawest is marketing more than just a place to ski. The company is selling experiences, and while these may be based on physical features such as magnificent mountain peaks, people keep coming back as much for the service as they do for the product. Thus, the chapter begins with a deceptively simple question: *What is a product?* Companies create offerings that may be *product dominated* or *service dominated*. We suggest that the package of benefits offered to customers by many firms is a subtle mix of product and service benefits. We then go on to describe ways to classify products sold to consumer and business markets. Next, we describe links between the way the product is classified and suitable marketing strategies for products in that particular classification. For product-dominated offerings, many decisions have to be made not only about product design, but also about *branding, packaging, labelling,* and *product-support services.* Marketing managers must also develop product lines and product mixes. The last section of the chapter deals with the challenges associated with marketing *service-dominated* products. Services present special marketing challenges since they are *simultaneously produced and consumed,* and are *intangible, perishable,* and *variable.*

Product
A cluster of benefits that can be offered to a market for attention, acquisition, use, or consumption that might satisfy a want or need. It includes physical objects, services, persons, places, organizations, and ideas.

◼ WHAT IS A PRODUCT?

A Sony CD player, a Supercuts haircut, a Celine Dion concert, a Jasper vacation, a GMC truck, H&R Block tax preparation services, and advice from an attorney are all products. We define a **product** as a cluster of benefits that can be offered to a market for attention, acquisition, use, or consumption and that might satisfy a want or need. Products include more than just tangible goods. Broadly defined, products include physical objects, services, persons, places, organizations, ideas, or mixes of these entities. **Services** are a form of product that consists of activities, benefits, or satisfactions that are offered for sale, such as haircuts, tax preparation, and home repairs. Services are essentially intangible and do not result in the ownership of anything tangible.

Service
Any activity or benefit that one party can offer to another that is essentially intangible and does not result in the ownership of anything tangible.

THE PRODUCT-SERVICE CONTINUUM

A company's offer to the marketplace often combines both tangible goods and intangible services. Each component can be a minor or a major part of the total offer. At one extreme, the offer may be product dominated and consist of a *pure tangible good*, such as soap, toothpaste, or salt—no services accompany the product. At the other extreme are service-dominated offerings—an intangible benefit is created for the customer but no physical product is exchanged. Examples include a doctor's exam, a university lecture, or financial services. Between these two pure extremes, however, many goods and services combinations are possible.

A company's offer may consist of a *tangible good with accompanying services.* For example, Ford offers more than just automobiles. Its offer also includes repair and maintenance services, warranty fulfilment, showrooms and waiting areas, and a host of other support services. A *hybrid offer* consists of equal parts of goods and services. For instance, people patronize restaurants both for their food and their service. A *service with accompanying goods* consists of a major service along with supporting goods. For example, Canadian Airline passengers primarily buy transportation service, but the trip also includes some tangibles, such as food, drinks, and an airline magazine. The service also requires a capital-intensive good—an airplane—for its delivery, but the primary offer is a service.

LEVELS OF PRODUCT

Product planners need to consider the product on three levels. The most basic level is the **core product,** which addresses the question: *What is the buyer really buying?* As Figure 8-1 illustrates, the core product stands at the centre of the total product. It consists of the problem-solving services or core benefits that consumers seek when they buy a product. A woman buying lipstick buys more than lip colour. Charles Revson of Revlon recognized this early: "In the factory, we make cosmetics; in the store, we sell hope." Theodore Levitt has pointed out that buyers "do not buy quarter-inch drills; they buy quarter-inch holes." Thus, when designing products, marketers must first define the core *benefits* the product will provide to consumers.

The product planner must next build an **actual product** around the core product. Actual products may have as many as five characteristics: a *quality level, features, design,* a *brand name,* and *packaging.* For example, Sony's Handycam Camcorder is an actual product. Its name, parts, styling, features, packaging, and other attributes have all been combined carefully to deliver the core benefit—a convenient, high-quality way to capture important moments.

Finally, the product planner must build an **augmented product** around the core and actual products by offering additional consumer services and benefits. Sony must offer more than just a camcorder. It must provide consumers with a complete solution to their picture-taking problems. Thus, when consumers buy a Sony Handycam, Sony and its dealers also might give buyers a warranty on parts and workmanship, free lessons on how to use the camcorder, quick repair services

Core product
The problem-solving services or core benefits that consumers are really buying when they obtain a product.

Actual product
A product's parts, quality level, features, design, brand name, packaging, and other attributes that combine to deliver core product benefits.

Augmented product
Additional consumer services and benefits built around the core and actual products.

FIGURE 8-1   *Three levels of product*

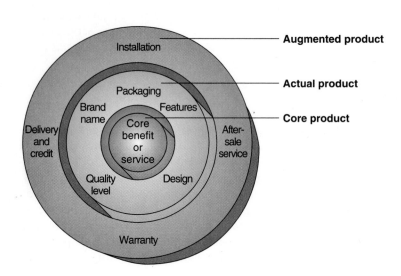

Core, actual, and augmented product: Consumers perceive this Sony camcorder as a complex bundle of tangible and intangible features and services that deliver a core benefit—a convenient, high-quality way to capture important moments.

when needed, and a toll-free telephone number to call if they have problems or questions. To the consumer, all of these augmentations become an important part of the total product.

Therefore, a product is more than a simple set of tangible features. Consumers tend to see products as complex bundles of benefits that satisfy their needs. When developing products, marketers first must identify the *core* consumer needs the product will satisfy. They must then design the *actual* product and find ways to *augment* it in order to create the bundle of benefits that will best satisfy consumers. Today, most competition occurs at the product augmentation level. Successful companies add benefits to their offers that not only will *satisfy*, but also will *delight* the customer.

PRODUCT CLASSIFICATIONS

Products and services fall into two broad classes based on the types of people that use them—*consumer products* and *industrial products*. Broadly defined, products also include other marketable entities such as organizations, persons, places, and ideas.

CONSUMER PRODUCTS

Consumer products
Products bought by final consumers for personal consumption.

Consumer products are those bought by final consumers for personal consumption. Marketers usually classify these goods further based on *how consumers go about buying them.* Consumer products include *convenience products, shopping products, specialty products,* and *unsought products.* These products differ in the ways consumers buy them; therefore they differ in how they are marketed (see Table 8-1).

Convenience products
Consumer products and services that the customer usually buys frequently, immediately, and with a minimum of comparison and buying effort.

Convenience products are consumer products and services that the customer usually buys frequently, immediately, and with a minimum of comparison and buying effort. They are usually low priced and are found in many types of retail outlets so they are available when customers need them. Convenience products can be divided further into *staples, impulse products,* and *emergency products. Staples* are products that consumers buy on a regular basis, such as ketchup, toothpaste, and electric power. *Impulse products* are purchased with little planning or search effort. These products are normally widely available. Thus, chocolate bars and magazines are placed next to checkout counters in many stores because shoppers may not otherwise think of buying them. Customers buy *emergency products* when their need is urgent—umbrellas during a rainstorm, travel insurance at an airport, or boots and shovels during the year's first snowstorm.

Shopping products
Consumer goods and services that the customer, in the process of selection and purchase, characteristically compares on such bases as suitability, quality, price, and style.

Shopping products are less frequently purchased consumer products and services that customers compare carefully on suitability, quality, price, and design. When buying shopping products and services, consumers spend much time and effort in gathering information and making comparisons. Examples

TABLE 8-1   *Marketing Considerations for Consumer Products*

MARKETING CONSIDERATIONS	TYPE OF CONSUMER PRODUCT			
	Convenience	**Shopping**	**Specialty**	**Unsought**
Customer buying behaviour	Frequent purchase, little planning, little comparison or shopping effort, low customer involvement	Less frequent purchase, much planning and shopping effort, comparison of brands on price, quality, style	Strong brand preference and loyalty, special purchase effort, little comparison of brands, low price sensitivity	Little product awareness, knowledge (or if aware, little or even negative interest)
Price	Low price	Higher price	High price	Varies
Distribution	Widespread distribution, convenient locations	Selective distribution in fewer outlets	Exclusive distribution in only one or a few outlets per market area	Varies
Promotion	Mass promotion by the producer	Advertising and personal selling by both producer and resellers	More carefully targeted promotion by both producer and resellers	Aggressive advertising and personal selling by producer and resellers
Examples	Toothpaste, magazines, laundry detergent	Major appliances, televisions, furniture, clothing	Luxury goods, such as Rolex watches or fine crystal	Life insurance, dental services

include furniture, clothing, vacations, and restaurants. Shopping products and services are offered through fewer outlets than convenience goods and services, but marketers provide more sales support to aid consumers in their comparisons.

Specialty products are consumer products and services with unique characteristics or brand identification for which a significant group of buyers is willing to make a special purchase effort. Examples include specific brands and types of cars, high-priced photographic equipment, and investment services. A Rolls-Royce, for example, is a specialty product because buyers are usually willing to travel great distances to buy one. Buyers normally do not compare specialty products. They invest only the time needed to reach dealers carrying the wanted products. Although these dealers do not need convenient locations, they still must let buyers know where to find them.

Unsought products are consumer products and services that the consumer either does not know about or knows about but does not normally think of buying. Most major innovations are unsought until the consumer becomes aware of them through advertising. Classic examples of known but unsought products are life insurance, encyclopedias, and blood donations. By their very nature, unsought products require a lot of advertising, personal selling, and other marketing efforts.

INDUSTRIAL PRODUCTS

Industrial products are those products and services purchased for further processing or for use in conducting a business. Thus, the distinction between a consumer product and an industrial product is based on the *purpose* for which the product is bought. If a consumer buys a lawn mower for use around home, the lawn mower is a consumer product. If the same consumer buys the same lawn mower for use in a landscaping business, the lawn mower is an industrial product.

There are three groups of industrial products: *materials and parts, capital items,* and *supplies and services.*

Materials and parts are industrial products that become part of the buyer's product, through further processing or as components. They include raw materials and manufactured materials and parts. *Raw materials* include farm products (wheat, cotton, livestock, fruits, vegetables) and natural products (fish, lumber,

Specialty products
Consumer products and services with unique characteristics or brand identification for which a significant group of buyers is willing to make a special purchase effort.

Unsought products
Consumer products and services that the consumer either does not know about or knows about but does not normally think of buying.

Industrial products
Products and services bought by individuals and organizations for further processing or for use in conducting a business.

Materials and parts
Industrial products that enter the manufacturer's product completely, including raw materials and manufactured materials and parts.

crude petroleum, iron ore). Farm products are supplied by many small producers who turn them over to marketing intermediaries that process and sell them. *Manufactured materials and parts* include component materials (iron, yarn, cement, wires) and component parts (small motors, tires, castings). Component materials usually are processed further—for example, pig iron is made into steel and yarn is woven into cloth. Most manufactured materials and parts are sold directly to industrial users. Price and service are the major marketing factors; branding and advertising tend to be less important.

Capital items
Industrial products that partly enter the finished product, including installations and accessory equipment.

Capital items are industrial products that aid in the buyer's production or operations. They include installations and accessory equipment. *Installations* consist of buildings (factories, offices) and fixed equipment (generators, drill presses, large computers, elevators). Because installations are major purchases, they usually are bought directly from the producer after a long decision period.

Accessory equipment includes portable factory equipment and tools (hand tools, lift trucks) and office equipment (fax machines, desks). They have a shorter life than installations and simply aid in the production process. Most sellers of accessory equipment use intermediaries because the market is spread out geographically, the buyers are numerous, and the orders are small.

Supplies and services
Industrial products that do not enter the finished product at all.

Supplies and services are industrial products that include operating supplies (lubricants, coal, computer paper, pencils) and repair and maintenance items (paint, nails, brooms). Supplies are the convenience products of the industrial field because they usually are purchased with a minimum of effort or comparison. *Business services* include maintenance and repair services (window cleaning, computer repair) and business advisory services (legal, management consulting, advertising). These services are usually supplied under contract. The factors associated with the successful marketing of professional services to industrial buyers were analyzed by de Brentani and Ragot of Concordia University.[4]

ORGANIZATIONS, PERSONS, PLACES, AND IDEAS

In addition to tangible products and services, in recent years marketers have broadened the concept of a product to include other "marketable entities"—namely, organizations, persons, places, and ideas.

Organizations often carry out activities to "sell" the organization itself. *Organization marketing* consists of activities undertaken to create, maintain, or change the attitudes and behaviour of target consumers toward an organization. Both profit and non-profit organizations practise organization marketing. Business firms sponsor public relations or corporate advertising campaigns to polish their images. Non-profit organizations, such as churches, universities, charities, museums, and performing arts groups, market their organizations to raise funds and attract members or patrons. *Image advertising* is a major tool that companies use to market themselves to various publics.

Marketing can also be used by individuals. *Person marketing* consists of activities undertaken to create, maintain, or change attitudes or behaviour toward particular people. All kinds of people and organizations practise person marketing. Prime ministers and provincial premiers skilfully marketed themselves, their parties, and their platforms to get needed votes and program support. Entertainers and sports figures such as Celine Dion and Tiger Woods use marketing to promote their careers and improve their impact and incomes. Professionals such as dentists, lawyers, accountants, and architects market themselves to build their reputations and increase business. Business leaders use person marketing as a strategic tool to develop their companies' fortunes as well as their own. Businesses, charities, sports teams, fine arts groups, religious groups, and other organizations also use person marketing. Creating or associating with well-known personalities often helps these organizations achieve their goals better.

This Street Teams advertisement is designed to stop child prostitution.

Social marketing
The creation and implementation of programs seeking to increase the acceptability of a social idea, cause, or practice within targeted groups.

Place marketing involves activities undertaken to create, maintain, or change attitudes or behaviour toward particular places. Examples include business site marketing and tourism marketing. *Business site marketing* involves developing, selling, or renting business sites for factories, stores, offices, warehouses, and conventions. Both provinces and municipalities try to sell companies on the advantages of locating new plants in their areas. Even entire nations, such as Indonesia, Ireland, Greece, Mexico, and Turkey have marketed themselves as good locations for business investment. *Tourism marketing* involves attracting vacationers to spas, resorts, cities, provinces, and nations. The effort is carried out by travel agents, airlines, motor clubs, oil companies, hotels, motels, and government agencies. Today almost every city, province, and country markets its tourist attractions. The government of Canada uses its web site (http://attractions.infocan.gc.ca) to inform residents and tourists about attractions and events. Saskatchewan markets itself as "clean, green, and welcoming." New Brunswick announces, "There's Fishing . . . and then there's New Brunswick's world-famous trophy fishing!"

Ideas also can be marketed. In one sense, all marketing is the marketing of an idea, whether it be the general idea of brushing your teeth or the specific idea that Crest provides the most effective decay prevention. Here, however, we narrow our focus to the marketing of *social ideas*, such as public health campaigns to reduce smoking, alcoholism, drug abuse, and overeating; environmental campaigns to promote wilderness protection, clean air, and conservation; and other campaigns such as family planning, human rights, and racial equality. This area has been called **social marketing**, and it includes the creation and implementation of programs seeking to increase the acceptability of a social idea, cause, or practice within targeted groups. For example, YWCAs across Canada promote a "week without violence," a Calgary group called Street Teams advertises to stop child prostitution, and the United Way runs ads to show how they help people in their local communities. But social marketing involves much more than just advertising. Many public marketing campaigns fail because they assign advertising the primary role and fail to develop and use all the marketing-mix tools.[5]

INDIVIDUAL PRODUCT DECISIONS

Figure 8-2 shows the important decisions in the development and marketing of products. We will focus on decisions about *product attributes, branding, packaging, labelling,* and *product-support services.*

FIGURE 8-2 *Individual product decisions*

PRODUCT ATTRIBUTES

Developing a product or service involves defining the benefits that the product will offer. These benefits are communicated and delivered by product attributes such as *quality, features,* and *design.*

Product Quality

Product quality
The ability of a product to perform its functions; it includes the product's overall durability, reliability, precision, ease of operation and repair, and other valued attributes.

Quality is one of the marketer's major positioning tools. **Product quality** has two dimensions—level and consistency. In developing a product, the marketer must first choose a quality level that will support the product's position in the target market. Here, product quality means *performance quality*—the level at which a product performs its functions. For example, a Rolls-Royce provides higher performance quality than a Chevrolet: it has a smoother ride, is made from more luxurious materials, handles better, and lasts longer. Companies rarely try to offer the highest possible performance quality level—few customers want or can afford the high levels of quality offered in products such as a Rolls-Royce, a Sub Zero refrigerator, or a Rolex watch. Instead, companies choose a quality level that matches target market needs and the quality levels of competing products.

Beyond quality level, high quality also can mean the *consistency* with which the quality is delivered. Here, product quality means *conformance quality*—freedom from defects and *consistency* or reliability, in delivering a targeted level of performance. All companies should strive for high levels of conformance quality. In this sense, a Chevrolet can have just as much quality as a Rolls-Royce. Although a Chevy doesn't perform as well as a Rolls, it can consistently deliver the quality that customers pay for and expect.

During the past two decades, a renewed emphasis on quality has spawned a global quality movement. Most firms implemented "Total Quality Management" (TQM) programs, efforts to constantly improve product and process quality in every phase of their operations. Recently, however, the total quality management movement has drawn criticism. Too many companies viewed TQM as a magic cure-all and created token total quality programs that applied quality principles only superficially. Today, companies are taking a "return on quality" approach, viewing quality as an investment and ensuring that quality improvements are tied to bottom-line results.[6]

Beyond simply reducing product defects, the ultimate goal of total quality is to improve customer value. For example, when Motorola first began its total quality program in the early 1980s, its goal was to reduce manufacturing defects drastically. In recent years, however, Motorola's quality concept has evolved into one of "customer-defined quality" and "total customer satisfaction." (See Marketing Highlight 8-1.) Thus, many companies today have turned quality into a potent strategic weapon. In fact, quality has now become a competitive necessity—in the coming century, only companies with the best quality will thrive.

Product Features

Product design
The process of designing a product's style and function: creating a product that is attractive; easy, safe, and inexpensive to use and service; and simple and economical to produce and distibute.

A product can be offered with varying features. A "stripped-down" model, one without any extras, is the starting point. The company can create higher-level models by adding more features. Features are a competitive tool for differentiating the company's product from competitors' products. Being the first producer to introduce a needed and valued new feature is one of the most effective ways to compete.

How can a company identify new features and decide which ones to add to its product? The company should periodically survey buyers who have used the product and ask these questions: How do you like the product? Which specific features of the product do you like most? Which features could we add to improve the product? The answers provide the company with a rich list of feature ideas. The company can then assess each feature's *value* to customers versus its *cost* to the company. Features that customers value little in relation to costs should be dropped; those that customers value highly in relation to costs should be added.

Product Design

The Canada Awards for Excellence are given to companies that have achieved outstanding performance.

Another way to add customer value is through distinctive **product design.** Some companies have reputations for outstanding design, such as Black & Decker in

MOTOROLA'S CUSTOMER-DEFINED, "SIX-SIGMA" QUALITY

Founded in 1928, Motorola introduced the first car radio—hence the name Motorola, suggesting "sound in motion." During World War II, it developed the first two-way radios ("walkie-talkies"), and by the 1950s, Motorola had become a household name in consumer electronics products. In the 1970s, however, facing intense competition mostly from Japanese firms, Motorola abandoned the radios and televisions that had made it famous. Instead, it focused on advanced telecommunications and electronics products—semiconductors, two-way radios, pagers, cellular telephones, and related gear. However, by the early 1980s, Japanese competitors were still beating Motorola to the market with higher-quality products at lower prices.

During the past decade, however, Motorola has come roaring back. It now leads all competitors in the global two-way mobile radio market and ranks number one in cellular telephones with a 45 percent worldwide market share. Motorola is the world's third-largest semiconductor producer, behind only Intel and NEC. Once in danger of being forced out of the pager business altogether, Motorola now dominates that market with an astonishing 85 percent global

market share. And rather than suffering at the hands of Japanese competitors, Motorola now has them on the run, even on their home turf. Motorola's sales in Japan now exceed $1.4 billion, accounting for almost seven percent of total company sales.

"Quality means the world to us," claims Motorola. An obsession with customer-driven quality has helped the company to achieve worldwide leadership in many product markets.

How has Motorola achieved such remarkable leadership? The answer is deceptively simple: an obsessive dedication to *quality.* In the early 1980s, Motorola launched an aggressive crusade to improve product quality, first by tenfold, then by a hundredfold. It set the unheard-of goal of "six-sigma" quality. Six sigma is a statistical term that means "six standard deviations from a statistical performance average." In plain English, the six-sigma standard means that Motorola set out to slash product defects to fewer than 3.4 per million components manufactured—99.9997 percent defect-free. "Six sigma" became Motorola's rallying cry. In 1988, it received one of the first annual Malcolm Baldrige National Quality Awards recognizing "preeminent quality leadership."

Motorola's initial efforts focussed on manufacturing improvements. This involved much more than simply increasing the number of quality control inspectors. The goal was to prevent defects from occurring in the first place. This meant *designing* products from the onset for quality and making things right the *first* time and *every* time. For example, Motorola's highly successful MicroTAC foldable, hand-held cellular phone has only

cordless appliances and tools, Steelcase in office furniture and systems, Bose in audio equipment, and Ciba Corning in medical equipment. Design can be one of the most powerful competitive weapons in a company's marketing arsenal.

Design is a larger concept than style. *Style* simply describes the appearance of a product. Styles can be eye-catching or yawn-inspiring. A sensational style may grab attention, but it does not necessarily make the product *perform* better. Unlike style, *design* is more than skin deep—it goes to the very heart of a product. Good design contributes to a product's usefulness as well as to its looks.

Good design can attract attention, improve product performance, cut production costs, and give and product a strong competitive advantage in the target market. For example, Braun, a German division of Gillette that has elevated design to a high art, has had outstanding success with its coffee markers, food processors, hair dryers, electric razors, and other small appliances. And Black & Decker has learned that innovative design can be very profitable.

What could be handier than a flashlight that you don't have to hold while you're probing under the sink for the cause of a leaky faucet? Black & Decker's flexible snakelight looks just like its namesake and attaches itself to almost anything, leaving your hands free. It can also stand up like an illuminated cobra to light your work space. The design won Black & Decker a gold medal in the Industrial Design Excellence Awards competition. More importantly, in a market where the average price is just $6, consumers are paying $30 for this flexible flashlight.[7]

one-eighth the number of parts contained in its original 1978 portable telephone; components snap together instead of being joined by screws or fasteners. This simpler design means fewer component defects and production errors.

Meeting the six sigma standard means that everyone in the organization must strive for quality improvement. Thus, total quality has become an important part of Motorola's basic corporate culture. Motorola spends $170 million annually to educate employees about quality, and then rewards people when they make things right. And because Motorola's products can be only as good as the components that go into them, the company forces its suppliers to meet the same exacting quality standards. Some suppliers grumble, but those that survive benefit greatly from their own quality improvements. As an executive from one of Motorola's suppliers puts it, "If we can supply Motorola, we can supply God."

More recently, as Motorola has developed a deeper understanding of the meaning of quality, its initial focus on preventing manufacturing defects has evolved into an emphasis on *customer-defined quality* and improving customer value. "Quality," notes

Motorola's vice-president of quality, "has to do something for the customer." Thus, the fundamental aim of the company's quality movement is "total customer satisfaction":

> Beauty is in the eye of the user. If [a product] does not work the way that the user needs it to work, the defect is as big to the user as if it doesn't work the way the designer planned it. Our definition of a defect is "if the customer doesn't like it, it's a defect."

Instead of focusing just on manufacturing defects, Motorola now surveys customers about their quality needs, analyses customer complaints, and studies service records in a constant quest to improve value to the customer. Motorola's executives routinely visit customers to gain better insights into their needs. As a result, Motorola's total quality management has done more than reduce product defects; it has helped the company to shift from an inwardly focused, engineering orientation to a market-driven, customer-focused one. The company has now expanded its quality program to all of its departments and processes, from manufacturing and product development to market research, finance, and even advertising.

Some skeptics are concerned that Motorola's obsession with quality might create problems. For example, the company's products sometimes have been late to the market. Others worry that building so much quality into a product might be too expensive. Not so, claims Motorola. In fact, the reverse is true—superior quality is the lowest-cost way to do things. The costs of monitoring and fixing mistakes can far exceed the costs of getting things right in the first place. Motorola estimates that its quality efforts have resulted in savings of more than $4.2 billion during the past six years.

And so Motorola's quest for quality continues. By the year 2001, Motorola is shooting for near perfection—a mind-boggling rate of just *one* defect per *billion*.

Sources: Quotations from "Future Perfect," *The Economist*, January 4, 1992, p. 61; Lois Therrien, "Motorola and NEC: Going for Glory," *Business Week*, Special issue on quality, 1991, pp. 60–61; and B. G. Yovovich, "Motorola's Quest for Quality," *Business Marketing*, September 1991, pp. 14–16. Also see Ronald Henkoff, "Keeping Motorola on a Roll," *Fortune*, April 18, 1994, pp. 67–78; and J. Ward Best, "The Making of Motorola," *Durham Herald Sun*, February 12, 1995, pp. A1, A11; www.mot.com/

BRANDING

Brand
A name, term, sign, symbol, or design, or a combination of these intended to identify the goods or services of one seller or group of sellers and to differentiate them from those of competitors.

Perhaps the most distinctive skill of professional marketers is their ability to create, maintain, protect, and enhance brands for their products and services. A **brand** is a name, term, sign, symbol, or design, or a combination of these that identifies the maker or seller of a product or service. Consumers view a brand as an important part of a product, they give products and services a personality that consumers can relate to, and branding can add value to a product. For example, most consumers would perceive a bottle of White Diamonds perfume as a high-quality, expensive product. But the same perfume in an unmarked bottle would likely be viewed as lower in quality, even if the fragrance were identical.

Branding has become so strong that today hardly anything goes unbranded. Salt is packaged in branded containers, and automobile parts—spark plugs, tires, filters—bear brand names that differ from those of the auto makers. Even fruits and vegetables are branded—Sunkist oranges, Dole pineapples, and Chiquita bananas. Intrawest is working to build recognition of its brand name. Services-dominated offerings such as mbanx, Fido, and Quik Copy strive to have widely recognized brands.

Branding helps buyers in many ways. Brand names help consumers identify products that might benefit them. Brands also tell the buyer something about product quality. Buyers who always buy the same brand know that they will get the same features, benefits, and quality each time they buy. Branding also gives the seller several advantages. The brand name becomes the basis on which a whole story can be built about a product's special qualities. The seller's brand name and trademark provide legal protection for unique product features that otherwise might be copied by competitors. And branding helps the seller to segment markets. For example, General Mills can offer Cheerios, Wheaties, Total, Lucky Charms, and many other cereal brands, not just one general product for all consumers.

A brand is a seller's promise to deliver consistently a specific set of features, benefits, and services to buyers. The best brands convey a warranty of quality. According to one marketing executive, a brand can deliver up to four levels of meaning:

- *Attributes.* A brand first brings to mind certain product attributes. For example, Mercedes suggests such attributes as "well engineered," "well built," "durable," "high prestige," "fast," "expensive," and "high resale value." The company may use one or more of these attributes in its advertising for the car. For years, Mercedes Benz advertised "Engineered like no other car in the world." This provided a positioning platform for other attributes of the car.

- *Benefits.* Customers do not buy attributes, they buy benefits. Therefore, attributes must be translated into functional and emotional benefits. For example, the attribute "durable" could translate into the functional benefit, "I won't have to buy a new car every few years." The attribute "expensive' might translate into the emotional benefit, "The car makes me feel important and admired." The attribute "well built" might translate into the functional and emotional benefit, "I am safe in the event of an accident."

- *Values.* A brand also says somthing about the buyers' values. Thus, Mercedes buyers value high performance, safety, and prestige. A brand marketer must identify the specific groups of car buyers whose values coincide with the delivered benefit package.

- *Personality.* A brand also projects a personality. Motivation researchers sometimes ask, "If this brand were a person, what kind of person would it be?" Consumers might visualize a Mercedes automobile as being a wealthy, middle-aged business executive. The brand will attract people whose actual or desired self-images match the brand's image.

Brand Equity

Brands vary in the amount of power and value they have in the marketplace. A powerful brand has high **brand equity.** Brands have higher brand equity to the extent that they have higher brand loyalty, name awareness, perceived quality, strong brand associations, and other assets such as patents, trademarks, and channel relationships.

Brand equity
The value of a brand, based on the extent to which it has high brand loyalty, name awareness, perceived quality, strong brand associations, and other assets such as patents, trademarks, and channel relationships.

A brand with strong brand equity is a valuable asset. Measuring the actual equity of a brand name is difficult. However, according to one estimate, the brand equity of Coca-Cola is $50 billion, IBM $25 billion, Disney $21 billion, and Kodak $18 billion.[8] The world's top brands include such superpowers as Harlequin, Campbell, Sony, Mercedes-Benz, and McDonald's. (See Marketing Highlight 8-2.)

High brand equity provides a company with many competitive advantages. A powerful brand enjoys a high level of consumer brand awareness and loyalty. Because consumers expect stores to carry the brand, the company has more leverage in bargaining with resellers. Because the brand name carries high credibility, the company can more easily launch line and brand extensions, such as when Coca-Cola leveraged its well-known brand to introduce Diet Coke or when Procter & Gamble introduced Ivory dishwashing detergent. Above all, a powerful brand offers the company some defence against fierce price competition. Some analysts view brands as *the* major enduring asset of a company, outlasting the company's specific products and facilities.

Branding poses challenging decisions to the marketer. Figure 8-3 shows the key branding decisions.

HARLEQUIN: ONE OF THE WORLD'S MOST POWERFUL BRAND NAMES

If you were asked to name the world's most powerful brand names, Coca-Cola, Toyota, McDonald's, Sony, Disney, Kodak, or BMW would probably spring to mind. But it may surprise you to learn that one of the leading world brands is a home-grown Canadian product—Harlequin romance novels. With revenues in excess of $470 million per year, Harlequin contributes over 45 percent of the operating revenues of its parent, Torstar Corp., publisher of The Toronto Star, and it remains phenomenally profitable. It makes 15 percent on every book it sells (three to four times the industry average), and it sells approximately 180 million books a year worldwide—almost six books per second.

The firm had humble beginnings. Founded in Winnipeg in 1949 by Richard Bonnycastle, Harlequin began by reprinting books sold in the United Kingdom or the United States. Harlequin's advance is another story of a woman being the power behind the throne. Bonnycastle's wife, Mary, first noticed how popular romances were with readers, and she suggested that the firm specialize in the genre. This, combined with another marketing insight led to much of Harlequin's future success. Rather than distributing its products in bookstores, Harlequin placed them where women shopped—in supermarkets and drugstores. The rest is history. The firm enjoyed growth rates in excess of 25 percent throughout the 1970s. However, many analysts thought that the women's movement of the 1980s would spell disaster for the company. How wrong they were! Harlequin has been labelled a company with products written for women, by women.

While many people have made fun of the romance genre, Harlequin attributes much of its success to having a high-quality marketing program. Quality begins with the product. The product, its books, are much higher quality than most literary critics care to admit, Harlequin

believes. They are written according to well-researched, carefully designed plotlines by over 1500 authors. Product quality is followed up with superb production capabilities and topped off by top-notch advertising.

Meticulous market research is conducted to understand the demographics and attitudes of the market. North American readers are mainly women whose average age is 39. They are well educated, with over

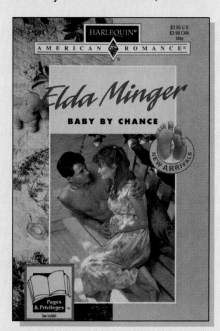

Harlequin's strong brand equity helps it sell books around the world.

half having some university education. They are employed and have household incomes of $35 000. Setting is important. While Texas is the most popular location for romance, readers do not like stories set in Washington, D.C., or other circus venues! Most of all, readers want happy endings. High-quality research has enabled Harlequin to target the segment of heavy users. While most Canadians buy only six books a year, Harlequin's romance readers spend $30 a month on books.

You might not consider packaging to be an important aspect of marketing when it comes to selling paperbacks, but it is also another of Harlequin's secrets of success. In Harlequin's case, the package is the book's cover. Careful research is again conducted to help Harlequin's 100 to 125-plus illustrators create the right cover to attract readers who may be searching through stores that carry hundreds of titles.

Another key to Harlequin's success is high repeat sales rates. This is where strong brand equity really helps. Readers know what to expect from Harlequin. This consumer confidence has made acceptance of the 72 new titles Harlequin introduces every month almost a certainty. Brand equity also lowers Harlequin's costs of advertising and promotion since its loyal readers are highly familiar with the brand and all that it stands for.

Harlequin's success is not confined to the North American market. It sells books in over 100 markets in 23 different languages. It keeps costs low by following its standardized marketing strategy. Harlequin also attributes its success to formulating alliances with overseas partners that help the firm establish a distribution system, gain access to the television and print media essential to build demand, and handle the repatriation of book royalties (i.e., ensure that Harlequin receives the profits generated by overseas book sales).

So the next time you think about powerful brands, think about Harlequin, a firm that has found success through branding and superior product management in an industry plagued by high failure rates.

Sources: Kevin Brown, "The Top 200 Mega-brands," *Advertising Age*, May 2, 1994, p. 33; and Gina Mallet, "The Greatest Romance on Earth," *Canadian Business*, August 1993, pp. 19–23. See also Paul Grescoe, *The Merchants of Venus* (Raincoat Books, 1996); www.romance.net

Brand Name Selection

A good name can add greatly to a product's success. However, finding the best brand name is a difficult task. It begins with a careful review of the product and its benefits, the target market, and proposed marketing strategies.

FIGURE 8-3 *Major branding decisions*

Service-dominated organizations, such as Outward Bound also have to build brand recognition in order to market their products.

YOU CAN'T RUN FROM YOUR PROBLEMS. YOU CAN, HOWEVER, CLIMB FROM THEM.

The best way to deal with life's problems is to, well, deal with them. We just think you should do it someplace incredible. Outward Bound is an exhilarating wilderness journey of self-discovery. A journey that provides you with challenges, skills training, and adventure that can help you deal with whatever life can throw at you. You'll spend your days hiking, climbing or canoeing, and your evenings reflecting and getting reacquainted with someone truly special. You. We provide all the equipment. All you need is an open mind. Because we believe that when you're 300 feet off the ground, chances are, your problems are going to look really small.

Call 1 800 268-7329 for a copy of our course brochure.

OUTWARD BOUND

Desirable qualities for a brand name include: (1) It should suggest something about the product's benefits and qualities. Examples: Beautyrest, Craftsman, Sunkist, Spic and Span, Snuggles. (2) It should be easy to pronounce, recognize, and remember. Short names help. Examples: Tide, Aim, Puffs. But longer ones are sometimes effective. Examples: "Love My Carpet" carpet cleaner, "I Can't Believe It's Not Butter" margarine, President's Choice "Too Good To Be True" products. (3) The brand name should be distinctive. Examples: Taurus, Kodak, Esso. (4) The name should translate easily into foreign languages. Before spending $100 million to change its name to Exxon, Standard Oil of New Jersey tested the name in 54 languages in more than 150 foreign markets. It found that the name Enco referred to a stalled engine when pronounced in Japanese. (5) It should be capable of registration and legal protection. A brand name cannot be registered if it infringes on existing brand names. Also, brand names that are merely descriptive or suggestive may be unprotectable. For example, Labatt registered the name Ice for its new beer and invested millions in establishing the name with consumers. But the courts later ruled that the term Ice is generic and that Labatt could not use the Ice name exclusively.

Once chosen, the brand name must be protected. Many firms try to build a brand name that will eventually become identified with the product category. Brand names such as Frigidaire, Kleenex, Levi's, Jell-O, Scotch Tape, Formica, and Fiberglas have succeeded in this way. However, their very success may threaten the company's rights to the name. Many originally protected brand names, such as cellophane, aspirin, nylon, kerosene, linoleum, yo-yo, trampoline, escalator, thermos, and shredded wheat, are now names that any seller can use.

Brand Sponsor

A manufacturer has four sponsorship options. The product may be launched as a **manufacturer's brand** (or national brand), as when Kellogg and IBM sell their output under their own manufacturer's brand names. Or the manufacturer may sell to resellers who give it a **private brand** (also called *store brand* or *distributor brand*). Although most manufacturers create their own brands, others market *licensed brands*. Finally, two companies can *co-brand* a product, such as when General Mills and Hershey Foods combined brands to create Reese's Peanut Butter Puffs cereal.

MANUFACTURER'S BRANDS VERSUS PRIVATE BRANDS. Manufacturers' brands have long dominated the retail scene. In recent times, however, an increasing number of department and discount stores, supermarkets, gas stations, clothiers, drugstores, and appliance dealers have their own brands. For example, Sears has created several names—Kenmore appliances, Diehard batteries, Craftsman tools, Weatherbeater paints—that buyers look for and demand. Canadian Tire's private-label tires are as well known as the manufacturers' brands of Goodyear and Bridgestone. Wal-Mart recently introduced its price-driven Great Value brand, which may eventually include more than 1000 items across most major food categories.[9]

Despite the fact that private brands are often hard to establish and are costly to stock and promote, private labels yield higher profit margins

Manufacturer's brand (national brand)
A brand created and owned by the producer of a product or service.

Private brand (distributor or store brand)
A brand created and owned by a reseller of a product or service.

Slotting fees
Payments demanded by retailers from producers before they will accept new products and find "slots" for them on the shelves.

for the intermediary. They also give intermediaries exclusive products that cannot be bought from competitors, resulting in greater store traffic and loyalty. For example, if Sears promotes General Electric appliances, other stores that sell GE products will also benefit. Further, if Sears drops the GE brand, it loses the benefit of its previous promotion for GE. But when Sears promotes its private brand of Kenmore appliances, Sears alone benefits from the promotion, and consumer loyalty to the Kenmore brand becomes loyalty to Sears.

The competition between manufacturers' and private brands is called the *battle of the brands*. In this battle, retailers have many advantages. They control what products they stock, where they go on the shelf, and which ones they will feature in local circulars. They charge manufacturers **slotting fees**—payments demanded by retailers before they will accept new products and find "slots" for them on the shelves. For example, Safeway required a payment of $25 000 from a small pizza roll manufacturer to stock its new product. Retailers price their store brands lower than comparable manufacturers' brands, thereby appealing to budget-conscious shoppers, especially in difficult economic times. Most shoppers know that store brands are often made by one of the larger manufacturers anyway.

As store brands improve in quality and as consumers gain confidence in their store chains, store brands are posing a strong challenge to manufacturers' brands. Loblaw, for example, is increasing the number of its store brands. Loblaw currently markets 1500 products under its President's Choice label.[10]

Since retailing is more concentrated in Canada than it is in the United States, store brands are more powerful. They account for almost 22 percent of the $30.5-billion annual supermarket sales in Canada compared to the 13.8 percent of sales of store brands in the United States. Currently, 100 percent of Canadian households buy at least some store brands. In fact, the average Canadian consumer buys 4.6 store branded products on each shopping trip. Store brands appeal to value-conscious consumers who note that these brands cost 10 to 40 percent less than nationally branded products.[11]

Store-brands' market share is expected to grow as more and more retailers launch and extend their lines of store brands. IGA and Food City, members of the Oshawa Group Ltd., recently launched 125 products under the store brand name Our Complements. A&P utilizes the name Master Choice to identify its high-end store brands, while Safeway Canada uses Stonehenge Farms to denote its store brands. Even regional retailers have entered the fray. Selection Zel is used by Provigo of Quebec and Sobeys Select is used by the Nova Scotia-based retailer.[12]

Private labels are even more prominent in Europe, accounting for as much as 32 percent of supermarket sales in Britain and 24 percent in France. French retail giant Carrefour sells more than 3000 in-house brands, ranging from cooking oil to car batteries.[13] Some marketing analysts predict that private brands eventually will knock out all but the strongest manufacturers' brands.

Private labels can become a powerful market force and can pose a threat to established national brands.

We cannot just assume, however, that national brands are doomed. Take the case of the "cola wars" in which Coke and Pepsi made a significant counter-attack against the private-label upstart, Cott. To fend off private brands, leading brand marketers will have to invest in R&D to bring out new brands, new features, and continuous quality improvements. They must design strong advertising programs to maintain high awareness and preference. And they must find ways to "partner" with major distributors in a search for distribution economies and improved joint performance.[14]

LICENSING.   Most manufacturers take years and spend millions to create their own brand names. However, some companies license names or symbols previously created by other

ALEXANDRA ACS-LOEWEN, PRODUCT MANAGER, KRAFT BRAND PROMOTIONS, KRAFT CANADA INC.

Kraft is a leader in the food industry both in Canada and abroad. It produces over 2500 products and markets them in over 140 countries. In Canada, Kraft manufactures and markets over 1500 products. Clearly, this a company that never stands still. In 1995 alone, it introduced over 30 new products and over 80 line extensions and product improvements to the Canadian marketplace. Kraft Canada not only builds successful businesses, but it also allows people to have great careers while having fun in the process. Alexandra Acs-Loewen believed this promise and has been with Kraft Canada for three years. She went to work at Kraft immediately after graduating from Queen's University. During her time with the company, she has worked on the Kraft salad-dressing business and on Post Kids' cereals.

Building Brand Equity

Alix's most recent challenge has been her new assignment to the team designed to market the Kraft name. While the company has always done some corporate marketing, this effort is focussed on the Kraft name, which is also the company's leading trademark. Kraft has a broad range of individual brands it has built successfully, including KRAFT DINNER, Cheez Whiz, and Miracle Whip. But the company also recognizes the value in its company name. This effort to market the Kraft name is part of the company's ongoing effort to maintain a rich relationship with its consumers. Research has shown that the Kraft name is the company's most valuable asset. In fact, Kraft is the most powerful food trademark in Canada and has the highest top-of-mind awareness among food brands. The brand is consistently associated with a number of images in the Canadian consumer's mind: reliability, concern for consumer, and quality.

Despite these strong associations, it is important for the company to keep the brand name relevant so that it can carry the company into the twenty-first century. Research also suggested to the team that Kraft has a traditional image. Consumers still remember advertising campaigns aired from the 1950s to 1970s, which showed only consumer's hands using Kraft products in recipe applications. Kraft believes that it is mandatory to be seen as keeping pace with today's society.

Kraft thinks that support of the corporate brand name achieves some notable benefits. For example, it allows the company to achieve some scale advantages since Kraft Canada has over 35 leading brands. Kraft uses the tagline "Good Food. Good Food Ideas." What this means is that Kraft provides consumers with both relevant and superior value food products as well as ideas and information related to these products and to food generally.

Integrated Marketing

In building brand equity, it is important that marketers ensure consistency across all product lines and integrated communications so that a unified image results, and the company is perceived by consumers as "speaking with one voice." For Kraft, the corporate logo is already prominent on brands' packaging, along with the company's promise of "satisfaction guaranteed" and a toll-free number for consumers to call to have their questions answered on products or to request additional information or help.

This consumer focus is also integrated into Kraft's *What's Cooking* magazine. This magazine has always been of great value to Kraft since it has made the company more approachable and helped to give Kraft a human face to consumers. It has thus helped Kraft build relationships with consumers, via a variety of useful recipes, ideas, and information on food topics. It also features its own toll-free number to increase direct communication with consumers. This, along with letters from real consumers, as well as tips from the Kraft Kitchens, all contribute to its value from the consumer's perspective, in Alix's view.

Kraft extends these concepts to the grocery store, where its message is seen by millions of consumers in programs such as in-store sampling and shelf-talkers, those little signs you see placed above products on grocery store shelves. Having a retail program integrated with other elements of the marketing mix is essential since so many consumers are making their purchase decisions within the store itself, rather than making pre-planned, out-of-store, choices.

Understanding the Consumer's Point of View

Developing these types of programs are not chance efforts. Kraft has long been known for its consumer focus and the extensive research upon which it bases its strategies. Kraft endeavours to understand its brands as consumers see them, which gives it valuable insights on how to continuously meet consumers' needs in food products. As Kraft's tagline is "Good Food. Good Food Ideas," it is also important for Kraft to understand what "food ideas" are most helpful and interesting to consumers. Research has allowed Kraft to know which products and appliances are actually in most consumers' kitchens. It has helped the company to understand how consumers prepare food, and what cooking techniques they are comfortable with, and those that they find intimidating. It has helped Kraft design recipes and products designed to make consumers' lives easier. All of this knowledge speaks of Kraft's market orientation, and is essential to understand food from the consumer's point of view.

It is easy to see why Alexandra Acs-Loewen is excited about these programs and believes in their power to help Kraft succeed.

Source: Alexandra Acs-Loewen was interviewed by P. Cunningham on April 19, 1996. We are grateful to her for taking the time to provide us with these insights.

Co-branding: The combined brands create broader consumer appeal and greater brand loyalty. Here, ConAgra joins Kellogg to offer Healthy Choice from Kellogg's cereals.

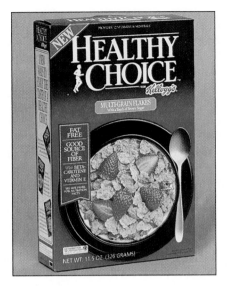

manufacturers, names of well-known celebrities, characters from popular movies and books—for a fee, any of these can provide an instant and proven brand name. Apparel and accessories sellers pay large royalties to adorn their products—from blouses to ties, and linens to luggage—with the names or initials of such fashion innovators as Alfred Sung, Calvin Klein, Pierre Cardin, Gucci, and Halston. Sellers of children's products attach an almost endless list of character names to clothing, toys, school supplies, linens, dolls, lunch boxes, cereals, and other items. The character names range from such classics as Disney, Peanuts, Barbie, and Flintstones characters, to the Muppets, Garfield, Batman, and the Simpsons.

Co-branding
The practice of using the established brand names of two different companies on the same product.

CO-BRANDING.   Although companies have been **co-branding** products for many years, there has been a recent resurgence in co-branded products. Co-branding occurs when two established brand names of different companies are used on the same product. For example, Pillsbury joined Nabisco to create Pillsbury Oreo Bars Baking Mix. And Kellogg joined forces with ConAgra to co-brand Kellogg's Healthy Choice cereals. In most co-branding situations, one company licenses another company's well-known brand to use with its own.

Co-branding offers many advantages. Because each brand dominates in a different category, the combined brands create broader consumer appeal and greater brand equity. Co-branding also allows companies to enter new markets with minimal risk or investment. For example, by licensing its Healthy Choice brand to Kellogg, ConAgra entered the breakfast segment with a solid product that was backed by Kellogg's substantial marketing support. In return, Kellogg could leverage the brand awareness of the Healthy Choice name in cereal.

Co-branding also has its limitations. Such relationships usually involve complex legal contracts and licences. Co-branding partners must carefully coordinate their advertising, sales promotion, and other marketing efforts. Finally, when co-branding, each partner must trust the other will take good care of its brand. As one Nabisco manager puts it, "Giving away your brand is a lot like giving away your child—you want to make sure everything is perfect."[15]

Line extension
Using a successful brand name to introduce additional items in a given product category under the same brand name, such as new flavours, forms, colours, added ingredients, or package sizes.

Brand Strategy

A company has four choices when it comes to brand strategy (see Figure 8-4). It can introduce *line extensions* (existing brand names extended to new forms, sizes, and flavours of an existing product category), *brand extensions* (existing brand names extended to new product categories), *multibrands* (new brand names introduced in the same product category), or *new brands* (new brand names in new product categories).

FIGURE 8-4   *Four brand strategies*

LINE EXTENSIONS.   **Line extensions** occur when a company introduces additional items in a given product category under the same brand name, such as new flavours, forms, colours, ingredients, or package sizes. Thus, Dannon recently introduced several line extensions, including seven new yogurt flavours, a fat-free yogurt, and a large economy-size yogurt. The vast majority of new product activity consists of line extensions. A company might introduce line extensions to

	Product Category	
	Existing	New
Existing Brand Name	Line extension	Brand extension
New	Multibrands	New brands

meet consumer desires for variety, to utilize excess manufacturing capacity, or to match a competitor's successful line extension. Some companies introduce line extensions simply to command more shelf space from resellers.

Line extensions involve some risks, however. An overextended brand name might lose its specific meaning or its unique selling proposition. As brand names are extended, they may be associated with products that do not possess the core qualities of the original branded offering. Line extensions will not sell enough to cover their development listing and promotion costs. Or, even when they sell enough, the sales may come at the expense of other items in the line. A line extension works best when it takes sales away from competing brands, not when it "cannibalizes" the company's other items.[16]

Brand extension
Using a successful brand name to launch a new or modified product in a new category.

Gap
www.gap.com/

Multibranding
A strategy under which a seller develops two or more brands in the same product category.

BRAND EXTENSIONS. A **brand extension** involves the use of a successful brand name to launch new or modified products in a new category. Fruit of the Loom launched new lines of socks, men's fashion underwear, women's underwear, and athletic apparel. Swiss Army Brand Sunglasses, Disney Cruise Lines, and Snackwell's Snackbar are all brand extensions.

There are many advantages to a brand extension strategy. A brand extension gives a new product instant recognition and faster acceptance. It also saves the high advertising costs usually required to build a new brand name. At the same time, a brand extension strategy involves some risk. Brand extensions such as Bic pantyhose, Heinz pet food, Life Savers gum, and Clorox laundry detergent met early deaths. The extension may dilute the image of the main brand. For example, when clothing retailer Gap saw competitors targeting its value-conscious customers with Gap-like fashions at lower prices, it began testing Gap Warehouse, which sold merchandise at a cut below Gap quality and price. However, the Gap connection confused customers and eroded the Gap image. As a result, the company renamed the stores Old Navy Clothing Company, a brand that has become enormously successful.[17]

If an extension brand fails, it may harm consumer attitudes toward the other products carrying the same brand name. Further, a brand name may not be appropriate to a particular new product, even if it is well made and satisfying—would you consider buying Texaco milk or Alpo chili? And a brand name may lose its special positioning in the consumer's mind through overuse. Companies that are tempted to transfer a brand name must research how well the brand's associations fit the new product.[18]

MULTIBRANDS. Companies often introduce additional brands in the same category. **Multibranding** offers a way to establish different features and appeal to different buying motives. Thus, Procter & Gamble (P&G) markets 11 different brands of laundry detergent. Multibranding also allows a company to lock up more reseller "shelf space." Or the company may want to protect its major brand by setting up *flanker* or *fighter brands*. For example, Seiko uses different brand names for its higher-priced watches (Seiko Lasalle) and lower-priced watches (Pulsar) to protect the flanks of its mainstream Seiko brand. Companies may also develop separate brand names for different regions or countries, perhaps to suit different cultures or languages. For example, P&G dominates the North American laundry detergent market with Tide, which in all its forms captures more than a 31 percent market share. In Europe, however, P&G leads with its Ariel detergent brand, whose annual sales of $2.1 billion make it Europe's number-two packaged-goods brand.

A major drawback of multibranding is that each brand might obtain only a small market share, and none may be very profitable. The company may end up spreading its resources over many brands instead of building a few brands to a highly profitable level. These companies should reduce the number of brands they sell in a given category and set up tighter screening procedures for new brands.

NEW BRANDS.   A company may create a new brand name when it enters a new product category for which none of the company's current brand names are appropriate. For example, Japan's Matsushita uses separate names for its different families of products: Technics, Panasonic, National, and Quasar. Or, the company might believe that the power of its existing brand name is waning and a new brand name is needed. Finally, the company may obtain new brands in new categories through acquisitions. For example, S. C. Johnson & Son, marketer of Pledge furniture polish, Glade air freshener, Raid insect spray, Edge shaving gel, and many other well-known brands, added several new powerhouse brands through its acquisition of Drackett Company, including Windex, Drano, and Vanish toilet bowl cleaner.

As with multibranding, offering many new brands can result in a company spreading its resources too thin. And in some industries, such as consumer packaged goods, consumers and retailers have become concerned that there are already too many brands, with too few differences between them. Thus, Procter & Gamble, Frito-Lay, and other large consumer product marketers are now pursuing *megabrand* strategies—weeding out weaker brands and focussing their marketing dollars only on brands that can achieve the number-one or -two market-share positions in their categories.[19]

PACKAGING

Packaging
The activities of designing and producing the container or wrapper for a product.

Packaging involves designing and producing the container or wrapper for a product. Some marketers have called packaging a fifth *P*, along with price, product, place, and promotion. The package may include the product's primary container (the tube holding Colgate toothpaste); a secondary package that is thrown away when the product is about to be used (the cardboard box containing the toothpaste); and the shipping package necessary to store, identify, and ship the product (a corrugated box carrying six dozen tubes of Colgate toothpaste). Labelling is also part of packaging and consists of printed information appearing on or with the package.

Traditionally, the primary function of the package was to contain and protect the product. In recent times, however, numerous factors have made packaging an important marketing tool. Increased competition and clutter on retail store shelves means that packages now must perform many sales tasks—from attracting attention, to describing the product, to making the sale. Designers can no longer ignore the psychological implications that packaging has for consumers. The package's shape, colour, symbols, and words drive how the consumer visualizes the product inside.[20]

Companies are realizing the power of good packaging to create instant consumer recognition of the company or brand. For example, in an average supermarket, which stocks 15 000 to 17 000 items, the typical shopper passes by some 300 items per minute, and 53 percent of all purchases are made on impulse. In this highly competitive environment, the package may be the seller's last chance to influence buyers. It becomes a "five-second commercial." The Campbell Soup Company estimates that the average shopper sees its familiar red-and-white can 76 times a year, creating the equivalent of $36 million worth of advertising.[21]

In recent years, product safety has also become a major packaging concern. We have all learned to deal with hard-to-open "childproof" packages. And after the rash of product tampering scares during the 1980s, most drug producers and food makers are now putting their products in tamper-resistant packages.

Packaging concept
What the package should *be* or *do* for the product.

Developing a good package for a new product requires making many decisions. The first task is to establish the packaging concept. The **packaging concept** states what the package should *be* or *do* for the product. Should the main functions of the package be to offer product protection, introduce a new dispensing method, suggest certain qualities about the product or the company, or something else? Decisions then must be made on specific elements of the package, such as

THE GERMAN PACKAGING ORDINANCE: MAKING THE POLLUTER PAY

The principle of "the polluter pays" once seemed far-fetched—a pipe dream of radical environmentalists. But as the rest of the world watches, the notion that sellers should be responsible for the environmental costs of their products is being put to the test in Germany. The Packaging Ordinance (Verpackungsordnung), enacted in June 1991, made private industry responsible for the collecting, sorting, and ultimate recycling packaging waste.

In Germany, as in Canada and the United States, packaging makes up a third of all solid waste. Everyone agrees that reducing it is a good idea, but the new German legislation is complex and controversial. It deals separately with three different kinds of packaging: *primary packaging*—the essential container that holds the product, like a perfume bottle; *secondary packaging*—outer material whose main function is point-of-purchase display and protection during shipping, like the box around the perfume bottle; and *transport packaging*—the carton or crate used to ship the perfume to stores. The ordinance decreed that all three types of packaging must be taken

back by retailers and returned to manufacturers—an onerous prospect for both parties. However, it allowed that if the industry could come up with an alternative, then retailers would not have to take back the first and largest category of waste, primary sales packaging.

The industry's solution was the Dual System (DSD), a non-profit

In Germany, sellers are now responsible for the environmental costs of their products. This widely used "green-dot" emblem indicates that a package is acceptable for industry collection systems.

company set up by German businesses that collects waste directly from consumers in addition to the country's municipal collection systems. DSD is funded by licensing fees for the now widely used *green dot:* a green arrow emblem indicating that a package is collectible by DSD. Now, rather than tossing their packaging out with the municipal trash, for which they must pay a fee, consumers can take it to a nearby yellow DSD bin to be collected for free.

Under the DSD system, although they must still collect secondary and transport packaging, stores are no longer required to take back huge mounds of primary sales packaging. However, there's a catch: To be eligible as DSD trash, a sales package must have the green dot. So, not surprisingly, retailers are reluctant to carry products without the green dot. Further, there is a growing preference among German consumers for recyclable packaging materials, and for less packaging in general. Thus, the Packaging Ordinance will strongly affect how companies package their products for the German market.

The ordinance puts the "polluter pays" principle to work by creating

size, shape, materials, colour, text, and brand mark. These various elements must work together to support the product's position and marketing strategy. The package must be consistent with the product's advertising, pricing, and distribution. In today's rapidly changing environment, most companies must recheck their packaging every two or three years to ensure its maximizing consumer impact.

In making packaging decisions, the company also must heed growing environmental concerns about packaging, and make decisions that serve society's interests as well as immediate customer and company objectives. Increasingly, companies will be asked to take responsibility for the environmental costs of their products and packaging (see Marketing Highlight 8-3).

LABELLING

Labels may range from simple tags attached to products to complex graphics that are part of the package. They perform several functions, and the seller must decide which ones to use. At the very least, the label *identifies* the product or brand, such as the name Sunkist stamped on oranges. The label might *describe* several things about the product—who made it, where it was made, when it was made, its contents, how it is to be used, and how to use it safely. Finally, the label might *promote* the product through attractive graphics.

incentives rather than through direct regulation. Unlike other European Union (EU) countries, Germany has no ban on specific packaging materials. Instead, green dot licence prices are based, in part, on the difficulty of recycling a particular material. This sets market mechanisms in motion. If a given packaging material is costly to recycle, the price of using it will rise and companies will switch to something else. Thus, the ordinance is forcing companies that do business in Germany to innovate and make their products more environmentally friendly.

The major problem with the landmark German recycling program is the lack of a market for recycled material. Notes one packaging expert:

> There seems to be widespread belief in the trash fairy, who comes overnight and turns garbage into gold for free. . . . Everything is recyclable, but that doesn't mean it's valuable. [The German ordinance] ignores the very essence of economics: supply and demand. When you're talking trash, it's difficult to believe that anyone will pay for it.

It's no secret that much of the packaging collected in DSD bins is not being recycled, but rather is piling up in warehouses or being exported. When German plastics turned up in French dumps and incinerators last year, it caused an EU-wide scandal.

All this leaves the German public sceptical. The green dot has little credibility with consumers—it's on almost all packaging, but everyone knows that the recycling structure is not yet in place. Moreover, some environmentalists are concerned that the green dot will give companies and consumers a licence not to care about environmental problems. For example, they fear that the ordinance will encourage Germans to use more one-way packaging rather than reusables, which don't carry the green dot.

Still, the ordinance serves as a wake-up call to both businesses and consumers, in Germany and around the world. It says, "Hey folks, we've got a problem, and something must be done about it." And despite its flaws, the ordinance does seem to be moving the country, however timidly, toward its goal of waste reduction. The German Environmental Ministry reports that packaging recycling is at 50 to 60 percent (except for plastics), the use of reusable shipping containers is on the rise, and secondary packages (boxes for toothpaste and liquor bottles, for instance) are starting to disappear from store shelves. Producers and retailers are now working together to help solve environmental problems.

France and Austria have passed similar legislation, and France has begun using the green dot, although with a different collection system. In Germany, new ordinances are on the horizon, including ones for mandating producer take-back of cars and electronic equipment. And the European community is now working on a directive that would set minimum standards for recycling in all of its member states. "It may take another year or two, but the train is running," assures one German ministry official. "The idea of product responsibility is spreading around the world."

Source: Adapted from Marilyn Stern, "Is This the Ultimate in Recycling?" *Across the Board,* May 1993, pp. 28–31. Also see Gene Bylinsky, "Manufacturing for Reuse," *Fortune,* February 6, 1995, pp. 102–112.

There has been a long history of legal and ethical concerns about labels. Labels can mislead customers, fail to describe important ingredients, or fail to include needed safety warnings. Currently, packages in Canada must only list nutritional information if they are making a specific dietary claim, such as low salt or low fat.[22] The *Consumer Packaging and Labelling Act* was passed to protect consumers from labelling or packaging that is false or misleading. The *Weights and Measures Act* deals with the units of measurement on labels. Consumer advocates are lobbying for additional legislation that would require such things as open dating (so that consumers can ascertain product freshness), unit pricing (so that consumers can compare products in standard measurement units), and percentage labelling (to reveal the percentage of ingredients such as sugar and fat).

PRODUCT-SUPPORT SERVICES

Product-support services
Services that augment actual products.

Customer service is another element of product strategy. A company's offer to the marketplace usually includes some services, which can be a minor or a major part of the total offer. Later in the chapter we discuss services as products in themselves. Here, we discuss **product-support services**—services that augment actual products. More and more companies are using product-support services as a major tool in gaining competitive advantage.

Cadillac
www.cadillac.com/

A company should design its product and support services to profitably meet the needs of target customers. The first step is to survey customers periodically to assess the value of current services and to obtain ideas for new ones. For example, Cadillac holds regular focus-group interviews with owners and carefully watches complaints that come into its dealerships. From this careful monitoring, Cadillac has learned that buyers are very upset by repairs that are not done correctly the first time.

Once the company has assessed the value of various support services to customers, it must next assess the costs of providing these services. It can then develop a package of services that will both delight customers and yield profits to the company. For example, based on its consumer interviews, Cadillac has set up a system directly linking each dealership with a group of 10 engineers who can help mechanics with difficult repairs. Such actions helped Cadillac jump, in one year, from fourteenth to seventh in independent rankings of service.[23]

PRODUCT LINE DECISIONS

Product line
A group of products that are closely related because they function in a similar manner, are sold to the same customer groups, are marketed through the same types of outlets, or fall within given price ranges.

We have looked at product strategy decisions such as branding, packaging, labelling, and services for individual products. But product strategy also calls for building a product line. A **product line** is a group of products that are closely related because they function in a similar manner, are sold to the same customer groups, are marketed through the same types of outlets, or fall within given price ranges. For example, General Motors produces several lines of cars, Nike produces several lines of athletic shoes, and Nortel produces several lines of telecommunications products. In developing product line strategies, marketers face a number of tough decisions.

The major product line decision is *line length*. The line is too short if the manager can increase profits by adding items; the line is too long if the manager can increase profits by dropping items. Product line length is influenced by company objectives. Companies that want to be positioned as full-line companies or that are seeking high market share and growth usually carry longer lines. Companies that are keen on high short-term profitability generally carry shorter lines consisting of selected items.

Product lines tend to lengthen over time. The sales force and distributors may pressure the manager for a more complete product line to satisfy their customers. Or, the product line manager may want to add items to the product line to increase sales and profits. However, as the manager adds items, several costs rise: design and

FIGURE 8-5 *Product line stretching decision*

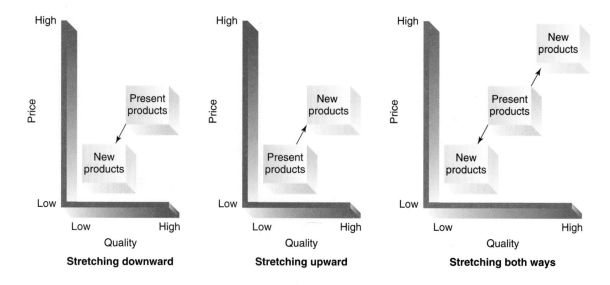

Stretching downward   Stretching upward   Stretching both ways

Ever wonder how an ordinary hotel room feels to a relocating family?

At Residence Inn, we haven't forgotten where relocating families are used to staying. In their homes. Their nice, big, comfortable homes. That's why our studio suites are much bigger than ordinary hotel rooms. And we not only give you more room, we also give you a living room where families can stretch out and relax. On top of that, our penthouse suites have an upstairs with an additional bedroom and bath. And most of our rooms have their own fireplaces.

Families won't go hungry for home cooked meals here, either. Every room comes with a full kitchen. We'll even do all of your grocery shopping for you.

But perhaps the biggest surprise of all is the affordable price: rooms are only $60-$90 a night.*

So call Residence Inn. Because families should be close. Not cramped. Toll-free 1-800-331-3131.

Residence Inn.

People who travel for a living, live here.

*Slightly higher in Los Angeles area. Based on 1-night stay. © 1991 Residence Inn by Marriott, Inc.

Product line stretching: Marriott stretched its hotel product line to include several branded hotels aimed at a different target market. Residence Inn, for example, provides a "home away from home" for people who travel for a living, who are relocating, or who are on temporary assignment and need inexpensive, temporary lodging.

Mercedes-Benz
www.mercedes-benz.com/

Marriott
www.marriott.com/

engineering costs, inventory costs, manufacturing changeover costs, order processing costs, transportation costs, and promotional costs to introduce new items. Eventually top management calls a halt to the mushrooming product line. Unnecessary or unprofitable items or services will be pruned from the line in an effort to increase overall profitability. This pattern of uncontrolled product line growth followed by heavy pruning is typical and may repeat itself many times.

The company must therefore extend its product lines carefully. It can systematically increase the length of its product line in two ways: by *stretching* its line and by *filling* its line. Every company's product line covers a certain range of the products offered by the industry as a whole. For example, BMW automobiles are located in the medium-high price range of the automobile market. Toyota focusses on the low-to-medium price range. *Product line stretching* occurs when a company lengthens its product line beyond its current range. Figure 8-5 shows that the company can stretch its line downward, upward, or both ways.

Stretching Downward

Many companies initially locate at the upper end of the market and later stretch their lines downward. A company may stretch downward to plug a market hole that otherwise would attract a new competitor, or to respond to a competitor's attack on the upper end. Or it may add low-end products because it finds faster growth taking place in the low-end segments. Mercedes stretched downward for all these reasons. Facing a slow-growth luxury car market and attacks by Japanese automakers on its high-end positioning, Mercedes introduced several smaller, lower-priced models. These included the sporty SLK hardtop convertible (priced at a modest $56 000) and the A-Class line ($28 000). And in a joint venture with Switzerland's Swatch watchmaker, Mercedes will soon launch the $14 000 Smart micro compact car, an environmentally correct second car.[24]

Stretching Upward

Companies at the lower end of the market may want to stretch their product lines upward. They may be attracted by a faster growth rate or higher margins at the higher end, or they may simply want to position themselves as full-line manufacturers or add prestige to their current products. For example, General Electric added its Monogram line of high-quality built-in kitchen appliances targeted at the select few households earning more than $140 000 a year and living in homes valued at over $550 000.

Stretching Both Ways

Companies in the middle range of the market may decide to stretch their lines in both directions. Marriott did this with its hotel product line. Along with regular Marriott hotels, it added the Marriott Marquis line to serve the upper end of the market, and the Courtyard and Fairfield Inn lines to serve the lower end. Each branded hotel line is aimed at a different target market. Marriott Marquis aims to attract and please top executives; Marriotts, middle managers; Courtyards, salespeople; and Fairfield Inns, vacationers and others on a low travel budget. The major risk with this strategy is that some travellers will trade down after finding that the lower-price hotels in the Marriott chain give them pretty much everything they want. However, Marriott would rather capture its customers who move downward than lose them to competitors.

Filling in the Product Line

An alternative to product line stretching is product line filling—adding more items within the present range of the line. There are several reasons for *product line filling:* reaching for extra profits, trying to satisfy dealers, trying to use excess capacity, trying to be the leading full-line company, and trying to plug holes to keep out competitors. Thus, Sony filled its Walkman line by adding solar-powered and waterproof Walkmans, and an ultralight model that attaches to a sweatband for joggers, bicyclers, tennis players, and other exercisers. However, line filling is overdone if it results in cannibalization and customer confusion. The company should ensure that new items are noticeably different from existing ones.

■ PRODUCT MIX DECISIONS

**Product mix
(or product assortment)**
The set of all product lines and items that a particular seller offers for sale to buyers.

An organization with several product lines has a product mix. A **product mix** (or **product assortment**) is the set of all product lines and items that a particular seller offers for sale. Avon's product mix consists of four major product lines: cosmetics, jewellery, fashions, and household items. Each product line consists of several sublines. For example, cosmetics breaks down into lipstick, blush, powder, and so on. Each line and subline has many individual items. Altogether, Avon's product mix includes 1300 items. In contrast, a large supermarket handles as many as 17 000 items; a typical Zellers stocks 15 000 items; and General Electric manufactures as many as 250 000 items.

A company's product mix has four important dimensions: width, length, depth, and consistency. Table 8-2 illustrates these concepts with selected Procter & Gamble consumer products.

The *width* of P&G's product mix refers to the number of different product lines the company carries. Table 8-2 shows a product mix width of six lines. (In fact, P&G produces many more lines, including mouthwashes, paper towels, disposable diapers, pain relievers, and cosmetics.)

The *length* of P&G's product mix refers to the total number of items the company carries. In Table 8-2, the total number of items is 42. We can also compute the average length of a line at P&G by dividing the total length (here 42) by

TABLE 8-2 *Product Mix Width and Product Line Length Shown for Selected Procter & Gamble Products*

	PRODUCT MIX WIDTH					
	Detergents	**Toothpaste**	**Bar Soap**	**Deodorants**	**Fruit Juices**	**Lotions**
PRODUCT LINE LENGTH	Ivory Snow	Gleem	Ivory	Secret	Citrus Hill	Wondra
	Dreft	Crest	Camay	Sure	Sunny Delight	Noxema
	Tide	Complete	Lava		Winter Hill	Oil of Olay
	Joy	Denquel	Kirk's		Texsun	Camay
	Cheer		Zest		Lincoln	Raintree
	Oxydol		Safeguard		Speas Farm	Tropic Tan
	Dash		Coast			Bain de Soleil
	Cascade		Oil of Olay			
	Ivory Liquid					
	Gain					
	Dawn					
	Ariel					
	Bold 3					
	Liquid Tide					

the number of lines (here 6). In Table 8-2, the average P&G product line consists of seven brands.

The *depth* of P&G's product mix refers to the number of versions offered of each product in the line. Thus, if Crest comes in three sizes and two formulations (paste and gel), Crest has a depth of six. By counting the number of versions within each brand, we can calculate the average depth of P&G's product mix.

The *consistency* of the product mix refers to how closely related the various product lines are in end use, production requirements, distribution channels, or in some other way. P&G's product lines are consistent insofar as they are consumer products that go through the same distribution channels. The lines are less consistent insofar as they perform different functions for buyers.

These product mix dimensions provide the handles for defining the company's product strategy. The company can increase its business in four ways. It can add new product lines, thus widening its product mix. In this way, its new lines build on the company's reputation in its other lines. The company can lengthen its existing product lines to become a more full-line company. Or it can add more product versions of each product and thus deepen its product mix. Finally, the company can pursue more product line consistency—or less—depending on whether it wants to have a strong reputation in a single field or in several fields.

SERVICES MARKETING

One of the major trends in North America in recent years has been the dramatic growth of services. Service jobs in Canada account for 72 percent of total employment. Services are growing even faster in the world economy, making up a quarter of the value of all international trade. Business services account for almost 30 percent of all Canadian exports, resulting in a substantial trade surplus for services, versus a large deficit for goods.[25]

Service industries vary greatly. The *governments* offer services through courts, employment services, hospitals, loan agencies, military services, police and fire departments, postal service, regulatory agencies, and schools. The *private non-profit organizations* offer services through museums, charities, churches, colleges, foundations, and hospitals. A large number of *business organizations* offer services—airlines, banks, hotels, insurance companies, consulting firms, medical and law practices, entertainment companies, real estate firms, advertising and research agencies, and retailers.

The convenience industry: Services that save you time—for a price.

Not only are there traditional service industries, but also new types keep popping up all the time. For example, the Canadian Imperial Bank of Commerce created a new banking service called Profile Banking (see Marketing Highlight 8-4).

Some North American service businesses are very large, with total sales and assets in the millions of dollars. Table 8-3 shows the largest service companies in Canada in various categories. There are also tens of thousands of smaller service providers. Selling services presents some special problems calling for special marketing solutions.

NATURE AND CHARACTERISTICS OF A SERVICE

A **service** is any activity or benefit that one party can offer to another that is essentially intangible and does

MARKETING HIGHLIGHT 8 - 4

CIBC's Profile Banking

"I never thought of designing a service innovation. I thought I was just doing my job." That's how Brad Baird modestly described his role in proposing, designing, and implementing a major service innovation—a new banking concept that became a significant profit centre for the Canadian Imperial Bank of Commerce.

When Brad first arrived for his assignment in the Lombard Place branch of CIBC in Winnipeg, he found an empty suite of offices tucked away on the mezzanine level. This space, he realized, was a potential gold mine. The downtown branch was located in an office tower that was connected by underground tunnels and covered walkways to a significant part of the city's business and shopping community, including Portage Place, Eaton Centre, Winnipeg Square, and The Bay. During Winnipeg's long winters, shoppers and businesspeople could access dozens of retail shops on the lower level as well as the Sheraton, the Westin, and three office towers. Hundreds of people walked by the branch every day. Many of these, Brad realized, were potential customers.

As Brad studied his customer base, he realized that the bank was not serving a potentially profitable customer segment. Thousands of professional people, aged 25 to 45, were earning good salaries. They were building substantial savings but were far from qualifying for the private banking service. What intrigued Brad about this segment was that they experienced what consumer researchers call "time poverty." These customers made money but had no time to investigate investment opportunities; they had trouble finding time to get to the bank to make deposits and pay their bills. They could benefit from some of the private banking services, and they might qualify for private banking some day, so the bank would be highly motivated to attract and hold these customers.

Brad proposed the development of a new profit centre that was ultimately called Profile Banking. The name derived from the fact that those using the centre had to meet specific requirements—that is, fit a profile. Customers in Profile Banking had to meet income and net worth levels. They dealt with account representatives in the Profile Banking office, not with branch officers. Brad realized that most of the customers didn't want to visit the branch in person; they were too busy and many of them travelled extensively. Therefore, all communication would be handled by voice mail and fax. While most customers dealt with the centre by phone, the office layout supported the high quality associated with the positioning strategy.

Employees of the centre were also screened. Not only did they have to demonstrate familiarity with the full range of banking functions, but they also had to have superb interpersonal and communication skills. Everyone who worked in the centre, including the secretaries, was licensed to sell mutual funds.

Promotion to clients was controlled. Profile Banking customers

---

TABLE 8-3 *The Largest Service Firms in Canada*

DIVERSIFIED SERVICES

Laidlaw
  (transportation, waste management)
Thimpear Corp.
  (diversified information services)

BANKS

Royal Bank
Bank of Montreal
Toronto-Dominion Bank
Canadian Imperial Bank of Commerce
Bank of Nova Scotia

FINANCIAL SERVICES

RBC Dominion Securities
Midland Walwyn
Burns Fry Holdings

TRANSPORTATION

CN Rail
Air Canada
Kleysen Transport
Purolator
Laidlaw

TELECOMMUNICATIONS

BCE Inc.
Bell Canada
Northern Telecom
Saskatchewan Telecommunications
Maritime Telephone
Newfoundland Telephone

INSURANCE

Great-West Life Assurance
Sun Life Assurance of Canada
Manulife Financial
London Life Insurance
Standard Life Assurance

UTILITIES

Manitoba Telephone
Centra Gas
Consumers Gas
Union Gas
TransAlta Utilities
Canadian Western Natural Gas

did not receive solicitations sent to other bank customers, but received occasional advertisements tailored to their specific segment.

To date, the centre has been an unqualified success. In fact, when Brad gave a presentation to a university class, one student commented, "Didn't he have any problems? Everything seemed perfect." A major factor in this smoothness was the unqualified support of Doneta Brotchie, senior vice-president, who was the top banking official for Manitoba and Saskatchewan. Brotchie's support allowed the centre to open, although a number of points had to be cleared with the bank's headquarters in Toronto. For example, banking centres had always been named by function at CIBC. Brad insisted on a name that would communicate the unique role of the centre.

Profile Banking has been overwhelmingly successful. The service has spread from Winnipeg to Toronto and is expected to be expanded to even more branches.

Customers who opened accounts in Winnipeg often prefer to remain with Profile Banking after they move to Calgary or Vancouver.

Still, managers realize that the following service concerns need to be addressed in future:

1. To identify customers for the Profile Banking centre, Brad developed a computer program that would print out lists of customers who met the criteria for profile banking, but who banked at another CIBC branch. By pulling these customers into the centre, Profile Banking was drawing profitable revenue sources away from the branches. At the same time, these customers might be lost to the bank altogether if they remained in the branches; Profile Banking clients showed significantly greater loyalty than average customers.

2. Competitors were trying to copy the centre. Like other service innovations, Profile Banking cannot be copyrighted and there are few

barriers to entry. Profile Banking had to find a way to compete against other centres once the uniqueness advantage was lost.

3. A smaller but significant problem was associated with maintaining customers. Every year, some customers failed to maintain the criteria required to remain clients of Profile Banking. Some clients suffered changes in economic status. Others simply did not use enough products—mutual funds, loans, credit cards—to justify the cost of personal service. Sometimes Brad would decide to retain a client who seemed to be weathering a bad patch, such as a senior executive who lost his or her job. In other instances, individual customers had to be de-marketed to the status of ordinary customers. These customers not only were likely to leave CIBC but also to retain negative feelings.

Source: This highlight was written by Cathy Goodwin, University of Manitoba.

TABLE 8-3 *continued*

FOOD SERVICES	RETAILING
Cara Operations	The Bay
Scott Hospitality	Eaton's
	Holt Renfrew
HEALTH CARE	Sears Canada
	Loblaw Companies
Extendicare	Jean Coutu Group
	Canadian Tire
BROADCASTING AND CABLE	Provigo
	Canada Safeway
Rogers Communications	Marks Work Wearhouse
Groupe Videotron	
WIC Western International Communications	
Canadian Broadcasting Corporation	
Shaw Communications	

not result in the ownership of anything. Its production may or may not be tied to a physical product. Activities such as renting a hotel room, depositing money in a bank, travelling on an airplane, visiting a psychiatrist, getting a haircut, having a car repaired, watching a professional sport, seeing a movie, having clothes cleaned at a dry cleaner, and getting advice from a lawyer all involve buying a service.

A company must consider four special characteristics of services when designing marketing programs: *intangibility, inseparability, variability,* and *perishability.* These characteristics are summarized in Figure 8-6 and discussed below.[26]

FIGURE 8-6 *Four service characteristics*

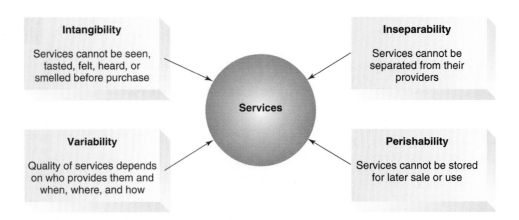

Intangibility
Services cannot be seen, tasted, felt, heard, or smelled before purchase

Inseparability
Services cannot be separated from their providers

Services

Variability
Quality of services depends on who provides them and when, where, and how

Perishability
Services cannot be stored for later sale or use

Service intangibility
A major characteristic of services—they cannot be seen, tasted, felt, heard, or smelled before they are bought.

Service inseparability
A major characteristic of services—they are produced and consumed at the same time and cannot be separated from their providers, whether the providers are people or machines.

Service variability
A major characteristic of services—their quality may vary greatly, depending on who provides them and when, where, and how they are provided.

Service perishability
A major characteristic of services—they cannot be stored for later sale or use.

Service intangibility means that services cannot be seen, tasted, felt, heard, or smelled before they are bought. For example, people undergoing cosmetic surgery cannot see the result before the purchase, and airline passengers have nothing but a ticket and the promise of safe delivery to their destinations.

To reduce uncertainty, buyers look for "signals" of service quality. They draw conclusions about quality from the place, people, price, equipment, and communication material that they can see. Therefore, the service provider's task is to make the service tangible in one or more ways. Whereas product marketers try to add intangibles to their tangible offers, service marketers try to add tangibles to their intangible offers.

Physical goods are produced, then stored, later sold, and still later consumed. In contrast, services are first sold, then produced and consumed at the same time. **Service inseparability** means that services cannot be separated from their providers, whether the providers are people or machines. If a service employee provides the employee service, then the employee is a part of the service. Because the customer is also present as the service is produced, *provider-customer interaction* is a special feature of services marketing. Both the provider and the customer affect the service outcome. Gerry Moore, Director of the CN Customer Support Centre, explains, "We're counting on our customers to help us move forward together . . . They work with us to provide accurate, timely information, such as bills of lading and short-term production forecasts."[27]

Service variability means that the quality of services depends on who provides them as well as when, where, and how they are provided. For example, some hotels, such as the Westin or Marriott, have reputations for providing better services than others. But within a given Marriott hotel, one registration-desk employee may be cheerful and efficient, whereas another standing just a few feet away may be unpleasant and slower. Even the quality of each employee's service varies according to his or her energy and frame of mind at the time of each customer encounter. Service firms can take several steps to help manage service variability. They can select and carefully train their personnel to give good service. They can provide employee incentives that emphasize quality, such as employee-of-the-month awards or bonuses based on customer feedback.

Service perishability means that services cannot be stored for later sale or use. Some dentists charge patients for missed appointments because the service value existed only at that point and disappeared when the patient did not show up. The perishability of services is not a problem when demand is steady. However, when demand fluctuates, service firms often have difficult problems. For example, public transport corporations have to own much more equipment than they would if demand were even throughout the day. Thus, service firms often design strategies for producing a better match between demand and supply. For instance, hotels and resorts charge lower prices in the off season to attract more guests. And restaurants hire part-time employees to serve during peak periods.

MARKETING STRATEGIES FOR SERVICE FIRMS

Just like manufacturing businesses, good service firms use marketing to position themselves strongly in chosen target markets. A&W Foods of Canada positions itself as combining fast foods with friendly service. The Westin Hotel chain positions itself to offer excellence, yet allows each hotel to retain its individual personality—for example, the Winnipeg Westin positions itself as "the finest hotel in our marketplace," with the goal of "exceeding all of our customers' expectations by delivering exceptional and caring service." A new airline, WestJet, positions itself to compete against the large carriers, such as Air Canada and Canadian Airlines. Modelling itself on the American innovator, Southwest Airlines, WestJet offers deep-discounted fares combined with no-frills service: no meals and no printed tickets.[28] These and other service firms establish their positions through traditional marketing mix activities.

However, because services differ from tangible products, they often require additional marketing approaches. In a product business, products are fairly standardized and can sit on shelves waiting for customers. But in a service business, the customer and frontline service employee *interact* to create the service. Thus, service providers must work to interact effectively with customers to create superior value during service encounters. Effective interaction, in turn, depends on the skills of frontline service employees, and on the service production and support processes backing these employees.

THE SERVICE-PROFIT CHAIN

Successful service companies focus their attention on both their employees and customers. They understand the *service-profit chain,* which links service firm profits with employee and customer satisfaction. This chain consists of five links:[29]

- ◆ *Healthy service profits and growth*—superior service firm performance, which results from . . .
- ◆ *Satisfied and loyal customers*—satisfied customers who remain loyal, repeat purchase, and refer other customers, which results from . . .
- ◆ *Greater service value*—more effective and efficient customer value creation and service delivery, which results from . . .
- ◆ *Satisfied and productive service employees*—more satisfied, loyal, and hard-working employees, which results from . . .
- ◆ *Internal service quality*—superior employee selection and training, a quality work environment, and strong support for those dealing with customers.

Therefore, reaching service profits and growth goals begins with taking care of those who take care of customers.

Internal marketing
Marketing by a service firm to train and effectively motivate its customer-contact employees and all the supporting service people to work as a team to provide customer satisfaction.

FIGURE 8-7 *Three types of marketing in service industries*

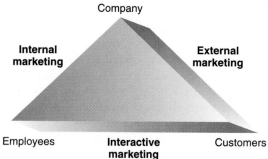

All of this suggests that service marketing requires more than just traditional external marketing using the four *P*s. Figure 8-7 shows that service marketing also requires both *internal marketing* and *interactive marketing.* **Internal marketing** means that the service firm must effectively train and motivate its customer-contact employees and all the supporting service people to work as a *team* to provide customer satisfaction. For the firm to deliver consistently high service quality, marketers must get everyone to practise customer orientation. In fact, internal marketing must *precede* external marketing.

Interactive marketing
Marketing by a service firm that recognizes that perceived service quality depends heavily on the quality of buyer-seller interaction.

Interactive marketing means that perceived service quality depends heavily on the quality of the buyer-seller interaction during the service encounter. In product marketing, product quality often depends little on how the product is obtained. But in services marketing, service quality depends on both the service deliverer and the quality of the delivery. Thus, service marketers cannot assume that they will satisfy the customer simply by providing good technical service. They must also master interactive marketing skills.[30]

Today, as competition and costs increase, and as productivity and quality decrease, more marketing sophistication is needed. Service companies face three major marketing tasks: They want to increase their *competitive differentiation, service quality,* and *productivity.*

Managing Service Differentiation

In these days of intense price competition, service marketers often complain about the difficulty of differentiating their services from those of competitors. To the extent that customers view the services of different providers as similar, they care less about the provider than the price.

To differentiate its service, British Airways offers international travellers such features as sleeping compartments and hot showers. As the comments in this ad show, customers really appreciate such services.

The solution to price competition is to develop a differentiated offer, delivery, and image. The *offer* can include *innovative features* that set one company's offer apart from competitors' offers. For example, airlines have introduced such innovations as in-flight movies, advance seating, air-to-ground telephone service, and frequent-flyer award programs to differentiate their offers. British Airways even offers international travellers a sleeping compartment, hot showers, and cooked-to-order breakfasts.

Service companies can differentiate their service *delivery* by having more able and reliable customer-contact people, by developing a superior physical environment in which the service product is delivered, or by designing a superior delivery process. For example, a bank might offer its customers electronic home banking as a better way to deliver banking services than having to drive, park, and wait in line.

Finally, service companies can differentiate their images through symbols and branding. Service marketers often find themselves challenged to find an intangible symbol of an intangible benefit. For example, Royal Bank's "Leo the Lion" shows a modernized version of the lion (although you have to look hard to see it!). Lions symbolize strength and power—desirable qualities of a large bank. Some credit unions in British Columbia have tried to differentiate themselves from the larger banks by showing humorous versions of the larger banks. BC Central Credit union chose to symbolize its virtues through peaceful wilderness settings, punctuated by the angry cry of bank customers who "can't take it anymore."

Managing Service Quality

One of the major ways a service firm can differentiate itself is by delivering consistently higher quality than its competitors do. Many companies are finding that outstanding service quality can give them a potent competitive advantage that leads to superior sales, profit performance, and customer retention.[31] A service firm's ability to hang on to its customers depends on how consistently it delivers value to them.

The key is to exceed the customers' service-quality *expectations*. As the chief executive at American Express puts it, "Promise only what you can deliver and deliver *more* than you promise!"[32] These expectations are based on past experiences, word of mouth, and service firm advertising. If *perceived service* of a given firm exceeds *expected service,* customers are apt to use the provider again.

Unfortunately, service quality is harder to define and judge than product quality. It is harder to get agreement on the quality of a haircut than on the quality of a hair dryer, for instance. People judge the quality of a service on five dimensions. They assess the *credibility* of the service. Strong brand names and guarantees increase consumers' perceptions of service credibility. They also want service providers to be *empathetic* and understand their needs and problems. Services must also be *reliable*. People expect that the service is delivered with consistent quality. People expect services to be *responsive* and to deal with them as individuals. Finally, people judge service quality using the *tangible cues* that surround service provision. Marketers carefully design the physical setting, or servicescape, where the customer receives the service to create particular perceptions. For example, in a store where the lighting is soft, the colour scheme is black, gold, and silver, and background classical music is played, people may perceive that they are receiving high-quality, prestigious service. Conversely, when they enter a store and see bare cement walls, tile floors, and smell popcorn, shoppers are likely to expect discount prices and limited service. Whatever the level of service provided, it is important that the service provider clearly define and communicate that level so that its employees know what they must deliver and customers know what they will get.

Many service companies have invested heavily to develop streamlined and efficient service-delivery systems. They want to ensure that customers will receive consistently high-quality service in every service encounter. Unlike product manufacturers who can adjust their machinery and inputs until everything is perfect, service quality always will vary since quality depends on the interactions between employees and customers. As hard as they try, even the best companies will have an occasional late delivery, burned steak, or grumpy employee. However, although a company cannot always prevent service problems, it can learn to recover from them. And good *service recovery* programs can turn angry customers into loyal ones. In fact, good recovery can win more customer purchasing and loyalty than if things had gone well in the first place.[33]

The first step is to *empower* frontline service employees—to give them the authority, responsibility, and incentives they need to recognize, care about, and tend to customer needs. At Marriott, for example, employees at all levels are given the authority to do whatever it takes to solve guests' problems on the spot while ferreting out the cause of those problems. At the CN Customer Support Centre, representatives are expected to take total ownership for their customers' requests: everything from daily car orders to billing issues. The centre combines high-tech with a human element. Toll-free numbers allow customers to access the centre. As soon as a call comes in, the customer's profile appears on the service representative's computer screen. Customers deal with the same service rep each time they call, providing a sense of continuity. The state-of-the-art communication lets customers save money by giving them information on empty rail cars available throughout the system.[34]

Studies of well-managed service companies show that they share a number of common virtues regarding service quality. They are "*customer obsessed*" and have a history of *top management commitment to quality*. For instance, the Canadian Imperial Bank of Commerce responds to customer telephone messages by the next business day and each branch has a Quality Representative assigned to train and monitor quality standards.

The best service providers also set high service-quality standards. Swissair, for example, aims to have 96 percent or more of its passengers rate its service as good or superior; otherwise, it takes action. A 98 percent accuracy standard may sound good, but using this standard, 64 000 Federal Express packages would be lost each day. Top service companies do not settle merely for "good" service, they aim for 100 percent defect-free service.[35]

The top service firms *watch service performance closely*—both their own and that of competitors. They use methods such as comparison shopping, customer surveys, and suggestion and complaint forms. For example, General Electric sends out 700 000 response cards each year to households who rate their service people's performance.

Good service companies also communicate their concerns about service quality to employees and provide performance feedback. At Federal Express, quality measurements are everywhere. When employees walk in the door in the morning, they see the previous week's on-time percentages. Then, the company's in-house television station gives them detailed breakdowns of what happened yesterday and any potential problems for the day ahead.[36]

Managing Productivity

With their costs rising rapidly, service firms are under great pressure to increase service productivity. They can do so in several ways. The service providers can train current employees better, or they can hire new ones who will work harder or more skilfully for the same pay. Or the service providers can increase the quantity of their service by giving up some quality. Doctors have moved toward handling more patients and giving less time to each. The provider can "industrialize the service" by adding equipment and standardizing production, as in McDonald's assembly-line approach to fast-food retailing. However, companies must avoid pushing productivity so hard that doing so reduces perceived quality. Attempts to industrialize a service or to cut costs can make a service company more efficient in the short run but reduce its longer-run ability to innovate, maintain service quality, or respond to consumer needs and desires.

Leading service providers have found that they can harness the power of technology to improve service quality while reducing costs. For example, many companies have used the Internet to improve customer access to information about their services. Skiers can visit the Whistler Mountain web site (http://www.whistler.net),

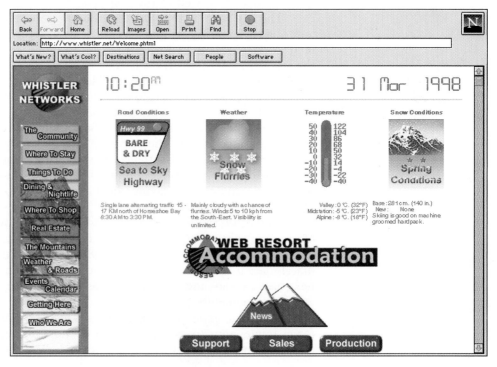

Whistler Mountain improves its customer service through use of its web page.

for instance, and find the answers to a wide range of questions that many skiers ask. Not only can they find out the hours of operation and current snow conditions, but they can also learn when it makes sense to buy a season pass versus buying individual day tickets. Provision of information online not only reduces the service providers' costs, but it also provides customers with more complete, readily accessible answers to their queries.

INTERNATIONAL PRODUCT AND SERVICES MARKETING

International product and service marketers face special challenges. First, they must figure out what products and services to introduce and in which countries. Then, they must decide how much to standardize or adapt their products and services for world markets. On the one hand, companies would like to standardize their offerings. Standardization helps a company to develop a consistent worldwide image. It also lowers manufacturing costs and eliminates duplication of research and development, advertising, and design efforts. On the other hand, consumers around the world differ in their cultures, attitudes, and buying behaviours. And markets vary in their economic conditions, competition, legal requirements, and physical environments. Companies usually must respond to these differences by adapting their product and service offerings. Something as simple as an electrical outlet can create big product problems:

> Those who have travelled across Europe know the frustration of electrical plugs, different voltages, and other annoyances of international travel. . . . Philips, the electrical appliance manufacturer, has to produce 12 kinds of irons to serve just its European market. The problem is that Europe does not have a universal [electrical] standard. The ends of irons bristle with different plugs for different countries. Some have three prongs, others two; prongs protrude straight or angled, round or rectangular, fat, thin, and sometimes sheathed. There are circular plug faces, squares, pentagons, and hexagons. Some are perforated and some are notched. One French plug has a niche like a keyhole; British plugs carry fuses.[37]

Packaging also presents new challenges for international marketers. Packaging issues can be subtle. For example, names, labels, and colours may not translate easily from one country to another. Packaging may also have to be tailored to meet the physical characteristics of consumers in various parts of the world. For instance, soft drinks are sold in smaller cans in Japan to better fit the smaller Japanese hand. Thus, although product and package standardization can produce benefits, companies usually must adapt their offerings to the unique needs of specific international markets.

Service marketing also face special challenges when going global. Some service industries have a long history of international operations. For example, banks had to provide global services in order to meet the foreign exchange and credit needs of their home-country clients wanting to sell overseas. In recent years, many banks have become truly global operations; Germany's Deutsche Bank, for example, has branches in 53 countries.

The travel industry also moved naturally into international operations. North American hotel chains have expanded internationally. Air Canada and Canadian Airlines are forming alliances with other world carriers so they can fly tourists and business travellers around the world. The early worldwide dominance of American Express has now been matched by Visa and MasterCard.

Professional and business services industries such as accounting, engineering, management consulting, and advertising only recently have globalized. The international growth of these firms followed the globalization of the manufacturing companies they serve. For example, as their client companies began to use global marketing and advertising strategies, advertising agencies and other marketing services firms responded by globalizing their own operations.

Retailers are among the latest service businesses to go global. As their home markets become saturated with stores, retailers such as Wal-Mart, Kmart, Toys 'R' Us, Office Depot, Saks Fifth Avenue, and Disney are expanding into faster-growing markets abroad. Japanese retailer Yaohan now operates the largest shopping centre in Asia, the 21-storey Nextage Shanghai Tower in China, and Carrefour of France is the leading retailer in Brazil and Argentina. Asian shoppers now buy North American products in Dutch-owned Makro stores, now Southeast Asia's biggest store group with sales in that region of more than $2.8 billion.[38]

Service companies wanting to operate in other countries are not always welcomed with open arms. Whereas manufacturers usually face straightforward tariff, quota, or currency restrictions when attempting to sell their products in another country, service providers are likely to face more subtle barriers. In some cases, rules and regulations affecting international service firms reflect the host country's traditions. In others, they appear to protect the country's own fledgling service industries from large global competitors with greater resources. In still other cases, however, the restrictions seem to have little purpose other than to make entry difficult for foreign service firms.

A new Turkish law, for example, forbids international accounting firms from bringing capital into the country to set up offices and requires them to use the names of local partners in their marketing rather than their own internationally known company names. In Buenos Aires, an accountant must have the equivalent of a high school education in Argentinean geography and history. In New Delhi, India, international insurance companies are not allowed to sell property and casualty policies to the country's fast-growing business community or life insurance to its huge middle class.[39]

Despite such difficulties, the trend toward growth of global service companies will continue, especially in banking, airlines, telecommunications, and professional services. Today service firms are no longer simply following their manufacturing customers. Instead, they are taking the lead in international expansion.

Summary of Chapter Objectives

A product is more than a simple set of tangible features. In fact, many marketing offers consist of combinations of both tangible goods and service. Offerings range from *pure tangible goods* at one extreme to *pure services* at the other. Each product or service offered to customers can be viewed on three levels. The *core product* consists of the core, problem-solving benefits that consumers seek when they buy a product. The *actual product* exists around the core and includes the quality level, features, design, brand name, and packaging. The *augmented product* is the actual product plus the various services and benefits offered with it, such as warranty, free delivery, installation, and maintenance.

1. **Define *product* and the major classifications of products and services.**

Products encompass more than simply tangible goods. Broadly defined, a *product* is anything that can be offered to a market for attention, acquisition, use, or consumption that might satisfy a want or need. Products include physical objects, services, persons, places, organizations, ideas, or mixes of these entities. Services are products that consist of activities, benefits, or satisfactions offered for sale that are essentially intangible, such as banking, hotel, tax preparation, and home repair services.

Products and services fall into two broad classes based on the types of consumers that use them. *Consumer products*—those bought by final consumers—are usually classified according to consumer shopping habits (convenience products, shopping products, specialty products, and unsought products). *Industrial products*—purchased for further processing or use in conducting a business—are classified according to their cost and the way they enter the production process (materials and parts, capital items, and supplies and services). Other marketable entities—such as organizations, persons, places, and ideas—can also be thought of as products. *Organizations* are marketed to create, maintain, or change the attitudes or behaviour of target audiences toward the organization. *Person marketing* consists of activities undertaken to create, maintain, or change attitudes or behaviour toward particular people. Some places are marketed (through *place marketing*) with the same basic goals. *Idea marketing* involves efforts to market ideas. A specific segment of idea marketing, *social marketing*, consists of the design, implementation, and control of programs seeking to increase the acceptability of a social idea, cause, or practice among a target group.

2. **Describe the roles of product and service branding, packaging, labelling, and product-support services.**

Companies develop strategies for items in their product lines by making decisions about product attributes, branding, packaging, labelling, and product-support services. *Product attribute* decisions involve the quality, features, and design the company will offer. *Branding* decisions include selecting a brand name, garnering brand sponsorship, and developing a brand strategy. *Packaging* provides many key benefits, such as protection, economy, convenience, and promotion. Package decisions often include designing *labels* that identify, describe, and possibly promote the product. Companies also develop *product-support services* that enhance customer service and satisfaction and safeguard against competitors.

3. **Explain the decisions that companies make when developing product lines and mixes.**

Most companies produce a product line rather than a single product. A *product line* is a group of products that are related in function, customer-purchase needs, or distribution channels. In developing a product line strategy, marketers face a number of tough decisions. *Line stretching* involves extending a line downward, upward, or in both directions to occupy a gap that might otherwise be filled by a competitor. In contrast, *line filling* involves adding items within the present range of the line. The set of product lines and items offered to customers by a particular seller comprise the *product mix*. The mix can be described by four dimensions: width, length, depth, and consistency. These dimensions are the tools for developing the company's product strategy.

4. **Identify the four characteristics that affect the marketing of a service.**

As we move toward a *world service economy*, marketers need to know more about marketing services. *Services* are characterized by four key characteristics. First, services are *intangible*—they cannot be seen, tasted, felt, heard, or smelled. Services are also *inseparable* from their service providers. Services are *variable* because their qualtiy depends on the service provider as well as the environment surrounding the service delivery. Finally, services are *perishable*. As a result, they cannot be inventoried, built up, or back ordered. Each characteristic poses problems and marketing requirements. Marketers work to find ways to make the service more tangible, to increase the productivity of providers who are inseparable from their products, to standardize the quality in the face of variability, and to improve demand movements and supply capacities in the face of service perishability.

5. **Discuss the additional marketing considerations that services require.**

Good service companies focus attention on *both* customers and employees. They understand the *service-profit chain* that links service firm profits with employee and customer satisfaction. Services marketing strategy calls not only for external marketing but also for *internal marketing* to motivate employees and *interactive marketing* to create service delivery skills among service providers. To succeed, service marketers must create *competitive differentiation*, offer high *service quality*, and find ways to increase *service productivity*.

Key Terms

Actual product *(p. 266)*
Augmented product *(p. 266)*
Brand *(p. 273)*
Brand equity *(p. 274)*
Brand extension *(p. 280)*
Capital items *(p. 269)*
Co-branding *(p. 279)*
Consumer products *(p. 267)*
Convenience products *(p. 267)*
Core product *(p. 266)*
Industrial products *(p. 268)*
Interactive marketing *(p. 292)*
Internal marketing *(p. 291)*
Line extension *(p. 279)*

Manufacturer's brand
  (or national brand) *(p. 277)*
Materials and parts *(p. 268)*
Multibranding *(p. 280)*
Packaging *(p. 281)*
Packaging concept *(p. 281)*
Private brand (or store brand)
  (p. 277)
Product *(p. 265)*
Product design *(p. 271)*
Product line *(p. 284)*
Product mix (or product
  assortment) *(p. 286)*
Product quality *(p. 271)*

Product-support services *(p. 283)*
Service *(p. 265)*
Service inseparability *(p. 290)*
Service intangibility *(p. 290)*
Service perishability *(p. 290)*
Service variability *(p. 290)*
Shopping products *(p. 267)*
Slotting fees *(p. 277)*
Specialty products *(p. 268)*
Social marketing *(p. 270)*
Supplies and services *(p. 269)*
Unsought products *(p. 268)*

Discussing the Issues

1. List and explain the core, tangible, and augmented products of the education experience that universities offer.

2. What is Intrawest's core, tangible product? How has it augmented this product? What service offerings does it combine with its core product? Has this combination of physical products and services created a competitive advantage for the firm relative to its competitors? Would you buy Intrawest stock given the prediction by David Foot that participation in active sports such as skiing will decline? Are demographics alone sufficient to explain buyer behaviour?

3. In recent years, automakers have tried to reposition many of their brands to the high-quality end of the market. Analyse how well they have succeeded. What else could

they do to change consumers' perceptions of their cars.

4. Evaluate why so many people are willing to pay more for branded products than for unbranded products. What does this tell you about the value of branding?

5. For many years there was one type of Coca-Cola, one type of Tide, and one type of Crest (in mint and regular). Now we find Coke in six or more varieties, Ultra, Liquid, and Unscented Tide, and Crest Gel with sparkles for kids. List some of the issues these line extensions raise for manufacturers, retailers, and consumers.

6. Illustrate how a theatre can deal with the intangibility, inseparability, variability, and perishability of the service it provides. Give specific examples.

Applying the Concepts

1. Different areas of a town may attract different sorts of businesses. (a) Go to your local mall and find the direction kiosk. Look at the map and count the number of retail outlets for each type of consumer good: convenience, shopping, specialty, or unsought goods. (Often the map index is organized into categories that are helpful for this task.) (b) Drive down the road that serves as you local commercial "strip" and do a quick count in the same categories. (c) Calculate

what percentage of businesses fall into each category for the two areas. Do you see any differences? If so, why do you think these differences exist?

2. Describe a service experience that left you highly satisfied. Think of another service experience that left you dissatisfied. Using what you learned by comparing these two experiences, develop a list of recommendations that would help marketing managers better manage service quality.

References

1. 1997 Annual Report, Intrawest, Vancouver, B.C.

2. 1997 Annual Report, Intrawest, Vancouver, B.C.

3. Ann Gibbon, "Big Seens as Best for Ski Resorts," *Globe and Mail*, September 17, 1996, pp. B1, B4; Patti Summerfield, 'Special Report: Top Database Marketers: Top in Hotels and Tourism: Intrawest Delivers Multi-resort Message," *Strategy: The Canadian Marketing Report*, July 21, 1997, p. DR12; Steve Threndyle, "Turning the Corner: Canada's Ski Industry Grows for the Future," *Supplement to the Financial Post Magazine*, October 1996, pp. 1–8; Konrad Yarabuski, "Intrawest Plans Peak Success," *Globe and Mail*, September 29, 1997, pp. B1, B11; Erica Zlomislic, "Whistler Targets American Skiers," *Strategy: The Canadian Marketing Report*, August 18, 1997, p. 8.

4. De Brentani, Ulrike, and Emmanuel Ragot, "Developing New Business-to-Business Professional Services: What Factors Impact Performance?, *Industrial Marketing Management*, November 1996, pp. 517-30.

5. See Roland T. Rust, Anthony J. Zahorik, and Timothy L. Keiningham, "Return on Quality (ROQ): Making Service Quality Financially Accountable," *Journal of Marketing*, April 1995, pp. 58–70; Valerie A. Zeithamel, Leonard L. Berry, and A. Parasuraman, "The Behavioral Consequences of Service Quality," *Journal of Marketing*, April 1996, pp. 31–46; and Otis Port, "The Baldrige's Other Reward," *Business Week*, March 10, 1997, p. 75.

6. Joseph Weber, "A Better Grip on Hawking Tools," *Business Week*, June 5, 1995, p. 99. For more on product design, see Peter H. Bloch, "Seeking the Ideal Form: Product Design and Consumer Response," *Journal of Marketing*, July 1995, pp. 16–29.

7. Kurt Badenhausen, "Blind Faith," *Financial World*, July 8, 1996, pp. 51–65. Also see David A. Aaker, *Managing Brand Equity* (New York: The Free Press, 1991); Terry Lefton and Weston Anson, "How Much Is Your Brand Worth?" *Brandweek*, January 26, 1996, pp. 43–44; and Don E. Schultz, "Brand Equity Has Become Oh So Fashionable," *Marketing News*, March 31, 1997, p. 9.

8. Emily DeNitto, "They Aren't Private Labels Anymore—They're Brands," *Advertising Age*, September 13, 1993, p. 8; and Warren Thayer, "Loblaws Exec Predicts: Private Labels to Surge," *Frozen Food Age*, May 1996, p. 1.

9. Jennifer Lawrence, "Brands Beware, Wal-Mart Adds Giant House Label," *Advertising Age*, April 5, 1993, pp. 1, 45.

10. Emily DeNitto, "They Aren't Private Labels Anymore—They're Brands," *Advertising Age*, September 13, 1993, p. 8; Marina Strauss, "Oshawa Group Plans to Fire Up Private-Label War," *Globe and Mail*, June 3, 1994, B1.

11. Marina Strauss, "Oshawa Group Plans to Fire Up Private-Label War," *Globe and Mail*, June 3, 1994, pp. B1-B2.

12. Bud Jorgensen, "Cott Cashes In, Makes Enemies," *Globe and Mail*, January 8, 1994, pp. B1, B6.

13. See Chip Walker, "What's in a Brand?" *American Demographics,* February 1991, pp. 54–56; Emily DeNitto, "No End to Private Label March," *Advertising Age*, November 1, 1993, p. S6; Patrick Oster, "The Eurosion of Brand Loyalty," *Business Week,* July 19, 1993, p. 22; and Marcia Mogelonsky, "When Stores Become Brands," *American Demographics,* February 1995, pp. 32–38.

14. See Silvia Sansoni, "Gucci, Armani, and . . . John Paul II?" *Business Week,* May 13, 1996, p. 61; Kate Fitzgerald, "License to Sell," *Advertising Age*, February 12, 1996, pp. S1–S10; and Cyndee Miller, "Seuss Characters Leap From Page into Licensing World," *Marketing News*, April 14, 1997, p. 2.

15. Kim Cleland, "Multimarketer Melange an Increasingly Tasty Option on the Store Shelf," *Advertising Age,* May 2, 1994, p. S10. Also see Maxine S. Lans, "To Enjoin or Not to Enjoin: A Tough Question," *Marketing News,* February 13, 1995, p. 5.

16. For more on line extensions, see Kevin Lane Keller and David A. Aaker, "The Effects of Sequential Introduction of Line Extensions," *Journal of Marketing Research*, February 1992, pp. 35–50; and Srinivas K. Reddy, Susan L. Holak, and Subodh Bhat, "To Extend or Not to Extend: Success Determinants of Line Extensions," *Journal of Marketing Research,* May 1994, pp. 243–262; James Pollock, "Between The Lines," *Marketing*, April 17, 1995, p. 14.

17. See Bill Abrams, "Marketing," *Wall Street Journal*, May 20, 1982, p. 33; and Bernice Kanner, "Package Deals," *New York*, August 22, 1988, pp. 267–68.

18. Robert M. McMath, "Chock Full of (Pea)nuts, *American Demographics*, April 1997, p. 60.

19. See Ira Teinowitz, "Brand Proliferation Attacked," *Advertising Age,* May 10, 1993, pp. 1, 49; and Jennifer Lawrence, "P&G Strategy: Build on Brands," *Advertising Age*, August 23, 1993, pp. 3, 31.

20. Jo Marney, "More Than a Pretty Surface," *Marketing*, April 10, 1995, p. 25.

21. See Bill Abrams, "Marketing," *Wall Street Journal,* May 20, 1982, p. 33; and Bernice Kanner, "Package Deals," *New York,* August 22, 1988, pp. 267–268.

22. Wallace Immen, "How to Judge a Food by Its Cover," *Globe and Mail,* May 31, 1994, p. A16.

23. See Ronald Henkoff, 'Service Is Everybody's Business," *Fortune*, June 27, 1994, pp. 48–60; Adrian Palmer and Catherine Cole, *Services Marketing: Principles and Practice* (Englewood Cliffs, NJ: Prentice Hall, 1995), pp. 56–60; and Fanglan Du, Paula Mergenhagen, and Marlene Lee, "The Future of Services," *American Demographics*, November 1995, pp. 30–47.

24. "Presto! The Convenience Industry: Making Life a Simpler," *Business Week*, April 27, 1987, p. 86; also see Ronald Henkoff, "Piety, Profits, and Productivity," *Fortune*, June 1992, pp. 84–85.

25. See Ronald Henkoff, "Service Is Everybody's Business," *Fortune*, June 27, 1994, pp. 48–60.

26. For more on definitions and classifications of services, see John E. Bateson, *Managing Services Marketing:*

Text and Readings (Hinsdale, IL: Dryden Press, 1989); and Christopher H. Lovelock, *Services Marketing* (Englewood Cliffs, NJ: Prentice Hall, 1991).

27. CN promotional brochure.

28. Terry Bullick, "No-Frills Airline Takes Flight in Western Canada," *Marketing*, February 19, 1996, p. 2.

29. See James L. Heskett, Thomas O. Jones, Gary W. Loveman, W. Earl Sasser, Jr., and Leonard A. Schlesinger, "Putting the Service-Profit Chain to Work," *Harvard Business Review*, March–April, 1994, pp. 164–174.

30. For more reading on internal and interactive marketing, see Christian Gronroos, "A Service Quality Model and Its Marketing Implications," *European Journal of Marketing*, Vol. 18, No. 4, 1984, pp. 36–44; and Leonard Berry, Edwin F. Lefkowith, and Terry Clark, "In Services, What's in a Name?" *Harvard Business Review*, September–October 1988, pp. 28–30.

31. For excellent discussion on defining and measuring service quality, see A. Parasuraman, Valerie A. Zeithaml, and Leonard L. Berry, "A Conceptual Model of Service Quality and Its Implications for Future Research," *Journal of Marketing*, Fall 1985, pp. 41–50; Zeithaml, Parasuraman, and Berry, *Delivering Service Quality: Balancing Customer Perceptions and Expectations* (New York: The Free Press, 1990); J. Joseph Cronin, Jr. and Steven A. Taylor, "Measuring Service Quality: A Reexamination and Extension," *Journal of*
Marketing, July 1992, pp. 55–68; and Parasuraman, Zeithaml, and Berry, "Reassessment of Expectations as a Comparison Standard in Measuring Service Quality: Implications for Further Research," *Journal of Marketing*, January 1994, pp. 111–124.

32. John Paul Newport, "American Express: Service That Sells," *Fortune*, November 20, 1989. Also see Frank Rose, "Now Quality Means Service Too," *Fortune*, April 22, 1991, pp. 97–108.

33. Christopher W. L. Hart, James L. Heskett, and W. Earl Sasser, Jr., "The Profitable Art of Service Recovery," *Harvard Business Review*, July–August 1990, pp. 148–156.

34. CN promotional brochure.

35. See James L. Heskett, W. Earl Sasser, Jr., and Christopher W. L. Hart, *Service Breakthroughs* (New York: Free Press, 1990).

36. Barry Farber and Joyce Wycoff, "Customer Service: Evolution and Revolution," *Sales & Marketing Management*, May 1991, pp. 44–51.

37. Philip Cateora, *International Marketing*, 8th ed. (Homewood, IL, Irwin, 1993), p. 270.

38. Carla Rapoport, "Retailers Go Global," *Fortune*, February 20, 1995, pp. 102–108.

39. Lee Smith, "What's at Stake in the Trade Talks," *Fortune*, August 27, 1990, pp. 76–77.

Company Case 8

THE SKISAILER (R)

Early in 1987, David Varilek was given the bad news about the worldwide sales of his invention, the Skisailer. The management at Mistral, the company that had invested in David's innovation, informed him that the first-year sales of Skisailer had failed to match the target and that the future of the product was in doubt. Only 708 Skisailers had been sold in the first season the product was on sale. Mistral, which manufacturered and marketed the product worldwide, had already invested more than half a million dollars in the project. The management was seriously considering dropping the product from its line next year.

Realizing that such an initial setback could jeopardize the future of his four-year-old invention, in March 1987 David asked a group of MBA students at a leading international school of management in Switzerland to study the market potential for Skisailer and recommend what needed to be done to revive sales. The students had recently completed the first phase of the project. They had presented David with their findings and the 23-year-old inventor was reviewing the information.

THE INVENTION

Skisailer was based on a concept that combined downhill skiing and windsurfing in a new sport: skisailing. As a Swiss native, David Varilek considered himself "born on skis." However, he had always been frustrated by not being able to ski on the flat snow fields that surrounded his home in the winter season.

In 1983, in his own garage, David invented a connection bar that could be fixed onto regular skis while still allowing them to be directed with great flexibility. A windsurfing rig, consisting of a connecting bar and a sail, could then be installed on the connection bar and, with enough wind, flat snow surfaces could become great fun for skiing. The idea was subsequently patented under the Swiss law. A major feature of the invention was that the Skisailer's unique design also allowed "windskiers" to use regular downshill skis and almost any type of windsurfing rig, an innovation that limited the buyer's expense. The connection bar and the sail were easy to instal. Lateral clamps used for attaching the connection bar to the skis did not damage them in any way except for small grooves on the side of each ski. Only 5 centimeters (2 inches) of the ski's length were held rigid and the rest retained normal flexibility. Safety had also been an important consideration when developing the Skisailer; three self-releasing safety mechanisms were installed on the product.

The Skisailer could be used on either smooth slopes or flat surfaces. The ideal surface for skisailing was on the kind of hard-packed snow usually found on groomed ski slopes, but the Skisailer could also be used on ice, where it could achieve speeds of up to 100 km/h. Skisailing in deep snow or slightly uphill required stronger wind. For use at high speeds, a safety helmet was recommended.

According to David Varilek, skisailing was as much fun as windsurfing even though it had to be done in cold weather. "For identical sensations, skisailing is easier to learn and handle than windsurfing," David claimed. "You can get on and get off the Skisailer easily, and you are always on your feet. Another great thing with the Skisailer is that you can take advantage of the terrain to perform the same kind of loopings as on sea waves. The Skisailers is a great vehicle for discovering variety in the surroundings."

MISTRAL WINDSURFING AG

In 1987, Mistral Windsurfing AG was a company affiliated with the ADIA Group, ADIA, a $1 billion conglomerate with headquarters in Lausanne, Switzerland, which had its activities centered around ADIA Interim, a company providing temporary personnel to companies around the world.

In 1980, ADIA had acquired Mistral as part of its diversification strategy. The acquisition was seen as an opportunity to enter a rapidly growing industry. Consistency in marketing and product policy over the past 10 years had made Mistral a leader in the worldwide windsurfing industry. This success was grounded in technological competence, permanent innovation, high quality standards, a selective international distribution policy, and strong financial backing. Thus, in a fiercely competitive market for windsurfing equipment, characterized by the rise and fall of brands and manufacturers, Mistral was occupying a leading position. To Martin Pestalozzi, the president of ADIA, the Skisailer represented a good opportunity to extend Mistral's product line at a time when Mistral management was increasingly concerned about the future of the windsurf market.

MISTRAL AND THE WINDSURF MARKET

The fathers of the modern windsurf were two Californians, Hoyle Schweitzer and James Drake, who had developed the concept and registered the Windsurfer brand.

They had applied for and received a patent in 1970 for their device, which was a cross between a surfboard and a sailboat.

In the early 1970s, Schweitzer bought out Drake and developed his firm, Windsurfing International, from a living-room operation into a multimillion-dollar corporation with branches in six countries. Due to its North American patents, Windsurfing International was able to hold a virtual monopoly in the United States and Canada until 1979 when a number of other firms entered the market.

Meanwhile, competition in the European windsurfing equipment market was years ahead of North America. First introduced to the European market by Ten Cate, a Dutch firm, windsurfing enjoyed an unprecedented growth, particularly in France and Germany. Even as the industry matured in the mid-1980s, it maintained growth in terms of dollar volume, though not in units. Interest in windsurfing had grown from a small pool of enthusiasts to a large and growing population, an estimated two to three million people internationally.

Established in 1976 in Bassersdorf near Zurich (Switzerland), Mistral rapidly won an international reputation among windsurfers. Its success was enhanced by two promotional strategies. First, from the start, Mistral had signed up Robby Naish, a young Californian who had won all the major distinctions and titles in this sport. Using Mistral equipment, Robby Naish had become the 1977 World Champion at age 12 and had dominated this sport ever since. In 1986, he won the world title for the tenth time in a row. Second, Mistral had promoted its brand by supplying several hundred windsurfs free of charge to such leisure organizations as Club Méditerranée that gave the brand visibility around the world.

Mistral also enjoyed an advantage over other windsurf manufacturers by concentrating on the upper price and quality range of the market. Worldwide, Mistral's equipment was considered the best. Robby Naish's name and the high quality and reliability of Mistral's products had helped build an extensive network of distributors in 30 countries. In 1980, the company had its own subsidiary in the United States, where it generated about one-third of its global sales and market share. Mistral was also directly represented in a number of European countries such as France, Germany and the Benelux. For the rest of the world, Mistral used exclusive agents who were responsible for selling Mistral products in specific regions.

RECENT MARKET DEVELOPMENTS IN WINDSURFING

Recently, a number of factors had combined to dampen the sales of windsurfs in the U.S. market. Patent infringement fights had led to the forced withdrawal of Bic and Tiga, both French manufacturers, from the market. With a total sales of 16 000 units, the two companies were among the major brands in the United States. Meanwhile, a number of European manufacturers had gone bankrupt, thus reducing even further the supply of and marketing expenditures on windsurfing equipment. Market saturation had also contributed to the decline of sales from 73 000 units in 1985 to 62 000 in 1986.

In Europe, where windsurfing had grown at spectacular rates over the years, the market was showing signs of a slowdown. According to the French market research group ENERGY, windsurfing equipment sales in France had risen from less than 600 units in 1974 to more than 115 000 units in early 1980s. However, cool weather conditions as well as general market saturation had reduced French sales to 65 000 units in 1986. In Germany, the second-largest market after France, sales had also declined to below 60 000 units from the high levels of the early 1980s. Sales had levelled off in Italy at around 35 000 units, in Holland at 45 000 units, and in Switzerland at 15 000 units.

European sales were dominated by European brands. In France, for example, Bic and Tiga together accounted for 45 000 sales. Mistral was the top imported brand. In Germany, Klepper was the leading local brand; Mistral was a distant fourth in market share. In 1986, the distribution of Mistral's global sales of 45 620 units was the United States, 25%; Europe, 30%; and the rest of the world, 45%. Windsurfing equipment accounted for 60% of the company's $52 million sales, while the rest was divided between sportswear (20%) and spare parts and accessories (20%).

THE SKISAILER AND MISTRAL'S DIVERSIFICATION POLICY

Mistral Windsurfing AG had contacted David Varilek at the beginning of 1984 after ADIA management learned about the Skisailer from a four-page article in a major Swiss magazine. David Varilek was interested in establishing a relationship with Mistral because the company was the world leader in windsurfing equipment.

The Skisailer seemed an appropriate product diversification for Mistral. The Skisailer could also fit in with the new line of winter sportswear and other ski-related products that Mistral's management was planning to develop. Mistral had full support from ADIA to launch the project.

In the spring of 1984, a contract for development, manufacturing, and distribution of the Skisailer was formally signed between David Varilek and Mistral. For the duration of the agreement, all Skisailer patent and trademark rights would be transferred to Mistral, but David would serve as technical adviser to the company and would receive in return a 2% royalty on sales. It was also agreed that David would demonstrate the Skisailer in competitions and exhibitions where Mistral was participating. Should total sales fall short of 5000 units by the end of 1986, either party could terminate the agreement, with trademarks and patents reverting back to David Varilek. Mistral could also counter any competitive offer made to David, a "first right of refusal."

INTRODUCING THE SKISAILER

During the summer of 1984, two prototypes of the Skisailer were developed at Mistral for presentation in November at ISPO, the largest European sports exhibition held annually in Munich, Germany. Between May and November 1984, the engineers developed several innovations that were added to the Skisailer. For example, the connecting bar and mounting blocks were strengthened to resist shocks and low temperatures. The equipment was also modified to accommodate the Mistral windsurf sailing rig.

In Munich at ISPO the Skisailer was widely acclaimed as a truly innovative product that would certainly win public enthusiasm. However, at this early stage of development, the product still lacked promotional support. No pamphlet, video, or pictures had been developed to present the product and educate potential users. David thought that the pictures used to introduce the product to Mistral's distributors were not attractive enough to trigger interest and buying. Nevertheless, some distributors liked the product and placed immediate orders.

The formal launch of Skisailer got under way in 1986. Mistral produced 2000 Skisailers, consisting of a mast foot, sail (available from its standard windsurf line), and the connecting bar. They were to be distributed worldwide through the company's network of wholesalers and independent sports shops in large and medium-sized cities. For example, in Lausanne, Switzerland, a city of 250 000 inhabitants with 30 skishops and three windsurf equipment stores, Skisailer was sold in three locations. Of the three stores, two specialized in ski equipment and the third sold windsurfing products.

Skisailer was priced at $410 retail; the price included the bar connection and its mounting blocks, but excluded the sail and mast, which cost an additional $590. Retail margins on the Skisailer and its rig were set at 35%. The wholesale margins were also 35%. The wholesale margins were also 35%. Skisailer cost Mistral $85 per unit to produce and ship to distributors; the cost for the sailing rig was around $200.

It seemed to David that the 1986 promotional budget of $15 000 set for Skisailer was too low. Mistral management had already turned down a $35 000 proposal from David to produce a promotional video showing Skisailer in action. Nevertheless, David decided to arrange for the shooting of such a video on his own at Mammoth Lake, California. Mistral later refunded David the $10 000 that the video had cost him.

As of early 1987, Mistral had invested more than half a million dollars in Skisailer:

Engineering and tooling	$214 000
Other costs	74 000
Development costs	**288 000**
Inventory: Assembled and spares	
At central warehouse	180 000
At distributors	68 000
Total	**$536 000**

MARKET RESEARCH FINDINGS

Because of his concern about the future of the Skisailer, David had commissioned the group of MBA students to study the global market for Skisailer and report on their findings. By early fall, the students had completed the first phase of their study, which dealt with estimating the market potential for Skisailer, competing products, ski market developments, and a survey of buyers, retailers, and wholesalers. A summary of the findings follows.

POTENTIAL MARKET

Based on interviews with buyers of the Skisailer, the team had learned that the potential customers were likely to be those who did both skiing and windsurfing. Building on industry reports suggesting a total worldwide population of 2 million windsurfers and 30 million skiers, the team estimated that a maximum of 60% of windsurfers, or a total of 1.2 million individuals, were also skiers. The "realizable market" for the Skisailer, according to the MBA students, was far below this maximum, however. They identified at least four "filters," which together reduced the realizable market potential to a fraction of the maximum:

Filter 1: Customer type. As a relatively new sport, Skisailer appealed to a group of enthusiasts whom the MBA students referred to as "innovators." Their study suggested that these buyers were in the 15 to 25 age bracket, liked sports but, for the most part, could not afford the price tag of the Skisailer. The next most likely group of buyers, called "early adopters," were older, less sporty, and more image conscious. The team believed that sufficient penetration of the first segment was necessary before the second group showed any interest in the new product.

Filter 2: Location. Users of the Skisailer reported that ideal skisailing conditions, such as flat ice- or snow-covered fields, were not always accessible. This location factor, the team believed, tended to reduce the potential for the product.

Filter 3: Climate. Climate, according to the MBA students, was another inhibiting factor. The Skisailer required not only suitable snow or ice, but also a good wind. The minimum required wind speed was around 20 kilometres/hour. The study identified a number of regions as meeting both the needed snow and wind conditions: Scandinavia and central Europe, certain parts of North America, and parts of Southern Australia.

Filter 4: Competing products. Four similar products were identified but, according to the student report, all lacked brand image, wide distribution, and product sophistication. Although information on competing products was scanty, the students had assembled the following information from different sources:

Brand (origin)	Retail Price	Total Units Sold	Main Sales Area
Winterboard (Finland)	$395	4000	Finland, United States
Ski Sailer (Australia)	$90	3500	Australia, United States
ArticSail (Canada)	$285	3000	Canada, United States
Ski Sailer (United States)	$220	300	United States

Based on their initial estimate of the maximum size of the potential market, as well as the limiting effects of the four filters, the students arrived at an estimate of 20 000 units as the total realizable market for Skisailer. This volume, they believed, could grow by as much as 10% per year. (Refer to Exhibit 2 for an estimate of the market potential and Exhibit 3 for the level of sales the students believed Skisailer could achieve over the next five years.)

Exhibit 2   *Skisailer Market Potential*

Market	Size	%	Filters
Potential market	1.2 million	100	Customer type
Available market	800 000	66	Location, climate
Qualified market	80 000	7	Indirect competition (monoski, skates, etc.)
Served market	40 000	3.5	Direct competition (Winterboard, ArticSail, etc.)
Realizable market	20 000	1.7	Customer type

COMPETING PRODUCTS

Winterboard

Winterboard, a light windsurfing board with skis, had been invented in Finland. It could be used on both ice and snow, and its performance was said to be impressive. Some rated the Winterboard as the best-performing windski after the Skisailer. In terms of sales, Winterboard had been the most successful windski

Exhibit 3   *Skisailer Achievable Sales Estimate*

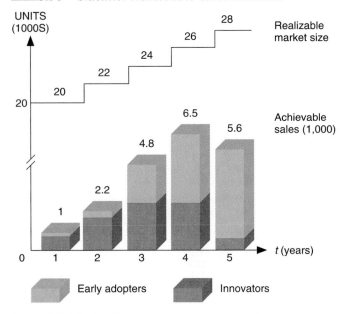

Source: MBA Student Report.

product. Over the last five years, 4000 units have been sold, mainly in Scandinavia and the United States, in regular sports shops. Winterboard was being sold at a retail price of $395, excluding the sailing rig. Retail margins were at 40%. The skis were already integrated into the board and did not need to be purchased as an extra.

According to the research team, Winterboard's management believed that prices, retail margins, and advertising expenditures were relatively unimportant in their marketing strategy. The key to success was organizing events, because people wanted sportive social gathering on weekends in the winter. When they had to go out snowsailing in the cold by themselves, they quickly lost interest.

Australian-made Ski Sailer

This product was essentially a simple bar with a mastfoot on it that could be attached to normal ski boots and used with either conventional skis or roller skates. The Ski Sailer had an equalizing slide and joint mechanism, so maneuvers such as parallel turns, jump turns, and snowplowing were possible. Any sailing rig could be fitted to the Ski Sailer's mast post.

The U.S. distributor for this product reported cumulative sales of about 3000 units (30% through ski shops, 70% through surf shops) at a retail price of $90 each. But he admitted that he had lost interest in the product when he realized that only customers who were tough and resistant to the cold enjoyed windsurfing in the wintertime. This meant a much smaller customer base than for his other leisure and sportswear products.

ArticSail Board

This product was essentially a W-shaped surfboard for use on snow, ice, or water. It was distributed by Plastiques L.P.A. Ltd. in Mansonville, Quebec, Canada, approximately 70 kilometres from the U.S.–Canadian border.

The ArticSail was especially designed for snow and ice, but it could also be used on water, in which case the rear filler plates would be replaced by two ailerons, also supplied with the board. Adjustable footstraps, included with the board, also had to be repositioned for use on water. The product was made of a special plastic, usable at both normal and very low temperatures. The producer warned users to watch for objects that could damage the underside of the sled.

The company reported a cumulative sales of approximately 3000 units (600 estimated for the winter of 1987–1988), mostly in Canada, at a retail price of $285 (including a 38% retail margin). Promotion expenses were about 15% on Canadian and U.S. sales, mainly spent on a two-person team demonstrating at skisailing resorts.

American-made Ski Sailer

Yet another Ski Sailer had been invented by a young Californian, Carl Meinberg. The American Ski Sailer also used a small board mounted on skis and was similar to the product developed by David Varilek. On his own, the inventory had sold about 50 Ski Sailers retailing at $220 each. During the winter season, Carl Meinberg toured a number of ski resorts, demonstrating the Ski Sailer; he spent the rest of the year selling his invention.

RECENT DEVELOPMENTS IN THE WORLD SKI MARKET

As background to their study, the research team also obtained information on the ski market. The 1986 sales of downhill (also called alpine) and cross-country skis are given in Exhibit 4.

The total world alpine skiing population was estimated at 30 million people in 1987. Competition in the ski market was intensive, and production capacity exceeded demand by an estimated 25% to 30% in 1987. Prices for skis were under pressure and retailers used discounts to build traffic. Retail profits were mostly made on sales of accessories and skiwear.

In distribution, specialty shops were losing market share to the large chains. Production was concentrated, with seven manufacturers controlling 80% of the market. The falling exchange rate for the U.S. dollar had put the large European producers such as Fischer and Kneissel at a disadvantage in the U.S. market.

Marketing skis depended heavily on successes in world championships and the image associated with the winning skis. In the mid-1980s, customers in the United

Exhibit 4 *World Market of Alpine and Cross-country Skis: 1985–1986 Season*

Ski Sales		Pairs Sold
Alpine		
Austria, Switzerland, Germany		1 450 000
Rest of Europe		1 550 000
United States and Canada		1 600 000
Japan		1 100 000
Other countries		300 000
	Total	6 000 000
Cross-country		
Austria, Switzerland, Germany		700 000
Scandinavia		800 000
Rest of Europe		400 000
United States and Canada		750 000
Other countries		150 000
	Total	2 800 000

States appeared to be losing interest in skiing, but these signs had not been observed in Europe and Japan, where the sport remained popular at a stable level.

A new innovation in skiing was the snowboard, a product with increasing popularity among younger customers. A snowboard was essentially a single large ski with two ski bindings positioned in a similar way as the footstraps on a windsurf.

The board had been available in the United States for many years, but had only recently been introduced in Europe. Snowboard's worldwide sales had doubled every year, reaching an estimated 40 000 in the 1986 season. One U.S. manufacturer, Burton, accounted for 50% of the market. Many manufacturers of winter products had taken advantage of the opportunity and had started producing their own versions of the snowboard. The product was very popular in the European distribution channels, and expectations for further growth were high.

BUYERS' SURVEY

The research team had interviewed a small number of Skisailer customers in Germany, Austria, the Benelux countries, the United States and Canada. Highlights of their comments on the advantages and disadvantages of the Skisailer follow:

Advantages of the Product

- Sure, skisurfing in winter is great; it's a lot of fun.
- You can do quick maneuvers, nice turns, beautiful power turns, and fast changes of the grips. It (the Skisailer) gives a good opportunity to train for windsurfing, as you have to drive the way you surf—with the pressure on the inner ski.
- I did not have any problem with turns.

- It is not difficult to learn if you have some feeling for sailing.
- It simulates surfing in your backyard.
- It is the right device if you want to do something on Sunday afternoon (with no time to drive somewhere in your car).
- Fun, different, new, good.
- It is the only thing with a mountain touch that you can use on the plain.
- It turns. That makes it much more fun than the other products on the market. You can do jives, curve jives, jumps . . . it is close to sailing a shore boat . . . it's a lot of fun.
- If the conditions are ideal, it's a lot of fun.

Disadvantages of the Product

- The feet get twisted; sailing on the wind requires exceptional twisting of the legs and knees.
- Both of the white caps at the end of the bar came off and it was virtually impossible to get spare parts.
- Difficult in heavy snow.
- Difficult to find the perfect conditions.
- You use it three or four times a season. For this, the price is too high.
- It is uncomfortable to use. You have to loosen up your boots; otherwise, the rim of the shoe cuts into your twisted leg.
- If the snow is too deep, you cannot use it. What you want is strong wind.
- The price is too high.
- My problem is that there is hardly any wind in winter.
- In the beginning, I was getting stiff in the unnatural position and my knees hurt, but later I got more relaxed and with time you have a lot of fun.
- In mid-winter, it is too cold to use it; spring is ideal.

RETAILERS' OPINIONS OF THE MISTRAL SKISAILER

A dozen retailers of the Skisailer—in Germany, Canada, Austria, and France—were also surveyed. Highlights of their comments follow:

Advantages of the Product

- You could sell a lot of them in the first year, but I do not see it as the absolute "barnstormer."
- It is a first-year novelty.
- It is a lot of fun in the snow . . . and for people with a lot of money. It is a new gimmick.
- It combines two favourite sports . . . skiing and windsurfing.
- It is better than all self-built products . . . you have full movability.
- Easy to use. It is an original idea.
- You can use your ski, it is flexible and easy to store.
- Very thoroughly constructed, very stable.

Disadvantages of the Product

- Unhappy product. Usable only under specific weather conditions.
- It is only a fad.
- You just don't drive with your ski to a lake and try it on the ice.
- Maybe it sells better in a winter shop.
- Your position on the skis is abnormal—the snowboard is a better alternative.
- We do not think that it will be a fast-turning product. . . .
- Impossible to sell—nobody tried it.
- In my environment, there is no space to do it, no lakes, no fields.
- For a backyard product, the price is too high. Even Mistral's good image doesn't help. Maybe this will change if the product is better known.
- Customers watched the video with enthusiasm, but when they learned the price, enthusiasm was nil. We are offering our last piece now at a discount of 40%.
- If you ski and windsurf, your hobbies cost you a lot of money. Often the early user is the sportive freak with a low income. How will you convince him about the product?

DISTRIBUTORS' COMMENTS

The research team interviewed Mistral distributors in 10 different countries in Europe and North America. Highlights of comments from five distributors follow:

Europe

- We first learned about the Skisailer at ISPO in Munich and ordered some.
- From Mistral we got some folders and the video. If you see it on the video, you want to use the Skisailer right away.
- We did not support the retailers very much because we felt that the Skisailer's marketing was not done professionally from the beginning. For instance, Skisailer deliveries were late.
- The product would have potential if the price were lower and the promotion were done professionally all the way through.
- We bought the Skisailer, which is good for use in our winter climate, after Mistral contacted us in 1985.
- The product is expensive and not really functional.
- Promotion was not good at all, only a few folders and a video, which was not free of charge. When there were product breakdowns, spare parts were not available.
- A Finnish competitor now has captured the market with a product that looks like a surfboard with two skis fitted into it. We have the right places for skisailing here!

- We used all our contracts and spent approximately $7500 in mid-1987 to promote this product on television.
- The retail price is too high for a product to be used only a few weekends in the winter.
- The snowboard, especially made for surfing on ski slopes, is much more fashionable.
- Surf and ski shops make higher margins on clothing and accessories that are sold in larger quantities.
- You don't create a product first and then look for the market; this is the wrong way around. The Skisailer is more a product for Scandinavia and similar regions in America or Canada.
- We didn't know the product but found the demonstration film to be convincing. Therefore, we organized ski resort demonstrations in the French Alps at racing events where there are many spectators. We also pushed about 40 Skisailers in several retail shops.
- For this product, finding suitable locations where you can have a training session with wind and snow is necessary.
- We estimate that the retailers have sold about half their inventory, but we do not want to get more involved and have the rest sent back to us. Retailers are looking for customer demand, which is lacking.

North America

- I cannot see further sales of the Skisailer without more product support. At low temperatures the rubber joints failed, but when we asked for replacements, there was no reply from Mistral. In the end, we had to strip other Skisailers to get the spare parts.
- We have good skisailing conditions (in South Ontario/Quebec) and a group of interested enthusiasts here. The product has been promoted to thousands of people! The folder and video are very good.
- On a trade show in Toronto, the product was well received except for the price, which is a problem.

CONCLUSION

In reviewing the research team's report, David was searching for clues that could explain the Skisailer's poor performance in its first selling season. Was it the product design that needed further refinement? Or the Skisailer's price, which was perceived by some as being high? Was the absence of high promotional support, which he always suspected to be a problem, a key factor? Or maybe Mistral's selective distribution was the core issue? What else could explain why his invention had failed to match everybody's expectations?

Country	UNIT SALES		
	To Distributors	To Retailers	To End Users
United States and Canada	233	98	45
Germany	250	50	10
Switzerland	42	30	1
France	56	40	20
Benelux	60	0	0
Others	67	12	4
Total shipped	708	230	80

An additional piece of information had heightened the need for immediate action. David had just received the final sales and inventory figures for the Skisailer from Mistral; while 708 units had been sold to the trade, only 80 units had been bought at retail.

David knew that Mistral management was about to review the future of the Skisailer. He feared that without a convincing analysis and action plan from him, the Skisailer would be dropped from Mistral's line. He was therefore impatiently waiting for the MBA research team's recommendations based on the data already collected.

QUESTIONS:

1. What type of product is the Skisailer? To whom does it appeal? Has the company properly identified the target market?

2. Define the main elements of the marketing program for the Skisailer. What are the programs strengths and weaknesses? What obstacles have limited the product's success?

3. Evaluate the research done by the MBA team. Do you agree with their methods and the conclusions arising from their study? How confident are you about the estimates of the product's market potential?

4. What are David's options? What criteria would you use to assess the various options? What should David do? Why have you made this recommendation?

Source: This case was written by Professors Dominique Turpin and Kamran Kashani as a basis for class discussion rather than to illustrate either effective or ineffective handling of an administrative situation. © Copyright 1991 by the International Institute for Management Development. Reprinted with permission.

Video Case 8
PORTELLO:
REPOSITIONING FOR GROWTH

In an industry dominated by such large companies as Coca-Cola and Pepsi, is there still room for small players in the soft-drink industry? Raj Rajerdiani believes so. He obtained the Canadian rights to a British soft drink called Portello, a beverage that has been sold around the world for more than 100 years in places such as the United Kingdom, India, Guyana, and Somalia. With just $30 000 as his start-up capital and an office in his basement, Raj started Bay Hill Impex, the company that would sell Portello in Canada. Within a short time the business became a family venture, employing his daughter, Natasha, his son, Neil, and his son-in-law, Amar.

Initially, Raj defined his target market as new immigrants to Canada since he believed that newcomers to Canada are often interested in finding some of the products they enjoyed in their homelands. Consequently, Raj established distribution agreements with small, ethnic grocery stores in the Toronto area whose clientele was consistent with his target market. This strategy was moderately successful: annual sales reached $750 000. But Raj believed that this market was limited and that true growth for his company would only be achieved by capturing larger markets. To broaden the target market and make the product available in mainstream distribution channels, he initiated discussions with some supermarkets, hoping to secure distribution arrangements.

In another attempt to reach additional target markets, Natasha and Neil tried to distribute Portello in nightclubs. They devised a cross-promotion strategy with a dance-format radio station that put the station's logo on the label of every bottle of Portello. In return, Portello received free advertising on the station. The promotion was ideal from Bay Hill's perspective since it didn't involve any additional costs. However, the idea of targeting nightclub patrons ended up being a risky strategy. Some nightclubs couldn't pay for the product as a result of unreliable club management and there seemed to be a poor match between the product and the consumers who frequented the clubs.

A year after abandoning the nightclub strategy, Portello is being repositioned to capture a broader target market. Armed with a strategic study conducted by three business students from the University of Western Ontario Business School, the management team at Bay Hill has significantly changed its marketing strategy in preparation for targeting a larger, mainstream market. For example, instead of carrying out discussions with one supermarket at a time, the company has signed an agreement with a food distributor who will sell the product to large supermarkets for a percentage of sales. They have also decided to increase the price of Portello slightly, a move that they believe consumers will not notice but that will help to pay for changes such as the purchase of a new labelling machine. Packaging changes will also be made with the objective of making the product more visible on competitive supermarket shelves.

The management team at Bay Hill is also looking forward to geographic expansion. While current business is centred in Ontario, they are now moving into the rest of Canada. A trade show in Vancouver offered the company an opportunity to talk to distributors in Western Canada and assess competition. The next challenge will be entering the U.S. market. Now that Raj has obtained the U.S. rights to Portello, he will be preparing a marketing strategy to enter that market, building on the lessons he has learned in Canada.

QUESTIONS

1. Do you think that the Portello brand name is an asset? Why or why not?
2. The packaging for Portello is going to be changed to target more of a mainstream market. What packaging changes would you recommend?
3. What changes, if any, should Raj and the Bay Hill Impex management team make to their current marketing strategy before introducing Portello in the United States?

Source: This case was prepared by Auleen Carson and is based on "Portello Repeat and Update," *Venture* (March 30, 1997).

C H A P T E R

NEW PRODUCT DEVELOPMENT AND LIFE CYCLE STRATEGIES

9

OBJECTIVES

When you finish this chapter, you should be able to

1. Explain how companies find and develop new-product ideas.

2. List and define the steps in the new-product development process.

3. Describe the stages of the product life cycle.

4. Describe how marketing strategies evolve during the product's life cycle.

"New products!" declares Gillette's Chairman and CEO Alfred M. Zeien, "that's the name of the game." Since its founding in 1901, Gillette's heavy commitment to innovation has kept the company razor-sharp. Gillette is best known for its absolute dominance of the razor-and-blades market. However, all of its divisions—Duracell batteries, Gillette toiletries and cosmetics (Right Guard, Soft & Dri), stationery products (Parker, Paper Mate, and Waterman pens), Oral-B toothbrushes, and Braun electrical appliances—share common traits: each is profitable, fast-growing, number one worldwide in its markets, and anchored by a steady flow of innovative new-product offerings. Last year, 40 percent of Gillette's sales came from products that didn't exist five years ago. "Gillette is a new product machine," says one Wall Street analyst.

New products don't just happen at Gillette. New-product success starts with a companywide culture that supports innovation. Whereas many companies try to protect their successful current products, Gillette encourages innovations that will cannibalize its established product hits. "They know that if they don't bring out a new zinger, someone else will," observes an industry consultant. Gillette also accepts blunders and dead ends as a normal part of creativity and innovation. It knows that it must generate dozens of new-product ideas to get just one success in the marketplace. The company scorns what CEO Zeien calls "putting blue dots in the soap powder"—attaching superficial frills to existing products and labelling them innovations. However, Gillette strongly encourages its people to take creative risks in applying cutting-edge technologies to find substantial improvements that make life easier for customers.

New-product development is complex and expensive, but Gillette's mastery of the process has put the company in a class of its own. For example, Gillette spent $275 million on designing and developing its Sensor family of razors, garnering 29 patents along the way. Although competing brands Bic and Wilkinson have significant shares of the disposable-razor market, and Shick, Norelco, and Remington compete effectively in the electric-razor market segment, Sensor dominates in the burgeoning cartridge-razor sector. Sensor's technological superiority gives it a global competitive advantage.

At Gillette, it seems that almost everyone gets involved in one way or another with new-product development. Even people who don't participate directly in the product design and development are likely to be pressed into service testing prototypes. Every working day at Gillette, 200 volunteers from various departments come to work unshaven, troop to the second floor of the company's gritty South Boston manufacturing and research plant, and enter small booths with a sink and mirror. There they take instructions from technicians on the other side of a small window as to which razor, shaving cream, or aftershave to use. The volunteers evaluate razors for sharpness of blade, smoothness of glide, and ease of handling. When finished, they enter their judgments into a computer. In a nearby shower room, women perform the same ritual on their legs and underarms. "We bleed so you'll get a good shave at home," says one Gillette employee.

This research supported Gillette's launch of its new shaving gel, Satin Care, into the Canadian marketplace. Aimed at women, the new gel is similar to Gillette's shaving gel for men, but with a few key differences: it has distinct packaging, a scent that women find more appealing, and extra moisturizers. Although 80 percent of women shave their legs regularly, the women's market is underdeveloped. Many women still use their partner's shaving products, a trend that Gillette hopes to reverse.

Gillette also excels at bringing new products to market. The company understands that, once introduced, fledgling products need generous manufacturing and marketing support to thrive in the hotly competitive consumer-products marketplace. To deliver the required support, Gillette has devised a formula that calls for R&D, capital investment, and advertising expenditures—which it refers to collectively as "growth drivers." Gillette's Cavalcade of Sports, one of Canada's best-known promotional campaigns, has acted as one of these drivers for more than 25 years. Retail partners such as Shoppers Drug Mart love the promotion because it brings business into their outlets. The $2-million annual campaign, which features giant in-store displays of sports celebrities and consumer contests, supports major brands such as Sensor. Moreover, it increases interest in new and smaller share brands such as Tame, Skin Care, and Trac II.

Thus, over the decades, superior new products have been the cornerstone of Gillette's amazing success. Since 1990, the company's earnings have grown at an annual rate of 17 percent, with an average annual return on equity of 33 percent. Among consumer-products companies, Gillette's return on sales is second only to Coca-Cola's. The company commands the loyalty of consumers in 200 countries around the globe. Gillette is still working to expand its global presence, however. For example, in the battery division, 45 percent of Duracell's sales are outside North America. Gillette plans to introduce its battery line in China—a country with huge potential. The Chinese purchase $4 billion in batteries annually compared to the $3 billion purchased by North American consumers.

Gillette's new-product prowess is so much a part of its image that it has even become the stuff of jokes. Quips down-home humourist Dave Barry: "One day soon the Gillette Company will announce the development of a razor that, thanks to a computer microchip, can actually travel ahead in time and shave beard hairs that don't even exist yet."[1]

As is the case with Gillette, new products have been the life blood of many firms and Canadians have had a long history as inventors in this process. For example, McIntosh apples, Pablum, frozen fish, and instant mashed potatoes are food products that all originated in Canada. Canadians are responsible for developing sports and leisure activities including basketball, five-pin bowling, table hockey, and Trivial Pursuit. Many of these inventions spawned entire industries. The modern-day communications industry was born with the invention of the telephone (Alexander Graham Bell). Reginald Fessenden, born near Sherbrooke, Quebec, was known as the father of radio after he invented amplitude modulation

Dr. Dennis Colonello designed the Abdomenizer in 1986 while practising as a chiropractor in northern Ontario.

(AM) radio and transmitted his first broadcast in 1900. Another Canadian, Charles Fenerty, with his ability to make paper from wood pulp, founded that industry. Modern air travel was made possible by another Canadian, Wallace Rupert Turnbull, who developed the variable-pitch propeller.

Consider just a few of the other products developed by Canadians. Dr. Cluny McPherson, of St. John's, Newfoundland, invented the gas mask used to save the lives of many allied soldiers in World War I. A quintessentially Canadian tool, the snowblower, was invented in 1925 by Quebec resident Arthur Sicard. Olivia Poole invented the Jolly Jumper, the internationally popular baby seat, in the 1950s, and Steve Pacjack of Vancouver invented the beer case with a tuck-in handle that helps you lug your beer home. Three Canadian Olympic sailors, Bruce Kirby, Hans Fogh, and Ian Bruce designed the world-class Laser sailboat in 1970. Wendy Murphy, a medical research technician, developed the Weevac 6—so named because it can carry six wee babies. Her idea was born when she realized, during the devastation of the 1985 Mexico City earthquake, that no apparatus existed to evacuate young children. Dr. Dennis Colonello designed the Abdomenizer in 1986 while practising as a chiropractor in northern Ontario. Before you laugh, remember that he has now rung up more than $100 million in sales. Dr. Frank Gunston, of Brandon, Manitoba, may have been one of the most philanthropic inventors. After developing and building a total knee-joint replacement, he decided not to patent his invention. This made it freely available to manufacturers and allowed patients needing the joint to benefit quickly from the technology and walk without pain. He received the prestigious Manning Principal Award in 1989 for his efforts.[2]

A company has to be good at developing and managing new products. Every product seems to go through a life cycle—it is born, goes through several phases, and eventually dies as newer products come along that better serve consumer needs. This product life cycle presents two major challenges. First, because all products eventually decline, the firm must be good at developing new products to replace aging ones (the problem of *new-product development*). Second, the firm must be good at adapting its marketing strategies in the face of changing tastes, technologies, and competition as products pass through life-cycle stages (the problem of *product life-cycle strategies*). We first look at the problem of finding and developing new products and then at the problem of managing them successfully over their life cycles.

NEW-PRODUCT DEVELOPMENT STRATEGY

New-product development
The development of original products, product improvements, product modifications, and new brands through the firm's own R&D efforts.

Given the rapid changes in consumer tastes, technology, and competition, companies must develop a steady stream of new products and services. A firm can obtain new products in two ways. One is through *acquisition*—by buying a whole company, a patent, or a licence to produce someone else's product. The other is through **new-product development** in the company's own research and development department. By *new products* we mean original products, product improvements, product modifications, and new brands that the firm develops through its own research and development efforts. In this chapter, we concentrate on new-product development.

Innovation can be very risky. Ford lost $485 million on its Edsel automobile; RCA lost $800 million on its SelectaVision videodisc player; and Texas Instruments lost a staggering $920 million before withdrawing from the home computer business. Other costly product failures from sophisticated companies include New Coke (Coca-Cola Company), VIM Micro Liquid (Unilever), Zap Mail electronic mail (Federal Express), Polarvision instant movies (Polaroid), Crystal Pepsi (PepsiCo), Clorox detergent (Clorox Company), and McLean Burgers (McDonald's).

New products continue to fail at a disturbing rate. One recent study estimated that new consumer packaged goods (consisting mostly of line extensions) fail at a rate of 80 percent. Another study found that about 33 percent of new industrial products fail at launch.[3] Why do so many new products fail? There are several reasons. Although an idea may be good, the market size may have been overestimated. Perhaps the actual product was not designed as well as it should have been. Or maybe it was incorrectly positioned in the market, priced too high, or advertised poorly. A high-level executive might push a favourite idea despite poor marketing research findings. Sometimes the costs of product development are higher than expected, and sometimes competitors fight back harder than expected.

Because so many new products fail, companies are anxious to learn how to improve their odds of new-product success. One way is to identify successful new products and determine what they have in common. One study found that the number-one success factor is a *unique superior product,* one with higher quality, new features, and higher value in use. Another key success factor is a *well-defined product concept* prior to development, in which the company carefully defines and assesses the target market, the product requirements, and the benefits before proceeding.[4] In all, to create successful new products, a company must understand its consumers, markets, and competitors, and develop products that deliver superior value to customers.

So companies face a problem—they must develop new products, but the odds weigh heavily against success. The solution lies in strong new-product planning. It must set specific criteria for new-product idea acceptance, based on the specific *strategic role* the product is expected to play. The product's role might be to help the company remain an innovator, to defend its market share, or to get a foothold in a new market. The company also requires a systematic *new-product development process* for finding and growing new products.

THE NEW-PRODUCT DEVELOPMENT PROCESS

The *new-product development process* for finding and growing new products consists of eight major steps (see Figure 9-1).

IDEA GENERATION

Idea generation
The systematic search for new-product ideas.

New-product development starts with **idea generation**—the systematic search for new-product ideas. A company typically has to generate many ideas in order to find a few good ones. At Gillette, of every 45 carefully developed new-product ideas, three make it into the development stage and only one eventually reaches the marketplace. A recent survey of product managers found that of 100 proposed new product ideas, 39 begin the product development process, 17 survive the development process, eight actually reach the marketplace, and only one eventually reaches its business objectives. Du Pont has found that it can take as many as 3000 raw ideas to produce just two winning commercial products. And pharmaceutical companies may require 6000 to 8000 starting ideas for every successful commercial new product.[5] The search for new-product ideas should be systematic rather than haphazard. Otherwise, although the company may find many ideas, most will not be good ones for its type of business. Top management can avoid this error by carefully defining its new-product

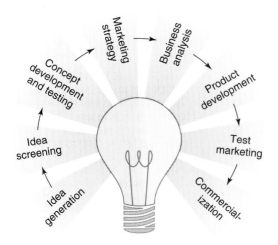

FIGURE 9-1 *Major stages in new-product development*

Kraft Canada used ideas from a variety of sources to develop its new line of herb dressings.

development strategy. Major sources of new-product ideas include internal sources, customers, competitors, distributors and suppliers, and others.

Many new product ideas come from *internal sources*. The company can find new ideas through formal research and development. It can pick the brains of its scientists, engineers, and manufacturing people. Or company executives can brainstorm new-product ideas. The company's salespeople are another good source because they are in daily contact with customers. Toyota claims that its employees submit two million ideas annually—about 35 suggestions per employee—and that more than 85 percent of these ideas are implemented.

Good new-product ideas result from watching and listening to *customers*. The company can conduct surveys or focus groups to learn about consumer needs and wants. It can analyse customer questions and complaints to find new products that better solve consumer problems. Company engineers or salespeople can meet with customers to get suggestions. Alcan has a product research centre in Kingston, Ontario, where company engineers work with automotive customers to discover ways of incorporating aluminum into cars. Use of more lightweight aluminum will enable manufacturers to increase cars' fuel efficiency.

Finally, consumers often create new products and uses on their own, and companies can benefit by finding these products and putting them on the market. The makers of WD-40, the multi-purpose lubricant, sponsor an annual contest to obtain ideas about new uses of the product from customer (see Marketing Highlight 9-1).

Competitors are another good source of new product ideas. O-Pee-Chee Co. Ltd., of London, Ontario, the bubble-gum, trading-card, and candy manufacturer, does no testing and no market research to uncover new products. Instead it signed licensing agreements with two of the leading U.S. confectionary companies. These companies send O-Pee-Chee progress reports on new products that O-Pee-Chee then uses to determine which products to introduce into Canada.[6]

Companies can also watch competitors' ads and other communications for clues about their new products. Companies buy competing new products, take them apart to see how they work, analyse their sales, and decide whether the company should introduce a new product of its own. For example, when designing its highly successful Taurus, Ford tore down more than 50 competing models, layer by layer, looking for things to copy or improve upon. It copied the Audi's accelerator-pedal "feel," the Toyota Supra fuel gauge, the BMW 528e tire and jack storage system, and 400 other such outstanding features.

Finally, *distributors and suppliers* can pass along information about consumer problems and new-product possibilities. Suppliers can tell the company about new concepts, techniques, and materials that can be used to develop new products. Other idea sources include trade magazines, shows, and seminars; government agencies; new-product

WD-40: SLICK WAYS TO CREATE NEW USES

Along with duct tape and the trusty hammer, WD-40 has become one of the truly essential survival items in most homes. Originally developed in 1953 to prevent rust and corrosion on Atlas missiles, it takes its name from the 40th and final attempt at creating a water displacement formula. Over the past 40 years, WD-40 has achieved a kind of "cult" status.

The WD-40 Company has shown a real knack for expanding the market by finding new uses for its popular substance. Many new ideas come from current users, who enter the company's annual contests. Winners of last year's "Invent Your Own Use" contest received cash prizes and many had their ideas featured in the company's "There's Always Another Use" advertising campaign.

Some entrants suggest simple and practical uses. The 1995 winning entry came from a teacher who used WD-40 to clean old chalkboards in her classroom. "Amazingly, the boards started coming to life again," she reports. "Not only were they restored, but years of masking and scotch tape residue came off as well." Other entrants report some pretty unusual uses. First place last year went to a woman whose parakeet, "Cookie," fell off her shoulder and landed on sticky mousetrap paper. When she tried to free the bird, she got both her hands stuck. The vet used good old WD-40 to free both victims. Still other reported uses seem highly improbable—one entrant claims that after spraying his Frisbee with WD-40, it flew out of sight, never to be seen again.

By now, almost everyone has discovered that WD-40 comes in handy for lubricating machinery, protecting tools from rust, loosening nuts and bolts, quieting squeaky hinges, and freeing stuck doors, drawers, windows, and zippers. And many fans know that you can use WD-40 to remove sticky-back labels from glassware, plastic, and metal items; bubble gum from hair and carpets; scuff marks from vinyl floors; and crayon marks from just about anywhere. Whether it be crayon or bubble gum on walls or in hair,

WD-40 is a lifesaver for the parents of precocious mess-makers. For example, when one user's two-year-old daughter took crayons in hand to create a colourful rainbow on the living room wall, a few squirts of WD-40 took care of the problem.

Such common uses make good sense, but did you hear about the nude burglary suspect who had wedged himself in a vent at a café in Denver? The fire department extracted him with a large dose of WD-40. Or how about the naval officer who used WD-40 to repel an

USE #722

WD-40® gets kid out of sticky situation. *A relieved mom (and daughter) from Washington state discovered that WD-40 is as good on stuck fingers as it is on stuck drawers. It's great for lubricating sliding glass doors, windows and anything else that sticks or squeaks.*

WD-40. THERE'S ALWAYS ANOTHER USE.

WD-40 Company has shown a real knack for expanding the market by finding new uses.

angry bear? Then there's the college student who wrote to say that a friend's nightly amorous activities in the next room were causing everyone in his dorm to lose sleep—he solved the problem by treating the squeaky bedsprings with WD-40.

Others report using WD-40 to clean paint brushes, renew old printer and typewriter ribbons, keep snow from sticking to snow shovels, and clean hard water stains and soap scum off shower doors and bathroom tiles. One inventive cemetery grounds keeper even uses WD-40 to clean and polish headstones. Many fishermen report that spraying a little WD-40 on bait helps them catch more fish. Some recreational users claim that spraying their golf clubs, golf balls, or bowling balls has greatly improved their games.

WD-40 has been used to unstick just about everything, including a repairman's finger from a toilet fitting, a little boy's head from his potty training seat, and a steer's head from a fence. Reports the farmer, "We just sprayed a little WD-40 on his head, and he slipped right out. . . ." Ranchers and race horse trainers say they use WD-40 to untangle manes and tails and to repel mud from hooves. And then there's the Florida man who found an entirely different way to use the product. When modern-day pirates boarded his boat, he hit one of the would-be hijackers over the head with a can of WD-40, which knocked him off the boat and saved the day.

Source: Numerous WD-40 Company press releases created by Phillips-Ramsey Advertising & Public Relations, San Diego, California. Also see John Hahn, "A Little Squirt Comes to the Rescue," *The Seattle Post-Intelligencer,* September 2, 1994, p. C2.

consultants; advertising agencies; marketing research firms; university and commercial laboratories; and inventors. Kraft Canada got the idea for its new line of herb dressings, which was launched in the summer of 1995, from a variety of sources. It observed that consumers were using herbs as a means of avoiding salt in their diets. It noted that sales of fresh herbs had risen dramatically in grocery stores. The company monitored food trends in restaurants and cooking shows and noted the addition of fresh herbs to many dishes. Finally, Kraft Canada worked with their own people in the KRAFT KITCHENS to determine what varieties of herbs would work best in their pourable dressings.

IDEA SCREENING

Idea screening
Screening new-product ideas in order to identify good ideas and drop poor ones as soon as possible.

The purpose of idea generation is to create a large number of ideas. The purpose of the succeeding stages is to *reduce* that number. The first idea-reducing stage is **idea screening.** The purpose of screening is to identify good ideas and drop poor ones as soon as possible. Product-development costs rise greatly in later stages. The company wants to proceed only with the product ideas that will turn into profitable products. As one marketing executive suggests, "Three executives sitting in a room can get 40 good ideas richocheting off the wall in minutes. The challenge is getting a steady stream of good ideas out of the labs and creativity campfires, through marketing and manufacturing and all the way to consumers."[7]

Many companies require their executives to write up new-product ideas on a standard form that can be reviewed by a new-product committee. The writeup describes the product, the target market, and the competition. It makes some rough estimates of market size, product price, development time and costs, manufacturing costs, and rate of return. The committee then evaluates the idea against a set of general criteria. For example, at Kao Company, the large Japanese consumer products company, the committee asks questions such as: Is the product truly useful to consumers and society? Is it good for our particular company? Does it mesh well with the company's objectives and strategies? Do we have the people, skills, and resources to make it succeed? Does it deliver more value to customers than competing products? Is it easy to advertise and distribute?

Surviving ideas can be screened further using a simple rating process such as the one shown in Table 9-1. The first column lists factors required for the successful launching of the product in the marketplace. In the next column, management rates these factors on their relative importance. Thus, management believes that marketing skills and experience are very important (.20), and purchasing and supplies competence is of minor importance (.05).

TABLE 9-1 *Product Idea Rating Process*

New-Product Success Factors	(A) Relative Importance	(B) Fit Between Product Idea and Company Capabilities											(A × B) Idea Rating
		.0	.1	.2	.3	.4	.5	.6	.7	.8	.9	1.0	
Company strategy and objectives	.20									X			.160
Marketing skills and experience	.20										X		.180
Financial resources	.15								X				.105
Channels of distribution	.15									X			.120
Production capabilities	.15									X			.120
Research and development	.10								X				.070
Purchasing and supplies	.05						X						.025
Total	1.00												.780*

*Rating scale: .00–.40, poor; .50–.75, fair; .76–1.00, good. Minimum acceptance level: .70

Next, on a scale of .0 to 1.0, management rates how well the new-product idea fits the company's profile on each factor. Here, management feels that the product idea fits very well with the company's marketing skills and experience (.9), but not too well with its purchasing and supplies capabilities (.5). Finally, management multiplies the importance of each success factor by the rating of fit to obtain an overall rating of the company's ability to launch the product successfully. Thus, if marketing is an important success factor, and if this product fits the company's marketing skills, this will increase the overall rating of the product idea. In the example, the product idea scored .74, which places it at the high end of the "fair idea" level.

The checklist promotes a more systematic product idea evaluation and basis for discussion—however, it is not designed to make the decision for management.

CONCEPT DEVELOPMENT AND TESTING

Product concept
A detailed version of the new-product idea stated in meaningful consumer terms.

An attractive idea must be developed into a **product concept.** It is important to distinguish among a *product idea,* a *product concept,* and a *product image.* A product idea is an idea for a possible product that the company can see itself offering to the market. A product concept is a detailed version of the idea stated in meaningful consumer terms. A product image is the way consumers perceive an actual or potential product.

Concept Development

Concept development
Concept development involves expanding the new-product idea into various alternative forms.

Concept testing
Testing new-product concepts with a group of target consumers to find out if the concepts have strong consumer appeal.

Concept development involves expanding the new-product idea into various alternative forms based on questions such as "Who will use the product?" "What primary benefit should the product provide?" "Which existing products will compete with the offering?" and "When and where will the product be used?" Suppose Toyota has a new product idea for developing a fuel-cell-powered electric car. The fuel cell has two major advantages compared to conventional engines and battery-powered cars. It causes less pollution, and, because it uses methane, it will have an unlimited range.[8]

Toyota's task is to develop this new product into alternative product concepts, find out how attractive each concept is to customers, and choose the best one. It might create the following product concepts for the fuel cell electric car:

Toyota's fuel-cell-powered electric car is a prime example of concept development.

◆ *Concept 1*   A moderately priced subcompact designed as a second family-car to be used around town. The car is ideal for running errands and visiting friends.

◆ *Concept 2*   A medium-cost sporty compact appealing to young people.

◆ *Concept 3*   An inexpensive subcompact "green" car appealing to environmentally conscious people who want practical transportation and low pollution.

Concept Testing

Concept testing calls for testing new-product concepts with groups of target consumers. The concepts may be presented to consumers symbolically or physically. Here, in words, is Concept 3:

An efficient, fun-to-drive, fuel-cell-powered subcompact car that seats four. This high-tech wonder runs on hydrogen created from methanol fuel, providing practical and reliable transportation with almost no pollution. It goes up to 130 km per hour and, unlike battery-powered electric cars, never needs recharging. It's priced, fully equipped, at $25 000.

TABLE 9-2 *Questions for Electric Car Concept Test*

1. Do you understand the concept of an electric car?

2. Do you believe the claims about the electric car's performance?

3. What are the major benefits of the electric car compared with a conventional car?

4. What improvements in the car's features would you suggest?

5. For what uses would you prefer an electric car to a conventional car?

6. What would be a reasonable price to charge for the electric car?

7. Who would be involved in your decision to buy such a car? Who would drive it?

8. Would you buy such a car? (Definitely, probably, probably not, definitely not)

For some concept tests, a word or picture description might be sufficient. However, a more concrete and physical presentation of the concept will increase the reliability of the concept test. Today, some marketers are finding innovative ways to make product concepts more real to concept-test subjects. For example, some are using virtual reality to test product concepts. Virtual reality programs use computers and sensory devices (such as gloves or goggles) to simulate reality. For example, a designer of kitchen cabinets can use a virtual reality program to help a customer "see" how his or her kitchen would look and work if remodelled with the company's products. Although virtual reality is still in its infancy, its applications are increasing daily.[9]

After being exposed to the concept, consumers then may be asked to react to it by answering the questions in Table 9-2. The answers will help the company decide which concept has the strongest appeal. For example, the last question asks about the consumer's intention to buy. Suppose 10 percent of the consumers said they "definitely" would buy and another 5 percent said "probably." The company could project these figures to the full population in this target group to estimate sales volume. Even then, the estimate is uncertain because people do not always carry out their stated intentions.

Many firms routinely test new product concepts with consumers before attempting to turn them into actual new products. For example, each month Richard Saunders Inc.'s Acu-POLL research system tests 35 new product concepts in person on 100 nationally representative grocery-store shoppers. The poll rates participants' interest in buying a given new product, their perceptions of how new and different the product idea is, and their judgment of the product's value compared with its price. In a recent poll, Nabisco's Oreo Chocolate Cones concept received a rare A+ rating, meaning that consumers think it is an outstanding concept that they would try and buy. Other product concepts didn't fare so well. Nubrush anti-bacterial toothbrush spray disinfectant, from Applied Microdontics, received an F. Consumers found Nubrush to be overpriced, and most don't think they have a problem with "infected" toothbrushes.[10]

MARKETING STRATEGY DEVELOPMENT

Marketing strategy development
Designing an initial marketing strategy for a new product based on the product concept.

Suppose Toyota finds that Concept 3 for the fuel-cell-powered car tests best. The next step is **marketing strategy development**—designing an initial marketing strategy for introducing this car to the market.

The *marketing strategy statement* consists of three parts. The first part describes the target market; the planned product positioning; and the sales, market share, and profit goals for the first few years. Thus:

The target market is younger, well-educated, moderate-to-high income individuals, couples, or small families seeking practical, environmentally responsible transportation. The car will be positioned as more economical to operate, more fun to drive, and less than today's internal combustion engine cars, and as less restricting than battery-powered electric cars that must be recharged regularly. The company will aim to sell 100 000 cars in the first year, at a loss of not more than $20 million. In the second year, the company will aim for sales of 120 000 cars and a profit of $36 million.

The second part of the marketing strategy statement outlines the product's planned price, distribution, and marketing budget for the first year:

The fuel-cell-powered electric car will be offered in three colours and will have optional air-conditioning and power-drive features. It will sell at a retail price of $25 000—with 15 percent off the list price to dealers. Dealers who sell more than 10 cars per month will receive an additional discount of five percent on each car sold that month. An advertising budget of $29 million will be divided equally between national and local advertising. Advertising will emphasize the car's fun and low emissions. During the first year, $140 000 will be spent on marketing research to find out who is buying the car and their satisfaction levels.

The third part of the marketing strategy statement describes the planned long-run sales, profit goals, and marketing mix strategy:

Toyota intends to capture a three percent long-run share of the total auto market and realize an after-tax return on investment of 15 percent. To achieve this, product quality will start high and improve over time. Price will be raised in the second and third years if competition permits. The total advertising budget will be raised each year by about 10 percent. Marketing research will be reduced to $86 000 per year after the first year.

BUSINESS ANALYSIS

Business analysis
A review of the sales, costs, and profit projections for a new product to determine whether these factors satisfy the company's objectives.

Once management has decided on its product concept and marketing strategy, it can evaluate the business attractiveness of the proposal. **Business analysis** involves a review of the sales, costs, and profit projections for a new product to determine whether they satisfy the company's objectives. If they do, the product can move to the product-development stage.

To estimate sales, the company should examine the sales history of similar products and should survey market opinion. It should estimate minimum and maximum sales to assess the range of risk. After preparing the sales forecast, management can estimate the expected product costs and profits, including marketing, R&D, manufacturing, accounting, and finance costs. The company then uses the sales and costs figures to analyse the new product's financial attractiveness.

PRODUCT DEVELOPMENT

Product development
Developing the product concept into a physical product to assure that the product idea can be turned into a workable product.

So far, the product may have existed only as a word description, a drawing, or perhaps a crude mockup. If the product concept passes the business test, it moves into **product development.** Here, R&D or engineering develops the product concept into a physical product. The product-development step, however, now calls for a large jump in investment. It will show whether the product idea can be turned into a workable product.

The R&D department will develop one or more physical versions of the product concept. R&D hopes to design a prototype that will satisfy and excite consumers and that can be produced quickly and at budgeted costs. Developing a successful prototype can take days, weeks, months, or even years. Often, products undergo rigorous functional tests to ensure that they perform safely and effectively. Here are some examples of such functional tests:[11]

Heinz Canada's Toddler Peach Cobbler took four years to develop.

A scuba-diving Barbie doll must swim and kick for 15 straight hours to satisfy Mattel that she will last at least one year. But because Barbie may find her feet in small owners' mouths rather than in the bathtub, Mattel has devised another, more tortuous test: Barbie's feet are clamped by two steel jaws to make sure that her skin doesn't crack—and choke—potential owners.

At Shaw Industries, temps are paid $5 an hour to pace up and down five long rows of sample carpets for up to eight hours a day, logging an average of 22 kilometres each. One regular reads three mysteries a week while pacing and shed 20 kilograms in two years. Shaw Industries counts walkers' steps and figures that 20 000 steps equal several years of average carpet wear.

Diana Yanik, co-ordinator of product development at the Heinz Company of Canada, sits tensely watching eight specially trained testers enter partitioned booths where they taste three small bowls with variations of Heinz's new product, Toddler Peach Cobbler. Reaching this point took four years and involved hundreds of decisions for Yanik, including finding a new type of peach that would withstand various processing methods. Careful testing is essential for Canada's most health-conscious and finicky consumers—small children who can barely hold a fork. The process began when Heinz's research revealed that mothers wanted a food to challenge children who were just beginning to develop teeth. Consequently, the product concept was born: a baby food with pieces that were large enough for a child to chew, but that did not pose a choking hazard. Prototypes were tested on 900 mothers and their children. Following dozens of recipe changes, $400 000 of specialized equipment, and weeks of rigid safety testing, the product was finally ready for supermarket shelves, where it soon became a hit.

The prototype must have the required functional features and also convey the intended psychological characteristics. The fuel-cell-powered car, for example, should strike consumers as being well built and safe. Management must learn what makes consumers decide that a car is well built. For some, this means having "solid-sounding" doors when they are slammed. For others, it is the result of independent crash tests.

TEST MARKETING

Test marketing
The stage of new-product development where the product and marketing program are tested in more realistic market settings.

If the product passes functional and consumer tests, the next step is **test marketing**, the stage at which the product and marketing program are introduced into more realistic market settings. Test marketing gives the marketer experience with marketing the product before going to the expense of full introduction. It lets the company test the product and its marketing program—positioning strategy, advertising, distribution, pricing, branding and packaging, and budget levels.

The amount of test marketing needed varies with each new product. Test marketing costs can be enormous, and test marketing takes time that may allow competitors to gain advantages. When the costs of developing and introducing the product are low, or when management is already confident about the new product, the company may do little or no test marketing. Companies often do not test market simple line extensions or copies of successful competitor products. For example, Procter & Gamble introduced its Folger's decaffeinated coffee crystals without test marketing, and Pillsbury rolled out Chewy granola bars and chocolate-covered Granola Dipps with no standard test market. However, when introducing a new product requires a big investment, or when management is not sure of the product or marketing program, a company may do a lot of test marketing. For instance, Lever spent two years testing its highly successful Lever 2000 bar soap before introducing it internationally.

One of the most interesting test market ideas to appear recently was Labatt Breweries' "Copper Vote '95." During a 17-day period, Labatt pitted two beers, identified only as Labatt X and Labatt Y, against each other. Consumers voted on their favourite. However, despite participation by 117 000 consumers, the product later failed.

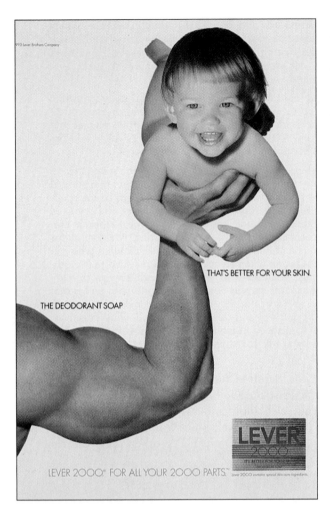

THAT'S BETTER FOR YOUR SKIN.

THE DEODORANT SOAP

LEVER 2000

LEVER 2000® FOR ALL YOUR 2000 PARTS.

Lever spent two years testing its highly successful Lever 2000 bar soap before introducing it internationally.

When using test marketing, consumer products companies usually choose one of three approaches—standard test markets, controlled test markets, or simulated test markets.

Standard Test Markets

Using standard test markets, the company finds a small number of representative test cities, conducts a full marketing campaign in these cities, and uses store audits, consumer and distributor surveys, and other measures to gauge product performance. The results are used to forecast national sales and profits, discover potential product problems, and fine-tune the marketing program.

Standard test markets have some drawbacks. They may be very costly—the average standard test market costs over $4 million, and they take a long time—some last as long as three years. Competitors often do whatever they can to make test-market results hard to read. They cut their prices in test cities, increase their promotion, or even buy up the product being tested. Finally, standard test markets give competitors a look at the company's new product well before it is introduced nationally. Thus, competitors may have time to develop defensive strategies, and may even beat the company's product to the market. For example, while Clorox was still test marketing its new detergent with bleach in selected markets, P&G launched Tide with Bleach nationally. Tide with Bleach quickly became the segment leader; Clorox later withdrew its detergent.

Despite these disadvantages, standard test markets are still the most widely used approach for major market testing. However, many companies today are shifting to quicker and cheaper controlled and simulated test-marketing methods.

Controlled Test Markets

Several research firms keep controlled panels of stores that have agreed to carry new products for a fee. The company with the new product specifies the number of stores and geographical locations it wants. The research firm delivers the product to the participating stores and controls shelf location, amount of shelf space, displays and point-of-purchase promotions, and pricing according to specified plans. Sales results are tracked to determine the impact of these factors on demand.

Controlled test-marketing systems such as Nielsen's Scantrack and Information Resources Inc.'s (IRI) BehaviorScan track individual behaviour from the television set to the checkout counter.[12] Controlled test markets take less time than standard test markets (six months to a year) and usually cost less (a year-long BehaviorScan test might cost from $275 000 to $2 750 000). However, some companies are concerned that the limited number of small cities and panel consumers used by the research services may not be representative of their products' markets or target consumers. And, as in standard test markets, controlled test markets allow competitors to get a look at the company's new product.

Simulated Test Markets

Companies also can test new products in a simulated shopping environment. The company or research firm shows ads and promotions for various products, including the new product being tested, to a sample of consumers. It gives consumers a small amount of money and invites them to a real or laboratory store where they may keep the money or use it to buy items. The researchers note how many consumers buy the new product and competing brands. This simulation provides a measure of the trial and the commercial's effectiveness against competing commercials. The researchers then ask consumers the reasons for their purchase or non-purchase. Some weeks later, they interview the consumers by phone to determine product attitudes, usage, satisfaction, and repurchase intentions. Using sophisticated computer models, the researchers then project national sales from results of the simulated test market. Recently, some marketers have begun to use new high-tech approaches to simulate test-market research, such as virtual reality and the Internet (see Marketing Highlight 9-2).

Simulated test markets overcome some of the disadvantages of standard and controlled test markets. They usually cost much less, can be run in eight weeks, and keep the new product out of competitors' view. Yet, because of their small samples and simulated shopping environments, many marketers do not consider simulated test markets to be as accurate or reliable as larger, real-world tests. Still, simulated test markets are used widely, often as "pre-test" markets. Because they are fast and inexpensive, one or more simulated tests can be run to quickly assess a new product or its marketing program. If the pre-test results are strongly positive, the product might be introduced without further testing. If the results are very poor, the product might be dropped or substantially redesigned and retested. If the results are promising but indefinite, the product and marketing program can be tested further in controlled or standard test markets.

Test Marketing Business Products

Business marketers use different methods for test marketing their new products. For example, they may conduct *product-use tests*. Here, the business marketer selects a small group of potential customers who agree to use the new product for a limited time. New industrial products also can be tested at *trade shows*. These shows draw a large number of buyers who view new products in a few concentrated days. The manufacturer sees how buyers react to various product features and terms, and can assess buyer interest and purchase intentions. Finally, some business marketers use *standard or controlled test markets* to measure the potential of their new products. They produce a limited supply of the product and give it to the sales force to sell in a limited number of geographical areas.

COMMERCIALIZATION

Commercialization
Introducing a new product into the market.

Test marketing gives management the information needed to make a final decision about whether to launch the new product. If the company goes ahead with **commercialization**—introducing the new product into the market—it will face high costs. The company will have to build or rent a manufacturing facility. And it may have to spend, in the case of a new consumer packaged good, between $14 million and $140 million for advertising and sales promotion in the first year.

The company launching a new product must first decide on introduction *timing*. If the electric car will eat into the sales of the company's other cars, its introduction may be delayed. If the electric car can be improved further, or if the economy is down, the company may wait until the following year to launch it.

Next, the company must decide *where* to launch the new product—in a single location, a region, the national market, or the international market. Few companies have the confidence, capital, and capacity to launch new products into full national or international distribution. They will develop a planned *market rollout* over time. In particular, small companies may enter attractive cities or regions one at a time. Larger companies, however, may quickly introduce new models into several regions or into the full national market.

VIRTUAL REALITY TEST MARKETING: THE FUTURE IS NOW

It's a steamy summer Saturday afternoon. Imagine that you're stopping off at the local supermarket to pick up some icy bottles of your favourite sports drink before heading to the tennis courts. You park the car, cross the parking lot, and walk through the store's automatic doors. You head for aisle five, passing several displays along the way, and locate your usual sports-drink brand. You pick it up, check the price, and take it to the check-out counter. Sounds like a pretty typical shopping experience, doesn't it? But in this case, the entire experience took place on your computer screen, not at the supermarket.

You've just experienced virtual reality—the wave of the future for test-marketing and concept-testing research—courtesy of Canada Market Research of Toronto. It has developed a research tool called Visionary Shopper, a CD-ROM virtual-reality approach that recreates shopping situations in which researchers can test consumers' reactions to such factors as product positioning, store layouts, and package designs. For example, suppose a cereal marketer wants to test reactions to a new package design and store-shelf positioning. Using Visionary Shopper on a standard desktop PC, test shoppers begin their shopping spree with a screen showing the outside of a grocery store. They click to enter the virtual store and are guided to the appropriate store section. Once there, they can scan the shelf, pick up various cereal packages, rotate them, study the labels—even look around to see what is on the shelf behind them. Using the touch screen, they can "purchase" the product or return it to the shelf. About the only thing they can't do is open the box and taste the cereal. The virtual shopping trip includes full sound and video, along with a guide who directs users through the experience and answers their questions.

Virtual reality testing can take any of several forms. For example, Alternative Realities Corporation (ARC) has created a virtual reality amphitheatre called the VisionDome. The Dome offers 360 by 160 degrees of film projection, allowing as many as 40 people to participate simultaneously in a virtual-reality experience.

The VisionDome is like an IMAX theatre, but with one big difference—it's interactive. "When you use a computer to generate an image . . . you have the advantage of making that image interactive," comments an ARC executive. When conducting research on a car, he suggests, "we can go into a VisionDome, see that car in three dimensions, look at it from every angle, take it out for a test drive, and allow the customer to configure that car exactly the way he wants it." Caterpillar foresees enomous potential for the Dome. "We can put one of our tractors in a VisionDome and actually have a customer sit in it and test it under whatever conditions they would use it for," says a Caterpillar design engineer. "The ability to immerse people in the product makes it a phenomenal [research and sales] tool."

Virtual reality as a research tool offers several advantages. For one, it's relatively inexpensive. For example, a firm can conduct a virtual store study for only about $36 000, including initial programming and the actual research on 75 to 100 people. This makes virtual reality research accessible to firms that can't afford full market-testing campaigns or the expense of creating actual mock-ups for each different product colour, shape, or size. Another advantage is flexibility. A virtual reality store can display an almost infinite variety of products, sizes, styles, and flavours in response to consumers' desires and needs. Research can be conducted in almost any simulated surrounding, ranging from food store interiors and new car showrooms to farm fields or the open road. The technique also offers great interactivity, allowing marketers and consumers to work together via computer on designs of new products and marketing programs.

Finally, virtual reality has great potential for international research, which has often been difficult for marketers to conduct. With virtual reality, researchers can use a single standardized approach to evaluate products and programs worldwide. Consider the following example:

One multinational company has begun to conduct virtual-shopping studies in North and South America, Europe, Asia, and Australia. Researchers create virtual stores in each country and region using the appropriate local products, shelf layouts, and currencies. Once the stores are online, a product concept can be quickly tested across locations. When the studies are completed, the results are communicated to headquarters electronically. The analysis reveals which markets offer the greatest opportunity for a successful launch.

Virtual reality research also has its limitations. The biggest problem: simulated shopping situations never quite match the real thing. Observes one expert, "Just because it's technically [feasible], that doesn't mean that when you put [people] behind a computer you're going to get true responses. Any time you simulate an experience you're not getting the experience itself. It's still a simulation."

So what's ahead for virtual reality in marketing? Some pioneers are extremely enthusiastic about the technology—not just as a research tool, but as a place where even real buying and selling can occur. They predict that the virtual store may become a major channel for personal and direct interactions with consumers—interactions that encompass not only research but also sales and service. They see great potential for conducting this type of research over the Internet, and virtual stores have become a reality on the Web. As one observer notes, "This is what I read about in science-fiction books when I was growing up. It's the thing of the future." For many marketers, that future is already a virtual reality.

Sources: Quotations and extracts from Raymond R. Burke, "Virtual Shopping: Breakthrough in Marketing Research," *Harvard Business Review*, March–April, 1996, pp. 120–131; Tom Dellacave, Jr., "Curing Market Research Headaches," *Sales & Marketing Management*, July 1996, pp. 85–85; and Brian Silverman, "Get 'em While They're Hot," *Sales & Marketing Management*, February 1997, pp. 47–48, 52; Jo Marney, "Design Testing Goes Digital," *Marketing*, March 24, 1997 (posted on their web site www.marketingmag.com).

Companies with international distribution systems may introduce new products through global rollouts. Colgate-Palmolive uses a "lead-country" strategy. For example, it launched its Palmolive Optims shampoo and conditioner first in Australia, the Philippines, Hong Kong, and Mexico, then rapidly rolled it out into Europe, Asia, Latin America, and Africa. International companies are increasingly introducing their new products in swift global assaults. Procter & Gamble did this with its Pampers Phases line of disposable diapers. In the past, P&G typically introduced a new product in the U.S. market. If it was successful, overseas competitors would copy the product in their home markets before P&G could expand distribution globally. With Pampers Phases, however, the company introduced the new product into global markets within one month of introducing it in the United States. It planned to have the product on the shelf in 90 countries within just 12 months of introduction. Such rapid worldwide expansion solidified the brand's market position before foreign competitors could react. P&G has since mounted worldwide introductions of several other new products.[13]

SPEEDING UP NEW-PRODUCT DEVELOPMENT

Many companies organize their new-product development process into an orderly sequence of steps, starting with idea generation and ending with commercialization. Under this **sequential product development** approach, one company department works individually to complete its stage of the process before passing the new product along to the next department and stage. This orderly, step-by-step process can help bring control to complex and risky projects. But it also can be dangerously slow. In fast-changing, highly competitive markets, such slow-but-sure product development can result in product failures, lost sales and profits, and crumbling market positions. "Speed to market" and reducing new product development "cycle time" have become pressing concerns to companies in all industries.

Sequential product development
A new-product development approach in which one company department works individually to complete its stage of the process before passing the new product along to the next department and stage.

Simultaneous (or team-based) product development
An approach to developing new products in which various company departments work closely together, overlapping the steps in the product-development process to save time and increase effectiveness.

Today, in order to get their new products to market more quickly, many companies are adopting a faster, team-oriented approach called **simultaneous (or team-based) product development**. Under the new approach, company departments work closely together, overlapping the steps in the product development process to save time and increase effectiveness. Instead of passing the new product from department to department, the company assembles a team of people from various departments that stays with the new product from start to finish. Such teams usually include people from the marketing, finance, design, manufacturing, and legal departments, and even supplier and customer companies.

Top management gives the product development team general strategic direction, but no clear-cut product idea or work plan. It challenges the team with stiff and seemingly contradictory goals—"turn out carefully planned and superior new products, but do it quickly"—and then gives the team whatever freedom and resources it needs to meet the challenge. In the sequential process, a bottleneck at one phase can seriously slow the entire project. In the simultaneous approach, if one functional area hits snags, it works to resolve them while the team moves on.

Black & Decker used the simultaneous approach—what it calls "concurrent engineering"—to develop its Quantum line of tools targeted toward serious do-it-yourselfers. B&D assigned a "fusion team," called Team Quantum and consisting of 85 Black & Decker employees from around the world, to get the right product line to customers as quickly as possible. The team included engineers, finance people, marketers, designers, and others from the United States, Britain, Germany, Italy, and Switzerland. From idea to launch, including three months of consumer research, the team developed the highly acclaimed Quantum line in only 12 months.

The simultaneous approach does have some limitations. Superfast product development can be riskier and more costly than the slower, more orderly sequential approach. Moreover, it often creates increased organizational tension and confusion.

BRUCE POPE, CEO
MOLSON BREWERIES LTD.

Bruce Pope joined Molson Breweries in 1988, and is the company's most recent president and CEO. Molson is the second-oldest company in Canada, preceded only by the Hudson Bay Company. The firm grew over time by acquiring a number of regional breweries across Canada. Molson diversified beyond the beer industry during the 1980s, buying such businesses as Diversey in the United States and Aikenheads and Beaver Lumber in Canada. During the 1990s, the firm decided to concentrate on its core business—beer—and has been divesting its other, unrelated companies.

In 1993, Molson entered into a 50/50 merger with the Carling Brewery. This was a unique merger in that neither firm took a controlling position in terms of being a majority shareholder. Not only did the merger allow the firms to share costs and achieve scope advantages that helped double its profitability, but it also positioned Molson to be a stronger player in the international marketplace.

Pope has a wealth of marketing experience in the consumer packaged-goods industry in addition to his experience at Molson. During his 18 years at Warner Lambert, he managed such products as Listerine, Schick, and Benedril, before becoming Regional President of the Mexico/Central America/Panama division. However, it was not until he moved into the brewing industry that he found he could utilize the full range of marketing tools.

First, in the beer industry everything is focused on the consumer. Second, segmentation is extremely important. Molson has 52 brands, which cannot all be targeted at males in the 19 to 23 age group. Whereas during his years at Warner Lambert Pope focused on mass advertising, display, and merchandising, at Molson he found that brand-image development, motivation of trade customers, the stimulation of trial, and sports and entertainment marketing are also extremely important.

Core Value Marketing
The most important facet of marketing at Molson, however, is the ability to get close to the customer and work to identify the company with customers' interests. To accomplish this task, Bruce Pope stresses that it is essential to develop an interaction with the customer and to develop a forum so that customers can speak to the firm. People today do not want to be treated as a

mass market, Pope warns. Instead they expect to be treated as individuals whose core values and needs are reflected by a company in a compelling fashion. This is what Molson did when trying to revitalize one of its brands, Canadian. Molson's "I am" campaign injected a sense of individual personality into the brand, touching consumers in a way that was relevant to them. This campaign helped Molson to turn around Canadian's sagging fortunes.

Bruce Pope

The question becomes, then, how do you respond to narrowly held interests and values and translate them into a "mass appeal" that is often so essential in consumer goods marketing? An even more troubling question, Pope noted, was the fact that Molson research uncovered the fact that many of the "Generation X" consumers, do not want to be marketed to, and do not like or trust advertising. Instead, they want to discover their own brands.

This was the dilemma faced by Molson when it was trying to find a beer to direct at the Generation-X target market. The solution was Molson's Red Dog beer. The bull dog that is the star of the ads exuded independence, and total disrespect for traditional behaviours.

Licensed establishments (bars and restaurants) represent another extremely important part of Molson's marketing effort. It is here that final consumers often try a new product for the first time. Thus, it is as important to market to the people running these establishments as it is to market to final consumers, Pope emphasizes. Molson has worked hard to also develop core-value marketing for this group.

Creating Customer Relationships
Another solution to developing an ongoing relationship with consumers is to create multiple avenues through which to contact and interact with them. These avenues must be important in the lives of the particular target audience. Thus, Molson uses a lot of event marketing. It sponsors "Molson Rocks" music concerts as well as "Molson's Hockey Night in Canada," and the "Molson Indy." It uses Internet marketing to inform consumers about concert and event schedules and sport scores as well as providing them with a contact point to talk to Molson's brewers. Tracking responses to its Internet site has revealed to Molson that consumers are highly involved with beer and highly informed about the product. They are savvy, literate, and knowledgeable. The important thing to understand, Pope stresses, is that you must respond to this consumer interest in a meaningful fashion. You also must make a connection with the consumer on his or her own terms.

This means that Molson's consumers do not just want to be marketed at. Rather, they also like to participate in the creation of programs. Molson found out how successful this tactic could be in its recent efforts with Brador beer in Quebec. It developed an ad and then asked consumers which one of two possible outcomes they would like as a conclusion to the ad story. They received over one million phone calls— five times the response they expected. In other words, Pope notes, all consumers need is the chance to participate.

In addition to the above programs, Molson has also turned to cause-related marketing to build more, and better, connections with its consumers. The brewery has affiliated itself with AIDS research since this is a highly relevant cause for its target market (see the Chapter 22 opening example for more details on Molson's program).

Such programs have positioned Molson as an important part of its consumers' lives. Molson touches people on multiple fronts and demonstrates that marketing beer is a multi-faceted, but rewarding task.

Source: Bruce Pope met with P. Cunningham and presented this material to her classes on March 26, 1996, and subsequently agreed to have it published in *Principles of Marketing*. We sincerely thank him for the insights he provided on the practice of marketing.

And the company must take care that rushing a product to market doesn't adversely affect its quality—the objective is not just to create products faster, but to create them *better* and faster. Despite these drawbacks, in rapidly changing industries facing increasingly shorter product life cycles, the rewards of fast and flexible product development far exceed the risks. Companies that get new and improved products to the market faster than competitors often gain a dramatic competitive edge. They can respond more quickly to emerging-consumer tastes and charge higher prices for more advanced designs. As one auto industry executive states, "What we want to do is get the new car approved, built, and in the consumer's hands in the shortest time possible . . . Whoever gets there first gets all the marbles."[14]

■ PRODUCT LIFE-CYCLE STRATEGIES

After launching the new product, management wants the product to enjoy a long and happy life. Although it does not expect the product to sell forever, management wants to earn a decent profit to cover all the effort and risk that went into launching it. Management is aware that each product will have a life cycle, although the exact shape and length is not known in advance.

Product life cycle (PLC)
The course of a product's sales and profits over its lifetime. It involves five distinct stages: product development, introduction, growth, maturity, and decline.

Figure 9-2 shows a typical **product life cycle (PLC)**, the course that a product's sales and profits take over its lifetime. The product life cycle has five stages:

1. *Product development* begins when the company finds and develops a new-product idea. During product development, sales are zero and the company's investment costs mount.

2. *Introduction* is a period of slow sales growth as the product is being introduced in the market. Profits are non-existent in this stage because of the heavy expenses of product introduction.

3. *Growth* is a period of rapid market acceptance and increasing profits.

4. *Maturity* is a period of slowdown in sales growth because the product has achieved acceptance by most potential buyers. Profits level off or decline because of increased marketing outlays to defend the product against competition.

5. *Decline* is the period when sales fall off and profits drop.

Not all products follow this S-shaped product life cycle. Some products are introduced and die quickly; others stay in the mature stage for a long, long time. Some enter the decline stage and are then cycled back into the growth stage through strong promotion or repositioning.

The PLC concept can describe a *product class* (gasoline-powered automobiles), a *product form* (minivans), or a *brand* (the Ford Taurus). The PLC concept applies differently in each case. Product classes have the longest life cycles—the sales of many product classes stay in the mature stage for a long time. Product forms, in contrast, tend to have the standard PLC shape. Product forms such as "cream deodorants," the "rotary telephone," and "phonograph records" passed through a regular history of introduction, rapid growth, maturity, and decline. A specific brand's life cycle can change quickly because of changing competitive attacks and responses. For example, although teeth-cleaning products (product class) and toothpastes (product form) have enjoyed fairly long life cycles, the life cycles of specific brands have tended to be much shorter.

FIGURE 9-2 *Sales and profits over the product's life from inception to demise*

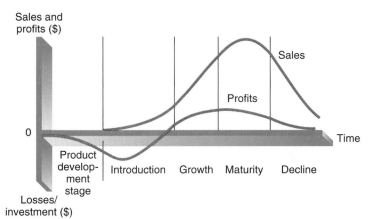

FIGURE 9-3 *Styles, fashions, and fads*

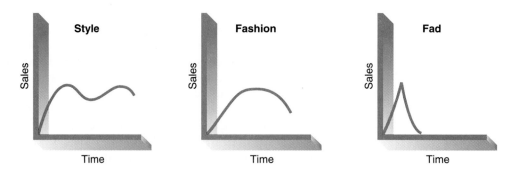

Style
A basic and distinctive mode of expression.

Fashion
A currently accepted or popular style in a given field.

Fads
Fashions that enter quickly, are adopted with great zeal, peak early, and decline very fast.

The PLC concept also can be applied to what are known as styles, fashions, and fads. Their special life cycles are shown in Figure 9-3. A **style** is a basic and distinctive mode of expression. For example, styles appear in homes (Victorian, ranch, modern); clothing (formal, casual); and art (realistic, surrealistic, abstract). Once a style is invented, it may last for generations, coming in and out of vogue. A style has a cycle showing several periods of renewed interest. A **fashion** is a currently accepted or popular style in a given field. For example, the "preppie look" in the clothing of the late 1970s gave way to the "loose and layered look" of the 1980s, which in turn yielded to the less conservative but more tailored look of the 1990s. Fashions tend to grow slowly, remain popular for a while, then decline slowly. **Fads** are fashions that enter quickly, are adopted with great zeal, peak early, and decline very fast. They last only a short time and tend to attract only a limited following. Examples include Rubik's Cubes, "pet rocks," Cabbage Patch dolls, or pogs. Fads do not survive for long because they normally do not satisfy a strong need or satisfy it well.

The PLC concept can be applied by marketers as a useful framework for describing how products and markets work. But using the PLC concept for forecasting product performance or for developing marketing strategies presents some practical problems.[15] For example, managers may have trouble identifying which stage of the PLC the product is in, identifying when the product moves into the next stage, and determining the factors that affect the product's movement through the stages. In practice, it is difficult to forecast the sales level at each PLC stage, the length of each stage, and the shape of the PLC curve.

Using the PLC concept to develop marketing strategy also can be difficult because strategy is both a cause and a result of the product's life cycle. The product's current PLC position suggests the best marketing strategies, and the resulting marketing strategies affect product performance in later life-cycle stages. Yet, when used carefully, the PLC concept can help in developing good marketing strategies for different stages of the product life cycle.

We looked at the product-development stage of the product life cycle in the first part of the chapter. We now look at strategies for each of the other life-cycle stages.

INTRODUCTION STAGE

Introduction stage
The product life-cycle stage when the new product is first distributed and made available for purchase.

The **introduction stage** starts when the new product is first launched. Introduction takes time, and sales growth is apt to be slow. Well-known products such as instant coffee, frozen orange juice, and powdered coffee creamers lingered for many years before they entered a stage of rapid growth.

In this stage, as compared to other stages, profits are negative or low because of the low sales and high distribution and promotion expenses. Much money is needed to attract distributors and build their inventories. Promotion spending is relatively high to inform consumers of the new product and get them to try it.

Because the market is not generally ready for product refinements at this stage, the company and its few competitors produce basic versions of the product. These firms focus their selling on those buyers who are most ready to buy.

A company, especially the *market pioneer,* must choose its launch strategy consistent with its intended product positioning. It should realize that the initial strategy is just the first step in a grander marketing plan for the product's entire life cycle. If the pioneer chooses its launch strategy to make a "killing," it will be sacrificing long-run revenue for the sake of short-run gain. As the pioneer moves through later stages of the life cycle, it will have to continuously formulate new pricing, promotion, and other marketing strategies. It has the best chance of building and retaining market leadership if it plays its cards correctly from the start.

GROWTH STAGE

Growth stage
The product life-cycle stage at which a product's sales start climbing quickly.

If the new product satisfies the market, it will enter a **growth stage,** in which sales will start climbing quickly. The early adopters will continue to buy, and later buyers will start following their lead, especially if they hear favourable word of mouth. Attracted by the opportunities for profit, new competitors will enter the market. They will introduce new product features, and the market will expand. The increase in competitors leads to an increase in the number of distribution outlets, and sales jump just to build reseller inventories. Prices remain where they are or fall only slightly. Companies keep their promotion spending at the same or a slightly higher level. Educating the market remains a goal, but now the company also must meet the competition.

Profits increase during the growth stage, as promotion costs are spread over a large volume and as unit-manufacturing costs fall. The firm uses several strategies to sustain rapid market growth as long as possible. It improves product quality and adds new product features and models. It enters new market segments and new distribution channels. It shifts some advertising from building product awareness to building product conviction and purchase, and it lowers prices at the right time to attract more buyers.

In the growth stage, the firm faces a trade-off between high market share and high current profit. By spending a lot of money on product improvement, promotion, and distribution, the company can capture a dominant position. In doing so, however, it gives up maximum current profit, which it hopes to make up in the next stage.

Discreet Logic Inc. of Montreal faces this quandary. It produces software that allows film-makers to generate special effects such as the huge break in the highway that confronts the racing bus in *Speed.* As the result of exploding demand, Discreet has experienced remarkable growth. Its owners, however, realize that it has to avoid "hitting the wall"—being unable to sustain the cash flow essential to support their growth.

Discreet Logic
www.discreet.com/

Discreet Logic faces the challenge of managing the growth phase of the product life cycle.

MATURITY STAGE

Maturity stage
The stage in the product life cycle where sales growth slows or levels off.

At some point, a product's sales growth will slow down, and the product will enter a **maturity stage.** This maturity stage normally lasts longer than the previous stages, and it poses strong challenges to marketing management. Most products are in the maturity stage of the life cycle, and therefore most of marketing management deals with the mature product.

The slowdown in sales growth results in many producers with many products to sell. In turn, this overcapacity leads to greater competition. Competitors begin marking down prices, increasing their advertising and sales promotions, and increasing their R&D budgets to find better versions of the product. These steps lead to a drop in profit. Some of the weaker competitors start dropping out, and the industry eventually contains only well-established competitors.

Although many products in the mature stage appear to remain unchanged for long periods, most successful ones are actually evolving to meet changing consumer needs (see Marketing Highlight 9-3). Product managers should do more than simply ride along with or defend their mature products—a good offence is the best defence. They should consider modifying the market, product, and marketing mix.

In *modifying the market*, the company tries to increase the consumption of the current product. It looks for new users and market segments, as when Johnson & Johnson targeted the adult market with its baby powder and shampoo, or when AirWave Canada Ltd., the company that markets Doc Martens footwear, began targeting older consumers in the 25 to 50 age bracket, with its message of quality and durability.[16] The manager also looks for ways to increase usage among present customers. Campbell does this by offering recipes and convincing consumers that "soup is good food." Or the company may want to reposition the brand to appeal to a larger or faster-growing segment, as Arrow did when it introduced its new line of casual shirts and announced, "We're loosening our collars."

The company might also try *modifying the product*—changing product characteristics such as quality, features, or style to attract new users and to inspire more usage. It might improve the product's quality and performance—its durability, reliability, speed, taste. Or it might add new features that expand the product's usefulness, safety, or convenience. For example, Sony keeps adding new styles and features to its Walkman and Discman lines, and Volvo adds new safety features to its

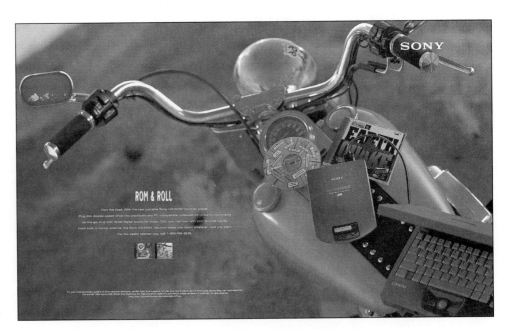

The maturity stage: To sustain growth, Sony keeps adding new features and models to its Walkman and Discman lines—here the CD-ROM Discman. "From rock to rocket science, the Sony Discman takes you down whatever road you want."

CRAYOLA CRAYONS: A LONG AND COLOURFUL LIFE CYCLE

Binney & Smith Company began making crayons near Easton, Pennsylvania, in 1903. Partner Edwin Binney's wife, Alice, named them Crayola crayons—after the French craie, meaning "stick of colour," and ola, meaning "oil." In the 90-odd years since, Crayola crayons have become a household staple, in more than 60 countries around the world, in boxes printed in 11 languages. If you placed all the Crayola crayons made in a single year end to end, they would circle the Earth four and a half times.

Few people can forget their first pack of "64s"—64 beauties neatly arranged in the familiar green-and-yellow flip-top box with a sharpener on the back. The aroma of a freshly opened Crayola box still drives kids into a frenzy and takes members of the older generation back to some of their fondest childhood memories. Binney & Smith, now a subsidiary of Hallmark, dominates the crayon market. Sixty-five percent of all North American children between the ages of two and seven pick up a crayon at least once a day and colour for an average of 28 minutes. Nearly 80 percent of the time, they pick up a Crayola crayon.

In some ways, Crayola crayons haven't changed much since 1903, when they were sold in an eight-pack for a nickel. Crayola has always been the number-one brand, and the crayons are still made by hand in much the same way as then. But a closer look reveals that Binney & Smith has made many adjustments in order to keep the Crayola brand in the mature stage and out of decline. Over the years, the company has added a steady stream of new colours, shapes, sizes, and packages. It increased the number of colours from the original eight in 1903 (red, yellow, blue, green, orange, black, brown, and white) to 48 in 1949, to 64 in 1958. In 1972, it added eight fluorescent colours—with hot names like Laser Lemon, Screamin' Green, and Atomic Tangerine; and in 1993, an additional 16 new colours, including Macaroni & Cheese and Purple Mountains Majesty. Most recently, it created a new line of glow-in-the-dark colours and crayons that change colours. In all, Crayola crayons now come in 96 colours and a variety of packages, including a 96-crayon attaché-like case.

Crayola has also recognized the need to change with the times and to reflect the changing composition of society. For example, in 1962, as a result of the Civil Rights Movement, Crayola renamed its "flesh" crayons—"peach." Similarly, in recent years, the company has introduced a "multicultural line," with colours representing the skin tones, hair tones, and eye colours of various ethnic groups.

Crayola's colourful lifecycle: Over the years, Binney & Smith has added a steady stream of new colours, shapes, sizes, and packages.

Over the years, the Crayola line also has grown to include many new sizes and shapes. In addition to the standard 10-centimetre crayon, it now includes flat, jumbo, and "So Big" crayons. Crayola Washable Crayons were added in 1991. Binney & Smith also extended the Crayola brand to new markets when it developed Crayola Markers and related products. Finally, the company has added several programs and services to help strengthen its relationships with Crayola customers. For example, in 1984 it began its Dream Makers art education program, a national elementary-school art program design to help students capture their dreams on paper and to support art schools. In 1986, it set up a toll-free 1-800-CRAYOLA hotline to provide better customer service.

Not all of Binney & Smith's life-cycle adjustments have been greeted with open arms by consumers. For example, facing flat sales throughout the 1980s, the company conducted market research that showed that children were ready to break with tradition in favour of some exciting new colours. They were seeing and wearing brighter colours and wanted to be able to colour with them as well. So, in 1990, Binney & Smith retired eight colours from the time-honoured box of 64—raw umber, lemon yellow, maize, blue grey, orange yellow, orange red, green blue, and violet blue—into the Crayola Hall of Fame. In their place, it introduced eight more-modern shades—Cerulean, Vivid Tangerine, Jungle Green, Fuchsia, Dandelion, Teal Blue, Royal Purple, and Wild Strawberry. The move unleashed a ground-swell of protest from loyal Crayola users, who formed such organizations as the RUMPS—the Raw Umber and Maize Preservation Society—and the National Committee to Save Lemon Yellow. Binney & Smith received an average of 334 calls a month from concerned customers. Company executives were flabbergasted—"We were aware of the loyalty and nostalgia surrounding Crayola crayons," a spokesperson says, "but we didn't know we [would] hit such a nerve." Still, fans of the new colours outnumbered the protestors, and the new colours are here to stay. However, the company did revive the old standards for one last hurrah in a special collectors' tin—it sold all of the 2.5 million tins made. Thus, the Crayola brand continues through its long and colourful life cycle.

Sources: Quotation from "Hue and Cry over Crayola May Revive Old Colors," *Wall Street Journal,* June 14, 1991, p. B1. Also see Margaret O. Kirk, "Coloring Our Children's World Since '03," *Chicago Tribune,* October 29, 1986, Sec. 5, p. 1; Catherine Foster, "Drawing Dreams," *Christian Science Monitor,* June 5, 1989, p. 13; Mike Christiansen, "Waxing Nostalgic: Crayola Retires a Colorful Octet," *Atlanta Constitution,* August 8, 1990, pp. B1, B4; and Ellen Neuborne, "Expansion Goes Outside Crayon Lines," *USA Today,* October 2, 1992, pp. B1, B2.

cars. Finally, the company can improve the product's styling and attractiveness. Thus, car manufacturers restyle their cars to attract buyers who want a new look. The makers of consumer food and household products introduce new flavours, colours, ingredients, or packages to revitalize consumer buying.

Finally, the company may decide to *modify the marketing mix*. Marketers also can try to improve sales by changing one or more marketing-mix elements. They can cut prices to attract new users and competitors' customers. They can launch a better advertising campaign or use aggressive sales promotions—trade deals, cents-off, premiums, and contests. The company can also move into larger market channels, using mass merchandisers, if these channels are growing. Finally, the company can offer new or improved services to buyers.

DECLINE STAGE

Decline stage
The product life-cycle stage at which a product's sales decline.

The sales of most product forms and brands eventually dip. The decline may be slow, as in the case of oatmeal cereal; or rapid, as in the case of phonograph records. Sales may plunge to zero, or they may drop to a low level where they continue for many years. This is the **decline stage**.

Sales decline for many reasons, including technological advances, shifts in consumer tastes, and increased competition. As sales and profits decline, some firms withdraw from the market. Those remaining may prune their product offerings. They may drop smaller market segments and marginal trade channels, or they may cut the promotion budget and reduce their prices further.

Carrying a weak product can be very costly to a firm, and not just in profits. There are many hidden costs. A weak product may take up too much of management's time. It often requires frequent price and inventory adjustments. It requires advertising and sales-force attention that might be better used to make "healthy" products more profitable. A product's failing reputation can cause customer concerns about the company and its other products. The biggest cost may well lie in the future. Keeping weak products delays the search for replacements, creates a lopsided product mix, hurts current profits, and weakens the company's foothold on the future.

For these reasons, companies need to pay more attention to their aging products. The firm's first task is to identify those products in the decline stage by regularly reviewing sales, market shares, costs, and profit trends. Then, management must decide whether to maintain, harvest, or drop each of these declining products.

Management may decide to *maintain* its brand without change in the hope that competitors will leave the industry. For example, Procter & Gamble made good profits by remaining in the declining liquid-soap business as others withdrew. Or management may decide to reposition the brand in hopes of moving it back into the growth stage of the product life cycle. For instance, after watching sales of its Tostitos tortilla chips plunge 50 percent from their mid-1980s high, Frito-Lay reformulated the chips by doubling their size, changing their shape from round to triangular, and using white corn flour instead of yellow. The new Tostitos Restaurant-Style Tortilla Chips have ridden the crest of the recent Tex-Mex food craze's record revenues.

Frito-Lay
www.fritolay.com/

Management may decide to *harvest* the product, which means reducing various costs (plant and equipment, maintenance, R&D, advertising, sales force) and hoping that sales hold up. If successful, harvesting will increase the company's profits in the short run. Or management may decide to *drop* the product from the line. It can sell it to another firm or simply liquidate it at salvage value. If the company plans to find a buyer, it will not want to run down the product through harvesting.

Table 9-3 summarizes the key characteristics of each stage of the product life cycle. The table also lists the marketing objectives and strategies for each stage.[17]

TABLE 9-3   *Summary of Product Life-Cycle Characteristics, Objectives, and Strategies*

	INTRODUCTION	**GROWTH**	**MATURITY**	**DECLINE**
Characteristics				
Sales	Low sales	Rapidly rising sales	Peak sales	Declining sales
Costs	High cost per customer	Average cost per customer	Low cost per customer	Low cost per customer
Profits	Negative	Rising profits	High profits	Declining profits
Customers	Innovators	Early adopters	Middle majority	Laggards
Competitors	Few	Growing number	Stable number beginning to decline	Declining number
Marketing Objectives				
	Create product awareness and trial	Maximize market share	Maximize profit while defending market share	Reduce expenditure and milk the brand
Strategies				
Product	Offer a basic product	Offer product extensions, service, warranty	Diversify brand and models	Phase out weak items
Price	Use cost-plus	Price to penetrate market	Price to match or best competitors	Cut price
Distribution	Build selective distribution	Build intensive distribution	Build more intensive distribution	Go selective: phase out unprofitable outlets
Advertising	Build product awareness among early adopters and dealers	Build awareness and interest in the mass market	Stress brand differences and benefits	Reduce to level needed to retain hard-core loyals
Sales Promotion	Use heavy sales promotion to entice trial	Reduce to take advantage of heavy consumer demand	Increase to encourage brand switching	Reduce to minimal level

Source: Philip Kotler, *Marketing Management: Analysis, Planning, Implementation, and Control,* 8th ed. (Englewood Cliffs, NJ: Prentice Hall, 1994), p. 365.

Summary of Chapter Objectives

Organizations must develop effective new product and service strategies. Their current products face limited life spans and must be replaced by newer products. But new products can fail—the risks of innovation are as great as the rewards. The key to successful innovation lies in a total-company effort, strong planning, and a systematic *new-product development* process.

1. **Explain how companies find and develop new-product ideas.**

Companies find and develop new-product ideas from various sources. Many new-product ideas stem from *internal sources.* Companies conduct formal research and development, "pick the brains" of their em-

ployees, and brainstorm at executive meetings. *Customers* are also a rich source of new-product ideas. By conducting surveys and focus groups and analysing customer questions and complaints, companies can generate new-product ideas that will meet specific consumer needs. *Competitors* are another source of new-product ideas. Companies track competitors' offerings and inspect new products, dismantling them, analysing their performance, and deciding whether to introduce a similar or improved product. Finally, *distributors and suppliers* may offer new-product ideas. Resellers are close to the market and can pass along information about consumer problems and new-product possibilities. Suppliers can tell the company about new concepts, techniques, and materials that can be used in new product development.

2. **List and define the steps in the new-product development process.**

    The new-product development process consists of eight sequential stages. A process starts with *idea generation*, which may draw inspiration from internal sources, customers, competitors, suppliers and others. Next comes *idea screening*, which reduces the number of ideas based on the company's own criteria. Ideas that pass the screening stage continue through *product concept development*, in which a detailed version of the new-product idea is stated in meaningful consumer terms. In the next stage, *concept testing*, new-product concepts are tested with a group of target consumers to determine whether the concepts have strong consumer appeal. Strong concepts proceed to *marketing strategy development*, in which an initial marketing strategy for the new product is developed from the product concept. In the *business analysis* stage, a review of the sales, costs, and profit projections for a new product is conducted to determine whether the new product is likely to satisfy the company's objectives. With positive results here, the ideas become more concrete through *test marketing* and finally are launched during *commercialization*.

3. **Describe the stages of the product life cycle.**

    Each product has a *life cycle* marked by a changing set of problems and opportunities. The sales of the typical product follow an S-shaped curve composed of five stages. The cycle begins with the *product-development stage* when the company finds and develops a new-product idea. The *introduction stage* is marked by slow growth and low profits as the product is distributed to the market. If successful, the product enters a *growth stage* that offers rapid sales growth and increasing profits. During this stage, the company tries to improve the product, enter new market segments and distribution channels, and reduce its prices slightly. Next comes a *maturity stage* when sales growth slows down and profits stabilize. The company seeks strategies to renew sales growth, including market, product, and marketing-mix modification. Finally, the product enters a *decline stage* in which sales and profits dwindle. The company's task during this stage is to recognize the decline, and to decide whether it should maintain, harvest, or drop the product. If the product is discontinued, it may be sold to another firm or liquidated for salvage value.

4. **Explain how marketing strategies change during the product's life cycle.**

    In the *introduction stage*, the company must choose a launch strategy consistent with its intended product positioning. Much money is needed to attract distributors and build their inventories, and to inform consumers of the new product and achieve trial. In the *growth stage*, companies continue to educate potential consumers and distributors. In addition, the company works to stay ahead of the competition and sustain rapid market growth by improving product quality; adding new product features and models; entering new market segments and distribution channels; shifting some advertising from building product awareness to building product conviction and purchase; and lowering prices at the right time to attract new buyers. In the *maturity stage*, companies continue to invest in maturing products and consider modifying the market, the product, and the marketing mix. When *modifying the market*, the company attempts to increase the consumption of the current product. When *modifying the product*, the company changes some of the product's characteristics—such as quality, features, or style—to attract new users or inspire more usage. When *modifying the market mix*, the company works to improve sales by changing one or more of the marketing-mix elements. Once the company recognizes that a product has entered the *decline stage*, management must decide whether to *maintain* the brand without change, hoping that competitors will drop out of the market; *harvest* the product, reducing costs and trying to maintaining sales; or *drop* the product, selling it to another firm or liquidating it at salvage value.

Key Terms

Business analysis *(p. 320)*
Commercialization *(p. 323)*
Concept testing *(p. 318)*
Decline stage *(p. 332)*
Fads *(p. 328)*
Fashion *(p. 328)*
Growth stage *(p. 329)*
Idea generation *(p. 314)*

Idea screening *(p. 317)*
Introduction stage *(p. 328)*
Marketing strategy development *(p. 319)*
Maturity stage *(p. 330)*
New-product development *(p. 313)*
Product concept *(p. 318)*
Product development *(p. 320)*

Product life cycle (PLC) *(p. 327)*
Sequential product development *(p. 325)*
Simultaneous product development *(p. 325)*
Style *(p. 328)*
Test marketing *(p. 321)*

Discussing the Issues

1. Labatt Breweries did careful market tests to launch its new Copper brand, yet the product failed. Discuss why you think the product flopped.

2. Less than one-third of new-product ideas come from the customer. Does this low percentage conflict with the marketing concept's philosophy of "find a need and fill it"? Why or why not?

3. Many companies have formal new product development systems and committees. Yet one recent study found that most successful new products were those that had been kept away from the formal system. Suggest reasons why might this be true.

4. List several factors you would consider in choosing cities for test marketing a new snack. Would where you live be a good test market? Why or why not?

5. Test market results for a new product are usually better than the business results the same brand achieves after it is launched. Name some reasons for this.

Applying the Concepts

1. List at least 10 new product ideas for your favourite fast-food chain. Out of all these ideas, which ones (if any) do you think would have a good chance of succeeding? What percentage of your ideas did you rate as having a good chance of success? [Divide the number of potentially successful ideas by the total number of ideas you listed, and multiply the result by 100 to get a percentage.] Can you explain why the potentially successful ideas seem stronger?

2. Go to the grocery store and list 15 items that appear to be new products. Rate each product for its level of innovation, with a 10 being extremely novel and highly innovative, and a 1 being a very minor change such as an improved package or fragrance. How truly new and innovative are these products overall? Do you think companies are being risk-averse because "pioneers are the ones who get shot"?

3. Divide your class into new-product teams. Develop a concept for a new product and a plan for launching it. Think about how well your team worked and how you could improve its performance.

References

1. Quotations from Lawrence Ingrassia, "Taming the Monster: How Big Companies Can Change," *The Wall Street Journal*, December 10, 1992, pp. A1, A6; William H. Miller, "Gillette's Secret to Sharpness," *Industry Week*, January 3, 1994, pp. 24–20; Linda Grant, "Gillette Knows Shaving—and How to Turn Out Hot New Products," *Fortune*, October 14, 1996, pp. 207–210; and Leslie Gevirtz, "Focus—Gillette

Posts Record Results in Quarter," Reuters Financial Service release, April 17, 1997; Alex Beckett, "Gillette to Debut Shaving Gel," *Strategy: The Canadian Marketing Report*, February 6, 1995, p. 1; Louise Gagnon, "Gillette Isn't About to Retire the Formula That Has Made Its Cavalcade of Sports Such a Success for 27 Years," *Marketing*, April 14, 1997, web site (marketingmag.com/search/gillette); "Duracell's Global Plans Charged by Gillette Purchase," *Marketing*, September 30, 1996, web site (marketingmag.com/search/gillette).

2. "Bright Ideas", *Royal Bank Reporter*, Fall 1992, pp. 6–15.

3. Kevin J. Clancy and Robert S. Shulman, *The Marketing Revolution: A Radical Manifesto for Dominating the Marketplace* (New York: Harper Business, 1991), p. 6; and Robert G. Cooper, "New Product Success in Industrial Firms," *Industrial Marketing Management*, 1992, pp. 215–223. Also see Gary Strauss, "Building on Brand Names: Companies Freshen Old Product Lines," *USA Today*, March 20, 1992, pp. B1, B2.

4. Robert G. Cooper and Elko J. Kleinschmidt, *New Product: The Key Factors in Success* (Chicago: American Marketing Association, 1990).

5. Jon Berry and Edward F. Ogiba, "It's Your Boss: Why New Products Fail," *Brandweek*, October 19, 1992, p. 16; Linda Grant, "Gillette Knows Shaving—and How to Turn Out Hot New Products," *Fortune*, October 14, 1996, pp. 207–210; Rosabeth Moss Kanter, "Don't Wait to Innovate," *Sales & Marketing Management*, February 1997, pp. 22–24; and Greg A. Stevens and James Burley, "3,000 Raw Ideas Equals 1 Commercial Success!" *Research-Technology Management*, May/June 1997, pp. 16–27.

6. Paul Sutter, "How to Succeed in Bubble Gum Without Really Trying," *Canadian Business*, Vol. 65, January 1992, pp. 48–50.

7. Brian O'Reilly, "New Ideas, New Products," *Fortune*, March 3, 1997, pp. 61–64.

8. See David Woodruff, "The Hottest Thing in 'Green Wheels,'" *Business Week*, April 28, 1997, p. 42.

9. See Raymond R. Burke, "Virtual Reality Shopping: Breakthrough in Marketing Research," *Harvard Business Review*, March–April 1996, pp. 120–131; and Brian Silverman, "Get 'Em While They're Hot," *Sales & Marketing Management*, February 1997, pp. 47–52.

10. Adrienne Ward Fawcett, "Orea Cones Make Top Grade in Poll," *Advertising Age*, June 14, 1993, p. 30.

Also see Linda Fitzpatrick, "Qualitative Concept Testing Tells Us What We Don't Know," *Marketing News*, September 23, 1996, p. 11.

11. See Faye Rice, "Secrets of Product Testing," *Fortune*, November 28, 1994, pp. 172–174; Simone Collier, "The Littlest Gourmet," *Report on Business*, April 1997, pp. 68–74.

12. See Howard Schlossberg, "IRI, Nielsen Slug It Out in 'Scanning Wars,'" *Marketing News*, September 2, 1991, pp. 1, 47.

13. Jennifer Lawrence, "P&G Rushes on Global Diaper Rollout," *Advertising Age*, October 14, 1991, p. 6; and Bill Saporito, "Behind the Tumult at P&G," *Fortune*, March 7, 1994, pp. 75–82.

14. See Hirotaka Takeuchi and Ikujiro Nonaka, "The New New-Product Development Game," *Harvard Business Review*, January-February 1986, pp. 137–46; Craig A. Chambers, "Transforming New Product Development," *Research-Technology Management*, November-December 1996, pp. 323–38; and Srikant Datar, C. Clark Jordan, Sunder Kekre, Surendra Rajiv, and Kannan Srinivasan, "Advantages of Time-Based New Product Development in a Fast-Cycle Industry," *Journal of Marketing Research*, February 1997, pp. 36–49. For a good review of research on new product development, see Shona L. Brown and Kathleen M. Eisenhardt, "Product Development: Past Research, Present Findings, and Future Directions," *Academy of Management Review*, April 1995, p. 343; and Jerry Wind and Vijay Mahajan, "Issue and Opportunities in New Product Development," *Journal of Marketing Research*, February 1997, pp. 1–12.

15. See George S. Day, "The Product Life Cycle: Analysis and Applications Issues," *Journal of Marketing*, Fall 1981, pp. 60–67; John E. Swan and David R. Rink, "Fitting Marketing Strategy to Varying Life Cycles," *Business Horizons*, January–February 1982, pp. 72–76; and Sak Onkvisit and John J. Shaw, "Competition and Product Management: Can the Product Life Cycle Help?" *Business Horizons*, July–August 1986, pp. 51–62.

16. Lara Mills, "Doc Martens Stepping Out to Reach an Older Market," *Marketing*, October 23, 1995, p. 2.

17. For a more comprehensive discussion of marketing strategies over the course of the product life cycle, see Philip Kotler, *Marketing Management*, 8th ed. (Englewood Cliffs, NJ: Prentice Hall, 1994), Chap. 14.

Company Case 9

INTRODUCING SPLENDA-BRAND SWEETENER

"An evolutionary ingredient that could dramatically change the food and beverage industry," is the bold opener for Redpath Specialty Products of Toronto's corporate brochure announcing the market launch of Splenda. Splenda is the first low-calorie sweetener actually created from sugar. Redpath Specialty Products hopes that manufacturers across Canada will incorporate Splenda into reduced-calorie versions of their products.

On September 5, 1991, Health and Welfare Canada granted regulatory approval for the new sweetener. Having received this clearance, Redpath hopes to challenge NutraSweet's hold on Canada's $25-million market for low-calorie foods.

Redpath hopes that Splenda offers food manufacturers a number of unique benefits that will encourage them to switch from the artificial sweeteners they are currently using. First, Splenda is 600 times sweeter than sugar. Redpath compares this to the fact that NutraSweet is only 180 times sweeter than sugar. Second, and even more importantly, Splenda leaves no unpleasant aftertaste.

Splenda, Redpath believes, will also be valuable to food manufacturers because it can withstand the high temperatures and severe processing conditions inherent to the manufacture of many food products. Furthermore, Splenda has durable properties. While NutraSweet only has a shelf life of six to eight weeks, Splenda does not break down over time.

MARKETPLACE POTENTIAL

As Canada's population ages, there has been increasing concern about health-related issues. More and more consumers are watching their weight. This has resulted in market growth rates for dietary-related products of over 230 percent over the last 10 years. Approximately 75 percent of Canadians consume calorie-reduced products on a regular basis. In fact, in certain product categories, low-calorie products have become the mainstream brand.

Because of the inability to include previous artificial sweeteners in many processed or baked-food products, and due to the inability of these products to retain their properties under high temperatures, Redpath believes that Splenda will result in rapid expansion of reduced-calorie products in a wider range of categories. If this occurs, Redpath expects the market to grow to over $50 million within the next five years.

THE MARKETING PLAN

A dual-pronged marketing effort is planned. Redpath believes that it must win over both manufacturers and consumers to make Splenda a success. However, the firm believes that a pull strategy will lead to eventual success. The market will grow as more and more consumers demand the inclusion of Splenda in the products they buy.

To create this consumer demand, Redpath plans to launch a major media campaign using heavy television advertising aimed at health-conscious women between the ages of 25 and 49. The Print Measurement Bureau estimates that 66.5 percent of all women and 33.5 percent of men are concerned about the nutritional content of the food they buy. In addition, the firm will use free-standing inserts in a number of consumer publications to create awareness of the product's benefits. This campaign is being launched with the objective of creating high product awareness among Canadian consumers.

Questions about which business segments to target have been heated. Some suggest that the soft-drink industry should be Splenda's prime target. Since consumers make frequent and heavy purchases of this product category, adoption of Splenda by soft-drink manufacturers would help it become well known in a short period. Others believe that NutraSweet is too well entrenched in this market and that manufacturers of baked goods would be a better target. They argue that the properties of Splenda shine in this application and that there is little competition from other sweeteners in this area.

Developing a positioning statement for the product has also been a difficult issue. Some managers believe that promoting the health benefits of Splenda should be the core of the campaign. Looking at the fact that almost one in five North Americans is overweight, and that one in 20 suffers from diabetes, these marketers believe that this market alone would be a substantial one for Splenda. Others disagree and suggest that Splenda should use a competition-based positioning strategy and focus on the claim that Splenda is a superior sweetener to NutraSweet. This positioning would appeal to both consumers and manufacturers in their view. The last group believes that Splenda is a unique product and that it should have a broad positioning statement to appeal to the many consumers who eat dietary products for cosmetic reasons or to maintain an active lifestyle.

Heavy promotional expenditures are considered necessary, not just to create awareness, but also to match the heavy advertising of Splenda's prime competitor, NutraSweet, a firm that spends up to $1.5 million annually on media advertising.

The media effort will be augmented by in-store promotions. Redpath plans to use couponing and sampling to promote trial of products made with Splenda. The company also hopes that the media will cover the product launch and that it will benefit from considerable public relations coverage.

QUESTIONS:

1. Which group should represent Splenda's primary target? Why?
2. How do you think NutraSweet will react to Splenda's entry into the market?
3. What specific tactics would you use to obtain trial of Splenda in both the consumer and manufacturer markets?
4. Should Redpath launch the product nationally or should it roll out the product gradually? If you decide for a gradual roll-out, which markets would you enter first?
5. What factors do you think will affect consumers' adoption of Splenda? How rapid will adoption be?

Sources: This case was written by P. Cunningham using the following sources: Barbara Aarsteinsen, "Approval for New Sweetener," *Toronto Star*, September 12, 1991; Marina Strauss, *Globe and Mail*, April 4, 1991, B1; *Redpath Specialty Products brochure: Introducing Splenda.*

Video Case 9

PROFITING FROM THE "NET"

Matt Harrop dropped out of high school in the mid 1990's to start his own business: Interlog, an Internet service provider (ISP) in Toronto. Although he knew his business, like the Internet itself, could grow fast, he had no idea how fast. For most of its first year of operation Interlog was experiencing growth of 15% per month. While this kind of growth is the envy of most business owners, managing that growth effectively turned out to be Matt's biggest business challenge.

Matt started Interlog in response to his own dissatisfaction as a customer of ISPs. ISPs are companies that provide a gateway to the Internet for computer users. ISPs generally have several phone lines and computer modems that allow easy access to the Internet for their customers. As a customer, Matt thought that existing ISPs were not doing a very good job and that he could do better. With a small bank loan, virtually no business plan and one phone line, Matt started Interlog.

There were only three other ISPs in business when Matt started, so competition was minimal. But demand was exploding as more and more businesses and consumers began to want access to the Internet. The resulting growth of Interlog was overwhelming. In the space of one year the company went from one phone line to 300 in order to service an end of the year customer base of 6,000 users. The company had to move twice during this time to keep up with the increased amount of hardware necessary to run the business and the increasing numbers of staff that were being hired to keep up with customer demand. During this first year, Matt recognized that he needed help with the management of the business. His strength was technical expertise, not management. He needed someone to help him effectively cope with the rate of growth that the company was experiencing. Matt's 26 year old brother, Lorian, a lawyer, was brought into the business as President to provide management leadership.

One of the problems caused by the rapid growth in the ISP industry was Interlog's inability to grow fast enough. An area that suffered was customer service. Interlog simply could not hire people fast enough to provide enough customer support. Matt and Lorian soon realized that service counts in the ISP business. Customers were demanding more and better service from all ISP service providers. If their phone connection was interrupted or if their software was not working properly while on the Internet, customers wanted to be able to talk to someone at their ISP who could solve the

problem. Increasing competition in the industry fuelled customer demands. At the end of Interlog's first year in business there were 80 ISP companies in business and customers were becoming more choosy. Interlog hired more employees to handle customer support so that by the end of the first year of operation there were twenty employees in the company, most in jobs related to customer technical support.

Financing the growth of Interlog has been another challenge. Despite their success, Matt and Lorian have had difficulty getting outside financing to help pay for the company's growth. Interlog is a profitable company in an otherwise unprofitable industry so getting investors has proven almost impossible. As a result the brothers have relied on bank lines of credit and leasing to see them through periods of growth.

The second year of business saw continuing rapid growth for Interlog: approximately 10% per month. The company was forced during this second year to become a larger, more formalized organization. At the end of year two of business there were 75 employees in the company servicing 30,000 customers. Since the systems in place for running the company were not developed for such a large organization, several changes were required. A new marketing department was created and the accounting and billing operation was completely revised to handle larger numbers of customers. The company offices had moved to the heart of the financial district in Toronto and now also included a storefront operation.

As Matt begins his third year of business he has not become complacent. He is well aware that the key to his success is the ability to change. Since the industry changes almost daily, both he and his organization have to be adaptable and creative. As Matt says, "If I can't think of something new and different, then I may as well not be in this business."

QUESTIONS:

1. What do you think the shape of the product life cycle for the ISP industry will look like?

2. What stage of the product life cycle is the ISP industry in right now? What implications does this have for the management of Interlog both now and in the future?

Source: This case was prepared by Auleen Carson and is based on the *Venture* series episode "Internet Geeks", which was first broadcast on March 30, 1997.

C H A P T E R 10

PRICING CONSIDERATIONS AND APPROACHES

Procter & Gamble (P&G), the huge consumer packaged-goods producer, is part of a complex food-industry distribution channel consisting of producers, wholesale food distributors, and grocery retailers. In 1992 and 1993, P&G's relations with many of its North American resellers took a decided turn for the worse. "We think that [P&G] will end up where most dictators end up—in trouble," fumed one reseller. Hundreds of kilometres away, another shared these harsh feelings: "We would obviously not delist P&G's products because they are too strong a player . . . but P&G's secondary brands might be given less prominence on the shelf than they received previously, and there would probably be a reluctance to list new items."

The cause of the uproar was P&G's new everyday fair pricing policy, tabbed "value pricing" by the company. Under this sweeping new plan, the company began phasing out most of the large promotional discounts that it had offered resellers in the past. At the same time, it lowered its everyday wholesale list prices for these products by 10 to 25 percent. P&G insists that price fluctuations and promotions had gotten out of hand. During the previous decade, average trade discounts had more than tripled. Some 44 percent of all marketing dollars spent by manufacturers went to trade promotions, up from 24 percent only a decade earlier.

Manufacturers had come to rely on price-oriented trade promotions to differentiate their brands and boost short-term sales. In turn, wholesalers and retail chains were conditioned to wait for manufacturers' "deals." While some Canadian supermarkets such as Loeb and the Price Club use everyday low pricing, others, like Food City, Loblaw, A&P, and Miracle Food Mart, are "high-low" retailers. These companies rely on short-lived promotions of select products to increase customer traffic. These promotions are funded by manufacturers who periodically sell goods to retailers at less than normal cost, so the retailer can then sell them to consumers at lower prices. These retailers also use "forward buying"—stocking up during manufacturer's price promotions on far more merchandise than they could sell, then reselling it to consumers at higher prices once the promotion was over. Such forward buying created costly production and distribution inefficiencies. P&G's factories

When you finish this chapter, you should be able to

1. Identify and define the internal factors affecting a firm's pricing decisions.

2. Identify and define the external factors affecting pricing decisions, including the impact of consumer perceptions of price and value.

3. Contrast the three general approaches to setting prices.

had to gear up to meet the resulting huge demand swings. Meanwhile, supermarkets needed more buyers to find the best prices and extra warehouses to store and handle merchandise that was bought "on deal." The industry's "promotion sickness" also infected consumers. Wildly fluctuating retail prices eroded brand loyalty by teaching consumers to shop for what's on sale, rather than to assess the merits of each brand.

Procter & Gamble
www.pg.com/

Through value pricing, P&G sought to restore the price integrity of its brands and to begin weaning the industry and consumers from discount pricing. But the strategy came into conflict with the pricing strategies of P&G's distribution channels. Discounts are the bread and butter of many retailers and wholesalers, who had used products that were purchased from P&G at special low prices for weekly sales to lure value-minded consumers into supermarkets or stores. In other cases, retailers and wholesalers relied on the discounts to pad their profits through forward buying. And although the average costs of products to resellers remained unchanged, resellers lost promotional dollars that they—not P&G—controlled. Thus, the new system gave P&G greater control over how its products are marketed, but reduced retailer and wholesaler pricing flexibility.

P&G's new strategy was risky. It alienated some of the very businesses that sell its wares to the public and it gave competitors an opportunity to take advantage of the ban on promotions by highlighting their own specials. P&G counted on its enormous market clout—retailers could ill afford, the company hoped, to eliminate heavily advertised and immensely popular brands such as Tide detergent, Crest toothpaste, Folger's coffee, Pert shampoo, and Ivory soap. But even P&G's size and power were sorely tested. Some large chains such as A&P and Safeway began pruning out selected P&G sizes or dropping marginal brands such as Prell and Gleem. And other chains considered moving P&G brands from prime, eye-level space to less visible shelves, stocking more profitable private-label brands and competitors' products in P&G's place.

Despite these strong reactions, P&G stayed the course with its bold new pricing approach, and the strategy appears to be paying off. After an initial drop in sales and market shares, P&G's products in most categories are again growing steadily and producing healthier profits. The company claims that it has cut list prices an average of six percent across its product portfolio, saving consumers over $8 billion during the past three years. Given this success at home, P&G introduced value pricing to its European markets in 1996. And it received the same blistering response from European retailers that it had received from North American retailers five years earlier. For example, Germany's largest retailer, Rewe, and its major supermarket chain, Spar, immediately "delisted" several P&G brands, including Ariel, Vizir, and Lenor laundry products, Bess toilet paper, and Tempo tissues. As happened in North America, initial European sales and market shares dipped as angry retailers responded.

P&G's struggle to reshape the industry's distorted pricing system demonstrates the dynamic forces shaping today's pricing decisions. Ideally, P&G should set its prices at the level that will reflect and enhance the value that consumers perceive in its brands. But such value is difficult to assess. Which offers more value: higher regular prices with frequent sales or lower everyday prices? And what impact will each pricing strategy have on consumer perceptions of brand quality? P&G's pricing decisions would be difficult enough if the company had only to set its own prices and gauge customer reactions. However, P&G's pricing decisions affect not only its own sales and profits, but also those of its marketing partners. Thus, P&G must work with resellers to find the pricing structure that is best for all. In the end, customers will judge whether prices accurately reflect the value they receive. Which is the best pricing strategy? Customers will vote with their food budget dollars.[1]

All profit organizations and many non-profit organizations must set prices on their products or services. *Price* goes by many names:

Price is all around us. You pay *rent* for your apartment, *tuition* for your education, and a *fee* to your ... dentist. The airline, railway, taxi, and bus companies charge you a *fare;* the local utilities call their price a *rate;* and the local bank charges you *interest* for the money you borrow. The price for driving your car on [the Rainbow bridge] is a *toll,* and the company that insures your car charges you a *premium.* The guest lecturer charges an *honorarium* to tell you about a government official who took a *bribe* to help a shady character steal *dues* collected by a trade association. Clubs or societies to which you belong may make a special *assessment* to pay unusual expenses. Your regular lawyer may ask for a *retainer* to cover her services. The "price" of an executive is a *salary,* the price of a salesperson may be a *commission,* and the price of a worker is a *wage.* Finally, although economists would disagree, many of us feel that *income taxes* are the price we pay for the privilege of making money.[2]

Price
The amount of money charged for a product or service, or the sum of the values that consumers exchange for the benefits of having or using the product or service.

In the narrowest sense, **price** is the amount of money charged for a product or service. More broadly, price is the sum of all the values that consumers exchange for the benefits of having or using the product or service.

How are prices set? Historically, prices usually were set by buyers and sellers bargaining with each other. Sellers would ask for a higher price than they expected to get, and buyers would offer less than they expected to pay. Through bargaining, they would arrive at an acceptable price. Individual buyers paid different prices for the same products, depending on their needs and bargaining skills.

Price is the only element in the marketing mix that produces revenue; all other elements represent costs. Price is also one of the most flexible elements of the marketing mix. Unlike product features and channel commitments, price can be changed quickly. At the same time, pricing and price competition is the number-one problem facing many marketing executives. Yet, many companies do not handle pricing well. The most common mistakes are pricing that is too cost oriented; prices that are not revised often enough to reflect market changes; pricing that does not take the rest of the marketing mix into account; and prices that are not varied enough for different products, market segments, and purchase occasions.

In this and the next chapter, we focus on the problem of setting prices. This chapter looks at the factors that marketers must consider when setting prices and at general pricing approaches. In the next chapter, we examine pricing strategies for new-product pricing, product mix pricing, price changes, and price adjustments for buyer and situational factors.

FACTORS TO CONSIDER WHEN SETTING PRICES

A company's pricing decisions are affected both by internal company factors and external environmental factors (see Figure 10-1).[3]

INTERNAL FACTORS AFFECTING PRICING DECISIONS

Internal factors affecting pricing include the company's marketing objectives, marketing-mix strategy, costs, and organization.

FIGURE 10-1 *Factors affecting price decisions*

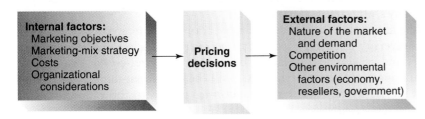

Marketing Objectives

Before setting price, the company must decide on its strategy for the product. If the company has selected its target market and positioning carefully, then its marketing-mix strategy, including price, will be fairly straightforward. For example, if General Motors decides to produce a new sports car to compete

Sub-Zero charges a premium price for its custom-made refrigerators to attain product-quality leadership.

Sub-Zero Refrigerators
www.yaleelectric.com/
refrig/sub/.htm

with European sports cars in the high-income segment, this suggests charging a high price. First Canada Inns, Best Value Inns, and Days Inn have positioned themselves as motels that provide economical rooms for budget-minded travellers; this position requires charging a low price. Thus, pricing strategy is largely determined by decisions on market positioning.

At the same time, the company may seek additional objectives. The clearer a firm is about its objectives, the easier it is to set price. Examples of common objectives are *survival, current profit maximization, market-share leadership,* and *product-quality leadership.*

Companies set *survival* as their major objective if they are troubled by too much capacity, heavy competition, or changing consumer wants. To keep a plant going, a company may set a low price, hoping to increase demand. In this case, profits are less important than survival. As long as their prices cover variable costs and some fixed costs, they can stay in business. However, survival is only a short-term objective. In the long run, the firm must learn how to add value or face extinction.

Many companies use *current profit maximization* as their pricing goal. They estimate what demand and costs will be at different prices and choose the price that will produce the maximum current profit, cash flow, or return on investment. In all cases, the company wants current financial results rather than long-run performance. Other companies want to obtain *market-share leadership.* They believe that the company with the largest market share will enjoy the lowest costs and highest long-run profit. To become the market-share leader, these firms set prices as low as possible. A variation of this objective is to pursue a specific market-share gain. Suppose the company wants to increase its market share from 10 percent to 15 percent in one year. It will search for the price and marketing program that will achieve this goal.

A company might decide that it wants to achieve *product-quality leadership.* This normally calls for charging a high price to cover such quality and the high cost of R&D. For example, Sub-Zero makes the Rolls-Royce of refrigerators—custom-made, built-in units that look more like hardwood cabinets or pieces of furniture than refrigerators. By offering the highest quality, Sub-Zero sells more than $70 million worth of fancy refrigerators a year worldwide, priced at up to $4000 each. Similarly, Pitney Bowes pursues a product-quality leadership strategy for its fax equipment. While Sharp, Canon, and other competitors fight over the low-price fax machine market with machines selling at around $700, Pitney Bowes targets large corporations with machines selling at about $7000. As a result, it captures some 45 percent of the large-corporation fax niche.[4]

A company also might use price to attain other more specific objectives. It can set prices low to prevent competition from entering the market or set prices at competitors' levels to stabilize the market. Prices can be set to keep the loyalty and support of resellers or to avoid government intervention. Prices can be reduced temporarily to create excitement for a product or to draw more customers into a retail store. One product may be priced to help the sales of other products in the company's line. Thus, pricing may play an important role in helping to accomplish the company's objectives at many levels.

Non-profit and public organizations may adopt a number of other pricing objectives. A university aims for *partial cost recovery,* knowing that it must rely on private gifts and government grants to cover the remaining costs. A non-profit theatre company may price its productions to fill the maximum number of theatre seats. A social service agency may set a *social price* geared to the varying income situations of different clients.

Marketing-Mix Strategy

Price is only one of the marketing-mix tools that a company uses to achieve its marketing objectives. Price decisions must be coordinated with product design, distribution, and promotion decisions to form a consistent and effective marketing program. Decisions made for other marketing-mix variables may affect pricing decisions. For example, producers using many resellers who are expected to support and promote their products may have to build larger reseller margins into their prices. The decision to position the product on high performance quality will mean that the seller must charge a higher price to cover higher costs.

Companies often make their pricing decisions first and then base other marketing-mix decisions on the prices they want to charge. Here, price is a crucial product positioning factor that defines the product's market, competition, and design. Many firms support such price-positioning strategies with a technique called *target costing,* a potent strategic weapon. Target costing reverses the usual process of first designing a new product, determining its cost, and then asking "Can we sell it for that?" Instead, it starts with an ideal selling price and targets, or controls costs, to ensure that the price is met.

Compaq Computer Corp.
www.compaq.com/

Compaq Computer Corporation calls this process "design to price." After being battered for years by lower-priced rivals, Compaq used this approach to create its highly successful, lower-priced Prolinea personal computer line. Starting with a price target set by marketing, and with profit-margin goals from management, the Prolinea design team determined what costs had to be in order to charge the target price. From this crucial calculation all else followed. To achieve target costs, the design team negotiated doggedly with all the company departments responsible for different aspects of the new product, and with outside suppliers of needed parts and materials. Compaq engineers designed a machine with fewer and simpler parts, manufacturing overhauled its factories to reduce production costs, and suppliers found ways to provide quality components at needed prices. By meeting its target *costs,* Compaq was able to set its target *price* and establish the desired price position. As a result, Prolinea sales and profits soared.[5]

Johnson Controls, Inc.
www.jci.com/

Other companies deemphasize price and use other marketing-mix tools to create *non-price* positions. Often, the best strategy is not to charge the lowest price, but rather to differentiate the marketing offer to make it worth a higher price. For example, for years Johnson Controls, a producer of climate-control systems for

Target costing: In creating its highly successful, lower-priced Prolinea line, Compaq started with a target price set by marketing and profit-margin goals from management. Then the design team determined what costs had to be in order to charge the target price.

office buildings, used initial price as its primary competitive tool. However, research showed that customers were more concerned about the total cost of installing and maintaining a system than about its initial price. Repairing broken systems was expensive, time-consuming, and risky. Customers had to shut down the heat or air conditioning in the whole building, disconnect a lot of wires, and face the dangers of electrocution. Johnson decided to change its strategy. It designed an entirely new system called Metasys. To repair the new system, customers need only pull out an old plastic module and slip in a new one—no tools required. Metasys costs more to make than the old system, and customers pay a higher initial price, but it costs less to install and maintain. Despite its higher asking price, the new Metasys system brought in $700 million in revenues in its first year.[6]

Thus, the marketer must consider the total marketing mix when setting prices. If the product is positioned on non-price factors, then decisions about quality, promotion, and distribution will strongly affect price. If price is a crucial positioning factor, then price will strongly affect decisions made about the other marketing-mix elements. However, even when featuring price, marketers need to remember that customers rarely buy on price alone. Instead, they seek products that give them the best value in terms of benefits received for the price paid. Thus, in most cases, the company will consider price along with all the other marketing-mix elements when developing the marketing program (see Marketing Highlight 10-1).

Costs

Costs set the floor for the price that the company can charge for its product. The company wants to charge a price that both covers all its costs for producing, distributing, and selling the product and delivers a fair rate of return for its effort and risk. A company's costs may be an important element in its pricing strategy. Many companies work to become the "low-cost producers" in their industries. Companies with lower costs can set lower prices that result in greater sales and profits.

Fixed costs
Costs that do not vary with production or sales level.

TYPES OF COSTS. A company's costs take two forms—fixed and variable. **Fixed costs** (also known as overhead) are costs that do not vary with production or sales level. For example, a company must pay each month's bills for rent, heat, interest, and executive salaries, whatever the company's output.

Variable costs
Costs that vary directly with the level of production.

Variable costs vary directly with the level of production. Each personal computer produced by Compaq involves a cost of computer chips, wires, plastic, packaging, and other inputs. These costs tend to be the same for each unit produced. They are called *variable* because their total varies with the number of units produced.

Total costs
The sum of the fixed and variable costs for any given level of production.

Total costs are the sum of the fixed and variable costs for any given level of production. Management wants to charge a price that will at least cover the total production costs at a given level of production. The company must watch its costs carefully. If it costs the company more than competitors to produce and sell a similar product, the company will have to charge a higher price or make less profit, putting it at a competitive disadvantage.

COSTS AT DIFFERENT LEVELS OF PRODUCTION. To price wisely, management needs to know how its costs vary with different levels of production. For example, suppose Texas Instruments (TI) has built a plant to produce 1000 hand-held calculators per day. Figure 10-2A shows the typical short-run average cost curve (SRAC). It shows that the cost per calculator is high if TI's factory produces only a few per day. But as production moves up to 1000 calculators per day, average cost falls. This is because fixed costs are spread over more units, with each one bearing a smaller fixed cost. TI can try to produce more than 1000 calculators per day, but average costs will increase because the plant becomes inefficient. Workers have to wait for machines, the machines break down more often, and workers get in each other's way.

OXYMORON: HIGH FASHION— DISCOUNT PRICE?

Will Canadian consumers believe that they can buy high-fashion clothing at discount prices? Winners thinks that this is a persuasive combination. And it has the sales figures to prove it. While the average fashion retailer generates sales of $250 per square foot, Winners manages a rate of $350. Moreover, its sales have climbed to over $100 million and management projects that growth will continue at an annual rate of 38 percent. These figures are even more amazing when one considers the number of bankruptcies occurring in fashion retailing.

Founded by David Margolis in 1982, Winners is a fashion discounter with retail outlets in Western Canada and Ontario. The company's success is reflected in its significant expansion plans. It is opening stores in Winnipeg, Calgary, and Edmonton to strengthen its western presence, and it plans to have over 100 stores in operation by 1997.

Margolis stresses that Winners isn't just another discount operation. Instead of selling low-quality clothing at low prices, the chain specializes in brand-name, high-quality, designer fashions. The company buys the excess inventory of design houses, or snaps up orders where retailers have defaulted on their line of credit. This allows Winners to offer clothing at

prices 40 percent below those charged by specialty retailers.

Quality and seasonality are features that set Winners apart from other off-price merchandisers. Part of Winners' strategy is to offer clothing in the appropriate season. Therefore it does not buy up slow-moving goods

Bargain prices combined with high-fashion merchandise have attracted a flood of shoppers to Winners.

at the end of the season. Being able to find the right fashion item at the right time of year has often been the winning strategy to bring back a first-time customer again and again.

You might also be surprised by who shops at Winners. While you might picture low-income, bargain-

conscious consumers as the stores' main clientele, you would be mistaken. Everyone from teenagers seeking leading-edge fashion to high-income career women stalk its aisles. Who can resist finding a T-shirt with a suggested retail price of $50 for $15? Such bargains give Winners shoppers

the feeling of being on a treasure hunt. There is a certain satisfaction, even among the wealthiest consumers, in saying what a bargain they found.

Source: Clayton Sinclair, "High Fashion at a Deep Discount," *Financial Times of Canada*, December 11, 1993, p. 12.

If TI believed it could sell 2000 calculators a day, it should consider building a larger plant. The plant would use more efficient machinery and work arrangements. Also, the unit cost of producing 2000 calculators per day would be lower than the unit cost of producing 1000 calculators per day, as shown in the long-run average cost (LRAC) curve (Figure 10-2B). In fact, a 3000-capacity plant would even be more efficient, according to Figure 10-2B. But a 4000 daily production plant would be less efficient because of increasing diseconomies of scale— too many workers to manage, paperwork slows things down, and so on. Figure 10-2B shows that a 3000 daily production plant is the best size to build if demand is strong enough to support this level of production.

COSTS AS A FUNCTION OF PRODUCTION EXPERIENCE. Suppose TI runs a plant that produces 3000 calculators per day. As TI gains experience in producing handheld calculators, it learns how to do it better. Workers learn shortcuts and become more familiar with their equipment. With practice, the work becomes better organized, and TI finds better equipment and production processes. With higher volume, TI becomes more efficient and gains economies of scale. As a result, average cost tends to fall with accumulated production experience. This is shown in Figure 10-3.[7] Thus, the average cost of producing the first 100 000 calculators is $10 per

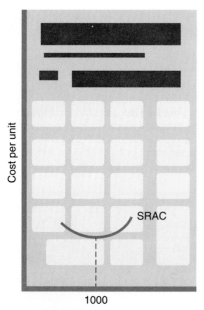

1000
Quantity produced per day
A. Cost behaviour in a fixed-size plant

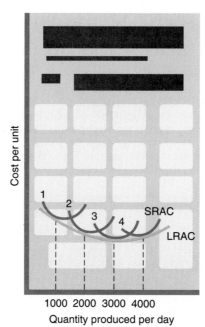

1000 2000 3000 4000
Quantity produced per day
B. Cost behaviour over different-size plants

FIGURE 10-2 *Cost per unit at different levels of production per period*

Experience curve (learning curve)
The drop in the average per-unit production cost that comes with accumulated production experience.

FIGURE 10-3 *Cost per unit as a function of accumulated production: the experience curve*

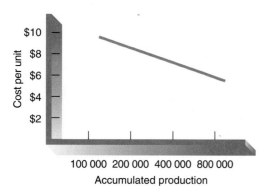

100 000 200 000 400 000 800 000
Accumulated production

calculator. When the company has produced the first 200 000 calculators, the average cost has fallen to $9. After its accumulated production experience doubles again to 400 000, the average cost is $7. This drop in the average cost with accumulated production experience is called the **experience curve** (or the **learning curve**).

If a downward-sloping experience curve exists, this is highly significant for the company. Not only will the company's unit production cost fall, but it will also fall faster if the company makes and sells more during a given period. But the market must stand ready to buy the higher output. And to take advantage of the experience curve, TI must get a large market share early in the product's life cycle. This suggests the following pricing strategy. TI should price its calculators low; its sales will then increase, and its costs will decrease through gaining more experience, and then it can lower its prices further.

Some companies have built successful strategies around the experience curve. For example, during the 1980s, Bausch & Lomb solidified its position in the soft contact lens market by using computerized lens design and steadily expanding its one Soflens plant. As a result, its market share climbed steadily to 65 percent. However, a single-minded focus on reducing costs and exploiting the experience curve will not always work. Experience curves became somewhat of a fad during the 1970s, and like many fads, the strategy was sometimes misused. Experience curve pricing carries some major risks. The aggressive pricing might give the product a cheap image. The strategy also assumes that competitors are weak and not willing to fight it out by meeting the company's price cuts. Finally, while the company is building volume under one technology, a competitor may find a lower-cost technology that lets it start at lower prices than the market leader, who still operates on the old experience curve.

Organizational Considerations
Management must decide who within the organization should set prices. Companies handle pricing in a variety of ways. In small companies, prices often are set by top management rather than by the marketing or sales departments. In large companies, pricing typically is handled by divisional or product line managers. In industrial markets, salespeople may be allowed to negotiate with customers within certain price ranges. Even so, top management sets the pricing objectives and policies, and it often approves the prices proposed by lower-level management or salespeople. In industries in which pricing is a key factor (aerospace, railways, oil companies), companies often will have a pricing department to set the best prices or help others in setting them. This department reports to the marketing department or top management. Others who have an influence on pricing include sales managers, production managers, finance managers, and accountants.

EXTERNAL FACTORS AFFECTING PRICING DECISIONS

External factors that affect pricing decisions include the nature of the market and demand, competition, and other environmental elements.

The Market and Demand

Whereas costs set the lower limit of prices, the market and demand set the upper limit. Both consumer and industrial buyers balance the price of a product or service against the benefits of owning it. Thus, before setting prices, the marketer must understand the relationship between price and demand for its product.

In this section, we explain how the price-demand relationship varies for different types of markets and how buyer perceptions of price affect the pricing decision. We then discuss methods for measuring the price-demand relationship.

PRICING IN DIFFERENT TYPES OF MARKETS.   The seller's pricing freedom varies with different types of markets. Economists recognize four types of markets, each presenting a different pricing challenge.

Pure competition
A market in which many buyers and sellers trade in a uniform commodity—no single buyer or seller has much effect on the going market price.

Under **pure competition,** the market consists of many buyers and sellers trading in a uniform commodity such as wheat, copper, or financial securities. No single buyer or seller has much effect on the going market price. A seller cannot charge more than the going price because buyers can obtain as much as they need at the going price. Nor would sellers charge less than the market price because they can sell all they want at this price. If price and profits rise, new sellers can easily enter the market. In a purely competitive market, marketing research, product development, pricing, advertising, and sales promotion play little or no role. Thus, sellers in these markets do not spend much time on marketing strategy. This lack of attention to marketing may be shortsighted, however. Marketing Highlight 10-2 outlines how a new marketing strategy changed the base of competition in the Canadian dairy industry.

Monopolistic competition
A market in which many buyers and sellers trade over a range of prices rather than a single market price.

Under **monopolistic competition,** the market consists of many buyers and sellers who trade over a range of prices rather than a single market price. A range of prices occurs because sellers can differentiate their offers to buyers. Either the physical product can be varied in quality, features, or style, or the accompanying services can be varied. Buyers see differences in sellers' products and will pay different prices for them. Sellers try to develop differentiated offers for different customer segments and, in addition to price, freely use branding, advertising, and personal selling to set their offers apart. For example, H.J. Heinz, Vlasic, Bick's, and several other national brands of pickles compete with dozens of regional and local brands, all differentiated by price and non-price factors. Because there are

Monopolistic competition: Canadian pickle marketer Bick's sets its pickles apart from dozens of other brands using both price and non-price factors.

REINVENTING MILK: SHAKING UP COMPETITION

Companies selling commodities in industries long regarded as purely competitive, struggle to free themselves from price-based competition. Consider the recent shake-up of the $2.5-billion dairy industry caused by Toronto-based Ault Foods Limited. Demand for milk has fallen in recent years as aging consumers switch to bottled waters and juices. For years grocery stores have used milk as a loss leader to generate customer traffic. Ault Food's introduction of Lactantia PürFiltre milk can be viewed as a strategy to differentiate its product and escape the limitations of pure price competition. The company hopes that its claims of fresher taste and longer shelf life will enable it to charge a premium price for its product. Ault Foods plans to charge 10 to 15 cents per litre more for its new product.

Developing a new form of milk wasn't an easy endeavour. It took Ault Foods four years to research the opportunity among consumers and to then develop the technology to meet consumer tastes. The company ran up bills of more than $8 million in the process. Ault was originally attempting to develop a cholesterol-free product, but realized that this technology was still years away. It decided, instead, to concentrate on the microfiltration process that eliminated the bacteria left behind by pasteurization.

The January 1995 launch caused considerable excitement in the staid dairy industry as witnessed by enthusiasm evident in a statement by Mike Pierce, director of product promotions at the Ontario Milk Marketing Board, "This move de-commodizes milk. Instead of just being the loss leader at grocery stores, milk could be brand-marketed and the processor could gain more margin."

Quebec producers didn't take long to recognize the power of the strategy. Natrel, the province's largest dairy company, launched Ultra'milk, a premium milk with extended shelf life. Premium milk has been popular in Quebec for some time, controlling 10 percent of the market. But launching such a new product is not cheap. Natrel accompanied the launch with a $1.3-million ad campaign.

Lactantia escaped price-based competition with its introduction of PürFiltre milk.

Competitive reaction to Ault's introduction of Lactantia PürFiltre was swift. Fearing that Ault's claims of a new, pure milk would turn away consumers from regular milk, other firms readied for battle. Cries of misleading marketing were heard throughout the marketplace. Beatrice Foods Ltd. led the attacks. First, it ran newspaper ads showing a mother nursing an infant with the headline: "With one exception, there's no milk more pure, more fresh, or more nutritious than Beatrice." It also conducted a series of taste tests that showed that consumers couldn't distinguish between Pürfiltre and Beatrice's milk and sought a court injunction to stop Ault from making its taste-based advertising claims. The courts, however, sided with Ault, viewing Beatrice's efforts as a rival's attempt to thwart competition.

Ault Foods had hoped to gain 15 percent of the market with its new product. However, its sales have been far from this target, reaching only 4.6 percent of the market in Ontario and 13 percent in Quebec. Ault Food's efforts to gain share have been stymied by its inability to gain intensive distribution for the product in Ontario. One of the main problems was its inability to get shelf space in the Loblaw chain. Loblaw is owned by George Weston Ltd., a firm that also owns a dairy firm, Neilson, a long-time competitor of Ault Foods. In August 1995, Neilson launched its own product, Trufiltre, which used microfiltering as well as an enrichment technique that gives its low-fat milk a rich taste. Trufiltre does not offer longer shelf life, however. The product has proven to be a popular with Loblaw shoppers and now accounts for 20 percent of Neilson's carton milk sales.

Sources: Laura Medcalf, "Cash Cow," *Marketing*, October 30, 1995, p. 10; Natrel Launches Premium Milk in Quebec," *Marketing*, October 23, 1995, p. 1; Laura Medcalf, "Trufiltre Joins High-Tech Milk Battle," *Marketing*, September 11, 1995, p. 4; James Pollock, "Ault Whips Up the Dairy Industry with PürFiltre, *Marketing*, March 13, 1995, p. 2; Marina Strauss, "Industry Cries Over Premium Milk," *Globe and Mail*, January 15, 1995, B1, B14; Natrel Launches Premium Milk in Quebec," *Marketing*, October 23, 1995, p. 1.

many competitors, each firm is less affected by competitors' marketing strategies than in oligopolistic markets.

Oligopolistic competition
A market in which there are a few sellers who are highly sensitive to each other's pricing and marketing strategies.

Under **oligopolistic competition,** the market consists of a few sellers who are highly sensitive to each other's pricing and marketing strategies. The product can be uniform (steel, aluminum) or non-uniform (cars, computers). There are few sellers because it is difficult for new sellers to enter the market. Each seller is alert to competitors' strategies and moves. If a steel company slashes its price by 10 percent, buyers will quickly switch to this supplier. The other steelmakers must respond by lowering their prices or increasing their services. An oligopolist is never sure that it will gain anything permanent through a price cut. In contrast, if an oligopolist raises its price, its competitors might not follow this lead. The oligopolist then would have to retract its price increase or risk losing customers to competitors.

Pure monopoly
A market in which there is a single seller—it may be a government monopoly, a private regulated monopoly, or a private nonregulated monopoly.

In a **pure monopoly**, the market consists of one seller. The seller may be a government monopoly (Canada Post), a private regulated monopoly (Trans Alta Utilities), or a private non-regulated monopoly (Du Pont when it introduced nylon). Pricing is handled differently in each case. A government monopoly can pursue a variety of pricing objectives. It might set a price below cost because the product is important to buyers who cannot afford to pay full cost. Or the price might be set either to cover costs or to produce good revenue. It can even be set quite high to slow down consumption. Until recently, this is how the Canadian government sought to decrease tobacco sales. In a regulated monopoly, the government permits the company to set rates that will yield a "fair return"—one that will let the company maintain and expand its operations as needed. Nonregulated monopolies are free to price at what the market will bear. However, they do not always charge the full price for a number of reasons: a desire not to attract competition, a desire to penetrate the market faster with a low price, or a fear of government regulation.

CONSUMER PERCEPTIONS OF PRICE AND VALUE. In the end, the consumer will decide whether a product's price is right. Pricing decisions, like other marketing-mix decisions, must be buyer oriented. When consumers buy a product, they exchange something of value (the price) to get something of value (the benefits of having or using the product). Effective, buyer-oriented pricing involves understanding how much value consumers place on the benefits they receive from the product and setting a price that fits this value.

A company often will find it hard to measure the values that customers will attach to its product. How do you value the way people feel when they wear brand-name or designer clothes, for example? But consumers do use these values to evaluate a product's price. If the perceived price is greater than the product's value, consumers will not buy the product. If the perceived price is below the product's value, they will buy it, but the seller loses profit opportunities. Marketers, therefore, must try to understand the consumer's reasons for buying the product and set price according to consumer perceptions of the product's value.

ANALYSING THE PRICE-DEMAND RELATIONSHIP. Each price the company might charge will lead to a different level of demand. The relation between the price charged and the resulting demand level is shown in the **demand curve** in Figure 10-4. The demand curve shows the number of units the market will buy in a given time period, at different prices that might be charged. In the normal case, demand and price are inversely related: That is, the higher the price, the lower the demand. Thus, the company would sell less if it raised its price from P_1 to P_2. In short, consumers with limited budgets probably will buy less of something if its price is too high.

In the case of prestige goods, the demand curve sometimes slopes upward. For example, one perfume company found that by raising its price, it sold more perfume rather than less. Consumers thought the higher price meant a better or more desirable perfume. However, if the company charges too high a price, the level of demand will be lower.

Demand curve
A curve that shows the number of units the market will buy in a given time period, at different prices that might be charged.

FIGURE 10-4 *Demand curves*

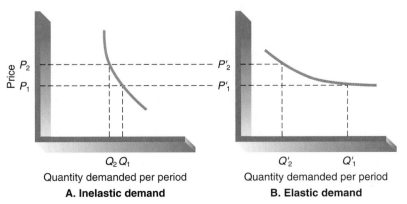

Quantity demanded per period
A. Inelastic demand

Quantity demanded per period
B. Elastic demand

Most companies try to measure their demand curves by estimating demand at different prices. The type of market makes a difference. In a monopoly, the demand curve shows the total market demand resulting from different prices. If the company faces competition, its demand at different prices will depend on whether competitors' prices stay constant or change with the company's own prices. Here, we will assume that competitors' prices remain constant. Later in this chapter, we will discuss what happens when competitors' prices change.

In measuring the price-demand relationship, the market researcher must not allow other factors affecting demand to vary. For example, if Sony increased its advertising at the same time as it lowered its television prices, we would not know how much of the increased demand was due to the lower prices and how much was due to the increased advertising. The same problem arises if a holiday weekend occurs when the lower price is set—more gift giving over the holidays causes people to buy more televisions. Economists show the impact of non-price factors on demand through shifts in the demand curve rather than movements along it.

Price elasticity
A measure of the sensitivity of demand to changes in price.

PRICE ELASTICITY OF DEMAND. Marketers also need to know **price elasticity**—how responsive demand will be to a change in price. Consider the two demand curves in Figure 10-4. In Figure 10-4A, a price increase from P_1 to P_2 leads to a relatively small drop in demand from Q_1 to Q_2. In Figure 10-4B, however, the same price increase leads to a large drop in demand from Q'_1 to Q'_2. If demand hardly changes with a small change in price, we say the demand is *inelastic*. If demand changes greatly, we say the demand is *elastic*. The price elasticity of demand is given by the following formula:

$$\text{Price Elasticity of Demand} = \frac{\text{\% Change in Quantity Demanded}}{\text{\% Change in Price}}$$

Suppose demand falls by 10 percent when a seller raises its price by 2 percent. Price elasticity of demand is therefore –5 (the minus sign confirms the inverse relation between price and demand) and demand is elastic. If demand falls by 2 percent with a 2 percent increase in price, then elasticity is –1. In this case, the seller's total revenue stays the same: The seller sells fewer items but at a higher price that preserves the same total revenue. If demand falls by 1 percent when price is increased by 2 percent, then elasticity is –1/2 and demand is inelastic. The less elastic the demand, the more it pays for the seller to raise the price.

What determines the price elasticity of demand? Buyers are less price-sensitive when the product they are buying is unique or when it is high in quality, prestige, or exclusiveness. They are also less price-sensitive when substitute products are hard to find or when they cannot easily compare the quality of substitutes. Finally, buyers are less price-sensitive when the total expenditure for a product is low relative to their income or when the cost is shared by another party.[8]

If demand is elastic rather than inelastic, sellers will consider lowering their price. A lower price will produce more total revenue. This practice makes sense as long as the extra costs of producing and selling more do not exceed the extra revenue.

Competitors' Costs, Prices, and Offers

Another external factor affecting the company's pricing decisions is competitors' costs and prices and possible competitor reactions to the company's own pricing moves. A consumer who is considering the purchase of a Canon camera will evaluate Canon's price and value against the prices and values of comparable products made by Nikon, Minolta, Pentax, and others. In addition, the company's pricing strategy may affect the nature of the competition it faces. If Canon follows a high-price, high-margin strategy, it may attract competition. A low-price, low-margin strategy, however, may stop competitors or drive them out of the market.

Canon needs to benchmark its costs against its competitors' costs to learn whether it is operating at a cost advantage or disadvantage. It also needs to learn the price and quality of each competitor's offer. Once Canon is aware of competitors' prices and offers, it can use them as a starting point for its own pricing.

If Canon's cameras are similar to Nikon's, it will have to price close to Nikon or lose sales. If Canon's cameras are not as good as Nikon's, the firm will not be able to charge as much. If Canon's products are better than Nikon's, it can charge more. Basically, Canon will use price to position its offer relative to the competition.

Other External Factors

When setting prices, the company also must consider other factors in its external environment. *Economic conditions* can have a strong impact on the firm's pricing strategies. Economic factors such as boom or recession, inflation, and interest rates influence pricing decisions because they affect both the costs of producing a product and consumer perceptions of the product's price and value. The company also must consider what impact its prices will have on other parties in its environment. How will *resellers* react to various prices? The company should set prices that give resellers a fair profit, encourage their support, and help them to sell the product effectively. The *government* is another important external influence on pricing decisions. Finally, *social concerns* may have to be considered. In setting prices, a company's short-term sales, market share, profit goals, as well as the ability of the vulnerable to afford them may have to be tempered by broader societal considerations.

GENERAL PRICING APPROACHES

The price the company charges will be somewhere between one that is too low to produce a profit and one that is too high to produce any demand. Figure 10-5 summarizes the major considerations in setting price. Product costs set a floor to the price; consumer perceptions of the product's value set the ceiling. The company must consider competitors' prices and other external and internal factors to find the best price between these two extremes.

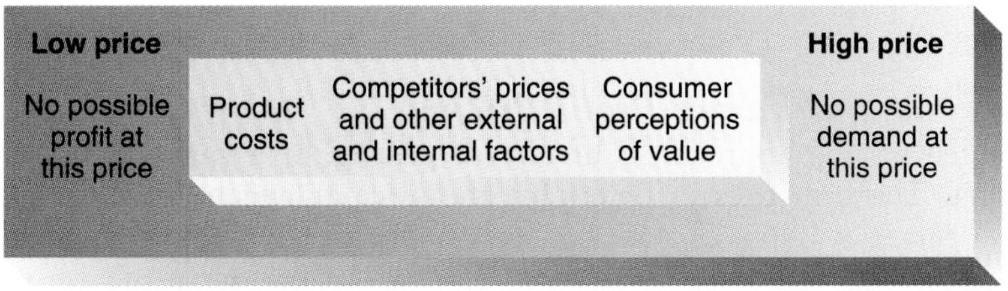

Companies set prices by selecting a general pricing approach that includes one or more of these three sets of factors. We will examine the following approaches: the *cost-based approach* (cost-plus pricing,

Low price				High price
No possible profit at this price	Product costs	Competitors' prices and other external and internal factors	Consumer perceptions of value	No possible demand at this price

FIGURE 10-5 *Major considerations in setting price*

breakeven analysis, and target profit pricing); the *buyer-based approach* (perceived-value pricing); and the *competition-based approach* (going-rate and sealed-bid pricing).

COST-BASED PRICING

Cost-Plus Pricing

Cost-plus pricing
Adding a standard markup to the cost of the product.

The simplest pricing method is **cost-plus pricing**—adding a standard markup to the cost of the product. Construction companies, for example, submit job bids by estimating the total project cost and adding a standard markup for profit. Lawyers, accountants, and other professionals typically price by adding a standard markup to their costs. Some sellers tell their customers they will charge cost plus a specified markup; for example, aerospace companies price this way to the government.

To illustrate markup pricing, suppose a toaster manufacturer had the following costs and expected sales:

Variable cost	$10
Fixed cost	$300 000
Expected unit sales	50 000

Then the manufacturer's cost per toaster is given by

$$\text{Unit Cost} = \text{Variable Cost} + \frac{\text{Fixed Costs}}{\text{Unit Sales}} = \$10 + \frac{\$300\,000}{50\,000} = \$16$$

Now suppose the manufacturer wants to earn a 20 percent markup on sales. The manufacturer's markup price is given by[9]

$$\text{Markup Price} = \frac{\text{Unit Cost}}{(1 - \text{Desired Return on Sales})} = \frac{\$16}{1 - .2} = \$20$$

The manufacturer would charge dealers $20 a toaster and make a profit of $4 per unit. The dealers, in turn, will mark up the toaster. If dealers want to earn 50 percent on sales price, they will mark up the toaster to $40 ($20 + 50% of $40). This number is equivalent to a *markup on cost* of 100 percent ($20/$20).

Does using standard markups to set prices make sense? Generally, no. Any pricing method that ignores demand and competitor prices is not likely to lead to the best price. Suppose the toaster manufacturer charged $20 but only sold 30 000 toasters instead of 50 000. Then the unit cost would have been higher since the fixed costs are spread over fewer units, and the realized percentage markup on sales would have been lower. Markup pricing only works if that price actually brings in the expected level of sales.

Still, markup pricing remains popular for many reasons. First, sellers are more certain about costs than about demand. By tying the price to cost, sellers simplify pricing—they do not have to make frequent adjustments as demand changes. Second, when all firms in the industry use this pricing method, prices tend to be similar and price competition is thus minimized. Third, many people believe that cost-plus pricing is fairer to both buyers and sellers. Sellers earn a fair return on their investment but do not take advantage of buyers when buyers' demand becomes great.

Breakeven Analysis and Target Profit Pricing

Breakeven pricing (target profit pricing)
Setting price to break even on the costs of making and marketing a product; or setting price to make a target profit.

Another cost-oriented pricing approach is **breakeven pricing,** or a variation called **target profit pricing.** The firm tries to determine the price at which it will break even or make the target profit it is seeking. Target pricing is used by General Motors, which prices its automobiles to achieve a 15 to 20 percent profit on its investment. This pricing method is also used by public utilities, which are constrained to make a fair return on their investment.

Target pricing uses the concept of a *breakeven chart,* which shows the total cost and total revenue expected at different sales volume levels. Figure 10-6 shows a breakeven chart for the toaster manufacturer discussed here. Fixed costs are $300 000 regardless of sales volume. Variable costs are added to fixed costs to form total costs, which rise with volume. The total revenue curve starts at zero and rises with each unit sold. The slope of the total revenue curve reflects the price of $20 per unit.

The total revenue and total cost curves cross at 30 000 units. This is the *breakeven volume.* At $20, the company must sell at least 30 000 units to break even; that is, for total revenue to cover total cost. Breakeven volume can be calculated using the following formula:

$$\text{Breakeven Volume} = \frac{\text{Fixed Cost}}{\text{Price} - \text{Variable Cost}} = \frac{\$300\,000}{\$20 - \$10} = 30\,000$$

If the company wants to make a target profit, it must sell more than 30 000 units at $20 each. Suppose the toaster manufacturer has invested $1 000 000 in the business and wants to set price to earn a 20 percent return, or $200 000. In that case, it must sell at least 50 000 units at $20 each. If the company charges a higher price, it will not need to sell as many toasters to achieve its target return. But the market may not buy even this lower volume at the higher price. Much depends on the price elasticity and competitors' prices.

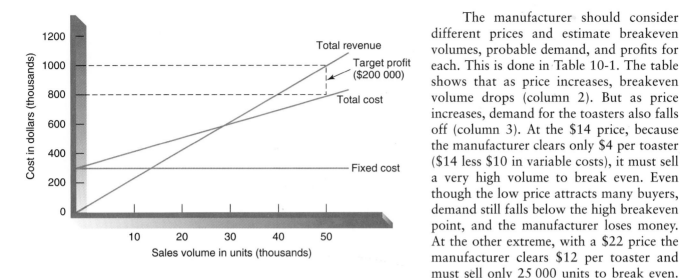

FIGURE 10-6 *Break-even chart for determining target price*

The manufacturer should consider different prices and estimate breakeven volumes, probable demand, and profits for each. This is done in Table 10-1. The table shows that as price increases, breakeven volume drops (column 2). But as price increases, demand for the toasters also falls off (column 3). At the $14 price, because the manufacturer clears only $4 per toaster ($14 less $10 in variable costs), it must sell a very high volume to break even. Even though the low price attracts many buyers, demand still falls below the high breakeven point, and the manufacturer loses money. At the other extreme, with a $22 price the manufacturer clears $12 per toaster and must sell only 25 000 units to break even. But at this high price, consumers buy too few toasters, and profits are negative. The table shows that a price of $18 yields the highest profits. Note that none of the prices produce the manufacturer's target profit of $200 000. To achieve this target return, the manufacturer will have to search for ways to lower fixed or variable costs, thus lowering the breakeven volume.

VALUE-BASED PRICING

Value-based pricing
Setting price based on buyers' perceptions of value rather than on the seller's cost.

An increasing number of companies are basing their prices on the product's perceived value. **Value-based pricing** uses buyers' perceptions of value, not the seller's cost, as the key to pricing. Value-based pricing means that the marketer cannot design a product and marketing program and then set the price. Price is considered along with the other marketing-mix variables *before* the marketing program is set.

Figure 10-7 compares cost-based pricing with value-based pricing. Cost-based pricing is product-driven. The company designs what it considers to be a good product, determines the costs of making the product, and sets a price that covers costs plus a target profit. Marketing must then convince buyers that the product's value at that price justifies its purchase. If the price turns out to be too high, the company must settle for lower markups or lower sales, both resulting in disappointing profits.

Value-based pricing reverses this process. The company sets its target price based on customer perceptions of the product value. The targeted value and price then drive decisions about product design and what costs can be incurred. As a result, pricing begins with analysing consumer needs and value perceptions, and the price is set to match consumers' perceived value.

TABLE 10-1 *Breakeven Volume and Profits at Different Prices*

(1) Price	(2) Unit Demand Needed to Break Even	(3) Expected Unit Demand at Given Price	(4) Total Revenues (1) × (3)	(5) Total Costs*	(6) Profit (4) − (5)
$14	75 000	71 000	$ 994 000	$1 100 000	−$ 32 000
16	50 000	67 000	1 072 000	970 000	102 000
18	37 500	60 000	1 080 000	900 000	180 000
20	30 000	42 000	840 000	720 000	120 000
22	25 000	23 000	506 000	530 000	−24 000

*Assumes fixed costs of $300 000 and constant unit variable costs of $10.

FIGURE 10-7 *Cost-based versus value-based pricing*

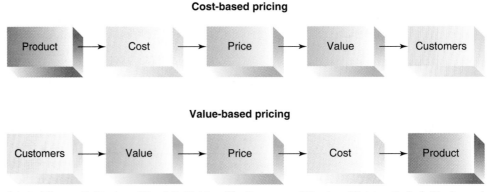

Source: Thomas T. Nagle and Reed K. Holden, *The Strategy and Tactics of Pricing,* 2nd ed. (Englewood Cliffs, NJ: Prentice Hall, 1995), p. 5.

A company using value-based pricing must find out what value buyers assign to different competitive offers. However, measuring perceived value can be difficult. Sometimes consumers are asked how much they would pay for a basic product and for each benefit added to the offer. Or a company might conduct experiments to test the perceived value of different product offers. If the seller charges more than the buyers' perceived value, the company's sales will suffer. Many companies overprice their products, and their products sell poorly. Other companies underprice. Underpriced products sell very well, but they produce less revenue than they would if prices were raised to the perceived-value level.

During the 1990s, marketers have noted a fundamental shift in consumer attitudes toward price and quality. Many companies have changed their pricing approaches to bring them into line with changing economic conditions and consumer price perceptions. More and more, marketers have adopted **value pricing** strategies—offering just the right combination of quality and good service at a fair price. In many cases, this has involved the introduction of less expensive versions of established, brand-name products. For example, Campbell introduced its Great Starts Budget frozen-food line, Holiday Inn opened several Holiday Express budget hotels, Revlon's Charles of the Ritz offered the Express Bar collection of affordable cosmetics, and fast-food restaurants such as Taco Bell and McDonald's offered "value menus." In other cases, value pricing has involved redesigning existing brands to offer more quality for a given price or the same quality for less.

In many business-to-business marketing situations, the pricing challenge is to find ways to adjust the value of the company's marketing offer in order to escape price competition and to justify higher prices and margins. This is especially true for suppliers of commodity products, which are characterized by little differentiation and intense price competition. In such cases, many companies adopt *value-added* strategies. Rather than cutting prices to match competitors, they attach value-added services to differentiate their offers and thus support higher margins (see Marketing Highlight 10-3).

An important type of value pricing at the retail level is *everyday low pricing (EDLP)*. EDLP involves charging a constant, everyday low price with few or no temporary price discounts. In contrast, *high-low pricing* involves charging higher prices on an everyday basis, but running frequent promotions to temporarily lower prices on selected items below the EDLP level.[10]

In recent years, high-low pricing has given way to EDLP in retail settings ranging from General Motors and Chrysler car dealerships to department stores such as Eatons. Retailers adopt EDLP for many reasons, the most important of which is that constant sales and promotions are costly and have eroded consumer confidence in the credibility of everyday shelf prices. Consumers also have less time

Value pricing
Setting price based on the right combination of quality and good service at a fair price.

THE VALUE OF VALUE-ADDED

When a company finds its major competitors offering a similar product at a lower price, the natural tendency is to try to match or beat that price. While the idea of undercutting competitors' prices and watching customers flock to you is tempting, dangers are associated with this approach. Successive rounds of price cutting can lead to price wars that erode the profit margins of all competitors in an industry. And price wars are numerous and bloody. For example, Molson and Labatt matched each others' price reductions in the summer of 1997 and finally called the battle a draw. McDonald's slashed its prices on Big Macs in an attempt to regain share from Wendy's and Burger King. Ultramar Ltée triggered one of Quebec's most dramatic gasoline price wars in the summer of 1996. Although it claims to have built awareness and increased traffic, Quebec's independent gas retailers claimed foul and asked the Federal Bureau of Competition to investigate Ultramar's price policy. A year-long price war that ensued between Sobeys and Superstore Atlantic not only squeezed the margins of the two combatants, but it also drove Wade Enterprises, a 78-year-old company, out of business. Thus, while numerous companies enter price wars with the intention of burying their competitors, such wars can easily backfire. Discounting a product can erode brand equity and cheapen it in the minds of customers. "It ends up being a losing battle," notes one marketing executive. "You focus away from quality, service, prestige—the things brands are all about." Another expert stresses that "pricing strategy requires the skilful manoeuvring of a diplomat, not the heavy, bloodied hand of a general. Unfortunately, all too many managers . . . know more about winning pricing battles than about preventing those that are not worth fighting."

So, what can a company do when a competitor undercuts its price? This was the question that Bell Canada had to ask itself when the $8-billion-a-year long-distance market was deregulated in 1994. Bell refused to enter a price war believing that, as the industry incumbent, it had the most to lose. While new competitors such as Sprint Canada offered promotions such as "15¢ a minute, anywhere, anytime!" Bell focused instead on winning back customers by emphasizing the service, support, and reliability that it could offer. Bell believes that focusing on price alone won't allow its competitors to forge ties with their customers. As one consultant noted, "If you tell consumers *price, price, price* all the time, that's what they'll think is important . . . and you will be rewarded with disloyalty as soon as your price isn't the lowest on the block."

Roughly the number of people who've switched back to Bell in the last month.

Rather than fighting an unprofitable price war, Bell stressed its service quality and reliability to win back customers.

Another strategy is to price above competitors and convince customers that the product is worth it. In this way, the company differentiates its offer and shifts the focus from price to value. But what if the company is operating as a supplier in a "commodity" business, where the products of all competitors seem similar? In such cases, the company must find ways to "decommoditize" its products. It can do this by developing value-added services that differentiate its offer and justify higher prices and margins.

Increasingly, today's winning suppliers are those who can provide value-added services for their customers. Here are some examples of how suppliers, both small and large, are using value-added services to give them a competitive edge:

◆ Jefferson Smurfit Corp. When General Electric expanded a no-frost refrigerator line in 1990, it needed more shipping boxes, and fast. Jefferson Smurfit Corporation, a $6.4-billion packaging supplier, assigned a coordinator to juggle production from three of its plants—and sometimes even divert product intended for other customers—to keep GE's plant humming. This kind of value-added hustling helped Jefferson Smurfit win the GE appliance unit's "Distinguished Supplier Award." It has also sheltered Smurfit from the bruising struggle of competing only on price. "Today, it's not just getting the best price but getting the best value—and there are a lot of pieces to value," says a vice president for procurement at Emerson Electric Company, a major Smurfit customer that has cut its supplier count by 65 percent.

◆ Microsystems Engineering Company. "The way we sell on value is by differentiating ourselves," says Mark Beckman, director of sales for Microsystems, a software company. "My product is twice as much as my nearest competitor, but we sell as much as—if not more than—our competition." Rather than getting into price wars, Microsystems adds value to its products by adding new components and services. "[Customers] get more for their money," says Beckman. 'We get the price because we understand what people want." When customers see the extra value, price becomes secondary. Ultimately,

Beckman asserts, "Let the customer decide whether the price you're charging is worth all the things they're getting." What if the answer is no? Beckman would suggest that dropping price is the last thing you want to do. Instead, look to the value of value-added.

Sources: Jim Morgan, "Value Added: From Cliché to the Real Thing," *Purchasing,* April 3, 1997, pp. 59–61; Richard A. Melcher, "The Middlemen Stay on the March," *Business Week,* January 9, 1995, p. 87; James E. Ellis, "There's Even a Science to Selling Boxes," *Business Week,* August 3, 1992, pp. 51–52; Erika Rasmusson, "The Pitfalls of Price Cutting," *Sales & Marketing Management,* May 1997, p. 17; David R. Henderson, 'What Are Price Wars Good For? Absolutely Nothing," *Fortune,* May 12, 1997, p. 156; Gail Chiasson, "Ultramar Shakes Up Quebec Gas Retailing,"*Marketing,* August 12, 1996, p. web site: marketingmag.com/search; Donalee Moulton, "Atlantic Canada Food Fight Claims First Casualty," *Marketing,* July 15, 1996, p. web site: marketingmag.com/search; Gayle MacDonald, "High Stakes in Burger Bargains," *Globe and Mail,* February 28, 1997, B11; Sean Silcoff, "The Price is (Rarely) Right," *Canadian Business,*February 1997, pp. 62–66; www.bell.ca/; www.smurfit. ie/; www.sprintcanada.ca/

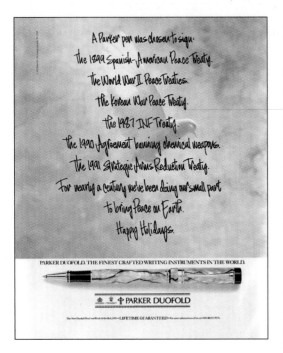

Perceived value: A less expensive pen might write as well, but some consumers will pay much more for the intangibles. This Parker model runs $250. Others are priced as high as $4800.

Going-rate pricing
Setting price based largely on following competitors' prices rather than on company costs or demand.

Sealed-bid pricing
Setting price based on how the firm thinks competitors will price rather than on its own costs or demand—used when a company bids for jobs.

and patience for such time-honoured traditions as watching for supermarket specials and clipping coupons.

The leader of EDLP is Wal-Mart, which practically defined the concept. Except for a few sale items every month, Wal-Mart promises everyday low prices on everything it sells. In contrast, Sears' attempts at EDLP failed. To offer everyday low prices, a company must first have everyday low costs. Wal-Mart's EDLP strategy works well because its expenses are only 15 percent of sales. When Wal-Mart first entered Canada, Zellers began a price war with the American giant in an attempt to defend its well-known slogan, "Where the lowest prices are the law!" However, Zellers soon learned that to win such a battle, lowest costs must also be the law! Since Zellers' operating costs were higher than Wal-Mart's, its profits were squeezed and the company had to abandon the fight.

COMPETITION-BASED PRICING

Consumers will base their judgments of a product's value on the prices that competitors charge for similar products. Here, we discuss two forms of competition-based pricing—*going-rate pricing* and *sealed-bid pricing*.

Going-Rate Pricing

In **going-rate pricing,** the firm bases its price largely on *competitors'* prices, with less attention paid to its *own* costs or to demand. The firm might charge the same, more, or less than its major competitors. In oligopolistic industries that sell a commodity such as steel, paper, or fertilizer, firms typically charge the same price. The smaller firms follow the leader: They change their prices when the market leader's prices change, rather than when their own demand or costs change. Some firms may charge a bit more or less, but they hold the amount of difference constant. Thus, minor gasoline retailers usually charge a few cents less than the major oil companies, without letting the difference increase or decrease.

Going-rate pricing is quite popular. When demand elasticity is hard to measure, firms feel that the going price represents the collective wisdom of the industry concerning the price that will yield a fair return. They also feel that holding to the going price will prevent harmful price wars.

Sealed-Bid Pricing

Competition-based pricing is also used when firms *bid* for jobs. Using **sealed-bid pricing,** a firm bases its price on how it believes competitors will price rather than on its own costs or on the demand. The firm wants to win a contract, and winning the contract requires pricing less than other firms.

TABLE 10-2 *Effect of Different Bids on Expected Profit*

Company's Bid	Company's Profit (1)	Probability of Winning With This Bid (Assumed) (2)	Expected Profit [(1) × (2)]
$ 9500	$ 100	.81	$ 81
10 000	600	.36	216
10 500	1100	.09	99
11 000	1600	.01	16

Yet the firm cannot set its price below a certain level. It cannot price below cost without harming its position. In contrast, the higher the company sets its price above its costs, the lower its chance of getting the contract.

The net effect of the two opposite pulls can be described in terms of the *expected profit* of the particular bid (see Table 10-2). Suppose a bid of $9500 would yield a high chance (say .81) of getting the contract, but only a low profit (say $100). The expected profit with this bid is therefore $81. If the firm bid $11 000, its profit would be $1600, but its chance of getting the contract might be reduced to .01. The expected profit would be only $16. Thus the company might bid the price that would maximize the expected profit. According to Table 10-2, the best bid would be $10 000, for which the expected profit is $216.

Using expected profit as a basis for setting price makes sense for the large firm that makes many bids. In playing the odds, the firm will make maximum profits in the long run. But a firm that bids only occasionally or needs a particular contract badly will not find the expected-profit approach useful. The approach, for example, does not distinguish between a $100 000 profit with a .10 probability and a $12 500 profit with an .80 probability. Yet the firm that wants to keep production going would prefer the second contract to the first.

Summary of Chapter Objectives

Price can be defined narrowly as the amount of money charged for a product or service, or more broadly as the sum of the values that consumers exchange for the benefits of having and using the product or service. Despite the increased role of non-price factors in the modern marketing process, price remains an important element in the marketing mix. It is the only element in the marketing mix that produces revenue; all other elements represent costs. Price is also one of the most flexible elements of the marketing mix. Unlike product features and channel commitments, price can be raised or lowered quickly. Even so, many companies are not good at handling pricing—pricing decisions and price competition are major problems for many marketing executives. Pricing problems often arise because prices are too cost oriented, not revised frequently enough to reflect market changes, not consistent with the rest of the marketing mix, or not varied enough for differing products, market segments, and purchase occasions.

1. Identify and define the internal factors affecting a firm's pricing decisions.

Many internal factors influence the company's pricing decisions, including the firm's *marketing objectives, marketing-mix strategy, costs,* and *organization for pricing.* The pricing strategy is largely determined by the company's *target market* and *positioning objectives.* Pricing decisions affect and are affected by product design, distribution, and promotion decisions. Therefore, pricing strategies must be carefully coordinated with the other marketing-mix variables when designing the marketing program.

Costs set the floor for the company's price—the price must cover all the costs of making and selling the product, plus a fair rate of return. Common pricing objectives include survival, current profit maximization, market-share leadership, and product-quality leadership.

In order to coordinate pricing goals and decisions, management must decide who within the organization is responsible for setting price. In large companies, some pricing authority may be delegated to lower-level managers and salespeople, but top management usually sets pricing policies and approves proposed prices. Production, finance, and accounting managers also influence pricing decisions.

2. **Identify and define external factors affecting pricing decisions, including the impact of consumer perceptions of price and value.**

   External factors that influence pricing decisions include the nature of the *market and demand*; *competitors' prices and offers*; and factors such as *the economy, reseller needs*, and *government actions*. The seller's pricing freedom varies with different types of markets. Pricing is especially challenging in markets characterized by monopolistic competition or oligopoly.

   Ultimately, the consumer decides whether the company has set the right price. The consumer weighs the price against the perceived values of using the product—if the price exceeds the sum of the values, consumers will not buy the product. The more *inelastic* the demand, the higher the company can set its price. Therefore, *demand* and *consumer value perceptions* set the ceiling for prices.

Consumers differ in the values they assign to different product features, and marketers often vary their pricing strategies for different price segments. When assessing the market and demand, the company estimates the demand curve, which shows the probable quantity purchased per period at alternative price levels. Consumers also compare a product's price to the prices of *competitors'* products. As a result, a company must learn the price and quality of competitors' offers and use them as a starting point for its own pricing.

3. **Contrast the three general approaches to setting prices.**

   A company can select one or a combination of three general pricing approaches: the *cost-based approach* (cost-plus pricing, breakeven analysis, and target profit pricing); the *value-based approach*; and the *competition-based approach*. Cost-based pricing sets prices based on the seller's cost structure while value-based pricing relies on consumer perceptions of value to drive pricing decisions. Competition-based pricing has two major variations. In *going-rate pricing*, the firm sets prices based on what competitors are charging. *Sealed-bid pricing* forces the company to set prices based on what they think the competition will charge.

Key Terms

Breakeven pricing (target profit pricing) *(p. 354)*
Cost-plus pricing *(p. 353)*
Demand curve *(p. 351)*
Experience curve (learning curve) *(p. 348)*
Fixed costs *(p. 346)*

Going-rate pricing *(p. 358)*
Monopolistic competition *(p. 349)*
Oligopolistic competition *(p. 350)*
Price *(p. 343)*
Price elasticity *(p. 352)*
Pure competition *(p. 349)*
Pure monopoly *(p. 351)*

Sealed-bid pricing *(p. 358)*
Total costs *(p. 346)*
Value-based pricing *(p. 355)*
Value pricing *(p. 356)*
Variable costs *(p. 346)*

Discussing the Issues

1. Certain "inexpensive" products that waste energy, provide few servings per container, or require frequent maintenance may *cost* much more to own and use than do products selling for a higher *price*. Discuss how marketers can use this information on "true

   cost" to gain a competitive edge in pricing and promoting their products.

2. Detergent A is priced at $2.19 for 900 mL, and detergent B is priced at $1.99 for 740 mL. Suggest which brand appears most attractive. Which is actually the better value,

assuming equal quality? Decide if there is a psychological reason to price in this way.

3. Procter & Gamble replaced its 450-gram packages of regular Folgers coffee with 365-gram "fast-roast" packages. Fast-roasting allows Procter & Gamble to use fewer coffee beans per pack with no impact on flavour or the number of servings per package. Determine which pricing approach was appropriate for setting the price for the fast-roast coffee—cost-based, buyer-based, or competition-based pricing?

4. Sales of Fleischmann's gin *increased* when prices were raised 22 percent over a two-year period. Explain what this tells you about the demand curve and the elasticity of demand for Fleischmann's gin. What does this suggest about using perceived-value pricing in marketing alcoholic beverages?

5. Genentech, a high-technology pharmaceutical company, has developed a clot-dissolving drug called TPA that will halt a heart attack in progress. TPA saves lives, minimizes hospital stays, and reduces damage to the heart itself. It was initially priced at $3060 per dose. Explain what pricing approach Genentech appeared to be using. Is demand for this drug likely to be elastic with price?

6. Columnist Dave Barry jokes that federal law requires this message under the sticker price of new cars: "Warning to stupid people: Do not pay this amount." Discuss why the sticker price is generally higher than the actual selling price of a car. Explain how you think car dealers set the actual prices of the cars they sell.

Applying the Concepts

1. Do a pricing survey of several gasoline stations in your town in different locations. If possible, check prices at stations at an exit ramp on a major highway, stations on your local strip, convenience stores and a smaller station that is not near any other stations. Write down the brand of gasoline, prices of regular and premium grades, type of location, distance to the nearest competitor, and the competitor's prices. (a) Is there a pattern to the pricing of gasoline at various outlets? (b) Do you think that these stations are using cost-based, buyer-based, or going-rate pricing?

2. You have inherited an automatic car wash where annual fixed costs are $50 000 and variable costs are $0.50 per car washed. You think people would be willing to pay $1 to have their car washed. Determine what the break-even volume would be at that price.

References

1. Portions adapted from Valerie Reitman, "Retail Resistance: Eliminated Discounts on P&G Goods Annoy Many Who Sell Them," *Wall Street Journal*, August 11, 1992, pp. A1, A3. Also see Zachary Schiller, 'Not Everyone Loves a Supermarket Special," *Business Week*, February 17, 1992, pp. 64–68; "P&G Plays Pied Piper on Pricing," *Advertising Age*, March 9, 1992, p. 6; Karen Benezra, "Beyond Value," *Brandweek*, October 7, 1996, pp. 14–16; and Dagmar Mussey, "Heat's on Value Pricing," *Advertising Age International*, January 1997, pp. i21–i22; Cathy Bond, "P&G's Gamble: Price or Promotion?" *Marketing*, February 13, 1997; and Patrick Allossery, "P&G Pricing Policy," *Strategy: The Canadian Marketing Report*, July 27, 1993, pp. 1, 15.

2. See David J. Schwartz, *Marketing Today: A Basic Approach*, 3rd ed. (New York: Harcourt Brace Jovanovich, 1981), pp. 270–273.

3. For an excellent discussion of factors affecting pricing decisions, see Thomas T. Nagle and Reed K. Holden, *The Strategy and Tactics of Pricing*, 2nd ed. (Englewood Cliffs, NJ: Prentice Hall, Inc., 1995), Chap. 1.

4. Norton Paley, "Fancy Footwork," *Sales & Marketing Management*, July 1994, pp. 41–42.

5. Christopher Farrell, "Stuck! How Companies Cope When They Can't Raise Prices," *Business Week*, November 15, 1993, pp. 146–155. Also see John Y. Lee, "Use Target Costing to Improve Your Bottom Line," *The CPA Journal*, January 1994, pp. 68–71.

6. Brian Dumaine, "Closing the Innovation Gap," *Fortune*, December 2, 1991, pp. 56–62.

7. Here accumulated production is drawn on a semi-log scale so that equal distances represent the same percentage increase in output.

8. See Nagle and Holden, *The Strategy and Tactics of Pricing*, Chap. 4.

9. The arithmetic of markups and margins is discussed in Appendix 1, "Marketing Arithmetic."

10. See Stephen J. Hoch, Xavier Drèze, and Mary E. Purk, "EDLP, Hi-Lo, and Margin Arithmetic," *Journal of Marketing*, October 1994, pp. 16–27.

Company Case 10

CANADIAN VS AIR CANADA: SURVIVING THE FARE WARS

A NEW FRONT

Joyce Harris and her daughter Dana pile suitcases in their car's trunk and prepare for the one-hour drive from their Pinoka, Alberta home to the Calgary Airport. Joyce and Dana are going to Vancouver to visit Joyce's sister, who just had a baby. Such visits normally would require a torturous car ride or an expensive plane trip. This morning, however, they will fly from Calgary to Vancouver for $99 each. Only $99! Moreover, they won't fly on the dominant airline in Western Canada, Canadian Airlines. They will fly Air Canada, the Montreal-headquartered giant that has just moved to further invade Canadian Airline's backyard.

Joyce and Dana are beneficiaries of the latest skirmish in the airline fare wars. However, the continuing fare wars have meant big trouble for the industry. Between 1990 and the end of 1992, the industry the world over carried 3.4 trillion passengers but still lost $22 billion—more than its total profits in its 60-year history. Since 1982, costs such as wages and fuel have doubled while the average price paid per mile flown has fallen 25 percent. Persistent overcapacity and the airlines' struggles to get out of bankruptcy have fuelled suicidal price wars.

But the battle for the western triangle represents more than just another fare-war episode. The attack represents round three of an all-out attack on the once-stable air-travel market.

ROUND ONE—THE BATTLE FOR OWNERSHIP

The war between the two giants of Canadian air travel began in earnest in 1992, when Air Canada's attempt to acquire Canadian was rebuffed. Canadian, fearful of losing many of its employees and its independent identity in a merger with Air Canada, began an affair with American Airlines of Fort Worth, Texas. In a lobbying effort of a magnitude never seen before in Canada, the two airlines began an advertising war to convince both politicians and the Canadian public of the merits of their respective positions. While Air Canada tried to convince politicians that only a single airline was financially viable in Canada, Canadian Airlines fought the war based on the merits of maintaining competition. In the two-week period just before the federal election, Air Canada ran $250 000 worth of newspaper ads, while Canadian countered with newspaper advertising costing $70 000. In the end, Canadian managed to out-lobby its rival and was allowed to strike a deal with American. American eventually acquired a 25 percent share of Canadian as well as the right for Canadian to hook into its computerized reservation system.

ROUND TWO—THE FIGHT FOR THE HIGH GROUND

Every general knows that dominating the high ground often leads to eventual success in battle. Similarly, two markets represent the high ground in terms of the lucrative operations. Two flight triangles account for close to 50 percent of air travel within Canada. The eastern triangle consists of flights between Toronto, Ottawa, and Montreal. The western triangle comprises routes between Calgary, Edmonton, and Vancouver. As both Air Canada and Canadian Airlines began to realize that their future success depended on winning over the business traveller, dominating these routes became more critical. Thus, each airline began to play in the other's backyard. Air Canada added 29 Rapid Air flights per day between Calgary and Vancouver to compete with Canadian's 31 flights on the same route. To counter this move, Canadian moved more resources into the eastern market, scheduling 41 flights between Toronto and Montreal, and 33 flights between Toronto and Ottawa. This compares with Air Canada's 61 flights per business day between Toronto and Montreal, and its 54 flights between Toronto and Ottawa.

Each airline is convinced that it can win over passengers in the other's home market. They cite the fact that business travel is finally rebounding after years of stagnation. Between 1991 and 1993, business travel in Canada fell by over 10 percent. Finally, in 1994 things began to improve, and 1995 saw growth of just under five percent. The average business traveller makes 17.3 round trips per year. Each airline added capacity to try and lure these travellers onto their planes, but the volume of air travel hasn't grown as fast as capacity. While Canadian's capacity grew by 12 percent, its volume expanded by only 4.6 percent. Air Canada fared better. It increased capacity by 12 percent and raised volume by almost the same amount, 11.7 percent.

The airlines have added services in an attempt to differentiate themselves, but each added service seems to be rapidly matched by the competitor. Both airlines welcome business travellers with newspapers and coffee. If nothing else, this service war illustrates the difficulty of creating strategic advantage in a services business. Each airline has added physical facilities such as designated departure lounges to try and attract the business traveller. Canadian has added gateside business centres that allow travellers to phone the office, send last-minute-faxes, run computer programs, and print reports.

Air Canada believes that Canadian is becoming increasingly vulnerable in its home market. Western Canadians have been fiercely loyal to Calgary-based Canadian airlines, but some believe that with the partnership with American, this loyalty is fading. Air Canada thus sees the opportunity to win over western passengers. Canadian, on the other hand, thinks it can make inroads into Air Canada's home turf. While Canadian has the luxury of operating out of the ultra modern Terminal 3, Air Canada flies out of the old Terminal 1 building at Toronto's Pearson airport. This crowded, aging facility is becoming increasingly less attractive to travellers.

ROUND THREE—RENEWED INVESTMENT AND SEAT SALES

Since both airlines carry heavy debt loads, maintaining or increasing cash flow is essential. Air Canada has $2.4 billion in long-term debt and Canadian owes $900 million, incurred largely when it bought out its western rival, Wardair. Air Canada, however, has more cash on hand, which may provide it with an edge in terms of adding routes or upgrading equipment.

It takes deep pockets to purchase new aircraft to fly additional routes. If you want to attract the business traveller, you must also incur heavy expenditures to upgrade aging equipment. Both airlines are attempting to make their aircraft more comfortable for weary road warriors. Older planes are being refitted with two seats (instead of the traditional three seats) to give travellers more leg room and work space. Telephones are being placed in seat backs and work stations are being provided on some aircraft models.

All this spending requires heavy influxes of cash. This is where the good news happens for travellers. To help fill excess capacity and to bring money into their cash-starved operations, Canadian announced deep discounts on 83 percent of its routes in Canada and the United States. Like Joyce and her daughter, many winter-weary Canadians jumped to grab $200 fares between Toronto and Orlando, or $300 seats between Vancouver and Toronto. Within a day, Air Canada announced matching fares.

Seat sales generate advance bookings since discount seats are offered only on certain flights at certain times. They provide the incentive for people to travel now rather than postponing a vacation to a later date. Since business travellers don't have the flexibility of other travellers, deep discounts, it is hoped, won't undermine the higher fares paid by this segment of customers. Whereas in the past, seat sales have resulted in a drain on profitability, Canadian thinks that this time the seat sale will improve its bottom line. It is relying on the new expertise it has gained from its partner, American, and its computerized "Sabre" reservation and data-tracking system, to help it cover its variable costs by filling unused capacity.

BATTLE TO THE DEATH?

Air Canada still takes the position that the Canadian market is only large enough for one major airline. It firmly believes that it is only a matter of time before it can take over Canadian or push it into bankruptcy. Furthermore, some analysts believe that neither airline is large enough to take on the American mega-carriers that are quickly moving into Canadian markets under the open skies agreement.

Industry analysts are concerned that the fare wars may cause history to repeat itself. In 1992, American Airlines followed a similar strategy to what Canadian is doing now. That year, American introduced its value-pricing program, which sparked a fare war that resulted in the industry losing US$2.5 billion in that year alone. Analysts' fears are compounded by the fact that Canadian airlines are adding to their cost structures with new routes and equipment at the same time as they are attempting to fight this fare war. They fear that slim margins will be unmercifully squeezed and that profitability from expected travel growth will evaporate.

The battle wages on and the press carries weekly reports of each competitor's salvos. The war is even fought on the Internet. When advertising its site (http://www.cdnair.ca), Canadian stressed that it was the first airline in the world to establish a home page. Air Canada (http://www.aircanada.ca) focusses more on its services and schedules, in addition to announcing information on its tourist destinations. Whether Canada will continue to have one or two national airlines remains to be seen.

QUESTIONS

1. What internal and external factors affect pricing decisions in the airline industry?

2. What marketing objectives have the various airline companies selected?

3. Which airline industry costs are fixed, and which are variable? What implications does this cost structure hold for airline operations?

4. What is the nature of demand and competition in the airline industry? Does demand differ for the business and leisure segments?

5. What pricing and other marketing recommendations would you make to U.S. Air to help it protect its markets?

Sources: This case was written by P. Cunningham based on the following sources: Adapted from M. J. McCarthy and B. O'Brian, "Lean, Nimble Airlines Head East, Targeting Region's Plump Prices," *Wall Street Journal,* February 28, 1994, p. A1. Used with permission of *Wall Street Journal.* Also see K. Labich, "What Will Save the U.S. Airlines," *Fortune,* June 14, 1993, pp. 98-101; Cecil Foster, "Tough Guys Don't Cuss," *Canadian Business,* February 1995, pp. 23-28; Jeff Heinrich, "Airlines Fate Up in the Air, *The Ottawa Citizen,* February 9, 1992; David Israelson, "No Love Lost in Battle for Skies," *Toronto Star,* January 6, 1996; Geoffrey Rowan, "Feuding Airlines Launch Ad War," *Globe and Mail,* August 18, 1993, B1; Andrew Tausz, "Airlines Wage a Turf War in the Clouds, *Globe and Mail,* February 13, 1996, C1, C8.

Video Case 10

SKEET AND IKE'S SPREADABLE ADVENTURE

Skeet and Ike's "Not Just Nuts" is the brand name of a line of spreadable products in the tradition of peanut butter, which was started by two young entrepreneurs in Vancouver. Jason Dorland, a recent art school graduate, and Ian Walker, an economics graduate, have developed nut spreads that are aimed at the segment of consumers who consider themselves gourmets. As the name of their product indicates, nuts are just one of the ingredients that the duo uses in their spreads. Among the other ingredients that flavour their products are M&Ms, coffee, yogurt, cinnamon, and Cajun spices.

The two partners began their business with limited means. As a result, they share production space with another food company and do everything themselves, from the hands-on production tasks of grinding the peanuts and taste-testing the product to management tasks such as negotiating deals with retailers who will stock the product. Even the label design depicting Dorland (nicknamed Skeet) and his dog, Ike, was drawn by Dorland as part of his graduate thesis for art school.

In Vancouver the Skeet and Ike's products retail in specialty stores that sell complementary products, such as bagels, and they sell for $5.50 to $6.00 per jar. While Dorland realizes that consumers often balk at the price, which is perceived as high for a "fun product," the costs of production are so high that offering a lower price to consumers is simply unrealistic. To help boost sales, Ian and Jason make personal visits to the stores to set up sampling booths. They have found that once consumers are given the opportunity to taste the product, they are more willing to make a purchase.

Walker and Dorland have tried to place their product in large retail grocery stores in Canada with limited success. They therefore turned their attention to the United States and landed their first major deal with a food retail chain located just three hours south of Vancouver in Seattle, Washington. Larry's supermarkets, a chain of five stores that target the gourmet consumer, agreed to stock 300 jars. Because of the large population that these stores service, the partners estimate that they will sell as much in those five stores as they would in 30 retail stores in Canada. In the U.S. market, the exchange rate allows the partners to charge a lower price: US$4.00 a jar. To help sell the product, the partners secured eye-level shelf space with large price stickers that draw attention to the product. They also continued their tradition of providing free samples to consumers and on the first day of their launch into the U.S. market, customer feedback was very positive.

QUESTIONS

1. What internal and external factors affect the pricing decisions made by Dorland and Walker?
2. Is the demand curve for "Not Just Nuts" elastic or inelastic?
3. What pricing approach are Walker and Dorland currently using? Would you suggest any changes to this approach?
4. Should the partners consider using a price incentive, such as coupons, to sell their product? What would be the advantages and disadvantages?

Source: This case was prepared by Auleen Carson and is based on "Skeet and Ike's," *Venture* (June 15, 1997).

CHAPTER 11

PRICING
STRATEGIES

Ever wonder why gas prices increase every Friday, or just before that long weekend when you plan to get away to the cottage? Or why every gas station in town seems to charge the same price? Ontario Premier Mike Harris created a furor in the summer of 1997 when he asked the same questions and implied that gas stations were colluding to gouge Ontario consumers. However, the report prepared by the federal departments of industry and natural resources, which was written to address these accusations, concluded that while the industry had a poor public image, no conspiracy of fixing prices existed.

Station owners, and their oil-refining parents, stress that rapid price movements and the almost instantaneous matching of prices by competitors bear witness to a purely competitive market where price must be matched or business will be lost. Consumer advocates, on the other hand, have long argued that price fixing must be a characteristic of the industry because changes in prices are not the result of changes in cost or demand. Demand for gasoline is constant with the exception of Fridays and the period just before major holidays. During these periods demand increases as consumers flee major cities or travel to visit distant relatives.

Have you ever wondered what factors make up the price of the gas you buy? You might be surprised by the answer. Almost 50 percent goes to taxes! Although taxation levels vary across Canada, the remaining costs associated with a litre of gasoline are the same nationwide. Take Vancouver as an example. The retail price might be $0.55/litre. Provincial tax is $0.14 and federal tax is $0.12. The cost of the crude from which the gasoline is produced is $0.15 and the costs of refining and marketing the gasoline are $0.12. This leaves a paltry $0.02 for the dealer from which he or she must cover the costs of their operation plus, hopefully, generate some profit. What does all this cost information mean? Simply put, at retail prices below $0.50, the station operator just isn't making any money. That is why the average price of gas across Canada hovers around 56.8 cents a litre.

1. Describe the major strategies for pricing imitative and new products.

2. Explain how companies find a set of prices that maximize the profits from the total product mix.

3. Discuss how companies adjust their prices to take into account different types of customers and situations.

4. Discuss the key issues related to initiating and responding to price changes.

The ability of a gasoline retailer to make any profit is influenced by the type of station he or she operates. Full-service stations incur more labour costs, and thus, are the most expensive to operate. These costs are compounded if the station has a service bay. Some stations have divided their pumps into self-serve and full-service areas. These have lower cost structures than the full-service operators. Not surprisingly, the lowest-cost outlets are those that have self-serve only. Costs and the economics of running gas stations have made high-volume sales increasingly important because the profit margin per sale is so low. This has sounded the death knell for many smaller stations or those offering additional services. It is becoming increasingly rare to have an attendant ask, "Can I check the oil for you?"

Finally, rural stations must have higher margins than their urban counterparts because they pump much lower volumes of gas. For example, in the Toronto area where a station may pump 5.1 million litres a year, the dealer margins of 3.06 cents a litre are the lowest in Canada. At the other extreme is a dealer in tiny Gaspé, Quebec, who marks up prices 14.17 cents a litre because they pump less than 700 000 litres a year. In between are dealers in Calgary and Victoria, who have markups just over 6.0 cents, and Regina dealers who have markups of 7.29 cents.

Why, you might ask, can't gasoline retailers escape from the vicious cycle of price competition? Overcapacity is one of the main reasons. Canada has too many stations, chasing too few consumers, who drive increasingly fuel-efficient cars. The major oil companies have been closing their less profitable stations to address this problem. In 1997, there were 15 500 service stations in Canada compared to 22 000 outlets in 1989. However, many analysts think the major oil companies haven't gone far enough in reducing retail capacity, and that overcapacity will continue to plague the industry.

Overcapacity remains a problem because the closures undertaken by the major oil companies have been matched by an increase in the number of independent operators. In fact, there are twice as many independents as there were just 10 years ago. Since independents have lower costs than franchised retailers, they can afford to shave just a little more off the price of a litre of gas.

So what happens in this oversaturated industry when one local operator changes his or her price of gas? In most neighbourhood markets, one station is recognized as the price-setter. By observing the behaviour of their fellow gas retailers over time, gas-station managers recognize that certain operators are first movers in setting particular trends. They are known for either trying to keep prices high or dropping them—"crashing the market." The franchises belonging to the national oil companies usually try to keep the prices high. The independents often try and get just a little more volume by dropping their price.

Gasoline is a commodity and consumers are highly price sensitive. You know from experience that you will drive across the street just to save half a cent on a litre of gas when you need to fill up. Thus, the stations must follow the lead of the price-setter. However, since no station can afford to keep prices below $0.50 for long, prices tend to rapidly rise back to the level of profitability after the market has briefly crashed.

This intense price competition surrounding station's core product, gas, explains why more and more stations are looking to sell higher-margin products. Even small gas bars are jamming themselves with impulse purchase items ranging from CDs and tapes to automotive accessories. Since these items allow the operator to generate higher margins, they offer a small window of profitability.

So next time you fill up and find yourself glaring at the operator because you have been charged such a high price, think about how little of your dollar actually goes into his or her pocket. Competitive markets with significant price competition aren't for the greedy or faint of heart![1]

In this chapter, we will look at complex dynamics of pricing. A company sets not a single price, but rather a *pricing structure* that covers different items in its line. This pricing structure changes over time as products move through their life cycles. The company adjusts product prices to reflect changes in costs and demand and to account for variations in buyers and situations. As the competitive environment changes, the company considers when to initiate price changes and when to respond to them. And as the gasoline pricing example demonstrates forcefully, pricing decisions are subject to an incredibly complex array of environmental and competitive forces.

This chapter examines the major dynamic pricing strategies available to management. In turn, we look at *new-product pricing strategies* for products in the introductory stage of the product life cycle, *product-mix pricing strategies* for related products in the product mix, *price-adjustment strategies* that account for customer differences and changing situations, and *strategies for initiating and responding to price changes.*[2]

NEW-PRODUCT PRICING STRATEGIES

FIGURE 11-1 *Price-quality strategies*

Pricing strategies usually change as the product passes through its life cycle. The introductory stage is especially challenging. We can distinguish between pricing a product that imitates existing products and pricing an innovative product that is patent-protected.

A company that plans to develop an imitative new product faces a product-positioning problem. It must decide where to position the product versus competing products in terms of quality and price. Figure 11-1 shows four possible positioning strategies. First, the company might decide to use a *premium pricing* strategy—producing a high-quality product and charging the highest price. At the other extreme, it might decide on an *economy pricing* strategy—producing a lower quality product but charging a low price. These strategies can co-exist in the same market as long as the market consists of at least two groups of buyers—those who seek quality and those who seek price. Thus, Rolex offers very high quality watches at very high prices, and Timex offers lower quality watches at more affordable prices.

The *good-value* strategy represents a way to attack the premium pricer. Its says, "We have high quality, but at a lower price." If this really is true, and quality-sensitive buyers believe the good-value pricer, they will sensibly buy the product and save money—unless the premium product offers more status or snob appeal. Using an *overcharging* strategy, the company overprices the product in relation to its quality. In the long run, however, customers will likely feel "taken." They will stop buying the product and will complain to others about it. Thus, this strategy should be avoided.

Companies that are introducing an innovative, patent-protected product face the challenge of setting prices for the first time. They can choose between two strategies: *market-skimming pricing* and *market-penetration pricing.*

MARKET-SKIMMING PRICING

Market-skimming pricing
Setting a high price for a new product to skim maximum revenues layer by layer from the segments willing to pay the high price; the company makes fewer but more profitable sales.

Many companies that invent new products initially set high prices to "skim" revenues layer by layer from the market. Intel is a prime user of this strategy, called **market-skimming pricing.** When Intel first introduces a new computer chip, it charges the highest price it can given the benefits of the new chip over competing chips. It sets a price that makes it *just* worthwhile for some segments of the market to adopt computers containing the chip. As initial sales slow down, and as competitors threaten to introduce similar chips, Intel lowers the price to draw in the next price-sensitive layer of customers.

Zellers practises market-penetration pricing. It stresses value and savings in its advertising stating, "Where the Lowest Price is the Law . . . Everyday!"

For example, when Intel first introduced its Pentium chips, it priced them at about $1400 each. As a result, computer producers priced their first Pentium PCs at $4800 or more, attracting as customers only serious computer users and business buyers. However, after introduction, Intel cut Pentium prices by 30 percent per year, eventually allowing the price of Pentium PCs to drop into the typical price range of home buyers. In this way, Intel skimmed a maximum amount of revenue from the various segments of the market.[3]

Market skimming makes sense only under certain conditions. First, the product's quality and image must support its higher price, and enough buyers must want the product at that price. Second, the costs of producing a smaller volume cannot be so high that they cancel the advantage of charging more. Finally, competitors should not be able to enter the market easily and undercut the high price.

MARKET-PENETRATION PRICING

Rather than setting a high initial price to *skim* off small but profitable market segments, some companies use **market-penetration pricing.** They set a low initial price in order to *penetrate* the market quickly and deeply—to attract a large number of buyers quickly and win a large market share. The high sales volume results in falling costs, allowing the company to cut its price even further. For example, Dell and Gateway used penetration pricing to sell high-quality computer products through lower-cost mail-order channels. Their sales soared when IBM, Compaq, Apple, and other competitors selling through retail stores could not match their prices. Home Depot, Zellers, and other discount retailers also use penetration pricing. They charge low prices to attract high volume. The high volume results in lower costs that, in turn, let the discounters keep prices low.

Several conditions favour setting a low price. First, the market must be highly price-sensitive so that a low price produces more market growth. Second, production and distribution costs must fall as sales volume increases. Finally, the low price must help keep out the competition—otherwise the price advantage may be only temporary, or, the new low price competitor must have a low-cost structure that existing competitors cannot, or will not, match. Marketing Highlight 11-1 illustrates how new competitors that combine low prices with great service are revolutionizing the auto industry.

■ PRODUCT-MIX PRICING STRATEGIES

Market-penetration pricing
Setting a low price for a new product to attract a large number of buyers and a large market share.

The strategy for setting a product's price often has to be changed when the product is part of a product mix. In this case, the firm looks for a set of prices that maximizes the profits on the total product mix. Pricing is difficult because the various products have related demand and costs and face different degrees of competition. We now take a closer look at five *product-mix pricing* situations summarized in Table 11-1.

PRODUCT LINE PRICING

Companies usually develop product lines rather than single products. For example, Toro makes many different lawn mowers, ranging from simple walk-behind versions priced at $259.95, $299.95, and $399.95, to elaborate riding mowers priced at

TABLE 11-1 *Product-Mix Pricing Strategies*

Strategy	Description
Product line pricing	Setting price steps between product line items
Optional-product pricing	Pricing optional or accessory products sold with the main product
Captive-product pricing	Pricing products that must be used with the main product
By-product pricing	Pricing low-value by-products to get rid of them
Product-bundle pricing	Pricing bundles of products sold together

Product line pricing
Setting the price steps between various products in a product line based on cost differences between the products, customer evaluations of different features, and competitors' prices.

$1000 or more. Each successive lawn mower in the line offers more features. Kodak offers not just one type of film, but an assortment including regular Kodak film, higher-priced Kodak Royal Gold film for special occasions, and a lower-priced, seasonal film called Funtime that competes with store brands. It offers each of these brands in a variety of sizes and film speeds. In **product line pricing**, management must decide on the price steps to set between the various products in a line.

The price steps should take into account cost differences between the products in the line, customer evaluations of their different features, and competitors' prices. If the price difference between two successive products is small, buyers usually will buy the more advanced product. This will increase company profits if the cost difference is smaller than the price difference. If the price difference is large, however, customers will generally buy the less advanced products.

In many industries, sellers use well-established *price points* for the products in their line. Thus, men's clothing stores might carry men's suits at three price levels: $185, $285, and $385. The customer probably will associate low-, average-, and high-quality suits with the three price points. Even if the three prices are raised a little, men typically will buy suits at their own preferred price points. The seller's task is to establish perceived quality differences that support the price differences.

OPTIONAL-PRODUCT PRICING

Optional-product pricing
The pricing of optional or accessory products along with a main product.

Many companies use **optional-product pricing**—offering to sell optional or accessory products along with their main product. For example, a car buyer may choose to order power windows, cruise control, and a radio with a CD player. Pricing these options is a sticky problem. Automobile companies have to decide which items to include in the base price and which to offer as options. Until recent years, General Motors' normal pricing strategy was to advertise a stripped-down model for, say, $17 000 to pull people into showrooms and then devote most of the showroom space to showing option-loaded cars at $19 000 or $21 000. The economy model was stripped of so many comforts and conveniences that most buyers rejected it. More recently, however, GM has followed the example of the Japanese auto makers and included in the sticker price many useful items previously sold only as options. The advertised price now often represents a well-equipped car.

CAPTIVE-PRODUCT PRICING

Captive-product pricing
Setting a price for products that must be used along with a main product, such as blades for a razor and film for a camera.

Companies that make products that must be used along with a main product are using **captive-product pricing**. Examples of captive products are razor blades, camera film, and computer software. Producers of the main products (razors, cameras, and computers) often price them low and set high markups on the supplies. Thus, Polaroid prices its cameras low because it makes its money on the film it sells. And Gillette sells low-priced razors but makes money on the replacement blades.

CARMAX: GOOD PRICES AND A WHOLE LOT MORE

Would you buy a used car from this . . . er, retail store? Circuit City, the leading consumer electronics and appliance retailer in the United States, thinks that you will. The company's new CarMax Auto Superstores are a far cry from the usual, sometimes less than reputable, used-car lot. CarMax Auto Superstores are located on sites filled with up to 1000 used but still gleaming cars, trucks, and minivans. As you might expect, given Circuit City's low-price guarantees, price figures prominently into CarMax's positioning—it promises "no-haggle, below-book prices." However, unlike Circuit City stores, CarMax does not claim to charge the lowest prices. Instead, price is only a part—and perhaps not even the most important part—of a broader mix of values that CarMax delivers to its customers.

More than a decade ago, when Circuit City first opened its large and modern stores, stocked with a wide selection of goods, staffed by knowledgeable salespeople, and offering liberal return policies and affordable financing, it brought new respectability to consumer electronics and appliance retailing.

Now, CarMax faces a similar situation with used cars—a highly fragmented industry and strong consumer concerns about reliability. Research shows that, when buying a used car, 40 percent of consumers question the dealer's reputation. Circuit City is bringing the same re-

spectability to used-car retailing that it brought to consumer electronics. It wants customers to be able to buy used cars from CarMax with the same ease and peace of mind that they purchase television sets, personal computers, camcorders, and refrigerators from Circuit City superstores.

Buying a used car from Car-Max is a dramatically different experience. CarMax offers a large

inventory for cars that meet the customer's specifications and budgets. The computer screen shows colour photographs of various choices, and the customer can receive a printout listing any car's specifications, features, kilometrage, and price, along with what has been done to prepare the car for sale. The sheet even contains a photo of the car and a map showing its location on the lot.

selection of cars, without a clunker in the bunch—most are less than five years old and sell for $11 000 to $21 000. Customers walk into a brightly lit showroom, where they are greeted by "sales associates" dressed in polo shirts, khakis, and running shoes. They use computer touch-screens to search the CarMax

When ready, customers visit the vast lot to see cars, while their children enjoy the latest toys and games in the supervised KidCare Centre. If the customer decides to purchase a car, financing can be arranged in less than 15 minutes through Circuit City's finance company. Moreover, CarMax will buy

---

Camera makers who do not sell film have to price their main products higher to make the same overall profit.

In the case of services, this strategy is called *two-part pricing*. The price of the service is broken into a *fixed fee* plus a *variable usage rate*. Thus, a telephone company charges a monthly rate—the fixed fee—plus charges for long distance calls—the variable usage rate. Amusement parks charge admission plus fees for food, midway attractions, and rides over a minimum. The service firm must decide how much to charge for the basic service and how much for the variable usage. The fixed amount should be low enough to induce usage of the service, and profit can be made on the variable fees.

BY-PRODUCT PRICING

In producing processed meats, petroleum products, chemicals, and other products, there are often by-products. If the by-products have no value and if getting rid of

the customer's old car for a set price, whether or not he or she buys a new one. The entire car-buying process, from rumbling in with the old clunker to purring out with a shiny previously loved model, can take less than an hour.

In addition to being quick and convenient, almost everything about CarMax inspires customer confidence. CarMax gives each car a 110-point quality inspection and backs it with a 30-day comprehensive warranty. It even offers a money-back guarantee—a customer who is not 100 percent satisfied can bring the car back within five days for a full refund. CarMax allows no high-pressure selling. Salespeople are carefully selected and trained to help customers find the car that's just right for them. They receive commissions based on how many cars they sell, but not on prices. This prevents commission-hungry salespeople from steering customers to more expensive cars.

Finally, at CarMax, a price is a price. Prices are marked right on the car and no haggling is allowed. CarMax prices aren't the lowest around, but they are usually competitive—right around book value. However, these slightly higher prices don't appear to bother customers. Recent studies have shown that many customers willingly pay more to avoid the hassle of negotiating for better deals, and to ensure that they get a good car and a fair price, backed by a reliable seller.

CarMax appears to have started a revolution in car retailing. The company now operates seven superstores and plans to open 55 more by the year 2000. Planning to enter every segment of the auto business from renting to servicing to financing, CarMax has also started selling new vehicles. In markets where it already operates, the company has driven out many smaller dealers. The big automakers worry that these superstores will erode their control over the retail channel. Their worries are justified, since two new chains—AutoNation, modelled after CarMax, and ValueStop, a chain that features older cheaper models—have just opened locations across the United States.

Thus, the big question for Canadian autodealers is whether the car superstore concept will move north. Since the "pre-used" vehicle market has been accelerating, they have reason to fret. Three million used cars are sold annually in Canada—more than double the number of new vehicles being sold. Canadian automotive consultant Dennis DesRosiers explains that the threat of entry by CarMax has motivated many complacent dealers to become better marketers. Consequently, many dealers are finally paying attention to customer satisfaction. They are replacing high-pressure sales tactics with "no-dicker" pricing in many areas. They are providing their salespeople with access to sophisticated databases so they can offer knowledge-based explanations of products and services for increasingly information-hungry buyers.

The big automakers are reinforcing dealers' efforts by using direct marketing to support their relationship-building efforts. They are using the World Wide Web to provide prospective buyers with an opportunity to browse without visiting a car lot (see www.bmw.ca; www.ford.ca; www.gmcanada.com; mercedes-benz.ca or www.nissancanada.com). Furthermore, Ford and GM are kicking off warranty programs that provide one-year guarantees on the mechanical fitness of used vehicles. Whether these efforts are sufficient to deter CarMax's entry into the Canadian market remains to be seen.

Sources: Quotations from Michael Janofsky, "Circuit City Takes a Spin at Used Car Marketing," *The New York Times*, October 25, 1993, p. D1. Also see Jean "Halliday, AutoNation and CarMax Gear Up for Used-Car Clash," *Advertising Age*, October 28, 1996, pp. 3, 50; Bradford Wernie, "Stigma Gone, Used Vehicles Defy the System," *Advertising Age*, April 7, 1997, p. s2; Gail DeGeorge and Keith Naughton, "Car Trouble," *Business Week*, May 5, 1997, pp. 34–35; Greg Keenan, "Revolution on the Car Lot," *Globe and Mail*, March 22, 1997, pp. B1, B4; Mariam Mesbah, "Used Car Marketing Revolution," *Strategy: The Canadian Marketing Report*, August 19, 1996, p. 1; Erica Zlomislic, "Special Report: Automotive Marketing: Superstore Threat Prompts New Customer Focus," *Strategy: The Canadian Marketing Report*, March 17, 1997, p. 29; www.circuitcity.pic.net/

By-product pricing
Setting a price for by-products in order to make the main product's price more competitive.

them is costly, this will affect the pricing of the main product. Using **by-product pricing**, the manufacturer will seek a market for these by-products and should accept any price that covers more than the cost of storing and delivering them. This practice allows the seller to reduce the main product's price to make it more competitive. By-products can even turn out to be profitable.

Sometimes companies don't realize how valuable their by-products are. For example, most zoos don't realize that one of their by-products—animal manure—can be an excellent source of additional revenue. But the Zoo-Doo Compost Company has helped many zoos understand the costs and opportunities involved with these by-products. Zoo-Doo licenses its name to zoos and receives royalties on manure sales. "Many zoos don't even know how much manure they are producing or the cost of disposing of it," explains president and founder Pierce Ledbetter. Zoos are often so pleased with any savings they can find on disposal that they don't think to move into active by-product sales. However, sales of the fragrant by-product can be substantial. So far novelty sales have been the largest,

Product line pricing: Infinity offers a line of home stereo speakers at prices ranging from $300 to $70 000 per pair.

Product-bundle pricing
Combining several products and offering the bundle at a reduced price.

with tiny containers of Zoo Doo (and even "Love, Love Me Doo" valentines) available in 160 zoo stores and 700 additional retail outlets. For the long-term market, Zoo-Doo looks to gardeners who buy seven to 30 kilograms of manure at a time. Zoo Doo is already planning a "dung of the month" club to reach this lucrative by-products market.[4]

PRODUCT-BUNDLE PRICING

Using **product-bundle pricing,** sellers often combine several of their products and offer the bundle at a reduced price. Thus, theatres and sports teams sell season tickets at less than the cost of single tickets; hotels sell specially priced packages that include room, meals, and entertainment; computer makers include attractive software packages with their personal computers. Price bundling can promote the sale of products that consumers might not otherwise buy, but the combined price must be low enough to get them to buy the bundle.[5]

Marketers must be cautious and avoid overbundling services. When new products are bundled with previous offers, and consumers are given no choice but to buy the new bundle of products or services, adverse consumer reaction may result. This was the situation faced by Rogers Cablesystems Ltd., Canada's largest cable-television provider, in early 1995. Rogers bundled its new specialty TV channels with existing cable-television packages and demanded an increased payment of $2 to $4 per month for the added services. The company used a technique called negative-option marketing. This occurs when services are automatically provided unless consumers notify the company that they do not want them. Consumer complaints caused Rogers to revise its marketing plan, but not before provincial legislators in British Columbia, Ontario, Nova Scotia, and Manitoba promised to investigate the negative-option practice.[6]

PRICE-ADJUSTMENT STRATEGIES

Rogers Cablesystems
www.rogerscable.com/

Companies usually adjust their basic prices to account for various customer differences and changing situations. Table 11-2 summarizes seven price-adjustment strategies: *discount and allowance pricing, segmented pricing, psychological pricing, promotional pricing, value pricing, geographical pricing,* and *international pricing.*

TABLE 11-2 *Price Adjustment Strategies*

Strategy	Description
Discount and allowance pricing	Reducing prices to reward customer responses such as paying early or promoting the product
Segmented pricing	Adjusting prices to allow for differences in customers, products, or locations
Psychological pricing	Adjusting prices for psychological effect
Promotional pricing	Temporarily reducing prices to increase short-run sales
Value pricing	Adjusting prices to offer the right combination of quality and service at a fair price
Geographical pricing	Adjusting prices to account for the geographic location of customers
International pricing	Adjusting prices for international markets

DISCOUNT AND ALLOWANCE PRICING

Most companies adjust their basic price to reward customers for certain responses, such as early payment of bills, volume purchases, and off-season buying. These price adjustments—called discounts and allowances—can take many forms.

Cash discount
A price reduction to buyers who pay their bills promptly.

A **cash discount** is a price reduction to buyers who pay their bills promptly. A typical example is "2/10, net 30," which means that although payment is due within 30 days, the buyer can deduct 2 percent if the bill is paid within 10 days. The discount must be granted to all buyers meeting these terms. Such discounts are customary in many industries and help to improve the sellers' cash situation and reduce bad debts and credit-collection costs.

Quantity discount
A price reduction to buyers who buy large volumes.

A **quantity discount** is a price reduction to buyers who buy large volumes. A typical example might be "$10 per unit for less than 100 units, $9 per unit for 100 or more units." Under the provisions of the Competition Act, quantity discounts must be offered equally to all customers and must not exceed the seller's cost savings associated with selling large quantities. These savings include lower selling, inventory, and transportation expenses. Discounts provide an incentive to the customer to buy more from one given seller, rather than from many different sources.

Functional discount
A price reduction offered by the seller to trade channel members who perform certain functions such as selling, storing, and recordkeeping.

A **functional discount** (also called a *trade discount*) is offered by the seller to trade channel members who perform certain functions, such as selling, storing, and record-keeping. Manufacturers may offer different functional discounts to different trade channels because of the varying services they perform, but manufacturers must offer the same functional discounts within each trade channel.

Seasonal discount
A price reduction to buyers who purchase merchandise or services out of season.

A **seasonal discount** is a price reduction to buyers who buy merchandise or services out of season. For example, lawn and garden equipment manufacturers will offer seasonal discounts to retailers during the fall and winter to encourage early ordering in anticipation of the heavy spring and summer selling seasons. Hotels, motels, and airlines will offer seasonal discounts in their slower selling periods. Seasonal discounts allow the seller to keep production steady during an entire year.

Allowance
Promotional money paid by manufacturers to retailers in return for an agreement to feature the manufacturer's products in some way.

Allowances are another type of reduction from the list price. For example, *trade-in allowances* are price reductions given for turning in an old item when buying a new one. Trade-in allowances are most common in the automobile industry, but are also given for other durable goods. *Promotional allowances* are payments or price reductions to reward dealers for participating in advertising and sales-support programs.

SEGMENTED PRICING

Segmented pricing
Selling a product or service at two or more prices, where the difference in prices is not based on differences in costs.

Companies often will adjust their basic prices to allow for differences in customers, products, and locations. In **segmented pricing,** the company sells a product or service at two or more prices, even though the difference in prices is not based on differences in costs (see Marketing Highlight 11-2). Segmented pricing takes several forms:

- *Customer-segment pricing.* Different customers pay different prices for the same product or service. Museums, for example, will charge a lower admission for students and senior citizens.

- *Product-form pricing.* Different versions of the product are priced differently, but not according to differences in their costs. For instance, Black & Decker prices its most expensive iron at $54.98, which is $10 more than the price of its next most expensive iron. The top model has a self-cleaning feature, yet this extra feature costs only a few more dollars to make.

- *Location pricing.* Different locations are priced differently, even though the cost of offering each location is the same. For instance, theatres vary their

THE RIGHT PRODUCT TO THE RIGHT CUSTOMER AT THE RIGHT TIME FOR THE RIGHT PRICE

Many companies would love to raise prices across the board—but fear losing business. Jimmy Legarreta, manager of a large opera company, decided there had to be a better way. He found one after carefully reviewing opera economics. Legarreta knew—and his computer system confirmed—that the company routinely turned away people for Friday and Saturday night performances, particularly for prime seats. Meanwhile, mid-week tickets went begging.

Legarreta also knew that not all seats were equal, even in the sought-after orchestra section. So the ticket manager and his staff sat in every one of the opera house's 2200 seats and gave each a value according to the view and the acoustics. With his revenue goal in mind, Legarreta played with ticket prices until he arrived at nine levels, up from the existing five. In the end, the opera raised prices for its most coveted seats by as much as 50 percent but also dropped the prices of some 600 seats. The gamble paid off in a nine percent revenue increase during the next season.

Although Legarreta didn't have a name for it, he was practising "segmented pricing," an approach that also has many other labels. Airlines call it "yield management" and practise it religiously. Robert Cross, a longtime consultant to the airlines, calls it "revenue management." In a book by that name, Cross argues that all companies should apply revenue-management concepts, which emphasize an aggressive micromarket approach to maximizing sales. "Revenue management," Cross writes, "assures that companies will sell the right product to the right consumer at the right time for the right price."

Cross's underlying premise: no two customers value a product or service exactly the same way.

Furthermore, the "perceived value" of a product results from many variables that change over time. Grand & Toy understands this premise and is implementing a direct marketing strategy that focuses on customizing pricing from specific segments of its customer base. The company uses "mini-catalogues" that feature products carefully matched to the needs of specific industry sectors, and customizes pricing by sector. IBM Canada follows a similar strategy for its new voice-recognition technology. Both products and their prices were tailored to the specific needs of various markets. IBM offers three products: *Simply Speaking Gold, Simply Speaking,* and *ViaVoice*. IBM's initial higher-priced products were targeted at the medical and legal markets. Next, IBM wanted to crack the consumer market with its *ViaVoice*. It priced the product more affordably for people wanting the product for home use.

Some of Cross's clients use sophisticated simulation modelling to predict sales at different price levels, but the technique doesn't have to be rocket science. If you understand your customers' motivation for buying and you keep careful sales records, it's possible to adjust prices to remedy supply-and-demand imbalances. Legarreta, for example, ended his mid-week slump by making opera affordable for more people, yet he accurately predicted that the weekend crowd would pay higher prices for the best seats.

Probably the simplest form of segmented pricing is off-peak pricing, which is common in the entertainment and travel industries. Both Air Canada and Canadian Airlines offer cheaper flights for people willing to travel over a weekend. Cellular phone companies such as Cantel use segmented "zone pricing." Users' fees are determined

using a combination of usage rates and geographic regions.

Many other companies could conceivably segment their prices to increase revenues and profits. Cross cites examples ranging from a one-chair barbershop, to an accounting firm, to a health centre. But there are risks. When you establish a range of prices, customers who pay the higher ones may feel cheated. "It can't be a secret that you're charging different prices for the same service," Cross advises. "Customers must know, so they can choose when to use a service."

Even so, promotions designed to shift customer traffic to offpeak times can backfire. Rick Johnson, owner of a car wash, describes his experience with a "Wonderful Wednesday" special: "The incentive was too good. It took away from the rest of the week and made Wednesday a monster day; it was a horrible strain on my facility and my people. I played around with the discount, but it was still a problem. So I finally dropped it."

The moral of the story? You can never know too much about your customers and the different values they assign to your product or service. With that customer knowledge comes power—to make the best pricing decisions.

Sources: Adapted with permission from Susan Greco, "Are Your Prices Right?" *Inc.,* January 1997, pp. 88–89. Copyright 1997 by Goldhirsh Group, Inc., 38 Commercial Wharf, Boston, MA 02110. David Bosworth, "Grand & Toy to Customize Offers, Pricing," *Strategy: The Canadian Marketing Report,* December 9, 1996, p. DR; Mark De Wolf, "IBM Brings Voice-Recognition to the Masses," *Strategy: The Canadian Marketing Report,* June 23, 1997, p. 5; Mikala Folb, "Cell Phones Taking Aim at New Targets," *Marketing,* May 26, 1997, Web site: marketingmag. com/search); www.grandandtoy.com/

seat prices because of audience preferences for certain locations, and universities charge higher tuition for overseas students.

◆ *Time pricing.* Prices vary by the season, the month, the day, and even the hour. Public utilities vary their prices to commercial users based on the time of day and weekend versus weekday. The telephone company offers lower "off-peak" charges, and resorts give seasonal discounts.

Segmented pricing: Ramada uses customer-segment and time pricing, and other incentives, to attract family travellers during the summer season. This summer, "four adults can stay in the same room for the cost of just one, and kids always stay free."

Psychological pricing
A pricing approach that considers the psychology of prices and not simply the economics; the price is used to say something about the product.

Reference prices
Prices that buyers carry in their minds and refer to when they look at a given product.

For segmented pricing to be an effective strategy, certain conditions must exist. The market must be segmentable, and the segments must show different degrees of demand. Members of the segment paying the lower price should not be able to turn around and resell the product to the segment paying the higher price. Competitors should not be able to undersell the firm in the segment being charged the higher price. Nor should the costs of segmenting and watching the market exceed the extra revenue obtained from the price difference. The practice should not lead to customer resentment and ill will. The segmented pricing must be legal and ethical, and segmented prices should reflect real differences in customers' perceived value.

PSYCHOLOGICAL PRICING

Price says something about the product. For example, many consumers use price to judge quality. A $100 bottle of perfume may contain only $3 worth of scent, but some people are willing to pay $100 because this price indicates something special.

In using **psychological pricing**, sellers consider the psychology of prices and not simply the economics. For example, one study of the relationship between price and quality perceptions of cars found that consumers perceive higher-priced cars as having higher quality.[7] By the same token, higher-quality cars are perceived to be even higher priced than they actually are. When consumers can judge the quality of a product by examining it or by calling on past experience with it, they use price less to judge quality. When consumers cannot judge quality because they lack the information or skill, price becomes an important quality signal (see Marketing Highlight 11-3).

Another aspect of psychological pricing is **reference prices**—prices that buyers carry in their minds and refer to when looking at a given product. The reference price might be formed by noting current prices, remembering past prices, or assessing the buying situation. Sellers can influence or use these consumers' reference prices when setting price. For example, a company could display its product next to more expensive ones in order to imply that it belongs in the same class. Department stores often sell women's clothing in separate departments differentiated by price: Clothing found in the more expensive department is assumed to be of better quality. Companies also can influence consumers' reference prices by stating high manufacturer's suggested prices, by indicating that the product was originally priced much higher, or by pointing to a competitor's higher price.

When marketers use reference pricing, they must ensure that they comply with both pricing and advertising regulations. Suzy Shier Ltd., one of Canada's largest retailers, was fined $300 000 in 1995 because of an illegal pricing and promotion practice. Suzy Shier is the firm that operates 375 stores across Canada including La Senza and L.A. Express.

In an attempt to influence consumers' reference pricing, Suzy Shier engaged in a practice known as double tagging. The company put two labels on clothing—one indicating an "original" price and the other showing a discount price of 50 to 70 percent lower. In and of itself this practice is not illegal. However, in order to comply with the Competition Act, the retailer must have sold the merchandise for a period of time at the original price. The 1994 investigation by the Competition Bureau revealed that Suzy Shier never sold merchandise at the original price, and that the goods were marked "special" even before they were shipped to retail stores. George Addy, director of investigation and research at the Competition Bureau stated, "The use of misleading comparison prices hurts consumers and makes it difficult to maintain healthy competition." Similar

HOW PRICE SIGNALS PRODUCT QUALITY

Heublein produces Smirnoff, North America's leading brand of vodka. Some years ago, Smirnoff was attacked by another brand. Wolfschmidt, priced at one dollar less per bottle, claimed to have the same quality as Smirnoff. Concerned that customers might switch to Wolfschmidt, Heublein considered several possible counter-strategies. It could lower Smirnoff's price by one dollar to hold on to market share; it could hold Smirnoff's price but increase advertising and promotion expenditures; or it could hold Smirnoff's price and let its market share fall. All three strategies would lead to lower profits, and it seemed that Heublein faced a no-win situation.

At this point, however, Heublein's marketers thought of a fourth strategy—and it was brilliant. Heublein *raised* the price of Smirnoff by one dollar! The company then introduced a new brand, Relska, to compete with Wolfschmidt. Moreover, it introduced yet another brand, Popov, priced even *lower* than Wolfschmidt. This product line-pricing strategy positioned Smirnoff as the elite brand and Wolfschmidt as an ordinary brand. Heublein's clever strategy produced a large increase in its overall profits.

The irony is that Heublein's three brands are pretty much the same in taste and manufacturing costs. Heublein knew that a product's price signals its quality. Using price as a signal, Heublein sells roughly the same product at three different quality positions.

Marketers should be aware that consumers and regulators sometimes regard such strategies as being exploitive. In 1995, there was an outcry among the 2.5 million Canadian contact lens users when it was revealed that Bausch & Lomb Canada Inc. had been selling the same contact lenses under different names for different prices. One version of the disposable contact lens is marketed under the name, SeeQuence 2, and is sold in packages of six for about $10 to $15 a pair. Users are instructed to dispose of the lenses after two weeks. The same lens is also sold under the brand name Medalist, but costs $25 to $30 a pair and usage instructions state that they can be worn for one month. A third brand name, Optima Frequent Wear, is also used for the lenses, but consumers pay $130 to $160 for them and are told that they can wear them for more than a year.

When questioned, Bausch and Lomb stated it didn't believe it was doing anything wrong. It claimed that consumers were paying for different wear, care, and replacement systems. The spokesperson also stated that the company offered options to the optometrists and opticians who distribute its products about which type of lens to prescribe.

In light of the above concerns, the federal Competition Bureau has been studying the case. In the United States, similar concerns have been raised. In November 1995, the District Court of Alabama ruled that buyers could pursue a class-action suit against the company for misrepresentation.

Source: Gay Abbate, "Same Contact Lens Priced Differently," *Globe and Mail*, January 10, 1995, p. A3; www.smirnoff.com/; www.bausch.com/

charges have been laid against Color Your World Inc. and the Hudson's Bay. The Bay is fighting the charges.[8]

Even small differences in price can suggest product differences. Consider a stereo priced at $300 compared to one priced at $299.95. The actual price difference is only five cents, but the psychological difference can be much greater. For example, some consumers will view the $299.95 as a price in the $200 range rather than the $300 range. Whereas the $299.95 will more likely be seen as a bargain price, the $300 price suggests more quality. Some psychologists argue that each digit has symbolic and visual qualities that should be considered in pricing. Thus, 8 is round and even and creates a soothing effect, whereas 7 is angular and creates a jarring effect.[9]

PROMOTIONAL PRICING

Promotional pricing
Temporarily pricing products below the list price, and sometimes even below cost, to increase short-run sales.

With **promotional pricing**, companies will temporarily price their products below list price and sometimes even below cost. Promotional pricing takes several forms. Supermarkets and department stores will price a few products as *loss leaders* to attract customers to the store in the hope that they will buy other items at normal markups. Sellers will also use *special-event pricing* in certain seasons to draw more customers. Thus, linens are promotionally priced every January to attract weary Christmas shoppers back into stores. Manufacturers will sometimes offer *cash rebates* to consumers who buy the product from dealers within a specified time; the manufacturer sends the rebate directly to the customer. Rebates have

This weekend, practically anything that fits in our new bag is 25% off.

Yes, we are sane.

EATON'S

We'd like to introduce you to our new bag. And to make sure you get the most out of it, this Saturday and Sunday, on Regular Priced Merchandise, we're offering 25% off practically anything you can fit into it, plus 15% off the stuff you can't. Because here at Eaton's, we're working on it.

Promotional pricing: Companies often reduce their prices temporarily to attract customers and boost sales.

FOB-origin pricing
A geographic pricing strategy in which goods are placed free on board a carrier; the customer pays the freight from the factory to the destination.

Uniform delivered pricing
A geographic pricing strategy in which the company charges the same price plus freight to all customers, regardless of their location.

recently been popular with automakers and producers of durable goods and small appliances. Some manufacturers offer *low-interest financing, longer warranties,* or *free maintenance* to reduce the consumer's "price." This practice has recently become a favourite of the auto industry. Or, the seller may simply offer *discounts* from normal prices to increase sales and reduce inventories. As the Procter & Gamble example illustrates, the promotional pricing can have adverse effects. Used too frequently and copied by competitors, they can create "deal-prone" customers who wait until brands go on sales before buying them. Or, constantly reduced prices can erode a brand's value in the eyes of customers.

GEOGRAPHICAL PRICING

A company also must decide how to price its products to customers located in different parts of the country or world. Should the company risk losing the business of more distant customers by charging them higher prices to cover the higher shipping costs? Or should the company charge all customers the same prices regardless of location? We will look at five geographical pricing strategies for the following hypothetical situation:

> The Peerless Paper Company is located in Fredericton, New Brunswick, and sells paper products to customers all over Canada. The cost of freight is high and affects the companies from whom customers buy their paper. Peerless wants to establish a geographical pricing policy. It is trying to determine how to price a $100 order to three specific customers: Customer A (Fredericton); Customer B (Winnipeg, Manitoba), and Customer C (Kamloops, British Columbia).

One option is for Peerless to ask each customer to pay the shipping cost from the Fredericton factory to the customer's location. All three customers would pay the same factory price of $100, with Customer A paying, say, $10 for shipping; Customer B, $15; and Customer C, $25. Called **FOB-origin pricing**, this practice means that the goods are placed *free on board* (hence, *FOB*) a carrier. At that point the title and responsibility pass to the customer, who pays the freight from the factory to the destination.

Because each customer picks up its own cost, supporters of FOB pricing feel that this is the fairest way to assess freight charges. The disadvantage, however, is that Peerless will be a high-cost firm to distant customers. If Peerless's main competitor happens to be in British Columbia, this competitor will no doubt outsell Peerless in British Columbia. In fact, the competitor would outsell Peerless in most of the West, whereas Peerless would dominate the East.

Uniform delivered pricing is the exact opposite of FOB pricing. Here, the company charges the same price plus freight to all customers, regardless of their location. The freight charge is set at the average freight cost. Suppose this is $15. Uniform delivered pricing therefore results in a higher charge to the Fredericton customer (who pays $15 freight instead of $10) and a lower charge to the Kamloops customer (who pays $15 instead of $25). On the one hand, the Fredericton customer would prefer to buy paper from another local paper company that uses FOB-origin pricing. On the other hand, Peerless has a better chance of winning over the British Columbia customer. Other advantages of uniform delivered pricing are that it is fairly easy to administer and it lets the firm advertise its price nationally.

Zone pricing
A geographic pricing strategy in which the company sets up two or more zones. All customers within a zone pay the same total price; the more distant the zone, the higher the price.

Zone pricing falls between FOB-origin pricing and uniform delivered pricing. The company sets up two or more zones. All customers within a given zone pay a single total price; the more distant the zone, the higher the price. For example, Peerless might set up an East Zone and charge $10 freight to all customers in this zone, a Prairie Zone in which it charges $15, and a West Zone in which it charges $25. In this way, the customers within a given price zone receive no price advantage from the company. For example, customers in Fredericton and Halifax pay the same total price to Peerless. The complaint, however, is that the Fredericton customer is paying part of the Halifax customer's freight cost. In addition, even though they may be located within a few kilometres of each other, a customer just barely on the west side of the line dividing the East and Prairie pays much more than does one just barely on the east side of the line.

Basing-point pricing
A geographic pricing strategy in which the seller designates some city as a basing point and charges all customers the freight cost from that city to the customer location, regardless of the city from which the goods are actually shipped.

Using **basing-point pricing,** the seller selects a given city as a "basing point" and charges all customers the freight cost from that city to the customer location, regardless of the city from which the goods actually are shipped. For example, Peerless might set Winnipeg as the basing point and charge all customers $100 plus the freight from Winnipeg to their locations. This means that an Fredericton customer pays the freight cost from Winnipeg to Fredericton, even though the goods may be shipped from Fredericton. Using a basing-point location other than the factory raises the total price for customers near the factory and lowers the total price for customers far from the factory.

If all sellers used the same basing-point city, delivered prices would be the same for all customers and price competition would be eliminated. Industries such as sugar, cement, steel, and automobiles used basing-point pricing for years, but this method has become less popular today. Some companies set up multiple basing points to create more flexibility: They quote freight charges from the basing-point city nearest to the customer.

Freight-absorption pricing
A geographic pricing strategy in which the company absorbs all or part of the actual freight charges in order to get the business.

Finally, the seller who is anxious to do business with a certain customer or geographical area might use **freight-absorption pricing.** Using this strategy, the seller absorbs all or part of the actual freight charges in order to get the desired business. The seller might reason that if it can get more business, its average costs will fall and more than compensate for its extra freight cost. Freight-absorption pricing is used for market penetration and to hold on to increasingly competitive markets.

INTERNATIONAL PRICING

Companies that market their products internationally must decide what prices to charge in the different countries in which they operate. In some cases, a company can set a uniform worldwide price. For example, Canadair sells its jetliners at about the same price everywhere, whether in the United States, Europe, or a Third World country. However, most companies adjust their prices to reflect local market conditions and cost considerations.

The price that a company should charge in a specific country depends on many factors, including economic conditions, competitive situations, laws and regulations, and development of the wholesaling and retailing system. Consumer perceptions and preferences also may vary among countries, calling for different prices. Or the company may have different marketing objectives in various world markets, which require changes in pricing strategy. For example, Sony might introduce a new product into mature markets in highly developed countries with the goal of quickly gaining mass-market share—this would call for a penetration pricing strategy. In contrast, it might enter a less developed market by targeting smaller, less price-sensitive segments—in this case, market-skimming pricing makes sense.

Costs play an important role in setting international prices. Travellers abroad are often surprised to find that goods that are relatively inexpensive at home may

International price escalation: A pair of Levi's selling for $42 in Canada goes for over $80 in a Levi's boutique in Korea and other Pacific Rim countries.

carry outrageously higher price tags in other countries. A pair of Levis selling for $42 in Canada goes for about $87 in Tokyo and $122 in Paris. A McDonald's Big Mac selling for a modest $2.25 here costs $7.99 in Moscow. Conversely, a Gucci handbag going for only $80 in Milan, Italy, fetches $340 in Canada. In some cases, such *price escalation* may result from differences in selling strategies or market conditions. In most instances, however, it is simply a result of the higher costs of selling in foreign markets—the additional costs of modifying the product, higher shipping and insurance costs, import tariffs and taxes, costs associated with exchange-rate fluctuations, and higher channel and physical distribution costs.

For example, Campbell found that its distribution costs in the United Kingdom were 30 percent higher than in the United States. North American retailers typically purchase soup in large quantities—48-can cases of a single soup by the dozens, hundreds, or carloads. In contrast, English grocers purchase soup in small quantities—typically in 24-can cases of *assorted* soups. Each case must be hand-packed for shipment. To handle these small orders, Campbell had to add a costly extra wholesale level to its European channel. The smaller orders also mean that English retailers order two or three times as often as their North American counterparts, which increases billing and order costs. These and other factors caused Campbell to charge much higher prices for its soups in the United Kingdom.[10]

Thus, international pricing presents some special problems and complexities. We discuss international pricing issues in more detail in Chapter 19.

PRICE CHANGES

After developing their pricing structures and strategies, companies often face situations in which they must initiate price changes or respond to price changes by competitors.

INITIATING PRICE CHANGES

In some cases, the company may find it desirable to initiate either a price cut or a price increase. In both cases, it must anticipate possible buyer and competitor reactions.

Initiating Price Cuts

Several situations may lead a firm to consider cutting its price. One such circumstance is excess capacity. In this case, the firm needs more business and cannot get it through increased sales effort, product improvement, or other measures. It may drop its "follow-the-leader pricing"—charging about the same price as their leading competitor—and aggressively cut prices to boost sales. But as the airline, construction equipment, and other industries have learned in recent years, cutting prices in an industry loaded with excess capacity may lead to price wars as competitors try to hold on to market share.

Another situation leading to price changes is falling market share in the face of strong price competition. Several North American industries—automobiles, consumer electronics, cameras, watches, and steel, for example—lost market share to Japanese competitors whose high-quality products carried lower prices than did their American counterparts. In response, North American companies resorted to more aggressive pricing action. General Motors, for example, cut its subcompact car prices by 10 percent on the West Coast of the United States, where Japanese competition was strongest.[11]

A company also may cut prices in a drive to dominate the market through lower costs. Either the company starts with lower costs than its competitors or it cuts prices in the hope of gaining market share that will further cut costs through larger volume. President's Choice used a low-cost, low-price strategy to introduce its private-label beer.

Initiating Price Increases

In contrast, many companies have had to *raise* prices in recent years. They do this knowing that the price increases may be resented by customers, dealers, and even their own sales force. Yet a successful price increase can greatly increase profits. For example, if the company's profit margin is three percent of sales, a one percent price increase will increase profits by 33 percent if sales volume is unaffected.

A major factor in price increases is cost inflation. Rising costs squeeze profit margins and lead companies to regular rounds of price increases. For example, in the face of rising pulp and paper costs, makers of newsprint and package-board have been forced to raise their prices across Canada. Companies often raise their prices by more than the cost increase in anticipation of further inflation. Another factor leading to price increases is overdemand: When a company cannot supply all its customers' needs, it can raise its prices, ration products to customers, or both.

Companies can increase their prices in a number of ways to keep up with rising costs. Prices can be raised almost invisibly by dropping discounts and adding higher-priced units to the line. Or prices can be pushed up openly. In passing on price increases to customers, the company should avoid the image of price gouging. The price increases should be supported with a company communication program telling customers why prices are being increased. The company sales force should help customers find ways to economize.

Where possible, the company should consider ways to meet higher costs or demand without raising prices. For example, it can shrink the product instead of raising the price, as chocolate bar manufacturers often do. Or it can substitute less expensive ingredients, or remove certain product features, packaging, or services. Or it can "unbundle" its products and services, removing and separately pricing elements that were formerly part of the offer. IBM, for example, now offers training and consulting as separately priced services.

Buyer Reactions to Price Changes

Whether the price is raised or lowered, the action will affect buyers, competitors, distributors, and suppliers and may interest government as well. Customers

The costliest perfume in the world.
NEIMAN-MARCUS

do not always interpret prices in a straightforward way. They may view a price *cut* in several ways. For example, what would you think if Sony were suddenly to cut its VCR prices in half? You might think that these VCRs are about to be replaced by newer models or that they have some fault and are not selling well. You might think that Sony is in financial trouble and may not stay in this business long enough to supply future parts. You might believe that quality has been reduced. Or you might think that the price will come down even further and that it will pay to wait and see.

Similarly, a price *increase*, which normally would lower sales, may have some positive meanings for buyers. What would you think if Sony *raised* the price of its latest VCR model? On the one hand, you might think that the item is very "hot" and may be unobtainable unless you buy it soon. Or you might think that the recorder is an unusually good value. On the other hand, you might think that Sony is greedy and charging what the traffic will bear.

Buyer reactions to price changes? What would you think if the price of Joy was suddenly cut in half?

Competitor Reactions to Price Changes

A firm considering a price change has to worry about the reactions of its competitors as well as its customers. Competitors are most likely to react when the number of firms involved is small, when the product is uniform, and when the buyers are well informed as was illustrated in the gasoline pricing example.

How can the firm determine the likely reactions of its competitors? If the firm faces one large competitor, and if the competitor tends to react in a set way to price changes, that reaction can be easily anticipated. But if the competitor treats each price change as a fresh challenge and reacts according to its self-interest, the company will have to determine just what makes up the competitor's self-interest at the time.

The problem is complex because, like the customer, the competitor can interpret a company price cut in many ways. It might think the company is trying to grab a larger market share, that the company is doing poorly and trying to boost its sales, or that the company wants the whole industry to cut prices to increase total demand.

When there are several competitors, the company must guess each competitor's likely reaction. If all competitors behave alike, this amounts to analysing only a typical competitor. In contrast, if the competitors do not behave alike—perhaps because of differences in size, market shares, or policies—then separate analyses are necessary. However, if some competitors will match the price change, there is good reason to expect that the rest also will match it.

RESPONDING TO PRICE CHANGES

Here we reverse the question and ask how a firm should respond to a price change by a competitor. The firm needs to consider several issues: Why did the competitor change the price? Was it to take more market share, to use excess capacity, to meet changing cost conditions, or to lead an industrywide price change? Is the price change temporary or permanent? What will happen to the company's market share and profits if it does not respond? Are other companies going to respond? And what are the competitor's and other firms' responses to each possible reaction likely to be?

Besides these issues, the company must make a broader analysis. It must consider its own product's stage in the life cycle, the product's importance in the company's product mix, the intentions and resources of the competitor, and the possible consumer reactions to price changes. The company cannot always make an extended analysis of its alternatives at the time of a price change, however. The competitor may have spent much time preparing this decision, but the company may

FIGURE 11-2 *Assessing and responding to competitor's price changes*

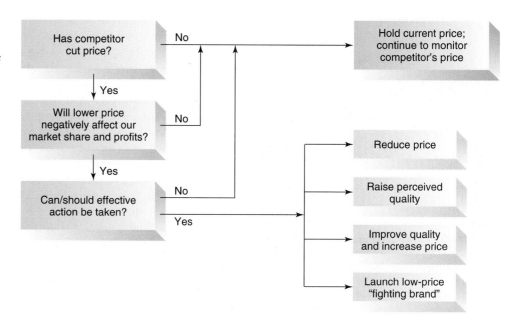

Fighting brands: When challenged on price by store brands and other low-priced entrants, Procter & Gamble turned a number of its brands into fighting brands, including Luvs disposable diapers.

have to react within hours or days. About the only way to cut down reaction time is to plan ahead for both possible competitor's price changes and possible responses.

Figure 11-2 shows the ways a company might assess and respond to a competitor's price cut. Once the company has determined that the competitor has cut its price and that this price reduction is likely to harm company sales and profits, it might simply decide to hold its current price and profit margin. The company might believe that it will not lose too much market share, or that it would lose too much profit if it reduced its own price. It might decide that it should wait and respond when it has more information on the effects of the competitor's price change. For now, it might be willing to hold on to good customers, while giving up the poorer ones to the competitor. The argument against this holding strategy, however, is that the competitor may get stronger and more confident as its sales increase, and that the company might wait too long to act.

If the company decides that effective action can and should be taken, it might make any of four responses. First, it could *reduce its price* to match the competitor's price. It may decide that the market is price-sensitive, and that it would lose too much market share to the lower-priced competitor. Or it might worry that recapturing lost market share later would be too hard. Cutting price will reduce the company's profits in the short run. Some companies might also reduce their product quality, services, and marketing communications to retain profit margins, but this ultimately will hurt long-run market share. The company should try to maintain its quality as it cuts prices.

Alternatively, the company might maintain its price but *raise the perceived quality* of its offer. It could improve its communications, stressing the relative quality of its product over that of the lower-price competitor. The firm may find it cheaper to maintain price and spend money to improve its perceived value than to cut price and operate at a lower margin.

Or, the company might *improve quality and increase price,* moving its brand into a higher price position.

PUBLIC POLICY AND PRICING

When Russia lifted controls on bread prices as part of its dramatic move toward a free-market economy, Moscow bakers phoned around each morning to agree on regular rounds of price increases. This caused the *Wall Street Journal* to comment: "They still don't get it!" Those who have grown up under a well-regulated, free-market economy understand that such price fixing is clearly against the rules of fair competition. Setting prices is an important element of a competitive marketplace.

Legal issues surrounding pricing are outlined in Sections 34, 36, and 38 of the Competition Act. Canadian pricing legislation was designed with two goals in mind: to protect consumers and to foster a competitive environment. Although pricing decisions made by firms do not generally require regulatory approval, Canadian marketers should be aware of three areas of concern: price fixing, price discrimination, and deceptive pricing (also called misleading price advertising).

Price Fixing. Federal legislation on price fixing states that sellers must set prices without talking to competitors. Otherwise, price collusion is suspected. Price fixing is illegal per se—that is, the government does not accept any excuses for price fixing. Even a simple conversation between competitors can have serious consequences. The legal charge under the Competition Act for offences of this nature is conspiracy. Recently six Ottawa hotels were each fined from $60 000 to $80 000 after they were convicted of colluding to fix prices offered to government employees. Bid rigging is another indictable offence under the clauses pertaining to price fixing. A number of cases in the construction industry have resulted in heavy fines being levied when competitors have been found guilty of rigging the prices of their bids. These cases have made most executives very reluctant to discuss prices in any way with competitors. In obtaining information on competitors' pricing, they rely only on openly published materials, such as trade association surveys and competitors' catalogues.

Price Discrimination. Section 34 of the Competition Act seeks to ensure that sellers offer the same price terms to a given level of trade. For example, every retailer is entitled to the same price terms whether the retailer is Sears or the local bicycle shop. However, price discrimination is allowed if the seller can prove that its costs are different when selling to different retailers—for example, that it costs less per unit to sell a large volume of bicycles to Sears than to sell a few bicycles to a local dealer. In other words, quantity or volume discounts are not prohibited. However, discriminatory promotional allowances (those not offered on proportional terms to all other competing customers) are illegal. Thus, large competitors cannot negotiate special discounts, rebates, and price concessions that are not made proportionally available to smaller competitors. For example, a small customer purchasing one-third as much as a larger competitor must receive a promotional allowance equal to one-third of what the large competitor was offered.

Although functional discounts (offering a larger discount to wholesalers than to retailers) are legal in the United States, they are illegal in Canada. In Canada, retailers and wholesalers are considered competing customers who must receive proportionally equal promotional allowances. Often Canadian marketers, who work for multinational firms, must explain the differences in the law to their American counterparts. Canadian marketers also must keep in mind that it is illegal for a buyer to knowingly benefit from any form of price discrimination. Price differentials also may be used to "match competition" in "good faith," provided the firm is trying to meet competitors at its own level of competition and the price discrimination is temporary, localized, and defensive rather than offensive.

Canadian marketers are allowed to offer price breaks for one-shot deals such as store-opening specials, anniversary specials, and stock-clearance sales. However, regional price differentials that limit competition are illegal. Canadian firms cannot price products unreasonably low in one part of the country with the intent of driving out the competition. Finally, resale price maintenance is also illegal. Canadian manufacturers can only suggest prices; it is illegal to require retailers to sell at a stipulated manufacturer's price.

Deceptive Pricing. Section 36 of the Competition Act covers areas where pricing and advertising practices converge. For example, firms cannot advertise a product at a low price, carry very limited stock, and then tell consumers they are out of the product so that they can entice them to switch to a higher-priced item. This is called "bait and switch" advertising, and is illegal in Canada. Firms must offer their customers "rain checks" to avoid legal sanctions if advertised items are not stocked in sufficient quantities to cover expected demand.

Deceptive pricing occurs when a seller states prices or price savings that are not actually available to consumers. Some deceptions are difficult for consumers to discern, such as when an airline advertises a low one-way fare that is available only with the purchase of a round-trip ticket, or when a retailer sets artificially high "regular" prices, then announces "sale" prices close to its previous everyday prices.

Ethical Issues. Being in compliance with the law is considered the minimum standard when judging whether pricing practices are ethical. For example, although charging inordinately high prices is not illegal, such a practice may lead to ethical concerns. Ethical criticisms have been levied when higher prices are charged for groceries in poor areas where consumers have limited access to transportation and have few choices in terms of retail outlets.

Other ethical questions centre on issues of whether consumers can understand prices and realistically compare them. For example, consumer advocates have condemned many car leasing contracts since the legal language used in the contracts prevents consumers from fully understanding the price they are paying for the car.

Ethical concerns regarding pricing also arise when consumers must negotiate prices. Often those who can least afford to pay a higher price (such as the poor, very young, elderly, or disabled), have the least ability to negotiate prices. These concerns arise when prices are not fixed. This is the case when people purchase cars, houses, professional services, or attend street markets. Many consumers are unaware that even when prices appear fixed, they may be subject to negotiation. For example, many consumers don't know that they can negotiate with their bank for more favourable terms on a consumer loan.

Sources: See the Competition Act, Sections 34–38, and N. Craig Smith and John A. Quelch, *Ethics in Marketing*, Boston: Irwin, pp. 389–404.

The higher quality justifies the higher price, which in turn preserves the company's higher margins. Or the company can hold its price on the current product and introduce a new brand at a higher price position.

Finally, the company might launch a low-price "fighting brand." Often, one of the best responses is to add lower-price items to the line or to create a separate lower-price brand. This is necessary if the particular market segment being lost is price-sensitive and will not respond to arguments of higher quality. Thus, when attacked on price by Fuji, Kodak introduced low-priced Funtime film. When challenged on price by store brands and other low-priced entrants, Procter and Gamble turned a number of its brands into fighting brands, including Luvs disposable diapers, Joy dishwashing detergent, and Camay beauty soap.[12]

Pricing strategies and tactics form an important element of a company's marketing mix. In setting prices, companies must carefully consider a great many internal and external factors before choosing a price that will give them the greatest competitive advantage in selected target markets. However, companies are not usually free to charge whatever prices they wish. Several laws restrict pricing practices, and a number of ethical considerations affect pricing decisions. Marketing Highlight 11-4 discusses the many public-policy and ethical issues surrounding pricing.

Summary of Chapter Objectives

Pricing decisions are subject to an incredibly complex array of environmental and competitive forces. A company sets not a single price, but rather a *pricing structure* that covers different items in its line. This pricing structure changes over time as products move through their life cycles. The company adjusts product prices to reflect changes in costs and demand and to account for variations in buyers and situations. As the competitive environment changes, the company considers when to initiate price changes and when to respond to them.

1. **Describe the major strategies for pricing imitative and new products.**

   Pricing is a dynamic process. Companies design a *pricing structure* that covers all their products. They change this structure over time and adjust it to account for different customers and situations. Pricing strategies usually change as a product passes through its life cycle. The company can decide on one of several price-quality strategies for in-troducing an imitative product, including premium pricing, economy pricing, good-value, or overcharging. In pricing innovative new products, it can follow a *skimming policy* by initially setting high prices to "skim" the maximum amount of revenue from various segments of the market. Or it can use *penetration pricing* by setting a low initial price to penetrate the market deeply and win a large market share.

2. **Explain how companies find a set of prices that maximizes the profits from the total product mix.**

   When the product is part of a product mix, the firm searches for a set of prices that will maximize the profits from the total mix. In *product line pricing*, the company decides on price steps for the entire set of products it offers. In addition, the company must set prices for *optional products* (optional or accessory products included with the main product), *captive products* (products that are required for use of the main product), *by-products* (waste or residual products produced when making the main product), and *product bundles* (combinations of products at a reduced price).

3. **Discuss how companies adjust their prices to take into account different types of customers and situations.**

   Companies apply a variety of *price-adjustment strategies* to account for differences in consumer segments and situations. One is *discount and allowance pricing*, whereby the company establishes cash, quantity, functional, or seasonal discounts, or varying types of allowances. A second strategy is *segmented pricing*, where the company sells a product at two or more prices to accommodate different customers, product forms, locations, or times. Sometimes companies consider more than economics in their pricing decisions, using *psychological pricing* to better communicate a product's intended position. In *promotional pricing*, a company offers discounts or temporarily sells a product below list price as a special event, sometimes even selling below cost as a loss leader. Another approach is *geographical pricing*, whereby the company decides how to price to distant customers, choosing from such alternatives as FOB pricing, uniform delivered pricing, zone pricing, basing-point pricing, and freight absorption pricing. Finally, *international pricing* means that the company adjusts its price to meet different conditions and expectations in different world markets.

4. **Discuss the key issues related to initiating and responding to price changes.**

   When a firm considers initiating a *price change*, it must consider customers' and competitors' reactions. There are different implications to *initiating price cuts* and *initiating price increases*. Buyer reactions to price changes are influenced by the meaning that customers see in the price change. Competitors' reactions flow from a set reaction policy or a fresh analysis of each situation.

   There are also many factors to consider in responding to a competitor's price changes. The company that faces a price change initiated by a competitor must try to understand the competitor's intent as well as the likely duration and impact of the change. If a swift reaction is desirable, the firm should preplan its reactions to different possible price actions by competitors. When facing a competitor's price change, the company might sit tight, reduce its own price, raise perceived quality, improve quality and raise price, or launch a fighting brand.

Key Terms

Allowances *(p. 375)*
Basing-point pricing *(p. 380)*
By-product pricing *(p. 373)*
Captive-product pricing *(p. 371)*
Cash discount *(p. 375)*
FOB-origin pricing *(p. 379)*
Freight-absorption pricing *(p. 380)*

Functional discount *(p. 375)*
Market-penetration pricing *(p. 370)*
Market-skimming pricing *(p. 369)*
Optional-product pricing *(p. 371)*
Product-bundle pricing *(p. 374)*
Product line pricing *(p. 371)*
Promotional pricing *(p. 378)*

Psychological pricing *(p. 377)*
Quantity discount *(p. 375)*
Reference prices *(p. 377)*
Seasonal discount *(p. 375)*
Segmented pricing *(p. 375)*
Uniform delivered pricing *(p. 379)*
Zone pricing *(p. 380)*

Discussing the Issues

1. When the dollar is weak, import prices rise, and Mercedes and Porsche prices rise with them. Yet when the dollar strengthens, the prices for these cars are kept high, yielding unusually large profits. Discuss whether Mercedes and Porsche should drop prices when

   the dollar rises. What effect would this have on used-car prices and trade-in values?

2. Describe which strategy—market skimming or market penetration—these companies use in pricing their products: (a) McDonald's, (b) Future Shop (television

and other home electronics), (c) Bic Corporation (pens, lighters, shavers, and related products), and (d) IBM. Are these the right strategies for these companies? Tell why or why not.

3. Carpet Fresh was the leading carpet deodorizer, priced at $3.49 for 370 grams. Arm & Hammer launched a competitive product priced at $2.75 for 740 grams and quickly became the number-one brand. Discuss the psychological aspects of this pricing. Does this superb-value strategy fit with Arm & Hammer's image?

4. The formula for chlorine bleach is virtually identical for all brands. Javex charges a premium price for this same product, yet remains the unchallenged market leader. Discuss what this implies about the value of a brand name. Analyse the ethical issues involved in this type of pricing.

5. Marketing Highlight 11-2 recommends that companies should use segmented pricing. Hold an in-class debate on this issue. Have half of the class resolve that segmented pricing is beneficial to buyers, the other half contends that segmented pricing exploits consumers.

6. A clothing store sells men's suits at three price levels—$180, $250, and $340. If shoppers use these price points as reference prices in comparing different suits, appraise the effect of adding a new line of suits at a cost of $280. Would you expect sales of the $250 suits to increase, decrease, or stay the same?

Applying the Concepts

1. List at least five examples of stores that use their pricing strategies as part of their marketing communications, such as a supermarket calling itself "the low-price leader" or even the name of Cost Plus Imports. Do any of your examples discuss offering average or high prices? Why not?

2. Go to your local supermarket and observe sizes and prices within product categories. Determine if the package sizes (the weight or number of units contained) are comparable across brands. Find at least two instances where a manufacturer seems to have made a smaller package in order to achieve a lower retail price. Does this appear effective? If your market has unit pricing labels, see whether the unit price is higher, lower, or the same as this brand's competitors. Does unit pricing information change your opinion about the effectiveness of this strategy?

References

1. Mathew Ingram, "Why Gasoline Prices Move so Crazily," *Financial Times of Canada*, October 2, 1993, pp. 6–7; Brent Jang, "Gasoline Plot a Myth, Report Says," *Globe and Mail*, October 11, 1997, pp. A1, A2.

2. For a comprehensive discussion of pricing strategies, see Thomas T. Nagle and Reed K. Holden, *The Strategy and Dynamics of Pricing*, 2nd ed. (Englewood Cliffs, NJ: Prentice Hall, 1995).

3. See David Kirkpatrick, "Intel Goes for Broke," *Fortune*, May 16, 1994, pp. 62–68; and Robert D. Hof, "Intel: Far Beyond the Pentium," *Business Week*, February 20, 1995, pp. 88–90.

4. Susan Krafft, "Love, Love Me Doo," *American Demographics*, June 1994, pp. 15–16.

5. See Nagle, *The Strategy and Tactics of Pricing*, pp. 225–228; and Manjit S. Yadav and Kent B. Monroe, "How Buyers Perceive Savings in a Bundle Price: An Examination of a Bundle's Transaction Value," *Journal of Marketing Research*, August 1993, pp. 350–358.

6. Ross Howard, "Rogers Caves In on Cable Channels," *Globe and Mail*, January 6, 1995, A1; Ross Howard, "Rogers Says New Channels in Jeopardy," *Globe and Mail*, January 7, 1995, pp. A1, A4.

7. Gary M. Erickson and Johnny K. Johansson, "The Role of Price in Multi-Attribute Product Evaluations," *Journal of Consumer Research*, September 1985, pp. 195–199.

8. Barrie McKenna, "Suzy Shier Fined $300,000," *Globe and Mail*, July 18, 1995, p. B5.

9. For more reading on reference prices and psychological pricing, see Nagle and Holden, *The Strategy and Tactics of Pricing*, Chapter 12; and K. N. Rajendran and Gerard J. Tellis, "Contextual and Temporal Com-

ponents of Reference Price," *Journal of Marketing,* January 1994, pp. 22–34.

10. Philip R. Cateora, *International Marketing,* 7th ed. (Homewood, IL: Irwin, 1990), p. 540.

11. For more on price cutting and its consequences, see Kathleen Madigan, "The Latest Mad Plunge of the Price Slashers, " *Business Week,* May 11, 1992, p. 36; and Bill Saporito, "Why the Price Wars Never End," *Fortune,* March 23, 1992, pp.68–78.

12. Jonathon Berry and Zachary Schiller, "Attack of the Fighting Brands," *Business Week,* May 2, 1994, p. 125.

Company Case 11

SWATCHMOBILE: IS THE TIME RIGHT FOR SMALL CARS?

If someone asked you what a Swatch watch and a Mercedes-Benz automobile have in common, you would probably answer, "not much." Perhaps you'd think the question was the lead-in to a joke. After all, the Swatch is a disposable $50 to $75 fashion watch made on assembly lines from plastic parts. Mercedes, by contrast, prides itself on making the "best engineered cars in the world"—highly complex machines designed by engineers who cut no corners and make no compromises.

AN UNLIKELY MARRIAGE

Well, that's all true, but the Swiss Corporation for Microelectronics and Watchmaking Industries (SMH) and Mercedes do have one thing in common—the Swatchmobile. In 1994, the two companies announced that they would jointly develop an innovative, subcompact, economy car designed to reach speeds of up to 150 km per hour while getting 130 km per gallon and costing about $21 000. The idea behind the joint venture was to combine Mercedes' knowledge of how to design and build automobiles with SMH's knowledge of microtechnology design and automated production.

FROM THE DRAWING BOARD

The Swatchmobile concept results from the work of several dozen young jeans-and-sweatshirt clad engineers who laboured around the clock for three years in a secret garage in Biel, Switzerland. They conceived a two-seater car that would combine the safety features of a Mercedes with the funkiness of a Swatch watch. Besides reaching high speeds and getting great fuel economy, the Swatchmobile would be about 20 percent smaller than a typical subcompact— you could park it sideways in a typical parking space!

To help accomplish all this, the engineers designed a 600cc, three-cylinder engine that would run on gasoline, electricity, or a combination of the two, and weigh one-tenth the amount of a typical gas engine while achieving equal power.

The unlikely marriage is also the result of market realities. Swatch, following its success in watches, was searching for something else on which to put its name. It had tried telephones, pager watches, and sunglasses—all without much success. In the meantime, Mercedes watched its sales plummet 11 percent in the early 1990s because of stiff Japanese competition in the luxury car market. Mercedes felt it needed to attract buyers who could not afford its traditional cars. It had already announced plans to introduce a compact, four-seat model called the "Vision A" at a price of about $36 000 in 1997.

In addition, many car companies were beginning to work on concepts for smaller cars. The companies feared that large cities might ban conventional cars due to pollution concerns. Thus, the companies wanted to begin designing smaller cars that produced less pollution. Most were examining cars powered with electric engines.

MICRO COMPACT CARS

Swatch and Mercedes formed a joint venture known as Micro Compact Car AG (MCC) to develop the new car. Nicolas Hayek, the man who led Swatch to its success, initially owned 49 percent of the company with Mercedes owning 51 percent. Mercedes has since increased its ownership to 81 percent. The company is headquartered in Biel where it has 80 people on its staff. It also has a technical centre in Renningen, Germany where it employs 170 people. By 1998, it expects to have 200 people in each location.

MCC has invested about $1 billion for research and development on the new car, and its suppliers have invested another $1 billion for new plant and equipment. MCC will produce the car in Hambach, France. At full capacity, the plant will employ 2000 people and produce 200 000 cars per year.

The Smart Car targets single people aged 18 to 36 and childless, dual-income couples living in urban areas who want a second car. The company wants to position the car as a fun but useful means of transportation in crowded cities.

Since the initial conception, the designers have abandoned the electric engine, because of the lack of adequate batteries, in favour of a small gasoline engine.

Instead of using a conventional assembly line, assemblers will snap the cars together, much as you would a child's toy model car, using five subassembly modules that come from suppliers' factories located immediately around the assembly site in Hambach. Because the car snaps together, the company will offer customers the ability to change the cars' features. For example, if after a month or so the customer does not like the car's colour, he or she can simply replace the panels with others of another colour. The car's overall length is 2.4 metres.

The company expects to begin selling the car in March 1998 at a price between $19 500 and $28 000. At this price, the dealer margin is 16 percent. Dealers will offer a leasing package that includes the rental of a larger car for two weeks per year when the customer might want more seats and room for luggage.

MCC began signing up dealers in 1997 with a target of signing up 100 in Europe (not including the United Kingdom) in the first phase of developing distribution. Although it will give preference to Mercedes dealers, it has also advertised for interested entrepreneurs. The second phase of distribution will cover the United Kingdom, the United States, and other right-hand-drive countries. The company has not indicated when this second phase will begin.

Dealers who want to distribute the Smart Car, as it is now called, will have to invest about $10 million to open a "Smart Centre." Of this amount, about $4 million is for real estate. MCC prefers that dealers build on land located near suburban shopping centres. The dealer will get an assigned geographic area capable of supporting sales of 1000 units per year with the expectation that sales will increase to 1300 units per year by 2001. The dealer will need a staff of 15 people initially with the expectation that it will sell 1000 units in the first year. Dealers will be allowed to determine the most appropriate compensation plan for their sales people and support staff.

The franchise agreement is much like a fast-food franchise in that there are tight restrictions on showroom design and customer service, and dealers who violate provisions in the agreement can lose their franchise quickly. The agreement requires that the dealer pay a fee of $140 per new car and $70 per used car to MCC to support marketing campaigns. They will also have to pay about $84 000 to support marketing research.

Dealers will also have to establish two other points where consumers can get information about the car. One point will have to be in an airport or railway station, and a second point will have to be in a shopping centre.

To promote the car's eventual introduction in France in 1998, MCC began a $100-million "street awareness" campaign in October 1997 that featured promotion teams handing out postcards that merely read, "Reduce to the max," without mentioning the car's name.

MCC projects that after five years the typical dealer will have sales of about $36 million with a gross profit on sales of 15 percent and a net return of four to five percent of sales, which equals about $1.4 million to $1.7 million.

WILL THE SMART CAR FLY?

Needless to say, there are plenty of skeptics who do not believe a tiny, two-seater car with almost no luggage space will make it in the highly competitive automobile market. However, other manufacturers are also targeting the minicar market. Ford believes that tiny cars will eventually account for about one-third of the market. It has a factory in Valencia, Spain that is already producing 200 000 Ka models per year, and it plans to increase capacity. Volkswagen, GM, and Rover all have microcar models under development. These companies are chasing Renault, which introduced its Twingo model minicar in 1993 and is selling 230 000 a year, about two percent of the West European car market.

It will be up to consumers to determine whether there is a market for these small cars or whether, like the Ford Edsel in the 1950s, the Smart Car will end up in museums as an example of one more time when car manufacturers missed the market.

QUESTIONS:

1. What core product is MCC offering in the Smart Car? What is the augmented product?

2. Into which consumer product classification does the Smart Car fall? What are the implications of this classification for MCC's marketing strategy?

3. What new product pricing strategy do you think MCC is using to introduce the car? What price adjustment strategies might the company want to use in the future? Do you think there is a price-quality relationship in people's mind when they purchase cars? What implications does this have for the pricing of the new Swatchmobile?

4. If you were a dealer examining MCC's proposal, what would you identify as the fixed and variable costs of doing business? How many cars will you have to sell to break-even on your investment (you have to make assumptions about salaries, etc. to perform this calculation).

5. Is the marketing plan for the Swatchmobile complete? What additional marketing recommendations would you make to MCC?

6. Is this a global product? What recommendations would you make to MCC if it decides to enter the North American market?

Sources: Thomas A. Sancton, "A Car, a Watch? Swatchmobile!," *Time*, March 28, 1994, p. 56; "Smaller Cars, Bigger Profits? European Cars," *The Economist*, November 9, 1996, p. 82; Luca Ciferri, "Smart to Get First Dealers This Spring," *Automotive News*, March 11, 1996, p. 20; Stefan Schlott, "Get Smart," *Automotive Industries*, August 1997, p. 75; Haig Simonian, "Mercedes-Benz May Play It Smart: Luxury Carmaker Hints at Developing Tiny Two-seater into a 'Second Brand'," *Financial Times*, London Edition, October 6, 1997, p. 1; "Smart Car Builds Street Awareness," *Euromarketing Via E-mail*, October 17, 1997.

Video Case 11

WEDDING BILLS

Companies can choose from a variety of methods when setting their prices. These range from adding a fixed amount to the cost of a product to taking into account the psychological value that consumers attach to the product. One of the best examples of this last method, and one that most of you will face someday, is the price charged for the products and services used in wedding celebrations.

When it comes to spending money for their wedding, many cautious consumers have spent far more than is rationally justified. The reason for this is that the wedding industry uses a series of techniques, some of which are unethical and others of which are illegal, to sell to this market. Salespeople work on "pushing the right buttons" to get the happy couple to spend more than required. One method they use is to sell the feeling. They talk to the couple about the fact that it is their special day and that everything should be story-book perfect. They tell the couple they should settle for nothing less than the best. This approach works best if the salesperson develops a strong rapport with the couple, and especially the bride, during the sales presentation. The bride is the most important party in this event because she has the greatest say in the products and services purchased.

The gown is one area where wedding planners and bridal shops have developed a variety of methods to get brides to spend more than necessary. One illegal method they use is to remove the manufacturer's labels from the gowns. This makes it impossible for the bride to do any comparison shopping because she does not know who made the gown. Another method is to have the bride order a gown one to two sizes larger than necessary. Brides are told that wedding dresses are often cut small and to get one that fits correctly requires ordering a larger size. The real purpose is to force the bride to pay for alterations. This can drive up the cost of a gown by an additional $200. Accessories for the gown such as veils, trains, and head dresses are aggressively sold. Why? They offer higher profit margins than the gown.

Premium prices are not limited to the gown. Caterers, halls, hotels, and printers that specialize in weddings have their own premium pricing methods. This includes everything from charging $50 for four litres of fruit punch that cost $3 in the grocery store to charging $14 for a coin, purported to bring good luck, which is only worth 10 cents. The bride and groom may also encounter service fees from the caterer. These fees reflect the royalty the caterer pays the reception hall to be listed as a recommended supplier. The florist industry has its own special method of setting prices for weddings. Consultants in the United States have nicknamed the practice the "Mercedes Syndrome." It involves the florist watching to see the brand of car the bride arrives in and setting the prices based on this observation. The more expensive the car, the higher the prices charged.

QUESTIONS

1. How would you describe the pricing strategy used by the wedding industry?

2. What are some examples of optional-product pricing in the case?

3. Do you think the wedding industry is engaging in psychological pricing? Why or why not?

4. In your opinion, do you think the pricing method used by the wedding industry is ethical? Why or why not?

Source: This case was prepared by Robert Warren and is based on the *Market Place* series episode "Wedding Bills," which was originally broadcast on April 2, 1996.

C H A P T E R 12

DISTRIBUTION
CHANNELS AND
LOGISTICS
MANAGEMENT

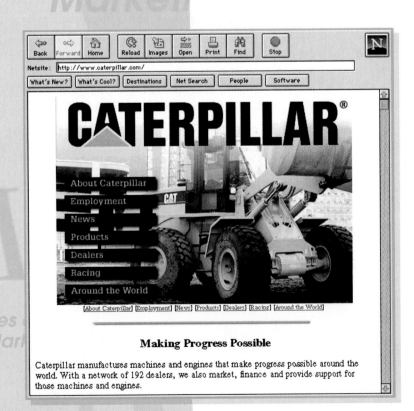

| ⟨ס□ | ס⟨ | 🏠 | 🌀 | 📑 | ⇒º | 🖨 | 🔍 | ● | N |
| Back | Forward | Home | Reload | Images | Open | Print | Find | Stop | |

Netsite: http://www.caterpillar.com/

| What's New? | What's Cool? | Destinations | Net Search | People | Software |

CATERPILLAR®

— About Caterpillar
Employment
News
Products
Dealers
Racing
Around the World

[About Caterpillar] [Employment] [News] [Products] [Dealers] [Racing] [Around the World]

Making Progress Possible

Caterpillar manufactures machines and engines that make progress possible around the world. With a network of 192 dealers, we also market, finance and provide support for those machines and engines.

For more than 50 years, Caterpillar has dominated the world's markets for heavy construction and mining equipment. Despite market swings and major competitive challenges, the big Cat keeps on purring. Its web site brags, "Caterpillar manufacturers machines and engines that make progress possible around the world." Its familiar yellow tractors, crawlers, loaders, and trucks are a common sight at construction sites in nearly 200 countries. With sales of $24 billion, Caterpillar is half again as large as its nearest competitor. It now captures more than a 40 percent share of the world's heavy construction-equipment market, and profits and returns stand at record levels.

Many factors contribute to Caterpillar's enduring success—high-quality products, flexible and efficient manufacturing, a steady stream of innovative new products, and a lean organization that is responsive to customer needs. Although Caterpillar charges premium prices for its equipment, its high-quality and trouble-free operation provides greater long-term value. Yet, according to Donald Fites, Caterpillar's chairman and CEO, these are not the most important reasons for Caterpillar's dominance. Instead, Fites contends, "the biggest reason for Caterpillar's success has been our system of distribution and product support and the close customer relationships it fosters . . . The backbone of that system is our 192 dealers around the world who sell and service our [equipment]."

Caterpillar's dealers provide a wide range of important services to customers. Fites summarizes:

> After the product leaves our door, the dealers take over. They are the ones on the front line. They're the ones who live with the product for its lifetime. They're the ones customers see. Although we offer financing and insurance, they arrange those deals for customers. They're out there making sure that when a machine is delivered, it's in the condition it's supposed to be in. They're out there training a customer's operators. They service a product frequently throughout its life, carefully monitoring a machine's health and scheduling repairs to prevent costly downtime. The customer . . . knows that there is a $24-billion-plus company called Caterpillar. But the dealers create the image of a company that doesn't just stand *behind* its products but *with* its products, anywhere in the world. Our dealers are the reason that our motto—Buy the Iron, Get the Company—is not an empty slogan.

OBJECTIVES

When you finish this chapter, you should be able to

1. Explain why companies use distribution channels and explain the functions that these channels perform.

2. Discuss how channel members interact and how they organize to perform the work of the channel.

3. Identify the major channel alternatives open to a company.

4. Explain how companies select, motivate, and evaluate channel members.

5. Discuss the nature and importance of physical distribution and integrated logistics management.

Caterpillar
www.caterpillar.com

Caterpillar's dealers build strong customer relationships in their communities. "Our independent dealer in Novi, Michigan, or in Bangkok, Thailand, knows so much more about the requirements of customers in those locations than a huge corporation like Caterpillar could," says Fites. Competitors often bypass their dealers and sell directly to big customers to cut costs or make more profits for themselves. However, Caterpillar wouldn't think of going around its dealers. "The knowledge of the local market and the close relations with customers that our dealers provide are worth every penny," Fites asserts. "We'd rather cut off our right arm than sell directly to customers and bypass our dealers."

Caterpillar and its dealers work in close harmony to find better ways to bring value to customers. Says Fites, "We genuinely treat our system and theirs as one." The entire system is linked by one worldwide computer network. For example, working at his desk computer, Fites can check to see how many Caterpillar machines in the world are waiting for parts. Closely linked dealers play a vital role in almost every aspect of Caterpillar's operations, from product design and delivery, to product service and support financing and insurance, to market intelligence and customer feedback.

In the heavy-equipment industry, where equipment downtime can mean big losses, Caterpillar's exceptional service gives it a huge advantage in winning and keeping customers. For example, consider Freeport-McMoRan, a Caterpillar customer that operates one of the world's largest copper and gold mines, 24 hours a day, 365 days a year. Located high in the mountains of Indonesia, the mine is accessible only by aerial cableway or helicopter. Freeport-McMoRan relies on more than 500 pieces of Caterpillar mining and construction equipment—worth several hundred million dollars—including loaders, tractors, and mammoth 24-ton, 2000-plus horsepower trucks. Many of these machines cost more than $1 million apiece. When equipment breaks down, Freeport-McMoRan loses money fast. Thus, Freeport-McMoRan gladly pays a premium price for machines and service it can count on. And it knows that it can count on Caterpillar and its outstanding distribution network for superb support.

The close working relationship between Caterpillar and its dealers comes down to more than just formal contracts and business agreements. According to Fites, the powerful partnership rests on a handful of basic principles and practices:

♦ *Dealer Profitability.* Caterpillar's rule: "Share the gain as well as the pain." When times are good, Caterpillar shares the bounty with its dealers rather than trying to grab all the riches for itself. When times are bad, Caterpillar protects its dealers. For example, in the mid-1980s, facing a depressed global construction-equipment market and cut-throat competition, Caterpillar sheltered its dealers by absorbing much of the economic damage. The company lost almost $1 billion dollars in just three years but didn't lose a single dealer. In contrast, competitors' dealers struggled and many failed. As a result, Caterpillar emerged with its distribution system intact and a stronger competitive position than ever.

♦ *Extraordinary Dealer Support.* Nowhere is this support more apparent than in the company's parts-delivery system—the fastest and most reliable in the industry. Caterpillar maintains 22 parts facilities around the world, which stock 320 000 different parts and ship 84 000 items per day, about one per second every day of the year. In turn, dealers have made huge investments in inventory, warehouses, fleets of trucks, service bays, diagnostic and service equipment, and information technology. Together, Caterpillar and its dealers guarantee parts delivery within 48 hours anywhere in the world. The company ships 80 percent of parts orders immediately, and 99 percent on the same day the order is received. In contrast, it's not unusual for competitors' customers to wait four or five days for a part.

♦ *Communications.* Caterpillar communicates with its dealers—fully, frequently, and honestly. According to Fites, "There are no secrets between us and our dealers. We have the financial statements and key operating data of every dealer in the world. . . . In addition, virtually all Caterpillar and dealer employees have real-time access to continually updated databases of service information, sales trends and forecasts, customer satisfaction surveys, and other critical data. . . . [Moreover,] virtually everyone from the youngest design engineer to the CEO now has direct contact with somebody in our dealer organizations."

◆ *Dealer Performance.* Caterpillar does all it can to ensure that its dealerships are run well. It closely monitors each dealership's sales, market position, service capability, financial situation, and other performance measures. It genuinely wants each dealer to succeed, and when it identifies a problem, it jumps in to help. As a result, Caterpillar dealerships, many of which are family businesses, tend to be stable and profitable. The average Caterpillar dealership has remained in the hands of the same family for more than 50 years. Some actually predate the 1925 merger that created Caterpillar.

◆ *Personal Relationships.* In addition to more formal business ties, Caterpillar forms close personal ties with its dealers in a kind of family relationship. Fites relates the following example: "When I see Chappy Chapman, a retired executive vice president. . . , out on the golf course, he always asks about particular dealers or about their children, who may be running the business now. And every time I see those dealers, they inquire, "How's Chappy?" That's the sort of relationship we have. . . . I consider the majority of dealers [to be] personal friends."

Thus, Caterpillar's superb distribution system serves as a major source of competitive advantage. The system is built on a firm foundation of mutual trust and shared dreams. Caterpillar and its dealers feel a deep pride in what they are accomplishing together. As Fites puts it, "There's a camaraderie among our dealers around the world that really makes it more than just a financial arrangement. They feel what they're doing is good for the world because they are part of an organization that makes, sells, and tends to the machines that make the world work."[1]

Marketing channel decisions are among the most important decisions that management faces. A company's channel decisions directly affect every other marketing decision. The company's pricing depends on whether it uses mass merchandisers or high-quality specialty stores. The firm's sales force and advertising decisions depend on how much persuasion, training, and motivation the dealers need. Whether a company develops or acquires certain new products may depend on how well those products fit the abilities of its channel members.

Companies often pay too little attention to their distribution channels, however, sometimes with damaging results. For example, automobile manufacturers have lost large shares of their parts and service business to companies like NAPA, Midas, Goodyear, and others because they have resisted making needed changes in their dealer franchise networks. In contrast, many companies have used imaginative distribution systems to *gain* a competitive advantage. Federal Express's creative and imposing distribution system made it the leader in the small-package delivery industry. General Electric gained a strong advantage in selling its major appliances by supporting its dealers with a sophisticated computerized order-processing and delivery system. And Dell Computer revolutionized its industry by selling direct rather than through retail stores.

Distribution channel decisions often involve long-term commitments to other firms. For example, companies like Ford, IBM, or Pizza Hut can easily change their advertising, pricing, or promotion programs. They can scrap old products and introduce new ones as market tastes demand. But when they set up distribution channels through contracts with franchisees, independent dealers, or large retailers, they cannot readily replace these channels with company-owned stores if conditions change. Therefore, management must design its channels carefully, with an eye on tomorrow's likely selling environment as well as today's.

This chapter examines four major questions concerning distribution channels: *What is the nature of distribution channels? How do channel firms interact and organize to do the work of the channel? What problems do companies face in designing and managing their channels? What role does physical distribution play in attracting and satisfying customers?* In Chapter 13, we will look at distribution channel issues from the perspective of retailers and wholesalers.

THE NATURE OF DISTRIBUTION CHANNELS

Distribution channel (marketing channel)
A set of interdependent organizations involved in the process of making a product or service available for use or consumption by the consumer or business user.

Most producers use intermediaries to bring their products to market. They try to forge a **distribution channel**—a set of interdependent organizations involved in the process of making a product or service available for use or consumption by the consumer or business user.[2]

WHY ARE MARKETING INTERMEDIARIES USED?

Why do producers give some of the selling job to intermediaries? After all, doing so means giving up some control over how and to whom the products are sold. The use of intermediaries results from their greater efficiency in making goods available to target markets. Through their contacts, experience, specialization, and scale of operation, intermediaries usually offer the firm more than it can achieve on its own.

Figure 12-1 shows how using intermediaries can provide economies. Part A shows three manufacturers, each using direct marketing to reach three customers. This system requires nine different contacts. Part B shows the three manufacturers working through one distributor, who contacts the three customers. This system requires only six contacts. In this way, intermediaries reduce the amount of work that must be done by both producers and consumers.

From the economic system's point of view, the role of marketing intermediaries is to transform the assortments of products made by producers into the assortments wanted by consumers. Producers make narrow assortments of products in large quantities, but consumers want broad assortments of products in small quantities. In the distribution channels, intermediaries buy the large quantities of many producers and break them down into the smaller quantities and broader assortments wanted by consumers. Thus, intermediaries play an important role in matching supply and demand.

FIGURE 12-1 *How a marketing intermediary reduces the number of channel transactions*

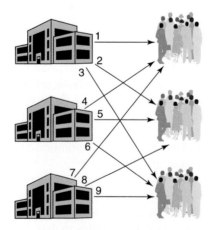

A. Number of contacts without a distributor
M x C = 3 x 3 = 9

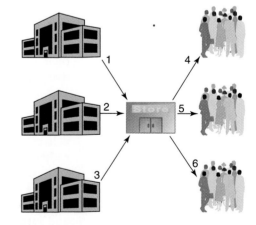

B. Number of contacts with a distributor
M + C = 3 + 3 = 6

 = Manufacturer   = Customer   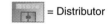 = Distributor

The concept of distribution channels is not limited to the distribution of tangible products. Producers of services and ideas also face the problem of making their output *available* to target populations. In the private sector, retail stores, hotels, banks, and other service providers take great care to make their services conveniently available to target customers. In the public sector, service organizations and agencies develop "educational distribution systems" and "health-care delivery systems" for reaching sometimes widely spread populations. Hospitals must be located to serve various patient populations, and schools must be located close to the children who need to be taught. Communities must locate their fire stations to provide rapid coverage of fires, and polling stations must be placed where people can vote conveniently.

University of Calgary
www.ucalgary.ca/

Queen's University
info.queensu.ca/index.html

Innovative universities are finding that they have to go to students if students are unable to come to them. For example, the University of Calgary forecasts that in just a few years, many of its students will be older, working, and taking classes off-campus. The university has joined a consortium of international universities that use computers to share professors, students, and ideas.[3] The term "distance education" has been coined to describe these programs. Queen's University has one of the most advanced systems of distance education. It was the first university to develop a national MBA Program. Students work in study groups and are linked to professors through interactive video-conferencing facilities in 16 cities across Canada from Victoria to St. John's. Other universities, such as the University of Western Ontario, were quick to follow suit.

DISTRIBUTION CHANNEL FUNCTIONS

A distribution channel moves goods from producers to consumers. It overcomes the major time, place, and possession gaps that separate goods and services from those who would use them. Members of the marketing channel perform many key functions. Some help to complete transactions:

- *Information:* gathering and distributing marketing research and intelligence information about actors and forces in the marketing environment needed for planning and aiding exchange.
- *Promotion:* developing and spreading persuasive communications about an offer.
- *Contact:* finding and communicating with prospective buyers.
- *Matching:* shaping and fitting the offer to the buyer's needs, including such activities as manufacturing, grading, assembling, and packaging.
- *Negotiation:* reaching an agreement on price and other terms of the offer so that ownership or possession can be transferred.

Others help to fulfil the completed transactions:

- *Physical distribution:* transporting and storing goods.
- *Financing:* acquiring and using funds to cover the costs of the channel work.
- *Risk taking:* assuming the risks of carrying out the channel work.

The question is not *whether* these functions need to be performed—they must be—but rather *who* is to perform them. All the functions have three things in common: They use up scarce resources, they often can be performed better through specialization, and they can be shifted among channel members. To the extent that the manufacturer performs these functions, its costs go up and its prices have to be higher. At the same time, when some of these functions are shifted to intermediaries, the producer's costs and prices may be lower, but the intermediaries must charge more to cover the costs of their work. In dividing the work of the

*Direct marketing channels:
Mountain Equipment
Co-op sells direct through
mail order and by
telephone.*

Tilley Endurables Inc.
www.tilley.com/

Channel level
A layer of intermediaries
that performs some work in
bringing the product and its
ownership closer to the final
buyer.

Direct marketing channel
A marketing channel that has
no intermediary levels.

Indirect marketing channels
Channels containing one or
more intermediary levels.

channel, the various functions should be assigned to the channel members who can perform them most efficiently and effectively to provide satisfactory assortments of goods to target consumers.

NUMBER OF CHANNEL LEVELS

Distribution channels can be described by the number of channel levels involved. Each layer of marketing intermediaries that performs some work in bringing the product and its ownership closer to the final buyer is a **channel level.** Because the producer and the final consumer both perform some work, they are part of every channel. We use the number of intermediary levels to indicate the length of a channel. Figure 12-2A shows several consumer distribution channels of different lengths.

Channel 1, called a **direct marketing channel,** has no intermediary levels. It consists of a company selling directly to consumers. For example, Avon, Amway, and Tupperware sell their products door to door or through home and office sales parties; Mountain Equipment Co-op sells clothing direct through mail order and by telephone; as well as through its own stores. Tilley Endurables Inc., makers of the famous, floppy Tilley hat sported by sailors, was among the award winners at the 12th Annual Catalogue Conference. The catalogue was praised because it uses no phony layout tricks. Instead, it uses real people—staff members of Tilley Endurables and Tilley customers—to model its clothing. The catalogue helps to differentiate the company since the owner's personality comes through every product description.

The remaining channels in Figure 12-2A are **indirect marketing channels.** Channel 2 contains one intermediary level. In consumer markets, this level is typically a retailer. For example, the makers of televisions, cameras, tires, furniture, major appliances, and many other products sell their goods directly to large retailers such as Leon's and Sears, which then sell the goods to final consumers. Channel 3 contains two intermediary levels, a wholesaler and a retailer. This channel often is used by small manufacturers of food, drugs, hardware, and other products. Channel 4 contains three intermediary levels. In the meat-packing industry, for example, jobbers usually come between wholesalers and retailers. The jobber buys from wholesalers and sells to smaller retailers who generally are not served by larger wholesalers. Distribution channels with even more levels are sometimes found, but less often. From the producer's point of view, a greater number of levels means less control and greater channel complexity.

Figure 12-2B shows some common business distribution channels. The business marketer can use its own sales force to sell directly to business customers. It also can sell to industrial distributors, who in turn sell to business customers. It can sell through manufacturer's representatives or its own sales branches to business customers, or it can use these representatives and branches to sell through industrial distributors. Thus, business markets commonly include multi-level distribution channels.

All of the institutions in the channel are connected by several types of *flows.* These include the *physical flow* of products, the *flow of ownership,* the *payment flow,* the *information flow,* and the *promotion flow.* These flows can even make channels with only one or a few levels very complex.

■ CHANNEL BEHAVIOUR AND ORGANIZATION

Distribution channels are more than simple collections of firms tied together by various flows. They are complex behavioural systems in which people and companies

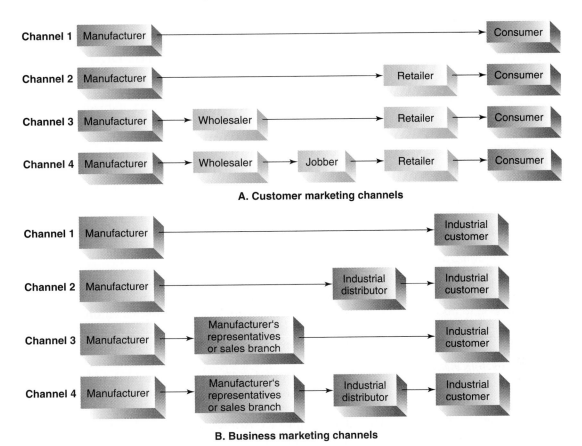

FIGURE 12-2   *Consumer and business marketing channels*

interact to accomplish individual, company, and channel goals. Some channel systems consist only of informal interactions among loosely organized firms; others consist of formal interactions guided by strong organizational structures. Moreover, channel systems do not stand still—new types of intermediaries surface, and whole new channel systems evolve. Here we look at channel behaviour and at how members organize to do the work of the channel.

CHANNEL BEHAVIOUR

A distribution channel consists of firms that have banded together for their common good. Each channel member depends on the others. For example, a Ford dealer depends on the Ford Motor Company to design cars that meet consumer needs. In turn, Ford depends on the dealer to attract consumers, persuade them to buy Ford cars, and service cars after the sale. The Ford dealer also depends on other dealers to provide good sales and service that will uphold the reputation of Ford and its dealer body. In fact, the success of individual Ford dealers depends on how well the entire Ford distribution channel competes with the channels of other auto manufacturers.

Each channel member plays a role in the channel and specializes in performing one or more functions. For example, IBM's role is to produce personal computers that consumers will like and to create demand through national advertising. Future Shop's role is to display these IBM computers in convenient locations, to answer buyers' questions, to close sales, and to provide service. The channel will be most effective when each member is assigned the tasks it can do best.

Ideally, because the success of individual channel members depends on overall channel success, all channel firms should work together smoothly. They should understand and accept their roles, coordinate their goals and activities,

Channel conflict
Disagreement among marketing channel members on goals and roles—who should do what and for what rewards.

Conventional distribution channel
A channel consisting of one or more independent producers, wholesalers, and retailers, each a separate business seeking to maximize its own profits even at the expense of profits for the system as a whole.

Vertical marketing system (VMS)
A distribution channel structure in which producers, wholesalers, and retailers act as a unified system. One channel member owns the others, has contracts with them, or has so much power that they all cooperate.

and cooperate to attain overall channel goals. By cooperating, they can more effectively sense, serve, and satisfy the target market.

However, individual channel members rarely take such a broad view. They are usually more concerned with their own short-run goals and their dealings with those firms closest to them in the channel. Cooperating to achieve overall channel goals sometimes means giving up individual company goals. Although channel members depend on one another, they often act alone in their own short-run best interests. They often disagree on the roles each should play—on who should do what and for what rewards. Such disagreements over goals and roles generate **channel conflict** (see Marketing Highlight 12-1).

Horizontal conflict occurs among firms at the same level of the channel. For instance, some Ford dealers complained about other dealers in their city who stole sales from them by being too aggressive in their pricing and advertising or by selling outside their assigned territories. Some Pizza Inn franchisees complained about other Pizza Inn franchisees cheating on ingredients, giving poor service, and hurting the overall Pizza Inn image.

Vertical conflict is even more common and refers to conflicts between different levels of the same channel. For example, General Motors came into conflict with its dealers some years ago by trying to enforce service, pricing, and advertising policies. Coca-Cola came into conflict with some of its bottlers who agreed to bottle competitor Dr. Pepper. And Goodyear caused conflict with its dealer network when it decided to sell tires through mass merchandisers.

Some conflict in the channel takes the form of healthy competition. Such competition can be good for the channel—without it, the channel could become passive and non-innovative. But sometimes conflict can damage the channel. For the channel as a whole to perform well, each channel member's role must be specified and channel conflict must be managed. Cooperation, role assignment, and conflict management in the channel are attained through strong channel leadership. The channel will perform better if it includes a firm, agency, or mechanism that has the power to assign roles and manage conflict.

VERTICAL MARKETING SYSTEMS

Historically, distribution channels have been loose collections of independent companies, each showing little concern for overall channel performance. These *conventional distribution channels* have lacked strong leadership and have been troubled by damaging conflict and poor performance. One of the biggest recent channel developments is the *vertical marketing systems* that have emerged to challenge conventional marketing channels. Figure 12-3 contrasts the two types of channel arrangements.

A **conventional distribution channel** consists of one or more independent producers, wholesalers, and retailers. Each is a separate business seeking to maximize its own profits, even at the expense of profits for the system as a whole. No channel member has much control over the other members, and no formal means exists for assigning roles and resolving channel conflict. In contrast, a **vertical marketing system** (VMS), which consists of the same players—producers, wholesalers, and retailers—acts as a unified system since one channel member owns the others, has contracts with them, or wields so much power that all members of the system cooperate. The VMS can be dominated by the producer, wholesaler, or retailer. Vertical marketing systems came into being to control channel behaviour and manage channel conflict. They achieve economies through size, bargaining power, and elimination of duplicated services.

FIGURE 12-3 *A conventional marketing channel versus a vertical marketing system*

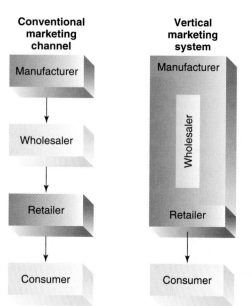

Conventional marketing channel	Vertical marketing system
Manufacturer	Manufacturer
Wholesaler	Wholesaler
Retailer	Retailer
Consumer	Consumer

GOODYEAR ROLLS, BUT OVER ITS DEALERS?

For more than 60 years, Goodyear Tire & Rubber Company, the company known for its famous blimp, sold replacement tires exclusively through its powerful network of independent Goodyear dealers. Both Goodyear and its 2500 dealers profited from this partnership. Goodyear received the undivided attention and loyalty of its single-brand dealers, and the dealers gained the exlusive right to sell the highly respected Goodyear tire line. In mid-1992, however, Goodyear shattered tradition and jolted its dealers by announcing that it would now sell Goodyear-brand tires through Sears auto centres, placing Goodyear dealers in direct competition with the giant retailer. This departure from the previously sacred dealer network left many dealers shaken and angry. Said one Goodyear dealer: "You feel like after 35 years of marriage, your [spouse] is stepping out on you." Said another, "I feel like they just stabbed me in the back."

Several factors forced the change in Goodyear's distribution system. During the late 1980s, massive international consolidation reshaped the tire industry, leaving only five competitors. Japan's Bridgestone acquired Firestone, Germany's Continental bought General Tire, Italy's Pirelli snapped up Armstrong, and France's Michelin acquired Uniroyal Goodrich. After six decades as the world's largest tire maker, Goodyear slipped to second behind Michelin. Instead of having its way with smaller North American rivals, Goodyear now found itself battling for market share against large and newly strengthened international competitors.

To add to Goodyear's woes, consumers were changing how and where they bought tires. Tires have become more of an impulse item, and value-minded tire buyers were increasingly buying from cheaper, multibrand discount outlets, department stores, warehouse clubs, and automotive centres such as Canadian Tire. The market share of these outlets had grown 30 percent in the previous five years, while that of tire dealers had fallen four percent. By selling exclusively through its dealer network, Goodyear simply wasn't putting its tires where many consumers were buying them.

The shifts in consumer buying were also causing problems for dealers. Although Goodyear offered an ample variety of premium lines, it provided its dealers with none of the lower-priced lines that many consumers were demanding. Thus, Goodyear was foundering and drastic measures were needed.

Goodyear may be facing some bumps on the road to good dealer relations.

Enter new management, headed by Stanley Gault, the miracle-working manager who had transformed Rubbermaid from a sleepy rubber company into one of North America's most admired market leaders. Gault took the helm in mid-1991 and moved quickly to streamline Goodyear, reducing its heavy debt, cutting costs, and selling off non-core businesses. But the biggest changes came in marketing. Under Gault, Goodyear speeded up new-product development and boosted advertising spending. For example, in late 1991, it introduced four new tires simultaneously— the innovative, non-hydroplaning Aquatred, the Wrangler line for pick-up trucks and vans, a fuel-efficient "green" tire, and a new high-performance Eagle model. In 1992, Goodyear introduced 12 more new tires—three times the usual number.

Gault also wasted little time in shaking up Goodyear's stodgy distribution system. In addition to selling its tires through Sears, the company began selling the Goodyear brand at Wal-Mart. Marketing research showed that one out of four Wal-Mart customers is a potential Goodyear

buyer, and that these buyers come from a segment unlikely to be reached by independent Goodyear dealers. The company also began drumming up new private-label business. It soon signed to sell private-label tires through Wal-Mart and warehouse clubs. Goodyear has since begun exploring other new distribution options as well.

Goodyear has recently developed new marketing initiatives. One such effort is the company's award-winning web site (http:// www.goodyear.com). While Internet surfers enjoy the site because of its car trivia and information about sporting events, Goodyear has also used its web site to bolster dealer sales. With a few clicks of their mouse, visitors to the site can enter their car model, model year, driving habits, and preferences in order to receive recommendations on the type of Goodyear tire that precisely meets their needs. The potential customers are then provided with the names and locations of Goodyear dealers in their area where they can purchase the tires. This information will not only bolster knowledge about dealers, but will also simplify the buying process for customers who can now arrive at the dealership fully informed about which tires to choose.

The expanded distribution system appeared to be a significant plus, at least in the short run. The marketing, distribution, and other changes got Goodyear rolling again. In its first year under Gault, Goodyear's sales and earnings soared, its market share increased one percent, and its stock price quadrupled. In 1993 and 1994, Goodyear made more profit than its nine direct competitors combined. By the time Gault stepped down in 1996, he'd delivered more than four years of heady profit gains, and his successor announced his intention to return Goodyear by the year 2000 to "its rightful position as the undisputed world leader."

In the long run, however, developing new channels risks eroding the loyalty and effectiveness of Goodyear's prized exclusive dealer network, one of the company's major competitive assets. To be fully effective, Goodyear and its dealers must work together in harmony for their mutual benefit. But the agreements with Sears and other retailers have created hard feelings and conflict between them. Some disgruntled dealers have struck back by taking on and aggressively promoting cheaper, private-label brands—brands that offered higher margins to dealers and more appeal to some value-conscious consumers. For example, shortly after the Sears announcement, one large Goodyear dealership in Florida adopted several lower-priced private brands, reducing its sales of Goodyear tires by 20 percent, but increasing its profit margins. The defiant dealer notes: "We [now] sell what we think will give the customer the best value, and that's not necessarily Goodyear."

Goodyear has taken steps to bolster anxious dealers. For example, it is now supplying dealers with a much-needed line of lower-priced Goodyear-brand tires. Goodyear sincerely believes that expanded distribution will help its dealers more than harm them. In the end, selling through Sears means better visibility for the Goodyear name, the company contends, and the resulting expansion of business will mean more money for dealer support. However, many dealers remain skeptical. In the long run, dealer defections could reduce Goodyear's market power and offset sales gains from new channels.

Sources: Quotations from Dana Milbank, "Independent Tire Dealers Rebelling Against Goodyear," *Wall Street Journal*, July 8, 1992, p. B1; Zachary Schiller, "Goodyear is Gunning Its Marketing Engine," *Business Week*, March 16, 1992, p. 42; Schiller, "Stan Gault's Designated Driver," *Business Week*, April 8, 1996; Charles Waltner, "Goodyear Rolls With The Market," *Advertising Age's Business Marketing*, January-February 1997, p. 58; and Al McGrath, "Managing Distribution Channels," *Business Quarterly*, Spring 1996, pp. 56–65.

FIGURE 12-4 *Major types of vertical marketing systems*

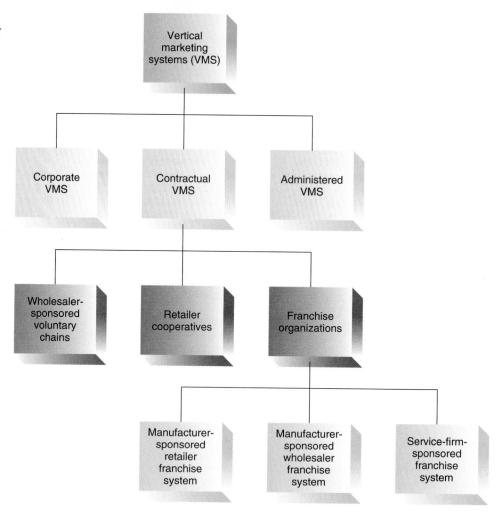

Goodyear Tire & Rubber Co.
www.goodyear.com/

We look now at the three major types of VMSs shown in Figure 12-4. Each type uses a different means for setting up leadership and power in the channel. In a *corporate VMS,* coordination and conflict management are attained through common ownership at different levels of the channel. In a *contractual VMS*, they are attained through contractual agreements among channel members. In an *administered VMS*, leadership is assumed by one or a few dominant channel members. We now take a closer look at each type of VMS.

Corporate VMS

Corporate VMS
A vertical marketing system that combines successive stages of production and distribution under single ownership—channel leadership is established through common ownership.

A **corporate VMS** combines successive stages of production and distribution under single ownership. In such corporate systems, cooperation and conflict management are handled through regular organizational channels. For example, Sears obtains more than 50 percent of its goods from companies that it partly or wholly owns. Bell markets telephones and related equipment through its own chain of Phonecentres. George Weston Inc, owner of Loblaw, operates a soft-drink bottling operation, an ice-cream-making plant, and a bakery that supplies stores with everything from bagels to birthday cakes.

Gallo, the world's largest winemaker, does much more than simply turn grapes into wine. It owns the trucking firm that transports the wines, the bottling company that makes the containers, and even a firm that makes the bottle caps. Whereas most wineries concentrate on production while neglecting marketing, Gallo participates in every aspect of selling "short of whispering in the ear of each imbiber."[4]

Contractual VMS

Contractual VMS
A vertical marketing system in which independent firms at different levels of production and distribution join together through contracts to obtain more economies or sales impact than they could achieve alone.

Wholesaler-sponsored voluntary chains
Contractual vertical marketing systems in which wholesalers organize voluntary chains of independent retailers to help them compete with large corporate chain organizations.

Retailer cooperatives
Contractual vertical marketing systems in which retailers organize a new, jointly owned business to carry on wholesaling and possibly production.

Franchise organization
A contractual vertical marketing system in which a channel member, called a franchiser, links several stages in the production-distribution process.

A **contractual VMS** consists of independent firms at different levels of production and distribution that join together through contracts to obtain more economies or sales impact than each could achieve alone. Contractual VMSs have expanded rapidly in recent years. There are three types of contractual VMSs: wholesaler-sponsored voluntary chains, retailer cooperatives, and franchise organizations.

Wholesaler-sponsored voluntary chains are systems in which wholesalers organize voluntary chains of independent retailers to help them compete with large chain organizations. The wholesaler develops a program in which independent retailers standardize their selling practices and achieve buying economies that let the group compete effectively with chain organizations. Examples include the Independent Grocers Alliance (IGA) and Western Auto.

Retailer cooperatives are systems in which retailers organize a new, jointly owned business to carry on wholesaling and possibly production. Members buy most of their goods through the retailer co-op and plan their advertising jointly. Profits are passed back to members in proportion to their purchases. Nonmember retailers also may buy through the co-op but do not share in the profits. Examples include the Co-op stores found in Western Canada and True Value Hardware.

In **franchise organizations**, a channel member called a *franchiser* links several stages in the production-distribution process. Franchising has been the fastest-growing retailing form in recent years. Canada has more than 50 000 franchise operations (four times more per capita than the United States) that ring up over $90 billion in sales. In fact, 40 percent of every dollar spent on retail items is spent at a franchise.[5] Almost every kind of business has been franchised—from motels and fast-food restaurants to dental centres and dating services, from wedding consultants and maid services to funeral homes and fitness centres. Although the basic idea is an old one, some forms of franchising are quite new.

There are three forms of franchises. The first form is the *manufacturer-sponsored retailer franchise system*, as found in the automobile industry. Ford, for example, licenses dealers to sell its cars; the dealers are independent businesspeople who agree to meet various conditions of sales and service. The second type of franchise is the *manufacturer-sponsored wholesaler franchise system*, as found in the soft-drink industry. Coca-Cola, for example, licenses bottlers (wholesalers) in various markets who buy Coca-Cola syrup concentrate and then carbonate, bottle, and sell the finished product to retailers in local markets. The third franchise form is the *service-firm-sponsored retailer franchise system,* in which a service firm licenses a system of retailers to bring its service to consumers. Examples are found in the auto-rental business (Hertz, Avis); the fast-food service business (Tim Horton Donuts); and the motel business (Holiday Inn, Ramada Inn).

The fact that most consumers cannot tell the difference between contractual and corporate VMSs shows how successfully the contractual organizations compete with corporate chains. Chapter 13 presents a fuller discussion of the various contractual VMSs.

Administered VMS

An **administered VMS** coordinates successive stages of production and distribution—not through common ownership or contractual ties but through the size and power of one of the parties. Manufacturers of a top brand can obtain strong trade cooperation and support from resellers. For example, General Electric, Procter and Gamble, Kraft, and Campbell Soup can command unusual cooperation from resellers regarding displays, shelf space, promotions, and price policies. And large retailers like The Bay and Toys 'R' Us can exert strong influence on the manufacturers that supply the products they sell.

Administered VMS
A vertical marketing system that coordinates successive stages of production and distribution, not through common ownership or contractual ties, but through the size and power of one of the parties.

Horizontal marketing systems
A channel arrangement in which two or more companies at one level join together to follow a new marketing opportunity.

HORIZONTAL MARKETING SYSTEMS

Another channel development is the **horizontal marketing system,** in which two or more companies at one level join together to follow a new marketing opportunity. By working together, companies can combine their capital, production capabilities, or marketing resources to accomplish more than any one company could alone.

Being a member of a horizontal marketing system helps Air Canada market its services efficiently worldwide.

As a business traveler, wouldn't it be great if the airline you fly most often was linked to other major airlines that could fly you anywhere you wanted to go. Smoothly. Effortlessly. Efficiently. Wouldn't it be great if you had more access to more airport lounges. And when flying on any of these major airlines, you could earn mileage that counts toward higher status in any of their frequent flyer programs. Wouldn't it be great if you could enjoy the same high standards of service whenever and wherever you fly. That's the idea behind Star Alliance, a network of Air Canada, Lufthansa, SAS, THAI and United Airlines. A partnership that signals a fundamental change in business travel. And these benefits are just the beginning. We will be offering even more in the months ahead. We know you have choices when you fly, and we're making sure Star Alliance is always your best choice. After all, there's no better way in the world to get around the world.

Imagine.

STAR ALLIANCE
The airline network for Earth.

Companies might join forces with competitors or non-competitors.[6] They might work with each other on a temporary or permanent basis, or they may create a separate company. The operations of the system may be confined to the domestic market or they may span the globe.

◆ Canada's two largest wineries, T.G. Bright & Co. Ltd. and Cartier & Inniskillin Vintners Inc., once major competitors, have merged. Together they have sales in excess of $130 million, placing them in the top 10 of North American wine marketers. Given the strength and size of large American vintners, such as Gallo described earlier, the two formed an alliance so that they could have the economies of scale and resources necessary to export into the U.S. market.

◆ Coca-Cola and Nestlé formed a joint venture to market ready-to-drink coffee and tea worldwide. Coke provided worldwide experience in marketing and distributing beverages and Nestlé contributed two established brand names—Nescafé and Nestea.[7]

◆ Forming successful horizontal marketing systems is absolutely essential in an era of global business and global travel. Air Canada is part of the Star Alliance whose partners include United Airlines, Lufthansa, SAS, and Thai Airways International. It battles Canadian Airlines, which has entered into partnerships with American Airlines, British Airways, Japan Airlines, and Quantas. These partnerships allow Air Canada to offer flights to 642 U.S. cities, for example, even though the airline has only 155 aircraft. It can link the routes that the different partners fly so that passengers can have seamless travel around the world. Air Canada benefits from the marketing efforts of its partners in their home countries and bookings they make for travellers coming to Canada. These alliances improve customer satisfaction since they ensure passengers have shorter layovers, more convenient connections, and less hassle transferring their baggage.[8]

The number of such horizontal marketing systems has increased dramatically in recent years, and the end is nowhere in sight.

Hybrid marketing channels Multichannel distribution systems in which a single firm sets up two or more marketing channels to reach one or more customer segments.

Hybrid channels: For years, IBM sold computers only through its sales force. However, it now serves the rapidly fragmenting market through a wide variety of channels, including its IBM Direct catalogue and telemarketing operation.

HYBRID MARKETING SYSTEMS

In the past, many companies used a single channel to sell to a single market or market segment. Today, with the proliferation of customer segments and channel possibilities, more and more companies have adopted *multichannel distribution systems*—often called **hybrid marketing channels.** Such multichannel marketing occurs when a single firm sets up two or more marketing channels to reach one or more customer segments. The use of hybrid channel systems has increased dramatically in recent years.

Figure 12-5 shows a hybrid channel. In the figure, the producer sells directly to consumer segment 1 using direct-mail catalogues and telemarketing, and reaches consumer segment 2 through retailers. It sells indirectly to business segment 1 through distributors and dealers, and to business segment 2 through its own sales force.

IBM provides a good example of a company that uses such a hybrid channel effectively. For years, IBM sold computers only through its own sales force. However, when the market for small, low-cost computers exploded, this single channel was no longer adequate. To serve the diverse needs of the many segments in the rapidly fragmenting computer market, IBM added 18 new channels in less than 10 years.[9]

FIGURE 12-5 *Hybrid marketing channel*

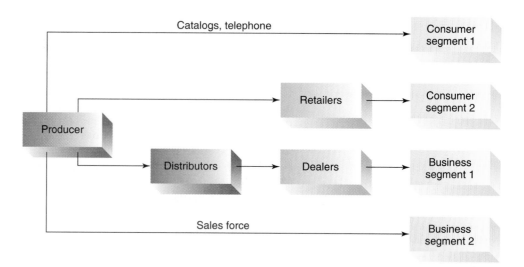

For example, in addition to selling through the vaunted IBM sales force, the company now sells its complete line of computers and accessories through IBM Direct, its catalogue and telemarketing operation. Consumers can also buy IBM personal computers from a network of independent IBM dealers, or from any of several large retailers, including Wal-Mart, Future Shop, and Business Depot. IBM dealers and value-added resellers sell IBM computer equipment and systems to a variety of special business segments.

Hybrid channels offer many advantages to companies facing large and complex markets. With each new channel, the company expands its sales and market coverage and gains opportunities to tailor its products and services to the specific needs of diverse customer segments. But such hybrid channel systems are harder to control, and they generate conflict as more channels compete for customers and sales. For example, when IBM began selling directly to customers at low prices through catalogues and telemarketing, many of its retail dealers cried "unfair competition" and threatened to drop the IBM line or to give it less emphasis.

CHANNEL DESIGN DECISIONS

We now look at several channel decisions facing manufacturers. In designing marketing channels, manufacturers struggle between what is ideal and what is practical. A new firm usually starts by selling in a limited market area. Because it has limited capital, it typically uses only a few existing intermediaries in each market—a few manufacturers' sales agents, a few wholesalers, some existing retailers, a few trucking companies, and a few warehouses. Deciding on the *best* channels might not be a problem: The problem might simply be how to convince one or a few good intermediaries to handle the line.

If the new firm is successful, it might branch out to new markets. Again, the manufacturer will tend to work through the existing intermediaries, although this strategy might mean using hybrid marketing channels. In smaller markets, the firm might sell directly to retailers; in larger markets, it might sell through distributors. In one part of the country, it might grant exclusive franchises because that is the way merchants normally work; in another, it might sell through all outlets willing to handle the merchandise.

Channels often evolve over time, and ongoing strategic analysis of channel decisions can help a firm maintain its competitive advantage. As markets mature, as is the case in the computer industry, distributors often become increasingly important. Sales through distributors account for about 45 percent of the information technology market, compared to 15 percent just four years ago. Industry pundits claim that there are "three things that make up a winning computer product: a product, corporate relationships and distributors. But without distributors, you can pretty well forget about the other two."[10]

Designing a channel system calls for analysing consumer service needs, setting the channel objectives and constraints, identifying the major channel alternatives, and evaluating them.

ANALYSING CONSUMER SERVICE NEEDS

Marketing channels can be thought of as *customer value delivery systems* in which each channel member adds value for the customer. Thus, designing the distribution channel starts with determining what values consumers in various target segments want from the channel.[11] Do consumers want to buy from nearby locations or are they willing to travel to more distant centralized locations? Would they rather buy over the phone or through the mail? Do they want immediate delivery or are they willing to wait? Do consumers value breadth of assortment or do they prefer specialization? Do consumers want many add-on services (delivery, credit, repairs, installation) or will they obtain these elsewhere? The more decentralized the channel, the faster the delivery; the greater the assortment provided, and the more add-on services supplied, the greater the channel's service level.

Consider the distribution channel service needs of business computer-system buyers. The delivery of service might include such things as demonstration of the product before the sale or provision of long-term warranties and flexible financing. After the sale, there might be training programs for using the equipment and a program to instal and repair it. Customers might appreciate "loaners" while their equipment is being repaired or technical advice over a telephone hotline.

But providing the fastest delivery, greatest assortment, and most services may not be possible or practical. The company and its channel members may not have the resources or skills needed to provide all the desired services. Also, providing higher levels of service results in higher costs for the channel and higher prices for consumers. The company must balance consumer service needs not only against the feasibility and costs of meeting these needs but also against customer price preferences. The success of off-price and discount retailing shows that consumers are often willing to accept lower service levels if this means lower prices.

SETTING THE CHANNEL OBJECTIVES AND CONSTRAINTS

Channel objectives should be stated in terms of the desired service level of target consumers. Usually, a company can identify several segments wanting different levels of channel service. The company should decide which segments to serve and the best channels to use in each case. In each segment, the company wants to minimize the total channel cost of meeting customer service requirements.

The company's channel objectives also are influenced by the nature of its products, company policies, marketing intermediaries, competitors, and the environment. *Product characteristics* greatly affect channel design. For example, perishable products require more direct marketing to avoid delays and too much handling. Bulky products, such as building materials or soft drinks, require channels that minimize shipping distance and the amount of handling.

Company characteristics also play an important role. For example, the company's size and financial situation determine which marketing functions it can handle itself and which it must give to intermediaries. And a company marketing strategy based on speedy customer delivery affects the functions that the company wants its intermediaries to perform, the number of its outlets, and the choice of its transportation methods.

The *characteristics of intermediaries* also influence channel design. The company must find intermediaries who are willing and able to perform the needed tasks. In general, intermediaries differ in their abilities to handle promotion, customer contact, storage, and credit. For example, manufacturer's representatives who are hired by several different firms can contact customers at a low cost per customer because several clients share the total cost. However, the selling effort behind the product is less intense than if the company's own sales force did the selling.

When designing its channels, a company also must consider its *competitors' channels*. In some cases, a company may want to compete in or near the same outlets that carry competitors' products. Thus, food companies want their brands to be displayed next to competing brands; Burger King wants to locate near McDonald's. In other cases, producers may avoid the channels used by competitors. Avon, for example, decided not to compete with other cosmetics makers for scarce positions in retail stores and instead set up a profitable door-to-door selling operation.

Finally, *environmental factors,* such as economic conditions and legal constraints, affect channel design decisions. For example, in a depressed economy, producers want to distribute their goods in the most economical way, using shorter channels and dropping unneeded services that add to the final price of the goods. Legal regulations prevent channel arrangements that "may tend to lessen competition substantially or tend to create a monopoly."

IDENTIFYING MAJOR ALTERNATIVES

When the company has defined its channel objectives, it should next identify its major channel alternatives in terms of *types* of intermediaries, *number* of intermediaries, and the *responsibilities* of each channel member.

Types of Intermediaries

A firm should identify the types of channel members available to carry out its channel work. For example, suppose a manufacturer of test equipment has developed an audio device that detects poor mechanical connections in any machine with moving parts. Company executives think this product would have a market in all industries where electric, combustion, or steam engines are made or used. This market includes industries such as aviation, automobile, railway, food canning, construction, and oil. The company's current sales force is small, and the problem is how best to reach these different industries. The following channel alternatives might emerge from management discussion:

♦ *Company sales force.* Expand the company's direct sales force. Assign salespeople to territories and have them contact all prospects in the area or develop separate company sales forces for different industries.

♦ *Manufacturer's agency.* Hire manufacturer's agents—independent firms whose sales forces handle related products from many companies—in different regions or industries to sell the new test equipment.

♦ *Industrial distributors.* Find distributors in the different regions or industries who will buy and carry the new line. Give them exclusive distribution, good margins, product training, and promotional support.

Sometimes a company must develop a channel other than the one it prefers because of the difficulty or cost of using the preferred channel. Still, the decision may turn out extremely well. For example, the U.S. Time Company first tried to sell its inexpensive Timex watches through regular jewellery stores, but most jewellery stores refused to carry them. The company then managed to get its watches into mass-merchandise outlets. This turned out to be a wise decision because of the rapid growth of mass merchandising. New forms of distribution also evolve for old products. The pharmacy industry in Canada has recently been challenged by a new type of intermediary—the emerging drugs-by-mail companies. Although less than one percent of prescriptions are filled by mail in Canada, the concept is catching on. Both government health plans and corporate benefit managers (who pay for most prescriptions) understand the lower costs that may result from the service. To save company drug plans money, large employers like Shell Canada, Dupont Canada, and the Toronto-Dominion Bank are including advertising literature provided by the mail-order drug companies in their internal corporate mailings to employees.[12]

Number of Marketing Intermediaries

Intensive distribution
Stocking the product in as many outlets as possible.

Exclusive distribution
Giving a limited number of dealers the exclusive right to distribute the company's products in their territories.

Selective distribution
The use of more than one, but fewer than all of the intermediaries who are willing to carry the company's products.

Companies also must determine the number of channel members to use at each level. Three strategies are available: intensive distribution, exclusive distribution, and selective distribution.

Producers of convenience products and common raw materials typically seek **intensive distribution**—a strategy in which they stock their products in as many outlets as possible. These goods must be available where and when consumers want them. For example, toothpaste, candy, and other similar items are sold in millions of outlets to provide maximum brand exposure and consumer convenience. Warner Lambert, Campbell, Coca-Cola, and other consumer goods companies distribute their products in this way.

By contrast, some producers deliberately limit the number of intermediaries handling their products. The extreme form of this practice is **exclusive distribution,** in which the producer gives only a limited number of dealers the exclusive right to distribute its products in their territories. Exclusive distribution often is found in the distribution of new automobiles and prestige women's clothing. For example, Rolls-Royce dealers are few and far between—even large cities may have only one or two dealers. By granting exclusive distribution, Rolls-Royce gains stronger distributor selling support and more control over dealer prices, promotion, credit, and services. Exclusive distribution also enhances the car's image and allows for higher markups.

Exclusive distribution: Rolls-Royce sells exclusively through a limited number of dealerships. Such limited distribution enhances the car's image and generates stronger dealer support.

Between intensive and exclusive distribution lies **selective distribution**—the use of more than one, but fewer than all of the intermediaries who are willing to carry a company's products. Most television, furniture, and small appliance brands are distributed in this manner. For example, Maytag, Whirlpool, and General Electric sell their major appliances through dealer networks and selected large retailers. By using selective distribution, they do not have to spread their efforts over many outlets, including many marginal ones. They can develop good working relationships with selected channel members and expect a better-than-average selling effort. Selective distribution gives producers good market coverage with more control and less cost than does intensive distribution.

Responsibilities of Channel Members

The producer and intermediaries must agree on the terms and responsibilities of each channel member. They should agree on price policies, conditions of sale, territorial rights, and specific services to be performed by each party. The producer should establish a list price and a fair set of discounts for intermediaries. It must define each channel member's territory, and it should be careful about where it places new resellers. Mutual services and duties need to be spelled out carefully, especially in franchise and exclusive distribution channels. For example, Tim Horton Donuts provides franchisees with promotional support, a record-keeping system, training, and general management assistance. In turn, franchisees must meet company standards for physical facilities, cooperate with new promotion programs, provide requested information, and buy specified food products.

EVALUATING THE MAJOR ALTERNATIVES

Suppose a company has identified several channel alternatives and wants to select the one that will best satisfy its long-run objectives. The firm must evaluate each alternative against economic, control, and adaptive criteria.

Using *economic criteria*, a company compares the likely profitability of different channel alternatives. It estimates the sales that each channel would produce and the costs of selling different volumes through each channel. The company must also consider *control issues*. Using intermediaries usually means giving them some control over the marketing of the product, and some intermediaries take more control than others. Other things being equal, the company prefers to retain as much control as possible. Finally, the company must apply *adaptive criteria*. Channels often involve long-term commitments to other firms, making it difficult to adapt the channel to the changing marketing environment. The company wants to keep the channel as flexible as possible. Thus, to be considered, a channel involving long-term commitment should be greatly superior on economic and control grounds.

DESIGNING INTERNATIONAL DISTRIBUTION CHANNELS

International marketers face many additional complexities in designing their channels. Each country has its own unique distribution system that has evolved over time and changes very slowly. These channel systems can vary widely from country to country. Thus, global marketers usually must adapt their channel strategies to the existing structures within each country. In some markets, the distribution system is complex and hard to penetrate, consisting of many layers and large numbers of intermediaries. Consider Japan:

> The Japanese distribution system stems from the early seventeenth century when cottage industries and a [quickly growing] urban population spawned a merchant class. . . . Despite Japan's economic achievements, the distribution system has remained remarkably faithful to its antique pattern. . . . [It] encompasses a wide range of wholesalers and other agents, brokers, and retailers, differing more in number than in function from their [North] American counterparts. There are myriad tiny retail shops. An even greater number of wholesalers supplies goods to them, layered tier upon tier, many more than most [North American] executives would think necessary. For example, soap may move through three wholesalers plus a sales company after it leaves the manufacturer before it ever reaches the retail outlet. A steak goes from rancher to consumers in a process that often involves a dozen middle agents. . . . The distribution network . . . reflects the traditionally close ties among many Japanese companies . . . [and places] much greater emphasis on personal relationships with users. . . . Although [these channels appear] inefficient and cumbersome, they seem to serve the Japanese customer well. . . . Lacking much storage space in their small homes, most Japanese homemakers shop several times a week and prefer convenient [and more personal] neighbourhood shops.[13]

Many Western firms have had great difficulty breaking into the closely knit, tradition-bound Japanese distribution network.

At the other extreme, distribution systems in developing countries may be scattered and inefficient, or altogether lacking. For example, China and India are huge markets, each containing hundreds of millions of people. In reality, however, these markets are much smaller than the population numbers suggest. Because of inadequate distribution systems in both countries, most companies can profitably access only a small portion of the population located in each country's most affluent cities.[14]

Thus, international marketers face a wide range of channel alternatives. Designing efficient and effective channel systems between and within various country markets poses a difficult challenge. We discuss international distribution decisions further in Chapter 19.

CHANNEL MANAGEMENT DECISIONS

Once the company has reviewed its channel alternatives and decided on the best channel design, it must implement and manage the chosen channel. Channel management calls for selecting and motivating individual channel members and evaluating their performance over time.

Selecting Channel Members

Producers vary in their ability to attract qualified marketing intermediaries. Some producers have no trouble signing up channel members. For example, Toyota had no trouble attracting new dealers for its Lexus line. In fact, it had to turn down many would-be resellers. In some cases, the promise of exclusive or selective distribution for a desirable product will draw plenty of applicants.

Nintendo
www.nintendo.com/

At the other extreme are producers who have to work hard to line up enough qualified intermediaries. For example, in 1986 when distributors were approached by a new, little-heard-of game called Nintendo, many refused to carry the product. They had recently been burned by the failure of Atari. But two Canadian distributors, Larry Wasser and Morey Chaplick, owners of Beamscope, accepted the product. Not a bad move considering that within one year after that decision, their sales went from next to nothing to $24 million![15]

When selecting intermediaries, the company should determine what characteristics distinguish the better ones. It will want to evaluate the channel member's years in business, other lines carried, growth and profit record, cooperativeness, and reputation. If the intermediaries are sales agents, the company will want to evaluate the number and character of other lines carried, and the size and quality of the sales force. If the intermediary is a retail store that wants exclusive or selective distribution, the company will want to evaluate the store's customers, location, and future growth potential.

Motivating Channel Members

Once selected, channel members must be continuously motivated to do their best. The company must sell not only *through* the intermediaries, but also *to* them. Most producers see the problem as finding ways to gain intermediary cooperation. They use the carrot-and-stick approach. At times they offer *positive* motivators such as higher margins, special deals, premiums, cooperative advertising allowances, display allowances, and sales contests. At other times they use *negative* motivators, such as threatening to reduce margins, to slow down delivery, or to end the relationship altogether. A producer using this approach usually has not done a good job of studying the needs, problems, strengths, and weaknesses of its distributors.

More advanced companies try to forge long-term partnerships with their distributors. This involves building a planned, professionally managed, vertical marketing system that meets the needs of both the manufacturer *and* the distributors.[16] Thus, Procter & Gamble and Wal-Mart work together to create superior

GENERAL ELECTRIC ADOPTS A "VIRTUAL INVENTORY" SYSTEM TO SUPPORT ITS DEALERS

Before the late 1980s, General Electric worked at selling through its dealers rather than to them or with them. GE operated a traditional system of trying to load up the channel with GE appliances, on the premise that "loaded dealers are loyal dealers." Loaded dealers would have less space to feature other brands and would recommend GE appliances to reduce their high inventories. To load its dealers, GE would offer the lowest price when the dealer ordered a full-truck load of GE appliances.

GE eventually realized that this approach created many problems, especially for smaller independent appliance dealers who could not afford to carry a large stock. These dealers were hard-pressed to meet price competition from larger multibrand dealers. Rethinking its strategy from the point of view of creating dealer satisfaction and profitability, GE created an alternative distribution model called the Direct Connect system. Under this system, GE dealers carry only display models. They rely on a "virtual inventory" to fill orders. Dealers can access GE's order-processing system 24 hours a day, check on model availability, and place orders for next-day delivery. Using the Direct Connect system, dealers also can get GE's best price, financing from GE Credit, and no interest charges for the first 90 days.

Dealers benefit by having much lower inventory costs while still having a large virtual inventory available to satisfy their customers' needs. In exchange for this benefit, dealers must commit to selling nine major GE product categories; generating 50 percent of their sales from GE products; opening their books to GE for review; and paying GE every month through electronic funds transfer.

As a result of Direct Connect, dealer profit margins have skyrocketed. GE also has benefited. Its dealers now are more committed and dependent on GE, and the new order-entry system has saved GE substantial clerical costs. GE now knows the actual sales of its goods at the retail level, which helps it to schedule its production more accurately. It now can produce in response to demand rather than to meet inventory replenishment rules. And GE has been able to simplify its warehouse locations so as to be able to deliver appliances to 90 percent of its customers within 24 hours. Thus, by forging a partnership, GE has helped both its dealers and itself.

Source: See Michael Treacy and Fred Wiersema, "Customer Intimacy and Other Discipline Values," *Harvard Business Review*, January–February 1993, pp. 84–93.

Creating dealer satisfaction and profitability: Using GE's Direct Connect system, dealers can access GE's order-processing system 24 hours a day, check on model availability, and place orders for next-day delivery. They can also get GE's best price, financing from GE Credit, and no interest.

value for final consumers. They jointly plan merchandising goals and strategies, inventory levels, and advertising and promotion plans. Similarly, General Electric works closely with its smaller independent dealers to help them be successful in selling the company's products (see Marketing Highlight 12-2). In managing its channels, a company must convince distributors that they can make their money by being part of an advanced vertical marketing system.

EVALUATING CHANNEL MEMBERS

The producer must regularly check each channel member's performance against standards such as sales quotas, average inventory levels, customer delivery time, treatment of damaged and lost goods, cooperation in company promotion and training programs, and services to the customer. The company should recognize and reward intermediaries who are performing well. Those who are performing poorly should be helped or, as a last resort, replaced.

A company may periodically "requalify" its intermediaries and prune the weaker ones. For example, when IBM first introduced its PS/2 personal computers, it reevaluated its dealers and allowed only the best ones to carry the new models. Each IBM dealer had to submit a business plan, send a sales and service employee to IBM training classes, and meet new sales quotas. Only about two-thirds of IBM's 2200 dealers qualified to carry the PS/2 models.[17]

Finally, manufacturers need to be sensitive to their dealers. Those who treat their dealers lightly risk not only losing their support but also causing some legal problems. Marketing Highlight 12-3 describes various rights and duties pertaining to manufacturers and their channel members.

PHYSICAL DISTRIBUTION AND LOGISTICS MANAGEMENT

Physical distribution (marketing logistics)
The tasks involved in planning, implementing, and controlling the physical flow of materials, final goods, and related information from points of origin to points of consumption to meet customer requirements at a profit.

In today's global marketplace, selling a product is sometimes easier than getting it to customers. Companies must decide on the best way to store, handle, and move their products and services so that they are available to customers in the right assortments, at the right time, and in the right place. Logistics effectiveness will have a major impact on both customer satisfaction and company costs. A poor distribution system can destroy an otherwise good marketing effort. Here we consider the *nature and importance of marketing logistics, goals of the logistics system, major logistics functions,* and the need for *integrated logistics management.*

NATURE AND IMPORTANCE OF PHYSICAL DISTRIBUTION AND MARKETING LOGISTICS

To some managers, physical distribution means only trucks and warehouses. But modern logistics is much more than this. **Physical distribution**—or **marketing logistics**—involves planning, implementing, and controlling the physical flow of materials, final goods, and related information from points of origin to points of consumption to meet customer requirements at a profit. In short, it involves getting the right product to the right customer in the right place at the right time.

Interlink's advertisement stresses the need to think of total solutions as a way of approaching logistics problems.

Traditional physical distribution has typically started with products at the plant and tried to find low-cost solutions to get them to customers. However, today's marketers prefer *market logistics* thinking, which starts with the marketplace and works backwards to the factory. Logistics addresses not only the problem of outbound distribution (moving products from the factory to customers), but also the problem of inbound distribution (moving products and materials from suppliers to the factory). It involves the management of entire *supply chains,* value-added flows from suppliers to final users, as shown in Figure 12-6. Thus, the logistics manager's task is to coordinate the whole-channel physical distribution system—the activities of suppliers, purchasing agents, marketers, channel members, and customers. These activities include forecasting, information systems, purchasing, production planning, order processing, inventory, warehousing, and transportation planning.

MARKETING HIGHLIGHT 12 - 3

PUBLIC POLICY AND DISTRIBUTION ETHICS

For the most part, companies are legally free to develop whatever channel arrangements suit them. In fact, the laws affecting channels seek to prevent the exclusionary tactics of some companies that might keep another company from using a desired channel. Of course, this means that the company must itself avoid using such exclusionary tactics. Most channel law deals with the mutual rights and duties of the channel members once they have formed a relationship.

The American Marketing Association (AMA) code of ethics (under which Canadian marketers also operate) focuses on issues of market power in the section dealing with distribution. Ethical marketers are advised not to manipulate product availability for purposes of exploitation, and not to use coercion in the marketing channel.

Full-Line Forcing

An agreement in which producers of a strong brand sometimes sell to dealers only if the dealers will take some or all of the rest of the line.

Exclusive Dealing

Many producers and wholesalers like to develop exclusive channels for their products. When the seller allows only certain outlets to carry its products, this strategy is called *exclusive distribution.* When the seller requires that these dealers not handle competitors' products, its

strategy is called *exclusive dealing.* Both parties benefit from exclusive arrangements: The seller obtains more loyal and dependable outlets, and the dealers obtain a steady source of supply and stronger seller support. But exclusive arrangements exclude other producers from selling to these dealers. They are legal as long as they do not substantially lessen competition or tend to create a monopoly and as long as both parties enter into the agreement voluntarily.

Exclusive Territories

Exclusive dealing often includes exclusive territorial agreements. The producer may agree not to sell to other dealers in a given area, or the buyer may agree to sell only in its own territory. The first practice is normal under franchise systems as way to increase dealer enthusiasm and commitment. It is also perfectly legal—a seller has no legal obligation to sell through more outlets than it wishes. The second practice, whereby the producer tries to keep a dealer from selling outside its territory, has become a major legal issue.

Tying Agreements

Producers of a strong brand sometimes sell it to dealers only if the dealers will take some or all of the rest of the line. This is called *full-line forcing.* Even though the practice isn't illegal, it causes considerable channel conflict.

Dealers' Rights

Producers are free to select their dealers, but their right to terminate dealers is somewhat restricted. In general, sellers can drop dealers "for cause." But they cannot drop dealers if, for example, the dealers refuse to cooperate in a doubtful legal arrangement, such as exclusive dealing or tying agreements.

Free Trade

With the advent of free trade, new public-policy issues have come to the fore. Many of these issues surround the distribution of Canadian cultural products. For example, in March 1995, it was announced in the new federal budget that the postal subsidy to Canadian magazine publishers was being cut. This subsidy had allowed Canadian publishers to mail out copies of magazines and newspapers for as little as $0.07 each. Free-trade advocates contend that this subsidy gives Canadian publishers an unfair advantage; however, Canadian publishers claim they cannot survive if the subsidy is cut. Although American publications dominate newsstands, Canadian magazines and newspapers overshadow their American competitors when it comes to mailed subscriptions. This case, as well as those associated with the distribution of agricultural products under Canada's marketing boards, will keep free-trade negotiators at the table for many long hours.

Full-line forcing
An agreement in which producers of a strong brand sometimes sell to dealers only if the dealers will take some or all of the rest of the line.

American Marketing Association
www.ama.org/

Companies today are placing greater emphasis on logistics for several reasons. First, customer service and satisfaction have become the cornerstones of marketing strategy in many businesses, and distribution is an important customer service element. More and more, effective logistics is becoming a key to winning and keeping customers. Companies are finding that they can attract more customers by giving better service or lower prices through better physical distribution. On the other hand, companies may lose customers when they fail to supply the right products on time.

Second, logistics is a major cost element for most companies. In one study, 10.5 percent of many countries' Gross Domestic Product is accounted for by functions such as wrapping, bundling, loading, unloading, sorting, reloading, and transporting goods."[18] About 15 percent of an average product's price is accounted for by shipping and transport alone. Poor physical distribution decisions result in high costs. Even large companies sometimes make too little use of modern decision tools for coordinating inventory levels; transportation modes; and plant, warehouse, and store locations. Improvements in physical distribution efficiency can yield tremendous cost savings for both the company and its customers.

FIGURE 12-6 *Marketing logistics: Managing supply chains*

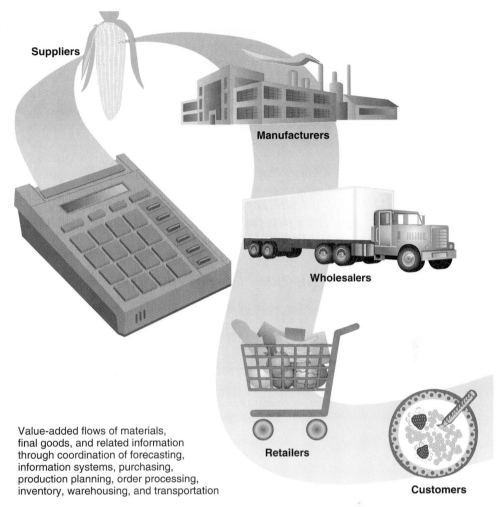

Suppliers

Manufacturers

Wholesalers

Retailers

Customers

Value-added flows of materials, final goods, and related information through coordination of forecasting, information systems, purchasing, production planning, order processing, inventory, warehousing, and transportation

Third, the explosion in product variety has created a need for improved logistics management. For example, in 1911, the typical A&P grocery store carried only 270 items. The shopkeeper could keep track of this inventory on about 10 pages of notebook paper. Today, the average A&P carries a bewildering stock of more than 16 700 items, some 62 times more than in 1911.[19] Ordering, shipping, stocking, and controlling such a variety of products presents a sizable logistics challenge.

Finally, improvements in information technology have created opportunities for major gains in distribution efficiency. The increased use of computers, point-of-sale scanners, uniform product codes, satellite tracking, electronic data interchange (EDI), and electronic funds transfer (EFT) has allowed companies to create advanced systems for order processing, inventory control and handling, and transportation routing and scheduling.

GOALS OF THE LOGISTICS SYSTEM

Some companies state their logistics objective as providing maximum customer service at the least cost. Unfortunately, no logistics system can *both* maximize customer service *and* minimize distribution costs. Maximum customer service implies rapid delivery, large inventories, flexible assortments, liberal returns policies, and other services—all of which raise distribution costs. In contrast, minimum distribution costs imply slower delivery, smaller inventories, and larger shipping lots—which represent a lower level of overall customer service.

The goal of the marketing logistics system should be to provide a targeted level of customer service at the least cost. A company must first research the importance of various distribution services to its customers, and then set desired service levels for each segment. The company typically will want to offer at least the same level of service as its competitors. But the objective is to maximize *profits,* not sales. Therefore, the company must weigh the benefits of providing higher levels of service against the costs. Some companies offer less service than their competitors and charge a lower price. Other companies offer more service and charge higher prices to cover higher costs.

The company ultimately must set logistics objectives to guide its planning. For example, service-response time is very important to buyers of large photocopy machines, so Xerox developed a service-delivery standard that can "put a disabled machine anywhere in North America back into operation within three hours after receiving the service request." Coca-Cola's distribution standard is "to put Coke within an arm's length of desire."

Major Logistics Functions

Given a set of logistics objectives, the company is ready to design a logistics system that will minimize the cost of attaining these objectives. The major logistics functions include *order processing, warehousing, inventory management,* and *transportation.*

Order Processing

Orders can be submitted in many ways—by mail or telephone, through salespeople, or via computer and electronic data interchange (EDI). In some cases, the suppliers might actually generate orders for their customers:

> One Kmart quick response program calls for selected suppliers to manage the retailer's inventory replenishment for their products. Kmart transmits daily records of product sales to the vendor, who analyzes the sales information, comes up with an order, and sends it back to Kmart through EDI. Once in Kmart's system, the order is treated as though Kmart itself created it. Says a Kmart executive, "We don't modify the order, and we don't question it. . . . Our relationship with those vendors is such that we trust them to create the type of order that will best meet our inventory needs."[20]

Once received, orders must be processed quickly and accurately. The order processing system prepares invoices and sends order information to those who need it. The appropriate warehouse receives instructions to pack and ship the ordered items. Products out of stock are back-ordered. Shipped items are accompanied by shipping and billing documents, with copies going to various departments.

Both the company and its customers benefit when the order-processing steps are carried out efficiently. Ideally, salespeople send in their orders daily, often using online computers. The order department quickly processes these orders, and the warehouse sends out the goods on time. Bills go out as soon as possible. Most companies now use computerized order-processing systems that speed up the order-shipping-billing cycle. For example, General Electric operates a computer-based system that, upon receipt of a customer's order, checks the customer's credit standing as well as whether and where the items are in stock. The computer then issues an order to ship, bills the customer, updates the inventory records, sends a production order for new stock, and relays the message back to the salesperson that the customer's order is on its way—all in less than 15 seconds.

Warehousing

Every company must store its goods while they wait to be sold. A storage function is needed because production and consumption cycles rarely match. For example, Toro and other lawn-mower manufacturers must produce all year long and store up

Automated warehouses: This sophisticated COMPAQ computer distribution centre can ship any of 500 different types of COMPAQ computers and options within four hours of receiving an order.

Distribution centre
A large, highly automated warehouse designed to receive goods from various plants and suppliers, fill them efficiently, and deliver goods to customers as quickly as possible.

their product for the heavy spring and summer buying season. The storage function overcomes differences in needed quantities and timing.

A company must decide on *how many* and *what types* of warehouses it needs, and *where* they will be located. The more warehouses the company uses, the more quickly goods can be delivered to customers. However, more locations mean higher warehousing costs. The company, therefore, must balance the level of customer service against distribution costs.

Some company stock is kept at or near the plant, with the rest located in warehouses around the country. The company might own private warehouses, rent space in public warehouses, or both. Companies have more control over warehouses they own, but that ties up their capital and is less flexible if desired locations change. In contrast, public warehouses charge for the rented space and provide additional services (at a cost) for inspecting goods, packaging them, shipping them, and invoicing them. By using public warehouses, companies also have a wide choice of locations and warehouse types.

Companies may use either *storage warehouses* or *distribution centres*. Storage warehouses store goods for moderate to long periods. **Distribution centres** are designed to move goods rather than just store them. They are large and highly automated warehouses designed to receive goods from various plants and suppliers, take orders, fill them efficiently, and deliver goods to customers as quickly as possible. For example, Wal-Mart operates huge distribution centres. One centre, which serves the daily needs of 165 Wal-Mart stores, contains some 28 acres of space under a single roof. Laser scanners route as many as 190 000 cases of goods per day along 18 kilometres of conveyer belts, and the centre's 1000 workers load or unload 310 trucks daily.[21]

Warehousing facilities and equipment technology have improved greatly in recent years. Older, multi-storied warehouses with slow elevators and outdated materials-handling methods are facing competition from newer, single-storied *automated warehouses* with advanced materials-handling systems under the control of a central computer. In these warehouses, only a few employees are necessary. Computers read orders and direct lift trucks, electric hoists, or robots to gather goods, move them to loading docks, and issue invoices. These warehouses have reduced worker injuries, labour costs, theft, and breakage and have improved inventory control.

Inventory

Inventory levels also affect customer satisfaction. The major problem is to maintain the delicate balance between carrying too much inventory and carrying too little. Carrying too much inventory results in higher-than-necessary inventory carrying costs and stock obsolescence. Carrying too little may result in stock-outs, costly emergency shipments or production, and customer dissatisfaction. In making inventory decisions, management must balance the costs of carrying larger inventories against resulting sales and profits.

Inventory decisions involve knowing both *when* to order and *how much* to order. In deciding when to order, the company balances the risks of running out of stock against the costs of carrying too much. In deciding how much to order, the company needs to balance order-processing costs against inventory carrying costs. Larger average-order size results in fewer orders and lower order-processing costs, but it also means larger inventory carrying costs.

During the past decade, many companies have greatly reduced their inventories and related costs through *just-in-time* logistics systems. Through such systems, producers and retailers carry only small inventories of parts or merchandise, often only enough for a few days of operations. New stock arrives exactly when needed, rather than being stored in inventory until being used. Just-in-time systems require accurate forecasting along with fast, frequent, and flexible delivery, so that new supplies will be available when needed. However, these systems result in substantial savings in inventory carrying and handling costs.

Transportation

Marketers need to take an interest in their company's *transportation* decisions. The choice of transportation carriers affects the pricing of products, delivery performance, and condition of the goods when they arrive—all of which will affect customer satisfaction.

In shipping goods to its warehouses, dealers, and customers, the company can choose among five transportation modes: rail, water, truck, pipeline, and air. Table 12-1 summarizes the characteristics of each transportation mode.

RAIL. Because most of Canada's population is contained in a belt that is only 300 km wide but 6400 km long, rail still carries most of the country's freight. Railways are one of the most cost-effective modes for shipping large amounts of bulk products—coal, sand, minerals, farm and forest products—over long distances. In addition, railways recently have begun to increase their customer services. Both CN and CP have designed new equipment to handle special categories of goods, provided flatcars for carrying truck trailers by rail (piggyback), and provided in-transit services such as the diversion of shipped goods to other destinations en route and the processing of goods en route. Thus, after decades of losing out to truckers, railways appear ready for a comeback.[22]

TRUCK. Trucks have increased their share of transportation steadily and now account for 25 percent of total cargo. They account for the largest portion of transportation *within* cities as opposed to *between* cities. Trucks are highly flexible in their routing and time schedules. They can move goods door to door, saving shippers the need to transfer goods from truck to rail and back again at a loss of time and risk of theft or damage. Trucks are efficient for short hauls of high-value merchandise. In many cases, their rates are competitive with railway rates, and trucks can usually offer faster service. Trucking firms have added many services in recent years. For example, Roadway Express now offers satellite

Roadway Express
www.roadway.com/

TABLE 12-1 *Characteristics of Major Transportation Modes*

Transportation Mode	Intercity Cargo Volume* (%)			Typical Products Shipped
	1970	1980	1991	
Rail	39.8%	37.5%	37.4%	Farm products, minerals, sand, chemicals, automobiles
Truck	21.3	22.3	26.3	Clothing, food, books, computers, paper goods
Water	16.5	16.4	16.0	Oil, grain, sand, gravel, metallic ores, coal
Pipeline	22.3	23.6	20.0	Oil, coal, chemicals
Air	0.17	0.19	0.3	Technical instruments, perishable products, documents

*In billions of cargo ton-miles.
Source: Statistical Abstract of the United States, 1993.

In today's business environment speed is critical. Roadway Express moves your shipment around the clock and communicates your shipment's location at the speed of light. Continuously tracked by satellite, our new sleeper tractors keep your shipment on the road and on time. You get reliable service and reliable information.

Just some of the ways we're changing to offer you exceptional service...with no exceptions.

tracking of shipments and sleeper tractors that move freight around the clock.

WATER.   A large amount of goods are moved by ships and barges on coastal and inland waterways. On the one hand, the cost of water transportation is very low for shipping bulky, low-value, non-perishable products such as sand, coal, grain, oil, and metallic ores. On the other hand, water transportation is the slowest transportation mode and is sometimes affected by the weather. Thus although many goods are shipped across the Great Lakes and through the St. Lawrence Seaway in the summer months, these routes are impassable in the winter.

PIPELINE.   Pipelines are a specialized means of shipping petroleum, natural gas, and chemicals from sources to markets. Pipeline shipment of petroleum products costs less than rail shipment, but more than water shipment. Most pipelines are used by their owners to ship their own products.

AIR.   Although air carriers transport less than one percent of the nation's goods, they are becoming more important as a transportation mode. Air-freight rates are much higher than rail or truck rates, but air freight is ideal when speed is needed or distant markets have to be reached. Among the most frequently air-freighted products are perishables (fresh fish, cut flowers) and high-value, low-bulk items (technical instruments, jewellery). Companies find

Roadway and other trucking firms have added many services in recent years, such as satellite tracking of shipments and sleeper tractors that keep freight moving around the clock.

Containerization
Putting the goods in boxes or trailers that are easy to transfer between two transportation modes.

that air freight also reduces inventory levels, packaging costs, and the number of warehouses needed.

The National Transportation Agency of Canada implements and administers transportation legislation in Canada. Information on the agency can be obtained from their web page (freenet.carleton.ca).

In choosing a transportation mode for a product, shippers consider as many as five criteria, as shown in Table 12-2. Thus, if a shipper needs speed, air and truck are the prime choices. If the goal is low cost, then water or pipeline might be best. Trucks appear to offer the most advantages—a fact that explains their growing share of the transportation market.

Thanks to *containerization*, shippers are increasingly combining two or more modes of transportation. **Containerization** consists of putting goods in boxes or trailers that are easy to transfer between two transportation modes. *Piggyback* describes the use of rail and trucks; *fishyback*, water and trucks; *trainship*, water and rail; and *airtruck*, air and trucks. Each combination offers advantages to the shipper. For example, not only is piggyback cheaper than trucking alone, but it also provides flexibility and convenience.

TABLE 12-2   *Rankings of Transportation Modes (1 = Highest Rank)*

	Speed (door-to-door delivery time)	Dependability (meeting schedules on time)	Capability (ability to handle various products)	Availability (no. of geographic points served)	Cost (per ton-mile)
Rail	3	4	2	2	3
Water	4	5	1	4	1
Truck	2	2	3	1	4
Pipeline	5	1	5	5	2
Air	1	3	4	3	5

Source: See Carl M. Guelzo, *Introduction to Logistics Management* (Englewood Cliffs, NJ: Prentice Hall, 1986), p. 46.

INTEGRATED LOGISTICS MANAGEMENT

Integrated logistics management
The logistics concept that emphasizes teamwork, both inside the company and among all the marketing channel organizations, to maximize the performance of the entire distribution system.

Today, more and more companies are adopting the concept of **integrated logistics management.** This concept recognizes that providing better customer service and trimming distribution costs requires *teamwork,* both inside the company and among all the marketing channel organizations. Inside the company, the various functional departments must work closely together to maximize the company's own logistics performance. The company must also integrate its logistics system with those of its suppliers and customers to maximize the performance of the entire distribution system.

Cross-Functional Teamwork Inside the Company

In most companies, responsibility for various logistics activities is assigned to many different functional units—marketing, sales, finance, manufacturing, purchasing. Too often, each function tries to optimize its own logistics performance without regard for the activities of the other functions. However, transportation, inventory, warehousing, and order processing activities interact, often in an inverse way. For example, lower inventory levels reduce inventory carrying costs. But they may also reduce customer service and increase costs from stockouts, back orders, special production runs, and costly fast-freight shipments. Because distribution activities involve strong trade-offs, decisions by different functions must be coordinated to achieve superior overall logistics performance.

Thus, the goal of integrated logistics management is to harmonize all of the company's distribution decisions. Close working relationships among functions can be achieved in several ways. Some companies have created permanent logistics committees composed of managers responsible for different physical distribution activities and transportation engineers. These committees meet often to set policies for improving overall logistics performance. Companies can also create management positions that link the logistics activities of functional areas. For example, Procter & Gamble has created "supply managers" who manage all of the supply chain activities for each of its product categories.[23] Many companies have a vice-president of logistics with cross-functional authority. In fact, according to one logistics expert, three-quarters of all major wholesalers and retailers, and a third of major manufacturing companies, have senior logistics officers at the vice president or higher level.[24] The location of the logistics functions within the company is a secondary concern. The important thing is that the company coordinate its logistics and marketing activities to create high market satisfaction at a reasonable cost.

Building Channel Partnerships

The members of a distribution channel are linked closely in delivering customer satisfaction and value. One company's distribution system is another company's supply system. The success of each channel member depends on the performance of the entire supply chain. For example, Zellers can charge the lowest prices at retail only if its entire supply chain—consisting of thousands of merchandise suppliers, transport companies, warehouses, and service providers—operates at maximum efficiency.

Companies must do more than improve their own logistics. They must also work with other channel members to improve whole-channel distribution. For example, it makes little sense for Levi Strauss to ship finished jeans to its own warehouses, then from these warehouses to Eaton's warehouses, from which they are then shipped to Eaton's stores. If the two companies can work together, Levi Strauss might be able to ship much of its merchandise directly to Eaton's stores, saving time, inventory, and shipping costs for both. Today, smart companies are coordinating their logistics strategies and building strong partnerships with suppliers and customers to improve customer service and reduce channel costs.

These channel partnerships can take many forms. Many companies have created *cross-functional, cross-company teams.* For example, Procter & Gamble has a team of almost 100 people living in Bentonville, Arkansas, home of Wal-Mart. The P&Gers work with their counterparts at Wal-Mart to jointly find ways to squeeze costs out of their distribution system. Working together benefits not only P&G and Wal-Mart, but also their final consumers.[25]

Other companies partner through *shared projects.* For example, many larger retailers are working closely with suppliers on in-store programs. Home Depot allows key suppliers to use its stores as a testing ground for new merchandising programs. The suppliers spend time at Home Depot stores watching how their product sells and how customers relate to it. They then create programs specially tailored to Home Depot and its customers.[26]

Channel partnerships may also take the form of *information sharing* and *continuous inventory replenishment* systems. Companies manage their supply chains through information. Suppliers link up with customers through electronic data interchange (EDI) systems to share information and coordinate their logistics decisions. Here is just one example:

> Increasingly, high-performance retailers are sharing point-of-sale scanner data with their suppliers through electronic data interchange. Wal-Mart was one of the first companies to provide suppliers with timely sales data. With its Retail Link system, major suppliers have "earth stations" installed, by which they are directly connected to Wal-Mart's information network. Now, the same system that tells Wal-Mart what customers are buying lets suppliers know what to produce and where to ship goods. For example, Wal-Mart sells millions of Wrangler jeans each year. Every night, Wal-Mart sends sales data collected on its scanners directly to VF Corporation (which makes Wrangler jeans), which then restocks automatically. So if a Wal-mart customer buys a pair of Wranglers on Tuesday morning, by the evening, records of the sales arrive in VF's central computer. If VF has a replacement pair in stock, it's shipped directly to the store the next day—and by Thursday, Wal-Mart's shelf is replenished. If not, VF's computers automatically order up a replacement—and a new pair of jeans is shipped within a week.[27]

Today, as a result of such partnerships, many companies have switched from *anticipatory-based distribution systems* to *response-based distribution systems.*[28] In anticipatory distribution, the company produces the amount of goods called for by a sales forecast. It builds and holds stock at various supply points such as the plant, distribution centres, and retail outlets. Each supply point reorders automatically when its order point is reached. When sales are slower than expected, the company tries to reduce its inventories by offering discounts, rebates, and promotions. For example, the auto industry produces cars far in advance of demand, and these cars often sit for months in inventory until the companies undertake aggressive promotion.

A response-based distribution system, in contrast, is *customer-triggered.* The producer continuously builds and replaces stock as orders arrive. It produces what is currently selling. For example, Japanese car makers take orders for cars, then produce and ship them within four days. Some large appliance manufacturers, such as Whirlpool and GE, are moving to this system. Benetton, the Italian fashion house, uses a *quick-response system,* dyeing its sweaters in the colours that are currently selling instead of trying to guess long in advance which colours people will want. Producing for order rather than for forecast substantially cuts down inventory costs and risks.

Third-Party Logistics

Third-party logistics
An integrated logistics company that performs any or all of the functions required to get their clients' product to market.

While most businesses perform their own logistics functions, a growing number of firms now outsource this function to **third-party logistics** providers such as Ryder Systems, UPS Worldwide Logistics, FedEx Logistics, Roadway Logistics

MARKETING HIGHLIGHT 12 - 4

GO RYDER, AND LEAVE THE DELIVERING TO US

Most big companies love to make and sell their products. But many hate the associated logistics grunt work—the bundling, loading, unloading, sorting, storing, reloading, transporting, and tracking required to supply their factories and to get products out to customers. They hate it so much that nearly one-third of Fortune 500 companies now outsource some or all of these functions. Increasingly, companies are handing over their logistics to specialists. Below are some examples:

Saturn. Saturn's just-in-time production system allows for almost no parts inventory at the plant. Instead, it relies on a world-class logistics system to keep parts flowing into the factory at precisely the times they're needed. Saturn is so adroit in managing its supply chain that in four years it has had to halt production just once—for only 18 minutes—because the right part failed to arrive at the right time. Most of the credit, however, goes to Ryder System, the logistics management firm. Ryder, best known for renting trucks, manages Saturn's far-ranging supply chain, moving the automaker's materials, parts, and products efficiently and reliably from supplier to factory to dealer showroom.

To keep Saturn's assembly lines humming, Ryder transports thousands of pre-inspected and presorted parts, hitting delivery windows as narrow as five minutes. Ryder's keeps its parts, people, and trucks in nearly constant blur of high-tech motion. This effective supply-chain management results in lower costs, improved operations, more productive dealers, and—in the end—more satisfied customers.

Cisco Systems. This vendor of computer networking equipment and network-management software ships tons of routers to Europe daily. It needs to know where each box is at any given time and may have to reroute orders on short notice to fill urgent customer requests. Moreover, Cisco's customers need to know exactly when orders will arrive. When Cisco handled its own logistics, deliveries took up to three weeks. Now, the company contracts its complex distribution process to UPS World-

wide Logistics. Leveraging its knowledge of international plane, train, and trucking schedules, UPS Worldwide can speed routers to European customers in fewer than four days. If its planes or trucks can't make the fastest delivery, UPS subcontracts the job to Lufthansa, KLM, or Danzas, a European trucking firm.

Cisco's reaps some additional advantages from the logistics partnership. For example, UPS Worldwide has extensive knowledge of local customs laws and import duties. It recently arranged with Dutch customs to aggregate Cisco's import

duties into a monthly bill, which is paid when customers receive shipments instead of each time the routers land at the airport. The result: even more savings in time and paperwork.

National Semiconductor. In the early 1990s, National Semiconductor—whose chips end up inside everything from cars and computers to telecommunications gear—faced a logistics nightmare. National produced and assembled chips in 13 plants located in the United States, Britain, Israel, and Southeast Asia. Finished products were then shipped to any array of large customers—IBM, Toshiba, Compaq, Ford, Siemens—each with factories scattered around the globe. On their way to customers, chips travelled any of 20 000 direct routes, mostly in the cargo holds of airplanes flown by 12 airlines, stopping along the way at 10 different warehouses. National's logistics performance left much to be desired: 95 percent of its products

were delivered within 45 days of the order. The other five percent took as long as 90 days. Because customers never knew which five percent would be late, they demanded 90 days worth of inventory in everything.

National's management set out to overhaul its global logistics network. It decided that all finished products would be transported to a central distribution centre in Asia, where they would be sorted and air-freighted to customers. Although strategically sound, the plan created some big practical problems: National knew a lot about making

chips but very little about air freight. "To do that," says the executive, "we would have had to make our company into FedEx." Instead, National *hired* FedEx, which now runs National's distribution centre in Singapore. The results have been startling. Within two years, National's distribution costs fell 27 percent. At the same time, sales jumped by $584 million and delivery performance improved dramatically. By outsourcing its distribution to a firm that specializes in efficient logistics, National Semiconductor has both cut its costs and improved its service to customers.

Sources: Quotations and other information from Ronald Henkoff, "Delivering the Goods," *Fortune*, November 28, 1994, pp. 74–77; Lisa H. Harrington, 'Special Report on Contract Logistics," *Transportation & Distribution*, September 1996, pp. A–N; and Scott Woolley, "Replacing Inventory with Information," *Forbes*, March 24, 1997, pp. 54–58; www.saturn.com/index.html; www.cisco.com/; www.national.com/

Services, or Emory Global Logistics (see Marketing Highlight 12-4). Such integrated logistics companies perform any or all of the functions required to get their clients' product to market. For example, Emory's Global Logistics unit provides clients with coordinated, single-source logistics services including supply chain management, customized information technology, inventory control, warehousing, transportation management, customer service and fulfilment, and freight auditing and control

Companies may use third-party logistics providers for several reasons. First, because getting the product to market is their main focus, these providers can often do it more efficiently and at lower cost than clients whose strengths lie elsewhere. According to a recent study, outsourcing warehousing alone typically results in 10 to 15 percent cost savings.[29] Second, outsourcing logistics frees a company to focus more intensely on its core business. Finally, integrated logistics companies understand the increasingly complex logistics environment. This can be especially helpful to companies attempting to expand their global market coverage. For example, companies distributing their products across Europe face a bewildering array of environmental restrictions that affect logistics, including packaging standards, truck size and weight limits, and noise and emissions pollution controls. By outsourcing its logistics, a company can gain a complete Pan-European distribution system without incurring the costs, delays, and risks associated with setting up its own system.[30]

Summary of Chapter Objectives

Marketing channel decisions are among the most important decisions that management faces. A company's channel decisions directly affect every other marketing decision. Each channel system creates a different level of revenues and costs and reaches a different segment of target consumers. Management must make channel decisions carefully, incorporating today's needs with tomorrow's likely selling environment. While some companies pay too little attention to their distribution channels, others have used imaginative distribution systems to gain competitive advantage.

1. **Explain why companies use distribution channels and explain the functions that these channels perform.**

    Most producers use intermediaries to bring their products to market. They try to force a *distribution channel*—a set of interdependent organizations involved in the process of making a product or service available for use or consumption by the consumer or business user. Through their contacts, experience, specialization, and scale of operation, intermediaries usually offer the firm more than it can achieve on its own. Distribution channels perform many key functions. Some help *complete* transactions by gathering and distributing *information* needed for planning and aiding exchange;

by *developing* and spreading persuasive communications about an offer; by performing *contact* work—finding and communicating with prospective buyers; by *matching*—shaping and fitting the offer to the buyer's needs; and by entering into *negotiation* to reach an agreement on price and other terms of the offer so that ownership can be transferred. Other functions help to *fulfil* the completed transactions by offering *physical distribution*—transporting and storing goods; *financing*—acquiring and using funds to cover the costs of the channel work; and *risk taking*—assuming the risks of carrying out the channel work.

2. **Discuss how channel members interact and how they organize to perform the work of the channel.**

    The channel will be most effective when each member is assigned the tasks it can do best. Ideally, because the success of individual channel members depends on overall channel success, all channel firms should work together smoothly. They should understand and accept their roles, coordinate their goals and activities, and cooperate to attain overall channel goals. By cooperating, they can more effectively sense, serve, and satisfy the target market.

In a large company, the formal organization structure assigns roles and provides needed leadership. But in a distribution channel composed of independent firms, leadership and power are not formally set. Traditionally, distribution channels have lacked the leadership needed to assign roles and manage conflict. In recent years, however, new types of channel organizations have appeared that provide stronger leadership and improved performance.

3. **Identify the major channel alternatives open to a company.**

Each firm identifies alternative ways to reach its market. Available means vary from direct selling to using one, two, three, or more intermediary *channel levels*. Marketing channels face continuous and sometimes dramatic change. Three of the most important trends are the growth of *vertical, horizontal,* and *hybrid marketing systems*. These trends affect channel cooperation, conflict, and competition. *Channel design* begins with assessing customer channel-service needs and company channel objective and constraints. The company then identifies the major channel alternatives in terms of the *types* of intermediaries, the *number* of intermediaries, and the *channel responsibilities* of each. Each channel alternative must be evaluated according to economic, control, and adaptive criteria. Channel management calls for selecting qualified intermediaries and motivating them. Individual channel members must be evaluated regularly.

4. **Discuss the nature and importance of physical distribution.**

Just as the marketing concept is receiving increased recognition, more business firms are paying attention to the *physical distribution*, or *marketing logistics*. Logistics is an area of potentially high cost savings and improved customer satisfaction. Marketing logistics involves coordinating the activities of the entire *supply chain* to deliver maximum value to customers. No logistics system can both maximize customer service and minimize distribution costs. Instead, the goal of logistics management is to provide a *targeted* level of service at the least cost. The major logistics functions include *order processing, warehousing, inventory management*, and *transportation*.

5. **Analyse integrated logistics, including how it may be achieved and its benefits to the company.**

The *integrated logistics concept* recognizes that improved logistics requires teamwork—in the form of close working relationships across functional areas inside the company and across various organizations in the supply chain. Companies can achieve logistics harmony among functions by creating cross-functional logistics teams, integrative supply manager positions, and senior-level logistics executives with cross-functional authority. Channel partnerships can take the form of cross-company teams, shared projects, and information-sharing systems. Through such partnerships, many companies have switched from *anticipatory-based distribution systems* to customer-triggered *response-based distribution systems*. Today, some companies are outsourcing their logistics functions to third-party logistics providers to save costs, increase efficiency, and gain faster and more effective access to global markets.

Key Terms

Discussing the Issues

1. The Book-of-the-Month Club (BOMC) has been successfully marketing books by mail for over 50 years. Discuss why so few publishers sell books directly by mail. How will competition from new companies like amazon.com affect BOMC?

2. Analyse why franchising is such a fast-growing form of retail organization. Why do you think franchising is a more popular way of doing business in Canada than it is in the United States?

3. Why have horizontal marketing arrangements become more common in recent years? Suggest several pairs of companies that you think could have successful horizontal marketing programs.

4. Describe the channel service needs of (a) consumers buying a computer for home use, (b) retailers buying computers to resell to individual consumers, and (c) purchasing agents buying computers for company use. What channels would a computer manufacturer design to satisfy these different service needs?

5. Decide which distribution strategies—intensive, selective, or exclusive—are used for the following products, and why? (a) Piaget watches (b) Acura automobiles, (c) Crispy-Crunch chocolate bars.

6. Identify several consequences of running out of stock that need to be considered when planning desired inventory levels.

Applying the Concepts

1. Discount malls and so-called "factory outlet centres" are increasing in popularity. Many of their stores are operated by manufacturers who normally sell only through intermediaries. If you have one of these malls nearby, visit it and study the retailers. Discuss what sort of merchandise is sold in these stores. Do any of them appear to be factory owned? If so, do these factory stores compete with the manufacturer's normal retailers? Appraise the pros and cons of operating these stores.

2. Go through a camera or computer magazine, and pay special attention to large ads for mail-order retailers. Look for ads for brand-name products that use selective distribution, such as Nikon cameras or Compaq computers. Locate an ad that is clearly from an authorized dealer, and one that appears not to be. How can you judge which channel is legitimate? Are there price differences between the legitimate and the unauthorized dealers, and if so, are they what you would expect? Now go online and search for the same product. Which firms use their web sites to support their dealer networks? Which ones seem to be in conflict with their dealers?

References

1. Quotations from Donald V. Fites, "Make Your Dealers Your Partners," *Harvard Business Review*, March-April 1996, pp. 84–95. Also see Peter Elstrom, "This Cat Keeps on Purring," *Business Week*, January 20, 1997, pp. 82–84.

2. Louis Stern and Adel I. El-Ansary, *Marketing Channels*, 4th. ed (Englewood Cliffs, NJ: Prentice Hall, 1992), p. 3.

3. Alanna Mitchell, "U of C Won't Go by Book," *Globe and Mail*, December 13, 1995, pp. A1, A14.

4. Jaclyn Fierman, "How Gallo Crushes the Competition," *Fortune*, September 1, 1986, p. 27.

5. See Richard C. Hoffman and John F. Preble, "Franchising Into the Twenty-First Century," *Business Horizons*, November–December, 1993, pp. 35–43; "Canada's Largest Franchise-only Show Returns," *Advertising Supplement, Globe and Mail*, September 24, 1997, p. 1.

6. This has been called "symbiotic marketing." For more reading, see Lee Adler, "Symbiotic Marketing," *Harvard Business Review*, November–December 1966, pp. 59–71; P. "Rajan" Varadarajan and Daniel Rajaratnam, "Symbiotic Marketing Revisited," *Journal of Marketing*, January 1986, pp. 7–17; and Gary Hamel, Yves L. Doz, and C. D. Prahalad, "Collaborate with Your Competitors—and Win," *Harvard Business Review*, January–February 1989, pp. 133–139.

7. See Allan J. Magrath, "Collaborative Marketing Comes of Age—Again," *Sales & Marketing Management*, September 1991, pp. 61–64; and Lois Therrien, "Cafe Au Lait, A Croissant—and Trix," *Business*

Week, August 24, 1992, pp. 50–51; Oliver Bertin, "Two Big Wineries to Merge," *Globe and Mail,* September 14, 1993, pp. B1, B22.

8. Peter Fitzpatrick, "Airlines of the World—Unite," *The Financial Post,* November 22, 1997, p. 8.

9. See Rowland T. Moriarity and Ursala Moran, "Managing Hybrid Marketing Systems," November–December 1990, pp. 146–155.

10. Geoffrey Rowan, "Distributors Play Key Role in Computer Firms Success," *Globe and Mail,* February 20, 1995, pp. B1-B2.

11. See Stern and Sturdivant, "Customer-Driven Distribution Systems," p. 35.

12. Angela Kryhul, "Prescription for Savings," *Marketing,* December 6, 1993, p. 11.

13. Subhash C. Jain, *International Marketing Management,* 3rd ed. (Boston, MA: PWS-Kent Publishing, 1990), pp. 489–491. Also see Emily Thronton, "Revolution in Japanese Retailing," *Fortune,* February 7, 1994, pp. 143–147.

14. See Philip Cateora, *International Marketing,* 7th ed. (Homewood, IL: Irwin, 1990), pp. 570–571.

15. Jennifer Wells, "We Can Get It for You Wholesale," *Report on Business,* March 1995, pp. 52-62.

16. See James A. Narus and James C. Anderson, "Turn Your Industrial Distributors into Partners," *Harvard Business Review,* March–April 1986, pp. 66–71; and Marty Jacknis and Steve Kratz, "The Channel Empowerment Solution," *Sales & Marketing Management,* March 1993, pp. 44–49.

17. See Katherine M. Hafner, "Computer Retailers: Things Have Gone from Worse to Bad," *Business Week,* June 8, 1987, p. 104.

18. Ronald Henkoff, "Delivering the Goods," *Fortune,* November 18, 1994, pp. 64–78. Also see Shlomo

Maital, "The Last Frontier of Cost Reduction," *Across the Board,* February 1994, pp. 51–52.

19. Ibid., p. 52.

20. "Linking with Vendors for Just-In-Time Service," *Chain Store Age Executive,* June 1993, pp. 22A–24A; and Joseph Weber, "Just Get It to the Stores on Time," *Business Week,* March 6, 1995, pp. 66–67.

21. John Huey, "Wal-Mart: Will It Take Over the World?" *Fortune,* January 30, 1989, pp. 52–64.

22. Shawn Tully, "Comeback Ahead for Railroads," *Fortune,* June 17, 1991, pp. 107–113.

23. "Managing Logistics in the 1990s," *Logistics Perspectives,* Anderson Consulting, Cleveland, OH, July 1990, pp. 1–6.

24. Maital, "The Last Frontier of Cost Reduction," p. 51.

25. Sandra J. Skrovan, "Partnering with Vendors: The Ties that Bind," *Chain Store Age Executive,* January 1994, pp. 6MH–9MH.

26. Ibid., p. 6MH.

27. See Joseph Weber, "Just Get It to the Store on Time," *Business Week,* March 6, 1995, pp. 66–67; and Gary Robbins, "Pushing the Limits of VMI (Vendor Managed Inventory)," *Stores,* March 1995, p. 42.

28. Based on an address by Professor Donald J. Bowersox at Michigan State University on August 5, 1992.

29. Ibid., p. 68; and Gail DeGeorge, "Ryder Sees the Logic of Logistics," *Business Week,* August 5, 1996, p. 56.

30. See Stern, El-Ansary, and Coughlan, *Marketing Channels,* p. 160; Patrick Byrne, "A New roadmap for Contract Logistics," *Transportation & Distribution,* April 1993, pp. 58–62; Ronald Henkoff, "Delivering the Goods," *Fortune,* November 18, 1994, pp. 64–77; and Scott Wooley, "Replacing Inventory with Information," *Forbes,* March 24, 1997, pp. 54–58.

Company Case 12

ICON ACOUSTICS: BYPASSING TRADITION

THE DREAM

Like most entrepreneurs, Dave Fokos dreams a lot. He imagines customers eagerly phoning Icon Acoustics in Ottawa to order his latest, custom-made stereo speakers. He sees sales climbing, cash flowing, and hundreds of happy workers striving to produce top-quality products that delight Icon's customers.

Like most entrepreneurs, Dave has taken a long time to develop his dream. While majoring in electrical engineering at Queen's University, Dave discovered that he had a strong interest in audio engineering. Following graduation, Dave landed a job as a speaker designer with Conrad-Johnson, a high-end audio-equipment manufacturer. Within four years, Dave had

designed 13 speaker models and decided to start his own company.

Dave identified a market niche that he felt other speaker firms had overlooked. The niche consisted of "audio-addicts"—people who love to listen to music and appreciate first-rate stereo equipment. These affluent, well-educated customers are genuinely obsessed with their stereo equipment. "They'd rather buy a new set of speakers than eat," Dave observes.

Dave faced one major problem—how to distribute Icon's products. He had learned from experience at Conrad-Johnson that most manufacturers distribute their equipment primarily through stereo dealers. Dave did not hold a high opinion of most such dealers; he felt that they too often played hardball with manufacturers, forcing them to accept thin margins. Furthermore, the dealers concentrated on only a handful of well-known producers who provided mass-produced models. This kept those firms that offered more customized products from gaining access to the market. Perhaps most disturbing, Dave felt that the established dealers often sold not what was best for customers, but whatever they had in inventory that month.

Dave dreamed of offering high-end stereo loudspeakers directly to the audio-obsessed, bypassing the established dealer network. By going directly to the customers, Dave could avoid the dealer markups and offer top-quality products and service at reasonable prices.

THE PLAN

At age 28, Dave set out to turn his dreams into reality. Some customers who had gotten to know Dave's work became enthusiastic supporters of his dream and invested $189 000 in Icon. With their money and $10 000 of his own, Dave started Icon in a rented facility in an industrial park.

The Market. Approximately 335 stereo-speaker makers compete for a $3-billion annual North American market for audio components. About 100 of these manufacturers sell to the low- and mid-range segments of the market, which account for 90 percent of the market's unit volume and about 50 percent of its value. In addition to competing with each other, U.S. manufacturers also compete with Japanese firms that offer products at affordable prices. The remaining 235 or so manufacturers compete for the remaining 10 percent of the market's unit volume and 50 percent of the value—the high end—where Dave hopes to find his customers.

Icon's Marketing Strategy. To serve the audio-addicts segment, Dave offers only the highest-quality speakers. He has developed two models: the Lumen and the Parsec. The Lumen stands 45 cm high, weighs 11 kg, and is designed for stand mounting. The floor-standing Parsec is 1.2 m high and weighs 43 kg. Both models feature custom-made cabinets that come in natural or black oak and walnut. Dave can build and ship two pairs of the Lumen speakers or one pair of the Parsec speakers per day by himself. In order to have an adequate parts inventory, he had to spend $50 000 of his capital on the expensive components.

Dave set the price of the Lumen and Parsec at $795 and $1795 per pair, respectively. He selected these prices to provide a 50 percent gross margin. He believes that traditional dealers would sell equivalent speakers at retail at twice those prices. Customers can call Icon on a toll-free 800 number to order speakers or to get advice directly from Dave. Icon pays for shipping and any return freight via Federal Express—round-trip freight for a pair of Parsecs costs $486.

Dave offers to pay for the return freight because a key part of his promotional strategy is a 30-day, in-home, no-obligation trial. In his ads, Dave calls this "The 43 200 Minute, No Pressure Audition." This trial period allows customers to listen to the speakers in their

EXHIBIT 12-1 *Icon Acoustics's pro-forma financials ($ in thousands)*

YEAR	1	2	3	4	5
Pairs of Speakers Sold	224	435	802	1256	1830
Total Sales Revenue	$303	$654	$1299	$2153	$3338
Cost of Sales:					
Materials and Packaging	$130	$281	$561	$931	$1445
Shipping	$43	$83	$157	$226	$322
Total Cost of Sales	$173	$364	$718	$1157	$1767
Gross Profit	$130	$290	$581	$996	$1571
Gross Margin	43%	44%	45%	46%	47%
Expenses:					
New Property and Equipment	$3	$6	$12	$15	$18
Marketing	$13	$66	$70	$109	$135
General and Administrative	$51	$110	$197	$308	$378
Loan Repayment	$31	$31	$0	$0	$0
Outstanding Payables	$30	$0	$0	$0	$0
Total Expenses	$128	$213	$279	$432	$531
Pretax Profit	$2	$77	$302	$564	$1040
Pretax Margin	1%	12%	23%	26%	31%

actual listening environment. In a dealer's showroom, the customer must listen in an artificial environment and often feels pressure to make a quick decision.

Dave believes that typical high-end customers may buy speakers for "non-rational" reasons: They want a quality product and good sound, but they also want an image. Thus, Dave has tried to create a unique image through the appearance of his speakers and to reflect that image in all of the company's marketing. He spent over $40 000 on distinctive stationery, business cards, a brochure, and a single display ad. He also designed a laminated label he places just above the gold-plated input jack on each speaker. The label reads: "This loudspeaker was handcrafted by [the technician's name who assembled the speaker goes here in his/her own handwriting]. Made in Canada by Icon Acoustics, Inc.

To get the word out, Dave concentrates on product reviews in trade magazines and on trade shows, such as the High End Hi-Fi show in New York. Attendees at the show cast ballots to select "The Best Sound at the Show." In the balloting, among 200 brands, Icon's Parsec speakers finished fifteenth. Among the top 10 brands, the least expensive was a pair priced at $2400, and six of the systems were priced from $8000 to $18 000. A reviewer in an issue of *Stereophile* magazine evaluated Icon's speakers and noted: "The overall sound was robust and dynamic, with a particularly potent low end. Parts and construction quality appeared to be first rate. Definitely a company to watch."

Dave made plans to invest in a slick, four-colour display ad in *Stereo Review,* the consumer magazine with the highest circulation (600 000). He also expected another favourable review in *Stereophile* magazine.

THE REALITY

Dressed in jeans and a hooded sweatshirt, Dave pauses in the middle of assembling a cardboard shipping carton, pulls up a chair, and leans against the concrete-block wall of his manufacturing area. Reflecting on his experiences during his first year in business, Dave realizes he's learned a lot in jumping all the hurdles the typical entrepreneur faces. Dave experienced quality problems with the first cabinet supplier. Then, he ran short of a key component after a mixup with a second supplier.

Despite his desire to avoid debt, he had to borrow $50 000 from a bank. Prices for his cabinets and some components had risen, and product returns had been higher than expected (19 percent for the past six months). These price and cost increases put pressure on his margins, forcing Dave to raise his prices (to those quoted earlier). Despite the price increases, his margins remained below his 50 percent target.

Still, Dave feels good about his progress. The price increase does not seem to have affected demand. The few ads and word-of-mouth advertising appear to be working. Dave receives about five phone calls per day, with one in seven calls leading to a sale. Dave also feels the stress of the long hours and the low pay, however. He is not able to pay himself a high salary—just $9500 this year.

Dave reaches over and picks up his most recent financial projections from a workbench (see Exhibit 13-1). He believes that this will be a breakeven year—then he'll have it made. As Dave sets the projections back on the workbench, his mind drifts to his plans to introduce two exciting new speakers—the Micron ($2495 per pair) and the Millennium ($7995 per pair). He also wonders if there is a foreign market for his speakers. Should he use his same direct marketing strategy for foreign markets, or should he consider distributors? The dream continues.

QUESTIONS

1. What functions do traditional stereo dealers perform?

2. Why has Dave Fokos decided to establish a direct channel? What objectives and constraints have shaped his decision?

3. What consumer service needs do Dave's customers have?

4. What problems will Dave face as a result of his channel decisions? What changes would you recommend in Dave's distribution strategy, if any? Will his strategy work in foreign markets?

5. What other changes would you recommend in Dave's marketing strategy?

Source: Adapted from "Sound Strategy," *INC.,* May 1991, pp. 46–56. © 1991 by Goldhirsh Group, Inc. Used with permission. Dave Fokos also provided information to support development of this case.

Video Case 12

SELLING EARTH'S SOUNDS

Kevin O'Leary, a sound engineer, is hoping to gain a piece of the $100 million a year nature recordings industry. He is the founder and President of Earth Noise, a new independent record label that features recordings of various nature sounds. The Earth Noise recordings have very high sound quality and Kevin is convinced that they have the potential to capture a significant share of the market. But Kevin is having trouble getting the recordings to customers. Identifying and securing distribution channels has been difficult and Kevin is considering what he can do to ensure that his product reaches potential customers.

Earth Noise was started in 1995 with the production of its first recording, The Sounds of Algonquin. After that recording was finished, Kevin immediately made plans to leave for Guatemala and the Queen Charlotte Islands in BC to make two more recordings. His goal was to get as many CDs produced as possible so that he could get a catalogue of recordings together. He felt that the way to make profits in this industry was to establish a good distribution network for the label, but getting distribution with just one recording was virtually impossible. Distributors were more interested in selling an entire product line.

While making more recordings was necessary, it was also expensive. Travel and equipment costs required that Kevin get cash from investors. He hired Kathy Meisler, a sales and marketing manager, to, among other things, arrange for an outside investor. The result was an alliance with Audio Products International (API), the makers of Mirage audio speakers. They provided $28,000 to finance Kevin's trip to Guatemala in return for the use of Kevin's recordings to demonstrate their speakers. Kevin was positioning his recordings as audiophile quality recordings. This distinguished his label from most of his competitors and was an excellent fit with API's positioning of its high end speakers.

The other way that Kevin was distinguishing his recordings was by packaging them with a travel guide, including photos and artwork from the location of the recording. While other nature recordings have mixed nature sounds with music, Kevin's recordings do not. He is more interested in providing a realistic recreation of the environment where the recordings were made. He plans to call his series of CDs "A Day in the Life of..." and promote the fact that they are not generic recordings but, instead, relate to a specific place.

The recording sessions in Guatemala and BC went very well. In fact, in Guatemala Kevin recorded sounds for an unplanned CD. He met a family of drummers in Guatemala and so he recorded what will be sold as a World Music CD in addition to his nature recording. However, when the mixing of the CDs was done back in Canada, some interference on the Guatemala recordings meant that more money and time were spent getting the recordings ready for launch.

To continue to finance the mixing of the Guatemala CDs and a launch party for them, Kathy went back to API for more money. Although they had originally said they would not provide more cash until the CDs were ready, they agreed to invest another $10,000 to ensure that the project was completed. Both Kathy and Kevin were anxious for the CDs to be launched before the Christmas season, the busiest time for CD sales. So the launch party was set for late October, 1996. Industry representatives, media people and potential investors were invited to the launch and the response to the recordings was very positive.

While the launch was seen as a way to get the product out into distribution, it didn't prove to be successful. Earth Noise missed the Christmas season and in January, 1997 still had no distributor. In addition, Kathy had left the company which meant that Kevin was back to doing everything himself. Short of cash to complete the mixing of the BC recording, Kevin began to try to find other investors. He visited The Upper Canada Brewing Company to explore the idea of a cross promotion.

With no distribution arrangements in place yet, Kevin approached Page Distribution in late January, 1997. Page Distribution supplies approximately 1,000 stores and they agreed to take 100 CDs. Denon, an even larger distributor, showed some interest but wanted to wait until March to distribute the CDs, arguing that stores are not interested in anything new until then. So two years after its initial recording was ready, Earth Noise is just starting to be distributed to customers. As Kevin waits for customer response to his CDs, he continues looking for investors and plans still other CDs for the Earth Noise product line.

QUESTIONS:

1. What are the options available to Kevin for getting the Earth Noise CDs distributed?

2. What would you recommend that Kevin do to increase the distribution of his products?

Source: This case was prepared by Auleen Carson and is based on the *Venture* series episode "CD Man", which was first broadcast on February 9, 1997.

C H A P T E R 13

RETAILING AND WHOLESALING

MOUNTAIN
EQUIPMENT
CO-OP
Fall & Winter 1997

"Take hard-as-nails consumers. Add murderous competition. What do you get? Some sizzling opportunities for radical retailers." These are the opening lines of an article printed in *Canadian Business* in May 1997 that discusses what it takes to thrive in Canada's turbulent retail environment —an environment marked by some dramatic failures including the recent closing of Consumers Distributing and the near-bankruptcy and restructuring of Eaton's, but also by some equally dramatic successes as discussed below. While retailers follow very different strategies, they all share one distinguishing feature—the ability to anticipate what their customers want and provide that product or service before their competitors. But product selection alone isn't enough. Consumers also want outstanding service and stimulating retail environments, provided at a reasonable price.

Another retailing expert, Dr. Len Berry, puts it this way. Successful retailers are committed to "the creation of a compelling value for their target customers." Value is created by pricing products and services fairly, providing exciting merchandising, offering respectful service, and saving customers' time and energy. Another key in an era of the time-pressed consumer is making shopping more convenient and more fun. Creating stores that both entertain and provide goods and services is important since "shopping is both a rational and an emotional experience," claims John Torella, a Toronto retail consultant. Retailers must understand how to stimulate consumers' senses to make shopping a more enjoyable and satisfying experience.

If any one retailer in Canada understands and practises the principles discussed above, it is Victoria's Thrifty Foods. The company's 13 stores have won accolades from industry analysts and customers alike. Its state-of-the art products and personal service have made it the fastest-growing medium-sized supermarket chain in Canada. Customer satisfaction has always been the firm's mantra, and employees pride themselves on getting customers exactly what they want. Thrifty Foods strives to find products that will pique their customers' interest. Not only does the company understand the needs of its varied customers, but it also has the ability to turn something as banal as grocery shopping into a fun experience for the whole family. And entire families come to the stores: moms and dads and kids. The owners of the stores, the Campbell family, have

When you finish this chapter, you should be able to

1. Explain the roles of retailers and wholesalers in the distribution channel.

2. Describe the major types of retailers and give examples of each.

3. Identify the major types of wholesalers and give examples of each.

4. Explain the marketing decisions facing retailers and wholesalers.

spent a lot of time working with designers to develop the decor of its outlets. The stores are designed to blend into their surrounding neighbourhoods. They are a far cry from the barren brick and mortar stores of many of their rivals. You are more likely to find garden archways than cinder blocks. The one thing that binds the design of all the stores together is the desire to make customers feel comfortable and at home.

Thrifty also knows that if you treat your staff well, they will treat customers well—and they do! The firm spends an unprecedented $1 million annually on training to upgrade employees' skills. In fact the staff are so satisfied that Thrifty has low staff turnover rates that are the envy of the industry. Through its staff and the constant presence of the owners in the stores, Thrifty builds long-term relationships with its clientele.

Since 25 percent of Thrifty's clientele are young families, the grocery chain has created many products just for these time-pressed consumers. They also make their stores family-friendly. Not only do they provide cookies for the children and offer child-sized grocery carts that kids push around the store, but Thrifty also features changing rooms and nurseries. Also, instead of placing candy by the cash register, Thrifty makes the area "kid-friendly" by stocking cash-register displays with fresh fruit, nutritious snacks, and toothpaste.

Young families aren't their only target, however. Thrifty Foods also focuses on seniors. Their Sendial program, staffed by 230 volunteers, provides seniors and disabled customers with dial-in grocery order and delivery service. Tapping into the concerns of the communities in which they are located, Thrifty Foods strives to make its stores and products environmentally friendly. The company also aims to be a good corporate citizen in other ways. The company donates to dozens of causes but doesn't do so as part of its marketing efforts. Does all this goodwill translate into profit? It certainly does! Thrifty's sales per square metre are considerably above the industry average and the firm and its franchisees now dominate the Vancouver Island grocery trade.

Mountain Equipment Co-op
www.mec.ca

Mountain Equipment Co-operative (MEC) is another of Canada's outstanding retailing firms. A non-profit cooperative, MEC sells goods aimed at the weekend adventurer. It is highly focused and has only four stores, which are located in Vancouver, Calgary, Toronto, and Ottawa. However, the company also has a catalogue operation that serves members across Canada and from 130 countries around the world. The firm uses technology to its advantage using an online merchandising management system that allows MEC to be a truly quick-response retailer. Whereas it once took the firm seven days to process a catalogue order, MEC now sends out goods within 24 hours. The system allows the firm to fine-tune its inventory to the needs of its demanding clientele.

From 1992 to 1997, the company's sales have soared by an outstanding 285 percent during a period when expenditures on retail goods in Canada have grown at a rate of only two percent. MEC has ridden the wave of interest in sports such as climbing, kayaking, and back-country camping. Its customers are young, affluent, well educated, and dedicated to the company. In fact, they own the company. Each has purchased a $5 share to become a member of the co-op and each has an emotional bond with the company. Shareholders vote for MEC's directors and thus directly influence the direction of the business. MEC offers high-quality, genuine equipment at reasonable prices. The company pays its staff well and thus attracts some of the best people in the industry. Their service personnel provide outstanding service. Many of the people who work for the company are sports fanatics and thus are knowledgable about their products. They know the stores like the back of their hands and can help customers locate products quickly and effectively. A time-pressed consumer rushed into the Toronto store recently with only 10 minutes to shop before she had to catch a train home. In that period, staff helped her find a fleece jacket, water bottle, and hiking socks, pay for her purchases and get out the door. "For service like that, I wait until I can travel the 250 km to come here!" she exclaimed.

Retailers aren't just restricted to firms that sell products. Retailers also sell services. When we look at services retailing, one truly outstanding firm is Montreal-based Air Transat. Nothing makes their CEO angrier than to hear the firm classified as an airline. They are a tour operator, he insists, and airplanes are just one of their tools. This is a firm that uses a vertical marketing system (see Chapter 12). Founded in 1987, Air Transat followed the example set by firms in the European travel industry. Their business concept linked the three key pillars of the holiday travel industry: travel agencies, vacation packages, and airlines. When someone visits one of its 321 travel agents, they are offered both an airline ticket and an exciting vacation package. Since Air Transat brings so many people to a location, it can negotiate with quality resorts to receive very competitive prices. Air Transat's ability to pre-book its flights means that it only flies its planes when they are booked to capacity. In periods of low demand, it can leave the planes on the ground and not incur the heavy expenses of half-full flights. Their vertical integration approach has been a competitive advantage for the firm. Air Transat has a unique model, the only one of its kind in North America. In fact, it has been so successful that today it has the leading share (36 percent) in the Canadian charter holiday market.

Air Transat is highly profitable in an industry that has been plagued by failure. Since 1989, 10 other independent charter airlines companies started up—only to go out of business. From its inception, Air Transat was able to offer affordable vacations to exotic locations in the Caribbean and Europe. It pioneered trips to many areas, such as the Dominican Republic, before any of its competitors had recognized the potential of the region. The company books Canadians on flights to Europe and flies its planes back to Canada full of Europeans who are anxious to visit what Air Transat markets as a "New World Experience with an Old World Charm." Air Transat can keep its prices low because it is a stickler about costs. The company has expanded globally by purchasing troubled companies at bargain-basement prices and then integrating them into the Air Transat family. It flies cheaper, older aircraft that it packs with passengers. For Air Transat, providing high-quality services at reasonable prices brings vacationers back again and again. Not a bad formula for success![1]

The three examples exemplify the dramatic changes taking place today in Canada's retailing industry. While there is no single formula for success, all of the retailers described above have adapted to a rapidly changing environment to provide the exceptional customer value that binds customers to these firms. In addition to working with customers, all these firms also work to develop exceptional relationships with all members of their channels, from suppliers to wholesalers. In the first section of this chapter, we look at the nature and importance of retailing, major types of store and non-store retailers, the decisions retailers make, and the future of retailing in Canada and abroad. In the second section, we discuss these same topics as they relate to wholesalers.

RETAILING

Retailing
All activities involved in selling goods or services directly to final consumers for their personal, non-business use.

Retailers
Businesses whose sales come *primarily* from retailing.

What is retailing? We all know that Wal-Mart, Eaton's, and The Bay are retailers, but so are Avon representatives, the local Holiday Inn, and Internet marketers. **Retailing** includes all the activities involved in selling goods or services directly to final consumers for their personal, non-business use. Many institutions—manufacturers, wholesalers, and not-for-profit organizations—do retailing. But most retailing is done by **retailers**: businesses whose sales come *primarily* from retailing—reselling goods to end consumers. And although most retailing is done in retail stores, in recent years non-store retailing—selling by mail, telephone, door-to-door contact, vending machines, and numerous electronic means—has grown tremendously. Because store retailing accounts for most of the retail business, we discuss it first. We then look at non-store retailing.

STORE RETAILING

Retail stores come in all shapes and sizes, and new retail types keep emerging. They can be classified by one or more of several characteristics: *amount of service, product line, relative prices, control of outlets,* and *type of store cluster.* Table 13-1 shows these classifications and the corresponding retailer types.

AMOUNT OF SERVICE

Different products require different amounts of service, and customer service preferences vary. Retailers may offer one of three levels of service—self-service, limited service, and full service.

Self-service retailers increased rapidly in Canada during the Great Depression of the 1930s. Customers were willing to perform their own "locate-compare-select" process to save money. Today, self-service is the basis of all discount operations and typically is used by sellers of convenience goods (such as supermarkets) and nationally branded, fast-moving shopping goods (such as The Future Shop).

Limited-service retailers, such as Sears or Saan stores, provide more sales assistance because they carry more shopping goods about which customers need information. Their increased operating costs result in higher prices. In *full-service retailers,* such as specialty stores and first-class department stores, salespeople assist customers in every phase of the shopping process. Full-service stores usually carry more specialty goods for which customers like to be "waited on." They provide more liberal return policies, various credit plans, free delivery, home servicing, and extras such as lounges and restaurants. More services result in much higher operating costs, which are passed along to customers as higher prices.

PRODUCT LINE

Retailers also can be classified by the length and breadth of their product assortments. Some retailers, such as **specialty stores**, carry a narrow product line with a deep assortment within that line. Examples include stores selling sporting goods, furniture, books, electronics, flowers, or toys. Today, specialty stores are flourishing for several reasons. The increasing use of market segmentation, market targeting, and product specialization has resulted in a greater need for stores that focus on specific products and segments.

In contrast, **department stores** carry a wide variety of product lines. Department stores grew rapidly through the first half of this century. However, over the past few decades, department stores have been squeezed between more focused and flexible specialty stores on the one hand, and more efficient, lower-priced discounters on the other. In response, many have added "bargain basements" and promotional events to meet the discount threat. Others have set up store

Specialty store
A retail store that carries a narrow product line with a deep assortment within that line.

Department store
A retail organization that carries a wide variety of product lines—typically clothing, home furnishings, and household goods; each line is operated as a separate department managed by specialist buyers or merchandisers.

Today, specialty stores are flourishing: they offer high-quality products, convenient locations, good hours, and excellent service.

TABLE 13-1   *Major Types of Retailers*

Type	Description	Examples
Speciality Stores	Carry a narrow product line with a deep assortment within that line; apparel stores, sporting-goods stores, furniture stores, florists, and bookstores. Speciality stores can be subclassified by the degree of narrowness in their product line. A clothing store would be a *single-line store*; a men's clothing store would be a *limited-line store*; and a men's custom-shirt store would be a *superspecialty store*.	Tall Men (tall-men's clothing); The Limited (women's clothing); The Body Shop (cosmetics and bath supplies)
Department Stores	Carry several product lines—typically clothing, home furnishings, and household goods—with each line operated as a separate department managed by specialist buyers or merchandisers.	Sears, Eaton's, The Bay
Supermarkets	Relatively large, low-cost, low-margin, high-volume, self-service operations designed to serve the consumer's total needs for food, laundry, and household-maintenance products.	Safeway Foods, A&P, Loblaws, Sobeys, Thrifty
Convenience Stores	Relatively small stores that are located near residential areas, operate long hours seven days a week, and carry a limited line of high-turnover convenience products. Their long hours and their use by consumers mainly for "fill-in" purchases make them relatively high-price operations.	7-11, Beckers, Mac's, Couche-Tard, Provi-Soir
Superstores	Larger stores that aim at meeting consumers' total needs for routinely purchased food and non-food items. They include *supercentres*, combined supermarket and discount stores, which feature cross merchandising. They also include so-called *"category killers"* that carry a very deep assortment of a particular line. Another superstore variation is *hypermarkets*, huge stores that combine supermarket, discount, and warehouse retailing to sell routinely purchased goods as well as furniture, large and small appliances, clothing, and many other items.	*Supercentres:* Wal-Mart Supercentres; *Category killers:* Toys 'R' Us (toys), Petsmart (pet supplies), Chapters (books), Home Depot (home improvement), Best Buy (consumer electronics); *Hypermarkets:* Carrefour (France); Pycra (Spain), Meijer's (Netherlands)
Discount Stores	Sell standard merchandise at lower prices by accepting lower margins and selling higher volumes. A true discount store *regularly* sells its merchandise at lower prices, offering mostly national brands, not inferior goods. Discount retailers include both general merchandise and speciality merchandise stores.	*General discount stores:* Wal-Mart, Zellers; *Speciality discount stores:* Future Shop (electronics), Crown Bookstores (books)
Off-Price Retailers	Sell a changing and unstable collection of higher-quality merchandise, often leftover goods, overruns, and irregulars obtained at reduced prices from manufacturers or other retailers. They buy at less than regular wholesale prices and charge consumers less than retail. They include three main types:	
Independent off-price retailers	Owned and run by entrepreneurs or by divisions of larger retail corporations.	T.J.Maxx, Winners
Factory Outlets	Owned and operated by manufacturers and normally carry the manufacturer's surplus, discontinued, or irregular goods. Such outlets increasingly group together in *factory outlet malls*, where dozens of outlet stores offer prices as much as 50 percent below retail on a broad range of items.	Dansk (dinnerware), Dexter (shoes), Ralph Lauren and Liz Claiborne (upscale apparel)
Warehouse clubs (or wholesale clubs)	Sell a limited selection of brand-name grocery items, appliances, clothing, and a hodgepodge of other goods at deep discounts to members who pay $25 to $50 annual membership fees. They serve small businesses and other club members out of huge, low-overhead, warehouse-like facilities and offer few frills or services.	Wal-Mart-owned Sam's Club, Max Clubs, Price-Costco, BJ's Wholesale Club
Catalogue Showrooms	Sell a broad selection of high-markup, fast-moving, brand-name goods at discount prices. These include jewellery, power tools, cameras, luggage, small appliances, toys, and sporting goods. Customers order the goods from a catalogue in the showroom, then pick them up from a merchandise pick-up area in the store.	Service Merchandise, Best Products

brand programs, "boutiques" and "designer shops" (such as Tommy Hilfiger or Polo shops within department stores), and other store formats that compete with specialty stores. Still others are trying mail-order, telephone, and web site selling. Service and outstanding product assortments remain the key differentiating factors.

Supermarkets are large, low-cost, low-margin, high-volume, self-service stores that carry a wide variety of food, laundry, and household products. They are the most frequently shopped type of retail store. Most Canadian supermarket stores are owned by supermarket chains such as Safeway, Loblaw, A&P, Dominion, and Penner Foods. Chains account for almost 70 percent of all supermarket sales.

Today, most supermarkets are facing slow sales growth because of slower population growth and an increase in competition from convenience stores, discount food stores, and superstores. They also have been hit hard by the rapid growth of out-of-home eating. Thus, supermarkets are looking for new ways to build their sales. Most chains now operate fewer but larger stores. They practise "scrambled merchandising," and carry many non-food items—beauty aids, housewares, toys, prescriptions, appliances, videocassettes, sporting goods, garden supplies—hoping to find high-margin lines to improve profits. They also are improving their facilities and services to attract more customers. Many supermarkets are "moving upscale," providing "from-scratch" bakeries, gourmet deli counters, and fresh seafood departments. Others are cutting costs, establishing more efficient operations, and lowering prices to compete more effectively with food discounters.

Convenience stores are small stores that carry a limited line of high-turnover convenience goods. These stores locate near residential areas and remain open long hours, seven days a week. When supermarkets won the right to open for business on Sundays, and drugstore chains and gas station boutiques began selling grocery and snack foods, convenience stores lost their monopoly on their key differentiating variable—*convenience*. The result has been a huge industry shakeout and a tremendous repositioning effort for many of these 17 500 stores across Canada. While many "mom-and-pop" stores are closing, others are being purchased by the large chains that now dominate the industry. For example, Toronto's Silcorp owns Mac's, Mike's Mart, Becker's, and Daisy Mart for a total of 1083 stores. Quebec's Couche-Tard operates 635 Depan-Escompte, Provi-soir, and Wink outlets. 7-Eleven, headquartered in Dallas, has 456 stores across Canada.

Whereas once these stores sold overpriced emergency goods, they now are repositioning themselves as "destination" outlets that offer many types of conveniences ranging from automated teller and stamp machines, to faxes and photocopiers. Like their larger rivals, convenience-store chains have started branding their own food items. They are investing heavily to redesign their stores to match the needs of their local neighbourhoods. Those in upscale areas offer baked goods such as croissants that customers can eat at in-store cafés. Those who find themselves in areas frequented by male, blue-collar workers stock meat-laden Subway-brand sandwiches. Couche-Tard is investing heavily in employee training so that the chain of stores can offer service that rivals their larger competitors. The company sends out flyers announcing their specials just like the supermarkets, and they offer mouth-watering fresh-baked goods, all allowing them to significantly increase their profits.[2]

Superstores are much larger than regular supermarkets and carry a large assortment of routinely purchased food and nonfood items.

Supervalu is an excellent example of a superstore—it even calls itself "the real Canadian Superstore." With locations from Thunder Bay, Ontario west to Vancouver, British Columbia, they have locations in all of western Canada's major cities. They even have a location in Whitehorse to service consumers in the Yukon. Its stores carry everything from telephones and children's apparel to fresh fruits and seafood.

Recent years have also seen the advent of superstores that are actually giant specialty stores, the so-called *category killers*. These "big-box" retailers are the

---

Supermarkets
Large, low-cost, low-margin, high-volume, self-service stores that carry a wide variety of food, laundry, and household products.

Convenience store
A small store located near a residential area that is open long hours seven days a week and carries a limited line of high-turnover convenience goods.

Superstore
A store almost twice the size of a regular supermarket that carries a large assortment of routinely purchased food and non-food items and offers such services as dry cleaning, post offices, photo finishing, cheque cashing, bill paying, lunch counters, car care, and pet care.

Convenience stores, such as 7-Eleven, are usually located in residential areas and remain open for long hours, seven days a week.

megastores that have crossed the border from the United States during the last decade. They have stores the size of airplane hangers that carry a wide assortment of a particular line with a knowledgeable staff. Category killers are prevalent in a wide range of categories. Home Depot Canada, Chapters, Office Depot, The Sports Authority, and Michaels Crafts are among the many recent entrants into the Canadian marketplace.

Another superstore variation, *hypermarkets*, are huge superstores, perhaps as large as six football fields. Although hypermarkets have been very successful in Europe and other world markets, they have met with little success in North America. Despite their size, most hypermarkets have only limited product variety, and many people balk at the serious walking required to shop in them.

Service retailers
Retailers that sell services rather than products.

Finally, for some businesses, the "product line" is actually a service. **Service retailers** include hotels and motels, banks, airlines, universities, movie theatres, tennis clubs, bowling alleys, restaurants, repair services, hair-care shops, and dry cleaners. Service retailers in Canada are growing faster than product retailers, and each service industry has its own retailing drama. Banks look for new ways to distribute their services, including on-line banking, automatic tellers, direct deposit, and telephone banking. Professional service providers—firms composed of lawyers, architects, chartered accountants, physiotherapists, or dentists—are just beginning to understand the importance of marketing. And universities are battling as never before to attract students into their programs.

RELATIVE PRICES

The third way retailers can be classified is according to the prices they charge. Most retailers charge regular prices and offer normal-quality goods and customer service. Some offer higher-quality goods and service at higher prices. The retailers that feature low prices are discount stores, "off-price" retailers, and catalogue showrooms.

Discount store
A retail institution that sells standard merchandise at lower prices by accepting lower margins and selling at higher volume.

A **discount store** sells standard merchandise at lower prices by accepting lower margins and selling at higher volume. The early discount stores cut expenses by operating in warehouse-like facilities in low-rent, heavily travelled districts. In recent years, facing intense competition from other discounters and department stores, many discount retailers have "traded up." They have improved decor,

Off-price retailers
Retailers that buy at less than regular wholesale prices and sell at less than retail. They include factory outlets, independents, and warehouse clubs.

Factory outlets
Off-price retailing operations that are owned and operated by manufacturers and that normally carry the manufacturer's surplus, discontinued, or irregular goods.

Independent off-price retailers
Off-price retailers that are either owned and run by entrepreneurs or are divisions of larger retail corporations.

Warehouse club (wholesale club)
Off-price retailer that sells a limited selection of brand-name grocery items, appliances, clothing, and a hodgepodge of other goods at deep discounts to members who pay annual membership fees.

added new lines and services, and opened suburban branches, which has led to higher costs and prices.

When the major discount stores traded up, a new wave of **off-price retailers** moved in to fill the low-price, high-volume gap. Ordinary discounters buy at regular wholesale prices and accept lower margins to keep prices down. In contrast, off-price retailers buy at less than regular wholesale prices and charge consumers less than retail. Off-price retailers have made the biggest inroads in clothing, accessories, and footwear. But they can be found in all areas, from discount brokerages to food stores and electronics.

The three main types of off-price retailers are *factory outlets, independents,* and *warehouse clubs.* **Factory outlets** are owned and operated by manufacturers and normally carry the manufacturer's surplus, discontinued, or irregular goods. Examples are Arrow Shirts, the Nike Factory Outlet, and the Danier Leather Factory outlet. Such outlets sometimes group together in *factory outlet malls,* where dozens of outlet stores offer prices as low as 50 percent below retail on a wide range of items.

Independent off-price retailers are either owned and run by entrepreneurs or are divisions of larger retail corporations. Although many off-price operations are run by smaller independents, most large off-price retailer operations are owned by bigger retail chains. Examples include Winners, which is owned by U.S.-based TJX.

Warehouse clubs (or *wholesale clubs,* or *membership warehouses*) such as Price-Costco sell a limited selection of brand name grocery items, appliances, clothing, and a hodgepodge of other goods at deep discounts to members who pay annual membership fees. They operate in huge, warehouse-like facilities and offer few frills. Such clubs make no home deliveries and accept no credit cards, but they do offer rock-bottom prices. Warehouse clubs took the country by storm in the 1980s, but their growth slowed considerably in the 1990s as a result of growing competition among warehouse store chains and effective reactions by supermarkets.

In general, although off-price retailing blossomed during the 1980s, competition has stiffened as more and more off-price retailers have entered the market. The growth of off-price retailing slowed a bit recently because of effective counterstrategies by department stores and regular discounters. Still, off-price retailing remains a vital and growing force in modern retailing.

Warehouse clubs operate in huge, low-overhead, warehouse-like facilities, and customers must wrestle large items to the checkout line. But such clubs offer rock-bottom prices.

Catalogue showroom
A retail operation that sells a wide selection of high-markup, fast-moving, brand name goods at discount prices.

A **catalogue showroom** sells a wide selection of high-markup, fast-moving, brand-name goods at discount prices. These include jewellery, power tools, cameras, luggage, small appliances, toys, and sporting goods. Catalogue showrooms make their money by cutting costs and margins to provide low prices that will attract a higher volume of sales. Canada's catalogue showroom industry was led by Consumers Distributing, which declared bankruptcy in 1996. It and its counterparts have been struggling in recent years as off-price retailers consistently beat catalogue showroom prices.

CONTROL OF OUTLETS

The fourth way to classify a retailer is by asking "Who controls the outlet?" Is it independently owned or part of a chain? Forms or ownership include *independent, owner-operated* stores, *corporate chains, voluntary chains* and *retail cooperatives, franchise organizations,* and *merchandising conglomerates.* Retailing is more concentrated in Canada than it is in the United States. Over 40 percent of Canadian retailers belong to some type of chain compared to 20 percent in the United States. In some sectors, the average is even higher. In the grocery sector, for example, over 65 percent of the market is controlled by chain stores. Table 13-2 shows Canada"s top merchandisers.

Corporate chain stores
Two or more outlets that are commonly owned and controlled, have central buying and merchandising, and sell similar lines of merchandise.

Chain stores are two or more outlets that are commonly owned and controlled, employ central buying and merchandising, and sell similar lines of merchandise. **Corporate chains** appear in all types of retailing, but they are strongest in department stores, variety stores, food stores, drugstores, shoe stores, and women's clothing stores. Corporate chains have many advantages over independents. Their size allows them to buy in large quantities at lower prices. They can afford to hire corporate-level specialists to deal with areas such as pricing, promotion, merchandising, inventory control, and sales forecasting. And chains gain promotional economies because their advertising costs are spread over many stores and over a large sales volume. Table 13-3 shows the major types of retail organizations.

Voluntary chain
A wholesaler-sponsored group of independent retailers that engages in group buying and common merchandising.

Retailer cooperative
A group of independent retailers that bands together to set up a jointly owned central wholesale operation and conducts joint merchandising and promotion efforts.

The great success of corporate chains caused many independents to band together in one of two forms of contractual associations. One is the **voluntary chain**—a wholesaler-sponsored group of independent retailers that engages in group buying and common merchandising. The most recognizable examples of this form are the Independent Grocers Alliance (IGA) and Western Auto. The other form of contractual association is the **retailer cooperative**—a group of independent retailers that bands together to set up a jointly owned central wholesale operation and conducts joint merchandising and promotion efforts. True Value Hardware is an example of this contractual association. These organizations give

TABLE 13-2 *Canada's Top 10 Merchandisers*

Rank	Company	1996 Revenues ($ 000s)
1	George Weston Ltd.	12 966 000
2	The Oshawa Group	6 160 700
3	Hudson's Bay Co.	5 984 518
4	Provigo Inc.	5 725 200
5	Canada Safeway Ltd.	4 795 900
6	Sears Canada Ltd.	3 918 325
7	Canadian Tire Corp., Ltd.	3 771 304
8	Shoppers Drug Mart Ltd.	3 298 315
9	Métro-Richelieu Inc.	3 145 600
10	Empire Co. Ltd.	2 699 535

Source: Industry Leaders, The Financial Post 500, 1996, p. 148. Reprinted with permission.

TABLE 13-3 *Major Types of Retail Organizations*

Type	Description	Examples
Corporate Chain Stores	Two or more outlets that are commonly owned and controlled, employ central buying and merchandising, and sell similar lines of merchandise. Corporate chains appear in all types of retailing, but they are strongest in department stores, variety stores, drugstores, shoe stores, and women's clothing stores.	La Senze (lingerie), Sports Experts (sports goods), Loblaws (grocery)
Voluntary Chains	Wholesaler-sponsored groups of independent retailers engaged in bulk buying and common merchandising.	Independent Grocers Alliance (IGA), Western Auto, True Value Hardware
Retailer Cooperatives	Groups of independent retailers who set up a central buying organization and conduct joint promotion efforts.	Calgary Group (groceries), ACE (hardware), Mountain Equipment Co-op (outdoor goods)
Franchise Organizations	Contractual association between a *franchiser* (a manufacturer, wholesaler, or organization) and *franchisees* (independent businesspeople who buy the right to own and operate one or more units in the franchise system). Franchise organizations are normally based on some unique product, service, or method of doing business, or on a trade name or patent, or on goodwill that the franchiser has developed.	McDonald's, Subway, Pizza Hut, Jiffy Lube, 7-Eleven, Yogen Früz
Merchandising Conglomerates	A free-form corporation that combines several diversified retailing lines and forms under central ownership, along with some integration of their distribution and management functions.	Dayton-Hudson, F.W. Woolworth

Franchise
A contractual association between a manufacturer, wholesaler, or service organization (a franchiser) and independent businesspeople (franchisees) who buy the right to own and operate one or more units in the franchise system.

independents the buying and promotion economies they need to meet the prices of corporate chains.

A **franchise** is a contractual association between a manufacturer, wholesaler, or service organization (the franchiser) and independent businesspeople (the franchisees) who buy the right to own and operate one or more units in the franchise system. The main difference between a franchise and other contractual systems (voluntary chains and retail cooperatives) is that franchise systems typically are based on some unique product or service; on a method of doing business; or on the trade name, goodwill, or patent that the franchiser has developed. Franchising has been prominent in fast-food companies, motels, gas stations, video stores, health and fitness centres, auto rentals, hair-cutting salons, real estate and travel agencies, and dozens of other product and service areas. Franchising is described in detail in Marketing Highlight 13-1.

Merchandising conglomerates are corporations that combine several different retailing forms under central ownership and share some distribution and management functions. For example, F. W. Woolworth, in addition to its variety stores, operates 28 specialty chains, including the Northern group of stores, which is composed of Northern Reflections, Northern Traditions, Northern Elements, and Northern Getaway as well as Kinney Shoe Stores, and Foot Locker (sports shoes). Diversified retailing, which provides superior management systems and economies that benefit all the separate retail operations, is likely to increase through to the end of the 1990s.

NON-STORE RETAILING

Although most goods and services are sold through stores, non-store retailing has been growing much faster than store retailing. Traditional store retailers are facing increasing competition from non-store retailers who sell through catalogues, direct mail, telephone, home TV shopping shows, the Internet, home and office parties, and other direct retailing approaches. Non-store retailing may account for a third of all sales by the end of the century. Non-store retailing includes *direct marketing*, *direct selling*, and *automatic vending*.

FRANCHISE FEVER

Once considered upstarts among independent businesses, franchises now command 40 percent of all retail sales in Canada and 35 percent of those in the United States. There are 25 000 franchised establishments in Canada generating $30 billion in sales. These days, it's nearly impossible to stroll down a city block or drive on a suburban street without seeing a Wendy's, a McDonald's, a Jiffy Lube, or a 7-Eleven. One of the best-known and most successful franchisers, McDonald's, now has 21 000 stores worldwide and racks up more than $42 billion in systemwide sales. Gaining fast is Subway Sandwiches and Salads, one of the fastest-growing franchises, with more than 8500 shops in North America. Franchising is even moving into new areas such as education. For example, LearnRight Corporation franchises its methods for teaching students thinking skills.

How does a franchising system work? The individual franchises are a tightly knit group of enterprises whose systematic operations are planned, directed, and controlled by the operation's innovator, called a *franchisor*. Generally, franchises are distinguished by three characteristics:

1. *The franchisor owns a trade or service mark and licenses it to franchisees in return for royalty payments.*

2. *The franchisee is required to pay for the right to be part of the system.* Yet this initial fee is only a small part of the total amount that franchisees invest when they sign a franchising contract. Start-up costs include rental and lease of equipment and fixtures, and sometimes a regular licence fee. McDonald's franchisees may invest as much as $864 000 in initial start-up costs. The franchisee then pays McDonald's a service fee and a rental charge that equal 11.5 percent of the franchisee's sales volume. Subway's success is partly due to its low start-up cost of $65 000 to $100 000, which is lower than 70 percent of other franchise system start-up costs.

3. *The franchisor provides its franchisees with a marketing and oper-*

ations system for doing business. McDonald's requires franchisees to attend its "Hamburger University" in Oak Brook, Illinois, for three weeks to learn how to manage the business. Franchisees must also adhere to certain procedures in buying materials.

In the best cases, franchising is mutually beneficial to both franchisor and franchisee. Franchisors can cover a new territory in little more than the time it takes the franchisee to sign a contract. They can achieve enormous purchasing power (consider the purchase order that Holiday Inn is likely to make for bed linens, for instance). Franchisors also benefit from the franchisee's familiarity with local communities and conditions, and from the motivation and hard work of employees who are entrepreneurs rather than "hired hands." Similarly, franchisees benefit from buying into a proven business with a well-known and accepted brand name. And they receive ongoing support in areas ranging from marketing and advertising to site selection, staffing, and financing.

As a result of the franchise explosion in recent years, many types of franchisors are having difficulty. John Lorinc, author of *Opportunity Knocks: The Truth About Canada's Franchise Industry*, says 35 percent of all franchises fail and 80 percent may only break even. Subway, in particular, has been criticized for misleading its franchisees by telling them that it has only a two percent failure rate when the reality is much different. Some franchisees also believe that they've been misled by exaggerated claims of support, only to feel abandoned after the contract is signed and $100 000 is invested. Difficulties may arise due to hidden costs imposed on franchisees or the signing up of people who lack the resources to get the business off the ground. The most common complaint: Franchisors focused on growth above all else who "encroach" on existing franchisees' territory by bringing in another store. Or franchisees may object to parent-company marketing programs that may adversely affect their local operations. For instance, franchisees strongly resisted McDonald's promotion, in which the company reduced prices on Big Macs and Egg

McMuffins in an effort to revive stagnant sales. Many franchisees believed that the promotion might cheapen McDonald's image and unnecessarily reduce their profit margins.

There will *always* be a conflict between the franchisors, who seek systemwide growth, and the franchisees, who want to earn a good living from their individual franchises. Some new directions that may deliver both franchisor growth and franchisee earnings are:

◆ *Strategic alliances, co-branding, and twinning.* The newest trend in franchising is the marriage between two independent franchises at a single location. Tim Hortons, for example, can often be found sharing facilities with Wendy's; Baskin-Robbins teams up with Dunkin Donuts; Second Cup partners with Harvey's. Since the largest costs borne by franchises are for land and staff, forming a alliance with another franchisee to share a location makes economic sense and can draw a more broad-based market to the joint outlets.

◆ *New Code of Ethics.* Each member of the Canadian Franchise Association is bound by a code of ethics designed to overcome some areas of difficulty. The code stipulates the following conditions: there will be a full and accurate written disclosure of all information considered material to the franchise relationship; the company selling the franchise will provide reasonable guidance, training, and supervision for franchisees; fairness shall characterize all dealings between the franchisor and its franchisees; and the franchisor shall make every effort to resolve complaints, grievances and disputes through fair and reasonable negotiation.

◆ *Expansion abroad.* Fast-food franchises have become very popular around the world. For example, Domino's has entered Japan with master franchisee Ernest Higa, which owns 106 stores in Japan with combined sales of $140 million. Part of Higa's success can be attributed to adapting Domino's product to the Japanese market, where food presentation is everything.

Higa carefully charted the placement of pizza toppings and made cutmark perforations in the boxes for perfectly uniform slices.

♦ *Non-traditional site locations.* Franchises are opening in airports, sports stadiums, university campuses, hospitals, gambling casinos, theme parks, convention halls, and even river boats.

Thus, it appears, franchise fever will not cool down soon. Experts expect that by the turn of the century,

franchises will capture more almost 50 percent of all North American sales.

Sources: Norman D. Axelrad and Robert E. Weigand, "Franchising—A Marriage of System Members," in Sidney Levy, George Frerichs, and Howard Gordon, eds., *Marketing Managers Handbook*, 3d ed. (Chicago: Darnell, 1994), pp. 919–934; Lawrence S. Welch, "Developments in International Franchising," *Journal of Global Marketing*, Vol. 6, Nos. 1–2, 1992, pp. 81–96; Andrew E. Serwer, "McDonald's Conquers the World," *Fortune*, October 17, 1994, pp. 103–116; "Trouble in Franchise

Nation," *Fortune*, March 6, 1995, pp. 115–129; Robert Maynard, "The Decision to Franchise," *Nation's Business*, January 1997, pp. 49–53; Cliff Edwards, "'Campaign 55' Flop Shows Growing Power of Franchisees," *Marketing News*, July 7, 1997, p. 9; "Canadian Franchise Association Code of Ethics," Advertising Supplement, *Globe and Mail*, September 18, 1996, p. 6; Jennifer Lanthier, "How Franchises Seduce Those with the Most to Lose," *The Financial Post*, April 22, 1997, p. 28, Susan Noakes, "Creating Marriages of Convenience," *The Financial Post*, February 14, 1997, p. 16; www.cfa.ca/

DIRECT MARKETING

Direct marketing
Marketing through various advertising media that interact directly with consumers, generally calling for the consumer to make a direct response.

Direct marketing uses various media to interact directly with consumers, generally calling for the consumer to make a direct response. While mass marketing and advertising typically reach an unspecified number of people, most of whom are not in the market for a product or will not buy it until some future date, direct-advertising vehicles are used to obtain immediate orders directly from targeted consumers. Although direct marketing initially consisted mostly of direct mail and mail-order catalogues, it has taken on several additional forms in recent years, including telemarketing, direct radio and television marketing, and on-line computer shopping and Internet shopping.

Direct marketing has boomed in recent years. All kinds of organizations use direct marketing: manufacturers, retailers, service companies, catalogue merchants, and non-profit organizations, to name a few. Its growing use in consumer marketing is largely a response to the increasing fragmentation of the world's mass markets into subsegments with distinct needs and wants. Direct marketing allows sellers to focus efficiently on these minimarkets with offers that better match specific consumer needs. It allows the seller to build continuous customer relationships by tailoring a steady stream of offers to a regular customer's specific needs and interests.

Other environmental and technological forces have also contributed to the rapid growth of direct marketing. For example, an increasingly complex, busy, and hassle-filled shopping environment has made shopping from home more attractive. New computer and communications technologies have given marketers the ability to keep better track of customers and their needs, to customize their offers, and to communicate individually with customers. Direct marketing also has grown rapidly in business-to-business marketing, as sellers look for new ways to market their goods and services more quickly, inexpensively, and conveniently.

The most rapidly growing area of direct marketing is online marketing—selling conducted through interactive online computer systems that link consumers with sellers electronically. As more and more buyers have gained access to the Internet, the use of online marketing by both consumer and business-to-business marketers has grown dramatically. We discuss direct marketing and the burgeoning field of online marketing fully in Chapter 17.

DIRECT SELLING

Door-to-door retailing
Selling door to door, office to office, or at home-sales parties.

Door-to-door retailing, which started centuries ago with roving peddlers, has grown into a huge industry. More than 600 companies sell their products door to door,

Door-to-door and in-home selling provide customers with convenience and personal attention, but higher costs result in higher prices.

office to office, or at home-sales parties. The pioneers in door-to-door selling are the Fuller Brush Company, vacuum cleaner companies like Electrolux, and book-selling companies, such as World Book. The image of door-to-door selling improved greatly when Avon entered the industry with its Avon representative—the homemaker's friend and beauty consultant. Tupperware and Mary Kay Cosmetics helped to popularize home sales parties, in which several friends and neighbours attend a party at a private home where products are demonstrated and sold.

The advantages of door-to-door selling are consumer convenience and personal attention. But the high costs of hiring, training, paying, and motivating the sales force result in higher prices. Although some door-to-door companies are still thriving, door-to-door selling has a somewhat uncertain future. The increase in the number of single-person and working-couple households decreases the chances of finding a buyer at home. Home-party companies are having trouble finding non-working women who want to sell products part time. And with recent advances in interactive direct-marketing technology, the door-to-door salesperson may well be replaced in the future by the household telephone, television, or home computer.

AUTOMATIC VENDING

Automatic vending
Selling through vending machines.

Automatic vending is not new—in 215 B.C. Egyptians could buy sacrificial water from coin-operated dispensers. But this method of selling soared after World War II. There are now over half a million vending machines in Canada—approximately one machine for every 55 people. Today's automatic vending uses space-age and computer technology to sell a wide variety of convenience and impulse goods—cigarettes, beverages, candy, newspapers, foods and snacks, hosiery, cosmetics, paperback books, T-shirts, insurance policies, pizza, audio tapes and videocassettes, and even shoeshines and fishing worms. Vending machines are even more popular in Japan, where they dispense everything from $100 Armani ties (gift wrapped), boxer shorts, beer, and sausages to pearls, stuffed animals, and $8 health drinks.[3]

Vending machines are found everywhere—in factories, offices, lobbies, retail stores, gasoline stations, airports, and train and bus terminals. Automatic teller machines provide bank customers with chequing, savings, withdrawal, and funds-transfer services. Compared to store retailing, vending machines offer consumers greater convenience (available 24 hours, self-service) and fewer damaged goods. But the expensive equipment and labour required for automatic vending make it a costly channel, and prices of vended goods are often 15 to 20 percent higher than those in retail stores. Customers also must put up with aggravating machine breakdowns, out-of-stock items, and the fact that merchandise cannot be returned.[4]

◼ RETAILER MARKETING DECISIONS

Retailers are searching for new marketing strategies to attract and hold customers. In the past, retailers attracted customers with unique products, more or better services than their competitors offered, or credit cards. Today, national brand manufacturers, in their drive for volume, have placed their branded goods everywhere. Thus, stores offer more similar assortments—national brands are found not only in department stores, but also in mass-merchandise and off-price discount stores. As a result, stores are looking more and more alike; they have become "commoditized." In any city, a shopper can find many stores, but few assortments.

FIGURE 13-1 *Retailer marketing decisions*

Service differentiation among retailers has also eroded. Many department stores have trimmed their services, whereas discounters have increased theirs. Customers have become smarter and more price-sensitive. They see no reason to pay more for identical brands, especially when service differences are shrinking. And because bank credit cards are now accepted at most stores, consumers no longer need credit from a particular store. For all these reasons, many retailers today are rethinking their marketing strategies.[5]

As shown in Figure 13-1, retailers face major marketing decisions about their *target markets and positioning, product assortment and services, price, promotion,* and *place.*

TARGET MARKET AND POSITIONING DECISION

Retailers first must define their target markets and then decide how they will position themselves in these markets. Should the store focus on upscale, midscale, or downscale shoppers? Do target shoppers want variety, depth of assortment, convenience, or low prices? Until they define and profile their markets, retailers cannot make consistent decisions about product assortment, services, pricing, advertising, store decor, or any of the other decisions that must support their positions.

Too many retailers fail to define their target markets and positions clearly. They try to have "something for everyone" and end up satisfying no market well. In contrast, successful retailers define their target markets well and position themselves strongly. For example, in 1963, Leslie H. Wexner borrowed $7000 to create *The Limited,* which started as a single store targeted to young, fashion-conscious women. All aspects of the store—clothing assortment, fixtures, music, colours, personnel—were orchestrated to match the target consumer. He continued to open more stores, but a decade later his original customers were no longer in the "young" group. To catch the new "youngs," he started the Limited Express. Over the years, he started or acquired other highly targeted store chains, including Victoria's Secret and others to reach new segments. Today The Limited, Inc. operates more than 4000 stores in seven different segments of the market, with sales of more than $9.6 billion.

Even large stores such as Wal-Mart and Sears must define their major target markets in order to design effective marketing strategies. In fact, in recent years, thanks to strong targeting and positioning, Wal-Mart has exploded to the point where its sales are almost equal to those of General Motors (see Marketing Highlight 13-2).

PRODUCT ASSORTMENT AND SERVICES DECISION

Retailers must decide on three major product variables: *product assortment, services mix,* and *store atmosphere.*

The retailer's *product assortment* must match target shoppers' expectations. The retailer must determine both the product assortment's *width* and its *depth.* Thus, a restaurant can offer a narrow and shallow assortment (small lunch counter), a narrow and deep assortment (delicatessen), a wide and shallow assortment

WAL-MART: THE NATION'S NEWEST RETAILER

In 1962, Sam Walton and his brother opened the first Wal-Mart discount store in small-town Rogers, Arkansas. It was a big, flat, warehouse-type store that sold everything from apparel to automotive supplies to small appliances at very low prices. Experts gave the fledgling retailer little chance—conventional wisdom suggested that discount stores could succeed only in large cities. Yet, from these modest beginnings, the chain expanded rapidly, opening new stores in one small southern town after another.

By the mid-1980s, Wal-Mart had exploded onto the national retailing scene. Incredibly, by 1997, Wal-Mart's annual sales exceeded $140 billion—more than those of Sears, Kmart, and JC Penney combined—making it the world's largest retailer and eleventh-largest company. In 1996, the company sold a Timex watch every 7.4 seconds and a Barbie Doll every two seconds. Wal-Mart's phenomenal growth shows fews signs of slowing. The company is now well established in both large and small centres. It has expanded into Latin and South America as well as Asia. The company entered Canada in 1995 when it purchased Woolco. Such sparkling performance has rewarded investors handsomely. An investment of $2300 in Wal-Mart stock in 1970 would be worth a whopping $4 million today!

What are the secrets behind this spectacular success? Wal-Mart listens to and takes care of its customers, treats employees as partners, and keeps a tight rein on costs.

Listening to and Taking Care of Customers

Wal-Mart positioned itself strongly in a well-chosen target market. Initially, Sam Walton focused on value-conscious consumers in small towns. The chain built a strong everyday low-price position long before it became fashionable in retailing. It grew rapidly by bringing the lowest possible prices to towns ignored by national discounters.

Wal-Mart knows its customers and takes good care of them. As one analyst puts it, "The company gospel . . . is relatively simple: Be an agent for customers, find out what they want, and sell it to them for the lowest possible price." Thus, the company listens carefully—for example, all top Wal-Mart executives go where their customers hang out. Each spends at least two days a week visiting stores, talking directly with customers, and getting a firsthand look at operations. Then, Wal-Mart delivers what customers want: a broad selection of carefully selected goods at unbeatable prices.

But the right merchandise at the right price isn't the only key to Wal-Mart's success. Wal-Mart also provides outstanding service that keeps customers satisfied. A sign reading "Satisfaction Guaranteed" hangs prominently at each store's entrance. Another sign inside the store

A Wal-Mart "people greeter" lends a helping hand.

reads "At Wal-Mart, our goal is: You're always next in line!" Customers are often welcomed by "people greeters" eager to lend a helping hand or just to be friendly. And, sure enough, the store opens extra checkout counters to keep waiting lines short.

Wal-Mart not only cares for customers in its stores, but it also supports their communities. The company supports everything from local sporting events to local charities. According to Steve Arnold, a professor at Queen's University, being a good corporate citizen reinforces consumers' attachment to the retailer. And he should know. He's conducted over 400 studies on Wal-Mart.

Treating Employees as Partners

Wal-Mart believes that, in the final accounting, the company's people are what really makes it better. Thus, it works hard to show employees that it cares about them. Wal-Mart calls employees "associates," a practice now widely copied by competitors. The associates work as partners, become deeply involved in operations, and share rewards for good performance.

Everyone at Wal-Mart [is] an associate—from [the CEO] . . . to a cashier . . . . "We," "us," and "our" are the operative words. Wal-Mart department heads, hourly associates who look after one or more of 30-some departments ranging from sporting goods to electronics, see figures that many companies never show general managers: costs, freight charges, profit margins. The company sets a profit margin for each store, and if the store exceeds it, then the hourly associates share part of the additional profit.

The partnership concept is deeply rooted in the Wal-Mart corporate culture. It is supported by open-door policies and grass-roots meetings that give employees a say in what goes on and encourage them to bring their problems to management. Wal-Mart's concern for its employees translates into high employee satisfaction, which in turn translates into greater customer satisfaction.

Keeping a Tight Rein on Costs

Wal-Mart has the lowest cost structure in the industry: Operating expenses amount to only 16 percent of sales, compared to 23 percent at Kmart. Thus, Wal-Mart can charge lower prices but still reap higher profits, allowing it to offer better service. This creates a "productivity loop." Wal-Mart's lower prices and better service attract more shoppers, producing more sales, making the company more efficient, and enabling it to lower prices even more.

Wal-Mart's low costs result in part from superior management and more sophisticated technology. Its Bentonville, Arkansas, headquarters contains "a computer-communications system worthy of the Defence Department," giving managers instant access to sales and operating information. And its huge, fully automated distribution centres employ the latest technology to supply stores efficiently. Wal-Mart also spends less than competitors on advertising—only 0.5 percent of sales, compared to 2.5 percent at Kmart and 3.8 percent at Sears. Because Wal-Mart has what customers want at the prices they'll pay, its reputation has spread rapidly by word of mouth. It has not needed more advertising.

Finally, Wal-Mart keeps costs down through good old "tough buying." Whereas the company is known for the warm way it treats customers, it is equally well known for the cold, calculated way it wrings low prices from suppliers. The following passage describes a visit to Wal-Mart's buying offices.

Don't expect a greeter and don't expect friendly. . . . Once you are ushered into one of the spartan little buyers' rooms, expect a steely eye across the table and be prepared to cut your price. "They are very, very focussed people, and they use their buying power more forcefully than anyone else . . . ," says the marketing vice president of a major vendor. "All the normal mating rituals are [forbidden]. Their highest priority is making sure everyone at all times in all cases knows who's in charge, and it's Wal-Mart. They talk softly, but they have piranha hearts, and if you aren't totally prepared when you go in there, you'll have your [head] handed to you."

Some observers wonder whether Wal-Mart can continue to grow at such a torrid pace and still retain its focus and positioning. They wonder if an ever-larger Wal-Mart can stay close to its customers and employees. The company's managers are betting on it. Says one top executive: "We'll be fine as long as we never lose our responsiveness to the consumer."

Sources: Quoted material from Bill Saporito, "Is Wal-Mart Unstoppable?" *Fortune,* May 6, 1991, pp. 50–59; and John Huey, "Wal-Mart: Will It Take Over the World?" *Fortune,* January 30, 1989, pp. 52–61. Also see Christy Fisher, "Wal-Mart's Way," *Advertising Age,* February 18, 1991, p. 3; Bill Saporito, "David Glass Won't Crack Under Fire," *Fortune,* February 8, 1993, pp. 75–80; and Bill Saporito, "And the Winner Is Still . . . Wal-Mart," *Fortune,* May 2, 1994, pp. 62–70; www.wal-mart.com/

(cafeteria), or a wide and deep assortment (large restaurant). Another product assortment element is the *quality* of the goods: The customer is interested not only in the range of choice but also in the quality of the products available.

No matter what the store's product assortment and quality level, there always will be competitors with similar assortments and quality. Therefore, the retailer must find other ways to *differentiate* itself from similar competitors. It can use any of several product-differentiation strategies. For one, it can offer merchandise that no other competitor carries—its own private brands or national brands on which it holds exclusives. Many of Canada's best-performing fashion retailers—Club Monaco, Roots Canada, and the Northern Group—not only stock their stores with their own brands of clothing, but they are also extending these brands into new lines of accessories and cosmetic products. Items such as jewellery, belts, backpacks, perfume, and toiletries are used to reinforce the store's brand image.[6] Second, the retailer can feature blockbuster merchandising events—Ben Moss Jewellers is known throughout Western Canada for their promotions involving celebrities. Finally, the retailer can differentiate itself by offering a highly targeted product assortment—Pennington and Cotton Ginny Plus carry goods for larger women; The It Store offers an unusual assortment of gadgets in what amounts to an adult toy store.

Retailers also must decide on a *services mix* to offer customers. The old "mom and pop" grocery stores offered home delivery, credit, and conversation—services that today's supermarkets ignore. The services mix is one of the key tools of non-price competition for setting one store apart from another.

The *store's atmosphere* is another element in its product arsenal. Every store has a physical layout that makes moving around in it either hard or easy. Paco Underhill, a retailing consultant, captures the importance of perceived crowding in a store with his "bum-brush" theory. He suggests that the possibility of a shopper making a purchase decreases significantly every time his or her posterior is accidentally brushed by another passerby.[7] Every store has a "feel"; one store is cluttered, another charming, a third plush, a fourth sombre. The store must have a planned atmosphere that suits the target market and moves customers to buy.

Many of today's successful new retailers, like Virgin, create entertaining shopping experiences in addition to deep product selection.

Increasingly, retailers are turning their stores into theatres that transport customers into unusual, exciting shopping environments. For example, New York's famous toy store, F.A.O. Schwartz, has customers lining up to get in. Customers ride escalators through a toy kingdom, and make their way through various boutiques with elaborate animated displays and spectacular exhibits, featuring Lego toys, Barbie Dolls, giant stuffed zoo animals, and even a talking tree. Virgin Group (the company that includes Virgin Atlantic Airways, Virgin Hotels, Virgin Megastore, and Virgin Communications) has just entered retailing. The new music and entertainment Virgin Megastore in downtown Vancouver is the epitome of stores combining shopping and entertainment. The 40 000-square-foot facility has a wealth of interactive features including an in-store DJ booth, individual listening stations, booths for viewing movies, and a café where people can sip expresso. In-store performances encourage shoppers to spend more time and, of course, more money. Careful attention was paid to store design. Wide aisles, escalators, and careful signage allow for easy movement throughout the store. Metal and marble are used in some sections to give them a modern look; fresco-like murals are used in others to create a completely different atmosphere.[8]

Indigo Books and Music, the Canadian upstart bookseller that was recently founded to take on "'big-box" retailers such as Barnes & Noble and Chapters, uses atmospherics to turn shopping for books into entertainment. It knows that shopping is a social activity for many consumers. People shop not only to make purchases, but also to mingle with others, see what's new, and treat themselves to something interesting or unexpected. Thus, Indigo Books and Music stores are designed using rich colours and wood accents. They feature special events and appearances by authors. They also offer plenty of space, where people can meet and feel at home.[9]

All of this confirms that retail stores are much more than simply assortments of goods. They are environments to be experienced by the people who shop in them. Store atmospheres offer a powerful tool by which retailers can differentiate their stores from those of competitors.

PRICE DECISION

A retailer's price policy is a crucial positioning factor and must be decided in relation to its target market, its product and service assortment, and its competition. All retailers would like to charge high markups and achieve high volume, but the two seldom go together. Most retailers seek *either* high markups on lower volume (most specialty stores) *or* low markups on higher volume (mass merchandisers and discount stores). Thus, Winnipeg-based Hanford Drewitt prices men's suits starting at $1000 and shoes at $400—it sells a low volume but makes a hefty profit on each sale. At the other extreme, Winners sells brand-name clothing at discount prices, settling for a lower margin on each sale but selling at a much higher volume.

Retailers also must pay attention to pricing tactics. Most retailers will put low prices on some items to serve as "traffic builders" or "loss leaders." On some

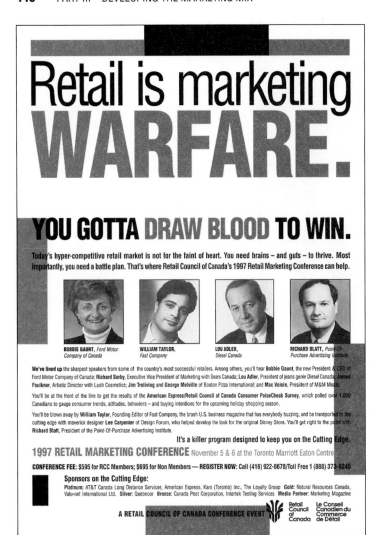

The dynamic, intense competition inherent in retail makes it a challenging business environment.

Central business districts Clusters of businesses and retail outlets, usually in the city core.

Shopping centre A retail location planned, developed, owned, and managed as a unit.

occasions, they run storewide sales. On others, they plan markdowns on slower-moving merchandise. For example, shoe retailers may expect to sell 50 percent of their shoes at the normal markup, 25 percent at a 40 percent markup, and the remaining 25 percent at cost.

PROMOTION DECISION

Retailers use the normal promotion tools—advertising, personal selling, sales promotion, and public relations—to reach consumers. They advertise in newspapers, magazines, radio, television, and the Internet. Advertising may be supported by circulars and direct-mail pieces. Personal selling requires careful training of salespeople in how to greet customers, meet their needs, and handle their complaints. Sales promotions may include in-store demonstrations, displays, contests, and visiting celebrities. Public relations activities, such as press conferences and speeches, store openings, special events, newsletters, magazines, and public service activities, are always available to retailers.

PLACE DECISION

Retailers often cite three critical factors in retailing success: *location, location,* and *location!* A retailer's location is key to its ability to attract customers. And the costs of building or leasing facilities have a major impact on the retailer's profits. Thus, site-location decisions are among the most important the retailer makes. Small retailers may have to settle for whatever locations they can find or afford. Large retailers usually employ specialists who select locations using advanced methods.

One of the savviest location experts in recent years has been toy-store giant Toys 'R' Us. Most of its new locations are in rapidly growing areas where the population closely matches their customer base. In an ever-intensifying war for the grocery consumer, Loblaw and Provigo battle for the best locations to pre-empt each other's expansion plans. The undisputed winner in the "place race" has been Wal-Mart, whose strategy of being the first mass merchandiser to locate in small and rural markets was been one of the key factors in its phenomenal success.

Most stores today cluster together to increase their customer pulling power and to give consumers the convenience of one-stop shopping. The main types of store clusters are the *central business district* and *shopping centre*.

Central business districts were the main form of retail cluster until the 1950s. Every large city and town had a central business district. When people began to move to the suburbs, however, these central business districts began to lose business. In recent years, many cities have joined with merchants to try to revive downtown shopping areas.

A **shopping centre** is a retail location that is planned, developed, owned, and managed as a unit. A *regional shopping centre*, the largest and most dramatic type, contains from 40 to over 200 stores. The Eaton Centre in Toronto, Place Ville Marie in Montreal, and West Edmonton Mall are shopping cities featuring a mix

The West Edmonton Mall is the largest mall in the world. Besides containing over 800 shops and services, it features the world's largest indoor amusement park and the world's largest indoor lake.

of large department stores and many small specialty stores. They attract customers from a wide area. A *community shopping centre* contains 15 to 40 retail stores. It normally contains a branch of a department store or variety store, a supermarket, specialty stores, professional offices, and sometimes a bank. Most shopping centres are *neighbourhood shopping centres* or strip malls that generally contain five to 15 stores. They are close and convenient for consumers. They usually contain a supermarket, perhaps a discount store, and several service stores—dry cleaner, self-service laundry, drugstore, video-rental outlet, barber or beauty shop, hardware store, or other stores.

According to the International Council of Shopping Centres, 80 percent of Canadian retail sales occur in shopping centres. But shopping centres may have reached their saturation point. For example, between 1991 and 1995, the number of malls increased from 3997 to 4164. But the number of shoppers going to malls every month grew only three percent. Thus, many areas contain too many malls, and as sales per square foot are dropping, vacancy rates are climbing. Some experts predict a shopping mall "shakeout," with as many as 20 percent of the regional shopping malls now operating in Canada closing by the year 2000. Despite the development of a few new "megamalls," such as the West Edmonton Mall, the current trend is toward smaller malls located in medium-size and smaller cities in fast-growing areas such as British Columbia and southern Alberta.[10]

Why are people using shopping malls less? First, with more women in the workforce and the baby boomers spending more time with their children, people have less time to shop. Second, shoppers appear to be tiring of traditional malls that are too big, too crowded, and too much alike. Today's large malls offer great selection but are less comfortable and convenient. Finally, today's consumers have many alternatives to traditional malls, such as online shopping.

THE FUTURE OF RETAILING

Retailers operate in a harsh and fast-changing environment that offers both threats and opportunities. For example, the industry suffers from chronic overcapacity. There is just too much retail space—about six square metres for every man, woman, and child, more than double that of 30 years ago—resulting in fierce competition for customer dollars. Consumer demographics, lifestyles, and shopping patterns are changing rapidly, as are retailing technologies. Moreover, quickly rising costs make more efficient operation and smarter buying essential. To be successful, then, retailers will have to choose target segments carefully and position themselves strongly. They will have to take into account the following retailing developments as they plan and execute their competitive strategies.

NEW RETAIL FORMS AND SHORTENING RETAIL LIFECYCLES

New retail forms continue to emerge to meet new situations and consumer needs. But the life cycle of new retail forms is becoming shorter. Department stores took

Eaton's
www.eatons.com

Wheel of retailing concept
A concept of retailing that states that new types of retailers usually begin as low-margin, low-price, low-status operations but later evolve into higher-priced, higher-service operations, eventually becoming like the conventional retailers they replaced.

about 100 years to reach the mature stage of the life cycle; more recent forms, such as catalogue showrooms and furniture warehouse stores, reached maturity in about 10 years. Internet retailing is still in its infancy, but remember, the concept was unknown just a few years ago. In such an environment, seemingly solid retail positions can crumble quickly. One of Canada's most venerable retailers, Eaton's, knows this only too well. The 127-year-old retailing veteran dominated the headlines of the business press for much of 1997 as it hovered on the brink of bankruptcy. The fall of such a retailing giant "serves as a stark reminder to mass-market retailers that past success means little in a fiercely competitive and rapidly changing industry."[11] Retailers can no longer sit back and rely on a once-successful formula—they must keep adapting.

Many retailing innovations are partially explained by the **wheel of retailing** concept.[12] According to this concept, many new types of retailing forms begin as low-margin, low-price, low-status operations. They challenge established retailers that have become "fat" by letting their costs and margins increase. The new retailers' success leads them to upgrade their facilities and offer more services. In turn, their costs increase, forcing them to increase their prices. Eventually, the new retailers become like the conventional retailers they replaced. The cycle begins again when still newer types of retailers evolve with lower costs and prices. The wheel of retailing concept seems to explain the initial success and later troubles of department stores, supermarkets, and discount stores and the recent success of off-price retailers.

GROWTH OF NON-STORE RETAILING

Although most retailing still takes place the old-fashioned way—across countertops in stores—consumers now have an array of alternatives, including mail-order, television, phone, and online shopping (see Marketing Highlight 13-3). Although such advances may threaten some traditional retailers, they offer exciting opportunities for others. Most store retailers are now actively exploring direct retailing channels.

INCREASING INTERTYPE COMPETITION

There has been a blurring of the traditional lines of retailing. Whereas only a few years ago, grocery retailers sold groceries, today they carry everything from books to pharmacy items to lawn furniture. Consumers can purchase a CD in specialty music stores, discount music stores, electronics superstores, video rental outlets, drugstores, and through dozens of web sites. And when it comes to brand-name appliances, department stores, discount stores, off-price retailers, catalogue showrooms, or electronics superstores all compete for the same customers. Today's retailers are beginning to focus on share of wallet rather than share of a particular product-market. "If [a store] can entice you, add value and be more convenient, [it's] going to get more out of your wallet than [its] competitor."[13]

Competition between chain superstores and smaller, independently owned stores has become particularly heated. Because of their bulk buying power and high sales volume, chains can buy at lower costs and thrive on smaller margins. The arrival of a superstore can quickly force nearby independents out of business. Yet the news is not all bad for smaller companies. Many small independent retailers are thriving. Independents are finding that sheer size and marketing muscle are often no match for the personal touch that small stores can provide or the specialty niches that small stores fill for a devoted customer base.

THE RISE OF MEGA-RETAILERS

The rise of huge mass-merchandisers and specialty superstores, the formation of vertical marketing systems and buying alliances, and a rash of retail mergers and

RETAILING GOES ONLINE

Most of us still make most of our purchases the old-fashioned way. We go to the store, find what we want, wait patiently in line to plunk down our cash or credit card, and bring home the goods. However, a growing number of online retailers are providing an attractive alternative—one that lets us browse, select, order, and pay with little more effort than it takes to apply an index finger to a mouse button. They sell a rich variety of goods ranging from flowers, CDs, books, and food to stereo equipment, kitchen appliances, airplane tickets, auto parts, and bags of cement. Here are just a few examples.

Music: *CDNow*'s cyberstore (www.cd-now.com) offers web shoppers more than 165 000 CD titles. Customers place their orders on line, CDNow contacts the distributor, and customers receive their music within 24 hours. Its site is so popular, CD-Now is making money from other companies that advertise on the site—something traditional music stores cannot do. The best news: CDNow spent only $3600 to build its web site but the site earned an estimated $8 million last year.

Books: *Amazon.com* (www.amazon.com), which offers 1.1 million books on line and discounts bestsellers up to 30 percent, has sales of about $24 million. The company orders books from publishers and has no store, no inventory. Most customers receive books two to three days after ordering. Although Amazon.com can't offer couches and coffee, it has authors post comments on their books, encourages customers to share opinions on books, and recommends titles to individual customers based on each customer's profile. The company even tracks down hard-to-find books. "Businesses can do things on the Web that simply cannot be done any other way," says founder and CEO Jeff Bezos. "We are changing the way people buy books."

Flowers: One-fourth of all flowers sold in the United States are now ordered on the Internet. *1-800-FLOWERS* (WWW.1-800-flower.com) president and owner Jim McCann, who created a $360-million company from one that was $10 million in debt in 1987, started selling flowers online in 1992. Now customers can find

1-800-FLOWERS on such interactive services as America Online, eWorld, and the Plaza on the Microsoft Network. In Arthur Andersen's latest *International Trends in Retailing*, McCann discusses taking the shopping experience on line. He writes, "For many businesses—for flowers, certainly—moving that [shopping] experience to an electronic medium is a bear. It just doesn't translate that directly. . . . We learned that to achieve the result we want, we would have to think about marketing in a new way. . . . Where we [used to

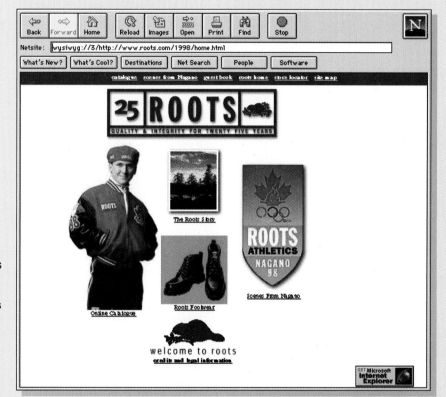

have] actual conversations, we now would have to provide a constant, changing stream of relevant information and entertainment. What has to happen, in other words, is that retailers must learn how to recreate the physical retail experience online."

Apparel: Many basic apparel items already move like wildfire via catalogues. And most catalogue retailers—L.L. Bean, Tilley Endurables, J. Crew, and others—have already put their catalogues online. However, other non-catalogue specialty retailers are also setting up to sell online. For example, the Gap plans soon to use its

web site (www.gap.com) to sell a limited line of merchandise, such as T-shirts, socks, sweaters, and other products that don't require trying on for size. Regular Gap shoppers, who know their Gap sizes, could order an even wider range of goods from the site. Since launching its web site, the Gap has mapped visitor usage patterns and found that, on average, people stayed 50 percent longer at the Gap site than at other sites. This statistic bodes well for the chain's chances at online retailing. The Gap's entry into online retail is a

natural, asserts one industry analyst. "It's about time," says the analyst. "The Gap is a marquee brand and an excellent demographic fit" with web users. The challenge will be to develop ways to spark impulse buys, which often add significantly to sales.

Food: Consumers could buy most of their groceries without touching them. Half of European food retailers surveyed recently by the *Financial Times* believe that home delivery will represent 20 percent of volume by 2005. A few online food retailers have already sprung up in Canada and the United States. Kentucky Fried Chicken

Canada (www.kfc-canada.com) has an interactive ordering system that's "finger-licking good." Panzerotta Pizza (pizza.idirect.com) will let you order pizza delivered to your door in the Greater Toronto area. And Quebec's maple syrup producers have a site that lets you learn more about the product and its suppliers (www.vir.com/~maplesyrup/sirop.htm). Peapod (www.peapod.com) has

teamed with supermarkets in Boston, Chicago, San Francisco, and Ohio.

Still, succeeding online is anything but a given. "The online success stories in retail are few and far between," cautions another analyst. Those who fare well tend to be catalogue companies with internal structures and staff to deal with orders. However, he admits, with each pass-

ing day, technological advances make it a bit easier for retailers to make their bottom lines online.

Source: Portions adapted from Jay A. Scansaroli and Vicky Eng, "Interactive Retailing: Marketing Products," *Chain Store Age*, January 1997, pp. 9A–10A. Gap examples and quotations from Alice Z. Cuneo, "The Gap Readies Electronic Commerce Plan for Web Site," *Advertising Age*, June 23, 1997, p. 18.

acquisitions have created a core of superpower mega-retailers. Through their superior information systems and buying power, these giant retailers can offer better merchandise selections, good service, and strong price savings to consumers. As a result, they grow even larger by squeezing out their smaller, weaker competitors. The mega-retailers also are shifting the balance of power between retailers and producers. A relative handful of retailers now control access to enormous numbers of consumers, giving them the upper hand in their dealings with manufacturers. For example, Wal-Mart's revenues are more than three times those of Procter & Gamble (P&G). Wal-Mart can, and often does, use this power to wring concessions from P&G and other suppliers.[14]

GROWING IMPORTANCE OF RETAIL TECHNOLOGY

Retail technologies are becoming critically important as competitive tools. Progressive retailers are using computers to produce better forecasts, control inventory costs, order electronically from suppliers, send e-mail between stores, and even sell to customers within stores. They are adopting checkout scanning systems, online transaction processing, electronic funds transfer, electronic data interchange, in-store television, and improved merchandise-handling systems.

Technology recently helped the managers of the newly renovated A&P in Hamilton, Ontario to unravel a mystery. Their scanner data revealed that five percent of the store clientele who used frequent-buyer cards were purchasing less—expenditures went from $80 per week to as low as $35. Concerned about this situation, the managers sent a letter to these card-holders asking them for reasons why they had changed their shopping habits. Customer responses revealed that although most people like the store's new look, they didn't like the new self-serve deli. Consequently they had started going elsewhere to buy their deli meats, and while in other stores, they did some shopping as well. As a result of this customer feedback, the store was remodelled again, and purchasing levels went back up. Not only did technology help the managers of the Hamilton store, but it also prevented A&P from making a chain-wide blunder.[15]

GLOBAL EXPANSION OF MAJOR RETAILERS

Retailers with unique formats and strong brand positioning are increasingly moving into other countries. Many are expanding internationally to escape mature and saturated home markets. Over the years, several giant North American retailers—The Gap, Toys 'R' Us, Wal-Mart—have become globally prominent as a result of their great marketing prowess. Wal-Mart, which now operates more than 300 stores in six countries, sees exciting potential abroad. For example, here's what happened when it recently opened two new stores in Shenzhen, China:

> [Customers came] by the hundreds of thousands—up to 175 000 on Saturdays alone—to China's first Wal-Mart Supercenter and Sam's Club. They broke the display glass to snatch out chickens at one store and carted off all of the big-screen televisions before the other store had been open an hour. The two outlets...were packed on Day One and have been bustling ever since.[16]

However, North American retailers are still significantly behind Europe and Asia when it comes to global expansion. Less than 20 percent of the top North American retailers operate globally, compared with 40 percent of European retailers and 31 percent of Asian retailers. There are a few global superstars among Canadian retailers, however. Roots Canada Ltd. has pursued growth outside Canada ever since its inception in 1973. In addition to its 95 Canadian stores, it has six outlets in the United States and 15 franchises in Asia where its Canadian wilderness image has brought it increasing popularity. Yogen Früz, born in Markham, Ontario in 1986, is now the world leader in the frozen yogurt market. Its 3300 stores in countries as diverse as Bosnia and El Salvador generate $420 million in sales. In fact, 90 percent of the company's revenues come from outside Canada.[17]

Among foreign retailers that have gone global are Britain's Marks and Spencer, Italy's Benetton, France's Carrefour hypermarkets, Sweden's IKEA home-furnishings stores, and Japan's Yaohan supermarkets.[18] Marks and Spencer, which started out as a penny bazaar in 1884, grew into a chain of variety stores over the decades and now has a thriving string of 150 franchised stores around the world. IKEA's well-constructed but fairly inexpensive furniture has proven very popular in North America.

RETAIL STORES AS "COMMUNITIES" OR "HANGOUTS"

With the rise in the number of people living alone, working at home, or living in isolated and sprawling suburbs, there has been a resurgence of establishments that, regardless of the product or service they offer, also provide a place for people to meet. These places include cafés, tea shops, juice bars, bookshops, superstores, children's play spaces, brew pubs, and urban greenmarkets. This is a North American-wide phenomenon. Brew pubs such as the Kingston Brew Pub offer tastings and a place to pass the time. Denver's two Tattered Covered Bookstores host more than 250 events annually, from folk dancing to women's meetings. The Discovery Zone, a chain of children's play spaces, offers indoor spaces where kids can go wild without breaking anything while stressed-out parents exchange stories. And, of course, there are the now-ubiquitous coffee houses and espresso bars, such as Starbucks, whose numbers have grown from 2500 in 1989 to a forecasted 10 000 by 1999.[19]

WHOLESALING

Wholesaling
All activities involved in selling goods and services to those buying for resale or business use.

Wholesaler
A firm engaged *primarily* in wholesaling activity.

Wholesaling includes all activities involved in selling goods and services to those buying for resale or business use. A retail bakery is engaging in wholesaling when it sells pastry to the local hotel. We call **wholesalers** those firms engaged *primarily* in wholesaling activity.

Wholesalers buy mostly from producers and sell mostly to retailers, industrial consumers, and other wholesalers. But why are wholesalers used at all? For example, why would a producer use wholesalers rather than selling directly to retailers or consumers? Quite simply, wholesalers are often better at performing one or more of the following channel functions:

◆ *Selling and promoting.* Wholesalers' sales forces help manufacturers reach any small customers at a low cost. The wholesaler has more contacts and is often more trusted by the buyer than the distant manufacturer.

◆ *Buying and assortment building.* Wholesalers can select items and build assortments needed by their customers, thereby saving the consumers much work.

◆ *Bulk-breaking.* Wholesalers save their customers money by buying in carload lots and breaking bulk (breaking large lots into small quantities).

◆ *Warehousing.* Wholesalers hold inventories, thereby reducing the inventory costs and risks of suppliers and customers.

◆ *Transportation.* Wholesalers can provide quicker delivery to buyers because they are closer than the producers.

◆ *Financing.* Wholesalers finance their customers by giving credit, and they finance their suppliers by ordering early and paying bills on time.

◆ *Risk bearing.* Wholesalers absorb risk by taking title and bearing the cost of theft, damage, spoilage, and obsolescence.

◆ *Market information.* Wholesalers give information to suppliers and customers about competitors, new products, and price developments.

◆ *Management services and advice.* Wholesalers often help retailers train their sales clerks, improve store layouts and displays, and set up accounting and inventory control systems.

TYPES OF WHOLESALERS

Merchant wholesalers
Independently owned businesses that take title to the merchandise they handle.

Broker
A wholesaler who does not take title to goods and whose function is to bring buyers and sellers together and assist in negotiation.

Agent
A wholesaler who represents buyers or sellers on a relatively permanent basis, performs only a few functions, and does not take title to goods.

Manufacturers' sales branches and offices
Wholesaling by sellers or buyers themselves rather than through independent wholesalers.

Wholesalers fall into three major groups (see Table 13-4): *merchant wholesalers, brokers and agents,* and *manufacturers' sales branches and offices.*

Merchant wholesalers are the largest single group of wholesalers, accounting for roughly 50 percent of all wholesaling. Merchant wholesalers include two broad types: *full-service wholesalers* and *limited-service wholesalers.* Full-service wholesalers provide a full set of services, whereas the various limited-service wholesalers offer fewer services to their suppliers and customers. The several different types of limited-service wholesalers perform varied specialized functions in the distribution channel.

Brokers and agents differ from merchant wholesalers in two ways: they do not take title to goods, and they perform only a few functions. Like merchant wholesalers, they generally specialize by product line or customer type. A **broker** brings buyers and sellers together and assists in negotiation. **Agents** represent buyers or sellers on a more permanent basis. *Manufacturers' agents* (also called manufacturers' representatives) are the most common type of agent wholesaler. Together, brokers and agents account for 11 percent of the total wholesale volume.

The third major type of wholesaling is that done in **manufacturers' sales branches and offices** by sellers or buyers themselves rather than through independent wholesalers. Manufacturers' offices and sales branches account for about 31 percent of all wholesale volume.

WHOLESALER MARKETING DECISIONS

Wholesalers have experienced mounting competitive pressures in recent years. They have faced new sources of competition, more demanding customers, new technologies, and more direct-buying programs on the part of large industrial, institutional, and retail buyers. As a result, they have had to improve their strategic decisions on target markets and positioning, and on the marketing mix—product assortments and services, price, promotion, and place (see Figure 13-2).

TABLE 13-4   *Major Types of Wholesalers*

Type	Description
Merchant Wholesalers	Independently owned businesses that take title to the merchandise they handle. In different trades they are called *jobbers, distributors*, or *mill supply houses*. Include full-service wholesalers and limited-service wholesalers:
Full-service wholesalers	Provide a full line of services: carrying stock, maintaining a sales force, offering credit, making deliveries, and providing management assistance. There are two types:
Wholesale merchants	Sell primarily to retailers and provide a full range of services. *General-merchandise wholesalers* carry several merchandise lines, while *general-line wholesalers* carry one or two lines in greater depth. *Specialty wholesalers* specialize in carrying only part of a line. (Examples: health-food wholesalers, seafood wholesalers.)
Industrial distributors	Sell to manufacturers rather than to retailers. Provide several services, such as carrying stock, offering credit, and providing delivery. May carry a broad range of merchandise, a general line, or a specialty line.
Limited-service wholesalers	Offer fewer services than full-service wholesalers. Limited-service wholesalers are of several types:
Cash-and-carry wholesalers	Carry a limited line of fast-moving goods and sell to small retailers for cash. Normally do not deliver. Example: A small fish store retailer may drive to a cash-and-carry fish wholesaler, buy fish for cash, and bring the merchandise back to the store.
Truck wholesalers (or truck jobbers)	Perform primarily a selling and delivery function. Carry a limited line of semiperishable merchandise (such as milk, bread, snack foods), which they sell for cash as they make their rounds of supermarkets, small groceries, hospitals, restaurants, factory cafeterias, and hotels.
Drop shippers	Do not carry inventory or handle the product. Upon receiving an order, they select a manufacturer, who ships the merchandise directly to the customer. The drop shipper assumes title and risk from the time the order is accepted to its delivery to the customer. They operate in bulk industries, such as coal, lumber, and heavy equipment.
Rack jobbers	Serve grocery and drug retailers, mostly in non-food items. They send delivery trucks to stores, where the delivery people set up toys, paperbacks, hardware items, health and beauty aids, or other items. They price the goods, keep them fresh, set up point-of-purchase displays, and keep inventory records. Rack jobbers retain title to the goods and bill the retailers only for the goods sold to consumers.
Producers' cooperatives	Owned by farmer members and assemble farm produce to sell in local markets. The co-op's profits are distributed to members at the end of the year. They often attempt to improve product quality and promote a co-op brand name, such as Sun Maid raisins, Sunkist oranges, or Diamond walnuts.
Mail-order wholesalers	Send catalogues to retail, industrial, and institutional customers featuring jewellery, cosmetics, specialty foods, and other small items. Maintain no outside sales force. Main customers are businesses in small outlying areas. Orders are filled and sent by mail, truck, or other transportation.
Brokers and Agents	Do not take title to goods. Main function is to facilitate buying and selling, for which they earn a commission on the selling price. Generally specialize by product line or customer types.
Brokers	Chief function is bringing buyers and sellers together and assisting in negotiation. They are paid by the party who hired them, and do not carry inventory, get involved in financing, or assume risk. Examples: food brokers, real estate brokers, insurance brokers, and security brokers.
Agents	Represent either buyers or sellers on a more permanent basis than brokers do. There are several types:
Manufacturers' agents	Represent two or more manufacturers of complementary lines. A formal written agreement with each manufacturer covers pricing, territories, order-handling, delivery service and warranties, and commission rates. Often used in such lines as apparel, furniture, and electrical goods. Most manufacturers' agents are small businesses, with only a few skilled salespeople as employees. They are hired by small manufacturers who cannot afford their own field sales forces, and by large manufacturers who use agents to open new territories or to cover territories that cannot support full-time salespeople.

TABLE 13-4 *continued*

Type	Description
Selling agents	Have contractual authority to sell a manufacturer's entire output. The manufacturer either is not interested in the selling function or feels unqualified. The selling agent serves as a sales department and has significant influence over prices, terms, and conditions of sale. Found in such product areas as textiles, industrial machinery and equipment, coal and coke, chemicals, and metals.
Purchasing agents	Generally have a long-term relationship with buyers and make purchases for them, often receiving, inspecting, warehousing, and shipping the merchandise to the buyers. They provide helpful market information to clients and help them obtain the best goods and prices available.
Commission merchants	Take physical possession of products and negotiate sales. Normally, they are not employed on a long-term basis. Used most often in agricultural marketing by farmers who do not want to sell their own output and do not belong to producers' cooperatives. The commission merchant takes a truckload of commodities to a central market, sells it for the best price, deducts a commission and expenses, and remits the balance to the producer.
Manufacturers' and Retailers' Branches and Offices	Wholesaling operations conducted by sellers or buyers themselves rather than through independent wholesalers. Separate branches and offices can be dedicated to either sales or purchasing.
Sales branches and Offices	Set up by manufacturers to improve inventory control, selling, and promotion. *Sales branches* carry inventory and are found in such industries as lumber and automotive equipment and parts. *Sales offices* do not carry inventory and are most prominent in dry-goods and notions industries.
Purchasing offices	Perform a role similar to that of brokers or agents but are part of the buyer's organization. Many retailers set up purchasing offices in major market centers such as New York and Chicago.

FIGURE 13-2
Wholesaler marketing decisions

TARGET MARKET AND POSITIONING DECISION

Like retailers, wholesalers must define their target markets and position themselves effectively—they cannot serve everyone. They can choose a target group by size of customer (only large retailers), type of customer (convenience food stores only), need for service (customers who need credit), or other factors. Within the target group, they can identify the more profitable customers, design stronger offers, and build better relationships with them. They can propose automatic reordering systems, set up management-training and advising systems, or even sponsor a voluntary chain. They can discourage less profitable customers by requiring larger orders or adding service charges to smaller ones.

MARKETING MIX DECISIONS

Like retailers, wholesalers must decide on product assortment and services, prices, promotion, and place. The wholesaler's "product" is the assortment of *products and services* that it offers. Wholesalers are under great pressure to carry a full line and to stock enough for immediate delivery. But this practice can damage profits. Wholesalers today are cutting down on the number of lines they carry, choosing to carry only the more profitable ones. Wholesalers also are rethinking which services count most in building strong customer relationships and which should be dropped or charged for. The key is to find the mix of services most valued by their target customers.

Price is also an important wholesaler decision. Wholesalers usually mark up the cost of goods by a standard percentage—say, 20 percent. Expenses may run 17 percent of the gross margin, leaving a profit margin of three percent. In grocery wholesaling, the average profit margin is often less than two percent. Wholesalers are trying new pricing approaches. They may cut their margin on some lines in order to win important new customers. They may ask suppliers for special price breaks when they can turn them into an increase in the supplier's sales.

Although *promotion* can be critical to wholesaler success, most wholesalers are not promotion-minded. Their use of trade advertising, sales promotion, personal selling, and public relations is largely scattered and unplanned. Many are behind the times in personal selling—they still see selling as a single salesperson talking to a single customer instead of as a team effort to sell, build, and service major accounts. Wholesalers also need to adopt some of the non-personal promotion techniques used by retailers. They need to develop an overall promotion strategy and to make greater use of supplier promotion materials and programs.

Finally, *place* is important—wholesalers must choose their locations and facilities carefully. Wholesalers typically locate in low-rent, low-tax areas and tend to invest little money in their buildings, equipment, and systems. As a result, their materials-handling and order-processing systems are often outdated. In recent years, however, large and progressive wholesalers are reacting to rising costs by investing in automated warehouses and on-line ordering systems. Orders are fed from the retailer's system directly into the wholesaler's computer, and the items are picked up by mechanical devices and automatically taken to a shipping platform where they are assembled. Winnipeg-based Coghlan's Limited provides camping accessories to the largest retailers in Canada, including Canadian Tire and Wal-Mart. To continue supplying these firms, they have had to invest in several technology and efficiency measures. For example, Coghlan's introduced an electronic data interchange (EDI) system with its customers. This system allows their customers to electronically submit orders, thus shortening the retailer's reorder time. They have also invested in a quick response (QR) system that allows Coghlan's to fill an order and have it on the customer's loading dock within 72 hours. Most large wholesalers employ computers to carry out accounting, billing, inventory control, and forecasting. Modern wholesalers are adapting their services to the needs of target customers and finding cost-reducing methods of doing business.

TRENDS IN WHOLESALING

As the thriving wholesaling industry moves into the next century, it faces considerable challenges. The industry remains vulnerable to one of the most enduring trends of the 1990s—fierce resistance to price increases and the winnowing-out of suppliers based on cost and quality. Progressive wholesalers constantly watch for better ways to meet the changing needs of their suppliers and target customers. They recognize that, in the long run, their only reason for existence comes from adding value by increasing the efficiency and effectiveness of the entire marketing channel. To achieve this goal, they must constantly improve their services and reduce their costs.

McKesson, North America's leading wholesaler of pharmaceuticals and healthcare products, provides an example of progressive wholesaling. To survive, McKesson had to remain more cost effective than manufacturers' sales branches. Thus, the company automated its 36 warehouses, established direct computer links with 225 drug manufacturers, designed a computerized accounts-receivable program for pharmacists, and provided drugstores with computer terminals for ordering inventories. Retailers can even use the McKesson computer system to maintain medical profiles on their customers. Thus, McKesson has delivered better value to both manufacturers and retail customers.

One study predicts several developments in the wholesaling industry.[20] Geographic expansion will require that distributors learn how to compete effectively over wider and more diverse areas. Consolidation will significantly reduce the number of wholesaling firms. Surviving wholesalers will grow larger, primarily through acquisition, merger, and geographic expansion. The trend toward vertical integration, in which manufacturers try to control their market share by owning the intermediaries that bring their goods to market, remains strong. In the health-care sector, for instance, drugmakers have purchased drug-distribution and pharmacy-management companies. This trend began in 1993 when drug-industry giant Merck acquired Medco Containment Services, a drug-benefits manager and mail-order distributor. The surviving wholesaler-distributors in this sector and in others will be bigger and will provide more services for their customers.[21]

The distinction between large retailers and large wholesalers continues to blur. Many retailers now operate formats such as wholesale clubs and hypermarkets that perform many wholesale functions. In return, many large wholesalers are setting up their own retailing operations. SuperValu, a leading food wholesaler, now operates its own retail outlets.

Wholesalers will continue to increase the services they provide to retailers—retail pricing, cooperative advertising, marketing and management information reports, accounting services, online transactions, and others. Rising costs on the one hand, and the demand for increased services on the other, will put the squeeze on wholesaler profits. Wholesalers who do not find efficient ways to deliver value to their customers will soon drop by the wayside. However, the increased use of computerized and automated systems will help wholesalers to contain the costs of ordering, shipping, and inventory-holding, boosting their productivity. By 1990, more than 75 percent of all wholesalers were using online order systems.

Finally, facing slow growth in their domestic markets and such developments as the North American Free Trade Agreement, many large wholesalers are now going global and will begin to generate much of their revenue outside their home country.

Summary of Chapter Objectives

Although most retailing is conducted in retail stores, in recent years, non-store retailing has increased enormously. In addition, although many retail stores are independently owned, an increasing number are now banding together under some form of corporate or contractual organization. Wholesalers have also experienced recent environmental changes, most notably mounting competitive pressures. They have faced new sources of competition, more demanding customers, new technologies, and more direct-buying programs on the part of large industrial, institutional, and retail buyers.

1. **Explain the roles of retailers and wholesalers in the distribution channel.**

   Retailing and wholesaling consist of many organizations bringing goods and services from the point of production to the point of use. Retailing includes all activities involved in selling goods or services directly to final consumers for their personal, non-business use.

Wholesaling includes all the activities involved in selling goods or services to those who are buying for the purpose of resale or for business use. Wholesalers perform many functions, including selling and promoting, buying and assortment building, bulk-breaking, warehousing, transporting, financing, risk bearing, supplying market information, and providing management services and advice.

2. **Describe the major types of retailers and give examples of each.**

   Retailers can be classified as store retailers and non-store retailers. Store retailers can be further classified by the amount of service they provide (self-service, limited service, or full service); product line sold (specialty stores, department stores, supermarkets, convenience stores, superstores, and service businesses); and relative prices (discount stores, off-price retailers, and catalogue showrooms). Today, many retailers are banding together in corporate and contractual retail organizations (corporate chains, voluntary chains and retailer cooperatives, franchise organizations, and merchandising conglomerates).

Although most goods and services are sold through stores, non-store retailing has been growing much faster than store retailing. Non-store retailers now account for more than 14 percent of all consumer purchases, and they may account for a third of all sales by the end of the century. Non-store retailing consists of direct marketing, direct selling, and automatic vending.

3. **Identify the major types of wholesalers and give examples of each.**

Wholesalers fall into three groups. First, merchant wholesalers take possession of the goods. They include full-service wholesalers (wholesale merchants, industrial distributors) and limited-service wholesalers (cash-and-carry wholesalers, truck wholesalers, drop shippers, rack jobbers, producers' cooperatives, and mail-order wholesalers). Second, brokers and agents do not take possession of the goods but are paid a commission for aiding buying and selling. Finally, manufacturers' sales branches and offices are wholesaling operations conducted by non-wholesalers to bypass the wholesalers.

4. **Explain the marketing decisions facing retailers and wholesalers.**

Each retailer must make decisions about its target markets, product assortment and services, price, promotion, and place. Retailers must choose target markets carefully and position themselves strongly. Today, wholesaling is holding its own in the economy. Progressive wholesalers are adapting their services to the needs of target customers and are seeking cost-reducing methods of doing business. Facing slow growth in their domestic markets and developments such as the North American Free Trade Association, many large wholesalers are also now going global.

Key Terms

Agent *(p. 454)*
Automatic vending *(p. 443)*
Broker *(p. 454)*
Catalogue showroom *(p. 439)*
Central business districts *(p. 448)*
Chain stores *(p. 439)*
Convenience store *(p. 436)*
Corporate chains *(p. 439)*
Department store *(p. 434)*
Direct marketing *(p. 442)*
Discount store *(p. 437)*
Door-to-door retailing *(p. 442)*

Factory outlets *(p. 438)*
Franchise *(p. 440)*
Independent off-price retailers *(p. 438)*
Manufacturers' sales branches and offices *(p. 454)*
Merchant wholesalers *(p. 454)*
Off-price retailers *(p. 438)*
Retailer cooperative *(p. 439)*
Retailers *(p. 433)*
Retailing *(p. 433)*
Service retailer *(p. 437)*

Shopping centre *(p. 448)*
Specialty store *(p. 434)*
Supermarkets *(p. 436)*
Superstore *(p. 436)*
Voluntary chain *(p. 439)*
Warehouse club (or wholesale club) *(p. 438)*
Wheel of retailing concept *(p. 450)*
Wholesaler *(p. 453)*
Wholesaling *(p. 453)*

Discussing the Issues

1. Convenience stores have lost their monopoly on convenience. Explain what you would do to increase a convenience store's sales.

2. Warehouse clubs that are restricted to members only, such as Price/Costco, are growing rapidly. They offer a very broad but shallow line of products, often in institutional packaging, at very low prices. Some members buy for resale, others buy to supply a business, and still others buy for personal use. Decide whether these stores

are wholesalers or retailers. How can you make a distinction?

3. Off-price retailers provide tough price competition to other retailers. Do you think that large retailers' growing power in channels of distribution will affect manufacturers' willingness to sell to off-price retailers at below regular wholesale rates? Suggest what policy Sony should have regarding selling to off-price retailers.

4. Postal-rate hikes make it more expensive to send direct mail, catalogues, and purchased products to consumers. Identify ways you

would expect direct mail and catalogue marketers to respond to an increase in postage rates.

5. Few Canadian retailers have gone global. Why has this occurred? What changes in today's marketing environment encourage global expansion?

6. Compare the fundamental differences between retailers, wholesalers, and manufacturers in the types of marketing decisions they make. Give examples of the marketing decisions made by the three groups which show their similarities and differences.

Applying the Concepts

1. Collect all the catalogues that you have received in the mail recently. (a) Sort them by type of product line. Is there some pattern to the types of direct marketers that are targeting you? (b) Where do you think these catalogue companies got your name? (c) How do you think a company that was selling your name and address to a direct marketer would describe your buying habits?

2. Watch a cable television shopping channel, or tune into an infomercial (often found on cable stations). (a) How are these shows attempting to target buyers? Do they mix hockey equipment and fine china in the same program, or are they targeting more carefully? (b) How much of the merchandise shown appears to be close-outs? How can you tell?

References

1. Information on Thrifty Foods Inc. from Sarah Cox, "Emerald Aisles," *Report on Business*, August 1996, pp. 52–59. Information on Mountain Equipment Co-op from David Chilton, "Special Report: Quick Response Retailing," *Strategy: The Canadian Marketing Report*, June 12, 1995, p. 22; and Brian Hutchinson, "Merchants of Boom," *Canadian Business*, May 1997, pp. 38–48. Information on Air Transat from Julie Barlow, "Spreading Its Wings," *Report on Business*, February, 1997, pp. 48–52; and Luis Millan, "If It Ain't Broke, Don't Buy It," *Canadian Business*, pp. 36–40. Also see "Special Report: Store-level Marketing," *Strategy: The Canadian Marketing Report*, May 26, 1997, p. 25 for quotations on retailing by L. Berry and J. Torella.

2. Anita Lahey, "Cornered Stores," *Marketing*, August 4, 1997, pp. 10–11; Luis Millan, "King of the Corner Store," *Canadian Business*, September 26, 1997, pp. 101–103.

3. See "Vending your Way," *Training and Development*, September 1996, p. 72; and Maxim Lenderman, "Vending Machines: Hot, Hot, Hot," *Beverage World*, February 1997, pp. 58–62.

4. See J. Taylor Buckley, "Machines Start New Fast-Food Era," *USA Today*, July 19, 1991, pp. B1, B2;

and Laurie McLaughlin, "Vending Machines Open to New Ideas," *Advertising Age*, August 19, 1991, p. 35.

5. For a fuller discussion, see Lawrence H. Wortzel, "Retailing Strategies for Today's Mature Marketplace," *The Journal of Business Strategy*, Spring 1987, pp. 45–56.

6. Mariam Mesbah, "Special Report: Fashion Retailers Branch Into Cosmetics," *Strategy: The Canadian Marketing Report*, January 20, 1997, p. 20.

7. Wendy Cuthbert, "Environment Plays Major Role in Purchase Decision: Expert," *Strategy: The Canadian Marketing Report*, September 29, 1997, p. 14.

8. Erica Zlomislic, "Special Report: Store-level Marketing: Virgin's Megahit," *Strategy: The Canadian Marketing Report*, May 26, 1997, p. 24.

9. Laura Campbell, "Ending Not Yet Written in Cutthroat Bookstore War," *The Financial Post*, October 7, 1997, p. 10; Myron Magnet, "Let's Go for Growth," *Fortune*, March 7, 1994, pp. 60–72; Val Ross, "Indigo Books Stakes Out Kingston," *Globe and Mail*, February 7, 1997, p. C3. Also see Dierdre Donahue, "Bookstores: A Haven for the Intellect," *USA Today*, July 10, 1997, pp. D1, D2.

10. See Francesca Turchiano, "The Unmalling of America," *American Demographics,* April 1990, pp. 36–42; Kate Fitzgerald, "Mega Malls: Built for the '90s, or the '80s?" *Advertising Age,* January 27, 1992, pp. S1, S8; Eric Wieffering, "What Has the Mall of America Done to Minneapolis?" *American Demographics,* February 1994, pp. 13–15; and Kenneth Labich, "What It Will Take to Keep People Hanging Out at the Mall," *Fortune,* May 29, 1995, pp. 102–106.

11. Amy Barrett, "A Retailing Pacesetter Pulls Up Lame," *Business Week,* July 12, 1993, pp. 122–23.

12. See Malcolm P. McNair and Eleanor G. May, "The Next Revolution of the Retailing Wheel," *Harvard Business Review,* September-October 1978, pp. 81–91; Stephen Brown, "The Wheel of Retailing: Past and Future," *Journal of Retailing,* Summer 1990, pp. 143–47; Stephen Brown, "Variations On a Marketing Enigma: The Wheel of Retailing Theory," *The Journal of Marketing Management* 7 (2), 1991, pp. 131–155; and Stanley C. Hollander, "The Wheel of Retailing," reprinted in *Marketing Management,* Summer 1996, pp. 63–66.

13. "Special Report: Store-level Marketing: Loblaw Combines Sizzle and Sell," *Strategy: The Canadian Marketing Report,* May 26, 1997, p. 25.

14. See Nirmalya Kumar, "The Power of Trust in Manufacturer-Retailer Relationships," *Harvard Business Review,* November-December 1996, pp. 92-106.

15. David Menzies, "Retail and High-tech," *Marketing,* August 5, 1996, website: www.marketingmag.com/search.

16. James Cox, "Red-letter Day as East Meets West in the Aisles," *USA Today,* September 11, 1996, p. B1. Also see Wendy Zellner, Louisa Shepard, Ian Katz, and David Lindorff, "Wal-Mart Spoken Here," *Business Week,* June 23, 1997, pp. 138–143.

17. Brian Hutchinson, "Merchants of Boom," *Canadian Business,* May 1997, pp. 38–47; Neil Morton, "Some Like It Cold," *Canadian Business,* September 1997, pp. 99–103.

18. Shelby D. Coolidge, "Facing Saturated Home Markets, Retailers Look to Rest of World," *Christian Science Monitor,* February 14, 1994, 7:1; and Carla Rapoport, "Retailers Go Global," *Fortune,* February 20, 1995, pp. 102–108.

19. See Gherry Khermouch, "Third Places," *Brandweek,* March 13, 1995, pp. 36–40; and Dierdre Donahue, "Bookstores: A Haven for the Intellect," *USA Today,* July 10, 1997, pp. D1, D2.

20. See Arthur Andersen & Co., *Facing the Forces of Change: Beyond Future Trends in Wholesale Distribution* (Washington, DC: Distribution Research and Education Foundation, 1987), p. 7. Also see Joseph Weber, "Its 'Like Somebody Had Shot the Postman,'" *Business Week,* January 13, 1992, p. 82; and Michael Mandel, "Don't Cut Out the Middleman," *Business Week,* September 16, 1996, p. 30.

21. Richard A. Melcher, "The Middlemen Stay On the March," *Business Week,* January 9, 1995, p. 87.

Company Case 13

CANADIAN RETAILING: AN INDUSTRY IN CHAOS

"Retailing is like the ocean. It shifts with the tide in and the tide out . . . you're going to have to keep changing all the time." These words, uttered by John Craig Eaton to a *Canadian Business* interviewer, certainly describe the state of the industry today. There may be no industry in Canada experiencing as much turmoil as the retailing sector. However, questions remain about whether the tide is coming in or has gone out for Canadian retailers.

Nineteen ninety-five has been called the bleakest year in Canadian retailing in decades. Part of the reason is consumers' nervousness about the economy and their ability to keep their jobs. Another is that many consumers have "maxed" out their credit cards and are facing a payment crunch. Others suggest that consumers are just becoming more savvy and are increasingly demanding better value for their money. New labels have been developed for 1990s consumers, such as "strident consumers," "cash-strapped shoppers," "value-driven buyers," and "shoppers from hell"—reflecting the attitudes of the retailers who serve them.

Whereas consumers in the 1980s often purchased $1000 suits and $200 scarves, some now seem to be focussing on purchases for their homes when they reluctantly part with their hard-earned dollars. Many shoppers rank convenience as their number-one criteria for store choice, which is not surprising given that 69 percent of mothers with children under 16 years of age also work outside the home. In addition, 1.3 million Canadians are now working extended hours, with an estimated 13.5 percent working more than a 50-hour week.

Parallelling the changes in consumer behaviour, the retailing industry itself has been evolving. Traditional department stores are being challenged on all sides. Whereas once they were the only venue that promised one-stop shopping, now this claim has been made meaningless by the presence of large shopping malls. Department stores like Eaton's and The Bay are being challenged by discounters, like Zellers and Wal-Mart, in a battle more fierce than any fought before. New competitors, known as "category killers,"—stores that offer everything a consumer could want in a limited product market, such as toys or furniture—have taken away share from traditional retailers that offered wide versus deep product assortments. Store like Toys 'Я' Us, Leon's, The Brick Warehouse, and Business Depot fall into this category. New retailing formats, such as televised shopping networks and Internet-based virtual shopping malls, have taken on more traditional venues.

Every lesson in competitive strategy is being played out before the eyes of every Canadian consumer. We see stores vying for the position of cost leader so that they can win consumers over with lower prices. We glimpse others carving out specialized niches offering product assortments to narrow groups of purchasers. We view the remainder trying desperately to differentiate themselves from the pack by focusing on specific categories of goods that appeal to wider groups of consumers. Let us now examine some of the players in each category.

DISCOUNT DEPARTMENT STORES

The major discounters operating in the Canadian market are Zellers, Wal-Mart, and Kmart. Kmart began its Canadian operations in 1963. Even though it began an ambitious store renewal plan in 1990, along with a focus on private-label fashions such as Basic Editions and Jaclyn Smith, it was doing poorly in recent years and in 1998 was bought out by the Hudson Bay Co. Wal-Mart, on the other hand, stormed onto the Canadian market like a stampede from its American homeland, trampling many others in its path. Bringing with it the know-how gained in the highly competitive U.S. marketplace, its success begins with a superb inventory management and distribution system. It relies heavily on an Electronic Data Interchange system that feeds information from its checkouts via satellite to its suppliers. The technology helps the company to recognize those items that are selling like hot cakes while enabling it to drop those that are slow movers. This system not only explains why Wal-Mart is rarely out of stock, it also enables it to lower costs by two or three percent below the industry average. Its ability to make large-volume purchases in conjunction with its American operations, adds to its ability to keep costs low.

While Wal-Mart claims to be a price discounter, it has developed a strategy of only offering the best prices on about 500, frequently purchased items. These are the items where the consumer recognizes a bargain as soon as he or she sees the price. This creates the impression of great prices throughout Wal-Mart stores even though the remainder of its stock may actually be sold at the same or even higher prices than at other retailers. This strategy has allowed Wal-Mart to achieve sales of $400/square foot that are the envy of the entire North American retailing industry.

Zellers

Allowing Wal-Mart to purchase the 122 Woolco stores in 1994 was viewed by some analysts as Zellers's biggest mistake. Letting the American giant into its backyard has caused Zellers a number of apparently unexpected problems. It seems ironic that in May 1994, investors and the press alike hung on the words of Hudson Bay's CEO, George Kosich. Decrying the fall in Canadian retail stock prices, Kosich called this a "huge overreaction." His words were echoed in the next few minutes by another executive who called it an "enormous over-reaction" and then by a third spokesperson who said it was a "tremendous overreaction"! The phrases reflected the confidence these managers had in Zellers' position as a truly "Canadian" retailer, and in its Club Z programs to weather the onslaught from Wal-Mart.

Zellers' spokespeople are not using these words any longer. The Hudson Bay Co., which owns Zellers, announced in March 1996 that it was closing Zellers' Montreal headquarters and merging it with the Toronto operations in an effort to avoid duplication and cut operating costs. Remember that this was just two years after the speeches described above!

Zellers' 300 stores make it Canada's largest department store and the stores account for approximately 23 percent of the $15-billion discount department-store market. It competes head-to-head with Wal-Mart Canada. Targeting low-income females in the age group 25 to 49 years of age with children, Zellers has long been known in Canada for its famous slogan, "Where the lowest price is the law." Zellers used its loyalty program, Club Z, to differentiate itself from other Canadian retailers. Its displays were designed to convey an image of merchandise abundance and to maximize store traffic. While it was behind the industry in terms of incorporating technology, such as checkout scanners into its stores, it did have a state-of-the-art distribution centre. However, the mismatch between the two parts of the organization often caused bottlenecks at the store loading ramps.

In the second half of 1995, Zellers began to live its low price slogan with a passion. It entered into a price-matching battle with Wal-Mart. As a result, operating profit fell from $215.6 million to $106.7 million. Although 1995 wasn't a good year for most retailers, many analysts believed it was more than economic conditions that caused Zellers' poor showing. Some though its single-minded focus on prices blinded it from considering other important factors such as cutting costs, improving its distribution system, reducing stock-outs, and improving forecasting.

MAJOR DEPARTMENT STORES

Three retailers comprise this category in Canada: Sears Canada with 41 percent of this segment, The Bay with a 31 percent share, and Eaton's, which is believed to control 28 percent. Departments stores account for approximately $6.5 billion in annual retail sales. These stores have been losing share of market. In 1991, Statistics Canada reported their sales at $7.1 billion.

To try and recover their positions and prevent further loss of share, each retailer is struggling with the question of what it means to consumers in the new world of the 1990s. The Bay has begun renovating its stores and has started re-emphasizing hardware while focussing on fashion and cosmetics. It uses sales and heavy promotion to attract consumers. Similarly, Sears, following its U.S. parent's lead of focussing on "the softer side of Sears," is also stressing clothing, but has aimed at a more casual market of slightly lower-income consumers. Building on its traditional roots, it has started developing new freestanding stores called "Whole Home Furniture Stores" to better compete with category killers like the Brick and Leon's.

Eaton's

Founded in 1869, Eaton's is one of Canada's oldest businesses. Today it operates 93 stores across Canada. It is still a family-owned enterprise and management has passed down through four generations of the family. By the 1950s, it was Canada's favourite store, accounting for 50 percent of department-store spending in Canada. Founded by an Irish immigrant, Eaton revolutionized Canadian retailing with the promise, "Goods satisfactory or money refunded." Such a promise was unheard of in an age when retailing was very much a case of "buyer beware." Integrity and a sense of social responsibility have long marked this veteran business. When its staff members were sent to World War I and II, Eaton's continued to pay their wages. During the Depression of the 1930s, it refused to lay off employees. Not surprisingly, employees have expressed deep loyalty for the company and its owners. The Eaton family is revered as much as Sam Walton was by members of his organization.

Even though tradition has been the backbone of the company, it may also have been part of its downfall. Eaton's clung to traditional parts of the business long after market forces dictated dropping them from the store's portfolio. For example, long after specialty retailers, like Shoppers Drug Mart, took away the majority of the business, Eaton's still refused to drop drug departments from its stores. It refused to shut down many of its small-town operations, even though the economics of maintaining them seemed insurmountable.

Although it has been on the edge of bankruptcy, Eaton's is showing new signs of life. In an effort to win back consumers, Eaton's has been trimming its staff, modernizing its information systems, and improving its distribution. There is some evidence that it is moving away from its strategy of "everyday low pricing" to one that uses occasional promotions. Its stores now have state-of-the-art systems for tracking goods from supplier to store floor. The company can now move goods from its distribution centre in less that two days whereas, just four years ago, it took eight days. It has begun working more closely with its suppliers and, like discounter, Wal-Mart, has demanded more from them. If suppliers do not follow its strict rules on packaging, labelling, and shipment accuracy, the face stiff fines. It is also dealing with fewer suppliers who provide top quality and service rather than the many diverse companies as was its policy previously.

Eaton's is also one of the first retailers to recognize the need for more professional retail managers. It has gone beyond developing its own in-house training program (which was based on best practices of companies like Motorola and General Electric), to founding the Eaton School of Retailing at Ryerson University (http://www.ryerson.cal-retailed/), which opened in 1994. By forming partnerships with other universities, it now offers courses in Montreal, Edmonton, Winnipeg, and Vancouver, in addition to those offered in Toronto.

Eaton's has begun to focus its merchandising on areas in which it faces no competition from discounters. It features store-within-stores and one has the sense of visiting boutiques full of designer-label apparel like Ralph Lauren, Nautica, and Hugo Boss, as well as Eaton's own brands such as Retreat and Distinction.

Eaton's has begun to renovate its stores, earmarking $300 million for the facelift. The purpose of the renovation is to make shopping easier for its time-pressed consumers. Eaton's pictures its consumers to be mainly women, even for menswear. The company believes that 60 to 70 percent of menswear purchases are made by women. Many of them are struggling to balance hectic lives with careers, husbands, homes, and kids. Thus, Eaton's believes that they must be able to find what they are looking for quickly, and receive rapid customer assistance, both in making their choices and in paying their bills. The new concentric floor plans have been designed with this purpose in mind.

SPECIALITY RETAILERS

The remainder of Canada's retail industry is made up of speciality retailers. One can find specialty stores that cater to almost every imaginable need or interest of Canadian consumers. There are speciality stores for power-boat and yacht enthusiasts, cooking stores for the would-be gourmet, clothing boutiques for the fashion conscious, bookstores for those with alternative lifestyles, retailers who cater to swimmers and rowers, cat shops for feline lovers, personal care stores like the Body Shop, and bird-watching stores, just to name a few.

THE FUTURE

Turmoil and change seem to be the best words to describe retailing in Canada. While the tide may be coming in for some retailers, there is no doubt that it is going out for others. Many believe that there are currently just too many stores for the size of the Canadian population and that some of the major urban markets are seriously over-saturated. Mergers and acquisitions are expected to consolidate parts of the industry, but the death and decline of players in other sectors will surely occur as the industry shake-out continues. Remember that names like Birks and Woodwards were once well-recognized parts of the Canadian retailing scene.

QUESTIONS

1. Can the concept "the wheel of retailing," be used to describe the current state of retailing in Canada?

2. Develop a profile for the "typical" customer you think regularly shops at a major department store like Eaton's, Sears, or The Bay; another for people who shop discounters like Zellers, Wal-Mart, or Kmart; and a third for those who frequent speciality retailers like Sports Chek, the Body Shop, or Birders World. Which group of stores attracts the most loyal customers? The least loyal? What does this tell you about the way people cross-shop retailers?

3. Some analysts believe that the demographics of the Canadian market are very different form those of the United States. In the United States, they claim, there are four distinct groups of consumers: the rich, the near rich, the not-so-rich, and the poor. In response, there are four classes of retailers that serve these distinct segments. These analysts believe that in Canada there is only a "middle class" market that is fragmented across widely dispersed urban areas. As a result, all retailers in Canada target the same consumer using virtually identical positioning strategies. Give the reasons why you agree or disagree with this analysis.

4. Describe the consumer of the 1990s. Which of the retailers described in the case do you think has best responded to the needs of this consumer?

5. Choose one of the retailers described in this case. If you were hired as a consultant to give them advice on how to improve their operations, what would you recommend they do? Be sure to include a description of the primary target market, the positioning you would recommend, and recommendations for modifications to their marketing mix.

Sources: Peggy Cunningham wrote this case based on the following source: Paul Brent, "Bay Shakes Up Zellers," *The Financial Post*, March 15, 1996, pp. 1–2; John Heinzl, "Did Zellers Discount the Wal-Mart Threat?" *Globe and Mail*, March 8, 1996; John Heinzl, "Playoff Pressure," *Report of Business Magazine*, April 1995, pp. 91–98; Ian McGugan, "Eaton's on the Brink," *Canadian Business*, March 1996, pp. 39–73; Mark Stevenson, "The Store to End All Stores," *Canadian Business*, May 1994, pp. 20–24; Wal-Mart Integrated Case Exercise, Wilfrid Laurier University, 1994.

Video Case 13

CASHING IN ON THE BOOK BOOM

The face of book retailing in Canada is changing. As has happened in many retail markets in Canada recently, the advent of large superstores, or category killers, in this retail sector is having a profound effect on small, independent retailers. With the entrance of Chapters and other large bookstores across the country, several small retailers have been forced to close. Still others, like Sandpiper Books in Calgary, intend to fight it out with their giant competitors.

Recent growth in the demand for books has made book retailing an attractive market. Over two billion books are sold every year in Canada, more than the sales of CDs and the rental of videos combined. This demand, which is expected to grow even more in the future, has led companies like Chapters to recognize profitable opportunities in the book selling business. Chapters is a company that carries over 100 000 book titles and hundreds of magazines in over 40 000 square feet of retail space per store. The Chapters concept, closely modelled after Barnes and Noble, a U.S. company that owns 20 percent of Chapters, features discounted books in a relaxed, upscale environment. As Larry Stevenson, CEO of Chapters, says, he wants to provide books in an environment that is conducive to browsing. Comfortable couches and an in-store cafe are just two of the features that support this positioning.

Three of Chapters' recent store openings have been in Calgary. Even before the second store was open, one of Calgary's oldest bookstores was forced to close. Treehouse Books, a children's bookstore located in a mall, was asked to close by mall management after Chapters was chosen as an anchor store for the mall. Remaining small bookstores in Calgary are facing still more competition from Bollum's books, a large book retailer started in Vancouver, which has opened a superstore in Calgary as well.

Sandpiper Books is a well-known independent bookstore in Calgary. President Kerry Longpre recognizes the competitive threat from the large book retailers but is prepared to meet the competition head on through a series of improvements to her store and a refocus of her retail strategy. She has changed locations, tripled her floor space, hired more staff, opened a cafe, and increased advertising for her store. She is also prepared to offer a superior level of service than is available in the superstores. She feels that service is key to her survival and as a result has hired very specialized staff to sell books. For example, a travel writer is working in the travel section and business people are selling business books. In addition, she is sponsoring special events for her customers, such as readings given by prominent writers.

As Sandpiper prepares to fight for survival in the Calgary market, Chapters has gone public to finance more expansion across the country. And even more competition is about to arrive in the Canadian book retail business. Indigo Books and Music is a book superstore concept that businesswoman Heather Reismann will soon be launching and that will serve, as Reismann claims, "true book lovers." With the entrance of Indigo, independent book retailers will again have to determine how to compete against yet another book superstore.

QUESTIONS:

1. Which consumers do you think Chapters is targeting? What aspects of a category killer like Chapters would consumers find appealing? Are there aspects of a category killer like Chapters that consumers would find unappealing?

2. What suggestions can you make to independent retailers like Sandpiper Books regarding the retail strategies (target market and positioning) and marketing mix (product and service assortment, prices, promotion and location) they can use to compete effectively with category killers like Chapters?

3. What impact, if any, do you think Chapters and other book superstores will have on non-store retailers of books (such as book clubs and Internet bookstores like amazon.com)?

Source: This case was prepared by Auleen Carson and is based on the *Venture* series episode "Book Biz," which was first broadcast on December 8, 1996.

Principles of
Marketing

Principles of
Marketi

ciples
Mark

CHAPTER 14

INTEGRATED
MARKETING
COMMUNICATION
STRATEGY

ALWAYS SEE
HOW LATE YOU ARE.
TIMEX INDIGLO

With bated breath, Canada's top advertising executives at the 1997 Marketing Awards waited to hear those magic words, "And the winner is...." While some attendees were confident they knew the advertising campaign that would take the honours, they didn't expect to hear the same name quite so many times. Timex Canada's Indiglo ads took an unprecedented number of awards: six gold awards—one each for the prestigious multimedia campaign, television campaign, television single ad under 30 seconds, television ad with a production cost under $50 000, newspaper campaign, and newspaper single-ad category. It also won eight silver medals including one for its magazine campaign, a bronze medal, and a certificate of honour in the outdoor/out-of-home single category.

Not bad for a series of ads that are deceptively simple. Each ad features little more than a wavy blue line on a black background. Each line captures the movement made by an Olympic athlete wearing an Indiglo watch while performing in his or her event: a rower, a diver, a runner, and the Canadian men's relay team. The ads have little text other than the brand and company name and the acknowledgment that the firm sponsors Canada's Olympic athletes. Bringing home the hardware didn't stop with the Marketing Awards for Indiglo, however. The ads also won *Strategy* magazine's top client award and the best media plan competition. Even more impressive was the Gold Lion awarded to the campaign at the International Advertising Festival held in Cannes, France.

The way the ads were judged speaks volumes about advertising today. For the Marketing Awards, the panel of judges looked for exceptional creativity combined with powerful persuasiveness. Ads couldn't be bland or boring; they had to be imaginative, engaging, and involving. The judges for the best media plan at *Strategy* magazine looked for the high quality of thinking that must go into an integrated media effort. They assessed the challenges and objectives that were presented to the agency by the client and how the creators of the media plan addressed these challenges both strategically and creatively. Finally, the media plan had to be effective, as evidenced by sales results and tracking studies.

OBJECTIVES

When you finish this chapter, you should be able to

1. Name and define the four tools of the promotion mix.

2. Outline the steps in developing effective marketing communication.

3. Explain the methods for setting the promotion budget and factors that affect the design of the promotion mix.

4. Identify the major factors that are changing today's marketing communications environment.

5. Discuss the process and advantages of integrated marketing communications.

Ogilvy & Mather
www.ogilvy.com/

Toronto's Ogilvy & Mather agency created the campaign for Timex. Timex had a new proprietary technology that it was incorporating into its watch line: the Timex Indiglo Night Light. Ogilvy & Mather had to create a campaign to launch the product. It needed to create awareness among the target audience of 18- to 49-year-olds across Canada. Ogilvy & Mather had to find the best media to demonstrate the technology in an impactful, innovative, and relevant way.

While choosing television as the media to build national awareness was the first and easiest choice, Ogilvy & Mather knew that other promotional materials would be needed to reinforce the television campaign. The agency therefore added print media, including newspapers and magazines. But even this was not enough. Since the technology in the new watch was groundbreaking, the media chosen had to be equally innovative. For this reason, Ogilvy & Mather also chose outdoor advertising that used custom-built backlights as well as electronic superboards to round out the campaign.

The Indiglo campaign is unique not only for the simplicity of its creative, but also because it went against some tried and true rules of advertising. It has always been the traditional view that the same creative will not work successfully in multi-media. That is, different executions are required for television, newspapers, and magazines. Conventional wisdom states that newspapers lend themselves best to price and sales messages because newspapers are printed and read daily. Magazines, however, are better suited to brand building. Steven Landsberg, creative director for the campaign, stressed that such general rules don't matter, but rather that the idea underpinning the execution must be inherently linked to the medium. "We try not to do ads. We try to create ideas that happen to be ads," he stresses. The ad must also be noticed by consumers and this requires more than just a strong selling idea. "It has to arouse curiosity," Landsberg adds.

Timex
www.timex.com/

When developing the Indiglo campaign, Landsberg knew that people first seeing the ads would wonder what the curious blue line slithering across their television screen actually was. Viewers' attention would be captured because they would have to determine that it was a Timex Indiglo watch worn by an Olympic athlete during his or her event. He noted that the idea of the simple blue line was so strong that it would work in almost any medium. But there were limits. The concept of the blue line wasn't suitable for the outdoor campaign. For this reason, he chose an Indiglo watch that actually kept time with the headline "Always see how late you are" for the outdoor superboards. According to Landsberg, because the medium was active, "the message becomes an event." Five superboards were placed in Timex's top three markets: Montreal, Vancouver, and Toronto. Not only did they catch the public eye, but they became "entertainment on the road," said Timex's marketing manager, Leo Fournier. As you can see, the campaign was both strategic and effective despite being developed on a limited budget.[1]

Modern marketing calls for more than just developing a good product, pricing it attractively, and making it available to target customers. Companies also must *communicate* with their customers, and what they communicate should not be left to chance. For most companies, the question is not *whether* to communicate, but *how much to spend* and *in what ways*.

Marketing communications mix (or Promotion mix)
The specific mix of advertising, personal selling, sales promotion, and public relations a company uses to pursue its advertising and marketing objectives.

■ THE MARKETING COMMUNICATIONS MIX

A company's total **marketing communications mix**—called its **promotion mix**—consists of the specific blend of advertising, personal selling, sales promotion, and public relations tools that the company uses to pursue its advertising and marketing objectives. Definitions of the four major promotion tools follow:

Advertising
Any paid form of nonpersonal presentation and promotion of ideas, goods, or services by an identified sponsor.

◆   **Advertising:** Any paid form of non-personal presentation and promotion of ideas, goods, or services by an identified sponsor.

Personal selling
Personal presentation by
the firm's sales force for the
purpose of making sales and
building customer relationships.

Sales promotion
Short-term incentives to
encourage purchase or sales
of a product or service.

Public relations
Building good relations with
the company's various publics
by obtaining favourable
publicity, building up a good
"corporate image," and
handling or heading off
unfavourable rumours,
stories, and events.

Direct marketing
Direct communications with
carefully targeted individuals
to obtain an immediate
response.

◆ **Personal selling:** Personal presentation by the firm's sales force for the purpose of making sales and building customer relationships.

◆ **Sales promotion:** Short-term incentives to encourage the purchase or sale of a product or service.

◆ **Public relations:** Building good relations with the company's various publics by obtaining favourable publicity, building up a good "corporate image," and handling or heading off unfavourable rumours, stories, and events.[2]

◆ **Direct marketing:** Direct communications with carefully targeted individual consumers to obtain an immediate response—the use of mail, telephone, fax, e-mail, and other non-personal tools to communicate directly with specific consumers or to solicit a direct response.

Each category consists of specific tools. For example, advertising includes print, broadcast, outdoor, and other forms. Personal selling includes sales presentations, trade shows, and incentive programs. Sales promotion includes point-of-purchase displays, premiums, discounts, coupons, specialty advertising, and demonstrations. Direct marketing includes catalogues, telemarketing, fax transmissions, the Internet, and more. Thanks to technological breakthroughs, people can now communicate through traditional media (newspapers, radio, telephone, and television), as well as newer media forms (fax machines, cellular phones, pagers, and computers). These new technologies have encouraged more companies to move from mass communication to more targeted communication and one-to-one dialogue.

At the same time, communication goes beyond these specific promotion tools. The product's design, its price, the shape and colour of its package, and the stores that sell it—*all* communicate something to buyers. Thus, although the promotion mix is the company's primary communication activity, the entire marketing mix—promotion *and* product, price, and place—must be coordinated for greatest communication impact.

In this chapter, we begin by examining three questions: First, *how does the communication process work?* Second, *what are the major steps in developing effective marketing communication?* Third, *how should the promotion budget and mix be determined?* We then look at recent dramatic changes in marketing communications that have resulted from shifting marketing strategies and advances in computers and information technologies. Next, we summarize the legal, ethical, and social responsibility issues in marketing communications. In Chapter 15, we look at *mass-communication tools*—advertising, sales promotion, and public relations. Chapter 16 examines the *sales force* as a communication and promotion tool, and Chapter 17 reviews developments in *direct and online marketing*.

A VIEW OF THE COMMUNICATION PROCESS

Too often, marketing communications has a short-term outlook focused on overcoming awareness, image, or preference problems in the target market. But this approach to communication has limitations: it is too short term and too costly, and most messages of this type fall on deaf ears. Today's marketers are moving toward viewing communications as the management of the customer buying process over time, during the pre-selling, selling, consuming, and post-consumption stages. Because customers differ, communications programs must be developed for specific segments, niches, and even individuals. And, given the new interactive communications technologies, companies must ask not only "How can we reach our customers?" but also "How can we find ways to let our customers reach us?"

Thus, the communications process should start with an audit of all the potential interactions that target customers may have with the product and company. For example, someone purchasing a new computer may talk to others, see

FIGURE 14-1
Elements in the communication process

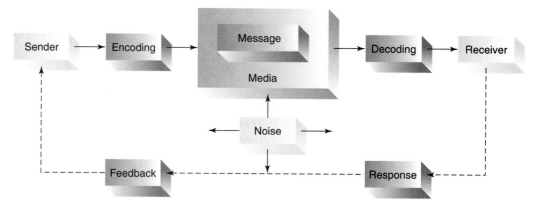

television commercials, read articles and ads in newspapers and magazines, and try out computers in the store. The marketer must assess the influence that each of these communications experiences will have at different stages of the buying process. This understanding will help marketers to allocate their communication dollars more efficiently and effectively.

To communicate effectively, marketers need to understand how communication works. Communication involves the nine elements shown in Figure 14-1. Two of these elements are the major parties in a communication—the sender and receiver. Another two are the major communication tools—the message and the media. Four more are major communication functions—encoding, decoding, response, and feedback. The last element is noise in the system. Definitions of these elements follow and are applied to an ad for Hewlett Packard colour copiers.

An understanding of the concerns of home-business owners helps Hewlett-Packard communicate effectively.

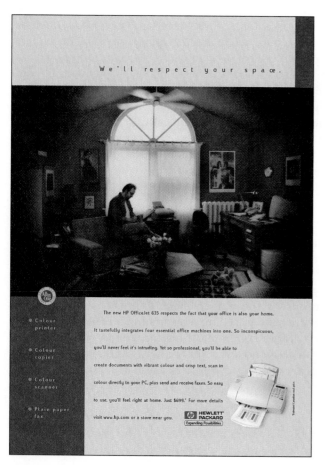

- ◆ *Sender:* The party sending the message to another party—here, Hewlett Packard.
- ◆ *Encoding:* The process of putting thought into symbolic form—Hewlett Packard's advertising agency assembles words and illustrations into an advertisement that will convey the intended message.
- ◆ *Message:* The set of symbols that the sender transmits—the actual HP copier ad.
- ◆ *Media:* The communication channels through which the message moves from sender to receiver—in this case, the specific magazines that Hewlett Packard selects.
- ◆ *Decoding:* The process by which the receiver assigns meaning to the symbols encoded by the sender—a consumer reads the HP copier ad and interprets the words and illustrations it contains.
- ◆ *Receiver:* The party receiving the message sent by another party—the home office or business customer who reads the HP copier ad.
- ◆ *Response:* The reactions of the receiver after being exposed to the message—any of hundreds of possible responses, such as the consumer is more aware of the attributes of HP copiers, actually buys an HP copier, or does nothing.
- ◆ *Feedback:* The part of the receiver's response communicated back to the sender—Hewlett Packard research shows that consumers are struck by and remember the ad, or consumers write or call HP praising or criticizing the ad or HP's products.

◆ *Noise:* The unplanned static or distortion during the communication process, which results in the receiver's getting a different message than the one the sender sent—the consumer is distracted while reading the magazine and misses the Hewlett Packard ad or its key points.

For a message to be effective, the sender's encoding process must mesh with the receiver's decoding process. Thus, the best messages consist of words and other symbols that are familiar to the receiver. The more the sender's field of experience overlaps with that of the receiver, the more effective the message is likely to be. Marketing communicators may not always share their consumer's field of experience. For example, an advertising copywriter from one social stratum might create ads for consumers from another stratum—say, blue-collar workers or wealthy business owners. However, to communicate effectively, the marketing communicator must understand the consumer's field of experience.

This model points out several key factors in good communication. Senders need to know what audiences they wish to reach and what responses they want. They must be good at encoding messages that take into account how the target audience decodes them. They must send messages through media that reach target audiences, and they must develop feedback channels so that they can assess the audience's response to the message.

STEPS IN DEVELOPING EFFECTIVE COMMUNICATION

We now examine the steps in developing an effective integrated communications and promotion program. The marketing communicator must do the following: identify the target audience; determine the response sought; choose a message; choose the media through which to send the message; select the message source; and collect feedback.

IDENTIFYING THE TARGET AUDIENCE

Buyer-readiness stages
The stages consumers typically pass through on their way to purchase, including awareness, knowledge, liking, preference, conviction, and purchase.

A marketing communicator starts with a clear target audience in mind. The audience may be potential buyers or current users, those who make the buying decision or those who influence it. The audience may be individuals, groups, special publics, or the general public. The target audience will heavily affect the communicator's decisions on *what* will be said, *how* it will be said, *when* it will be said, *where* it will be said, and *who* will say it.

DETERMINING THE RESPONSE SOUGHT

FIGURE 14-2 *Buyer-readiness stages*

Once the target audience has been defined, the marketing communicator must decide what response is sought. Of course, in most cases, the final response is *purchase*. But purchase is the result of a long process of consumer decision-making. The target audience may be in any of six **buyer-readiness stages**, the stages that consumers typically pass through on their way to making a purchase. The marketing communicator needs to know where the target audience now stands and to what stage it needs to be moved. These stages include *awareness, knowledge, liking, preference, conviction,* or *purchase* (see Figure 14-2).

The marketing communicator's target market may be totally unaware of the product, know only its name, or know one or a few things about it. The communicator must first build *awareness* and *knowledge*.

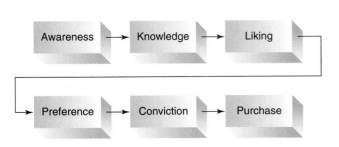

JAY WHITESIDE—ENTREPRENEUR

Jay has been involved in one form of marketing or another for most of his career. He took his degree from Western University with a major in social sciences. Jay's marketing experiences are really eclectic. He has worked as a marketing manager and marketing instructor. He began his career with Black & Decker, went next to Harlequin Books, and then moved on to McDonald's Restaurants. He moved on again to become the head of Sport and Entertainment sponsorships for Labatt Breweries and was involved with developing the Toronto Olympic bid before becoming an independent businessperson. He is currently working on a number of ventures including his ice gardens concept.

Give Marketing Some Respect!

Despite all of his experience in marketing, it wasn't until Jay read Regis McKenna's article, "Marketing is Everything," that he felt he didn't have to apologize for his profession. McKenna's article reinforced and confirmed Jay's personal view that marketing is a process-driven activity in which an analytical approach is key. Like McKenna, Jay believes that everything an organization does is marketing. He stresses, however, that there is much more to marketing than just the notion of the marketing mix. The ultimate consumer benefit may be the result of good financial controls just as much as it can arise from superior advertising. In other words, Jay says, marketing is a general management function, not a specialty.

Jay has always liked marketing because it appeals to his "split personality." Marketing has allowed him to use two very different sets of skills. First, he brings a systematic approach to marketing problems, working methodically from one issue to the next so that he can thoroughly understand consumers and base his strategies on them. This is where Jay wrestles with one of the profound paradoxes of marketing. He has to use his analytical skills to understand how the product or services history is written, but then he must use this evidence from the past to predict outcomes in the future. Now he can focus on opportunities, on influencing the future, and on being creative.

The New Venture—Ice Gardens

Jay has been able to bring all of the above thinking to bear on his new business venture, the Ice Garden.™ This venture will instal four to six ice rinks in one location. They will attract a more diverse set of users than any one venue could possibly draw, and as a result of their economies of scale, they will be able to offer a range of services not possible in stand-alone facilities. Although the first Ice Garden installation is being planned for York University, Jay believes that the concept will enjoy its greatest success in the United States.

Jay Whiteside

In the United States, the rinks will be used as part of the NHL venue, as well as creating a value-added location. Not only will Ice Gardens allow teams to expand their franchises, but they will also allow developers and corporate sponsors to tap into the exponential growth in youth ice sports such as hockey and figure skating. Each Ice Garden will act as a family entertainment centre, and will feature dry-land training facilities, provide day care, enable customized coaching and tutorials, as well as providing a pro shop and food services. Such a wide range of activities are offered that the Ice Gardens will attract 18 different market segments. Delivery of a substantial consumer benefit is at the heart of the strategy since Jay firmly believes that if you do well by consumers, they will do well by you.

In marketing the Ice Garden concept to potential corporate sponsors such as Bell Canada, Pepsi, Nike, Hostess-Frito Lay, or Imperial Oil, Jay notes the importance of branding as well as a targeted communications strategy. While many people looking for sponsorships have held out their hands and focused on what the sponsor can do for them, Jay stresses that it is more important to focus on what the venue can do for the sponsor. Sponsors value factors such as the ability to achieve marketing objectives, deliver a particular target audience, or transfer a unique image to the firm.

Understanding the Canadian Marketplace

While Canadian and American managers are equally knowledgeable and capable, some differences can be noted. Jay believes Canadian managers are slower to make decisions, often make fewer decisions, and sometimes are not as committed to thoroughness in their analysis. Americans, on the other hand, tend to "own" problems and take responsibility for their solution, pay more attention to detail, and have a higher service orientation than Canadians. Jay attributes this to our different histories. Whereas Americans came from a frontier society where individuals had to rely on themselves, Canadians were part of a colonial structure, where people turned to government to solve problems. This has led to differences in the way firms try to raise venture capital as well as the way they approach business. For example, Canadians turn to governments and banks for funding, whereas American entrepreneurs are more likely to go to their personal networks of families, friends, key customers, or neighbours to solicit investment. Jay also notes that our recent histories have been shaped by radically different influences. Much of the U.S. mindset has been influenced by the experiences of the Vietnam War. This is especially noticeable in government hierarchies, where the networks formed during the Vietnam conflict now link many senior managers today.

Jay's experience and vision will undoubtedly take his new venture forward to success. Whether he is passing the puck to his American teammates or working on strength building at home, his experience, insight, and knowledge of marketing will serve him well.

Source: Jay Whiteside was interviewed by P. Cunningham for *Principles of Marketing* on April 9, 1996. We sincerely wish to thank him for the insights he provided on the practice of marketing.

For example, when Nissan introduced its Infiniti automobile line, it began with an extensive "teaser" advertising campaign to create name familiarity. Initial ads for the Infiniti created curiosity and awareness by showing the car's name but not the car. Later ads created knowledge by informing potential buyers of the car's high quality and many innovative features.

Assuming target consumers *know* the product, how do they *feel* about it? Once potential buyers know about the Infiniti, Nissan's marketers want to move them through successively stronger stages of feelings toward the car. These stages include *liking* (feeling favourable about the Infiniti), *preference* (preferring Infiniti to other car brands), and *conviction* (believing that Infiniti is the best car for them). Infiniti marketers can use a combination of the promotion mix tools to create positive feelings and conviction. Advertising extols the Infiniti's advantages over competing brands. Press releases and other public relations activities stress the car's innovative features and performance. Dealer salespeople tell buyers about options, value for the price, and after-sale service.

Finally, some members of the target market might be convinced about the product, but not quite get around to making the *purchase.* Potential Infiniti buyers may decide to wait for more information, or for the economy to improve. The communicator must lead these consumers to take the final step. Actions might include offering special promotional prices, rebates, or premiums. Salespeople might call or write to selected customers, inviting them to visit the dealership for a special showing.

Of course, marketing communications alone cannot create positive feelings and purchases for Infiniti. The car itself must provide superior value for the customer. In fact, outstanding marketing communications can actually speed the demise of a poor product. The more quickly potential buyers learn about the poor product, the more quickly they become aware of its faults. Thus, good marketing communication calls for "good deeds followed by good words."

DESIGNING A MESSAGE

Having defined the desired audience response, the communicator turns to developing an effective message. Ideally, the message should get *Attention,* hold *Interest,* arouse *Desire,* and obtain *Action* (a framework known as the *AIDA model*). In practice, few messages take the consumer all the way from awareness to purchase, but the AIDA framework suggests the qualities of a good message.

In putting together the message, the marketing communicator must solve three problems: what to say (*message content*), how to say it logically (*message structure*), and how to say it symbolically (*message format*).

Message Content

Rational appeals
Message appeals that relate to the audience's self-interest and show that the product will produce the claimed benefits; examples include appeals of product quality, economy, value, or performance.

The communicator must identify an appeal or theme that will produce the desired response. There are three types of appeals: rational, emotional, and moral.

Rational appeals relate to the audience's self-interest. They show that the product will produce the desired benefits. Examples are messages showing a product's quality, economy, value, or performance. Thus, in its ads, Mercedes offers cars that are "engineered like no other car in the world," stressing engineering design, performance, and safety. Buckley's Mixture took its most recognizable quality, the bad taste of its cough syrup, and recently turned it into an award-winning campaign linked by the tag line, "It tastes awful. And it works."

Emotional appeals
Message appeals that attempt to stir up negative or positive emotions that will motivate purchase; examples include fear, guilt, shame, love, humour, pride, and joy appeals.

Emotional appeals attempt to stir up either negative or positive emotions that can motivate purchase. Communicators may use positive emotional appeals such as love, pride, joy, and humour. For example, advocates for humorous messages claim that they attract more attention and create more liking and belief in the sponsor. Cliff Freeman, the advertiser responsible for Little Caesars' humorous

"Pizza, Pizza" ads, contends that "Humour is a great way to bound out of the starting gate. When you make people laugh, and they feel good after seeing the commercial, they like the association with the product." But others maintain that humour can detract from comprehension, wear out its welcome fast, and overshadow the product.[3]

Communicators can also use negative emotional appeals such as fear, guilt, and shame, which get people to do things they should (brush their teeth, buy new tires), or to stop doing things they shouldn't (smoke, drink too much, eat fatty foods). For example, a Crest ad invokes mild fear when it claims, "There are some things you just can't afford to gamble with" (cavities). Etonic ads ask "What would you do if you couldn't run?" They go on to note that Etonic athletic shoes are designed to avoid injuries—they're "built so you can last." So does a Michelin tire ad that features cute babies and suggests, "Because so much is riding on your tires."

Moral appeals are directed to the audience's sense of what is "right" and "proper." They often are used to urge people to support social causes such as a cleaner environment and aid to the needy, or combat social problems such as drug abuse, discrimination, sexual harassment, and spousal abuse. An example of a moral appeal is the March of Dimes appeal: "God made you whole. Give to help those He didn't."

Message Structure

The communicator also must decide how to handle three message-structure issues. The first is whether to draw a conclusion or leave it to the audience. Early research showed that drawing a conclusion was usually more effective. More recent research, however, suggests that in many cases the advertiser is better off asking questions and letting buyers draw their own conclusions. The second message-structure issue is whether to present a one-sided argument (mentioning only the product's strengths), or a two-sided argument (touting the product's strengths while also admitting its shortcomings). Thus, Heinz ran the message "Heinz Ketchup is *slow good*" and Listerine ran the message "Listerine tastes bad twice a day." Usually, a one-sided argument is more effective in sales presentations—except when audiences are highly educated, negatively disposed, or likely to hear opposing claims. In these cases, two-sided messages can enhance the advertiser's credibility and make buyers more resistant to competitor attacks. The third message-structure issue is whether to present the strongest arguments first or last. Presenting them first gets strong attention, but may lead to an anti-climactic ending.[4]

Message Format

The marketing communicator also needs a strong *format* for the message. In a print ad, the communicator has to decide on the headline, copy, illustration, and colour. To attract attention, advertisers can use novelty and contrast; eye-catching pictures and headlines; distinctive formats; message size and position; and colour, shape, and movement. If the message will be carried over the radio, the communicator must choose words, sounds, and voices. The "sound" of an announcer promoting banking services should be different from one promoting quality furniture.

If the message is to be carried on television or in person, then all these elements plus body language have to be planned. Presenters plan their facial

---

Moral appeals
Advertising messages directed to the audience's sense of what is "right" or "proper."

WEB LINKS

March of Dimes
www.modimes.org/

A mild fear appeal:
"When you get a cavity,
there's no second chance."

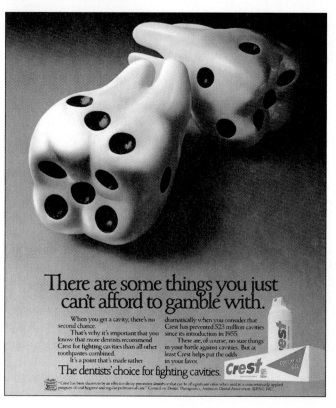

There are some things you just can't afford to gamble with.

When you get a cavity, there's no second chance.
That's why it's important that you know that more dentists recommend Crest for fighting cavities than all other toothpastes combined.
It's a point that's made rather

dramatically when you consider that Crest has prevented 523 million cavities since its introduction in 1955.
There are, of course, no sure things in your battle against cavities. But at least Crest helps put the odds in your favor.

The dentists' choice for fighting cavities. **Crest**

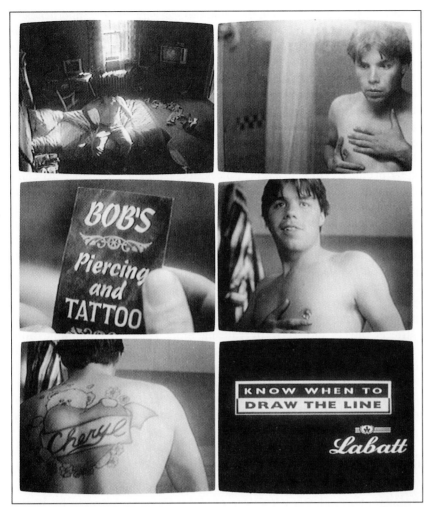

Labatt's award-winning "Know When to Draw the Line" television campaign captured attention and communicated a serious message in a persuasive and humorous manner.

Personal communication channels
Channels through which two or more people communicate directly with each other, including face to face, person to audience, over the telephone, or through the mail or e-mail.

Word-of-mouth influence
Personal communication about a product between target buyers and neighbours, friends, family members, and associates.

expressions, gestures, dress, posture, and hair style. If the message is carried on the product or its package, the communicator has to watch texture, scent, colour, size, and shape. For example, colour plays a major communication role in food preferences. When consumers sampled four cups of coffee that had been placed next to brown, blue, red, and yellow containers (all the coffee was identical, but the consumers did not know this), 75 percent felt that the coffee next to the brown container tasted too strong; nearly 85 percent judged the coffee next to the red container to be the richest; nearly everyone felt that the coffee next to the blue container was mild; and the coffee next to the yellow container was seen as weak. Thus, if a coffee company wants to communicate that its coffee is rich, it should probably use a red container along with label copy boasting the coffee's rich taste.[5]

CHOOSING MEDIA

The communicator now must select *channels of communication*. There are two broad types of communication channels—*personal* and *non-personal*.

Personal Communication Channels

In **personal communication channels,** two or more people communicate directly with each other. They might communicate face to face, over the telephone, or even through the mail or e-mail. Personal communication channels are effective because they allow for personal addressing and feedback.

Some personal communication channels are controlled directly by the company. For example, company salespeople contact buyers in the target market. But other personal communications about the product may reach buyers through channels not directly controlled by the company. These might include independent experts—consumer advocates, consumer buying guides, and others—making statements to target buyers. Or they might be neighbours, friends, family members, and associates talking to target buyers. This last channel, known as **word-of-mouth influence,** has considerable effect in many product areas.

Personal influence carries great weight for products that are expensive, risky, or highly visible. For example, buyers of automobiles, home decor, and fashion often go beyond mass-media sources to seek the opinions of knowledgeable people.

Companies can take several steps to put personal communication channels to work for them. They can devote extra effort to selling their products to well-known people or companies, who may in turn influence others to buy. They can create *opinion leaders*—people whose opinions are sought by others—by supplying certain people with the product on attractive terms. For example, companies can work through community members such as local radio personalities, class presidents, and heads of local organizations. And they can use influential people in their advertisements or develop advertising that has high "conversation value."

Non-personal Communication Channels

Non-personal communication
channels
Media that carry messages without personal contact or feedback, including major media, atmospheres, and events.

Campbell Soup Company
www.campbellsoup.com/

Using a celebrity,
Shaquille O'Neil, helped
Pepsi score with
consumers.

Non-personal communication channels are media that carry messages without personal contact or feedback. They include major media, atmospheres, and events. Major *media* include print media (newspapers, magazines, direct mail); broadcast media (radio, television); and display media (billboards, signs, posters). *Atmospheres* are designed environments that create or reinforce the buyer's leanings toward buying a product. Thus, lawyers' offices and banks are designed to communicate confidence and other qualities that might be valued by their clients. *Events* are staged occurrences that communicate messages to target audiences. For example, public relations departments arrange press conferences, grand openings, shows and exhibits, public tours, and other events. Many Canadian companies sponsor sporting events that draw audiences that match the firm's target market. For example, the Bank of Montreal is the lead sponsor for equestrian events held at Spruce Meadows in Calgary and at the Royal Winter Fair in Toronto. Molson Breweries holds two annual Indy races: one in Vancouver, the other in Toronto.

Non-personal communication affects buyers directly. In addition, using mass media often affects buyers indirectly by causing more personal communication. Communications first flow from television, magazines, and other mass media to opinion leaders and then from these opinion leaders to others. Thus, opinion leaders step between the mass media and their audiences and carry messages to people who are less exposed to media. This suggests that mass communicators should aim their messages directly at opinion leaders, letting them carry the message to others.

BETTER GET YOURS BEFORE SHAQ GETS IT ALL.

SELECTING THE MESSAGE SOURCE

The message's impact on the audience also is affected by how the audience views the sender. Messages delivered by highly credible sources are more persuasive. For example, pharmaceutical companies want doctors to tell about their products' benefits because doctors are very credible figures. Many food companies now are promoting to doctors, dentists, and other health-care providers to motivate these professionals to recommend their products to patients.

Campbell Soup Company did this to promote its new Intelligent Cuisine meal plan program of prepackaged, healthy frozen entrées and snacks that are delivered weekly via UPS to customers' homes. The 40 or so meals are tailored to nutritional guidelines limiting fat, cholesterol, and salt. To win the support of physicians, Campbell consulted with the Heart and Stroke Association and Canadian Diabetes Association, and sponsored research on the program's effectiveness. Campbell's salespeople visit health-care professionals regularly, urging them to recommend the Intelligent Cuisine program to their patients.[6]

Marketers also hire celebrity endorsers—well-known athletes, actors, and even cartoon characters—to deliver their messages (see Marketing Highlight 14-1). Runner Donovan Bailey flies around the track wearing Adidas, basketball star Michael Jordan soars for Nike, rower Marnie McBean shampoos with Pert, Shaquille O'Neal is "Mr. Big"

CELEBRITY ENDORSERS

"Kid, you've got the talent, but you've got a problem," barks Bill Laimbeer, one of basketball's all-time dirtiest players, at young superstar Grant Hill during a commercial for Fila. "You're too nice." A series of drills follows in which Laimbeer tries to teach Hill elbowing, tripping, referee abuse, cameraman pushing, nose piercing—all the skills needed for today's modern athletes to make big money off the court and playing field. But the joke is on Laimbeer. A follow-up spot shows Hill calling his mom, asking her to rescue him. The next commercial in the series depicts Hill finally breaking free of Laimbeer's hold, despite 52 days of brainwashing at "Camp Tough Guy." "I've got to play with decency, honesty," he says as a ray of light dawns upon him. "I've got to play clean." Clean is now cool. Clean is also lucrative. For endorsing Fila's running shoes, Hill will receive about $36 million over five years.

Companies today are paying big bucks to have their products associated with big-name athletes. North American companies this year put more than $1 billion into the pockets of perhaps 2000 athletes for endorsement deals and licensing rights—a tenfold increase from just a decade ago. With so much money riding on athletes as spokespersons, companies are taking great care to put their money on endorsers with the right stuff. In fact, of the $290 million earned in endorsements and licensing income listed by *Forbes* magazine's Super 40 list of top-earning athletes last year, $250 million went to athletes with sterling reputations.

Choosing the wrong salesperson can result in embarrassment and a tarnished image. Hertz discovered this when it entrusted its good name to the care of spokesmen like O.J. Simpson. Kellogg Canada Inc. is still feeling the agony over its sponsorship of sprinter Ben Johnson, who was stripped of his gold medal after the 1988 Olympics for taking an illegal substance.

Manufacturers and advertisers seek an endorser's "halo effect"—the positive association that bathes the product in good vibes after a popular sports celebrity has pitched it. The trend toward nice is very good news for brand names that are marketed

globally. Tennis star Michael Chang has emerged as the most popular athlete in Asia by far. Reebok is basing its entire Asian strategy around him, as is Procter & Gamble's Rejoice (Pert Plus) shampoo line. What makes Asia so crazy about Chang? It's not just his heritage. It's also his persona. On a continent where family is considered paramount, Chang is coached by his brother, and they travel frequently with their parents. He's properly humble and soft-spoken as well. "We've always been a very close-knit family, and I think that's pretty characteristic of Asian families, period," says Chang.

Olympic sponsorship is a significant marketing vehicle for many firms.

Professional athletes aren't the only ones drawing sponsorship dollars. Amateur athletes, especially those training for the Olympics, are receiving increased attention. Olympic sponsorship is a significant marketing vehicle, whether it is of the Games themselves, the teams that compete in them, or individual athletes. People aren't as jaded in their views of Olympic athletes as they are about their professional counterparts. Although Olympic athletes may not be household names, people believe that these athletes compete for the love of the sport. Thus, the goodwill that adheres to a company that supports Olympic athletes is greater than that associated with support of a professional sports celebrity. Since the Olympics draw both international and national audiences, they provide

sponsoring companies with the opportunity to speak to the world.

The power of the Games has led Kellogg to re-enter the sponsorship game. Runner Donovan Bailey will grace the front of the Corn Flakes box. Swimmer Joanne Malar, who projects an image of fitness and health-consciousness, was chosen as the perfect fit for Special K. Divers Anne Montminy and Annie Pelletier will also receive Kellogg's support.

Kellogg certainly isn't alone in its sponsorship of Canadian Olympic athletes. Home Depot Canada has a unique program in which it provides jobs for 10 Olympians in training. Panasonic runs breakthrough advertising showing the women's rowing team tearing up the pavement of Canadian cities. Nike Canada supports the snowboarding and hockey teams. Roots Canada was one of Canada's official clothing providers for the Games, and also sponsors individual athletes such as skater Elvis Stojko. Tim Hortons supports the Canadian Cycling Association, while Procter & Gamble supports the Spirit of Sport Foundation.

Olympic sponsorship is not without risks, however. When firms endorse an individual athlete, they run the risk that the person might not perform as well as hoped. They may say something unfortunate in their excitement over victory. They may even bring disrepute as when Canadian snowboarder Ross Rebagliati was temporarily stripped of his win after testing positive for marijuana. Many sponsors are now making their sponsored athletes sign codes of conduct and morality.

Rather than sponsoring individual competitors, many firms are now endorsing teams. Ken McGovern, a Vancouver researcher who specializes in sponsorship says, "When you're endorsing a team, what you're really doing is endorsing the spirit of the Games, the excitement of competition and the national pride that comes with that." Corporations that help make all this happen reap a tremendous harvest of goodwill.

Although the sponsorship arena has long been dominated by male athletes, not only men's teams are drawing sponsorship dollars. In 1998, women's hockey was an Olympic event for the first time, and the Canadian team attracted a number of sponsors including Imperial Oil.

While some corporations focus their sponsorship efforts on just the athletes, other firms such as McDonald's of Canada take a more integrated approach. The company begins by sponsoring the CBC, the official broadcaster of the games. Each of its 950 Canadian restaurants is designated an "official headquarters." All of McDonald's in-restaurant materials feature Olympic themes from tray liners to sandwich wraps to a special magazine touting Olympic values. Olympic watches are offered as the featured premium and the company sends coupon booklets bearing Olympic logos to every Canadian household. Sales of the watches alone raise $1 million for the Canadian Olympic team. So that people watching the television coverage of the Games don't get bored with watching a single ad aired again and again, McDonald's is creating 11 commercials. McDonald's believes that it is better to be associated with the spirit of the Games than it is to sponsor an individual athlete.

Sources: Portions adapted from Lane Randall, "Nice Guys Finish First," *Forbes*, December 16, 1996, pp. 236–242. Also see Susan Chandler, "Michael Jordan's Full Corporate Press," *Business Week*, April 7, 1997; and Roy S. Johnson, "Tiger!" *Fortune*, May 12, 1997, pp. 73–84; John Heinzl, "Logos an Olympic event," *Globe and Mail*, October 20, 1997, B1, B4; Lara Mills, "Women get in the Game," *Marketing*, April 7, 1997, pp. 10–11; James Walker, "Ben Johnson on their minds," *The Financial Post*, July 13, 1996; www. kelloggs.com/index_nite.html

for Cadbury Chocolate Canada, skaters Isabelle Brasseur and Lloyd Eisler are fuelled by beef, and Jerry Seinfeld stumps for American Express. In fact, *Advertising Age* magazine recently named the entire cast of the "Seinfeld" television series as its Star Presenter of the Year.[7]

COLLECTING FEEDBACK

After sending the message, the communicator must research its effect on the target audience. This involves asking the target audience members whether they remember the message, how many times they saw it, what points they recall, how they felt about the message, and their past and present attitudes toward the product and company. The communicator also would like to measure behaviour resulting from the message—how many people bought a product, talked to others about it, or visited the store.

Feedback on marketing communications may suggest changes in the promotion program or in the product offer itself. For example, when the new Boston Market restaurant chain enters new market areas, it uses television advertising and coupons in newspaper inserts to inform area consumers about the restaurant and to lure them in. Suppose feedback research shows that 80 percent of all consumers in an area recall seeing Boston Market ads and are aware of what the restaurant offers. Sixty percent of those who are aware of it have eaten at the restaurant, but only 20 percent of those who tried it were satisfied. These results suggest that although the promotion program is creating *awareness,* the restaurant isn't giving consumers the *satisfaction* they expect. Therefore, Boston Market needs to improve its food or service while staying with the successful communication program. In contrast, suppose the feedback research shows that only 40 percent of area consumers are aware of the restaurant, that only 30 percent of those aware of it have tried it, but 80 percent of those who have tried it return. In this case, Boston Market needs to strengthen its promotion program to take advantage of the restaurant's power to create customer satisfaction.

SETTING THE TOTAL PROMOTION BUDGET AND MIX

We have examined the steps in planning and sending communications to a target audience. But how does the company decide on the total *promotion budget* and its division among the major promotional tools to create the *promotion mix?* We now look at these questions.

SETTING THE TOTAL PROMOTION BUDGET

One of the hardest marketing decisions facing a company is how much to spend on promotion. John Wanamaker, the department-store magnate, once said: "I know that half of my advertising is wasted, but I don't know which half. I spent $2 million for advertising, and I don't know if that is half enough or twice too much." Thus, it is not surprising that industries and companies vary widely in how much they spend on promotion. Promotion spending may be 20 to 30 percent of sales in the cosmetics industry and only two or three percent in the industrial machinery industry. Within a given industry, both low and high spenders can be found.

How does a company decide on its promotion budget? We look at four common methods used to set the total budget for advertising: the *affordable method,* the *percentage-of-sales method,* the *competitive-parity method,* and the *objective-and-task method.*[8]

Affordable Method

Affordable method
Setting the promotion budget at the level management thinks the company can afford.

Some companies use the **affordable method:** They set the promotion budget at the level they think the company can afford. Small businesses often use this method, reasoning that the company cannot spend more on advertising than it has. They start with total revenues, deduct operating expenses and capital outlays, and then devote some portion of the remaining funds to advertising.

Unfortunately, this method of setting budgets completely ignores the effects of promotion on sales. It tends to place advertising last among spending priorities, even in situations where advertising is critical to the firm's success. It leads to an uncertain annual promotion budget, which makes long-range market planning difficult. Although the affordable method can result in overspending on advertising, it more often results in underspending.

Percentage-of-Sales Method

Percentage-of-sales method
Setting the promotion budget at a certain percentage of current or forecasted sales or as a percentage of the sales price.

Other companies use the **percentage-of-sales method,** setting their promotion budget at a certain percentage of current or forecasted sales. Or they budget a percentage of the unit sales price. The percentage-of-sales method has a number of advantages. First, using this method means that promotion spending is likely to vary with what the company can "afford." It also helps management think about the relationship between promotion spending, selling price, and profit per unit. Finally, this method supposedly creates competitive stability because competing firms tend to spend about the same percentage of their sales on promotion.

Despite these claimed advantages, however, the percentage-of-sales method has little to justify it. It wrongly views sales as the *cause* of promotion rather than as the *result.* "A study in this area found good correlation between investments in advertising and the strength of the brands concerned—but it turned out to be effect and cause, not cause and effect...The strongest brands had the highest sales and could afford the biggest investments in advertising!"[9] The budget is based on availability of funds rather than on opportunities. It may prevent the increased spending sometimes needed to turn around falling sales. Because the budget varies with year-to-year sales, long-range planning is difficult. Finally, the method does not provide any basis for choosing a *specific* percentage, except what has been done in the past or what competitors are doing.

Competitive-Parity Method

Competitive-parity method
Setting the promotion budget to match competitors' outlays.

Still other companies use the **competitive-parity method,** setting their promotion budgets to match competitors' outlays. They monitor competitors' advertising or get

Chrysler Canada used the objective-and-task method to differentiate its product and create awareness of its sliding doors on both sides of its minivans using this campaign.

industry promotion-spending estimates from publications or trade associations, and then set their budgets based on the industry average.

Two arguments support this method. First, competitors' budgets represent the collective wisdom of the industry. Second, spending what competitors spend helps prevent promotion wars. Unfortunately, neither argument is valid. There are no grounds for believing that the competition has a better idea of what a company should be spending on promotion than does the company itself. Companies differ greatly, and each has its own special promotion needs. Finally, there is no evidence that budgets based on competitive parity prevent promotion wars.

Objective-and-Task Method

The most logical budget setting method is the **objective-and-task method**, whereby the company sets its promotion budget based on what it wants to accomplish with promotion. This budgeting method entails (1) defining specific promotion objectives, (2) determining the tasks needed to achieve these objectives, and (3) estimating the costs of performing these tasks. The sum of these costs is the proposed promotion budget.

The objective-and-task method forces management to spell out its assumptions about the relationship between dollars spent and promotion results. But it is also the most difficult method to use. Often, it is hard to determine which specific tasks will achieve specific objectives. For example, suppose Sony wants 95 percent awareness for its latest camcorder model during the six-month introductory period. What specific advertising messages and media schedules should Sony use to attain this objective? How much would these messages and media schedules cost? Sony management must consider such questions, even though they are hard to answer.

SETTING THE PROMOTION MIX

The company now must divide the total promotion budget among the major promotion tools—advertising, personal selling, sales promotion, and public relations. It must blend the promotion tools carefully into a coordinated *promotion mix*. Companies within the same industry differ greatly in the design of their promotion mixes. For example, Avon spends most of its promotion funds on personal selling and direct marketing, whereas Revlon spends heavily on consumer advertising. Toronto-based M.A.C (Make-up Art Cosmetics), on the other hand, has rocketed onto the world stage with almost no traditional advertising. Instead, M.A.C has relied on demonstrating its products at major fashion shows, using

Objective-and-task method
Developing the promotion budget by (1) defining specific objectives; (2) determining the tasks that must be performed to achieve these objectives; and (3) estimating the costs of performing these tasks. The sum of these costs is the proposed promotion budget.

point-of-purchase displays featuring its spokespersons RuPaul and k.d. lang, in addition to personal selling, and cause-related marketing. These tactics have resulted in 1995 sales of approximately $150 million, along with $4 million raised for AIDS recognition and research as part of the company's cause-marketing efforts.[10] We now look at the many factors that influence the marketer's choice of promotion tools.

The Nature of Each Promotion Tool

Each promotion tool—*advertising, personal selling, sales promotion,* and *public relations*—has unique characteristics and costs. Marketers must understand these characteristics in selecting their tools.

ADVERTISING.   The many forms of advertising contribute uniquely to the overall promotion mix. Advertising can reach masses of geographically dispersed buyers at a low cost per exposure. It enables the seller to repeat a message many times, and it lets the buyer receive and compare the messages of various competitors. Because of advertising's public nature, consumers tend to view advertised products as standard and legitimate—buyers know that purchasing advertised products will be understood and accepted publicly. Large-scale advertising says something positive about the seller's size, popularity, and success.

Advertising is also very expressive—it allows the company to dramatize its products through the artful use of visuals, print, sound, and colour. On the one hand, advertising can be used to build a long-term image for a product (such as Coca-Cola ads). On the other hand, advertising can trigger quick sales (as when Sears advertises a weekend sale).

Advertising also has some shortcomings. Although it reaches many people quickly, advertising is impersonal and cannot be as persuasive as company salespeople. For the most part, advertising can carry on only a one-way communication with the audience, and the audience does not feel that it must pay attention or respond. In addition, advertising can be very costly. Although some advertising forms, such as newspaper and radio advertising, can be done on small budgets, other forms, such as network TV advertising, require very large budgets.

PERSONAL SELLING.   Personal selling is the most effective tool at certain stages of the buying process, particularly in building up buyers' preferences, convictions, and actions. Compared to advertising, personal selling has several unique qualities. It involves personal interaction between two or more people, so each person can observe the other's needs and characteristics and make quick adjustments. Personal selling also allows all kinds of relationships to develop, ranging from a matter-of-fact selling relationship to a deep personal friendship. The effective salesperson keeps the customer's interests at heart in order to build a long-term relationship. Finally, with personal selling the buyer usually feels a greater need to listen and respond, even if the response is a polite "no thank you."

These unique qualities come at a cost, however. A sales force requires a longer-term commitment than does advertising—advertising can be turned on and off, but sales-force size is harder to change. Personal selling is also the company's most expensive promotion tool, costing industrial companies an average of over $275 per sales call.[11] North American firms spend up to three times as much on personal selling as they do on advertising.

SALES PROMOTION.   Sales promotion includes a wide assortment of tools—coupons, contests, cents-off deals, premiums such as "buy 10 products, get one free," and others—all of which have many unique qualities. They attract consumer attention and provide information that may lead to a purchase. They offer strong incentives to purchase by providing inducements or contributions that give additional value to consumers. And sales promotions invite and reward quick response. Whereas advertising says "buy our product," sales promotion says "buy it now."

Companies use sales-promotion tools to create a stronger and quicker response. Sales promotion can be used to dramatize product offers and to boost sagging sales. Sales promotion effects are usually short-lived, however, and are not effective in building long-run brand preference.

PUBLIC RELATIONS.   Public relations offers several unique qualities. It is very believable—news stories, features, and events seem more real and believable to readers than ads do. Public relations also can reach many prospects who avoid salespeople and advertisements—the message gets to the buyers as "news" rather than as a sales-directed communication. And, like advertising, public relations can dramatize a company or product.

Marketers tend to underuse public relations or to use it as an afterthought. Yet a well-planned public relations campaign used with other promotion mix elements can be very effective and economical.

DIRECT MARKETING.   Although there are many forms of direct marketing—direct mail, telemarketing, electronic marketing, online marketing, and others—they all share four distinctive characteristics. Direct marketing is non-public: the message is normally addressed to a specific person. Direct marketing is also immediate and customized: messages can be prepared very quickly and can be tailored to appeal to specific consumers. Finally, direct marketing is interactive: it allows a dialogue between the marketer and consumer, and messages can be altered depending on the consumer's response. Thus, direct marketing is well suited to highly targeted marketing efforts and to building one-to-one customer relationships.

Promotion Mix Strategies

Marketers can choose from two basic promotion mix strategies—*push* promotion or *pull* promotion. Figure 14-3 contrasts the two strategies. A **push strategy** involves "pushing" the product through distribution channels to final consumers. The producer directs its marketing activities (primarily personal selling and trade promotion) toward channel members to induce them to carry the product and to promote it to final consumers. Using a **pull strategy**, the producer directs its marketing activities (primarily advertising and consumer promotion) toward final consumers to induce them to buy the product. If the pull strategy is effective, consumers then will demand the product from channel members, who will in turn demand it from producers. Thus, under a pull strategy, consumer demand "pulls" the product through the channels.

Some small industrial goods companies use only push strategies; some direct-marketing companies use only pull. Most large companies use some combination of

Push strategy
A promotion strategy that calls for using the sales force and trade promotion to push the product through channels. The producer promotes the product to wholesalers, the wholesalers promote to retailers, and the retailers promote to consumers.

Pull strategy
A promotion strategy that calls for spending a lot on advertising and consumer promotion to build up consumer demand. If the strategy is successful, consumers will ask their retailers for the product, the retailers will ask the wholesalers, and the whole-salers will ask the producers.

FIGURE 14-3   *Push versus pull promotion strategy*

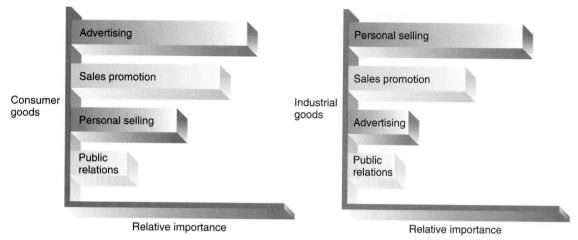

FIGURE 14-4   *Relative importance of promotion tools in consumer versus industrial markets*

both. For example, Frito-Lay uses mass-media advertising to pull its products, and a large sales force and trade promotions to push its products through the channels. In recent years, consumer goods companies have been decreasing the pull portions of their promotion mixes in favour of more push (see Marketing Highlight 14-2).

Companies consider many factors when developing their promotion mixes, including type of product/market, the use of a push or pull strategy, the buyer readiness stage, and the product life-cycle stage.

TYPE OF PRODUCT/MARKET.   The importance of different promotion tools varies between consumer and business markets (see Figure 14-4). Consumer goods companies usually "pull" more, putting more of their funds into advertising, followed by sales promotion, personal selling, and then public relations. In contrast, industrial goods companies tend to "push" more, putting most of their funds into personal selling, followed by sales promotion, advertising, and public relations. In general, personal selling is used more heavily with expensive and risky goods and in markets with fewer and larger sellers.

Although advertising is less important than sales calls in business markets, it still plays an important role. Business-to-business advertising can build product awareness and knowledge, develop sales leads, and reassure buyers. Similarly, personal selling can add a lot to consumer goods marketing efforts. It is simply not the case that "salespeople put products on shelves and advertising takes them off." Well-trained consumer goods salespeople can sign up more dealers to carry a particular brand, convince them to give the brand more shelf space, and urge them to use special displays and promotions.

BUYER READINESS STAGE.   The effects of the promotional tools vary for the different buyer readiness stages. Advertising, along with public relations, plays the major role in the awareness and knowledge stages, more important than that played by "cold calls" from salespeople. Customer liking, preference, and conviction are more affected by personal selling, which is closely followed by advertising. Finally, closing the sale is mostly done with sales calls and sales promotion. Clearly, personal selling, given its high costs, should focus on the later stages of the customer buying process.

PRODUCT LIFE-CYCLE STAGE.   The effects of different promotion tools also vary with stages of the product life cycle. In the introduction stage, advertising and public relations are good for producing high awareness, and sales promotion is useful in promoting early trial. Personal selling must be used to get the trade to carry the product. In the growth stage, advertising and public relations continue

ARE CONSUMER GOODS COMPANIES GETTING TOO "PUSHY"?

Consumer packaged-goods companies such as Kraft/General Foods, Procter & Gamble, RJR/Nabisco, Campbell, and Gillette grew into giants by using mostly pull promotion strategies. They used massive doses of national advertising to differentiate their products, build market share, and maintain customer loyalty. But during the past two decades, these companies have become more "pushy," de-emphasizing national advertising and putting more of their promotion budgets into personal selling and sales promotions. Trade promotions (trade allowances, displays, cooperative advertising) now account for about 60 to 75 percent of total consumer product company marketing spending. That leaves only 40 percent of total marketing spending for media advertising and consumer spending.

Why have these companies shifted so heavily toward push strategies? One reason is that mass-media campaigns have become more expensive and less effective in recent years. Network television costs have risen sharply while audiences have fallen off, making national advertising less cost-effective. Companies also have increased their market segmentation efforts and are tailoring their marketing programs more narrowly, making national advertising less suitable than localized retailer promotions. And in these days of brand extensions and me-too products, companies sometimes have trouble finding meaningful product differences to feature in advertising. So they have differentiated their products through price reductions,

premium offers, coupons, and other push techniques.

Another factor speeding the shift from pull to push has been the greater strength of retailers. Today's retailers are larger and have more access to product sales and profit information. They now have the power to demand and get what they want—and what they want is more push. Whereas national advertising bypasses them on its way to the masses, push promotion benefits them directly. Consumer promotions give retailers an immediate sales boost, and cash from trade allowances pads retailer profits. Thus, producers often must use push just to obtain good shelf space and advertising support from important retailers.

However, many marketers are concerned that the reckless use of push will lead to fierce price competition and a never-ending spiral of price slashing and deal making. This situation would mean lower margins, and companies would have less money to invest in the research and development, packaging, and advertising needed to improve products and maintain long-run consumer preference and loyalty. If used improperly, push promotion can mortgage a brand's future for short-term gains. Sales promotion buys short-run reseller support and consumer sales, but advertising builds long-run brand value and consumer preference. By robbing the advertising budget to pay for more sales promotion, companies might win the battle for short-run earnings but lose the war for long-run consumer loyalty and market share.

Thus, many consumer companies now are rethinking their promotion strategies and reversing the trend by shifting their promotion budgets back slightly toward advertising. Push strategies remain very important. In packaged-goods marketing, short-run success often depends more on retailer support than on the producer's advertising. But many companies have realized that it's not a question of sales promotion versus advertising, or of push versus pull. Success lies in finding the best mix of the two: consistent advertising to build long-run brand value and consumer preference, and sales promotion to create short-run trade support and consumer excitement. The company needs to blend both push and pull elements into an integrated promotion program that meets immediate consumer and retailer needs as well as long-run strategic needs.

Sources: James C. Schroer, "Ad Spending: Growing Marketing Share," *Harvard Business Review*, January–February 1990, pp. 44–48; John Philip Jones, "The Double Jeopardy of Sales Promotions," *Harvard Business Review*, September– October 1990, pp. 145–152; Zachary Schiller, "Not Everyone Loves a Supermarket Special," *Business Week*, February 17, 1992, pp. 64–68; Lois Therrien, "Brands on the Run," *Business Week*, April 19, 1993, pp. 26–29; and 16th Annual Survey of Promotional Practices, Donnelly Marketing Inc., Oakbrook Terrace, IL, June 1994, p. 9; Andrea Haman, "Causes of the Conundrum," *Marketing, Promo Report*, August 21, 1995, p. S8; Lara Mills, "The Trade-Promotion Trap," *Marketing, Promo Report*, August 21, 1995, p. S4.

to be powerful influences, whereas sales promotion can be reduced because fewer incentives are needed. In the mature stage, sales promotion again becomes important relative to advertising. Buyers know the brands, and advertising is needed only to remind them of the product. In the decline stage, advertising is kept at a reminder level, public relations is dropped, and salespeople give the product only a little attention. Sales promotion, however, might continue strong.

THE CHANGING FACE OF MARKETING COMMUNICATIONS

During the past several decades, companies around the world have perfected the art of mass marketing—selling highly standardized products to masses of customers. In the process, they have developed effective mass-media advertising techniques to support their mass-marketing strategies. These companies routinely invest millions of dollars in the mass media, reaching tens of millions of customers with a single ad. However, as we move toward the twenty-first century, marketing managers are facing some new marketing communications realities.

THE CHANGING COMMUNICATIONS ENVIRONMENT

Two major factors are changing the face of today's marketing communications. First, as mass markets have fragmented, marketers are shifting away from mass marketing. More and more, they are developing focussed marketing programs designed to build closer relationships with customers in more narrowly defined micromarkets. Second, vast improvements in computer and information technology are speeding the movement toward segmented marketing. Today's information technology helps marketers to keep closer track of customer needs—more information about consumers at the individual and household levels is available than ever before. New technologies also provide new communications avenues for reaching smaller customer segments with more tailored messages.

The shift from mass marketing to segmented marketing has had a dramatic impact on marketing communications. Just as mass marketing gave rise to a new generation of mass media communications, the shift toward one-on-one marketing is spawning a new generation of more specialized and highly targeted communications efforts.[12]

Given this new communications environment, marketers must rethink the roles of various media and promotion mix tools. Mass-media advertising has long dominated the promotion mixes of consumer product companies. However, although television, magazines, and other mass media remain very important, their dominance is now declining. *Market* fragmentation has resulted in *media* fragmentation—in an explosion of more focused media that better match today's targeting strategies. For example, in 1975, what used to be called the three major TV networks (ABC, CBS, and NBC) attracted 82 percent of the 24-hour viewing audience. By 1995, that number had dropped to only 35 percent, as cable television and satellite broadcasting systems now offer advertisers dozens or even hundreds of alternative channels that reach smaller, specialized audiences. And it's expected to drop even further, to 25 percent by 2005.[13] Similarly, the relatively few mass magazines of the 1940s and 1950s—*Look, Life, National Geographic*—have been replaced by more than 11 000 special-interest magazines reaching smaller, more focussed audiences. And, beyond these channels, advertisers are making increased use of new, highly targeted media, ranging from e-mail and fax marketing to on-line computer services and CD-ROM catalogues.

More generally, advertising appears to be giving way to other elements of the promotion mix. In the glory days of mass marketing, consumer product companies spent a lion's share of their promotion budgets on mass-media advertising. Today, media advertising captures only about 23 percent of total promotion spending.[14] The rest goes to various sales promotion activities, which can be focused more effectively on individual consumer and trade segments. In all, companies are doing less *broadcasting* and more *narrowcasting*. They are using a richer variety of focused communication tools in an effort to reach their many and diverse target markets.

INTEGRATED MARKETING COMMUNICATIONS

The recent shifts from mass marketing to targeted marketing, and the corresponding use of a richer mixture of communication channels and promotion tools, pose a problem for marketers. Consumers are being exposed to a greater variety of marketing communications from and about the company from a broader array of sources. However, customers don't distinguish between message sources the way marketers do. In the consumer's mind, advertising messages from different media such as television, magazines, or online sources blur into one. Messages delivered via different promotional approaches—such as advertising, personal selling, sales promotion, public relations, or direct marketing—all become part of a single overall message about the company. Conflicting messages from these different sources can result in confused company images and brand positions.

All too often, companies fail to integrate these various communications channels. The result is a hodgepodge of communications to consumers. Mass advertisements say one thing, a price promotion sends a different signal, a product label creates still another message, company sales literature says something altogether different, and the company's web site seems out of sync with everything else.

The problem is that these communications often come from different company sources. Advertising messages are planned and implemented by the advertising department or advertising agency. Personal selling communications are developed by sales management. Other functional specialists are responsible for public relations, sales promotion, direct marketing, and other forms of marketing communications. Moreover, members of various departments often differ in their views on how to divide the promotion budget. The sales manager would rather hire a few more salespeople than spend $200 000 on a single television commercial. The public relations manager feels that he or she can do wonders with some money shifted from advertising to public relations.

In the past, no one person was responsible for thinking through the communication roles of the various promotion tools and coordinating the promotion mix. Today, however, more companies are adopting the concept of **integrated marketing communications (IMC)**. Under this concept, the company carefully integrates and coordinates its many communications channels—mass-media advertising, personal selling, sales promotion, public relations, direct marketing, packaging, and others—to deliver a clear, consistent, and compelling message about the organization and its products.[15] (See Marketing Highlight 14-3 for examples.) As one marketing executive puts it, "IMC builds a strong brand identity in the marketplace by tying together and reinforcing all your images and messages. IMC means that all your corporate messages, positioning and images, and identity are coordinated across all [marketing communications] venues. It means that your PR materials say the same thing as your direct mail campaign, and your advertising has the same 'look and feel' as your web site."[16]

The company identifies the roles that the various promotional tools will play and the extent to which each will be used. It carefully coordinates the promotional activities and the timing of when major campaigns occur. It keeps track of its promotional expenditures by product, promotional tool, product life-cycle stage, and observed effect in order to improve future use of the promotion mix tools. Finally, to help implement its integrated marketing strategy, the company appoints a marketing communications director who has overall responsibility for the company's communications efforts. To integrate its external communications effectively, the company must first integrate its internal communications activities.

Integrated marketing communications produces better communications consistency and greater sales impact. It places the responsibility in someone's hands—where none existed before—to unify the company's image as it is shaped by thousands of company activities. It leads to a total marketing communication strategy aimed at showing how the company and its products can help customers solve their problems.

Integrated marketing communications
The concept under which a company carefully integrates and coordinates its many communications channels to deliver a clear, consistent, and compelling message about the organization and its products.

INTEGRATED MARKETING COMMUNICATIONS: TOMMY,

An ever-increasing number of companies are learning that carefully integrated marketing communications can pay big dividends. Here are just three examples.

Tommy: Integrated Consumer Services Marketing

Although marketing certainly isn't new in the entertainment business, the demands being put on programs are growing as markets become more competitive. As more and more theatres open in major Canadian cities, competition to attract audiences is growing. Some business analysts believe that the Toronto market, for example, is now overpopulated with mega-productions. Thus, in the face of intense competitive rivalry, it is the job of marketing to build an audience to attend these expensive productions.

Consider the integrated marketing program utilized by the musical *Tommy* when it first opened in Toronto. Five months before the production opened, mass-media advertising was used to create awareness about the musical for residents of Toronto and the surrounding areas. As curtain time approached, live radio broadcasts were scheduled to coincide with the opening of ticket sales. These broadcasts were designed to attract a younger audience than the one that traditionally goes to the theatre. American Express added weight to the campaign by targeting its cardholders with its "Front-of-the-Line" program— an effort that allows members to get first access to scarce tickets. Direct mail, corporate tie-ins, and tourist-trade marketing were also employed as part of the effort to fill the theatre. Despite all these efforts, attendance didn't reach the producers' expectations and *Tommy* was forced to close prematurely.

Hewlett-Packard: Integrated Business-to-Business Marketing

Hewlett-Packard puts integrated marketing communications to work in its business-to-business markets. H-P uses a closely coordinated mix of advertising, event marketing, direct marketing, and personal selling to sell workstations to high-level corporate buyers. At the broadest level, corporate image television ads, coupled with targeted ads in trade magazines, position H-P as a supplier of high-quality solutions to customers' workstation problems. Beneath this broad advertising umbrella, H-P then uses direct marketing to polish its image, update its customer database, and generate leads for the sales force. Finally, company sales reps follow up to close sales and build customer relationships.

Integrated Marketing Communications: To rebuild relationships with working women, Hallmark developed a major marketing effort called "The Very Best." Hallmark's most frequent and loyal customers receive personalized mailings with product information.

H-P's highly successful program of "interactive audio teleconferences" illustrates the company's mastery of integrated communications. These teleconferences are like mammoth conference calls in which H-P representatives discuss key industry issues and H-P practices with current and potential customers. To garner participation in the program, H-P employs a five-week, seven-step "registration process." First, four weeks before a teleconference, H-P mails out an introductory direct-mail package, complete with a number and business reply cards. One or two days after the mail package is received, H-P telemarketers call prospects to register them for the conference,

and registrations are confirmed immediately by direct mail. A week before the teleconference, H-P mails out detailed briefing packages, and three days before the event, calls are made again to confirm participation. A final confirmation call is made the day before the teleconference. Finally, one week after the event, H-P uses follow-up direct mail and telemarketing to qualify sales leads and develop account profiles for sales reps.

What is the result of this integrated marketing communications effort? A response rate of 12 percent, compared with just 1.5 percent using a traditional mail and telemarketing approach. Moreover, 82 percent of those who say they'll participate actually take part, compared with only 40 percent for past, non-synchronized efforts. The program has generated qualified sales leads at 200 percent above the forecasted level, and the average workstation sale has increased 500 percent.

Not surprisingly, Hewlett-Packard is sold on integrated marketing communications. However, H-P managers warn that integrated marketing requires great dedication and practical rigour. Perhaps the toughest challenge is the fact that success results from the intense and detailed coordination of the efforts of many company departments. To achieve coordination, H-P assigns cross-functional teams composed of representatives from sales, advertising, marketing, production, and information systems to oversee its integrated communications efforts.

Hallmark Cards: Integrated Consumer Products Marketing

Hallmark's general brand advertising and program sponsorship are well known. Over the years, the company has relied heavily on mass-media television and print advertising to position Hallmark as the card to give "When you care enough to send the very best." It has also sponsored the highly regarded *Hallmark Hall of Fame* TV specials to reinforce its wholesome, family-oriented image.

Over the past five years, however, Hallmark has transformed

itself from a traditional advertiser to a leader in state-of-the-art integrated marketing communications. Hallmark now uses a well-engineered combination of network TV, print advertising, newspaper-distributed coupons, in-store promotions, point-of-sale materials, and direct marketing to lure customers into its stores.

In the late 1980s, the number-one greeting-card marketer realized that its core group of consumers—working women—was changing. These women had become busier than ever and therefore harder to reach through traditional mass-media advertising. Also, Hallmark's product line had expanded beyond greeting cards to include gifts, collectibles, and home entertaining and decorating products. To rebuild relationships with working women, Hallmark developed a major database marketing effort called "The Very Best," which tied directly into its overall advertising program.

"The Very Best" cultivates Hallmark's most frequent and loyal customers, who receive regular personalized mailings filled with information about new products, including coupons and incentives to pull them into Hallmark's 5000 Gold Crown stores. "The Very Best" mailings also provide information about holiday entertaining and gift-giving. Hallmark's goal is to build closer, more personal relationships with important customers. "We want our communications to be very warm and relevant," says Ira Stolzer, Hallmark's director of advertising. "We want each woman on our 'Very Best' list to feel like she's getting a mailing from her sister." According to Mr. Stolzer, the results have been "absolutely phenomenal. People really enjoy being on our mailing lists, and in focus groups we've had incredible feedback from them." In each mailing, Hallmark invites comments about the program. This has created a positive dialogue between Hallmark and its customers.

Hallmark is careful to see that all the different parts of its marketing communications work together. The same team oversees media advertising, in-store marketing, and direct mailings. The integrated effort has put many new weapons in Hallmark's communications arsenal. "In the old days we might have said, 'Here's a marketing problem, let's solve it with some TV and print advertising,' and that was all there was to it," Mr. Stolzer says. "Today, we have . . . multiple solutions and [can be] extremely creative [in finding] effective ways to reach our target customers."

Sources: Portions based on Mark Suchecki, "Integrated Marketing: Making It Pay," *Direct,* October 1993, p. 43; and Kate Fitzgerald, "In Line for Integrated Hall of Fame," *Advertising Age,* November 8, 1993, p. S12. Also see Kate Fitzgerald, "Hallmark Alters Focus as Lifestyles Change," *Advertising Age,* October 31, 1994, p. 4; Lara Mills, "Tommy Rocks with High-Volume Marketing," *Marketing,* March 13, 1995, p. 3.

SOCIALLY RESPONSIBLE MARKETING COMMUNICATION

Whoever is in charge, people at all levels of the organization must be aware of the growing body of legal and ethical issues surrounding marketing communications. Most marketers work hard to communicate openly and honestly with consumers and resellers. Still, abuses may occur, and public policy-makers have developed a substantial body of laws and regulations to govern advertising, personal selling, and direct marketing activities. In this chapter we discuss issues regarding advertising and personal selling. Issues relating to direct marketing are addressed in Chapter 17.

Advertising

By law, companies must avoid false or deceptive advertising. Advertisers must not make false claims, such as stating that a product cures something when it does not. They must avoid false demonstrations, as when a soup marketer put clear marbles in the bottom of the bowl to make the soup appear to have more noodles in advertising.

Advertisers must not create ads that have the capacity to deceive, even though no one actually may be deceived. A car cannot be advertised as giving 14 km per litre unless it does so under typical conditions, and a diet bread cannot be advertised as having fewer calories simply because its slices are thinner. The problem is how to tell the difference between deception and "puffery"—simple acceptable exaggerations not intended to be believed.

Sellers must avoid bait-and-switch advertising that attracts buyers under false pretenses. For example, a large retailer advertised a sewing machine at $179.

Toys 'R' Us helped both parents and disabled children with its new toy guide.

However, when consumers tried to buy the advertised machine, the seller downplayed its features, placed faulty machines on showroom floors, downplayed the machine's performance, and took other actions in an attempt to switch buyers to a more expensive machine. Such actions are both unethical and illegal.

A company's trade promotion activities also are closely regulated. For example, under the Competition Act, sellers cannot favour certain customers through their use of trade promotions. They must make promotional allowances and services available to all resellers on proportionately equal terms.

Beyond simply avoiding legal pitfalls, such as deceptive or bait-and-switch advertising, companies can use advertising to encourage and promote socially responsible programs and actions. For example, Toys 'R' Us (Canada) was recently praised by a number of groups for its new *Toy Guide for Differently Abled Kids!* This 16-page catalogue, featuring 50 toys designed for disabled children, was distributed through the company's 56 Canadian locations as well as through agencies such as Easter Seals and the Canadian National Institute for the Blind. Although none of the toys displayed in the catalogue was specifically designed for disabled children, the publication informed parents about which toys were suitable for their children and how the toys might help their children develop certain skills.[17]

PERSONAL SELLING

The company's salespeople must follow the rules of "fair competition." For example, salespeople may not lie to consumers or mislead them about the advantages of buying a product. To avoid bait-and-switch practices, salespeople's statements must match advertising claims.

Different rules apply to consumers who are called on at home versus those who go to a store in search of a product. Because people called on at home may be taken by surprise and may be especially vulnerable to high-pressure selling techniques, most provincial governments have stipulated a *three-day cooling-off rule* to give special protection to customers who are not seeking products. Under this rule, customers who agree in their own homes to buy something have 72 hours in which to cancel a contract or return merchandise and get their money back, no questions asked.

Much personal selling involves business-to-business trade. In selling to businesses, salespeople may not offer bribes to purchasing agents or to others who can influence a sale. They may not obtain or use technical or trade secrets of competitors through bribery or industrial espionage. Finally, salespeople must not disparage competitors or competing products by suggesting things that are not true.[18]

Summary of Chapter Objectives

Modern marketing calls for more than just developing a good product, pricing it attractively, and making it available to target customers. Companies also must communicate with current and prospective customers, and what they communicate should not be left to chance. For most companies, the question is not whether to communicate, but how much to spend and in what ways.

1. **Name and define the four tools of the promotion mix.**

    A company's total marketing communications mix—also called its promotion mix—consists of the specific blend of advertising, personal selling, sales promotion, public relations, and direct marketing tools that the company uses to pursue its advertising and marketing objectives. Advertising includes any paid form of non-personal presentation and promotion of ideas, goods, or services by an identified sponsor. In contrast, public relations focuses on building good relations with the company's various publics by obtaining favourable unpaid publicity. Firms use sales promotion to provide short-term incentives to encourage the purchase or sale of a product or service. Personal selling is any form of personal presentation by the firm's sales force for the purpose of making sales and building customer relationships. Finally, firms seeking immediate response from targeted individual customers use non-personal direct marketing tools to communicate with customers.

2. **Outline the steps in developing effective marketing communication.**

    In preparing marketing communications, the communicator's first task is to identify the target audience and its characteristics. Next, the communicator must define the response sought, whether it be awareness, knowledge, liking, preference, conviction, or purchase. Then a message should be constructed with an effective content and structure. Media must be selected, both for personal and non-personal communication. Finally, the communicator must collect feedback by watching how much of the market becomes aware, tries the product, and is satisfied in the process.

3. **Explain the methods for setting the promotion budget and factors that affect the design of the promotion mix.**

    The company must decide how much to spend for promotion. The most popular approaches are to spend what the company can afford, to use a percentage of sales, to base promotion on competitors' spending, or to base it on an analysis and costing of the communication objectives and tasks.

    The company must divide the promotion budget among the major tools to create the promotion mix. Companies can pursue a push or a pull promotional strategy, or a combination of the two. What specific blend of promotion tools is best depends on the type of product/market, the desirability of the buyer's readiness stage, and the product life-cycle stage.

4. **Identify the major factors that are changing today's marketing communications environment.**

    Recent shifts in marketing strategy from mass marketing to targeted or one-on-one marketing, coupled with advances in computers and information technology, have had a dramatic impact on marketing communications. Although still important, the mass media are giving way to a profusion of smaller, more focused media. Companies are doing less broadcasting and more narrowcasting.

    People at all levels of the organization must be aware of the many legal and ethical issues surrounding marketing communications. Companies must work hard and proactively to communicate openly, honestly, and agreeably with their customers and resellers.

5. **Discuss the process and advantages of integrated marketing communications.**

    As marketing communicators adopt richer but more fragmented media and promotion mixes to reach their diverse markets, they risk creating a communications hodgepodge for consumers. To prevent this, more companies are adopting the concept of integrated marketing communications, which demands the careful integration of all sources of company communication to deliver a clear and consistent message to target markets.

    To integrate its external communications effectively, the company must first integrate its internal communications activities. The company then works out the roles that the various promotional tools will play and the extent to which each will be used. It carefully coordinates the promotional activities and the timing of when major campaigns occur. Finally, to help implement its integrated marketing strategy, the company appoints a marketing communications director who has overall responsibility for the company's communications efforts.

Key Terms

Advertising *(p. 468)*

Affordable method *(p. 479)*

Buyer-readiness stages *(p. 471)*

Direct marketing *(p. 469)*

Emotional appeals *(p. 473)*

Integrated marketing communications *(p. 486)*

Marketing communications mix (or Promotion mix) *(p. 468)*

Moral appeals *(p. 474)*

Non-personal communication channels *(p. 476)*

Objective-and-task method *(p. 480)*

Percentage-of-sales method *(p. 479)*

Personal communication channels *(p. 475)*

Personal selling *(p. 469)*

Public relations *(p. 469)*

Pull strategy *(p. 482)*

Push strategy *(p. 482)*

Rational appeals *(p. 473)*

Sales promotion *(p. 469)*

Word-of-mouth influence *(p. 475)*

Discussing the Issues

1. Name which form of marketing communications each of the following represents: (a) a U2 T-shirt sold at a concert, (b) a *Rolling Stone* interview with Eric Clapton arranged by his manager, (c) a scalper auctioning tickets at a Pearl Jam concert, and (d) a record store selling Boyz II Men albums for $2 off the week their latest music video debuts on network television.

2. Many firms advertising in Canada use American rather than Canadian celebrities to endorse their products. For example, Sprint Canada uses Candice Bergen (who plays Murphy Brown on the self-titled sitcom) to promote its service. Why do you think they made this choice? Identify a product or service that has made effective use of a celebrity endorser. Identify another where you think the use of a celebrity endorser was inappropriate. What criteria did you use to differentiate between a successful and unsuccessful use of a celebrity endorser?

3. How can an organization get feedback on the effects of its communication efforts? Describe how (a) the March of Dimes and (b) Procter & Gamble can get feedback on the results of their communications.

4. Companies spend billions of dollars on advertising to build a quality image for their products. At the same time they spend billions more on discount-oriented sales promotions, offering lower price as a main reason to purchase. Discuss whether promotion is enhancing or reducing the effect of advertising. Can you find an example where they enhance one another?

5. Recently, pharmaceutical companies have begun to communicate directly with consumers via the mass media, even though they cannot mention prescription product names and benefits in the same television ad. Ads promise that doctors have some unspecified help available for baldness. Nicoderm, Habitrol, and Prostep nicotine patches battle for consumers' awareness, but they cannot mention cigarette addiction. Decide whether you consider this to be advertising or public relations. Do you think it would be effective?

6. Why do some business-to-business marketers advertise on national television, when their target audience is only a fraction of the people they have paid to reach with their message? List some non-consumer-oriented commercials you have seen on TV and describe what the marketers were trying to accomplish with them.

Applying the Concepts

1. Think of a nationally advertised product or service that has been running a consistent advertising message for a number of years. Go to the library and copy several examples of print advertising for this brand from back issues of magazines. (a) When you examine these ads closely, how consistent are the message content, structure, and format? (b) Which response(s) do you think this campaign is seeking: awareness,

knowledge, liking, preference, conviction, or purchase? (c) Do you think the advertising campaign is successful in getting the desired response? Why or why not?

2. Consider an automobile brand you are familiar with. (a) List examples of how this brand uses advertising, personal selling, sales promotion, direct marketing, and public relations. (Public relations examples may be difficult to spot, but consider how cars are used in movies or television programs, or as celebrity vehicles for sports tournaments or parades.) (b) Does this auto maker use promotion tools in a coordinated way that builds a consistent image, or are the efforts fragmented? Explain.

References

1. Joanne Ingrassia, "Digital Alternatives," *Marketing*, November 18, 1996, web site: www.marketingmag.com/search; Steven Landsberg, "Crossing Media Boundaries," *Marketing*, April 28, 1997, web site: www.marketingmag.com/search; Laura Medcalf, "Timex, O&M Shine at '97 Marketing Awards," *Marketing*, March 31, 1997, p. 2; "Special Report: Best Media Plan Competition," *Strategy: The Canadian Marketing Report*, March 31, 1997, p. 34.

2. For these and other definitions, see Peter D. Bennett, *Dictionary of Marketing Terms* (Chicago: American Marketing Association, 1988).

3. Kevin Goldman, "Advertising: Knock, Knock. Who's There? The Same Old Funny Ad Again," *The Wall Street Journal*, November 2, 1993, p. B10; and Marc G. Weinberger, Harlan Spotts, Leland Campbell, and Amy L. Parsons, "The Use and Effect of Humour in Different Advertising Media," *Journal of Advertising Research*, May-June 1995, pp. 44–55.

4. For more on message content and structure, see Leon G. Schiffman and Leslie Lazar Kanuk, *Consumer Behavior*, 5th ed. (Englewood Cliffs, NJ: Prentice Hall, 1994), Chap. 10; Alan G. Sawyer and Daniel J. Howard, "Effects of Omitting Conclusions in Advertisements to Involved and Uninvolved Audiences," *Journal of Marketing Research*, November 1991, pp. 467–474; Cornelia Pechmann, "Predicting When Two-Sided Ads Will Be More Effective Than One-Sided Ads: The Role of Correlational and Correspondent Inferences," *Journal of Marketing*, November 1992, pp. 441–453; and Ayn E. Crowley and Wayne D. Hoyer, "An Integrative Framework for Understanding Two-Sided Persuasion," *Journal of Consumer Research*, March 1994, pp. 561–574.

5. Philip Kotler and Ronald E. Turner, *Marketing Management: Analysis, Planning, Implementation, and Control*, ninth ed. (Scarborough, ON: Prentice Hall Canada, 1998), pp. 612–613.

6. Joseph Weber, "Now Campbell's Makes House Calls," *Business Week*, June 16, 1997, pp. 144–146.

7. Joe Mandese, "Star Presenter of the Year," *Advertising Age*, September 25, 1995, pp. 1, 6; and Elizabeth Lesly, "The Economics of a TV Supershow and What It Means to NBC and the Industry," *Business Week*, June 2, 1997, pp. 121.

8. For a more comprehensive discussion on setting promotion budgets, see J. Thomas Russell and W. Ronald Lane, *Kleppner's Advertising Procedure* (Englewood Cliffs, NJ: Prentice Hall, 1993), pp. 138–141.

9. David Allen, "Excessive Use of the Mirror," *Management Accounting*, June 1966, p. 12. Also see Laura Petrecca, "4A's Will Study Financial Return On Ad Spending," *Advertising Age*, April 7, 1997, pp. 3, 52.

10. Lara Mills, "That Old M.A.C Magic," *Marketing*, February 5, 1996, pp. 1, 11.

11. See "Median Costs Per Call By Industry," *Sales & Marketing Management*, June 28, 1993, p. 65.

12. Michael Kubin, "Simple Days of Retailing on TV Are Long Gone," *Marketing News*, February 17, 1997, pp. 2, 13.

13. For more discussion, see Don E. Schultz, Stanley I. Tannenbaum, and Robert F. Lauterborn, *Integrated Marketing Communication* (Chicago, IL: NTC Publishing, 1992), pp. 11, 17.

14. *16th Annual Survey of Promotional Practices*, Donnelly Marketing Inc., Oakbrook Terrace, IL, June 1994, p. 9.

15. See Schultz, Tannenbaum, and Lauterborn, *Integrated Marketing Communication*, Chaps. 3 and 4; and Don Schultz, "It's Time to Come Up with Strategies, Not Just Tactics," *Marketing News*, August 20, 1990, p. 11.

16. P. Griffith Lindell, "You Need Integrated Attitude to Develop IMC," *Marketing News*, May 26, 1997, p. 6.

17. James Pollock, "Toys 'R' Us Reaches Out to Differently-Abled Kids," *Marketing*, October 16, 1995, p. 2.

18. For more on the legal aspects of promotion, see Louis W. Stern and Thomas I. Eovaldi, *Legal Aspects of Marketing Policy* (Englewood Cliffs, NJ: Prentice Hall, 1984), Chaps. 7 and 8; Robert J. Posch, *The Complete Guide to Marketing and the Law* (Englewood Cliffs, NJ: Prentice Hall, 1988), Chaps. 15 to 17; and Kevin Kelly, "When a Rival's Trade Secret Crosses Your Desk . . ." *Business Week*, May 20, 1991, p. 48.

Company Case 14

FIERCE CREATURES: INSECTS, DOGS, AND OTHER AMIGOS WORK TO RING UP PCS SALES

In 1997, the sector that spent the most on advertising was the telecommunications industry. Here's a short test that will tell you whether you've spent your time hitting the books or watching too much TV:

(A) Which telephone company uses television character Murphy Brown (Candice Bergen) as its spokesperson?

(B) Which company uses an ad showing a young baseball player in Japan calling home for encouragement?

(C) Which campaign uses insects?

(D) Which phone brands itself using the name of a dog?

(E) Who has a chirpy 12-year-old who is always syrupy sweet?

(And the answers are: A - *Sprint Canada*, B - *AT&T Canada*, C - *Clearnet*, D - *Microcell's FIDO*, E - *Bell Mobility*).

If you can answer all of the above questions, then you had better start spending more time studying! All of the above examples are prime-time ads that have inundated audiences in Canada as the telecommunications firms battle for market share and strive to launch new products. In 1997 alone, Canada's largest advertiser, BCE, parent of the Bell companies, spent a cool $99 million on advertising. Rogers Cantel dug deep and found $35.5 million for its communications budget. Sprint Canada splurged with another $17.6 million, AT&T budgeted $16.6 million, and Unitel coughed up an additional $13.8 million. Even the newest players had huge expenditures: Microcell and Clearnet spent $400 000 and $800 000 respectively.

Part of the above expenditures went to support the launch of the industry's newest products—personal communications services or PCS—those funky little handsets that handle everything from e-mail to voice-mail to actual telephone calls. The fight for market share is being fought with a vengeance and, if this market follows the history of cell phones, it won't be an easy battle. Even after years on the market, cell phones have penetrated a meagre 12 to 15 percent of Canadian market.

It may not be surprising that consumers have been so slow on the uptake. They have been barraged with ads and sales pitches, yet they find it impossible to compare prices and total costs of the services since most of the companies were subsidizing the cost of the phone by making consumers sign long-term service contracts and charging them premium per-minute usage rates. At least that was the case until Clearnet, of Pickering, Ontario, entered the scene.

Clearnet is one of the four firms vying for share in this superheated market. While the telecommunications giants, Bell and Rogers Cantel, are marketing their PCS products to existing customers as upgrades for their current products, the upstarts, Clearnet and Microcell, want consumers to see PCS as a totally new product class that will give consumers control over their personal and business communications. Thus, Rogers Cantel used promotions that extended Amigo brand into the PCS arena shouting, "Lets get digital!" and Bell uses the same 12-year-old spokesperson for both its Bell Mobility and PCS spots to tie the two product lines together. Microcell has built its strategy around faithful FIDO.

When planning its strategy, Clearnet believed it faced a three-fold challenge: it had to introduce a completely new technology, it needed to establish a unique brand identify for its product, and it had to provide potential buyers with enough information so that they would be comfortable making a purchase decision.

Research conducted by Clearnet and its agency, TAXI Advertising and Design, showed that consumers were concerned about rampant technological change and the constant product variations it created. Thus, the team knew that focusing on the technology itself would be a mistake. Unlike the other companies, Clearnet decided to offer national coverage from day one instead of rolling out its products on an area-by-area basis. It also decided to simultaneously aim its product at both the end-consumer and the business marketplaces. Unlike the other competitors, Clearnet's pricing strategy is simplicity itself. Consumers pay $149.99 for their PCS phone and sign up for one of two talk-time plans. George Cope, Clearnet President says, "We've finally made wireless telephoning accessible and affordable. No more 60¢-a-minute charges." In addition to simplicity in pricing, Clearnet made its phones widely available. Customers can use one of over 600 outlets across Canada as well as non-traditional phone sales outlets such as Blockbuster Video, Business Depot, Future Shop, Grand & Toy, Battery Depot, and The Telephone Booth.

Given Clearnet's cross-country launch and non-traditional distribution channels, it needed a communications strategy that would be as meaningful in Amherstview as it was in the Okanagan. Moreover, Clearnet, a small player facing industry giants, only had a small communications budget to launch the product, $800 000 compared to the $10 million used by Bell to launch its PCS service. Thus, Clearnet had to carefully integrate its efforts so that it could speak to consumers with one voice.

In the face of these daunting challenges, Clearnet decided to create a human face for its brand that would link all of the elements of their campaign. This thinking gave birth to Mike, the 'buddy' that can handle all forms of communication including two-way radio. Mike is an unassuming guy meant to typify to potential users that the service is a practical way to save users both time and money. Clearnet put Mike everywhere. Clearnet decided it was important to use a shotgun approach, believing it could only reach key buyers with this type of campaign. Thus, Mike appeared in a teaser campaign placed in newspapers, on television, in direct-mail pieces, at special events, and in news releases.

Clearnet's initial campaign was aimed at generating awareness. Its next task was to provide potential buyers with more information to move them through the decision-making process. This is where newspaper advertising really came into its own. According to Rick Seifeddine, Clearnet's director of communications and advertising, "Newspapers allow you to touch a lot of people, but [they] give you a little more time to deliver a complex message."

The secondary objective of the campaign was to generate leads about people most interested in the product so that Clearnet could follow up with more personal, targeted sales methods. Being able to explore niche markets overlooked by the two big players is an important part of Clearnet's strategy. It plans to use a direct marketing program that will target small firms and home businesses in which internal and external communications is essential to getting their work done. As part of its direct marketing efforts, Clearnet will make use of the Web, telemarketing, direct mail, and direct television.

Clearnet's "Mike" campaign helped turn the company into the mouse that roared. It currently is the industry leader, selling 30 000 units. It has grown rapidly since its birth in 1994 when it had only 11 employees. Today its staff exceeds 1600. In an effort to continue to grow sales, Clearnet has just begun the second phase of its plan. It will spend between $10 and $20 million on this effort. The most recent Clearnet ads are variations on the theme "the hidden life of insects" and its "nature-based" campaign features dung beetles and fly-catching plants. The focus of the campaign is simplicity, and ads contain the message that buying PCS technology is as easy and hassle-free as "buying a toaster." Whether Clearnet can escape the competitive jungle and overcome the predators remains to be seen. Watching just a little TV will allow you to follow this safari.

QUESTIONS:

1. When launching a new product based on a new technology, is the presence of competition a good or bad thing?

2. Which strategy do you think is most viable for the PCS product launch—the one followed by the big telecommunications companies that position their products as line extensions, or the one used by the upstart firms that position their products as breakthrough, new-to-the world offerings? Which one is easier to communicate to prospective customers? Which one offers the biggest payback?

3. Describe the unique selling proposition around which Clearnet's integrated communication program was built.

4. While Clearnet's shotgun approach may give the firm the volume it needs to cover the huge costs of launching the product, do you think this strategy is viable for the future?

5. The communications task facing marketers of the new PCS technology is complex. They have to convey messages to consumers that range from the benefits associated with the product, to the capabilities of the new technologies. They must explain how PCS differs from cell phones, and what the various price-points will be. The firms also have to move consumers step-by-step through the decision-making process. What media vehicles would you recommend for people at different decision-making stages? Can you use the same media for end-consumers and business customers?

6. The huge amount of ad spending in the telecommunications market may have caused considerable consumer confusion. Did Clearnet's advertising campaign differentiated the firm from its competition? Before you read this case, did you recall Clearnet's ads? Did you understand the benefits of its products?

7. As consumers become more comfortable with PCS technology, what do you think are the communication challenges that Clearnet will face in the future?

Sources: Quotations from Terence Belford, "Dial-up goes digital," *The Financial Post*, November 20, 1997, p. P5; David Bosworth, "Special report: Mike packs wallop with media splash," *Strategy: The Canadian Marketing Report*, March 3, 1997, p. 30. Also see David Chilton, "Clearnet—Meet Mike," *Strategy: The Canadian Marketing Report*, September 30, 1996, p. 5; Lesley Daw and Bobbi Bulmer, "The Telco Barrage," *Marketing*, October 20, 1997, pp. 22–25; Mark De Wolf, "PCS products a natural for direct marketing," *Strategy: The Canadian Marketing Report*, July 21, 1997, p. DR1; Lara Mills, "Clearnet PCS adopts 'natural' strategy," *Marketing*, October 6, 1997, p. 3; Patti Summerfield, "Bell Mobility launches PCS Plus," *Strategy: The Canadian Marketing Report*, October 13, 1997, p. 2; web site: www.clearnet.com/

Video Case 14

EXPOSING ADVERTISING'S DARK SIDE

Not everyone is enthusiastic about the way companies use advertising to market their products. *Adbusters* is a Vancouver-based magazine dedicated to exposing the "darker" side of advertising. Editor Kalle Lassn uses satire and authentic-looking phony ads to show how advertisers manipulate the public into being dissatisfied with themselves, and how they encourage consumers to buy goods and services they do not really need.

One reason the ads look so real is the fact that Lassn has some high-profile help. Professional photographers, animators, and writers who normally command top dollar in their fields lend their talents to *Adbusters* for nothing; and their expert work rivals the real thing. Absolut Vodka, the target of one of *Adbusters'* fake ads, took the joke seriously enough to threaten legal action.

In spite of being a thorn in the side of big companies, the magazine supports itself without any advertising at all; instead, it relies on 10 000 subscribers in Canada and 15 000 in the United States. Some of that revenue also goes into Lassn's other organization, The Media Foundation, to purchase airtime for national commercials encouraging people to consume less. And *Adbusters'* annual calendar has become a big hit with top ad executives throughout North America.

QUESTIONS:

1. How does *Adbusters* use a brand's recognizable images against the advertiser?

2. Why would someone start a magazine like *Adbusters*?

3. Do you believe the magazine's "ads" are really advertising? If yes, would they be considered informative, persuasive, or comparison advertising?

4. Why would this project be done in the print magazine medium? Discuss why the message would, or would not be, as effective for other mediums such as radio, TV, newspapers, the Internet, direct mail, or outdoor?

5. Do you think the ads are effective? Why?

Source: This case was prepared by Kim Coghill and is based on "Adbusters," *Undercurrents*, (November 13, 1995).

CHAPTER 15

ADVERTISING, SALES PROMOTION, AND PUBLIC RELATIONS

When you finish this chapter, you should be able to

1. Define the roles of advertising, sales promotion, and public relations in the promotion mix.

2. Describe the major decisions involved in developing an advertising program.

3. Explain how sales promotion campaigns are developed and implemented.

4. Explain how companies use public relations to communicate with their publics.

Santa Cruz Hughes knew she was onto something when she received a call from her daughter at school. It seems that the children in her daughter's class were picking up the phrase, "Not going anywhere for a while? Grab a Snickers." This was music to her ears, since Hughes is senior marketing manager at M&M/Mars and the woman behind the now highly successful Snickers advertising campaign.

In its "Not going anywhere for a while?" theme, Snickers has found the elusive "big idea"—a creative approach that turns a solid advertising strategy into a great advertising campaign. The line has become the basis for a series of wonderfully engaging commercials that spill over with brand personality. Such engaging commercials are crucial in today's cluttered and chaotic TV advertising environment, in which the average adult is exposed to as many as 247 ads a day. Before an ad can even start to communicate a selling proposition, it must first break through the din of commercials and other distractions to capture viewer attention. Humour is often the best clutter-buster, and the Snickers ads are delightfully funny.

The campaign consists of several humorous variations on a central premise: through circumstances beyond their control, characters in the ads find themselves stuck in one place for a long time, without access to real food. The first spot in the campaign featured Buffalo Bills coach Marv Levy—who had taken teams to the Super Bowl four times without a win—lecturing his players that none of the players could leave until they figured out how to win the big game. The ad was funny, but it was also very expensive—football stars don't come cheap. So the creative team at BBDO Worldwide, the Snickers ad agency, set out reduce production expenses. "We have a great idea," said the ad agency's creative director to his team. "Let's simplify it." The team came back with five new spots costing only about $1 million, a modest sum compared to some of the agency's lavish, Cecil B. DeMille-type productions for other clients. The lower budget created a kind of modesty and simplicity in the Snickers campaign that made the new ads even more appealing than the original.

One of these ads, set in a football locker room, takes a good-natured poke at political correctness. A gruff, crew-cut head coach announces, "Listen up. This year we gotta be a little more 'politically correct' with the team prayer." He turns to a priest standing behind him and says, "Hit it, Padre." The priest begins his prayer, but before he can go on, the coach interrupts to introduce a second clergyman. "All right, Rabbi. Let's go." Then the rabbi is also interrupted, this time in favour of a Native spiritualist, who in turn gives way to a Buddhist priest. "That was very touching," growls the coach. As the camera pans the room to reveal a long line of spiritual leaders waiting to bless the team, the voice-over says, "Not going anywhere for a while? Grab a Snickers."

Snickers
www.snickers.com/

Some may take the Snickers campaign as comedy for comedy's sake, but beneath the funny lines is a serious selling proposition. The stakes are high and so is the investment. M&M/Mars spent more than $57 million last year on advertising for Snickers, a brand that generates almost $400 million in annual sales. The campaign's objective is to advance Snickers' long-time hunger-satisfaction positioning—it's the chocolate bar to eat when no "real food" is available. Previous advertising portrayed idealized role models such as fire fighters and investigative reporters devouring Snickers bars before carrying out nougat-fortified acts of heroism. Those ads were neither entertaining nor relevant to the brand's primary target market of males aged 18 to 22. The new ads, however, meet both criteria and have worked to reposition the product. They give Snickers a less serious tone, and give the brand more credibility and believability as a hunger-relieving stop-gap measure. "We moved [our positioning] from [damping] a preoccupying hunger to satisfying hunger in an enjoyable way," explains Hughes.

It appears that lots of consumers are grabbing Snickers. The aggressive ad campaign has helped make Snickers one of the best-performing candy and snack brands in North America. Snickers sales have grown more than 10 percent since the campaign was introduced, about double the growth rate of the category. The campaign seems to have captured the minds and imaginations of North American consumers. "Enjoyability, memorability, and awareness of the thing have gone through the roof," says Peter Littlewood, director of marketing for the brand.

Thus, the Snickers advertising campaign amounts to much more than just funny ads. Bob Garfield, ad reviewer for *Advertising Age*, concludes: "The annals of advertising record very few...enduring 'big ideas,' but soon you may add to the list 'Not going anywhere for a while? Grab a Snickers.' ...As the campaign inexorably develops—and it will, over many years—this [big] idea will be revealed to have more than charm. It will have depth, scope, and the endless power of surprise. So grab a Snickers and enjoy. This advertising isn't going away for a long, long time."[1]

Companies must do more than make good products—they must inform consumers about product benefits and carefully position products in consumers' minds. To do this, they must skilfully use the mass-promotion tools of *advertising, sales promotion,* and *public relations.* We take a closer look at each of these tools in this chapter.

ADVERTISING

Advertising can be traced to the very beginnings of recorded history. Archeologists working in the countries around the Mediterranean Sea have dug up signs announcing various events and offers. The Romans painted walls to announce gladiator fights, and the Phoenicians painted pictures promoting their wares on large rocks along parade routes. A Pompeii wall painting praised a politician and asked for votes. During the Golden Age in Greece, town criers announced the sale of cattle, crafted items, and even cosmetics. An early "singing commercial" went as follows:

TABLE 15-1   *Canada's Top Ten National Advertisers*

Rank	Company	Total $ (000s)
1	General Motors of Canada	111.4
2	BCE	94.2
3	Procter & Gamble	84.2
4	Hudson Bay Company	72.3
5	Vycom Electronics	67.8
6	Government of Canada	67.6
7	Sears Canada	67.2
8	Chrysler Canada	58.2
9	Viacom Enterprises	57.8
10	Kraft Canada	57.3

Source: Adapted from "Top 10 Advertisers boost spending in'95" *Marketing*, April 15, 1996,p. 1.

"For eyes that are shining, for cheeks like the dawn / For beauty that lasts after girlhood is gone / For prices in reason, the woman who knows / Will buy her cosmetics from Aesclyptos."

Modern advertising, however, is a far cry from these early efforts. Advertising is a significant industry in Canada, employing more than 196 000 people. It is almost as important to the Canadian economy as the tourism industry. Over $8 billion is spent annually on advertising in Canada. This equates to $267 spent on advertising for every man, woman, and child in Canada.[2] In the United States, advertisers run up an annual advertising bill of more than $250 billion; worldwide advertising spending is approximately $600 billion. Although advertising is used mostly by business firms, it is also used by a wide range of non-profit organizations, professionals, and social agencies that advertise their causes to various target publics. In fact, the sixth-largest advertising spender is a non-profit organization—the Canadian government. Advertising is a good way to inform and persuade, whether the purpose is to sell Coca-Cola worldwide or to get consumers in a developing nation to drink milk or use birth control.

When one examines the categories with the heaviest advertising expenditures, one finds that retailing leads the list. Retailing accounts for one of every five advertising dollars spent in Canada. The next four leading categories are automotive, food, business equipment and services, and entertainment. These five categories account for 54 percent of all Canadian advertising. The fastest-growing category is toys and games. Table 15-1 lists 10 companies that spent the most on advertising in 1995. General Motors of Canada is the leader. Although Procter & Gamble ranks third in Canada, it is the *world's* largest advertiser, spending a whopping $4 billion globally.

Made-in-Canada ads, like this one created by J. Walter Thompson's for Kraft Canada, significantly boosted sales of Philadelphia cream cheese.

MAJOR DECISIONS IN ADVERTISING

Marketing management must make five important decisions when developing an advertising program (see Figure 15-1).

SETTING OBJECTIVES

The first step in developing an advertising program is to set *advertising objectives*. These objectives should be based on past decisions about the target market,

MARKETERS SPEAK OUT

SANDRA HAWKEN, ASSISTANT ACCOUNT EXECUTIVE, LEO BURNETT COMPANY

Sandra Hawken, a 1995 commerce graduate, can't believe how exciting every working day is. Leo Burnett opened the doors of its Canadian operation in 1952. Since she joined Leo upon graduating from Queen's University, Sandra has been involved in a number of advertising-related projects ranging from planning new brand strategies to creating new commercials. The Toronto office offers a full range of integrated marketing services and includes the disciplines of direct and event marketing, sales promotion, and public relations in addition to traditional media advertising. Major clients serviced by the Toronto office include Bell Canada, Kellogg's Canada Inc., Procter & Gamble Inc., Cadbury Chocolate Canada Inc., and Kraft Canada Inc.

The Toronto office of the Leo Burnett Company Ltd. is one of 72 full-service offices that comprise the chain of agencies that now operates in 62 different markets worldwide. Leo Burnett also has an office in Montreal called RTA that handles the translation of advertising materials into French. Leo Burnett employs 6950 people worldwide. It has been called one of the world's finest and oldest agencies, and it is one of the remaining few privately held global advertising companies. It has produced award-winning advertising that has helped build the businesses of some of the world's largest packaged-goods firms and services companies. Leo Burnett commercials are as familiar to all of us as members of our own families. Tony the Frosted Flakes tiger, the Pillsbury Dough Boy, the lonely Maytag repairman, and the monk searching for the Cadbury secret are all Leo Burnett creations.

Leo Burnett still operates under the principles and philosophies handed down by its founder. Leo Burnett first opened his agency in Chicago in 1935, using visionary statements such as, "When you reach for the stars, you may not quite get one, but you won't come up with a handful of mud either." All Leo Burnett agencies worldwide are imbued with this culture. This philosophy is captured in the firm's corporate logo—a hand reaching for a star-strewn firmament.

As part of the celebration surrounding the Leo Burnett's 60 years of operation, *Marketing* reprinted a speech

made by Leo Burnett to his staff in 1967. Excerpts from the speech entitled "When to take my name off the door," demonstrate not only Leo Burnett's commitment to his business, but also his belief in the importance of character and integrity. He would demand that his name be removed from the agency under the following circumstances:

When you stop rededicating yourselves every day to the idea that better advertising is what the Leo Burnett Company is all about.

When you are no longer what Thoreau called a 'corporation with a conscience'—which means to me, a corporation of conscientious men and women.[2]

Sandra Hawken

This strong culture first attracted Sandra Hawken to the company. As Sandra notes, "The advertising industry seemed more exciting and interesting than most of the other options available through on-campus recruiting. But more importantly, Leo Burnett felt like a family that truly cared about its employees. It was a place that fostered wonderful traditions."

Leo Burnett is also remembered for saying, "You can grow up in the advertising business, but you don't have to grow old in it." And growing up in the business is exactly what Sandra is doing. After only six months with Leo Burnett, 23-year-old Sandra has just begun to get her feet wet. She is learning something new every day and is only beginning to realize that working in client service in a multinational advertising agency provides many challenges as well as a whole lot of fun.

Her job with Leo Burnett began with an intense six-week training program. Sandra is now an Assistant Account Executive. In this position she has learned how to brief creative teams. She shares responsibility for bringing together a number of agency functions ranging from media planning, accounting, and research. She works as part of a team that develops strategies, creative ideas, and media plans for the client brand group. She works as the client's representative during the commercial-making process. Sandra's job has her in jeans one day feverishly analysing competitive media plans, and in a business suit the next, leading a meeting as part of the agency team. "There's no typical day for me—each one offers new excitement and challenges. Big ideas are our product, and hopefully, I play a part in the process of making ideas happen."

Sandra has been involved in developing a proposal to identify alternatives to traditional advertising, such as cause-related marketing, grassroots programs, and sponsorships for one client. This project has brought her into brainstorming sessions with members from across all disciplines in the agency. She has had to read countless articles and research reports, and she has been asked questions of almost anyone who would listen. One of Sandra's brands has had a longstanding television campaign that is now poised for change. Sandra is really excited about this project, "It is incredible being part of the team that was confronted with the task of getting inside the heads of our consumers to come up with a strategy to make them see our product in an entirely new light." You may have noticed that Sandra uses the word "team" a lot. That is because the team environment at Leo Burnett has made Sandra's need to learn something new every day manageable. When talking to Sandra, one has no doubt how much she loves her work. Her excitement at being part of the fast-paced advertising industry will keep her "reaching for the stars" for a long while yet.

Sandra Hawken, Assistant Account Executive, Leo Burnett Company (Toronto) wrote this vignette especially for *Principles of Marketing*, 3rd Canadian edition. "When to take my name off the door," speech by Leo Burnett delivered to his staff December 1, 1967, reprinted in "Leo Burnett at 60," *Marketing*, July 31/August 7, 1995, p. S18.

FIGURE 15-1 *Major advertising decisions*

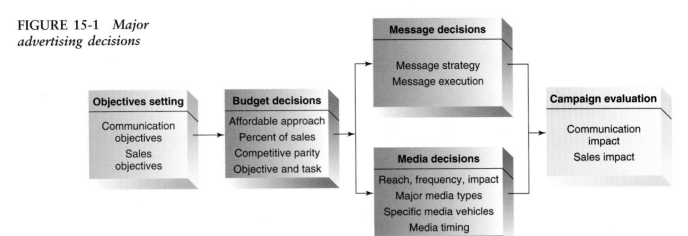

Advertising objective
A specific communication *task* to be accomplished with a specific *target* audience during a specific period of *time*.

Informative advertising
Advertising used to inform consumers about a new product or feature and to build primary demand.

Persuasive advertising
Advertising used to build selective demand for a brand by persuading consumers that it offers the best quality for their money.

Comparison advertising
Advertising that compares one brand directly or indirectly to one or more other brands.

positioning, and marketing mix. The marketing positioning and mix strategy define the job that advertising must do in the total marketing program.

An **advertising objective** is a specific communication *task* to be accomplished with a specific *target* audience during a specific period of *time*. Advertising objectives can be classified by primary purpose—whether the aim is to *inform, persuade,* or *remind.* Table 15-2 lists examples of each of these objectives.

Informative advertising is used heavily when introducing a new product category. In this case, the objective is to build primary demand. Thus, producers of compact-disc players first informed consumers of the sound and convenience benefits of CDs. **Persuasive advertising** becomes more important as competition increases. Here, the company's objective is to build selective demand. For example, when compact-disc players became established, Sony began trying to persuade consumers that its brand offered the best quality for their money.

Some persuasive advertising has become **comparison advertising,** in which a company directly or indirectly compares its brand with one or more other brands. For example, in its classic comparison campaign, Avis positioned itself against market-leading Hertz by claiming, "We're number two, so we try harder." Procter & Gamble positioned Scope mouthwash against Listerine, claiming that

TABLE 15-2 *Possible Advertising Objectives*

To Inform	
Telling the market about a new product	Describing available services
Suggesting new uses for a product	Correcting false impressions
Informing the market of a price change	Reducing buyers' fears
Explaining how the product works	Building a company image

To Persuade	
Building brand preference	Persuading buyers to purchase now
Encouraging switching to your brand	Persuading buyers to receive a sales call
Changing buyer perceptions of product attributes	

To Remind	
Reminding buyers that the product may be needed in the near future	Keeping the product in buyers' minds during off seasons
Reminding buyers where to buy the product	Maintaining top-of-mind product awareness

Yak Attack

The competition is yakking so much about 0¢/minute evenings and weekends, we just have to call them on it.

CANTEL AMIGO LEISURE PLAN

0¢ a minute

EVENINGS AND WEEKENDS

The competition is doing too much yakking and not enough listening. Because Cantel Amigo Leisure Plan customers have enjoyed unlimited evening and weekend calling since July. All across Canada.

THE AMIGO LEISURE PLAN

It's 0¢ a minute evenings from 6 pm until 8 am. And weekends from 6 pm Friday until 8 am Monday. Other times are just 65¢ a minute. The basic rate for our Amigo Leisure Plan is only $35.95 a month. Even better, our Amigo Leisure Plan now comes with the Motorola 910 cellular phone at no extra charge.

THE MOTOROLA 910

It's lightweight (9.8 oz) and state of the art, with 100 minutes talktime or 18 hours standby time. It features speed dialing and one-touch emergency dialing. And you can store in memory the 30 numbers you dial most often.

So remember, next time the competition goes yak-yak-yak: we were there first.

When we say Cantel gives you superior cellular, we're not just yakking.

CANTEL

SUPERIOR CELLULAR

Sometimes a company will compare its product or service directly to those of its competitors. This Cantel "Yak Attack" ad compares itself to Bell Mobility's "Yak" campaign.

Reminder advertising
Advertising used to keep consumers thinking about a product.

minty-fresh Scope "fights bad breath and doesn't give medicine breath." In 1995, the *Toronto Star* told prospective advertisers that it attracted more business readers than the *Globe and Mail*. Comparison advertising also has been used for products such as soft drinks, computers, deodorants, toothpastes, automobiles, pain relievers, and long-distance telephone service.[3]

The Competition Act stipulates that an advertisement using competitive claims must be based on an adequate and proper test that supports it. For example, a recent case between Duracell and its arch-rival, Eveready, resulted in Duracell having to change its advertising. Duracell had performed advanced tests on both companies' batteries, however, the tests were not deemed to be adequate since they hadn't included Eveready's newest battery, which was on retailers' shelves when the ad aired.[4]

Reminder advertising is important for mature products—it keeps consumers thinking about the product. Stanfield's reminded consumers about the benefits of their long underwear in an award-winning outdoor campaign.

SETTING THE ADVERTISING BUDGET

After determining its advertising objectives, the company next sets its *advertising budget* for each product. The role of advertising is to affect demand for a product. The company wants to spend the amount needed to achieve the sales goal. Four commonly used methods for setting the advertising budget are discussed in Chapter 14. Here we describe some specific factors that should be considered when setting the advertising budget:

◆ *Stage in the product life cycle.* New products typically need large advertising budgets to build awareness and to gain consumer trial. Mature brands usually require lower budgets as a ratio to sales.

◆ *Market share.* High-market-share brands usually need more advertising spending as a percentage of sales than low-share brands. Building the market or taking share from competitors requires larger advertising spending than simply maintaining current share.

◆ *Competition and clutter.* In a market with many competitors and high advertising spending, a brand must advertise more heavily to be heard above the noise in the market.

◆ *Advertising frequency.* When many repetitions are needed to present the brand's message to consumers, the advertising budget must be larger.

◆ *Product differentiation.* A brand that closely resembles other brands in its product class (beer, soft drinks, laundry detergents) requires heavy advertising to set it apart. When the product differs greatly from competitors, advertising can be used to point out the differences to consumers.[5]

Setting the advertising budget is no easy task. How does a company know if it is spending the right amount? Some critics charge that large consumer packaged-goods firms tend to spend too much on advertising and business-to-business marketers generally underspend on advertising. They claim that, on the one hand, the large consumer companies use lots of image advertising without really knowing its effects. They overspend as a form of "insurance" against not spending enough. On the other hand, business-to-business advertisers tend to rely too heavily on their sales forces to bring in orders. They underestimate the power of company and product image in preselling industrial customers. Thus, they do not spend enough on advertising to build customer awareness and knowledge.

How much impact does advertising really have on consumer buying and brand loyalty? A research study analysing household purchases of frequently bought consumer products came up with the following surprising conclusion:

> Advertising appears effective in increasing the volume purchased by loyal buyers but less effective in winning new buyers. For loyal buyers, high levels of exposure per week may be unproductive because of a levelling off of ad effectiveness.... Advertising appears unlikely to have some cumulative effect that leads to loyalty.... Features, displays, and especially price have a stronger impact on response than does advertising.[6]

These findings did not sit well with the advertising community, and several people attacked the study's data and methodology. They claimed that the study measured mostly short-run sales effects. Thus, it favoured pricing and sales-promotion activities, which tend to have more immediate impact. In contrast, most advertising takes many months, or even years, to build strong brand positions and consumer loyalty. These long-run effects are difficult to measure. However, a more recent study of BehaviorScan data over a 10-year period found that advertising does produce long-term sales growth, even two years after a campaign ends.[7] This debate underscores the fact that measuring the results of advertising spending remains a poorly understood subject.

Kellogg's developed a campaign that broke through the advertising clutter and repositioned Special K as a food that is part of a balanced diet.

ADVERTISING STRATEGY

Advertising strategy consists of two major elements—creating advertising *messages* and selecting advertising *media*. In the past, most companies developed messages and media plans independently. Media planning often was viewed as secondary to

THE ASHANTIS OF GHANA THINK A WOMAN'S BODY GETS MORE ATTRACTIVE AS SHE AGES.

Please contact your travel agent for the next available flight.

A 50 year old's body more attractive than a 20 year old's? Why not? It's only perception, after all. In every culture, our bodies change as we age. Wouldn't it be nice if ours were to celebrate the process? Exercise. Establish a healthy routine. Start with a balanced breakfast every morning and go from there. Kellogg's Special K cereal is fat free and a source of nine essential nutrients so it's a light, sensible way to help start your day. At any age, looking your best is about being strong and healthy. Which is important if you expect to be travelling in the near future.

Kellogg's Special K
specialk.kelloggs.ca

Look good on your own terms.

the message creation process. The creative department first created good advertisements, then the media department selected the best media for carrying these advertisements to desired target audiences. This often caused friction between creatives and media planners.

Today, however, media fragmentation, soaring media costs, and more focussed target marketing strategies have promoted the importance of the media-planning function. In some cases, an advertising campaign might start with a great message idea, followed by the choice of appropriate media. In other cases, however, a campaign might begin with a good media opportunity, followed by advertisements designed to take advantage of that opportunity. Increasingly, companies are realizing the benefits of planning these two important elements *jointly*. Messages and media should blend harmoniously to create an effective overall advertising campaign. This realization has resulted in greater cooperation between the creative and media functions. (See Marketing Highlight 15-1.)

Creating the Advertising Message

A large advertising budget does not guarantee a successful advertising campaign. Two advertisers can spend the same amount on advertising, yet have very different results. No matter how big the budget, advertising can succeed only if commercials gain attention and communicate well.

THE CHANGING MESSAGE ENVIRONMENT.   Good advertising messages are especially important in today's costly and cluttered advertising environment. While almost every Canadian household is equipped with a television (99 percent), and over 77 percent of Canadians watch television at least once a day, the increasing number of choices available to viewers with the advent of cable has resulted in fragmentation of the television audience. Seventy-six percent of Canadian homes report that they subscribe to cable. Canada has French and two English national television networks as well as 14 regional networks. Add to this number the 21 national specialty networks and seven Pay-TV channels. Not only have the number of Canadian channels increased, but so have the number of American signals, which are picked up by people in large border cities as well as cable users. In 1995, Canadians spent 17 percent of their viewing time watching U.S. stations.

In addition to television, there are 817 radio stations in Canada, 110 daily newspapers, over 900 community newspapers, and over 500 consumer magazines. Advertisers can also use outdoor advertising, transit advertising, bench advertising, elevator advertising, theatre screen advertising, and more novel media such as aerial advertising (balloons, skywriting), product placement in films and television shows, and washroom advertising. According to one estimate, adults are exposed to almost 250 ads per day, and this figure doesn't include signs or billboards!

When you look at the number of advertising alternatives you should begin to understand why the development of media plans to reach Canadians has become more difficult.[8] Consider the situation facing network television advertisers. They typically pay up to $50 000 for each 30 seconds of advertising time on a Canadian network—even more if it's an especially popular U.S. program such as "ER" ($720 000 per spot), "Friends" ($650 000), or "Home Improvement" ($485 000); or an event like the Super Bowl ($1.4 million). In such cases, their ads are sandwiched in with a clutter of some 60 other commercials, announcements, and network promotions per hour.

But things get even worse. Until recently, television viewers were pretty much a captive audience for advertisers. Viewers had only a few channels from which to choose. Those who found the energy to get up and change channels during boring commercial breaks usually found only more of the same on the other channels. But with the growth in cable TV, VCRs, and remote-control units, today's viewers have many more options. Take, for example, what happened to the viewing habits of

THE MEDIUM AND THE MESSAGE: A NEW HARMONY

Renowned Canadian author Marshall McLuhan wrote in the 1960s that "the medium is the message." McLuhan was a writer far in advance of his time. His belief that the medium was a more powerful influence on the viewer than the message is only beginning to be understood by advertisers today. Understanding the importance of the medium has resulted in the creative revolution taking place in ad agencies today, but it isn't necessarily coming from the creatives. More and more, creative directors are turning to the media departments to make their best ideas work harder. Media planning is no longer an after-the-fact complement to a new ad campaign. Media planners are now working more closely than ever with creatives to allow media selection to help shape the creative process, often before a single ad is written. In some cases, media people are even initiating ideas for new campaigns.

Among the more noteworthy ad campaigns based on tight media-creative partnerships is the one for Vin & Sprit AB's Absolut vodka. V&S and TBWA, its ad agency, meet once each year with a slew of magazines to set Absolut's media schedule. The schedule consists of up to 100 magazines, ranging from consumer and business magazines to theatre playbills. The agency's creative department is charged with creating media-specific ads.

The result is a wonderful assortment of very creative ads for Absolut, tightly targeted to audiences of the media in which they appear. For example, an "Absolut Bravo" ad in playbills has roses adorning a clear bottle, while business magazines contain an "Absolut Merger" foldout. In the Atlantic provinces, an Absolut bottle is shown with a model of the Bluenose inside. In 1997, Absolut's sponsorship of a Mordecai Richler short story in *Saturday Night* magazine provoked controversy in Canada over the blurring of editorial

Media planners for Absolut Vodka work with creatives to design ads targeted to specific media audiences. "Absolut Bravo" appears in theatre playbills. "Absolut Chicago" targets consumers in the Windy City.

and advertising content—text on one page of the story was formatted to reveal the outline of an Absolut bottle.

At a time of soaring media costs and cluttered communication channels, increased creative-media harmony can pay big dividends. The Absolut experience has had a positive impact on TBWA's approach to the advertising creative process. Says the agency's CEO, "What V&S has done for us is to give us a more open mind and put more demand on all departments to be creative in their ideas than might be the case otherwise." And closer cooperation between creative and media people has paid off handsomely for V&S. Largely as a result of its breakthrough advertising, V&S now captures a 58 percent share of the imported vodka market. Sales rocketed from just 12 000 cases in 1980 to more than 2.7 million cases in 1990.

Sources: Adapted from Gary Levin, " 'Meddling' in Creative More Welcome," *Advertising Age*, April 9, 1990, pp. S4, S8; "*Saturday Night* runs Absolut-sponsored Fiction," *Marketing*, July 14, 1997, p. 27. Also see William Wells, John Burnett, and Sandra Moriarty, *Advertising: Principles and Practice*, 2nd ed. (Englewood Cliffs, NJ: Prentice Hall, 1992), p. 266; Marshall McLuhan, *Understanding Media*, Scarborough: New American Library, 1964, p. ix.

Absolut Vodka
www.absolutvodka.com/

Canadian children following the release of the *Lion King* in 1995. Children aged two to 11, who normally spent 16.4 percent to 18.7 percent of their time viewing material on the VCR, now spent approximately 20 percent of their time watching videos on the VCR. The trend continued for over three months, when normal viewing habits resumed.[9] Viewers can also avoid ads by watching commercial-free cable channels. They can "zap" commercials by pushing the fast-forward button during taped programs. With remote control, they can instantly turn off the sound during a commercial or "zip" around the channels to see what else is on.[10]

Thus, just to gain and hold attention, today's advertising messages must be better planned, more imaginative, more entertaining, and more rewarding to

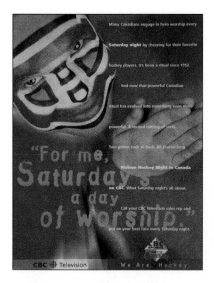

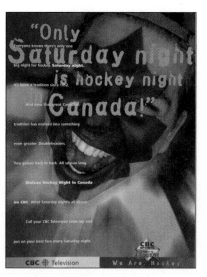

Ads for Hockey Night in Canada *target young people and position hockey as part of the Canadian life experience.*

Environics
environics.net

consumers. "Today we have to entertain and not just sell, because if you try to sell directly and come off as boring or obnoxious, people are going to press the remote on you," points out one advertising executive. "When most TV viewers are armed with remote channel switchers, a commercial has to cut through the clutter and seize the viewers in one to three seconds, or they're gone," comments another.[11] Creative strategy therefore will play an increasingly important role in advertising success.

MESSAGE STRATEGY. The first step in creating effective advertising messages is to decide what general message will be communicated to consumers—to plan a *message strategy*. The purpose of advertising is to get consumers to think about or react to the product or company in a certain way. People will react only if they believe that they will benefit from doing so. Thus, developing an effective message strategy begins with identifying customer *benefits* that can be used as advertising appeals. In the search for benefits to feature, many creative people start by talking to consumers, dealers, experts, and competitors. Others try to imagine consumers buying or using the product to figure out the benefits they seek. Ideally, advertising message strategy will follow directly from the company's broader positioning strategy.

Message strategy statements tend to be plain, straightforward outlines of benefits and positioning points that the advertiser wants to stress. These strategy statements must be turned into advertisements that will persuade consumers to buy or believe something. The advertiser must now develop a compelling *creative concept*—or *"big idea"*—that will bring the message strategy to life in a distinctive and memorable way. At this stage, simple message ideas become great ad campaigns. Usually, a copywriter and art director will team up to generate many creative concepts, hoping that one of these concepts will turn out to be the big idea. The creative concept may emerge as a visualization, a phrase, or a combination of the two.

The creative concept will guide the choice of specific appeals to be used in an advertising campaign. Advertising appeals should have three characteristics. First, they should be meaningful, pointing out benefits that make the product more desirable or interesting to consumers. Second, appeals must be believable—consumers must believe that the product or service will deliver the promised benefits. A recent survey, Environics 3SC Monitor of Social Values, revealed that 53 percent of Canadians believed that advertising lies most of the time.[12] If advertising is to be effective, viewers must view it as a credible source that communicates to them with integrity. Advertising messages must also be in line with communication generated through word of mouth if they are to be believed since people use multiple sources of information, notes Canadian consultant Richard Kelly.[13] Appeals should also be distinctive—they should tell how the product is better than the competing brands. For example, the most meaningful benefit of owning a wristwatch is that it keeps accurate time, yet few watch ads feature this benefit. Instead, based on the distinctive benefits they offer, watch advertisers might select any of a number of advertising themes. For years, Timex has been the affordable watch that "Took a lickin' and kept on tickin'." In contrast, Swatch has featured style and fashion, whereas Rolex stresses luxury and status.

MESSAGE EXECUTION.   The impact of the message depends not only on *what* is said, but also on *how* it is said. The advertiser now has to turn the "big idea" into an actual ad execution that will capture the target market's attention and interest. The creative people must find the best style, tone, words, and format for executing the message. Any message can be presented in different *execution styles,* such as the following:

- *Slice of life.* This style shows one or more "typical" people using the product in a normal setting. For example, a series of ads shows young Canadians with their faces painted, ready to attend Molson's *Hockey Night in Canada.*

- *Lifestyle.* This style shows how a product fits in with a particular lifestyle. For example, The Ontario Milk Marketing Board shows how active Canadians get their energy.

- *Fantasy.* This style creates a fantasy around the product or its use. Perfume ads are famous for this type of advertising. The Gap even introduced a perfume named Dream. Ads show a woman sleeping blissfully and suggests that the scent is "the stuff that clouds are made of."

- *Mood or image.* This style builds a mood or image around the product, such as beauty, love, or serenity. No claim is made about the product except through suggestion. Bermuda tourism ads create such moods.

- *Musical.* This style shows one or more people or cartoon characters singing a song about the product. For example, one of the most famous ads in history is a Coca-Cola ad built around the song, "I'd like to teach the world to sing."

- *Personality symbol.* This style creates a character that represents the product. The character might be *animated* (the Jolly Green Giant, Cap'n Crunch, Garfield the Cat) or *real* (Morris the 9-Lives Cat).

- *Technical expertise.* This style shows the company's expertise in making the product. Thus, Maxwell House shows one of its buyers carefully selecting the coffee beans, and Titleist explains its ability to make a better golf ball.

- *Scientific evidence.* This style presents survey or scientific evidence that the brand is better or better liked than one or more other brands. For years, Crest toothpaste has used scientific evidence to convince buyers that Crest is better than other brands at fighting cavities.

- *Testimonial evidence.* This style features a highly believable or likable source that endorses the product. It could be celebrities like Canadian figure skating pair Brasseur and Eisler (beef) or ordinary people saying how much they like a given product ("My doctor said Mylanta").

The advertiser also must choose a *tone* for the ad. Procter & Gamble always uses a positive tone: Its ads say something very positive about its products. P&G also avoids humour that might detract from the message. In contrast, Little Caesar's "pizza, pizza" ads use humour—in the form of the comical Little Caesar character—to drive home the advertiser's "two for the price of one" message.

The advertiser must use memorable and attention-getting *words* in the ad. For example, the following themes on the left would have much less impact without the creative phrasing on the right:

Message Theme	Creative Copy
7-Up is not a cola.	"The Uncola."
A BMW is a well-engineered automobile.	"The Ultimate Driving Machine."
If you want a light beer with taste, Blue Light is a good beer to drink.	"Beer not water."
We don't rent as many cars, so we have to do more for our customers.	"We're number two, so we try harder." (Avis)
London Life can help you plan for a comfortable retirement.	Freedom 55.
Red Rose Tea has superior taste.	"Only in Canada you say—Pity!"

Finally, *format* elements make a difference on an ad's impact as well as its cost. A small change in ad design can make a big difference on its effect. The *illustration* is the first thing the reader notices—it must be strong enough to draw attention. Next, the *headline* must effectively entice the right people to read the copy. Finally, the *copy*—the main block of text in the ad—must be simple but strong and convincing. Moreover, these three elements must effectively work *together*. Even then, less than 50 percent of the exposed audience might notice a truly outstanding ad; 30 percent might recall the main point of the headline; 25 percent might remember the advertiser's name; and less than 10 percent might have read most of the body copy. Less than outstanding ads, unfortunately, will not achieve even these results.

Selecting Advertising Media

The major steps in media selection are (1) deciding on *reach, frequency,* and *impact;* (2) choosing among major *media types;* (3) selecting specific *media vehicles;* and (4) deciding on *media timing.*

DECIDING ON REACH, FREQUENCY, AND IMPACT.   To select media, the advertiser must decide what reach and frequency are needed to achieve advertising objectives. **Reach** is a measure of the *percentage* of people in the target market who are exposed to the ad campaign during a given period of time. For example, the advertiser might try to reach 70 percent of the target market during the first three months of the campaign. **Frequency** is a measure of how many *times* the average person in the target market is exposed to the message. For example, the advertiser might want an average exposure frequency of three. The advertiser also must decide on the desired **media impact**—the *qualitative value* of a message exposure through a given medium. For example, for products that need to be demonstrated, messages on television may have more impact than messages on radio because television uses sight *and* sound. The same message in one magazine (say, *Maclean's*) may be more believable than in another (say, *The National Enquirer*). In general, the more reach, frequency, and impact the advertiser seeks, the higher the advertising budget will have to be.

CHOOSING AMONG MAJOR MEDIA TYPES.   The media planner must know the reach, frequency, and impact of each of the major media types. As summarized in Table 15-3, the major media types are newspapers, television, direct mail, radio, magazines, and outdoor. Each medium has advantages and limitations.

Media planners consider many factors when making their media choices. The *media habits of target consumers* will affect media choice—for example, radio and television are the best media for reaching teenagers. So will the *nature of the product*—fashions are best advertised in colour magazines, and Polaroid cameras are best demonstrated on television. Different *types of messages* may require different media. A message announcing a major sale tomorrow will require radio or newspapers; a message with a lot of technical data might require magazines or direct mailings. *Cost* is

VISA uses humour to set the right tone for its student market.

Reach
The percentage of people in the target market exposed to an ad campaign during a given period.

The media buyer for BC Hot House made it impossible to miss these ads placed on every bus within 300 kilometres of Vancouver.

TABLE 15-3 *Profiles of Major Canadian Media Types*

Medium	Number	% Advertising Revenues (1995-1996)	Exposures	Advantages	Limitations
Newspapers	110 daily 939 community	25	Daily circulation 4.6 million copies; 67% read a newspaper every day	Flexibility; timeliness; good local market coverage; broad acceptance; high believability.	Short life; poor reproduction quality; small pass-along audience.
Television	3 national 14 regional 21 specialty 7 Pay TV	25	77% of Canadians view at least once daily; 23.1 hours (English Canada); 27.7 hours (French Canada) per week	Combines sight, sound, and motion; high attention; high reach.	High absolute cost; high clutter; fleeting exposure; less audience selectivity.
Direct Mail	N/A	14	All Canadian households can be reached	High selectivity and flexibility. Personalization.	High cost/exposure. Junk-mail image.
Radio	817 stations	10	Reaches 95% of all Canadians 12+ once weekly Teens: 10.6 hrs/week Adults: 21 hrs/week	Mass use; high geographic and demographic selectivity; low cost.	Audio presentation only; lower attention; non-standardized rate structures; fleeting exposure.
Magazines	500+ consumer magazines	3	Readership varies with magazine type. High circulation magazines like *Homemakers* reaches 1.6 million readers; specialty magazines like *B.C. Outdoors* may only have circulations of 37 000.	High geographic and demographic selectivity; credibility and prestige; high-quality reproduction; long life; good pass-along readership.	Long ad purchase lead time; some waste circulation; no guarantee of ad placement position within magazine.
Outdoor/ Transit	Available in 90+ markets	3	Wide exposure in urban areas	Flexibility; high repeat exposure; low cost; llow competition.	No audience selectivity; creative limitations.
Online	N/A	4	37% of Canadian adults have access	High selectivity. Low cost. Immediate. Interactive.	Demographically skewed audience. Audience controls exposure.

Source: Information compiled from Canadian Media Directors' Council 1997–98 *Media Digest* and Justin Smallbridge, "Outdoor led 1996 ad revenue growth," *Marketing,* Oct. 6, 1997, p. 4.

Frequency
The number of times the average person in the target market is exposed to an advertising message during a given period.

Media impact
The qualitative value of a message exposure through a given medium.

Media vehicles
Specific media within each general media type, such as specific magazines, television shows, or radio programs.

also a major factor in media choice. Whereas television is very expensive, for example, newspaper advertising costs much less. The media planner considers both the total cost of using a medium and the cost per thousand exposures—the cost of reaching 1000 people using the medium.

Media impact and cost must be re-examined regularly. For a long time, television and magazines have dominated in the media mixes of national advertisers, with other media often neglected. Recently, however, the costs and clutter of these media have gone up, audiences have dropped, and marketers are adopting strategies beamed at narrower segments. As a result, advertisers are increasingly turning to alternative media, ranging from cable TV and outdoor advertising to parking meters and shopping carts (see Marketing Highlight 15-2).

SELECTING SPECIFIC MEDIA VEHICLES. The media planner now must choose the best **media vehicles**—specific media within each general media type. For example,

MARKETING HIGHLIGHT 15 - 2

ADVERTISERS SEEK ALTERNATIVE MEDIA

As network television costs soar and audiences shrink, many advertisers are looking for new ways to reach consumers. And the move toward micromarketing strategies, focussed more narrowly on specific consumer groups, also has fuelled the search for alternative media to replace or supplement network television. Advertisers are shifting larger portions of their budgets to media that cost less and target more effectively.

Two media benefitting most from the shift are outdoor advertising and cable television. Billboards have undergone a resurgence in recent years. Although outdoor advertising spending recently has levelled off, advertisers now spend more than $813 million annually on outdoor media, a 68 percent increase over 10 years ago. Gone are the ugly eyesores of the past; in their place we now see cleverly designed, colourful attention-grabbers. Outdoor advertising provides an excellent way to reach important local consumer segments.

Cable television is also booming. Today, more than 76 percent of all Canadian households subscribe to cable. The recent launch of new specialty channels is the biggest change in Canadian broadcasting. While the major channels still earn 90 percent of advertising revenues, the new specialty channels, such as Bravo, The Discovery Channel, Life Network, the New Country Music, Showcase Television, and WTN are each now earning revenues in excess of $5 million. Moreover, they are continuing to attract an ever-larger audience and, even more importantly, their ad revenue growth is increasing at a rate of 9.3 percent compared to the three percent gain experienced by conventional TV. These channels are expected to penetrate 60 percent of Canadian households in the near future. Not only do these stations offer the benefit of delivering highly targeted audiences, but their audiences may also have been difficult to reach by traditional means. MuchMusic, for example, presents an avenue to communicate with hard-to-reach teens, while stations like Bravo attract upscale female audiences.

Specialty channels are a bargain compared to many other forms of media advertising. Not only are they 25 to 50 percent cheaper than national television, but they are also giving magazines a run for their money. An advertiser can run a month-long campaign on a specialty channel for about the price of buying a full-page colour ad in some print media. These low prices have attracted many new advertisers to television. YTV, for example, has begun targeting small toy manufacturers that previously could not consider television advertising because of the prohibitive costs.

Cable television and outdoor advertising seem to make good sense. But, increasingly, ads are popping up in far less likely places. In their efforts to find less costly and more highly targeted ways to reach consumers, advertisers have discovered a dazzling collection of "alternative media." As consumers, we're used to ads on television, in magazines and newspapers, on the radio, and along the roadways. But these days, no matter where you go or what you do, you probably will run into some new form of advertising.

You escape to the ballpark, only to find billboard-size video screens running Labatt Blue ads while a blimp with an electronic message board circles lazily overhead. You pay to see a movie at your local theatre, but first you see a two-minute science-fiction fantasy that turns out to be an ad for General Electric portable stereo boxes. Then the movie itself is full of not-so-subtle promotional plugs for Pepsi, Domino's Pizza, Alka-Seltzer, MasterCard, Fritos, or any of a dozen other products. You sit down to rest your weary feet in the eating area of your local mall only to find the table top covered by an ad. An even bigger surprise is that the sponsor is the Body Shop, which, up until now, has avoided advertising and relied on publicity. In Guelph, Ontario, you pass school buses carrying exterior ads with social messages. Boats cruise along public beaches flashing advertising messages for Sundown Sunscreen or Gatorade to sunbathers. Advertisers seeking a really out-of-this-world alternative can pay $500 000 for 58 feet of prime advertising space on the hull of a Conestoga 1620 expendable rocket launched by NASA.

Some of these alternative media seem a bit far-fetched, and they sometimes irritate consumers. But for many marketers, these media can save money and provide a way to hit selected consumers where they live, shop, work, and play. Of course, this may leave you wondering if there are any commercial-free havens remaining for ad-weary consumers. The back seat of a taxi, perhaps, or public elevators, or stalls in a public restroom? Forget it! Each has already been invaded by innovative marketers.

Sources: See Alison Leigh Cowan, "Marketers Worry as Ads Crop Up in Unlikely Places," *Raleigh News and Observer,* February 21, 1988, p. 11; Kathy Martin, "What's Next? Execs Muse Over Boundless Ad Possibilities," *Advertising Age,* August 27, 1990; John P. Cortez, "Ads Head for the Bathroom," *Advertising Age,* May 18, 1992, p. 24; Ronald Grover, Laura Zinn, and Irene Recio, "Big Brother is Grocery Shopping with You," *Business Week,* March 29, 1993, p. 60; Richard Szathmary, "The Great (and not so great) Outdoors," *Sales & Marketing Management,* March 1992, pp. 75–81; Riccardo A. Davis, "More Ads Go Outdoors," *Advertising Age,* November 9, 1992, p. 36; and "Special Report: Cable TV," *Advertising Age,* March 27, 1995, pp. 51–53; "Redrawing the TV Map," *Marketing,* October 30, 1995, p. 13; Jim McElgunn, "Who's Watching What?" *Marketing,* May 29, 1995, pp. 14-15; Andrea Haman, "Boom Still On for Specialties," *Marketing,* October 30, 1995, pp. 30-31; Marina Strauss, "Is There no Hiding Place Left?" *Globe and Mail,* January 18, 1996, p. B12; Canadian Media Directors' Council *95-96 Media Digest.*

television vehicles include *North of 60, Market Place, Friends,* and *Hockey Night in Canada.* Magazine vehicles include *Maclean's, Equinox,* and *Chatelaine.* The media planner ultimately decides which vehicles give the best reach, frequency, and impact for the money.

Media planners also compute the cost per thousand persons reached by a vehicle. For example, if a full-page, four-colour advertisement in *Maclean's* costs $28 580 and *Maclean's* readership is 519 472 people, the cost of reaching each group of 1000 persons is about $55. The same advertisement in *Ski Canada* may cost only $5245 but reach only 47 908 persons—at a cost per thousand of about $111. The media planner would rank each magazine by cost per thousand and favour those magazines with the lower cost per thousand for reaching target consumers.

The media planner also must consider the costs of producing ads for different media. Whereas newspaper ads may cost very little to produce, flashy television ads may cost millions. On average, advertisers must pay $309 000 to produce a single 30-second television commercial. Nike recently paid a cool $2.8 million to make a single ad called "The Wall."[14]

In selecting media vehicles, the media planner must balance media cost measures against several media impact factors. First, the planner should balance costs against the media vehicle's *audience quality.* For a baby lotion advertisement, for example, *New Mother* magazine would have a high-exposure value; *The Hockey News* would have a low-exposure value. Second, the media planner should consider *audience attention.* Readers of *Flare,* for example, typically pay more attention to ads than do *The Economist* readers. Third, the planner should assess the vehicle's *editorial quality—Maclean's* and *Canadian Business* are more believable and prestigious than *The National Enquirer.*

DECIDING ON MEDIA TIMING. The advertiser also must decide how to schedule the advertising over the course of a year. Suppose sales of a product peak in December and drop in March. The firm can vary its advertising to follow the seasonal pattern, to oppose the seasonal pattern, or to be the same all year. Most firms do some seasonal advertising. Some do *only* seasonal advertising: For example, Hallmark advertises its greeting cards only before major holidays.

Finally, the advertiser must choose the pattern of the ads. *Continuity* means scheduling ads evenly within a given period. *Pulsing* means scheduling ads unevenly over a given time period. Thus, 52 ads could either be scheduled at one per week during the year or pulsed in several bursts. The idea is to advertise heavily for a short period to build awareness that carries over to the next advertising period. Those who favour pulsing feel that it can be used to achieve the same impact as a steady schedule, but at a much lower cost. However, some media planners believe that although pulsing achieves minimal awareness, it sacrifices depth of advertising communications.

ADVERTISING EVALUATION

The advertising program should evaluate both the *communication effects* and the *sales effects* of advertising regularly. Measuring the communication effect of an ad—*copy testing*—tells whether the ad is communicating well. Copy testing can be done before or after an ad is printed or broadcast. Before the ad is placed, the advertiser can show it to consumers, ask how they like it, and measure recall or attitude changes resulting from it. After the ad is run, the advertiser can measure how the ad affected consumer recall or product awareness, knowledge, and preference.

But what sales are caused by an ad that increases brand awareness by 20 percent and brand preference by 10 percent? The sales effect of advertising is often harder to measure than the communication effect. Sales are affected by many factors besides advertising—such as product features, price, and availability.

One way to measure the sales effect of advertising is to compare past sales with past advertising expenditures. Another way is through experiments. For example, to test the effects of different advertising spending levels, Pizza Hut could vary the amount it spends on advertising in different market areas and measure the differences in the resulting sales levels. It could spend the normal amount in one market area, half the normal amount in another area, and twice the normal amount in a third area. If the three market areas are similar, and if all other marketing efforts in the area are the same, then differences in sales in the three cities could be related to advertising level. More complex experiments could be designed to include other variables, such as difference in the ads or media used.

ORGANIZING FOR ADVERTISING

Different companies organize in different ways to handle advertising. In small companies, someone in the sales department might handle advertising. Large companies set up advertising departments whose job it is to set the advertising budget, work with the ad agency, and handle direct-mail advertising, dealer displays, and other advertising not done by the agency. Most large companies use outside advertising agencies because they offer several advantages.

How does an advertising agency work? Advertising agencies were started in the mid- to late 1800s by salespeople and brokers who worked for the media and received a commission for selling advertising space to companies. As time passed, the salespeople began to help customers prepare their ads. Eventually, they formed agencies and grew closer to the advertisers than to the media. Today's agencies employ specialists who can often perform advertising tasks better than the company's own staff. Agencies also bring an outside perspective to solving the company's problems, along with lots of experience from working with different clients and situations. Thus, today, even companies with strong advertising departments use advertising agencies.

Some ad agencies are huge—BBDO Canada Inc., the country's largest agency, has annual billings (the dollar amount of advertising placed for clients) of $56.7 million. Like many other agencies, it has grown by gobbling up smaller firms. Other agencies operate on a much smaller scale, but can still win big accounts. Such is the case with Gee Jeffery & Partners, a diminutive firm that surprised the industry when it won the giant Canadian Airlines account. Advertising agencies are an important facet of Canadian business. A recent survey revealed that 45 percent of English-Canadians say they care a lot about whether the commercials they view on television are created in Canada. This percentage is even higher when one turns to Quebec. In that province, 58 percent of the respondents stressed that they want commercials especially designed for them. Canadian viewers also believe that they can tell whether a commercial is Canadian-made.[15]

Most large advertising agencies have the staff and resources to handle all phases of an advertising campaign for their clients, from creating a marketing plan to developing ad campaigns and preparing, placing, and evaluating ads. Agencies usually have four departments: creative, which develops and produces ads; media, which selects media and places ads; research, which studies audience characteristics and wants; and business, which handles the agency's business activities. Each account is supervised by an account executive, and people in each department are usually assigned to work on one or more accounts.

Ad agencies traditionally have been paid through commissions and fees. In the past, the agency typically received 15 percent of the media cost as a rebate. Consider, for example, that the agency bought $60 000 of magazine space for a client. The magazine would bill the advertising agency for $51 000 ($60 000 less 15 percent), and the agency then billed the client for $60 000, keeping the

$9000 commission. If the client purchased space directly from the magazine, it would have paid $60 000 because commissions are only paid to recognized advertising agencies.

However, both advertisers and agencies have become increasingly dissatisfied with the commission system. Larger advertisers complain that they pay more for the same services received by smaller ones simply because they place more advertising. Advertisers also believe that the commission system drives agencies away from low-cost media and short advertising campaigns. Agencies are dissatisfied because they perform extra services for an account without receiving additional pay. As a result, the trend is now toward paying either a straight fee or a combination of commission and fee. Some large advertisers are now linking agency compensation with the performance of the agency's advertising campaigns. Today, only about 35 percent of companies still pay their agencies on a commission-only basis.[16]

Another trend is affecting the advertising agency business. Ad agencies are being attacked by new competitors—management consulting firms such as Andersen Consulting Canada, McKinsey, KPMG, and Ernst & Young. Increasing numbers of these firms are developing expertise in what was always regarded as the domain of advertising agencies: effective target marketing and brand image management. The threat is even greater for advertising agencies that have cut back their strategic resources with the recent economic downturn.[17] As a result, some agencies have begun offering a full range of integrated marketing services under one roof, including strategic planning and marketing research, in addition to their traditional promotion mix activities of advertising, sales promotion, public relations, direct marketing, and sales training. Other agencies have responded by becoming more specialized and focused such as the "creative boutiques"—smaller, independent agencies that specialize only in creative campaigns.

INTERNATIONAL ADVERTISING DECISIONS

International advertisers face many complexities not encountered by domestic advertisers. The most basic issue concerns the degree to which global advertising should be adapted to the unique characteristics of various country markets. Some large advertisers have attempted to support their global brands with highly standardized worldwide advertising, with campaigns that work as well in Bangkok as they do in Burlington. For example, brands such as Nike, Pepsi, and Jeep are advertised in much the same way globally. Jeep has created a worldwide brand image of ruggedness and reliability. Pepsi uses standardized appeals to target the world's youth. And Nike urges North Americans, Africans, Asians, and Europeans alike to "Just do it." Standardization produces many benefits—lower advertising costs, greater coordination of global advertising efforts, and a more consistent worldwide company or product image. However, standardization also has drawbacks. Most importantly, it ignores the fact that country markets differ greatly in their cultures, demographics, and economic conditions. Thus, most international advertisers think globally but act locally. They develop global advertising *strategies* that bring efficiency and consistency to their worldwide advertising efforts. Then they adapt their advertising *programs* to make them more responsive to consumer needs and expectations within local markets.

Companies vary in the degree to which they adapt their advertising to local markets. For example, Kellogg's Frosted Flakes commercials are almost identical worldwide, with only minor adjustments for local cultural differences. For example, one advertisement uses a tennis theme that has worldwide appeal and features teenage actors with generic good looks—neither identifiably Northern European nor Latin American. Of course, Kellogg translates the commercials into different languages. In the English version, for example, Tony growls "They're Gr-r-reat!" whereas in the German version it's "Gr-r-rossartig!" Other adaptations are more

Kellogg's Frosted Flakes commercials are almost identical worldwide, with only minor adjustments for local cultural differences.

subtle. In the North American ad, after winning the match, Tony leaps over the net in celebration. In other versions, he simply "high fives" his young partner. The reason: Europeans do not jump over the net after winning at tennis.[18]

In contrast, other firms, like Parker Pen Company, change their advertising substantially from country to country.

> Print ads in Germany simply show the Parker Pen held in a hand that is writing a headline—"This is how you write with precision." In the United Kingdom, where it is the brand leader, [ads emphasize] the exotic processes used to make pens, such as gently polishing the gold nibs with walnut chips. . . . In the United States, the ad campaign's theme is status and image. The headlines are . . . "Here's how you tell who's boss," and "There are times when it has to be Parker." The company considers the different themes necessary because of different product images and . . . customer motives in each market.[19]

Global advertisers face several additional problems. For instance, advertising media costs and availability differ considerably from country to country. Some countries have too few media to handle all of the advertising offered to them. Other countries are peppered with so many media that an advertiser cannot gain national coverage at a reasonable cost. Media prices often are negotiated and may vary greatly. For example, one study found that the cost of reaching 1000 consumers in 11 different European countries ranged from $2.20 in Belgium to $8.22 in Italy. For women's magazines, the advertising cost per page ranged from $3.49 per thousand circulation in Denmark to $15.11 in Germany.[20]

Countries also differ in the extent to which they regulate advertising practices. Many countries have extensive systems of laws restricting how much a company can spend on advertising, the media used, the nature of advertising claims, and other aspects of the advertising program. Such restrictions often require that advertisers adapt their campaigns from country to country. Consider the following example:

> A 30-second Kellogg commercial produced for British TV would have to have [several] alterations to be acceptable [elsewhere] in Europe: Reference to iron and vitamins would have to be deleted in the Netherlands. A child wearing a Kellogg's T-shirt would be edited out in France where children are forbidden from endorsing products on TV. In Germany, the line "Kellogg makes cornflakes the best they've ever been" would be cut because of rules against making competitive claims. After alterations, the 30-second commercial would be [only] about five seconds long.[21]

Sales promotion
Short-term incentives to encourage purchase or sales of a product or service.

Thus, although advertisers may develop global strategies to guide their overall advertising efforts, specific advertising programs usually must be adapted to meet local cultures and customs, media characteristics, and advertising regulations.

SALES PROMOTION

Advertising is joined by two other mass-promotion tools—*sales promotion* and *public relations*. **Sales promotion** consists of short-term incentives to encourage purchase or sales of a product or service. Whereas advertising offers reasons to buy a product or service, sales promotion offers reasons to buy *now*. Examples are found everywhere. A freestanding insert in the weekend newspaper contains a coupon offering 50 cents off Organics shampoo. The end-of-the-aisle display in the local supermarket tempts impulse buyers with a wall of Coke cartons. An executive buys a new Compaq laptop computer and gets a free carrying case, or a family buys a new Taurus and receives a rebate cheque for $500. A hardware store chain receives a 10 percent discount on selected Black & Decker portable power tools if it agrees to advertise them in local newspapers.

Sales promotion includes a wide variety of promotion tools designed to stimulate earlier or stronger market response. It includes **consumer promotion**—samples, coupons, rebates, prices-off, premiums, contests, and others; **trade promotion**—buying allowances, free goods, merchandise allowances, cooperative advertising, push money, dealer sales contests; and **sales-force promotion**—bonuses, contests, sales rallies.

RAPID GROWTH OF SALES PROMOTION

Sales-promotion tools are used by most organizations, including manufacturers, distributors, retailers, trade associations, and non-profit institutions. They are targeted toward final buyers (consumer promotions), business customers (business promotions), retailers and wholesalers (trade promotions), and members of the sales force (sales-force promotions). Today in many consumer packaged-goods companies, sales promotion accounts for 75 percent or more of all marketing expenditures. Sales-promotion expenditures have been increasing 12 percent annually, compared to advertising's increase of only 7.6 percent.[22]

Several factors have contributed to the rapid growth of sales promotion, particularly in consumer markets. First, inside the company, product managers face greater pressures to increase their current sales, and promotion now is accepted more by top management as an effective sales tool. Second, externally, the company faces more competition, and competing brands are less differentiated. Competitors are using more promotions, and consumers have become more deal oriented. Third, advertising efficiency has declined because of rising costs, media clutter, and legal restraints. Finally, retailers are demanding more deals from manufacturers.

The growing use of sales promotion has resulted in *promotion clutter*, similar to advertising clutter. Consumers are increasingly tuning out promotions, weakening their ability to trigger immediate purchase. In fact, the extent to which North American consumers have come to take promotions for granted was illustrated dramatically by the reactions of Eastern European consumers when Procter & Gamble recently gave out samples of a newly introduced shampoo. To P&G, the sampling campaign was just business as usual. To consumers in Poland and Czechoslovakia, however, it was little short of a miracle:

> With nothing expected in return, Warsaw shoppers were being handed free samples of Vidal Sassoon Wash & Go shampoo. Just for the privilege of trying the new product; no standing in line for a product that may not even be on the shelf. Some were so taken aback that they were moved to tears. In a small town in Czechoslovakia, the head of the local post office was so pleased to be part of the direct-mail sampling program, he sent the P&G staffer roses to express his thanks. The postmaster told the P&G'er: "This is the most exciting thing that's ever happened in this post office—it's a terrific experience to be part of this new market economy that's coming."[23]

Although no sales promotion is likely to create such excitement among promotion-prone consumers in North America and other Western countries, manufacturers now are searching for ways to rise above the clutter, such as offering larger coupon values or creating more dramatic point-of-purchase displays.

Consumer promotion
Sales promotion designed to stimulate consumer purchasing, including samples, coupons, rebates, prices-off, premiums, patronage rewards, displays, and contests and sweepstakes.

Trade promotion
Sales promotion designed to gain reseller support and to improve reseller selling efforts, including discounts, allowances, free goods, cooperative advertising, push money, and conventions and trade shows.

Sales-force promotion
Sales promotion designed to motivate the sales force and make sales-force selling efforts more effective, including bonuses, contests, and sales rallies.

PURPOSE OF SALES PROMOTION

Sales-promotion tools vary in their specific objectives. For example, a free sample stimulates consumer trial; a free management advisory service cements a long-term relationship with a retailer. Sellers use sales promotions to attract new users, to reward loyal customers, and to increase the repurchase rates of occasional users.

Many sellers think of sales promotion as a tool for breaking down brand loyalty and advertising as a tool for building up brand loyalty. Thus, an important issue for marketing managers is how to divide the budget between sales promotion and advertising.

Sales promotions typically are used together with advertising or personal selling. Consumer promotions usually must be advertised and can add excitement and pulling power to ads. Trade and sales-force promotions support the firm's personal selling process. In using sales promotion, a company must set objectives, select the right tools, develop the best program, pretest and implement it, and evaluate the results.

SETTING SALES-PROMOTION OBJECTIVES

Sales-promotion objectives vary widely. Sellers may use *consumer promotions* to increase short-term sales or to help build long-term market share. The objective may be to entice consumers to try a new product, lure away consumers from competitors' products, get consumers to "load up" on a mature product, or hold and reward loyal customers. Objectives for *trade promotions* include getting retailers to carry new items and more inventory, getting them to advertise the product and give it more shelf space, and getting them to buy ahead. For the *sales force*, objectives include getting more sales-force support for current or new products or getting salespeople to sign up new accounts.

In general, sales promotions should aim at *consumer relationship building*. Rather than creating only short-term sales volume or temporary brand switching, they should help to reinforce the product's position and build long-term relationships with consumers. This is what Kraft Canada has done with its magazine *What's Cooking*. Included in newspapers as a freestanding insert, the booklet contains letters from consumers, cooking tips, information on maintaining a healthy diet, and recipes based on Kraft products. It contains information on Kraft's toll-free number that consumers can call to get more "good food ideas." Consumers look forward to receiving the magazine and many keep it and refer to it for years to come. In this way marketers are avoiding "quick-fix," price-only promotions in favour of promotions designed to build brand equity. Another example comes from France where Nestlé set up roadside Relais Bébé centres, where travellers can stop to feed and change their babies. At each centre, Nestlé hostesses provide free disposable diapers, changing tables, high chairs, and free samples of Nestlé baby food. Each summer, 64 hostesses welcome 120 000 baby visits and dispense six million samples of baby food. This ongoing promotion provides real value to parents and an ideal opportunity to build relationships with customers. At key meal-time moments, Nestlé hostesses are in direct contact with mothers in a unique, brand-related relationship. Nestlé also provides a toll-free phone number for free baby-nutrition counselling.[24]

Even price promotions can be designed to help build customer relationships. Examples include all of the "loyalty marketing programs" that have mushroomed in recent years. For instance, the Second Cup sponsors a "frequent buyer" program whereby regular customers receive free cups of coffee as well as coffee beans. Thus, if properly designed, every sales-promotion tool has consumer-relationship-building potential.

SELECTING SALES-PROMOTION TOOLS

Many tools can be used to accomplish sales-promotion objectives. Descriptions of the main consumer- and trade-promotion tools follow.

Consumer-Promotion Tools

The main consumer-promotion tools include samples, coupons, cash refunds, price packs, premiums, advertising specialties, patronage rewards, point-of-purchase displays and demonstrations, and contests, sweepstakes, and games.

Samples are offers of a trial amount of a product. Some samples are free; for others, the company charges a small amount to offset its cost. The sample might be delivered door to door, sent by mail, handed out in a store, attached to another product, or featured in an ad. Sampling is the most effective—but most expensive—way to introduce a new product. For example, the recent Canadian introduction of Time Out chocolate bars and Barq's Root Beer involved the distribution of samples as well as a heavy television-, newspaper-, and magazine-advertising campaigns.

Sampling has grown rapidly in Canada. Recent research has shown that when given a choice between a free sample and a coupon, 92 percent of consumers prefer a sample. Since aging consumers are less likely to try new products, manufacturers like sampling because it provides a risk-free way for consumers to try a new product. Since a person is hired to conduct most in-store sampling programs, consumers can also ask for more information about a product. Retailers also like sampling programs because they add excitement to the in-store shopping experience. Sampling is becoming so popular, however, that manufacturers must become increasingly creative and targeted with their sampling programs. Grocery shoppers, for example, may be offered up to 10 samples each time they enter a store. Provigo tripled the number of sampling programs in its stores from 5000 to 15 000 annually.[25]

Coupons are certificates that give buyers a saving when they purchase specified products. They are supposed to generate excitement and competition among brands, but an increasing number of manufacturers believe that coupons are costly and inefficient. The U.S. market is saturated: American households receive 3000 coupons annually compared to only 400 directed at Canadian households. Redemption rates are low, often only two percent, and are declining due to increased clutter. Thus, major consumer-goods companies, led by Procter & Gamble, are issuing fewer coupons and targeting them more carefully.

Heaviest coupon users in Canada tend to be females, between the ages of 35 to 49, with families and incomes of $35,000+. Quebec residents use more coupons than do consumers in the other provinces. In the past, marketers have relied almost exclusively on mass-distributed coupons delivered through the mail or those printed in newspaper or magazine ads. Today, however, they're sending out coupons to carefully targeted households known to use specific brands. Marketers are also distributing coupons through shelf dispensers at the point of sale, by electronic point-of-sale coupon printers, or through "paperless coupon systems" that dispense personalized discounts to targeted buyers at the checkout counter in stores. Some companies are now offering coupons on their web sites or through online coupon services such as Interactive Coupon Network's CoolSavings site (http://www.coolsavings.com) and Money Mailer's H.O.T. Coupons site (http://www.hotcoupons.com). In a recent week-long promotion using the Cool-Savings site, H&R Block offered a coupon for 25 percent savings on premium tax preparation. Ten percent of consumers who downloaded the coupon redeemed it, significantly higher than the two percent average redemption for traditional coupons.[26]

Cash refund offers (or **rebates**) are like coupons except that the price reduction occurs after the purchase rather than at the retail outlet. The consumer sends

---

Samples
Offers to consumers of a trial amount of a product.

Coupons
Certificates that give buyers a saving when they purchase a specified product.

Cash refund offers (rebates)
Offers to refund part of the purchase price of a product to consumers who send a "proof of purchase" to the manufacturer.

Drink Pepsi and get scads of stuff to wear.

And 'cause it's you,
we'll include
the heels to match.

Run out and get a Pepsi Stuff catalogue anywhere you can score Pepsi. Then collect points when you buy specially marked bottles, cans and fountain cups (a.k.a. movie theatre cups) of Pepsi. When you have enough points fill out the order form at the back of the catalogue, using your real name of course, and send away. Next thing you know the mailman's tugging Pepsi Stuff to your door. With your neighbour's pitbull on his heels. P.S. Are you still there? Offer ends October 31, 1996.

PEPSI STUFF
DRINK IT. GET IT.

The Pepsi Stuff program was heralded as the most successful promotional campaign to run in Canada in 40 years.

Price packs (cents-off deals)
Reduced prices that are marked by the producer directly on the label or package.

Premiums
Goods offered either free or at low cost as an incentive to buy a product.

Advertising specialties
Useful articles imprinted with an advertiser's name, given as gifts to consumers.

Patronage rewards
Cash or other awards for the regular use of a certain company's products or services.

a "proof of purchase" to the manufacturer, who then refunds part of the purchase price by mail. For example, Toro ran a clever pre-season promotion on some of its snowblower models, offering a rebate if the snowfall in the buyer's market area turned out to be below average. Competitors were not able to match this offer on such short notice, and the promotion was very successful.

Price packs (also called **cents-off deals**) offer consumers savings off the regular price of a product. The reduced prices are marked by the producer directly on the label or package. Price packs can be single packages sold at a reduced price (such as two for the price of one), or two related products banded together (such as a toothbrush and toothpaste). Price packs are very effective—even more so than coupons—in stimulating short-term sales.

Premiums are goods offered either free or at low cost as an incentive to buy a product. A premium may come inside the package (in-pack) or outside the package (on-pack). If reusable, the package itself may serve as a premium—such as a decorative tin. Premiums are sometimes mailed to consumers who have sent in a proof of purchase, such as a box top. "Drink it. Get it." was the slogan for the Pepsi Stuff premium offer that one industry analyst called the "most successful promotion run in Canada in the last 40 years." Pepsi added value to a purchase of their product in a highly "youth-relevant" way by letting people redeem points of specially marked packaged for "must-be-seen" merchandise from the Pepsi stuff catalogue. Eighty-one percent of soft-drink users were aware of the offer. The promotion increased Pepsi's market share by seven percent. While 53 percent of the gain came from people switching brands, the remainder came because heavy Pepsi drinkers consumed more product. Although the share gains are impressive, the program also improved consumer attitude and imagery measures of Pepsi.[27]

Advertising specialties are useful articles imprinted with an advertiser's name given as gifts to consumers. Typical items include baseball caps, pens, calendars, key rings, matches, shopping bags, T-shirts, caps, nail files, and coffee mugs. Such items can be very effective. In a recent study, 63 percent of all consumers surveyed were either carrying or wearing an ad specialty item. More than three-quarters of those who had an item could recall the advertiser's name or message before showing the item to the interviewer.[28]

Patronage rewards are cash or other awards offered for the regular use of a certain company's products or services. For example, airlines offer "frequent flyer plans," awarding points for miles travelled that can be turned in for free airline trips. Marriott Hotels has adopted an "honoured guest" plan that awards points to users of their hotels. Baskin-Robbins offers frequent-purchase awards—for every 10 purchases, customers receive a free litre of ice cream.

Point-of-purchase (POP) promotions include displays and demonstrations that occur at the point of purchase or sale. An example is a five-foot-high cardboard display of Cap'n Crunch next to Cap'n Crunch cereal boxes. Unfortunately, many retailers do not like to handle the hundreds of displays, signs, and posters

Point-of-purchase (POP) promotions
Displays and demonstrations that take place at the point of purchase or sale.

Contests, sweepstakes, games
Promotional events that give consumers the chance to win something—such as cash, trips, or goods—by luck or through extra effort.

they receive from manufacturers each year. Manufacturers have responded by offering better POP materials, tying them in with television or print messages, and offering to set them up.

Contests, sweepstakes, and games such as Tim Horton's "roll up the rim to win," give consumers the chance to win something, such as cash, trips, or goods, by luck or through extra effort. A *contest* calls for consumers to submit an entry—a jingle, guess, suggestion—to be judged by a panel that will select the best entries. A *sweepstakes* calls for consumers to submit their names for a drawing. A *game* presents consumers with something—bingo numbers, missing letters—every time they buy, which may or may not help them win a prize. A sales contest urges dealers or the sales force to increase their efforts, with prizes going to the top performers.

Online contests are one of the newest promotion tools, but the industry is still in its infancy. Marketers view the potential of using promotions on the Internet as a means of attracting attention to their web pages and fostering interactivity—the first element in building a relationship with a web-site visitor. Bayshore Trust did just that with its recent online scavenger hunt. DealerNet (http://www.dealernet.com), a partnership that resembles a virtual auto mall that provides information on new and used cars, attracted visitors to its site using contests that range from cash prizes to car giveaways.

Trade-Promotion Tools

More sales-promotion dollars are directed to retailers and wholesalers (69 percent) than to consumers. Trade promotion can persuade retailers or wholesalers to carry a brand, give it shelf space, promote it in advertising, and push it to consumers. Shelf space is so scarce these days that manufacturers often have to offer price-offs, allowances, buy-back guarantees, or free goods to retailers and wholesalers to get on the shelf and, once there, to stay on it.

Manufacturers use several trade-promotion tools. Many of the tools used for consumer promotions—contests, premiums, displays—also can be used as trade promotions. Or the manufacturer may offer a straight **discount** off the list price on each case purchased during a stated period of time (also called a *price-off, off-invoice, or off-list*). The offer encourages dealers to buy in quantity or to carry a new item. Dealers can use the discount for immediate profit, for advertising, or for price reductions to their customers.

Discount
A straight reduction in price on purchases during a stated period of time.

Manufacturers also may offer an **allowance** (usually so much off per case) in return for the retailer's agreement to feature the manufacturer's products in some way. An *advertising allowance* compensates retailers for advertising the product. A *display allowance* compensates them for using special displays.

Allowance
Promotional money paid by manufacturers to retailers in return for an agreement to feature the manufacturer's products in some way.

Manufacturers may offer *free goods,* which are extra cases of merchandise, to intermediaries who buy a certain quantity or who feature a certain flavour or size. They may offer *push money*—cash or gifts to dealers or their sales force to "push" the manufacturer's goods. Manufacturers may give retailers free *specialty advertising items* that carry the company's name, such as pens, pencils, calendars, paperweights, matchbooks, and memo pads.

Business-Promotion Tools

Companies spend billions of dollars each year on promotion to industrial customers. These business promotions are used to generate business leads, stimulate purchases, reward customers, and motivate salespeople. Business promotion includes many of the same tools used for consumer or trade promotions. Here, we focus on two major business-promotion tools—conventions and trade shows, and sales contests.

Many companies and trade associations organize *conventions and trade shows* to promote their products. Firms selling to the industry show their products at the trade show. More than 5800 trade shows occur every year, drawing approximately 80 million people. John Treleaven, director of trade planning and operations for the

The FITT program is designed to help Canadian students acquire the skills to sell products and services in international markets.

International Business Development Bureau at the Department of Foreign Affairs and International Trade in Ottawa says, "Trade fairs are the most powerful marketing tool at the disposal of Canadian exporters."[29] The success of trade shows is revealed in the bottom lines of many Canadian companies. Recently, the 400 Canadian firms that displayed their wares at the 40 largest German trade fairs rang up more than $250 million in sales. Vendors receive many benefits, such as opportunities to find new sales leads, contact customers, introduce new products, meet new customers, sell more to present customers, and educate customers with publications and audiovisual materials. Trade shows also help companies reach many prospects not reached through their sales forces. In emerging economies, such as Russia, where conventional marketing and media channels are underdeveloped, trade fairs are the only means of reaching potential buyers.

Business marketers may spend as much as 35 percent of their annual promotion budgets on trade shows. They face several decisions, including which trade shows to participate in, how much to spend on each trade show, how to build dramatic exhibits that attract attention, and how to follow up on sales leads effectively.[30]

A *sales contest* is a contest for salespeople or dealers to motivate them to increase their sales performance over a given period. Called "incentive programs," these contests motivate and recognize good company performers, who may receive trips, cash prizes, or other gifts. Some companies award points for performance, which the receiver can turn in for any of a variety of prizes. Sales contests work best when they are tied to measurable and achievable sales objectives (such as finding new accounts, reviving old accounts, or increasing account profitability).

DEVELOPING THE SALES-PROMOTION PROGRAM

The marketer must make several other decisions in order to define the full sales-promotion program. First, the marketer must decide on the *size of the incentive*. A certain minimum incentive is necessary if the promotion is to succeed; a larger incentive will produce more sales response. The marketer also must set *conditions for participation*. Incentives might be offered to everyone or only to select groups.

The marketer must decide how to *promote and distribute the promotion* program itself. A 50-cents-off coupon could be given out in a package, at the store, by mail, or in an advertisement. Each distribution method involves a different level of reach and cost. Increasingly, marketers are blending several media into a total campaign concept. The *length of the promotion* is also important. If the sales-promotion period is too short, many prospects (who may not be buying during that time) will miss it. If the promotion runs too long, the deal will lose some of its "act now" force. Finally, the marketer must determine the *sales-promotion budget*. The most common way is to use a percentage of the total budget for sales promotion. A better way is the objective-and-task method discussed in the previous chapter.

Evaluation is also very important. Yet many companies fail to evaluate their sales-promotion programs, and others evaluate them only superficially. Manufacturers can use one of many evaluation methods. The most common method is to compare sales before, during, and after a promotion. Suppose a company has a six percent market share before the promotion, which jumps to 10 percent during the promotion, falls to five percent right after, and rises to seven percent later on. The promotion seems to have attracted new users and more buying from current customers. After the promotion, sales fell as consumers used up their inventories. The long-run rise to seven percent means that the company gained some new users. If the brand's share had returned to the old level, then the promotion would have changed only the *timing* of demand rather than the *total* demand.

Consumer research also would show the kinds of people who responded to the promotion and what they did after it ended. *Surveys* can provide information on how many consumers recall the promotion, what they thought of it, how many took advantage of it, and how it affected their buying. Sales promotions also can be evaluated through *experiments* that vary factors such as incentive value, length, and distribution method.

Clearly, sales promotion plays an important role in the total promotion mix. To use it well, the marketer must define the sales-promotion objectives, select the best tools, design the sales-promotion program, pre-test and implement the program, and evaluate the results.

PUBLIC RELATIONS

Public relations
Building good relations with the company's various publics by obtaining favourable publicity, building up a good "corporate image," and handling or heading off unfavourable rumours, stories, and events. Major PR tools include press relations, product publicity, corporate communications, lobbying, and counselling.

Another major mass-promotion tool is **public relations**—building good relations with the company's various publics by obtaining favourable publicity, building up a good "corporate image," and handling or heading off unfavourable rumours, stories, and events. Public relations departments may perform any or all of the following functions:

◆ *Press relations or press agentry:* Creating and placing newsworthy information in the media to attract attention to a person, product, or service. If you check the Canada Newswire web site (http://www.newswire.ca) you will see many examples of different firms' press releases.

◆ *Product publicity:* Publicizing specific products.

◆ *Public affairs:* Building and maintaining national or local community relations.

◆ *Lobbying:* Building and maintaining relations with legislators and government officials to influence legislation and regulation.

◆ *Investor relations:* Maintaining relationships with shareholders and others in the financial community.

◆ *Development:* Public relations with donors or members of non-profit organizations to gain financial or volunteer support.[31]

Public relations is used to promote products, people, places, ideas, activities, organizations, and even nations. Marketing boards have used public relations to rebuild interest in declining commodities such as eggs, apples, milk, and potatoes. The Canadian Dietetic Association credits effective public relations for the nearly 15 000 calls it received during its March Nutrition Month program—a number 34 percent higher than expected.[32] New York City turned around its image when its "I Love New York" campaign took root, attracking millions more tourists to the city. Johnson & Johnson's masterly use of public relations played a major role in saving Tylenol from extinction after its product-tampering scare. Nations have used public relations to attract more tourists, foreign investment, and international support.

Public relations can have a strong impact on public awareness at a much lower cost than advertising (see Marketing Highlight 15-3). The company does not pay for the space or time in the media. Rather, it pays for a staff to develop and circulate information and to manage events. If the company develops an

PUBLIC RELATIONS: STRETCHING THE MARKETING BUDGET

Italian sports-car maker Lamborghini sells less than 100 of its cars each year in North America. Marketing Lamborghinis is no simple matter. The car is pure poetry in motion—but at a steep price. The Diablo VT's 492-horsepower engine delivers a top speed of 323 km/hr and goes from 0 to 95 km/hr in just 4.1 seconds. The price: $344 000. Just to lease a Diablo VT runs $4318 a month with a $74 000 down payment. Moreover, because so few Lamborghinis are sold, most people rarely see one. Thus, to gain exposure and persuade would-be buyers, the company must invest its modest US$ 850 000 marketing budget carefully.

Lamborghini's eventual goal is to sell 1500 to 2000 units a year in North America. This goal is based partly on expanding its product line-up to include a sport-utility vehicle priced in the $110 000 to $145 000 range. To reach this ambitious sales goal, however, the carmaker will need to increase its exposure and awareness. It currently advertises in several selective business, travel, and lifestyle magazines, emphasizing the car's speed and sensual beauty. In addition, the company recently fielded a direct-mail campaign to 50 000 prospective buyers with media household incomes of $2.0 million.

When it comes to advertising, however, $850 000 doesn't go far. So Lamborghini stretches its limited marketing budget with an assortment of less expensive public relations efforts. The company actively courts the press. For example, it makes the car available to auto journalists for test drives. This resulted in a recent *New York Times* review describing the car as "kinetic sculpture, proof of affluence, and amusement-park ride wrapped into one." After a test drive, a *Fortune* journalist wrote, "On the beauty meter, the screaming lemon-yellow Diablo rates right up there with a roomful of Matisse originals. . . . Neighbours I have

never met come rushing out of their homes to get a closer look." And after riding with Lamborghini's chief U.S. test driver, another journalist reported, "He fired up the engine and shot out of Lamborghini's vast and immaculate garage. He slammed the car sideways through the parking lot [and] a split second later straightened the Diablo out with a snap and hammered ahead. No swaying, no rolling, no hesitation, just unadultered energy. It was an

all-sensory extravaganza." Lamborghini also sponsors tasteful public relations events. For example, it recently held a cocktail party for 200 people at a Giorgio Armani store in Boston, with an invitation list put together by the store and *The Robb Report*, a publication devoted to the lifestyles of the wealthy.

Lamborghini is constantly seeking new ways to expose the car to its affluent audience. As a result of good public relations efforts, the Lamborghini Diablo VT was designated as a pace car for the 1995 PPG Indy Car World Series. This gave Lamborghini exposure at 15 race sites

and allowed local dealers to give prospective buyers a ride around the track in the days before a race. Says a Lamborghini executive, "We sold three cars by doing that last year at the Detroit Grand Prix." Also, for the first time, Lamborghini is making a demonstrator available to its North American dealers, so that prospects can test-drive the car without the dealer worrying about kilometrage and insurance costs.

Lamborghini's total annual sales amount to only a tiny fraction of the advertising budgets of the major carmakers. However, through the innovative use of public relations, the company successfully stretches its modest marketing budget to gain exposure among affluent buyers.

Sources: Quotations from Raymond Serafin, "Even Lamborghini Must Think Marketing," *Advertising Age*, May 1, 1995, p. 4; Faye Rice, "Lamborghini's Sales Drive," *Fortune*, June 12, 1995, p. 13; and Sue Zesiger, "Driving with the Devil," *Fortune*, February 17, 1997, pp. 170–171; home.lamborghini.com/

interesting story, it could be picked up by several different media, having the same effect as advertising that would cost millions of dollars. And it would have more credibility than advertising. Public relations results can sometimes be spectacular.

It can also be used to help overcome corporate crisis. Whistler Mountain Resort Association recently faced just such a crisis when its Quicksilver chair failed, detaching several chairs from the cable and injuring several skiers and killing one.

Whistler's marketing director, David Perry, developed Whistler's public relations policy when he joined the organization in 1992. He believed Whistler should be proactive in providing the media with information if a crisis occurred and that the organization should never appear to be hiding anything. On December 23, 1995, Perry had to put his plan into action. To ensure consistency in their messages, Whistler appointed two people to address media queries—Perry and the president of Whistler, Doug Forseth. Their first priority was to control information flow and keep panic under control. They quickly informed parents waiting at the bottom of the hill that their kids were safe. David Perry also opened up a media centre from which reporters could work. He laboured to find out the reason underlying the failure of the lift and he strived to keep government ministers informed in an attempt to avoid an inquiry. He recruited senior managers to call all of the skiers who had been on the lift that day and arranged for counselling for employees affected by the stress of the accident. Whistler ran ads thanking the community for its support during the crisis and Perry appeared on a local talk show. When asked about what he would have done differently to improve the situation, Perry noted that he wished he had made earlier contact with the victim's family. His policy had proven effective in handling the operations side of the incident, but lacked insight into dealing with the human side of the accident.[33]

Despite its potential strengths, public relations often is described as a marketing stepchild because of its limited and scattered use. The public relations department is usually located at corporate headquarters. Its staff is so busy dealing with various publics—stockholders, employees, legislators, city officials—that public relations programs to support product marketing objectives may be ignored. And marketing managers and public relations practitioners do not always talk the same language. Many public relations practitioners view their job as simply communicating. In contrast, marketing managers tend to be much more interested in how advertising and public relations affect sales and profits.

This situation is changing, however. Many companies now want their public relations departments to manage all of their activities with a view toward marketing the company and improving the bottom line. Some companies are setting up special units called *marketing public relations* to support corporate and product promotion and image-making directly. Many companies hire marketing public relations firms to handle their PR programs or to assist the company public relations team.

MAJOR PUBLIC RELATIONS TOOLS

Public relations professionals use several tools. One of the major tools is *news.* Public relations professionals find or create favourable news about the company and its products or people. Sometimes news stories occur naturally, and sometimes the PR person can suggest events or activities that would create news. *Speeches* can also create product and company publicity. Increasingly, company executives must field questions from the media or give talks at trade associations or sales meetings, and these events can either build or hurt the company's image. Another common PR tool is *special events,* ranging from news conferences, press tours, grand openings, and fireworks displays to laser shows, hot-air balloon releases, multimedia presentations, and star-studded spectaculars designed to reach and interest target publics.

Public relations people also prepare *written materials* to reach and influence their target markets. These materials include annual reports, brochures, articles, and company newsletters and magazines. *Audiovisual materials,* such as films, slide-and-sound programs, and video and audio cassettes, are being used increasingly as communication tools. *Corporate-identity materials* also can help create a corporate identity that the public immediately recognizes. Logos, stationery, brochures, signs, business forms, business cards, buildings, uniforms, and company cars and trucks—all become marketing tools when they are attractive, distinctive, and memorable.

Companies also can improve public goodwill by contributing money and time to *public-service activities*. For example, Procter & Gamble and Publishers' Clearing House held a joint promotion to raise money for the Special Olympics. The Publishers' Clearing House mailing included product coupons, and Procter & Gamble donated 10 cents per redeemed coupon to the Special Olympics.

A company's web site can also be a good public relations vehicle. Consumers and members of other publics can visit the site for information and entertainment. Such sites can be extremely popular. For example, Butterball's site (http://www.butterball.com), which features cooking and carving tips, received 550 000 visitors on one day during Thanksgiving week last year. Web sites can also be ideal for handling crisis situations. For example, when several bottles of Odwalla apple juice sold on the West Coast were found to contain E coli bacteria, Odwalla initiated a massive product recall. Within just three hours, the company set up a web site laden with information about the crisis and Odwalla's response. Company staffers also combed the Internet looking for newsgroups discussing Odwalla and posted links to the site. In another example, American Home Products quickly set up a web site to distribute accurate information and advice after a model died, reportedly after inhaling its Primatene Mist. The Primatene site, up less than 12 hours after the crisis, remains in place today (http://www.primatene.com).[34]

MAJOR PUBLIC RELATIONS DECISIONS

In considering when and how to use product public relations, management should set PR objectives, choose the PR messages and vehicles, implement the PR plan, and evaluate the results.

Setting Public Relations Objectives

The first task is to set *objectives* for public relations. Planet Hollywood, the U.S. movie-themed restaurant chain that recently opened in Toronto and Vancouver, hired two public relations firms to co-ordinate the activities associated with their Canadian launch. Planet Hollywood's objective was to have PR firms use their knowledge of the unique cultural and physical conditions in the two cities to adapt the elements of a typical U.S. opening to suit the Canadian marketplace. The Toronto agency, Langdon Starr Ketchum, organized everything for the celebrity-studded opening—from a media preview to charity nights that benefited the Heart and Stroke Foundation and the Variety Club, two charities deemed important by potential Toronto patrons. The agency created a successful Hollywood-style street party in the dead of Toronto winter that drew a crowd of more than 5000 including personnel from 12 radio stations, the *Toronto Star*, and CityTV. The event caused quite a stir and generated 80 minutes of radio and 150 minutes of television coverage. The Vancouver-based public relations agency, Barr & Wilcox Group, took a different approach. They coordinated contests that ran in Vancouver's newspapers, on television, and on 12 radio stations. The opening in Vancouver drew 15 000 fans and was covered by the international media including U.S.-based *Entertainment Tonight*.[35]

Choosing Public Relations Messages and Vehicles

The organization next selects its major public relations message themes and the PR tools it will use. Message themes should be guided by the organization's overall marketing and communications strategies. Public relations is an important part of the organization's overall integrated marketing communications program. Thus, public relations messages should be carefully integrated with the organization's advertising, personal selling, direct marketing, and other communications. In some cases, the choices of public relations messages and tools will be clear-cut. In others, the organization will have to create news rather than find it.

Creating events is especially important in publicizing fund-raising drives for non-profit organizations. Fund-raisers have developed a large set of special events such as art exhibits, auctions, benefit evenings, book sales, contests, dances, dinners, fairs, fashion shows, phonathons, telethons, rummage sales, tours, and walkathons. No sooner is one type of event created, such as a walkathon, than competitors create new versions, such as readathons, bikeathons, and jogathons.

Implementing the Public Relations Plan

Implementing public relations requires care. Take the matter of placing stories in the media. A *great* story is easy to place—but most stories are not great and may not get past busy editors. Thus, one of the main assets of public relations people is their personal relationships with media editors. In fact, PR professionals are often former journalists who know many media editors and know what they want. They view media editors as a market to be satisfied so that editors will continue to use their stories.

Evaluating Public Relations Results

Public relations results are difficult to measure because PR is used with other promotion tools and its impact is often indirect. If PR is used before other tools come into play, its contribution is easier to evaluate.

The easiest measure of publicity effectiveness is the number of exposures in the media. Public relations people give the client a "clippings book" showing all the media that carried news about the product. Such exposure measures are not very satisfying, however. They do not tell how many people actually read or heard the message, nor what they thought afterward. In addition, because the media overlap in readership and viewership, it does not give information on the *net* audience reached.

A better measure is the change in product awareness, knowledge, and attitude resulting from the publicity campaign. Assessing the change requires measuring the before-and-after levels of these measures. The U.S. Potato Board learned, for example, that the number of people who agreed with the statement "Potatoes are rich in vitamins and minerals" went from 36 percent before its public relations campaign to 67 percent after the campaign. That change represented a large increase in product knowledge.

Sales and profit impact, if obtainable, is the best measure of public relations effort. For example, 9-Lives sales increased 43 percent at the end of a major "Morris the Cat" publicity campaign. However, advertising and sales promotion also had been stepped up, and their contribution has to be considered.

Summary of Chapter Objectives

Companies must do more than make good products—they must inform consumers about product benefits and carefully position products in consumers' minds. To do this, they must skilfully use three mass-promotion tools in addition to personal selling, which targets specific buyers. The three mass-promotion tools are advertising, sales promotion, and public relations.

1. **Define the roles of advertising, sales promotion, and public relations in the promotion mix.**

Advertising—the use of paid media by a seller to inform, persuade, and remind about its products or organization—is a strong promotion tool. Canadian marketers spend more than $8 billion each year on advertising, and it takes many forms and has many uses. Sales promotion covers a wide variety of short-term incentive tools—coupons, premiums, contests, buying allowances—designed to stimulate final and business consumers, the trade, and the company's own sales force. In recent years, sale-promotion spending has been growing faster than advertising spending. Public relations—gaining favourable publicity and creating a favourable company image—is the least used of the major promotion tools, although it has great potential for building consumer awareness and preference.

2. **Describe the major decisions involved in developing an advertising program.**

   Advertising decision making involves decisions about the objectives, the budget, the message, the media, and, finally, the evaluation of results. Advertisers should set clear objectives as to whether the advertising is intended to inform, persuade, or remind buyers. The advertising budget can be based on sales, on competitors' spending, or on the objectives and tasks.

   The message decision calls for planning a message strategy and executing it effectively. The media decision involves defining reach, frequency, and impact goals; choosing major media types; selecting media vehicles; and deciding on media timing. Message and media decisions must be closely coordinated for maximum campaign effectiveness. Finally, evaluation calls for evaluating the communication and sales effects of advertising before, during, and after the advertising is placed.

3. **Explain how sales promotion campaigns are developed and implemented.**

   Sales promotion campaigns call for setting sales-promotion objectives (in general, sales promotions should be consumer relationship-building); selecting tools; developing and implementing the sales-promotion program by using trade promotion tools (discounts, allowances, free goods, push money) and business-promotion tools (conventions, trade shows, sales contests) as well as deciding on such elements as the size of the incentive, the conditions for participation, how to promote and distribute the promotion package, and the length of the promotion. After this process is completed, the company evaluates the results.

4. **Explain how companies use public relations to communicate with their publics.**

   Companies use public relations to communicate with their publics by setting PR objectives; choosing PR messages and vehicles; implementing the PR plan; and evaluating PR results. To accomplish these goals, public relations professionals use several tools such as news, speeches, and special events. They also prepare written, audiovisual, and corporate-identity materials and contribute money and time to public-relations activities.

Key Terms

Advertising objective *(p. 501)*
Advertising specialties *(p. 518)*
Allowance *(p. 519)*
Cash refund offers (rebates) *(p. 517)*
Comparison advertising *(p. 501)*
Consumer promotion *(p. 515)*
Contests, sweepstakes, games *(p. 519)*
Coupons *(p. 517)*

Discount *(p. 519)*
Frequency *(p. 509)*
Informative advertising *(p. 501)*
Media impact *(p. 509)*
Media vehicles *(p. 509)*
Patronage rewards *(p. 518)*
Persuasive advertising *(p. 501)*
Point-of-purchase promotions (POP) *(p. 519)*

Premiums *(p. 518)*
Price packs (cents-off deals) *(p. 518)*
Public relations *(p. 521)*
Reach *(p. 508)*
Reminder advertising *(p. 502)*
Sales promotion *(p. 514)*
Sales-force promotion *(p. 515)*
Samples *(p. 517)*
Trade promotion *(p. 515)*

Discussing the Issues

1. Contrast the benefits and drawbacks of comparison advertising. Which has more to gain from using comparison advertising—the leading brand in a market or a lesser brand? Why?

2. Surveys show that many North Americans are sceptical of advertising claims. Do you mistrust advertising? Analyse why or why not. Suggest some things advertisers could do to increase credibility.

3. Explain what factors call for more *frequency* in an advertising media schedule, and what factors call for more *reach*. How can you increase one without sacrificing the other or increasing the advertising budget?

4. An ad states that Almost Home cookies are the "moistest, chewiest, most perfectly baked cookies the world has ever tasted," besides homemade cookies. If you think some other brand of cookies is moister or chewier, is the Almost Home claim false? Should this type of claim be regulated?

5. Companies often run advertising, sales promotion, and public relations efforts at the same time. Can their effects be separated? Discuss how a company might evaluate the effectiveness of each element in this mix.

6. Assess why many companies are spending more on trade promotions and consumer promotions than on advertising. Is heavy spending on sales promotions a good strategy for long-term profits? Why or why not?

Applying the Concepts

1. Buy a weekend paper and sort through the colour advertising and coupon inserts. Find several examples that combine advertising, sales promotion, and/or public relations. For instance, a manufacturer may run a full-page ad that also includes a coupon and information on its sponsorship of a charity event, such as Easter Seals or Special Olympics. (a) Do you think these approaches using multiple tools are more or less effective than a simple approach? Why? (b) Try to find ads from two direct competitors. Are these brands using similar promotional tools in similar ways?

2. Find two current television advertisements that you think are particularly effective, and two more that you feel are ineffective. (a) Describe precisely why you think the better ads are effective, and why the ineffective ads fall short. (b) How would you improve the less effective ads? If you feel they are too poor to be improved, write a rough draft of an alternate ad for each.

References

1. Portions adapted from "The Marketing 100: Snickers' Santa Cruz Hughes," *Advertising Age*, June 30, 1997, p. S32; Bob Garfield, "Snickers Ads Grab the Elusive 'Big Idea,'" *Advertising Age*, September 2, 1996, p. 37; and Garfield, "Best TV: Snickers," *Advertising Age*, May 26, 1997, p. S1. Also see Edward A. Robinson, "Frogs, Bears, and Orgasms: Think Zany If You Want to Reach Today's Consumers," *Fortune*, June 9, 1997, pp. 153-156; and Jennifer Harrison, "Advertising Joins the Journal of the Soul," *American Demographics*, June 1997, p. 25.

2. Leo-Rice Barker, "Study Measures Quebec Canadian Ad Industries," *Strategy: The Canadian Marketing Report*, May 26, 1997, p. 6; Justin Smallbridge, "Outdoor Led 1996 Ad Revenue Growth," *Marketing*, October 6, 1997, p. 4.

3. Larry Jabbonsky, "The Return of a Lightning Rod," *Beverage World*, August 1993, p. 6. For more on the development of the Always Coca-Cola campaign, see "Soda-Pop Celebrity," *The Economist*, September 14, 1991, pp. 75–76; Betsy Sharkey, "CAA's Casting Call for Coke," *Adweek*, February 8, 1993, pp. 38–40;

Melanie Wells and Marcy Magiera, "Coke Features Classic Images," *Advertising Age*, February 14, 1994, p. 5; Melanie Wells, "No Cataclysm, Just Hollywood Dabble-On," *Advertising Age*, January 16, 1995, pp. 1, 8; and Dottie Enrico, "Coca-Cola's Polar Bears Make for Hottest Ads," *USA Today*, March 17, 1995, p. 2.

4. Eric Swetsky, "Death of a Sales Bunny," *Marketing*, January 22, 1996, p. 18; "Marketers Move From Stores to Courts," *Marketing*, January 18, 1996, p. 5.

5. Leah Rickard, "New Ammo for Comparative Ads," *Advertising Age*, February 14, 1994, p. 26.

6. See Donald E. Schultz, Dennis Martin, and William P. Brown, *Strategic Advertising Campaigns* (Chicago: Crain Books, 1984), pp. 192–197; and Philip Kotler, *Marketing Management: Analysis, Planning, Implementation, and Control*, 8th ed. (Englewood Cliffs, NJ: Prentice Hall, 1994), pp. 630–631.

7. Gerard J. Tellis, "Advertising Exposure, Loyalty, and Brand Purchase: A Two-Stage Model of Choice," *Journal of Marketing Research*, May 1988, pp.

134–135. For counterpoints, see Magid M. Abraham and Leonard M. Lodish, "Getting the Most Out of Advertising and Promotion," *Harvard Business Review,* May–June 1990, pp. 50–60.

8. The statistics in this section were taken from the *Canadian Media Directors' Council Media Digest 1997-98,* which is published by *Marketing* magazine.

9. "Freeze Frame: A Marketing-Nielsen Update on television," *Marketing,* June 5, 1995, p. 26.

10. See Mark Landler, "Neck and Neck at the Networks," *Business Week,* May 20, 1991, pp. 36–37; Faye Rice, "A Cure for What Ails Advertising," *Fortune,* December 16, 1991, pp. 119–122; and Allan J. Magrath, "The Death of Advertising Has Been Greatly Exaggerated," *Sales & Marketing Management,* February 1992, pp. 23–24.

11. Edward A. Robinson, "Frogs, Bears, and Orgasms: Think Zany If You Want to Reach Today's Consumers," *Fortune,* June 9, 1997, pp. 153–156.

12. Joe Mandese, "Cost to Make TV Ad Nears Quarter Million," *Advertising Age,* July 4, 1994, pp. 3, 6.

13. Richard Kelly, "Is There a Future in Advertising, *Marketing,* June 5, 1995, p. 12.

14. Joe Mandese, "Cost to Make TV Ad Nears Quarter Million," *Advertising Age,* July 4, 1994, pp. 3, 6.

15. Jim McElgunn, "Who Cares Where an Ad's Made?" *Marketing,* May 8, 1995, p. 20; "Canada's Top Agencies," *Marketing,* July 24, 1995, p. 11.

16. Iris Cohen Selinger, "Big Profits, Risks with Incentive Fees," *Advertising Age,* May 15, 1995, p. 3.

17. Lara Mills, "Stealing Business," *Marketing,* June 22, 1997, p. 18.

18. Michael Lev, "Advertisers Seek Global Messages," *New York Times,* November 18, 1991, p. D9.

19. Philip R. Cateora, *International Marketing,* 7th ed. (Homewood, IL: Irwin, 1990), p. 462.

20. Ibid., p. 475.

21. Cateora, *International Marketing,* pp. 466–467.

22. Alison Fahey, "Shops See Surge in Promotion Revenues," *Advertising Age,* February 20, 1989, p. 20; Scott Hume, "Sales Promotion: Agency Services Take on Exaggerated Importance for Marketers," *Advertising Age,* May 4, 1992, pp. 29, 32; and *16th Annual Survey of Promotional Practices,* Donnelly Marketing Inc., Oakbrook Terrace, IL, June 1994, p. 9.

23. Jennifer Lawrence, "Free Samples Get Emotional Reception," *Advertising Age,* September 30, 1991, p. 10.

24. "Nestlé Banks on Databases," *Advertising Age,* October 25, 1993, pp. S6–S10.

25. Lesley Daw, "The Tasting Race," *Marketing,* August 18/25, 1997, pp. S1–S2; David Mudie, "The Sampling Menu," *Marketing,* August 18/25, 1997, p. S3.

26. Kate Fitzgerald, "Coupons Expand on Web," *Advertising Age,* March 31, 1997, p. 24.

27. Jeff Lobb, "Stuff-ing It to Coke," *Marketing,* January 27, 1997, p. 15.

28. See "Power to the Key Ring and T-Shirt," *Sales & Marketing Management,* December 1989, p. 14; and J. Thomas Russell and W. Ronald Lane, *Kleppner's Advertising Procedure,* 12th ed. (Englewood Cliffs, NJ: Prentice Hall, 1993), pp. 408–410.

29. "International Trade Fairs," an advertising supplement to the January 1994 issue of *Canadian Business.*

30. See Thomas V. Bonoma, "Get More Out of Your Trade Shows," *Harvard Business Review,* January–February 1983, pp. 75–83; Jonathan M. Cox, Ian K. Sequeira, and Alissa Eckstein, "1988 Trade Show Trends: Shows Grow in Size; Audience Quality Remains High," *Business Marketing,* June 1989, pp. 57–60; and Richard Szathmary, "Trade Shows," *Sales & Marketing Management,* May 1992, pp. 83–84.

31. Adapted from Scott M. Cutlip, Allen H. Center, and Glen M. Brown, *Effective Public Relations,* 7th ed. (Englewood Cliffs, NJ: Prentice Hall, 1994), pp. 8–21.

32. "The Agency Perspective," *Marketing,* February 13, 1995, pp. 16-17.

33. Gail Chiasson, "PR in Action: When the Media Come Calling," *Marketing,* February 12, 1996, p. 23.

34. Mark Gleason, "Edelman Sees Niche in Web Public Relations," *Advertising Age,* January 20, 1997, p. 30.

35. Lesley Daw, "Hands Across the Border," *Marketing,* May 26, 1997, p. 23.

Company Case 15

UNIVERSITY OF OTTAWA INTERCOLLEGIATE SPORTS

The phone rang in the office of Luc Gelineau, the Director of Sports Services at the University of Ottawa. He had just finished a meeting with the Sports Services Advisory Council outlining the recent budget cuts to the "Big 5" intercollegiate programs and strategies to acquire alternative funding.[1] On the line was John Goldfarb, the manager of the local branch of the Royal Bank of Canada. The bank was recently approached as a potential sponsor of intercollegiate sports and Mr. Goldfarb was calling to update Luc on the reaction of the bank executives. He summarized the situation:

"Well Luc, I've spoken to several of the executives and it seems like we might be interested in getting involved. We're excited at the possibilities and would like to sit down and discuss the details. Specifically, we would like to know what type of exposure your teams can offer us."

Mr. Gelineau understood what Mr. Goldfarb was getting at, but after recently attending a football game and being surrounded by empty seats, he realized that he could provide few of the exposure incentives that he felt the bank was looking for (see Exhibit 1 for attendance records). He got off the phone, turned to his MBA interns and said:

"Dammit guys, we have a quality product! Our soccer team won the National Championships, our football team is ranked third in the nation, we've produced athletes that have competed internationally at the Olympics and professionally. How come we still can't get fans out to watch these stars of tomorrow! Set up another meeting with the Advisory Council. We need to look at intercollegiate sports and investigate ways we can increase attendance at games and make it more attractive for sponsors to become involved."

BACKGROUND

Established in 1976, Sports Services at the University of Ottawa is a subsidiary of Student Affairs. They manage and operate all of the sporting facilities on campus, including the university's gymnasiums, hockey arena, and football field. In addition to offering recreational, instructional, and intramural activities to students, Sports Services provides the necessary training environment for student-athletes, enabling them to represent the university on an intercollegiate level. Presently, eight men's and seven women's teams compete at Canadian Intercollegiate Athletic Union (C.I.A.U.) or Ontario University Athletic Association/Ontario Women's Intercollegiate Athletic Association (OUAA/OWIAA) sanctioned events. Of these 15 intercollegiate teams, the five highest profile sports are classified as the "Big 5."

Historically, Sports Services has relied on money raised through their recreational, instructional, and intramural programs, along with funds from student auxiliary fees, to operate each of the intercollegiate teams effectively. The 1994–95 overall intercollegiate budget was approximately $650 000.

The budgets for the "Big 5" teams were more than adequate to run their respective programs effectively prior to and including the 1994–95 season. However, more recently, several factors have caused significant reductions to each of the team's operating budgets and have raised the need to investigate alternative methods of funding.

Gender Equity

The issue of gender equity in sports has become a "hot" topic, not only on the campuses of Canadian universities, but across the United States as well. In March 1994, the then Director of Sports Services, Michel Leduc, appointed a committee on gender equity to study the status of women's involvement in Sports Services. In order to establish a policy of gender equity in intercollegiate sports, the committee recommended that financing and membership in men's and women's interuniversity programs

Exhibit 1   *Ticket Sales Analysis Seasons 1991-1996 (Average Attendance)*

Team	1991-92 Tickets	1992-93 Tickets	Δ%	1993-94 Tickets	Δ%	1994-95 Tickets	Δ%	1995-96 Tickets	Δ%
Football	970	1163	20%	815	-30%	531	-35%	625	18%
Hockey	103	189	46%	196	4%	228	17%	180	-21%
Volleyball	58	138	140%	147	7%	124	-16%	181	14%
Basketball	154	281	82%	213	-24%	220	3%	201	-9%
Total Tickets	1312	1771	35%	1371	-23%	1103	-20%	1147	4%

[1] The big five teams are basketball (male and female), hockey, football, and volleyball.

should reflect the gender distribution of the student population: Women = 56%; Men = 44%. In response to the above recommendation, Sports Services granted intercollegiate status to women's soccer and reduced the ratio of men's to women's financing from 2.66 in 1994–95 to 1.96 for the 1996–97 season. This decrease in funding for male-dominated teams (e.g., football) led to a chain of events that resulted in decreases to all intercollegiate teams.

Mass Participation

Increased enrolment in sports services is transforming the traditional competitive environment into a more recreational atmosphere. That is, more participation in recreational activities is occurring instead of traditional competitive intercollegiate sports.

Financial Constraints

In January 1996, the University of Ottawa outlined proposed cuts to the 1996–97 budget that would eliminate over $7 million from university services including a 14 percent or $435 000 reduction to the budget of Student Affairs. Increases to students' tuition fees and resulting demonstrations held by the Student Federation Union Organization (SFUO) have made it unrealistic for Sports Services to increase athletic auxiliary fees to compensate for the budget cuts. In addition, recent renovations to Sports Services' athletic facilities have resulted in a further strain on funds.

ENVIRONMENT

Student Life at the University of Ottawa

The University of Ottawa, North America's oldest and largest bilingual university, is located in the downtown core of the city. Student enrolment for the 1996–97 academic year totalled nearly 25 000 full-time and part-time students (see Exhibit 2 for specific breakdowns). In addition, 77 percent of the University's graduates remain in the Ottawa area.

The university school year begins with one week of activities for the new students (freshmen). These activities are organized by senior students that serve as floor reps in the residences, and executives of the faculty associations. Recently, these activities have included games, pub crawls, talent contests and other events. Freshmen look to their senior peers for guidance and direction. At the same time, new students are looking to maximize their freedom and explore new activities and interests. Although the transition can be rough, active involvement in student life can smooth out the bumps in the adjustment period.

At the conclusion of this week, students move to the usual routine of courses and homework. Approximately 2000 students live in the university residences. Events are sporadically planned throughout the year, arranged by various associations and clubs, coinciding

Exhibit 2 *Student Composition at the University of Ottawa*

	Graduate	Undergraduate	Total
Full Time	2147	14 150	16 297
Part Time	1378	6074	7452
Total	3525	20 224	23 749

	Graduate	Undergraduate	Total
English Program	2363	12 350	14 713
French Program	1162	7874	9036
Total	3525	20 224	23 749

	Graduate	Undergraduate	Total
Female	1759	11 985	13 744
Male	1766	8239	10 005
Total	3525	20 224	23 749

	Graduate	Undergraduate	Total
Graduate Students	3525		3525
		22	22
Freshmen		8480	8480
Sophomores		4511	4511
Juniors		4846	4846
Seniors		2365	2365
Total	3525	20 224	23 749

	Full Time	Part Time	Total
	Age	Age	Age
	Mean	Mean	Mean
Graduate Students	32.0	35.5	33.4
Undergraduate Students	24.2	33.7	27.1
Total	25.2	34.0	28.0

	Graduate	Undergraduate	Total
Faculty of Administration	861	2199	3060
Faculty of Arts	500	4873	5373
Common Law		561	561
Civil Law	67	516	583
Faculty of Education	541	1503	2044
Faculty of Engineering	372	1357	1729
Faculty of Medicine	232	852	1084
Faculty of Science	359	2031	2390
Registrar's Office		30	30
Faculty of Health Sciences	152	1781	1933
Faculty of Social Science	441	4521	4962
Total	3525	20 224	23 749

with calendar events such as Halloween, Christmas, Valentines Day, etc. A vast majority of these activities are organized by the faculty associations and are extremely popular with the students. However, faculty activities are rarely directed to the intercollegiate sports program. Currently there are nine faculties at the University of Ottawa (see appendix B for more details), each of which has its own student association.

The school year is divided into two semesters, fall and winter. The fall semester is broken up by the Thanksgiving long weekend in early October and University of Ottawa day (where regular students have the day off and prospective students visit the campus) at some point in late October. The Christmas break ends the month of December. The winter semester is highlighted by the study break in late February and the four-day weekend in the beginning of April, before exams. The typical student has 15 hours of class time a week plus additional homework time. In general, students will usually have some time to participate in extracurricular activities during the week.

Activities in Ottawa/Hull Region

With a relatively small and young population, the people of Ottawa have traditionally been strong supporters of all sporting events and activities. As of 1996, the region is home to two major junio hockey teams (Hull Olympiques, Ottawa 67's); three Interuniversity Athletic Programs (Algonquin College, Carleton University, University of Ottawa); a triple A baseball team (Ottawa Lynx); and three other professional sports franchises (Ottawa Rough Riders Football Club, Ottawa Senators Hockey Club, and Ottawa Loggers Roller Hockey Club).

Although all of the professional teams have been well supported in the past, recently they have been experiencing significant attendance problems. This decline in attendance is threatening the very existence of the 126-year-old tradition of Rough Rider Football in Ottawa. As of Monday, November 4, 1996, the Canadian Football League revoked the Ottawa Rough Riders franchise. Although there is talk of starting a new franchise, Ottawa fans are still left without football to satisfy their gridiron needs. Similarly, after initial enthusiasm for the introduction of the Senators in 1991, filling the newly constructed 19 000 seat Corel Centre has become a problem. Many of the supporters of these tems cite the high ticket prices and poor competitive performance as reasons for their absence.

Although attendance has demonstrated a sharp decline, there is still a strong base of potential supporters in the region. Ottawa residents are very active and according to the last census, spend more money on entertainment than the average Canadian. Thus, instead of sporting events, people have turned to other entertainment options such as the numerous theatres, museums, and art galleries that are located in the city.

The Game Experience

The "Big 5" varsity teams compete throughout the school year, with the seasons of different teams beginning and ending at different times. The football team "kicks off" the varsity season usually with the first game taking place at the end of the first week of class. While the football season ends in November, the hockey, basketball, and volleyball teams compete throughout both the fall and winter semester.

Getting Students to Attend

Before deciding what should be done to alleviate the problem, the group of MBA interns decided to go to a game themselves.

Jeff, the most outgoing of the group, attempted to encourage some of his classmates to come. He approaches them and said: "Hey guys, a bunch of us are going to the game this weekend, why don't you come?"

Tara, usually a sports enthusiast, responded: "What game? I haven't heard a thing about it!"

Jeff exclaimed: "How can you say that? There are posters in every buliding on campus and a pep rally was held at the campus bar."

"Oh. Is that what that was?" asked Adam sarcastically. "I thought it was a little get-together for the physics club."

"O.K., O.K!, so a lot of people didn't show up, but I heard other promotions such as ticket giveaways and Rowdy Challenges[2] are being attempted to bring more fans out," responded Jeff.

In an attempt to stay away from the game, Adam interjected: "I was at a game last year and although the play was exciting, it just wasn't made into an event."

Jeff replied: "Well guys, Sports Services apparently hires students to run promotions during the game and they hold contests at half-time. You would win a pizza or even drive home with a new car for a year."

"Hey! I like pizza," exclaimed Tara enthusiastically. "I'm willing to give the game a chance if the price is right. What is it going to cost us?"

"Well," Jeff explained. "There are different ticket prices depending on whether you are a student or not and whether you're interested in seeing more than one game." (See Exhibit 3 for a description of ticket prices.)

Tara replied: "You know, I've always wanted to go to a Gee-Gees game, but I never know where the games are played. Where are the games played and how do you get. . . ."

Interrupting Tara, Adam began to chuckle and said: "Yeah, the reason you don't know where to go is because the football games are a half-hour walk from campus."

---

[2] A Rowdy Challenge is a competition between two groups on campus, usually within residence, to see who has more spirit at a sporting event.

Exhibit 3   *Intercollegiate Ticket Price Structure*

	Students	**Adults**
Regular Season:		
Hockey Basketball Volleyball	$2	$4
Football	$4	$7
Playoffs:		
Hockey Basketball Volleyball	$3	$5
Football	$4	$7
Season Pass:		
(Admits individual to all home games)	$20	$30

Jeff acknowledged the distance to the football stadium but said: 'All of the other teams play their games right on campus, so there's no excuse!"

Finally, after realizing that the game might be an opportunity to have a good time and meet new people, Adam agreed to go to the game, with Jeff and some of his classmates.

The Game as an Event

In the spring of 1994, a marketing survey was conducted in an attempt to understand students' perceptions of Sports Services. As part of their survey, an analysis of intercollegiate sports revealed that while the majority of students were interested in sports, only a small percentage were drawn into supporting the Gee-Gees. With regard to those students who attended football games, a majority of the respondents (31 percent) answered that they went to the games to be with their friends. Interestingly, only 15 percent of the respondents who attended did so to see the game.

In addition to the above findings, an informal survey conducted by the promotions officer of Sports Services revealed that in order to make the games more attractive, more than just the game would need to be offered. In fact, this finding was consistent with past attendance records. Games with high attendance were often associated with an event outside of the game itself. The survey also identified that students have the perception that the quality of the games is poor, even though past successes are numerous.

The annual Panda Game between Ottawa and Carleton is a good example of game-related events resulting in elevated attendance. This historical game always attracts a large number of students, as events leading up to the game promote rivalries between the two universities. While attendance for the Panda game has ranged from 2000 to 5000 in recent years, Sports Services has had a difficult time carrying these numbers over to other regular season games. In contrast, several other Canadian universities have been able to maintain a respectable number of spectators at all of their games by making them an event and part of the university tradition. However, this has not occurred at the University of Ottawa.

Sports Services' Dilemma

Back in his office, Luc was getting ready for the meeting with the Advisory Council when he turned to his interns:

"You know, guys, I am so damn frustrated! I have been working like mad to get a sponsorship deal with the Royal Bank and I'm not sure if it is going to happen. I would love to invite some of their managers out to the game on Saturday and show them the outstanding product that we have to offer. However, how could I if our fan support is typical of most games? They would probably no longer be interested in working out a deal! How do I get more people to attend our games?"

Luc reflected on a game he had attended at the University of Michigan between the Wolverines and the Buckeyes from Ohio State where the stands were filled to the rafters with over 100 000 fans. He thought how nice it would be to get even a small percentage of those numbers to come out to a game. If only the University of Ottawa could cultivate this type of environment, then attaining the support of students, alumni, local residents, companies, and sponsors would be easy.

Although Luc knew what they wanted, he did not know how it should be accomplished. Out of frustration he turned to his interns and said: "What should we do?"

QUESTIONS

1. What does Luc Gelineau have to do before a sponsorship deal with the Royal Bank (or another firm) can be undertaken? When developing your answer, think about the things that make a sponsorship attractive for a corporation.

2. Corporate sponsorship of educational programs in public schools and universities has been a controversial topic. What are the pros and cons of entering into a sponsorship arrangement?

3. What market segments does Luc have to consider when developing his plans? Which is the most important segment? Can Luc attract multiple segments to the games? Will the presence of one segment detract from the experience of the others?

4. What role will the different elements of the promotion mix play in helping Luc revitalize Sports Services at the University of Ottawa?

5. Design a promotion plan that will help Luc solve his problems. Be specific about the objectives of your plan, the target audience, the media you will use, and the creative strategy you will employ.

Source: This case was written by David S. Litvack, University of Ottawa. It was reproduced with permission of the author.

Video Case 15

IMAGE MAKING:
THE CASE OF HARRY ROSEN

When Harry Rosen, men's clothing retailer, decided to remake the image of his stores to attract a new target market, he chose Roche Macaulay and Partners, an ad agency in Toronto, to help him. Considered a "hip" agency in the industry, Roche Macaulay and Partners bills approximately $50 million a year. Since the Harry Rosen account could be worth $1 million a year, it represented a substantial account. The agency was therefore anxious to provide a campaign that was acceptable to the Harry Rosen management team within the eight-week deadline they had been given.

There are 22 Harry Rosen stores in Canada, which together generate $100 million in sales a year. Although successful at serving existing customers, Harry Rosen was concerned that the business was not attracting young men, which could have serious implications for the future of his business. While the new image was necessary to attract new clients, Rosen wanted to ensure that this new image would be acceptable to his existing, core customers. The first task for the ad agency then, was to compare customers to non-customers to determine why younger men were not shopping at Harry Rosen stores. To do this they used one of the most common research methods in advertising: focus groups. Three groups, costing $10 000, were run. One group was composed of regular Harry Rosen customers, the other two of young men who don't shop at Harry Rosen.

The focus groups revealed that younger men associated Harry Rosen stores with their fathers, not themselves. They viewed themselves as individuals and did not believe that Harry Rosen could outfit them to maintain that individuality. Among the questions asked in the focus groups was, "If Harry Rosen was a car, what type of car would it be?" The answers to this question included adjectives like, "bigger and conservative." Participants also thought the Harry Rosen "car" would be driven by a 55-year-old, confirming the association of the stores with older men. While each group was in session, Harry Rosen and his management team, along with agency personnel, were watching behind a one-way mirror to try to better understand the younger demographic group they hoped to target.

One goal of focus groups is to identify what is known in advertising as the "consumer insight." If properly identified, this consumer insight can be used to develop a powerful advertising campaign that is meaningful to targeted consumers. In this case, two of the key insights from the focus groups, as identified by the agency personnel, were that time was a precious commodity for the younger demographic group and that they hated to shop. The agency people tried to develop a campaign to build on these findings, including tag lines such as, "The average man would rather get out than shop for clothes," "When you shop at Harry Rosen it is time well spent," and "Harry Rosen takes the hassle out of shopping." After Harry Rosen saw these initial ideas, he was unconvinced. He questioned the findings of the focus groups and did not believe that time was an important enough issue to focus on. Additionally, he believed that the campaign focused too much on negative concepts such as "hassle."

The Roche Macaulay team started again from scratch to develop another series of ad ideas. This time they developed a campaign that focused on recognizable people wearing clothes from Harry Rosen. The headline of the ad would include the person's name and proclaim that the outfit they were shown in is what they will be wearing on a particular day. These ads would then be run in newspapers across Canada on the date mentioned in the ad. The people used in the ads would be an eclectic mix of personalities such as sports figures, authors, artists, and business people. They would also represent different styles and sizes to emphasize the fact that Harry Rosen can help customers maintain their individuality.

Harry Rosen was pleased with the new idea. He felt that the campaign built a strong identity that would bring in new customers but would also be meaningful to his existing customers. In the fall of 1996, the campaign was run in newspapers across Canada.

QUESTIONS:

1. Describe the characteristics of the agency-client relationship in this case. Based on this case, what observations would you make about the way this relationship works?

2. Discuss the advantages and disadvantages of using focus-group research to develop advertising. What role did the focus groups play in developing the campaign for Harry Rosen?

Source: This case was prepared by Auleen Carson and is based on "Harry Rosen," *Venture,* (September 22, 1996).

Principles of
Marketing

M

rinciples of
Marketing

ciples
Mark

CHAPTER 16

PERSONAL SELLING AND SALES MANAGEMENT

Fifteen years ago, the Eastman Chemical Company began a deceptively simple, customer-driven quality program called "Customers and Us." The program is focused on doing everything possible to improve the quality of the company's relationships with its customers. Not surprisingly, Eastman's 500 salespeople have played a prominent role in the company's customer-driven quality program, a program that has won several prestigious business awards. Eastman knows that its salespeople must be skilled at performing the basic selling tasks—finding qualified customers, presenting Eastman's products, and getting orders. And its sales managers must excel at hiring outstanding sales prospects, training them to sell effectively, and motivating them to perform at a high level. Each year, the sales force generates more than $7 billion in sales for Eastman's 10 business units, ranging from packaging plastics and coatings to fine chemicals. However, at Eastman, salespeople do more than simply travel their territories, hawking the company's wares. What makes Eastman's sales force special is its penchant for building long-term, mutually profitable relationships with the company's 7000 customers worldwide.

Eastman's carefully selected, extensively trained salespeople excel at keeping customers satisfied. They work tirelessly to build strong customer relationships. They are thoroughly trained so that they understand Eastman's products, listen to customers, understand their expectations, and respond to their problems and complaints.

The sales force forms a critical link between Eastman and its customers. Given the company's deep dedication to customer satisfaction, the sales force often finds itself in the position of co-ordinating many of Eastman's 18 000 employees in team efforts that are focused on improving customer relationships. The acronym for Eastman's customer-driven, team-oriented problem-solving approach is MEPS, which stands for "Making Eastman the Preferred Supplier." The objective of the MEPS program is to improve the processes that link Eastman to its customers. When specific customer problems are found, MEPS teams are formed to solve them. Although MEPS projects vary widely, they are all sales driven and customer focused.

OBJECTIVES

When you finish this chapter, you should be able to

1. Discuss the role of a company's salespeople in creating value for customers and building customer relationships.

2. Identify the six major sales-force management steps.

3. Explain how companies design sales-force strategy and structure.

4. Explain how companies recruit, select, and train salespeople.

5. Describe how companies compensate and supervise salespeople, and how they evaluate sales-force effectiveness.

6. Discuss the personal selling process, distinguishing between transaction-oriented marketing and relationship marketing.

One Eastman sales rep, for instance, initiated a MEPS project when a customer was experiencing persistent problems with the presence of black specks in one of its chemical products. The sales rep organized a cross-functional team to study the problem, including people from Eastman's supply and distribution, manufacturing, and product support services groups. The MEPS team solved the problem by recommending that new equipment be installed at the customer's facility. Another MEPS project arose when customers complained that they found Eastman's standard "conditions of sale," which were printed on the back of order sheets, somewhat offensive. The conditions made it sound as though Eastman was saying, "We know you're out to get us, and we're going to make sure you don't." The MEPS team refined and shortened the terms of sale and made them more reader-friendly.

To resolve customer problems, Eastman must first know what the problems are. Consequently, the company tries to make it easy for customers to complain by conducting frequent customer satisfaction surveys, encouraging salespeople to ask about problems, and providing a 24-hour, toll-free number for receiving complaints. The sales organization is responsible for managing the customer satisfaction survey, which is printed in nine languages and administered to customers around the world. On the survey, customers rate both Eastman and its closest competitor on 25 performance factors, including issues such as product quality, pricing practices, on-time and correct delivery, sales expertise, and sharing market information. Salespeople take the survey seriously. Trainees are taught that "the second most important thing they have to do is get their customer satisfaction surveys out to and back from customers," says Eastman's sales training manager. "Number one, of course, is getting orders."

The customer survey provides important feedback for the organization as a whole, but it has also become one of the sales force's most powerful marketing tools. Salespeople hand-deliver the survey, and then review the survey results on follow-up sales calls. The sales reps are responsible for discussing survey results with customers and for informing customers of how Eastman plans to resolve any problems identified by the survey. According to Bill Barnes, Eastman's director of customer satisfaction, "We want to show customers that the survey will be a working tool to build our relationship." Customers appreciate the survey—it shows that Eastman is listening to them, and working hard to satisfy their needs. As one customer notes, "The survey is just a piece of paper.... What I value is the professional courtesy, the fact that [Eastman] follows up continually."

Thus, Eastman's salespeople have learned that the best way to keep getting orders is to build long-term relationships with customers. The company's focus on quality and customer satisfaction has given its sales force both renewed energy and a new sense of purpose.[1]

It's no wonder that companies like Eastman Chemical work diligently to improve their sales forces. Sales are the lifeblood of every compant. Robert Louis Stevenson noted that "everyone lives by selling something." While everyone has experience with the sales personnel you meet in every retail establishment, you are probably less familiar with the sales forces used by business organizations to sell products and services to customers around the world. In fact, companies such as IBM Canada and Xerox are famous for the quality of their sales staff. Procter & Gamble, Warner Lambert, and Wrigley's Canada all hire university graduates into sales jobs since having highly educated, professional sales personnel is essential for building strong relationships with channel members. Sales forces are also found in many other kinds of organizations. Canada Post uses an extensive sales force to help launch new products such as its direct-mail offerings and courier services. Universities use recruiters to attract new students. Agriculture Canada sends specialists into the field to convince farmers to use new agricultural methods and

Eastman Chemical Company
www.eastman.com/

products. You will have to take on a sales role when you have to sell your knowledge and expertise to prospective employers.

The sales force may be one of the company's largest investments. Many of today's business executives believe that quality salespeople can act as a sustainable point of difference versus the competition.[2] However, many also believe that the era of the lone salesperson is coming to an end and that team selling will take its place. Customers are more demanding and retailers' power is increasing. The technology on which many products is based is so complex that no one individual can be an expert in all of its aspects. Add to this the fact that product life cycles are shortening and cost-to-sales ratios are too high. This has led to increasing demands to make costly personal sales more efficient. Thus, the overriding concern for many firms is integration—the merging of sales and marketing, the coordination of customer relationships and communication, and the development of a comprehensive information database that tracks buyer behaviour as well as product purchases.[3] In this chapter, we examine the role of personal selling in the organization, sales-force management decisions, and basic principles of personal selling.

THE ROLE OF PERSONAL SELLING

There are many types of personal selling jobs, and the role of personal selling can vary greatly from one company to another. Here, we look at the nature of personal selling positions and at the role the sales force plays in modern marketing organizations.

THE NATURE OF PERSONAL SELLING

Selling is one of the oldest professions in the world. The people who do the selling go by many names: *salespeople, sales representatives, account executives, sales consultants, sales engineers, agents, district managers,* and *marketing representatives,* to name just a few.

People hold many stereotypes of salespeople—including some unfavourable ones. "Salesman" may bring to mind the image of Arthur Miller's pitiable Willy Loman in *Death of a Salesman.* Or you might think of Meredith Willson's cigar-smoking, back-slapping, joke-telling Harold Hill in *The Music Man.* Both examples depict salespeople as loners, travelling their territories trying to foist their wares on unsuspecting or unwilling buyers.

However, modern salespeople are a far cry from these unfortunate stereotypes. Today, most salespeople are well-educated, well-trained professionals who work to build and maintain long-term relationships with customers. They build these relationships by listening to their customers, assessing customer needs, and organizing the company's efforts to solve customer problems and satisfy customer needs. For example, consider Boeing, the aerospace giant that dominates the worldwide commercial aircraft market with a 55 percent market share. It takes more than a friendly smile and a firm handshake to sell expensive airplanes:

> Selling high-tech aircraft at $70 [$90] million or more a copy is complex and challenging. A single big sale can easily run into the billions of dollars. Boeing salespeople head up an extensive team of company specialists—sales and service technicians, financial analysts, planners, engineers—all dedicated to finding ways to satisfy airline customer needs. The salespeople begin by becoming experts on the airlines, much like Wall Street analysts would. They find out where each airline wants to grow, when it wants to replace planes, and details of its financial situation. The team runs Boeing and competing planes through computer systems, simulating the airline's routes, cost per seat, and other factors to show that their planes are most efficient. Then the high-level negotiations begin. The selling process is nerve-rackingly slow—it can take two or three years from the first sales presentation to the day the sale is announced.

The term "salesperson" covers a wide range of positions, from the clerk selling in a retail store to the engineering salesperson who consults with client companies.

Salesperson
An individual acting for a company by performing one or more of the following activities: prospecting, communicating, servicing, and information-gathering.

Sometimes top executives from both the airline and Boeing are brought in to close the deal. After getting the order, salespeople then must stay in almost constant touch to keep track of the account's equipment needs and to make certain the customer stays satisfied. Success depends on building solid, long-term relationships with customers, based on performance and trust. According to one analyst, Boeing's salespeople "are the vehicle by which information is collected and contacts are made so all other things can take place."[4]

The term **salesperson** covers a wide range of positions. At one extreme, a salesperson might be largely an *order taker,* such as the department-store salesperson standing behind the counter. At the other extreme are *order getters*—salespeople whose positions demand the *creative selling* of products and services ranging from appliances, industrial equipment, or airplanes to insurance, advertising, or consulting services. Other salespeople engage in *missionary selling:* These salespeople are not expected or permitted to take an order, but only build goodwill or educate buyers. An example is a salesperson for a pharmaceutical company who calls on doctors to educate them about the company's drug products and to urge them to prescribe these products to their patients.[5] In this chapter, we focus on the more creative types of selling and on the process of building and managing an effective sales force.

THE ROLE OF THE SALES FORCE

Personal selling is the interpersonal arm of the promotion mix. Advertising consists of one-way, non-personal communication with target consumer groups. In contrast, personal selling involves two-way, personal communication between salespeople and individual customers—whether face-to-face, by telephone, through video conferences, or by other means. This means that personal selling can be more effective than advertising in more complex selling situations. Salespeople can probe customers to learn more about their problems. They can adjust the marketing offer to fit the special needs of each customer and can negotiate terms of sale. They can build long-term personal relationships with key decision-makers.

The role of personal selling varies from company to company. Some firms have no salespeople at all—for example, companies that sell only through mail-order catalogues, or companies that sell through manufacturer's representatives, sales agents, or brokers. In most firms, however, the sales force plays a major role. In companies that sell business products, such as Xerox or Du Pont, the company's salespeople work directly with customers. In fact, to many customers, salespeople may be the only contact. To these customers, the sales force *is* the company. In consumer product companies such as Procter & Gamble or Wilson Sporting Goods that sell through intermediaries, final consumers rarely meet salespeople or even know about them. Still, the sales force plays an important behind-the-scenes role. It works with wholesalers and retailers to gain their support and to help them be more effective in selling the company's products.

The sales force serves as a critical link between a company and its customers. In many cases, salespeople serve both masters—the seller and the buyer. First, they *represent the company to customers*. They find and develop new customers and communicate information about the company's products and services. They sell products by approaching customers, presenting their products, answering objections, negotiating prices and terms, and closing sales. In addition, salespeople provide services to customers, carry out market research and intelligence work, and fill out sales call reports.

At the same time, salespeople *represent customers to the company*, acting inside the firm as "champions" of customers' interests. Salespeople relay customer concerns about company products and actions back to those who can handle them. They learn about customer needs, and work with others in the company to develop greater customer value. Thus, the salesperson often acts as an "account manager" who manages the relationship between the seller and buyer.

As companies move toward a stronger market orientation, their sales forces are becoming more market focused and customer oriented. The old view was that salespeople should worry about sales and the company should worry about profit. However, the current view holds that salespeople should be concerned with more than just producing *sales*—they also must know how to produce *customer satisfaction* and *company profit*. They should be able to examine sales data, measure market potential, gather market intelligence, and develop marketing strategies and plans. They should know how to orchestrate the firm's efforts toward delivering customer value and satisfaction. A market-oriented rather than a sales-oriented sales force will be more effective in the long run. Beyond winning new customers and making sales, it will help the company to create long-term, profitable relationships with customers.

■ MANAGING THE SALES FORCE

Sales-force management
The analysis, planning, implementation, and control of sales-force activities. It includes designing sales-force strategy and structure; and recruiting, selecting, training, compensating, supervising, and evaluating the firm's salespeople.

We define **sales-force management** as the analysis, planning, implementation, and control of sales-force activities. It includes designing sales-force strategy and structure, and recruiting, selecting, training, compensating, supervising, and evaluating the firm's salespeople. These major sales-force management decisions are shown in Figure 16-1 and are discussed in the following sections.

DESIGNING SALES-FORCE STRATEGY AND STRUCTURE

Marketing managers face several sales-force strategy and design questions. How should salespeople and their tasks be structured? How large should the sales force be? Should salespeople sell alone or work in teams with other people in the company? Should they sell in the field or by telephone? We address these issues below.

Sales-Force Structure

A company can divide sales responsibilities along any of several lines. The decision is simple if the company sells only one product line to one industry with customers in many locations. In that case the company would use a *territorial sales-force structure*. However, if the company sells many products to many types of

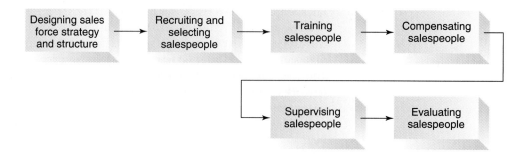

FIGURE 16-1 *Major steps in salesforce management*

customers, it might need a *product sales-force structure,* a *customer sales-force structure,* or a combination of the two.

TERRITORIAL SALES-FORCE STRUCTURE.   In the **territorial sales-force structure,** each salesperson is assigned to an exclusive geographic territory and sells the company's full line of products or services to all customers in that territory. This sales organization has many advantages. It clearly defines the salesperson's job, and because only one salesperson works the territory, he or she gets all the credit or blame for territory sales. The territorial structure also increases the salesperson's desire to build local business relationships that, in turn, improve selling effectiveness. Finally, because each salesperson travels within a limited geographic area, travel expenses are relatively small.

A territorial sales organization often is supported by many levels of sales management positions. For example, Campbell Soup recently changed from a product sales-force structure to a territorial one, whereby each salesperson is now responsible for selling all Campbell Soup products. Starting at the bottom of the organization, *sales merchandisers* report to *sales representatives,* who report to *retail supervisors,* who report to *directors of retail sales operations,* who report to *regional sales managers.* Regional sales managers, in turn, report *general sales managers,* who report to a *vice-president and general sales manager.*[6]

PRODUCT SALES-FORCE STRUCTURE.   Salespeople must know their products—especially when the products are numerous and complex. This need, together with the trend toward product management, has led many companies to adopt a **product sales-force structure,** in which the sales force sells along product lines. For example, Kodak uses different sales forces for its film products than for its industrial products. The film products sales force deals with simple products that are distributed intensively, whereas the industrial products sales force deals with complex products that require technical understanding.

The product structure can lead to problems, however, if a single large customer buys many different company products. For example, Baxter International, a hospital supply company, has several product divisions, each with a separate sales force. Several Baxter salespeople might end up calling on the same hospital on the same day. This means that the salespeople travel over the same routes and wait to see the same customer's purchasing agents. These extra costs must be compared with the benefits of better product knowledge and attention to individual products.

CUSTOMER SALES-FORCE STRUCTURE.   More and more companies are now using a **customer sales force structure,** in which they organize the sales force along customer or industry lines. Separate sales forces may be set up for different industries, for serving current customers versus finding new ones, and for major accounts versus regular accounts. IBM Canada recently reorganized its sales force so that its 1000-plus members could become specialist in selling computers, software, and services to narrow industry sectors such as banks, insurance companies, and resource-based firms such as petroleum companies.[7]

Territorial sales-force structure
A sales force organization that assigns each salesperson to an exclusive geographic territory in which that salesperson carries the company's full line.

Product sales-force structure
A sales-force organization under which salespeople specialize in selling only a portion of the company's products or lines.

Kodak Canada
www.kodak.com/
aboutKodak/regions/kci/
kciHomePage.shtml

Customer sales-force structure
A sales-force organization under which salespeople specialize in selling only to certain customers or industries.

IBM
www.ibm.com/

Organizing the sales force around customers can help a company become more customer focused and build closer relationships with important customers. IBM recently made a shift from a product-based structure to a customer-based one. Before this shift occurred, droves of salespeople representing different IBM software, hardware, and services division might call on a single large client, creating confusion and frustration. Such large customers wanted a "single face"—one point of contact for all of IBM's vast array of products and services. Now, following the restructuring, a single IBM "client executive" works with each large customer and manages a team of IBM staff—product representatives, systems engineers, consultants, and others— who work with the customer. The client executive becomes an expert in the customer's industry. Greg Buseman, a client executive in the distribution industry who spends most of his time working with a major consumer packaged-goods customer, describes his role this way: "I am the owner of the business relationship with the client. If the client has a problem, I'm the one who pulls together software or hardware specialists or consultants. At the customer I work most closely with, we usually have 15 to 20 projects going at once, and I have to manage them."[8] Such an intense focus on customers is widely credited for IBM's dramatic turnaround in recent years.

Pyramid sales-force structure
A sales-force organization under which salespeople recruit others into the network so that the organization constantly expands.

PYRAMID STRUCTURES. Some successful firms, such as Amway, Tupperware, and Mary Kay, use **pyramid sales-force structures**, or multi-level plans. In Canada alone, these organizations generate $1.3 billion in annual sales and employ 600 000 salespeople. Pyramid firms rely on current salespeople to recruit others into the network so that the organization constantly expands. When a salesperson recruits a new sales rep, the recruiter receives a small commission on all the sales that the new recruit generates. Weekenders of Toronto is one of the most successful organizations of this type. Boasting a sales force of 15 000, it rang up sales of $70 million, and as it expands into new territories such as Chile, Germany, and Australia, is expected to hit $250 million. Sales reps convince their friends to hold "parties" where six to eight people view and buy a line of coordinated knit clothing. The average Weekenders sales rep rings up $17 000 per year in sales compared to an industry average of $2000. For those at the top of the pyramid, it can be a lucrative business. Lia Keeping, queen of the Weekenders sales force, takes home a monthly cheque of approximately $64 000. This type of organization has long been tarred with an unsavoury image since many scams have used this type of structure. However, they are completely legal if they don't charge an entry fee to join the organization, don't force sales representatives to stock up on products at rates above those it costs plan operators, and are honest about what a typical salesperson earns.[9]

Complex sales-force structure
A sales-force organization that combines several types of sales-force structures.

COMPLEX SALES-FORCE STRUCTURES. Today's sales forces are often composed of people with different skills, who are employed to accomplish different tasks ranging from merchandisers who help retailers, such as Shoppers Drug Mart get the most out of their displays, to telemarketers, like those at Kodak Canada who help customers get more timely service, to information managers, like those at Lotus Canada who help customers solve complex networking problems.[10] When a company sells a wide variety of products to many types of customers over a broad geographical area, it often combines several types of sales-force structures. Salespeople can be specialized by customer and territory, by product and territory, by product and customer, or by territory, product, and customer. No single structure is best for all companies and situations. Each company should select a sales-force structure that best serves the needs of its customers and fits its overall marketing strategy.

Sales-Force Size

Once the company has set its structure, it is ready to consider sales-force size. Salespeople constitute one of the company's most productive—and most expensive— assets. Therefore, increasing their number will increase both sales and costs. Many companies, like the Adams Brands division of Warner-Lambert Canada, whose sales force sells Chiclets, Rolaids, and Halls to Canadian retailers, are concerned with cutting the cost of selling. The firm now employs as many salespeople working three days a week as it does full-time sales staff.[11]

Many companies use some form of **workload approach** to set sales-force size. Using this approach, a company first groups accounts into different classes according to size, account status, or other factors related to the amount of effort required to maintain them. It then determines the number of salespeople needed to call on each class of accounts the desired number of times. The company might think as follows: Suppose we have 1000 Type-A accounts and 2000 Type-B accounts. Type-A accounts require 36 calls a year and Type-B accounts require 12 calls a year. In this case, the sales force's *workload*—the number of calls it must make per year—is 60 000 calls [(1000 × 36) + (2000 × 12) = 36 000 + 24 000 = 60 000]. Suppose our average salesperson can make 1000 calls a year. Thus, the company needs 60 salespeople (60 000 ÷ 1000).

Other Sales-Force Strategy and Structure Issues

Sales management must also decide who will be involved in the selling effort and how various sales and sales-support people will work together.

OUTSIDE AND INSIDE SALES FORCES.   The company may have an **outside sales force** (or *field sales force*), an **inside sales force**, or both. Outside salespeople travel to call on customers. Inside salespeople conduct business from their offices via telephone, e-mail, and fax or visits from prospective buyers.

To reduce time demands on their outside sales forces, many companies have increased the size of their inside sales forces. Inside salespeople include technical support people, sales assistants, and telemarketers. *Technical support people* provide technical information and answers to customers' questions. *Sales assistants* provide clerical backup for outside salespeople. They call ahead and confirm appointments, conduct credit checks, follow up on deliveries, and answer customers' questions when outside salespeople cannot be reached. *Telemarketers* use the phone to find new leads and qualify prospects for the field sales force, or to sell and service accounts directly.

The inside sales force frees outside salespeople to spend more time selling to major accounts and finding major new prospects. Depending on the complexity of the product and customer, a telemarketer can make from 20 to 33 decision-maker contacts a day, compared to the average of four that an outside salesperson can see. And for many types of products and selling situations, **telemarketing** can be as effective as a personal call but much less expensive. For example, whereas a typical personal sales call can cost well over $275, a routine industrial telemarketing call costs only about $7 and a complex call about $28.[12] Telemarketing can be used successfully by both large and small companies:

> Kodak Canada recently began placing new emphasis on telemarketing. While it has always employed an inside sales staff to serve small or distant customers, it has now begun encouraging customers to call its telemarketers to receive faster service—whether it be improved inventory replenishment, or updates on upcoming special offers and events. To retain the personal touch with customers using telemarketing services, Kodak has begun sending its customers photographs of its telesales reps along with flow charts so that customers can better understand how requests for service move through the company. Similarly, Molson Breweries has hired six telesales people to manage inventory, promotions and merchandising for its smaller clients, allowing it to shrink its Ontario salesforce from 125 salespeople to 70. Canadian telemarketing guru, Jim Domanski, stresses that telemarketing costs about

Workload approach
An approach to setting sales force size in which the company groups accounts into different size classes and then determines how many salespeople are needed to call on them the desired number of times.

Outside sales force
(or *field sales force*) Outside salespeople who travel to call on customers.

Inside sales force
Salespeople who conduct business from their offices via telephone, e-mail, and fax or visits from prospective buyers.

Telemarketing
Using the telephone to sell directly to consumers.

Experienced telemarketers sell complex chemical products by phone at DuPont's Corporate Telemarketing Centre. Says one: "I'm more effective on the phone . . . and you don't have to outrun the dogs."

one-tenth the rate for making a personal sales call and that a good telemarketer can reach as many companies in a day as a field sales rep can contact in a week.[13]

TEAM SELLING. The days when a single salesperson handled a large and important customer are vanishing rapidly. Today, as products become more complex, and as customers grow larger and more demanding, one person simply cannot handle all of a large customer's needs anymore. Instead, most companies now are using **team selling** to service large, complex accounts. Sales teams might include people from sales, marketing, engineering, finance, technical support, and even upper management. For example, Procter & Gamble assigns teams consisting of salespeople, marketing managers, technical service people, and logistics and information-systems specialists to work closely with large retail customers such as Shoppers Drug Mart, Zellers, and Loblaw. In such team-selling situations, salespeople become "orchestrators" who help coordinate a whole-company effort to build profitable relationships with important customers (see Marketing Highlight 16-1).[14]

Team selling
Using teams of people from sales, marketing, engineering, finance, technical support, and even upper management to service large, complex accounts.

Yet companies recognize that just asking their people for teamwork does not produce it. They must revise their compensation and recognition systems to give credit for work on shared accounts, and they must set up better goals and measures for sales-force performance. They must emphasize the importance of teamwork in their training programs while at the same time honouring the importance of individual initiative.

RECRUITING AND SELECTING SALESPEOPLE

At the heart of any successful sales-force operation is the recruiting and selection of good salespeople. In order to "weed out mediocrity," Warner-Lambert Canada has begun hiring undergraduate and graduate students to improve the skill level of those people it sends into the field.[15] The performance difference between an average salesperson and a top salesperson can be substantial. According to one study, sales superstars sell an average of 1.5 to 2 times more than the average salesperson.[16] In a typical sales force, the top 30 percent of the salespeople might bring in 60 percent of the sales. Thus, careful salesperson selection can greatly increase overall sales-force performance.

Beyond the differences in sales performance, poor selection results in costly turnover. One study found an average annual sales-force turnover rate of 27 percent for all industries. The costs of high turnover can be great. When a salesperson quits, the costs of finding and training a new salesperson—plus the costs of lost sales—can run as high as $70 000 to $105 000. And a sales force with many new people is less productive.[17]

What Makes a Good Salesperson?
Selecting salespeople would not be a problem if the company knew what traits to look for. If it knew that good salespeople were outgoing, aggressive, and energetic, for example, it could simply check applicants for these characteristics. But many successful salespeople are also bashful, soft-spoken, and laid-back. Some are tall and others are short; some speak well and others poorly; some dress fashionably and others shabbily.

Still, the search continues for the magic list of traits that spells sure-fire sales success. One survey suggests that good salespeople have a lot of enthusiasm, persistence, initiative, self-confidence, and job commitment. They are committed to sales as a way of life and have a strong customer orientation. Another study suggests that good salespeople are independent and self-motivated, and are excellent listeners. Still another study advises that salespeople should be a friend to the customer as well as persistent, enthusiastic, attentive, and—above all—honest. They must be internally motivated, disciplined, hard-working, and able to build strong relationships with customers.[18]

MARKETING HIGHLIGHT 16 - 1

TEAM SELLING: SHIFTING SALESPEOPLE FROM "SOLOISTS" TO "ORCHESTRATORS"

For years, the customer has been solely in the hands of the salesperson. The salesperson identified the prospect, arranged the call, explored the customer's needs, created and proposed a solution, closed the deal, and turned cheerleader as others delivered what he or she promised. For selling relatively simple products, this approach can work well. But if the products are more complex and the service requirements greater, the salesperson simply can't go it alone. Consider the following example from MCI, a provider of telecommunications:

This was Michael Quintano's big chance. The 23-year-old, up-and-coming MCI sales rep had only called on customers billing less than $2500 a month. Then, from out of the blue, he hit upon Nat Schwartz and Company (NS&C), a china and crystal retail-telemarketer with monthly telephone billings exceeding $10 000. In over his head, he offered MCI veteran Al Rodriguez a split on the commission in return for some help. When the pair visited NS&C headquarters, they found a store filled with nothing but china and crystal. "No way does this store bill $10 000. We'll close this deal in one or two calls," Quintano thought. However, when they were led to a bustling back room filled with telemarketers working the phones, their visions of a quick close were swiftly put on hold.

Quintano and Rodriguez realized they would have to expand their sales team. They called on sales manager Stephen Smith and MCI Telecommunications consultant Tom Mantone, who during two meetings with NS&C cleared up questions about technical details such as phone-line installations. That smoothed the way for Quintano and Rodriguez to close the deal. Thus, by relying on team selling, Michael Quintano landed the largest account of his career.

Lotus Development Canada Ltd. has discovered the power of selling seminars.

More and more, companies are finding that sales teams can unearth problems, solutions, and sales opportunities that no individual salesperson could. Such teams might include experts from any area or level of the selling firm—sales, marketing, technical and support services, R&D, engineering, operations, finance, and others. In team-selling situations, the salesperson shifts from "soloist" to "orchestrator." One such salesperson puts it in sports terms. "It's my job to be the quarterback. [Taking care of a large customer] gets farmed out to different areas of the company, and different questions have to be answered by different people. We set up a game plan and then go in and make the call."

Some companies, like IBM and Xerox, have used teams for a long time. Others have only recently reorganized to adopt the team concept. John Hancock, for example, a large U.S. insurance firm, recently set up sales-and-service teams in six territories. Each team is led by a director of sales who acts as a mini-CEO, managing all aspects of customer contact: sales, service, and technical support. The result is an informed, dedicated team that is closer to the customer.

When a customer's business becomes so complex that a single company's sales organization can't provide a complete solution, firms might even create multi-company sales teams. For example, teams from MCI, IBM, and Rohm recently joined forces in an effort to provide solutions to a large customer that was setting up a complex data-application network. MCI's team provided information on data

---

How can a company determine what traits salespeople in its industry should have? Job *duties* suggest some of the traits a company should look for. Is a lot of planning and paperwork required? Does the job call for much travel? Will the salesperson face a lot of rejections? Will the salesperson be working with high-level buyers? The successful salesperson should be suited to these duties. The company also should look at the characteristics of its most successful salespeople for clues to needed traits.

Recruiting Procedures

After management has decided on needed traits, it must *recruit* salespeople. The human resources department looks for applicants by getting names from current salespeople, using employment agencies, placing classified ads, and contacting university students. Until recently, companies sometimes found it hard to sell university students on selling. Many thought that selling was a job and not a profession, that salespeople had to be deceitful to be effective, and that selling involved too much insecurity and travel. In addition, some women believed that selling was a man's

communication, IBM's on computer hardware and software, and Rohm's on switching equipment. "The meeting provided the customer with one point of contact to solve a variety of needs," said an MCI sales executive.

Some companies have even opened special sites for team sales meetings, called *executive briefing centres.* Xerox runs six of these centres. Xerox sales teams invite key people from important accounts to one of the centres, where centre staff conduct briefings, arrange video conferences with experts in other parts of the country, and provide other services that help the team build business and improve customer service.

Team selling does have some pitfalls. For example, selling teams can confuse or overwhelm customers who are used to working with only one saleperson. Salespeople who are used to having customers all to themselves may have trouble learning to work with and trust others on a team. Finally, difficulties in evaluating individual contributions to the team-selling effort can create some sticky compensation issues.

Still, team selling can produce dramatic results. For example, Dun & Bradstreet, the world's largest marketer of business information and related services, recently established sales teams composed of representatives from its credit, collection, and marketing business units, which up until then had worked separately. Their mission was to work as a team to call on more senior-level staff in customer organizations, learn about customer needs, and offer solutions. The teams concentrated on D&B's top 50 customers. When one of the D&B sales teams asked to meet with the chief financial officer of a major telecommunications company, the executive responded, "I'm delighted you asked, but why talk?" He found out after a one-hour meeting. The D&B team listened as he discussed problems facing his organization, and by the end of the information-seeking session, the team had come up with several solutions for the executive, and had identified $2 million in D&B sales opportunities from what had been a $900 000 customer. More teams met with more clients, creating more opportunities. About a year after the program started, D&B's marketing department had targeted $275 million in sales opportunities, about half of which would not have been found under the old system. Now these teams are getting together with D&B's top 200 customers.

Other companies, particularly in the high-tech arena, have moved away from sending sales reps to customers, and moved towards selling seminars, during which customers come to them. Using the seminar format, teams of functional specialists and sales reps act as instructors, informing current and prospective clients of new technological developments, product improvements, and upcoming product introductions. Microsoft Canada Inc., IBM Canada Ltd., Geac Computer Corp. Ltd., and Lotus Development Canada Ltd. have begun to use this technique to target their specialized audiences more effectively. Using this format, the high-tech firm rents space in a large hotel's conference facilities, sets up massive projection screens, and then demonstrates how the firm's technology can assist the firm's business customers solve common business problems. Such venues draw up to 700 customers, allowing high-tech firms to increase their sales productivity while at the same time reducing selling costs. A contact made through seminar selling costs approximately $20, while a personal sales call costs more than $200.

Sources: Portions adapted from Joseph Conlin, "Teaming Up," *Sales & Marketing Management,* October 1993, pp. 98–104; and Richard C. Whiteley, "Orchestrating Service," *Sales & Marketing Management,* April 1994, pp. 29–30. Also see Christopher Meyer, "How the Right Measures Help Teams Excel," *Harvard Business Review,* May–June 1994, pp. 95–103; Mark Stevenson, "The Lean, Mean Sales Machine," *Canadian Business,* January 1994, p. 34; www.dnb.com/

career. To counter such objections, recruiters now offer high starting salaries and income growth and tout the fact that many of the presidents of large North American corporations started out in marketing and sales. They point out that more than 28 percent of the people now selling industrial products are women. Women account for a much higher percentage of the sales force in some industries, such as textiles and apparel (61 percent), banking and financial services (58 percent), communications (51 percent), and publishing (49 percent).

Selecting Salespeople

Recruiting will attract many applicants, from which the company must select the best. The selection procedure can vary from a single informal interview to lengthy testing and interviewing. Many companies give formal tests to sales applicants. Tests typically measure sales aptitude, analytical and organizational skills, personality traits, and other characteristics. Test results count heavily in such companies as IBM, Prudential, Procter & Gamble, and Gillette. Gillette claims that tests have reduced turnover by 42 percent and that test scores have correlated well with the later performance of new salespeople. But test scores provide only one piece of information in a set that includes personal characteristics, references, past employment history, and interviewer reactions.[19]

TRAINING SALESPEOPLE

Many companies used to send their new salespeople into the field almost immediately after hiring them. They would be given samples, order books, and general instructions ("sell in Manitoba and Saskatchewan"). Training programs were luxuries. To many companies, a training program translated into much expense for instructors, materials, space, and salary for a person who was not yet selling, and a loss of sales opportunities because the person was not in the field.

Today's new salespeople, however, may spend anywhere from a few weeks or months to a year or more in training. The average training period is four months. Norton Company, the industrial abrasives manufacturer, puts its new salespeople through a 12-month training program. The first six months are spent at company headquarters, with the remaining time spent in the field. Rob Granby, vice-president of sales at Cadbury Beverages Canada, believes that training and a supportive corporate culture are essential. "If your corporate culture isn't one that nourishes and helps salespeople flourish, then no matter what you layer on in terms of bonus programs and special incentives, it won't make a difference," he says.[20]

Training programs have several goals. Salespeople need to know and identify with the company, so most training programs begin by describing the company's history and objectives, its organization, its financial structure and facilities, and its chief products and markets. Salespeople also need to know the company's products, so sales trainees are shown how products are produced and how they work. They also need to know customers' and competitors' characteristics, so the training program teaches them about competitors' strategies and about different types of customers and their needs, buying motives, and buying habits. Since more and more firms are using technology to help the sales force accomplish their tasks more effectively and efficiently, firms must train their sales forces to use technology effectively. Firms such as Xerox Canada, Clearly Canadian, and the Mutual Group insurance company provide their sales reps with notebook computers that run sophisticated software. Sales reps can access client lists, order forms, price lists, and product specifications—in other words, all the information in the firm's database, directly from the field. The electronic links also help salespeople provide feedback to the firm to help it keep its database up to date.[21] Because salespeople must know how to make effective presentations, they are trained in the principles of selling. Finally, salespeople need to understand field procedures and responsibilities. They learn how to divide time between active and potential accounts and how to use an expense account, prepare reports, and route communications effectively.

COMPENSATING SALESPEOPLE

To attract salespeople, a company must have an appealing compensation plan. These plans vary greatly both by industry and by companies within the same industry. The level of compensation must be close to the "going rate" for the type of sales job and needed skills. For example, the average earnings of an experienced, middle-level industrial salesperson amount to about $65 000.[22] To pay less than the going rate would attract too few quality salespeople; to pay more would be unnecessary.

Compensation is composed of several elements—a fixed amount, a variable amount, expenses, and fringe benefits. The fixed amount, usually a salary, gives the salesperson some stable income. The variable amount, which might be commissions or bonuses based on sales performance, rewards the salesperson for greater effort. Expense allowances, which repay salespeople for job-related expenses, let salespeople undertake needed and desirable selling efforts. Fringe benefits, such as paid vacations, sickness or accident benefits, pensions, and life insurance, provide job security and satisfaction.

Management must decide what *mix* of these compensation elements makes the most sense for each sales job. Different combinations of fixed and variable compensation give rise to four basic types of compensation plans—straight salary, straight commission, salary plus bonus, and salary plus commission. A study of sales-force compensation plans showed that 70 percent of all companies surveyed use a combination of base salary and incentives. The average plan consisted of about 60 percent salary and 40 percent incentive pay.[23]

The sales-force compensation plan can be designed both to motivate salespeople and to direct their activities. For example, if sales management wants salespeople to emphasize new account development, it might pay a bonus for opening new accounts. Thus, the compensation plan should direct the sales force toward activities that are consistent with overall marketing objectives.

Table 16-1 illustrates how a company's compensation plan should reflect its overall marketing strategy. For example, if the overall strategy is to grow rapidly and gain market share, the compensation plan should reward high sales performance and encourage salespeople to capture new accounts. This might suggest a larger commission component coupled with new account bonuses. By contrast, if the marketing goal is to maximize profitability of current accounts, the compensation plan might contain a larger base salary component, with additional incentives based on current account sales or customer satisfaction. In fact, more and more companies are moving away from high commission plans that may drive salespeople to make short-term grabs for business. Notes one sales-force expert, "The last thing you want is to have someone ruin a customer relationship because they're pushing too hard to close a deal." Instead companies are designing compensation plans that reward salespeople for building customer relationships and growing the long-run value of each customer.[24] Thus, firms such as Astra Pharma have not used a commission plan for some time. Instead they reward their representatives for their level of understanding their industry, gained through company training and outside courses, and their involvement in it. And this involvement means more than a "nine-to-five" job. Reps offer evening presentations to groups that influence patients' treatment decisions, such as the Heart and Stroke Foundation and the Canadian Lung Association. They work with hospitals and drug stores to organize patient seminars.[25] (See Marketing Highlight 16-2.)

TABLE 16-1   *The Relationship Between Overall Marketing Strategy and Sales-Force Compensation*

	STRATEGIC GOAL		
	To Rapidly Gain Market Share	**To Solidify Market Leadership**	**To Maximize Profitability**
Ideal Salesperson	• An independent self-starter	• A competitive problem-solver	• A team player • A relationship manager
Sales Focus	• Deal making • Sustained high effort	• Consultative selling	• Account penetration
Compensation Role	• To capture accounts • To reward high performance	• To reward new and existing account sales	• To manage the product mix • To encourage team selling • To reward account management

Source: Adapted from Sam T. Johnson, "Sales Compensation: In Search of a Better Solution," *Compensation & Benefits Review,* November–December 1993, pp. 53–60.

PAYING FOR CUSTOMER VALUE

For years, companies have paid their salespeople based on sales volume and dollar sales. Both are worthy goals, as long as the primary objective is selling the product. However, as the emphasis shifts to adding customer value, retaining customers and building strong relationships, and building "share-of-customer" (percentage of the customer's total business captured), companies are adding a new set of measures to their sales compensation equations. More and more, salespeople are being evaluated and compensated based on the following kinds of measures:

Long-term customer satisfaction. This requires a salesperson not to oversell customers in the short run in order to satisfy a sales quota, but to look out for customers' best interests and focus on helping them achieve their goals.

Full customer service. This requires that the salesperson provide whatever customers need, by working within the firm as well as building alliances with other companies that offer complementary products and services needed by customers. The goal: to never send a customer out the door to become someone else's customer.

Retention rates. Salespeople strive to ensure that once a customer buys from the company, the customer doesn't buy from anyone else.

Compensation plans are being redesigned to motivate salespeople to build real relationships with customers.

SUPERVISING SALESPEOPLE

New salespeople need more than a territory, compensation, and training—they need *supervision*. Through supervision, the company *directs* and *motivates* the sales force to do a better job.

Directing Salespeople

How much should sales management be involved in helping salespeople manage their territories? It depends on everything from the company's size to the experience of its sales force. Thus, companies vary widely in how closely they supervise their salespeople.

Many companies help their salespeople in identifying customer targets and setting call norms. They classify customers based on sales volume, profit, and growth potential, and then they set call norms accordingly. Companies may also specify how much time their sales forces should spend prospecting for new accounts. If left alone, many salespeople will spend most of their time with current customers, who are better-known quantities. Moreover, whereas a prospect may never deliver any business, salespeople can depend on current accounts for some business.

Companies also direct salespeople in how to use their time efficiently. One tool is the annual call plan, which outlines the customers and prospects to call on during certain months and identifies activities to carry out. Activities include participating in trade shows, attending sales meetings, and carrying out marketing research. Another tool is time-and-duty analysis. In addition to time spent selling, the salesperson spends time travelling, waiting, eating, taking breaks, and performing administrative chores.

Growth of customer value. This involves increasing each customer's value to the company by increasing the customer's overall volume of business and capturing a greater share of that business. To make this happen, they must build strong relationships based on real value and customer success.

To see how including such measures in the compensation formula might affect a salesperson's performance, imagine rewarding a car salesperson differently. Most car dealerships reward salespeople for moving cars. Each car sale results in a commission. Once the commission is paid, the salesperson turns to finding a new customer for the next sale. But what if, in addition to a token commission, the dealership rewarded the sales associate for long-term customer satisfaction, such as high 18-month satisfaction scores? Such rewards would motivate the salesperson to follow up with the customer, to ensure that the service department was handling the customer well, and to identify and resolve a host of other problems that might upset the customer.

Suppose the dealership further rewarded the sales associate for share-of-customer. The associate would then find out what else is in the customer's garage and concentrate on ways to use the dealership's products to build "share-of-garage." If rewarded for such smart selling, the associate would find service, repair, and accessories for a customer, and get them all under the dealership's roof. The dealership would know what the customer wanted next, and when. In addition, the sales associate would feed customer information into the dealership's database, so that the customer would be served well even when the associate was on a well-earned vacation. Then, the dealership and the associate could work together to track customer needs electronically.

Most importantly, suppose that the dealership rewarded this salesperson for increasing long-term customer value to the dealership—perhaps by paying a tiny percentage of every dollar ever spent at the dealership by the customer on cars, financing, insurance, service, and repair. The salesperson would thus be motivated not just to make the sale, but to ensure that each customer returned to this dealership for everything, forever.

To be sure, reaching this level of sophistication in sales-force compensation will not be easy. Such measures are difficult to track and apply. However, salespeople usually do what they are rewarded for doing. Sales compensation plans can help to motivate salespeople to build real relationships between customers and the company, increasing the value of each customer to the company.

Source: Adapted from Don Peppers and Martha Rogers, "The Money Trap," *Sales & Marketing Management*, May 1997, pp. 58–60.

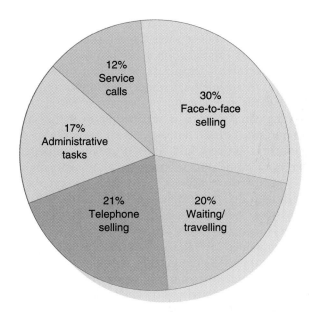

FIGURE 16-2
How salespeople spend their time

Source: Dartnell Corporation; 27th Survey of Sales Force Compensation. © 1992; Dartnell Corporation

Figure 16-2 shows how salespeople spend their time. On average, actual face-to-face selling time accounts for only 30 percent of total working time! If selling time could be raised from 30 percent to 40 percent, this would be a 33 percent increase in the time spent selling. Companies always are looking for ways to save time—using phones instead of travelling, simplifying record-keeping forms, finding better call and routing plans, and supplying more and better customer information.

Many firms have adopted sales-force automation systems that computerize sales-force operations for more efficient order-entry transactions, improved customer service, and better salesperson decision-making. One recent study of 100 large companies found that 48 percent are "actively pursuing" sales-force automation, while another 34 percent are planning or considering it. In another study, 70 percent of companies reported that their sales reps now carry notebook computers.[26] Salespeople use computers to profile customers and prospects, analyse and forecast sales, manage accounts, schedule sales calls, enter orders, check inventories and order status, prepare sales and expense reports, process correspondence, and carry out many other activities. Sales-force automation not only lowers sales-force costs and improves productivity, but it also improves the quality of sales management decisions. Here is an example of successful sales-force automation:[27]

Owens-Corning recently put its sales force on line with FAST—its newly developed Field Automation Sales Team system. This system provides Owens-Corning

Owens Corning
www.owenscorning.com/

Sales quotas
Standards set for salespeople, stating the amount they should sell and how sales should be divided among the company's products.

Sales-force incentives: Many companies award cash, merchandise, trips, or other gifts as incentives for outstanding sales performance.

salespeople with a constant supply of information about their company and the people they're dealing with. Using laptop computers, each salesperson can access three types of programs. First, FAST gives them a set of generic tools, with everything from word processing to fax transmission to creating presentations on-line. Second, it provides product information—tech bulletins, customer specifications, pricing information, and other data that can help close a sale. Finally, it offers up a wealth of customer information—buying history, types of products ordered, and preferred payment terms. Reps previously stored such information in loose-leaf books, calendars, and account cards. FAST makes working directly with customers easier than ever. Salespeople can prime themselves on backgrounds of clients; call up pre-written sales letters; transmit orders and resolve customer-service issues on the spot during customer calls; and have samples, pamphlets, brochures, and other materials sent to clients with a few keystrokes.

Perhaps the fastest-growing sales-force technology tool is the Internet. In a recent survey by Dartnell Corporation of 1000 salespeople, nearly 20 percent reported using the Internet regularly in their daily selling activities. The most common uses include gathering competitive information, monitoring customer Web sites, and researching industries and specific customers. More than half of those not yet online reported that they soon will be. As more and more companies provide their salespeople with web access, experts expect explosive growth in sales-force Internet usage.[28]

Motivating Salespeople

Some salespeople will do their best without any special urging from management. To them, selling may be the most fascinating job in the world. But selling can also be frustrating. Salespeople often work alone, and they must sometimes travel away from home. They may face aggressive, competing salespeople and difficult customers. They sometimes lack the authority to do what is needed to win a sale and may thus lose large orders they have worked hard to obtain. Therefore, salespeople often need special encouragement to do their best.

Management can boost sales-force morale and performance through its *organizational climate, sales quotas,* and *positive incentives.* Organizational climate describes the feeling that salespeople have about their opportunities, value, and rewards for a good performance within the company. Some companies treat salespeople as if they are not very important. Other companies treat their salespeople as their prime movers and allow virtually unlimited opportunity for income and promotion. Not surprisingly, a company's attitude toward its salespeople affects their behaviour. If they are held in low esteem, there is high turnover and poor performance. If they are held in high esteem, there is less turnover and higher performance.

Many companies set **sales quotas** for their salespeople—standards stating the amount they should sell and how sales should be divided among the company's products. Compensation often is related to how well salespeople meet their quotas. Sales quotas are set at the time the annual marketing plan is developed. The company first decides on a sales forecast that is reasonably achievable. Based on this forecast, management plans production, work-force size, and financial needs. It then sets sales quotas for its regions and territories. Generally, sales quotas are set higher than the sales forecast to encourage sales managers and salespeople to give their best effort. If they fail to make their quotas, the company may still make its sales forecast.

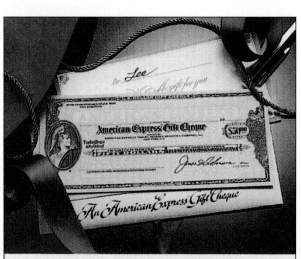

Motivate your sales force by showing them there's gold at the end of the rainbow.

All salespeople are motivated by money. But that's not necessarily the best way to reward them for a job well done. After all, once they put that cash in their wallets, it will probably be spent on everyday bills and groceries.

That's why there's no better way to reward a sales force than with the American Express® Gift Cheque. It's every bit as flexible as cash. But it's more valuable, because it encourages people to go out and get something they truly want. And that makes it a more memorable incentive.

American Express Gift Cheques are also

easy to order and administer. They can be purchased in bulk at special corporate rates and delivered right to you. Or we can help you design a direct fulfillment program, custom-tailored to fit your company's needs.

So when it's time for a sales push, let your sales force know it's also a golden opportunity for them. With the American Express Gift Cheque.

For more information about American Express Gift Cheques and how to get them, call 1-800-777-7337.

Gift Cheques

Companies also use several incentives to increase sales force effort. *Sales meetings* provide social occasions, breaks from routine, chances to meet and talk with "company brass," and opportunities to air feelings and to identify with a larger group. Companies also sponsor *sales contests* to spur the sales force to make a selling effort above what would normally be expected. Other incentives include honours, merchandise and cash awards, trips, and profit-sharing plans. Pierre Généreux, of St-Jean de Matha, won a continent-wide sales contest at the annual Ski-Doo dealers' convention, in a unique manner. He made a presentation in French to several hundred American and English-Canadian colleagues, none of whom understood anything he said. Généreux, who is unilingual Francophone, used a combination of showmanship, authoritative tone, and passion to "bring the heart out" of his product. His "romancing of the machine" was so convincing that he won the "best salesperson" competition.[29]

EVALUATING SALESPEOPLE

We have thus far described how management communicates what salespeople should be doing and how it motivates them to do it. This process requires good feedback. And good feedback means getting regular information from salespeople to evaluate their performance.

Sources of Information

Management gets information about its salespeople in several ways. The most important source is the *sales report*. Additional information comes from personal observation, customers' letters and complaints, customer surveys, and discussions with other salespeople.

Sales reports are divided into plans for future activities and summaries of completed activities. The best example of the plan for future activities is the *work plan* that salespeople submit a week or month in advance. The work plan describes intended calls and routing. From this report, the sales force plans and schedules activities. It also informs management of the salespeople's whereabouts and provides a basis for comparing plans and performance. Salespeople can then be evaluated on their ability to "plan their work and work their plan." Sometimes, managers contact individual salespeople to suggest improvements in work plans.

Companies also are beginning to require their salespeople to draft *annual territory marketing plans* in which they outline their plans for building new accounts and increasing sales from existing accounts. Formats vary greatly—some ask for general ideas on territory development; others ask for detailed sales and profit estimates. Such reports cast salespeople as territory marketing managers. Sales managers study these territory plans, make suggestions, and use the plans to develop sales quotas.

Salespeople write up their completed activities on *call reports*. Call reports keep sales management informed of the salesperson's activities, show what is happening with each customer's account, and provide information that might be useful in later calls. Salespeople also submit *expense reports* for which they are partly or wholly repaid. Some companies also ask for reports on new business, lost business, and local business and economic conditions.

These reports supply the raw data from which sales management can evaluate sales-force performance. Are salespeople making too few calls per day? Are they spending too much time per call? Are they spending too much money on entertainment? Are they closing enough orders per hundred calls? Are they finding enough new customers and holding onto enough old customers?

Formal Evaluation of Performance

Using sales-force reports and other information, sales management formally evaluates members of the sales force. Formal evaluation produces four benefits.

First, management must develop and communicate clear standards for judging performance. Second, management must gather well-rounded information about each salesperson. Third, salespeople receive constructive feedback that helps them to improve future performance. Finally, salespeople are motivated to perform well because they know they will have to sit down with the sales manager and explain their performance.

COMPARING SALESPEOPLE'S PERFORMANCE.   One type of evaluation compares and ranks the sales performance of different salespeople. Such comparisons can be misleading, however. Salespeople may perform differently because of differences in territory potential, workload, level of competition, company promotion effort, and other factors. Furthermore, sales are not usually the best indicator of achievement. Management should be more interested in how much each salesperson contributes to net profits—a concern that requires looking at each salesperson's sales mix and expenses.

COMPARING CURRENT SALES WITH PAST SALES.   A second type of evaluation is to compare a salesperson's current performance with past performance. Such a comparison should directly indicate the person's progress. Table 16-2 provides an example.

The sales manager can learn many things about Chris Bennett from this table. Bennett's total sales increased every year (line 3). This does not necessarily mean that Bennett is doing a better job. The product breakdown shows that Bennett has been able to push the sales of product B further than those of product A (lines 1 and 2). According to the quotas for the two products (lines 4 and 5), the success in increasing product B sales may be at the expense of product A sales. According to gross profits (lines 6 and 7), the company earns twice as much gross profit (as a ratio to sales) on A as it does on B. Bennett may be pushing the higher-volume, lower-margin product at the expense of the more profitable product. Although Bennett increased total sales by $1100 between 1992 and 1993 (line 3), the gross profits on these total sales actually decreased by $580 (line 8).

TABLE 16-2   *Evaluating Salespeople's Performance*

Territory: Midland	Salesperson: Chris Bennett			
	1992	1993	1994	1995
1. Net sales product A	$251 300	$253 200	$270 000	$263 100
2. Net sales product B	$423 200	$439 200	$553 900	$561 900
3. Net sales total	$674 500	$692 400	$823 900	$825 000
4. Percent of quota product A	95.6	92.0	88.0	84.7
5. Percent of quota product B	120.4	122.3	134.9	130.8
6. Gross profits product A	$ 50 260	$ 50 640	$ 54 000	$ 52 620
7. Gross profits product B	$ 42 320	$ 43 920	$ 53 390	$ 56 190
8. Gross profits total	$ 92 580	$ 94 560	$109 390	$108 810
9. Sales expense	$ 10 200	$ 11 100	$ 11 600	$ 13 200
10. Sales expense to total sales (%)	1.5	1.6	1.4	1.6
11. Number of calls	1675	1700	1680	1660
12. Cost per call	$ 6.09	$ 6.53	$ 6.90	$ 7.95
13. Average number of customers	320	324	328	334
14. Number of new customers	13	14	15	20
15. Number of lost customers	8	10	11	14
16. Average sales per customer	$ 2108	$ 2137	$ 2512	$ 2470
17. Average gross profit per customer	$ 289	$ 292	$ 334	$ 326

Sales expense (line 9) shows a steady increase, although total expense as a percentage of total sales seems to be under control (line 10). The upward trend in Bennett's total dollar expenses does not seem to be explained by any increase in the number of calls (line 11), although it may be related to success in acquiring new customers (line 14). However, there is a possibility that in prospecting for new customers, Bennett is neglecting present customers, as indicated by an upward trend in the annual number of lost customers (line 15).

The last two lines on the table show the level and trend in Bennett's sales and gross profits per customer. These figures become more meaningful when they are compared with overall company averages. If Chris Bennett's average gross profit per customer is lower than the company's average, Chris may be concentrating on the wrong customers or may not be spending enough time with each customer. Looking back at the annual number of calls (line 11), Bennett may be making fewer calls than the average salesperson. If distances in the territory are not much different, this may mean Chris is not putting in a full workday, is poor at planning routing or minimizing waiting time, or spends too much time with certain accounts.

QUALITATIVE EVALUATION OF SALESPEOPLE. A *qualitative evaluation* usually examines a salesperson's knowledge of the company, products, customers, competitors, territory, and tasks. Personal traits—manner, appearance, speech, and temperament—can be rated. The sales manager also can review any problems in motivation or compliance. Each company must decide what would be most useful to know. It should communicate these criteria to salespeople so that they understand how their performance is evaluated and can make an effort to improve it.

PRINCIPLES OF PERSONAL SELLING

We now turn from designing and managing a sales force to the actual personal selling process. Personal selling is an ancient art that has spawned a large literature and many principles. Effective salespeople operate on more than just instinct—they are highly trained in methods of territory analysis and customer management.

THE PERSONAL SELLING PROCESS

Companies spend hundreds of millions of dollars on seminars, books, cassettes, and other materials to teach salespeople the "art" of selling. Millions of books on selling are purchased every year, with tantalizing titles such as *How to Sell Anything to Anybody* and *Winning Through Intimidation*. One of the most popular and enduring books on selling is Dale Carnegie's *How to Win Friends and Influence People*.

Most companies take a *customer-oriented approach* to personal selling. They train salespeople to identify customer needs and to find solutions. This approach assumes that customer needs provide sales opportunities, that customers appreciate good suggestions, and that customers will be loyal to salespeople who have their long-term interests at heart. One recent survey found that purchasing agents appreciate salespeople who understand their needs and meet them. As one purchasing agent states:

> My *expectation* of salespeople is that they've done their homework, uncovered some of our needs, probed to uncover other needs, and presented convincing arguments of mutual benefits for both organizations. . . . [The problem is that] I don't always see that.[30]

The problem-solver salesperson fits better with the marketing concept than does the hard-sell salesperson. The qualities that purchasing agents *dislike most* in salespeople included being pushy, late, and unprepared or disorganized. The qualities they *value most* included honesty, dependability, thoroughness, and follow-through.

FIGURE 16-3 *Major steps in effective selling*

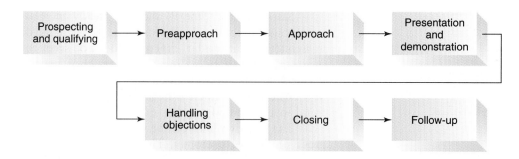

STEPS IN THE SELLING PROCESS

Selling process
The steps that the salesperson follows when selling, which include prospecting and qualifying, pre-approach, approach, presentation and demonstration, handling objections, closing, and follow-up.

Most training programs view the **selling process** as consisting of several steps that the salesperson must master (see Figure 16-3). These steps focus on the goal of getting new customers and obtaining orders from them. However, most salespeople spend much of their time maintaining existing accounts and building long-term customer *relationships*. We discuss the relationship aspect of the personal selling process in the final section of the chapter.

Prospecting and Qualifying

Prospecting
The step in the selling process in which the salesperson identifies qualified potential customers.

The first step in the selling process is **prospecting**—identifying qualified potential customers. The salesperson often must approach many prospects to get just a few sales. In the insurance industry, for example, only one out of nine prospects becomes a customer. In the computer business, 125 phone calls result in 25 interviews leading to five demonstrations and one sale.[31] Although the company supplies some leads, salespeople need skill in finding their own. They can ask current customers for the names of prospects. They can build referral sources, such as suppliers, dealers, non-competing salespeople, and bankers. They can join organizations to which prospects belong or can engage in speaking and writing activities that will draw attention. They can search for names in newspapers or directories and use the telephone and mail to track down leads. Or they can drop in unannounced on various offices (a practice known as "cold calling").

Salespeople need to know how to *qualify* leads—that is, how to identify the good ones and screen out the poor ones. Prospects can be qualified by evaluating their financial ability, volume of business, special needs, location, and possibilities for growth.

Preapproach

Preapproach
The step in the selling process in which the salesperson learns as much as possible about a prospective customer before making a sales call.

Before calling on a prospect, the salesperson should learn as much as possible about the organization (what it needs, who is involved in the buying) and its buyers (their characteristics and buying styles). This step is known as the **preapproach.** The salesperson can consult standard sources (*Scott's Directory, Moody's, Standard & Poor's, Dun & Bradstreet*), acquaintances, and others to learn about the company. The salesperson should set *call objectives*, which may be to qualify the prospect, to gather information, or to make an immediate sale. Another task is to decide on the best approach, which might be a personal visit, a phone call, or a letter. The best timing should be considered carefully because many prospects are busiest at certain times. Finally, the salesperson should consider an overall sales strategy for the account.

Approach

Approach
The step in the selling process in which the salesperson meets and greets the buyer to get the relationship off to a good start.

During the **approach** step, the salesperson should know how to meet and greet the buyer and to get the relationship off to a good start. This step involves the salesperson's appearance, opening lines, and the follow-up remarks. The opening lines should be positive, such as "Mr. Johnson, I am Chris Bennett from the All-

In the sales presentation, the salesperson tells the product story to the buyers.

tech Company. My company and I appreciate your willingness to see me. I will do my best to make this visit profitable and worthwhile for you and your company." This opening might be followed by some key questions to learn more about the customer's needs or the showing of a display or sample to attract the buyer's attention and curiosity.

Presentation and Demonstration

During the **presentation** step of the selling process, the salesperson tells the product "story" to the buyer, showing how the product will make or save money. The salesperson describes the product features but concentrates on presenting customer benefits. Using a *need-satisfaction approach,* the salesperson starts with a search for the customer's needs by getting the customer to do most of the talking. This approach calls for good listening and problem-solving skills.[32]

Sales presentations can be improved with demonstration aids, such as booklets, flip charts, slides, videotapes or videodiscs, and product samples. If buyers can see or handle the product, they will better remember its features and benefits.

Presentation
The step in the selling process in which the salesperson tells the product "story" to the buyer, showing how the product will make or save money for the buyer.

Handling objections
The step in the selling process in which the salesperson seeks out, clarifies, and overcomes customer objections to buying.

Closing
The step in the selling process in which the salesperson asks the customer for an order.

Handling Objections

Customers almost always have objections during the presentation or when asked to place an order. The problem can be either logical or psychological, and objections are often unspoken. In **handling objections,** the salesperson should use a positive approach, seek out hidden objections, ask the buyer to clarify any objections, take objections as opportunities to provide more information, and turn the objections into reasons for buying. Every salesperson needs training in the skills of handling objections.

Closing

After handling the prospect's objections, the salesperson now tries to close the sale. Some salespeople do not get around to **closing** or do not handle it well. They may lack confidence, feel guilty about asking for the order, or fail to recognize the right moment to close the sale. Salespeople should know how to recognize closing signals from the buyer, including physical actions, comments, and questions. For example, the customer might sit forward and nod approvingly or ask about prices and credit terms. Salespeople can use one of several closing techniques. They can ask for the order, review points of agreement, offer to help write up the order, ask whether the buyer wants this model or that one, or note that the buyer will lose out if the order is not placed now. The salesperson may offer the buyer special reasons to close, such as a lower price or an extra quantity at no charge.

Follow-up
The last step in the selling process in which the salesperson follows up after the sale to ensure customer satisfaction and repeat business.

Follow-Up

The last step in the selling process—**follow-up**—is necessary if the salesperson wants to ensure customer satisfaction and repeat business. Right after closing, the salesperson should complete any details on delivery time, purchase terms, and other matters. The salesperson then should schedule a follow-up call when the initial order is received to ensure that there is proper installation, instruction, and servicing. This visit would reveal any problems, assure the buyer of the salesperson's interest, and reduce any buyer concerns that might have arisen since the sale.

GREAT SALESPEOPLE: DRIVE, DISCIPLINE, AND RELATIONSHIP-BUILDING SKILLS

What sets great salespeople apart from all the rest? What separates the masters from the merely mediocre? In an effort to profile top sales performers, Gallup Management Consulting, a division of the well-known Gallup polling organization, has interviewed as many as a half million salespeople. Its research suggests that the best salespeople possess four key talents: intrinsic motivation, disciplined work style, the ability to close a sale, and, perhaps most importantly, the ability to build relationships with customers.

Intrinsic Motivation

"Different things drive different people—pride, happiness, money, you name it," says one expert. "But all great salespeople have one thing in common: an unrelenting drive to excel." This strong, internal drive can be shaped and molded, but it can't be taught. The source of the motivation varies—some are driven by money, some by hunger for recognition, some by a yearning to build relationships. The Gallup research revealed four general personality types, all high performers, but each with different sources of motivation. *Competitors* are people who not only want to win, but crave the satisfaction of beating specific rivals—other companies *and* their fellow salespeople. They'll come right out and say to a colleague, "With all due respect, I know you're salesperson of the year, but I'm going after your title." The *ego-driven* are salespeople who just want to experience the glory of winning. They want to be recognized as being the best, regardless of the competition. *Achievers* are a rare breed who are almost completely self-motivated. They like accomplishment, and routinely set goals that are higher than what is expected of them. They often make the best sales managers because they don't mind seeing other people succeed, as long as the

organization's goals are met. Finally, *service-oriented* salespeople are those whose strength lies in their ability to build and cultivate relationships. They are generous, caring, and empathetic. "These people are golden," says the national training manager of Minolta Corporation's business equipment division. "We need salespeople who will take the time to follow up on the 10 questions a customer might have, salespeople who love to stay in touch."

No one is purely a competitor, an achiever, ego-driven, or service-driven. There's at least some of each in most top performers. "A *competitor* with a strong sense of *service* will probably bring in a lot of business, while doing a great job of taking care of customers," observes the managing director of the Gallup Management Consulting Group. "Who could ask for anything more?"

Disciplined Work Style

Whatever their motivation, if salespeople aren't organized and focussed, and if they don't work hard, they can't meet the ever-increasing demands that customers are making these days. Great salespeople are tenacious about laying out detailed, organized plans, then following through in a timely, disciplined way. There's no magic here, just solid organization and hard work. "Our best sales reps never let loose ends dangle," says the president of a small business equipment firm. "If they say they're going to make a follow-up call on a customer in six months, you can be sure that they'll be on the doorstep in six months." Top sellers rely on hard work, not luck or gimmicks. "Some people says it's all technique or luck," notes one sales trainer. "But luck happens to the best salespeople when they get up early, work late, stay up till two in the morning working on a proposal, or keep making calls when everyone is leaving at the end of the day."

The Ability to Close the Sale

Other skills mean little if a seller can't ask for the sale. No close, no sale. Period. So what makes for a great closer? For one thing, an unyielding persistence, say managers and sales consultants. Claims one, "Great closers are like great athletes. They're not afraid to fail, and they don't give up until they close." Part of what makes the failure rate tolerable for top performers is their deep-seated belief in themselves and what they are selling. Great closers have a high level of self-confidence and believe that they are doing the right thing. And they've got a burning need to make the sale happen—to do whatever it takes within legal and ethical standards to get the business.

The Ability to Build Relationships

Perhaps most important in today's relationship-marketing environment, top salespeople are customer problem-solvers and relationship-builders. They have an instinctive understanding of their customers' needs. Talk to sales executives and they'll describe top performers in these terms: Empathetic. Patient. Caring. Responsive. Good listeners. *Honest.* Top sellers can put themselves on the buyer's side of the desk and see the world through their customers' eyes. Today, customers are looking for business partners, not golf partners. "At the root of it all," says a Dallas sales consultant, "is an integrity of intent. High performers don't just want to be liked, they want to add value." High-performing salespeople, he adds, are "always thinking about the big picture, where the customer's organization is going, and how they can help them get there."

Source: Adapted from Geoffrey Brewer, "Mind Reading: What Drives Top Salespeople to Greatness?" *Sales & Marketing Management,* May 1994, pp. 82–88.

RELATIONSHIP MARKETING

The principles of personal selling as just described are *transaction oriented*—their aim is to help salespeople close a specific sale with a customer. But in many cases,

Relationship marketing
The process of creating, maintaining, and enhancing strong, value-laden relationships with customers and other stakeholders.

the company is not seeking simply a sale: it has targeted a major customer that it would like to win and serve. The company would like to show the customer that it has the capabilities to serve the customer's needs in a superior way over the long haul, in a mutually profitable *relationship*.

Most companies today are moving away from transaction marketing, with its emphasis on making a sale. Instead, they are practising **relationship marketing,** which emphasizes building and maintaining profitable long-term relationships with customers by creating superior customer value and satisfaction. Recognition of the importance of relationship marketing has increased rapidly in the past few years. Companies are realizing that when operating in maturing markets and facing stiffer competition, it costs a lot more to wrest new customers from competitors than to keep current customers.

Today's customers are large and often global. They prefer suppliers who can sell and deliver a coordinated set of products and services to many locations; who can quickly solve problems that arise in their different parts of the nation or world; and who can work closely with customer teams to improve products and processes. For these customers, the sale is only the beginning of the relationship.

Unfortunately, some companies are not set up for these developments. They often sell their products through separate sales forces, each working independently to close sales. Their technical people may not be willing to lend time to educate a customer. Their engineering, design, and manufacturing people may have the attitude that "it's our job to make good products and the salesperson's to sell them to customers." However, companies increasingly are recognizing that winning and keeping accounts requires more than making good products and directing the sales force to close lots of sales. It requires a carefully coordinated, whole-company effort to create value-laden, satisfying relationships with important customers.

Relationship marketing is based on the premise that important accounts need focussed and continuous attention. Studies have shown that the best salespeople are those who are highly motivated and good closers, but more than this, they are customer-problem solvers and relationship builders (see Marketing Highlight 16-3). Good salespeople working with key customers do more than call when they think a customer might be ready to place an order. They also study the account and understand its problems. They call or visit frequently, work with the customer to help solve the customer's problems and improve its business, and take an interest in customers as people.

Summary of Chapter Objectives

Selling is one of the world's oldest professions. People who do the selling are known by a variety of names, including salespeople, sales representatives, account executives, sales consultants, sales engineers, agents, district managers, and marketing representatives. Regardless of their titles, members of the sales force play a key role in modern marketing organizations.

The term salesperson covers a wide spectrum of positions. Salespeople may be order takers, such as the department-store salesperson who stands behind the counter. Or they may be order getters—salespeople engaged in the creative selling of products and services such as appliances, industrial equipment, advertising, or consulting services. Other salespeople perform

missionary selling, in which they are not involved in taking an order but in building goodwill or educating buyers. To be successful in these more creative forms of selling, a company must first build and then manage an effective sales force.

1. **Discuss the role of a company's salespeople in creating value for customers and building customer relationships.**

Most companies use salespeople, and many companies assign them an important role in the marketing mix. For companies selling business products, the firm's salespeople work directly with customers. Often the sales force is the customer's only direct contact with the company and therefore may be viewed by customers as representing the company itself. In contrast, for consumer product companies that sell through intermediaries, consumers usually do not meet salespeople or even know about them. But the sales force works behind the scenes, dealing with wholesalers and retailers to obtain their support and help them become effective in selling the firm's products.

As an element of the marketing mix, the sales force is very effective in achieving certain marketing objectives and carrying out such activities as prospecting, communicating, selling and servicing, and information gathering. But with companies becoming more market-oriented, a marketed-focused sales force also works to produce customer satisfaction and company profit. To accomplish these goals, the sales force needs not only traditional skills but also skills in marketing analysis and planning.

2. **Identify the six major sales-force management steps.**

The high cost of the sales force calls for an effective sales management process consisting of six steps: designing sales-force strategy and structure; recruiting and selecting; training; compensating; supervising; and evaluating salespeople.

3. **Explain how companies design sales-force strategy and structure.**

In designing a sales force, sales management must address issues such as what type of sales-force structure will work best (territorial, product, customer, pyramid, or complex structure); how large the sales force should be; who will be involved in the selling effort and how its various sales and sales-support people will work together (inside or outside sales forces and team selling).

4. **Explain how companies recruit, select, and train salespeople.**

To hold down the high costs of hiring the wrong people, salespeople must be recruited and selected carefully. In recruiting salespeople, a company may look to job duties and the characteristics of its most successful salespeople to suggest the traits it wants in its sales force and then look for

applicants through recommendations of current salespeople, employment agencies, classified ads and by contracting university students. In the selection process, the procedure can vary from a single informal interview to lengthy testing and interviewing. Once the selection process is complete, training programs familiarize new salespeople not only with the art of selling, but also with the company's history, its products and policies, and the characteristics of its market and competitors.

5. **Describe how companies compensate and supervise salespeople, and how they evaluate sales-force effectiveness.**

The sales-force compensation system helps to reward, motivate, and direct salespeople. In compensating salespeople, companies try to offer an appealing compensation plan that is typically close to the going rate for the type of sales job and needed skills. In addition to compensation, all salespeople need supervision, and many need continuous encouragement because they must make many decisions and face many frustrations. Furthermore, the company must evaluate their performance periodically to help them do a better job. In evaluating salespeople the company relies on receiving regular information gathered through sales reports, personal observations, customers' letters and complaints, customer surveys, and conversations with other salespeople.

6. **Discuss the personal selling process, distinguishing between transaction-oriented marketing and relationship marketing.**

The art of selling involves a seven-step selling process: prospecting and qualifying; preapproach; approach; presentation and demonstration; handling objections; closing; and follow-up. These steps help marketers to close a specific sale and as such are transaction oriented. However, a seller's dealings with customers should be guided by the larger concept of relationship marketing. The company's sales force should help to orchestrate a whole-company effort to develop profitable long-term relationships with key customers based on superior customer value and satisfaction.

Key Terms

Approach *(p. 554)*
Closing *(p. 555)*
Complex sales-force structure
   (p. 541)
Customer sales-force structure
   (p. 540)
Follow-up *(p. 555)*
Handling objections *(p. 555)*
Inside sales force *(p. 542)*

Outside sales force *(p. 542)*
Preapproach *(p. 554)*
Presentation *(p. 555)*
Product sales-force structure
   (p. 540)
Prospecting *(p. 554)*
Pyramid sales-force structure
   (p. 541)
Relationship marketing *(p. 557)*

Sales force management *(p. 539)*
Salesperson *(p. 538)*
Sales quotas *(p. 550)*
Selling process *(p. 554)*
Team selling *(p. 543)*
Telemarketing *(p. 542)*
Territorial sales-force structure
   (p. 540)
Workload approach *(p. 542)*

Discussing the Issues

1. Grocery stores require their suppliers' salespeople not only to sell but also to serve as aisle clerks. These salespeople must restock shelves, build displays, and set up point-of-purchase material. Decide whether it is important for a manufacturer to meet these demands. Are there creative ways to free the salesperson's time for more productive uses?

2. Explain why so many sales-force compensation plans combine salary with bonus or commission. What are the advantages and disadvantages of using bonuses as incentives, rather than using commissions?

3. More than 60 pyramid companies currently operate in Canada, selling everything from vitamins to cleaning products. Many people are attracted to these organizations because there are no costs to join, they have no educational requirements, and no sales experience is necessary. As pyramid selling becomes more competitive, what will these types of firms have to do to be successful? What training methods would work best for these types of organizations? If they are go-

ing to invest in training, what can pyramid organizations do to reduce turnover, which currently averages 75 percent in most of these organizations?

4. Many analysts predict that firms will begin to merge their sales and marketing departments. Traditionally, marketing departments dealt with issues relating to the behaviour of end customers while salespeople developed relationships with distributors and retailers. Why do you think firms are moving in this direction? What problems will they have implementing this tactic?

5. The surest way to become a sales-force manager is to be an outstanding salesperson. Name some advantages and disadvantages of promoting top salespeople to management positions. Why might an outstanding salesperson refuse to be promoted?

6. Good salespeople are familiar with their competitors' products as well as their own. Analyse what you would do if your company expected you to sell a product that you thought was inferior to the competition's. Why?

Applying the Concepts

1. Experience a sales pitch. Go to a retailer. Find out whether the salespeople are likely to be working on commission, such as a car dealership, or salary such as an appliance and electronics dealer. (a) Rate your salesperson. Was their approach, presentation, and demonstration effective? (b) Was the salesperson knowledge-

able, and able to answer your questions in a helpful and believable way? (c) Did you feel the salesperson's expertise added value to the product, or not? (d) Consider your emotional response to the sales pitch. Did you enjoy the experience, or find it hard to endure? Why did you react this way?

2. Rent a video such as *The Tin Men, Wall Street, Used Cars, Cadillac Man, Edward Scissorhands*, or *Glengarry Glen Ross*. These videos all use unflattering portrayals of salespeople. Why do you think the stereotype portrayed in the film has evolved?

What does the film say about the ethics of selling? If you were a recruiter for a sales position, how would you overcome these stereotypes among prospective job candidates at your university?

References

1. Based on William Keenan, Jr., "What's Sales Got To Do With It?" See also Melissa Campanelli, "Eastman Chemical: A Formula For Quality," *Sales & Marketing Management*, October 1994, p. 88; and Kenan, "Plugging Into Your Customers' Needs," *Sales & Marketing Management*, January 1996, pp. 62-66.

2. Mariposa Communications Group, "Special Report: Motivating the Salesforce: Mariposa" four perspectives on life in sales, *Strategy: The Canadian Marketing Report*, August 21, 1995, p. 25.

3. Barbara Canning Brown, "Sales Is Where the Rubber Hits the Road," *Strategy: The Canadian Marketing Report*, May 29, 1995, p. 21.

4. See Bill Kelley, "How to Sell Airplanes, Boeing-Style," *Sales & Marketing Management*, December 9, 1985, pp. 32–34. Also see Dori Jones Yang and Andrea Rothman, "Boeing Cuts Its Altitude as the Clouds Roll In," *Business Week*, February 8, 1993, p. 25.

5. For a comparison of several classifications, see William C. Moncrief III, "Selling Activity and Sales Position Taxonomies for Industrial Sales Forces," *Journal of Marketing Research*, August 1986, pp. 261–270.

6. See Rayna Skolnik, "Campbell Stirs Up Its Sales Force," *Sales & Marketing Management*, April 1986, pp. 56–58.

7. Carolyn Leitch, "IBM Reorganizing Sales Force," *Globe and Mail*, May 7, 1994, p. B3.

8. Geoffrey Brewer, "Love the Ones You're With," *Sales & Marketing Management*, February 1997, pp. 38–45.

9. Kenneth Kidd, "Clothes Encounters," *Report on Business*, October 1996, pp. 58–71.

10. Mark Stevenson, "The Lean, Mean Sales Machine," *Canadian Business*, January 1994, pp. 32-36.

11. Ibid, p. 32.

12. See Rudy Oetting and Geri Gantman, "Dial 'M' for Maximize," *Sales & Marketing Management*, June 1991, pp. 100–106; and "Median Costs Per Call By Industry," *Sales & Marketing Management*, June 28, 1993, p. 65.

13. Mark Stevenson, "The Lean, Mean Sales Machine," *Canadian Business*, January 1994, pp. 34, 36.

14. See Frank V. Cespedes, Stephen X. Doyle, and Robert J. Freedman, "Teamwork for Today's Selling," *Harvard Business Review*, March–April 1989, pp. 44–54, 58; Joseph Conlin, "Teaming Up," *Sales & Marketing Management*, October 1993, pp. 98–104; and Richard C. Whiteley, "Orchestrating Service," *Sales & Marketing Management*, April 1994, pp. 29–30.

15. Mark Stevenson, "The Lean, Mean Sales Machine," *Canadian Business*, January 1994, p. 32.

16. See Perri Capel, "Are Good Salespeople Born or Made?" *American Demographics*, July 1993, pp. 12–13.

17. See George H. Lucas, Jr., A. Parasuraman, Robert A. Davis, and Ben M. Enis, "An Empirical Study of Sales Force Turnover," *Journal of Marketing*, July 1987, pp. 34–59; Lynn G. Coleman, "Sales Force Turnover Has Managers Wondering Why," *Marketing News*, December 4, 1989, p. 6; and Thomas R. Wotruba and Pradeep K. Tyagi, "Met Expectations and Turnover in Direct Selling," *Journal of Marketing*, July 1991, pp. 24–35.

18. See Geoffrey Brewer, "Mind Reading: What Drives Top Salespeople to Greatness?" *Sales & Marketing Management*, May 1994, pp. 82–88.

19. See "To Test or Not to Test," *Sales & Marketing Management*, May 1994, p. 86.

20. Mark De Wolf, "Special Report: Motivating the Salesforce," *Strategy: The Canadian Marketing Report*, August 18, 1997, p. 19.

21. David Chilton, "Special Report: Technology for Marketers: Laptop Has Simplified the Work of the Salesforce," *Strategy: The Canadian Marketing Report*, January 6, 1997, p. 20.

22. See *1993 Sales Manager's Budget Planner, Sales & Marketing Management*, June 28, 1993, p. 72.

23. Christen P. Heide, "All Levels of Sales Reps Post Impressive Earnings," press release, http://www.dartnellcorp.com, May 5, 1997.

24. Geoffrey Brewer, "Brain Power," *Sales & Marketing Management*, May 1997, pp. 39– 48; and Don Peppers and Martha Rogers, "The Money Trap," *Sales & Marketing Management*, May 1997, pp. 58– 60.

25. "Editorial: New Motivational Ideas Reflect New Breed of Rep," *Strategy: The Canadian Marketing Report*, August 21, 1995, p. 14.

26. Thayer C. Taylor, "SFA: The newest orthodoxy," *Sales & Marketing Management*, February 1993, pp. 26–28; Tom Dellecave, Jr., "How do you stack up?" *Sales and Marketing Technology*, December 1996, pp. 34–36; and Ken Dulaney, "The automated sales force," *Marketing Tools*, October 1996, pp. 57–63.

27. Tony Seideman, "Who Needs Managers?" *Sales & Marketing Management*, Part 2, June 1994, pp. 15–17.

28. Christen P. Heide, "Nearly 20 Percent of Salespeople Are Now Online," http://www.dartnellcorp.com, May 5, 1997. Also see Alan Horowitz, "Why, when and

how to implement SFA," *Sales & Marketing Management,* May 1997, pp. 7a–8a.

29. B.J. Del Conte, "Language is No Barrier When it Comes to Sales," *The Financial Post Magazine,* April 1996, p. 14.

30. Derrick C. Schnebelt, "Turning the Tables," *Sales & Marketing Management,* January 1993, pp. 22–23.

31. Vincent L. Zirpoli, "You Can't 'Control' the Prospect, So Manage the Presale Activities to Increase Performance," *Marketing News,* March 16, 1984, p. 1.

32. Thayer C. Taylor, "Anatomy of a Star Salesperson," *Sales & Marketing Management,* May 1986, p. 50. Also see Barry J. Farber and Joyce Wycoff, "Relationships: Six Steps to Success," *Sales & Marketing Management,* April 1992, pp. 50–58; and Stephen B. Castleberry and C. David Shepherd, "Effective Interpersonal Listening and Personal Selling," *Journal of Personal Selling and Sales Management,* Winter 1993, pp. 35–49.

Company Case 16

IBM: RESTRUCTURING THE SALES FORCE

TAKING OVER

In early 1993, IBM's Board of Directors decided the time was right for dramatic action. The once-proud company had seen its sales fall from almost $96 billion in 1990 to $90 billion in 1992. Moreover, in the same period, profits had plunged from $8.2 billion to a loss of $6.89 billion. In April, the Board hired Louis V. Gerstner, Jr., a former McKinsey Company consultant and R. J. Reynolds CEO, to serve as its new Chairman and Chief Executive Officer and to turn the company around.

In July 1993, just three months into his new job, Gerstner announced his first major strategic decision. Gerstner identified IBM's sales force as a key source of the company's problems. Many observers had expected that he would restructure the sales force in his efforts to refocus the company. These observers felt that IBM's sales force was too large and unwieldy and that it was too slow to change to meet changing customer needs. However, Gerstner surprised many people by announcing that he would postpone his decision as to what to do about IBM's sales force.

In an internal memo to his 13 top managers, Gerstner concluded that, "It is clear to me that our current [marketing] organization doesn't always function well, *i.e.,* doesn't always permit us to serve our customer in the most efficient and effective way." However, he noted, "I don't want to undertake a major reorganization of IBM at this time." Gerstner argued that radical reform would pose unacceptable risks to customer loyalty. Therefore, he had decided to try to make IBM's current sales and marketing systems work better.

GETTING INTO TROUBLE

You might wonder how IBM, one of the largest and most successful companies in the world, had gotten into

such a fix. In early 1994, in his introduction to the *1993 IBM Annual Report,* Gerstner wrote that IBM's problems resulted from the company's failure to keep pace with rapid industry change. He also argued that IBM had been too bureaucratic and too preoccupied with its own view of the world. He suggested that the company had been too slow to take new products to market and had missed the higher profit margins that are typical of the computer industry early in a product's life cycle.

Although bureaucracy and slowness were significant problems, IBM's customers and industry observers identified IBM's preoccupation with its own view of the world as the real problem. They argued that the company stopped listening to its customers. It peddled mainframe computers to customers who wanted midrange systems and personal computers. It pushed products when customers wanted solutions. One former salesperson noted that, "We were so well trained, we could sell anything, good or bad. So, under quota pressures, we sold systems that our customers didn't need, didn't want, and couldn't afford."

IBM had designed its sales compensation system to encourage and reward selling mainframe systems. Another former salesperson observed that, "You could sell a PC and get a pat on the back. You could sell a midrange system and get a lot of dollars. But when you sold a mainframe, you would walk on water. You were a hero."

The salespeople also often insisted that customers buy all of their products from IBM and became indignant when a customer used another vendor. Also, the salespeople were often inflexible. They made "one-size-fits-all" presentations using canned, off-the-shelf marketing programs. One customer added, "They wouldn't tailor their programs to what you needed as a customer." It was ". . . this is our canned package. We know this works. Trust us."

TURNING THINGS AROUND

Despite these problems, Gerstner's decision not to make strategic changes to the 40 000-person sales force meant that he would continue to carry out changes that former CEO John Akers had begun. Beginning in 1991, Akers had restructured the sales force using a geographic focus. Senior managers acted as account executives for the top IBM clients in their regions. These account executives managed the full breadth of client relationships including understanding the customer's company and its industry. These managers could call on a pool of regional product specialists and service representatives to satisfy customer needs. The account executives reported to branch managers who reported to "trading area" managers who ultimately reported to regional managers. In foreign countries, a country manager had full control over that country's sales force.

Some executives at IBM Canada are worried that changes to the sales-force structure will diminish their power and authority. Under the new sales-force plan, sales personnel will be organized by industry rather than geography or products. Industry sectors include banking, insurance, manufacturing, petroleum, transportation, health care, communications, distribution, education, government, travel, and utilities. What worries Canadian managers is that its 1000-plus commissioned sales staff will report to industry-sector leaders based in the United States. Canadian reps, however, will also report to one of five regional managers based in Western Canada, Quebec or Toronto. Those who support the plan note that the restructuring will gradually allow salespeople to make more decisions.

Akers' approach continued IBM's traditional focus on presenting "one face to the customer." The account executive structure allowed the customer to deal with one IBM interface rather than dealing with salespeople from each of IBM's product and service areas. Gerstner's reluctance to make changes probably resulted from a meeting where the company's top 200 customers told him they did not want to be confused by 20 different IBM salespeople calling on them. However, it was also hard for any IBM salesperson to be familiar with the wide range of products and services the company offered. One manager pointed out that, "We have an awfully broad sales manual. . . .You can't be a generalist."

Nevertheless, IBM had already begun to tinker with its sales approach. In response to increasing competition, declining sales, and changing corporate buying habits, the company had already developed "fighter pilots." These salespeople were specialists who tried to increase sales by pushing neglected products. Further, Akers had allowed some product lines, like the personal computer and printer divisions, to develop their own sales forces. He had also allowed some experimentation with salespeople who specialized in certain industries.

As for compensating the sales force, IBM adjusted the compensation plan each January. The company modified the plan to promote sales of certain products or increase market share in targeted areas. One analyst noted that it was not unusual for a branch manager to have 240 separate measurements because different product groups would set quotas to encourage salespeople to sell their offerings. Until 1993, only six percent of a salesperson's salary above the base salary (the bulk of a person's pay) reflected the profitability of his or her sales. In 1993, the company increased the portion based on profitability to 20 percent.

PURSUING THE IDEAL SALES FORCE

Many industry observers argued that Gerstner's decision to forego any major sales-force changes merely reflected his desire to continue to study the problem. One consultant noted that Gerstner wanted to wait until the dust settled from personnel cutbacks that had reduced IBM's employment from 344 000 to 256 000 between 1991 and 1993. Microsoft Chairman William Gates suggested that although IBM was known for its unified sales force, ". . . I think it's inevitable that they'll get rid of it."

The question was: What sales-force strategy should IBM use to revive its sagging sales and profits while satisfying customer and employee requirements?

QUESTIONS

1. What problems do you see in IBM's sales force's objectives, strategy, structure, and compensation?

2. Which industry sectors do you believe require the most local or Canadian knowledge on the part of sales personnel? Do you believe the move to make salespeople industry specialists is a wise one? Why or why not?

3. What objectives would you set for IBM's sales force, and what strategy, structure, and compensation plan would you establish to accomplish your objectives? Identify the tradeoffs involved as you make each of these decisions.

4. Given your recommendations, how would you recruit, train, supervise, motivate, and evaluate IBM's sales force?

Sources: Laurie Hays, "IBM's Gerstner Holds Back from Sales Force Shake-Up," *Wall Street Journal*, July 7, 1993, p. B1. Used with permission of *Wall Street Journal*. Also see Geoffrey Brewer, "Abort, Retry, Fail?" *Sales and Marketing Management*, October 1993, pp. 80–86; and IBM Corporation, *1993 Annual Report*; Carolyn Leitch, "IBM Reorganizing Sales Force," *Globe and Mail*, May 7, 1994, p. B3.

Video Case 16

CANADA'S HOTTEST HOME SELLER

Real estate agent Craig Procter has become ReMax's top seller in Canada and changed the face of the real estate business in the process. In a field where most agents sell 10 or 20 homes each year, Procter sells over 200.

His secret? Procter specializes in sales promotion—but instead of promoting his company, he's become an expert at promoting himself. All of his moves are carefully planned to build name recognition, loyalty, and publicity, from getting his name emblazoned on everything from bus benches to milk jugs, to paying his clients' long-distance telephone bill to call Toronto on his special phone line, to offering to buy your house with cash if you want to buy a different home from him.

Just 32 years old, the seven-year real estate veteran now commands $1000 a day from people who want the privilege of following him around to learn his secrets.

But putting those secrets to use is not cheap; Procter may gross over $1.2 million a year, but almost a quarter of that is spent on promotions, and after other expenses and taxes, his net is only about $150 000. And if he wants to keep that up, Procter knows he cannot sit

back for an instant. His competition is hot on his heels, imitating his marketing gimmicks and forcing Procter to continually come up with new ideas to keep competitors from catching up with him.

QUESTIONS:

1. Describe the marketing tactics used by Procter. How effective are they?

2. Do you think he is spending too much on promotions? Why or why not?

3. Why do other salespeople sell under the Procter name instead of using his strategy themselves? Has Procter turned his name into a brand name?

4. What makes Procter a good salesperson?

5. Using the sales steps described in the chapter, how does Procter assign the various tasks in the sales process?

Source: This case was prepared by Kim Coghill and is based on "Top Sellers," *Venture*, (May 21, 1995).

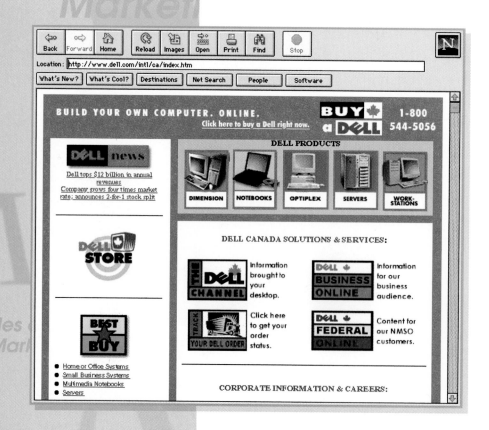

Principles of
Marketing

rinciples of
Marketi

ciples
Marl

C H A P T E R 17

DIRECT AND
ONLINE MARKETING

When 19-year-old Michael Dell began selling personal computers out of his university dorm room in 1984, few would have bet on his chances for success. In those days, most computer makers sold their PCs through an extensive network of all-powerful distributors and resellers. Even as the fledgling Dell Computer Corporation began to grow, competitors and industry insiders scoffed at the concept of mail-order computer marketing. PC buyers, they contended, needed the kind of advice and hand-holding that only full-service channels could provide. Mail-order PC sales, like mail-order clothing, would never amount to more than 15 percent of the market.

Yet young Michael Dell has proved the skeptics wrong. In little more than a decade, he has turned his dorm-room mail-order business into a burgeoning, $11-billion computer empire. Dell Computer is now the world's largest direct marketer of computer systems and the world's fastest-growing computer manufacturer. Dell Canada is the third bestselling computer maker in the country. Last year, U.S. unit sales jumped 71 percent, five times the industry average. Profits skyrocketed 91 percent and the company's stock price tripled. Direct buyers now account for nearly a third of all PC sales and Dell's once-skeptical competitors are now scrambling to build their own direct marketing systems.

What's the secret to Dell's stunning success? Dell's direct marketing approach delivers greater customer value through an unbeatable combination of product customization, low prices, fast delivery, and award-winning customer service. A customer can talk by phone with a Dell representative on Monday morning; order a fully customized, state-of-the-art PC to suit his or her special needs; and have the machine delivered to his or her doorstep by Wednesday—all at a price that's 10 percent to 15 percent below competitors' prices. Dell backs its products with high-quality service and support. As a result, Dell consistently ranks among the industry leaders in product reliability and service, and its customers are routinely among the industry's most satisfied.

OBJECTIVES

When you finish this chapter, you should be able to

1. Discuss the benefits of direct marketing to customers and companies and the trends fuelling its rapid growth.

2. Define a customer database and list the four ways that companies use databases in direct marketing.

3. Identify the major forms of direct marketing.

4. Compare the two types of online marketing channels and explain the effect of the Internet on electronic commerce.

5. Identify the benefits of online marketing to consumers and marketers and the four ways that marketers can conduct online marketing.

6. Discuss the public policy and ethical issues facing direct marketers.

Dell customers receive exactly the machines they need. Michael Dell's initial idea was to serve individual buyers by allowing them to customize machines with the special features they wanted at low prices. However, this one-to-one approach also appeals strongly to corporate buyers, because Dell can so easily preconfigure each computer to precise requirements. Dell routinely preloads machines with a company's own software and even undertakes such tedious tasks as pasting inventory tags on each machine so that computers can be delivered directly to an employee's desk. As a result, about 90 percent of Dell's sales now come from large corporate, government, and educational buyers.

Direct selling results in more efficient selling and lower costs, which translate into lower prices for customers. Because Dell builds machines to order, the company carries barely any inventory. Dealing one-to-one with customers helps the company to react immediately to shifts in demand, so Dell doesn't get stuck with PCs no one wants. Finally, by selling directly, Dell has no dealers to pay off. As a result, on average, Dell's costs are 12 percent lower than those of Compaq, its leading PC competitor.

Dell knows that time is money, and the company is obsessed with "speed." For example, Dell has long been a model of just-in-time manufacturing and efficient supply-chain management. It has also mastered the intricacies of today's lightning-fast electronic commerce. This combination makes Dell a lean and very fast operator. "Dell calls it 'velocity'—squeezing time out of every step in the process—from the moment an order is taken to collecting the cash. [By selling direct, manufacturing to order, and] tapping credit cards and electronic payment, Dell converts the average sale to cash in less than 24 hours. By contrast, Compaq Computer Corp., which sells primarily through dealers, takes 35 days, and even mail-order rival Gateway 2000 takes 16.4 days." Such blazing speed results in more satisfied customers and still lower costs. For example, customers are often delighted to find their new computers arriving within as few as 36 hours of placing an order. And because Dell doesn't order parts until an order is booked, it can take advantage of ever-falling component costs. On average, its parts are 60 days newer than those in competing machines, and hence 60 days further down the price curve. This gives Dell a six percent profit advantage from parts costs alone.

Flush with success, Dell is taking its direct-marketing formula a step further. It's again doing what once seemed impossible: selling PCs on the Internet. Now, by simply clicking the "Buy a Dell" icon at Dell's web site, customers can design and price customized computer systems electronically. Then, with a click on the "purchase" button, they can submit an order, choosing from online payment options that include a credit card, company purchase order, or corporate lease. Dell dashes out a digital confirmation to customers within five minutes of receiving the order. After receiving confirmation, customers can check the status of the order online at any time.

Dell Computer Corp.
www.dell.com/

The Internet is a perfect extension of Dell's direct-marketing model. Customers who are already comfortable buying direct from Dell now have an even more powerful way to do so. "The Internet," says Michael Dell, "is the ultimate direct model. . . . [Customers] like the immediacy, convenience, savings, and personal touches that the [Internet] experience provides. Not only are some sales done completely online, but people who call on the phone after having visited dell.com are twice as likely to buy."

If initial sales are any indication, it looks as though Dell has once again rewritten the book on successful direct marketing. The direct marketing pioneer now sells more than $3 million worth of computers daily from its web site, and Internet sales are growing at 20 percent each month. Some 225 000 browsers visit Dell's site each week, and buyers range from individuals purchasing home computers to large business users buying high-end $40 000 servers. Use of the Internet has allowed Dell to cut costs while offering buyers more services and information. Dell has 35 000 pages of service and support information on its site. Michael Dell sees online marketing as the next great conquest in the company's direct marketing crusade. "The Internet is like a booster rocket on our sales and growth," he proclaims. "Our vision is to have *all* customers conduct *all* transactions on the Internet, globally."

This time, competitors aren't scoffing at Michael Dell's vision of the future. It's hard to argue with success, and Michael Dell has been very successful. By following his hunches, at the tender age of 32, he has built one of the world's hottest computer companies. In the process, he's amassed a personal fortune exceeding $6.2 billion.[1]

Many of the marketing tools we examined in previous chapters were developed in the context of *mass marketing*: targeting broadly with standardized messages and marketing offers. Today, however, with the trend toward more narrowly targeted or one-to-one marketing, more and more companies are adopting *direct marketing* as a primary marketing approach or as a supplement for other approaches. Increasingly, companies are turning to direct marketing in an effort to reach carefully targeted customers more efficiently and to build stronger, more personal, one-to-one relationships with them.

In this chapter, we examine the nature, role, and growing applications of direct marketing and its newest form, online, or Internet, marketing. We address the following questions: What is direct marketing? What are its benefits to companies and their customers? How do customer databases support direct marketing? What channels do direct marketers use to reach individual prospects and customers? What marketing opportunities do online channels provide? How can companies use integrated direct marketing for competitive advantage? What public and ethical issues do direct and online marketing raise?

■ WHAT IS DIRECT MARKETING?

Direct marketing
Direct communications with carefully targeted individual consumers to obtain an immediate response.

Mass marketers have typically sought to reach millions of buyers with a single product and a standard message delivered through the mass media. Thus, Procter & Gamble (P&G) originally launched Crest toothpaste in one version with a single message ("Crest fights cavities"), hoping that 300 million North Americans would

Loyalty programs, such as the Airmiles program, provide added value for customers while allowing firms to build extensive customer databases.

learn the message and buy the brand. P&G did not need to know its customers' names or anything else about them, only that they wanted to take good care of their teeth. Most marketing communications consisted of one-way communication directed *at* consumers, not two-way communication *with* them.

In contrast, **direct marketing** consists of direct communications with carefully targeted individual consumers to obtain an immediate response. Thus, direct marketers communicate directly with customers, often on a one-to-one, interactive basis. They closely match their marketing offers and communications to the needs of narrowly defined segments or even individual buyers. Direct marketing can help firms build the value of their brands. As Judy Elder, president of Ogilvy & Mather Direct, stresses, "Clients that come to us now are brand marketers first and foremost, and they are looking at direct-marketing techniques because they understand that the ability to target precisely can deliver more effective results."[2] And beyond brand and image building, they usually seek a direct, immediate, and measurable consumer response.

Early direct marketers—catalogue companies, direct mailers, and telemarketers—gathered customer names and sold their goods mainly through the mail and by telephone. Today, improved database technologies and new media—computers, modems, fax machines, e-mail, the Internet, and online services—permit more sophisticated direct marketing. Their availability and reasonable costs have greatly enlarged direct marketing opportunities.

Today, most marketers see direct marketing as playing an even broader role than simply selling products and services. They view it as an effective tool for interfacing with customers to build long-term customer relationships. Thus, catalogue companies send birthday cards, information on special events, or small gifts to select members of their customer bases. Airlines, hotels, and other businesses build strong customer relationships through frequency award programs (for example, frequent-flyer miles) and club programs. Company web sites provide ways for customers to "visit" companies, learn about their products and services, interact with company personnel, and participate in entertaining events and activities. In this way, direct marketing becomes *direct relationship marketing*.

GROWTH AND BENEFITS OF DIRECT MARKETING

Reflecting the trend toward more targeted and one-to-one marketing, direct marketing is now the fastest-growing form of marketing. In this section, we discuss the benefits of direct marketing to customers and sellers and the reasons for its rapid growth.

THE BENEFITS OF DIRECT MARKETING

Direct marketing benefits customers in many ways. Consumers report that home shopping is fun, convenient, and hassle-free. It saves time and introduces them to a larger selection of merchandise. They can do comparative shopping by browsing through mail catalogues and online shopping services, and then order products for themselves or others. Industrial customers can learn about available products and services without waiting for and tying up time with salespeople.

Sellers also benefit. Direct marketers can develop an internal database or buy mailing lists containing names of almost any group: millionaires, new parents, left-handed people, or recent university graduates. They can then personalize and customize their messages. With today's technology, a direct marketer can select small groups or even individual consumers, customize offers to their special needs and wants, and promote these offers through individualized communications.

Direct marketers can build closer relationships with their customers. For example, Friskies pet care maintains a database of cat owners and communicates directly with Friskies Cat Club mailings. Direct marketing also can be timed to reach prospects at just the right moment. And because they reach more interested consumers at the best time, direct-marketing materials receive higher readership and response. Unlike traditional communications methods, such as television advertising, direct marketers have the advantage of being able to measure the type and rate of response for people targeted by direct marketing campaign. They can compile databases using geographic, demographic and psychographic characteristics for those people who respond to a campaign, those who request more information, or those who actually buy a product or service. They can thereby determine groups with a high propensity to respond or assess the types of media and messages that work best when trying to reach a particular target audience. Finally, direct marketing provides security—the direct marketer's offer and strategy may be less visible to competitors.

THE GROWTH OF DIRECT MARKETING

Sales through traditional direct-marketing channels (catalogues, direct mail, and telemarketing) have been growing rapidly. Whereas North American retail sales grow around three percent annually, catalogue and direct-mail sales are growing at around seven percent. Canadians buy over $10 billion in goods and services through direct-marketing channels. A recent Canadian Direct Marketing Association study discovered that 64 percent of the firms surveyed used some form of direct marketing each year, that they all expected to increase expenditures on direct marketing, and that many use their direct marketing efforts as a means to collect information on customers and prospects to help drive better database-driven marketing programs. Despite these positive attitudes about direct marketing, many businesses also have some concerns. Canada Post recently adopted a policy whereby consumers can post signs on their mail boxes to indicate that they don't want any "junk" mail. They expect that five to 10 percent of consumers will take this action. Furthermore, over 60 percent of the service and manufacturing firms surveyed believe that customers "only tolerate or dislike" direct marketing. Those firms that don't use direct marketing cite the cost of the effort and lack of knowledge about database-marketing techniques as the reasons why they don't use this technique.[3]

Canadian Direct Marketing Association
www.cdma.org/

The Canadian Direct Marketing Association intends to address the latter concern. It believes that Canadian universities are not currently producing students who understand the direct-marketing industry or who are aware of the tremendous employment opportunities in it. Although some universities, such as York and Dalhousie, offer direct-marketing courses, no Canadian university offers degrees or certificates the way that more than 25 U.S. universities do. The Canadian Direct Marketing Association is currently developing a model for a Canadian direct-marketing program to encourage universities to develop these skills in their students.

While direct marketing through traditional channels is growing rapidly, online marketing is growing explosively. The creation of the "information superhighway" promises to revolutionize commerce. Today more than 36 percent of the 11.6 million Canadian households have a PC. It is estimated that 31 percent of Canadians use the Internet. In business-to-business marketing alone, annual North American revenues on the Internet exceed $850 million, and that number could go as high as $95 billion by the year 2000.[4] We will examine online marketing more closely later in this chapter.

In the consumer market, the extraordinary growth of direct marketing is a response to the new marketing realities discussed in previous chapters. Market "demassification" has resulted in an ever-increasing number of market niches with distinct preferences. Direct marketing allows sellers to focus efficiently on these mini-markets with offers that better match specific consumer needs.

Other trends have also fuelled the rapid growth of direct marketing in the consumer market. Higher costs of driving, traffic congestion, parking headaches, lack of time, a shortage of retail sales help, and lines at checkout counters all

What's in a logo?

I n our case, some of the most trusted names in Canadian business.

We're the CDMA, The Canadian Direct Marketing Association.

Our members offer you goods and services through the mail, the telephone, television, and in some cases, the computer. We're the industry that brings you the convenience of home shopping.

And when you see our logo, or are contacted by one of our members, you know you've found a professional organization.

Everyone of our over 450 member companies adheres to a Code of Ethics and Standards of Practice, tough environmental policies, and a comprehensive set of guidelines that demand honesty, truth, accuracy and

fairness in all customer dealings.

Our members also follow a comprehensive Privacy Code that gives you full control over how information, such as your name and address, is used.

And we have a Do Not Mail / Do Not Call Service that lets you add or remove your name from our members' mailing or calling lists. To activate this service, just drop a postcard with your name, address (including postal code) and telephone number to: Do Not Mail / Do Not Call Service, 1 Concorde Gate, Suite 607, Don Mills, Ontario, M3C 3N6. It helps our members communicate more effectively with people who enjoy shopping from home.

So look closely, there's a lot in our logo.

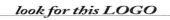 **look for this LOGO** →   CDMA Member   Canadian Direct Marketing Association

encourage at-home shopping. Consumers are responding favourably to direct marketers' toll-free phone numbers, their willingness to accept telephone orders 24 hours a day, seven days a week, and their growing commitment to customer service. The growth of 24-hour and 48-hour delivery via Purolator, CanPar, Federal Express, UPS, DHL, and other express carriers has made direct shopping fast and easy. Finally, the growth of affordable computer power and customer databases has enabled direct marketers to single out the best prospects for any product they wish to sell.

Direct marketing has also grown rapidly in business-to-business marketing, partly in response to the ever-increasing costs of reaching business markets through the sales force. Since personal sales calls often cost $360 per contact, they should be made only when necessary and to high-potential customers and prospects. Lower cost-per-contact media—such as telemarketing, direct mail, and the newer electronic media—often prove more cost-effective in reaching and selling to more prospects and customers.

CUSTOMER DATABASES AND DIRECT MARKETING

Table 17-1 lists the main differences between mass marketing and so-called *one-to-one marketing*.[5] Companies that know about individual customer needs and characteristics can customize their offers, messages, delivery modes, and payment methods to maximize customer value and satisfaction. And today's companies have a very powerful tool for accessing the names, addresses, preferences, and other pertinent information about individual customers and prospects: the customer database.

Customer database
An organized collection of comprehensive data about individual customers or prospects, including geographic, demographic, psychographic, and behavioural data.

A **customer database** is an organized collection of comprehensive data about individual customers or prospects, including geographic, demographic, psychographic, and behavioural data. The database can be used to locate good potential customers, tailor products and services to the special needs of targeted consumers, and maintain long-term customer relationships. *Database marketing* is the process of building, maintaining, and using customer databases and other databases (products, suppliers, resellers) for the purpose of contacting and transacting with customers.

Many companies confuse a customer mailing list with a customer database. A customer mailing list is simply a set of names, addresses, and telephone numbers. A customer database contains much more information. In business-to-business marketing, the salesperson's customer profile might contain information such as the

TABLE 17-1 *Mass Marketing vs. One-to-One Marketing*

Mass Marketing	One-to-One Marketing
Average customer	Individual customer
Customer anonymity	Customer profile
Standard product	Customized market offering
Mass production	Customized production
Mass distribution	Individualized distribution
Mass advertising	Individualized message
Mass promotion	Individualized incentives
One-way message	Two-way messages
Economies of scale	Economies of scope
Share of market	Share of customer
All customers	Profitable customers
Customer attraction	Customer retention

Source: Adapted from Don Peppers and Martha Rogers, *The One-to-One Future* (New York: Doubleday/Currency, 1993).

Introducing Canadian
Wildlife Federation's
Lasting Legacy.

*Many non-profits, such
as the Canadian Wildlife
Federation, use database
marketing to raise funds.*

products and services the customer has bought; past volumes and prices; key contacts (and their ages, birthdays, hobbies, and favourite foods); competitive suppliers; status of current contracts; estimated customer expenditures for the next few years; and assessments of competitive strengths and weaknesses in selling and serving the account. In consumer marketing, the customer database might contain a customer's demographics (age, income, family members, birthdays), psychographics (activities, interests, and opinions), buying behaviour (past purchases, buying preferences), and other relevant information. For example, the catalogue company Fingerhut maintains a database containing some 1300 pieces of information about each of the 30 million households (see Marketing Highlight 17-1). And Ritz-Carlton's database holds more than 500 000 individual customer preferences.

Database marketing is most frequently used by charities and non-profit marketers, business-to-business marketers, and service retailers (hotels, banks, and airlines). Increasingly, however, consumer packaged-goods companies and retailers are also using database marketing. A recent survey found that almost two-thirds of all large consumer-products companies are currently using or building such databases for targeting their marketing efforts.[6] Armed with the information in their databases, these companies can identify small groups of customers to receive fine-tuned marketing offers and communications. Procter & Gamble uses its database to market Pampers disposable diapers, using such tactics as "individualized" birthday cards for babies and reminder letters to move up to the next size. Kraft Foods has amassed a list of more than 30 million users of its products who have responded to coupons or other Kraft promotions. Based on their interests, the company sends these customers tips on such issues as nutrition and exercise, as well as recipes and coupons for specific Kraft brands. Blockbuster, the massive entertainment company, uses its dataase of 36 million households and two million daily transactions to help its video-rental customers select movies and to steer them to other Blockbuster subsidiaries.[7]

More and more small companies are also starting to use direct marketing both nationally and internationally. Harry Wicken, general manager of Mailfast Canada, stresses that small companies cannot afford to neglect the vast opportunities that the international marketplace represents. He uses the example of a program developed for a small company that markets educational materials. Mailfast first developed a profile of the company's products. These profiles were then matched to consumer preferences and purchasing activities in a number of international markets. In markets where there was a match between customer tastes and the company's products, Mailfast acquired mailing lists of consumers whom the company could target effectively.[8]

Companies use their databases in four ways:

1. *Identifying prospects.* Many companies generate sales leads by using advertising that has some sort of response feature, such as a business reply card or toll-free number. The database is built from these responses. The company identifies the best prospects, then reaches them by mail, phone, or personal calls in an attempt to convert them into customers.

2. *Deciding which customers should receive a particular offer.* Companies identify the profile of an ideal customer for an offer. Then they search their databases for individuals most closely resembling the ideal type to improve its targeting precision over time. Following a sale, it can set up an automatic sequence of activities: one week later, send a thank-you note; five weeks later, send a new offer; 10 weeks later (if customer has not responded), phone the customer and offer a special discount.

3. *Deepening customer loyalty.* Companies can build customers' interest and enthusiasm by remembering their preferences and by sending appropriate

DATABASE MARKETING: FINGERHUT BUILDS STRONG CUSTOMER RELATIONSHIPS

As Betty Holmes of Detroit, Michigan, sifts through the day's stack of mail, one item in particular catches her eye. It's only a catalogue, but it's speaking directly to her. A laser-printed personal message on the catalogue's cover states: "Thank you, Mrs. Holmes, for your recent purchase of women's apparel. To show our thanks, we are offering you up to five free gifts, plus deferred payment until July 31st." The note goes on, with amazing accuracy, to refer Betty to specific items in the catalogue that will likely interest her.

The catalogue is from Fingerhut, the giant direct-mail retailer and master database marketer. A typical Fingerhut catalogue offers products ranging from $20 toy phones to $2000 big-screen televisions. Fingerhut operates on a *huge* scale: It sends out some 558 million mailings each year—more than 1.5 million per day. When new customers first respond to a direct-mail offer, Fingerhut asks them to fill out a questionnaire about the kinds of products that interest them. Using information from this questionnaire and from other sources, along with information about later purchases, Fingerhut has built an impressive marketing database. The database contains some 1300 pieces of information on each of 30 million active and potential customers. It's filled to the brim with the usual demographic details such as address, age, marital status, and number of children, but also tracks hobbies, interests, birthdays, and other seemingly obscure facts.

The database allows Fingerhut to target the most likely buyers with products that interest them most. Instead of sending out the same catalogues and letters to all of its customers, Fingerhut tailors its offers based on what each customer is likely to buy. Moreover, promotions such as the Birthday Club provide opportunities to create special offers that sell more products. A month before a child's birthday, Birthday Club customers receive a free birthday gift for their child if they agree to try any one of the products Fingerhut offers in an accompanying mailing. A customer who responds to these and other offers might become one of millions of "promotable" customers who receive Fingerhut mailings. As a result of such skilful use of its database, Fingerhut achieves direct-mail response rates that are three times the industry average. Says one retailing consultant, "Fingerhut is one of those pioneering companies that is making intense knowledge of their customer a core competency."

Fingerhut uses its database to build long-term customer relationships that go well beyond its merchandise. It stays in continuous touch with preferred customers through regular special promotions—an annual sweepstakes, free gifts, a deferred-billing promotion, and others. These special offers are all designed with one goal in mind: to create a reason for Fingerhut to be in the customer's mailbox. Once in the mailbox, the personalized messages and targeted offers get attention.

Credit is an important cornerstone of Fingerhut's relationship with customers. The average Fingerhut customer has a household income of just $35 000. Whereas many retailers and credit companies are reluctant to extend credit to this moderate-income group, Fingerhut encourages credit. Catalogues list monthly payments in bold type, and actual prices in fine print. Customers can spread a $40 running shoe purchase over 13 months with payments of just $4.79 per month. Thus, Fingerhut regularly extends credit to people who would otherwise have to pay cash. "When I started out, Fingerhut was the only place that would give me credit," says Marilyn Gnat from Eagle River, Wisconsin, a loyal Fingerhut customer who raised nine children on a modest income.

Despite selling to consumers of modest means, Fingerhut turns credit into a competitive advantage by using its huge database to effectively control credit risks. Some 40 percent of Fingerhut customers have had so little credit that they don't even have credit reports. Thus, the company's extensive database helps it to do a better job than competitors can of predicting customers' creditworthiness. Fingerhut further controls credit risks by what it offers to whom. When a new customer makes a first order, the amount of credit allowed may be limited to $50. If the customer pays promptly, the next mailing offers higher-ticket items. Good customers, who pay their bills regularly, receive cards and rewards to reinforce this behaviour. For example, an award envelope cheers "Congratulations! You've been selected to receive our 'exceptional customer award!'" and contains a certificate suitable for framing.

Recently, Fingerhut has begun applying its database touch to the Internet. Customers can now log onto the Fingerhut Online web site (www.fingerhut.com) and order products from the catalogue using an online order form. The company's popular Andy's Garage Sale site (www.andys-garage.com) even customizes its interactions with web customers. "If you are repeatedly buying golfing equipment and I'm buying boat supplies, it'll show you golf bags, and it'll show me life jackets," explains Fingerhut's vice president of marketing.

The skilful use of database marketing and relationship building have made Fingerhut one of the largest direct-mail marketers in the United Staes. Founded in 1948 by brothers Manny and William Fingerhut, it now sells more than $2.8 billion worth of mail-order merchandise each year, making it the second-largest consumer catalogue company in the United States behind J.C. Penney. In fact, one in every six U.S. households has *bought* something from the company. Fingerhut's success is no accident. "Most of our competitors use a full catalogue; they could care less about what the individuals want," notes a Fingerhut executive. "Fingerhut finds out what each customer wants and builds an event around each promotion."

Sources: Quotations from Eileen Norris, "Fingerhut Gives Customers Credit," *Advertising Age*, March 6, 1986, p. 19; Susan Chandler, "Data is Power. Just Ask Fingerhut," *Business Week*, June 3, 1996, p. 69; and Mitch Wagner, "Repeat Traffic is Goal of Customerized Web Sites," *Computer World*, November 25, 1996, p. 48. Also see John N. Frank, "A Finger in the Card Pie," *Credit Card Management*, July 1996, pp. 22–28; and Rob Yoegel, "Fingerhut's Penny Mailing," *Target Marketing*, April 1997, pp. 53–55.

information, gifts, or other materials. For example, Mars, a market leader in pet food as well as candy, compiled the names of virtually every German family that owns a cat by contacting veterinarians and by offering the public a free booklet entitled *How to Take Care of Your Cat*. People who request the booklet fill out a questionnaire, providing their cat's name, age, birthday, and other information. Mars then sends a birthday card to each cat along with a new cat food sample and money-saving coupons for Mars brands. The result is a lasting relationship with the cat's owner.

4. *Reactivating customer purchases.* The database can help a company make attractive offers of product replacements, upgrades, or complementary products just when customers might be ready to act. For example, a General Electric customer database contains each customer's demographic and psychographic characteristics along with an appliance purchasing history. Using this database, GE marketers assess how long specific customers have owned their current appliances and which past customers might be ready to purchase again. A rich customer database allows GE to build profitable new business by locating good prospects, anticipating customers' needs, cross-selling products and services, and rewarding loyal customers.[9]

Like many other marketing tools, database marketing requires a special investment. Companies must invest in computer hardware, database software, analytical programs, communication links, and skilled personnel. Companies need to plan their data-gathering efforts carefully. Many firms gather a wealth of consumer information only to find that they are at a loss regarding how to use this resource effectively. The database system also must be user friendly and available to various marketing groups, including those in product and brand management, new-product development, advertising and promotion, direct mail, telemarketing, field sales, order fulfilment, and customer service. A well-managed database should lead to sales gains that will more than cover its costs. Royal Caribbean cruises, for example, has had success in this area. Database marketing allows it to offer spur-of-the-moment cruise packages that help to fill all the berths on its ships. Fewer unbooked rooms mean maximized profits for the cruise line.

As more companies move into database marketing, the nature of marketing will change. Mass marketing and mass retailing will continue, but their prevalence and power may diminish as more buyers turn to non-retail shopping. More consumers will use electronic shopping to search for the information and products they need. Online services will provide more objective information about the comparative merits of different brands. Marketers will need to think of new ways to create effective online messages, as well as new channels for delivering products and services efficiently.

■ FORMS OF DIRECT MARKETING COMMUNICATION

The major forms of direct marketing—as shown in Figure 17-1—include *face-to-face selling, direct-mail marketing, catalogue marketing, telemarketing, direct-response television marketing, kiosk marketing,* and *online marketing.*

FACE-TO-FACE SELLING

The original and oldest form of direct marketing is the sales call, which we examined in Chapter 16. Today most business-to-business marketers rely heavily on a professional sales force to locate prospects, develop them into customers, build lasting relationships, and grow the business. Or they hire manufacturers' representatives and agents to carry out the direct selling task. In addition, many consumer companies use a direct selling force to reach final consumers: insurance

FIGURE 17-1 *Forms of direct marketing*

Direct-mail marketing
Sending an offer, announcement reminder, or other item to a person at a particular address.

agents, stockbrokers, and salespeople working part- or full-time for direct-sales organizations such as Avon, Amway, Mary Kay, Tupperware, and Please Mum.

DIRECT-MAIL MARKETING

Direct-mail marketing involves sending an offer, announcement, reminder, or other item to a person at a particular address. Using highly selective mailing lists, direct marketers send out millions of mail pieces each year—letters, ads, samples, foldouts, and other "salespeople with wings." Direct mail is well suited to direct, one-to-one communication. It permits high target-market selectivity, can be personalized, is flexible, and allows easy measurement of results. Whereas the cost per thousand people reached is higher than with mass media such as television or magazines, the people who are reached are much better prospects.

Direct mail has proved successful in promoting all kinds of products, from books, magazine subscriptions, and insurance to gift items, clothing, gourmet foods, and industrial products. Direct mail also is used heavily by charities, which use it to raise billions of dollars each year.

The direct-mail industry seeks new methods and approaches. For example, videocassettes have become one of the fastest-growing direct mail media. With VCRs now in 85 percent of North American homes, marketers mailed out an estimated 85 million tapes in 1995. For instance, to introduce its Donkey Kong Country video game, Nintendo created a 13-minute MTV-style video and sent two million copies to avid video-game players. This direct-mail video helped Nintendo sell 6.1 million units of the game in only 45 days, making it the fastest-selling game in industry history.[10] Some direct marketers even mail out computer disks. For example, Ford sends a computer disk called "Disk Drive Test Drive" to consumers responding to its ads in computer publications. The diskette's menu provides technical specifications and attractive graphics about Ford cars, and answers frequently asked questions.

Until recently, all mail was paper-based and handled by Canada Post, telegraphic services, or for-profit mail carriers such as Purolator, Federal Express, DHL, or Airborne Express. Recently, however, three new forms of mail delivery have become popular:

◆ *Fax mail.* Fax machines allow delivery of paper-based messages over telephone lines. Fax mail has one major advantage over regular mail: The message can be sent and received almost instantaneously. Marketers now routinely send fax mail announcing offers, sales, and other events to prospects and customers with fax machines. Fax numbers of companies and individuals are now available through published directories. However, some prospects and customers resent receiving unsolicited fax mail, which clutters their machines and consumes their paper.

◆ *E-mail.* E-mail (short for *electronic mail*) allows users to send messages or files directly from one computer to another. Messages arrive almost instantly and are stored until the receiving person retrieves them. Many marketers now send sales announcements, offers, product information, and other messages to e-mail addresses—sometimes to a few individuals, sometimes to large groups. As people begin to receive more e-mail messages, including unimportant ones, they may look for an "agent" software program to sort out the more important messages from those that can be ignored or discarded. Unsolicited e-mail may anger some users so much they *SPAM* the sender by sending a return message designed to jam the sender's system.

◆ *Voice mail.* Voice mail is a system for receiving and storing oral messages at a telephone address. Telephone companies sell this service as a substitute for answering machines. The person with a voice-mail account can check messages by dialling into the voice-mail system and punching in a personal code. Some marketers have set up programs that will dial a large number of telephone numbers and leave the selling messages in the recipients' voice mailboxes.

These new forms delivery direct mail at incredible speeds, compared to the post office's "snail mail" pace. Yet, much like mail delivered through traditional channels, they may be resented as "junk mail" if sent to people who have no interest in them. For this reason, marketers must carefully identify appropriate targets so as not to waste their money and recipients' time.

CATALOGUE MARKETING

Catalogue marketing
Selling through catalogues mailed to a select list of customers or made available in stores.

Sears Canada
www.sears.ca

Catalogue marketing involves selling through catalogues mailed to a select list of customers or made available in stores. Some huge general-merchandise retailers, such as Sears Canada, which has 1700 catalogue stores across the country, traditionally used their catalogues as a "general store" mass-marketing tool. Today, facing challenges from thousands of specialty catalogues aimed at market niches, Sears has changed its strategy and has begun to send out more targeted, cost-effective catalogues. In an attempt to win back women who were no longer active catalogue shoppers, Sears developed a 124-page women's apparel catalogue. When Consumers Distributing went into bankruptcy, Sears mailed a 36-page jewellery catalogue to people living in the area surrounding a former Consumers Distributing store. To augment its catalogue sales, Sears launched a new special occasions gift registry. More than the traditional bride registry, Sears aims the service at anyone celebrating a special occasion. People celebrating special events ranging from anniversaries to christenings to graduations can compile gift lists from the more than 50 000 products and services offered in Sears catalogues and retail stores. The new strategies have given Sears double-digit sales increases.[11]

Over 14 billion copies of more than 8500 different consumer catalogues are mailed out annually. Last year, catalogue sales accounted for more than $125 billion in sales. While catalogue sales account for almost four percent of retail sales in the United States, they represent six percent of sales in Canada. Almost 30 percent of Canadians annually order merchandise from their homes, and according to the Canadian Direct Marketing Association, catalogue sales were equivalent to $68 for every

Sears Canada's 1997 fall and winter catalogue, aimed at 4 million mostly rural customers, featured country singers Michelle Wright for English Canada and Julie Masse for Quebec.

THE FLAGSHIP STORE 900 Don Mills Road 416-441-6141
QUEEN'S QUAY TERMINAL 207 Queen's Quay W. 416-203-0463
MAIL ORDER CATALOGUE www.tilley.com 1-800-363-8737
POUR LE SERVICE EN FRANÇAIS 1-800-465-4249

Tilley's customers can shop for products online.

Telemarketing
Using the telephone to sell directly to customers.

Tilley Endurables
www.tilley.com

person living in Canada.[12] Consumers can buy just about anything from a catalogue. The Canadian Olympic Association developed a catalogue of team-branded merchandise to raise funds and increase support of the Canadian Olympic Team participating at the Winter Games in Nagano, Japan. Bridgehead, the retailing arm of Oxfam Canada, targets socially conscious coffee buyers who want to purchase beans from democratically run coffee co-operatives in developing countries. The Best Catalog Company of Toronto brings together 12 different merchandisers in its Hampshire Collection catalogue, which is targeted at affluent Christmas shoppers.[13]

Most consumers enjoy receiving catalogues and will sometimes even pay to get them. Many catalogue marketers are now even selling their catalogues at book stores and magazine stands. Some companies, such as Royal Silk, Neiman Marcus, Sears, and Spiegel, are also experimenting with videotape, computer disk, CD-ROM, and Internet catalogues. Many retailers have also put their catalogues on the World Wide Web. For example, Tilley Endurables shoppers can visit the company's web site and check whether a product is in-stock, order online, or send a free "virtual" Tilley hat to anyone around the world.

Many business-to-business marketers also rely heavily on catalogues. Whether in the form of a simple brochure, three-ring binder, book, or encoded on a videotape or computer disk, catalogues remain one of today's hardest-working sales tools. For some companies, in fact, catalogues have even taken the place of salespeople. In all, companies mail out more than 1.1 *billion* business-to-business catalogues each year, reaping more than $72 billion worth of catalogue sales.[14]

TELEMARKETING

Telemarketing—using the telephone to sell directly to consumers—has become the major direct-marketing communication tool. Marketers use *outbound* telephone marketing to sell directly to consumers and business. *Inbound* toll-free numbers are used to receive orders from television and radio ads, direct mail, or catalogues. The average household receives 19 telephone calls each year and makes 16 calls to place orders. In 1996, toll-free telephone numbers generated $680 million for Canadian phone companies. Some industry analysts boldly predict that by the turn of the century, half of all retail sales will be completed by telephone.[15]

Many firms also use toll-free numbers for their customer service lines. A recent survey by *Marketing* magazine found that most customer service lines were staffed by well-informed people who could provide an impressive amount of information. People conducting the survey were impressed with the fact that Toyota Canada (1-888-Toyota8) made information available to callers in English, French, or Chinese. They also praised Heinz (1-800-565-2100) for its bilingual service where callers can access a wealth of nutritional information for Heinz products, learn about its Baby Club, or how to direct labels to its cause-related marketing program with the Children's Miracle Network.[16]

Some marketers use 900 numbers to sell consumers information, entertainment, or the opportunity to voice an opinion on a pay-per-call basis. For example, for a charge, consumers can obtain pet care information from Quaker Oats or golf lessons from *Golf Digest*. In addition to its 800 number and Internet site, Nintendo offers a 900 number, for $1.50 per minute, for gameplayers wanting assistance with the company's video games. Overall, the use of 900 numbers has grown by more than 10 percent a year over the past five years.[17]

Business-to-business marketers use telemarketing extensively. In fact, more than $165 billion worth of business products were marketed by phone last year.

For example, Raleigh Bicycles uses telemarketing to reduce the amount of personal selling needed for contacting its dealers; in the first year, sales-force travel costs were reduced 50 percent, and sales in a single quarter increased 34 percent.[18]

Most consumers appreciate many of the offers they receive by telephone. Properly designed and targeted telemarketing provides many benefits, including purchasing convenience and increased product and service information. However, the recent explosion in unsolicited telephone marketing has annoyed many consumers who object to the almost daily "junk phone calls" that pull them away from the dinner table or clog up their answering machines.

DIRECT-RESPONSE TELEVISION MARKETING

Direct-response television marketing
Television spots that persuasively describe a product and give customers a toll-free number for ordering.

Direct-response television marketing takes one of two major forms. The first is *direct-response advertising*. Direct marketers air commercials, often 60 or 120 seconds long, that persuasively describe a product and give customers a toll-free number for ordering. Television viewers also encounter 30-minute advertising programs, or *infomercials*, for a single product. Such direct-response advertising works well for sellers of magazines, books, small appliances, tapes and CDs, collectibles, and many other products.

For years, infomercials have been associated with somewhat questionable pitches for juicers, get-rich-quick schemes, and nifty ways to stay in shape without working very hard at it. Recently, however, a number of top marketing companies—GTE, Johnson & Johnson, MCA Universal, Sears, Procter & Gamble, Revlon, Apple Computer, Toyota, and others—have begun using infomercials to sell their wares over the phone, refer customers to retailers, or send out coupons and product information. In all, infomercials produced almost $1.4 billion in sales in 1994.[19]

Home shopping channels, another form of direct-response television marketing, are television programs or entire channels dedicated to selling goods and services. Some home shopping channels, such as the Canadian Home Shopping Network, recently relaunched as The Shopping Channel, broadcast 24 hours a day. The program's hosts offer bargain prices on products ranging from jewellery, lamps, collectible dolls, and clothing to power tools and consumer electronics—usually obtained by the home shopping channel at closeout prices. Viewers of The Shopping Channel tend to be female (70%) and over the age of 25. Sales through North American home shopping channels grew from $650 million in 1986 to an estimated $2.8 billion in 1994. Sears, Kmart, J.C. Penney, Spiegel, and other major retailers are now looking into the home shopping industry. Many experts think that advances in two-way, interactive television and linkages with Internet technology will eventually make video shopping one of the major forms of direct marketing.[20]

Driver Net helps truck drivers plan their routes.

KIOSK MARKETING

Some companies place information and ordering machines—called *kiosks* (in contrast to vending machines, which dispense actual products)—in stores, airports, and other locations. Hallmark and American Greetings use kiosks to help customers create personalized cards. Lee jeans stores use a kiosk called Fit Finder to provide women with a quick way to determine the size and style of Lee jeans that fit their personal preference. Toyota Canada used kiosks to target younger buyers. The Liquor Control Board of Ontario installed interactive kiosks to run advertisements for featured products and to enhance customer service. IKEA Canada is allowing Unicef to set up fundraising kiosks in its stores.[21]

Business marketers also use kiosks. For example, Investment Canada placed a kiosk at an Atlanta trade show to introduce Canadian telecommunications and computer products to international buyers. Dow Plastics also places kiosks at trade shows to collect sales leads and to provide information on its 700 products. The kiosk system reads customer data from encoded registration badges and produces technical data sheets that can be printed at the kiosk or faxed or mailed to the customer. The system has resulted in a 400 percent increase in qualified sales leads.[22]

The most recent and fastest-growing form of direct marketing involves online channels and electronic commerce. We discuss these channels in detail in the next section.

WINDOW ON THE FUTURE: ONLINE MARKETING AND ELECTRONIC COMMERCE

Staying in touch is the watchword of the 1990s. Thus, it is not surprising that the 1990s have been labelled the Information Age, and that both marketers and consumers are touting the phrase "Knowledge is power." The Internet is the tool by which both consumers and companies are tapping into this theme and making it part of their daily lives.

The Internet is an exciting business resource and marketing tool. It has brought consumers into contact with marketers as never before. The Net has allowed people to be creators of information on products and services instead of mere consumers of them. Jim Carroll, co-author of *The Canadian Internet Advantage* and other Internet publications, said: "Today, the opportunity is marketing. Tomorrow, the opportunity will be access to the corporate system to support more direct interaction with the customer. And I think the third phase will be some type of transaction being performed by the customer."[23]

Online marketing
The use of interactive online computer systems, which link consumers with sellers.

Commercial online services
The provision of online information and marketing services to subscribers who pay a monthly fee.

Internet (or the Net)
A vast and burgeoning global web of computer networks.

Online marketing is conducted through interactive online computer systems, which link consumers with sellers electronically. There are two types of online marketing channels: commercial online services and the Internet.

Commercial online services offer online information and marketing services to subscribers who pay a monthly fee. The best-known online services are American Online, CompuServe, Sympatico, and Prodigy. These online services provide subscribers with information (news, libraries, education, travel, sports, reference), entertainment (fun and games), shopping services, dialogue opportunities (bulletin boards, forums, chat boxes), and e-mail.

After growing rapidly through the mid-1990s, the commercial online services are now being overtaken by the **Internet** as the primary online marketing channel. In fact, all of the online service firms now offer Internet access as a primary service. The Internet is a vast and burgeoning global web of computer networks. The Internet was created by the U.S. Defense Department during the 1960s, initially to link goverment labs, contractors, and military installations. Today, this huge, public computer network links computer users of all types all around the world. Anyone with a PC, a modem, and the right software can browse the Internet to obtain or share information on almost any subject and to interact with other users.[24]

Internet usage has surged with the recent development of the user-friendly World Wide Web access standard and Web browser software such as Netscape Navigator, Microsoft Internet Explorer, and Mosaic. Now, even novices can surf the Net with fully integrated text, graphics, images, and sound. Users can send e-mail, exchange views, shop for products, and access news, food recipes, art, and business information. The Internet itself is free, although individual users usually must pay a commercial access provider to be hooked up to it.

NICK JONES,
NEW MEDIA EVANGELIST
COMMUNIQUÉ, TORONTO

Yes, Nick's official business title is "New Media Evangelist." He has the business card to prove it, but it is somewhat of an understatement to say that Nick Jones took an indirect route into business and marketing. The son of a Canadian diplomat, Nick is a child of the global era, living in South Africa, Germany, and Iraq before returning to Canada. When selecting universities, Nick went to his father for advice. Although his dad had a B.Com. degree, he advised Nick to do something creative first. This advice sent Nick in pursuit of an undergraduate degree in fine arts. In addition to doing his degree, Nick was an active member of the student body and also played in the band. Although he was highly creative, Nick was also an organizer—he led a fundraising project that resulted in the establishment of a student art gallery, called the Union Gallery, in the main library building.

Nick thought his best career bet would be as an administrator of an arts organization, but not being able to tear himself away from campus life, Nick decided to take an MBA as a means of accomplishing his goal. He did a summer internship with Warner Lambert only to be convinced that he wasn't the packaged-goods type. He shifted gears again and took a Masters of Public Administration only to discover that he was not destined to be a bureaucrat, but was very much a businessperson after all.

Nick's first job after graduation brought him to Toronto where he joined a friend who was running a fledgling baseball magazine. Nick took on the role of marketing and sales manager. He did everything from developing advertising to running events. He even developed their award-winning "DUGOUT" web site, writing the code by hand. Nick learned that the big trick to being successful in publishing is getting what you print to people who will pay for it. Like many start-up organizations, the magazine was incurring heavy production and distribution costs. Although the magazine had national and international subscribers, there just weren't enough buyers and the magazine went into bankruptcy.

Nick moved on to a company called Incontext, a software company that specialized in HTML editing software. The company was doing well, until Microsoft came on the scene and merged with one of Incontext's chief competitors. The result: closure number two.

Not to be daunted, Nick moved on to Southern New Media, the interactive media arm of Southern newspaper group. Southam's president gave the group the mandate to experiment and learn about new media and find new ways to deliver information to

Nick Jones

consumers in a profitable manner. Southam's president was convinced that just being a newspaper company wouldn't be sufficient to allow the firm to survive into the 21st century. Nick was in heaven. He could freely explore a vast array of services just to learn what they were doing and how they were doing it. But, the summer of 1996 brought Conrad Black onto the scene. He purchased Southern and had quite a different view of new media. He saw the new media group as a "figment of previous management's overheated imagination." Surprise, Nick was de-hired once again.

He landed briefly at Grey Advertising's Interactive Group, but when things didn't work out, Nick decided to take a time-out. Although he did some consulting, he spent most of his time biking, sailing, and reading. He sat down and wrote a personal mission statement to clarify his goals and then he set out to find

the position that would meet the mission statement. He found it at Communiqué—an integrated communications company formed by the joining together of several independent companies. Communiqué is a highly entrepreneurial firm full of energy, karma, and excitement. It is a very technology-driven company—one that uses technology to drive performance. If someone needs a tool to better perform their job, they get it along with the training required to use the technology effectively.

When Communiqué takes on a client, it does a communications audit for them. It looks at everything the client uses to communicate to its publics—everything from its letterhead to its web site. The aim of the audit is to determine if the company is using the right tools to create the integrated image and position that the client desires. This approach has given Communiqué an edge—so much that it recently won the Microsoft and A&W accounts.

Now for Nick's role as the New Media Evangelist. Communiqué's clients know about TV and radio and what these media can do for them, but they are uncomfortable with newer technologies like interactive kiosks, e-mail, and web sites. Nick attends presentations to prospective clients to assess which vehicles are the best ones to obtain the results that client wants to achieve. He sells the necessity of having a Net presence with religious zeal. He stresses that two million people in Canada go online one to four times a week and the numbers are growing at a rate of 100 percent per year. He emphasizes that the Net will be a big part of marketing communication in the future. It is open 24 hours a day, 365 days a year. It is a sales centre that never closes and, Nick stresses, if you design your site well, people will use it. Nick can't think of a company that shouldn't use the Internet, unless there is one out there whose target group has no Internet access. If a client is doubtful that the Internet represents a significant opportunity, Nick only has to show them what their competitors are doing. It only takes a short, interactive presentation to convince most clients that they need to get moving. Now it is Nick's job to give clients the information they need to start competing on-line and beat their competitors.

Taking advantage of Internet marketing opportunities is no easy task, however. Creating a web site takes a lot of insight and analysis. The design, function, and aesthetics of the site have to be carefully planned and integrated. The client has to think carefully about what services it wants to provide and what the potential interaction with their customer will be. In addition, firms using the Internet have to understand that while Canada is a very regional country, they are communicating to the planet when they post a site on the Internet. Firms have to build a web site where anyone in the world can comfortably get information about what the company does. But the job doesn't stop there. Even though you have to think globally, you can't forget about the local, home market. You have to balance the content of your site—if there is too much local content, it is perceived as honky and unsophisticated; if there is too much global emphasis, you create the impression you don't care about local customers. Nick suggests you look at the Jack Daniel's site (www.jackdaniels.com) if you want to see a company that really understands how to perform this balancing act. If you want to see a project that is keeping Nick and his team busy, go to microsoft.com/canada.

Nick couldn't be happier than he is now in his new position. He has the privilege of managing a great team. They all work very long hours, but that is what it takes to deliver outstanding work. If you want to be converted, go see (or better yet, e-mail) Nick!

RAPID GROWTH OF ONLINE MARKETING

Sony has developed an impressive web site that promotes its artists and music. The site supplied artist profiles and information about new releases, as well as an online order form.

Although still in their infancy, Internet usage and online marketing are growing explosively. According to a recent study, 23 percent of people 16 or older in North America—more than 50 million people—have used the Internet in the last month, up from just one million people in late 1994. An additional 12 percent of adults use commercial online services such as America Online or CompuServe. A Statistics Canada survey revealed that in 1997 1.5 million Canadian households had access to the Internet—almost double the 1996 rate.[25] Internet usage is increasing at a rate of 12 000 new users per day, and some analysts predict that there will be more than a billion users by the year 2000.[26] There may now be as many as four to six million web sites worldwide, and this number is growing by as many as 400 new sites each week.[27]

This explosion of Internet usage heralds the dawning of a new world of *electronic commerce*. **Electronic commerce** is the general term for a buying and selling process that is supported by electronic means. *Electronic markets* are "marketspaces" in which sellers offer their products and services electronically, and buyers search for information, identify what they want, and place orders using a credit card or other means of electronic payment.

The electronic commerce explosion is all around us. Here are just two examples:

A reporter wants to buy a 35 mm camera. He logs onto the Shopper's Advantage web site (www.cuc.com/ctg/cgi-bin/sashopper/), clicks on cameras, then clicks on 35-mm cameras. A list of all the major brands appears, along with information about each brand. He can retrieve a photo of each camera and reviews by

Electronic commerce
A buying and selling process that is supported by electronic means.

experts. Finding the camera he wants, he places an order by typing in his credit-card number, address, and preferred shipping mode.

An executive is planning a trip to London and wants to locate a hotel that meets her needs. She signs onto the Travelocity web site (www.travelocity.com) and inputs her criteria (rate, location, amenities, safety). The computer produces a list of appropriate hotels, and she can book a room once she has made her choice.

Canadians are leaders in the use of this new medium. A 1997 survey by A.C. Neilsen found that 53 percent of Internet users in Canada used information they found on the Internet before making a purchase compared to 39 percent in the United States. Fifteen percent of Net users have purchased a product or service online, and the percentage is growing daily.[28]

UNDERSTANDING EMPOWERED CONSUMERS

The fundamental principle that businesspeople must understand when considering marketing on the Internet is that consumers have greater control over the marketing process than ever before. People who use the Net value information and tend to respond negatively to messages aimed only at selling. Whereas traditional marketing focused on the delivery of goods and services to a somewhat passive audience, electronic marketers must recognize that people who surf the Net exert discretion over the information that is presented to them by marketers. The Net puts the consumer, not the marketer, in control of communication. Consumers now seek information about products and services under conditions they set. As in traditional venues, consumers ignore much of the material presented and focus only on those pieces that capture their imagination and interest.

Surfers are knowledgeable, expert consumers, who are less likely to fall for "hype" and require evidence of the merits of an offer. The Web gives consumers access to multiple sources from which to seek information. They no longer have to rely on the marketer alone as the main source of information about a product. Such information-search activities are viewed as a problem by some site holders. These site providers have found that while many browsers visit the sites for online shopping, few actually make purchases. However, this "window-shopping" is viewed as a positive first step by others, who believe that it is the first stage that potential consumers go through as they build up their knowledge base and confidence in the Web.[29]

Richmond BC Savings Credit Union knows that offbeat humour appeals to many web users.

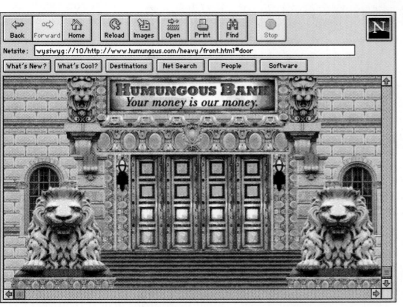

Even more importantly, buyers will increasingly become creators of product information, not just consumers of it. As web users join interest groups that share information on products, more inter-consumer product information will be generated. Thus, the Internet has started to provide a new vehicle for consumer activism. Marketers must be aware that consumers can now use the Internet to instantaneously communicate their dissatisfaction with a particular product or service to thousands of people around the world.

WHO USES THE NET?

What is your image of people who use the Web? Do you visualize them as computer nerds and hackers with big glasses and pasty faces? As social misfits who rarely get a date, who live off junk food, and hole up in the rec rooms late at night pounding on their keyboards? If this is your image, it is generally wrong![30]

A.C. Nielsen's 1997 Canadian Internet Survey revealed that one in three Canadians (29 percent of the population) over age 18 uses the Internet. Only 22 percent of Canadians used the Internet a year ago. These figures, however, don't mean that there is an ever-present, constant user community. Some people go online frequently, others only occasionally. Heavy users, those people who use the Internet daily, account for 35 percent of all Internet users. Frequent users, people who go online at least once a week, are the next largest group representing 34 percent of Internet users. The remainder are composed of casual users—people who only use the Internet once or twice a month. While heavy users are largely males who began using the Internet at least two years ago, casual users tend to be female and have less Internet experience. Internet usage also varies by province. Ontario has the largest number of households with Internet access. British Columbia, Quebec, and Alberta have the next largest number of households.[31]

What else characterizes these users? First, they are young (53 percent range in age from 16 to 34). Second, they are affluent; 25 percent have household incomes over $110 000. Third, they are highly educated and professional. Sixty-four percent of users report that they have at least four years of university education, and 51 percent list themselves as professionals or managers. Finally, while 22 percent of English-speaking respondents to a Deloitte and Touche survey said they used the Net in a single month, only 12 percent of French-speaking respondents had.[32]

While the figures provided above describe the "average" Net user, one has to remember that Net users come from all age groups. For example, the population of more than four million "Net kids" (predicted to reach almost 20 million by the year 2000) has attracted a host of online marketers. Sympatico offers a "Kids Only" area where kids can have fun and be as silly as they want to be. They can also find online magazines along with the usual games, software, and chat rooms as well as the Kids Help Phone.[33]

Autonet Canada's web site gives customers specifications and prices for more than 600 new cars, as well as other information of interest to car owners.

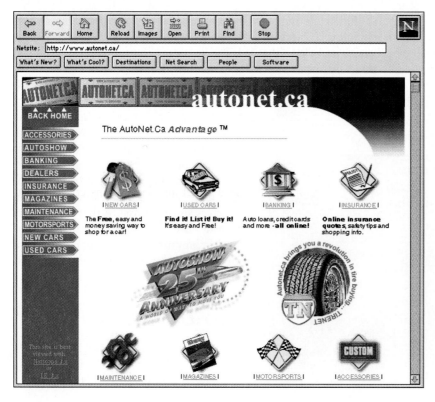

THE BENEFITS OF ONLINE MARKETING

Why have online services become so popular? Online marketing yields benefits to both consumers and marketers.

Benefits to Consumers

Online buying provides the same basic benefits to consumers as other forms of direct marketing. It is *convenient*. Customers don't have to battle traffic, find a parking space, and walk through seemingly countless stores and aisles to find and examine products. They can compare brands, check out prices, and order merchandise 24 hours a day from any location. Online buying is *easy* and *private*: customers face fewer buying hassles and don't have to face salespeople or open themselves up to persuasion and emotional pitches.

Given that most consumers would prefer to visit the dentist than visit a car showroom, it is not surprising that new automobile-related web sites pop up almost weekly. For example, Big 3 Employee Vehicles (www.big3vehicles.com) gives people information about used cars sold by employees of the big auto makers. It is predicted that such sites will allow 20 percent of Canadians to purchase cars over the Net in the near future.[34]

Online buying offers consumers some additional advantages. The commercial online services and the Internet give consumers access to an abundance of comparative *information*—information about companies, products, and competitors. In addition, online buying is *interactive* and *immediate*. Consumers often can interact with the seller's site to find exactly the information, products, or services they desire, then order or download them on the spot. For example, Black Photo Corp. (www.blackphoto.com) allows customers to see their photos online. For $5.49, Black notifies customers via e-mail once their pictures are ready. Using a confidential password provided by Black, customers can view their photos on the company's web site. They can then send their pictures to anyone around the world if they choose to do so.[35]

Benefits to Marketers

Online marketing also yields many benefits to marketers. Rather than just being another communication tool, it helps companies reinforce their core strategy. Because of its one-to-one, interactive nature, online marketing is a good tool for *customer relationship building*. It brings companies and their customers closer together. Companies can interact with customers to learn more about specific customer needs and wants and to build customer databases. In turn, online customers can ask questions and volunteer feedback. Based on this ongoing interaction, companies can increase customer value and satisfaction through product and service refinements. They can also tailor their communications and offers to the requirements of specific customers. George Fisher, CEO of Eastman Kodak Company, sums it up this way: "Online activity gives us a way to meet customer needs and desires that is unparalleled since the days of the door-to-door [salesperson].[36]

Online marketing can *reduce costs* and *increase efficiency*. Online marketers avoid the expense of maintaining a store and the accompanying costs of rent, insurance, and utilities. Because customers deal directly with sellers, online marketing often results in lower costs and improved efficiencies for channel and logistics functions such as order processing, inventory handling, delivery, and trade promotion. Finally, communicating electronically often costs less than communicating on paper through the mail. For instance, a company can produce digital catalogues for much less than the cost of printing and mailing paper ones. While many people originally thought that the relatively low costs of setting up an online marketing operation would mean that both small and large firms could afford it, Internet marketing doesn't come cheap. Molson found that its "I Am" web site cost about the same as it does to purchase 30 seconds of commercial time on prime-time network television. Recent research showed that the median cost of setting up a web site was $25 000. However, some firms report that they spend as much as $50 000 to $100 000 to establish their sites. The costs of maintaining and updating sites are not included in these figures.[37]

Richmond BC Savings Credit Union knows that offbeat humour appeals to many web users.

Online marketing also offers greater *flexibility*, allowing the marketer to adjust its offers and programs continually. For example, once a paper catalogue is mailed, the products, prices, and other catalogue features are fixed until the next catalogue is sent. However, an online catalogue can be adjusted continously, adapting product assortments, prices, and promotions to match changing market conditions.

Finally, the Internet is a truly *global* medium that allows buyers and sellers to click from one country to another in seconds. A Web surfer from Paris or Istanbul can access Roots Canada's impressive Internet shop (www.roots.com), or even book a motor home to travel through the Canadian Rockies. Canada West R V Vacations (www.motorhome.com).[38] Even small online marketers find that they have ready access to global markets. Despite these many benefits, however, online marketing is not for every company nor for every product. Careful thought has to be given to if, when, and how it should be done.

ONLINE MARKETING CHANNELS

Marketers can conduct online marketing in four ways: by creating an electronic storefront; by placing ads online; by participating in Internet forums, news groups, or "web communities"; or by using online e-mail or webcasting.

Creating an Electronic Storefront

In opening an electronic storefront, a company has two choices: it can buy space on a commercial online service or it can open its own web site. Crabtree & Evelyn Ltd., for example, is linked through Sympatico (www.atmarket.sympatico.ca). The online services typically design the storefront for the company and introduce it to their subscribers. For these services, the company pays the online service an annual fee plus a small percentage of the company's online sales.

Corporate web site
Sites designed to handle interactive communication initiated by the consumer.

In addition to buying a location on an online service, or as an alternative, thousands of companies have now created their own web sites. These sites vary greatly in purpose and content. The most basic type is a **corporate web site**. In early 1997, there were 4.5 million sites in the .com domain, the area of the Internet reserved for companies. In the first six months of 1997, 600 000 new sites came online in this domain.[39] These sites are designed to handle interactive communication *initiated by the consumer*. They seek to build customer goodwill and to supplement other sales channels rather than to sell the company's products directly (see Marketing Highlight 17-2). Corporate web sites typically offer a rich variety of information and other features in an effort to answer customer questions, build closer customer relationships, and generate excitement about the company. Corporate web sites generally provide information about the company's history, its mission and philosophy, and the products and services that it offers. They might also tell about current events, company personnel, financial performance, and employment opportunities. Many corporate web sites also provide exciting entertainment features to attract and hold visitors. Finally, the site might also provide opportunities for customers to ask questions or make comments through e-mail before leaving the site.

Marketing Web Site
A site designed to engage consumers in an interaction that will move them closer to a purchase or other marketing outcome.

Other companies create a **marketing web site**. These sites are designed to engage consumers in an interaction that will move them closer to a purchase or other marketing outcome. With a marketing web site, communication and interactions are *initiated by the marketer*. Such a site might include a catalogue, shopping tips, and promotional features such as coupons, sales events, or contests. Companies aggressively promote their marketing web sites in print and broadcast advertising, and through "banner-to-site" ads that pop up on other web sites. Consumers can find a web site for buying almost anything. Wal-Mart Canada recently established a site so people living in remote areas in Canada could have

PILLSBURY CENTRAL: INFORMATION AND A WHOLE LOT MORE TO KEEP CUSTOMERS COMING BACK

Pillsbury Central does everything that a good corporate web site should do. No, you can't use the site to order up products bearing one of the company's familiar brands—Pillsbury, Green Giant, Hungry Jack, LeSueur, Progresso, Old El Paso, Totino's, Haagen-Dazs, or one of a dozen others. Pillsbury Central isn't designed to be a direct selling channel. Instead, it's meant to be a one-to-one communication tool for enhancing Pillsbury's relationships with customers.

Pillsbury Central provides interesting and useful information—*lots* of information—that keeps consumers coming back again and again. A click on the "Pillsbury Story" icon provides access to detailed information on everything from the company's history, mission, and values; to its environmental and community involvement efforts; to its products, brand logos, and facts about familiar characters like Poppin Fresh, the Pillsbury Doughboy, and the Jolly Green Giant. For example, did you know that the Green Giant brand was originally named for the company's new "Green Giant" pea hybrid, and that the giant was originally white? When the company's trademark attorney suggested a switch to the more distinctive green, management responded with the argument "who ever heard of a green giant?" Obviously, everyone has by now.

Tap the "Bake-Off Contest" icon and you'll find out all you ever wanted to know about the Pillsbury Bake-Off—history, winning recipes, rules, tips, even an online entry form. The "Mealtime Solutions" icon provides a gateway to recipes and entertaining ideas—hundreds of them—for every season. Feeding a group? Try the "Casual Gatherings" icon to see plans for a patio party, backyard summer social, or football fiesta open house.

Pillsbury Central contains a bulletin board that lets you interact with other site surfers to post and share cooking shortcuts, tips on saving time and money, or requests for longlost recipes. For example, a visitor named Donya recently posted: "Please help me! I lost a favourite recipe for Hungry Jack Biscuits Coffee Cake Dessert that

Pillsbury printed about 10 years ago on those little 3x5 cards they used to put out. Has anyone got this recipe? Please post ASAP." Another visitor posted the requested recipe the very next day.

company explains, the information will help them build a better site. In fact, using this information, Pillsbury has built an impressive consumer database. It uses the database to prepare individualized e-mail dis-

Pillsbury Central does all that a good corporate web site should do. No, you can't use it to order one of the company's familiar brands. However, as this web page suggests, it's a good means of enhancing Pillsbury's relationships with consumers.

The Pillsbury Central web site also offers visitors an opportunity to subscribe to Pillsbury's Digital Dispatch, a periodic e-mail bulletin sent automatically to subscribers containing cooking and entertaining tips, recipes, and time-saving ideas to make life easier. To receive the bulletins, you fill out an online form with your name and address, age, and other demographic information, and indicate your cooking interests and the kinds of information you'd like to receive. Providing this information is optional—"You don't have to answer every question . . . for instance, if you're worried that we're going to pester you or send you a bunch of junk mail (we won't)." However, the

patches tailored to the specific demographics and expressed interests of these self-selected and very receptive consumers. For example, in late 1997, Pillsbury sent a dispatch to parents of school-aged children containing recipes for easy to prepare school-day meals and instructions on how to receive e-mailed recipes for "Snacks to Pack: Portable Munchies for Kids of All Ages." The dispatch also contained links to Pillsbury web sites filled wth menu ideas and quick-to-make recipes suited for the busy family's back-to-school schedule.

According to Michael Lundeby, president of Creative Resource Center, the marketing communications agency that created and manages the site, Pillsbury Central has been a huge success. The site draws millions of hits each month, and Pillsbury's digital dispatch has attracted tens of thousands of subscribers whose demographics closely match Pillsbury's target market. E-mail responses to the newsletter suggest that members appreciate not only the Information it contains, but also the personal interaction with Pillsbury. By tracking which recipes site visitors access most frequently, Pillsbury obtains valuable information about current consumer desires and cooking habits. All of these benefits come at a surprisingly low cost. The annual budget for the site totals less than the amount the company spends for a single advertisement on prime-time television.

According to Lundeby, web technology is changing rapidly, as are consumer usage and buying patterns. Thus, Pillsbury Central remains a work in constant process. "That's the beauty of the Internet as a communication form," says Lundeby. "As our audience—and what they want—change, so will the site."

Pillsbury Central
www.pillsbury.com

access to some of its products. Mbanx gives people access to all of the services provided by the Bank of Montreal. IBM Canada encourages people to think of them when they do "e-business."

Despite the tremendous hype about the Internet, many retailers who have developed web sites are saying, "Show me the money!" Even widely praised sites such as Amazon.com, the online bookseller, have yet to turn a profit. In 1996, only 0.1 percent of total Canadian retail sales (or less than $25 million) came from people actually making online purchases. Computer-related products and services head the list of products actually purchased. People also use the Net to make travel reservations, do their banking, purchase books, small gifts, flowers, toys, and games. For organizations such as the Royal Canadian Mint, (www.rcmint.ca), Internet marketing makes sense. Sixty percent of their sales come from outside Canada and they can interact with these distant customers.[40]

Business-to-business marketers also make good use of marketing web sites. For example, corporate buyers can visit Sun Microsystems' web site, (www.sun.com), select detailed descriptions of Sun's products and solutions, request sales and service information, and interact with staff members. And FedEx's web site (www.fedex.com) allows customers to schedule their own shipments, request a courier, and track their packages in transit.

While some firms such as Air Canada and Bank of Montreal's Mbanx have done a superb job of integrating online technology into their core business, much business-to-business marketing using the Internet is still in its infancy. A recent survey conducted by the consulting firm A.T. Kearney Ltd. found that while many firms use the Internet to gather and share information, 80 percent of Canadian companies neither buy or sell products or services over the Net. Barriers to growth for online business commerce include the belief that firms are not offering the right products or services and that there are security and privacy issues. To solve these problems, many firms are now using extranets: extensions of their internal computer networks that allow them to link with their suppliers, members of their distribution channels, and corporate customers.[41]

Placing Advertisements Online

Companies can place online advertisements in any of three ways. First, they can place classified ads in special sections offered by the major commercial online services. The ads are listed according to when they arrived, with the latest ones heading the list. Second, ads can be placed in certain Internet newsgroups that are set up for commercial purposes. Finally, the company can buy **online ads** that pop up while subscribers are surfing online services or web sites. Such ads include banner ads, pop-up windows, "tickers" (banners that move across the screen), and "roadblocks" (full-screen ads that users must pass through to reach the other screens they wish to view). For example, a web user or America Online subscriber who

Online ads
An advertisement that pops up while subscribers are surfing online services or web sites.

is looking up airline schedules or fares might find a flashing banner on the screen exclaiming "Rent a car from Alamo and get up to two days free!"

Web advertising is on the increase. However, many marketers still question its value as an effective advertising tool. Costs are reasonable compared with those of other advertising media. For example, web advertising on ESPNet SportZone, which attracts more than 500 000 web surfers and 20 million "hits"—the number of times the site is accessed—per week, costs about $430 000 per year. Netscape, the popular web-browser site, charges about $520 000 per year and delivers an estimated one million impressions. Still, web surfers can easily ignore these banner ads, and often do. Web locations that sell advertising space are still working to develop good measures of advertising impact. Thus, although many firms are experimenting with web advertising, it still plays only a minor role in their promotion mixes.

Participating in Forums, Newsgroups, and Web Communities

Companies may decide to participate in or sponsor Internet forums, newsgroups, and bulletin boards that appeal to specific special interest groups. Such activities may be organized for commercial or non-commercial purposes. *Forums* are discussion groups located on commercial online services. A forum may operate a library, a "chat room" for real-time message exchanges, and even a classified ad directory. For example, America Online boasts some 14 000 chat rooms, which account for a third of its members' online time.[42] Most forums are sponsored by interest groups. Thus, as a major musical instruments manufacturer, Yamaha might start a forum on classical music.

Newsgroups are the Internet version of forums, where people post and read messages on a specified topic. *Bulletin board systems (BBSs)* are specialized online services that centre on a specific topic or group. Marketers might want to identify and participate in newsgroups and BBSs that attract subscribers who fit their target markets. However, newsgroups and BBS users often resent commercial intrusions on their Net space, so marketers must tread carefully, participating in subtle ways that provide real value to participants.

Tripod is an online hangout for twenty-somethings, offering chat rooms and free home pages for posting job résumés.

The popularity of forums and newsgroups has resulted in a rash of commercially sponsored web sites called *web communities*. Such sites provide a place where members can congregate online and exchange views on issues of common interest. They are "the cyber-space equivalent to the bar at TV's *Cheers*, where everybody knows your e-mail name."[43] For example, Women's Wire is a web community where career-oriented women can engage in discussion forums and celebrity chats on women's issues.

Visitors to these Net neighbour-hoods develop a strong sense of community. Such communities are attractive to marketers because they represent clearly defined market segments since they draw consumers with common interests and well-defined demographics. For example, Parent Soup provides an ideal environment for the web ads of Johnson & Johnson, Gerber's, and other makers of children's products.

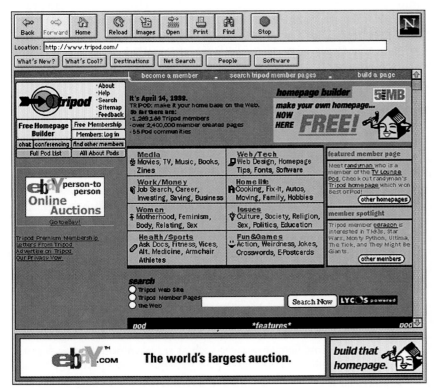

Tripod® is a registered trademark of Tripod, Inc. All rights reserved.

Moreover, cyberhood consumers visit frequently and stay online longer, increasing the chance of meaningful exposure to the advertiser's message.

Using E-mail and Webcasting

A company can encourage prospects and customers to send questions, suggestions, and even complaints to the company via e-mail. Customer service representatives can quickly respond to such messages. The company may also develop Internet-based electronic mailing lists of customers or prospects. Such lists provide an excellent opportunity to introduce the company and its offerings to new customers and to build ongoing relationships with current ones. Using the lists, online marketers can send out customer newsletters, special product or promotion offers based on customer purchasing histories, reminders of service requirements or warranty renewals, or announcements of special events.

Webcasting
A service that automatically downloads customized information to recipients' PCs.

Companies can also sign on with any of a number of "**webcasting**" services, which automatically download customized information to recipients' PCs. For a monthly fee, subscribers to these services can specify the topics they're interested in. Then, rather than spending hours scouring the Internet, they can sit back while the webcaster automatically delivers information of interest to their desktops. Webcasting, also known as "push" programming, affords an attractive channel through which online marketers can deliver their Internet advertising or other information content.

> Now, instead of waiting for Web surfers to stumble onto their sites and banner ads, marketers can send animated ads directly to the desktops of target customers. Retailers such as Lands' End and Virtual Vineyards are dabbling with such in-your-face methods to notify subscribers of promotions and even send them order forms. Merchants can approach live sales prospects and not just couch potatoes.[44]

Webcasting services such as PointCast and Ifusion are growing quickly and attracting increasing numbers of advertisers. The major commercial online services are also beginning to offer webcasting to their members. However, as with other types of online marketing, companies must be careful that they don't cause resentment among Internet users who are already overloaded with "junk e-mail." Warns one analyst, "There's a fine line between adding value and the consumer feeling that you're being intrusive."[45]

Online users gather at an Internet café. How does the demographic and psychographic profile of this group differ from the general population?

THE PROMISE AND CHALLENGES OF ONLINE MARKETING

Online marketing offers great promise for the future. Yet despite all the hype and promise, online marketing may be years away from realizing its full potential and has yet to carve out a central role in consumers' lives. As one analyst comments, "The Web is hip. The Web is cool. And increasingly, the Web is way frustrating," for both marketers and the Internet users they wish to reach. Here are just some of the challenges that online marketers face:

◆ *Limited consumer exposure and buying:* Although expanding rapidly, online marketing still reaches only a limited marketplace. Moreover, web users appear to do more window browsing than actual buying. Only an estimated 10 to 15 percent of web surfers actually use the web regularly for shopping or to obtain commercial services such as travel information. Less than six million people have ever made an online purchase.[46]

◆ *Skewed user demographics and psychographics:* Online users tend to be more upscale and technically oriented than the general population. This makes online marketing ideal for marketing computer hardware and software, consumer electronics, financial services, and certain other classes of products. However, it makes online marketing less effective for selling mainstream products.

◆ *Chaos and clutter.* The Internet offers up millions of web sites and a staggering volume of information. Thus, navigating the Internet can be frustrating, confusing, and time-consuming for consumers. In this chaotic and cluttered environment, many web ads and sites go unnoticed or unopened. Even when noticed, marketers will find it difficult to hold consumer attention. One study found that a site must capture web surfers' attention within eight seconds or lose them to another site. That leaves very little time for marketers to promote and sell their goods.

◆ *Security:* Consumers worry that unscrupulous snoopers will eavesdrop on their online transactions or intercept their credit-card numbers and make unauthorized purchases. In turn, companies doing business online fear that others will use the Internet to invade their computer systems for the purposes of commercial espionage or even sabotage. Online marketers are developing solutions to such security problems. However, there appears to be a "never-ending competition between the technology of security systems and the sophistication of those seeking to thwart them."[47]

◆ *Ethical concerns:* Privacy is a primary concern. Marketers can easily track web-site visitors, and many consumers who participate in web-site activities provide extensive personal information. This may leave consumers open to information abuse if companies make unauthorized use of the information in marketing their products or exchanging electronic lists with other companies. There are also concerns about segmentation and discrimination. The Internet currently serves upscale consumers well. however, poorer consumers have less access to the Net, leaving them increasingly less informed about products, services, and prices.[48]

Despite these challenges, both large and small companies are quickly integrating online marketing into their marketing mixes.

INTEGRATED DIRECT MARKETING

Integrated direct marketing
A direct-marketing approach that involves using multiple-vehicle, multiple-stage campaigns.

Although direct marketing and online marketing have boomed in recent years, many companies still try "one-shot" efforts that relegate these tactics to minor roles in their marketing and promotion mixes. A more powerful approach is **integrated direct marketing**, which involves using multiple-vehicle, multiple-stage campaigns. Such campaigns can greatly improve response. Whereas a direct-mail piece alone might generate a two percent response, adding a toll-free number can raise the response rate by 50 percent. A well-designed outbound telemarketing effort might increase response by another 500 percent. Suddenly, a two percent response has grown to 13 percent or more by adding interactive marketing channels to a regular mailing.[49]

More elaborate integrated direct marketing campaigns can be used. Consider the multimedia, multistage campaign shown in Figure 17-2. Here, the paid ad creates awareness of a product, provides information on the corporate web site, and stimulates inquiries. The company immediately sends direct mail to those who inquire. Within a few days, the company follows up with a phone call seeking an order. Some prospects will order by phone, others might request a face-to-face sales call. In such a campaign, the marketer seeks to improve response rates and

FIGURE 17-2 *An integrated direct marketing campaign*

profits by adding media and stages that contribute more to additional sales than to additional costs (see Marketing Highlight 17-3).

PUBLIC POLICY AND ETHICAL ISSUES IN DIRECT MARKETING

Direct marketers and their customers usually enjoy mutually rewarding relationships. Occasionally, however, a darker side emerges. The aggressive and sometimes shady tactics of a few direct marketers can bother or harm consumers, casting a shadow over the entire industry. Abuses range from simple excesses that irritate consumers to instances of unfair practices or even outright deception and fraud. During the past few years, the direct marketing industry also has faced growing concerns about invasion of privacy issues.[50]

IRRITATION, UNFAIRNESS, DECEPTION, AND FRAUD

Direct marketing excesses sometimes annoy or offend consumers. Most of us dislike direct-response TV commercials that are too loud, too long, and too insistent. Especially bothersome are dinnertime or late-night phone calls. Beyond irritating consumers, some direct marketers have been accused of taking unfair advantage of impulsive or less sophisticated buyers. Television shopping shows and program-long "infomercials" seem to be the worst culprits. They feature smooth-talking hosts, elaborately staged demonstrations, claims of drastic price reductions, "while they last" time limitations, and unequalled ease of purchase to inflame buyers who have low sales resistance.

Worse yet, so-called "heat merchants" design mailers and write copy intended to mislead buyers. Other direct marketers pretend to be conducting research surveys when they are actually asking leading questions to screen or persuade consumers. Fraudulent schemes, such as investment scams or phony collections for charity, have also multiplied in recent years. Crooked direct marketers can be hard to catch: direct-marketing customers often respond quickly, do not interact personally with the seller, and usually expect to wait for delivery. By the time buyers realize that they have been bilked, the thieves are usually somewhere else plotting new schemes.

INVASION OF PRIVACY

Invasion of privacy is perhaps the toughest public policy issue now confronting the direct-marketing industry. These days, it seems that almost every time consumers order products by mail or telephone, enter a sweepstakes, apply for a credit card, or take out a magazine subscription, their names are entered into some company's already bulging database. Using sophisticated computer technologies, direct marketers can use these databases to "micro-target" their selling efforts.

Consumers often benefit from such database marketing—they receive more offers that are closely matched to their interests. However, many critics worry that marketers may know *too* much about consumers' lives, and that they may use this knowledge to take unfair advantage of consumers. At some point, they claim, the extensive use of databases intrudes on consumer privacy. For example, they ask, should Bell be allowed to sell marketers the names of customers who frequently call the 800 numbers of catalogue companies? Is it right for credit bureaus to compile and sell lists of people who have recently applied for credit cards—people who are considered prime direct-marketing targets because

AMERICAN STANDARD'S INTEGRATED DIRECT MARKETING: ANYTHING BUT STANDARD

You probably haven't thought much about your bathroom—it's not something that most of us get all that inspired about. But as it turns out, you probably have a relationship with your bathroom unlike that with any other room in your house. It's where you start and end your day, primp and preen and admire yourself, escape from the rigours of everyday life, and do some of your best thinking. The marketers at American Standard, the plumbing fixtures giant, understand this often-overlooked but special little room. And they've set out upon a mission to help people design bathrooms worthy of their finest moments.

Working with its ad agency, Carmichael Lynch, American Standard has created a wonderfully warm and highly effective but not-so-standard integrated marketing campaign. The campaign, called "We want you to love your bathroom," targets men and women aged 25 to 54 from households planning to remodel bathrooms or replace fixtures. The campaign employs a carefully integrated mix of brand image and direct-response media ads, direct mailings, and personal contracts to create a customer database, generate sales leads, gently coax customers into its retail showroom, and build sales and market share.

The campaign begins with a series of humorous, soft-sell brand image ads in home and shelter magazines like *Home, House Beautiful*, and *Country Living*, which have a high percentage of readers undertaking remodelling products. Featuring simple but artistic shots of ordinary bathroom fixtures and scenes, the ads position American Standard as a company that understands the special relationships we have with our bathroom. For example, one ad shows a white toilet and a partially unwound roll of toilet paper, artfully arranged in a corner against plain blue-grey walls. "We're not in this business for the glory," proclaims the headline. "Designing a toilet or sink may not be as glamorous as, say, designing a Maserati. But to us, it's every bit as important. After all, more

people will be sitting on our seats than theirs."

Another ad shows the feet of a man standing on a white tile bathroom floor wearing his goofy-looking floppy-eared dog slippers. "The rest of the world thinks you're a genius," notes the ad. But "after a long day of being brilliant, witty, and charming, it's nice just to be comfortable. The right bathroom understands. And accepts you unconditionally." Each simple but engaging ad includes a toll-free phone number and urges readers to call for a free guidebook "overflowing with products, ireas, and inspiration."

American Standard has created a wonderfully warm and effective but not-so-standard integrated marketing campaign. It all starts with ads like these.

Whereas the brand image ads position American Standard and its products, when it comes to generating inquires, the real workhorses are the one-third-page, coupon-like "direct-response" ads that run in the same magazines. One such ad notes, "You will spend seven years of your life in the bathroom. You will need a good book." Readers can obtain the free guidebook by mailing in the coupon or calling the toll-free number listed in the ad.

Consumers who respond find that they've taken the first step in a

carefully orchestrated relationship building venture. First, they receive the entertaining, highly informative, picture-filled 30-page guidebook titled *We Want You to Love Your Bathroom*, along with a folksy letter thanking them for their interest and noting the locations of nearby American Standard dealers.

The guidebook is chock full of helpful tips on bathroom design, starting with answers to some simple questions: What kind of lavatory—what colour? The bathtub—how big, big enough for two? The toilet—sleek one-piece or familiar two-piece?

The faucet? You'll fumble for it every morning, so be particular about how it operates. To spice things up, the guidebook also contains loads of entertaining facts and trivia. An example: During the Middle Ages, Christianity preached that to uncover your skin, even to bathe it, was an invitation to sin. Thank heavens for perfume. These days, we average about four baths or 7.5 showers a week." And, of course, the booklet contains plenty of information on American Standard products, along with a tear-out card that prospective customers can return to obtain more detailed guides and product catalogues.

In addition to the guidebook, customers receive a carefully coordinated stream of communications from American Standard, starting with a series of "Bathroom Reading" bulletins, each containing information on specific bathroom design issues. For example, one issue contains information and tips on how to make a bathroom safer, another issue offers "10 neat ways to save water."

Meanwhile, information about prospective customers and their remodelling projects collected by the 1-800 operator or from the coupon goes into American Standard's customer database. The database generates leads for salespeople at American Standard's showrooms throughout North America. The company markets the program to key distributors and kitchen and bath

dealers, motivating them to follow up on leads and training them how to do it effectively. The key is to get customers who've made inquiries to come into the showroom. Not long after making their inquiries, prospective customers typically receive a hand-written postcard—or perhaps even a phone call—from a local dealer's Showroom Consultant, who extends a personal invitation to visit, see American Standard products first hand, and discuss bathroom designs. Thus, the integrated direct marketing program builds relationships not just with buyers, but with dealers as well.

American Standard's integrated direct marketing campaign has done wonders for the company's positioning and performance. Since the campaign began, American Standard's plumbing division has experienced steady

increases in sales and earnings—earnings last year tripled those of the previous year. The campaign generates tens of thousands of qualified leads per year for local showrooms—more than a half million qualified leads so far. Research confirms significant shifts in consumer perceptions of American Standard and its products—from "boring and institutional" to well designed and loaded with "personal spirit." According to Bob Srenaski, Group Vice President of Marketing at American Standard, the campaign has "totally repositioned our company and established a momentum and winning spirit that is extraordinary." "The campaign has been incredible. It's given American Standard and its products a more personal face, one that's helped us to build closer relationships with customers and dealers.

of their spending behaviour? Or is it right for provinces to sell the names and addresses, gender and birth date of driver's licence holders?

In their drive to build databases, companies sometimes get carried away. For example, Microsoft caused substantial privacy concerns when it introduced its Windows 95 software. It used a "Registration Wizard" that allowed users to register their new software online. However, when users went online to register, without their knowledge, Microsoft took the opportunity to "read" the configurations of their PCs. Thus, the company gained instant knowledge of the major software products running on each customer's system. When users learned of this invasion, they protested publicly and Microsoft abandoned the practice. However, such actions have spawned a quiet but determined "privacy revolt" among consumers and public policy makers.[51]

In a recent survey of consumers, 79 percent of respondents said that they were concerned about threats to their personal privacy. In another survey, *Advertising Age* magazine asked advertising industry executives how they felt about database marketing and the privacy issue. The responses of two executives show that even industry insiders have mixed feelings.[52]

There are profound ethical issues relating to the marketing of specific household data—financial information, for instance. . . . For every household . . . the computer can guess with amazing accuracy . . . things like credit use, net worth, and investments, the kind of information most people would never want disclosed, let alone sold to any marketer.

It doesn't bother me that people know I live in a suburb . . . and have X number of kids. It [does] bother me that these people know the names of my wife and kids and where my kids go to school. They . . . act like they know me when the bottom line is they're attempting to sell me something. I do feel that database marketing has allowed companies to cross the fine line of privacy. . . . [And] in a lot of cases, I think they know they have crossed it.

The direct-marketing industry is addressing issues of ethics and public policy. Direct marketers know that, left untended, such problems will lead to increasingly negative consumer attitudes, lower response rates, and calls for more restrictive provincial and federal legislation. More importantly, most direct marketers want the same things that consumers want: honest and well-designed marketing offers targeted only toward consumers who will appreciate and respond to them. Direct marketing is just too expensive to waste on consumers who don't want it.

Summary of Chapter Objectives

Mass marketers have typically tried to reach millions of buyers with a single product and a standard message communicated via the mass media. Consequently, most mass marketing communications were one-way communications directed *at* consumers rather than two-way communications *with* consumers. Today, many companies are turning to direct marketing in an effort to reach carefully targeted customers more efficiently and to build stronger, more personal, one-to-one relationships with them.

1. **Discuss the benefits of direct marketing to customers and companies and the trends fuelling its rapid growth.**

   Customers benefit from direct marketing in many ways. For consumers, home shopping is fun, convenient, hassle free, saves time, and gives them a bigger selection of merchandise. It allows them to comparison shop using mail catalogues and online shopping services, and then order products and services without dealing with salespeople. Sellers also benefit. Direct marketers can buy mailing lists containing names of nearly any target group, customize offers to special wants and needs, and then use individualized communications to promote these offers. Direct marketers can also build a continuous relationship with each customer; time offers to reach prospects at the right moment, thereby receiving higher readership and response; and easily test alternative media and messages. Finally, direct marketers gain privacy because their offer and strategy are less visible to competitors.

   Various trends have led to the rapid growth of direct marketing. Market "demassification" has produced a constantly increasing number of market niches with specific preferences. Direct marketing enables sellers to focus efficiently on these minimarkets with offers that better match particular consumer wants and needs.

Other trends encouraging at-home shopping include higher costs of driving, traffic congestion, parking headaches, lack of time, a shortage of retail sales help, and long lines at checkout counters. Consumers like the convenience of direct marketers' toll-free phone numbers, their acceptance of orders round the clock, and their commitment to customer service. The growth of quick delivery via express carriers has also made direct shopping fast and easy. The increased affordability of computers and customer databases has allowed direct marketers to single out the best prospects for each of their products. Finally in business-to-business marketing, lower cost-per-contact media has proven more cost-effective in reaching and selling to more prospects and customers than if a sales force were used.

2. **Define a customer database and list the four ways companies use databases in direct marketing.**

   A *customer database* is an organized collection of comprehensive data about individual customers or prospects, including geographic, demographic, psychographic, and behavioural data. Companies use databases to identify prospects; decide which customers should receive a particular offer, deepen customer loyalty, and reactivate customer purchases.

3. **Identify the major forms of direct marketing.**

   The main forms of direct marketing include *face-to-face selling, direct-mail marketing, catalogue marketing, telemarketing, direct-response television marketing, kiosk marketing*, and *online, or Internet, marketing*. Most companies today continue to rely heavily on *face-to-face selling* through a professional sales force, or they hire manufacturers' representatives and agents. *Direct mail marketing* consists of the company sending an offer, announcement, reminder, or other item to a person at a specific address. Recently, three new forms of mail delivery have become popular—*fax mail, e-mail*, and *voice mail*. Some marketers rely on *catalogue marketing*, or selling through catalogues mailed to a select list of customers or made available in stores. *Telemarketing* consists of using the telephone to sell directly to consumers. *Direct-response television marketing* has two forms—(1) *direct-response advertising* or *infomercials*, and (2) *home shopping channels*. *Kiosks* are information and ordering machines that direct marketers place in stores, airports, and other locations. *Online marketing* involves online channels and electronic commerce and is usually conducted through interactive online computer systems, which electronically link consumers with sellers.

4. **Compare the two types of online marketing channels and explain the effect of the Internet on electronic commerce.**

The two types of online marketing channels are *commercial online services* and the *Internet*. *Commercial online services* provide online information and marketing services to subscribers for a monthly fee. The *Internet* is a vast global and public web of computer networks. In contrast to commercial online services, use of the Internet is free—anyone with a PC, a modem, and the right software can browse the Internet to obtain or share information on almost any subject and to interact with other users.

The explosion of Internet usage has created a new world of *electronic commerce*, a term that refers to the buying and selling process that is supported by electronic means. In this process, *electronic markets* become "marketspaces" in which sellers offer products and services electronically, while buyers search for information, identify their wants and needs, and then place orders using a credit card or other form of electronic payment.

5. **Identify the benefits of online marketing to consumers and marketers and the four ways that marketers can conduct online marketing.**

For consumers, online marketing is beneficial for many reasons. It is *interactive, immediate*, and provides access to an abundance of comparative *information* about products, companies, and competitors. Marketers also benefit from on line marketing. For them, it helps *consumer relationship building, reduces costs, increases efficiency*, provides more *flexibility*, and is, in the form of the Internet, a *global* medium that enables buyers and sellers in different countries to interact with each other in seconds. Marketers can conduct online marketing by creating an electronic storefront; placing ads online; participating in Internet forums, newsgroups, or "web communities"; or by using online e-mail or webcasting.

6. **Discuss the public policy and ethical issues facing direct marketers.**

Direct marketers and their customers have typically forged mutually rewarding relationships. However, there remains a potential for customer abuse, ranging from irritation and unfair practices to deception and fraud. In addition, there have been growing concerns about invasion of privacy, perhaps the most difficult public policy issue currently facing the direct marketing industry.

Key Terms

Catalogue marketing *(p. 575)*
Commercial online services *(p. 578)*
Corporate web site *(p. 584)*
Customer database *(p. 570)*
Direct marketing *(p. 567)*
Direct-mail marketing *(p. 574)*
Direct-response television marketing *(p. 577)*
Electronic commerce *(p. 581)*
Integrated direct marketing *(p. 589)*
Internet (or the Net) *(p. 578)*
Marketing web site *(p. 584)*
Online ads *(p. 586)*
Online marketing *(p. 578)*
Telemarketing *(p. 576)*
Webcasting *(p. 588)*

Discussing the Issues

1. As demonstrated in the chapter, direct marketing consists of direct communication with carefully targeted individual consumers to obtain an immediate response. Contact one of the personal computer direct marketers (such as Dell Computer—www.del.com). Answer the following questions about your contact: (a) How do they make it easy to order their products? (b) What differentiates them from traditional retailers or manufacturers? (c) What are their chief advantages and disadvantages? (d) How is security provided (or not)? (e) Based on your experience, what is your opinion of online marketers?

2. It has been said that direct marketing benefits in the customer in many ways. After reviewing the material about this subject in your text, provide three examples of direct marketers that demonstrate strong marketing benefits for their customers. Describe and explain the benefits.

3. Companies that know about individual customer needs and characteristics can customize their offers, messages, delivery modes, and payment methods to maximize customer value and satisfaction. Answer the following questions about these companies: (a) State Farm Insurance; (b) IBM; (c) The Museum of Civilization; (d) Canadian Cancer Society; and (e) Lexus. How could the organizations create customer databases that would reveal significant information about their customers or supporters? Where would they get their information? Do you think the cost of building a database would be significant? What do you think would be the most significant demographic information that should be part of the individual databases?

4. Direct mail marketing used to mean sending an offer, announcement, reminder, or item to a person through the mail. Today, new forms of direct communication are emerging. Critique (a) Fax mail, (b) E-mail, and (c) Voice mail as forms of direct mail. Examine the advantages, disadvantages, customer profile, competitive advantage, cost, and future of these forms.

5. Using either a direct-response television commercial or an infomercial, compare the product or service against how the product might be sold in the traditional ways (such as radio, newspapers, magazines, in-store display, or outdoor). To make your evaluation consider answering the following questions: (a) Under what circumstances do you think the two forms of direct-response work best? (b) What type of products seem naturally suited to the direct-response form? (c) What do you see as the greatest disadvantage to the direct-response approach?

6. For marketing purposes, what do we really know about the typical Internet user? Using the information in Figure 17-2 as a springboard, prepare a brief profile of the typical Internet user. What additional information would you like to know (and how might you obtain the information) about the Internet user for (a) a music distributor desiring to design an attractive web site for the first time; (b) a university wishing to attract new students; and (c) an airline wishing to expand its customer base.

7. Online marketing offers great promise for the future. Assume that you are the sales manager for a local travel agency. Make a case that would persuade your superiors that going "online" would be a good investment. Cite both positive and negative consequences. Explain how you will integrate this effort into the other parts of your promotion mix.

Applying the Concepts

1. List your three favourite web sites (if you are familiar with the Web—go online and explore). Answer the following questions about your chosen sites and your Internet experiences: (a) What makes the site(s) attractive to you? (b) Have you ever ordered products or services via the Internet (if so, describe the experience)? (c) What are your

fears about using the Internet for commerce (if any)? (d) If one thing could be changed on each of your favourite sites, what would it be? (e) What do you foresee for the Internet in the next 10 years (and how will this affect your favourite sites)?

2. The primary purpose of creating a marketing web site is to engage the customers in an interaction that will move them closer to a purchase or other marketing outcome. Go to your university's web site. Put the site under your personal microscope and critically examine the marketing aspects of the site (if your university does not have a site, design one for them by outlining what you think would be critical points of consumer interest). Write a brief report that outlines your thoughts and criticisms on how well the site meets what you perceive to be the marketing objectives of the site.

References

1. Quotations from Amanda Long, "Dell Canada Proves the Power of the Web," *The Financial Post*, October 15, 1997, p. 13; Gary McWilliams, "Whirlwind on the Web," *Business Week*, April 7, 1997, pp. 132–136; and Bill Robbins and Cathie Hargett, Dell Internet Sales Top $1 Million a Day," Press Release, Dell Computer Corporation, March 4, 1997. Also see, "Dell PC Sales Via Internet Doubling," Reuters Ltd., June 18, 1997; Eryn Brown, "Could the Very Best PC Marker Be Dell Computer? *Fortune*, April 14, 1997, pp. 26–27; "Michael Dell's Plan for the Rest of the Decade," *Fortune*, June 9, 1997, p. 138; and Andrew E. Serwer, "The Hottest Stock of the '90s," *Fortune*, September 8, 1997, p. 16.

2. Brendan Christie, "Direct Marketing Agencies, Ogilvy & Mather Direct," *Strategy: The Canadian Marketing Report*, April 28, 1997, p. DR22.

3. Lesley Daw, "Adoption of 'No Junk Mail' Option Law," *Marketing*, July 21, 1997, p. 2; Mark De Wolf, "CDMA Taps Into Education," *Strategy: The Canadian Marketing Report*, May 26, 1997, p. 2; David Foley, "Speaking Directly: Direct Marketing Growing," *Strategy: The Canadian Marketing Report*, June 12, 1995, p. 19.

4. James Champy, "The Cyber-Future Is Now," *Sales & Marketing Management*, September 1997, p. 28; Geoffrey Roan, "Internet Home Access Almost Doubles," Statscan, *Globe and Mail*, November 28, 1997, B6.

5. See Don Peppers and Martha Rogers, *The One-to-One Future* (New York: Doubleday/Currency, 1993).

6. *18th Annual Survey of Promotional Practices*, Carol Wright Promotions, Inc., Naperville, IL, 199, p. 36.

7. See Jonathan Berry, "A Potent New Tool for Selling: Database Marketing," *Business Week*, September 4, 1994, pp. 56–62; "How to Turn Junk Mail into a Gold Mine," *The Economist*, April 1, 1995, p. 51; and Weld F. Royal, "Do Databases Really Work?" *Sales & Marketing Management*, October 1995, pp. 66–74.

8. Harry Wicken, "Opinion: Small Firms Can Do International DM," *Strategy: The Canadian Marketing Report*, February 5, 1996, p. 18.

9. See Joe Schwartz, "Databases Deliver the Goods," *American Demographics*, September 1989, pp. 23–25; Gary Levin, "Database Draws Fevered Interest," *Advertising Age*, June 8, 1992, p. 31; Jonathan Berry, "A Potent New Tool for Selling: Database Marketing: Database Marketing," *Business Week*, September 5, 1994, pp. 56–62; and Richard Cross and Janet Smith, "Customer Bonding and the Information Core," *Direct Marketing*, February 1995, p. 28.

10. Junu Bryan Kim, "Marketing with Video: The Cassette Is in the Mail," *Advertising Age*, May 22, 1995, p. S-1.

11. David Bosworth, "New Database System Helps Sears Canada Improve Catalogue Sales," *Strategy: The Canadian Marketing Report*, February 17, 1997, p. DR1; David Chilton, "New Sears Gift Registry Services Branches Out From Weddings," *Strategy: The Canadian Marketing Report*, June 24, 1996, p. 3; Wendy Cuthbert, "Sears Goes New Country," *Strategy: The Canadian Marketing Report*, June 9, 1997, p. 6.

12. Jane Hodges, "Direct Marketing Tackles Benefits of New Media," *Advertising Age*, November 4, 1996, p. 22; Alex Beckett, "Spiegel Catalogue Invades Canada," *Strategy: The Canadian Marketing Report*, January 22, 1997, p. 8; Mariam Mesbah, "Hose by Phone Service: Pantyhose for Busy Executives, Rural Women," *Strategy: The Canadian Marketing Report*, August 19, 1996, p. 7.

13. Alex Beckett, "Best Catalogue Adds Two New Books," *Strategy: The Canadian Marketing Report*, February 5, 1996, p. 6; Mark DeWolf, "COA Tries Fundraising Catalogue," *Strategy: The Canadian Marketing Report*, September 15, 1997, p. SDR6; Erica Zlomislic, "Bridgehead Brews Up Fairly Traded Coffee Club," *Strategy: The Canadian Marketing Report*, September 15, 1997, p. SDR2.

14. Bristol Voss, "Calling All Catalogs! *Sales & Marketing Management*, December 1990, pp. 32–37; and Thayer C. Taylor, "Catalogues Come of Age," *Sales & Marketing Management*, December 1993, pp. 39–41.

15. Robert Wasserman, "How to Evaluate the Results of Your Call Center's Efforts," *Telemarketing*, March 1995, p. 77; and "Telemarketing Cited as Chief Form of Direct Marketing," *Marketing News*, January 1, 1996, p. 9.

16. Astrid Van Den Broek, "On the Line," *Marketing*, September 29, 1997, pp. 14–15.

17. Kevin R. Hopkins, "Dialing in to the Future," *Business Week*, July 28, 1997, p. 90.

18. See Richard L. Bencin, "Telefocus: Telemarketing Gets Synergized," *Sales & Marketing Management*, February 1992, pp. 49–57; Martin Everett, "Selling by Telephone," *Sales & Marketing Management*, December 1993, pp. 75–79; and John F. Yarbrough, "Dialing for Dollar$," *Sales & Marketing Management*, January 1997, pp. 61–67.

19. Jim Auchmute, "But Wait There's More!" *Advertising Age*, October 17, 1985, p. 18; Kathy Haley, "Infomercials Lure More Top Marketers," *Advertising Age*, May 9, 1994, pp. IN2, IN8; Chad Rubel, "Infomercials Evolve as Major Firms Join Successful Format," *Marketing News*, January 2, 1995, pp. 1, 36; and Jacqueline M. Graves, "The Fortune 500 Opt for Infomercials," *Fortune*, March 6, 1995, p. 20.

20. See Rebecca Piirto, "The TV Beast," *American Demographics*, May 1993, pp. 34–42; Frank Rose, "The End of TV as We Know It," *Fortune*, December 23, 1996, pp. 58–68; Elizabeth Lesly and Robert D. Hof, "Is Digital Convergence for Real?" *Business Week*, June 23, 1997, pp. 42–43; Amy Cortese, "Not @Home Alone: Bill Comes Knocking," *Business Week*, July 14, 1997, p. 24; Patti Summerfield, "Home Shopping Network Gets New Name, Look," *Strategy: The Canadian Marketing Report*, February 5, 1996, p. 7.

21. M.R. Kropko, "Card Markers Struggling with Computer Kiosks," *Marketing News*, June 3, 1996, p. 6; Bruce Fox, "Levi's Personal Pair Prognosis Positive," *Chain Store Age*, March 1996, pp. 35–36; Kathleen Kerwin, "Used-Car Fever," *Business Week*, January 22, 1996, pp. 34–35; David Chilton, "LCBO Installs Interactive Kiosks," *Strategy: The Canadian Marketing Report*, January 24, 1997, p. 13; Wendy Cuthbert, "Cineplex Gets Ad Kiosks," *Strategy: The Canadian Marketing Report*, March 31, 1997, p. 4; "For the Record: UNICEF Kiosks at Ikea," *Strategy: The Canadian Marketing Report*, November 24, 1997, p. 15.

22. "Interactive: Ad Age Names Finalists," *Advertising Age*, February 27, 1995, pp. 12–14.

23. "Focus on the Internet," *Globe and Mail*, January 8, 1995, p. 3.

24. For more on the basics of using the Internet, see Raymond D. Frost and Judy Strauss, *The Internet: A New Marketing Tool* (Upper Saddle River, NJ: Prentice Hall, 1997).

25. Statistics Canada, *Household Facilities and Equipment Survey*, 1997 (64-202-XPB).

26. Brad Edmondson, "The Wired Bunch," *American Demographics*, June 1997, pp. 10–15; and Amy Cortese, "A Census in Cyberspace," *Business Week*, May 5, 1997, p. 84. For the most recent statistics, check the results of an ongoing survey of Internet usage conducted by CommerceNet and Nielsen Media Research, www.commerce.net/nielsen/.

27. See John Deighton, "The Future of Interactive Marketing," *Harvard Business Review*, November-December 1996, pp. 151–162; and Philip Kotler, Gary Armstrong, Peggy H. Cunningham, and Robert Warren, *Principles of Marketing*, Third Canadian Edition (Scarborough, Ontario: Prentice Hall Canada, 1996), p. 525.

28. Brendan Christie, "Sympatico: The Internet Service for Everyone," *Strategy: The Canadian Marketing Report*, May 26, 1997, p. SS1.

29. Tim Grantham, "Window Shopping is Big on the Web," *Globe and Mail*, November 14, 1995, p. C2.

30. Fabrice Taylor, "Portrait of a Hacker," *Globe and Mail*, February 27, 1996, p. C1.

31. Bronskill, "Canadians Enter Cyberspace Cautiously," *Kingston Whig Standard*, January 3, 1997, pp. 1, 11; Randy Carr, "Opinion: Quantity, Not Quality, Fuelling Internet Growth," *Strategy: The Canadian Marketing Report*, August 18, 1997, p. 13.

32. "Small Business Briefs," *Globe and Mail*, March 4, 1996, p. B3.

33. Paul M. Eng, "Cybergiants See the Future—and It's Jack and Jill," *Business Week*, April 14, 1997, p. 44.

34. Simon Avery, "Taking a Test Drive in Your Living Room," *The Financial Post*, November 5, 1997, p. 7.

35. Geoffrey Rowan, "Black Photo Offers to Post Pictures On-line," *Globe and Mail*, June 5, 1997, p. B7.

36. John Deighton, "The Future of Interactive Marketing," pp. 151–162.

37. Marina Strauss, "Web Sites Don't Boost Sales, Survey of Retailers Says," *Globe and Mail*, October 7, 1997, p. B8.

38. Ian Gray, "Unique Address Brings in Customers," *The Financial Post*, March 22, 1997, p. 52.

39. Michael Parent, "Joining the Millions Already on the Net," *Globe and Mail*, November 14, 1997, p. C6.

40. Catherine Harris, "Shopping on the Net Catches on Slowly," *The Financial Post*, March 22, 1997, p. 58; Amanda Lang, "Still Searching for the Holy Grail," *The Financial Post*, June 19, 1997, p. 17; David Menzies, "New Media at Royal Canadian Mint," *The Financial Post Magazine*, November 1997, p. 130.

41. Louise Kehoe, "Caught in the Web of Electronic Commerce," *The Financial Post*, March 27, 1997, p. 23; Gayle MacDonald, "The Internet is Overrated, Survey Shows," *Globe and Mail*, July 3, 1997, p. B9.

42. Robert D. Hof, "Internet Communities," *Business Week*, May 5, 1997, pp. 64–80.

43. *Ibid.*, p. 66.

44. Amy Cortese, "It's Called Webcasting, and It Promises to Deliver the Info You Want, Straight to Your PC," *Business Week*, February 24, 1997, pp. 95–104; "Anna Zornoas: PointCast," *Advertising Age*, July 14, 1997, p. 4; and Mary J. Cronin, "Using the Web to Push Key Data to Decision Makers," *Fortune*, September 29, 1997, p. 254.

45. *Ibid.*, p. 98. Also see Randi Feigenbaum, "Garbage In—and In and In," *Business Week*, September 9, 1996, p. 110; and Hoag Levins, "Growing Impact of E-Mail," *Editor & Publisher*, March 1, 1997, pp. 26–27.

46. John Deighton, "The Future of Interactive Marketing," p. 156; and CNN Headline News, June 9, 1997.

47. *Ibid.*, p. 158.

48. See Ira Teinowitz, "Internet Privacy Concerns Addressed," *Advertising Age*, June 16, 1997, p. 6; and Teinowitz, "Net Privacy Debate Spurs Self-Regulation," *Advertising Age*, June 9, 1997, p. 36.

49. See Ernan Roman, *Integrated Direct Marketing* (New York: McGraw-Hill, 1988), p. 108; and Mark Suchecki, "Integrated Marketing: Making It Pay," *Direct*, October 1993, p. 43.

50. Portions of this section are based on Terrence H. Witkowski, "Self-Regulation Will Suppress Direct Marketing's Downside," *Marketing News*, April 24, 1989, p. 4. Also see Cyndee Miller, "Privacy vs. Direct Marketing," *Marketing News*, March 1, 1993, pp. 1,

14; Judith Waltrop, "The Business of Privacy," *American Demographics*, October 1994, pp. 46–55; and Katie Muldoon, "The Industry Must Rebuild Its Image," *Direct*, April 1995, p. 106; and Jim Castelli, "How to Handle Personal Information," *American Demographics*, March 1996, pp. 50–57.

51. John Hagel III and Jeffrey F. Rayport, "The Coming Battle for Customer Information," *Harvard Business Review*, January-February 1997, pp. 53–65.

52. Melanie Rigney, "Too Close for Comfort, Execs Warn," *Advertising Age*, January 13, 1992, p. 31. Also see "Summary of '1992 Harris-Equifax Consumer Privacy Survey,'" *Marketing News*, August 16, 1993, p. A18; and Laura Hanson, "A Short List of Telemarketing No-Nos," *Marketing Tools*, January/February 1997, p. 50.

Company Case 17

AMAZON.COM: BOOKING ON THE INTERNET

PONDERING THE INTERNET

When Canadians think of buying books, they might plan to visit an independent bookstore, such as Frog Hollow in Halifax or Audreys in Edmonton; a member of a small chain, such as Toronto-based Lichtman's; or even one of the new Chapters or Indigo Books superstores across the country. However, thanks to the Internet you can now buy a book without leaving your home. Amazon.com is a category-killer that transcends borders and has changed bookselling not only in the United States but internationally as well.

The Amazon.com story began in the early 1990s, when Jeff Bezos, like many other potential entrepreneurs, pondered how he might use the Internet for business purposes. Bezos, then a senior vice president at a Wall Street hedge fund, believed that an Internet company would have to offer a greatly superior product or service if it were going to get customers to jump through the technological hoops involved in Internet commerce.

Bezos drew up a list of 20 Internet business possibilities ranging from magazines to PC hardware or software. After analysing the list, however, he settled on selling books. He had always loved books and bookstores, but he had never considered starting a bookstore of his own.

Bezos knew that the book printing and selling industry in the United States was very fragmented. Hundreds of publishers churn out about 50 000 books per year on every imaginable subject. They then distribute those books through hundreds of distribution companies, which in turn sell to hundreds of bookstores. This fragmentation had already resulted in industry consolidation. Giants such as Barnes & Noble, Borders,

Books-A-Million, and Crown operated about 800 book superstores and controlled almost 50 percent of all bookstore sales in the United States. These chains had already driven many independent bookstores out of business.

Bezos realized, however, that even the biggest individual bookstore could offer only a fraction of the 50 000 books published each year, not to mention all the previous books in print. Theoretically, he recognized that a "virtual" bookstore could offer every book in print—a mighty river of text. Thus, the name Amazon.

AT THE HEADWATERS

Bezos understood that the giants such as Barnes & Noble or Borders, with their strength in dealing with publishers and book distributors, would eventually turn to the Internet. He believed that in any product category customers could remember two or three brand names. "In shoes, there's Nike, Reebok, maybe Adidas, and then there's everyone else," he argues. Thus, he insists, Amazon.com had to win the third slot in online book selling by becoming established first and building a brand name. In the normal world of retailing, a newcomer has a chance because customers can visit the stores and look for themselves. But web pages can't offer such tangible assurance. Therefore, the brand name becomes especially important. Customers are more likely to visit the several sites they know rather than searching for and evaluating lots of unknown sites.

Therefore, Bezos envisioned a big business from the beginning. He had to capture as much of the market as quickly as possible. Rather than setting up shop in

New York, Bezos moved to Seattle, which has a rich pool of software talent and is located near one of the world's largest book warehouses. He also knew that to grow quickly, he would need lots of money for marketing. Thus, he launched into networking, looking for computer industry investors and venture capitalists who could understand his vision.

The interesting aspect of Bezos' bookstore vision was that there would be no actual bookstore. At Amazon.com's headquarters in a modern Seattle office building, there are no books for sale or even in sight. The few books that Amazon.com actually stocks are in a warehouse in south Seattle. Amazon.com functions almost entirely as an intermediary. It takes customers' requests over the Web and zips them electronically to one of a dozen distributors, which fills the order. Ingram Book Group, the largest U.S. book wholesaler with seven strategically located warehouses, fills about 60 percent of Amazon.com's orders. The distributor ships the books to Amazon.com, which then sends them to the customer. Customers pay a $3.00 shipping charge per order plus $.95 per book shipped in the United States.

In July 1994, when Amazon.com opened for business at its www.Amazon.com web address, it offered customers the opportunity to select from one million books. Because it was aware that many people were still unsure about using their credit cards to order over the Internet, Amazon.com offered software encryption to ensure the privacy of transactions. It also offered to pay up to $50 of any unauthorized charges that a credit-card company might fail to waive.

Two Challenges

Bezos understood that it was not enough simply to launch the business and offer books and the information-system infrastructure to handle customers' requests. Customers had to enjoy visiting the Amazon.com site. Just like an actual retail store, Amazon.com had to make its site a destination.

Unlike traditional bookstores, however, Amazon.com could not offer an intimate café or coffee shop, helpful clerks, lounge chairs or inviting displays. In fact, the site did not even offer sophisticated graphics or animation. So, what could Amazon.com offer?

First, it offered discounts. Like many other bookstores, Amazon.com offered discounts on books reviewed by or included on a number of established book reviews—discounts of up to 40 percent. It also offered discounts of 30 percent on hardbacks and 20 percent on paperbacks.

Second, it offered an easy-to-use site that made it relatively simple to search for books by author, title, subject, or keyword. But at a traditional store, clerks can help the customer search for books in the same ways. However, Amazon.com supplemented its searches with excerpts from book reviews by both professional reviewers, by Amazon.com customers, and even by the book's author.

It also set up amusing contests and provided information in lots of different ways. Customers could click on icons to find lists of the latest bestsellers, books that had won awards, or books reviewed by the media. Customers could also indicate their interests or favourite authors, and Amazon.com would e-mail them when books in that area or from that author became available.

Given all this, Amazon.com's second challenge was to make consumers aware of its site and encourage them to visit and use it. Unlike many other online marketers, however, Amazon.com has been willing to spend the money to build awareness among the blizzard of Internet start-ups.

For example, in early July 1997, Amazon.com announced a series of multimillion-dollar deals with America Online (AOL), Excite, and Yahoo. Like other Internet providers, Amazon.com realizes the growing importance of these "gateway" providers. The company signed a $19-million agreement with AOL to gain access to its 8.5 million subscribers, who represent 46 percent of home Internet users. AOL agreed to provide an Amazon.com button on its Internet page in return for up-front commission on purchases made by its customers. Likewise, Amazon.com will add book reviews to search results on Yahoo! in return for banner ads on Yahoo! sites. Yahoo! customers represent 37 percent of home Internet users. Finally, Amazon.com offered Excite a three-year advertising commitment in return for Excite making the company its exclusive bookseller. Yahoo! and Excite also bring access to at-work users of the Internet.

But Can You Make Money?

Many analysts cite Amazon.com as one of the few successful online businesses. But many critics question whether firms can make money over the Internet. Amazon.com announced that sales for its second quarter ending June 30, 1997 reached $39 million compared with just $3.1 million for the same period in 1996. However, its net loss for the second quarter reached $9.4 million versus a loss of $1.1 million for that period a year earlier. Amazon.com indicated that for the first six months of 1997, it had revenues of $61.5 million and lost $13.6 million while spending $16.4 million on marketing and sales efforts and $6.2 million on product development.

The company also indicated that its cumulative customer accounts totalled 610 000, with repeat customers accounting for more than 50 percent of its second-quarter orders. The company now offers customers the opportunity to select from 2.5 million books.

To help reduce costs and improve profitability, Bezos is rethinking his distribution strategy. He is expanding Amazon.com's Seattle warehouse, allowing the company to stock 200 000 to 300 000 titles and to buy most of its books directly from publishers rather than from distributors. This will allow the company to avoid the distributor markups.

However, no matter how Amazon.com gets its books, it still faces the expensive and challenging task of repackaging and reshipping the books to customers. As a result, even though Amazon.com's sales are now at the annual rate of $100 million, Bezos estimates that it must triple its sales to support the cost of its expanded inventory.

QUESTIONS:

1. How do customers and Amazon.com benefit from online marketing?

2. Outline Amazon.com's marketing strategy. What problems do you see with its strategy?

3. What marketing recommendations would you make to Amazon.com? Specifically, how can Amazon.com get more people to visit and use its site?

4. What marketing strategies can Canadian booksellers develop to compete with Amazon.com?

5. What ethical issues does Amazon.com face? How should it deal with those issues?

Sources: Amazon.com home page: www.Amazon.com; Patrick M. Reilly, "Booksellers Prepare to Do Battle in Cyberspace," *The Wall Street Journal*, January 28, 1997; Charles C. Mann, "Read Me," *Inc. Technology*, Vol. 2, 1997, pp. 54–61; Mitch Wagner, "E-commerce Shoppers Need Tools to Help Themselves," *Computerworld*, June 30, 1997, p. 6; Mitch Wagner, "Price of Web Poker Just Went Up," *Computerworld*, July 14, 1997, p. 4; Jim Milliot, "Amazon.com Sales Soar in Second Quarter," *Publishers Weekly*, July 28, 1997, p. 11; Jared Sandberg, "Retailers Pay Big for Prime Internet Real Estate," *The Wall Street Journal*, July 8, 1997, p. B1; Anthony Bianco, "Virtual Bookstores Start to Get Real," *Business Week*, October 27, 1997.

Video Case 17

VIRTUAL BANKING AT ING DIRECT

Canadians are world leaders in the use of new banking technologies. Debit cards, telephone banking, and banking over the Internet are now common banking practices in Canada. And it is Canadians' comfort with these new technologies that has encouraged ING, the world's third-largest bank, to start a bank in Canada without building even one branch. All of the banking transactions for customers of the ING bank will be done electronically.

Branchless banking is not new to Canada. VanCity, a credit union in British Columbia, established the branchless Citizens Bank of Canada in January 1997. However, the entrance of ING is significant because of the company's size and the resources it will have to direct toward the development and marketing of its new Canadian bank, ING Direct. The ING organization, which is headquartered in Amsterdam, operates worldwide and has twice the total assets of the Royal Bank of Canada, currently Canada's largest bank. With all of these assets at its disposal, ING Direct will be adding an unprecedented level of competition to the Canadian banking scene. In particular, its planned pricing tactics include cheaper rates, fewer service charges, and lower prices, all of which are available to consumers because the cost of providing the banking services will be so much less than if a branch system existed.

ING has become acquainted with the Canadian financial marketplace as a result of operating in the Canadian insurance industry for several years. Yves Brouillette, president and CEO of ING Canada, claims that ING is "much more entrepreneurial" than many firms in the financial sector and plans to be a significant presence in retail banking in Canada. Retail banking is worth hundreds of billions of dollars in Canada and the large, existing banks have posted record profits in recent years. These profits, combined with increased costs to consumers for banking services, have fuelled

consumer mistrust of the industry and the current players in it, possibly creating an opportunity for a new entrant such as ING Direct.

According to industry analysts, the existing banks in Canada have reason to be worried about ING Direct. The large banks have become accustomed to protection from legislation that limited competitive threats. But now several actions by existing Canadian banks show that they are taking the ING Direct threat seriously. All of the major banks now offer telephone and Internet banking, and have recently directed further resources to these electronic services. Additionally, the planned mergers between the Royal Bank and the Bank of Montreal and between TD and CIBC will mean that ING Direct faces competitors in Canada that are comparable to its size. Consumers may well benefit in this increasingly competitive market, but banks that fail to meet the competitive challenge may see their once comfortable market shares eroded by virtual competitors.

QUESTIONS

1. What challenges do virtual banks face in trying to gain consumer trust? What implications does this have for ING Direct as it enters the Canadian banking industry?

2. What factors would cause consumers to switch from their existing bank to ING Direct? How should existing banks counter the threat from virtual banks such as ING Direct?

3. Visit the ING Direct web site (www.ingdirect.ca) and the web site for the Citizens Bank of Canada (www.citizensbank.ca). What are the differences between the two sites? What is each organization attempting to achieve with its site?

Source: This case was prepared by Auleen Carson and is based on "Virtual Banks," *Venture* (September 22, 1996).

C H A P T E R 18

COMPETITIVE STRATEGIES:

Building Lasting Customer Relationships

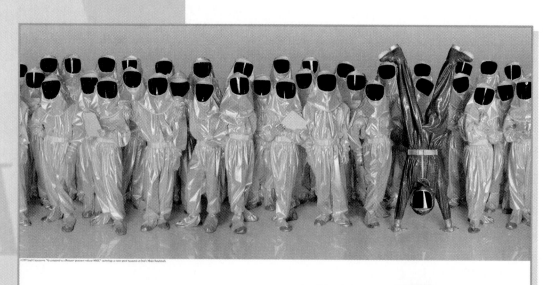

Guess who makes the Pentium processor even more fun?

Among the highly trained technicians who manufacture Intel Pentium processors, a certain group stands out. They work in the MMX media enhancement technology department and have been specially trained to do one thing: add fun to the Pentium processor. PCs that have a Pentium processor with

MMX technology give you richer color, fuller sound, smoother video and faster graphics.* And when combined with software designed for MMX technology, you'll get the most from your multimedia. MMX technology from Intel. It's the technical term for fun. ▶ www.intel.com

The Computer Inside.™

For more than 25 years, Intel, the company that figured out how to brand something as inconspicuous as a computer chip, has dominated the microprocessor market for personal computers. The company's sales and profits have soared accordingly. In just over a decade, the chip giant's sales have jumped nearly twentyfold to more than $30 billion. Its share of the microprocessor market now tops 90 percent, dominating competitors such as Advanced Micro Devices (AMD) and Cyrix. During the past 10 years, with gross margins hovering at around 60 percent, Intel's average annual return has been an astounding 44 percent. The company's earnings exceed the total profits of the top 10 PC manufacturers combined.

Intel's stunning success results from its relentless dedication to a simple competitive marketing strategy: provide the most value and satisfaction to customers through product leadership. Some companies deliver superior value through convenience and low prices; others by coddling their customers and tailoring products to meet the special needs of precisely defined market niches. By contrast, Intel delivers superior value by creating a continuous stream of leading-edge products. The result is intense customer loyalty and preference, both from the computer and software producers who add ever-more features that require increasingly brawny microprocessors, and from final PC buyers who want their PCs to do ever-more cool things.

Intel's microprocessors are true wonders of modern technology. Its Pentium II microprocessor is a veritable one-chip mainframe, and the technology is improving at nearly the speed of light. Intel invests heavily to develop state-of-the-art products and bring them quickly to market. In 1996 alone, the company spent a whopping $7 billion on research and development and capital spending. The result is a rapid succession of ever-better chips that no competitor can match.

In fact, Intel has innovated at such a torrid pace that its microprocessors have at times outpaced market needs and capabilities. For example, in the early 1990s, the speed of Intel's chips began to overtake that of other PC components. The industry's existing "bus" system—the internal network that directs the flow of electrons within a computer—served up data at a far slower rate than Intel's new Pentium could handle it. So why would producers buy the faster chips

When you finish this chapter, you should be able to

1. Define customer value and satisfaction, and discuss how companies attract new customers and retain current ones through relationship marketing.

2. Explain the role of a company value chain and the value delivery network in meeting customer needs.

3. Clarify the concept of total quality marketing and its relationship to customer value and satisfaction.

4. Discuss the need to understand competitors as well as customers through competitor analysis.

5. Explain the fundamentals of competitive marketing strategies based on creating value for customers.

6. Illustrate the need for balancing customer and competitor orientations in becoming a truly market-centred organization.

if existing PC architecture couldn't take advantage of it? Bus designs had always come from PC makers, but no new faster designs appeared to be on the horizon. Instead of waiting, Intel quickly designed a new bus called PCI, and shared the design with computer makers. The PCI became the standard bus on PCs, paving the way for Intel's faster chips.

Intel's growth depends on increasing demand for microprocessors, which in turn depends on growth in PC applications and sales. Thus, Intel has taken product leadership a step further. Rather than sitting back and relying on others to create new market applications requiring its increasingly powerful microprocessors, the company now develops such applications itself. The situation is analogous to the early days of electricity, when makers of generating equipment began making appliances to stimulate the demand for electrical power. According to one account, to ensure continued growth in the demand for its microprocessors, Intel has set out "to make the PC the central appliance in our lives. In [Intel's] vision, we will use PCs to watch TV, to play complex games on the Internet, to store and edit family photos, to manage the appliances in our homes, and to stay in regular video contact with our family, friends, and co-workers." Of course, at the heart of all of these applications will be the latest Intel-powered PC. To realize this vision, Intel has invested heavily in market development. The company has established the Intel Architecture Labs (IAL), with 600 employees working to expand the market for all PC-related products, not just Intel products.

Intel has also invested in dozens of small companies working on projects that might spark demand for the processing power that only Intel can supply. The company's widely varied investments include the Palace, which creates virtual Web communities; Citrix Systems, which makes software to link Internet users; and CyberCash, which is developing an online payment system. "The next killer app," says the former head of Intel's Internet and communications group, "is use of the Internet for online socialization." He foresees the day when individuals can use computers in their own homes to watch a ball game or movie as a group, making comments through their online three-dimensional characters as they watch. Again, such applications will require far more computing power the today's personal computers afford. And new Intel chips will provide the needed power.

Looking ahead, Intel's growth and industry dominance will depend on its ability to produce a steady flow of state-of-the-art chips and irresistible new applications that will lure new consumers into PC ownership and encourage current owners to trade up their machines. Intel's top executives don't foresee any slowing of the pace. Says Intel president Craig Barrett, "We picture ourselves going down the road at 120 miles an hour. Somewhere there's going to be a brick wall...but our view is that it's better to run into the wall than to anticipate it and fall short."[1]

Today's companies face their toughest competition ever. In previous chapters, we have argued that to succeed in today's fiercely competitive marketplace, companies will have to move from a *product and selling philosophy* to a *customer and marketing philosophy.* This chapter spells out in more detail how companies can go about winning customers and outperforming competitors. The answer lies in doing a better job of *meeting and satisfying customer needs.* They must become adept in *building customers,* not just *building products.* Bob Stephen, owner of Scarborough's Infiniti Nissan Store, has taken this challenge as an opportunity. He knows that most people dread visiting a dealership, so he advertises his new, customer-focused way of doing business. He knows that *building a customer* begins with the first transaction. This is a car dealer's best opportunity to establish a long-term, profitable relationship with a customer. The experience must be satisfying since the provision of parts and service over the lifetime of the vehicle makes the dealer profitable. No dealer can make enough just selling cars, Bob stresses. He provides his customers with informative, no-hassle service and a money-back guarantee when they buy a vehicle. After the purchase, Bob knows that customers hate waiting while their cars are serviced. Inspired by executive lounges in airports, he has solved this problem by providing upscale waiting rooms equipped with phones and hook-ups for laptop computers so busy executives don't have downtime while they wait. Bob's customer-oriented approach keeps people returning to his dealership.[2]

In this chapter, we discuss strategies for gaining competitive advantage by building customer relationships based on superior customer value, satisfaction, and quality. First, we address several important questions relating to these key relationship building-blocks: What are customer value and customer satisfaction? How do leading companies organize to create and deliver high value and satisfaction? How can companies keep current customers as well as get new ones? How can companies practise total quality marketing? In the second half of the chapter, we focus on issues of how a company can accomplish the above tasks better than its competitors.

DEFINING CUSTOMER VALUE AND SATISFACTION

More than 35 years ago, Peter Drucker insightfully observed that a company's first task is "to create customers." However, creating customers can be a difficult task. Today's customers face a vast array of product and brand choices, prices, and suppliers. The company must answer a key question: How do customers make their choices?

The answer is that customers choose the marketing offer that gives them the most value. They form expectations of value and act upon them. Whether the offer delivers the expected value affects customers' satisfaction and repurchase behaviour.

CUSTOMER VALUE

Customer delivered value
The consumer's assessment of the product's overall capacity to satisfy his or her needs. The difference between total customer value and total customer cost of a marketing offer—"profit" to the customer.

Caterpillar
www.cat.com/

Total customer value
The total of all of the product, services, personnel, and image values that a buyer receives from a marketing offer.

Total customer cost
The total of all the monetary, time, energy, and psychic costs associated with a marketing offer.

Consumers buy from the firm that they believe offers the highest **customer delivered value**—the difference between *total customer value* and *total customer cost* (see Figure 18-1). For example, suppose that a large construction firm wants to buy a bulldozer to use in residential construction work. It wants a reliable, durable bulldozer that performs well. It can buy the bulldozer from either Caterpillar or Komatsu. The salespeople for the two companies carefully describe their respective offers to the buyer.

The construction firm now evaluates the two competing bulldozer offers to assess which one offers the greatest value. It adds all the values from four sources—*product, services, personnel,* and *image*. First, it judges that Caterpillar's bulldozer provides higher reliability, durability, and performance. It also decides that Caterpillar has better accompanying services—delivery, training, and maintenance. The customer views Caterpillar personnel as more knowledgeable and responsive. Finally, it places higher value on Caterpillar's reputation. Thus, the customer decides that Caterpillar offers more **total customer value** than does Komatsu.

Does the construction firm buy the Caterpillar bulldozer? Not necessarily. The firm also will examine the **total customer cost** of buying Caterpillar's bulldozer versus Komatsu's. First, the buyer will compare the prices it must pay for each of the competitors' products. If Caterpillar's bulldozer costs a lot more than Komatsu's does, the higher price might offset the higher total customer value. Moreover, total customer cost consists of more than just monetary costs. As Adam Smith observed more than two centuries ago, "The real price of anything is the toil and trouble of acquiring it." Total customer cost also includes the buyer's

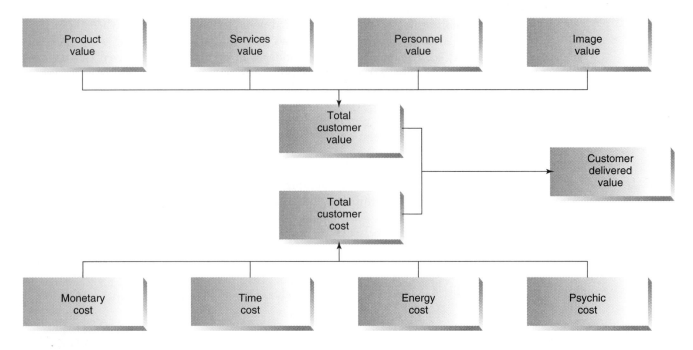

FIGURE 18-1 *Customer delivered value*

Caterpillar must convince customers that its products offer greater value than competitors' products. It makes "serious machines," and a "serious commitment" to customer satisfaction.

anticipated time, energy, and psychic costs. The construction firm will evaluate these costs along with monetary costs to form a complete estimate of its costs.

The buying firm now compares total customer value to total customer cost and determines the total delivered value associated with Caterpillar's bulldozer. In the same way, it assesses the total delivered value for the Komatsu bulldozer. The firm then will buy from the competitor that offers the highest delivered value.

Some marketers might rightly argue that this concept of how buyers choose among product alternatives is too rational. They might cite examples in which buyers did not choose the offer with an objectively measured highest delivered value. For example, suppose that the Caterpillar salesperson convinces the construction firm that, considering the benefits relative to the purchase price, Caterpillar's bulldozer offers a higher delivered value. The customer still might decide to buy the Komatsu bulldozer. Why would the buyer make this apparent non-value-maximizing purchase? There are many possible explanations. For example, perhaps the construction firm's buyers enjoy a long-term friendship with the Komatsu salesperson. Or the firm's buyers might be under strict company orders to buy at the lowest price. Or perhaps the construction firm rewards its buyers for short-term performance, causing them to choose the less expensive Komatsu bulldozer, even though the Caterpillar machine will perform better and be less expensive to operate in the long run.

Clearly, buyers operate under various constraints and sometimes make choices that give more weight to their personal benefit than to company benefit. However, the customer-delivered-value framework applies to many situations and yields rich insights. It suggests that sellers must first assess the total customer delivered value associated with their own and competing marketing offers to determine how their own offers stack up. If competitors deliver greater value, the firm must act.

How might Caterpillar use this concept of buyer decision making to help it succeed in selling its bulldozer to this buyer? It can improve its offer in one of two ways. First, it can increase total customer value by strengthening or augmenting the product, services, personnel, or image benefits of its offer. Second, it can reduce total customer cost by lowering its price or by lessening the buyer's time, energy, and psychic costs. In fact, although Caterpillar products cost more than competing brands, the company claims that its higher-quality, superior service and its strong reputation make its products a better value in the long run. The company's goal is to provide customers with the "lowest total cost per cubic [metre] of earth moved, ton of coal uncovered, or [kilometre] of road graded over the life of the product."[3]

CUSTOMER SATISFACTION

Thus, consumers form expectations about the value of marketing offers and make their buying decisions based upon these expectations. *Customer satisfaction* with a purchase depends on the product's performance relative to a buyer's expectations. A customer might experience various degrees of satisfaction. If the product's performance falls short of expectations, the customer is dissatisfied. If performance matches expectations, the customer is satisfied. If performance exceeds expectations, the customer is highly satisfied or delighted.

But how do buyers form their expectations? Expectations are based on the customer's past buying experiences, the opinions of friends and associates, and marketer and competitor information and promises. Marketers must be careful to set the right level of expectations. If they set expectations too low, they may satisfy those who buy but fail to attract enough buyers. In contrast, if they raise expectations too high, buyers are likely to be disappointed. For example, Holiday Inn ran a campaign a few years ago called "No Surprises," which promised consistently trouble-free accommodations and service. However, Holiday Inn guests still encountered problems, and the expectations created by the campaign only made customers more dissatisfied. Holiday Inn had to withdraw the campaign.

Indices that track customer satisfaction in the manufacturing and service industries show that overall customer satisfaction has declined slightly in recent years. It is unclear whether this has resulted from a decrease in product and service quality or from an increase in customer expectations. In either case, it presents an opportunity for companies that can deliver superior customer value and satisfaction.

Today's most successful companies are raising expectations—and delivering performance to match. These companies embrace total customer satisfaction. For example, Honda claims "One reason our customers are so satisfied is that we aren't." And Cigna vows "100% Satisfaction. 100% of the Time." Such companies track their customers' expectations, perceived company performance, and customer satisfaction (see Marketing Highlight 18-1). Highly satisfied customers produce several benefits for the company. Satisfied customers are less price sensitive, remain customers for a longer period, and speak favourably about the company and its products to other people.

Although the customer-centred firm seeks to deliver high customer satisfaction relative to competitors, it does not attempt to *maximize* customer satisfaction. A company can always increase customer satisfaction by lowering its price or increasing its services, but this may result in lower profits. Thus, the purpose of marketing is to generate customer value profitably. Ultimately, the company must deliver a high level of customer satisfaction while at the same time delivering at least acceptable levels of satisfaction to the firm's other stakeholders. This requires a very

Total customer satisfaction: Cigna vows, "We'll never be 100 percent satisfied until you are, too."

Are we aiming too high? Or is everyone else aiming too low?

At the CIGNA Group Pension Division, customer satisfaction is our number one priority. Sounds good in an ad. But how do we achieve it? By giving the customer a voice. And then listening to it. When our customers told us that simplifying participant financial statements was a major priority, we listened. Then, using their input we designed more user-friendly reports.

When customers told us they wanted more investment options, we listened, too. Responding to their request with new accounts—six investing in mutual funds. Including highly rated funds from well-known outside investment companies.

And because even a little thing can often be a big thing, we listen to everything. For example, when customers told us they preferred talking to people rather than computers, we eliminated recorded messages in our customer service areas.

The point is, when the customer talks, we listen. To find out precisely how well, call CIGNA Group Pension Division, 1-800-238-2525.

Of course, we're not saying that we're perfect. But what we are saying is that we'll never be 100% satisfied until you are, too.

100% SATISFACTION. 100% OF THE TIME.

CIGNA

TRACKING CUSTOMER SATISFACTION

Tools for tracking and measuring customer satisfaction range from the primitive to the sophisticated. Companies use the following methods to measure how much customer satisfaction they are creating.

Complaint and Suggestion Systems

A customer-centred organization makes it easy for customers to make suggestions or complaints. Restaurants and hotels provide forms on which guests can check off their likes and dislikes. Some customer-centred companies, such as P&G, General Electric, and Whirlpool, set up customer hotlines with 800 numbers to make it easy for customers to inquire, suggest, or complain. These call centres allow firms to listen to the voice of the customer on a wide variety of issues, says Stanley Brown, director of the Centre for Excellence in Customer Satisfaction at Toronto-based Coopers & Lybrand Consulting. Proactive listening allows organizations to understand what customers value most. Such systems not only help companies to act more quickly to resolve problems, but they also provide companies with many good ideas for improved products and service.

Customer Satisfaction Surveys

Simply running complaint and suggestion systems may not give the company a full picture of customer satisfaction and dissatisfaction.

Studies show that one of every four purchases results in consumer dissatisfaction, but that less than five percent of dissatisfied customers bother to complain—most customers simply switch suppliers. As a result, the company needlessly loses customers.

Tracking customer satisfaction: Each year Whirlpool mails its Standardized Appliance Measurement of Satisfaction survey to 180 000 households, asking them to rate all of its appliances.

A Coopers & Lybrand survey of more than 1800 companies revealed that successful organizations are more likely to survey customers on various issues including the effectiveness of complaint handling, how they compare to competitors on key customer values, customer satisfaction, conformance to standards, order fulfilment, customer needs, and new product ideas. They send questionnaires or make telephone calls to a sample of recent customers to find out how they feel about various aspects of the company's performance. They also survey buyers' views on competitor performance. Whirlpool surveys customer satisfaction on a massive scale, then acts on the results:

When customers talk, Whirlpool listens. Each year the company mails its Standardized Appliance Measurement of Satisfaction (SAMS) survey to 180 000 households, asking people to rate all its appliances on dozens of attributes. When a competitor's product ranks higher, Whirlpool engineers rip it apart to see why. The company [also] pays hundreds of consumers to fiddle with computer-simulated products at the company's Usability Lab while engineers record the users' reactions on videotape.

A company can measure customer satisfaction in a number of ways. It can measure satisfaction directly by asking: "How satisfied are you with this product? Are you highly dissatisfied, somewhat dissatisfied, neither satisfied nor dissatisfied, somewhat satisfied, or highly satisfied?" Or it can ask respondents to rate how much they expected of

delicate balance: the marketer must continue to generate more customer value and satisfaction but not "give away the house."[4]

RETAINING CUSTOMERS

Satisfied customers are more likely to be loyal customers. However, the relationship between customer satisfaction and loyalty varies greatly across industries and competitive situations.

CUSTOMER SATISFACTION AND CUSTOMER LOYALTY

Figure 18-2 shows the relationship between customer satisfaction and loyalty in five different markets.[5] In all cases, as satisfaction increases, so does loyalty. In highly

certain attributes and how much they actually experienced. Finally, the company can ask respondents to list any problems they have had with the offer and to suggest improvements.

While collecting customer satisfaction data, companies often ask additional useful questions. They often measure the customer's *repurchase intention;* this will usually be high if customer satisfaction is high. According to CEO John Young at Hewlett-Packard, nine out of ten customers in H-P surveys who rank themselves as highly satisfied say they would definitely or probably buy from H-P again.

A company also might ask about the customer's likelihood or willingness to recommend the company and brand to other people. Peter Zarry, York University's authority on customer satisfaction, believes that this is the best way to track and improve customer satisfaction. When companies ask their customers what they need to do so that customers would be willing to refer their products or services to their friends, they uncover the customer's key expectations. Revamping their business to meet these expectations not only allows companies to improve customer loyalty, but it also helps them to attract new customers.

Ghost Shopping
Another useful way of assessing customer satisfaction is to hire people to pose as buyers to report their experiences in buying the company's and competitors' products. These "ghost shoppers" can even present specific problems to test whether the company's personnel handle difficult situations well. For example, ghost shoppers can complain about a restaurant's food to see how the restaurant handles this complaint. Not only should companies hire ghost shoppers, but managers themselves should leave their offices from time to time and experience first-hand the treatment they receive as "customers."

Lost Customer Analysis
Companies should contact customers who have stopped buying, or those who have switched to a competitor, to learn why this happened. When IBM loses a customer, it mounts a thorough effort to learn how it failed: Was IBM's price too high, its service poor, or its products substandard? Not only should the company conduct such *exit interviews,* it should also monitor the *customer loss rate.* A rising loss rate indicates that the company is failing to satisfy its customers.

Some Cautions in Measuring Customer Satisfaction
Customer satisfaction ratings are sometimes difficult to interpret. When customers rate their satisfaction with some element of the company's performance, say delivery, they can vary greatly in how they define good delivery. It might mean early delivery, on-time delivery, order completeness, or something else. Yet, if the company tried to define every element in detail, customers would face a huge questionnaire.

Companies also must recognize that two customers can report being "highly satisfied" for different reasons. One might be easily satisfied most of the time, whereas the other might be hard to please but was pleased on this occasion. Further, managers and salespeople can manipulate their ratings on customer satisfaction. They can be especially nice to customers just before the survey or try to exclude unhappy customers from being included in the survey. Finally, if customers know that the company will go out of its way to please customers, even if they are satisfied, some customers may express high dissatisfaction in order to receive more concessions.

Source: Quotation from Sally Solo, "Whirlpool: How to Listen to Consumers," *Fortune,* January 11, 1993, pp. 77–79. Also see Howard Schlossberg, "Measuring Customer Satisfaction is Easy to Do—Until You Try It," *Marketing News,* April 26, 1993, pp. 5, 8; John W. Verity, "The Gold Mine of Data in Customer Service," *Business Week,* March 21, 1994, pp. 113–114; Stanley A. Brown, "Special Report: Call Centres: A New, Greater Focus on Customer Satisfaction," *Strategy: The Canadian Marketing Report,* May 1, 1995, p. CDMA-23; and David Foley, "Speaking Directly: The Myth of the Satisfied Customer," *Strategy: The Canadian Marketing Report,* April 17, 1995, p. 20.

Xerox
www.xerox.com/

competitive markets, such as those for automobiles and personal computers, there is surprisingly little difference between the loyalty of less satisfied customers and those who are merely satisfied. However, there is a tremendous difference between the loyalty of satisfied customers and completely satisfied customers.

Even a slight drop from complete satisfaction can create an enormous drop in loyalty. For example, one study showed that completely satisfied customers are almost 42 percent more likely to be loyal than merely satisfied customers. Another study by AT&T showed that 70 percent of customers who say they are satisfied with a product or service are still willing to switch to a competitor; customers who are highly satisfied are much more loyal. And Xerox found that its totally satisfied customers are six times more likely to repurchase Xerox products over the next 18 months than are its satisfied customers.[6] This means that companies must aim high if they want to retain their customers. Customer delight creates an emotional affinity for a product or service, not just a rational preference, and this creates high customer loyalty.

FIGURE 18-2 *The relationship between customer satisfaction and customer loyalty*

Source: Reprinted by permission of *Harvard Business Review*. From "Why Satisfied Customer Defect," by Thomas O. Jones and W. Earl Sasser, Jr., November-December 1995, pp. 91. Copyright © 1997 by the President and Fellows of Harvard College; all rights reserved.

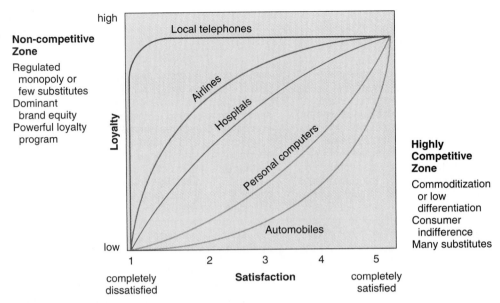

Figure 18-2 also shows that in non-competitive markets, such those served by regulated monopolies or those dominated by powerful or patent-protected brands, customers tend to remain loyal no matter how dissatisfied they are. This might seem like an ideal situation for the protected or dominant firm. However, such firms may pay a high price for customer dissatisfaction in the long run.

For example, during the 1960s and 1970s, Xerox flourished under the protection of patents on its revolutionary photocopy process. Customers had no choice but to remain loyal to Xerox, and sales and profits soared despite customer dissatisfaction over machine malfunctions and rising prices. In fact, customer dissatisfaction led to even greater short-run profits for Xerox: disgruntled customers were forced to pay for service when machines broke down, and some even leased extra machines as back-ups. But during the early 1980s, Xerox paid dearly for its failure to satisfy its customers. Japanese competitors skirted patents and entered the market with higher-quality copiers sold at lower prices. Dissatisfied customers gleefully defected to the new competitors. Xerox's share of the world copier market plunged from more than 80 percent to less than 35 percent in just five years.[7]

Thus, even highly successful companies must pay close attention to customer satisfaction and its relationship to customer loyalty. Xerox has now developed industry-leading, customer-driven quality and customer satisfaction programs. As a result, although it has lost its dominance, it is once again a profitable industry leader.

THE NEED FOR CUSTOMER RETENTION

Traditional marketing theory and practice have focused on attracting new customers rather than retaining existing ones. Today, however, the emphasis is shifting. Beyond designing strategies to attract new customers and create transactions with them, companies are striving to retain current customers and build lasting relationships with them.

Why the new emphasis on retaining customers? In the past, many companies took their customers for granted. Facing an expanding economy and rapidly growing markets, companies could practise a "leaky bucket" approach to marketing. Growing markets meant a plentiful supply of new customers. Companies could keep filling the marketing bucket with new customers without worrying about losing old customers through holes in the bottom of the bucket.

However, companies today are facing some new marketing realities. Changing demographics, a slow-growth economy, more sophisticated competitors, and overcapacity in many industries—all of these factors mean that there are fewer customers to go around. Many companies are now fighting for shares of flat or fading markets. Thus, the costs to attracting new consumers are rising. In fact, it costs five times as much to attract a new customer as it does to keep a current customer satisfied.[8]

Companies are also realizing that losing a customer means losing more than a single sale: it means losing the entire stream of purchases that the customer would make over a lifetime of patronage. For example, here is a dramatic illustration of customer lifetime value:

> Stu Leonard, who operates a highly profitable single-store supermarket, says that he sees $72 500 flying out of his store every time he sees a sulking customer. Why? Because his average customer spends about $145 a week, shops 50 weeks a year, and remains in the area for about 10 years. If this customer has an unhappy experience and switches to another supermarket, Stu Leonard has lost $72 500 in revenue. The loss can be much greater if the disappointed customer shares the bad experience with other customers and causes them to defect.

Similarly, the customer lifetime value of a Taco Bell customer exceeds $17 280. For General Motors, a customer's lifetime value might well exceed $490 000. Thus, working to retain customers makes good economic sense. A company can lose money on a specific transaction, but still benefit greatly from a long-term relationship.[9]

Attracting new customers remains an important marketing task. However, today's companies must also focus on retaining current customers and building profitable, long-term relationships with them. The key to customer retention is superior customer value and satisfaction.

THE KEY: CUSTOMER RELATIONSHIP MARKETING

Relationship marketing
The process of creating, maintaining, and enhancing strong, value-laden relationships with customers and other stakeholders.

Relationship marketing involves creating, maintaining, and enhancing strong relationships with customers and other stakeholders including suppliers, distributors, wholesalers, retailers, and even competitors with the objective of achieving higher levels of customer satisfaction through collaboration of all parties involved.[10] Canadian marketing writer John Dalla Costa contrasts his relationship model with the outmoded views of marketing shown in Table 18-1 below. Relationship marketing is oriented toward the long term. The goal is to deliver long-term value to customers. Relationship maketing requires that all of the company's departments and its partners work together with marketing as a team to serve the customer. It involves building relationships at many levels—economic, social, technical, and legal—resulting in high customer loyalty.

Companies form different levels of customer relationships depending on the nature of the target market. At one extreme, a company with many low-margin customers may seek to develop basic relationships with them. For example, H.J.

Table 18-1   *A Relationship Marketing Model*

Old Marketing Model	New Marketing Model
Focus on the product.	Focus on the process for serving customers.
Define the target group.	Feed and nourish the relationship.
Set brand objectives.	Extend respect and value to customers.
Opportunity comes from analysis.	Opportunity comes from synergy.
Focus on brand benefit.	Develop and refresh relevance.
Create strategic advertising.	Open the doors for dialogue.
Operate against a brand plan.	Improvize to sustain the relationship.
Driven by the marketing group.	A pervasive inter-disciplinary attitude.

Source: John Dalla Costa, "Towards a Model Relationship," *Marketing*, June 27, 1994, p. 12.

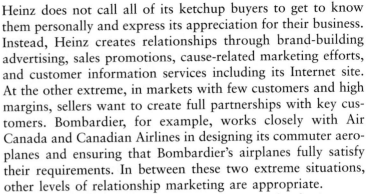

Relationship marketing: Increasingly, companies are moving away from a focus on individual transactions and toward a focus on building value-laden relationships with customers. Here PaineWebber declares, "We invest in relationships."

Federal Express
www.fedex.com

Heinz does not call all of its ketchup buyers to get to know them personally and express its appreciation for their business. Instead, Heinz creates relationships through brand-building advertising, sales promotions, cause-related marketing efforts, and customer information services including its Internet site. At the other extreme, in markets with few customers and high margins, sellers want to create full partnerships with key customers. Bombardier, for example, works closely with Air Canada and Canadian Airlines in designing its commuter aeroplanes and ensuring that Bombardier's airplanes fully satisfy their requirements. In between these two extreme situations, other levels of relationship marketing are appropriate.

Today, more and more companies are developing customer loyalty and retention programs. Beyond offering consistently high value and satisfaction, marketers can use a number of specific marketing tools to develop stronger bonds with consumers.[11] First, a company might build value and satisfaction by adding financial benefits to the customer relationship. For example, many companies now offer frequency marketing programs that reward customers who buy frequently or in large amounts. Airlines offer frequent-flyer programs, hotels provide room upgrades to their frequent guests, and supermarkets give patronage refunds.

Other companies sponsor club marketing programs that offer members special discounts and other benefits. For example, Reebok sponsors Club Reebok, which targets running-shoe-wearing kids by offering sports-related activities. Lladro, maker of fine porcelain figurines, sponsors a "Collectors Society" with an annual membership fee of $50. Members receive a free subscription to a quarterly magazine, a bisque plaque, free enrolment in the Lladro Museum, and member-only tours to visit the company and Lladro family in Valencia, Spain. And Harley-Davidson sponsors the Harley Owners Group (HOG), which now numbers 330 000 members—about one-third of all Harley owners.

A second approach is to add social benefits as well as financial benefits. Here the company increases its social bonds with customers by creating events that allow customers to socialize with each other as well as with the company. For example, to build better relationships with its customers, Saturn regularly invites all of its almost one million owners to a "Saturn Reunion." Canada's large brewers, Molson and Labatt, sponsor concerts and sporting events that attract their target audiences.

A third approach to building customer relationships is to add structural ties as well as financial and social benefits. For example, a business marketer might supply customers with special equipment or computer linkages that help them manage their orders, payroll, or inventory. McKesson Corporation, a leading pharmaceutical wholesaler, has invested millions of dollars in its electronic data interchange (EDI) system to help small pharmacies manage their inventory, order entry, and shelf space. And Federal Express offers its FedEx Ship program to thousands of its best corporate and individual customers to keep them from defecting to competitors such as UPS. The program provides free computer software that allows customers to link directly with Federal Express' computers. Customers can use the software to arrange shipments and to check the status of their Federal Express packages while en route to their destination.

Relationship marketing means that marketers must focus on managing their customers as well as their products. At the same time, they don't want relationships with every customer. In fact, there are undesirable customers for every company. The objective is to determine which customers the company can serve most effectively relative to competitors. Ultimately, marketing is the art of

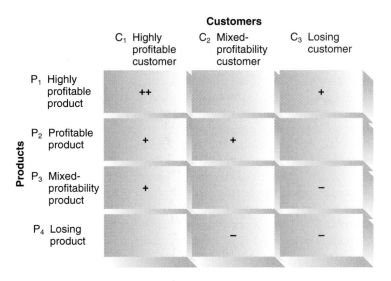

Customers

| | C_1 Highly profitable customer | C_2 Mixed-profitability customer | C_3 Losing customer |

FIGURE 18-3
Customer/product profitability analysis

attracting and keeping profitable customers. In some cases, companies may even want to "fire" customers that are too unreasonable or that cost more to serve than they are worth.

Companies should actively measure individual customer value and profitability. Figure 18-3 shows a useful type of profitability analysis.[12] Customers comprise the columns of the figure and products or services comprise the rows. Each cell contains a symbol for the profitability of selling a given product or service to a given customer. Customer C1 is very profitable—he or she buys three profit-making products—products P1, P2, and P3. Customer C2 yields mixed profitability, buying one profitable product and one unprofitable product. Customer C3 generates losses by purchasing one profitable product and two unprofitable ones ("loss leaders"). What can the company do about consumers such as C3? First, the company should consider raising the prices of its less profitable products or eliminating them altogether. Second, the company also can try to cross-sell its profit-making products to its unprofitable customers. If these actions cause customers such as C3 to defect, it may be for the good. In fact, the company would might benefit by encouraging its unprofitable customers to switch to competitors.[13]

DELIVERING CUSTOMER VALUE AND SATISFACTION

Customer value and satisfaction are important ingredients in the marketer's formula for success. However, marketers alone cannot deliver superior value and satisfaction. In fact, although it plays a leading role, marketing can be only a partner in attracting and keeping customers. The marketing department can be effective only in companies in which all departments and employees have teamed up to form a competitively superior customer value-delivery system.

Consider McDonald's. People do not swarm to the 21 000 McDonald's restaurants worldwide only because they love the chain's hamburgers. In fact, according to one national survey, consumers rank McDonald's food products behind Burger King and Wendy's in taste preference.[14] Still, McDonald's commands more than a 20 percent share of Canada's fast-food business—more than the shares of Burger King and Wendy's combined. Consumers flock to the McDonald's system, not just to its food products. Around the world, McDonald's finely tuned system delivers a high standard of what the company refers to as QSCV—quality, service, cleanliness, and value. McDonald's is effective only to the extent that it successfully partners with its employees, franchisees, suppliers, and others to jointly deliver exceptionally high customer value.

To fully meet customer needs, marketers must work closely with other company departments and with other marketing system organizations. In this section, we examine the concepts of a company value chain and value delivery network.

VALUE CHAIN

Each company department can be thought of as a link in the company's value chain.[15] That is, each department carries out value-creating activities to design, produce, market, deliver, and support the firm's products. The firm's success depends not only on how well each department performs its work, but also on how well the activities of various departments are coordinated.

For example, the goal of Ritz-Carlton Hotels is to deliver "a truly memorable experience" for its guests. Marketers comprise an important link in the Ritz-Carlton value chain that creates this experience. They conduct research to learn about customer needs, design services to meet these needs, advertise to inform guests about services and locations, and perform other value-creating activities. However, other departments must also perform well in order to make the Ritz-Carlton experience a reality. For example, the Ritz-Carlton housekeeping and maintenance staffs ensure that everything at the Ritz-Carlton looks and works just right, meeting customers' exacting standards for room cleanliness and repair. The human resources department hires people-oriented employees, trains them carefully, and motivates them to ferret out and attend to even the slightest customer want or need. For example, Ritz-Carlton employees treat customers as individuals, not as nameless, faceless members of a mass market. Whenever possible, employees refer to guests by name and offer each guest a warm welcome every day. Finally, the information systems department maintains an extensive customer database, which holds more than 500 000 individual customer preferences, accessible by all hotels in the worldwide Ritz chain. For example, a guest who requests a foam pillow at the Ritz in Montreal will be delighted to find one waiting in the room when he or she checks into the Atlanta Ritz months later.[16]

A company's value chain is only as strong as its weakest link, however. Success depends on how well each department performs its work of adding value for customers and on how well the activities of different departments are coordinated. At Ritz-Carlton, if customer-contact people are poorly selected or trained, or if rooms are anything less than spotless, marketers cannot fulfil their promise of a truly memorable experience.

VALUE DELIVERY NETWORK

Customer value delivery system
The system made up of the value chains of the company and its suppliers, distributors, and ultimately customers who work together to deliver value to customers.

In its search for competitive advantage, the firm needs to look beyond its own value chain and into the value chains of its suppliers, distributors, and ultimately customers. More companies today are "partnering" with the other members of the supply chain to improve the performance of the **customer value delivery network**. For example, Honda has designed a program for working closely with its suppliers to help them reduce their costs and improve quality. When Honda chose Donnelly Corporation to supply all of the mirrors for its North American-made cars, it sent engineers to visit Donnelly's plants, looking for ways to improve its products and operations. This helped Donnelly reduce its costs by two percent in the first year. As a result of its improved performance, Donnelly's sales to Honda have grown from $7 million annually to more than $85 million in less than 10 years. In turn, Honda has gained an efficient, low-cost supplier of quality components. And as a result of Honda's partnerships with Donnelly and other suppliers, Honda customers receive greater value in the form of lower-cost, higher-quality cars.[17]

An excellent value delivery network connects jeans maker Levi Strauss with its suppliers and distributors. One of Levi's major retailers is Sears. Every night, thanks to electronic data interchange (EDI), Levi's learns the sizes and styles of its blue jeans that sold through Sears and other major outlets. Levi's then electronically orders more fabric from the Milliken Company, its fabric supplier. In turn, Milliken relays an order for more fibre to Du Pont, its fibre supplier. In this way, the partners in the supply chain use the most current sales information to manufacture what is selling, rather than to manufacture based on potentially inaccurate sales forecasts. This is known as a quick response system, in which goods are pulled by demand, rather than pushed by supply.

MICHAEL HENAHAN, BUSINESS ANALYST, AND ROB SHIELDS, SPONSOR DEVELOPMENT CONSULTANT, LOYALTY MANAGEMENT GROUP CANADA

Although you might not recognize the name, Loyalty Management Group, or the name of their president and CEO, Craig Underwood, you will recognize their main product, the Air Miles card. Loyalty Management Group Canada is the firm that conceived this concept and marketed it in Canada. The firm does more, however, than just help people turn their purchasing behaviour into Travel Miles. It offers management consulting services to its partner firms as well as creating value-added marketing programs for them.

Building Value-Added Programs

Here is how the Loyalty Management program and the AIR MILES program work. Loyalty Management purchases excess capacity from a number of designated travel providers and hotels. These partners include Holiday Inn, Canadian Airlines, US AIR, United, and American Airlines, in addition to a number of hotels and car-rental companies. It issues free AIR MILES cards to final consumers. It signs up businesses that offer these cardholders AIR MILES Travel Miles towards free air travel, and/or accommodation as well as other entertainment options such as movie passes.

Loyalty Management Group Canada creates value for its three groups of major stakeholders. For the almost five million Canadian households that collect Travel Miles, the firm provides a means of increasing the value they receive for every purchasing dollar. While buying products and services they need every day, consumers accumulate points towards free goods and travel.

While free travel is the main benefit for consumers, there are also significant benefits for sponsoring firms, according to Mike and Rob. Sponsorship for the card helps a retailer differentiate itself from competitors. It also helps a firm attract new customers to its business. Once people start using a particular AIR MILES sponsor, they make more frequent purchases, which helps retailers build customer loyalty.

Loyalty Management Group also offers its sponsors a means to target their promotional material to consumers most interested in their products and services. It helps them understand consumer behaviour, and helps them target consumers who are using related services. For example,

Loyalty Management Group could tell Goodyear about a consumer who is buying a lot of gasoline using their AIR MILES card, but not buying Goodyear tires. This would give Goodyear the opportunity to market to an individual recognized as a heavy traveller and a prime prospect for a tire manufacturer.

Finally, Loyalty Management Group creates another stream of revenue for its travel, product, and leisure suppliers since it pays them for the capacity awarded to consumers. This is quite a different situation from what occurs with airlines' frequent-flyer programs. When a consumer collects enough frequent-flyer points from an airline, and then uses these points to obtain a free seat, the airline receives no revenue from the transaction. This is not the case with the AIR MILES card, since Loyalty Management Group purchases the seats from the airline before awarding them to consumers.

Michael Henahan, Craig Underwood, and Rob Shields.

While the AIR MILES card is far from a unique concept, it is one that demonstrates the success of a superior value position and an integrated marketing program. In comparison to stand-alone loyalty programs, such as Zellers' Club Z, AIR MILES allows sponsoring firms to form a coalition to share the administrative costs of the program, the costs of rewards, and the start-up costs rather than funding these charges individually. Since sponsors have exclusive rights to AIR MILES, it helps protect them from competitive attacks. Finally, since Loyalty Management Group maintains a detailed database on its cardholders, including their purchase behaviours, it helps firms understand their target audiences better, while allowing them to more effectively reach consumers with targeted promotional messages. In fact, Rob and

Mike claim that a direct-mail message sent out by a single firm costs at least $0.73 per piece, but a sponsor insert in the AIR MILES summary costs as little as $0.14 due to the benefits of sharing costs. What is more, consumers read the mail they receive from AIR MILES. Research has shown that 95 percent of consumers open their AIR MILES mail and over 48 percent of these people read all of the correspondence, while another 17 percent read at least half of it.[1]

Loyalty Management Group based its marketing program on sound research. When considering what types of consumer incentives to offer, it asked the question, "If you had some extra disposable income, which one of the following would you be most likely to spend it on: Travel/vacation, home improvement, or automobile? Travel and vacations was the clear winner with over 50 percent of their respondents making this choice.

Marketing Challenges

As other firms have discovered, Canada is characterized by marked regional differences. While the program is highly successful in Western Canada where it has penetrated 69 percent of households, it is less successful in Ontario and Quebec, where its household penetration is 38 percent and 30 percent respectively. It has done better in the Atlantic provinces, with almost 40 percent penetration, but this is still a far cry from its success in the West. One of the variables that explains this difference is that Loyalty has been successful at signing up a grocery sponsor in the West, but hasn't managed this feat, to date, in its eastern markets. A number of challenges face Loyalty Management. There is a need to differentiate LMGC's brand of AIR MILES from other programs offering "points" on various airlines. Furthermore, the demand for consulting services may grow beyond the firm's ability to supply the service. Now that many consumers have the AIR MILES card, the challenge will be to get them to use it more by frequenting a wider set of sponsors.

Source: Michael Henahan and Rob Shields met with P. Cunningham on March 1, 1996 and presented this material to her classes as well as making it available for use in *Principles of Marketing.* We sincerely wish to thank them for the insights they provided on the practice of value-added marketing.

---

[1] Usage and Attitude Survey, Tandemor Research, 1993.

Increasingly in today's marketplace, competition no longer occurs between individual competitors. Rather, it takes place between the entire value delivery networks created by these competitors. Thus, Levi's performance against another jeans maker—say Wrangler—depends on the quality of Levi's value-delivery network versus Wrangler's. Companies no longer compete—their entire marketing networks do.

IMPLEMENTING TOTAL QUALITY MARKETING

Customer satisfaction and company profitability are linked closely to product and service quality. Higher levels of quality result in greater customer satisfaction, while at the same time supporting higher prices and often lower costs. Therefore, *quality improvement programs* normally increase profitability. The well-known Profit Impact of Marketing Strategies (PIMS) studies show a high correlation between relative product quality and profitability.[18]

The striking global successes of many Japanese companies have resulted from their exceptional quality. Most customers will no longer accept or tolerate average quality. If companies want to remain in the race, let alone be profitable, they have no choice but to adopt quality concepts. According to GE's Chairman, John F. Welch, Jr., "Quality is our best assurance of customer allegiance, our strongest defence against foreign competition, and the only path to sustained growth and earnings."[19] A recent survey of 2000 people in 19 countries asked how consumers rated the quality of their country's manufactured products and those from other countries around the world. Almost 60 percent of Canadians believe that products manufactured here are very good to excellent. Only 41 percent rank Japanese products at the same quality level, and a mere 34 percent agree that products from the United States are good to excellent. Canadians' endorsement of the quality of their own products isn't shared worldwide, however. Canada ranks sixth among 14 countries in terms of global perceptions of the quality of manufactured products. Products from Canada may be less well known in some countries, and this may have caused this somewhat low rating. In countries where Canadian products are well known, such as the United States, Canada ranks fourth on the list trailing Japan, the United States, and Germany.[20]

But what exactly is quality? Various experts have defined quality as "fitness for use," "conformance to requirements," and "freedom from variation."[21] The American Society for Quality Control defines quality as the totality of features and characteristics of a product or service that bear on its ability to satisfy stated or implied needs. This is clearly a customer-centred definition of quality. It suggests that a company has delivered quality whenever its products and services meet or exceed customers' needs, requirements, and expectations.

A number of Canadian companies from the manufacturing and service sectors have improved their profitability by following this customer-oriented view of quality. Gedas A.

Nortel's commitment to quality has made it a world leader.

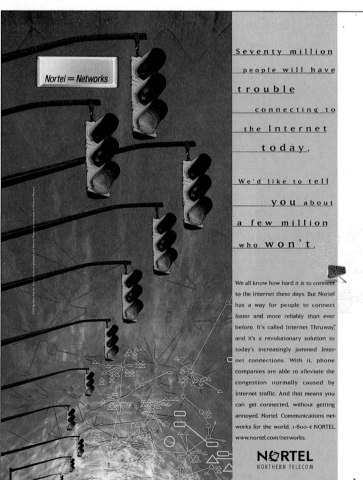

Nortel = Networks

Seventy million people will have **trouble** connecting to the Internet **today**.

We'd like to tell **you** about a few million who **won't**.

We all know how hard it is to connect to the Internet these days. But Nortel has a way for people to connect faster and more reliably than ever before. It's called Internet Thruway, and it's a revolutionary solution to today's increasingly jammed Internet connections. With it, phone companies are able to alleviate the congestion normally caused by Internet traffic. And that means you can get connected, without getting annoyed. Nortel. Communications networks for the world. 1-800-4 NORTEL. www.nortel.com/networks.

NORTEL
NORTHERN TELECOM

Sakus, president of Nortel's switch-manufacturing business, realized his company got into trouble in the early 1990s because "we took the view of what was good for us rather than what was good for the customer. To survive in the global economy, you have to put the customer first in everything that you do and you cannot do that unless you have an underpinning of quality." This insight allowed Nortel to move from a staggering loss of $884 million in 1993, to profits of over $100 million in 1996. Hank Stackhouse, general manager of the Delta Whistler Resort in British Columbia, has focused on the continual improvement of quality and customer satisfaction because "as a destination resort competing for tourist dollars against resorts the world over, an ability to deliver the highest possible customer satisfaction is a prerequisite for success." To improve quality and make customer feedback more relevant to service providers, Stackhouse held 15 guest focus groups. People from a number of functional areas witnessed the sessions, including the executive chef, director of human resources, and director of food and beverage services.[22]

It is important to distinguish between performance quality and conformance quality. *Performance quality* refers to the *level* at which a product performs its functions. For example, a Mercedes provides higher performance quality than a Volkswagen: it has a smoother ride, handles better, and lasts longer. It is more expensive and sells to a market with higher means and requirements. *Conformance quality* refers to freedom from defects and the *consistency* with which a product delivers a specified level of performance. Thus, a Mercedes and a Volkswagen can be said to offer equivalent conformance quality to their respective markets to the extent that each consistently delivers what its market expects. A $70 000 car that meets all of its requirements is a quality car; so is a $25 000 car that meets all of its requirements. But if the Mercedes handles badly, or if the Volkswagen gives poor fuel efficiency, then both cars have failed to deliver quality, and customer satisfaction suffers accordingly.

TOTAL QUALITY MANAGEMENT

Total quality management (TQM) swept the corporate boardrooms of the 1980s. Many companies adopted the language of TQM but not the substance. Others viewed TQM as a cure-all for all the company's problems. Still others became obsessed with narrowly defined TQM principles and lost sight of broader concerns for customer value and satisfaction. As a result, many TQM programs begun in the 1980s failed, causing a recent backlash against TQM. Still, when applied in the context of creating customer satisfaction, total quality principles remain a requirement for success. Although many firms don't use the TQM label anymore, for most top companies customer-driven quality has become a way of doing business. They apply the notion of "return on quality (ROQ)," and they ensure that the quality they offer is the quality that customers want. This quality, in turn, results in improved sales and profits.[23]

Total quality is the key to creating customer value and satisfaction. Just as marketing is everyone's job, total quality is everyone's job:

> Marketers who don't learn the language of quality improvement, manufacturing, and operations will become as obsolete as buggy whips. The days of functional marketing are gone. We can no longer afford to think of ourselves as market researchers, advertising people, direct marketers, marketing strategists—we have to think of ourselves as customer satisfiers—customer advocates focussed on whole processes.[24]

As you drive through the industrial sector of your city or town, you may have seen evidence of the continued focus on quality by many Canadian firms. Huge banners hang over their entrances declaring that they have been certified under the ISO 9000 series or 14000 series of standards. ISO is the acronym for the International Organization for Standardization, which is headquartered in Geneva,

Hunter Technology Inc. believes that a customer focus should drive an ISO 9000 program.

Switzerland. In Canada, the program is administered by the Quality Management Institute, which is a division of the Canadian Standards Association. The 9000 series is an internationally accepted standard for quality systems. It plays two primary roles: it establishes standards and systems for quality management within firms; and sets quality assurance benchmarks against which customers can evaluate a supplier's quality system. The 14000 series is an Environmental Management System (EMS) developed to help organizations implement effective environmental management systems. Van MacHaffley, vice president of Hunter Energy and Technologies, an Orillia, Ontario-based producer of gas fireplaces and heaters that recently underwent the approval process, believes that the product that the customer sees should be the real motivator behind seeking ISO accreditation. "Certification doesn't guarantee the impossible goal of 100% defect-free products. It does assure the consumer that the manufacturer gives product quality a high level of priority and allocates resources to maintain and improve that quality." Receiving ISO accreditation also helps firms compete worldwide since they can demonstrate that they have consistent, third-party verification of their quality procedures. Companies in more than 80 countries have voluntary adopted these standards. In Canada, almost 3000 firms have achieved registration.[25]

MARKETING'S ROLE IN TOTAL QUALITY

Marketing management has two responsibilities in a quality-centred company. First, marketing management must participate in formulating strategies and policies designed to help the company win through total quality excellence. Second, marketing must deliver marketing quality as well as production quality. It must perform each marketing activity—marketing research, sales training, advertising, customer service, and others—to high standards.

Marketers play several major roles in helping their companies define and deliver high-quality goods and services to target customers. First, marketers bear the major responsibility for correctly identifying the customers' needs and requirements and for communicating customer expectations correctly to product designers. Second, marketers must ensure that the customers' orders are filled correctly and on time, and must check that customers have received proper instructions, training, and technical assistance in the use of the product. Third, marketers must stay in contact with customers after the sale to ensure that they remain satisfied. Finally, marketers must gather and convey customer ideas for product and service improvements to the appropriate company departments.

Finally, marketers must gather and convey customer ideas for product and service improvements to the appropriate company departments. Marketers must be the customer's watchdog or guardian, complaining loudly for the customer when the product or the service is not right. Marketing Highlight 18-2 presents some important conclusions about total marketing quality strategy.

PURSUING A TOTAL QUALITY MARKETING STRATEGY

The Japanese have long taken to heart consultant W. Edwards Deming's lessons about winning through total quality management (TQM). This quest for quality paid off handsomely. Consumers around the world flocked to buy high-quality Japanese products, leaving many North American firms playing catch-up.

In recent years, many firms have closed the quality gap. Many have started their own quality programs in an effort to compete both globally and domestically with the Japanese. A growing number of companies have appointed a "Vice-President of Quality" to spearhead total quality. Total quality stems from the following premises about quality improvement:

1. *Quality is in the eyes of the customer.* Quality must begin with customer needs and end with customer perceptions. As Motorola's vice-president of quality suggests, "Quality has to do something for the customer. . . . Beauty is in the eye of the beholder. If [a product] does not work the way that the user needs it to work, the defect is as big to the user as if it doesn't work the way the designer planned it. Our definition of a defect is 'if the customer doesn't like it, it's a defect.'" Thus, the fundamental aim of today's quality movement has now become "total customer satisfaction." Quality improvements are meaningful only when they are perceived by customers.

2. *Quality must be reflected not just in the company's products, but in every company activity.* Leonard A. Morgan of GE says: "We are not just concerned with the quality of the product, but with the quality of our advertising, service, product literature, delivery, and after-sales support."

3. *Quality requires total employee commitment.* Quality can be delivered only by companies in which all employees are committed to quality and motivated and trained to deliver it. Successful companies remove the barriers between departments. Their employees work as teams to carry out core business processes and to create desired outcomes. Employees work to satisfy their internal customers as well as external customers. The Government of New Brunswick has been successful at attracting new business to the province partly because its employees have provided quality service to business.

4. *Quality requires high-quality partners.* Quality can be delivered only by companies whose value-chain partners also deliver quality. Therefore, a quality-driven company must find and align itself with high-quality suppliers and distributors.

Ford recognizes that quality requires a total employee commitment.

5. *A quality program cannot save a poor product.* The Pontiac Fiero launched a quality program, but because the car didn't have a performance engine to support its performance image, the quality program did not save the car. A quality drive cannot compensate for product deficiencies.

6. *Quality can always be improved.* The best companies believe in the Japanese concept of *kaizen,* "continuous improvement of everything by everyone." The best way to improve quality is to benchmark the company's performance against the "best-of-class" competitors or the best performers in other industries, striving to equal or even surpass them.

7. *Quality improvement sometimes requires quantum leaps.* Although the company should strive for continuous quality improvement, it must at times seek a quantum quality improvement. Companies sometimes can obtain small improvements by working harder. But large improvements call for fresh solutions and for working smarter. For example, John Young of Hewlett-Packard did not ask for a 10 percent reduction in defects, he asked for a *tenfold* reduction and got it.

8. *Quality does not cost more.* Managers once argued that achieving more quality would cost more and slow down production. But improving quality involves learning ways to "do things right the first time." Quality is not *inspected* in; it must be *designed* in. Doing things right the first time reduces the costs of salvage, repair, and redesign, not to mention losses in customer goodwill. Motorola claims that its quality drive has saved over $900 million in manufacturing costs during the last five years.

9. *Quality is necessary but may not be sufficient.* Improving a company's quality is absolutely necessary to meet the needs of more demanding buyers. At the same time, higher quality may not ensure a winning advantage, especially as all competitors increase their quality to more or less the same extent. For example, Singapore Airlines enjoyed a reputation as the world's best airline. However, competing airlines have attracted larger shares of passengers recently by narrowing the perceived gap between their service quality and Singapore's service quality.

Sources: Quotations from Lois Therrien, "Motorola and NEC: Going for Glory," *Business Week,* Special issue on quality, 1991, pp. 60–61. Also see David A. Garvin, "Competing on Eight Dimensions of Quality," *Harvard Business Review,* November–December 1987, p. 109; Frank Rose, "Now Quality Means Service Too," *Fortune,* April 22, 1992, pp. 97–108; Cyndee Miller, "TQM out; 'Continuous Process Improvement' in," *Marketing News,* May 9, 1994, pp. 5, 10; and David Greising, "Quality: How to Make It Pay," *Business Week,* August 8, 1994, pp. 54–59.

■ COMPETITIVE MARKETING STRATEGIES

Competitive advantage
An advantage over competitors gained by offering consumers greater value, either through lower prices or by providing more benefits that justify higher prices.

Today, understanding customers is crucial, but it's not enough. Under the marketing concept, companies gain **competitive advantage** by designing offers that satisfy target consumer needs *better than competitors' offers.* This dual focus is called **market orientation.** Thus, marketing strategies must consider not only the needs of target consumers, but also the strategies of competitors. The first step is **competitor analysis,** the process of identifying and assessing key competitors. The second step is developing **competitive marketing strategies** that strongly position the company against competitors and give it the greatest possible competitive advantage.

■ COMPETITOR ANALYSIS

FIGURE 18-4 *Steps in analysing competitors*

To plan effective competitive marketing strategies, the company needs to find out all it can about its competitors. It must constantly compare its products, prices, channels, and promotion with those of close competitors. In this way the company can find areas of potential competitive advantage and disadvantage.

As shown in Figure 18-4, competitor analysis involves first identifying and assessing competitors, and then selecting which competitors to attack or avoid.

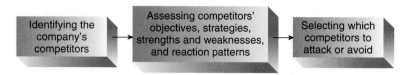

IDENTIFYING COMPETITORS

Market orientation
A simultaneous focus on customers and competitors.

Competitor analysis
The process of identifying key competitors; assessing their objectives, strategies, strengths and weaknesses, and reaction patterns; and selecting which competitors to attack or avoid.

Competitive marketing strategies
Strategies that strongly position the company against competitors and that give the company the strongest possible strategic advantage.

Normally, it would seem a simple task for a company to identify its competitors. Coca-Cola knows that Pepsi is its major competitor; and Caterpillar knows that it competes with Komatsu. At the narrowest level, a company can define its competitors as other companies offering a similar product and services to the same customers at similar prices. Thus, Buick might view Ford as a major competitor, but not Mercedes or Hyundai.

But companies actually face a much wider range of competitors. The company might define competitors as all firms making the same product or class of products. Thus, Buick would see itself as competing against all other automobile makers. Even more broadly, competitors might include all companies making products that supply the same service. Here Buick would see itself competing against not only other automobile makers, but also companies that make trucks, motorcycles, or even bicycles. Finally, and still more broadly, competitors might include all companies that compete for the same consumer dollars. Here Buick would see itself competing with companies that sell major consumer durables, new homes, or vacations abroad.

Companies must avoid "competitor myopia." A company is more likely to be "buried" by its latent competitors than its current ones. For example, Canada's largest banks are posing threats to a number of different businesses. Their huge customer base and intimate knowledge of these customers are viewed as a strategic advantage in selling a range of financial products and services. In just a few years, banks have added investment services such as RRSPs, mutual funds, discount and full-service brokerages, causing an erosion of the shares of the traditional players in these markets. Banks have waged an eight-year war to be allowed to sell insurance, claiming that consumers would benefit, in terms of lower rates, from a more competitive market. Canada's 150 life insurance and 220 property and casualty insurers have strongly opposed the banks' entry in an attempt to defend their ownership of the $48-billion market. For now, their market is safe. The banks were denied the mandate they need to sell insurance in the spring 1996 budget speech. However, the banks vow they will continue their fight. Banks have also been

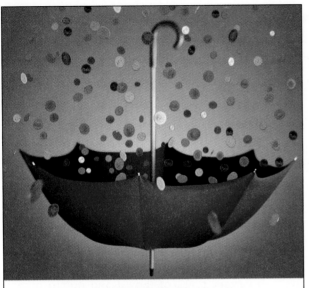

IF EARNING MONEY WERE THIS EASY, WE'D ALL CARRY AN UMBRELLA.

But life just isn't like that, is it? So instead, at TD Bank Financial Group® we've put together a team of professionals and services to help you make

WE'RE HERE TO HELP MAKE IT EASIER.

TD

more out of your money. We're not saying we can make it rain pennies from heaven, but we think we're close. Please take a look at the next page for details.

Banks, like TD Bank, are competing in many new fields and are new but formidable competitors for investment and insurance companies.

Strategic group
A group of firms in an industry following the same or a similar strategy.

Benchmarking
The process of comparing the company's products and processes to those of competitors or leading firms in other industries to find ways to improve quality and performance.

attempting to enter the lucrative automobile-leasing market. They want to offer customers lease options instead of being restricted to just offering car loans. Again, they are being strongly opposed by Canada's 3800 new-car dealerships. Currently, the $9-billion leasing industry is dominated by the credit subsidiaries of the big automakers.[26]

ASSESSING COMPETITORS

Having identified the main competitors, marketing management now asks: What does each competitor seek in the marketplace? What is each competitor's strategy? What are various competitors' strengths and weaknesses, and how will each react to actions that the company might take?

Each competitor has a mix of objectives, each with differing importance. The company wants to know the relative importance that a competitor places on current profitability, market-share growth, cash flow, technological leadership, service leadership, and other goals. Knowing a competitor's mix of objectives reveals whether the competitor is satisfied with its current situation and how it might react to different competitive actions. A company also must monitor its competitors' objectives for various product/market segments. If the company finds that a competitor has discovered a new segment, this might be an opportunity. If it finds that competitors plan new moves into segments now served by the company, it will be forewarned and, hopefully, forearmed.

The more that one firm's strategy resembles another firm's strategy, the more the two firms compete. In most industries, the competitors can be sorted into groups that pursue different strategies. A **strategic group** is a group of firms in an industry following the same or a similar strategy in a given target market. For example, in the major appliance industry, General Electric, Whirlpool, and Maytag all belong to the same strategic group. Each produces a full line of medium-price appliances supported by good service. Sub Zero and KitchenAid, on the other hand, belong to a different strategic group. They produce a narrower line of higher-quality appliances, offer a higher level of service, and charge a premium price.

Some important insights emerge from identifying strategic groups. For example, if a company enters one of the groups, the members of that group become its key competitors. Thus, the company needs to consider all of the dimensions that identify strategic groups within the industry. It needs to know each competitor's product quality, features, and mix; customer services; pricing policy; distribution coverage; sales-force strategy; and advertising and sales promotion programs. And it must study the details of each competitor's R&D, manufacturing, purchasing, financial, and other strategies.

Marketers need to carefully assess each competitor's strengths and weaknesses in order to answer the critical question: What *can* our competitors do? Companies normally learn about their competitors' strengths and weaknesses through secondary data, personal experience, and hearsay. They also can conduct primary marketing research with customers, suppliers, and dealers. Recently, a growing number of companies have turned to **benchmarking,** comparing the company's products and processes to those of competitors or leading firms in other industries to find ways to improve quality and performance. Benchmarking has become a powerful tool for increasing a company's competitiveness.

Expanding into a new strategy segment: General Electric offers a premium-quality, premium-price line of kitchen appliances.

Scott reacted to P&G's entry into the Canadian paper towel market with this ad called "the straight facts about paper towels."

Finally, the company wants to know: What *will* our competitors do? A competitor's objectives, strategies, and strengths and weaknesses go a long way toward explaining its likely actions, as well as its likely reactions to company moves such as price cuts, promotion increases, or new-product introductions. In addition, each competitor has a certain philosophy of doing business, a certain internal culture and guiding beliefs. Marketing managers need a deep understanding of a given competitor's mentality if they want to anticipate how the competitor will act or react.

Each competitor reacts differently. Some do not react quickly or strongly to a competitor's move. They may feel their customers are loyal; they may be slow in noticing the move; they may lack the funds to react. Some competitors react only to certain types of moves and not to others. They might always respond strongly to price cuts in order to signal that these will never succeed. But they might not respond at all to advertising increases, believing these to be less threatening. Other competitors react swiftly and strongly to any action. For example, Scott Paper Ltd. of Mississauga, Ontario spent little time hesitating when P&G entered the Canadian market with its Bounty paper towels. Scott, the market leader in the $200-million Canadian paper-towel market, believed that P&G unfairly compared its 27-cm towels to the 22-cm towels offered by competitors. Scott retaliated with a print ad campaign featuring the headline, "What are the straight facts about paper towels?" The ad stated that Scott's Ultra towels were 60 percent more absorbent than Bounty Jumbo towels and that Scott Ultra rolls were 24 percent longer. Scott hasn't just waged its war on the advertising front, however. It has pursued both marketing and legal weapons in its battle. It spent $1.5 million sending samples of its Ultra towels to Canadian households. It is also seeking punitive damages of $1 million from P&G in the Federal Court of Canada. In addition, in an effort to prevent P&G from using the Bounty slogan "Quicker Picker Upper," Scott asserts that P&G misled retailers and consumers by not making fair and complete comparisons.[27] Unlike Scott, some competitors show no predictable reaction pattern. They might or might not react on a given occasion, and there is no way to foresee what they will do based on their economics, history, or anything else.

In some industries, competitors live in relative harmony; in others, they fight constantly. Knowing how major competitors react gives the company clues on how best to attack competitors or how best to defend the company's current positions.[28]

SELECTING COMPETITORS TO ATTACK AND AVOID

A company has already largely selected its major competitors through prior decisions on customer targets, distribution channels, and marketing-mix strategy. These decisions define the strategic group to which the company belongs. Management now must decide which competitors to compete against most vigorously.

Most companies prefer to aim their shots at their weak competitors. This requires fewer resources and less time. But in the process, the firm may gain little. The argument could be made that the firm also should compete with strong competitors in order to sharpen its abilities.

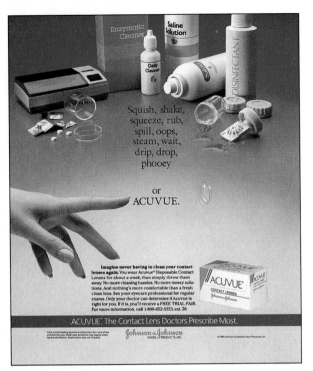

After driving smaller competitors from the market, Bausch & Lomb faced larger, more resourceful ones, such as Johnson & Johnson's Vistakon division. Vistakon's Acuvue disposable lenses forced Bausch & Lomb to take some of its own medicine.

Furthermore, even strong competitors have some weaknesses, and succeeding against them often provides greater returns.

Most companies will compete with competitors who resemble them most (i.e., close competitors versus distant competitors). Thus, Chevrolet competes more against Ford than against Jaguar. At the same time, the company may want to avoid trying to "destroy" a close competitor. For example, in the late 1970s, Bausch & Lomb moved aggressively against other soft lens manufacturers with great success. However, the conquests turned out to be questionable victories. One after another, competitors were forced to sell out to larger firms such as Revlon, Schering-Plough, and Johnson & Johnson. As a result, Bausch & Lomb now faced much larger competitors—and it suffered the consequences. Johnson & Johnson acquired Vistakon, a small nicher with only $28 million in annual sales, which served the tiny portion of the contact-lens market for people with astigmatism. Backed by J&J's deep pockets, however, Vistakon proved a formidable opponent. When the small but nimble Vistakon unit introduced its innovative Acuvue disposable lenses, the much larger Bausch & Lomb was forced to take some of its own medicine. According to one analyst, "The speed of the [Acuvue] rollout and the novelty of [J&J's] big-budget ads left giant Bausch & Lomb . . . seeing stars." By 1992, J&J's Vistakon was number one in the fast-growing disposable segment and had captured about 25 percent of the entire contact-lens market.[29] In this case, success in hurting a close rival brought in tougher competitors.

A company really needs and benefits from competitors. The existence of competitors results in several strategic benefits. Competitors may help increase total demand as illustrated in the opening example about the courier industry. They may share the costs of market and product development and help to legitimize new technologies. They may serve less attractive segments or lead to more product differentiation. Finally, they lower the antitrust risk and improve bargaining power versus labour or regulators.

However, a company may not view all of its competitors as beneficial. An industry often contains "well-behaved" competitors and "disruptive" competitors.[30] Well-behaved competitors play by the rules of the industry. They favour a stable and healthy industry, set reasonable prices in relation to costs, motivate others to lower costs or improve differentiation, and accept reasonable levels of market share and profits. Disruptive competitors, on the other hand, break the rules. They try to buy share rather than earn it, take large risks, and in general shake up the industry. For example, Canada Post and Purolator are accused by the Canadian Courier Association of being "disruptive" couriers that harm the whole industry. A company might be smart to support well-behaved competitors, aiming its attacks at disruptive competitors.

The implication is that "well-behaved" companies would like to shape an industry that consists of only well-behaved competitors. Through careful licensing, selective retaliation, and coalitions, they can shape the industry so that the competitors behave rationally and harmoniously, follow the rules, try to earn share rather than buy it, and differentiate to compete less directly.

COMPETITIVE STRATEGIES

Having identified and evaluated its major competitors, the company now must design broad competitive marketing strategies that will best position its offer against competitors' offers and give the company the strongest possible competitive advantage. But what broad marketing strategies might the company use? Which ones are best for a particular company, or for the company's different divisions and products?

No one strategy is best for all companies. Each company must determine what makes the most sense given its position in the industry and its objectives, opportunities, and resources. Even within a company, different strategies may be required for different businesses or products. Johnson & Johnson uses one marketing strategy for its leading brands in stable consumer markets and a different marketing strategy for its new high-tech health-care businesses and products. We now look at broad competitive marketing strategies that companies can use.

BASIC COMPETITIVE STRATEGIES

More than a decade ago, Michael Porter suggested four basic competitive positioning strategies that companies can follow—three winning strategies and one losing one.[31] The three winning strategies include:

◆ *Overall cost leadership.* Here the company works hard to achieve the lowest costs of production and distribution so that it can price lower than its competitors and win a large market share. Texas Instruments and Wal-Mart are leading practitioners of this strategy.

◆ *Differentiation.* Here the company concentrates on creating a highly differentiated product line and marketing program so that it comes across as the class leader in the industry. Most customers would prefer to own this brand if its price is not too high. IBM and Caterpillar follow this strategy in computers and heavy construction equipment, respectively.

◆ *Focus.* Here the company focuses its effort on serving a few market segments well rather than going after the whole market. Thus, Mountain Equipment Co-op offers products only to outdoor enthusiasts who favour non-motorized sports such as rock climbing or kayaking rather than to a broader mix of people who enjoy outdoor recreational activities such as power boating or the use of all-terrain vehicles.

Companies that pursue a clear strategy—one of the above—are likely to perform well. The firm that carries out that strategy best will make the most profits. But firms that do not pursue a clear strategy—*middle-of-the-roaders*—do the

These ads indicate that the two companies, Clearnet and Bell Mobility, are using different strategies to win customers for their new PCS technology. How would you describe the strategies each firm is using?

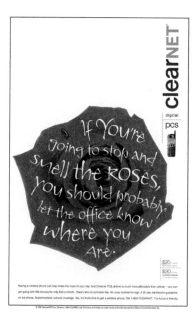

worst. Sears, Chrysler, and International Harvester all encountered difficult times because they did not stand out as the lowest in cost, highest in perceived value, or best in serving some market segment. Middle-of-the-roaders try to be good on all strategic counts, but end up being not very good at anything.

More recently, two marketing consultants, Michael Treacy and Fred Wiersema, offered a new classification of competitive marketing strategies.[32] They suggest that companies gain leadership positions by delivering superior value to their customers. Companies can pursue any of three strategies—called *value disciplines*—for delivering superior customer value. These are:

- ◆ *Operational excellence:* The company provides superior value by leading its industry in price and convenience. It works to reduce costs and to create a lean and efficient value delivery system. It serves customers who want reliable, good quality products or services, but who want them cheaply and easily. Examples include Wal-Mart and Dell Computer.

- ◆ *Customer intimacy:* The company provides superior value by precisely segmenting its markets and then tailoring its products or services to match exactly the needs of targeted customers. It builds detailed customer databases for segmenting and targeting, and empowers its marketing people to respond quickly to customer needs. It serves customers who are willing to pay a premium to get precisely what they want, and it will do almost anything to build long-term customer loyalty and to capture customer lifetime value. Examples include Tilley Endurables, Land's End outfitters, and Kraft Foods.

- ◆ *Product leadership:* The company provides superior value by offering a continuous stream of leading-edge products or services that make their own and competing products obsolete. It is open to new ideas, relentlessly pursues new solutions, and works to reduce cycle times so that it can get new products to market quickly. It serves customers who want state-of-the-art products and services, regardless of the costs in terms of price or inconvenience. Examples include Cognos and Corel.

Product leadership: Motorola provides superior value through a continuous stream of leading-edge products.

Some companies successfully pursue more than one value discipline at the same time. For example, Federal Express excels at both operational excellence and customer intimacy. However, such companies are rare—few firms can be the best at more than one of these disciplines. By trying to be *good at all* of the value disciplines, a company usually ends up being *best at none.*

Treacy and Wiersema have found that leading companies focus on and excel at a single value discipline, while meeting industry standards on the other two. They design their entire value delivery system to single-mindedly support the chosen discipline. For example, Wal-Mart knows that customer intimacy and product leadership are important. Compared with other discounters, it offers very good customer service and an excellent product assortment. Still, it offers less customer service and less depth in its product assortment than specialty and department stores that pursue customer intimacy or product leadership strategies. Instead, it focuses obsessively on operational excellence—on reducing costs and streamlining its order-to-delivery process to make it convenient for customers to buy just the right products at the lowest prices.

Classifying competitive strategies as value disciplines is appealing. It defines marketing strategy in terms of the single-minded pursuit of delivering value to customers. It recognizes that management must align

Daddy fought in the war.

The Motorola MicroTAC Ultra Lite™ comes from a long line of heroes. Like the original SCR 536 hand-held wireless radio, which cut our boys loose from the wires of war. Lives depended on us then. Busy lives depend on us now. Motorola. The best-selling, most-preferred cellular phones in the world.

Ⓜ **MOTOROLA**

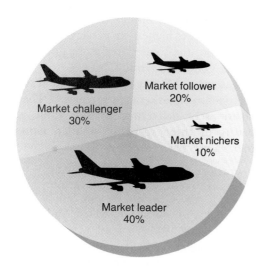

FIGURE 18-5
Hypothetical market structure

Market leader
The firm in an industry with the largest market share; it usually leads other firms in price changes, new product introductions, distribution coverage, and promotion spending.

Market challenger
A runner-up firm in an industry that is fighting hard to increase its market share.

Market follower
A runner-up firm in an industry that wants to hold its share without rocking the boat.

Market nicher
A firm in an industry that serves small segments that the other firms overlook or ignore.

every aspect of the company with the chosen value discipline—from its culture, to its organization structure, to its operating and management systems and processes.

COMPETITIVE POSITIONS

Firms competing in a given target market will, at any point in time, differ in their objectives and resources. Some firms will be large, others small. Some will have many resources, others will be strapped for funds. Some will be old and established, others new and fresh. Some will strive for rapid market share growth, others for long-term profits. And the firms will occupy different competitive positions in the target market.

We will adopt a classification of competitive strategies based on the roles firms play in the target market—that of leading, challenging, following, or niching. Suppose that an industry contains the firms shown in Figure 18-5. Forty percent of the market is in the hands of the **market leader,** the firm with the largest market share. Another 30 percent is in the hands of a **market challenger,** a runner-up that is fighting hard to increase its market share. Another 20 percent is in the hands of a **market follower,** another runner-up that wants to hold its share without rocking the boat. The remaining 10 percent is in the hands of **market nichers,** firms that serve small segments not being pursued by other firms.

We now look at specific marketing strategies that are available to market leaders, challengers, followers, and nichers (see Table 18-2). Remember, however, that these classifications often do not apply to a whole company, but only to its position in a specific industry. For example, large and diversified companies such as IBM, Sears, or Procter & Gamble might be leaders in some markets and nichers in others. For example, Procter & Gamble leads in many segments, such as dishwashing and laundry detergents, disposable diapers, and shampoo, but it challenges Lever in hand soaps. Such companies often use different strategies for different business units or products, depending on the competitive situations of each.

MARKET-LEADER STRATEGIES

Most industries contain an acknowledged market leader. The leader has the largest market share and usually leads the other firms in price changes, new product introductions, distribution coverage, and promotion spending. The leader may or may not be admired or respected, but other firms concede its dominance. Competitors focus on the leader as a company to challenge, imitate, or avoid. Some of the best-known market leaders are Purolator (courier services), General Motors (autos), Kodak (photography), IBM (computers), Caterpillar (earth-moving equipment),

Table 18-2 *Strategies for Market Leaders, Challengers, Followers, and Nichers*

Market-Leader Strategies	Market-Challenger Strategies	Market-Follower Strategies	Market-Nicher Strategies
Expand total market	Full frontal attack	Follow closely	By customer, market, quality-price, service
Protect market share	Indirect attack	Follow at a distance	Multiple niching
Expand market share			

Coca-Cola (soft drinks), Campbell's (soups), Sears Canada (retailing), McDonald's (fast food), and Gillette (razors and blades).

A leader's life is not easy. It must maintain a constant watch. Other firms keep challenging its strengths or trying to take advantage of its weaknesses. The market leader can easily miss a turn in the market and plunge into second or third place. A product innovation may come along and hurt the leader (as when Tylenol's non-aspirin painkiller took the lead from Bayer Aspirin). Or the leading firm might grow fat and slow, losing out against new and peppier rivals. Bell Canada knows this only too well. On July 1, 1994, the government ruled that Canada's largest phone company had to provide "equal access" to the telecommunication lines it owns. The result was an influx into the Canadian $7.5-billion long-distance phone market by almost 200 new competitors who challenged Bell in both the business and home telephone markets. For Bell, the results were not a pretty sight. By 1996, it had lost 27 percent of the lucrative long-distance market to competitors like Unitel and Sprint Canada. Bell's earnings dropped from $1.2 billion in 1994, to $782 million in 1995. Bell now thinks the worst is over. It has lobbied government and gained approval to increase local rates. It has developed break-through advertising. It has cut staff to make itself more cost-effective. It has developed value-added services for its customers such as call waiting, call identifiers, and message-answering services. It has allied itself with new partners to offer services over the Internet. It has even redesigned its long-standing brand logo to reflect that Bell is now a more dynamic company with a more human face.[33]

To remain number one, leading firms can take any of three actions. First, they can find ways to expand total demand. Second, they can protect their current market share through good defensive and offensive actions. Third, they can try to expand their market share further, even if market size remains constant.

EXPANDING THE TOTAL MARKET. The leading firm normally gains the most when the total market expands. If Canadians take more pictures, Kodak stands to gain the most because it sells more than 80 percent of this country's film. If Kodak can convince more Canadians to take pictures, or to take pictures on more occasions, or to take more pictures on each occasion, it will benefit greatly.

Market leaders can expand the market by developing new users, new uses, and more usage of the product. For example, Revlon might find new perfume users in its current markets by convincing women who do not use perfume to try it. It might find users in new demographic segments, such as by producing cologne for men. Or it might expand into new geographic segments, perhaps by selling its perfume in other countries.

Marketers can expand markets by discovering and promoting new uses for the product. For example, the makers of WD-40, the multi-purpose household lubricant and solvent, sponsors an annual contest to discover new uses. Another example of new-use expansion is Arm & Hammer baking soda. Its sales had flattened after 125 years. Then the company discovered that consumers were using baking soda as a refrigerator deodorizer. It launched a heavy advertising and publicity campaign focusing on this use and persuaded consumers to place an open box of baking soda in their refrigerators and to replace it every few months.

Finally, market leaders can encourage more usage by convincing people to use the product more often or to use more per occasion. Campbell encourages people to eat soup more often by running ads containing new recipes in *Canadian Living* and other home magazines. Years ago, the Michelin Tire Company found a creative way to increase usage per occasion. It wanted French car owners to drive more kilometres per year, resulting in more tire replacement. Michelin began rating French restaurants on a three-star system. It reported that many of the best restaurants were in the south of France, leading many Parisians to take weekend drives south. Today, a three-star Michelin rating is the ultimate accolade in fine cuisine. Michelin also

Today, you can

count on steel

for safer cars,

stronger houses

and

cleaner air.

We're not talking about the old steel your dad grew up with. Today's steel has changed not only the way we live, but also the role it plays in the environment.

Steel is produced in a way that's 80% cleaner than just 10 years ago. Not to mention steel is recycled more than plastic, aluminum, glass and paper, combined.

And now steel can even keep you safe at home. More and more families are building steel-frame homes for better protection against natural disasters like hurricanes.

Of course, along with these changes, the strength of steel remains unmatched. So you can rest easy knowing it's not just going to make a difference in your life today, it's going to make a difference tomorrow.

The New Steel
Feel the strength.

www.thenewsteel.org

©1997 ✦ The**Steel**Alliance

With this dramatic ad, the steel industry hopes to attract users away from competing products and get existing users to use more steel.

publishes guidebooks with maps and sights along the way to encourage additional travel.

PROTECTING MARKET SHARE. While trying to expand total market size, the leading firm also must constantly protect its current business against competitors' attacks. Coca-Cola must constantly guard against Pepsi-Cola; Gillette against Bic; Kodak against Fuji; McDonald's against Wendy's; General Motors against Ford.

What can the market leader do to protect its position? First, it must prevent or fix weaknesses that provide opportunities for competitors. It needs to keep its costs down and its prices in line with the value the customers see in the brand. The leader should "plug holes" so that competitors do not jump in. But the best defence is a good offence, and the best response is *continuous innovation*. The leader refuses to be content with the way things are and leads the industry in new products, customer services, distribution effectiveness, and cost cutting. It keeps increasing its competitive effectiveness and value to customers. It takes the offensive, sets the pace, and exploits competitors' weaknesses.

EXPANDING MARKET SHARE. Market leaders also can grow by increasing their market shares further. In many markets, small market share increases mean very large sales increases. For example, a one-percent increase in market share for a Canadian cosmetic firm is worth $2.3 million. A similar increase in share for a computer firm equals $20.3 million.[34]

Studies have shown that, on average, profitability rises with increasing market share.[35] Because of these findings, many companies have sought expanded market shares to improve profitability. General Electric, for example, declared that it wants to be at least number one or two in each of its markets or else get out. GE shed its computer, air-conditioning, small appliances, and television businesses because it could not achieve top-dog position in these industries.

Companies must not think, however, that gaining increased market share will improve profitability automatically. Much depends on their strategy for gaining increased share. There are many high-share companies with low profitability and many low-share companies with high profitability. The cost of buying higher market share may far exceed the returns. Higher shares tend to produce higher profits only when unit costs fall with increased market share, or when the company offers a superior-quality product and charges a premium price that more than covers the cost of offering higher quality.

MARKET-CHALLENGER STRATEGIES

Firms that are second, third, or lower in an industry are sometimes quite large, such as Colgate, Ford, Kmart, Avis, Westinghouse, and PepsiCo. These runner-up

Market challenger Nissan attacks more expensive competitors, claiming that the Nissan Altima can do what a more expensive car can do. Properly equipped, the Altima can "out-slalom an Acura Legend L Sedan," "out-brake a BMW 325si," and "provide more freeway power than a Mercedes-Benz 190E 2.3."

firms can adopt one of two competitive strategies. They can challenge the leader and other competitors in an aggressive bid for more market share (market challengers). Or they can play along with competitors and not rock the boat (market followers). We now look at competitive strategies for market challengers.

A market challenger must first define its strategic objective. The challenger can attack the market leader, a high-risk but potentially high-gain strategy that makes good sense if the leader is not serving the market well. To succeed with such an attack, a company must have some sustainable competitive advantage over the leader—a cost advantage leading to lower prices or the ability to provide better value at a premium price. In the construction equipment industry, Komatsu successfully challenged Caterpillar by offering the same quality at much lower prices. And Kimberly Clark's Huggies grabbed a big share of the disposable diaper market from P&G by offering a better-fitting diaper with reusable fasteners. If the company goes after the market leader, its objective may be to wrest a certain market share. Bic knows that it can't topple Gillette in the razor market—it simply wants a larger share. Or the challenger's goal might be to take over market leadership. IBM entered the personal computer market late, as a challenger, but quickly became the market leader.

Alternatively, the challenger can avoid the leader and instead challenge firms its own size, or smaller local and regional firms. These smaller firms may be underfinanced and not serving their customers well. Molson, Canada's second-oldest company, grew to its present size not by challenging large competitors, but by gobbling up small local or regional competitors. If the company goes after a small local company, its objective may be to put that company out of business. The important point remains: The challenger must choose its opponents carefully and have a clearly defined and attainable objective.

Choosing an Attack Strategy

How can the market challenger best attack the chosen competitor and achieve its strategic objectives? Figure 18-6 shows five possible attack strategies. In a full *frontal attack,* the challenger matches the competitor's product, advertising, price, and distribution efforts. It attacks the competitor's strengths rather than its weaknesses. The outcome depends on who has the greater strength and endurance. If the market challenger has fewer resources than the competitor, a frontal attack makes little sense.

Even great size and strength may not be enough to challenge a firmly entrenched, resourceful competitor successfully. For example, Unilever has twice the worldwide sales of Procter & Gamble and five times the sales of Colgate-Palmolive. Yet its North American subsidiary, Lever Brothers, trails P&G. A while back, Lever launched a full frontal assault against P&G in the detergent market. Lever's Wisk was already the leading liquid detergent. In quick succession, it added a barrage of new products—Sunlight dishwashing detergent, Snuggle fabric softener, Surf laundry powder—and backed them with aggressive promotion and distribution efforts. But P&G spent heavily to defend its brands and held on to most of its business. And it counterattacked with Liquid Tide, which came from nowhere in just 17 months to run neck-and-neck with Wisk. Lever did gain market share, but most of it came at the expense of smaller competitors.[36]

FIGURE 18-6 *Attack strategies*

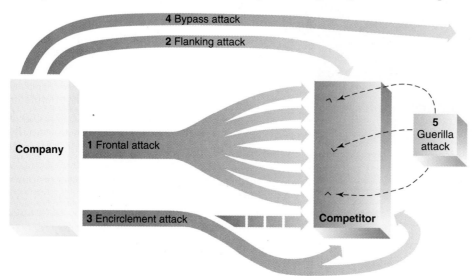

Rather than attacking head on, the challenger can launch a *flanking attack,* concentrating its strength against the competitor's weaker flanks or on gaps in the competitor's market coverage. For example, Netscape Communications Corp. has attempted to outflank giant competitor, Microsoft Corp., to gain dominance in the $5.5-billion market in software that provides access and application tools for the Internet. Netscape, although much smaller than Microsoft, has a technological edge in Web applications and has built up a credible brand name among "surfers." Although Microsoft is making huge investments to catch up to its feisty competitor, Netscape has won 85 percent of this sector of the software market. To retain its lead, Netscape recently signed a networking and marketing agreement that allows Compuserve's four million subscribers free use of Netscape's Navigator. Microsoft has countered with a similar partnership with America Online.[37] Flank attacks make good sense when the company has fewer resources than the competitor.

An *encirclement attack* involves attacking from the front, sides, and rear at the same time. The encirclement strategy makes sense when the challenger has superior resources and believes that it can break the competitor's hold on the market quickly. For example, Seiko attacked the watch market by gaining distribution in every major watch outlet and overwhelming competitors with constantly changing variety. It now makes and sells 2300 models worldwide.

Using a *bypass attack,* the challenger bypasses the competitor and targets easier markets. It might diversify into unrelated products, move into new geographic markets, or leapfrog into new technologies to replace existing products. With technological leapfrogging, instead of copying the competitor's product and mounting a costly frontal attack, the challenger passes by the competitor with the next technology. Thus, Minolta toppled Canon from the lead in the 35mm SLR camera market when it introduced its technologically advanced auto-focussing Maxxum camera. Canon's market share dropped toward 20 percent while Minolta's zoomed past 30 percent. It took Canon three years to introduce a matching technology.

Finally, smaller or poorly financed challengers can mount *guerrilla attacks.* These are small, periodic attacks to harass and demoralize the competitor, with the goal of eventually establishing permanent footholds. The challenger might use selective price cuts, executive raids, intense promotional outbursts, or assorted legal actions. Specific guerrilla actions can be cheap, but continuous guerrilla campaigns can be expensive. And they eventually must be followed up by stronger attacks if the challenger wishes to gain ground against competitors.

MARKET-FOLLOWER STRATEGIES

Not all runner-up companies want to challenge the market leader. Challenges are never taken lightly by the leader. If the challenger's lure is lower prices, improved service, or additional product features, the leader can quickly match these to defuse the attack. The leader probably has more staying power in an all-out battle for customers. A hard fight might leave both firms worse off. Thus, many firms prefer to follow rather than challenge the leader.

A follower can gain many advantages. The market leader often bears the huge expenses of developing new products and markets, expanding distribution, and educating the market. The market follower, on the other hand, can learn from the leader's experience and copy or improve on the leader's products and programs, usually with much less investment. Although the follower probably will not overtake the leader, it often can be as profitable. A good example of a follower is Dial Corporation, maker of such well-known brands as Dial, Tone, and Pure&Natural hand soaps, Armour Star canned meats, Purex laundry products, StaPuf fabric softener, SnoBol toilet cleaner, and Brillo scouring pads:

> Flashy it isn't. Dial doesn't try to come up with innovative new products. . . . It doesn't spend zillions to make its offerings household names across the nation. Instead, Dial prefers to coast in the slipstream of giant rivals, such as Procter & Gamble. [Its] lineup consists largely of me-too products and second-tier regional brands. . . . Instead of spending big on research and development or marketing, Dial leaves it to others. . . . And Dial lets other companies educate consumers about new products. P&G, for instance, introduced concentrated powder detergents in 1990. Dial followed over a year later with its own concentrated version, Purex—priced as much as one-third lower than P&G's Tide.[38]

Following is not the same as being passive or a carbon copy of the leader. The follower has to define a growth path, but one that does not create competitive retaliation. A market follower must know how to hold current customers and win a fair share of new ones. Each follower tries to bring distinctive advantages to its target market—location, services, financing. The follower is often a major target of attack by challengers. Therefore, the market follower must keep its manufacturing costs low and its product quality and services high. It must also enter new markets as they open up.

MARKET-NICHER STRATEGIES

Almost every industry includes firms that specialize in serving market niches. Instead of pursuing the whole market, or even large segments, these firms target subsegments, or niches. Nichers are often smaller firms with limited resources. But smaller divisions of larger firms also may pursue niching strategies. Firms with low shares of the total market can be highly profitable through smart niching (see Marketing Highlight 18-3).

One study of highly successful midsize companies found that, in almost all cases, these companies niched within a larger market rather than going after the whole market.[39] An example is A. T. Cross, which niches in the high-price pen and pencil market. It makes the famous gold writing instruments that many executives own or want to own. By concentrating in the high-price niche, Cross has enjoyed great sales growth and profit. Of course, the study found other features shared by successful smaller companies—offering high value, charging a premium price, and having strong corporate cultures and vision.

Why is niching profitable? The main reason is that the market nicher ends up knowing the target customer group so well that it meets their needs better than other firms that casually sell to this niche. As a result, the nicher can charge a substantial markup over costs because of the added value. Whereas the mass marketer achieves *high volume,* the nicher achieves *high margins.*

Nichers try to find one or more market niches that are safe and profitable. An ideal market niche is big enough to be profitable and has growth potential. It is one that the firm can serve effectively. Per-

Quality nicher: Hewlett-Packard specializes in the high-quality, high-price end of the hand-calculator market.

CONCENTRATED MARKETING: TERRY BIKES FIND SPECIAL NICHE

Is there room for a budding new competitor alongside the giants in the bicycle industry? Grayson Bain of Rocky Mountain Bicycle Co., and Georgena Terry of Terry Precision Bicycles for Women Inc. think so. Rocky Mountain Bicycle's Hammer racing bicycle was recently named bicycle of the year by California-based Mountain Biking magazine. Rocky Mountain sold 15 000 bikes in 1995, earning revenues of approximately $12 million. Long known for their quality, these bikes are performance machines that retail for $600 to $4000. They are the Cadillacs of the biking world, targeted at the top five percent of the market. Rocky Mountain's customers are bike enthusiasts who want nothing but the best, including features such as motorcycle-style suspension. This small, Delta, British Columbia company isn't just a local player. It exports 40 percent of its production to markets in 14 countries, including Europe and the United States. Germany is currently its largest overseas market. Rocky Mountain's success has been due to its reputation for quality products and its new focus on its core business. Whereas it experienced some difficulties when it started carrying accessories from other companies, it has been reborn with its concentration on its core bicycle business.

Georgena Terry is another entrepreneur who has developed a small but promising niche in the bicycle market—high-performance bikes for women.

There was nothing astonishing about the idea. Three years ago, Terry, then a 34-year-old MBA student, decided to start building bicycles. Oh, sure, she'd specialize in high-priced women's bikes, carving out a niche just as they had taught her at The Wharton Business School. But the US$1.3-billion bicycle industry didn't

Concentrated marketing: Georgena Terry has shown how a small company can succeed against larger competitors.

tremble at the thought of diminutive Terry picking up a wrench. True, she might have an interesting twist: her bikes would have a shorter top tube and a slightly smaller front wheel that would provide a more comfortable ride for women cyclists who put in 40 or 50 miles at a clip—but who rides that far? Most folks just use their bikes to pedal down to the Dairy Queen or tool around the neighbourhood on Sunday afternoons. Besides, if it turned out she had something, the industry could always wheel out a knockoff.

So when Terry set up shop, no one noticed. But they are noticing now. In its first year, Terry Precision Bicycles for Women, Inc., sold 20 bikes. In the second year it shipped 1300, and in the third year it sold 2500 more. Suddenly, her banker is more friendly, and the bicycle magazines are calling to see what she thinks of this or that. Terry has succeeded by concentrating on serving the special needs of serious women cyclists.

The idea began when Terry herself became interested in biking. She found that she had trouble finding a comfortable riding position. "The standard bicycle—even a woman's bike—is designed for a man. To fit women, who have longer legs and shorter torsos, bike shops shove the seat forward and tilt the handlebars back." That didn't help the

haps most importantly, the niche is of little interest to major competitors. And the firm can build the skills and customer goodwill to defend itself against a major competitor as the niche grows and becomes more attractive.

The key idea in nichemanship is specialization. A market nicher can specialize along any of several market, customer, product, or marketing mix lines. For example, it can specialize in serving one type of *end-user*, as when a law firm specializes in the criminal, civil, or business law markets. The nicher can specialize in serving a given *customer-size* group—many nichers specialize in serving small customers who are neglected by the majors. Some nichers focus on one or a few *specific customers*, selling their entire output to a single company, such as Wal-Mart or General Motors. *Geographic nichers* sell only in a certain locality, region, or area of the world. *Quality-price nichers* operate at the low or high end of the market. For example, Hewlett-Packard specializes in the high-quality, high-price end of the hand-calculator market. Finally, *service nichers* offer services not available from other firms. An example is a bank that takes loan requests over the phone and hand delivers the money to the customer.

Niching carries some major risks. For example, the market niche may dry up, or it might grow to the point that it attracts larger competitors. That is why many companies practise *multiple niching*. By developing two or more niches, the

five-foot-two, 98-pound Terry. She began wondering if shortening the frame would improve things. So she picked up a blowtorch—"a friend showed me how to use it so I wouldn't kill myself"—and headed for the basement. She came back up with a bike that had a smaller frame. Friends saw it, borrowed it, and asked if she'd make frames for them. Two years later she was still turning out frames and making a living—sort of.

Finally, she got tired of just getting by and started a company. Bicycling was undergoing a mini-boom and 70 percent of all new riders were women, so she'd specialize in women's bikes. She hauled seven or eight of her bikes to a New England Area Rally in Amherst, Massachusetts. "I figured we'd do very well or very badly. Women would either go 'who cares?' or love it." She sold three bikes that weekend (at US$775 each) and took orders for four more. Says Terry, "I have never been more excited in my life."

To her credit, Terry moved deliberately. Her major innovation was the frame, so she concentrated on that and didn't set out to reinvent the (bicycle) wheel. Her marketing plan was equally careful. As word spread, people would call up and ask to buy a bike. "We were thrilled, but always asked the name of their local bicycle shop. We'd then call the shop and say, 'Congratulations, you've just sold a Terry bike.'" Retailers, who found themselves making a quick couple of hundred dollars, usually asked for a few more bikes. That's how Terry put together a dealer network.

With almost no money for advertising, Terry concentrated on promotion. She hired a public relations firm that was quick to position her as a female David taking on bicycling's Goliaths. The approach paid off—the bicycle press discovered Terry and gave her bikes enthusiastic endorsements. That got customers into the stores and bikes out the door. Terry's professional business approach makes her stand out from competitors in a high-end bicycling industry filled with scores of tiny manufacturers that can take months to fill orders and are often unresponsive to both customers and shop owners. Terry, who ships on time, courts retailers, and answers questions from customers, quickly became a favourite.

But even as the marketing plan got her up and pedalling, Terry was moving to forestall competition. Recognizing that her high price would scare off many customers, Terry almost immediately began to segment. She was soon selling her high-end models for US$1200 and, to preempt the foreign competition that she knew would be coming, she signed two Asian companies to build versions of her bike that retail for US$450 to US$850. The strategy has worked so far. Although six companies, including Fuji America, now market bicycles to women, Terry is holding her own. Competitors' bikes just aren't as good. As one customer asserts, "Women can tell the difference on a ride around the block. My feet reach the pedals more comfortably, and it is easier to reach the hand brakes. You feel more in control on one of her bikes."

Continued success is far from assured. Over time, her competitors will improve their designs. And the more successful Terry becomes, the more competition she is likely to attract. Yet, she has shown how a company with fewer resources can succeed against larger competitors by concentrating on a small, high-quality segment. At some point, as with many small nichers, Terry may have to think about selling out or joining forces with a bigger company to survive. But that is still a long way off. For now, Terry says, "This is wonderful."

Source: Adapted from Paul B. Brown, "Spokeswoman," *Career Futures,* Spring–Summer 1989, pp. 30–32; Robert Williamson, "Bike Maker Rides Rebound," *Globe and Mail,* February 2, 1996, p. B8.

---

company increases its chances for survival. Even some large firms prefer a multiple-niche strategy to serving the total market. One large law firm has developed a national reputation in the three areas of mergers and acquisitions, bankruptcies, and prospectus development, and it does little else.

BALANCING CUSTOMER AND COMPETITOR ORIENTATIONS

Competitor-centred company
A company whose moves are mainly based on competitors' actions and reactions; it spends most of its time tracking competitors' moves and market shares and trying to find strategies to counter them.

Whether a company is a market leader, challenger, follower, or nicher, it must watch its competitors closely and find the competitive marketing strategy that positions it most effectively. And it must continually adapt its strategies to the fast-changing competitive environment.

This question now arises: Can the company spend too much time and energy tracking competitors, damaging its customer orientation? The answer is yes! A company can become so competitor-centred that it loses its even more important customer focus.

A **competitor-centred company** is one that spends most of its time tracking competitors' moves and market shares and trying to find strategies to counter

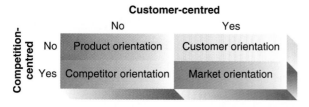

FIGURE 18-7 *Evolving company orientations*

Customer-centred company
A company that focuses on customer developments in designing its marketing strategies and on delivering superior value to its target customers.

Market-oriented company
A company that pays balanced attention to both customers and competitors in designing its marketing strategies.

them. This approach has some pluses and minuses. On the positive side, the company develops a fighter orientation. It trains its marketers to be on a constant alert, watching for weaknesses in their own position, and searching out competitors' weaknesses. On the negative side, the company becomes too reactive. Rather than carrying out its own customer-oriented strategy, it bases its own moves on competitors' moves. As a result, because so much depends on what the competitors do, the company does not move in a planned direction toward a goal.

A **customer-centred company**, by contrast, focusses more on customer developments in designing its strategies. Clearly, the customer-centred company is in a better position to identify new opportunities and set long-run strategies that make sense. By watching customer needs evolve, it can decide what customer groups and what emerging needs are the most important to serve, given its resources and objectives.

In practice, today's companies must be **market-oriented companies**, watching both their customers and their competitors. They must not let competitor watching blind them to customer focussing. Figure 18-7 shows that companies have moved through four orientations over the years. In the first stage, they were product-oriented, paying little attention to either customers or competitors. In the second stage, they became customer-oriented and started to pay attention to customers. In the third stage, when they started to pay attention to competitors, they became competitor-oriented. Today, companies need to be market-oriented, paying balanced attention to both customer and competitors. A market orientation pays big dividends—one recent study found a substantial positive relationship between a company's marketing orientation and its profitability, a relationship that held regardless of type of business or market environment.[40]

Summary of Chapter Objectives

Today's companies face their toughest competition ever. To survive, a company must win customers and outperform competitors, often by moving from a product and selling philosophy to a customer and marketing philosophy. Winning companies in today's marketplace have become adept at developing and implementing strategies for building customers, not merely building products.

1. **Define customer value and satisfaction, and discuss how companies attract new customers and retain current ones through relationship marketing.**

   Faced with a growing range of choices of products and services, consumers base their buying decisions on their perceptions of quality, value, and service. Companies must understand the determinants of customer value and satisfaction. Customer-delivered value is the difference between total customer value and total customer cost. Customers will usually choose the offer that maximizes their delivered value.

Customer satisfaction results when a company's performance has fulfilled a buyer's expectations. Customers are dissatisfied if performance is below expectations, satisfied if performance equals expectations, and delighted if performance exceeds expectations. Satisfied customers remain loyal longer, buy more, are less price sensitive, and talk favourably about the company to other people.

Companies not only strive to gain customers but, perhaps more importantly, to retain customers. Customer-relationship marketing is the key to retaining customers. Companies must decide the level at which they want to build relationships with different market segments and individual customers, ranging from basic relationships to full partnerships. Which is best depends on a customer's lifetime value relative to the costs required to attract and keep that customer. Today's marketers use a number of specific marketing tools to develop stronger bonds with customers by adding financial and social benefits or structural ties.

2.   Explain the role of a company value chain and the value delivery network in meeting customer needs.

To create customer value and satisfaction, and to retain customers, companies must manage their value chains and value delivery networks in a customer-oriented way. Each company department can be viewed as a link in the firm's value chain. That is, each department carries out value-creating activities to design, produce, market, deliver, and support the firm's products. The firm's success depends on how well each department performs its work and on how well the activities of various departments are coordinated.

In seeking a competitive advantage, a company must also look beyond its own value chain and into the customer value delivery network—the system composed of the value chains of its suppliers, distributors, and, ultimately, customers. Today most companies are "partnering" with the other members of the supply chain to improve the performance of the customer value delivery network.

3.   Clarify the concept of total quality marketing and its relationship to customer value and satisfaction.

Total quality management is a major approach to providing customer satisfaction and company profitability. Companies need to understand and meet consumer quality expectations. To be successful companies therefore must do a better job of meeting consumer quality expectations than competitors do. Besides measurement and reward systems, delivering quality requires total management and employee commitment. Marketers perform a critical role in their company's effort to achieve higher quality by helping design strategies and programs that help the company win through total quality excellence and by delivering market quality as well as production quality.

4.   Discuss the need to understand competitors as well as customers through competitor analysis.

To prepare an effective marketing strategy, a company must consider its competitors as well as its customers. It must continuously analyse competitors and develop competitive marketing strategies that position it effectively against competitors and provide it with the strongest possible competitive advantage.

Competitive analysis first involves identifying the company's major competitors. The company then assesses competitors' objectives, strategies, strengths and weaknesses, and reaction patterns. Using this information, it can select competitors to attack or avoid. Next, having identified and assessed its main competitor, the company must decide how it wants to deliver value to target customers and develop a broad competitive strategy by which it can gain competitive advantage.

5.   Explain the fundamentals of competitive marketing strategies based on creating value for customers.

Which competitive marketing strategy makes the most sense depends on the company's industry, and on whether it is a market leader, challenger, follower, or nicher. A market leader has to mount strategies to expand the total market, protect market share, and expand market share. A market challenger is a firm that tries aggressively to expand its market share by attacking the leader, other runner-up companies, or smaller firms in the industry. The challenger can select from a variety of direct or indirect attack strategies. A market follower is a runner-up firm that chooses not to rock the boat, usually from fear that it stands to lose more than it might gain. But the follower is not without a strategy and seeks to use its particular skills to gain market growth. Some followers enjoy a higher rate of return than the leaders in their industry. A market nicher is a smaller firm that is unlikely to attract the larger firms. Market nichers often become specialists in some end use, customer size, specific customer, geographic area, or service.

6.   Illustrate the need for balancing customer and competitor orientations in becoming a truly market-oriented organization.

A competitive orientation is important in today's markets, but companies should not overdo their focus on competitors.

Companies are more likely to be hurt by emerging consumer needs and new competitors than by existing competitors.

Market-driven companies that balance consumer and competitor considerations are practising a true market orientation.

Key Terms

Benchmarking *(p. 621)*
Competitive advantage *(p. 620)*
Competitive marketing strategies *(p. 620)*
Competitor analysis *(p. 620)*
Competitor-centred company *(p. 633)*

Customer-centred company *(p. 634)*
Customer delivered value *(p. 605)*
Customer value delivery system *(p. 614)*
Market-oriented company *(p. 634)*
Market challenger *(p. 626)*
Market follower *(p. 626)*

Market leader *(p. 626)*
Market nicher *(p. 626)*
Market orientation *(p. 620)*
Relationship marketing *(p. 611)*
Strategic group *(p. 621)*
Total customer cost *(p. 605)*
Total customer value *(p. 605)*

Discussing the Issues

1. Recall an activity in which you went beyond the normal effort and "gave your all" to produce the utmost in quality. How much of your improvement in quality did other people notice—all, some, or none? Analyse whether there is a balance point that provides the right mix of quality and effort.

2. Describe a situation in which you became a "lost customer." Did you leave because of poor product quality, poor service quality, or both?

3. Education reform remains a major issue in Canada. One concern is a lack of value: the costs of education often seem to outweigh the benefits. Propose some meaningful ways to measure education quality that could be used in efforts to improve value.

4. "Well-behaved" companies prefer well-behaved competition. Decide whether it should make any difference to consumers whether competition is "well behaved" or "disruptive." Why or why not?

5. Many medium-sized firms are in an unprofitable middle ground between large firms and smaller, more focussed firms. Discuss how medium-sized firms could use market nicher strategies to improve their profitability.

6. The goal of the marketing concept is to satisfy customer wants and needs. What is the goal of a competitor-centred strategy? Determine whether the marketing concept and competitor-centred strategy are in conflict.

Applying the Concepts

1. Remember the last time you complained about a product or service. Did you receive a refund or replacement product, a response letter, or no reply at all? How does the type of response affect your attitude toward the company?

2. Find a company, organization, or individual that has clearly established a strong relationship with its customers. Some examples include: BMW automobiles or Harley Davidson motorcycles; the Canadian Cancer Society, or Bare-Naked Ladies.

Talk to several customers who strongly identify with one such "product." How do they view their relationship to the product? What are the key values they receive? What, if anything, does the "manufacturer" do to maintain this relationship?

3. Market-leaders often attempt to expand the total market, especially in slower-growing, mature markets. Find examples in which manufacturers are attempting to expand total market demand for their products.

References

1. Quotations from David Kirkpatrick, "Intel's Amazing Profit Machine," *Fortune,* February 17, 1997, pp. 60–72; and Damon Darlin, "Intel's Palace," *Forbes,* September 9, 1996, pp. 42–43. Also see Wendy Cuthbert, "Intel Adds Humor to MMX," *Strategy: The Canadian Marketing Report,* February 3, 1997, p. 3; Andy Reinhardt, "Pentium: The Next Generation," *Business Week,* May 12, 1997, pp. 42–43; and Reinhardt, "Intel's Dreamers Make Room for a Details Man," *Business Week,* May 26, 1997, pp. 125–128.

2. Wendy Cuthbert, "Nissan Dealer Takes New Approach," *Strategy: The Canadian Marketing Report,* July 7, 1997, p. 5.

3. See Donald V. Fites, "Make Your Dealers Your Partners," *Harvard Business Review,* March-April 1996, pp. 84–95.

4. Thomas E. Caruso, "Got a Marketing Topic? Kotler Has an Opinion," *Marketing News,* June 8, 1992, p. 21.

5. Thomas O. Jones and W. Earl Sasser, Jr., "Why Satisfied Customers Defect," *Harvard Business Review,* November-December 1995, pp. 88–99. Also see Thomas A. Stewart, "A Satisfied Customer Isn't Enough," *Fortune,* July 21, 1997, pp. 112–113.

6. Ibid., p. 91. For other examples, see Roger Sant, "Did He Jump or Was He Pushed?" *Marketing News,* May 12, 1997, pp. 2, 21.

7. See Joseph Juran, "Made in the U.S.A.: A Renaissance in Quality," *Harvard Business Review,* July-August 1993, pp. 42–50.

8. Thomas A. Stewart, "After All You've Done for Your Customers, Why Are They Still Not Happy?" *Fortune,* December 11, 1995, pp. 178–182

9. For more on assessing customer value, see Gordon A. Wyner, "Customer Valuation: Linking Behavior and Economics," *Marketing Research,* Summer 1996, pp. 36–38; Wyner, "Which Customers Will Be Valuable in the Future?" *Marketing Research,* Fall 1996, pp. 44–46; and John O. Whitney, "Strategic Renewal for Business Units," *Harvard Business Review,* July-August 1996, pp. 84–98.

10. David W. Cravens, "Introduction to the Special Issue on Relationship Marketing," *Journal of the Academy of Marketing Science,* Fall 1995, 23 (4), p.235.

11. Leonard L. Berry and A. Parasuraman, *Marketing Services: Competing Through Quality* (New York: The Free Press, 1991), pp. 136–142.

12. See Thomas M. Petro, "Profitability: The Fifth `P' of Marketing," *Bank Marketing,* September 1990, pp. 48–52.

13. For example, see Bill Stoneman, "Banking on Customers," *American Demographics,* February 1997, pp. 37–41.

14. Jennifer Waters, "High-tech Test Restaurant Offers Customer Orders, More Efficiency," *Advertising Age,* April 14, 1997, p. 49.

15. Michael E. Porter, *Competitive Advantage: Creating and Sustaining Superior Performance* (New York: Free Press, 1985); and Michel E. Porter, "What Is Strategy?" *Harvard Business Review,* November-December 1996, pp. 61–78.

16. Edwin McDowell, "Ritz-Carlton's Keys to Good Service," *New York Times,* March 31, 1993, p. 1; Don Peppers, "Digitizing Desire," *Forbes,* April 10, 1995, p. 76; and Ginger Conlon, "True Romance," *Sales & Marketing Management,* May 1996, pp. 85–89.

17. Myron Magnet, "The New Golden Rule of Business," *Fortune,* February 21, 1994, pp. 60-63. Also see Jim Morgan and Robert M. Monczka, "Supplier Integration: A New Level of Supply Chain Management," *Purchasing,* January 11, 1996, pp. 110–113.

18. Robert D. Buzzell and Bradley T. Gale, *The PIMS Principles: Linking Strategy to Performance* (New York: The Free Press, 1987), Chapter 6.

19. Quality: The U.S. Drives to Catch Up," *Business Week,* November, 1982, pp. 66–80, here p. 68. For a recent assessment of progress, see "Quality Programs Show Shoddy Results," *Wall Street Journal,* May 14, 1992, p. B1.

20. Brian Milner, "Survey Finds Pride in Canadian Products High," *Globe and Mail,* December 4, 1996, p. B8.

21. See "The Gurus of Quality: American Companies are Heading the Quality Gospel Preached by Deming, Juran, Crosby, and Taguchi," *Traffic Management,* July 1990. pp. 35–39.

22. Gordon Arnaut, "Pursuing New Standards of Excellence," and "Reaching for New Heights," *Quality in Action: A Special Report from the National Quality Institute,* insert in *Report on Business,* July 1995.

23. See David Greising, "Quality: How to Make It Pay," *Business Week,* August 8, 1994, pp. 54–59; and Cyndee Miller, "TQM Out; 'Continuous Process Improvement' In," *Marketing News,* May 9, 1994, pp. 5, 10.

24. J. Daniel Beckham, "Expect the Unexpected in Health Care Marketing Future," in *The Academy Bulletin,* July 1992, p. 3.

25. Quotation from Johanna Power, "Raising the standard" in "ISO 9000: A Special Report," *The Financial Post,* August 23, 1996, p. 11. Other material from "Canada and ISO 9000," An Advertising Supplement to the *Globe and Mail,* December 16, 1996, pp. 1-2; and Rob Guilbronson and Paul Chahine, "ISO 9000 Implementation at Polysar (A)," Case 9-93-D019, Western Business School, p. 6.

26. John Geddes, "Auto Dealers Outgun Banks in Leasing Showdown," *Financial Post,* March 29, 1996, p. 1; Karen Howlette, Barrie McKenna, and John Partridge, "How the Banks Lost Big," *Globe and Mail,* March 9, 1996, pp. B1, B4; and Dennis Slocum, "Banks Forge Ahead with Plan to Sell Insurance Policies," *Globe and Mail,* March 20, 1996, pp. B1, B13.

27. "P&G and Scott Engage in Paper Towel Sampling Tussle," *Marketing,* April 10, 1995, p. 4; Scott Paper Challenges P&G Over Bounty Ads," *Marketing,* November 13, 1995, p. 1; "Paper Towel Duel Resumes on Ad Front," *Marketing,* December 11, 1995, p. 3.

28. For a good discussion of the underlying rules of competitive interaction and reaction, see Gloria P. Thomas and Gary F. Soldow, "A Rules-Based Approach to

Competitive Interaction," *Journal of Marketing,* April 1988, pp. 63–74. Also see Walter D. Brandt, Jr., "Profiling Rival Decision Makers," *The Journal of Business Strategy,* January/February 1991, pp. 8–11.

29. See Michael E. Porter, *Competitive Advantage* (New York: The Free Press, 1985), pp. 226–227; Joseph Weber, "How J&J's Foresight Made Contact Lenses Pay," *Business Week,* May 4, 1992, p. 132.

30. See Porter, *Competitive Advantage,* Chap. 6.

31. Michael E. Porter, *Competitive Strategy: Techniques for Analyzing Industries and Competitors* (New York: Free Press, 1980), Ch. 2.

32. Michael Treacy and Fred Wiersema, "Customer Intimacy and Other Value Disciplines," *Harvard Business Review,* January–February 1993, pp. 84–93; and Michael Treacy and Fred Wiersema, "How Market Leaders Keep Their Edge," *Fortune,* February 6, 1995, pp. 88–98.

33. Beppi Crosariol, "War of the Wires," *Report on Business,* May 1994, pp. 32-46; Philip Demont, "Bell Expects 40% Jump in Profit," *The Financial Post,* March 20, 1996, p. 1; Philip Demont, "Osborn's Reputation Put to the Test at BCE, *The Financial Post,* March 9, 1996, p. 1; Lee Jacobson, "Bell's New Face Looks For-

ward, *Globe and Mail,* March 21, 1996, p. B9; Lawrence Surtees, "Long-distance Battle Will Hit Home," *Globe and Mail,* June 28, 1994, pp. B1, B20; and Jill Vardy, "Bell Climbs on Internet Radio Bandwagon," *Financial Post,* March 15, 1996, p. 6.

34. *Financial Times of Canada,* December 11, 1993, p. 13.

35. See David M. Szymanski, Sundar G. Bharadwaj, and P. Rajan Varadarajan, "An Analysis of the Market Share-Profitability Relationship," *Journal of Marketing,* July 1993, pp. 1–18.

36. See Andrew C. Brown, "Unilever Fights Back in the U.S.," *Fortune,* May 26, 1986, pp. 32–38.

37. Mark Evans, "Tortoise, Hare Battle for First Place," *The Financial Post,* March 14, 1996, p. 8.

38. Amy Barrett, "Dial Succeeds by Stepping in Bigger Footsteps," *Business Week,* June 13, 1994, pp. 82–83.

39. Donald K. Clifford and Richard E. Cavanagh, *The Winning Performance: How America's High- and Midsize Growth Companies Succeed* (New York: Bantam Books, 1985).

40. See John C. Narver and Stanley F. Slater, "The Effect of a Market Orientation on Business Profitability," *Journal of Marketing,* October 1990, pp. 20–35.

Company Case 18

PROCTER & GAMBLE: MAKING IT SIMPLE

The last time Cindy Walters went shopping, she bought dandruff shampoo for her husband, Don. She'd planned to buy Head and Shoulders, since she had seen advertising for that. At the store, however, she found six variations of Head and Shoulders in three different sizes—all at different prices. The shelf was crowded with six other brands of dandruff shampoo—and she couldn't help but notice that one of these brands was on sale. Cindy was in a rush. She had to be to work in 15 minutes, and she didn't feel like reading all the labels—they had more information about dandruff than anyone cared to know! Next time, she thought, Don can buy his own shampoo! In desperation she grabbed the bottle that was on sale. "I can't spend forever making this decision," she thought.

Does this sound familiar? Have you ever arrived at the store and found yourself overwhelmed with the choices available? Ever had difficulty comparing prices, or found that the brand on sale or the one you had a coupon for wasn't exactly what you wanted? Ever thought "Why do they make it so complicated? Why don't they make one standard version and price it lower?" If you've had such experiences and thoughts, Procter & Gamble has finally read your mind.

When Durk Jager took over as president and chief operating officer at P&G, the company was making 55 price changes a day across 110 brands, offering 440 promotions a year, and tinkering with package sizes, colours, and contents. "We were confusing [customers]" admits Jager. "It's mind-boggling how difficult we've made it for them over the years." Six variations of Head and Shoulders seems like a lot, but P&G was actually offering 31 variations!

Today's average consumer (yes, it's usually a woman), takes just 21 minutes to do her shopping—from the moment she slams her car door in a supermarket parking lot to the moment she climbs back in with her purchases. In that time, she buys an average of 18 items out of the store's 30 000 to 40 000 choices. She spends 25 percent less time browsing than she did five years ago and often doesn't even bother to check prices. She wants the same product, at the same price, in the same row, week after week. And that's what Durk Jager wants to give her. P&G is now standardizing product formulas and packages, reducing trade promotions, easing up on coupons, dropping marginal brands, cutting product lines, and using similar ads worldwide. The result? P&G has drastically cut marketing costs, which enables it to boost sales with lower prices while at the same time increasing margins.

Making these changes has improved P&G's communications with both final consumers and the trade.

How have consumers reacted? Have they noticed that the number of product and brand variations has decreased? No. A study by Willard Bishop Consulting, Ltd. and Information Resources, Inc. found that 80 percent of consumers saw no difference when P&G eliminated marginal items and reduced the number of product variations. Some consumers even seem to think that there is more choice now than before. P&G's market share has increased by five percent. Perhaps in the past, consumers suffered so much sensory overload from the thousands of items on the shelves that they could not hope to make the best or even a good decision. With fewer product variations, they may be doing more comparison shopping and identifying the best buy.

Many stores are crammed with things that people never buy. A study by Kurt Salmon Associates, Inc. found that a quarter of the products in a typical supermarket sell fewer than one unit a month and that just 7.6 percent of all personal-care and household products account for 84.5 percent of sales. A lot of merchandise goes unnoticed by consumers and may actually be in their way, keeping them from making the best choice.

While the reductions in product lines make it easier for consumers to compare products, buyers may take a negative view of the loss of coupons and other promotions. P&G has decided that using coupons and price promotions, such as cents-off packs and refunds, simply taught consumers to wait until the product was on sale. Because these promotions were so frequent, many may not have purchased at the regular price in a long time. The effect of so much sales promotion was to reduce perceived prices. To combat this, P&G has introduced everyday low prices as it has eliminated the promotions. Even so, when comparing the new everyday low prices with coupon and promotional prices, many consumers perceive the everyday low prices as higher.

Another negative effect of couponing and promotional pricing is that they teach consumers to buy on the basis of price rather than on brand attributes or benefits. In the face of fewer coupons and price promotions, consumers may take one of several courses of action. First, they may simply change brands in order to buy a cheaper brand. Second, they may adopt different criteria upon which to base their purchase decisions, such as quality special product features. The first action is easier in that it involves less change in decision making. If consumers do begin to evaluate brands, other forms of communication, such as labelling and advertising, must be used to convince consumers of the brand's value.

Even as P&G is reducing couponing, it is also standardizing packaging and reducing the number of special labels on products. In Canada and other international marketplaces, it is printing information in several languages on the same label in order to reduce the cost of printing multiple labels in different languages. Thus,

labels for some products may contain less information in some countries.

To overcome the loss of coupons and promotions, P&G plans to use more in-store demonstrations and sampling. These forms of promotion actually cost more but focus on the product's attributes. They are, however, more complicated and time-consuming to plan and supervise, and they don't have the mass distribution and non-perishability that coupons offered. Coupons, however, had begun to lose their appeal with consumers. Redemption rates had fallen from four to two percent. Consumers were deluged with coupons—many found that the time to clip and save coupons was too costly, that they frequently forgot their coupons, or found coupons had expired by the time they tried to use them. So, perhaps consumers will not miss coupons all that much.

P&G usually considers its advertising budget to be sacrosanct, so it is not likely to cut that. However, P&G is moving toward more globally standardized advertising. An example is its recent promotion for Pringle's potato chips. Nearly everything in the ad—the rap music theme, the young people dancing around, the tag line—"Once you pop, you can't stop"—is as popular in Europe as in North America. But will it work in Japan or South America? How much product information can be put in standardized, global advertising? Products and brands that are well established in one country may be new in another country, so messages should be different. If advertising has to communicate more about the product and brand, that will be hard to do with standardized global messages.

P&G is also cutting marginal product lines, such as Lilt home permanents, Bain de Soleil, and Aleve. This allows it to concentrate on core products that sell well—laundry detergents, peanut butter, personal care products, and cosmetic items. In doing so, P&G hopes to send a clearer message about its products, but it faces a branding problem in communications. The company has traditionally used individual brand names rather than a company name or family brand. Not everyone realizes that P&G makes Crest, Jif and Cheer. Thus, the effect that the company wants—a clear message of simplicity in buying from P&G—may never materialize in the consumer's mind.

While making all these changes in its consumer marketing, P&G also dealt with problems in its channels of distribution. "P&G was the most hated and feared supplier we had" comments Davis Herrimon, senior vice president at Giant Food Inc. "If P&G told us they were dropping nine 'gazillion' coupons through advertisements all across the country, of course we had to buy because shoppers would come in with the coupons. P&G was a totally immovable object and wouldn't respond to anything we wanted." Consequently, retailers had to change displays and shelf facings frequently to introduce new products while changing prices and handling tons of coupons.

In addition P&G pushed large quantities of goods to retailers with the result that products might sit in inventory for a year. Rather than selling to retailers in smaller quantities, the company attempted to change product formulations to make them stay usable longer. These resulted in an increased need for warehouse and shelf space, lots of returns, and consumer dissatisfaction over stale goods. When coupled with promotional requirements, retailers' costs grew, damaging their cash flow. However, P&G was so big that retailers could not afford to lose it as a supplier.

Today, P&G has become one of the most liked consumer goods suppliers. Instead of dealing with multiple P&G salespeople as they did in the past (one for Charmin, one for Tide, another for Jif), retailers deal with one P&G rep who handles all truck schedules and can give an arrival time within 30 minutes. Trucks deliver only what is needed, based on data from checkout registers, indicating, for example, how many jars of Jif have sold.

Using sales data, P&G now knows how much of each good is selling, when, and where. It can analyze sales patterns in stores and help retailers determine which brands and how many units to stock. Sometimes it even recommends that a P&G brand be eliminated or that brands from other companies be added. For example, Giant had to eliminate Oxydol (which didn't sell) but found that the number of variations of Pringle's potato chips should be increased from two to five. As a result, retailers' stockturns have improved, and that means an increase in income for them. P&G has moved from being the enemy to becoming a trusted partner. It has established strong, positive relationships with retailers to the benefit of both parties.

Even though sales in general were increasing, in 1996 P&G found it necessary to revert to its old ways by using a two-for-one promotion for Crest to shore up declining market share. Actions such as this keep the message about lower prices and the focus on the brand's value from coming through to consumers. In addition, due to static sales, P&G has had to raise the price on Pampers—one of the brands used to herald the everyday low price strategy. While Durk Jager wants to "make the best choice crystal clear" to consumers, short run actions such as the one for Crest undermine the company's other actions. While retailers and other distributors have gotten a clear message from P & G, it's not clear that consumers have or will.

QUESTIONS

1. Review the different strategies described in the Chapter. What strategy is P&G using?

2. How does P&G's new strategy help the firm build relationships with retailers and final consumers? Can fewer brands create value for consumers? For retailers?

3. Does P&G understand the principles of total quality management? How does it use these principles in its new strategy?

4. How should P&G communicate its new programs to retailers and consumers. What message execution style(s) would you recommend? How would you measure the effect of the new campaigns?

Sources: Raju Narisetti, "P&G, Seeing shoppers were being confused, overhauls marketing," *Wall Street Journal*, January 15, 1997, p. B1; Raju Narisetti, "P&G to Stores: Keep the dented Crisco cans," *Wall Street Journal*, March 21, 1997, p. B1; Amanda Richards, "P&G retreat on price strategy," *Marketing*, February 13, 1997, p. 1; Zachary Schiller, "Make it simple," *Business Week*, September 9, 1996, pp. 96–104; Zachary Schiller, "An old coach with new discipline," *Business Week*, September 9, 1996, p. 104.

Video Case 18

WORD PROCESSING WARS: COREL VERSUS MICROSOFT

Corel, an Ottawa-based software firm, surprised the software industry in the spring of 1996 by purchasing the WordPerfect word processing product. The firm had no previous experience in word processing and by entering the market was going head to head with a formidable competitor: Microsoft. While most firms try to avoid competition with the industry leader, Corel, led by President and CEO Michael Cowpland, sought to capture some of Microsoft's market share by attacking the company directly.

Corel was extremely successful with its original product, Corel Draw, a computer graphics product. The company had developed a niche market and they enjoyed the luxury of being ignored by big players such as Microsoft. But when WordPerfect became available at a bargain price, Cowpland couldn't resist getting Corel into the word processing market-the most lucrative in the software industry. Ten years ago that market was dominated by WordPerfect, but when Corel purchased WordPerfect, Microsoft, with their Microsoft Office product, had 90 percent of the market. This 90 percent share was worth $4 billion and represented half of Microsoft's total revenues. Cowpland's goal on purchasing WordPerfect was to achieve 50 percent market share.

The first thing Cowpland did after purchasing WordPerfect was to revise it to become a suite of products like Microsoft Office. Leveraging their expertise in graphics, Corel added a presentations application as well as a spreadsheet. When the product was ready for launch, Cowpland spared no expense. The Corel Office suite was launched backed by a $100-million advertising campaign, and the messages in the campaign made no secret of the fact that Corel was pursuing Microsoft. Comparative ads were used with the tag lines, "Now it's Microsoft's turn to play catch up." Cowpland himself oversaw the entire WordPerfect revision and launch process.

Initially the Corel Office suite fared well in the retail market and in the summer of 1996 stole half of the retail market share. While the company was pleased with this achievement, they realized that attracting corporate buyers was critical to their long-term success.

These corporate buyers were targeted with company "road shows" and booths at trade shows that showcased the Corel Office suite. Aggressive discount pricing was also used to entice corporate buyers. The product was sold for half the price of Microsoft Office and in addition Corel was offering an upgrade to the WordPerfect product from any word processing package for $99. All of this aggressive pricing and the large ad budgets took their toll on Corel's cash reserves. While Microsoft has about $7 billion in cash, Corel has $2 million, down from $74 million in 1995.

All Corel products are updated annually, which is better than the industry standard. The company's promise is to always develop something new. In addition to revisions to Corel Draw and WordPerfect, Corel's 1500 employees are working on the development of 100 other software products, including videoconferencing software. Speed is critical in the software market where industry products and dynamics can change daily. So the challenge for Cowpland and Corel will be to continue to improve existing products such as Corel Office and develop new products, while also avoiding the wrath of the largest company in the software industry.

QUESTIONS:

1. What attack strategy (frontal, flank, encirclement, bypass, or guerrilla) has Corel used against Microsoft? What are the advantages and disadvantages of the strategy they chose?

2. What do you think Microsoft's reaction to Corel WordPerfect Suite will be?

3. What is Corel's competitive advantage in the word processing market?

4. Based on the launch of the WordPerfect Suite, would you classify Corel as a market-centred, customer-centred, or competitor-centred company? What are the benefits and dangers of following this orientation?

Source: This case was prepared by Auleen Carson and is based on "Corel," *Venture*, (October 27, 1996).

C H A P T E R 19

THE GLOBAL
MARKETPLACE

Basketball, the quintessential American game, is rapidly becoming a worldwide craze. For example, a recent *New York Times* survey of more than 45 000 teenagers on five continents asked "What are your favourite entertainment pursuits?" The top two answers: watching television and basketball. If you ask Canadian teenagers aged 12 to 17 to name their favourite athletes, Wayne Gretzky loses out to Michael Jordan, Shaquille O'Neal, and Damon Stoudamire. And no organization is doing more to promote worldwide basketball than the National Basketball Association (NBA), a truly global marketing enterprise. NBA games are televised around the world, and the league with its partners sold millions of dollars worth of NBA-licensed basketballs, backboards, T-shirts, and other merchandise both inside and outside North America last year. The NBA is now a powerful worldwide brand. A recent *Fortune* article summarizes:

> Forget about going to Disneyland. Now that the NBA season is over, basketball's big stars are headed for more exotic locales: Shaquille O'Neal to South Korea, Karl Malone to Hong Kong, Allen Iverson to Chile, and all the Chicago Bulls—including chief luminary Michael Jordan—to France. Deployed by global sponsors Coca-Cola, Reebok, and McDonald's, these well-paid travelling salesmen will hawk soda, sneakers, burgers, and basketball to legions of mostly young fans. That they are recognized from Santiago to Seoul says a lot about the soaring worldwide appeal of hoops—and about the marketing juggernaut known as the NBA. After watching their favourite stars swoop in and slam-dunk on their local TV stations, fans of the league now cheer the mate in Latin America, the trofsla in Iceland, and the smash in France. Care to guess the most popular basketball team in China? Why, it's the "Red Oxen" from Chicago, of course.

Like many other businesses, the NBA's primary motive for going global is growth. In North America the league now sells out most of its games, and licensing revenues have flattened in recent years. According to NBA Commissioner David Sterns, "There are just so many seats in an arena and so many hours of television

OBJECTIVES

When you finish this chapter, you should be able to

1. Discuss how the international trade system, economic, political-legal, and cultural environments affect a company's international marketing decisions.

2. Describe three key approaches to entering international markets.

3. Explain how companies adapt their marketing mixes for international markets.

4. Identify the three major forms of international marketing organization.

programming, period. The domestic business is becoming mature. That's why we're moving internationally." Compared with the NBA's overall yearly revenues of $2.2 billion, current international revenues are modest—estimated at a little more than $86 million from television rights fees, sponsorships, and the league's share of licensing sales. But the worldwide potential is huge, and the league is investing heavily to build its popularity and business abroad.

Professional and amateur leagues have been thriving for years in Europe and Asia, and basketball has been an Olympic sport since 1936. Broader historical forces have also helped to promote the NBA's efforts to go global: the collapse of communism and the growth of market economies, the globalization of consumer companies, and a revolution in worldwide television. Most recent is the explosion of the global Internet. The NBA's site (www.NBA.com) offers materials in several languages and draws almost a third of its visitors from outside North America. A survey conducted by a global advertising agency of 28 000 teenagers in 45 countries found that Michael Jordan was the world's favourite athlete by far. In China, which has its own professional basketball leagues, boys on the streets of Beijing and Shanghai wear Bulls gear because they want to be like Jordan.

Toronto Raptors
www.nba.com/raptors/

Entry into the Canadian market was a natural for the NBA since basketball, originally invented by a Canadian, was already a popular sport. Despite skilful marketing, the NBA's success in Canada is far from assured, however. Even though the Toronto Raptors won *Canadian Business* magazine's award for best product launch in 1996, and Canadian fans have been criticized for being too enthusiastic and noisy, game attendance has been waning for both the Grizzlies and the Raptors. When the games were a novelty act in Toronto, average attendance was about 18 300 fans per game—almost capacity. In Vancouver, the Grizzlies didn't fill the stadium, but drew 17 500 fans per game. Today, these numbers have declined by about 20 percent. There is no doubt that the NBA faces a considerable challenge in hockey-crazed Canada. Many people, therefore, question the Raptors' pricing strategy. While seats at a hockey game range between $43 to $85, the Raptors bill their fans $59 to $91. The Grizzlies, however, are lowering their prices to attract more families. They charge $11 to $22 for select seats at the game.

Vancouver Grizzlies
www.nba.com/grizzlies/

Merchandise sales are another story, however. The Raptors are currently fifth of 29 NBA teams in terms of merchandise sales while the Grizzlies are eleventh. Part of the Raptors' merchandising success story is due to the organization's careful attention to its logo development. Following a model used by the San Jose Sharks, the Raptors held a name-the-team contest that drew over 2000 entries. Once these were whittled down to 10, fans were asked to vote on their favourites. Issues including whether the name would appeal to young fans were also considered since the future success of the franchise is tied to attracting the 12- to 17-year-old audience. The name "Raptors" also won out because the marketing team knew that kids identified with the fast, smart, aggressive dinosaurs featured earlier in *Jurassic Park*. Furthermore, since the name held no specific tie to Toronto, it was as marketable in Halifax or Frankfurt as it was in Toronto.

Since NBA basketball is as much about spectacle and entertainment as it is about sport, television programming has always been viewed as key to a franchise's success. Televised games are only one part of the mix. An array of NBA-based programs, mostly targeted at kids and teenagers, also promote the league and its players. YTV's *Dunk Street*, a 30-minute hoop-show with a Canadian slant, for example, drew an average of 204 000 weekly viewers. NBA Canada also ran two advertising spots titled "I love this game," designed to further educate Canadians about basketball, and "I love this stuff," focused on promoting merchandise sales. The ads ran on television shows such as MuchMusic, which are popular among young fans.

Selling corporate sponsorships also brings tremendous revenues into the expansion team's coffers. NBA Canada has issued more than 60 licences to date. Air Canada and Shoppers Drug Mart were quick to jump on board. Air Canada, now the official airline of the Canadian teams, even has Raptors-emblazoned aircraft. Nestlé Canada also rushed to sign on. It invested in a chocolate-bar promotion called "Eat your way to the NBA." Kellogg Canada was another eager partner, and placed the phone number for season tickets on its boxes of Rice Krispies. Kellogg's Joanne Doyle, manager of product communications, not only believes that "we gain value from the association with a tremendous marketing machine," but also that "the demographics of the [NBA] broadcasts also show a good female viewership, important to us since most grocer shoppers are women." Coca-Cola, meanwhile, targets basketball-crazed teenagers by placing NBA and team logos on Sprite soft drink cans, which are sold in 30 countries.

Today in Canada, the NHL and Major League Baseball are still the two favourite leagues. And older fans are unwilling to give up their ties to Wayne Gretzky. But the NBA franchises are coming on fast. What is the outcome in this popularity contest here and abroad? Stay tuned.[1]

In the past, Canadian companies paid little attention to international trade. Even exporting to the United States was considered a big step. If they could pick up some extra sales through exporting, that was fine. But the main market was at home. The home market was also much safer. Managers did not need to learn other languages, deal with strange and changing currencies, face political and legal uncertainties, or adapt their products to different customer needs and expectations. Today, however, the situation is much different.

GLOBAL MARKETING INTO THE TWENTY-FIRST CENTURY

The world is shrinking rapidly with the advent of faster communication, transportation, and financial flows. Products developed in one country—Gucci purses, Mont Blanc pens, McDonald's hamburgers, Japanese sushi, Pierre Cardin suits, German BMWs—are finding enthusiastic acceptance in other countries. We would not be surprised to hear about a German businessman wearing an Italian suit meeting an English friend at a Japanese restaurant who later returns home to drink Russian vodka and watch *Traders* on television.

True, many companies have been carrying on international activities for decades. McCain, Bata, Coca-Cola, IBM, Kodak, Nestlé, Shell, Bayer, Toshiba, Sony, and other companies are familiar to most consumers around the world. But today global competition is intensifying. Foreign firms are expanding aggressively into new international markets, and domestic companies that never thought about foreign competitors suddenly find these competitors in their own backyards. The firm that stays at home to play it safe not only might lose its chance to enter other markets but also risks losing its home market.

In North America, names such as Sony, Toyota, Nestlé, Norelco, Mercedes, and Panasonic have become household words. Other products and services that appear to be domestic really are produced or owned by foreign companies: Bantam books, Cadbury chocolate, Baskin-Robbins ice cream, GE and RCA televisions, Firestone tires, Kiwi shoe polish, Lipton tea, Carnation milk, and Pillsbury products, to name just a few. North America also has attracted huge foreign investments in basic industries such as steel, petroleum, tires, and chemicals, and in tourist and real estate ventures, illustrated by Japanese land purchases in British Columbia and California. Few North American industries are now safe from foreign competition.

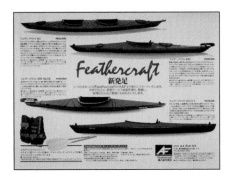

Many small Canadian firms such as Blitz Design Corp and Feathercraft Inc. have become successful international marketers.

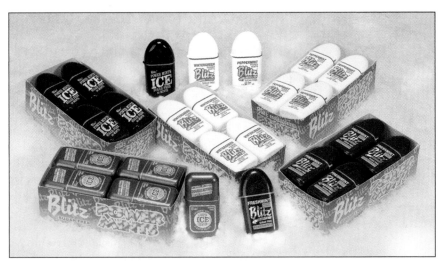

In an era of free trade, firms must learn how to enter foreign markets and increase their global competitiveness. Many Canadian companies have been successful at international marketing: Nortel, Mosaid, Corel, IMAX, Bombardier, CAE, Labatt, Moosehead, Northern Reflections, Alcan, Magna International, Barrick Gold Corp., Nova Corp., Newbridge Networks, and Atco, just to name a few. Order some french fries in Thailand, Russia, Costa Rica, Tunisia, Vietnam, or Syria, and chances are you will be biting into a product manufactured by McCain International Inc. of Florenceville, New Brunswick. But you don't have to be an industry giant to venture into overseas markets. The list of the 10 winners of the 1997 Canada Export Awards shows more small to medium-sized enterprises than large firms. Consider Blitz Design Corp. of Langley, British Columbia, for example. The company developed and markets "power" sugar-free breath mints to more than 15 countries around the world. Its largest market is the United States, where it is now among the top 10 in sales—not a bad accomplishment considering it took on giant brands such as Breathsavers, Tic Tac, Certs, and Clorets.[2] Exports sales are a mainstay of many Canadian businesses. In 1996, they comprised 38.42 percent of the gross domestic product. Throughout the 1990s, Canada's export sales have been growing at an annual rate of 11.5 percent. They went from $140 billion in 1991 to over $250 billion in 1995, a 75 percent increase.[3]

Despite these impressive figures, many firms are still hesitant about testing foreign waters. In 1992, the headline in the cover story from April's *Report on Business* dedicated to understanding Canadian international business proclaimed, "Fear of Trying: All that holds us back from conquering markets is . . .the private sector's timid approach to trade." The Liberal government and its "Team Canada" approach, the Canadian Export Development Corp. and the Department of Foreign Affairs and International Trade are helping both large and small Canadian businesses make inroads in overseas markets.[4]

As business continues to become more international in scope, companies will have to answer some basic questions: What market position should we try to establish in our country, in our economic region, and globally? Who will our global competitors be, and what are their strategies and resources? Where should we produce or source our products? What strategic alliances should we form with other firms around the world?

Ironically, although the need for companies to go abroad is greater today than in the past, so are the risks. Companies that go global confront several major problems. First, high debt, inflation, and unemployment in many countries have resulted in highly unstable governments and currencies, which limit trade

Many companies have made the world their market.

and expose firms to many risks. Second, governments are placing more regulations on foreign firms, such as requiring joint ownership with domestic partners, mandating the hiring of nationals, and limiting profits that can be taken from the country. Third, foreign governments often impose high tariffs or trade barriers to protect their own industries. Finally, corruption is an increasing problem—officials in several countries often award business not to the best bidder but to the highest briber.

Global industry
An industry in which the strategic positions of competitors in given geographic or national markets are affected by their overall global positions.

Global firm
A firm that, by operating in more than one country, gains R&D, production, marketing, and financial advantages that are not available to purely domestic competitors.

Companies selling in global industries have no choice but to internationalize their operations. A **global industry** is one in which the competitive positions of firms in given local or national markets are affected by their overall global positions. Therefore, a **global firm** is one that, by operating in more than one country, gains marketing, production, R&D, and financial advantages that are not available to purely domestic competitors. The global company sees the world as one market. It minimizes the importance of national boundaries and raises capital, source materials and components, and manufactures and markets its goods wherever it can do the best job. For example, Ford's "world truck" sports a cab made in Europe and a chassis built in North America. It is assembled in Brazil and imported for sale. Thus, global firms gain advantages by planning, operating, and coordinating their activities on a worldwide basis.

FIGURE 19-1 *Major decisions in international marketing*

Because firms around the world are globalizing at a rapid rate, domestic firms in global industries must act quickly before the window closes on them. This does not mean that small and medium-size firms must operate in a dozen countries to succeed. These firms can practise global nichemanship. In fact, companies marketing on the Internet may find themselves going global whether they intend it or not (see Marketing Highlight 19-1).

As shown in Figure 19-1, a company faces six major decisions in international marketing. Each decision will be discussed in detail in this chapter.

LOOKING AT THE GLOBAL MARKETING ENVIRONMENT

Before deciding whether to operate internationally, a company must thoroughly understand the international marketing environment. That environment has changed a great deal in the last two decades, creating both new opportunities and new problems. The world economy has globalized. World trade and investment have grown rapidly, with many attractive markets opening up in Western and Eastern Europe, China, India, the Pacific Rim, Russia, and elsewhere. There has been a growth of global brands in automobiles, food, clothing, electronics, and many other categories. The number of global companies has grown dramatically. Meanwhile, the dominant position of North American firms has declined. Other countries, such as Japan and Germany, have increased their economic power in world markets. The international financial system has become more complex and fragile, and North American companies face increasing trade barriers erected to protect domestic markets from outside competition.

THE INTERNATIONAL TRADE SYSTEM

A company looking abroad must start by understanding the international *trade system.* When selling to another country, the firm faces various trade restrictions. The most common is the **tariff,** which is a tax levied by a foreign government against certain imported products. The tariff may be designed either to raise revenue or to protect domestic firms. The exporter also may face a **quota,** which sets limits on the amount of goods the importing country will accept in certain product categories. The purpose of the quota is to conserve on foreign exchange and to protect local industry and employment. An **embargo,** or boycott, is the strongest form of quota, which totally bans some kinds of imports.

Firms may also face **exchange controls** that limit the amount of foreign exchange and the exchange rate against other currencies. The company also may face **non-tariff trade barriers,** such as biases against bids or restrictive product standards that go against North American product features. At the same time, certain forces *help* trade between nations. Examples are the General Agreement on Tariffs and Trade and various regional free trade agreements.

The World Trade Organization and GATT

The General Agreement on Tariffs and Trade (GATT) is a 50-year-old treaty designed to promote world trade by reducing tariffs and other international trade barriers. Since the treaty's inception in 1948, member nations (currently numbering 124) have met in eight rounds of GATT negotiations to reassess trade

---

Tariff
A tax levied by a government against certain imported products. Tariffs are designed to raise revenue or to protect domestic firms.

Quota
A limit on the amount of goods that an importing country will accept in certain product categories; it is designed to conserve on foreign exchange and to protect local industry and employment.

Embargo
A ban on the import of a certain product.

Exchange controls
Government limits on the amount of its foreign exchange with other countries and on its exchange rate against other currencies.

Non-tariff trade barriers
Non-monetary barriers to foreign products, such as biases against a foreign company's bids or product standards that go against a foreign company's product features.

THE INTERNET: A WHOLE NEW WORLD

As the Internet and online services attract ever-more users around the world, many marketers are taking advantage of the Internet's global reach. Major global marketers already on the Net range from automakers (General Motors) to publishers who put their magazines online (Brunico Inc.), to retailers who put catalogues online (J. Crew), to global wine shippers (Virtual Vineyards), to compact disc marketers (CDNow), to banks (ING). All are taking advantage of cyberspace's trivialization of national boundaries.

Whether or not they intend it, companies that sell or promote on the Internet have the whole world for a market. For some of these companies, the global market has largely been a hit-or-miss affair. They present their content in English for the North American market, and if any international users stumble across it and end up buying something, so much the better. CompuServe's Electronic Mail, for example, reports that 40 percent of some merchants' sales come from overseas members, who are largely attracted to merchandise that previously had been available only in the United States.

Other marketers have made a more strategic decision to enter the global market. They're using the Web and online services to reach new customers outside their home countries, support existing customers who reside abroad, and build global brand awareness. Some of these companies adapt their web sites to provide country-specific content and services to their best potential international markets, ideally in the local language. They may also provide local sales support and, where applicable, bill in local currencies. Other marketers choose to use an online service such as CompuServe, Europe On-line, America Online, Microsoft Network in Europe, or services such as NiftyServe or PC Van in Japan. Such online services can form "partnerships" with the marketer, helping to perform transactions and other services abroad.

For the most part, marketers have targeted the countries or regions with the largest potential online populations. Europe and Japan are prime targets. International Data Corporation, a European market-research firm, estimates that in Europe alone by the year 2000, some 35 million users—both businesses and consumers—will be logging onto the Web, buying more than $4 billion worth of goods and services.

can run over $5 per hour, with long-distance calling and data surcharges in rural areas running as high as $23 per hour.

In addition, depending on the country, the global marketer may also run up against governmental restrictions on electronic commerce. France, for instance, has laws against providing encrypted content.

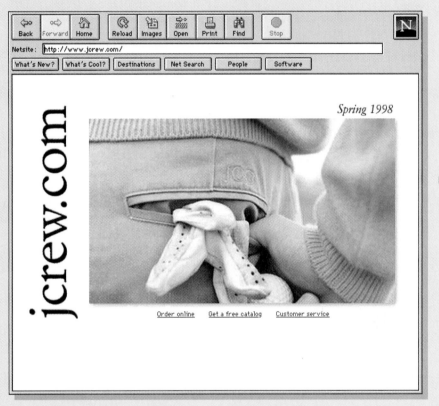

Despite these encouraging numbers, Internet marketers sometimes become caught up in the hype and overstate the Web's seemingly sure-fire global opportunities. The reality of the global Internet market depends on each country's economic, technical, cultural, political, and regional dynamics. Many countries remain technologically underdeveloped and have a low-income citizenry that lacks PCS or even phone connections. Other countries have acceptable phone and PC penetrations, but high connection costs sharply restrict casual uses such as surfing on the Internet. For example, even in advanced countries such as the United Kingdom, connection rates

In Germany, it is illegal for credit-card companies and direct-marketing firms to gather certain types of data on potential applicants—a precaution taken by the country to prevent the massive abuses of centralized information experienced during the Nazi era. Such restrictions, sometimes combined with underdeveloped banking systems, have limited credit-card and direct-mail usage in many countries. Subsequently, marketers outside North America sometimes must find alternative marketing and collection approaches.

Finally, there is the problem faced by any new medium in any country—just getting recognition. Given the cyberspace hype in

North America, many marketers are surprised to learn that familiarity with the Internet among the masses overseas is still very low. Affluent, information-intensive residents are catching on to the Internet, but mainstream consumers remain clueless.

Despite these barriers, global Internet enterprise is growing rapidly. In fact, a whopping 83 percent of managers surveyed recently by management consulting firm KPMG said that electronic commerce will be a major export vehicle by the year 2000. For companies that wish to go global, the Internet and online services can represent an easy way to get started, or to reinforce other efforts. For large companies, casting an international Web is a natural. For example, L.L. Bean sells via the Web to customers around the world. Hewlett-Packard uses a web site to deal with its resellers Europe-wide, offering information in many languages. And Texas Instruments' (TI) European Semiconductor group uses an English-only "TI & Me" site to sell and support its signal processors, logic devices, and other chips across the European continent. TI receives 100 to 150 inquiries per day over the Web.

But small companies can also market globally on the Web. Take compact-disc marketer CDNow. Although only two years old, this virtual company now has a global market and multimillion-dollar revenues. And it exists only on the Web.

Sources: Portions adapted from Peter Krasilovsky, "A Whole New World," Marketing Tools Supplement, *American Demographics*, May 1996, pp. 22–25. Also see Richard N. Miller, "The Year Ahead," *Direct Marketing*, January 1997, pp. 42–44; and Jack Gee, "Parlez-vous Inter-Net?" *Industry Week*, April 21, 1997, pp. 78–79.

barriers and set new rules for international trade. The first seven rounds of negotiations reduced the average worldwide tariffs on manufactured goods from 45 percent to just five percent.

The most recent GATT negotiations, dubbed the Uruguay Round, dragged on for seven long years before concluding in 1993. Although the benefits of the Uruguay Round won't be felt for many years, the new accord should promote robust long-term global trade growth. It reduces the world's remaining merchandise tariffs by 30 percent, which could boost global merchandise trade by up to 10 percent, or $375 billion in current dollars, by the year 2002. The new agreement also extends GATT to cover trade in agriculture and a wide range of services, and it toughens international protection of copyrights, patents, trademarks, and other intellectual property.[5] Beyond reducing trade barriers and setting standards for trade, the Uruguay Round established the World Trade Organization (WTO) to police and enforce GATT rules. One of the WTO's first major tasks was to host negotiations on the General Agreement on Trade in Services, which deals with worldwide trade in banking, securities, and insurance services. In general, the WTO will act as an umbrella organization, overseeing GATT, the General Agreement on Trade in Services, and a similar agreement governing intellectual property. In addition, the WTO mediates global disputes and imposes trade sanctions—authorities that the previous GATT organization never possessed.

World Trade Organization
www.wto.org/

Regional Free Trade Zones

Economic community
A group of nations organized to work toward common goals in the regulation of international trade.

Certain countries have formed *free trade zones* or **economic communities**—groups of nations organized to work toward common goals in the regulation of international trade. One such community is the *European Union (EU)*. Formed in 1957, the European Union—then called the Common Market—set out to create a single European market by reducing barriers to the free flow of products, services, finances, and labour among member countries and developing policies on trade with non-member nations. Today, the European Union represents one of the world's single largest markets. Its 15-member countries contain more than 370 million consumers and account for 20 percent of the world's exports. By the year 2000, as more European nations seek admission, the EU could contain as many as 450 million people in 28 countries.

European unification offers tremendous trade opportunities for North America and other non-European firms. However, it also poses threats. As a result of increased unification, European companies will grow bigger and more

Celebrating 1997 as
Canada's Year of Asia Pacific

Export Development Corporation is proud to sponsor the 1997 Asia Pacific Economic Cooperation Forum.

For more than 50 years EDC has helped Canadian companies export to Asian and other world markets by providing them with risk management services including insurance, financing and guarantees.

Our experience and knowledge of foreign markets enables us to provide new and seasoned exporters with a window to the world – to make the most of export opportunities. Last year alone, EDC helped Canadian companies export to more than 135 markets, including Asia Pacific. That is more than any other Canadian financial institution.

When it comes to exporting, every year can be a year of opportunity.

Call us today at **1-800-532-2220** for more information or visit us on the web at: **http://www.edcinfo.com**

Minimize risk.
Export with
confidence.

EDC
SEE

Organizations, such as the Export Development Corporation (EDC) supported Canada's trade initiatives in the Asia-Pacific region.

NAFTA Secretariat
www.nafta-sec-alena.org/

APEC Secretariat
www.apeccsec.org.sg/

competitive. Perhaps an even bigger concern, however, is that lower barriers inside Europe will only create thicker outside walls. Some observers envision a "Fortress Europe" that heaps favours on firms from EU countries but hinders outsiders by imposing obstacles such as stiffer import quotas, local content requirements, and other non-tariff barriers.

Progress toward European unification has been slow—many doubt that complete unification ever will be achieved. For example, in December 1991, European Union leaders approved the Maastricht Treaty, an amendment to the original EU charter, which called for establishing a central bank and single European currency—dubbed the "Euro"—by 1999. However, after much bitter squabbling, the EU has set a new implementation schedule, which now delays the complete conversion to the Euro until 2002. Despite a detailed implementation schedule, some analysts remain sceptical that EU countries will ever agree on the Euro.

Even if the European Union manages to standardize its general trade regulations, from a marketing perspective, creating an economic community will not create a homogeneous market. With 14 languages and distinctive national customs, it is unlikely that the EU will ever become a homogeneous whole. Although economic and political boundaries may fall, social and cultural differences will remain, and companies marketing in Europe will face a daunting mass of local rules. Still, even if only partly successful, European unification will make a more efficient and competitive Europe a global force with which to be reckoned.[6]

In North America, the United States and Canada phased out trade barriers in 1989. In January 1994, the *North American Free Trade Agreement (NAFTA)* established a free trade zone with the United States, Mexico, and Canada. The agreement creates a single market of 360 million people who produce and consume $9.3 trillion worth of goods and services. As it is implemented over the next 15 years, NAFTA will eliminate all trade-barrier and investment restrictions among the three countries.

Canada is also a member of APEC—the Asian-Pacific Economic Cooperation. The 18-member economies began their association in 1989. APEC is currently composed of members from Australia, Brunei, Chile, China, Hong Kong, Indonesia, Korea, Japan, Malaysia, Mexico, New Zealand, the Philippines, Papua New Guinea, Singapore, Taiwan, Thailand, and the United States. As part of Canada's year of Asia Pacific, these economies met in Vancouver in 1997. The association hopes to foster free trade in a region that now accounts for 45 percent of world trade. While the more developed countries want to set a timeline for the implementation of tariff reductions, less developed countries, such as Indonesia, Malaysia, and Thailand, have been more cautious, fearing that such actions will harm industries just in their infancy.[7]

Other free trade areas are forming in Latin America and South America. For example, MERCOSUL now links Brazil, Colombia, and Mexico, and Chile and Mexico have formed a successful free trade zone. Venezuela, Colombia, and Mexico—the "Group of Three"—are also negotiating a free trade area. It is likely

ARTHUR SOLER, PRESIDENT
CADBURY CHOCOLATE CANADA INC.

Even though Arthur Soler, the President of Cadbury Chocolate Canada Inc., won't tell us the "Caramilk Secret," he can tell us a lot about the challenges associated with Canadian marketing. Arthur did not begin his career as a marketer, however. He graduated from Ryerson Polytechnical Institute in 1965 and first went to Procter and Gamble as a Financial Analyst. In 1970, he joined Warner Lambert as a Financial Planning Manager, but soon moved into marketing with Adams Brands, the division that markets Trident Gum, Halls, and Clorets. In 1990, he ended his 20 years with Warner Lambert to become the President of Neilson Cadbury, Canada's largest chocolate-bar company. In January 1996, the firm was acquired by Cadbury Schweppes UK, making it part of the world's sixth-largest confectionery company. It is from this position that Arthur speaks to us today.

The Challenges of Marketing to Trade Customers

Arthur Soler has no doubts about what constitute the major challenges facing marketers in the 1990s. Marketers must do at least as good a job of marketing to the trade as they do marketing to final consumers. Whereas we can segment consumers into relatively homogeneous groups, and then market to them using one program, no similar strategy is possible with trade customers, Arthur stresses. Thus, programs must be tailored to meet the needs of each retailer.

Another lesson that has to be learned when marketing to the trade, Mr. Soler stresses, is understanding that it is not brands that are important to trade customers, but rather it is the category that they care about. Trade customers do not care if you sell a lot of just one brand, or divide the sales among 10 brands. What they want, Arthur emphasizes, is the best means to improve their business.

This need to understand the trade, in addition to marketing to final consumers, has changed the way marketing departments operate and the way marketers and salespeople are trained, Mr. Soler notes. For example, his Marketing Vice President has two years in sales, and his Sales VP has eight years in marketing. This cross-training is important because

Sales needs to understand the consumer element, and Marketing needs to appreciate the complexities of marketing to the trade.

The reality of the 1990s, says Mr. Soler, is that the trade is driving the business. If you want to have a powerful retailer, like one of the warehouse clubs, carry even one of your major brands, you have to package the product in the manner dictated by the retailer.

Arthur Soler

Mr. Soler believes that the power of the trade in Canada is mindboggling. This power arises from high levels of concentration. He also makes the point that you no longer sell to the retailer—he or she sells to you. Manufacturers are asked to buy end-of-aisle displays, space in the retailer's flyers, a portion of the retailer's cooperative advertising, and a position on the shelf. Focussing so much attention on the trade has resulted in many marketers losing their focus on the consumer, Mr. Soler believes.

This can be a fatal mistake, in his view. Despite the dire predictions several years ago that brands were dying, this is far from the truth. Brands have sometimes become weaker, however. Some marketers became arrogant about the power of their brands, believing that consumers would always pay more for branded products. The introduction of high-quality private-label products put this assumption into question. Consumers quickly saw that they could get good value for lower prices.

This inability to raise prices has resulted in a renewed focus on controlling costs. When prices could go up indiscriminately, marketers

became lazy about monitoring overhead expenses and waste. This is not the case today! The focus at Cadbury Chocolate has been to eliminate waste right across the supply chain. Concentrating on achieving greater efficiency has allowed Cadbury to use less working capital, carry less inventory, and still improve customer service.

Global Marketing?

Changing tack, Mr. Soler moved our discussion along to the issue of global marketing. While he notes that competition is global, brands aren't! He thinks there is too much emphasis on global competition. While companies may have global power in terms of the resources, knowledge, and research that they can bring to the marketplace, market competition is fought at the brand level. To make his point, Arthur stresses that there are only a few truly global brands—McDonald's, Coca-Cola, Gillette—but there are many powerful domestic brands.

In this sense, marketing in the 1990s has not changed. You still use the same fundamentals—establishing clear objectives, linking consumer behaviour to strategy, segmenting the market, and integrating the elements of the marketing mix. In other words, you have to get the fundamentals right on a region-by-region basis. Mr. Soler makes his point by noting that while CrispyCrunch is the number-one brand in English Canada, it is number 23 in Quebec, where consumers just do not like its peanut-butter taste. Cadbury is also beginning to think more about segmenting further to meet the needs of multicultural segments, especially those of the Asian market. In addition to regional and cultural differences, you also must understand the trade.

In closing, Mr. Soler stresses his optimism about marketing in Canada. While many bemoan the difficulties of marketing here, Arthur notes that it is a country with stable growth, consumers with disposable income, and where a number of companies are growing even though others are going. The trick, he advises, is to know the difference between the two!

Source: Arthur Soler was interviewed by P. Cunningham on April 18, 1996 for *Principles of Marketing*. We sincerely wish to thank him for the insights he provided on the practice of marketing.

that NAFTA will eventually merge with this and other arrangements to form an all-Americas free trade zone.[8]

Although the recent trend toward free trade zones has caused great excitement and new market opportunities, this trend also raises some concerns. For example, groups of countries that trade freely among themselves may tend to increase barriers to outsiders (for example, creating a "Fortress Europe"). Stricter local-content rules may add a new kind of bureaucracy and will once again limit international trade. In Canada and the United States, unions fear that NAFTA will lead to the further exodus of manufacturing jobs to Mexico, where wage rates are much lower. And environmentalists worry that companies that are unwilling to invest in environmentally safe practices will relocate in Mexico, where pollution regulation has been lax.

A recent poll revealed that 44 percent of Canadians believed that NAFTA had harmed the economy. In fact, nothing could be further from the truth. Since the inception of the agreement, the export of Canadian products to the United States has doubled to nearly $220 billion. Exports account for over 25 percent of our total national output and provide work for over two million Canadians. Exports have also grown faster than imports from the United States. Canada's trade surplus has tripled since NAFTA's inception and is now more than $41 billion. Growth has been evident even in industries that doomsayers forecast would die after the inception of free trade. Take the textile industry, for example. Exports to the United States went from $474 million in 1988 to $1.9 billion in 1996. Some jobs were lost and plants closed as firms sought greater cost efficiencies, however.

Many analysts worry that Canada is too dependent on trade with the United States. As Gordon Ritchie, one of the chief architects of the free trade agreement, notes, "Now for the bad news: while this base is very solid, we would prefer it to be much broader. These export results have been achieved by too few companies, in too few sectors, selling into a single, albeit huge, market." For example, the automobile industry alone accounts for 22.6 percent of Canada's exports and most of these go to the United States. Two surveys conducted in 1996 and 1997 revealed that 75 percent of exporting firms target their international marketing efforts at the United States, compared to the 38 percent directed at Western Europe. Another 38 percent concentrate on Asia, and 27 percent focus on Latin America. The percentages don't add to 100 since some companies enter multiple markets. Thus, it isn't surprising that many experts believe that Canada must continue to diversify its trade base if the country is to make a mark in the global arena.[9]

Despite NAFTA's many successes, a number of challenges are posed to maintaining smooth trade relations between Canada and the United States. Salmon fishing and water access rights are being disputed along the Inside Passage between Vancouver Island and the mainland. The U.S. government has presented a number of challenges to Canada's policies regarding protection of its dairy and poultry industries. Canada also wants special protection for its cultural industries. This dispute has been brought to a head by *Sports Illustrated*'s efforts to produce a split run for Canada—a magazine with American content, but that runs Canadian ads. Another dispute arose as a result of Canada's trading status with Cuba.[10]

Whether conducting business in North America, or venturing further afield, Canadian businesspeople must realize that each nation has unique features that must be understood. A nation's readiness for different products and services and its attractiveness as a market to foreign firms depend on its economic, political-legal, ethical, and cultural environments.

ECONOMIC ENVIRONMENT

The international marketer must study each country's economy. Two economic factors reflect the country's attractiveness as a market: the country's industrial structure and its income distribution.

The country's *industrial structure* shapes its product and service needs, income levels, and employment levels. The four types of industrial structures are as follows:

◆ *Subsistence economies.* In a subsistence economy, the vast majority of people engage in simple agriculture. They consume most of their output and barter the rest for simple goods and services. They offer few market opportunities.

◆ *Raw-material-exporting economies.* These economies are rich in one or more natural resources but poor in other ways. Much of their revenue comes from exporting these resources. Examples are Chile (tin and copper); Zaire (copper, cobalt, and coffee); and Saudi Arabia (oil). These countries are good markets for large equipment, tools and supplies, and trucks. If there are many foreign residents and a wealthy upper class, they are also a market for luxury goods. For example, the Canadian firm, Crystal Fountains, has received orders of approximately $1 million from the United Arab Emirates where people are willing to pay $150 000 to $200 000 for fountains.[11]

◆ *Industrializing economies.* In an industrializing economy, manufacturing accounts for 10 to 20 percent of the country's economy. Examples include Egypt, the Philippines, India, and Brazil. As manufacturing increases, the country needs more imports of raw textile materials, steel, and heavy machinery, and fewer imports of finished textiles, paper products, and automobiles. Canada's 1996 trade mission to India, for example, resulted in the signing of agreements worth $444 million. Industrialization typically creates a new rich class and a small but growing middle class, both demanding new types of imported goods.[12]

◆ *Industrial economies.* Industrial economies are major exporters of manufactured goods and investment funds. They trade goods among themselves and also export them to other types of economies for raw materials and semifinished goods. The varied manufacturing activities of these industrial nations and their large middle class make them rich markets for all sorts of goods.

The second economic factor is the country's *income distribution.* Countries with subsistence economies may consist mostly of households with very low family incomes. In contrast, industrialized nations may have low-, medium-, and high-income households. Still other countries may have only households with either very low or very high incomes. However, marketers must not form stereotypes based on average income alone. Even people in low-income countries may find ways to buy products that are important to them. For example,

Income distribution: Even poorer countries may have small but wealthy segments. Although citizens of Budapest, Hungary have relatively low annual incomes, well-dressed shoppers flock to elegant stores like this one, stocked with luxury goods.

In the United States, the first satellite dishes sprang up in the poorest parts of the Appalachian mountains. . . . The poorest slums of Calcutta are home to 70 000 VCRs. In Mexico, homes with colour televisions outnumber those with running water. Low average-income figures may conceal a lively luxury market. In Warsaw (average annual income: $3600), well-dressed shoppers flock to elegant boutiques stocked with Christian Dior perfume and Valentino shoes. . . . In China, where per-capita income is less than $850, the Swiss company Rado is selling thousands of its $1000 watches.[13]

Thus, international marketers face many challenges in understanding how the economic environment will affect decisions about which global markets to enter and how.

POLITICAL-LEGAL AND ETHICAL ENVIRONMENT

Nations differ greatly in their political-legal environments. At least four political-legal factors should be considered in deciding whether to do business in a given country: attitudes toward international buying, government bureaucracy, political stability, and monetary regulations.

In their attitudes toward international buying, some nations are quite receptive to foreign firms, and others are quite hostile. For example, India has bothered foreign businesses with import quotas, currency restrictions, and limits on the percentage of the management team that can be non-nationals. As a result, many North American companies left India because of all the hassles. In contrast, neighbouring Asian countries such as Singapore, Thailand, Malaysia, and the Philippines woo foreign investors and shower them with incentives and favourable operating conditions.

A second factor is *government bureaucracy*—the extent to which the host government runs an efficient system for helping foreign companies: efficient customs handling, good market information, and other factors that support conducting business. North Americans are often shocked by demands for bribes to make these trade barriers disappear even though such demands are illegal and unethical. These issues are discussed in Marketing Highlight 19-2.

Political stability is another issue. Governments change hands, sometimes violently. Even without a change, a government may decide to respond to new popular feelings. The foreign company's property may be taken, its currency holdings may be blocked, or import quotas or new duties may be set. International marketers may find it profitable to do business in an unstable country, but the unsteady situation will affect how they handle business and financial matters.

Finally, companies must also consider a country's *monetary regulations*. Sellers want to take their profits in a currency of value to them. Ideally, the buyer can pay in the seller's currency or in other world currencies. Short of this, sellers might accept a blocked currency—one whose removal from the country is restricted by the buyer's government—if they can buy other goods in that country that they need themselves or can sell elsewhere for a needed currency. Besides currency limits, a changing exchange rate also creates high risks for the seller.

Countertrade
International trade involving the direct or indirect exchange of goods for other goods instead of cash. Forms include barter, compensation (buyback), and counterpurchase.

Most international trade involves cash transactions. Yet many nations have too little hard currency to pay for their purchases from other countries. They may want to pay with other items instead of cash, which has led to a practice called **countertrade**. Countertrade takes several forms. *Barter* involves the direct exchange of goods or services. Another form is *compensation* (or *buyback*), whereby the seller sells a plant, equipment, or technology to another country and agrees to take payment in the resulting products. *Counterpurchase* occurs when the seller receives full payment in cash but agrees to spend some portion of the money in the other country within a stated time period. Countertrade deals can be very complex. For example, Daimler-Benz recently agreed to sell 30 trucks to

THE GREY ZONE:
INTERNATIONAL MARKETING ETHICS

A well-known business ethics scholar, Richard De George, wrote that, "Business ethics is as national, international, or global as business itself, and no arbitrary geographical boundaries limit it." International business ethics is increasingly becoming front-page news, but the topic isn't a new one or even one born of modern times. For centuries, trade has brought people and cultures into direct conflict. The exploitation of numerous countries in the colonial periods of France, England, and Spain illustrate extreme cases of unethical marketing practice. Exchanges in which worthless beads were traded for gold and silver make some of the scandals presented in the modern press pale in comparison.

Marketing has long been associated with questions of ethics, both nationally and internationally. Marketing and ethics are closely aligned since the element of trust is inherent in the creation of ongoing exchange relationships that lie at the heart of marketing. It cannot be denied that firms operating in international markets face a growing number of ethical issues. Business is increasingly global in nature, firms operate in multiple national markets, and they seek to raise capital from multiple international sources. Moreover, since foreign market growth outpaced North American market growth, the mandate for understanding how to manage international ethical behaviour is growing.

Decisions that marketers must make while working within the context of any corporation are complex and are often fraught with conflicts of values. Such conflicts are at the heart of many ethical dilemmas even in

national business enterprises. They become seemingly insurmountable problems in the arena of international businesses where people from different cultures, political systems, economies, value systems, and ethical standards must interact. In other words, ethical concerns involve more than black-and-white decisions; they involve many shades of grey where the values of people from one country conflict with those from another. For example, in some countries, giving and receiving gifts is customary at the close of business transactions. However, for many North American firms, acceptance of gifts, other than mere tokens of appreciation such as chocolates or flowers, is viewed as unethical or may even be illegal.

Ethical issues surround all of the functional areas of international business and are centred on a number of business strategy questions including market-entry decisions, bribery and gift-giving, contract negotiations, human resource issues, crisis-management situations, product policy, advertising practices, pricing and transfer pricing, information systems management and privacy, grey markets, environmental concerns, accounting, finance and taxation, and production. Many of these areas are of specific concern to marketers. International advertising, for example, often raises ethical concerns. While many European countries use nudity and sexual innuendo in their advertising, some North Americans often find this offensive. In countries such as India, showing people kissing is objectionable.

Offering certain products for sale in some countries has also raised ethical criticisms. North American

companies have been criticized for marketing harmful chemicals overseas that are banned from use in their home markets. Avon has been criticized for selling cosmetics to people in countries where many people cannot afford enough food. Even though a product itself may not be inherently harmful, ethical criticisms have been directed at companies that did not take measures to prevent harm arising to consumers who incorrectly used products (like baby formula, drugs, or pesticides), due to high rates of illiteracy and inability to understand product-use instructions. There are also ethical issues associated with packaging in international markets. In some countries, such as Germany, manufacturers must recycle all packaging. In others, due to lack of disposal facilities, packaging adds to pollution problems.

Pricing raises yet another set of ethical concerns. Sometimes higher prices must be charged due to the increased costs of marketing overseas, but when overly high prices are levied just because a firm has a monopoly in a foreign country, ethical questions have to be asked. Ethical criticisms have been levied at firms for their refusal to send female sales representatives or managers into countries with adverse gender stereotypes even though this hampers women's chances for advancement or higher earnings.

Bribery is always a thorny issue in international markets. While it is undeniable that in some countries, it is viewed as a "normal" way of doing business, this is not universally the case. Marketers should be aware that in most countries bribery is an illegal practice. North Americans should also

Romania in exchange for 150 Romanian jeeps, which it then sold to Ecuador for bananas, which were in turn sold to a German supermarket chain for German currency. Through this roundabout process, Daimler-Benz finally obtained payment in German money.[14]

CULTURAL ENVIRONMENT

Each country has its own folkways, norms, and taboos. The seller must examine the way consumers in different countries think about and use certain products before planning a marketing program. There are often surprises. For example, the

be sensitive to the fact that because we hold the stereotypical belief that bribes are expected overseas, we often make the mistake of offering such a payment when we perceive the slightest hesitation in signing a business deal. Rather than expecting a bribe, the foreign official may just be more risk-averse or want more information. The offering of a bribe, in these cases, will not only cause offence but it will often terminate the relationship.

When discussing international business ethics, North Americans believe that we take the moral highroad. We've all read reports of companies being blocked from doing business in South America because of rigged bidding systems, or losing sales in China or Korea because firms cannot legally pay the bribes necessary to get the business. However, we have to be aware that some countries may have higher moral standards than we do. For example, one survey showed that fewer Japanese executives will cheat on their expense sheets than will a comparable group of North American executives. Other surveys of Canadian businesspeople have shown that most ethical problems are not faced when one tries to do business in exotic locales, but rather when dealing with our closest neighbour, the United States. While this may be due to the fact that we do more business with the United States than with any other country, problems such as industrial espionage, product safety concerns, sales practices, and hiring practices have been areas of growing ethical concern.

Despite the rising number of ethical issues faced by marketers, there are often few guidelines to help them come to terms with these issues. International marketers must be aware, however, that they have multiple responsibilities to the firms and their customers. They must avoid knowingly harming any of their constituents. They must sell safe products, ensure truthful advertising, and charge fair prices. As a minimum, marketers working for Canadian companies must abide by the laws of the countries in which they operate. It is stressed, however, that being an ethical marketer often means going beyond the mere provisions of a legal system. Marketers also must consider what is right or wrong. Such considerations involve respecting the human rights of people, no matter what country they reside in. It involves avoidance of exploitation of individuals or their environment.

More and more companies, such as Imperial Oil and Warner Lambert, have codes of ethics that have been developed to guide their employees' decisions. A 1995 survey of the CEOs of the top 500 companies in Canada revealed that 80 percent of these firms have codes of ethics. What is more important is that many of these firms also require that the principles outlined in the code be applied unilaterally, no matter what country the firm is operating in. In other words, the rules applying to conducting the business in Canada also apply to subsidiaries of the business operating overseas.

In Canada, it is the responsibility of top levels of management to set ethics policy and to ensure that it is implemented throughout their firms. Leading scholars in the field of marketing ethics emphasize that planning for ethical behaviour must begin at the same time as the rest of the strategic international market-planning effort. Thinking about ethics cannot be an afterthought! This type of planning includes decisions such as which international markets to enter, since some areas are known for their inherent ethical challenges. For example, does the firm want to enter markets dominated by totalitarian and military regimes, or those known for their record of human-rights violations or ongoing environmental damage? Other questions include what types of products to market. The marketing of pesticides, tobacco, liquor, and pharmaceuticals, for example, all have unique ethical questions associated with them.

In addition to a code of ethics, firms must actively train their employees to be more sensitive to ethical issues, especially as they send their employees overseas. While less than 40 percent of firms offer ethics training, surveys indicate that employees want this type of training, that it has a positive effect in reducing unethical behaviour, and that it heightens ethical issue recognition and sensitivity.

Thus, although international marketing can be one of the most exciting and rewarding areas of the profession, be aware that it also presents some of the most difficult ethical problems and issues.

Source: This highlight is based on an article written by Peggy Cunningham entitled "Managing Marketing Ethics in International Business: Literature Review and Directions for Future Research," published in the Proceedings of the ASAC Conference, Windsor, June 1995.

average French man uses almost twice as many cosmetics and beauty aids as his wife. The Germans and the French eat more packaged, branded spaghetti than do Italians. Italian children like to eat chocolate bars between slices of bread as a snack. Japanese people will not eat chocolate and peanuts together because they believe that it will cause nose bleeds.

Companies that ignore such differences can make some very expensive and embarrassing mistakes. Here's an example:

> McDonald's and Coca-Cola managed to offend the entire Muslim world by putting the Saudi Arabian flag on their packaging. The flag's design includes a passage from the Koran (the sacred text of Islam), and Muslims feel very strongly that their Holy Writ should never be wadded up and tossed in the garbage.[15]

Business norms and behaviour also vary among countries. Business executives need to be briefed on these factors before conducting business in another country. Here are some examples of different global business behaviour:

◆ South Americans like to sit or stand very close to each other when they talk business—in fact, almost nose-to-nose. The North American business executive tends to keep backing away as the South American moves closer. Both may end up being offended.

◆ In face-to-face communications, Japanese business executives rarely say no. Thus, North Americans tend to be frustrated, and they may not know where they stand. However, when North Americans come to the point quickly, Japanese business executives may find this behaviour pushy and offensive.

◆ In France, wholesalers don't want to promote a product. They ask their retailers what they want and deliver it. If a company builds its strategy around the French wholesaler's cooperation in promotions, it is likely to fail.

◆ When North American executives exchange business cards, each usually gives the other's card a cursory glance and stuffs it in a pocket for later reference. In Asia, however, executives dutifully study each other's cards during a greeting, carefully noting company affiliation and rank. They use both hands to give their card to the most important person first.

Thus, each country and region has cultural traditions, preferences, and behaviours that the marketer must study.

DECIDING WHETHER TO GO INTERNATIONAL

While many firms view themselves only as local businesses serving their immediate communities, they must also be increasingly aware of the globalization of competition even if they never plan to go overseas themselves. Too many of these firms have realized the dangers too late and have gone out of business when faced with new competitors such as the category killers from the United States or abroad. Companies that operate in global industries, where their strategic positions in specific markets are affected strongly by their overall global positions, have no choice but to think and act globally. Thus, Nortel must organize globally if it is to gain purchasing, manufacturing, financial, and marketing advantages. Firms in a global industry must be able to compete on a worldwide basis if they are to succeed.

Any of several factors might draw a company into the international arena. Global competitors might attack the company's domestic market by offering better products or lower prices. The company might want to counterattack these competitors in their home markets to tie up their resources. Or the company might discover foreign markets that present higher profit opportunities than the domestic market does. The company's domestic market might be shrinking or the company might need an enlarged customer base to achieve economies of scale. Or it might want to reduce its dependence on any one market so as to reduce its risk. Finally, the company's customers might be expanding abroad and require international servicing.

Before going abroad, the company must weigh several risks and answer many questions about its ability to operate globally. Can the company learn to understand the preferences and buyer behaviour of consumers in other countries? Can it offer competitively attractive products? Will it be able to adapt to other countries' business cultures and deal effectively with foreign nationals? Do the company's managers have the necessary international experience? Has management considered the impact of regulations and the political environments of other countries?

Because of the risks and difficulties of entering international markets, most companies do not act until some situation or event thrusts them into the global arena. Someone—a domestic exporter, a foreign importer, a foreign government—may ask the company to sell abroad. Or the company may be saddled with overcapacity and must find additional markets for its goods.

DECIDING WHICH MARKETS TO ENTER

Before going abroad, the company should try to define its international *marketing objectives and policies*. First, it should decide what *volume* of foreign sales it wants. Most companies start small when they go abroad. Some plan to stay small, seeing international sales as a small part of their business. Other companies have bigger plans, seeing international business as equal to or even more important than their domestic business.

The company must choose *how many* countries it wants to market in. Generally, it makes sense to operate in fewer countries with deeper commitment and penetration in each. For example, the Bulova Watch Company decided to operate in many international markets and expanded into more than 100 countries. As a result, it spread itself too thin, made profits in only two countries, and lost around $55 million.

Next, the company must decide on the *types* of countries to enter. A country's attractiveness depends on the product, geographical factors, income and population, political climate, and other factors. The seller may prefer certain country groups or parts of the world. In recent years, many major markets have emerged, offering both substantial opportunities and daunting challenges (see Marketing Highlight 19-3).

After listing possible international markets, the company must screen and rank each one. PepsiCo, found the People's Republic is especially enticing: it is the most populous country in the world, and Coca-Cola does not yet dominate it.[16] In addition to selling Pepsi soft drinks, the company hopes to build many of its Pizza Hut restaurants in China. Yet we still can question whether market size *alone* is reason enough for selecting China. PepsiCo also must consider other factors: Will the Chinese government be stable and supportive? Does China provide for the production and distribution technologies needed to produce and market Pepsi products profitably? Will Pepsi and pizza fit Chinese tastes, means, and lifestyles? For example, when considering an entry by Pizza Hut, PepsiCo. should consider that cheese has not been part of the traditional Chinese diet and many Chinese people do not care to eat it.

Possible global markets should be ranked on several factors, including market size, market growth, cost of doing business, competitive advantage, and risk level. The goal is to determine the potential of each market, using indicators like those shown in Table 19-1 on page 662. Then the marketer must decide which markets offer the greatest long-run return on investment.

General Electric's appliance division uses what it calls a "smart-bomb" strategy for selecting global markets to enter. GE's executives examine each potential country microscopically, measuring such factors as strength of local competitors, market-growth potential, and availability of skilled labour. The company then targets only markets where it can earn more than 20 percent on its investment. The goal: "to generate the best returns possible on the smallest investment possible." Once targets are selected, GE Appliances zeros in with marketing "smart bombs"—products and programs tailored to yield the best performance in each market. As a result of this strategy, GE is trouncing competitors such as Whirlpool and Maytag in Asian markets.[17]

DECIDING HOW TO ENTER THE MARKET

Once a company has decided to sell in a foreign country, it must determine the best mode of entry. Its choices are *exporting, joint venturing,* and *direct investment.*

THE LAST MARKETING FRONTIERS: EASTERN EUROPE, CHINA, AND VIETNAM, AND CUBA

As communist and formerly communist countries reform their markets, and trade barriers are dismantled, North America companies are eagerly anticipating the profits that await them. Here are "snapshots" of the opportunities and challenges that marketers face in three of the world's global marketing frontiers.

Eastern Europe: A Market Ready to Harvest

As Central and Eastern Europe continue the transition to free-marked economies, the market for Canadian goods and services is expanding. Rapid economic growth and the privatization of state-owned companies point the way to increasing opportunities. Within 1996 alone, Canadian exports to this region climbed by more than 50 percent. The Canadian Development Corporation (CDC), a Crown corporation, has helped Canadian firms expand in the region by providing them with financial and risk management services. Other federal government programs designed to help firms ease their way into these markets are those run by the Canadian International Development Agency (CIDA).

Russia, a challenging market, nonetheless boasts 250 Canadian companies that have thrived in the oil and gas, agricultural, housing/construction, and telecommunications markets, selling more than $319 million in goods and services. Poland is Canada's second-largest trade partner in the area. Canada has long enjoyed an excellent reputation in Poland. While charting a course through Poland's business channels is no

easy task, perseverance pays off and Canadian firms exported $154 million to the country in 1996. Since the Czech Republic is one of the most stable and fastest-growing former communist countries in Europe, Canadians firms have been working diligently to build relationships there.

Pepsi in China—a huge marketing opportunity?

Hungary is another target of Canadian firms. The new airport in Budapest was built by a Canadian-led consortium and this project bears witness to the country's more open and friendly business environment. Canadian exports to Hungary have increased by 500 percent in a 10-year period.

China: 1.2 Billion Consumers

In Guangdong province, Chinese "yuppies" walk department-store aisles to buy $140 Nike or Reebok running shoes or think nothing of spending $6 on a jar of Skippy peanut butter in the supermarket section. Although Chinese consumers might make as little as $190 a month, they still have plenty of spending money because of subsidized housing and health care, and lots of savings under the mattress. In Shenzen, the Guangdong's second-largest city, consumers have the highest disposable income in all of China—$5600 annually. With purchasing power like this, a population of 1.2 billion, and the fastest-growing economy in the world, China is encouraging companies from around the world to set up shop there. Instead of the communist propaganda of yore, modern Chinese billboards exclaim, "Give China a chance."

Since the Prime Minister's highly publicized "Team Canada" trade delegation to China in 1994, Canadian exports to China have grown by 50 percent. Business with China should continue to escalate through the Hong Kong gateway. Hong Kong reverted to Chinese control on July 1, 1997. Canada and Hong Kong have a long trade history.

FIGURE 19-2 *Market entry strategies*

Figure 19-2 shows three market entry strategies, along with the options each one offers. As the figure shows, each succeeding strategy involves more commitment and risk, but also more control and potential profits.

Exporting	**Joint venturing**	**Direct investment**
Indirect Direct	Licensing Contract manufacturing Management contracting Joint ownership	Assembly facilities Manufacturing facilities

Amount of commitment, risk, control, and profit potential

EXPORTING

The simplest way to enter a foreign market is through **exporting.** The company may passively export its surpluses from time to time, or it may make an active commitment

Exports to Hong Kong have grown at a rate of 20 percent per year and more than 150 Canadian companies have offices in the city.

Yet for all the market potential in Hong Kong and China, there are many hurdles to jump, especially when entering mainland China and marketing to the Chinese. For example, even firms that have been highly successful in the Chinese market, such as Nortel or Bombardier, still face prolonged and difficult negotiations. Firms are often unsure about who has the authority to close a deal or make a final decision. Moreover, China is not one market, but many, and regional governments may discriminate against certain goods. Distribution channels are undeveloped, consisting of thousands of tiny mom-and-pop stores that can afford to stock only a few bottles or packages at a time. And China's dismal infrastructure can turn a rail shipment travelling from Guanzhou to Beijing into a month-long odyssey. As Canadian firms expand from Hong Kong into mainland China, *guanxi*, or connections, have become one of the keys to doing business. Many believe that businesses will need a Chinese partner with local political connections in order to be successful. Others acquire Chinese business partners who can help them penetrate distribution channels and hire experienced personnel. Another major concern is China's distressing human-rights record. Levi Strauss has turned its back on China's vast market for blue jeans because of such concerns. But other firms counter that industry can

be part of the solution. "Supporting the business sector will result in economic and political freedoms for the Chinese people," says a 3M spokesperson.

Vietnam: An Untapped Market

Vietnam seems like a marketer's dream: 72 million consumers, 80 percent of whom are younger than 40; loads of natural resources, including oil, gold, gas, and timber; and a coastline of pristine beaches that could turn out to be the hot new tourist spot. Vietnam is the world's twelfth most populous nation, and southeast Asia's second-largest market.

Amid all the excitement, however, there are some notes of caution. The per-capita income of most Vietnamese is $280 a year, and like China, Vietnam's transportation and communication systems rank among the world's worst. While the country and its markets develop, marketers are spending their money cautiously. Because most consumers are seeing products for the first time ever, companies are investing most of their marketing dollars in very simple advertising campaigns. For this reason, radio and billboards are fruitful venues for advertising. One billboard in Ho Chi Minh City boasts a single word: Sony.

Cuba: Watching and Waiting

The U.S.-led embargo against Cuba has not only dampened the country's economic prospects, but the American political pressure has also caused problems for Canadian firms doing business there. Since Cuba is one of the lushest Caribbean islands, the

main business opportunities have been the booming hotels built or managed by Canadian, Spanish, and Mexican operators. Some 800 000 tourists crammed Cuba's shores last year, and tourism overtook sugar exports as Cuba's top hard-currency earner.

Cuba's consumer market consists of 11 million people. As with the emerging markets of China and Vietnam, Cuba's infrastructure needs years of rebuilding. Some places have no running water, gasoline, sewer systems, and energy sources. "They'll have to take care of the basic concept of survival before they can think about pizza and Pepsi," says Joe Zubizarreta, a Cuban-born advertising executive.

Sources: Nattalia Lea, "Passage to the China Market," *Marketing*, September 12, 1994, pp. 8–8; Marlene Piturro, "Capitalist China?" *Brandweek*, May 16, 1994, pp. 24–27; Mark L. Clifford, "How You Can Win in China," *Business Week*, May 26, 1997, pp. 66–69; Cyndee Miller, "U.S. Firms Rush to Claim Share of Newly Opened Vietnam Market," *Marketing News*, March 14, 1994, p. 11; Thomas A. Kissane, "What Are We Doing in Vietnam?" *Sales & Marketing Management,*, May 1996, pp. 96–97; Christy Fisher, "U.S. Marketers Wait for Opening in Cuba," *Advertising Age*, August 29, 1994, pp. 1, 6' Sean Mehegan, "Is Castro Convertible?" *Restaurant Business*, May 1, 1996, pp. 36–38; Melana Zyla, "Polish your Connections to Prosper in Business," *Globe and Mail*, July 1, 1997, p. C13; and "Central and Eastern Europe: A Market Ready to Harvest," *Advertising Supplement, Canadian Business*, July 1997; "Hong Kong Means Business," *The Financial Post*, June 30, 1997, p. HK4.

Exporting
Entering a foreign market by sending products and selling them through international marketing intermediaries (indirect exporting) or through the company's own department, branch, or sales representatives or agents (direct exporting).

to expand exports to a particular market. In either case, the company, like Feathercraft kayaks, produces all its goods in its home country. It may or may not modify them for the export market. Exporting involves the least change in the company's product lines, organization, investments, or mission.

Companies typically start with *indirect exporting*, working through independent international marketing intermediaries. Indirect exporting involves less investment because the firm does not require an overseas sales force or set of contacts. It also involves less risk. International marketing intermediaries—domestic-based export merchants or agents, cooperative organizations, and export-management companies—bring know-how and services to the relationship, so the seller normally makes fewer mistakes.

Sellers may eventually move into *direct exporting*, whereby they handle their own exports. The investment and risk are somewhat greater in this strategy, but

TABLE 19-1 *Indicators of Market Potential*

1. Demographic Characteristics	4. Technological Factors
Size of population Rate of population growth Degree of urbanization Population density Age structure and composition of the population	Level of technological skill Existing production technology Existing consumption technology Education levels
2. Geographic Characteristics	**5. Sociocultural Factors**
Physical size of a country Topographical characteristics Climate conditions	Dominant values Lifestyle patterns Ethnic groups Linguistic fragmentation
3. Economic Factors	**6. National Goals and Plans**
GNP per capita Income distribution Rate of growth of GNP Ratio of investment to GNP	Industry priorities Infrastructure investment plans

Source: Susan P. Douglas, C. Samuel Craig, and Warren Keegan, "Approaches to Assessing International Marketing Opportunities for Small and Medium-Sized Business," *Columbia Journal of World Business*, Fall 1982, pp. 26–32.

so is the potential return. A company can conduct direct exporting in several ways. It can set up a domestic export department that carries out export activities. It can also set up an overseas sales branch that handles sales, distribution, and perhaps promotion. The sales branch gives the seller more presence and program control in the foreign market and often serves as a display centre and customer service centre. The company also can send home-based salespeople abroad at certain times in order to find business. Finally, the company can do its exporting either through foreign-based distributors who buy and own the goods or through foreign-based agents who sell the goods on behalf of the company.

JOINT VENTURING

Joint venturing
Entering foreign markets by joining with foreign companies to produce or market a product or service.

A second method of entering a foreign market is **joint venturing**—joining with domestic or foreign companies to produce or market products or services. By forming a joint venture and partnerships with their Chinese counterparts, Blewett Dodd Ching Lee Ltd., a Vancouver-based architectural firm, has been able to win lucrative contracts in China's booming building industry.[18] Joint venturing differs from exporting in that the company joins with a partner to sell or market abroad. It differs from direct investment in that an association is formed with someone in the foreign country. There are four types of joint ventures: licensing, contract manufacturing, management contracting, and joint ownership.

Licensing

Licensing
A method of entering a foreign market in which the company enters into an agreement with a licensee in the foreign market, offering the right to use a manufacturing process, trademark, patent, trade secret, or other item of value for a fee or royalty.

Licensing is a simple way for a manufacturer to enter international marketing. The company, as was the case with BCE's entry into India, forms an agreement with a licensee in the foreign market. For a fee or royalty, the licensee buys the right to use the company's manufacturing process, trademark, patent, trade secret, or other item of value. The company thus gains entry into the market at little risk; the licensee gains production expertise or a well-known product or name without having to start from scratch.

Coca-Cola markets internationally by licensing bottlers around the world and supplying them with the syrup needed to produce the product. Tokyo Disneyland

夜がきれい、君もきれい、スターライト★デート。

Tokyo Disneyland.

Licensing: Tokyo Disneyland is owned and operated by the Oriental Land Co., Ltd. (a Japanese development company), under licence from Walt Disney Company.

Contract manufacturing
A joint venture in which a company contracts with manufacturers in a foreign market to produce the product.

Management contracting
A joint venture in which the domestic firm supplies the management know-how to a foreign company that supplies the capital; the domestic firm exports management services rather than products.

Joint ownership
A joint venture in which a company joins investors in a foreign market to create a local business in which the company shares joint ownership and control.

Direct investment
Entering a foreign market by developing foreign-based assembly or manufacturing facilities.

is owned and operated by Oriental Land Company under licence from the Walt Disney Company.

Licensing has potential disadvantages, however. The firm has less control over the licensee than it would over its own production facilities. Furthermore, if the licensee is very successful, the firm has given up these profits, and if and when the contract ends, it may find it has created a competitor.

Contract Manufacturing

Another option is **contract manufacturing**—the company contracts with manufacturers in the foreign market to produce its product or provide its service. Sears used this method in opening up department stores in Mexico and Spain, where it found qualified local manufacturers to produce many of the products it sells. The drawbacks of contract manufacturing are the decreased control over the manufacturing process and the loss of potential profits on manufacturing. The benefits are the chance to start faster, with less risk, and the later opportunity either to form a partnership with or to buy out the local manufacturer.

Management Contracting

Under **management contracting,** the domestic firm supplies management know-how to a foreign company that supplies the capital. The domestic firm exports management services rather than products. A number of Canadian engineering firms, such as Acres International and Agra Monenco, use management contracting.

Management contracting is a low-risk method of getting into a foreign market, and it yields income from the beginning. The arrangement is even more attractive if the contracting firm has an option to buy some share in the managed company later on. The arrangement is not sensible, however, if the company can put its scarce management talent to better uses or if it can make greater profits by undertaking the whole venture. Management contracting also prevents the company from setting up its own operations for a period of time.

Joint Ownership

Joint ownership ventures consist of one company joining forces with foreign investors to create a local business in which they share joint ownership and control. A company may buy an interest in a local firm, or the two parties may form a new business venture. Magna, the Canadian auto-parts manufacturer, recently acquired much of a U.K. firm, Marley PLC, to expand its business into the European Common Market.[19] Joint ownership may be needed for economic or political reasons. The firm may lack the financial, physical, or managerial resources to undertake the venture alone, or a foreign government may require joint ownership as a condition for entry.

Joint ownership has certain drawbacks. The partners may disagree over investment, marketing, or other policies. Whereas many U.S. firms like to reinvest earnings for growth, local firms often like to take out these earnings. Furthermore, whereas U.S. firms emphasize the role of marketing, local investors may rely on selling.

DIRECT INVESTMENT

The biggest involvement in a foreign market comes through **direct investment**—the development of foreign-based assembly or manufacturing facilities. If a company has gained experience in exporting and if the foreign market is large enough, foreign production facilities offer many advantages. The firm may have lower costs in the form of cheaper labour or raw materials, foreign government investment incentives, and freight savings. The firm may improve its image in the host country because it creates jobs. Generally, a firm develops a deeper relationship with government, customers, local suppliers, and distributors, allowing it to better adapt its products to the local market. Finally, the firm keeps full control over the investment and therefore can develop manufacturing and marketing policies that serve its long-term international objectives.

The main disadvantage of direct investment is that the firm faces many risks, such as restricted or devalued currencies, falling markets, or government takeovers. In some cases, a firm has no choice but to accept these risks if it wants to operate in the host country. These lessons were only too clear when Toronto-based Bata Shoes decided to return to its Czech homeland, and begin operations through the route of direct investment. The route, however, wasn't an easy one. Negotiations with government officials to re-establish the family shoe business took years of wrangling. Legal and political hurdles represented only half the battle, as marketing manager, former Calgarian, Jeanne Milne, quickly learned. She faced problems ranging from lack of customer research to redesigning window displays. She discovered that offering sales didn't work since consumers in the Czech Republic equate discounts with inferior quality. Service providers had to be trained since providing service had become a foreign concept. As one Czech employee complained, "Why should I smile at customers?" They don't smile at me." Even customers had to be re-educated. When employees went to the stockroom to search for correct sizes, customers followed them, believing that shoe clerks were going elsewhere just to avoid serving them. The struggle has been worth it. Bata is held up as an exemplar of one of the few truly successful privatization efforts in Eastern Europe.

DECIDING ON THE GLOBAL MARKETING PROGRAM

Standardized marketing mix
An international marketing strategy for using basically the same product, advertising, distribution channels, and other elements of the marketing mix in all the company's international markets.

Adapted marketing mix
An international marketing strategy for adjusting the marketing-mix elements to each international target market, bearing more costs but hoping for a larger market share and return.

Companies that operate in one or more foreign markets must decide how much, if at all, to adapt their marketing mixes to local conditions. At one extreme are companies that use a **standardized marketing mix** worldwide. Proponents of global standardization claim that it results in lower production, distribution, marketing, and management costs, letting companies offer consumers higher-quality and more reliable products at lower prices. This is the thinking behind Coca-Cola's decision that Coke should taste about the same around the world and Ford's production of a "world car" that suits the needs of most consumers in most countries.

At the other extreme is an **adapted marketing mix**. In this case, the producer adjusts the marketing mix elements to each target market, bearing more costs but hoping for a larger market share and return. Nestlé, for example, varies its product line and its advertising in different countries. Proponents argue that consumers in different countries vary greatly in their geographic, demographic, economic, and cultural characteristics, resulting in different needs and wants, spending power, product preferences, and shopping patterns. Therefore, companies should adapt their marketing strategies and programs to fit the unique consumer needs in each country.

The question of whether to adapt or standardize the marketing mix has been much debated in recent years. However, global standardization is not an all-or-nothing proposition, but rather a matter of degree. Companies should look for more standardization to help keep down costs and prices and to build greater global brand power. But they must not replace long-run marketing thinking with short-run financial thinking. Although standardization saves money, marketers must ensure that they offer what consumers in each country want.[20]

Many possibilities exist between the extremes of standardization and complete adaptation. For example, Coca-Cola sells virtually the same Coke beverage worldwide, and it pulls advertisements for specific markets from a common pool of ads designed to have cross-cultural appeal. However, the company sells a variety of other beverages created specifically for the tastebuds of local markets. Prices and distribution channels may also vary widely from market to market.

PRODUCT

Five strategies allow for adapting products and promotions to a foreign market (see Figure 19-3).[21] We first discuss the three product strategies and then turn to the two promotion strategies.

Straight product extension
Marketing a product in a foreign market without any change.

Straight product extension means marketing a product in a foreign market without any change. Top management tells its marketing people: "Take the product as is and find customers for it." The first step, however, should be to find out whether foreign consumers use that product and what form they prefer.

Straight extension has been successful in some cases and disastrous in others. Coca-Cola, Kellogg cereals, Heineken beer, and Black & Decker tools are all sold successfully in about the same form around the world. But General Foods introduced its standard powdered Jell-O in the British market only to find that British consumers prefer a solid-wafer or cake form. Straight extension is tempting because it involves no additional product-development costs, manufacturing changes, or new promotion. But it can be costly in the long run if products fail to satisfy foreign consumers.

Product adaptation
Adapting a product to meet local conditions or wants in foreign markets.

Product adaptation involves changing the product to meet local conditions or wants. For example, McDonald's serves beer in Germany and coconut, mango, and tropic mint shakes in Hong Kong. General Foods blends different coffees for the British (who drink their coffee with milk), the French (who drink their coffee black), and Latin Americans (who prefer a chicory taste). In Japan, Mister Donut serves coffee in smaller and lighter cups that better fit the fingers of the average Japanese consumer; even the doughnuts are a little smaller. In Brazil, Levi's developed its Femina jeans featuring curvaceous cuts that provide the ultra-tight fit traditionally favoured by Brazilian women. Campbell serves up soups that match unique tastes of consumers in different countries. For example, it sells duck-gizzard soup in the Guangdong Province of China; in Poland, it features *flaki*, a peppery tripe soup. And IBM adapts its worldwide product line to meet local needs. For example, IBM must make dozens of different keyboards—20 for Europe alone—to match different languages.[22]

Product invention
Creating new products or services for foreign markets.

Product invention consists of creating something new for the foreign market. This strategy can take two forms. It might mean reintroducing earlier product forms that happen to be well adapted to the needs of a given country. For example, the National Cash Register Company reintroduced its crank-operated cash register at half the price of a modern cash register and sold large numbers in Asia, Latin America, and Spain. Or a company might create a new product to meet a need in another country. For example, an enormous need exists for low-cost, high-protein foods in less developed countries. Companies such as Maple Leaf Foods, McCain, Quaker Oats, Swift, and Monsanto are researching the nutrition needs of these countries, creating new foods, and developing advertising campaigns to gain product trial and acceptance. Product invention can be costly, but the payoffs are worthwhile.

FIGURE 19-3 *Five international product and promotion strategies*

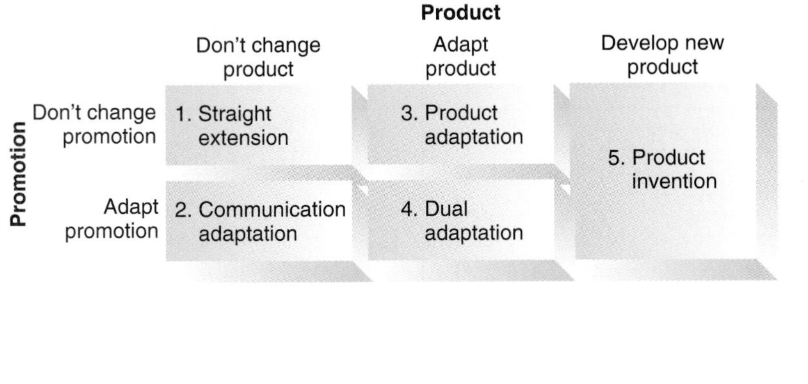

	Product		
	Don't change product	Adapt product	Develop new product
Promotion — Don't change promotion	1. Straight extension	3. Product adaptation	
Promotion — Adapt promotion	2. Communication adaptation	4. Dual adaptation	5. Product invention

PROMOTION

Companies can either adopt the same promotion strategy they used in the home market or change it for each local market. Consider advertising messages. Some global companies use a standardized advertising theme around the world. Exxon and its 70 percent-owned Canadian subsidiary, Imperial Oil, used "Put a tiger in your tank," which gained international recognition. Of course, the copy may be varied in minor ways to adjust for language differences. In Japan, for instance, where consumers have trouble pronouncing "snap, crackle, pop," the little Rice Krispies critters say "patchy, pitchy, putchy." Colours also are changed sometimes to avoid taboos in other countries. Purple is associated with death in most of Latin America; white is a mourning colour in Japan; and green is associated with jungle sickness in Malaysia. Wal-Mart had to change its advertising after its initial launch in Canada. It quickly discovered the need to learn some French and translated its all-English advertising directed at Quebec. Even names must be changed. In Sweden, Helene Curtis changed the name of its Every Night Shampoo to Every Day because Swedes usually wash their hair in the morning. Kellogg also had to rename Bran Buds cereal in Sweden, where the name roughly translates as "burned farmer." (See Marketing Highlight 19-4 for more on language blunders in international marketing.)

Communication adaptation
A global communication strategy of fully adapting advertising messages to local markets.

Canadian advertisers have produced award-winning ads that have successfully promoted products and services around the world.

Other companies follow a strategy of **communication adaptation,** fully adapting their advertising messages to local markets. Kellogg ads in North America promote the taste and nutrition of Kellogg's cereals versus competitors' brands. In France, where consumers drink little milk and eat little for breakfast, Kellogg's ads must convince consumers that cereals are a tasty and healthful breakfast.

Media also need to be adapted internationally because media availability varies from country to country. Television advertising time is very limited in Europe, for instance, ranging from four hours a day in France to none in Scandinavian countries. Advertisers must buy time months in advance, and they have little control over airtimes. Magazines also vary in effectiveness. For example, magazines are a major medium in Italy and a minor one in Austria. Newspapers are national in the United Kingdom but are only local in Spain.

The Institute of Canadian Advertising, which represents most of Canada's major agencies, launched a 1997 marketing initiative aimed at

WATCH YOUR LANGUAGE!

Many multinationals have had difficulty crossing the language barrier, with results ranging from mild embarrassment to outright failure. Seemingly innocuous brand names and advertising phrases can take on unintended or hidden meanings when translated into other languages. Careless translations can make a marketer look downright foolish to foreign consumers. We've all run across examples when buying products from foreign countries—here's one from a firm in Taiwan attempting to instruct children on how to install a ramp on a garage for toy cars:

> Before you play with, please fix the waiting plate by yourself as per below diagram. But after you once fixed it, you can play with as is and no necessary to fix off again.

Many North American firms are guilty of similar errors when marketing abroad.

The classic language blunders involve standardized brand names that do not translate well. When Coca-Cola first marketed Coke in China in the 1920s, it developed a group of Chinese characters that, when pronounced, sounded like the product name. Unfortunately, the characters actually translated to mean "bite the wax tadpole." Today, the characters on Chinese Coke bottles translate as "happiness in the mouth."

Several car makers have had similar problems when their brand names crashed into the language barrier. Chevy's Nova translated into Spanish as no va—"It doesn't go." GM changed the name to Caribe and sales increased. Ford introduced its Fiera truck only to discover that the name means "ugly old woman" in Spanish. And it introduced its Comet car in Mexico as the Caliente—slang for "streetwalker." Rolls-Royce avoided the name Silver Mist in German markets, where "mist" means "manure." Sunbeam, however, entered the German market with its Mist-Stick hair curling iron. As should have been expected, the Germans had little use for a "manure wand."

One well-intentioned firm sold its shampoo in Brazil under the name Evitol. It soon realized it was claiming to sell a "dandruff contraceptive." An American company reportedly had trouble marketing Pet milk in French-speaking areas. It seems that the word "pet" in French means, among other things, "to break wind."

Advertising themes often lose—or gain—something in the translation. The Coors beer slogan "get loose with Coors" in Spanish came out as "get the runs with Coors." Coca-Cola's "Coke adds life" theme in Japanese translated into "Coke brings your ancestors back from the dead."

Such classic infractions are soon discovered and corrected, and they may result in little more than embarrassment for the marketer. But countless other more subtle blunders may go undetected and damage product performance in less obvious ways. The multinational company must carefully screen its brand names and advertising messages to guard against those that might damage sales, make it look silly, or offend consumers in specific international markets.

Sources: Some of these and many other examples of language blunders are found in David A. Ricks, "Products That Crashed into the Language Barrier," *Business and Society Review,* Spring 1983, pp. 46–50. Also see Marty Westerman, "Death of the Frito Bandito," *American Demographics,* March 1989, pp. 28–32; and David W. Helin, "When Slogans Go Wrong," *American Demographics,* February 1992, p. 14.

---

achieving better recognition of the strong track record and worldwide capabilities of Canadian agencies. In an effort that integrated public relations, ads in trade publications, direct marketing, a web site (www.goodmedia.com/ica), and a 126-page book titled, *Canadian Advertising, Push the Boundaries,* the Institute worked to convey the message that Canadian-produced advertising travels well beyond Canada's borders. The campaign featured work done by Canadian agencies such as a promotion for the Turkish Office of Tourism designed to increase recognition of Turkey as a safe tourist destination; the Dove advertisements run in 34 countries that positioned the soap as the mildest alternative; the Duracell ads that have bolstered the product's superiority image in Mexico, Venezuela, Spain, and Hong Kong; and the Visa ads that helped to reinforce the leadership position of the card in Canada and South America.[23]

PRICE

Companies also face many problems in setting their international prices. For example, how might Black & Decker price its power tools globally? It could set a uniform price all around the world, but this amount would be too high a price in poor countries and not high enough in rich ones. It could charge what consumers in each country would bear, but this strategy ignores differences in the actual costs from country to country. Finally, the company could use a standard mark-up of its costs everywhere, but this approach might price Black & Decker out of the market in some countries where costs are high.

Regardless of how companies go about pricing their products, their foreign prices probably will be higher than their domestic prices. Makers of Feathercraft kayaks have discovered the problem of price escalation as they market in Japan. Even though the kayaks cost the Japanese consumer twice as much as they do Canadian purchasers, the firm makes its lowest margins on Japanese sales. The problem results from Japan's multi-level distribution system. A kayak may have to pass through five intermediaries before reaching the consumer, and each intermediary gets a cut of the price pie. High prices have become more problematic as Japanese consumers become more value conscious.[24]

Another problem involves setting a price for goods that a company ships to its foreign subsidiaries. If the company charges a foreign subsidiary too much, it may end up paying higher tariff duties even while paying lower income taxes in that country. If the company charges its subsidiary too little, it can be charged with *dumping*. Dumping occurs when a company either charges less than its costs or less than it charges in its home market. Thus, Harley-Davidson accused Honda and Kawasaki of dumping motorcycles on the U.S. market.[25] Canadian farmers have been charged with dumping wheat on the U.S. market. The U.S. International Trade Commission also ruled recently that Japan was dumping computer memory chips in the United States and laid stiff duties on future imports. Various governments are always watching for dumping abuses, and they often force companies to set the price charged by other competitors for the same or similar products.

DISTRIBUTION CHANNELS

Whole-channel view
Designing international channels that take into account all the necessary links in distributing the seller's products to final buyers, including the seller's headquarters organization, channels between nations, and channels within nations.

The international company must take a **whole-channel view** of the problem of distributing products to final consumers. Figure 19-4 shows the three major links between the seller and the final buyer. The first link, the *seller's headquarters organization*, supervises the channels and is part of the channel itself. The second link, *channels between nations*, moves the products to the borders of the foreign nations. The third link, *channels within nations*, moves the products from their foreign entry point to the final consumers. Some North American manufacturers may think their job is done once the product leaves their hands, but they would do well to pay more attention to its handling within foreign countries.

Channels of distribution within countries vary greatly from nation to nation. First, there are the large differences in the *numbers and types of intermediaries* serving each foreign market. For example, a Canadian company marketing in China must operate through a frustrating maze of state-controlled wholesalers and retailers. Chinese distributors often carry competitors' products and frequently refuse to share even basic sales and marketing information with their suppliers. Hustling for sales is an alien concept to Chinese distributors, who are used to selling all they can obtain. Working with or getting around this system sometimes requires substantial time and investment. When Coke and Pepsi first entered China, for example, customers bicycled up to bottling plants to get their soft drinks. Now, both companies have set up direct-distribution channels, investing heavily in trucks and refrigeration units for retailers.[26]

FIGURE 19-4 *Whole-channel concept for international marketing*

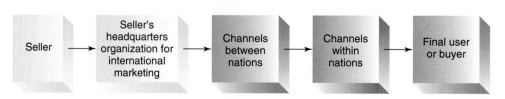

Another difference lies in the *size and character of retail units* abroad. Whereas large-scale retail chains dominate the North American scene, much retailing in other countries is done by many small independent retailers. In India, millions of retailers operate tiny shops or sell in open markets. Their markups are high, but the actual price is lowered through price haggling. Supermarkets could offer lower prices, but supermarkets are difficult to build and open because of many economic and cultural barriers. Incomes are low, and people who lack refrigeration prefer to shop daily for small amounts rather than weekly for large amounts. Packaging is not well developed because it would add too much to the cost. These factors have kept large-scale retailing from spreading rapidly in developing countries.

DECIDING ON THE GLOBAL MARKETING ORGANIZATION

Companies manage their international marketing activities in at least three different ways. Most companies first organize an export department, then create an international division, and finally become a global organization.

A firm normally gets into international marketing by simply shipping out its goods. If its international sales expand, the company organizes an *export department* with a sales manager and a few assistants. As sales increase, the export department then can expand to include various marketing services so that it can actively pursue business. If the firm moves into joint ventures or direct investment, the export department no longer will be adequate.

Many companies become involved in several international markets and ventures. A company may export to one country, license to another, have a joint ownership venture in a third, and own a subsidiary in a fourth. Sooner or later it will create an *international division* or subsidiary to handle all its international activity.

International divisions are organized in a variety of ways. The international division's corporate staff consists of marketing, manufacturing, research, finance, planning, and personnel specialists. They plan for and provide services to various operating units, which can be organized in one of three ways. They may be *geographical organizations,* with country managers who are responsible for salespeople, sales branches, distributors, and licensees in their respective countries. Or the operating units can be *world product groups,* each responsible for worldwide sales of different product groups. Finally, operating units can be *international subsidiaries,* each responsible for its own sales and profits.

Several firms have passed beyond the international division stage and become truly *global organizations.* They stop thinking of themselves as national marketers who sell abroad and start thinking of themselves as global marketers. The top corporate management and staff plan worldwide manufacturing facilities, marketing policies, financial flows, and logistical systems. The global operating units report directly to the chief executive or executive committee of the organization, not to the head of an international division. Executives are trained in worldwide operations, not just domestic *or* international. The company recruits management from many countries, buys components and supplies where they cost the least, and invests where the expected returns are greatest.

Consider the history of Nortel Ltd., Canada's premium high-tech manufacturer, for example. In the early 1970s, it sold most of its production to another member of the BCE family, Bell Canada. By the 1980s, with its state-of-the-art digital switching technology, it was making over 50 percent of its sales to the United States, and five percent to other world markets. By 1994, however, 32 percent of Nortel's $8.9 billion in revenue came from global markets and the company has set the goal of increasing this percentage to 50 percent by the year 2000.[27]

Moving into the twenty-first century, major companies must become more global if they hope to compete. As foreign companies successfully invade their domestic markets, companies must move more aggressively into foreign markets. They will have to change from companies that treat their international operations as secondary concerns to companies that view the entire world as a single borderless market.[28]

Summary of Chapter Objectives

In the past, North American companies paid little attention to international trade. If they could pick up some extra sales through exporting, that was fine. But the big market was at home, and it teemed with opportunities. Companies today can no longer afford to focus only on their domestic market, regardless of its size. Many industries are global industries, and firms that operate globally achieve lower costs and higher brand awareness. At the same time, global marketing is risky because of variable exchange rates, unstable governments, protectionist tariffs and trade barriers, and several other factors. Given the potential gains and risks of international marketing, companies need a systematic way to make their international marketing decisions.

1. **Discuss how the international trade system, economic, political-legal, and cultural environments affect a company's international marketing decisions.**

   A company must understand the global marketing environment, especially the international trade system. It must assess each foreign market's economic, political-legal, and cultural characteristics. The company must then decide on the volume of international sales it wants, how many countries it wants to market in, and which specific markets it wants to enter. This decision calls for weighing the probable rate of return on investment against the level of risk.

2. **Describe three key approaches to entering international markets.**

   The company must decide how to enter each chosen market—whether through exporting, joint venturing, or direct investment. Many companies start as exporters, move to joint ventures, and finally make a direct investment in foreign markets. In exporting, the company enters a foreign market by sending and selling products through international marketing intermediaries (indirect exporting) or the company's own department, branch, or sales representative or agent (direct exporting). When establishing a joint venture, a company enters foreign markets by joining with foreign companies to produce or market a product or service. In licensing, the company enters a foreign market by contracting with a licensee in the foreign market, offering the right to use a manufacturing process, trademark, patent, trade secret, or other item of value for a fee or royalty. Many companies start as exporters, move to joint ventures, and finally make a direct investment in foreign markets.

3. **Explain how companies adapt their marketing mixes for international markets.**

   Companies must also decide how much their products, promotion, price, and channels should be adapted for each foreign market. At one extreme, global companies use a standardized marketing mix worldwide. Others use an adapted marketing mix, in which they adjust the marketing mix to each target market, bearing more costs but hoping for a larger market share and return.

4. **Identify the three major forms of international marketing organization.**

   The company must develop an effective organization for international marketing. Most firms start with an export department and graduate to an international division. A few become global organizations, with worldwide marketing planned and managed by the top officers of the company. Global organizations view the entire world as a single, borderless market.

Key Terms

Adapted marketing mix *(p. 664)*	Exporting *(p. 661)*	Product adaptation *(p. 665)*
Communication adaptation *(p. 666)*	Global firm *(p. 647)*	Product invention *(p. 665)*
Contract manufacturing *(p. 663)*	Global industry *(p. 647)*	Quota *(p. 648)*
Countertrade *(p. 655)*	Joint ownership *(p. 663)*	Standardized marketing mix
Direct investment *(p. 663)*	Joint venturing *(p. 662)*	*(p. 664)*
Economic community *(p. 650)*	Licensing *(p. 662)*	Straight product extension *(p. 665)*
Embargo *(p. 648)*	Management contracting *(p. 663)*	Tariff *(p. 648)*
Exchange controls *(p. 648)*	Non-tariff trade barriers *(p. 648)*	Whole-channel view *(p. 668)*

Discussing the Issues

1. With all the problems facing companies that "go global," explain why so many companies are choosing to expand internationally. What are the advantages of expanding beyond the domestic market?

2. Canadians have widely diverging opinions about the pros and cons of the North American Free Trade Agreement (NAFTA). Conduct a debate with your classmates. Do you think the agreement should be expanded or dropped?

3. Some marketers argue that bribery is wrong no matter what the circumstances. Others believe that it is the only way companies can successfully do business in some countries. Debate this issue in your class.

4. Many companies have manufacturing plants overseas that they use to produce goods later marketed in North America. They are often accused of exploiting labour in these countries by paying extremely low wages and condoning poor working conditions, while at the same time they pay millions to advertise their products with highly paid celebrities. Companies such as Nike, which manufacture overseas, defend themselves saying that they pay above-average wages and enforce labour codes above those generally found in lesser developed countries. Many also claim that their companies work diligently to improve conditions. Do you think international business improves world conditions or exploits lesser developed economies?

5. "Dumping" leads to price savings to the consumer. Determine why governments make dumping illegal. What are the *disadvantages* to the consumer of dumping by foreign firms?

6. Which type of international marketing organization would you suggest for the following companies? (a) Cannondale Bicycles, selling three models in the Far East; (b) a small Canadian manufacturer of toys, marketing its products in Europe; and (c) Dodge, planning to sell its full line of cars and trucks in Kuwait.

Applying the Concepts

1. Marketing Highlight 19-3 describes some emerging economies that might be of interest to marketers. Think of an area not covered in this highlight (South Africa, Peru, Korea, Finland, etc.). Gather information on this country that you might use if you were a marketing manager of a small Canadian software firm that produces games designed for children aged 7 to 12. Be sure to use the Internet in your search (for example, the site pacific.commerce.ubc.ca/ keith.Lectures/mktg.html describes the decisions faced by a company contemplating entry into a new country. Ciber.bus.msu.edu/busres/ tradeshow.htm lists international trade shows nd events). Organize the information you find, noting if it is important or an unimportant factor in your decision to enter the market you've chosen to study.

2. Tourism is one of Canada's fastest-growing industries. Its lifeblood depends on being

able to attract foreign tourists. Go to your university library and find several foreign magazines. Locate pictures, stories, or ads featuring Canadian travel destinations. Study what you find. Look at the size and layout of the stories and ads, and see if you can understand basically what is being said. How is Canada trying to differentiate itself as a travel destination? What regions are advertising most? What is the basis of their appeals? How would you promote tourism in your area?

References

1. Quotations from Stuart Foxman, "Sponsored Supplement: The NBA in Canada: Celebrating Season II," *Strategy: The Canadian Marketing Report*, January 6, 1997, p. 31; Marc Gunther, "They All Want to Be Like Mike," *Fortune*, July 21, 1997, pp. 51–53; (Time Inc. All rights reserved.) Also see David Berman, "Mr. Big," *Canadian Business*, June 1997, pp. 59–70; David Berman, "Just Wave Money," *Canadian Business*, June 1996, pp. 80–88; Lesley Goodson, "MBA Canada: Marketing Debut, Grizzlies & Raptors Tip Off," *Strategy: The Canadian Marketing Report*, February 19, 1996, pp. 30, 35; Eve Lazarus, "Grizzlies Take Their Marketing Personally," *Marketing*, November 10, 1997, p. 3; Bob Ryan, "Hoop Dreams," *Sales & Marketing Management*, December 1996, pp. 48–53; and Jeff Jensen, "'Experiential Branding' Makes It to the Big Leagues," *Advertising Age*, April 14, 1997, pp. 20, 14.

2. "1997 Canada Export Awards," Department of Foreign Affairs and International Trade, insert in *Report on Business*, July 1997.

3. "Exports, Eh?" *and Canadian Business*, January 1997, p. 21; and "Canada: An Olympian of International Trade," an advertising supplement, Department of Foreign Affairs and International Trade, insert in *Canadian Business*, January 1997.

4. Wayne Gooding, "Fear of Trying," *Report on Business*, April 1992, pp. 33-40; Michael Salter, "Gone Global," *Report on Business*, January 1996, p. 87.

5. Douglas Harbrecht and Owen Ullmann, "Finally GATT May Fly," *Business Week*, December 29, 1993, pp. 36–37. Also see Cateora, *International Marketing*, pp. 49–51; and Louis S. Richman, "What's Next After GATT's Victory?" *Fortune*, January 10, 1994, pp. 66–70.

6. For more on the European Union, see Andrew Hilton, "Mythology, Markets, and the Emerging Europe," *Harvard Business Review*, November-December 1992, pp. 50–54; Rebecca Piirto Heath, "Think Globally," Marketing Tools Supplement, *American Demographics*, October 1996, pp. 49–54; "Ever More Complicated Union," *The Economist*, March 30, 1996, pp. 47–49; and "Around Europe in 40 Years," *The Economist*, May 31, 1997, p. S4.

7. Alan Freeman, "Leaders Aim for Free Trade at APEC Forum," *Globe and Mail* November 12, 1994, p. B3; "The Vancouver Summit," *Globe and Mail*, November 19, 1997, pp. D1–D4.

8. For more reading on free-trade zones, see Blayne Cutler, "North American Demographics," *American Demographics*, March 1992, pp. 38–42; Andrew Hilton, "Mythology, Markets, and the Emerging Europe," *Harvard Business Review*, November–December 1992, pp. 50–54; Geoffrey Brewer, "New World Orders," *Sales & Marketing Management*, January 1994, pp. 59–63; Roberto E. Batres, "Benefiting from NAFTA: New Opportunities in North America," *Prizm*, Arthur D. Little, Inc., Cambridge, MA, First Quarter, 1994, pp. 17–29; and William C. Symonds, "Meanwhile, to the North, NAFTA Is a Smash," *Business Week*, February 27, 1995, p. 66.

9. Gayle MacDonald, "Consultant Warns of Short Trade Vision," *Globe and Mail*, October 16, 1997, p. B15; Gordon Ritchie, "Sitting on Top of the World," in "Post 2000," *Report on the Nation, The Financial Post*, October 4, 1997, p. 4; Konrad Yarkabuski, "Textile Entrepreneurs Thriving on Free Trade," *Globe and Mail*, November 24, 1997, pp. B1, B4.

10. Earl Fry, "In Spite of Trade Frictions, NAFTA's Been a Success," *The Financial Post*, March 23, 1996, p. 21; Peter Morton, "The Never-Ending Story," *The Financial Post*, March 16, 1996, p. 21; and Peter Morton, "Canadian Firms Face Cuba Fallout," *The Financial Post*, March 13, 1996, p. 1.

11. Gordon Pitts, "Waters for the World," *Globe and Mail*, September 19, 1994, p. B4.

12. John Stackhouse, "Trade Team Signs Indian Deals," *Globe and Mail*, January 11, 1996, pp. B1, B8.

13. Bill Saporito, "Where the Global Action Is," *Fortune*, Special Issue on "The Tough New Consumer," autumn-winter 1993, pp. 62–65. Also see Keegan and Green, *Principles of Global Marketing*, pp. 39–44.

14. For these and other examples, see Louis Kraar, "How to Sell to Cashless Buyers," *Fortune*, November 7, 1988, pp. 147–154; Cyndee Miller, "Worldwide Money Crunch Fuels More International Barter," *Marketing News*, March 2, 1992, p. 5; and Nathaniel Gilbert, "The Case for Countertrade," *Across the Board*, May 1992, pp. 43–45.

15. Rebecca Piirto Heath, "Think Globally," *Marketing Tools*, October 1996, pp. 49–54.

16. Louis Kraar, "Pepsi's Pitch to Quench Chinese Thirsts," *Fortune*, March 17, 1986, p. 58. Also see Alan Farnham, "Ready to Ride Out China's Turmoil," *Fortune*, July 3, 1989, pp. 117–118; and Pete Engardio, "China Fever Strikes Again," *Business Week*, March 29, 1993, pp. 46–47.

17. Lidna Grant, "GE's 'Smart Bomb' Strategy," *Fortune*, July 21, 1997, pp. 109–110.

18. Robert Williamson, "Architects Draw on Friendship," *Globe and Mail*, September 7, 1993, pp. B1, B9.

19. Greg Keenan, "Magna Buys U.K. Business," *Globe and Mail*, March 21, 1996, p. B1.

20. See George S. Yip, "Global Strategy . . . In a World of Nations?" *Sloan Management Review,* Fall 1989, pp. 29–41; Kamran Kashani, "Beware the Pitfalls of Global Marketing," *Harvard Business Review,* September–October 1989, pp. 91–98; Saeed Saminee and Kendall Roth, "The Influence of Global Marketing Standardization on Performance," *Journal of Marketing,* April 1992, pp. 1–17; David M. Szymanski, Sundar G. Bharadwaj, and Rajan Varadarajan, "Standardization versus Adaptation of International Marketing Strategy: An Empirical Investigation," *Journal of Marketing,* October 1993, pp. 1–17; and Ashish Banerjee, "Global Campaigns Don't Work; Multinationals Do," *Advertising Age,* April 18, 1994.

21. See Keegan, *Global Marketing Management,* 4th ed. (Englewood Cliffs, NJ: Prentice Hall, 1989), pp. 378–381. Also see Peter G. P. Walters and Brian Toyne, "Product Modification and Standardization in International Markets: Strategic Options and Facilitating Policies," *Columbia Journal of World Business,* Winter 1989, pp. 37–44.

22. For these and other examples, see Andrew Kupfer, "How to Be a Global Manager," *Fortune,* March 14, 1988, pp. 52–58; Maria Shao, "For Levi's: A Flattering Fit Overseas," *Business Week,* November 5, 1990, 76–77; and Joseph Weber, "Campbell: Now It's M-M-Global," *Business Week,* March 15, 1993, pp. 52–53.

23. "The Showcase," *Marketing,* October 20, 1997, pp. 14–19.

24. Alan Freeman, "B.C.'s Feathercraft Kayaks Making Waves in Japan," *Globe and Mail,* July 25, 1994, pp. B1, B2.

25. See Michael Oneal, "Harley-Davidson: Ready to Hit the Road Again," *Business Week,* July 21, 1986, p. 70.

26. See Shao, "Laying the Foundation for the Great Mall of China," p. 69.

27. Michael Salter, "Gone Global," *Report on Business,* January 1996, p. 87.

28. See Kenichi Ohmae, "Managing in a Borderless World," *Harvard Business Review,* May–June 1989, pp. 152–161; William J. Holstein, "The Stateless Corporation," *Business Week,* May 14, 1990, pp. 98–105; and John A. Byrne and Kathleen Kerwin, "Borderless Management," *Business Week,* May 23, 1994, pp. 24–26.

Company Case 19

BURGER KING: SELLING WHOPPERS IN JAPAN

"International is where it's at," explains Ron Paul, a Technomic consultant. "The fast-food burger category is going to find its better growth opportunity overseas. We're close to saturation in the United States. That's why McDonald's has been so aggressive in overseas markets."

That's also why Burger King must be so aggressive in Japan. McDonald's entered the Japanese market 25 years ago and now has 2000 outlets there generating $3.6 billion in sales—that's *half* of the entire fast-food burger market in Japan. In addition, McDonald's generates 47 percent of its corporate profits from its 7000 units overseas, whereas Burger King generates only 19 percent of company sales from its 1600 units overseas. Worldwide, Burger King ranks fourth behind McDonald's, KFC, and Pizza Hut. With North American markets saturated, and the mad-cow disease scare slowing sales in Europe, Burger King must find new areas to expand.

In Japan, Burger King will face stiff competition. Not only is McDonald's well entrenched there, but KFC also has 1040 stores in Japan, making it number two in the Japanese fast-food market. Between them, McDonald's and KFC create a formidable barrier to the entry of other firms. These big players have taken most of the good locations, leaving only marginal sites for would-be competitors.

Just ask the folks at Wendy's, which made a major push in Japan in the 1980s, but after 16 years has only 67 outlets in the region. Wendy's is facing difficulty finding deep-pocket players who want to open fast-food restaurants. Even local officials of Daiei, Inc., which licenses Wendy's in Japan, concede that the entry attempt has been a failure.

Burger King tried to enter the Japanese market once before. It began selling franchises there 20 years ago; franchisees paid an initial franchise fee plus royalties to the parent corporation. However, the royalties were too high and the operation failed. If that weren't enough, the second-ranked burger place in Japan is a *local* competitor, Mos Burger, which accounts for 25 percent of the market.

In addition to Burger King's previous failure, the near saturation of the Japanese market, and stiff foreign and local competition, the company faces another problem in Japan. Burger wars have plagued the entire fast-food industry and almost eliminated profits—even for McDonald's. Burger King figures that this could be an advantage, because the competitors' pockets are less full than usual. However, as a result of the burger wars, Japanese consumers are accustomed to getting "cheap burgers," and Burger King's Whoppers tend to cost more.

Burger King recognizes that this time it must find an innovative way to enter the market. It must attract attention and obtain good locations in an almost saturated market. It will not be an easy task. Due to the limited amount of land in Japan, real estate costs much more than in North America. Finding good sites will be difficult. Burger King will also have to convince Japanese consumers to pay more for a burger. Yet Japanese customers tend to be careful purchasers and to look for good value for their yen.

The solution? Joint ventures. Burger King joined with Japan Tobacco Inc. to form Burger King Japan. Because Japan Tobacco is two-thirds owned by the Japanese Ministry of Finance, it has deep pockets. Its first move was to buy out Morinaga Love Hamburger chain and immediately convert the 36 Morinaga Love restaurants to Burger King outlets. Now, other struggling burger chains have expressed an interest in being acquired by Burger King Japan. Even big retailers such as Ito-Yokado are inquiring about the possibility of opening Burger King restaurants in their shopping centres as an alternative to McDonald's.

In addition, the Japanese government has relaxed restrictions on how gasoline is sold, and Burger King hopes to place stores in gas-and-burger outlets. Such an arrangement provides advantages for both parties. Gas companies get a new competitive weapon with which to attract customers, and Burger King avoids the high cost of developing stand-alone sites. Furthermore, Burger King already operates gas-and-burger stations in New Zealand and Australia, so it has experience with this kind of operation. And Burger King is talking to Shell Sekiyu K.K., a unit of Royal Dutch/Shell Group.

While some observers believe that Burger King's lack of name recognition in Japan is a disadvantage, Burger King thinks it can capitalize on this void to create an upscale image. It believes that a high-class image will help to set it apart from McDonald's.

To appeal to affluent Japanese teenagers, nearly all Burger King restaurants will have a "retro look" of 1950s and 1960s pop culture. Sales for Burger King have jumped 40 percent to 50 percent with the pop theme.

For parents, the appeal may be somewhat different. Whereas McDonald's sells teriyaki burgers and fried rice in Japan, Burger King wants to focus on its traditional burgers. "There were not enough vegetables at most other places," says approving mother Midori Morisaka, who brought her five-year-old son to a Tokyo Burger King. Consequently, the Whopper with its healthy serving of tomatoes and lettuce, has strong appeal for her.

For Japanese consumers in general, Mr. Yuji Kagohashi, president of Burger King Japan, wants to capitalize on Burger King's big competitive advantage—flame broiling. He reasons, "Japanese restaurants often put the kitchen's flames up front to lure in customers, and we can do the same. Why does Burger King hide its biggest weapon against McDonald's in the back of the restaurant?"

Putting the flames up front may be a good idea for Burger King for another reason—lack of promotional funds. With so many outlets to open, Burger King lacks

funds to engage in the heavy promotional campaigns that McDonald's and KFC usually launch. Instead, it relies on promotional events such as grand openings, which generate publicity and are promoted through circulars that are distributed in the local market.

Is the competition concerned? Not really—not now. "McDonald's is the king of burgers," says Shinji Minakata, managing director of Dairy Queen, a firm that has cut back its product line to coffee and ice cream because of its inability to sell burgers in Japan. "McDonald's has ushered us into the age of 80-yen hamburgers," says Sumeo Yokokawa, a manager at KFC Japan. "A burger is a burger for most people now; flame-broiling and extra vegetables are at best an incremental difference most customers don't really care about."

McDonald's isn't afraid. The industry leader is moving ahead with plans to have 10 000 outlets in Japan by the year 2006. Even if Burger King opens 200 a year for the next decade, it will still remain far behind McDonald's in number of locations, and that can really make a difference. Remember Midori Morisaka? There's no Burger King in suburban Chiba where her family lives. To get a Burger King Whopper, she and her son had to make a long trip downtown. The question is, how many customers will build a preference for a burger that is so hard to get to?

"We don't see them as a threat at all," adds Jun Fujita, assistant manager of a McDonald's in Tokyo's Setagaya neighbourhood, where a Burger King will open in March. "Who's ever heard of Burger King?"

QUESTIONS

1. What aspects of Japan's economic, political-legal, and cultural environments are important for Burger King to understand? How will Japan's recent stock-market woes affect Burger King's strategy?

2. Why have Burger King and other companies in the case decided to enter foreign markets? Why have they chosen Japan? Do you agree with their decisions?

3. Contrast Burger King's entry strategy 20 years ago with its present entry strategy. What are the differences? Is the new entry strategy likely to be more successful? If so, why?

4. Evaluate Burger King's proposed marketing strategy and program for Japan. Which elements of its marketing program do you think will be successful? Which ones are likely to be less successful?

Sources: Alina Matas, "Burger King Corp. plans 200 stores for Japan," *Miami Herald*, July 16, 1996, p. 7; Jack Russell, "Burger King vs. giants in Japan," *Advertising Age*, August 1, 1996, p. 34; Norihiko Shirouzu, "Whoppers face entrenched foes in Japan: Big Macs," *Wall Street Journal*, February 4, 1997, pp. B1 and B6; Edith Hill Updike, "Burger King wants to build a kingdom in Asia," *Business Week*, November 25, 1996, p. 52.

Video Case 19

AIR TRANSAT'S GLOBAL TOUR

Air Transat, headquartered in Montreal, is the only surviving Canadian-owned tour operator in the $5-billion Canadian tour industry. While just a few years ago there were several other Canadian operators, they have either been bought out by European firms or have gone bankrupt. Jean Marc Eustache, the owner of Transat, is now trying to become an international player himself by expanding into Europe. He has already purchased a French tour operator and is considering the purchase of a British firm, which will give him even more access to the European tourist market.

Eustache started in the travel industry over 20 years ago when he was a university student. At the time he was a Marxist and a student leader in Quebec. He believed that travel should be accessible to all so he started a travel company specializing in affordable student travel, even though he was afraid of flying. Although still in the travel business, his philosophical orientation has changed significantly. Eustache is now a capitalist who is not afraid of making profits. His company boasts three percent margins, which are among the highest in the industry. He is, however, still afraid of flying.

In the tour industry, size is important. The larger the firm, the more cost advantages it can enjoy. For example, as the firm becomes larger it has more power with hotels and other suppliers to negotiate better deals. These cost advantages are important in an industry that has regular price wars between operators. Consumers often hold out for last-minute specials, which forces the tour operators to sell below cost. To compete effectively in this industry, Transat has grown through the purchase of other firms and has become vertically integrated. In addition to purchasing two Canadian tour operators, it owns its own travel agency, baggage-handling organization and planes. Eustache hopes to eventually purchase hotels and ships to achieve even greater size and further vertical integration. He thinks of his company as a "leisure group," a perspective that presents several opportunities for growth.

Transat's recent moves to expand to Europe will provide not only cost advantages but they will also allow the company to better manage consumer demand cycles in North America. The consumer purchase cycles of vacations are different in Europe and North America. While Canadians want to travel in the winter and not in the summer, consumers in European countries such as the United Kingdom and France want to travel in the summer, not the winter. By servicing both markets, Transat Air will be able to avoid overcapacity during the traditional, North American non-peak times.

As Eustache looks at companies to purchase, he must be careful that Transat does not itself become the target of a takeover. A few years ago a larger company tried, unsuccessfully, to take over Transat Air. Eustache's goal is to become one of the five or six largest tour companies in the world. But as he strives to achieve that goal, Eustache will need to be one step ahead of competitive moves in the global tourism marketplace.

QUESTIONS:

1. What mode of entry is Air Transat using to enter international markets?

2. How is the choice of mode of entry into international markets different for a service firm such Air Transat, as compared to a manufacturing firm?

3. As Air Transat expands globally, what factors should they consider in deciding whether to standardize or adapt aspects of their marketing mix?

Source: This case was prepared by Auleen Carson and is based on "Transat Air," *Venture,* (March 16, 1997).

CHAPTER 20

MARKETING AND SOCIETY

Social Responsibility and Marketing Ethics

HOW TO BE A LOCAL HERO

BE PICKY Do you ever feel overwhelmed by all the good causes that ask for donations? You'd like to help every one, but it's just not possible. Local Heroes know that the answer is to be picky. ❦ Review the causes you already support and be sure that your experience with each of them is rewarding. ❦ Then think about other issues you feel are critical to you and your community. ❦ Now look for the organizations that work in these areas. Call them up, visit their offices, or write for their brochures and find out all you can about what they do. The more involved you get, the more satisfaction you'll get back. ❦ Nobody expects you to say yes all the time, but you can be a Local Hero by making some causes, "Your Causes". So be picky. And be a Local Hero.

IMAGINE
A New Spirit
of Giving

A national program to encourage giving and volunteering.

"New models of philanthropy [are emerging that emphasize] a far closer relationship among business, individuals and communities ... corporations are not just giving donations to charity but are entering partnerships that exemplify the best creative approaches to meeting community needs." With these words, Courtney Pratt, president of Noranda Inc. and chair of Imagine, opened the 1997 New Spirit of Community awards celebration held to recognize companies that actively and productively support a range of social causes. Imagine is a program designed to encourage firms to invest at least one percent of their pretax profits in the charities and non-profit organizations of their choice and to encourage employee volunteerism. The program currently has more than 400 corporate members and is administered by the Canadian Centre of Philanthropy. Their web site (http://www.ccp.ca) contains a wealth of information to guide both firms and non-profit organizations in these efforts.

Courtney Pratt's words are the hallmark of an era where corporations are looking for new ways to demonstrate their social responsibility. Rather than just focusing on business problems, many organizations also strive to improve social welfare by donating human resources, expertise and knowledge, products, services, and money to resolve a wide range of social dilemmas. These efforts range from cause-related marketing programs (in which firms donate a portion of the sales revenue from a product to a specific cause), to what is becoming known as strategic philanthropy and social alliances, in which firms join with non-profit organizations to resolve complex, long-term social issues.

The top award winner in 1997 was the partnership between Bell Canada and Kids Help Phone. Kids Help Phone is a national, not-for-profit fundraising organization dedicated to the health and well-being of Canadian children. Bell, the founding sponsor of the organization, has been working with Kids Help Phone for over seven years. There was a natural fit between the telecommunications company and a charity that helps young people over phone lines. The program also fits with Bell's renewed positioning and focus on youth and community commitment.

When you finish this chapter, you should be able to

1. Identify the major social criticisms of marketing.

2. Define consumerism and environmentalism and explain how they affect marketing strategies.

3. Describe the principles of socially responsible marketing.

4. Explain the role of ethics in marketing.

5. List the major principles for public policy toward marketing.

Kids Help Phone currently receives over 4000 calls a day from young people who need to discuss problems or are reaching out for help. The bilingual toll-free service (1-800-668-6868) provides professional counselling to kids in need—24 hours a day, 365 days a year. Kids Help Phone has answered more than 1.2 million calls. Even with its $5-million budget, it can handle only one-third of the calls it receives. Kids Help Phone was also increasingly concerned that it was not reaching part of the population it was established to help. Since 78 percent of the calls come from females, Kids Help Phone believed that males were facing social obstacles when it came to sharing their problems and concerns with others. Kids Help Phone believed that the Internet might be a better avenue for addressing the needs of male youth.

Bell quickly responded to the need and committed $1.5 million to the project. Working with its online provider, MediaLinx Interactive, Bell and Kids Help Phone designed and launched a 130-page web site aimed at providing youth with information on topics ranging from AIDS to physical/sexual abuse, from eating disorders to divorce, from pregnancy to suicide, drugs and alcohol (kidshelp. sympatico.ca). In addition to the funding, Bell provides technological resources and management personnel to the program. Its advertising agency, BBDO, developed an integrated print, television, outdoor, and transit campaign to build awareness of the site. The web site has been a tremendous success and has won a number of awards. The pride that Bell employees take in the program is another benefit derived from the effort.

Is Bell alone in its social responsibility and social marketing efforts? Hardly! Firms of all shapes and sizes are adopting social marketing programs as part of their arsenal. Molson Breweries has a long history of social marketing. Molson and its co-sponsors have raised over $4 million for AIDS research through programs such as Dancers for Life. Molson stresses that a number of important principles have to be followed when undertaking this type of effort. First, the company must select a cause that is relevant to its target audience. Next, the firm must make a substantial contribution to the cause and should be prepared to commit for the long term. Finally, a firm can generate favourable publicity for its brands in conjunction with this type of effort if it doesn't exploit the cause.

McDonald's Restaurants of Canada is another social marketer. It has a long-standing program whereby it raises funds for Ronald McDonald houses—places where families of critically ill children can stay while their child is hospitalized. During McHappy Days, its over 700 Canadian restaurants donate $1 from the sale of every Big Mac. Under the umbrella of its Always brands, Procter & Gamble acts as a national sponsor of the Canadian Breast Cancer Foundation. Like many firms that advocate social marketing, P&G didn't just contribute funds, it also encourages its employees to join the effort by participating in fundraising activities such as the "Run for a Cure." Nissan Canada partners with Meals on Wheels to deliver hot lunches to the elderly and shut-ins. Sears Canada has joined with Industry Canada to provide 100 000 refurbished computers and printers to classrooms and libraries across Canada. After a survey of its customers revealed that the well-being of children was the primary issue among Sears' diverse customer base, the firm settled on this program, titled Computers for Schools. Sears not only donated 1000 computers from its own headquarters, but it also used its 110 outlets and 1800 catalogue offices to create awareness of the program, act as drop-off sites for companies wishing to donate their computers, and used its fleet of trucks to transport donated PCs to refurbishment centres.

It's not just large companies that are responding to calls for help. Wascana Energy of Regina responded to the school board's appeal for assistance. Volunteers from the company adopted a school in a low-income district. They participate in a breakfast program, supply and distribute Christmas gifts, run a "job shadowing" program, host sports activities, and sponsor an awards program that helped the school address major issues including students' poor attitudes toward education and low attendance rates.

Why are companies taking on these expanded roles and responsibilities? Many businesses see social marketing as another means of reaching their target customers and enhancing the value of their brands. They align themselves with not-for-profit organizations in order to break through the clutter of traditional advertising and add distinctiveness and value to their offerings. Molson, for example, believes its program helped build stronger relationships with customers, enhanced its corporate image, and created a sense of pride among its employees. Sears believes it is reinforcing its position as Canada's family store and its reputation as a company that supports communities. Other firms want to create lifestyle associations between themselves and the causes they support. They develop social marketing programs to address corporate or brand image problems, build brand loyalty, and address issues of low employee morale and productivity. Being a socially responsible corporate citizen may even help firms deal with regulatory threats. It also must be stressed that many marketers involved in these programs are sincerely involved in the causes they choose as partners. They work diligently with their not-for-profit partner to resolve the social issue. The final, and perhaps most important reason corporations are becoming more socially responsible is that their customers are demanding more from corporations. A recent survey revealed that 20 percent of Canadians believe business should work to address social problems.

Thus, social marketing appears to be here to stay according to 82 percent of Canadian executives recently surveyed. Almost two-thirds of companies polled utilize some form of social marketing and many firms plan to expand these efforts.[1]

Responsible marketers discover what consumers want and respond with the right products, priced to give good value to buyers and profit to the producer. The *marketing concept* is a philosophy of customer service and mutual gain.

Not all marketers follow the marketing concept, however. In fact, some companies use questionable marketing practices, and some marketing actions that seem innocent in themselves strongly affect society. Consider the sale of cigarettes. Theoretically, companies should be free to sell cigarettes, and smokers should be free to buy them. But this transaction affects the public interest. First, the smoker may be shortening his or her own life. Second, smoking places a health-care burden on the smoker's family and on society at large. Third, other people around the smoker may suffer discomfort and harm from second-hand smoke. Thus, private transactions may involve larger questions of public policy.

This chapter examines the social effects of marketing practices. We examine several questions: What are the most frequent social criticisms of marketing? What steps have private citizens taken to curb marketing ills? What steps have legislators and government agencies taken to curb marketing ills? What steps have enlightened companies taken to carry out socially responsible and ethical marketing? We examine how marketing affects and is affected by each of these issues.

■ SOCIAL CRITICISMS OF MARKETING

Marketing receives much criticism. Some of this criticism is justified; much is not. Social critics claim that certain marketing practices hurt individual consumers, society as a whole, and other business firms.

MARKETING'S IMPACT ON INDIVIDUAL CONSUMERS

Consumers have many concerns about how well the marketing system serves their interests. Surveys usually show that consumers hold mixed or even slightly unfavourable attitudes toward marketing practices.[2] Consumer advocates, government agencies, and other critics have accused marketing of harming consumers through high prices, deceptive practices, high-pressure selling, shoddy or unsafe products, planned obsolescence, and poor service to disadvantaged consumers.

High Prices

Many critics charge that the marketing system causes prices to be higher than they would be under more "sensible" systems. They point to three factors—*high costs of distribution, high advertising and promotion costs*, and *excessive markups*.

HIGH COSTS OF DISTRIBUTION. A longstanding charge is that greedy intermediaries mark up prices beyond the value of their services. Critics charge either that there are too many intermediaries or that intermediaries are inefficient and poorly run, that they provide unnecessary or duplicate services, and that they practise poor management and planning. As a result, distribution costs too much, and consumers pay for these excessive costs in the form of higher prices.

How do retailers answer these charges? They argue as follows: First, intermediaries do work that would otherwise have to be done by manufacturers or consumers. Second, markups reflect services that consumers themselves want—more convenience, larger stores and assortment, longer store hours, return privileges, and others. Third, the costs of operating stores keep rising, forcing retailers to raise their prices. Fourth, retail competition is so intense that margins are actually quite low. For example, after taxes, supermarket chains are typically left with one to three percent profit on their sales. If some resellers try to charge too much relative to the value they add, other resellers will step in with lower prices. Low-price stores such as The Dollar Store, Zellers, Wal-Mart, and other discounters pressure their competitors to operate efficiently and keep their prices down.

HIGH ADVERTISING AND PROMOTION COSTS. Modern marketing also is accused of pushing up prices because of heavy advertising and sales promotion. For example, a dozen tablets of a heavily promoted brand of aspirin sell for the same price as 100 tablets of less promoted brands. Differentiated products—cosmetics, detergents, toiletries—include promotion and packaging costs that can amount to 40 percent or more of the manufacturer's price to the retailer. Critics charge that much of the packaging and promotion adds only psychological value to the product rather than functional value. Retailers use additional promotions—advertising, displays, and sweepstakes—that add several cents more to retail prices.

Some retailers use high markups, but the higher prices cover services that consumers want.

Marketers answer these charges in several ways. First, consumers want more than the merely functional qualities of products. They also want psychological benefits—they want to feel wealthy, beautiful, or special. Consumers usually can buy functional versions or products at lower prices but often are willing to pay more for products that also provide desired psychological benefits. Second, branding gives buyers confidence. A brand name implies a certain quality, and consumers are willing to pay for well-known brands even if they cost a little more. Third, heavy advertising is needed to inform millions of potential buyers of the merits of a brand. If consumers want to know what is available on the market, they must expect manufacturers to spend large sums of money on advertising. Fourth, heavy advertising and promotion may be necessary for a firm to match competitors' efforts. The business

would lose "share of mind" if it did not match competitive spending. At the same time, companies are cost-conscious about promotion and try to spend their money wisely. Finally, heavy sales promotion is needed to time to time because goods are produced ahead of demand in a mass-production economy. Special incentives have to be offered in order to sell inventories.

EXCESSIVE MARKUPS.   Critics also charge that some companies mark up goods excessively. They point to the drug industry, where a pill costing five cents to make may cost the consumer 40 cents to buy. They point to the pricing tactics of funeral homes that prey on the emotions on bereaved relatives and to the high charges for television and auto repair.

Marketers respond that most businesses try to deal fairly with consumers because they want repeat business. Most consumer abuses are unintentional. When shady marketers do take advantage of consumers, they should be reported to the police, Better Business Bureaus, and to provincial ministries of Consumer and Commercial Relations. Marketers also respond that consumers often don't understand the reason for high markups. For example, pharmaceutical markups must cover the costs of purchasing, promoting, and distributing existing medicines plus the high research and development costs of finding new medicines.

Better Business Bureau
www.bbb.org/

Deceptive Practices

Marketers sometimes are accused of deceptive practices that lead consumers to believe they will get more value than they actually do. Deceptive practices fall into three groups: deceptive pricing, promotion, and packaging. *Deceptive pricing* includes practices such as falsely advertising "factory" or "wholesale" prices or a large price reduction from a phony high retail list price. The Competition Bureau has taken action against merchants who advertise false values, sell old merchandise as new, or charge too much for credit. For example, Montreal-based Suzy Shier Ltd., which operates 375 outlets across Canada, was fined $300 000 in 1995 by the Federal Bureau of Competition after it was found guilty of misleading advertising. The firm, which also operates La Senza and L.A. Express stores, was found to be double-tagging merchandise. While double-tagging, the practice of placing a sales ticket showing an original price and another ticket showing a sales price of a piece of clothing, it is not in and of itself illegal, Suzy Shier violated the law because it had not sold a substantial volume of goods at the original price. In fact, it was found that much of the double-tagging was done at the factory. Color Your World has also been found guilty of this practice; The Bay is fighting similar charges. When defending themselves, these companies claim that double-tagging is widely practised and that consumers know nothing is ever sold at the original price anymore.[3]

Deceptive promotion includes practices such as overstating the product's features or performance, luring the customer to the store for a bargain that is out of stock, or running rigged contests. *Deceptive packaging* includes exaggerating package contents through subtle design, not filling the package to the top, using misleading labelling, or describing size in misleading terms.

Deceptive practices have led to industry self-regulation standards as well as legislation and other consumer-protection actions. The Competition Act forbids many of the practices. The Advertising Standards Council has published several guidelines listing deceptive practices. The toughest problem is defining what is "deceptive." For example, some years ago, Shell Oil advertised that Super Shell gasoline with platformate gave more mileage than the same gasoline without platformate. Although this was true, what Shell did not say is that almost *all* gasoline includes platformate. Its defence was that it had never claimed that platformate was found only in Shell gasoline. But even though the message was literally true, it was ruled that the ad's *intent* was to deceive.

Taxi Advertising and Design created controversy as well as a new position for Manager Jeans with its 'X-rated' billboards.

Marketers argue that most companies avoid deceptive practices because such practices harm their business in the long run. If consumers do not get what they expect, they will switch to more reliable products. In addition, consumers usually protect themselves from deception. Most consumers recognize a marketer's selling intent and are careful when they buy, sometimes to the point of not believing completely true product claims.

High-Pressure Selling

Salespeople are sometimes accused of high-pressure selling that persuades people to buy goods they had no intention of buying. It is often said that encyclopedias, insurance, real estate, cars, and jewellery are *sold*, not *bought*. Salespeople are trained to deliver smooth, canned talks to entice purchase. They sell hard because sales contests promise big prizes to those who sell the most.

Marketers know that buyers often can be talked into buying unwanted or unneeded things. Laws require door-to-door salespeople to announce that they are selling a product. Buyers also have a "three-day cooling-off period" in which they can cancel a contract after rethinking it. In addition, consumers can complain to Better Business Bureaus or to provincial ministries when they feel that undue selling pressure has been applied.

Shoddy or Unsafe Products

Another criticism is that products lack the quality they should have. One complaint is that many products are not made well or services did not perform well. Such complaints have been lodged against products and services ranging from home appliances, automobiles, and clothing to home and auto repair services.

A second complaint is that many products deliver little benefit. For example, some consumers are surprised to learn that many of the "healthy" foods being marketed today, ranging from cholesterol-free salad dressings and low-fat frozen dinners to high-fibre bran cereals, may have little nutritional value. In fact, they may even be harmful.

> [Despite] sincere efforts on the part of most marketers to provide healthier products, ... many promises emblazoned on packages and used as ad slogans continue to confuse nutritionally uninformed consumers and ... may actually be harmful to that group.... [Many consumers] incorrectly assume the product is "safe" and eat greater amounts than are good for them.... For example, General Foods' ... new ... "low-cholesterol, low-calorie" cherry coffee cake ... may confuse some consumers who shouldn't eat much of it. While each serving is only 90 calories, not everyone realizes that the suggested serving is tiny [one-thirteenth of the small cake]. Although eating half a ... cake may be better than eating half a dozen Dunkin Donuts ... neither should be eaten in great amounts by people on restrictive diets.[4]

A third complaint concerns product safety. Product safety has been a problem for several reasons, including manufacturer indifference, increased production complexity, poorly trained labour, and poor quality control. For years, Consumers Union—the organization that publishes *Consumer Reports*—has reported various hazards in tested products: electrical dangers in appliances, carbon-monoxide poisoning from room heaters, injury risks from lawn mowers, and faulty automobile design, among many others. The organization's testing and other activities have helped consumers make better buying decision and encouraged businesses to eliminate product flaws (see Marketing Highlight 20-1).

Consumer Reports
www.consumer.org/

However, most manufacturers *want* to produce quality goods. The way a company deals with product quality and safety problems can damage or help its reputation. Companies selling poor-quality or unsafe products risk damaging conflicts with consumer groups and regulators. Moreover, unsafe products can result in product-liability suits and large awards for damages. More fundamentally, consumers who are unhappy with a firm's products may avoid future purchases and talk other consumers into doing the same. Today's marketers know that customer-driven quality results in customer satisfaction, which in turn creates profitable customer relationships.

Planned Obsolescence

Critics also have charged that some producers follow a program of planned obsolescence, causing their products to become obsolete before they actually should need replacement. For example, critics charge that some producers continually change consumer concepts of acceptable styles to encourage more and earlier buying. An obvious example is constantly changing clothing fashions. Other producers are accused of holding back attractive functional features, then introducing them later to make older models obsolete. Critics claim that this occurs in the consumer electronics and computer industries. Still other producers are accused of using materials and components that will break, wear, rust, or rot sooner than they should.

Marketers respond that consumers *like* style changes; they get tired of the old goods and want a new look in fashion or a new design in cars. No one has to buy the new look, and if too few people like it, it will simply fail. Companies frequently withhold new features when they are not fully tested, when they add more cost to the product than consumers are willing to pay, and for other good reasons. But they do so at the risk that a competitor will introduce the new feature and steal the market. Moreover, companies often put in new materials to lower their costs and prices. They do not design their products to break down earlier, because they do not want to lose customers to other brands. Instead, they implement total quality programs to ensure that products will consistently meet to exceed customer expectations. Thus, much of so-called planned obsolescence is the working of the competitive and technological forces in a free society—forces that lead to ever-improving goods and services.

Poor Service to Disadvantaged Consumers

Finally, the marketing system has been accused of poorly serving disadvantaged consumers. Critics claim that the urban poor often have to shop in smaller stores that carry inferior goods and charge higher prices. A recent Consumers Union study compared the food shopping habits of low-income consumers and the prices they pay relative to middle-income consumers in the same city. The study found that the poor do pay more for inferior goods. The results suggested that the presence of large national chain stores in low-income neighbourhoods made a big difference in keeping prices down. However, the study also found evidence of "redlining," a type of economic discrimination in which major chain retailers avoid placing stores in disadvantaged neighbourhoods.[5] Banks have been accused of similar practices when they refuse credit or loans to low-income people.

Clearly, better marketing systems must be built in low-income areas—one hope is to get large retailers to open outlets in low-income areas. Moreover, low-income people and other vulnerable groups clearly need consumer protection.

MARKETING'S IMPACT ON SOCIETY AS A WHOLE

The marketing system has been accused of adding to several "evils" in society at large. Advertising has been a special target—so much so that the American

WHEN *CONSUMER REPORTS* TALKS, BUYERS LISTEN

For more than 60 years, *Consumer Reports* has given buyers the lowdown on everything from sports cars to luggage to lawn sprinklers. Published by

several times that many borrowers, as dog-eared library copies will attest, *Consumer Reports* is one of North America's most-read magazines. It's also one of the most influential. In

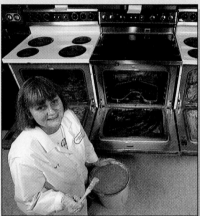

month. In 1992, when it raved about Saucony's Jazz 3000 sneakers, sales doubled, leading to nationwide shortages.

Although non-readers may view *Consumer Reports* as a deadly dull shopper's guide to major household appliances, the magazine does a lot more than rate cars and refrigerators. In recent issues, it has looked at mutual funds, prostate surgery, home mortgages, retirement communities, and public health policies. In the 1930s Consumers Union was one of the first organizations to urge a boycott of products imported from Nazi Germany. In the 1950s it warned that fallout from U.S. nuclear tests was contaminating milk supplies. In the 1960s and 1970s it prodded carmakers to install seat belts, then air bags.

Yet the magazine is rarely harsh or loud. Instead, it's usually understated, and it can even be funny. Lifebuoy soap was itself so smelly that it simply overwhelmed your B.O. with L.O. And what reader didn't delight to find in a 1990 survey of soaps that the most expensive bar, Eau de Gucci at 31 cents per hand-washing, wound up dead last in a blind test?

Consumers Union carries out its testing mission: Suitcases bang into one another inside the huge "Mechanical Gorilla," and a staffer coats the interior of self-cleaning ovens with a crusty concoction called "Monster Mash."

Consumers Union, the non-profit product-testing organization, the magazine's mission can be summed up by CU's motto: Test, Inform, Protect. With more than five million subscribers and

1988, when its car-testers rated Suzuki's topple-prone Samurai as "not acceptable"—meaning don't even take one as a gift—sales plunged 70 percent the following

---

Association of Advertising Agencies launched a campaign to defend advertising against what it felt to be common but untrue criticisms.

False Wants and Too Much Materialism

Critics, led by Professor Rick Pollay of the University of British Columbia, have charged that the marketing system urges too much interest in material possessions. Professor Pollay wrote an article published in the *Journal of Marketing* that outlined the unintended consequences of advertising. The article documented the work of a wide range of social critics who claim that advertising promoted materialism, undermined family values, reinforced negative stereotypes, and created a class of perpetually dissatisfied consumers.[6] People are judged by what they *own* rather than by who they *are*. To be considered successful, people must own a large home, two cars, and the latest consumer electronics. This drive for wealth and possessions hit new highs in the 1980s, when phrases such as "greed is good" and "shop till you drop" seemed to characterize the times. In the 1990s, although many social scientists have noted a reaction against the opulence and waste of the 1980s and a return to more basic values and social commitment, our infatuation with material things continues. For example, when asked in a recent poll what they value most in their lives, subjects listed enjoyable work (86 percent), happy children (84 percent), a good marriage (69 percent), and contributions to society (66 percent). However, when asked what most symbolizes success, 85 percent said money and the things it will buy.[7]

Consumer Reports readers clearly appreciate CU and its magazine. It is unlikely that any other magazine in the world could have raised $24 million toward a new building simply by asking readers for donations. To avoid even the appearance of bias, CU has a strict no-ads, no-freebies policy. It buys all of its product samples on the open market, and anonymously. A visit to CU's maze of labs confirms the thoroughness with which CU's testers carry out their mission. A chemist performs a cholesterol extraction test on a small white blob in a beaker; a ground-up piece of turkey enchilada, you are told. Elsewhere you find the remains of a piston-driven machine called Fingers that added 1 + 1 on pocket calculators hundreds of thousands of times or until the calculators failed, whichever came first. You watch suitcases bang into one another inside a huge contraption—affectionately dubbed the "Mechanical Gorilla"—that looks like a three-metre-wide clothes dryer.

Down the hall in the appliance department a pair of "food soilers" will soon load 20 dishwashers with identical sets of dirty dishes. A sample dinner plate is marked with scientific precision in eight wedge-shaped sections, each with something different caked to it—dried spaghetti, spinach, chipped beef, or something else equally difficult to clean. Next door, self-cleaning ovens are being tested, their interiors coated with a crusty substance—called "Monster Mash" by staffers—that suggests month-old chili sauce. The recipe includes tapioca, cheese, lard, grape jelly, tomato sauce, and cherry pie filling—mixed well and baked one hour at 425 degrees. If an oven's self-cleaning cycle doesn't render the resulting residue into harmless-looking ash, five million readers will be so informed.

Some of the tests that CU runs are standard tests, but many others are not. Several years ago, in a triumph of low-tech creativity, CU's engineers stretched paper towels across embroidery hoops, moistened the centre of each with exactly ten drops of water, then poured lead shot into the middle. The winner held seven pounds of shot; the loser, less than one. Who could argue with that? There is an obvious logic to such tests, and the results are plainly quantifiable.

From the start, Consumers Union has generated controversy. The second issue dismissed the Good Housekeeping Seal of Approval as nothing more than a fraudulent ploy by publisher William Randolph Hearst to reward loyal advertisers. *Good Housekeeping* responded by accusing CU of prolonging the depression. To the business community, *Consumer Reports* was at first viewed as a clear threat to business. During its early years, more than 60 advertising-dependent publications, including the *New York Times, Newsweek,* and the *New Yorker,* refused to accept CU's subscription ads.

Through the years, many manufacturers have filed suit against CU, challenging findings unfavourable to their products. However, the controversy has more often helped than hurt subscriptions, and to this day Consumers Union has never lost or settled a libel suit.

Source: Adapted from Doug Stewart, "To buy or not to buy, that is the question at *Consumer Reports," Smithsonian,* September 1993, pp. 34–43.

The critics do not view this interest in material things as a natural state of mind but rather as a matter of false wants created by marketing. Businesses hire advertisers to stimulate people's desires for goods, and advertisers use the mass media to create materialistic models of the good life. People work harder to earn the necessary money. Their purchases increase the output of American industry, and industry in turn uses advertisers to stimulate more desire for the industrial output. Thus, marketing is seen as creating false wants that benefit industry more than they benefit consumers.

Others believe these criticisms overstate the power of business to create needs, however. People have strong defences against advertising and other marketing tools. Marketers are most effective when they appeal to existing wants rather than when they attempt to create new ones. Furthermore, people seek information when making important purchases and often do not rely on single sources. Even minor purchases that may be affected by advertising messages lead to repeat purchases only if the product performs as promised. Finally, the high failure rate of new products shows that companies are not able to control demand.

On a deeper level, our wants and values are influenced not only by marketers, but also by family, peer groups, religion, ethnic background, and education. If North Americans are highly materialistic, these values arose out of basic socialization processes that go much deeper than business and mass media could produce alone.

*Cultural pollution:
People's senses are
sometimes assaulted by
commercial messages.*

Too Few Social Goods

Business has been accused of overselling private goods at the expense of public goods. As private goods increase, they require more public services that are usually not forthcoming. For example, an increase in automobile ownership (private good) requires more highways, traffic controls, parking spaces, and police services (public goods). The overselling of private goods results in "social costs." For cars, the social costs include traffic congestion, air pollution, and deaths and injuries from car accidents.

A way must be found to restore a balance between private and public goods. One option is to make producers bear the full social costs of their operations. For example, the government could require automobile manufacturers to build cars with even more safety features and better pollution-control systems. Auto makers would then raise their prices to cover extra costs. If buyers found the price of some cars too high, however, the producers of these cars would disappear, and demand would move to those producers that could support the sum of the private and social costs.

Cultural Pollution

Critics charge the marketing system with creating *cultural pollution*. Our senses are being assaulted constantly by advertising. Commercials interrupt serious programs; pages of ads obscure printed matter; billboards mar beautiful scenery. These interruptions continuously pollute people's minds with messages of materialism, sex, power, or status. Although most people do not find advertising overly annoying (some even think it is the best part of television programming), some critics call for sweeping changes.

Marketers answer the charges of "commercial noise" with these arguments: First, they hope that their ads reach primarily the target audience. But because of mass-communication channels, some ads are bound to reach people who have no interest in the product and are therefore bored or annoyed. People who buy magazines addressed to their interests—such as *Harrowsmith* or *Canadian Business*—rarely complain about the ads because the magazines advertise products of interest. Second, ads make it possible for consumers to receive commercial television and radio free of charge and keep down the costs of magazines and newspapers. Many people think commercials are a small price to pay for these benefits.

Too Much Political Power

Another criticism is that business wields too much political power. "Oil," "tobacco," "auto," and "pharmaceuticals" firms lobby government to promote their interests against the public interest. Advertisers are accused of holding too much power over the mass media, limiting their freedom to report independently and objectively. One critic has asked: "How can *Life*...and *Reader's Digest* afford to tell the truth about the scandalously low nutritional value of most packaged foods...when these magazines are being subsidized by such advertisers as General Foods, Kellogg's, Nabisco, and General Mills? ...The answer is *they cannot and do not*."[8]

North American industries promote and protect their interests. They have a right to representation in Parliament and the mass media, although their influence can become too great. Fortunately, many powerful business interests once thought to be untouchable have been tamed in the public interest. For example, Petro-Canada was formed to give Canadians greater control over the oil industry. Ralph Nader caused legislation that forced the automobile industry to build more safety into its cars. Amendments to the Tobacco Products Control Act made it necessary for cigarette manufacturers to place stronger warnings on their packages about the dangers of smoking. Warnings, which must appear in black type on a white background on the top of the package, include messages such as: "Cigarettes cause strokes and heart disease" and "Smoking reduces life expectancy."[9] Because the media receive advertising revenues from many different advertisers, it is easier to resist the influence of one or a few of them. Too much business power tends to result in counterforces that check and offset these powerful interests.

MARKETING'S IMPACT ON OTHER BUSINESSES

Critics also charge that a company's marketing practices can harm other companies and reduce competition. Three problems are involved: acquisitions of competitors, marketing practices that create barriers to entry, and unfair competitive marketing practices.

Critics claim that firms are harmed and competition reduced when companies expand by acquiring competitors rather than by developing their own new products. During the past decade, Corel bought out WordPerfect; Interbrew SA, a Belgian company, acquired Labatt in a $2.7-billion takeover in the summer of 1995; Procter & Gamble gobbled up Richardson-Vicks, Noxell, and parts of Revlon. Acquisition is a complex subject. Acquisitions can sometimes be good for society. The acquiring company may gain economies of scale that lead to lower costs and lower prices. A well-managed company may take over a poorly managed company and improve its efficiency. An industry that was not very competitive might become more competitive after the acquisition. But acquisitions also can be harmful and, therefore, are closely regulated by the government.

Critics also have charged that marketing practices bar new companies from entering an industry. Large marketing companies can use patents and heavy promotion spending, and can tie up suppliers or dealers to keep out or drive out competitors. Nowhere are these issues more apparent than in Canada's pharmaceutical industry. In 1993, Canada revised the regulations dealing with patent protection for drugs. Patent protection was extended from 17 years to 20 years. Manufacturers of branded drugs claimed that this increased protection has made the Canadian pharmaceutical industry more competitive internationally. The report is hotly disputed, however. The generic manufacturers want patent protection reduced to 10 years. They claim that the branch of the pharmaceutical industry composed of branded drug firms has cut jobs since being granted extended protection.

Finally, some firms have in fact used unfair competitive marketing practices with the intention of hurting or destroying other firms. They may set their prices below costs, threaten to cut off business with suppliers, or discourage the buying of a competitor's products. Various laws work to prevent such predatory competition. It is difficult, however, to prove that the intent or action was really predatory. For example, in recent years, Wal-Mart and American Airlines have been accused of predatory pricing—setting prices that could not be profitable to drive out smaller or weaker competitors. The question is whether this was unfair competition or the healthy competition of a more efficient company against the less efficient.

CITIZEN AND PUBLIC ACTIONS TO REGULATE MARKETING

Because some people view business as the cause of many economic and social ills, grass-roots movements have arisen from time to time to keep business in line. The two major movements have been *consumerism* and *environmentalism*.

CONSUMERISM

The first consumer movements took place in the early 1900s and in the mid-1930s. Both were sparked by an upturn in consumer prices. Another movement began in the 1960s. Consumers had become better educated, products had become more complex and hazardous, and people were questioning the status quo. Many accused big business of wasteful and unethical practices. Since then, many consumer groups have been organized, and several consumer laws have been passed. The consumer movement has spread beyond North America and is especially strong in Europe.[10]

Consumerism
An organized movement of citizens and government agencies to improve the rights and power of buyers in relation to sellers

But what is the consumer movement? **Consumerism** is an organized movement of citizens and government agencies to improve the rights and power of buyers in relation to sellers. The Consumers' Association of Canada (CAC), (http://www.ccn.dal.ca/CAC/cacwhatis:html) has acted as a consumer advocate and has provided information to Canadian consumers for 47 years. It is a volunteer-based, non-governmental organization dedicated to representing the interests of Canadian consumers. Founded in 1947, it is the only nationally organized group of consumers in Canada. With the exception of Prince Edward Island, there are CAC associations in every province. The association lobbies government to secure consumer rights in areas of food, health care, environment, consumer products and services, regulated industries (phone, electricity, telecommunications, cable), financial institutions, taxation, trade, and any other issue of concern to Canadians facing complex buying decisions. The association establishes annual priorities. Some of the most recent issues include health-care reform; the Information Highway; interprovincial trade barriers; consumer education and purchasing literacy; GST reform; price visibility; package downsizing; and environmental rights and responsibilities. The association has also outlined the following as fundamental consumer rights:

♦ *The right to safety.* Consumers have the right to be protected against the marketing of goods that are hazardous to health or life.

♦ *The right to be informed.* Consumers must be protected against fraudulent, deceitful, or grossly misleading information, advertising, labelling or other practices. They are to be given the facts needed to make an informed choice.

♦ *The right to choose.* Consumers have the right to choose, wherever possible, among a variety of products and services at competitive prices. In industries where competition is not workable and government regulation is substituted, consumers must be assured of satisfactory quality and service at fair prices.

♦ *The right to be heard.* It is important that consumers' voices be heard. Thus, they must receive full and sympathetic consideration in the formulation of government policy, and fair and expeditious treatment in its administrative tribunals.

♦ *The right to redress against damage.* Consumers have the right to seek redress from a supplier of goods and services for any loss or damage suffered because of bad information, or faulty products or performance, and shall have easy and inexpensive access to settlement of small claims.

♦ *The right to consumer education.* Canadian consumers have the right to be educated as school children so that they will be able to act as informed consumers through their lives. Adults also have the right to consumer education.[11]

Each proposed right has led to more specific proposals by consumerists. The right to be informed includes the right to know the true interest on a loan (truth in lending), the true cost per unit of a brand (unit pricing), the ingredients in a product (ingredient labelling), the nutrition in foods (nutritional labelling), product freshness (open dating), and the true benefits of a product (truth in advertising).

Consumer desire for more information led to putting ingredients, nutrition, and dating information on product labels.

Proposals related to consumer protection include strengthening consumer rights in cases of business fraud, requiring greater product safety, and giving more power to government agencies. Proposals relating to the quality of life include controlling the ingredients that go into certain products (detergents) and packaging (soft-drink containers), reducing the level of advertising "noise," and appointing consumer representatives to company boards to protect consumer interests.

In addition to the Canadian Consumers Association, some Better Business Bureaus, such as the one for mainland British Columbia, offer tips whereby consumers can protect themselves from fraud or shady business practices. For example, it provides information on the dangers of advertisements that promise consumers easy ways of earning money at home, explains the rules about the cooling-off periods, how to differentiate between legitimate and fraudulent requests for charitable contributions, and the legality of pyramid schemes.

Consumers have not only the *right* but also the *responsibility* to protect themselves instead of leaving this function to someone else. Consumers who believe they got a bad deal have several remedies available, including writing to the company president or to the media; contacting federal, provincial or local agencies; and going to small-claims courts.

ENVIRONMENTALISM

Environmentalism
An organized movement of concerned citizens and government agencies to protect and improve people's living environment.

Environmentalism is an organized movement of concerned citizens, businesses, and government agencies to protect and improve people's living environment. Environmentalists are not against marketing and consumption; they simply want people and organizations to operate with more care for the environment. The marketing system's goal should not be to maximize consumption, consumer choice, or consumer satisfaction, but rather to maximize life quality. And "life quality" means not only the quantity and quality of consumer goods and services, but also the quality of the environment. Environmentalists want environmental costs included in both producer and consumer decision making.

In response to these concerns, the Canadian government has undertaken a number of initiatives to improve the environment. It froze production levels of chlorofluorocarbons (CFCs), the major cause of ozone layer depletion, at 1986 levels, and committed itself to reducing production by a further 50 percent by the year 2000. Canada's environment ministers established a voluntary program intended to reduce excessive packaging by 50 percent by the year 2000. Patterning itself after the successful Blue Angel program in West Germany, the Canadian government developed an environmentally friendly labelling program and endorsed the goal of sustainable development put forward by the World Commission on Environment and Development. The Canadian Environmental Assessment Act is one piece of legislation developed to promote its goal.

Just say "the lake"

and it conjures up all that is peaceful, beautiful and well, just right in our lives. Just saying it can transport you to a better frame of mind. A better place that's clean and natural and away from it all.

When you're there it's the best place on Earth to be. Just knowing it has existed, virtually unchanged, for thousands of years and will go on being the best place on earth for your children and theirs. That's the real magic of the lake.

Clean... The U.S. Environmental Protection Agency recently awarded Honda's 4-stroke outboard engines (25 & 30 horse-power) with the 1998 Certification for reduced emissions. What's more, these advanced engines **already meet the strict standard for 2006**, which requires further **emission reductions of 75% over current standards.** Honda also expects to have its entire line of clean-running outboards, from 2 hp to 90 hp, approved before the end of the year.

Long before we built our first 4-stroke outboard in 1964, respect for the environment was one of our fundamental corporate policies. And with this ongoing commitment, we'll continue to lead the way in preserving what is truly magic.

Many companies, such as Chrysler Canada and Honda, are responding positively to Canadians' concerns about environmental issues.

Marketers cannot ignore the urgency of environmental issues or be blind to the fact that governments are increasingly willing to take action and pass regulations restricting marketing practices. All parts of the marketing mix are affected. Advertisers are accused of adding to the solid waste problem when they use direct mail or newspaper inserts. Manufacturers are criticized for making products that incorporate materials that increase pollution or cannot be recycled. Excess packaging is constantly under fire. The average Canadian family "rips its way through one tonne of packaging a year"[12] and 80 percent of this material ends up in landfill sites or incinerators. Distribution systems have been cited for adding to air pollution as trucks move products from the factory to the store. Critics claim that even when environmentally friendly products are available, they are priced too high for many consumers to afford.

Buying behaviour has changed as sensitivity to this issue grew. In the late 1980s, a new product attribute was borne—"environmentally friendly." According to a recent survey conducted by the Grocery Product Manufacturers of Canada, 80 percent of respondents said they would be willing to pay more for "green" products. Companies began to respond to these changes in demand. Seventy percent of Procter & Gamble's paper packaging is now made from recycled paper and they have been marketing their "enviro paks" to reduce plastic waste. Retailers in both Canada and the United States are demanding more environmentally sensitive products. Wal-Mart has asked its suppliers to provide more of these products. Loblaw has developed an entire line of products under its "green" President's Choice label.[13] Governments are demanding that newsprint be made with a high proportion of recycled paper. The City of Toronto has stated that it will favour products that are "green." To this end, the purchasing director for the city conducted extensive research to develop a list of green suppliers, published as the *Directory of Environmentally Sound Products*.[14]

Marketers should be cautioned, however, not to take unfair advantage of consumers' environmental concerns. The Consumer Association of Canada and a number of environmental groups are afraid that public concern about the environment, and their desire and willingness to take action, may be used against them.[15]

The growing concern with environmental issues need not be a threat to businesses, however. More and more firms are accepting their responsibility to protect the environment. David Buzzelli, CEO of Dow Chemical Company Canada Inc., has explicitly taken such a stand:

> Industry has an ethical responsibility to protect the health and safety of people and the environment throughout the lifecycle of its products ... And it has more technological capability than individuals and governments, so it has the ethical responsibility to help find practical solutions.[16]

As we move into the twenty-first century, more and more companies are adopting policies of *environmental sustainability*—developing strategies that both sustain the environment and produce profits for the company. According to one strategist, "The challenge is to develop a sustainable global economy: an economy that the planet is capable of supporting indefinitely. ... [It's] an enormous challenge—and an enormous opportunity."[17] Figure 20-1 shows a grid that companies can use to gauge their progress toward environmental sustainability.[18] At the most basic level, a company can practise pollution prevention. This involves more than pollution control—cleaning up waste after it has been created. Pollution prevention means eliminating or minimizing waste before it is created. Companies have developed ecologically safer products, recyclable and biodegradable packaging, better pollution controls, and more energy-efficient operations (see Marketing Highlight 20-2). They are finding that they can be both green and competitive. Consider how the Dutch flower industry has responded to its environmental problems:

> Intense cultivation of flowers in small areas was contaminating the soil and groundwater with pesticides, herbicides, and fertilizers. Facing increasingly strict regulation, ...the Dutch understood that the only effective way to address the problem would be to develop a closed-loop system. In advanced Dutch greenhouses, flowers now grow in re-circulated water and rock wool, not in soil. This lowers the risk of infestation, and reduces the need for fertilizers and

FIGURE 20-1
The environmental sustainability grid

Source: Reprinted by permission of *Harvard Business Review*. From "Beyond Greening: Strategies for a Sustainable World," by Stuart L. Hart, January-February 1997, pp. 74. Copyright © 1997 by the President and Fellows of Harvard College; all rights reserved.

	Internal	External
Tomorrow	**New Environmental Technology** Is the environment performance of our products limited by our existing technology base? Is there potential to realize major improvements through new technology?	**Sustainability Vision** Does our corporate vision direct us toward the solution of social and environmental problems? Does our vision guide the development of new technologies, markets, products, and processes?
Today	**Pollution Prevention** Where are the most significant waste and emission streams from our current operations? Can we lower costs and risks by eliminating waste at the source or by using it as useful input?	**Product Stewardship** What are the implications for product design and development if we assume responsibility for a product's entire life cycle? Can we add value or lower costs while simultaneously reducing the impact of our products?

THE NEW ENVIRONMENTALISM AND "GREEN MARKETING"

On Earth Day 1970, a newly emerging environmentalism movement made its first large-scale effort to educate people about the dangers of pollution. This was a tough task: At the time, most folks weren't all that interested in environmental problems. By 1990, however, Earth Day had become an important cause across North America, punctuated by articles in major magazines and newspapers, prime-time television extravaganzas, and countless events. It turned out to be just the start of an entire "Earth Decade" in which environmentalism has become a massive worldwide force.

These days, environmentalism has broad public support. People hear and read daily about a growing list of environmental problems—global warming, acid rain, depletion of the ozone layer, air and water pollution, hazardous waste disposal, the buildup of solid wastes—and they are calling for solutions. The new environmentalism is causing many consumers to rethink what products they buy and from whom. These changing consumer attitudes have sparked a major new marketing thrust—*green marketing*—the movement by companies to develop and market environmentally responsible products. Committed "green" companies pursue not only environmental cleanup but also pollution prevention. True "green" work requires companies to practise the three R's of waste management: reducing, reusing, and recycling waste.

Northern Telecom has developed a program in which the company examines all of the components it designs into products to help ensure that they are made from more environmentally responsible materials, and that finished products can be recycled once their life cycle is complete.

Corporate environmentalism: Enlightened companies are taking action not because someone is forcing them to, but because it is the right thing to do.

reduced inclusion of superfluous information. Not only did they improve the environmental sensitivity of their products, but they also found that they produced clearer, more concise, and more memorable messages in the

Spencer Francey Group, a Toronto-based communications firm, is developing more environmentally friendly media kits, trade-show displays, and information packages.In developing more environmentally friendly advertising and promotion materials for their clients, they reduced the amount of materials used, incorporated recycled materials whenever possible, and

process. One of their programs was so successful that it was named by *Time* as one of the best designs of the year.

Specialized products and services have been developed to meet the demands of green consumers. Such products are even being offered on the financial market. Ethical Funds, the largest family of "green funds" in Canada, invests only in firms that pass

pesticides. The...closed-loop system also reduces variation in growing conditions, thus improving product quality. Handling costs have also gone down... The net result is not only dramatically lower environmental impact but also lower costs, better product quality, and enhanced global competitiveness.[19]

At the next level, companies can practise *product stewardship*—minimizing not only pollution from production, but all environmental impacts throughout the full product life cycle. Many companies, such as Nortel, are adopting *design for environment* (DFE) practices, which involve thinking ahead in the design stage to create products that are easier to recover, reuse, or recycle. DFE practices not only help to sustain the environment, but they can also be highly profitable:

Consider Xerox Corporation's Asset Recycle Management (ARM) program. A well-developed [process] for taking back leased copiers combined with a sophisticated remanufacturing process allows...components to be reconditioned, tested, and then reassembled into "new" machines. Xerox estimates that ARM savings

an ethical screening process that includes criteria such as records of good labour relations and charitable giving, as well as sound environmental policies.

McDonald's provides another good example of green marketing. It used to purchase Coca-Cola syrup in plastic bags encased in cardboard, but now the syrup is delivered as gasoline is, pumped directly from tank trucks into storage vats at restaurants. The change saved 34 million kilograms of packaging a year. All napkins, bags, and tray liners in McDonald's restaurants are made from recycled paper, as are its carry-out drink trays and even the stationery used at headquarters. For a company the size of McDonald's, even small changes can make a big difference. For example, just making its drinking straws 20 percent lighter saved the company 500 000 kilograms of waste per year. Beyond turning its own products green, McDonald's purchases recycled materials for building and remodelling its restaurants, and it challenges its suppliers to furnish and use recycled products.

Producers in a wide range of industries are responding to environmental concerns. For example, 3M runs a *Pollution Prevention Pays* program, which has led to substantial pollution and cost reduction. Dow built a new ethylene plant in Alberta that uses 40 percent less energy and releases 97 percent less waste water.

During the early phase of the new environmentalism, promoting environmentally improved products and actions ballooned into a big business. In fact, environmentalists and regulators became concerned that companies were going overboard with their use of terms like *recyclable, degradable,* and *environmentally responsible.* Perhaps of equal concern was that, as more and more marketers used green marketing claims, more and more consumers would view them as little more than gimmicks.

Responsible green marketing is not an easy task and is full of many contradictions. Even companies like The Body Shop, while admired for increasing awareness of issue such as degradation of the rain forests and the use of animal testing, are criticized for exaggerating their progressive practices. However, as we close out the century, environmentalism appears to be moving into a more mature phase. Gone are the hastily prepared environmental pitches and products designed to capitalize on, or even exploit, growing public concern. The new environmentalism is now going mainstream—broader, deeper, and more sophisticated. In the words of one analyst:

> Dressing up ads with pictures of eagles and trees will no longer woo an environmentally sophisticated audience. People want to know that companies are incorporating environmental values into their manufacturing processes, products, packaging, and the very fabric of their corporate cultures. They...want to know that companies will not compromise the ability of future generations to enjoy the quality of life that we enjoy today.

... As a result, we're seeing the marriage of performance benefits and environmental benefits...one reinforces the other.

In all, some companies have responded to consumer environmental concerns by doing only what is required to avert new regulations or to keep environmentalists quiet. Others have rushed to make money by catering to the public's mounting concern for the environment. But enlightened companies are taking action not because someone is forcing them to, or to reap short-run profits, but because it is the right thing to do. They believe that environmental farsightedness today will pay off tomorrow—for both the customer and the company.

Sources: Quotation from Robert Rehak, "Green Marketing Awash in Third Wave," *Advertising Age,* November 22, 1993, p. 22. Also see Joe Schwartz, "Earth Day Today," *American Demographics,* April 1990, pp. 40–41; Eric Wieffering, "Wal-Mart Turns Green in Kansas," *American Demographics,* December 1993, p. 23; David Woodruff, "Herman Miller: How Green is My Factory," *Business Week,* September 16, 1991, pp. 54–56; Jacquelyn Ottman, "Environmentalism Will Be *The* Trend of the '90s," *Marketing News,* December 7, 1992, p. 13; Peter Stisser, "A Deeper Shade of Green," *American Demographics,* March 1994, pp. 24–20; Jon Entine, "In Search of Saintly Stock Picks," *Report on Business,* October 1995, p. 45; and Carolyn Leitch, "PR Firm Delivers Fewer Pounds in the Ruff, in the Aid of Less Waste," *Report on Environmental Protection, Globe and Mail,* Tuesday, February 27, 1990, p. C1.

Ethical Funds
www.ethicalfunds.com/

Monsanto Company
www.monsanto.com/
monsanto/indexb.html

in raw materials, labour, and waste disposal in 1995 alone were in the $400-million to $500-million range...Xerox has discovered a way to add value and lower costs. It can continually provide lease customers with the latest product upgrades, giving them state-of-the-art functionality with minimum environmental impact.[20]

At the third level of environmental sustainability, companies look to the future and plan for *new environmental technologies.* Although many organizations have made significant headway in pollution prevention and product stewardship, they are limited by existing technologies and need to develop new technologies. Monsanto, for example, is tackling this problem with biotechnology. By controlling plant growth and pest resistance through bioengineering rather than through the application of pesticides or fertilizers, it hopes to find an environmentally sustainable path to increased agricultural yields.[21]

Finally, companies can develop a *sustainability vision,* which serves as a guide to the future. It shows how the company's products and services, processes, and policies must evolve and what new technologies must be developed to get there. This vision of sustainability provides a framework for pollution control, product stewardship, and environmental technology.

Most companies today invest most heavily in pollution prevention. Some forward-looking companies practise product stewardship and are developing new environmental technologies. Few companies have well-defined sustainability visions. However, emphasizing only one or a few cells in the environmental sustainability grid in Figure 20-1 can be shortsighted. While investing only in the bottom half of the grid puts a company in a good position today, it will be vulnerable in the future. In contrast, undue emphasis only on the top half suggests good environmental vision, but without the skills needed to implement it. Thus, companies should work at developing all four dimensions of environmental sustainability.

Environmentalism creates some special challenges for global marketers. As international trade barriers come down and global markets expand, environmental issues are having an ever-greater impact on international trade. Countries in North America, Western Europe, and other developed regions are developing stringent environmental standards. A side accord to the North American Free Trade Agreement (NAFTA) also sets up a commission for resolving environmental matters. And the European Union's Eco-Management and Audit Regulation provides guidelines for environmental self-regulation.[22]

However, environmental policies will vary widely from country to country, and uniform worldwide standards are not expected for another 15 years or more.[23] Although countries such as Canada, Denmark, Germany, Japan, and the United States have fully developed environmental policies and high public expectations, major countries such as China, India, Brazil, and Russia are in only the early stages of developing such policies. Moreover, environmental factors that motivate consumers in one country may have no impact on consumers in another. For example, PVC soft-drink bottles cannot be used in Switzerland or Germany. However, they are preferred in France, which has an extensive recycling process for them. Thus, international companies are finding it difficult to develop standard environmental practices that work around the world. Instead, they are creating general policies, and then translating these policies into tailored programs that meet local regulations and expectations.

PUBLIC ACTIONS TO REGULATE MARKETING

Citizen concerns about marketing practices usually will lead to public attention and legislative proposals. New bills will be debated—many will be defeated, others will be modified, and a few will become workable laws.

Many of the laws that affect marketing are listed in Chapter 3. The task is to translate these laws into the language that marketing executives understand as they make decisions about competitive relations, products, price, promotion, and channels of distribution. Figure 20-2 illustrates the major legal and ethical issues facing marketing management.

BUSINESS ACTIONS TOWARD SOCIALLY RESPONSIBLE MARKETING

At first, many companies opposed consumerism and environmentalism. They thought the criticisms were either unfair or unimportant. But by now, most companies have grown to accept the new consumer rights, at least in principle. They might oppose certain pieces of legislation as inappropriate ways to solve certain consumer problems, but they recognize the consumer's right to information and

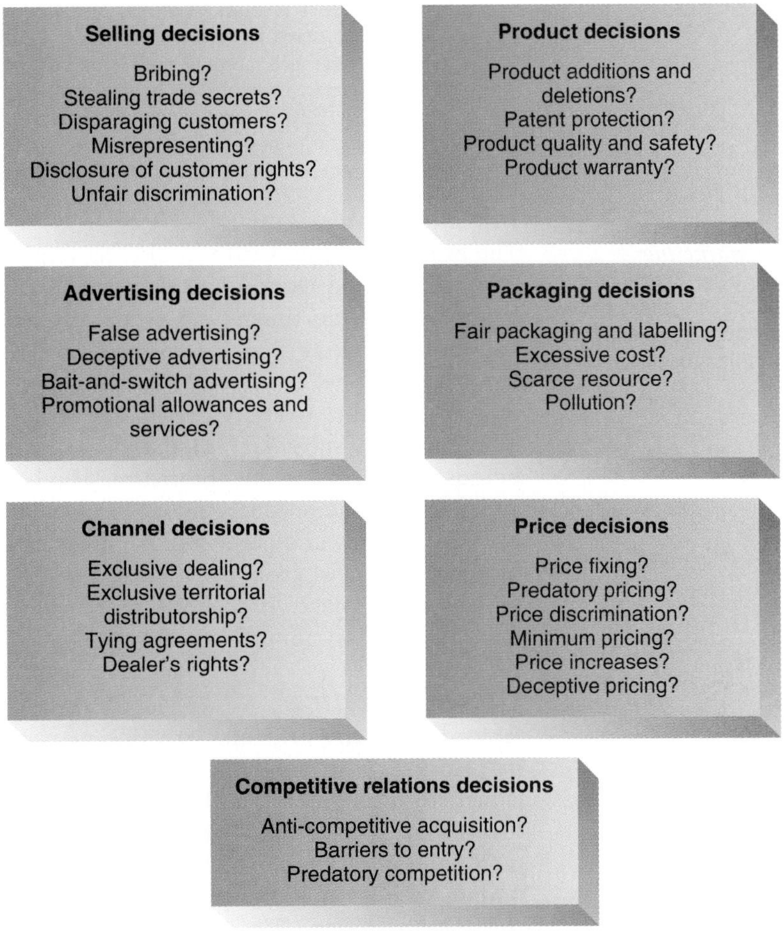

FIGURE 20-2 *Legal issues facing marketing management*

Selling decisions

Bribing?
Stealing trade secrets?
Disparaging customers?
Misrepresenting?
Disclosure of customer rights?
Unfair discrimination?

Product decisions

Product additions and deletions?
Patent protection?
Product quality and safety?
Product warranty?

Advertising decisions

False advertising?
Deceptive advertising?
Bait-and-switch advertising?
Promotional allowances and services?

Packaging decisions

Fair packaging and labelling?
Excessive cost?
Scarce resource?
Pollution?

Channel decisions

Exclusive dealing?
Exclusive territorial distributorship?
Tying agreements?
Dealer's rights?

Price decisions

Price fixing?
Predatory pricing?
Price discrimination?
Minimum pricing?
Price increases?
Deceptive pricing?

Competitive relations decisions

Anti-competitive acquisition?
Barriers to entry?
Predatory competition?

protection. Many of these companies have responded positively to consumerism and environmentalism in order to serve consumer needs better.

ENLIGHTENED MARKETING

Enlightened marketing
A marketing philosophy holding that a company's marketing should support the best long-run performance of the marketing system; its five principles include consumer-oriented marketing, innovative marketing, value marketing, sense-of-mission marketing, and societal marketing.

Consumer-oriented marketing
A principle of enlightened marketing that holds that a company should view and organize its marketing activities from the consumers' point of view.

The philosophy of **enlightened marketing** holds that a company's marketing should support the best long-run performance of the marketing system. Enlightened marketing consists of five principles: *consumer-oriented marketing, innovative marketing, value marketing, sense-of-mission marketing,* and *societal marketing.*

Consumer-Oriented Marketing

Consumer-oriented marketing means that the company should view and organize its marketing activities from the consumer's point of view. It should work hard to sense, serve, and satisfy the needs of a defined group of customer. Consider the following example:

Montreal-based Walsh Integrated Environmental Systems Inc. focused on solving the waste management problems of hospitals. The owner, David Walsh, fresh out of business school, wanted to found his own business. After conducting a 12-week waste audit at Montreal's Royal Victoria Hospital, he realized what a huge waste management problem hospitals faced. Disposing of biohazardous waste costs 20 times as much as getting rid of regular waste and can result in bills of over $450 000 per year. Yet Walsh also saw that other materials, from pop cans to newspapers, were thrown in the biohazardous containers the hospital was using. In fact, about 65 percent of the material in the garbage could go into the regular waste stream. Walsh's new business developed a system called the Waste Tracker that allows hospital staff to track the waste from each department, identify how much is biohazardous, and uncover who is misusing the system. His system now saves hospitals over $200 000 per year. Walsh is confident that his focus on solving hospitals' problems will be as valuable to U.S. hospitals as it is to Canadian institutions so he plans to expand his business. He hopes his new Internet site (http://www.cam.org/~walsh/index.html) that allows users to download a sample system as well as video material will help crack this market.[24]

Innovative Marketing

Innovative marketing
A principle of enlightened marketing that requires that a company seek real product and marketing improvements.

The principle of **innovative marketing** requires that the company continuously seek real product and marketing improvements. The company that overlooks new and better ways to do things will eventually lose customers to another company that has found a better way. Cosmair Canada Inc.'s ability to be an innovative marketer has enabled it to retain its lead in the $2.5-billion Canadian cosmetic and fragrance market over its two major rivals, Procter & Gamble and Lever-Ponds. The Canadian subsidiary of Paris-based Cosmair markets well-known consumer brands L'Oréal, Lancôme, Biotherm, Maybelline, Ralph Lauren, and Drakkar Noir, and professional products in its Redken and L'Oréal lines. It carefully monitors consumer trends and competitors' offerings so that it can launch a constant stream of successful new products designed to fill every niche of the cosmetic and fragrance marketplace. It dominates the channels of distribution, and spends more than $20 million annually on advertising.[25]

Value Marketing

Value marketing
A principle of enlightened marketing that holds that a company should put most of its resources into value-building marketing investments.

According to the principle of **value marketing**, the company should put most of its resources into value-building marketing investments that build long-run consumer loyalty by continually improving the value that consumers receive from the firm's marketing offer. Lowering costs and prices, making services more convenient, and improving product quality are some value-adding strategies. The value-adding strategy of Canada's Forrec Limited has made it a leader in international theme-park design. While the company name isn't exactly a household word, it has been responsible for the creation of Canada's Wonderland north of Toronto and the new casino in Niagara Falls. It also brought a South Pacific beach to the

Creating value for clients, like Universal City, has made Canada's Forrec Limited a world-leader in attraction design.

Vancouver ad agency Lanyon Phillips Partners created this award-winning ad for Friends of Animals, to help them to fulfil their mission of preventing the use of fur for fashion.

Sense-of-mission marketing
A principle of enlightened marketing that holds that a company should define its mission in broad social terms rather than narrow product terms.

Societal marketing
A principle of enlightened marketing that holds that a company should make marketing decisions by considering consumers' long-run interests, and society's long-run interests.

Loblaw's President's Choice "Too Good to Be True" soups, developed to meet specialized needs, also appeal to a wider group of consumers.

middle of Edmonton, created the Streets of San Francisco in the heart of Florida, added a rooftop waterpark to the Bangkok horizon, built a theme park at the edge of the Pyramids of Giza, and is developing an aquarium in Shanghai. Steve Moorehead reveals the secret of his company's success as follows, "We make the site a place where people want to be, and provide a sense of enjoyment, where they know that they're not being ripped off, and we entice them to come back again and again."[26]

Sense-of-Mission Marketing

Sense-of-mission marketing means that the company should define its mission in broad *social* terms rather than narrow *product* terms. When a company defines a social mission, employees feel better about their work and have a clearer sense of direction. For example, defined in narrow product terms, ice-cream marketer Ben & Jerry's mission might be "to sell ice cream and frozen yogurt." However, on its web page (www.benjerry.com), the company states its mission more broadly as one of "linked prosperity":

> Our mission consists of three related parts: *Product*: To make, distribute, and sell the finest quality all natural ice cream and related products in a wide variety of innovative flavours made from Vermont dairy products. *Economic*: To operate the company on a sound financial basis of profitable growth, increasing value for our shareholders, and creating career opportunities and financial rewards for our employees. *Social*: To operate the company in a way that actively recognizes the central role that business plays in the structure of society by initiating innovative ways to improve the quality of life of a broad community—local, national, and international. The underlying mission of Ben & Jerry's is the determination to seek new and creative ways of addressing all three parts, while holding a deep respect for the individuals, inside and outside the company, and for the communities of which they are a part.

Reshaping the basic task of selling consumer products into the larger mission of serving the interests of consumers, employees, and others in the company's various "communities" has allowed the firm to grow and prosper while simultaneously accomplishing a social agenda.

Many not-for-profit and special interest organizations also use mission marketing. Vancouver ad agency Lanyon Phillips Partners helped Friends of Animals, a New York-based group opposed to the wearing of fur for fashion, when it developed an award-winning 1995 campaign.[27]

Societal Marketing

Following the principle of **societal marketing**, an enlightened company makes marketing decisions by considering consumers' wants and interests, the company's requirements, and society's long-run interests. The company is aware that neglecting consumer and societal long-run interests is a disservice to consumers and society. Alert companies view societal problems as opportunities.

Hewlett-Packard Canada is proud of its commitment to the local communities in which it operates. In

FIGURE 20-3 *Societal classification of products*

Deficient products
Products that have neither immediate appeal nor long-run benefits.

Pleasing products
Products that give high immediate satisfaction but may hurt consumers in the long run.

Salutary products
Products that have low appeal but may benefit consumers in the long run.

Desirable products
Products that give both high immediate satisfaction and high long-run benefits.

fact, it points out that citizenship is one of its seven corporate objectives. Hewlett-Packard articulates this belief as follows, "HP Canada sees its contribution to societal needs as creating better places for Canadians to live, including HP employees and our customers." This sense of citizenship is more than corporate public relations. The company works to translate its words into practice. It actively works to protect the environment carefully following the 3 Rs (reduce, recycle, reuse), and it supports important causes such as education and health care since it believes "that the betterment of our society is not a job to be left to a few; it is a responsibility to be shared by all."[28]

A societally oriented marketer wants to design products that are not only pleasing but also beneficial. The difference is shown in Figure 20-3. Products can be classified according to their degree of immediate consumer satisfaction and long-run consumer benefit. **Deficient products**, such as bad-tasting and ineffective medicine, have neither immediate appeal nor long-run benefits. **Pleasing products** give high immediate satisfaction but may hurt consumers in the long run. An example is cigarettes. **Salutary products** have low appeal but benefit consumers in the long run. Insurance is a salutary product. **Desirable products** give both high immediate satisfaction and high long-run benefits. President's Choice "Too Good to Be True" soup mixes have been cited as healthful products. Developed for people with special dietary needs, they have been welcomed by a range of consumers who want good-tasting, high-fibre, low-fat, easy-to-prepare, healthful food.

The challenge posed by pleasing products is that they sell very well but may end up hurting the consumer. The product opportunity, therefore, is to add long-run benefits without reducing the product's pleasing qualities. For example, Sears developed a phosphate-free laundry detergent that was also very effective. The challenge posed by salutary products is to add some pleasing qualities so that they will become more desirable in the consumers' minds. For example, synthetic fats and fat substitutes, such as NutraSweet's Simplesse and P&G's Olestra, promise to improve the appeal of more healthful low-calorie and low-fat foods.

MARKETING ETHICS

Conscientious marketers face many moral dilemmas. The best thing to do is often unclear. Because not all managers have fine moral sensitivity, companies need to develop *corporate marketing ethics policies*—broad guidelines that everyone in the organization must follow. These policies should cover distributor relations, advertising standards, customer service, pricing, product development, and general ethical standards.

The finest guidelines cannot resolve all the difficult ethical situations the marketer faces. Table 20-1 lists some difficult ethical situations that marketers could face during their careers. If marketers choose immediate sales-producing actions in all these cases, their marketing behaviour might well be described as immoral or even amoral. If they refuse to go along with *any* of the actions, they might be ineffective as marketing managers and unhappy because of the constant moral tension. Managers need a set of principles that will help them to determine the moral importance of each situation and decide how far they can go in good conscience.

But *what* principle should guide companies and marketing managers on issues of ethics and social responsibility? One philosophy is that such issues are decided by the free market and legal system. Under this principle, companies and their managers are not responsible for making moral judgments. Companies can in good conscience do whatever the system legally allows.

A second philosophy puts responsibility not in the system, but in the hands of individual companies and managers. This more enlightened philosophy suggests that a company should have a "social conscience." Companies and managers

Table 20-1 *Some Morally Difficult Situations in Marketing*

1. You work for a cigarette company and up until now have not been convinced that cigarettes cause cancer. A report comes across your desk that clearly shows the link between smoking and cancer. What would you do?

2. Your R&D department has changed one of your products slightly. It is not really "new and improved," but you know that putting this statement on the package and in advertising will increase sales. What would you do?

3. You have been asked to add a stripped-down model to your line that could be advertised to attract customers to the store. The product won't be very good, but salespeople will be able to switch buyers up to higher-priced units. You are asked to give the green light for this stripped-down version. What would you do?

4. You are considering hiring a product manager who just left a competitor's company. She would be more than happy to tell you all the competitor's plans for the coming year. What would you do?

5. One of your top dealers in an important territory has had recent family troubles and his sales have slipped. It looks like it will take him a while to straighten out his family trouble. Meanwhile you are losing many sales. Legally, you can terminate the dealer's franchise and replace him. What would you do?

6. You have a chance to win a big account that will mean a lot to you and your company. The purchasing agents hints that a "gift" would influence the decision. Your assistant recommends sending a fine colour television set to the buyer's home. What would you do?

7. You have heard that a competitor has a new product feature that will make a big difference in sales. The competitor will demonstrate the feature in a private dealer meeting at the annual trade show. You can easily send a snooper to this meeting to learn about the new feature. What would you do?

8. You have to choose between three ad campaigns outlined by your agency. The first (A) is a soft-sell, honest information campaign. The second (B) uses sex-loaded emotional appeals and exaggerates the product's benefits. The third (C) involves a noisy, irritating commercial that is sure to gain audience attention. Pretests show that the campaigns are effective in the following order: C, B, and A. What would you do?

9. You are interviewing a capable woman applicant for a job as a salesperson. She is better qualified than the men just interviewed. Nevertheless, you know that some of your important customers prefer dealing with men, and you will lose some sales if you hire her. What would you do?

10. You are a sales manager in an encyclopedia company. Your competitor's salespeople are getting into homes by pretending to take a research survey. After they finish the survey, they switch to their sales pitch. This technique seems to be very effective. What would you do?

should apply high standards of ethics and morality when making corporate decisions, regardless of "what the system allows." History provides an endless list of examples of company actions that were legal and allowed but were highly irresponsible. Consider the following example:

> Prior to the [U.S.] Pure Food and Drug Act, the advertising for a diet pill promised that a person taking this pill could eat virtually anything at any time and still lose weight. Too good to be true? Actually the claim was quite true; the product lived up to its billing with frightening efficiency. It seems that the primary active ingredient in this "diet pill" was tapeworm larvae. These larvae would develop in the intestinal tract and, of course, be well fed; the pill taker would in time, quite literally, starve to death.[29]

Each company and marketing manager must work out a philosophy of socially responsible and ethical behaviour. Under the social marketing concept, companies and managers must look beyond what is legal and allowed and develop standards based on personal integrity, corporate conscience, and long-run consumer welfare. According to a recent survey of the CEOs of Canada's Top 500

SUSAN YOUNG, TREASURER, IMPERIAL OIL FOUNDATION

Imperial Oil has been cited by *Report on Business* (April 1995) as Canada's best firm in terms of Corporate Social Responsibility. Susan Young, Treasurer of the Imperial Oil Foundation, is an integral part of the team that has made this distinction possible. She took her first degree from McMaster University, and followed this with a stint at the Ontario Institute of Education. She was a primary-school teacher for seven years, but then joined Imperial Oil as a member of the marketing department. She also worked in Human Resources at Imperial, before she joined the public affairs department. Despite the hectic pace of her job, Susan still finds time to sit on the boards of a number of charitable foundations, act as a partner in two businesses, and jaunt around the countryside on her Harley-Davidson motorcycle.

Imperial Oil has been Canada's largest oil and gas company for more than a century. Its mission is to create value for its shareholders through the development and sale of hydrocarbon energy and related products. It is the country's largest producer of crude oil, a major producer of natural gas, and a significant supplier of petrochemicals. It is also the largest refiner and marketer of products, under the Esso brand name.

A History of Giving

Imperial Oil has a long history as one of the most philanthropic firms in Canada. This tradition goes back to 1894 when Imperial gave its first donation of $100 to a Newfoundland fishermen's mission. Imperial has also worked long and hard to foster the mission of the Imagine campaign, an effort designed by the Canadian Centre for Philanthropy, to encourage companies to donate one percent of pre-tax earnings to charity.

Imperial has several programs aimed at teens.

For the last eight years, Imperial has focused its social marketing efforts on children. Beginning in 1996, it allocated 65 percent of its budget, or $4 million, to children- and youth-centred causes. Susan Young states that Imperial's social mission is one of acting as an advocate for children in society. In the past, Imperial was very quiet about its support of not-for-profit endeavours. Today, it is making its voice heard. It is using its marketing arm to communicate Imperial's and Esso's support of children's causes with the aim of enhancing the image of the corporation.

Social marketing efforts are designed with two purposes in mind. The first involves a long-term commitment to the resolution of social problems. The second purpose is the enhancement of the business objectives of a sponsoring firm. Thus, while Imperial has worked hard to create positive change in the lives of children, it is also seeking to improve its business through its social marketing programs. In other words, Susan Young stresses that gone are the days when firms undertook social marketing efforts merely in the hopes of image enhancement. Today's programs not only have to help the bottom line in terms of increased sales, but they also have to accomplish such important tasks as the building of brand equity, improving employee productivity, and instilling customer loyalty.

One of the first programs that Imperial supported, as part of its focus on children's well-being, was *Safe Kids Canada*. This program was aimed at improving the physical safety of young children. Its objective was to reduce injuries by educating people about the

companies, 84 percent agreed that there was a good understanding of ethics in their companies, and 90 percent said that ethics was a priority for senior managers. Many Canadian companies (80 percent) have developed codes of ethics to help their managers make better decisions. Even more importantly, 70 percent of the codes were written to develop standards that go beyond mere legal compliance. However, only 27 percent of the firms surveyed offered ethics training programs and only 25 percent have ethics compliance officers. Nonetheless, 75 percent of the companies studied reported that employees of their firms had been disciplined because of lack of ethical behaviour.[30]

As with environmentalism, the issue of ethics provides special challenges for international marketers. Business standards and laws vary widely from one country to the next. For example, while Levi Strauss, Nike, and the Gap have forward-thinking human relations policies in North America, these firms have been accused of exploiting workers working for their subcontractors in Latin America and Southeast Asia. Like many other international firms, Nike has responded by developing a code of ethics that applies to their international businesses as well as to their domestic operations.

Gift giving, always a thorny issue in international business negotiations, is often covered under these codes. Some firms, such as General Motors and Bata

importance of using such preventive devices as children's car seats, and helmets for biking or skating.

This program, however, was not wide enough in scope to accomplish all of Imperial's aims. It did not allow Imperial to address the very real needs of older children and youth. Thus, Imperial divided children's safety problems into distinct areas and is working to develop specific programs to address the important issues in each area. For example, Imperial is considering a program entitled "Transition to Life," aimed at creating awareness of home safety issues for children from newborn to age two. It has a "Transition to School" program, which focuses on issues of early mental development. It has youth hockey programs and Medals of Achievement aimed at children seven to 12 years of age. It has broadened the focus of these programs beyond ice hockey to road hockey. Imperial is trying to build a culture of sportsmanship by educating both children and parents about fair play and the importance of having fun versus just winning the game.

Imperial also has several programs aimed at teens. One program it is considering is focused on the development of math and science skills, especially among young girls. Imperial realizes that developing these skills is essential for there to be an adequate pool of young women entering engineering and earth sciences. Another program addresses the transition period between the teenage years and adulthood. Imperial realizes this is an age when young people thrive on risk, but that taking risks often has disastrous consequences. This concern led to the support of the Smart Risk program. Imperial knows it cannot prevent risk-taking among teens, but it can make teens more aware of the differences between good risks and disastrous ones. Imperial has provided support to its Hero and Party programs under this umbrella to promote messages such as avoiding drinking and driving. Imperial also founded the KAPOW program (Kids and the Power of Work), through which it provides summer job training with not-for-profit organizations for high-risk youth.

One of the major things Susan Young stresses is that social problems cannot be solved merely by throwing money at them. While Imperial has undoubtedly given considerable financial support to many youth-related activities, it has also used its corporate power to draw attention to the issues. It has worked to leverage the expertise with these efforts to attract other corporate partners to help support them. Imperial is attempting to get other existing programs and government incentives aligned behind these efforts. It has also involved its own employees, their spouses, and retirees in the programs. These people provide time and management expertise instead of money to youth programs. Not only does this involvement help Esso people develop their skills, but it also facilitates the delivery of programs and the communication of their benefits.

Trying to resolve social issues is not an easy task. Since Imperial is one of Canada's leading companies, its every move is scrutinized. It cannot afford any missteps with these programs. Despite its successes, Imperial is working on leading-edge programs to proactively prevent problems, rather than just trying to reactively resolve issues. This is an incredible challenge. Being the first firm to take on many of these initiatives, Imperial is inventing strategy without the benefit of historical research and data to support its efforts. Few other companies have the experience, concern, or drive to take on the social challenges being addressed by Imperial.

Source: Susan Young was interviewed by P. Cunningham for *Principles of Marketing* on April 22, 1996. We sincerely wish to thank her for the insights she provided on the practice of social marketing.

Industries Ltd., have very strict codes that forbid the acceptance of gifts, entertainment, or other gratuity. The codes rule out acceptance of any token including tickets to the football game, birthday presents from suppliers, or even a watch sent through the mail. GM realizes that in some countries, like China, where gift giving is part of the business culture, refusal to accept a gift would have significant negative implications. Thus, GM's representatives working here can accept a gift as long as they do it in the name of the company and turn it over for display on the company premises. Bata believes that such a strict policy is necessary because it is impossible to differentiate between a gift and a bribe. Either can lead a decision-maker into a conflict of interest and an inability to make a purchase decision that represents the best value for the company.[31]

While it is both illegal and unethical for a Canadian firm to bribe a Canadian government official, Canada currently has no law that prevents firms from paying bribes when they operate overseas. Thus, Canadian managers working in international marketplaces often have to ask themselves whether they should apply a different legal and ethical standard to business practices when they are overseas than they do at home. This situation may change rapidly. In May 1997, the Organization for Economic Co-operation and Development (OECD) made a recommendation to its member countries, including Canada, that domestic legislation be

OECD
www.oecd.org/

Table 20-2 *American Marketing Association Code of Ethics*

Members of the American Marketing Association are committed to ethical, professional conduct. They have joined together in subscribing to this Code of Ethics embracing the following topics:

Responsibilities of the Marketer

Marketers must accept responsibility for the consequences of their activities and make every effort to ensure that their decisions, recommendations, and actions function to identify, serve, and satisfy all relevant publics: customers, organizations, and society.

Marketers' professional conduct must be guided by:

1. The basic rule of professional ethics: not knowingly to do harm;
2. The adherence to all applicable laws and regulations;
3. The accurate representation of their education, training, and experience; and
4. The active support, practice, and promotion of this Code of Ethics.

Honesty and Fairness

Marketers shall uphold and advance the integrity, honour, and dignity of the marketing profession by:

1. Being honest in serving consumers, clients, employees, suppliers, distributors, and the public;
2. Not knowingly participating in conflict of interest without prior notice to all parties involved; and
3. Establishing equitable fee schedules including the payment or receipt of usual, customary, and/or legal compensation for marketing exchanges.

Rights and Duties of Parties in the Marketing Exchange Process

Participants in the marketing exchange process should be able to expect that:

1. Products and services offered are safe and fit for their intended uses;
2. Communications about offered products and services are not deceptive;
3. All parties intend to discharge their obligations, financial and otherwise, in good faith; and
4. Appropriate internal methods exist for equitable adjustment and/or redress of grievances concerning purchases.

It is understood that the above would include, but is not limited to, the following responsibilities of the marketer:

In the area of product development and management,

♦ disclosure of all substantial risks associated with product or service usage;

♦ identification of any product component substitution that might materially change the product or impact on the buyer's purchase decision;
♦ identification of extra cost-added features.

In the area of promotions,

♦ avoidance of false and misleading advertising;
♦ rejection of high-pressure manipulations, or misleading sales tactics;
♦ avoidance of sales promotions that use deceptions or manipulation.

In the area of distribution,

♦ not manipulating the availability of a product for purpose of exploitation;
♦ not using coercion in the marketing channel;
♦ not exerting undue influence over the reseller's choice to handle a product.

In the area of pricing,

♦ not engaging in price fixing;
♦ not practising predatory pricing;
♦ disclosing the full price associated with any purchase.

In the area of marketing research,

♦ prohibiting selling or fundraising under the guise of conducting research;
♦ maintaining research integrity by avoiding misrepresentation and omission of pertinent research data;
♦ treating outside clients and suppliers fairly.

Organizational Relationships

Marketers should be aware of how their behaviour may influence or impact on the behaviour of others in organizational relationships. They should not demand, encourage, or apply coercion to obtain unethical behaviour in their relationships with others, such as employees, suppliers, or customers.

1. Apply confidentiality and anonymity in professional relationships with regard to privileged information;
2. Meet their obligations and responsibilities in contracts and mutual agreements in a timely manner;
3. Avoid taking the work of others, in whole, or in part, and represent this work as their own or directly benefit from it without compensation or consent of the originator or owner;
4. Avoid manipulation to take advantage of situations to maximize personal welfare in a way that unfairly deprives or damages the organization of others.

Any AMA member found to be in violation of any provision of this Code of Ethics may have his or her Association membership suspended or revoked.

Canadian Occidental Petroleum Ltd.
www.cdnoxy.com/

passed that criminalizes bribery in international transactions. In June, the recommendation was endorsed by Canada and the other G7 members at their annual meeting. The new law banning bribery is expected to be passed in 1998.

In September 1997, a coalition of companies, headed by Calgary-based Canadian Occidental Petroleum Ltd. and Errol Mendes of the University of Ottawa, published a voluntary code designed to guide international business practices. In addition to prohibiting bribery, the new code advocates the protection of human rights, worker health and safety, and the environment. It also encourages firms to be actively involved in the welfare of the local communities in which they operate. The code has been supported by the federal government, Business Council on National Issues, Alliance of Manufacturers and Exporters Canada, Canadian Chamber of Commerce, and Conference Board of Canada. Canadian government officials note, however, that while the new voluntary code is an important first step that acts as a catalyst for action, firms must work diligently to implement and enforce the code if it is to have a meaningful effect.[32]

The future holds many challenges and opportunities for marketing managers as they move into the twenty-first century. Technological advances in solar energy, personal computers, interactive television, modern medicine, and new forms of transportation, recreation, and communication provide abundant marketing opportunities. However, forces in the socioeconomic, cultural, and natural environments increase the limits under which marketing can be carried out. Companies that are able to create new values in a socially responsible way will have a world to conquer.

Canada's 74 000 plus charities and not-for-profit organizations use marketing extensively for two prime purposes: working toward rectifying a pressing social problem and fundraising. For example, the YMCA has a national one-week campaign aimed at stopping domestic violence. Health Canada runs programs aimed at reducing smoking and increasing people's levels of physical activity. While few question the importance of these worthy causes, there has been growing criticism about some of the fundraising methods employed by charities. Two major concerns have surfaced. more and more charities are using lotteries to raise funds. These not only add to the pressures on people to gamble, they may often jeopardize the welfare of the non-profit. Some lotteries have not raised enough funds through ticket sales to cover the cost of prizes that have to be awarded and funds, that should be earmarked to help the needy, are used to cover lottery expenses. Third party fundraisers, usually professional telemarketers, are another source of ethical concern. They raise funds on the part of non-profit organizations, but the charity may only see a small portion of the money raised.[33] In the face of growing public scrutiny, not-for-profits have to be as ethically aware and socially responsible as their for-profit counterparts.

PRINCIPLES FOR PUBLIC POLICY TOWARD MARKETING

Finally, we want to propose several principles that might guide the formulation of public policy toward marketing. These principles reflect assumptions underlying much of modern marketing theory and practice.

◆ *The principle of consumer and producer freedom.* Freedom for producers and consumers is the cornerstone of a dynamic marketing system. Marketing freedom is important if a marketing system is to deliver a high standard of living. People can achieve satisfaction in their own terms rather than in terms defined by someone else. This leads to greater fulfilment through a closer matching of products to desires. But more principles are needed to implement this freedom and prevent abuses.

◆ *The principle of curbing potential harm.* As much as possible, transactions freely entered into by producers and consumers are their private business. The political system curbs producer or consumer freedom only to prevent transactions that harm or threaten to harm the producer, consumer, or third parties. Transactional harm is widely recognized grounds for government intervention. The major issue is whether there is sufficient actual or potential harm to justify the intervention.

♦ *The principle of meeting basic needs.* The marketing system should serve disadvantaged consumers as well as affluent ones. In a free-enterprise system, producers make goods for markets that are willing and able to buy. Certain groups who lack purchasing power may go without needed goods and services, causing harm to their physical or psychological well-being. While preserving the principle of producer and consumer freedom, the marketing system should support economic and political actions to solve this problem. It should strive to meet the basic needs of all people, and all people should share to some extent in the standard of living it creates.

♦ *The principle of economic efficiency.* The marketing system strives to supply goods and services efficiently and at low prices. The extent to which a society's needs and wants can be satisfied depends on how efficiently its scarce resources are used. Free economies rely on active competition and informed buyers to make a market efficient. To make profits, competitors must watch their costs carefully while developing products, prices, and marketing programs that serve buyer needs. Buyers get the most satisfaction by finding out about different competing products, prices, and qualities, and choosing carefully. The presence of active competition and well-informed buyers keeps quality high and prices low.

♦ *The principle of innovation.* The marketing system encourages authentic innovation to bring down production and distribution costs and to develop new products to meet changing consumer needs. Much innovation is really imitation of other brands, with a slight difference to provide a selling point. But an effective marketing system encourages real product innovation and differentiation to meet the wants of different market segments.

♦ *The principle of consumer education and information.* An effective marketing system invests heavily in consumer education and information to increase long-run consumer satisfaction and welfare. The principle of economic efficiency requires this investment, especially in cases where products are confusing because of their numbers and conflicting claims. Ideally, companies will provide enough information about their products. But consumer groups and the government can also give out information and ratings. Students in public schools can take courses in consumer education to learn better buying skills.

♦ *The principle of consumer protection.* Consumer education and information cannot do the whole job of protecting consumers. The marketing system also must provide consumer protection. Modern products are so complex that even trained consumers cannot evaluate them with confidence. Consumers do not know whether a mobile phone gives off cancer-causing radiation, whether a new automobile has safety flaws, or whether a new drug product has dangerous side effects. A government agency must review and judge the safety levels of various foods, drugs, toys, appliances, fabrics, automobiles, and housing. Consumers may buy products but fail to understand the environmental consequences, so consumer protection also covers production and marketing activities that might harm the environment. Finally, consumer protection prevents deceptive practices and high-pressure selling techniques where consumers would be defenceless.

These seven principles are based on the assumption that marketing's goal is not to maximize company profits or total consumption or consumer choice, but rather to maximize life quality. Life quality means meeting basic needs, having available many good products, and enjoying the natural and cultural environment. Properly managed, the marketing system can help to create and deliver a higher quality of life to people around the world.

Summary of Chapter Objectives

Responsible marketers discover what consumers want and respond with the right products, priced to give good value to buyers and profit to the producer. A marketing system should sense, serve, and satisfy consumer needs and improve the quality of consumers' lives. In working to meet consumer needs, marketers may take some actions that are not to everyone's liking or benefit. Marketing managers should be aware of the main criticisms of marketing.

1. **Identify the major social criticisms of marketing.**

   Marketing's impact on individual consumer welfare has been criticized for its high prices, deceptive practices, high-pressure selling, shoddy or unsafe products, planned obsolescence, and poor service to disadvantaged consumers. Marketing's impact on society has been criticized for creating false wants and too much materialism, too few social goods, cultural pollution, and too much political power. Critics have also criticized marketing's impact on other businesses for harming competitors and reducing competition through acquisitions, practices that create barriers to entry, and unfair competitive marketing practices.

2. **Define consumerism and environmentalism and explain how they affect marketing strategies.**

   Concerns about the marketing system have led to citizen-action movements. Consumerism is an organized social movement intended to strengthen the rights and power of consumers relative to sellers. Alert marketers view it as an opportunity to serve consumers better by providing more consumer information, education, and protection. Environmentalism is an organized social movement seeking to minimize the harm done to the environment and quality of life by marketing practices. The first wave of modern environmentalism was driven by environmental groups and concerned consumers, whereas the second wave was driven by government, which passed laws and regulations governing industrial practices impacting the environment. Moving into the twenty-first century, the first two environmentalism waves are merging into a third and stronger wave in which companies are accepting responsibility for doing no environmental harm. Companies now are adopting policies of environmental sustainability—developing strategies that both sustain the environment and produce profits for the company.

3. **Describe the principles of socially responsible marketing.**

   Many companies originally opposed these social movements and laws, but most of them now recognize a need for positive consumer information, education, and protection. Some companies have followed a policy of enlightened marketing, which holds that a company's marketing should support the best long-run performance of the marketing system. Enlightened marketing consists of five principles: consumer-oriented marketing, innovative marketing, value marketing, sense-of-mission marketing, and societal marketing.

4. **Explain the role of ethics in marketing.**

   Increasingly, companies are responding to the need to provide company policies and guidelines to help their managers deal with questions of marketing ethics. Of course, even the best guidelines cannot resolve all of the difficult ethical decisions that firms must make. But there are some principles that marketers can choose among. One principle states that such issues should be decided by the free market and legal system. A second, and more enlightened, principle puts responsibility not in the system but in the hands of individual companies and managers. Each firm and marketing manager must develop a philosophy of socially responsible and ethical behaviour. Under the societal marketing concept, managers must look beyond what is legal and allowable and develop standards based on personal integrity, corporate conscience, and long-term consumer welfare.

   Because business standards and practices vary among countries, the issue of ethics poses special challenges for international marketers. The growing consensus among today's marketers is that it is important to make a commitment to a common set of shared standards worldwide.

5. List the major principles for public policy toward marketing.

To maximize life quality for all peoples, public policy toward marketing might be guided by seven principles. These principles are (1) the principle of consumer and producer freedom; (2) the principle of curbing potential harm; (3) the principle of meeting basic needs; (4) the principle of economic efficiency; (5) the principle of innovation; (6) the principle of consumer education and information; and (7) the principle of consumer protection.

Key Terms

Consumerism *(p. 688)*
Consumer-oriented marketing *(p. 695)*
Deficient products *(p. 698)*
Desirable products *(p. 698)*
Enlightened marketing *(p. 695)*
Environmentalism *(p. 689)*
Innovative marketing *(p. 696)*
Pleasing products *(p. 698)*
Salutary products *(p. 698)*
Sense-of-mission marketing *(p. 697)*
Societal marketing *(p. 697)*
Value marketing *(p. 696)*

Discussing the Issues

1. Many firms, like Molson, Canada Trust, Procter & Gamble, Bell Canada, and Imperial Oil, have been practising cause-related marketing as a means of fulfilling their social responsibilities. Cause-related marketing is the practice of associating a for-profit firm's products or services with a not-for-profit cause. While the primary purpose of the program is the accomplishment of marketing objectives, the not-for-profit also achieves significant benefits from these campaigns. Describe some of the cause-related campaigns you have seen. Do you think they are a legitimate means for firms to fulfil part of their social responsibility?

2. Does marketing *create* barriers to entry or *reduce* them? Describe how a small manufacturer of household cleaning products could use advertising to compete with Procter & Gamble.

3. If you were a marketing manager at Dow Chemical Company, tell which you would prefer: government regulations on acceptable levels of air and water pollution, or a voluntary industry code suggesting target levels of emissions. Why?

4. Go to a web site of a Canadian business publication that places their current editions online (for example, Brunico Communications Inc. http://www.brunico.com, publishers of *KidScreen*, and *Strategy: The Canadian Marketing Report*; *Marketing* magazine (http://www.marketingmag.ca); *The Financial Post* (http://www.canoe.ca/fp); or the *Globe and Mail* (http://www.globeandmail.ca). Look through the online edition(s) of one of these magazines. Classify the articles on specific companies according to whether they have unethical marketing practices, environmental sustainability practices, or enlightened marketing practices. In what classification do most of the companies fall? What does this tell you about Canadian business practices today?

5. Compare the marketing concept with the principle of societal marketing. Do you think marketers should adopt the societal marketing concept? Why or why not?

6. If you had the power to change our marketing system in any way feasible, decide what improvements you would make. What improvements could you make as a consumer or entry-level marketing practitioner?

Applying the Concepts

1. Changes in consumer attitudes, especially the growth of consumerism and environmentalism, have led to more societal marketing—and to more marketing that is

supposedly good for society, but is actually closer to deception. (a) List three examples of marketing campaigns that you feel are genuine societal marketing. If possible, find examples of advertising or packaging that supports these campaigns. (b) Find three examples of deceptive or borderline imitations of societal marketing. How are you able to tell which campaigns are genuine and which are not? (c) What remedies, if any, would you recommend for this problem?

2. As a society, Canadians have many things to be proud of—and many areas where there is more work to be done. (a) Make a list of 10 important social issues in Canada. Your list may include economic issues, education, health care, environment, politics, or any other significant sphere. (b) Pick one issue that is especially important to you from the list above. Using what you have learned from this course, make a list of ways in which marketing principles and tools could be used to help on your issue.

References

1. Speech by Bruce Pope, CEO Molson Breweries, Queen's University, School of Business, March 27, 1996; Jon Entine, "Rain-forest Chic," *Report on Business Magazine*, October 1995, pp. 41–52; Janet MacPhail, "Event Marketing: Social Marketing a Process, Not a Program," *Strategy: The Canadian Marketing Report*, September 29, 1997, p. 20; David Menzies, "All For a Good Cause," *Marketing*, September 26, 1994, pp. 13–15; Erica Zlomislic, "Sears backs PC donation effort," *Strategy: The Canadian Marketing Report*, November 24, 1997, p. 1; "And the Winners Are ...," *Inter Sector: A Newsletter for Imagine's Community Partners*, Vol. 3, No. 6, p.1; Bell Canada's web site (www.bell.ca), "Bell Sponsorships"; "Editorial" Social Marketing Passes Test," *Strategy: The Canadian Marketing Report*, March 3, 1997, p. 10; "For the Record: Kids Help Ads," *KidScreen*, February 3, 1997, p. 7; "Wascana Energy Gives Kids a Head Start," *New Directions*, Vol. 1(2), pp. 1–2.

2. See John F. Gaski and Michael Etzel, "The Index of Consumer Sentiment Toward Marketing," *Journal of Marketing*, July 1986, pp. 71–81; Faye Rice, "How to Deal with Tough Customers," *Fortune*, December 3, 1990, pp. 38–48; and Richard W. Pollay and Banwari Mittal, "Here's the Beef: Factors, Determinants, and Segments in Consumer Criticism of Advertising," *Journal of Marketing*, July 1993, pp. 99–114.

3. Barrie McKenna, "Suzy Shier Fined $300 000," *Globe and Mail*, July 18, 1995, p. B7.

4. Sandra Pesmen, "How Low Is Low? How Free Is Free?" *Advertising Age*, May 7, 1990, p. S10.

5. See Judith Bell and Bonnie Maria Burlin, "In Urban Areas: Many More Still Pay More for Food," *Journal of Public Policy and Marketing*, Fall 1993, pp. 268–270; and Alan R. Andreasen, "Revisiting the Disadvantages: Old Lesson and New Problems," *Journal of Public Policy and Marketing*, Fall 1993, pp. 270–275.

6. Richard W. Pollay, "The Distorted Mirror: Reflections on the Unintended Consequences of Advertising," *Journal of Marketing*, April 1986, pp. 18–36.

7. See Anne B. Fisher, "A Brewing Revolt Against the Rich," *Fortune*, December 17, 1990, pp. 89–94; and Norval D. Glenn, "What Does Family Mean?" *American Demographics*, June 1992, pp. 30–37.

8. From an advertisement for *Fact* magazine, which does not carry advertisements.

9. Ann Gibbon, "Smoking's Labelling Perils," *Globe and Mail*, May 5, 1994, pp. B1–B2.

10. For more details, see Paul N. Bloom and Stephen A. Greyser, "The Maturing of Consumerism," *Harvard Business Review*, November-December 1981, pp. 130–139; Robert J. Samuelson, "The Aging of Ralph Nader," *Newsweek*, December 16, 1985, p. 57; Douglas A. Harbrecht, "The Second Coming of Ralph Nader," *Business Week*, March 6, 1989, p. 28.

11. Consumers' Association of Canada, Box 9300, Ottawa, Ontario K1G 3T9, web page (http://www.ccn.dal.ca/cac/cacwhatis:html).

12. Ken MacQueen, "Ministers Declare War on Excess Packaging," *The Whig-Standard*, March 22, 1990, p. 11.

13. Helen Kohl, "Are They Nature's Choice," *The Financial Post*, April 11, 1990, p. 18.

14. Tony Martin, "The Call to Go Green Gets a Hearing in Corporate Boardrooms," *Report on Environmental Protection, Globe and Mail*, February 27, 1990, p. C8.

15. "How Green is Green?" *Canadian Consumer*, Vol. 19, No. 9, 1989, p. 6.

16. David Buzzelli, "Corporate Ethics and the Environment: The Challenge for Business Leaders," *Agenda for Action: A Report on Business and the Environment: An Ethical Solution*, Canadian Centre for Ethics and Corporate Policy, Toronto, February 1990, pp. 13–16.

17. Stuart L. Hart, "Beyond Greening: Strategies for a Sustainable World," *Harvard Business Review*, January-February 1997, pp. 66–76.

18. Ibid, p. 74.

19. Michael E. Porter and Claas van de Linde, "Green and Competitive: Ending the Stalemate," *Harvard Business Review*, September-October 1995, pp. 120–134.

20. Stuart Hart, "Beyond Greening," p. 72.

21. Ibid, p. 83; and Linda Grant, 'Monsanto's Bet: There's Gold in Going Green," *Fortune*, April 14, 1997, pp. 116–118.

22. S. Noble Robinson, Ralph Earle III, and Ronald A.N. McLean, "Transnational Corporations and Global Environmental Policy," *Prizm*, Arthur D. Little, Inc., Cambridge, MA, First Quarter, 1994, pp. 51–63.

23. Ibid, p. 56.

24. Linda Sutherland, "Brothers Find Focus in Waste," *Globe and Mail*, January 6, 1997, p. B8.

25. Louise Gagnon, "Cosmetic Changes," *Marketing*, July 21/28, 1997, p. 18.

26. Ian Cruickshank, "Fun Factory," *Report on Business Magazine*, August 1997, pp. 30–34.

27. Michael McCullough, "Vancouver's LPB Creates for the Animals," *Marketing*, November 20, 1995, p. 6.

28. "Getting Involved in the Community: The HP Way," supplement sponsored by Hewlett-Packard (Canada) Ltd., *Report on Business*, April 1996, p. 30.

29. Dan R. Dalton and Richard A. Cosier, "The Four Faces of Social Responsibility," *Business Horizons*, May-June 1982, pp. 19–27.

30. Survey data collected by Peggy Cunningham and Derek Gent, Queen's University, School of Business, May 1995.

31. Janet McFarland, "When Is a Gift a Bribe?" *Globe and Mail*, January 15, 1996; "GM's Gift Policy Covers the Bases—From Football to Prickly Plants," *Globe and Mail*, September 11, 1997, p. B17.

32. Laurence Hebb, "Foreign Bribes Test Laws at Home," *Globe and Mail*, October 16, 1997, B2; Ijeoma Ross, "New Ethics Code Is Just a Start," *Globe and Mail*, September 9, 1997, p. B17; Jeff Sallot, "Ottawa Takes Middle Road on Ethics," *Globe and Mail*, September 6, 1997.

33. Simone Collier, "Chump Change," *Report on Business Magazine*, October 1996, pp. 90-100.

Company Case 20

DIET PILLS: TOO GOOD TO BE GOOD FOR YOU

The old adage "Perception is reality" certainly applies to body image. A recent survey found that 90 percent of respondents believe that they weigh too much, even though only 25 percent of the survey population was deemed to be medically overweight. Even more troubling is the fact that this number includes women who are actually underweight, but who still view themselves as fat. North Americans spend almost $60 billion a year trying to stay thin. It is a strange industry. What other industry sector could keep selling products and services that fail to perform as promised? People buy diet pills, join health clubs, and use weight management services, but they keep gaining weight.

No one denies that being medically overweight is a serious medical problem. The number of people in this category is growing as the population ages. Some analysts believe that the cost of the overweight North American population is approaching $150 billion a year. The medical community considers obesity to be the second-greatest health hazard—right behind smoking. But there is a difference between those people who are actually overweight, and those who perceive themselves to be in this category despite the fact they are well within their recommended weight limits.

Perceptions of obesity may make people susceptible to unscrupulous marketing tactics. They purchase premium-priced products that have dubious benefits. For example, a single can of Slim Fast powder that lasts only one week costs $13.99. Products sold by Weight Watchers are priced significantly higher than other food items in the same product category, yet people purchasing these diet foods keep cash registers humming. Programs such as Jenny Craig promise people new figures and more fulfilling lives.

While these products and services may eat up consumers' dollars, they probably don't result in significant long-term harm. The same isn't true for a diet pill named Redux. After receiving approval by the U.S. Federal Drug Administration (FDA), the product was launched with a major promotional program. In just five years, sales of Redux soared to an estimated $1.4 billion annually. It wasn't long, however, before serious questions were raised about Redux. The prestigious *New England Journal of Medicine* published a study linking the main ingredient in Redux to a rare but fatal lung disorder. Even though sales declined and the FDA removed Redux from the market, it was already too late for consumers who suffered and died from taking a seemingly harmless item—diet pills.

Why do such tragedies occur? Are consumers to blame with their obsession with being thin? Certainly this obsession has driven sales of diet soft drinks to a level of $25 billion a year. Health clubs rake in an additional $14 billion; exercise-equipment manufacturers have sales of $6 billion a year; and commercial weight-loss programs, such as Weight Watchers, earn more than $3 billion a year. Not only is this a large market, but it has also been experiencing considerable growth potential. If nothing else, it is almost guaranteed repeat business. Almost all of the North Americans who shed pounds each year put them back on eventually, and the dieting-exercising cycle starts all over again.

Dieting and exercising require effort and time. People must forego what they want most—lots of tasty food—and suffer the pain and discomfort of exercise in order to lose only a pound or two a week. Doctors and public health officials frequently caution against losing too much weight too quickly. Consequently, the deprivation and suffering can go on for a long time. No wonder diet pills look so good. Taking pills is easy, requires no immediate or obvious pain, and doesn't force you to give up what you want.

Redux was a prescription drug, but certainly word-of-mouth had its effect and taking a pill is easier than exercising. Moreover, Redux succeeded in curbing people's appetites. Users of Redux found that they would sit down to a normal meal but never finish it. They felt full and satisfied before eating everything on their plate. As a result, they ate less. Some users lost as much as 40 pounds in just two months—instant success with little effort or pain! Given news of the product's success, it's not surprising that overweight North Americans were flooding doctors' offices seeking prescriptions for the product.

But why would medical practitioners who are concerned with people's health recommend or prescribe such a product? Some of the blame can be placed at the door of manufacturers, who were overly zealous in their attempts to sell the product. Pharmaceutical salespeople pitched the drug to family physicians, psychiatrists, cardiologists, interns, and even gynecologists—people who are less likely to be familiar with the drug or treatment of obesity. According to one analysis, Redux salespeople logged 140 000 doctor visits in the first three months alone—making it one of the largest drug launches in 1996. Doctors received patient starter kits that contained coupons for joining Weight Watchers and Jenny Craig diet centres. Consultants believed that receipt of the kits encouraged doctors to prescribe the drug without monitoring a patient's weight loss.

While some health risks were known at the time of the launch, some salespeople either were unaware of them or neglected to mention them during their sales calls. One physician, Dr. Gary Huber, says that the salesperson who called on him touted Redux as safe for lifetime use—even though the company's own brochures admit that the drug had been tested for only one year—and hardly addressed the lung disease risk. "I was amazed at how little the salesman knew," Dr. Huber said. Thus, poorly prepared or overly aggressive salespeople were calling on doctors who might be unfamiliar with either weight-loss methods or drugs, and who in turn might prescribe the product to people whose weight loss they did not monitor.

Although many doctors believe that an approved drug is a safe drug, Redux was initially approved with a caveat. Doctors were to prescribe it only for use by obese patients—individuals who were at least 15 to 20 pounds overweight. The FDA knew that pulmonary hypertension (a constriction of blood vessels near the heart that can lead to heart failure) was associated with Redux. An international study indicated that use of Redux could lead to the death of as many as 46 people per million when taken for just three months. However, ordinary aspirin can kill more individuals per million than Redux. For obese persons, the risk of death or debilitation from Redux was acceptable precisely because the risk of death or debilitation from obesity is higher. Consequently, some of the risk associated with Redux was known to the FDA and was considered acceptable under certain conditions.

The major problem, however, was not with medically obese people who were closely supervised by their doctors. Rather, it occurred with the millions of individuals who were only a few pounds overweight, or not even overweight at all, and wanted Redux to shed a few pounds so that they would look better. For these people, Redux raised the risks of death to unacceptable levels. Some knew the risks and wanted the drug anyway, but others did not. Again, the obsession with being thin, coupled with the willingness of doctors to prescribe a heavily marketed drug, led to use of Redux by the wrong market segment.

When one reads of cases such as Redux, one wonders who is to blame for such tragic occurrences. Was it government regulators who approved a drug with known side effects? Was it salespeople who were motivated to earn their commissions regardless of the consequences for final consumers? Was it harried doctors who were too busy to follow up with their patients? Or was it consumers themselves who pursue an elusive body image that few can actually attain?

QUESTIONS

1. Think through the traditional buyers' and sellers' rights listed in this chapter. Which rights were violated in the Redux case?

2. The Redux case is an example of a product that caused extreme harm. While the outcomes may be less severe, do you think other products with diet positionings exploit consumers in the same way (think of the products you see labelled as "lite," cholesterol free, or calorie reduced).

3. Many critics blame advertising for people's obsession with thinness. Do you think these criticisms are valid? Can you find specific ads that help support your claim? What is the effect of campaigns like the one recently featured by Body Shop showing a model with a rounded figure, or Special K's efforts to make women more aware of the need

for a healthy diet? While women are most often viewed as the victims of poor body images, do men feel pressured by images of slim, muscular male models in ads?

4. If you were the marketing manager for a firm marketing a diet pill, what methods could you develop that would prevent a case like Redux from repeating itself? What would a code of ethics for such a firm look like?

Sources: L. Davis, A. Gardiner, D. Greene, K. Harness, and S. Mickle, "The Ethics of the Diet Industry," case written for Comm 338, Queen's University; Robert Langreth, "Is Marketing of Diet Pill too Aggressive?" *Wall Street Journal*, November 21, 1996, p. B1; Robert Langreth, "Diet-drug Mix May Damage Heart Valves," *Wall Street Journal,* July 9 1997, p. B1; Robert Langreth, "Eminent Journal Urges Moratorium on Diet-drug Use," *Wall Street Journal,* August 28, 1997, p. B1; Michael D. Lemonick, "The Miracle Drug?" *Time,* September 23, 1996, from Time web site, www.pathfinder.com/time/magazine/domestic/1996/960923/test.html; and Jay Palmer, "Hey, Fatso!" *Barron's,* July 1, 1996, p. 25–29.

Video Case 20

Classrooms for Sale

Public schools, like many public-sector organizations, are facing cutbacks in government funding. As a result, some have started considering partnerships with businesses to generate cash to maintain expensive programs like sports and buy costly equipment such as computers. Art Kelly, principal of Assumption Catholic Secondary School in Brampton, Ontario, has encouraged business partnerships in his school. A basketball scoreboard sponsored by Coca-Cola for about $500 a month is just one of his partnership programs that critics claim is exposing his students to subtle and unethical methods of persuasion.

Business involvement in schools was evident in Canada as far back as the 1920s when Ivory soap sponsored soap-carving contests and provided songbooks to schools containing "company" songs. While there was little questioning of such activities at that time, the anti-establishment sentiments that characterized the 1960s put an end to corporate involvement in schools until recently. With fiscal pressures mounting on schools, many administrators are faced with the choice of seeking out business financing or not being able to offer what many would consider important school programs.

Some of the most vocal critics of school and business partnerships are teachers. Some teacher associations have opposed the influence of corporations in schools, arguing that schools are a place of learning and should be a shelter for children against commercialization. To answer this criticism, Kelly wonders why we would want to protect students from the very world they have to live in.

The business/school partnership often goes beyond providing capital or equipment. At Kelly's school, for example, several local entrepreneurs and business people are brought into the classroom to assist in curriculum delivery. In one class, a local car dealer discusses the differences between buying and leasing a car. While some students and teachers claim that these guest lectures enhance the learning that students will experience, others recognize that from the business person's perspective, students and/or their parents are a lucrative target market. By giving a lecture to students, the business person has the opportunity to influence perceptions about the company and its products or services. While that opportunity may cost thousands of dollars to purchase in mass media such as television or magazines, the guest lecture offers that opportunity free of charge.

Art Kelly has no problem providing his students as marketing opportunities for business people. "I'm a business person," he says, "involved in running, if you like, a school, but also a franchise. You are going to have to be able to draw in corporate dollars to keep your schools going." As he looks at his school's Coca-Cola scoreboard, he is open about the fact that he is not loyal to Coca-Cola. If Pepsi or another competitor in the industry came in with more money, he would displace the Coca-Cola logo. "They are going to drink something," says Kelly.

Questions:

1. Is there a difference between the ethics of guest lectureships compared to corporate sponsorships in public schools?

2. Do partnerships between businesses and schools violate the "principle of consumer education and information" and the "principle of consumer protection," which are two of the principles for public policy toward marketing outlined in the text? Do they violate the "right to consumer education" outlined by the Consumers' Association of Canada?

3. Why don't more corporations donate money to schools without having their name associated with that donation?

4. What is the nature of corporate sponsorships in universities? Are these sponsorships ethical?

Source: This case was prepared by Auleen Carson and is based on "Marketing in the Classroom," *Undercurrents,* (March 14, 1997).

KRAFT CANADA INC. NEW PRODUCT DEVELOPMENT— CHILDREN'S CEREAL

In November 1995, Susan Morrison, Product Manager, New Product Development (Children's Cereals), sat at her desk in the Toronto headquarters of Kraft Canada Inc. working on a new product development proposal for a Peanut Butter & Jam (PB&J) cereal. Susan had joined KCI in 1993, after graduating from Queen's University with an honours bachelor of commerce degree. Her performance record to date had been outstanding, and she had progressed rapidly through the company, receiving her latest promotion to her present position only two months ago. This was her first big project as a product manager, and she was eager for the challenges that lay ahead.

PB&J cereal had just completed a six-month test market trial in British Columbia with mixed results. It was up to her to come up with a detailed launch recommendation for this new product. Whether she chose to launch or not, she needed to justify her reasons—especially considering the fact that Tom Johnson, Vice President of Marketing for Breakfast Cereals, was a strong proponent of PB&J.

Susan was particularly concerned with how to allocate her limited dollars for new product development in order to address what she perceived to be the key areas: advertising, trade support, in-store promotions, and manufacturing. The maximum amount that Susan could spend on this project was $4 million. If the product was to be a success, it would need a careful balancing of these elements. As well, these decisions needed to take into consideration the present competitive environment. Susan's position had been created out of a corporate mandate to focus on and foster new products (which presently made up over 20 percent of the total cereal category volume), in order to grow share and volume in a fast-growing cereal market, Susan's time had come to turn opportunity into success.

In 1988, Philip Morris, the leading consumer-products company in the world, purchased Kraft for $13 billion dollars and subsequently merged it with General Foods, which Philip Morris already owned, to create Kraft General Foods. In 1989, it announced that Kraft and General Foods Canadian operations would be merged, with the head office personnel located in Toronto and the operations and technology group located in Montreal. Exhibits 1 and 2 contain the organizational structure of Philip Morris and KGFC.

As a result of the merger, KGFC became the largest packaged-goods company in Canada, with 1992 sales of $1.8 billion (Procter & Gamble was second with 1992 sales of $1.75 billion). The company sold a wide variety of food products to Canadian consumers, a sample list of which is included in Exhibit 3. Along with its strong brand portfolio and size, KGFC had well-established positions in food distribution channels and an excellent reputation for its food technology and food applications (such as recipes). The company had also pursued a program of strategic acquisitions in order to grow the business. In January 1993, KGFC had acquired NABISCO cereals to add to its own POST[1] cereals portfolio. In February 1995,

---

[1] Unless indicated otherwise, a brand name in capital letters denotes a registered trade-mark of Kraft Canada Inc.

Exhibit 1 *Kraft Canada Inc.: Structure of Philip Morris*

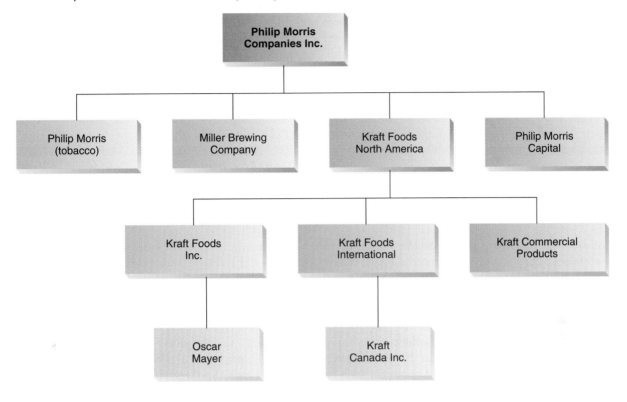

Exhibit 2 *Kraft Canada Inc.: Structure of Kraft Canada Inc.*

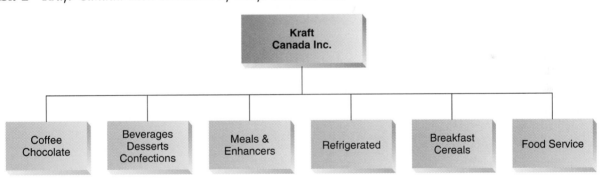

Exhibit 3 *Kraft Canada Inc.*

List of Major Food Brands Marketed by Kraft Foods	
CRACKER BARREL cheddar cheese	KOOL-AID beverages
KRAFT SINGLES process cheese	MINUTE rice
MAXWELL HOUSE coffee	SHAKE'N BAKE coating mixes
SANKA decaffeinated coffee	STOVE TOP stuffing mixes
GENERAL FOODS INTERNATIONAL COFFEE	MAGIC MOMENTS puddings
instant coffee mix	PHILADELPHIA cream cheese
NABOB coffee	TOBLERONE[2] chocolate
POST cereals (e.g., HONEYCOMB, ALPHA-BITS,	CRYSTAL LIGHT beverages
SUGAR-CRISP)	KRAFT pourable dressings
SHREDDIES, GOLDEN HONEY, SHREDDIES,	BAKER'S chocolates
NABISCO SHREDDED WHEAT	KRAFT DINNER
JELL-O desserts	CHEEZ WHIZ
TANG breakfast drink	

[2] TOBLERONE is a registered trademark of Chocolat Tobler Ltd. used under license by Kraft Canada Ltd.

reflecting the strong equity and heritage associated with the Kraft trademark amongst consumers, Kraft General Foods announced plans to change the corporate name to Kraft Foods Inc., with the Canadian subsidiary becoming known as Kraft Canada Inc. (KCI). Additionally, KCI had established a strong leadership mission, which required its operations to achieve outstanding quality, to obtain excellent financial results and to foster innovation. Six overall strategies had been developed focusing on using the company's competitive strengths to achieve its goals. Exhibit 4 outlines the six strategies.

THE CHILDREN'S CEREAL MARKET IN CANADA

The children's cereal market in Canada included all "pre-sweetened" cereals and represented approximately 23 percent of the growing $350-million total retail ready-to-eat[3] cereal market in 1994. In 1995, the children's cereal market was forecast to grow by over five percent, compared with 1.5 percent for the overall cereal category. The average retail selling price for a box of children's cereal was $3.80 in 1994. Although children sometimes ate adult-oriented products such as

SHREDDIES cereal, they usually chose a children's brand when given a choice. Retailers generally placed children's cereals on the bottom shelves in the cereal aisle so that children could reach them easily. Exhibit 5 provides a list of major children's cereals available in Canada in 1994.

In 1995 Kraft marketed cereals under the POST trademark. POST children's cereals included three major brands (HONEYCOMB, SUGAR-CRISP, and ALPHA-BITS) and three minor brands (Fruity PEBBLES,[4] Cocoa PEBBLES and Marshmallow ALPHA-BITS). The major POST brands were sold in both small and large pack sizes (250–275g and 400–450g respectively) through supermarkets and convenience stores, while the minor brands only came in one size (375g and 400g respectively). In 1994, these brands held a strong number 2 position in the children's cereal market. Exhibit 6 provides a breakdown of POST children's cereal shares by brand.

POST children's cereals were aimed at children aged 3 to 12. There was no "over-all" positioning for POST children's cereals, instead they were individually positioned to provide unique consumer benefits. Exhibit 7 provides a table of brand positionings for POST cereals. Spokescharacters were used to provide

Exhibit 4 *Kraft Foods Inc.*

Corporate Strategies
1. Focus resources on high-priority, high-growth and high-return potential businesses; harvest/divest others.
2. Aggressively manage new business development activities while avoiding undue risk and vigorously defend established businesses.
3. Exploit all synergies across Kraft Foods and other Philip Morris companies.
4. Pursue maximum productivity.
5. Manage with global perspective.
6. Be organizationally flexible.

Exhibit 5 *Kraft Canada Inc.*

1994 Major Children's Cereal Brands in Canada			
POST	**KELLOGG'S**	**GENERAL MILLS**	**QUAKER OATS**
SUGAR CRISP	FROSTED FLAKES	CINNAMON TOAST CRUNCH	CAP'N CRUNCH
HONEYCOMB	FROOT LOOPS	Monster Cereals (COUNT CHOCULA, FRANKEN-BERRY, etc.)	
ALPHA-BITS	MARSHMALLOW KRISPIES	LUCKY CHARMS	
Fruity PEBBLES	CORN POPS	COCOA PUFFS	
Cocoa PEBBLES		GOLDEN GRAHAMS	
Marshmallow ALPHA-BITS		PRO*STARS	
		TRIX	

[3] as opposed to cereal which require cooking, such as oatmeal.

[4] PEBBLES is a registered trade-mark of Hanna-Barbara Productions, Inc. used under license by Kraft Canada Inc.

Exhibit 6   *Kraft Canada Inc.*

	POST Children's Cereal Brand Shares				
	1990	**1991**	**1992**	**1993**	**1994**
HONEYCOMB Share	8.2	8.8	9.0	9.1	9.4
ALPHA-BITS Share	7.8	8.1	8.1	8.2	8.4
SUGAR-CRISP Share	6.3	6.8	6.9	7.1	7.2
PEBBLES Share	4.1	4.4	4.5	4.4	4.3
Marshmallow ALPHA-BITS Share	0.0	1.1	1.6	1.7	2.0
Total POST Children's Share	**26.4**	**29.2**	**30.1**	**30.5**	**31.3**

Exhibit 7   *Kraft Canada Inc.*

	Brand Positioning		
Brand	**Target Ages**	**Positioning**	**Key Consumer Benefit**
SUGAR-CRISP	6-11	The great tasting cereal that Sugar Bear loves and can't get enough of.	The fun of experiencing Sugar Bear's "cool" as he fulfils his craving for SUGAR-CRISP cereal.
ALPHA-BITS	3-7	The letter shaped cereal.	The fun of creating "magical" experiences using ALPHA-BITS letter shapes.
HONEYCOMB	3-12	The "big" cereal—big in size, big in taste enjoyment, and big on life's adventures.	Larger-than-life adventures while enjoying the "big" taste of HONEY-COMB cereal.
Marshmallow ALPHA-BITS	3-7	The letter shaped cereal with marshmallow vowels.	The fun taste of marshmallow vowels.
PEBBLES	3-7	Fred and Barney's favourite cereal because it has a distinctive, flavourful taste.	The Bedrockian fun of enjoying the flavourful taste of PEBBLES cereal.

Source: The Globe & Mail, Thursday, October 13, 1994

an emotional link between the product and children. For example, the Honeycomb Kid impressed children with larger-than-life adventures while enjoying the "big" taste of HONEYCOMB cereal.

Any launch strategy that Susan devised would not include Quebec. Quebec law restricted advertising to children such that advertising was not a viable marketing alternative in that province. As a result, a business plan for Quebec would not be required of Susan at this time.

THE COMPETITION

The children's cereal market in Canada was made up of several large brand-name manufacturers. Although private-label store brands did exist, their market share was presently insignificant. Kellogg's was the leader in the

children's cereal market in 1994 primarily due to the strength of its two major brands—FROSTED FLAKES[5] and FROOT LOOPS.[6] Kellogg's had changed its business objective to aggressive volume growth in early 1991. As a result, they had placed increased emphasis on new product development and expansion. The KCI sales force had recently noticed a number of new products being tested in various regions across Canada. Exhibit 8 contains a market share breakdown by manufacturer, as well as a breakdown of marketing expenditures for POST children's cereals.

The other two competitors in the market were General Mills and Quaker Oats. General Mills' major brands included CINNAMON TOAST CRUNCH,[7] PRO*STARS,[8] and LUCKY CHARMS.[9] General Mills'

[5] FROSTED FLAKES is a registered trade-mark of Kellogg Canada Inc.

[6] FROOT LOOPS is a registered trade-mark of Kellogg Canada Inc.

[7] CINNAMON TOAST CRUNCH is a registered trade-mark of General Mills Canada, Inc.

[8] PRO*STARS is a registered trade-mark of General Mills Canada, Inc.

[9] LUCKY CHARMS is a registered trade-mark of General Mills Canada, Inc.

Exhibit 8 *Kraft Canada Inc.*

					Children's Cereal Market Statistics				
	1987	**1988**	**1989**	**1990**	**1991**	**1992**	**1993**	**1994**	**1995**[11]
% Market Volume Growth	+3	+5	+4	+3	+5	−5	+6	+4	+5
Market Sales ($000,000)	103	109	114	118	125	132	140	145	152
POST CHILDREN'S CEREALS									
Share	26	27	26	26	29	30	30	31	32
Trade as a % of Revenue	7	7	9	11	10	12	13	14	14
Advertising as a % of Revenue	18	17	16	17	24	18	18	18	20
Premiums as a % of Revenue	2	2	4	3	3	5	5	4	4
Manufacturing & Overheads as a % of Revenue	64	65	64	61	55	56	54	52	5—
KELLOGG's Share	52	51	51	52	50	51	48	45	44
GENERAL MILL's Share	12	11	12	12	10	9	10	10	11
QUAKER OAT's Share	8	8	8	7	7	6	7	7	5
OTHER Share	2	3	3	3	4	4	5	7	9

strategy had always been to launch new products to take advantage of popular children's trends. In the past nine years, General Mills had launched 10 new children's cereal brands, many of them being simple line extensions. Information indicated that General Mills was ready to step up its new product launches as well, attempting to capitalize on such trends as the recent dinosaur craze. Quaker Oats' only major children's brand was CAP'N CRUNCH,[10] and they had not launched any new children's products (other than a line extension) in the past decade.

Consumer Attitudes and Behaviour

It is generally accepted that children do have a good deal of influence over food purchase decisions—especially children's cereal purchases. In fact, research had shown that children, when physically in the store, choose the cereal 85 percent of the time, although parents usually retain the right to "veto" the purchase decision. Although product taste (and associated attributes, like texture) has the greatest influence on children's cereal preferences, two other factors also influence this: advertising and in-pack premiums. Advertising plays a significant role in impacting children's awareness levels and the degree of influence they exert on their parents. Television is the most influential medium, particularly among older children, likely the result of diminished parental restrictions. About three-quarters of mothers claim that their children's product preferences are influenced by television advertising. As such, television has always been the

advertising medium of choice by major children's cereal manufacturers.

In-pack premiums also play a major role in influencing children's decisions. Premiums such as stickers, small toys, and markers are added to the package of the product. POST children's cereals have always made a point of offering the "best" premiums, those with the highest degree of "value." Children view premiums as a bonus or surprise. Generally, retail price and a child's preference play an equal role in a mother's purchase decision. Recent evidence suggested that a cereal's nutritional content was starting to play a more significant role in a mother's decision to buy a cereal for her children. Things such as in-pack premiums, premiums, advertising, and point-of-purchase displays played a less important role in a mother's cereal purchase decision.

New Product Opportunity

PB&J cereal presented an interesting opportunity for KCI. One of the unique benefits of PB&J was that it could be made with KRAFT Peanut Butter and KRAFT Jam. PB&J provided children with a healthy alternative to sugar-coated cereals, without sacrificing taste. If Susan decided to launch this product nationally, senior management would want to see a comprehensive positioning strategy for this new brand before there would be any approval to proceed. History had shown that products that were poorly positioned or had their target weakly defined were doomed to failure.

In order to get some expert recommendations, Susan had asked Richard Murray, Account Director at

---

[10] CAP'N CRUNCH is a registered trade-mark of The Quaker Oats Company of Canada Limited.

[11] Forecasted figures from the 1995 Children's Cereal Marketing Plan.

the advertising agency, for some advice. Richard had worked on POST cereals for over eight years, and thus was extremely knowledgeable about the POST business and its advertising. In a recent conversation with Susan about PB&J he had said:

> I would strongly recommend positioning this product as the "wacky and wild cereal that is sure to gross out your parents." It's true that kids will only eat cereal if it tastes good to them, however a little "far-out" appeal goes a long way with them too. Kids will not beg their parents to buy a cereal that is healthy and nutritious.

On the other hand, Sheila Jones, Home Economist,[12] had commented that the 1990s were going to be the decade of healthier eating, with consumers making more informed choices about what they put in their mouths. She had suggested that PB&J be positioned as an all-natural children's cereal, which would certainly appeal to mothers. As she had said:

> Parents are watching more closely what they feed their children. PB&J provides us with the opportunity to enter an underdeveloped segment of the children's cereal market. Research from the B.C. test indicates that there is great potential for a "healthy" children's cereal. After all, the mother is the one who makes the ultimate decision.

One other issue for Susan to consider was the name of this new cereal. While it has been launched in B.C. as POST PB&J, some people, including her assistant Dave Beaton, Associate Product Manager, New Product Development (Children's Cereals), had suggested that perhaps one of the factors contributing to PB&J's less-than-spectacular test launch was its name:

> The name PB&J just isn't that exciting. It does not inspire anyone to want to try it. We need a name that will jump out at consumers, especially children, so that they will want to try it. Once they try it, the taste will sell them—our job is to get them to take it off the shelf.

ADVERTISING MIX

There were a number of issues to consider when trying to determine the appropriate advertising mix for the new product. Just yesterday, Richard Murray had emphasized how important advertising was in attempting to launch a new product:

> Advertising plays an important role in generating awareness of new products within the highly competitive cereal market. Dozens of new products are launched each year, but only a handful withstand the test of time. Television is the best medium to create awareness of a new product simply because of its mass nature. Television advertising leads to awareness of brands amongst an ever-changing target audience. In the case of POST children's cereals, we have created compelling, unique brand images that leverage brand value and build long-term brand equity.

Television advertising had long been the primary driver of generating awareness and expanding sales volume, but it was not cheap. Generally, TV flights lasted from four to six weeks at a time, and their residual value could be expected to last anywhere from one and a half to two months. Excluding Quebec, a national children's television campaign could run between $550 000 to $700 000 depending upon the coverage weight and frequency. Production costs were not included in this figure, and could run from $100 000 to $200 000 depending upon how elaborate the commercial was. The B.C. test market had not included TV advertising, as it was simply too expensive to produce a commercial for such a small market.

The placement of any television advertising used would be determined by the positioning of the product. This placement would then determine the cost. An ad shown during prime time could cost four to five times more than one shown during Saturday-morning cartoons. Thus a healthy positioning to moms would result in more expensive television advertising.

There were other forms of advertising to consider as well. Barb Johnson, Marketing Research Associate, (Children's Cereals), had been recommending some alternative forms of advertising:

> Don't forget, almost 80% of mom's purchase decisions take place in the store—money that has been traditionally spent on television advertising could be better spent on point-of-purchase advertising. It's a waste of money to spend all of your advertising dollars before the customer gets in the door—it's simply not worth it.

One of the possible forms of point-of-purchase advertising available was Infoshelf, an on-shelf display that projected perpendicularly from the shelf above or below the product and would hold a card displaying any of a number of things, from a coupon to a small version of a current print ad. It was essentially a print advertisement on the shelf. Attached would be coupons to save money on the purchase of the product. Infoshelf generally cost between $55 000 to $75 000 for a four-week national flight, plus the costs of coupon redemption, which could run anywhere from $50 000 to $90 000 depending upon the value and redemption rate of the offer. Another very successful in-store tool was in-store sampling, in which a booth was set up and shoppers were offered the product to sample. Couponing was often undertaken at the same time to provide an additional incentive to purchase the

---

[12] Home Economists were the "food experts" at KCI with extensive knowledge of nutrition, food preparation, and consumer tastes.

Exhibit 9   *Kraft Canada Inc. Infoshelf Sample—Infoflag & Ad Pad*

Exhibit 10   *Kraft Canada Inc. Infoshelf Sample—"Shelf Talker"*

Exhibit 11 *Kraft Canada Inc. In-Store Sampling*

In-store Sampling & Demonstration

Fully customized events provide one-on-one selling to a receptive, buying public.

In-store sampling and demonstration carries your advertising in-store and converts consumers with one-on-one contact right at the point where two thirds of all purchase decisions are made!

ACTMEDIA has become the largest product sampling and demonstration company in Canada by building enduring partnerships with a wide cross-section of clients.

What makes our programs so effective?

Experience:

We pride ourselves in finding a creative solution to your promotion challenges. From basic table top sampling, to mall tours and trade shows, to full blown theme demonstrations complete with characters, contests and other forms of creative consumer involvement, we can do it all - turn-key hassle free!

Unique Management System:

Our Account Managers are responsible for planning, directing, managing and executing the entire program, and ensuring your Sales Force maximizes the program's potential.

Unique Operation Structure:

In every major marketplace, our Operations Group provides a full-time manager, a team of supervisors, individual store communication with pre-event booking and confirmation, in-depth training of field staff, and a telephone hotline for fast answers to any questions that arise. They also facilitate the collection of program information.

Unique Information System:

Our computerized information system can generate customized store lists to your specification, monitor your program on a weekly basis, provide regular program reports, and produce a final results report detailing sales, inventory levels, coupon distribution and consumer reaction. We can report by item, store, chain or region ... by any break you wish. Most importantly, we report on a timely basis!

Trained Field Staff:

As the largest in our industry with over 3,600 field staff, we can ensure employment consistency, thereby attracting and retaining top-calibre, trained field personnel across the country. We can execute programs in any number of stores, anytime, for any duration! Challenge us!

ACTMEDIA
THE IN-STORE MARKETING NETWORK

product. However, in-store sampling was fairly expensive. On average, an eight-week national campaign (excluding Quebec) that covered approximately 20 percent of stores would cost $300 000 to $350 000. The B.C. test launch had included an initial four-week run of in-store sampling, followed by a four-week Infoshelf program. Exhibits 9, 10 and 11 show examples of both Infoshelf and in-store sampling.

Other forms of advertising included FSIs (free standing inserts), and door-to-door sampling. An FSI was a one-page ad which generally included a product coupon, and was distributed through local newspapers along with other FSIs in a flyer format. There were three companies nationally which produced FSI flyers, and a one-page ad in these flyers typically cost $50 000 for each week of national distribution. Door-to-door sampling was a very effective but expensive method of generating trial of a new product. Typically, a sample size of the product was mailed to a house, along with some coupons to entice the consumer to purchase the product at the store. An average price for door-to-door sampling was $1.50 per household, product (raw material) costs not included. There were roughly four million households in Canada (excluding Quebec), of which 35 percent were estimated to contain children under the age of 15.

TRADE SUPPORT

Securing trade support for a product launch was essential for any new product to succeed. The KCI sales force recognized the value of strong manufacturer-trade relationships, and had invested a great deal of time and energy into fostering these relationships. Their work had not gone unnoticed—the KCI sales force was widely recognized as the best in the industry. Over the past few years, the dollars spent on trade, primarily in trade deals,[13] had gradually been increasing, up to the point where this year it was estimated that trade spending would equal 50 percent of total advertising expenditures. Richard Lemond, Regional Sales Manager, Ontario, summed up the importance of trade support:

> Spending money on the trade motivates the trade to promote POST cereal. Retailers will be more likely to feature our product in retail advertising or display our product in the store, which will in turn increase our sales. The average cereal aisle is 60 feet long. After walking 20 feet, consumers generally recognize one brand they like, pick it up, and then not even look at the rest. When our cereal is promoted in the store, it builds on the awareness generated by our advertising investment.

Recently, Kellogg's and General Mills had increased their number of trade deals from three to four per year per brand. In addition, the value of these deals had also been increased significantly to support more store display and co-op (flyer) advertising. Richard advocated increasing the money available for deals with the trade on this new product, remarking:

> There are over 100 brands of cereal and only one or two are promoted by supermarkets each week. If Kellogg's has increased the number of times their brands are promoted, then some other cereal manufacturer will be promoted less. By increasing trade funds, I can ensure that POST cereal will get its fair share of trade support.

Presently, trade spending on a brand would amount to roughly $350 000 per trade deal. If Susan decided to increase trade spending, she could do one of two things. The first option would be to increase the number of deals that PB&J cereal offered. This could be somewhat risky because if another manufacturer offered retailers a better deal, PB&J cereal could lose out. Alternatively, as a second option, Susan could increase the depth of the discount offered on each deal (i.e., a greater percent reduction in price per case). This would likely ensure that PB&J would be promoted over other brands. However, this would not address the increase in trade deals from both Kellogg's and General Mills.

MANUFACTURING ISSUES

Production of PB&J on a national level would require refitting an old cereal line that was presently not being used. Modification to this line was estimated to cost $850 000. PB&J was a slightly more expensive product to produce than average children's cereals, given the higher price of its ingredients. Although product costs vary widely by brand depending upon the ingredients, average variable manufacturing costs (VMCs included raw materials, packaging, and labour costs directly associated with the manufacture of the product) of children's cereals were in the $0.75–$0.80/lb range. In total, it was estimated that PB&J would be five to seven percent more expensive to manufacture than other POST children's cereals. POST cereals typically strived to maintain a 10% to 15% margin on their selling price to retailers. In turn, retailers typically took an additional 20–25% margin at-shelf. Given the slightly higher manufacturing costs, Susan would have to decide whether to absorb the increased costs, or pass them on to the retailer, who in turn would undoubtedly increase the selling price.

MARKET RESEARCH

Although pre-launch test results had indicated that PB&J would be a success (as seen in Exhibit 12), test

---

[13] A trade deal was usually a combination of reduced factory selling prices and extra funds used to encourage the retail trade to promote a manufacturer's products. Most manufacturers divided the year into thirteen four-week deal periods.

Exhibit 12   *Kraft Canada Inc.*

	Purchase Intent—PB&J		
	Would Buy (%)	Might/Might Not Buy (%)	Would Not Buy (%)
1. After Viewing the Concept	30	38	32
2. After (1) and tasting the product	45	28	27
3. After (2) and being told it would sell for $3.95	18	35	47

Exhibit 13   *Kraft Canada Inc.*

	Purchase Intent—PB&J		
	Share Performance (%)		
	Objective	Actual	Variance
Sept '93	4.0	3.1	(0.9)
Aug '93	4.5	4.2	(0.3)
July '93	5.0	5.2	(0.2)
June '93	4.5	4.6	0.1
May '93	4.0	4.3	0.3
Apr '93	5.0	4.8	(0.2)

Exhibit 14   *Kraft Canada Inc.*

Market Research Results—B.C. Screening		
Suggested Advantages PB&J Has Over Other Children's Cereals		
	Pre-Test Focus Groups (N=250)	B.C. Consumer Test Groups (N=150)
PRODUCT RELATED		
New Product	14%	15%
Good/great taste	12%	10%
"Peanutty" flavour	14%	15%
"All natural" ingredients	20%	16%
PRICE/PACKAGING RELATED		
Cheaper/reasonable price	2%	1%
Appropriate size	15%	17%
Good premiums	16%	14%
IMAGE/MEDIA RELATED		
Name	14%	16%
Like concept of a PB&J cereal	9%	8%
Kids like/love it	15%	16%
All others	8%	7%
None/no advantage	38%	35%
Don't know/not stated	24%	21%

Exhibit 15 *Kraft Canada Inc.*

Market Research Results—B.C. Screening (cont'd)		
Suggested Advantages PB&J Has Over Other Children's Cereals		
	Pre-Test Focus Groups (N=250)	B.C. Consumer Test Groups (N=150)
PRODUCT RELATED		
New Product/not well known	5%	12%
"Funny" taste	9%	16%
Not enough flavour	6%	11%
Bad colour	2%	2%
PRICE/PACKAGING RELATED		
Price/too expensive	14%	19%
Small Package	3%	3%
Poor premiums	2%	3%
IMAGE/MEDIA RELATED		
Name	11%	19%
Poorly advertised/supported	—	10%
Don't like concept of a PB&J cereal	11%	9%
Kids don't like it	4%	4%
Don't like "healthy" image	7%	10%
All others	6%	5%
None/no advantage	45%	33%
Don't know/not stated	22%	18%

market performance had been mixed. Total share performance was below target figures, despite the fact that awareness was relatively high. Exhibit 13 provides a breakdown of month-by-month share figures for the B.C. test. Consumer research groups had commented on inconsistent product quality, but production had attributed much of this to difficulties in producing small quantities on a pilot-scale (small-batch) line. The plant had made assurances that product quality would be greatly improved with a national launch because production would take place on a continuous, high-volume line, leading to much more consistent results. Exhibits 14 and 15 provide a summary of market research results.

One of the possible reasons put forth for the lower than expected share results was that PB&J was launched at an average retail price of $3.95 in British Columbia, approximately $0.15 above the national average, and almost $0.30 above the B.C. average for children's cereals. As previously mentioned, this raised the question of whether to hold prices consistent with national averages and absorb the decreased margins, or increase the price to account for higher manufacturing costs.

CONCLUDING COMMENTS

As Susan set out to determine whether to launch PB&J nationally, she remembered Tom's remarks to her yesterday:

> I'm really excited about this PB&J cereal. Although the B.C. test results are somewhat mixed, I don't think this means we should be throwing in the towel on PB&J just yet. I believe the concept is a good one, and that it has tremendous potential to increase both our volume and share. On top of that, I think kids will love it—my kids can't get enough of it!

If Susan decided to go ahead with a launch, positioning was clearly the first most important question to answer. Would it make more sense to appeal to kids, or increasingly health-conscious parents? And how would she allocate her limited dollars to satisfy all of the important elements of the marketing mix? Spending was further constrained by the fact that senior management had recently decided that all new product opportunities should provide a positive return on investment within three years of launch.

Although the challenges were large, the opportunities for Susan were equally great. A successful launch would only add to her already outstanding record at KCI. With excitement, Susan set out to consider her options.

QUESTIONS

1. Is this an important market for Kraft?
2. What factors would you consider when making the launch/no launch decision?
3. How would you explain the test market results. Do they result from poor strategy (i.e., the wrong product aimed at the wrong market), or are they the result of poor implementation (i.e., failure to execute the marketing plan effectively)?
4. Perform a break-even analysis for the new cereal. How do these results affect your decision?
5. Develop a marketing plan to successfully launch this product. Stipulate when and how the plan should be evaluated once it starts to be executed.
6. What reaction do you expect from your competitors?

LIPTON MONARCH
PMG

*This case study was prepared by Stephen Burns, Kevin Orbinski and Pamela Heaney
with guidance from Dr. Peggy Cunningham of Queen's University. Certain proprietary data have been disguised. We want to express our thanks to Unilever Canada
for their writing of the case. This case is a shared property of Unilever Canada Ltd.*

*No part of this publication may be reproduced, stored in a retrieval system,
or transmitted in any form or by any means—electronic, mechanical, photocopying,
recording or otherwise—without the permission of Queen's University School of
Business.*

In 1993, Lipton Monarch Professional Markets Group (PMG) president and
executives developed and strategized the company's second five-year, long-term
plan (LTP) since the company's formation. This LTP was for the period
1994–1999. It was now July 1994 and the executives were assessing the viability
of meeting first-year objectives of the company's LTP. With PMG being young and
resources limited, it was important for management to continually reassess product portfolio and business structure options so that LTP objectives could be met
and PMG could continue to have overall support from its shareholder.

Lipton Monarch PMG was the result of the natural evolution of Lipton
Food Service Division at Thomas J. Lipton retail company and the Bakery and
Food Processing Division of Monarch Fine Foods retail company. With these two
divisions joined together in July 1991, the goal of the new company—Lipton
Monarch PMG—was to specifically address the needs of the out-of-home food
industry customers. This merger occurred because the specific needs of their marketplace were not adequately addressed in the retail structure and yet both divisions had shown excellent results under the circumstances. Consumer trends were
such that away-from-home consumption would remain flat or slightly increase
over the years 1991–2000.

Lipton Monarch PMG was dedicated to providing Canadian out-of-home
food operators with value-added food products of unsurpassed quality based on a
thorough understanding of the operator needs and the company's ability to meet
those needs through use and application of resources put in place to support the
new company. These resources included the ability to market branded products and
to design and manufacture "signature" products (products designed with large
clients to meet exacting needs of the client) for the industry. The focus of these
products was to broaden operators' menu appeal and to ease operational pressure.
PMG's core product categories included soups, beverages, edible fats/oils (margarines, cooking and salad oils), bakery products, and sauces. Brand names include
Red Rose tea, Becel margarine, Ragu sauces, Mexicasa and Soup Du Jour.

The company's philosophy was "customer-driven," where customer needs
were clearly identified and succinctly met through constant communication. PMG
was the only national company with a retail linkage that focused exclusively on
out-of-home industry and operated as a separate entity from its retail counterpart.
Competitors such as H.J. Heinz, Kraft, Nestle and Campbell's companies were primarily retail based, meaning that all food service business was conducted based
on retail management and production systems and sales/marketing ideologies. In
relation to PMG's positioning in the industry, these competitors' food service business was considered to be secondary to their retail business.

As the parent company and shareholder of PMG, Unilever operated as one
of the world's largest purveyors of consumer packaged goods, with famous brand

names such as Dove soap, Becel margarine, Popsicle novelty foods, Sunlight detergent, Brooke Bond and Lipton teas. Other significant brands owned and marketed by Unilever in Canada included Calvin Klein and Elizabeth Arden personal care products, Lepage's glues and Dickie Dee ice cream.

Unilever had invested large amounts of capital in supporting the founding of PMG as the need to wholly dedicate resources to the out-of-home industry was apparent. While Lipton Monarch PMG had achieved its plan requirements since 1991, the Long-Term Plan (LTP) completed in April 1993 was aggressive at both the top and bottom line.

PMG's business represented approximately 10 percent of Unilever's top line in Canada and eight percent of its bottom line. Over the life of LTP, it was expected that those figures would be increased to 14 percent of Unilever's top line and 15 percent of its bottom line. In relation to other Unilever companies in Canada, PMG was expected to show significant growth over the LTP.

period. Volume growth of 44 percent and profit growth of 90 percent over the 1994–1999 period in a market that had been continually plagued by recession and GST meant PMG executives had to reconsider the product portfolio and business structure required to meet the LTP. The company strongly believed the business concept and strategy were sound through LTP.

CANADIAN FOOD INDUSTRY

In 1993, receipts for the Canadian out-of-home market reached $26.8 billion. Sales projected for 1994 were expected to reach $27.8 billion. Wholesale food purchases represented $9.07 billion in 1993 with an approximate $9.21 billion expected in 1994 (see Exhibit 1). The industry was expected to continue a slow recovery over the following 12 to 24 months with real growth for sales receipts projected at 1.8 percent in 1995 and 2.5 percent in 1996.

Much of the growth in the industry tended to follow U.S. trends; the same held true for product

Exhibit 1 *Food Service Market Overview Comparison 1992 (actual) versus 1993-1994 (projected)*

Wholesale Purchases	1992 (actual) ($B)	1993 (proj.) ($B)	1994 (proj.) ($B)
Commercial Food Services			
Restaurants, unlicensed			
Quick Service	$1.56	$1.65	$1.73
Restaurants, licensed	2.48	2.62	2.72
Family Dining	1.86*	1.99	2.08
Fine Dining	.62	.63	.64
Take-Out	1.25*	1.30*	1.33*
Hotels/Motels	1.07	1.07	1.07
Vending	.07	.07	.07
Retail Hosts			
Department Stores	.07	.07	.07
Convenience Stores	.10	.104	.109
Supermarket Delis	.10	.10	.10
Transportation	.09	.09	.9
Other Commercial	.68	.54	.52
Total Commercial	$7.47	$7.61	$7.80

*Some double counting may have occurred as many restaurants also offer take-out.

Wholesale Purchases	1992 (actual) ($B)	1993 (proj.) ($B)	1994 (proj.) ($B)
Institutional Food Service			
Health Care	$.67	$.603	$.55
Hospitals	(.33)	(.30)	(.27)
Long Term Care	(.34)	(.303)	(.28)
Government	.19	.18	.18
Management Services	.68*	.68*	.68*
Total Institutional	$1.54	$1.46	$1.41

*Some receipts may be included in above numbers.

Wholesale Purchases	1992 (actual) ($B)	1993 (proj.) ($B)	1994 (proj.) ($B)
Total Food Service Market	$9.01	$9.07	$9.21

formats. In 1993, American food service operators' purchases from distributors represented 42 percent for perishable foods, 29 percent for frozen foods, 19 percent and 10 percent for dry/canned foods and non-foods respectively.

As a result of sluggish economic times and lingering effects of the GST, the industry's share of the total Canadian food dollar in 1993 was 37 percent compared to 42 percent in 1989. As Canada began to exit the recession and as consumers were expected to have less time but increased purchasing power, more disposable income was expected to be spent in the out-of-home industry. Particularly, large growth was expected from the 45- to 54-year-olds considering they held the highest household incomes and traditionally spent approximately 55 percent of their food dollar on food away from home.

In 1993, 55 percent of the U.S. food service dollar was spent with a larger or medium-sized chain account. This percentage slightly increased from 52 percent in 1991. In Canada, this same measurement was 42 percent in 1993. While this was a significant increase from 36 percent in 1991, it was predicted to be closer to the American number by 1997–1998. This significant trend was expected to occur at the expense of the independent operator.

Exhibit 2 *Segment Trend Analysis & Impact on Manufacturer*

Analysis	Operators				
	Quick Service	**Family Dining**	**Fine Dining**	**Take-Out**	**Management Services**
Operator Trends	◆ Limited menu offerings, but enticing. ◆ Dicount pricing. ◆ Decreased labour costs. ◆ Near to home.	◆ Out-of-home experience. ◆ Multi-concepts, multi-units. ◆ Variety of ethnic foods on menu. ◆ Fastest growing segment.	◆ Restructuring to become more upscale casual dining. ◆ Declining segment.	◆ Home eating. ◆ "Traditional" meals are popular with consumers.	◆ Provide quality food at low prices. ◆ Provide good customer service. ◆ Growth of multi-unit, multi-concept operator.
Food Preparation & Purchasing	◆ Systematic operations. ◆ Strict specifications for food products and preparation. ◆ Portion control. ◆ Limited storage space (smaller back-of-house & larger front-of-house). ◆ Frozen and/or ambient prepared foods.	◆ More operational flexibility than QSR. ◆ RTU foods becoming more popular to help decrease labour costs back-of-house & increase service in front-of-house.	◆ Executive chefs still make food from scratch but using more prepared sauces, soups and gravies.	◆ Convenient food products. ◆ Systematic operations. ◆ Fast service. ◆ Environmentally friendly packaging. ◆ Frozen foods and or ambient. ◆ Hand held and portable.	◆ High quality, flavourful foods, nutritional value.
Impact On Manufacturing	◆ High quality prepared foods. ◆ Products "fit" with operational capacities. ◆ Technologically advanced packaging/ environmentally friendly products. ◆ Flavourful products with nutritional value.	◆ Supply chains with signature products. ◆ Create strong relationship with key players. ◆ Unique and ethnically rich foods.	◆ Focus on supplying high quality prepared products for chef to use as basis for most dishes.	◆ Ability to provide products that resemble "homestyle" cooking. ◆ Technologically advanced packaging.	◆ Build relationship on national basis with key players. ◆ Increase yield for product for low price. ◆ Traditional menu offerings.

In researching industry needs, PMG was able to reconfirm the importance of the labour problem in the industry. Labour made up on average 32 to 35 percent total costs and had potential to worsen as provincial minimum wages crept up. Equally as important was the overall quality of the labour pool. A serious lack of skilled labour presented a major and costly problem to out-of-home operators. Most employees were part-time or were working to supplement family income; a very small number had any actual "skill" in preparing and presenting food. Operators wanted to move to semi-prepared and/or fully prepared foods as a way to deal with this major problem, which was expected to worsen as the economy picked up. Significant too was the increasing consumer preference for fresh, additive-free food and this trend's impact on operator requirements. Most operators wanted these semi/fully prepared foods in a ready-to-use (RTU) format with as few additives as possible. RTU products blended ingredients so that the result would be a homemade style product that would require the operator to pour out of the container, heat, and serve without having to add significant complexity in the kitchen. These types of product provided the operator with consistency from day to day and from location to location. RTUs were often referred to as "one-step" products. This important trend confirmed PMG's belief in new technology as a key driving force in achieving LTP.

The food service industry included a variety of commercial and non-commercial operators who purchased either from distributors or direct from the manufacturers. Commercial operators, made up of Quick Service, Family Dining, Fine Dining, Hotels/Motels and Take-Out establishments accounted for 82 percent of food service receipts in 1993. Non-commercial operators, mainly healthcare and management services, accounted for the remaining 18 percent. PMG executives grouped operators into five main categories according to their buying behaviour (see Exhibit 2).

Commercial Operators

QUICK SERVICE—This segment was characterized by high-speed service at the front counter/cashier where there was usually a limited menu offered at reasonably low price points, i.e., McDonald's, Harvey's, Tim Horton's. This sector was highly volatile to economic activity and it was a key objective of most operators to control costs. With the fastest growth in competition, operators in this segment were focusing on implementing technologically advanced operational systems in order to better control costs. As more quick service establishments moved in this direction, manufacturers were forced to understand the limits of each operational system so that products could be supplied to meet exacting standards and specifications. As operational systems were adopted, packaging and portion control was the main concern of quick service operators. This segment was the largest in the business and was expected to grow at a rate of three to four percent per year in the next five years.

FAMILY DINING—This segment offered good-value table service in a casual and entertaining setting, i.e., Red Lobster, Olive Garden, Kelsey's Restaurants. Establishments in this segment ranged from coffee house to "casual dining" in a more upscale environment. Family dining represented a significant opportunity for manufacturers because of the broad range of menu items and the degree of operational flexibility. This segment was dominated by independent operators where relationships with suppliers had a significant impact on buying decisions. Further trends dictated that the multi-unit, multi-concept chains would quickly grow, and the independent operator would decline. An opportunity existed for those manufacturers who were able to build strong relationships, provide high-quality products and innovative marketing support.

FINE DINING—This segment was typically classified as a white tablecloth restaurant that served premium-quality food at a price greater than family dining. The "away-from-home" experience for the customer encompassed a high level of service and unique menu offerings, i.e., french cuisine. Qualified chefs took pride in creating food from scratch and tended to frown upon ready-to-use products. This sector was expected to decline in size by five percent per year due to economic pressures and the growing popularity of upscale family dining establishment. As such, many fine dining establishments appeared to be restructuring towards a more casual setting.

TAKE-OUT—This segment typically provided food that was fully prepared and packaged for removal from the premises, i.e., Swiss Chalet, drive thrus, Pizza Pizza. Take-out customers were demanding more "home-style" and "healthy" meals at a valued price. Operators in this segment emphasized environmentally friendly packaging and systematic operations. Those manufacturers who provided prepared products with technologically advanced packaging invited success.

Non-Commercial Operators

MANAGEMENT SERVICES—Operators in this segment managed the food services operation within facilities such as government buildings, corporations, health-care locations and educational institutions. The sector was dominated by three major players—Versa Services Limited, Marriott, and Beaver Foods Limited. Purchasing of products for individual units was done on a national basis through contracts with their head offices, with flexibility given to some individual units.

to remain abreast of changes and continuously evaluate competition and opportunities. Future growth depended on the identification and exploration of profitable niches that matched PMG's capabilities and strategies for the next five years.

FOOD SERVICE DISTRIBUTORS

In 1993, food service distribution in Canada remained fragmented, but consolidation was occurring. There were 500 distributors who serviced 42,000 customers where total purchases accounted for $9.07 billion. Of these purchases, 60 percent were shipped by full-service and local distributors and the remaining 40 percent were shipped by specialty distributors and those manufacturers who shipped direct to the customer.

Two major buying groups, Associated Food Distributors (AFD) and Federated Foods, accounted for over 70 percent of full-service distributors' volume nationally. The remaining 30 percent were system specialists and all other (see Exhibit 3). Distributors averaged a 17 percent margin on sales to operators. A typical distributor carried 1,500 to 7,500 items. Decisions to carry products were based on operator needs and requests and the strength of relationship between the manufacturer and distributor.

Purchasing decisions were based on factors such as value-added marketing, product specification, nutritional value, consistent quality, yield, and price. These operators tended to serve food that resembled the food people ate at home. The one percent annual growth that was projected for this segment presented an opportunity to those manufacturers who were able to build strong relationships nationally and execute locally.

Industry-wide developments included the demand for a variety of ethnic foods. Seventy-one percent of customers believed that "chain menus were increasingly alike" and offered little ethnic variety in their meals. As the chain business was expected to continue its significant growth at the expense of the independent operator, this type of consumer perception would have to be addressed by both the chain operator and manufacturers supporting these clients.

Customers were also focusing on the nutritional value of their "out-of-home" meal and preferred to eat flavour-enhanced foods with less salt and fat. With the aging population, operators were more attentive to specialized dietary needs and the nutritional content of the products they chose to use.

The rate of change and innovation in the industry was faster than ever before. PMG was challenged

Exhibit 3   Distribution Channel: 1993 Overview

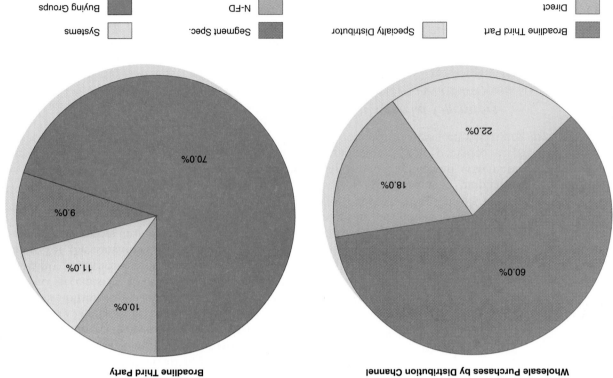

Wholesale Purchases by Distribution Channel

60.0%

18.0%

22.0%

Broadline Third Part   Specialty Distributor   Direct

1993 Purchases: $9.07 Billion

Broadline Third Party

70.0%

9.0%

11.0%

10.0%

Systems   Buying Groups

N-FD   Segment Spec.

1993 Purchases: $5.4 Billion

Types of Distributors

Full Service distributors carried a variety of products, including national brands, operator private label, and distributor/buying group private label. These distributors offered sales and customer support in addition to distribution. They would operate regionally and service multi-unit and independent accounts.

"**Local**" **Full Service** distributors operated within a smaller region or metropolitan area which typically specialized in a single market segment.

System Specialists were vertically integrated with one or more chain accounts and a majority of the products stocked were operator private label.

Specialty distributors carried a wide range of related products that catered to specific needs (i.e, paper, produce, protein, or bakery products only).

Products shipped from the manufacturer to the chain, multi-unit, or independent accounts would represent **Direct Shipments**. Some companies who ship direct may also use a full service or local distributor for the same products.

Distribution: Key Issues and Implications

Consolidation of distributors was fast approaching the industry as competition from U.S. alliances and Free Trade/GATT impacted product sourcing and purchasing power. With U.S. super distributors entering the Canadian market, this forced out many mid-sized distributors and forced large full-service distributors to focus on controlling costs and increasing customer service. Smaller or specialty distributors were forced to find niche markets and take advantage of the opportunity to provide increased customer service over larger, volume-driven distributors.

The opening-up of markets also began to increase competition for the Canadian manufacturer as product sourcing through American suppliers, where prices were often lower, was more readily available.

The emergence of large-scale warehousing operations like The Price Club and Costco enabled operators to buy commodities at savings over distributor prices. Though these warehouses competed with some distributors, they catered to the smaller independent operators who did not make up a large market for mid- to large-scale distributors.

Retail ownership of food service distributors also had begun to impact the Canadian manufacturer. Where many food service distributors tended to belong to large buying groups but were owned by retail companies such as Safeway Canada and Oshawa Foods, some business decisions that were made for the food service side were based on a retail business focus. Specifically, the retail philosophy on private label was expected to impact the food service distributor over

time. With the growth of private label, (i.e., private label made up 20 percent of distributor sales), competition for manufacturers' branded products was increasing in a shrinking market.

As the out-of-home market continued to be extremely competitive, the role of the distributor was becoming more and more important. Manufacturers using a "Push" strategy, or filling the distribution channel and relying on distributors to sell through to the operator, accepted that the distributor would have substantial leverage over what product was made available for sale to operators. Manufacturers using a "Pull" strategy, or ensuring that operators' needs were properly addressed by the manufacturer and that distributors were used to distribute product only, accepted that leverage over which products were designed and made available had to rest with them, especially as the market became even more competitive.

Typically, independent operators purchased from a set list of available products through distributors. They did not have a large degree of clout in telling distributors what to make available. Conversely, large chain operators dictated to distributors what to make available to their units. These same product selections were generally made available to independent operators by distributors.

The role of distributor was to take on significant strategic relevance to manufacturers. Choosing a "Pull" versus a "Push" strategy would dramatically alter the structure of a business in Canada. A fundamental question seemed to be: Who is selling to the operator—the distributor or the manufacturer?

Some manufacturers such as Nestle and Kraft had an alternative route and invested in their own distribution centres, as well as shipping through the third-party distribution channel already outlined. Historically, Lipton Monarch PMG had not considered moving into the direct shipment business but rather focused on utilizing the available resources of the already established Canadian distributor network.

Food Service Suppliers

Historically, food service suppliers had fallen into two categories, as follows:

1. Large organizations whose main focus was retail grocery but who had augmented that business with food service unit accounting for approximately one-third of total volume and profit while adding little complexity to the core retail business. Examples of these suppliers included Best Foods, H.J. Heinz, Nestle, Campbell's, and Kraft General Foods. These organizations were characterized by food service personnel supply products either designated for retail or slightly altered for

food service. Companies such as H.J. Heinz and Kraft regarded the presence of their products on restaurant tables as highly credible, low-cost advertising that helped retail sales. The retail company usually had large and value-added resources to support the retail focus; these resources were not wholly applied to the food service business as sales from this business were viewed as "plus business" rather than as a profit source of equivalent importance to retail sales.

2. Small outfits dealing exclusively within food service, usually on a regional basis. Examples of these suppliers were Lynch Foods, Pepes, and Nalley's. Companies in this category typically relied either on a small sales group and the distributive trade or exclusively on the distributive trade through a third party (or separate) broker network. Typical of those groups was a lack of resources to bring significant value to the marketplace, but a willingness to be flexible as per customer product needs if the volume/profit opportunity existed.

In light of trends already mentioned, some large organizations had shown more interest in the industry through application of dedicated resources, i.e., product development, marketing, and supply chain management. Still, however, most industry suppliers relied on low price propositions to build volume and offset total company—retail and food service—costs.

The profit opportunity existed for those organizations who were willing to take the best of both types of categories, i.e., effectively applying resources to bring valued products to the operator with premium margins through innovation, supported by low cost production. This could be achieved by ensuring the organization had a solid and thorough understanding of the industry and the customer.

LIPTON MONARCH PROFESSIONAL MARKETS GROUP

In 1994, PMG still had two divisions—Food Service and Bakery/Food Processors—operating autonomously. Each had a vice president of sales/marketing and its own profit/volume targets. 1993 sales of the combined businesses were in excess of $120M. 1994 targets called for 11 percent growth in volume/profit.

PMG had 100 employees at head and central region office and 32 in the eastern and western regions. PMG's own manufacturing facility in Belleville, Ontario employed a total of 85 people. Unique in the industry was that PMG's president and two vice presidents of sales/marketing had spent their entire careers in the out-of-home food business; their combined experience totalled 70 years.

The functional groups were staffed as follows: sales/marketing had 79 employees, the balance of the head office staff—product development/quality control and assurance, logistics, customer service, information technology, finance and human resources—numbered 32. Significant in the sales/marketing structure was that there were six layers between entry level and the president.

PMG had an excellent reputation in the industry as a company whose sales and marketing people understood the issues of the operator very well and built business strategies around them. The primary focus of PMG was soups, sauces, beverages—included in beverages were a small coffee business and large drink crystal, hot and cold tea, and Cup-A-Soup businesses—edible fats in food service and edible fats/oils in bakery products in bakery/food processors. PMG had capitalized well on innovative application of mature product technologies. Examples of this were seen in the soup/gravy and bakery product areas where a mature dry-mix technology was used with interesting and unique ingredients to create upscale, premium products in each category. These products had carved out a niche in their categories and were very profitable to the company. In the sauce area, PMG had led the industry in using innovative packaging systems (plastic jugs, tetra-pak) to deliver Ready to Use (RTU), high-quality product to the operator at a high margin to the company. The operator need for RTU/reduced additive product was a significant part of the success of these products. PMG knew it had to move more into these areas while maintaining the profit flow from mature technology categories. Unilever North America had approved investment in new technology if the required payback could be substantiated in an approved business plan.

The food service sales group was national in its coverage and focused primarily on the operators with secondary support of the distributor. The sales force had solid penetration with independent operators across Canada and as a result had good distribution of core products on a national basis. Each salesperson was responsible for a geographic area and reported to a zone manager, who in turn reported to a regional function. The sales force was composed of business generalists; there were no segment or product specialists. Food service had a large sales force for the size of its business but had felt its strategy of operator focus with top-quality product and support required these numbers.

The bakery/food processors had sales support in Montreal, central Ontario and Vancouver. They focused on distributors and small- to medium-sized operators. Each sales person reported to a regional function.

To further support the business, the food service group had a qualified chef and dietitian to work with sales/marketing in proper application of product. The bakery/food processor group had qualified bakers working in technical support functions at the customer level.

When part of the retail companies however, PMG had a reputation as a "branded" only group whose industry programs were inflexible and non-negotiable. Product and pricing decisions were made through marketing at head office. In fact, when part of the retail group, PMG did not have a dedicated function looking after the large chain accounts in Canada. This meant clients like McDonald's and Swiss Chalet/Harvey's had little or no contact with the company.

A significant reason for PMG's formation was the dedication of resources to the needs of larger customers and distributors across Canada. Controlling manufacturing and dedicated product development meant PMG could deal directly with the specific needs of large clients. Dedicated logistics and information technology meant the company could build industry programs suited to the needs of the distributive trade as well.

One of the first things done when PMG was formed was the introduction of a dedicated function to deal with the varied needs of the large chain customer on a national basis in the food service area. As 1993 ended, this function accounted for 23 percent of company revenues, still markedly underdeveloped versus the industry. Where PMG controlled manufacturing and dedicated marketing support and bring Unilever resources to these important customers, it was believed that significant opportunity existed in the short and long term.

PMG had to recognize the ever-increasing role of the distributor in the business. The previous reputation of inflexibility had to be overcome if PMG was to leverage these distributors to achieve LTP targets. It was generally agreed that PMG must work with the distributive trade to better understand their role in the business and to capitalize on opportunities. A dedicated "trade marketing" function was established during 1993 to focus on properly liaising with the distributive trade.

PMG was involved in 18 categories with over 680 SKUs. These categories could be broken down into seven groupings (see Exhibit 4). Edible fats/oils accounted for 46 percent of volume; tea accounted for six percent. These categories were Unilever Worldwide "starred" categories, which meant they were seen as very strategic to Unilever and thus attracted large resources to further their success around the world.

Canamera was the major competitor in the edible fats/oils category. Canamera held 80 percent of the Canadian market and focused on a low-cost production strategy. PMG held approximately 12 percent of the market and focused on low-cost production with a technology-driven approach to the business. The main beverage competitors were Kraft (excluding coffee) and Mother Parker's (excluding coffee). (Both these companies had large coffee businesses; their other beverages businesses were not nearly as large or successful as PMG's.) Both companies were low-cost producers and distribution driven. Mother Parker's was fully dedicated to the food service industry, Kraft General Foods had both retail and food service business. PMG's differentiation between these two major beverage competitors involved a product-driven approach targeted toward operators, not distributors.

Exhibit 4 *Lipton Monarch Product Chart Relative Importance Per Category*

Product/Category	Format	Category As Percentage of PMG Revenue	Number of Products In Category	Number of Products Equalling 75% Or More Of Category Revenue
Edible Fats/Oils	◆ Liquid ◆ Cubes	46.0	19	6
Beverages	◆ Sugar Based ◆ Leaves ◆ Beans	23.0	148	34
Soups	◆ Dry Mix	10.0	90	32
Sauces	◆ Wet ◆ RTU	6.0	22	8
Bakery	◆ Dry Mix	6.0	76	48
Other	◆ Sugar Based ◆ Canned	3.5	66	17
Ethnic	◆ Wet ◆ RTU	3.0	19	4
Health Care	◆ Dry Mix ◆ Canned	2.5	61	24
		100.0	684	173

Exhibit 5 *Lipton Monarch PMG Category Trend Overview*

Product/Category	Format	Percentage Of PMG Total Revenue	Category Trend	PMG Priority	Manufactured By
Edible Fats/Oils	56.4	46	Flat	Starred Unilever	PMG
Beverages	28.2	23	Decline	Tea: Starred Unilever	PMG
				Other: High PMG	PMG
Soups/Sauces	19.6	16	Growth	High PMG	PMG
Bakery	7.4	6	Growth	High PMG	Co-Packed
Other	4.3	3.5	Decline	Rationalize	Co-Packed
Ethnic	3.7	3	Growth	Medium PMG	PMG, Co-Packed
Health Care	3.07	2.5	Growth	High PMG	PMG, Co-Packed
	122.6M	100%			

Soups/sauces totalled 33 percent of volume, were manufactured by PMG and contributed significantly to the profit of the business (see Exhibit 5). Although bakery products only accounted for six percent of revenues in 1993, it was seen as an area with large growth potential.

Of the remaining groupings: Ethnic and Health Care accounted for six percent of volume and were expected to achieve growth over the life of LTP. The last category: "Other" was onerous and in need of rationalization. It accounted for three percent of volume.

In the soup/sauces category, the major competitors were Campbell's, Nestle, H.J. Heinz and E.D. Smith. All the major competitors, with the exception of Nestle, held a larger percent of the market over PMG in each category. None of the companies was fully dedicated to the out-of-home food industry. The major strategic focus of these categories for the competitors was low-cost production, distribution "push" and technology driven. On the other hand, PMG's strategic focus for these categories was both market and customer driven, again targeted towards the operator.

The major bakery competitors were IDL and Multifoods. Each company held a larger share of the market over PMG and both had a market driven approach to the business. Where IDL was dedicated to the out-of-home industry, Multifoods focused more on the retail businesses. In comparison to the competitors' approaches to business, PMG executives decided a product- and customer-driven approach fit better with company objectives.

Outside of these existing categories, PMG was considering investment in Unilever "emerging" categories (categories deemed to be large opportunities in future): namely Frozen Dough including buns, cookies, breads and Ambient (product not requiring freezing) stable meals/sauces that were ready to use. These categories were seen to have huge potential as they addressed customer needs **and** were being supported by Unilever Worldwide. Current competition in the frozen baked-goods category existed with Heinz and Corporate Foods where strategic focus was market and distribution driven. Both companies held a larger share of the market than PMG due to their time in the somewhat developed but still growing category. The main competitive advantage for PMG in this category was its ability to be a fully dedicated manufacturer and supplier, supported by significant technological advantages from Unilever around the world.

PMG had a dedicated manufacturing site in Belleville that manufactured soups, beverages and co-packed (i.e., produced and packaged on Lipton's behalf by other manufacturers) for the retail company. PMG also shared manufacturing facilities with retail on some soups and oils and all edible fats. Sauces were manufactured in a shared facility. Other items were co-packed either in Canada or in the United States by manufacturing facilities that were not owned by PMG. PMG had a small but growing export business in the soup and sauces category.

STRATEGY MEETING

PMG executives met to discuss product portfolio and business structure opinions that focused on Unilever "starred" and "emerging" categories. They also discussed operator needs. The amalgamation of both groups' sales and marketing functions into one was debated.

The entire session was focused on what product portfolio and business structure options would assist PMG in meeting the volume and profit growth targets of its LTP.

Some executives believed PMG should dissipate and rejoin the retail organizations of Thomas J. Lipton and Monarch Fine Foods to take advantage of resources at reduced cost. This would put less pressure on indirect costs and thus the profit picture. These executives stated that reliance and focus on the leading retail brands being marketed in the grocery business would also attract resources from the retail management group.

Other executives believed that PMG should remain a separate entity but that an amalgamation of the Food Service and Bakery divisions should take place. This would remove duplication and free up resources to better focus on growing areas of the business. These executives stated that the real need in the business was for qualified business people who understood the issues relevant to their customers and who were properly supported and empowered to address them directly.

By bringing both groups together, joint attention could be focused on large and medium chains who deal both with Food Service and Bakery. Resources could be reallocated and used more efficiently and product/marketing applications for customers may be better assembled for the larger customer. Discussion involved the introduction of a research function spending all its time on understanding customer needs and potential application of Unilever technologies in meeting these needs.

Anther option involved bringing together both groups to support specific industry segments. This approach had at its core the belief that each business segment, i.e., Quick Service, Family Dining, etc., was unique and needed its own focus.

Another option considered was to focus attention on the distributive trade as they could control distribution at a lesser cost to PMG. This argument supported the focus on retail brands as a key point of leverage with the distributors rather than focusing sales efforts on end-users or operators who would then pull the Lipton products from the distributors. This "push" rather than "pull" channel strategy would be a new approach to doing business for Lipton Food Service but not for the Monarch Bakery/Food Processors. This suggestion would to be less costly in terms of people investment, particularly salespeople required to "sell" the operator.

During the afternoon coffe break, the president of the Lipton Monarch Professional Group left the meeting shaking his head. Decisions about the structure of the company would affect the entire business—from resources it received to the types of products it developed. He knew that some companies were merging their sales and marketing functions but wondered if this was the best approach for PMG. Traditionally, sales people focused on distributors while marketing staff gave their attention to customers. Merging the functions would significantly affect current and future relationships with out-of-home food operators and distributors. Given all the debate in the meeting, he was in a quandary about the best course of action for the division. In fact, he wondered if there would be a separate division for him to manage.

CASE STUDY LEGEND

Out-Of-Home Industry Any food establishment serving food for consumption away from home or serving food from in-home consumption via home delivery.

Food Operator Person(s) operating establishments as above.

Canadian Food Dollar Total of **all** money spent on food in Canada, both grocery and out-of-home.

Chain Account Restaurant (or other establishment) with three or more locations. Included in this definition are examples such as Kelsey's (42 locations), McDonald's (659 locations) or Lime Rickey's (4 locations), etc.

Independent Operator Restaurant (or other establishment) with only one location. Usually run by owners. Often called "Mom & Pop" style operator.

Semi-Prepared & Fully Prepared Foods (or Ready To Use) Food items that come to a restaurant from a distributor literally semi-prepared (needing little work to finish) or fully prepared (ready to use).

Commercial Operator Operating for profit.

Non-Commercial Operator Non-profit, subsidized operations.

QUESTIONS

1. What trends in the marketing environment are affecting out-of-home food operators (i.e., fast food restaurants, family dining establishments, and upscale restaurants)? What new needs have these trends created for out-of-home operators? How well do the products currently offered by Lipton Professional Marketing Group (PMG) meet these needs?

2. What segment of the market represents the best target for PMG? What types of new products would be valued by this segment. What quality and pricing levels should they have (e.g., high price/high quality; low price/low quality, etc.).

3. Why are distributors so important for both PMG and out-of-home operators? Is a "push" or a "pull" strategy aimed at distributors more viable?

4. At the strategy meeting, some executives make the case that the Professional Marketing Group should be merged back into the retail organization. Should the managers of PMG resist this suggestion? Why or why not? If PMG remains a separate division, what are the advantages and disadvantages of merging the sales and marketing groups within PMG?

FEMSA CERVEZA:
SOL IN THE UK

David Agar prepared this case under the supervision of Professor Carlos Ruy Martinez and Professor John Hulland solely to provide material for class discussion. The case is not intended to illustrate either effective or ineffective handling of a managerial situation. Certain names and other identifying information may have been disguised to protect confidentiality. The Wester Business School wishes to acknowledge the participation of the Instituto Technológico y de Estudios Superviores de Monterrey, Nuevo León, México in the development of this case. Partial funding for the development of this case was received from the Donald F. Hunter Professorship in International Business.

This material is not covered under authorization from CanCopy or any reproduction rights organization. Any form of reproduction, storage or transmittal of this material is prohibited without written permission from Western Business School. Copies or permission to reproduce may be obtained by contacting Case and Publication Services, Western Business School, The University of Western Ontario, London, Ontario, N6A 3K7, or by calling (519) 661–3208, or faxing (519) 661–3882.

Copyright © 1995 The University of Western Ontario 95/11/01

In October 1994, Señor Victor Padilla, the Export Director for Cerveceria Cuauhtemoc Moctezuma (FEMSA Cerveza) was reviewing the most recent report on the brewery's European export volumes. He was particularly concerned about the collapse in exports to the United Kingdom (UK). The UK represents FEMSA Cerveza's second-largest export market after the United States (US), and was a critical element of the company's export strategy, which sought to use export markets to protect or even increase the company's revenues. Because of the high fixed costs inherent in the brewing industry, one determinant of a brewer's success was its ability to maintain high sales volumes that translated into large revenues.

Although FEMSA Cerveza exported two brands of beer to the UK (SOL and Dos Equis), Señor Padilla was particularly concerned by the recent collapse in the sales of the SOL brand. Although SOL had originally done very well in the UK (on a volume basis), more recently, sales had declined sharply.

Señor Padilla wondered whether sales volumes could be improved by repositioning the product. He knew that to do this would require a new marketing plan, in which advertising would likely play a prominent role. There was also the question of whether it would be necessary to change the packaging, the bottle, or the colour and flavour of the beer. He was also worried about the distribution channels and whether or not the company's current distribution arrangement gave it access to its target market or the group it might wish to target should it decide to reposition the product. He also wondered whether it might be more prudent for FEMSA Cerveza to abandon the UK altogether and to focus on other European and global markets. The declining volumes were an indication that Mexican beer might have no future in the UK. Señor Padilla set out to review information on the UK market, wondering what FEMSA Cerveza's next move should be.

Fomento Economico Mexicano, S.A. de C.V. (FEMSA)

Mexico had a rich history in the production and sale of beer. The first brewery established in North America was founded in Mexico on December 12, 1543, through a concession granted by the King of Spain to the Spanish conquistador Alonso de Herrera. In contrast, the first US brewery was founded in 1623 in Manhattan, and the first Canadian brewery was founded in 1668 in Quebec City.

From 1543 through to the late 1980s, many small breweries were established throughout Mexico, most in Mexico City or in the immediate area surrounding it. In 1890, Mexico's first large scale brewery was constructed in Monterrey, Nuevo Leon. La Fabrica de Hielo y Cerveza Cuauhtemoc, S.A., was built at a cost of 100,000 pesos.

Over the next 10 years, Cerveceria Cuauhtemoc added several local businesses to support the brewing operation. In 1899, Cerveceria Cuauhtemoc established Vidrios y Cristales de Monterrey, S.A., to manufacture glass bottles. In 1900, Fierro y Acero (later named Fundidora Monterrey) was established to manufacture steel and other metals used in the bottling (bottle caps) and packaging divisions of the company. Cerveceria Cuauhtemoc also owned factories that produced malt, corrugated carton and paper, and it founded two banks—Banco de Nuevo Leon and Banco Mercantil—to help finance its investments.

In 1936, all the company's interests were consolidated under one holding company named Valores Industriales, S.A. (VISA). By 1994, VISA had become Mexico's fifth-largest publicly traded company. FEMSA was a sub-entity of VISA, responsible for VISA's food-related activities: the production and distribution of beer and soft drinks, and the production of packaging materials used mainly in the bottled beverage industry. FEMSA was organized into four divisions: Beer, Retail, Coca-Cola FEMSA, and Packaging (see Exhibit 1).

The Retail division was responsible for the management of OXXO convenience stores throughout Mexico. At the end of 1993, the company owned and operated over 700 of these stores, making it the leading operator of convenience stores in Mexico's retail sector. OXXO was also the leading distributor of beer, handling 2 per cent of the total sold in Mexico. Unlike most other small retail operations, OXXO convenience stores offered a broad range of products and services to Mexican consumers.

Coca-Cola FEMSA was the largest Coca-Cola franchise in the world, and was responsible for the production and distribution of Coca-Cola, Sprite, and Fanta Orange throughout Mexico. The mission of the packaging division was to provide the Mexican beverage and food industries with containers and packages, at prices

Exhibit 1 *Femsa Profile (all figures are in US dollars)*

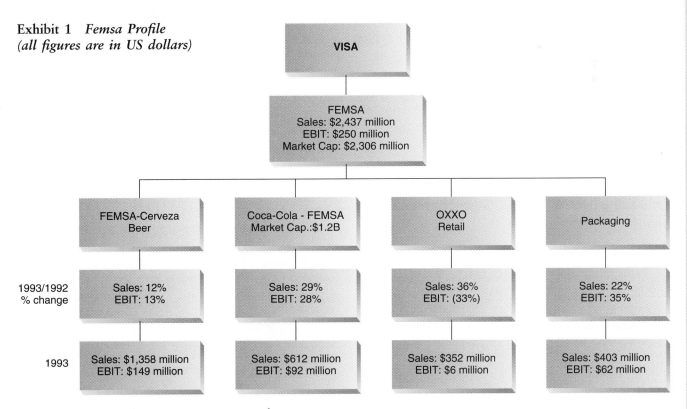

Source: A Winning North American Brewing Partnership

that were cost competitive at international levels. The packaging division's major products were beverage cans, crown bottle caps, glass bottles, labels, and cardboard boxes. The beer division, FEMSA Cerveza, was responsible for the production and distribution of beer throughout both Mexico and the rest of the world. FEMSA Cerveza's major brands in Mexico were Carta Blanca, Superior, Tecate, Tecate Light, XX Lager, Bohemia, SOL, Indio, and Heineken beers, which it distributed in Mexico on behalf of Heineken Breweries of Germany.

FEMSA Cerveza produced 20.4 million hL[1] of beer in the fiscal year ended December 31, 1993, although the division had the capacity to produce 24.4 million hL. The company operated an international beer division that exported beer to the US and Europe, but more than 95 per cent of its production continued to be sold in Mexico. The principle objectives of the export division were to generate volume for the company and to provide a source of foreign currency. The latter was important because some of the company's inputs needed to be acquired from outside the country. This, combined with the instability of the Mexican peso, created a need for FEMSA to develop a stable source of foreign currency.

FEMSA's consolidated net sales were N$7.571 billion[2] for fiscal year ended December 31, 1993, an increase of almost 7 per cent over the previous fiscal year when consolidated sales totalled N$7.090 million. The brewing division contributed N$4.089 billion in sales, up slightly from N$4.072 billion in the previous year. FEMSA's net income for 1993 was N$684 million compared to N$552 in 1992.

FEMSA Cerveza's Export Activities

FEMSA Cerveza operated an export division that distributed the company's products in over 55 countries around the world. FEMSA Cerveza's portfolio of brands of beer that it exported throughout the world was extensive. A list and description of the company's major export brands appears in Exhibit 3. Exhibit 4 presents the brewery's export volumes to England since 1986 and growth in volume, in per cent, for selected European countries.

THE UK BREWING INDUSTRY

UK consumers spent £13.6 billion and consumed 35.3 million barrels[3] of beer in 1993. The UK beer industry employed 127,630 people in beer production, 9,650 in distribution, and 622,350 in the management and operation of clubs and pubs.

There were 65 brewers in the UK, operating 95 breweries, although only nine of these were considered to operate nationally. The remainder were regional brewers, or in some cases local brewers that sold draught products to one or two small establishments. Draught beer was beer packaged and sold in a keg, drawn and delivered to the glass as needed. It was estimated that there were in excess of 1,000 brands of beer available in the UK, although many were available exclusively in certain localities. The six largest brewers in the UK in 1994 were Bass, Allied, Grand Metropolitan, Whitbread, Scottish & Newcastle, and Courage. Collectively these six brewers controlled over 75 per cent of the market. This was unusual, because in many countries, such as Mexico and Canada, two national brewers controlled in excess of 90 per cent of the domestic market.

Despite the appearance of a competitive environment, in reality the UK brewing industry had evolved into what had been termed a "complex monopoly". Brewers had vertically integrated their operations to include not only beer production but also wholesale and retail outlets for beer distribution. Though organizational structures known as "tied estates," brewers owned and operated over 50 per cent of all on-licence[4] and less than 10 per cent of all off-licence[5] premises in the UK. The tied relationship was most pervasive in the public house (pub) trade, the most preferred venue for the consumption of beer in the UK, where nearly 75 per cent of all pubs were owned by brewers.

Tied estates ranged in size from in excess of 7,000 establishments to as few as two. The tied relationship allowed brewers to control the products that were offered for sale and their prices, as well as the services, amenities, and appearances of the various premises. The result was that independent suppliers faced difficulties in marketing their products. Brewers were in turn able to keep prices high, resulting in higher margins and profits.

While beer was sold in several different formats in the UK, draught had traditionally been the most preferred format. This phenomenon was the result of a long tradition of consuming beer in pubs. However, despite an overall increase in leisure spending in the

---

[1] hL is the abbreviation for hectolitre. A hectolitre is equivalent to 100 litres, or 293 bottles of beer.

[2] N$ = New Peso. To help simplify foreign exchange transactions, the Mexican government introduced a new peso on January 1, 1993. The new peso was worth 1,000 of the old pesos. See Exhibit 2 for currency exchange rates between Mexico, Canada, the United States, and the United Kingdom in October, 1994.

[3] 1 barrel = 1.65 hectolitres.

[4] On-licence refers to all outlets licenced to sell beer for consumption on the premises, including pubs (public houses), clubs, hotels, and restaurants.

[5] Off-licence refers to all outlets licenced to sell beer to the take-home market (e.g., wine and spirits stores).

UK, pub-going had declined over the past four years and was expected to continue to do so in the future. With the deterioration in the UK economy in the early 1990s, many people had switched from consuming beer at the pub to consuming beer at home. Most of the beer consumed at home was packaged and was lower priced. The switch to at-home consumption had also led to a decline in overall consumption nationally, since the social environment of the pub led people to drink more than they would at home. Furthermore, although in a pup people generally seemed to prefer beer, at home some broadened their choices to include wine and spirits. Anti-drink-and-drive campaigns had also contributed to the decrease in beer consumption, which in 1993 was approximately 173 pints per head, down from 180 pints per head a year earlier.

Despite these trends, the on-licence trade remained the predominant distribution segment for the consumption of beer in the UK. In 1993, over 81 per cent of all beer consumed in the UK was purchased at on-licence establishments.

Imports
Imports represented approximately 6 per cent of all beer consumed in the UK: Guinness from Ireland accounted for 3 per cent, Holsten from Germany accounted for 1.5 per cent, and 300 different brands competed for the remaining 1.5 per cent or 529,825 barrels[6]. SOL and Dos Equis were among the 300 brands, representing FEMSA's key exports to the UK.

The majority of imported beer was consumed in London and the South East of the UK, where over 25 per cent of the population lived. This area of the UK was the site of most of the country's tourism and accounted for a disproportionate number of the country's fashion-conscious, urban professionals.

Most foreign beers available for sale in the UK were sold at premium prices and were lagers. Although they were of little significance in terms of market size, their general popularity with the UK consumer had increased, particularly with the fashion-conscious sector. Many had gained a foothold through the restaurant trade, including Kingfisher (India), Tiger (Singapore), and Dos Equis (Mexico), where customers expected to drink something exotic and authentic with their food.

Varieties of Beer
Several different types of beer were available in the UK. The most common types were: lager, ale, stout, and lite, with the latter not enjoying the same success in the UK as it had in the US. Lager was golden in colour, clear and sparkling, with a crisper, more delicate flavour. The lager market in the UK was sub-divided into standard and premium. Generally, premium lagers had a higher alcohol content than standard lagers, although the increasingly competitive environment in the UK prompted some brewers to market what was technically a standard lager brand as a premium lager. More hops[7] were added when brewing an ale, giving it a distinctive fruitiness, acidity, and a pleasantly bitter seasoning. In all, ales had a more assertive, individual personality than lagers. Stouts were characterized by darkness and profundity, were either dry or sweet, and varied dramatically in alcohol content. Lite beers were low carbohydrate, low alcohol content beers.

BEER CONSUMPTION IN THE UK

The Pub
In the UK, the pub had long been the preferred venue for the consumption of beer. In 1994, the major consideration for consumers in selecting a pub was its location. Consumers chose an outlet because it was close to home or work. Also, for many, visits to the pub were an opportunity to meet friends, and people often frequented their local (preferred establishment) to maintain social ties.

The largest segment of the pub-going population was between the ages of 18 and 34, and 61 per cent of this segment had a preference for a particular locale (i.e. a regular establishment which they patronized). Exhibit 5 indicates the drink preferences of pub-goers, along with a more general profile of the drinking preferences of people in the UK. Exhibit 6 compares the popularity of the pub with other leisure activities.

The Lager Market
By 1993, the lager market in the UK had grown by 10 per cent versus 1983, despite a 5 per cent decrease in overall beer sales in the UK over the same period. Exhibit 7 illustrates beer consumption in the UK, by type, between 193 and 1993. The lager market was broken down into five segments according to alcohol by volume (A.B.V.): No alcohol beer/Low alcohol beer (0%–1.2%); commodity lager (1.3%–3.3%); standard lager (3.4%–4.2%); premium lager (4.3%–7.5%); SOL was positioned and competed in the premium lager segment of the market.

Premium lager had increased in significance in the UK beer market from 20 to 30 per cent of the lager market. Within the premium segment, the majority of growth had come from premium bottle lager versus canned or draught, which in 1988 represented 23 per cent of the premium lager market and in 1993 represented 32 per cent of the premium lager market.

The premium bottled lager market represented the fastest-growing segment of the UK brewing industry,

---

[6] 1 barrel = 1.65 hectolitres and 1 hectolitre = 176 pints.

[7] Hops are one main ingredient in beer. The others are malt barley, yeast, and water.

and was expected to represent 35 to 40 per cent of all premium lager beer sales by the year 2000. As a result, there were many new entrants into this segment of the market, although over time very few survived. Those that did survive became stable brands and enjoyed high margins, high volumes, less diverse competition and a long life.

A study of those brands that were considered to be stable and those products that were considered to be fads ("ephemeral") resulted in a set of characteristics for each group (see Exhibit 8).

Distribution was critical to the success of any brand in this segment of the market, particularly because of the "tied estate" arrangements. Exhibit 9 presents purchase trends for the off-licence trade and Exhibit 10 presents purchase trends for the on-licence trade in the UK.

The Consumer

The premium bottled lager drinker was most often a male, between the ages of 18 and 35, whose leisure activities included cinema, shopping and socializing in bars, clubs and restaurants. This person was well dressed and groomed, and tended to watch television programs and read magazines that kept up with recent trends.

This individual had specific ideas about the various beer product types and formats available in the market. Draught beer was perceived as cheaper but low in taste, watery, weak and bloating. Non-premium bottle lager was perceived as reliable, but weak, low in taste, poor in value and boring. Premium-bottled lager was perceived as being stronger and better flavoured.

Beer that was consumed at home was purchased from off-licence establishments such as liquor stores and supermarkets where brand choice was usually influenced by consumer familiarity and special promotional offers. As well, cans were preferred over bottles because they offered better value and were more convenient.

Outside of the home, the predominant location of beer consumption for this group was the club. Here premium bottled lager was preferred for several reasons:

◆ It provided an alternative to draught beer that was less bloating, more refreshing, more reliable (unlike draught that could be watered down) and consistent, a cleaner drink less liable to yield a hangover.

◆ A bottle was much more convenient and practical than a drink in a glass for the crowded situations of clubs. The narrow mouth of a bottle reduced the amount spilled if the container was knocked over. A person could carry several by their narrow necks using hands and pockets, making it easier to buy a round for friends. They were safer, because typically the drinker held the bottle, instead of putting it down where it might get taken or knocked over.

◆ In clubs the customers were more quickly served at the bar because they did not need to wait for a tap to be free and the beer to be poured out.

◆ Bottles remained colder longer.

◆ Because bottled premium lager was stronger, it created the mood for socializing and dancing more quickly. The same intoxicating effect was achieved by drinking less volume, and the resulting decrease in bloating left the imbibers more comfortable for dancing.

Product and Brand Attributes

Alcoholic strength was seen as the most important attribute of premium bottled lager. Strength was what most drinkers first looked for when assessing a brand. Rather than looking for the Alcohol by Volume (A.B.V.) designated on the bottle, most people looked for other clues, in particular bottle colour. Dark bottles were perceived to contain stronger beer than clear glass bottles, and brands in brown glass were perceived to be stronger that those in green glass.

Strength was viewed as important because beer was being drunk to relax and enliven the consumer, to get him or her into the right mood to cope with various social situations. Because premium bottled lager provided the same effect as draught or non-premium bottled lager, with less volume, so it could be consumed more quickly and with less bloating. Stronger beer was also thought to have a better taste and the higher strength justified the higher price. Finally, beer was being consumed primarily for intoxication; therefore, higher alcohol content delivered the desired benefit more quickly.

Although flavour was less important than strength to many beer consumers, it was more important to older drinkers and was used by all to discriminate between brands. Most drinkers were looking for a clean, crisp, smooth-tasting beer. The attribute drinkers liked least in terms of flavour was a weak or unpleasant after-taste.

Price was a low priority except for beer bought to drink at home, in which case special offers could influence choice. Most UK club goers said that the point of going out was to have a good time and that they expected to pay for this. Cheap beer was thought to be a waste of money and likely to be weaker and poor in taste.

FEMSA CERVEZA PRODUCTS IN THE UK

Dos Equis

The first FEMSA Cerveza product available in the UK was Dos Equis. In the early 1980s, Cerveceria Moctezuma (which became part of FEMSA Cerveza in 1985 after it was merged with Cerveceria Cuauhtemoc) was approached by an English person who had vacationed in Mexico, planned to open his own beer importing company in the UK, and wanted to offer a Mexican beer as part of his product line.

Cerveceria Moctezuma granted this importer the exclusive right to import and sell Dos Equis in the UK. As the volume of Dos Equis being sold in the UK increased, the importer sold his right to Maison Caurette, a large alcoholic beverage distributor in London. Maison Caurette imported and distributed some beer products, although its primary strength was wine. As a result of this, its primary distribution strength was in the bar and club trade. In addition, Maison Caurette operated almost exclusively in the London area.

Dos Equis had maintained steady sales volumes in the UK since its 1982 introduction. FEMSA representatives believed that the beer was consumed by people who weren't trying to be different, who maintained a portfolio of beers from which they drank as opposed to those people who were loyal to one brand, and was mainly drunk when people went out to eat Mexican food. Advertising of Dos Equis was limited to on-premise promotions.

Market research had shown that the brand was relatively unknown, except in the occasional off-licence establishment. Its Spanish-sounding name led many people to conclude that the product was from Spain. Finally, although people thought that the label looked dated and cheap, they also thought that the two Xs on the beer's label suggested strength.

SOL

In 1988, Maison Caurette approached FEMSA Cerveza looking for "something bigger for the UKs." It was at this time that a rival Mexican brewer's Corona brand was reaching the height of its popularity in the US. Maison Caurette explained that FEMSA Cerveza's SOL brand was sold in a clear bottle with a painted-on label, similar to the packaging of Corona. The UK distributor suggested that FEMSA should consider introducing SOL into the UK in order "to beat Corona to the punch." This recommendation made a great deal of sense, given that in the past whichever beer, SOL or Corona, had entered a particular market first, it subsequently retained the leadership position in that market. FEMSA Cerveza agreed to proceed, and in late 1988 the first cases of SOL arrived in the UK.

The first task of Maison Caurette was to create brand awareness of SOL. The strategy used to introduce SOL to the UK was straightforward. Trend-setting venues in London were selected: winebars, brass clubs[8], discos, and restaurants, places frequented by UK "Yuppies" and places with which Maison Caurette had an established relationship. On-premise promotions such as SOL parties, free t-shirts and caps, and happy hours with SOL were used to encourage patrons to try SOL.

The product was positioned as a distinctive, exotic, high-priced item. It was drunk out of a bottle with a wedge of lime positioned in the bottle's neck. In the UK market, SOL was a unique product and its price was integral to its image. Maison Caurette's management believed it was important for people to perceive SOL as:

> Something I can drink because I earn enough money to be able to pay the price for the product. This is a product that not everyone can afford.

In late 1989, the marketing strategy was intensified, and television advertisements teaching people how to drink the product were developed and aired almost exclusively in the London area. The Export Director commented:

> We did more advertising on the lime side than on the SOL side. In fact, I believe we sold more limes than beer.

The result was that SOL became equated with lime, and anyone who wanted a beer with a lime ordered a SOL.

Sales volumes in the UK began to increase rapidly in the early 1990s, with demand at times outstripping supply. In one extreme case, demand was so great that FEMSA Cerveza sent a full container of SOL by airplane from Mexico to the UK in order to avoid being unable to supply a key customer. Although the company had not undertaken any market research, the Export Director speculated that the principal reason for SOL's success in the UK was that the product was different. In fact, it was the only premium bottle lager available in a clear bottle. All other premium-priced lagers were available either in cans, or in green or brown glass bottles. In addition, SOL's introduction into the UK coincided with a movement among 18- to 35-year-olds, who, having developed a mistrust of brewers in general, had abandoned traditional draught products and the pubs that their parents and grandparents frequented.

Advertising Proposals for SOL

By the end of 1993, the sales picture was much less encouraging. In response to declining sales volumes of SOL, in early 1994 FEMSA Cerveza hired a large global advertising agency to study the decline, and to help the company decide whether the product was salvageable. Furthermore, if SOL had a future in the UK market, the agency was asked to recommend to FEMSA Cerveza how it might go about restoring the product to its former glory.

The advertising agency undertook focus group studies to attempt to understand how SOL was per-

---

[8] A brass club was a restaurant/bar that also provided an area for dancing.

ceived in the market. The following responses were those more commonly used to depict SOL:

Gimmicky	Feel like I'm drinking a Babycham
Yesterday's Fad	Not the beer to be seen drinking
Just another import	I only drink it at home
Weak	You don't hear about it anymore
Cocktail lager	Not as popular as it was two years ago when everyone drank it
A "soft" drink	You can only get it in certain bars
Drunk by "trendies"	I drink it when I can get it
For posers	

When questioned about the product, two London pub patrons commented on SOL:

I got the mick taken out of me by my friends last night because I ordered a SOL.

SOL is a bit superficial. It got really popular and people went away from it.

The advertising agency presented its findings to FEMSA executives, and both groups concluded that it was necessary to establish/reposition SOL less as a gimmick (i.e. something that was fashion oriented) and more as a stable brand in that premium bottled lager market. FEMSA's export group decided that they should highlight the following qualities of SOL in attempting to reposition the product: the beer was refreshing, light, easy-to-drink, it had a good, clean taste, and it came from a tropical country.

The advertising agency was convinced that it was possible to establish SOL as a stable brand within the premium bottled lager segment of the brewing industry. It had developed several advertising campaigns for television, scripts for which are found in Exhibit 11. The campaigns were intended to position SOL as a high quality, premium product with a premium price, that was authentically Mexican.

However, soon after viewing these proposals, FEMSA management in Mexico decided to discontinue their relationship with the advertising agency and these advertising campaigns were never used. Instead, they decided that they would conduct market research on the SOL brand in-house, and, provided that their research indicated a future for SOL in the UK, they would work with a new advertising company to develop an appropriate campaign for SOL.

Results of In-house Market Research

The in-house marketing research indicated that SOL was a well-known, previously trendy brand, widely consumed four years earlier. SOL was still closely associated with the quarter of lime that was its trademark. However, the decline in awareness because of lack of promotion and distribution had become critical as the number of alternative brands available in the market continued to increase.

Although most people believed that SOL originated from Mexico, or possibly Spain, this fact appeared to be an unimportant component of its personality. In terms of the future viability of the product, greater importance was given to its other characteristics: good tasting, crisp, clean, smooth, refreshing, low in gas (but not flat), light in character, lacking aftertaste, and suitable for refreshment and intoxication. Exhibit 12 presents brand image data collected from male consumers by FEMSA regarding SOL and some of the other leading premium lagers in the premium bottled lager segment of the market. Exhibit 13 presents some brand image characteristics of SOL obtained through an informal survey of both males and females.

The marketing research also revealed that a product's country of origin had relevance only when it was Northern Europe or the US, as both regions had a strong brewing reputation with the British.

Unfortunately, the British attributed no special significance to the fact that a beer originated from Mexico. They did not perceive the country as particularly attractive, but as exotic, lively, colourful, and offering popular and interesting Mexican food. The British also saw Mexico as poor and underdeveloped, as well as unclean and dangerous. The emphasis on the Mexican origin of a product might initially have intrigued consumers, but did little in the longer term to entice them to continue consuming the product.

Competitive Reaction

In the early 1990s, Corona had entered the UK market, but was not particularly successful since SOL had already established itself as the bottled Mexican beer in the UK. Some UK brewers developed imitations of SOL, and marketed these brands as Mexican-type beer. However, according the FEMSA Cerveza, these brands met with little success.

As the popularity of premium bottled lager continued to increase, so did the number of products available to consumers. It was estimated that by the end of 1994, UK consumers would be able to choose from over 400 brands in this category of the market. Ten years earlier no more than four brands of premium bottled lager had been available. Competition for a place in this market segment was fierce, with millions of pounds sterling being spent annually on media.

Exhibit 14 presents a media expenditure index for the more prominent premium price lagers in the UK. Exhibit 15 presents a penetration index for the leading premium priced bottled lagers available in the UK.

THE DECISION

SOL has experienced some trying times after its entry into the UK brewing market, which was the world's most dynamic and competitive beer market. After having reviewed the information presented to him, Señor Padilla concluded that future opportunities existed in the UK for SOL, but realized that success would not come easily. With so many companies from around the world competing for a small fraction of this market, Señor Padilla knew that FEMSA Cerveza would need to develop a sophisticated marketing strategy if it planned to earn a permanent place for its SOL brand among UK beer consumers. As he studied the material that had been collected over the previous months, he recognized that there were a number of different ways in which he could proceed. Specifically, he needed to decide how he would position the brand; what characteristics of SOL, in any, he would modify; what new distribution channels, if any, he should pursue; and finally, what type of advertising and promotional campaign would be necessary in order to give UK consumers a reason to once again buy SOL.

Exhibit 2 *Currency Exchange Rates October 1994*

	Canadian dollars	US dollars	New Mexican Pesos	British Pounds
1 Canadian dollar =	1.00	0.7416	2.5291	0.4689
1 US dollar =	1.3484	1.00	3.4094	0.6323
1 new Mexican Peso =	0.3954	0.2933	1.00	0.1854
1 British Pound =	2.1325	1.5815	5.3929	1.00

Source: The Globe & Mail, Thursday, October 13, 1994

Exhibit 3 *FEMSA Cerveza Brands Available for Export*

Product	Description	Alcohol by Volume (based on 12oz. serving)
Tecate	◆ first brewed in 1947 ◆ traditionally served in a can topped with a squeeze of lime and a sprinkle of salt ◆ designed to quench big thirsts ◆ rated the #1 imported canned beer in the US in 1994 ◆ available in bottles	4.55%
Tecate Light	◆ brewed since 1992 ◆ Mexico's first low-calorie beer ◆ light beer with real flavour and character ◆ a light extension of Tecate beer, one of Mexico's top-selling brands ◆ available in long-neck bottles and fluted, silver cans	4.10%
SOL	◆ brewed since 1899 ◆ golden lager beer with a smooth mellow flavour ◆ clear long-neck bottle with a painted on label	4.10%
Bohemia	◆ brewed since 1900 ◆ a classic European-style lager beer ◆ full body, rich flavour	4.80%
Dos Equis	◆ brewed since 1900 ◆ beautiful amber-coloured beer with a rich, creamy head and smooth, mellow flavour ◆ excellent example of a traditional Vienna-style beer ◆ #1 selling imported amber beer in the US	4.75%
Dos Equis Special Lager	◆ brewed since 1983 ◆ mellow tasting, refreshing, golden lager beer ◆ unique green glass bottle	4.45%

Source: FEMSA Cerveza marketing brochure, December 1994

Exhibit 4 *FEMSA Cerveza Export Volumes to the UK (thousands of cases)*

	1986	1987	1988	1989	1990	1991	1992	1993	1994[9]
England	12	44	69	249	1,206	2,535	2,177	1,983	1,124

FEMSA Cerveza Growth in Export Volumes
Selected Countries in Europe (per cent)

	1991	1992	1993	1994[9]
France	41.3	110.3	1.7	22.5
Germany	58.8	101.9	11.9	33.1
Spain	n/a	n/a	121.4	35.5

[9] The 1994 figure is year to date as of end of September, 1994.

Exhibit 5 *Drink Preference of UK Pub-Goers*

	Men	Women
Beer	83%	37%
Spirits	10%	26%
Soft drinks	7%	37%

Source: The Brewer's Society

Where People in the UK go to get a Beer

When?	Where?	What?	Atmosphere?
Weekdays	Local Pub	Draught	Relaxed Smaller Groups Cheaper Easy Going
Weekends	Clubs	Bottled Beer (brands important)	Portable Convenient Know what you're drinking Party Atmosphere

Source: S.G. Warburg Securities Study on Pub Retailing, March 1994

Exhibit 6 *Most Popular Leisure Activities in the UK in 1992*

Activity	% who visited at least once a quarter
Pub	71%
Cinema	39%
Theatre	26%
Spectator Sports Event	23%

Source: S.G. Warburg Securities Study on Pub Retailing, March 1994

Exhibit 7 *Percentage Sales of All Beer Types in the UK*

	1983	1988	1992	1993
Draught	76.5	73.3	69.5	68.5
Packaged	21.5	26.7	30.5	31.5
Total Ale and Stout	64.1	51.4	48.7	48.0
Total Lager	35.9	48.6	51.3	52.0

Source: Brewers and Licensed Retailers Association, London, UK

Exhibit 8 *Characteristics of Beer Brands in the UK Market*

Ephemeral		Stable	
◆ Novelty	◆ Discreet	◆ Trusted	◆ Open
◆ Special	◆ One-off	◆ Accessible	◆ Original
◆ Fast burn	◆ Commodity	◆ Constant	◆ Brand
◆ Difficult	◆ Exotic	◆ Authentic	◆ Easy

Exhibit 9 *Purchase Trends*
          Off-Trade - Great Britain - 1993

Point of Purchase	Total Lager (%)	Premium Lager (%)	Premium Bottled Lager (%)	SOL (%)	Average Number of Brands[5] Stocked
Multiple Grocers[1]	46.9	43.9	59.7	50.1	16.9
Multiple Specialists[2]	20.4	27.7	22.7	29.5	12.4
Independent Specialists[3]	10.9	12.4	8.1	12.5	8.5
Independent Grocers[4]	16.9	13.2	7.2	6.7	5.4
Co-ops	5.0	2.8	2.3	1.2	7.2

[1] Operate more than five outlets

[2] Operate more than five outlets and sell only alcohol

[3] Operate fewer than five outlets

[4] Operate fewer than five outlets and sell only alcohol

[5] Brands refers to premium bottled lager brands

Note: These indicate, by per cent, the volume of lager, premium lager, premium bottle lager, and SOL being purchased at each of the various off-trade segments. They also show the average number of premium bottled lager brands stocked by each of the off-trade distribution segments.

Source: STATS MR

Exhibit 10 *Purchase Trends*
           On-Trade - Great Britain - 1993

Point of Purchase	Premium Priced Lager (%)	SOL (%)	Average Number of Brands[2] Stocked
Big 5[1] - Managed	19.5	12.5	5.8
Big 5 - Non-Managed	13.7	1.8	4.5
Regionals	13.7	3.8	3.4
Independent Pubs	22.2	14.4	4.7
Clubs	14.4	2.7	2.6
Hotels	5.9	3.9	5.0
Other Bars	7.9	15.1	4.7
Restricted (Restaurants)	11.4	49.8	3.3

[1] Big 5 refers to the top five brewers in the U.K.

[2] Brands refers to premium bottled lager brands.

Note: These data indicate, by per cent, the volume of premium priced lager and SOL being purchased at each of the various on-trade segments. They also show the average number of premium bottled lager brands stocked by each of the off-trade distribution segments.

Source: STATS MR

Exhibit 11 *Television Advertising Script*

"The Usual"

Throughout this commercial, we would hear a swirling abstract piece of music that rises higher and higher in pitch and ends in cacophony.

This music accompanies a series of brightly coloured surreal images that celebrate the unseen side of Mexico.

As the pitch of the music gets higher and higher, the cuts between the images get faster and faster.

We see people in bizarre masks.
We see a shelf stacked with candy skulls.
We see a woman with live iguanas in her hair.

Exhibit 11 *continued*

We see a man in a bizarre devil mask drinking a bottle of SOL.

We see two rattlesnakes fighting.

We see three Mexican Elvis impersonators.

We see a toothless old lady laughing.

We see an old bicycle turn a corner, mounted on the front is the stuffed head of a bull.

We see a cemetery at night with colourful gifts and candles placed on every grave.

We see a group of men dancing in skeleton suits.

We see two women in a bar, arm wrestling, people surround them drinking SOL.

We see a man dressed as a woman and wearing a crown.

We see a woman dressed as a man and wearing another crown.

We see someone in a bar, clutching a bottle of SOL and grinning at us, displaying green teeth cut out of lime peel.

We see a 1962 Mercedes on fire.

We see a ghost.

We see people laughing as they try to lap some beer from a glass like a dog.

We see two wrestlers fighting in Mexican wrestling masks.

We see four young women dressed as Angels.

The music stops and we cut to a title:

THE USUAL

We cut to a second title:

IN ORIZABA, MEXICO

We cut to a chilled bottle of SOL.

"Burro"

This commercial is set outside a home in a Mexican suburb. Parked in the driveway is a well-kept classic American car. It's a very hot, dry day.

A Mexican man, aged 30 and dressed in normal everyday clothes, steps into frame. He holds a chilled, open bottle of SOL. He speaks directly to the camera:

"SOL is my favourite beer, the favourite beer of my father, and of his father."

He turns his head momentarily to look proudly at his bottle of beer, then looks back toward the camera:

"And for all you people who might want to be disrespectful towards it, we have a message for you."

We pull back to see the man is standing in front of two other men. Behind him on his left is an old man. Behind him on his right is an extremely old man. They begin to sing along to a rhythm played on a guitar, while performing an awkward little dance routine.

They sing:

"If you don't like the beer, kiss my burro . . ."

We cut to the face of the old man singing the last three words:

"If you don't like the beer, kiss my burro . . ."

We cut back to the men dancing, then we see the last three words sung by the young man:

"If you don't like the beer, kiss my burro . . ."

We cut back to the men dancing. This time we see the last three words sung by the oldest man.

The music stops, and we return to a close-up of the face of the youngest Mexican, who toasts us with a bottle of SOL and says:

"Remember Hombre, it's not what you think of the beer, it's what the beer thinks of you."

We super: Brewed in Orizaba, Mexico, since 1899.

"Scorpion"

In this commercial we open on a hot day outside the SOL brewery in Mexico. A worker is stacking boxes of SOL. He accidentally knocks one of them over. The box drops onto its side and the top falls open. We see a close-up of a big black scorpion scuttling across the dust and into the open box. The man, unaware, carries on stacking. Then, noticing the fallen box, he rights it, seals it and casually places it with the other boxes.

We cut to the boxes on a dockside in Mexico waiting to be loaded onto a ship.

Then we see the boxes unloaded at a British port, and cut to them on a truck being driven down a motorway.

We then see a close-up of a single box of SOL. It's now open and resting on the bar of a typical English pub. A man is taking the bottles out two by two and putting them onto the cool shelf behind the bar. From a view inside of the box, we see his hand coming in, reaching for bottles. Two by two the bottles come out until eventually it's completely empty.

Exhibit 11 *continued*

We move to a view of the pub at night. It's very busy. We see the barman's hand reach up to the shelf above the bar. We see a close-up of his fingers fumbling to reach a glass and see that his hand is about an inch away from a big, black scorpion. It's alive and well and watching the man's hand. We cut to the scorpion's view of the pub. Its tail twitches slightly.

We cut to black and see the words: SOL. Imported from Orizaba, Mexico.

"SOL Destroying"

The commercial is set in the apartment of a 25-year-old man. It is stylish, but obviously male in its decor.

We open on a room of people.

We hear the sound of music and laughing voices so there is obviously a party going on.

We view the action through a camera's eye view from the floor looking skyward. The camera is focused close-up—the distant images appear out of focus.

We span the room and see the images of people.

We focus on a man whose arm comes into focus as his hand reaches out to a table and picks up and drinks from a bottle of beer. As he replaces the almost full bottle, it misses the edge and falls.

We focus on a bottle of SOL and follow it closely as it falls to the floor.

Dramatically, it explodes in slow motion just before it hits the camera.

We freeze the picture on the shattered glass.

On a fragment of it we can clearly make out the word SOL.

Alongside this word DESTROYING fades up.

Followed by a voice over:

MEXICAN BORN AND BREWED SINCE 1899.

"SOL Survivor"

The commercial opens on a smoke-filled room.

Dust fills the screen. We hear two men coughing.

As the dust clears we see an old-fashioned fridge charred and covered in soot.

A dirty hand open the fridge to reveal a single bottle covered in white dust. The light in the fridge flickers as the hand brushes off the dust to reveal the SOL label.

The bottle is removed. We hear it being opened off screen and one of the men says, "Don't ever, ever do that again . . ."

The bottle is put into the screen again, a drink having been taken. Alongside the word SOL on the bottle the word SURVIVOR fades up.

This is followed by a voice-over:

MEXICAN BORN AND BREWED SINCE 1899.

"SOL Witness"

It's midnight and we're in a darkened room. The only light creeps through some slatted blinds and onto a woman's hands. She is slowly, deliberately removing black leather gloves. A lone cello or violin is playing a single, menacing tone.

She is being watched. We don't know by whom or by what, but whoever or whatever it is can see her shape distorted through a drinking glass.

She drops her glove into her bag, snaps it shut and leaves. Odd that. Don't most people put on gloves when they leave?

A drinks cabinet moves slowly and slightly ajar. The light from within illuminates the edge of a bottle. The door opens a little bit more to reveal a bottle of SOL. It's almost as if the bottle is peeking out of the cabinet.

Alongside the word SOL on the bottle, the word WITNESS fades up on the screen.

This is followed by a voice-over:

MEXICAN BORN AND BREWED SINCE 1899.

Exhibit 12 *Brand Image (Males Only)*

	Is a clean tasty beer %	Is a smooth beer %	Is worth paying extra for %	Is good quality %	Is an upmarket beer %	Is attractively packaged %
SOL	7	12	7	13	16	12
Becks	55	49	32	50	37	30
Budweiser	57	47	28	52	28	36
Dos Equis	4	2	5	1	7	4
Grolsch	17	14	20	26	20	24
Holsten Pils	17	13	14	19	14	12
Labatts Ice	21	17	9	15	12	12
Michelob	14	10	12	18	20	15
Molson	8	9	8	12	11	12

Note: Sample size was 250

Source: Moctezuma & Cuauhtemoc Imports Ltd.

Exhibit 13 *Image of SOL*

	Gender		Age			
	Male %	Female %	18-22 %	23-27 %	28-31 %	32-34 %
I would drink with friends	22	20	30	22	14	19
Is an upmarket beer	16	16	17	17	16	13
Is always available where you drink	14	17	16	13	15	16
Is good quality	13	15	17	12	15	10
Is a smooth beer	12	18	14	13	13	15
Is attractively packaged	12	15	17	13	17	6
Is for people who know about good lager	9	9	8	7	9	11
Is a clean, tasty beer	7	11	11	7	4	12
Is worth paying extra for	7	8	5	5	10	8
Used to be fashionable	7	5	5	6	8	6
Is a 'football'[10] lager	2	2	1	3	2	1

[10] A 'football' lager is a beer that you would drink with friends while watching a football game.

Note: Sample size was 250

Source: Moctezuma & Cuauhtemoc Imports Ltd.

Exhibit 14   *Media Expenditure Index[1]*
              Premium Price Lagers - Great Britain

Brand	1991	1992	1993	1994[2]
Becks	12.3	4.7	2.3	11.5
Budweiser	66.0	98.4	98.6	100.0
Grolsch	24.8	18.5	8.3	20.6
Holsten	70.8	33.7	63.0	79.1
Kronenberg	n/a	54.8	22.6	18.8
SOL	13.8	6.6	5.1	5.4
Stella Artois	n/a	48.4	58.6	57.9

[1] Index is chosen so that Budweiser's spending in 1994 is equal to 100.

[2] 1994 numbers are an estimate based on figures as of October 1994

Source: Moctezuma & Cuauhtemoc Imports Ltd.

Exhibit 15   *Penetration Trends Index[1] For Premium Lager Brands*
              Great Britain - On Trade

Brand	1991	1992	1993	1994[2]
Becks	30.6	35.6	58.6	55.0
Budweiser	36.0	61.3	82.9	100.0
Grolsch	12.6	5.4	10.4	6.8
Holsten	112.2	106.0	87.8	85.1
Kronenberg	7.7	9.0	10.8	6.3
SOL	16.2	22.6	11.3	8.1
Stella Artois	7.7	9.0	13.5	18.5

[1] Index is chosen so that Budweiser's spending in 1994 is equal to 100.

[2] 1994 numbers are an estimate based on figures as of October 1994

Source: Moctezuma & Cuauhtemoc Imports Ltd.

THE CANADIAN LIVING FOUNDATION: CREATING A NATIONAL MARKETING STRATEGY

On a Wednesday morning in May 1997, Martha O'Connor, executive director of the Canadian Living Foundation (CLF), arrived early at her office in Toronto. CLF is an organization devoted to developing, providing and sponsoring food programs for needy children. It also provides dietary knowledge essential to promoting the well-being of low-income Canadian families.

Martha began working with CLF in 1992, and has since been the driving force and vision behind the organization, enabling it to provide 18 million meals to kids through school and community programs supported by the Foundation. For the past few months, she has been developing some ideas for increasing donation revenue to the Foundation, but a major restructuring at the organization had prevented her from being able to dedicate time to boosting marketing efforts. But this morning her mind, and her calendar, were clear. She sat down at her desk to formulate her objectives and to begin planning for a national marketing strategy.

Martha was pleased with the donation revenues that the Foundation generated in Ontario. However, she felt that the organization was almost an unknown entity in the other provinces and the donations that the Foundation received from corporations and private citizens outside Ontario were minimal. As with most not-for-profit organizations, CLF has a minimal budget for advertising. Martha wondered what the most effective and efficient way to increase nationwide gifts to the Foundation would be. The Foundation's primary method of communication was through *Canadian Living* magazine. The magazine donates editorial and advertising space to the Foundation. This space has allowed it to recognize its donors and sponsors of events as well as publicize its fundraising appeals.

Event marketing was the primary tool utilized by the Foundation to generate both funds and publicity. Many types of organizations create events ranging from international athletic competitions to community barbecues. When organizations develop events they hope to attract corporate sponsors who pay to have their name associated with the event in return for the advertising and communication opportunities that the event affords them. Gate admissions and donations can be another source of revenue generated by the event.

Event marketing has allowed the Foundation to create news about itself. The Foundation tailors its events so that they appeal to specific audiences. Benefit evenings, auctions, walkathons and contests are all examples of event marketing that appeal to very different target markets. If an event succeeds in captivating the attention of the media, the publicity generated by the event serves to educate the public about the mission of the Foundation, and thereby helps it to raise funds. The CLF has a successful history of creating or participating in events in Toronto, such as food festivals and golf tournaments. The events have been well attended and thus have raised money and attracted corporate sponsorship.

However, since the Foundation had no offices and few contacts in other cities, event marketing on behalf of the Foundation was non-existent in other parts of Canada. Thus, Martha wondered if this tactic would be feasible in cities where the Foundation had no staff or offices. Perhaps it would be better to spend precious advertising dollars to create awareness via a national television commercial, and then follow up by increasing the pre-existing direct mail campaign. The possibilities were endless. Another thought always came to Martha as she considered spending precious Foundation dollars: "Should we be investing in marketing with money that could be used to create more nutrition programs to feed Canada's hungry children?"

This question was one that Martha constantly struggled with as the head of a not-for-profit organization. She was aware that she had a great responsibility: to ensure that the funds donated to the Foundation were used in a way that was most beneficial to children. Martha was aware that the direction in which she steered the Foundation was under the constant scrutiny of the public eye, and that not-for-profit organizations are often accused by the media of failing to act in the best interests of the cause they support. This type of accusation can be debilitating for a charity or foundation. People's trust in the organization is vital if the Foundation is to fulfil its mission.

To maintain the outstanding reputation of the CLF, Martha always focused on the priorities of all the Foundation's stakeholders when making strategic decisions. She believed in making choices that were optimal for the communities across Canada, corporate donors and sponsors, the media, not-for-profit partners and governments at the national, provincial, and municipal levels. However, maximizing the benefits accruing to all stakeholders was always a difficult task. Different groups often had quite different agendas. Martha could only estimate the effect that an increase in marketing and advertising efforts would have on donations. Without a direct correlation between spending more money on promoting the Foundation and greater donation revenues, Martha believed that many of the Foundation's stakeholders would prefer that the money be used for grants to start new nutrition programs.

Martha was also critically aware that the Foundation had been accused by people in provinces other than Ontario of having a "myopic" vision: of focusing its efforts on Ontario, and more specifically, on Toronto. She knew that something had to be done to correct this perception.

BACKGROUND

The Canadian Living Foundation, originally called The Holly Street Foundation for Families, was founded in 1992 after a group of editors at *Canadian Living* magazine uncovered the shocking statistic that one in five Canadian children lived in poverty. Many of these children did not receive adequate nutritious food every day. Since research indicated that there is a positive correlation between proper nutrition and learning, it was obvious that a program was needed as an alter-native to sending kids to school with empty stomachs. The editors channelled their concern for the welfare of Canadian children into creating the mandate for the Canadian Living Foundation. The mandate, which remains unchanged in 1997, was to help develop and maintain children's nutrition programs via funding, start-up information and nutritional counselling.

Once the Foundation was formed, it was decided that the organization's mission should be to help communities help themselves. This premise was intended to create a proactive alternative to food banks, which provide handouts that are inevitably depleted. Instead, the Foundation would offer start-up grants (usually between $500 and $2500) to partially fund food, equipment, and other initial costs. Then, with a grant as seed money, parents, community groups, and schools would build partnerships in the community to get the additional resources and support they need for a nutrition program. Since it began in September 1992, *Breakfast for Learning* (as the program came to be called) has assisted more than 1700 groups to start or improve nutrition programs in their communities and schools.

The Foundation has always been hesitant to turn down requests for help; however the overwhelming number of schools and community groups asking for assistance has led to the evolution of certain guidelines that must be met before any nutrition program is granted funding. A board of directors was assembled to incorporate the Foundation. They are responsible for ensuring that any proposed program will be accessible to all children, without discrimination and will meet nutritional guidelines established by *Canada's Food Guide to Healthy Eating*. The programs must also prove that they will encourage parental involvement, and be funded in part by sources other than those from the Foundation. These guidelines are not only in place for the welfare of the nutrition program participants; but they are also crucial to the marketing of the Foundation to the public, as they guard against any potential bad press with respect to the fairness of the allocation of funds to nutrition programs.

The CLF's admirable goal of ensuring that no child in Canada goes to school hungry has created an abundance of favourable attention for the Foundation. In the fiscal year of 1997 (see Exhibit 1), the Foundation generated revenues of $785 239 from donations and fundraising. They spent $190 274 raising these funds. The ability of the Foundation to increase donations over the years has undoubtedly been due in part to Martha O'Connor's conviction that the Foundation will not be run or marketed as a charity. As Martha explains, "We don't want to support a *'doing for'* mentality. The objective is always to leave ownership of a program, and the decision-making process, to the parents and partners of any given community."

Martha has fought the media's tendency to sensationalize poverty and children's suffering, and to create the image that the poor and downtrodden are the only people who need nutritional aid. In reality, there are many reasons that kids go to school hungry. It may be due to poverty, the fact that working parents have insufficient time, or they may just have poor dietary habits. The key to CLF's philosophy has always been to portray the child hunger problem as a challenge for all members of a community—poor or otherwise.

PROGRAM OVERVIEW

The CLF employs seven full-time staff members, including Martha O'Connor. Exhibit 2 depicts how CLF is organized. As with most not-for-profit organizations, there is always more work to be done at the CLF than there is money to hire adequate staff. Fortunately, there are also over 100 dedicated volunteers who work for the Foundation on a regular basis, assisting with office administration, event planning and execution.

Over the past five years, the Foundation has grown and evolved to offer two distinct areas of concentration. The first program, Nutrition Program Grants and Resources, is responsible for collecting, reviewing, and granting applications for nutrition program funding. This arm of the Foundation is also responsible for educating communities about how to set up effective nutrition programs. *The Breakfast Program Information Kit*, a guide to setting up a nutrition program, as well as healthy eating information for parents and posters, games and other activities for kids are distributed to any person or group who contacts the Foundation to request them. With over 2000 requests per year from across Canada, the people who work for this area of the Foundation are constantly attempting to keep up with the demands for information.

The Community Partners Program (CPP) is also a vital arm of the Foundation. This program was developed to play the role of building key partnerships in the community and creating a network of support for children and families. Partnerships, by developing linkages and pooling resources, are the most efficient vehicle for allocating scarce resources, increasing the effectiveness of a group or organization and enhancing its impact on the cause it supports. Tracey Robertson, the CPP National Coordinator, works to bring together representatives from government, business, volunteer groups, and community agencies who can influence and change policies, create funding priorities and reallocate existing resources to support child nutrition programs at the community level. The Community Partners Program (CPP) also publishes its own literature, called *The Community Partners Program Guide*, which outlines topics such as identifying influ-

ential partners and leaders within the community, using community resources creatively, developing tools for building successful community partnership programs and case studies of existing programs.

A pilot program with Nissan Canada's head office exemplifies the purpose of the CPP. Nissan staff had decided that they would like to focus their charitable efforts on children's nutrition programs in the Peel Region of Toronto as well as become involved in the community. With the help of CLF, the people at Nissan chose to support a breakfast program at Havenwood Public School. Nissan pays to feed the 70 children who attend the breakfast program each day, and the employees volunteer to help cook and serve breakfast on a rotating basis. Nissan also supports 25 other nutrition programs in the Peel region.

THE CHARITABLE ORGANIZATION INDUSTRY

Recession and unemployment in Canada, and the human suffering they inflict, have created a need for the development of charitable organizations to ease the ever-increasing strain on social and human services. The sectors of education, health, social services and arts and culture have all recently had their funding significantly (or entirely) cut by government, as deficits are severely restricting the amount of money that the public sector has to contribute. Without the social safety net that used to exist in Canada, private organizations are responding by endeavouring to create new solutions for almost every social problem.

While many Canadians have responded to this increased need, there has been such rapid growth in the number of charitable organizations that the demand for funds has often outstripped supply. Between 1982 and 1992, Canada averaged an annual increase of 2204 registered charities. In 1996, there were 75 000 registered charities nationwide and this figure continues to climb. In 1997, all these new players are attempting to share the original "pie" provided by core funders such as the United Way and the few corporations that have traditionally donated money to charities. As a result, funds are being spread very thinly, requiring charitable foundations to become increasingly resourceful and business-minded in order to deal with the fierce competition and to tap into new sources for donations.

While donations from the general public continue to be heavily solicited, the corporate sector has become the target for charities' increased funding drives. Many corporations have "deep pockets" and a vested interest in contributing to a cause, as a firm's charitable associations can have a positive impact on consumer decisions to buy its product or service. In 1993, the Institute of Donations and Public Affairs Research (IDPAR) estimated that Canadian companies donated a total of $476 million in 1993, with a focus on education, social services, and health.

COMPETITION

Martha believes that many people confuse the Canadian Living Foundation with an organization called Feed the Children. This organization is an Oklahoma-based charity with offices in 19 other countries, including Canada. It is an 18-year-old Christian organization that provides emergency relief, medical supplies, and food for needy families in North America and overseas. Feed the Children has built public awareness through the use of TV advertisements developed by the Oklahoma headquarters. These ads flash the sad faces of helpless, poverty stricken children into millions of living rooms across North America. It has also used a direct-mail campaign, telemarketing (to previous donors), and 12 canvassing offices that send representatives door-to-door in communities across the country. In Canada, Feed the Children currently provides only minimal aid to children's programs.

Martha is concerned about donor confusion because Feed the Children recently received unfavourable press coverage in a number of Canada's leading newspapers. While Feed the Children successfully raised funds from private citizens, it has not been particularly successful in securing donations from the corporate sector. Corporations that have supported Feed the Children do so in the form of gifts-in-kind or services rendered, instead of cash donations.

Martha's Challenge

Martha believes that one of CLF's most difficult marketing challenges is to differentiate the Foundation from Feed the Children and other charities that provide basic supplies. Martha wants to position the Foundation as one that contributes more than food. She believes that the Foundation is a catalyst that supports communities that are working to build more and better nutrition programs.

While Martha knows that the Feed the Children campaign has been successful at building awareness, she is concerned with the image that the ads create. She is uncomfortable with the paternalistic view that the poor are incapable of helping themselves even when they are given the right resources. She believes that this attitude is outdated. Furthermore, she thinks such ads stigmatize the poor. The CLF works to show how positive things can be accomplished. Martha tries to shift people into the mindset that poverty is every Canadian's responsibility. Thus, ads such as those run by Feed the Children are inconsistent with the Foundation's goal of helping communities to help themselves. However, Martha realizes the effectiveness of television advertising and, despite the huge cost, frequently considers the possibility of creating an ad campaign to promote the

Foundation, which has not been done before. The difficulty is, she ponders "How do I make people understand that there is a child poverty problem in Canada without using shock tactics that arouse people's pity?"

PAST AND CURRENT FUNDRAISING EFFORTS

In the past, fundraising efforts by the Foundation have been directed at two target markets: corporate and individual donors. Each market segment has very different reasons for giving to a cause, and, therefore, CLF has developed distinct fundraising initiatives for each group.

Corporate Donors

Until recently, many companies have chosen to keep their contribution to charities or Foundations quiet. However, in the competitive, image-conscious 1990s, corporations are realizing the benefits of aligning themselves with a charitable organization. Gone are the days when companies provided "free money"—corporations now want clearly defined benefits, value, and return on their investment. Most businesses are embracing "specialization funding" whereby they carefully choose a Foundation or charity that is in some way affiliated with their industry or target market. In addition, firms focus on "marketing-driven awareness," which is a strategy for creating customer loyalty via charitable support. The Canadian Living Foundation recognizes this and has developed several initiatives for allowing corporations to contribute to *Breakfast for Learning* in ways that are mutually beneficial for both the firms and the Foundation.

An annual corporate campaign is launched every September, which sends out mailings to businesses across the country. A solicitation letter and package (which includes information on the Foundation's mission and endeavours) requesting cash contributions is delivered to corporations that have previously donated to the Foundation. CLF also solicits companies that have listed children's causes as ones they support. The Foundation's target groups for corporate fundraising and promotion include food companies, mass merchandisers, food service companies, drug chains, growers and primary producers, toy retailers, and airlines. These types of companies have been targeted because they are known to generate large profits or have core competencies that are affiliated in some way with children. A vital tool in the marketing of the Foundation to corporations is a database of all previously solicited corporation donors, which includes details on the amount of a donation (if one was made) or reasons for opting not to donate, conditions (if any) of the gift, and the contact name, address, and phone number.

Another option for contributing to the Foundation that is presented to corporations is the Corporate Sponsorship/Partnership Program. For each fundraising event that the Foundation organizes, a wide variety of appropriate sponsors/partners within the corporate community are identified by Jane Rogers, the Foundation's director of fundraising and communications. Following this identification of potential sponsors, proposals are created that include several levels of sponsorship and recognition. These proposals are then sent to the potential sponsors, suggesting a range of sponsorship options from contributing in a small way (perhaps paying for employees to attend the event) to making a large cash donation to promote the event. Once a firm agrees to participate in the organization of an event, Jane tailors each partnership program to meet the corporate partner's specific needs and goals.

The CLF has organized and executed, or participated in, many kinds of events, promotions, and contests over the past five years. All of the events have been made possible entirely or in part by corporate sponsors who provided funds, celebrities who have volunteered to draw crowds, or individuals that have generously donated their time, money, or services. While the support of so many different parties had definitely been cost-effective for the Foundation, it has led to an opportunistic, rather than a strategic, approach to fundraising. The CLF had not attempted to build recognition for its name and mission via any one marketing vehicle, therefore the public had not developed an association of the Foundation with any one person, company or positioning statement. In Exhibit 3, a list and description of the events and promotions the Foundation has undertaken is provided.

Individual Donors

According to the 1995 Goldfarb Report, 29 percent of Canadian citizens donate to charities because of sympathy or affiliation to the charitable organization. *Canadian Living* has played a major role in soliciting donations from individuals by promoting the Foundation in the publication, thereby providing readers of the magazine with an affiliation with the Foundation. Since the Foundation was formed in 1992, a *CLF Update* has been included in each monthly edition of the magazine, outlining the most recent endeavours and achievements of the Foundation. At the end of each CLF Update, readers are encouraged to make a $20 tax-deductible donation to Breakfast for Learning.

Thanks to this initial promotion by *Canadian Living*, CLF has been able to generate enough funds to increase its campaigns directed at individual donors. In addition to a quarterly newsletter that is sent to anyone requesting information on the Foundation (which includes a coupon that suggests predetermined donation values of $20, $35 and $50), the individual donor campaign consists of merchandising and direct mail.

MERCHANDISING

The CLF's merchandising raises funds via the mail-order sale of Elizabeth Berry (a well-known Canadian artist) prints and Christmas cards produced by the Cornerstone 52 Foundation. The Foundation pays a distribution company to handle all orders for the prints and Christmas cards, and Elizabeth Berry and Cornerstone 52 Foundation forward a percentage of the profits to the Foundation on a monthly basis. The sale of the Elizabeth Berry prints has been an especially lucrative initiative, generating $93 726 for the Breakfast for Learning program between 1994 and 1997. Over the next year, it is planned that more merchandise will be sold to raise money for the Foundation, with the next addition to the line being diaries produced by Cornerstone 52, the same company that manufactures the Christmas cards. (See Exhibit 4 for a financial summary of fundraising efforts.)

The Foundation maintains a database of all purchasers of CLF merchandise and past corporate donors, and uses this as a mailing list to target people for repeat sales of prints and cards.

DIRECT MAIL

The 1996-1997 fiscal year was the first time the CLF used a direct-mail campaign. Martha met with a direct-mail consultant in early 1996 to decide the specifics of the letter and envelope. They also had to decide the number of letters to be mailed and to whom they would be sent. *Canadian Living* generously donated mailing lists compiled of the names and addresses of anyone who had ever bought anything from Marketplace, the magazine's mail order division, so that CLF could add these names to its own database of previous donors and merchandise purchasers.

The letter itself was created in a very personal style, with a small envelope opposed to a business size one to make the appeal seem less commercial and more friendly. The content of the letter was written and signed by Martha O'Connor herself, and explained the mission and objectives of the Foundation. Much thought and planning, as well as $30 000, went into the first direct-mail effort and hundreds of people from across the country sent back their 'postage paid' envelopes. However, the response was not great enough for the Foundation to reach the direct-mail breakeven point and the loss from the campaign amounted to $5996.

Despite the disappointing results from the initial direct-mail effort, Martha believed that this tactic was an excellent way to educate Canadians about the Foundation's cause in addition to soliciting donations. Immediately following the release of the results for the first campaign, motions were made to learn from the past mistakes and organize the direct mail initiative for 1997-1998. Armed with more mailing lists, including names of magazine subscribers, participants in events, contests, and displays, The CLF would launch its second campaign at an expense of $50 000. Profits were forecasted to be $55 000. Three personalized mailings were scheduled for 1997-1998, with specially designed direct-mail packages and solicitation letters sent to existing donors. The letters sent to potential new donors would also be tailored specifically to target people who had no previous involvement with the Foundation.

PROVINCIAL CHILD NUTRITION PROGRAM

There was another issue to complicate Martha's decision regarding how to increase awareness and donations for the Foundation in provinces other than Ontario: the Provincial Child Nutrition Program. In May 1996, CLF entered into a three-way partnership with the Province of Ontario and GIFT (the Grocery Industry Foundation) for the purpose of supporting communities that were developing and expanding nutrition programs aimed at elementary school-age children. The Province of Ontario agreed to contribute $4.4 million over two years to eliminate child hunger in Ontario. As part of this contribution, $174 710 was allocated for communications during the two-year period, to be used *only* in Ontario. An elaborate marketing strategy was prepared to meet the goals, which were jointly set by the Foundation and the government. These goals included the establishment of 500 to 700 new nutrition programs and providing 70 communities with support through the Community Partners Program. Some of the specific communication tasks outlined in the partnership agreement were to establish a separate "Ontario" identity for the program, provide a toll-free number to facilitate community inquiries, and create video, radio, and print public service announcements to be used in news reports and as stand-alone stories on television, radio, and in print advertisements.

Of course, Martha was overjoyed with the support that the Province of Ontario and GIFT provided. The amount of money they were jointly contributing was staggering—especially when one considers that most not-for-profit organizations were having their government funding seriously reduced or cut altogether. It was obvious that the government of Ontario was impressed with the Foundation's work and wanted to ensure that it was continued. However, with all money being spent and work being done on the Ontario communications plan, Martha became increasingly concerned about how to ensure that the other provinces were receiving the Foundation's key messages.

One clear benefit of the Provincial Child Nutrition program was that the communications plan for Ontario was subsidized. This meant that now more funds were available to dedicate to improving the campaigns in the other provinces and territories. Martha now had to determine the best way to spend the money. She truly believed that the event marketing that had been done in Ontario had been critical to the Foundation's success. Fundraising with events may have even been instrumental in securing the government of Ontario's support, because it demonstrated that the organization is proactive, well managed and capable of making things happen. Martha's mind always began to race when she thought of the possibilities of event marketing in other regions of Canada. "Perhaps if we begin building a stronger concept of what the Foundation does in the minds of Canadians living outside Ontario with event marketing, the other provinces will stand up and take notice of what Ontario has done. Then, the CLF could work on forming partnerships with the governments in all the provinces, similar to the Provincial Child Nutrition Program."

However, Martha was well aware that much of Ontario's event marketing had been funded and organized by a large support network of volunteers and corporations that existed for the Foundation in Toronto, most importantly *Canadian Living*. She knew that significantly more money would have to be dedicated to ensuring the success of events in other provinces to compensate for the lack of support networks, sponsorship and staff, which were vital to the event marketing that had been done in Toronto. If it was decided that event marketing was an area of importance, the question would be which of the pre-existing events could be translated into a country-wide campaign.

1997 MARKETING OPTIONS

After considering the Foundation's fundraising and marketing history, Martha was still unsure about what the most viable and profitable marketing options were for 1997, but one thing was clear: CLF could not continue to rely on random fundraising opportunities—the competition for donation dollars had become too intense. Martha was certain that in order to successfully penetrate provinces outside Ontario it was imperative that a strategic focus for "branding" the Foundation and building recognition though marketing and planning special events be developed. Her gut feeling was that a national advertising campaign or event marketing on a country-wide scale were the two best strategic directions to take, but how to most effectively capture the attention of individuals, corporations, and governments in each province was not an easy question to answer. Martha knew, however, that she had to be open to all possible options. Martha sat back in her chair and sighed. She knew that formulating a successful national marketing strategy for CLF would be a difficult, but the challenges she faced were worth the struggle. If the right choices were made, the outcome would be more healthy and happy Canadian children.

Questions

1. What special conditions or factors must be considered when marketing a charitable foundation, which differ from what should be considered when marketing a for-profit business?

2. What steps would you take to ensure the profitability of the second direct-mail campaign to individual donors? How could the direct-mail efforts be used in conjunction with a marketing strategy for national event marketing or advertising?

3. If you had to choose one company or celebrity endorser to represent the CLF in a national campaign, who would it be? What qualities would that person or corporation have to have in order to be an effective advocate for the CLF?

4. If the Foundation was to use marketing research to determine how best to solicit more donations from provinces other than Ontario, what type of research would you recommend?

5. What criteria would you use to evaluate Martha's options of either using national event marketing or national advertising (or any other option you consider to be viable)? What are the pros and cons of each?

6. If a national advertising campaign was decided upon, what subject matter (images, voice over) would you use to effectively communicate The CLF's message without using shock tactics aimed at arousing people's pity?

7. If Martha decided to implement either national event marketing or national advertising, how could *Canadian Living* be utilized as a partner in the marketing efforts? What other corporate partners does the Foundation currently have that could assist with a national campaign?

8. Are there other alternatives Martha should explore to build her national marketing strategy?

9. Develop a set of recommendations, an implementation summary and a time line to help Martha O'Connor solve her marketing strategy dilemma.

Source: This case was written by Lindsey Davis under the supervision of Peggy Cunningham. We are extremely grateful to Martha O'Connor and the Canadian Living Foundation for helping us to develop this case.

Bibliography

Citations

1. Khoury, G. *From Patrons to Partners: Strategies for the 90's* Canadian Business Review Summer 1993, pg. 28

2. http://charityvillage/research/rsta14.html

3. http://charityvillage/research/rep1.html

References

Canadian Living Foundation Financial Statements March 31, 1996

Fundraising Plan for Breakfast for Learning Canadian Living Foundation June 1997

Provincial Child Nutrition Program - Two Year Communications Strategy November 1996

http://feedthechildren.com

http://charityvillage.com

Interview with Kathy Johnstone, Feed the children

Exhibit 1   *Canadian Living Foundation - Core 5 Year Financial Summary*

	FY93	FY94	FY95	FY96	FY97	FY98 Budget
FR Revenue	77 028	66 899	345 610	541 366	785 239	892 000
FR Costs	36 632	1043	79 207	146 708	190 274	216 500
Net Revenue	40 396	65 856	266 403	394 658	594 965	675 500
Charitable Prg Cost	17 803	74 391	99 301	401 590	486 237	500 895
Admin Costs	49	201	12 223	34 631	40 618	63 770
Total Costs	17 852	74 592	111 524	436 221	536 855	564 665
Surplus (Deficit)	22 544	(8736)	154 879	(41 563)	58 110	185 835

Exhibit 2 *Organizational Structure*

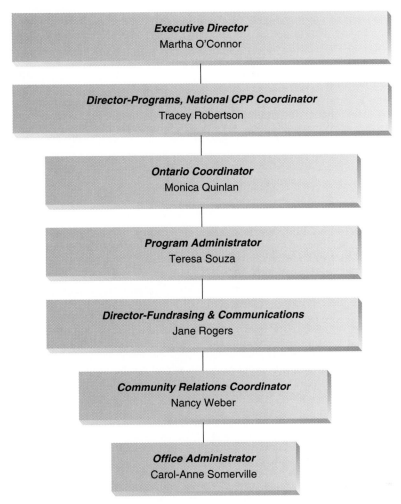

Executive Director
Martha O'Connor

Director-Programs, National CPP Coordinator
Tracey Robertson

Ontario Coordinator
Monica Quinlan

Program Administrator
Teresa Souza

Director-Fundrasing & Communications
Jane Rogers

Community Relations Coordinator
Nancy Weber

Office Administrator
Carol-Anne Somerville

Exhibit 3 *Summary of Event and Promotion Activities for Corporate Fundraising*

Women's Corporate Golf Tournament

Supported by the rising popularity of golf among women, and the statistic that the majority of the donations to the CLF are made by women, the foundation made the decision to host the First Annual Women's Golf Classic in September 1996. The green fee was $1000 per foursome, and included a banquet after the day of golf. The golf tournament was paid for in part by corporate partners, who were given the option of being platinum ($25 000), gold ($15 000), or silver ($10 000) sponsors. The golf tournament attracted some high profile companies, such as American Airlines, Pepsi and The Dairy Farmers of Ontario, which all donated money or products to be raffled off. Many other companies offered $1500 to be a "Hole Sponsor" or paid the $1000 entry fee and sent four lucky staff members to Spring Lakes Golf Course, just outside of Toronto, for the day.

In 1996, the majority of the sponsorship money was needed to cover the expenses of the golf tournament. However, in 1997 the Golf Classic is forecasted to make a profit and the CLF has set a goal for the tournament to earn $30 000.

Newman's Own Recipe Contest

The Newman's Own Recipe Contest is made possible by *Canadian Living* Magazine, and Newman's Own, Inc. (a California-based food company owned by actor Paul Newman).

The contest, which is run annually in the May issue of *Canadian Living* Magazine, invites readers to submit their favorite recipes which use Newman's Own products. The Canadian Living chefs prepare and judge the recipes, and the winning entrant is sent to New York to dabble in a kitchen with Paul Newman himself. Funds are raised for the CLF when people buy Newman's Own products for the duration of the contest, as a percentage of the cost

Exhibit 3 *continued*

of each product sold is donated to the foundation. In 1996, the purchase of Newman's Own products in Canada resulted in a \$25 000 contribution. The target for the earnings of the 1997 Newman's Own contest is \$34 000.

A similar contest in the Quebec magazine *Coup de Pouce* is also planned for the near future.

Dragon Boat Racing Competition

In the summer of 1996, the foundation was approached by a company who was organizing an annual Dragon Boat Racing Competition which raised money for charity. The Dragon Boat organizing committee had chosen the Canadian Living Foundation as one of the charities who were worthy of being a beneficiary of the proceeds raised by the race. Each Dragon Boat would be oared by teams of employees who would be sponsored by their employer firms in Toronto. Martha immediately agreed to participate in the Dragon Boat Festival, by allowing the foundation's logo and information to be featured on promotional material for the race. This was a good decision for the foundation: corporate teams paddled together to raise more than \$34 000!

Celebrity Baseball Tournament

On Labour Day weekend in 1994 and 1995, the foundation staff, numerous volunteers and the wives of the Toronto Blue Jays and Toronto Maple Leafs joined forces to play ball to raise money and awareness for the CLF. The admission to the tournament was free for spectators, but money was generated via sponsorships from companies such as Coca-Cola, Jane's Foods and Black and Decker.

The third annual Jays vs. Leafs wives game was scheduled to be played on August 30th, 1996. However, it had to be cancelled two weeks before the set date because many of the players had other commitments that took priority over the foundation's fundraiser. The cancellation was extremely disappointing to the committee who had been in charge of organizing the game, as well as the many families who had planned on attending. The companies who had sponsored the baseball game were also irritated by the fact that they did not receive the publicity they were promised. Overall, the cancellation created negative attention for the foundation, and the staff was aware that this could not be afforded. It was decided that the baseball game would not be continued in 1997, and the lesson was learned that events must be better organized in the future to avoid any future problems that could tarnish the CLF's public image.

Shania Twain

In the summer of 1996, discussions began between foundation staff and Shania Twain, the popular Canadian country singer, about ways that Shania could contribute to the CLF's cause. Shania had expressed an interest in the work the foundation does, and Martha felt that she would be an excellent celebrity for raising awareness of the CLF. Shania was raised in poverty herself and often suffered hunger as a child, and as a result feels a strong sense of empathy for all children facing hunger. It was arranged with Shania's management that proceeds from the sales in Canada of her single "God Bless the Child" would be donated to the foundation's Breakfast for Learning program.

One of the objectives of the foundation's 1997–1998 marketing and communications plan was to approach Shania Twain to investigate the possibility of the singer becoming the official spokesperson for the foundation. Shania Twain is renowned across Canada, and Martha thought her national popularity would be beneficial for increasing the profile of the CLF in all provinces. It was decided, and mutually agreed upon by Martha and Shania Twin and her management, that Shania would be used for special events and the development of promotional materials whenever possible.

Lois Lilienstein

Lois Lilienstein, of the musical group Sharon, Lois and Bram, is also a spokesperson for the foundation. Lois, through her decades of work performing to children and work on behalf of UNICEF, is a knowledgeable and appropriate celebrity endorser for the foundation. Lois assists the foundation by signing thank-you letters for classes of school children who raise money for the CLF, and posing for pictures that were featured on healthy eating posters.

Bell 1 (900) Numbers

In 1995, Bell Canada offered to assist the CLF with the set up and cost of a 1-900 donation line. This new fundraising premise worked by having Bell customers call the 1-900 line in order to indicate that they would like to contribute to a charity or not-for-profit organization by adding the sum of money to be donated to their phone bill. Bell would then forward the proceeds of the fundraising campaign to the not-for-profit organization. The 1995–1996 1-900 donation was not widely accepted by Bell customers, and in fact amounted to a loss of \$4558 for the foundation. However, after a year had gone by, it appeared that the public had gained more experience in dealing with 1-900 donation lines. It was decided that the foundation's 1-900 number would be reinstated. The main source of advertising for the 1-900 donation line is the CLF web site, which can be accessed via the *Canadian Living* Magazine web site (www.canadianliving.com). The web site lists three phone numbers; one to be called to make a \$20

Exhibit 3 *continued*

donation, one for a $35 donation and one for a $50 donation. When a potential donor calls, they are greeted with a message from the foundation which includes information about the CLF's programs. Jane Rogers is very optimistic about the success of the new donation line and has budgeted for $10 000 in revenues from the project in 1997–1998.

Exhibit 4 *Summary Fund Raising Activities*

Activity	Year	Revenue $	Costs $	Net $
Merchandising Elizabeth Berry	1994-95	66 873	39 445	27 428
	1995-96	81 852	44 761	37 091
	1996-97	61 699	32 492	29 207
	1997-98 (Budgeted)	50 000	25 000	25 000
Cornerstone 52	1995-96	18 825	6422	12 403
	1996-97	3100	526	2574
	1997-98	3000	1500	1500
Events	1994-95	19 040	5168	13 872
	1995-96	22 401	10 383	12 018
	1996-97	84 690	41 996	42 694
	1997-98	127 000	57 000	70 000
Newman's Own Recipe Contest	1995-96	67 998	16 370	51 628
	1996-97	34 625	8040	26 585
	1997-98	13 000	4500	8500
Direct Mail	1996-97	24 004	30 000	(5996)
	1997-98	55 000	50 000	5000
Corporations	1995-96	91 026	24 245	66 781
	1996-97	270 766	-	270 766
	1997-98	360 000	-	360 000
Bell 1-900	1995-96	636	5194	(4558)
	1996-97	0	0	0
	1997-98	10 000	3000	7000

MEASURING AND FORECASTING DEMAND

When a company finds an attractive market, it must estimate that market's current size and future potential carefully. This appendix presents the principles and tools for measuring and forecasting market demand.

To develop effective targeting strategies, and to manage their marketing efforts effectively, companies must be good at both measuring *current* market demand and forecasting *future* demand. Overly optimistic estimates of current or future demand can result in costly overcapacity or excess inventories. Under-estimating demand can mean missed sales and profit opportunities.

MEASURING CURRENT MARKET DEMAND

Marketers will want to estimate three aspects of current market demand—*total market demand, area market demand,* and *actual sales and market shares.*

ESTIMATING TOTAL MARKET DEMAND

The **total market demand** for a product or service is the total volume that would be bought by a defined consumer group in a defined geographic area in a defined time period in a defined marketing environment under a defined level and mix of industry marketing effort.

Total market demand is not a fixed number, but a function of the stated conditions. For example, next year's total market demand for ice cream in Canada will depend on how much the makers of Sealtest, Haagen-Dazs, Parlour, President's Choice, and other brands spend on marketing. It will also depend on many environmental factors, ranging from the level of consumer health concerns to the weather in key market areas. The demand for the premium ice-cream brands will be affected by economic conditions.

FIGURE A2-1 *Market demand*

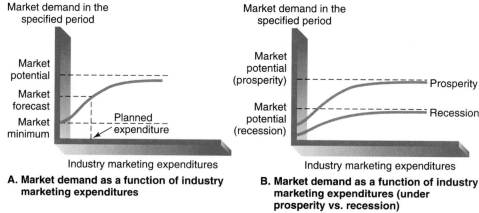

A. Market demand as a function of industry marketing expenditures

B. Market demand as a function of industry marketing expenditures (under prosperity vs. recession)

Part A of Figure A2-1 shows the relationship between total market demand and various market conditions. The horizontal axis shows different possible levels

Estimating total market demand for a new product like RCA's Digital Satellite System presents a difficult challenge.

Total market demand
The total volume of a product or service that would be bought by a defined consumer group in a defined geographic area in a defined time period in a defined marketing environment under a defined level and mix of industry marketing effort.

Market potential
The upper limit of market demand.

Primary demand
The level of total demand for all brands of a given product or service—for example, the total demand for motorcycles.

Selective demand
The demand for a given brand of a product or service.

of industry marketing expenditures in a given time period. The vertical axis shows the resulting demand level. The curve shows the estimated level of market demand at varying levels of industry marketing effort. Some minimum level of sales would occur without any marketing expenditures. Greater marketing expenditures would yield higher levels of demand, first at an increasing rate, and then at a decreasing rate. Marketing efforts above a certain level would not cause much more demand. This upper limit of market demand is called market potential. The industry market forecast shows the expected level of market demand corresponding to the planned level of industry marketing effort in the given environment.[1]

Companies selling in mature, non-expandable markets often take **primary demand**—total demand for all brands of a given product or service—as given. They concentrate their marketing resources on building **selective demand**—demand for *their* brand of the product or service. For example, in North America, where it faces a mature and largely non-expandable total soft drink market, Coca-Cola directs most of its marketing energies toward building consumer preference for Coke, Diet Coke, Sprite, and its other brands. However, in countries such as China or Russia, which are characterized by huge but largely untapped market potential, Coca-Cola attempts to build the primary demand for soft drinks, as well as preference for its own brands.

Companies have developed various practical methods for estimating total market demand. We will illustrate two here. Suppose Warner Communications Company wants to estimate the total annual sales of recorded compact discs. A common way to estimate total market demand is as follows:

$$Q = n \times q \times p$$

where

Q = total market demand

n = number of buyers in the market

q = quantity purchased by an average buyer per year

p = price of an average unit

Thus, if there are 100 million buyers of compact discs each year, the average buyer buys six discs a year, and the average price is \$17, then the total market demand for discs is \$10.2 billion (= 100 000 000 × 6 × \$17).

A variation of this approach is the *chain ratio method*. This method involves multiplying a base number by a chain of adjusting percentages. For example, suppose Thompson Consumer Electronics (TCE) wants to estimate the market potential for its new RCA Digital Satellite System. This system uses a small 18-inch wide home satellite dish mounted on a rooftop, windowsill, or porch railing to receive digital television signals relayed from two high-power satellites in space. System prices start at \$975 for the satellite dish, decoder box, and remote control. Customers can subscribe to more than 150 channels, all with crystal-clear digital quality pictures and CD-quality sound. Initially, TCE will target households in small towns and rural areas where cable TV is limited or lacking. TCE can make a Canadian demand estimate for the RCA Digital Satellite System using a chain of calculations like the following:

Total number of Canadian households

♦ The percentage of Canadian households located in small towns and rural areas not served well by cable television

♦ The percentage of these small town and rural households with moderate or heavy television usage

♦ The percentage of moderate or heavy usage households with enough discretionary income to buy RCA's home satellite dish

This simple chain of calculations would provide only a rough estimate of potential demand. However, more detailed chains involving additional segments and other qualifying factors would yield more accurate and refined estimates.[2]

ESTIMATING AREA MARKET DEMAND

Companies face the problem of selecting the best sales territories and allocating their marketing budget optimally among these territories. Therefore, they need to estimate the market potential of different cities, provinces, and countries. Two major methods are available: the *market-buildup method,* which is used primarily by business goods firms, and the *market-factor index method,* which is used primarily by consumer goods firms.

Market-Buildup Method

Market-buildup method
A forecasting method that calls for identifying all the potential buyers in each market and estimating their potential purchases.

The **market-buildup method** calls for identifying all the potential buyers in each market and estimating their potential purchases. Suppose a manufacturer of mining instruments developed an instrument that can be used in the field to test the actual proportion of gold content in gold-bearing ores. By using it, miners would not waste their time digging deposits of ore containing too little gold to be commercially profitable. The manufacturer wants to price the instrument at $1000. It sees each mine as buying one or more instruments, depending on the mine's size. The company wants to determine the market potential for this instrument in each mining province or territory. It would hire a salesperson to cover each area that has a market potential of over $300 000. The company wants to start by finding the market potential in the Northwest Territories.

To estimate the market potential in the N.W.T., the manufacturer can consult the Standard Industrial Classification (SIC) developed by Statistics Canada. The SIC is the government's coding system that classifies industries, for purposes of data collection and reporting, according to the product produced or operation performed. Each major industrial group is assigned a two-digit code—metal mining bears the code number 06. Within metal mining are further breakdowns into four-digit SIC numbers (the gold category has the code number 0611).

Next, the manufacturer can turn to the *Financial Post Survey of Mines* to determine the number of gold-mining operations in each territory and province, their locations within the territory and province, and the number of employees, annual sales, and net worth. Using the data on the N.W.T., the company can prepare a market potential estimate.

An examination of the SIC data reveals that the N.W.T. has 220 gold mines. It is projected that large mines have the potential to purchase four instruments each, while small mines will purchase only one instrument. Fifty percent of the mining operations are large mines. Therefore, the total market for potential instrument sales in the N.W.T. equals $(220 \times .50 \times 4) + (220 \times .50 \times 1)$ 550 instruments. Since each instrument sells for $1000, the market equals $550 000. Thus, the company would need to hire two salespeople to cover the N.W.T.

Market-Factor Index Method

Consumer goods companies also have to estimate area market potentials. Consider the following example: A manufacturer of men's dress shirts wishes to evaluate its sales performance relative to market potential in several major market areas, starting with Vancouver. It estimates total national potential for dress shirts at about $200 million per year. The company's current nationwide sales are $14 million, about a seven percent share of the total potential market. Its sales in the Vancouver metropolitan area are $1 200 000. It wants to know whether its share of the Vancouver market is higher or lower than its national seven percent market share. To determine this, the company first needs to calculate market potential in the Vancouver area.

Market-factor index method
A forecasting method that identifies market factors that correlate with market potential and combines them into a weighted index.

A common method for calculating area market potential is the **market-factor index method,** which identifies market factors that correlate with market potential and combines them into a weighted index. An excellent example of this method is called the *market rating index*, which is published each year by *The Financial Post* in its *Canadian Markets* publication. This survey estimates the market rating for each province and metropolitan area of Canada. The market rating index is based on two factors: the area's share of Canada's *population*, and *retail sales*. The market rating index (MRI) for a specific area is given by

MRI = percentage of national retail sales in the area ÷ percentage of national population in the area.

Using this index, the shirt manufacturer looks up the Vancouver metropolitan area and finds that this market has 5.77 percent of the nation's population, and 7.03 percent of the nation's retail sales. Thus, the market rating index for Vancouver is

$$MRI = 7.03/5.77 = 122$$

Vancouver has a market rating index that is 22 percent higher than the national average. Because the total national potential is $200 million nationally each year, total potential in Vancouver equals $200 million × 1.22 × .0577 = $14 078 000. Thus, the company's sales in Vancouver of $1 200 000 amount to a $1 200 000 ÷ $14 078 800 = 8.5 percent share of area market potential. Comparing this with its seven percent national share, the company appears to be doing better in Vancouver than in other areas of Canada.

The weights used in the buying power index are somewhat arbitrary. They apply mainly to consumer goods that are neither low-priced staples nor high-priced luxury goods. Other weights can be used. Also, the manufacturer would want to adjust the market potential for additional factors, such as level of competition in the market, local promotion costs, seasonal changes in demand, and unique local market characteristics.

Many companies compute additional area demand measures. Marketers now can refine province-by-province and city-by-city measures down to census tracts or postal codes. Census tracts are small areas about the size of a neighbourhood, and postal code areas (designated by Canada Post) can be used to identify particular streets, neighbourhoods, or communities within larger cities.

ESTIMATING ACTUAL SALES AND MARKET SHARES

Besides estimating total and area demand, a company will want to know the actual industry sales in its market. Thus, it must identify its competitors and estimate their sales.

Industry's trade associations often collect and publish total industry sales, although not individual company sales. In this way, each company can evaluate its performance against the industry as a whole. Suppose the company's sales are increasing at a rate of five percent a year and industry sales are increasing at 10 percent. This company actually is losing its relative standing in the industry.

Another way to estimate sales is to buy reports from marketing research firms that audit total sales and brand sales. For example, A.C. Nielsen, IRI, and other marketing research firms use scanner data to audit the retail sales of various product categories in supermarkets and drugstores, and they sell this information to interested companies. A company can obtain data on total product category sales as well as brand sales. It can compare its performance with that of the total industry or any particular competitor to see whether it is gaining or losing in its relative standing.[3]

FORECASTING FUTURE DEMAND

Forecasting
The art of estimating future demand by anticipating what buyers are likely to do under a given set of conditions.

Forecasting is the art of estimating future demand by anticipating what buyers are likely to do under a given set of future conditions. Very few products or services lend themselves to easy forecasting. Those that do generally involve a product with steady sales, or sales growth, in a stable competitive situation. But most markets do not have stable total and company demand, so good forecasting becomes a key factor in company success. Poor forecasting can lead to overly large inventories, costly price markdowns, or lost sales due to items being out of stock.

Companies commonly use a three-stage procedure to arrive at a sales forecast. First they make an *environmental forecast,* followed by an *industry forecast,* followed by a *company sales forecast.* The environmental forecast calls for projecting inflation, unemployment, interest rates, consumer spending and saving, business investment, government expenditures, net exports, and other environmental events important to the company. The result is a forecast of gross domestic product, which is used along with other indicators to forecast industry sales. Then the company prepares its sales forecast by assuming that it will win a certain share of industry sales.

Companies use several specific techniques to forecast their sales. Table A2-1 lists many of these techniques.[4] All forecasts are built on one of three information bases: what people say, what people do, or what people have done. The first basis—*what people say*—involves surveying the opinions of buyers or those close to them, such as salespeople or outside experts. It includes three methods: surveys of buyer intentions, composites of sales-force opinions, and expert opinion. Building a forecast on *what people do* involves putting the product into a test market to assess buyer response. The final basis—*what people have done*—involves analysing records of past buying behaviour or using time-series analysis or statistical demand analysis.

TABLE A2-1 *Common Sales Forecasting Techniques*

Based on:	Methods
What people say	Surveys of buyers' intentions
	Composite sales force opinions
	Expert opinion
What people do	Test markets
What people have done	Time-series analysis
	Leading indicators
	Statistical demand analysis

SURVEY OF BUYERS' INTENTIONS

One way to forecast what buyers will do is to ask them directly. This suggests that the forecaster should survey buyers. Surveys are especially valuable if the buyers have clearly formed intentions, will carry them out, and can describe them to interviewers. However, this is sometimes not the case, and marketers must be careful when using consumer survey data to make forecasts.

Several research organizations conduct periodic surveys of consumer buying intentions. These organizations ask questions such as the following:

Do you intend to buy a car within the next six months?

0	.1	.2	.3	.4	.5	.6	.7	.8	.9	1.0
No chance		Slight chance		Fair chance		Good chance		Strong chance		For certain

Forecasting is the art of estimating future demand, generally no easy task. When Burger King licensed action figures from the hit Disney movie, The Lion King, *demand was triple the forecasted amount. At the same time, McDonald's featured Happy Meal toys from* The Flintstones *movie, a failure at the box office.*

This is called a *purchase probability scale.* In addition, the various surveys ask about the consumer's present and future personal finances, and his or her expectations about the economy. The various bits of information are combined into a *consumer sentiment measure* (Survey Research Center of the University of Michigan) or a *consumer confidence measure* (Sindlinger and Company). Consumer durable goods companies subscribe to these indexes to help them anticipate major shifts in consumer buying intentions so that they can adjust their production and marketing plans accordingly.

For *business buying,* various agencies and consulting firms carry out intention surveys about plant, equipment, and materials purchases.

COMPOSITE OF SALES-FORCE OPINIONS

When buyer interviewing is impractical, the company may base its sales forecasts on information provided by the sales force. The company typically asks its salespeople to estimate sales by product for their individual territories. It then adds up the individual estimates to arrive at an overall sales forecast.

Few companies use their sales force's estimates without some adjustments. Salespeople are biased observers. They may be naturally pessimistic or optimistic, or they may go to one extreme or another because of recent sales setbacks or successes. Furthermore, they are often unaware of larger economic developments and they do not always know how their company's marketing plans will affect future sales in their territories. They may understate demand so that the company will set a low sales quota. They may not have the time to prepare careful estimates or may not consider it worthwhile.

Assuming these biases can be countered, a number of benefits can be gained by involving the sales force in forecasting. Salespeople may have better insights into developing trends than any other group. After participating in the forecasting process, the salespeople may have greater confidence in their quotas and more incentive to achieve them. Also, such "grassroots" forecasting provides estimates broken down by product, territory, customer, and salesperson.[5]

EXPERT OPINION

Companies can also obtain forecasts by turning to experts. Experts include dealers, distributors, suppliers, marketing consultants, and trade associations. Thus,

In 1943, then-IBM chairman Thomas Watson forecast a worldwide market for about five computers.

auto companies survey their dealers periodically for their forecasts of short-term demand. Dealer estimates, however, are subject to the same strengths and weaknesses as salesforce estimates.

Many companies buy economic and industry forecasts from well-known firms such as Andersen Consulting. These forecasting specialists are in a better position than the company to prepare economic forecasts because they have more data available and more forecasting expertise.

Expert opinion is often captured in a number of academic journals, including the *Canadian Business Review*, which publishes information on economic conditions and indicators that affect Canadian business. For example, it was recently projected that Canada's exports to the United States would continue to perform well given predictions that the U.S. economy would remain strong, and not be threatened by interest rate increases.[6] Canada's export success was attributed to its mix of exports as well as the low dollar.

Occasionally companies will invite a special group of experts to prepare a forecast. The experts may be asked to exchange views and develop a group estimate (group discussion method). Or they may be asked to supply their estimates individually, with the company analyst combining them into a single estimate. Finally, they may supply individual estimates and assumptions that are reviewed by a company analyst, revised, and followed by further rounds of estimation (called the Delphi method).

Experts can provide good insights upon which to base forecasts, but they can also be wrong. For example, in 1943, IBM Chairman Thomas J. Watson predicted, "I think there's a world market for about five computers." And in 1946, Daryl F. Zanuck, head of 20th Century-Fox, made this pronouncement: "TV won't be able to hold on to any market it captures after the first six months. People will soon get tired of staring at a plywood box every night."[7] In 1981, Bill Gates, founder of Microsoft, proclaimed "640 K ought to be enough for anybody." Thus, where possible, the company should substantiate experts' opinions with estimates obtained using other methods.

TEST MARKETING

Where buyers do not plan their purchases carefully or where experts are not available or reliable, the company may want to conduct a direct test market. A direct test market is especially useful in forecasting new-product sales or established-product sales in a new distribution channel or territory. Test marketing is discussed in Chapter 11.

TIME-SERIES ANALYSIS

Time-series analysis
Breaking down past sales into its trend, cycle, season, and erratic components, then recombining these components to produce a sales forecast.

Many firms base their forecasts on past sales. They assume that the causes of past sales can be uncovered through statistical analysis. Then, analysts can use the causal relations to predict future sales. **Time-series analysis** consists of breaking down the original sales into four components—trend, cycle, season, and erratic components—then recombining these components to produce the sales forecast.

Trend is the long-term, underlying pattern of growth or decline in sales resulting from basic changes in population, capital formation, and technology. It is found by fitting a straight or curved line through past sales. *Cycle* captures the medium-term, wavelike movement of sales resulting from changes in general economic and competitive activity. The cyclical component can be useful for medium-range forecasting. Cyclical swings, however, are difficult to predict because they do not occur on a regular basis. *Season* refers to a consistent pattern of sales movements within the year. The term *season* describes any recurrent hourly, weekly, monthly, or quarterly sales pattern. The seasonal component may be related to weather, holidays, and trade customs. The seasonal pattern provides a norm for forecasting short-range sales. Finally, *erratic events* include fads, strikes, snow storms, earthquakes, riots, fires, and other disturbances. These components, by definition, are unpredictable and should be removed from past data to see the more normal behaviour of sales.

Suppose an insurance company sold 12 000 new life insurance policies this year and wants to predict next year's December sales. The long-term trend shows a five percent sales growth rate per year. This information alone suggests sales next year of 12 600 (= 12 000 × 1.05). However, a business recession is expected next year and probably will result in total sales achieving only 90 percent of the expected trend-adjusted sales. Sales next year will more likely be 12 600 × .90 = 11 340. If sales were the same each month, monthly sales would be 11 340 ÷ 12 = 945. However, December is an above-average month for insurance policy sales, with a seasonal index standing at 1.30. Therefore December sales may be as high as 945 × 1.3 = 1228.5. The company expects no erratic events, such as strikes or new insurance regulations. Thus, it estimates new policy sales next December at 1228.5 policies.

LEADING INDICATORS

Leading indicators
Time series that change in the same direction but in advance of company sales.

Distribution requirements planning
A system that starts with a forecast of end-user demand and calculates how long it will take to manufacture and move products through a distribution network to the customer.

Many companies try to forecast their sales by finding one or more **leading indicators**—other time series that change in the same direction but in advance of company sales. Automotive repair shops, for example, can use the previous year's car sales as an indicator of demand for their services. For example, after-sales service is an important factor in increasing customer satisfaction. As anyone knows who has owned a speciality foreign car, getting after-sales service can often be problematic due to the difficulties in obtaining spare parts. A solution to this problem was developed by Abbott Canada. The firm developed a system called **Distribution Requirements Planning** (DRP) for its own manufacturing and materials management. DRP starts with a forecast of end-user demand and calculates how long it will take to manufacture and move products through a distribution network to the customer. A manufacturing and distribution schedule is then created to meet that demand. This customer-based scheduling system has proven so powerful that many manufacturers, including upscale manufacturers such as Rolls-Royce Motor Cars Ltd., are increasingly turning to DRP as globalization of production and marketing creates extended supply chains. The systems allows Rolls-Royce to manufacture spare parts in its factory in England and ship them to three distribution centres, which service dealers worldwide. The forecast allows development of long-term plans detailing the timing and quantity of parts production.[8]

STATISTICAL DEMAND ANALYSIS

Statistical demand analysis
A set of statistical procedures used to discover the most important real factors affecting sales and their relative influence; the most commonly analysed factors are prices, income, population, and promotion.

Time-series analysis treats past and future sales as a function of time, rather than as a function of any real demand factors. But many real factors affect the sales of any product. **Statistical demand analysis** is a set of statistical procedures used to discover the most important real factors affecting sales and their relative influence. The factors most commonly analysed are prices, income, population, and promotion.

Statistical demand analysis consists of expressing sales (Q) as a dependent variable and trying to explain sales as a function of a number of independent demand variables $X_1, X_2, \ldots, X_n$. That is:

$$Q = f(X_1, X_2, \ldots, X_n)$$

Using a technique called *multiple-regression analysis,* various equation forms can be statistically fitted to the data in the search for the best predicting factors and equation.[9]

For example, forecasting the demand for personal computer printers worldwide is a challenging process. At the Vancouver Division of Hewlett-Packard Co., where several models of DeskJet printers are produced, factory orders for printers are forecast by product number, option, and region. Regression models are preferred because they provide a "causal" structure similar to Hewlett-Packard's current expert judgment models and allow for "what-if" scenarios to be developed based on the forecasts. Regression models can also be used to determine what changes would be most successful. The major elements taken into consideration when developing the long-range forecast include historical trends, primary research, secondary research, and management judgment.[10]

Statistical demand analysis can be very complex, and the marketer must take care in designing, conducting, and interpreting such analysis. Yet constantly improving computer technology has made statistical demand analysis an increasingly popular approach to forecasting.

Key Terms

Distribution requirements planning (p. 765)
Forecasting (p. 762)
Leading indicators (p. 765)

Market-buildup method (p. 760)
Market-factor index method (p. 761)
Market potential (p. 759)
Primary demand (p. 759)

Selective demand (p. 759)
Statistical demand analysis (p. 765)
Time-series analysis (p. 764)
Total market demand (p. 759)

References

1. For further discussion, see Gary L. Lilien, Philip Kotler, and K. Sridhar Moorthy, *Marketing Models* (Eaglewood Cliffs, NJ: Prentice-Hall, 1992).

2. For more on forecasting total market demand, see F. William Barnett, "Four Steps to Forecast Total Market Demand," *Harvard Business Review*, July–August 1988, pp. 28–34; and "Forecasting the Potential for New Industrial Products," *Industrial Marketing Management*, no. 4, 1989, pp. 307–312.

3. For a more comprehensive discussion of measuring market demand, see Philip Kotler, *Marketing Management: Analysis, Planning, Implementation, and Control*, 8th ed. (Englewood Cliffs, NJ: Prentice Hall, 1994), Chapter 10.

4. For a listing and analysis of these and other forecasting techniques, see David M. Georgoff and Robert G. Murdick, "Manager's Guide to Forecasting," *Harvard Business Review*, January–February 1986, pp. 110–120; and Donald S. Tull and Del I. Hawkins, *Marketing Research: Measurement and Method*, 6th ed.

(New York: Macmillan, 1990), Chapter 21. For a listing of common forecasting problems, see John B. Mahaffie, "Why Forecasts Fail," *American Demographics*, March 1995, pp. 34–40.

5. For more on the salesforce composite method, see Tull and Hawkins, *Marketing Research: Measurement and Method*, pp. 705–706.

6. James G. Frank, "Outside Forces Set Back the Outlook," *Canadian Business Review*, Vol. 21 (4), Winter 1994, pp. 4–6.

7. See "Sometimes Expert Opinion Isn't All It Should Be," *Go*, September–October 1985, p. 2.

8. Donald Davis, "Tough Customers," *Manufacturing Systems*, November, 1994, pp. 16–27.

9. See Tull and Hawkins, *Marketing Research: Measurement and Method*, pp. 686–691.

10. Joel Bryant and Kim Jensen, "Forecasting Inkjet Printers at Hewlett-Packard," *Journal of Business Forecasting*, Vol. 13 (2), Summer 1994, pp. 27–28.

MARKETING ARITHMETIC

One aspect of marketing not discussed within the text is marketing arithmetic. The calculation of sales, costs, and certain ratios is important for many marketing decisions. This appendix describes three major areas of marketing arithmetic: the *operating statement, analytic ratios,* and *markups and markdowns.*

OPERATING STATEMENT

The operating statement and the balance sheet are the two main financial statements used by companies. The **balance sheet** shows the assets, liabilities, and net worth of a company at a given time. The **operating statement** (also called **profit-and-loss statement** or **income statement**) is the more important of the two for marketing information. It shows company sales, cost of goods sold, and expenses during a specified time period. By comparing the operating statement from one time period to the next, the firm can identify favourable or unfavourable trends and take appropriate action.

Table A3-1 shows the 1995 operating statement for Dale Parsons Men's Wear, a specialty store in the Prairies. This statement is for a retailer; the operating statement for a manufacturer would be somewhat different. Specifically, the section on purchases within the "cost of goods sold" area would be replaced by "costs of goods manufactured."

The outline of the operating statement follows a logical series of steps to arrive at the firm's $25 000 net profit figure:

Net sales	$300 000
Cost of goods sold	−175 000
Gross margin	$125 000
Expenses	−100 000
Net profit	$ 25 000

The first part details the amount that Parsons received for the goods sold during the year. The sales figures consist of three items: *gross sales, returns and allowances,* and *net sales.* **Gross sales** is the total amount charged to customers during the year for merchandise purchased in Parsons's store. As expected, some customers returned merchandise because of damage or a change of mind. If the customer gets a full refund or full credit on another purchase, we call this a *return.* Or the customer may decide to keep the item if Parsons will reduce the price. This is called an *allowance.* By subtracting returns and allowances from gross sales, we arrive at net sales—what Parsons earned in revenue from a year of selling merchandise:

Gross sales	$325 000
Returns and allowances	−25 000
Net sales	$300 000

The second major part of the operating statement calculates the amount of sales revenue Dale Parsons retains after paying the costs of the merchandise. We start with the inventory in the store at the beginning of the year. During the year, Parsons bought $165 000 worth of suits, pants, shirts, ties, jeans, and other goods. Suppliers gave the store discounts totalling $15 000, so that net purchases were $150 000. Because the store is located away from regular shipping routes, Parsons had to pay an additional $10 000 to get the products delivered, giving the firm a net cost of $160 000. Adding the beginning inventory, the cost of goods available

TABLE A3-1 *Operating Statement Dale Parsons Men's Wear*
Year Ending December 31, 1995

Gross sales			$325 000
Less: Sales returns and allowances			25 000
Net sales			$300 000
Cost of goods sold			
Beginning inventory, January 1, at cost		$ 60 000	
Gross purchases	$165 000		
Less: Purchase discounts	15 000		
Net purchases	$150 000		
Plus: Freight-in	10 000		
Net cost of delivered purchases		$160 000	
Cost of goods available for sale		$220 000	
Less: Ending inventory, December 31, at cost		$ 45 000	
Cost of goods sold			$175 000
Gross margin			$125 000
Expenses			
Selling expenses			
Sales, salaries, and commissions	$ 40 000		
Advertising	5 000		
Delivery	5 000		
Total selling expenses		$ 50 000	
Administrative expenses			
Office salaries	$ 20 000		
Office supplies	5 000		
Miscellaneous (outside consultant)	5 000		
Total administrative expenses		$ 30 000	
General expenses			
Rent	$ 10 000		
Heat, light, telephone	5 000		
Miscellaneous (insurance, depreciation)	5 000		
Total general expenses		$ 20 000	
Total expenses			$100 000
Net profit			$ 25 000

for sale amounted to $325 000. The $45 000 ending inventory of clothes in the store on December 31 is then subtracted to come up with the $175 000 **cost of goods sold.** Here again we have followed a logical series of steps to figure out the cost of goods sold:

Amount Parsons started with (beginning inventory)	$ 60 000
Net amount purchased	+150 000
Any added costs to obtain these purchases	+ 10 000
Total cost of goods Parsons had available for sale during the year	$220 000
Amount Parsons had left over (ending inventory)	− 45 000
Cost of goods actually sold	$175 000

The difference between what Parsons paid for the merchandise ($175 000) and what he sold it for ($300 000) is called the **gross margin** ($125 000).

In order to show the profit Parsons "cleared" at the end of the year, we must subtract from the gross margin the *expenses* incurred while doing business. *Selling expenses* included two sales employees, local newspaper and radio advertising, and the cost of delivering merchandise to customers after alterations. Selling expenses totalled $50 000 for the year. *Administrative expenses* included the salary for an office manager, office supplies such as stationery and business cards, and miscellaneous expenses including an administrative audit conducted by an outside consultant. Administrative expenses totalled $30 000 in 1995. Finally, the general expenses of rent, utilities, insurance, and depreciation came to $20 000. Total expenses were therefore $100 000 for the year. By subtracting expenses ($100 000) from the gross margin ($125 000), we arrive at the net profit of $25 000 for Parsons during 1995.

ANALYTIC RATIOS

The operating statement provides the figures needed to compute some crucial ratios. Typically these ratios are called **operating ratios**—the ratio of selected operating statement items to net sales. They let marketers compare the firm's performance in one year to that in previous years (or with industry standards and competitors in the same year). The most commonly used operating ratios are the *gross margin percentage*, the *net profit percentage*, the *operating expense percentage*, and the *returns and allowances percentage*.

Ratio		Formula		Computation From Table A3-1	
Gross margin percentage	=	$\dfrac{\text{gross margin}}{\text{net sales}}$	=	$\dfrac{\$125\,000}{\$300\,000}$	= 42%
Net profit percentage	=	$\dfrac{\text{net profit}}{\text{net sales}}$	=	$\dfrac{\$25\,000}{\$300\,000}$	= 8%
Operating expense percentage	=	$\dfrac{\text{total expenses}}{\text{net sales}}$	=	$\dfrac{\$100\,000}{\$300\,000}$	= 33%
Returns and allowances percentage	=	$\dfrac{\text{returns and allowances}}{\text{net sales}}$	=	$\dfrac{\$25\,000}{\$300\,000}$	= 8%

Another useful ratio is the *stockturn rate* (also called *inventory turnover rate*). The stockturn rate is the number of times an inventory turns over or is sold during a specified time period (often one year). It may be computed on a cost, selling price, or units basis. Thus the formula can be

$$\text{Stockturn rate} = \frac{\text{cost of goods sold}}{\text{average inventory at cost}}$$

or

$$\text{Stockturn rate} = \frac{\text{selling price of goods sold}}{\text{average selling price of inventory}}$$

or

$$\text{Stockturn rate} = \frac{\text{sales in units}}{\text{average inventory in units}}$$

We will use the first formula to calculate the stockturn rate for Dale Parsons Men's Wear:

$$\frac{\$175\,000}{(\$60\,000 + \$45\,000)/2} = \frac{\$175\,000}{\$52\,500} = 3.3$$

That is, Parsons's inventory turned over 3.3 times in 1995. Normally, the higher the stockturn rate, the higher the management efficiency and company profitability.

Return on investment (ROI) is frequently used to measure managerial effectiveness. It uses figures from the firm's operating statement and balance sheet. A commonly used formula for computing ROI is

$$\text{ROI} = \frac{\text{net profit}}{\text{sales}} \times \frac{\text{sales}}{\text{investment}}$$

You may have two questions about this formula: Why use a two-step process when ROI could be computed simply as net profit divided by investment? And what exactly is "investment"?

To answer these questions, let's look at how each component of the formula can affect the ROI. Suppose Dale Parsons Men's Wear has a total investment of $150 000. The ROI can be computed as follows:

$$\text{ROI} = \frac{\$25\ 000\ \text{(net profit)}}{\$300\ 000\ \text{(sales)}} \times \frac{\$300\ 000\ \text{(sales)}}{\$150\ 000\ \text{(investment)}}$$
$$8.3\% \qquad \times \qquad 2 \qquad = 16.6\%$$

Now suppose that Parsons had worked to increase his share of market. He could have had the same ROI if his sales doubled while dollar profit and investment stayed the same (accepting a lower profit ratio to get higher turnover and market share):

$$\text{ROI} = \frac{\$25\ 000\ \text{(net profit)}}{\$600\ 000\ \text{(sales)}} \times \frac{\$600\ 000\ \text{(sales)}}{\$150\ 000\ \text{(investment)}}$$
$$4.16\% \qquad \times \qquad 4 \qquad = 16.6\%$$

Parsons might have increased his ROI by increasing net profit through more cost cutting and more efficient marketing:

$$\text{ROI} = \frac{\$50\ 000\ \text{(net profit)}}{\$300\ 000\ \text{(sales)}} \times \frac{\$300\ 000\ \text{(sales)}}{\$150\ 000\ \text{(investment)}}$$
$$16.6\% \qquad \times \qquad 2 \qquad = 33.2\%$$

Another way to increase ROI is to find some way to get the same levels of sales and profits while decreasing investment (perhaps by cutting the size of Parsons's average inventory):

$$\text{ROI} = \frac{\$25\ 000\ \text{(net profit)}}{\$300\ 000\ \text{(sales)}} \times \frac{\$300\ 000\ \text{(sales)}}{\$75\ 000\ \text{(investment)}}$$
$$8.3\% \qquad \times \qquad 4 \qquad = 33.2\%$$

What is "investment" in the ROI formula? *Investment* is often defined as the total assets of the firm. But many analysts now use other measures of return to assess performance. These measures include *return on net assets (RONA), return on shareholders' equity (ROE),* or *return on assets managed (ROAM).* Because investment is measured at a point in time, we usually compute ROI as the average investment between two time periods (say, January 1 and December 31 of the same year). We can also compute ROI as an "internal rate of return" by using discounted cash-flow analysis (see any finance textbook for more on this technique). The objective in using any of these measures is to determine how well the company has been using its resources. As inflation, competitive pressures, and cost of capital increase, such measures become increasingly important indicators of marketing and company performance.

■ MARKUPS AND MARKDOWNS

Retailers and wholesalers must understand the concepts of **markups** and **markdowns**. They must make a profit to stay in business, and the markup percentage affects profits. Markups and markdowns are expressed as percentages.

There are two different ways to compute markups—on *cost* or on *selling price*:

$$\text{Markup percentage on cost} = \frac{\text{dollar markup}}{\text{cost}}$$

$$\text{Markup percentage on selling price} = \frac{\text{dollar markup}}{\text{selling price}}$$

Dale Parsons must decide which formula to use. If Parsons bought shirts for $15 and wanted to mark them up $10, his markup percentage on cost would be $10/$15, or 67.7 percent. If Parsons based markup on selling price, the percentage would be $10/$25, or 40 percent. In figuring markup percentage, most retailers use the selling price rather than the cost.

Suppose Parsons knew his cost ($12) and desired markup on price (25 percent) for a man's tie and wanted to compute the selling price. The formula is:

$$\text{Selling price} = \frac{\text{cost}}{1 - \text{markup}}$$

$$\text{Selling price} = \frac{\$12}{.75} = \$16$$

As a product moves through the channel of distribution, each channel member adds a markup before selling the product to the next member. This "markup chain" is shown for a suit purchased by a Parsons customer for $200:

		$ Amount	% of Selling Price
Manufacturer	Cost	$108	90%
	Markup	12	10%
	Selling price	$120	100%
Wholesaler	Cost	$120	80%
	Markup	30	20%
	Selling price	$150	100%
Retailer	Cost	$150	75%
	Markup	50	25%
	Selling price	$200	100%

The retailer whose markup is 25 percent does not necessarily enjoy more profit than a manufacturer whose markup is 10 percent. Profit also depends on how many items with that profit margin can be sold (stockturn rate), and on operating efficiency (expenses).

Sometimes a retailer wants to convert markups based on selling price to markups based on cost, and vice versa. The formulas are

$$\text{Markup percentage on selling price} = \frac{\text{markup percentage on cost}}{100\% + \text{markup percentage on selling cost}}$$

$$\text{Markup percentage on cost} = \frac{\text{markup percentage on selling price}}{100\% - \text{markup percentage on selling price}}$$

Suppose Parsons found that his competitor was using a markup of 30 percent based on cost and wanted to know what this would be as a percentage of selling price. The calculation would be

$$\frac{30\%}{100\% + 30\%} = \frac{30\%}{130\%} = 23\%$$

Because Parsons was using a 25 percent markup on the selling price for suits, he felt that his markup was suitable compared with that of the competitor.

Near the end of the summer Parsons still had an inventory of summer slacks in stock. Therefore, he decided to use a *markdown,* a reduction from the original selling price. Before the summer he had purchased 20 pairs at $10 each, and he had since sold 10 pairs at $20 each. He marked down the other pairs to $15 and sold five pairs. We compute his *markdown ratio* as follows:

$$\text{Markdown percentage} = \frac{\text{dollar markdown}}{\text{total net sales in dollars}}$$

The dollar markdown is $25 (five pairs at $5 each) and total net sales are $275 (10 pairs at $20 + five pairs at $15). The ratio, then, is $25/$275, or 9 percent.

Larger retailers usually compute markdown ratios for each department rather than for individual items. The ratios provide a measure of relative marketing performance for each department and can be calculated and compared over time. Markdown ratios can also be used to compare the performance of different buyers and salespeople in a store's various departments.

Key Terms

Balance sheet *(p. 768)*	Markdown *(p. 772)*	Operating statement
Cost of goods sold *(p. 769)*	Markup *(p. 772)*	(or profit-and-loss statement
Gross margin *(p. 769)*	Operating ratios *(p. 770)*	or income statement) *(p. 768)*
Gross sales *(p. 768)*		Return on investment (ROI) *(p. 771)*

CAREERS IN MARKETING

Now that you have completed your first course in marketing, you have a good idea of what the field entails. You may have decided that you want to pursue a marketing career because it offers constant challenge, stimulating problems, the opportunity to work with people, and excellent advancement opportunities. Marketing is a very broad field with a wide variety of tasks involving the analysis, planning, implementation, and control of marketing programs. You will find marketing positions in all types and sizes of institutions. This appendix describes entry-level and higher-level marketing opportunities and lists steps you might take to select a career path and better market yourself.

MARKETING CAREERS TODAY

Almost a third of all North Americans are employed in marketing-related positions. Thus, the number of possible marketing careers is enormous. Because of the knowledge of products and consumers gained in these jobs, marketing positions provide excellent training for the highest levels in the organization. A recent study by an executive recruiting firm found that more top executives have come out of marketing than any other area.

Marketing salaries vary by company and position. Beginning salaries usually rank only slightly below those for engineering and chemistry but equal or exceed those for economics, finance, accounting, general business, and the liberal arts. If you succeed in an entry-level marketing position, you will quickly be promoted to higher levels of responsibility and salary.

This appendix can be used alone. But to aid you in your job search, you may also want to consult some of the supplements to the fourth edition of *Principles of Marketing*. The *Career Paths* CD-ROM guides you through a self-test to identify the marketing paths that suit your skills and interests, and describes the main types of marketing jobs. The Prentice-Hall Web site **www.prenhall.com** also provides regularly updated information on marketing careers. Click business publishing, scroll to the bottom of the page, and click PHLIP.

OVERALL MARKETING FACTS AND TRENDS

In conducting your job search, consider the following facts and trends that are changing the world of marketing:

TECHNOLOGY. Technology is altering the way marketers work. For example, price coding allows instantaneous retail inventorying. Software for marketing training, forecasting, and other functions is changing the way we market. And the Internet is creating new jobs and new recruiting rules. Consider the explosive growth in new media marketing. Whereas advertising firms have traditionally recruited "generalists" in account management, "generalist" has now taken on a whole new meaning—advertising account executives must now have both broad and specialized knowledge.

DIVERSITY. The number of women and minorities in marketing continues to rise. Traditionally, women were mainly in retailing. Now women and minorities are rapidly moving into all industries. They also are rising rapidly into marketing management. For example, women now outnumber men by nearly two to one as advertising account executives. As marketing becomes more global, the need for diversity in marketing positions will continue to increase, opening new opportunities.

GLOBAL. Companies like Coca-Cola, McDonald's, MTV, and Procter & Gamble have become multinational, with offices and manufacturing operations in hundreds of countries. Indeed, such corporations often make more profit from sales outside the United States than from within. And it's not just the big companies that are involved in international marketing. Organizations of all sizes have moved into the global arena. Many new marketing opportunities and careers will be directly linked to the expanding global marketplace. The globalization of business also means that you will need more cultural, language, and people skills in the marketing world of the twenty-first century.

NON-PROFIT ORGANIZATIONS. Increasingly, universities, arts organizations, libraries, hospitals, and other non-profit organizations are recognizing the need for effectively marketing their "products" and services to their specific public. This awareness has led to new marketing positions—with these organizations hiring their own marketing directors and marketing vice presidents or using outside marketing specialists.

LOOKING FOR THE RIGHT JOB IN TODAY'S MARKETING WORLD

To choose and find the right job, you will need to apply the marketing skills you've learned in this course, especially marketing analysis and planning. Follow these nine steps for marketing yourself: (1) conduct a self-assessment and seek career counseling; (2) examine job descriptions; (3) develop job search objectives; (4) explore the job market and assess opportunities; (5) develop search strategies; (6) prepare a resume; (7) write a cover letter and assemble supporting documents; (8) interview for jobs; and (9) follow up.

CONDUCT A SELF-ASSESSMENT AND SEEK CAREER COUNSELLING

If you're having difficulty deciding what kind of marketing position is the best fit for you, start out by doing some self-testing or receive some career counselling. Self-assessments require that you honestly and thoroughly evaluate your interests, strengths, and weaknesses. What do you do well (your best and favourite skills) and not so well? What are your favourite interests? What are your career goals? What makes you stand out from other job seekers? The answers to such questions may suggest which marketing careers to seek or avoid. For help in making an effective self-assessment, look at the following book in your local bookstore: Richard Bolles, *What Color Is Your Parachute?* (Berkeley, CA: Ten Speed Press, published annually).

This book can also help you find a career counsellor. (Some counsellors can help you in your actual job search, too.) You can also consult the career counselling, testing, and placement services at your university or college.

Career Counselling on the Internet

Today an increasing number of universities and commercial career counsellors offer career guidance on the Internet. In general, university sites are by far the best. But one useful commercial site you might look at is JobSmart (jobsmart.org/tools/resume/index.htm).

EXAMINE JOB DESCRIPTIONS

After you have identified your skills, interests, and desires, you need to see which marketing positions are the best match for them. Human Resources Development

Canada maintains a national job bank that includes job openings in business and management (http://ein.ccia.st-thomas.on.ca/agencies/cec/jobs/jobbank.html).

Your initial career shopping list should be broad and flexible. Look for different ways to achieve your objectives. For example, if you want a career in marketing management, consider the government and non-profit sectors as well as the private sector, and regional as well as national firms. Be open initially to exploring many options, then focus on specific industries and jobs, listing your basic goals as a way to guide your choices. Your list might include the following: "a job in a start-up company, near a big city, on the West Coast, doing new product planning, with a computer software firm."

EXPLORE THE JOB MARKET AND ASSESS OPPORTUNITIES

At this stage, you need to look at the market and see what positions are actually available. You do not have to do this alone. Any of the following may assist you.

University Placement Centres

Your university placement centre is an excellent place to start. Besides posting specific job openings, placement centres have the current edition of *College Placement Annual*, which lists job openings for hundreds of companies seeking college graduates for entry-level positions, as well as openings for people with experience or advanced degrees. More and more, Canadian universities and colleges are also going on the Internet. Many of these sites allow you to access the campus placement service.

In addition, find out everything you can about the companies that interest you by consulting business magazines, annual reports, business reference books, faculty, career counsellors, and so forth. Try to analyse the industry's and the company's future growth and profit potential, advancement opportunities, salary levels, entry positions, travel time, and other factors of significance to you.

Job Fairs

Placement offices often work with corporate recruiters to organize on-campus job fairs. You might also use the Internet to check on upcoming career fairs in your region. The Career Fairs site has such listings (www.cyberplex.com/hitech).

Networking and the Yellow Pages

Networking, or asking for job leads from friends, family, people in your community, and career centres is one of the best ways to find a marketing job. The idea is to spread your net wide, contacting anybody and everybody.

The phone book's yellow pages are another effective way to job search. Check out employers in your field of interest in whatever region you want to work, then call and ask if they are hiring for the position of your choice. You can also find the yellow pages online.

Summer Jobs and Internships

In some parts of the country, one in seven students gets a job where they interned. Many Canadian packaged goods companies have summer internship programs. Non-profit organizations also hire summer interns. *The Back Door Guidebook* (Ten Speed Press, 1997) lists 1000 short-term work experiences around the world. On the Internet, look at the National Internship Directory (www.tripod.com/work/internship) for U.S. internships. In addition, the major job listing sites such as the Monster Board (www.monster.com), have separate areas for internships. If you know a company for which you wish to work, visit that company's corporate web side, enter the personnel area, and check for internships. If there are none listed, try e-mailing the personnel department to inquire if internships are offered.

The Internet

A constantly increasing number of sites on the Internet deal with job hunting. The book, *Get Wired, You're Hired: The Canadian Guide to Job Hunting On-line* by Mark Swartz can be a valuable resource. You can also use the Internet to make contacts with people who can help you gain information on companies and research companies that interest you. The Can Work Net (http://www.canworknet.ca) was developed so that Canadians would have comprehensive information at their fingertips to facilitate their job searches. The Riley Guide offers another great introduction to what jobs are available (www.jobtrak.com/jobguide/). In addition, Job Search and Employment Opportunities: Best Bets on the Net provides a very comprehensive listing (http:asa.ugl.lib.umich.edu/chdoc/employment/).

Most companies have their own Web sites on which they post job listings. This may be helpful if you have a specific and fairly limited number of companies that you are watching for job opportunities. But if this is not the case, remember that to find out what interesting marketing jobs the companies themselves are posting, you may have to visit hundreds of corporate sites.

DEVELOP SEARCH STRATEGIES

Once you've decided which companies you are interested in, you need to contact them. One of the best ways is through on-campus interviews. But not every company you are interested in will visit your school. In such instances, you can write (this includes e-mail) or phone the company directly or ask marketing professors or school alumni for contacts.

PREPARE RESUMES

A resume is a concise yet comprehensive written summary of your qualifications, including your academic, personal, and professional achievements, that showcases why you are the best candidate for the job. Many organizations use resumes to decide which candidates to interview.

In preparing your resume, remember that all information on it must be accurate and complete. Resumes typically begin with the applicant's full name, telephone and fax numbers, and traditional mail and e-mail addresses. A simple and direct statement of career objectives generally appear next, followed by work history and academic data (including awards and internships), and then by personal activities and experiences applicable to the job sought. The resume usually ends with a list of references whom the employer may contact. If your work or internship experience is limited, non-existent, or irrelevant, it is a good idea to emphasize your academic and non-academic achievements, showing skills related to those required for excellent job performance.

There are three types of resumes. *Chronological* resumes, which emphasize career growth, are organized in reverse chronological order, starting with your most recent job. They focus on job titles within organizations, describing the responsibilities required for each job. *Functional* resumes focus less on job titles and work history and more on assets and achievements. This format works best if your job history is discontinuous or characterized by job moves or shifts. *Mixed*, or *combined*, resumes include elements from each of the other two formats. First, the skills used for a specific job are listed, then the job title is stated. This format works best for applicants whose past jobs are in other fields or seemingly unrelated to the position.

Your local bookstore or library has many books that can assist you in developing your resume. Two popular guides are Tom Jackson, with Ellen Jackson, *The New Perfect Resume* (Garden City, NY: Anchor Press/Doubleday, revised, 1996) and Yana Parker, *The Damn Good Resume Guide* (Berkeley, CA: Ten Speed Press, 1996). Computer software programs such as *WinWay Resume*, provides hundreds of sample resumes and ready-to-use phrases while guiding you through the resume-preparation process.

Online Resumes

♦ Today more and more job seekers are posting their resumes on the Internet. Preparing an electronic resume is somewhat different from preparing a traditional resume. For example, you need to know the relevant rules about scanning (including the concern that your computer will be unable to scan the attractive fonts you used in your original resume) and keywords. Moreover, if you decide to post your resume in a public area such as a Web site, then for security purposes you might not want to include your street or business address or the name of previous employers or references. (This information can be mailed later to employers after you have been contacted by them.) The following sites might assist you in writing your online resume: Job Smart (http://jobsmart.org/tools/resume/index.htm) and ResumixResumeBuilder (http://www.resmix.com/resume-form.html). In addition, college placement centres usually assist you in developing a resume. (Placement centres can also help with your cover letter and provide job-interview workshops.)

RESUME TIPS

♦ Communicate your worth to potential employers in a concrete manner, citing examples whenever possible.

♦ Be concise and direct.

♦ Use verbs to show you are a doer.

♦ Do not skimp on quality or use gimmicks. Spare no expense in presenting a professional resume.

♦ Have someone critique your work. A single typo can eliminate you from being considered.

♦ Customize your resume for specific employers. Emphasize your strengths as they pertain to your targeted job.

After you have written your resume, you need to post it. The following sites may be good locations to start: Online Career Center, the biggest job bank in the world (www.occ.com); The World Wide Web Employment Center, an international listing of sites by occupation (www.harbornet.com/biz/office/annex.html); and Yahoo! Resume Services, a listing narrowed to business and economy companies (www.yahoo.com/Business_and_Economy/Companies/Employment/resume_services/).

WRITE COVER LETTER AND ASSEMBLE SUPPORTING DOCUMENTS

Cover Letter

You should include a cover letter informing the employer that a resume is enclosed. But a cover letter does more than this. It also serves to summarize in one page the contents of your resume and explains why you think you are the right person for the position. The goal is to persuade the employer to look at the more detailed resume. A typical cover letter is organized as follows: (1) the name and position of the person you are contacting; (2) a statement identifying the position you are applying for, how you heard of the vacancy, and the reasons for your interest; (3) a summary of your qualifications for the job; (4) a description of what follow-up action you intend to take, such as phoning in two weeks to see whether the resume has been received; (5) an expression of gratitude for the opportunity of being a candidate for the job.

Letters of Recommendation and Other Supporting Documents

Letters of recommendation are written references by professors, former and current employers, and others that testify to your character, skills, and abilities. A good reference letter tells why you would be an excellent candidate for the position. In choosing someone to write a letter of recommendation, feel confident that the person will give you a good reference. In addition, do not assume that the person knows everything about you or the position you are seeking. Rather, provide the person with your resume and other relevant data. As a courtesy, allow the reference writer at least one month to complete the letter and enclose a stamped, addressed envelope with your materials.

In the packet containing your resume, cover letter, and letters of recommendation, you may also want to attach other relevant documents that support your candidacy, such as academic transcripts, graphics, portfolios, and samples of writing.

INTERVIEW FOR JOBS

The job interview offers you an opportunity to gather more information about the organization, while at the same time allowing the organization to gather more information about you. Obviously, you'll want to present yourself in a positive way. The interview process consists of three parts: before the interview, the interview itself, and after the interview. If you successfully pass through these stages, you will be called back for the follow-up interview.

Before the Interview

In preparing for your interview, do the following:

1. Understand that interviewers have diverse styles, including the "Chitchat," let's-get-to-know-each-other style; the interrogation style of question after question; and the tough-probing "why, why, why" style, among others. So be ready for anything.

2. With a friend, practise being interviewed and then ask for a critique. Or videotape yourself in a practice interview so that you can critique your performance youself. Your university placement service may also offer "mock" interviews to help you.

3. Prepare at least five good questions whose answers are not easily found in the company literature such as, "What is the future direction of the firm?" "How does the firm differentiate itself from competitors?" "Do you have a new-media division?"

4. Anticipate possible interview questions, such as "Why do you want to work for this company?" or "Why should we hire you?" Prepare solid answers before the interview. Have a clear idea of why you are interested in joining the company and the industry to which it belongs.

5. Avoid back-to-back interviews—they can be exhausting.

6. Dress conservatively and professionally. Be neat and clean.

7. Arrive 10 minutes early to collect your thoughts and review the major points you intend to cover. Check your name on the interview schedule, noting the name of the interviewer and the room number. Be courteous and polite to office staff.

8. Approach the interview enthusiastically. Let your personality shine through.

During the Interview
During the interview, do the following:

1. Shake hands firmly in greeting the interviewer. Introduce yourself, using the same form the interviewer uses. Focus on creating a good initial impression.

2. Keep your poise. Relax, smile when appropriate, be upbeat throughout.

3. Maintain eye contact, good posture, and speak distinctly. Don't clasp your hands or fiddle with jewellery, hair, or clothing. Sit comfortably in your chair. Do not smoke, even if asked.

4. Carry extra copies of your resume with you.

5. Have your background down pat. Present your selling points. Answer questions directly. Avoid one-word or too wordy answers.

6. Let the interviewer take the initiative, but don't be passive. Find an opportunity to direct the conversation to things about yourself that you want the interviewer to hear.

7. To end on a high note, make your most important point or ask you most pertinent question during the past part of the interview.

8. Don't hesitate to "close." You might say, "I'm very interested in the position, and I have really enjoyed this interview."

9. Obtain the interviewer's business card or address and phone number so you can follow up later.

♦ *A Tip for "Acting" the Interview:* Before you open your mouth, find out *what it's like* to be a brand manager, sales representative, market researcher, advertising account executive, or other position for which you're interviewing.

After the Interview
After the interview, do the following:

1. After leaving the interview, record the key points that arose. Note who will follow up and when to expect a decision.

2. Analyse the interview objectively, including the questions asked, the answers to them, your overall interview presentation, and the interviewer's responses to specific points.

3. Immediately send a thank-you letter, mentioning any additional items and your willingness to supply further information.

4. If you do not hear within the specified time, write or call the interviewer to determine your status.

FOLLOW-UP

If you are successful, you will be invited to visit the organization. The in-company interview will probably run from several hours to an entire day. The organization will examine your interest, maturity, enthusiasm, assertiveness, logic, and company and functional knowledge. You should ask questions about issues of important to you. Find out about the working environment, job role, responsibilities, opportunities for advancement, current industrial issues, and the company's personality. The company wants to discover if you are the right person for the job, whereas you want to find out if it is the right job for you. The key is to determine if the right fit exists between you and the company.

■ MARKETING JOBS

This section describes some of the key marketing positions.

ADVERTISING

Advertising is one of today's hottest fields in marketing. In fact, *Money* magazine lists a position in advertising as among the 50 best jobs in North America.

Job Descriptions

Key advertising positions include copywriter, art director, production manager, account executive, and media planner/buyer. *Copywriters* write advertising copy and help find the concepts behind the written words and visual images of advertisements. *Art directors*, the other part of the creative team, help translate the copywriters' ideas into dramatic visuals called "layouts." Agency artists develop print layouts, package designs, television layouts (called "storyboards"), corporate logotypes, trademarks, and symbols. *Production managers* are responsible for physically creating ads, in-house or by contracting through outside production houses. *Account executives* serve as a liaison between clients and agencies. They coordinate the planning, creation, production, and implementation of an advertising campaign for the account. *Media planners* determine the best mix of television, radio, newspaper, magazine, and other media for the advertising campaign.

Skills Needed, Career Paths, and Typical Salaries

Work in advertising requires strong people skills in order to interact closely with an often difficult and demanding client base. In addition, advertising attracts people with high skills in planning, problem solving, creativity, communication, initiative, leadership, and presentation. Advertising involves working under high levels of stress and pressure created by continual deadlines. Advertisers frequently must work long hours to meet deadlines for a presentation. But work achievements are very apparent, with the results of creative strategies observed by thousands or even millions of people.

Because they are so sought after, positions in advertising sometimes require an MBA. But many jobs are open for business and liberal arts undergraduates. Advertising positions often serve as gateways to higher-level management. Moreover, with large advertising agencies opening offices all over the world, there is the possibility of eventually working on global campaigns.

Starting advertising salaries are relatively low compared to some other marketing jobs because of strong competition for entry-level advertising jobs. You may even want to consider working for free to break in. Compensation will increase quickly as you move into account executive or other management positions. For more facts and figures, see the Web pages of *Advertising Age*, a key ad industry publication (www.adage.com, Click on the Job Bank button) or *Marketing* magazine (www.marketingmag.ca/careers).

BRAND AND PRODUCT MANAGEMENT

Brand and product managers plan, direct, and control business and marketing efforts for their products. They are involved with research and development, packaging, manufacturing, sales and distribution, advertising, promotion, market research, and business analysis and forecasting.

Job Descriptions

A company's brand management team consists of people in several positions. The *brand manager* guides the development of marketing strategies for a specific brand.

The *assistant brand manager* is responsible for certain strategic components of the brand. The *product manager* oversees several brands within a product line or product group. The *product category manager* directs multiple product lines in the product category. The *market analyst* researches the market and provides key strategic information to the project managers. The *project director* is responsible for collecting market information on a marketing or product project. The *research director* oversees the planning, gathering, and analysing of all organizational research.

Skills Needed, Career Paths, and Typical Salaries

Brand and product management requires high problem-solving, analytical, presentation, communication, and leadership skills, as well as the ability to work well in a team. Product management requires long hours and involves the high pressure of running large projects. The newcomer joins a brand team as an assistant and learns the ropes by doing numerical analysis and watching senior brand people. This person can eventually head the team and later move on to manage a larger brand, and then several brands. Many industrial goods companies also have product managers. Product management is one of the best training grounds for future corporate officers while providing good opportunities to move into international marketing. Product managers command relatively high salaries. Because this job category encourages or requires an MBA, many companies encourage their employees to return to university for this degree.

SALES AND SALES MANAGEMENT

Sales and sales management opportunities exist in a wide range of profit and non-profit organizations and in product and service organizations, including financial, insurance, consulting, and government organizations.

Job Descriptions

Key jobs include consumer sales, industrial sales, national account manager, service support, sales trainers, sales management, and teleseller. *Consumer* sales involves selling consumer products and services through retailers. *Industrial sales* includes selling products and services to other businesses. The *national account manager (NAM)* oversees a few very large accounts. *Service support* personnel support salespeople during and after the sale of a product. The *sales trainer* trains new hires and provides refresher training for all sales personnel. *Sales management* includes a sequence of positions, ranging from district manager to vice-president of sales. The *teleseller* (not to be confused with the home consumer telemarketer) offers service and support to field salespeople.

Salespeople enjoy active professional lives, working outside the office and interacting with others. They manage their own time and activities. Competition for top jobs can be intense. Every sales job is different, but some positions involve extensive travel, long work days, and working under pressure, which can negatively impact personal life. Expect also to be transferred more than once between company headquarters and regional offices.

Skills Needed, Career Paths, and Typical Salaries

Selling is a people profession, in which you will work with people every day, all day long. Besides people skills, sales professionals need sales and communication skills. Most sales positions also require high problem-solving, analytical, presentation, and leadership ability as well as creativity and initiative. Teamwork skills are increasingly important.

Career paths lead from salesperson to district, regional, and higher levels of sales management and, in many cases, to the top management of the firm. Today, most entry-level sales management positions require a university or college degree. More and more people seeking selling jobs are acquiring sales experience in an internship capacity or from a part-time job before graduating. Although there is a high turnover rate (one in four people leave their jobs in a year), sales positions are great springboards to leadership positions, with more CEOs starting in sales than in any other entry-level position. Possibly this explains why competition for top sales jobs is intense.

Starting base salaries in sales may be moderate, but compensation is often supplemented by significant commission, bonus, or other incentive plans. In addition, many sales jobs include a company car or car allowance. Successful sales people are among most companies' highest paid employees. *Strategy* magazines' web site posts brand management and sales positions (www.strategymag.com/careers).

RETAILING

Retailing provides an early opportunity to assume marketing responsibilities. Key jobs include store manager, regional manager, buyer, department manager, and salesperson. The *store manager* directs the management and operation of an individual store. The *regional manager* manages groups of stores across several provinces and reports performance to headquarters. The *buyer* selects and buys the merchandise stores carry. The *department manager* acts as store manager of a department like clothing but on the department level. The *salesperson* sells merchandise to retail customers.

JOB DESCRIPTIONS
Retailing can involve relocation, but generally there is little travel, unless you are a buyer. Retailers work long hours, but their daily activities are often more structured than some types of marketing positions.

SKILLS NEEDED, CAREER PATHS, AND TYPICAL SALARIES
Retailing requires high levels of people and sales skills because retailers are constantly in contact with customers. Enthusiasm, willingness, and communication skills are very helpful for retailers, too. A typical career path in retailing is to start as trainees or assistant buyers. In large stores, university graduates are often sought. Rising in the ranks usually occurs as a result of performance in various positions, with buyers typically working in more prestigious departments or becoming merchandise managers with the responsibility of overseeing buyers working under them. Starting salaries in retailing tend to be low, but pay increases as you move into management or some retailing speciality jobs.

NON-PROFIT ORGANIZATIONS

The key jobs in non-profits include marketing director, director of development, event coordinator, publication specialist, and intern-volunteers. The *marketing director* is in charge of all marketing activities for the organization. The *director of development* organizes, manages, and directs the fund-raising campaigns that keep a non-profit in existence. An *event coordinator* directs all aspects of fundraising events, from initial planning through implementation. The *publication specialist* oversees publications designed to promote awareness of the organization. Although usually an unpaid position, the *intern/volunteer* performs various marketing functions, and this work can be an important step to gaining a full-time position.

SKILLS NEEDED, CAREER PATHS, AND SALARIES. Non-profits look for people with a strong sense of community spirit and the desire to help others. The non-profit

sector is typically not for someone who is money-driven. Starting pay is usually lower than in other marketing fields. However, the bigger the non-profit, the better your chance of rapidly increasing your income when moving into upper management.

OTHER MARKETING JOBS

Marketing Research

Marketing researchers interact with managers to define problems and identify the information needed to resolve them. They design research projects, prepare questionnaires and samples, analyse data, prepare reports, and present their findings and recommendations to management. They must understand statistics, consumer behaviour, psychology, and sociology. MBA degrees help. Career opportunities exist with manufacturers, retailers, some wholesalers, trade and industry associations, marketing research firms, advertising agencies, and governmental and private non-profit agencies.

New-Product Planning

People interested in new-product planning can find opportunities in many types of organizations. They usually need a good background in marketing, marketing research, and sales forecasting; they need organizational skills to motivate and coordinate others; and they may need a technical background. Usually, these people work first in other marketing positions before joining the new-product department.

Marketing Logistics (Physical Distribution)

Marketing logistics, or physical distribution, is a large and dynamic field, with many career opportunities. Major transportation carriers, manufacturers, wholesalers, and retailers all employ logistic specialists. Increasingly, marketing teams include logistics specialists, and marketing managers career paths include marketing logistics assignments. Course work in quantitative methods, finance, accounting, and marketing will provide you with the necessary skills for entering the field.

Public Relations

Most organizations have a public relations staff to anticipate problems with publics, handle complaints, deal with media, and build the corporate image. People interested in public relations should be able to speak and write clearly and persuasively, and they should have a background in journalism, communications, or the liberal arts. The challenges in this job are highly varied and very people oriented.

COMPANY/BRAND/NAME INDEX

Pages printed in boldface contain margin Weblinks for organizations and companies.

SUBJECT INDEX

PHOTO/AD CREDITS

Chapter 1 Page 2, courtesy of Nike Canada and Cossette Communication - Marketing; Page 10, courtesy of Patriot Computer Corporation; creative by Miller Williams Interactive Advertising Inc.;Page 10, reprinted with permission of USTA NOR CAL; Page 11, reprinted with permission of Bell Canada; Page 12 , reprinted with permission of Ford Motor Company; Page 19, courtesy Johnson & Johnson; PAGE 20, photo by Alex Meyboom, courtesy International Study Centre, Queen's University; PAGE 21, courtesy of the Sisters of Charity of Quebec. Marketing Conception: Martial Ménard, Klaxon et Méchant Boris; PAGE 25, Bettmann; PAGE 26, reprinted with permission of Metro Works, Province of Ontario and The Upper Canada Brewing Company; PAGE 27, Robert Johnston

Chapter 2 PAGE 36, courtesy of Canadian Tire Corporation Limited; PAGE 43, reprinted with permission of 3M; PAGE 50, courtesy of Cirque du Soleil; PAGE 53 (left), reprinted with permission of Choice Hotels Canada Inc.; PAGE 53 (right), reprinted with permission of Four Seasons Hotels; PAGE 56, courtesy of Jollibee Foods Corporation; PAGE 60, Robert Johnston; PAGE 62, Mark Seliger/Campbell Soup Company

Chapter 3 PAGE 74, courtesy of Eli Lilly Canada Inc. and Cossette Communication - Marketing; PAGE 78, reprinted with permission of Credit Suisse; PAGE 80, courtesy of Wal-Mart Canada and Communicorp Studios; PAGE 83, reprinted with permission of Toys "R" Us; PAGE 84, reprinted with permission of Houston Effler Herstek Favat; PAGE 87, reprinted with permission of Kraft Canada Inc.; PAGE 90, courtesy of Air Canada; PAGE 91, courtesy of IBM Canada and Ogilvy & Mather; PAGE 95 (left), courtesy of Microsell and Graphiques M & H; PAGE 95 (right), courtesy of Clearnet and TAXI Advertising & Design; PAGE 98, reprinted with permission of Farmers Dairy/Page & Wood Design; PAGE 100, courtesy of Imperial Oil Limited and Deer Park Design; PAGE 101, "Whale," a commercial produced by the Canadian Heritage Commission for its "The World Needs More Canada" campaign, reprinted with permission of Canadian Tourism Commission

Chapter 4 PAGE 110, courte sy of Molson Breweries and MacLaren McCann; PAGE 118, reprinted with permission of Porsche Cars North America, Inc.; PAGE 121, courtesy of Direct Protect; PAGE 123, © Roger Ressmeyer/Starlight; PAGE 127, reprinted with permission of Nielsen North America; PAGE 128, © Rick Friedman/Black Star; PAGE 129, reprinted with permission of Information Resources Inc.; PAGE 132, courtesy Focus Suites/Quirks Marketing Research Review; PAGE 137, courtesy of YOUtv Inc.; PAGE 139, © Ken Kerbs; PAGE 140, Robert Johnston

Chapter 5 PAGE 152, courtesy of Harley-Davidson; PAGE 157, courtesy of Bank of Montreal; PAGE 159, courtesy of Air Canada and Hamazaki Wong; PAGE 161, courtesy of Fred Deeley Imports and Larter Creative; PAGE 164, courtesy of Chronometric Co. Ltd. and The O'Rourke Group; PAGE 167, courtesy of General Motors of Canada Ltd. and MacLaren McCann Canada Inc.; PAGE 173, reprinted with permission of Joseph E. Seagram & Sons, Inc.; PAGE 177, Robert Johnston; PAGE 178, reprinted with permission of McNeil Consumer Products Company; PAGE 182, courtesy of GE; PAGE 185, © Arthur Meyerson/Reproduced with permission of The Coca-Cola Company

Chapter 6 PAGE 196, courtesy of Bombardier; PAGE 201, courtesy of Canadian Air Cargo; PAGE 202, reprinted by permission of the Dow Chemical Company; PAGE 205, reprinted with permission of Nokia Products Ltd.; PAGE 207 (left), © Jim Feingersh/Stock Market; PAGE 207 (right), © R. Steedman/Stock Market; PAGE 209, reprinted with permission of PMAC; PAGE 211, courtesy of UUNet Canada Inc.; PAGE 214, reprinted with permission of Computing Devices Canada; PAGE 215, courtesy of Sikorsky, a United Technologies Company

Chapter 7 PAGE 222, courtesy of Roche Macaulay & Partners Advertising Inc.; PAGE 230, created by Atlantic Progress Magazine,

reprinted with permission; PAGE 232 (left), reprinted with permission of Johnson & Johnson; PAGE 232 (right), reprinted with permission of Toyota Motor Sales U.S.A., Inc.; PAGE 234, reprinted with permission of Fruit of the Loom Canada, Inc.; PAGE 234, courtesy Eastman Kodak; PAGE 237, reprinted with permission of Steelcase Canada; PAGE 241, © Jeff Greenberg/Photo Researchers; PAGE 243, reprinted with permission of Altamira Investment Services Inc.; PAGE 245, courtesy of Cadbury Chocolate Canada Inc.; PAGE 247, reprinted with permission of Volvo Canada Ltd.; PAGE 249, reprinted with permission of Canada Post Corporation; PAGE 250, courtesy of EDS Canada; PAGE 253, reprinted with permission of Schott Corporation

Chapter 8 PAGE 262, courtesy of Intrawest Corporation; PAGE 264, courtesy of Intrawest Corporation; PAGE 267, reprinted with permission of Aaron Jones Studios; PAGE 270, courtesy of Parallel Strategies; PAGE 271, courtesy National Quality Institute; PAGE 272, courtesy of Motorola, Inc.; PAGE 275, reprinted with permission of Harlequin Enterprises Limited; PAGE 276, courtesy of Roche Macaulay & Partners Advertising Inc.; PAGE 277, photo by Bob Carroll, reprinted with permission of Loblaw Brands Limited; PAGE 278, reprinted with permission of Kraft Canada Inc.; PAGE 279, courtesy Kellogg Co.; PAGE 282, © Regis Bossu/Sygma; PAGE 285, reprinted with permission of Residence Inn, Marriott; PAGE 287, John C. Hillery; PAGE 292, reprinted with permission of British Airways; PAGE 294, courtesy of Whistler Mountain PAGE 294, Fig. 8-22, © 1998 - Whistler Networks Corp.

Chapter 9 PAGE 310, courtesy of Gillette; PAGE 313, © Neil Graham; PAGE 315, courtesy of Kraft Canada Inc.; PAGE 316, reprinted with permission of WD-40 Company; PAGE 318, courtesy of Toyota Canada Inc.; PAGE 320, courtesy of H.J. Heinz Company of Canada; PAGE 322, courtesy of Lever Brothers Company; PAGE 326, courtesy Molson Breweries; PAGE 329, courtesy of Discreet Logic; PAGE 330, reprinted with permission of Sony Corporation of America; PAGE 331, Binney & Smith

Chapter 10 PAGE 340, courtesy of Procter & Gamble; PAGE 344, Subzero Freezer Co.; PAGE 345, reprinted with permission of Compaq Computers Corp. and Ammirati & Puris/Lintas; PAGE 347, courtesy of Winners; PAGE 349, reprinted with permission of Bick's Pickles; PAGE 351, courtesy Ault Foods; PAGE 357, courtesy of Bell Canada and BBDO; PAGE 358, reprinted with permission of Parker Pen USA Ltd.

Chapter 11 PAGE 366, courtesy of Petro-Canada; PAGE 370, reprinted with permission of Zellers; PAGE 372, courtesy of CarMax Auto Superstores Inc.; PAGE 374, reprinted with permission of Infinity Systems, Inc.; PAGE 377, reprinted with permission of Ramada Franchise Systems, Inc.; PAGE 379, courtesy of Roche Macaulay & Partners Advertising Inc.; PAGE 381, © Kim Newton/Woodfin Camp; PAGE 383, reprinted with permission of Jean Patou, Inc.; PAGE 384, reprinted with permission of Leo Burnett Company, Inc. and The Procter & Gamble Company

Chapter 12 PAGE 392, courtesy of Caterpillar; PAGE 394, Fig. 12-1, ©1998 Caterpillar Inc.; PAGE 398, reprinted with permission of Mountain Equipment Co-op; PAGE 401, © Will Crocker; PAGE 404, courtesy of Air Canada; PAGE 405, reprinted with permission of IBM Corporation; PAGE 409, © Dan Rubin/The Stock Shop; PAGE 412, reprinted with permission of GE Appliances; PAGE 413, reprinted with permission of INTERLINK Freight Systems, Creative design by The Greaves & Allen Advertising Studios, Willowdale, Ontario; PAGE 417, reprinted with permission of Compaq Computer Corp. All rights reserved; PAGE 419, reprinted with permission of Roadway Express, Inc.; PAGE 422, courtesy of Ryder Truck Rental Canada Ltd. and Ideasmiths Co.

Chapter 13 PAGE 430, courtesy of Mountain Equipment Co-op; PAGE 434, courtesy Eddie Bauer, Inc.; PAGE 437, courtesy 7-Eleven Canada; PAGE 443, courtesy Tupperware Home Parties; PAGE 445 (left and right), courtesy National Public Relations (Toronto) Limited; PAGE 447, courtesy of Virgin Megastore, Vancouver; PAGE 448, courtesy of Retail Council of Canada and MacDonald Design; PAGE 449, West Edmonton Mall; PAGE 451, courtesy of Roots; PAGE 451, Fig. 13-18, courtesy of Roots Canada, Ltd.

Chapter 14 PAGE 466, courtesy of Ogilvy & Mather; PAGE 470, courtesy of Hewlett Packard and Saatchi & Saatchi Advertising Inc.; PAGE 473, © Bernard Clark; PAGE 474, © The Procter & Gamble Company; PAGE 475, courtesy of Labatt Breweries and Axmith, McIntyre, Wicht; PAGE 476, reprinted with permission of Pepsi-Cola Company; PAGE 477, Used with permission of Kellogg Canada Inc. © 1996; PAGE 480, courtesy of Chrysler Canada and BBDO Windsor; PAGE 487, courtesy Hallmark Cards Inc.; PAGE 489, reprinted with permission of Toys "R" Us

Chapter 15 PAGE 498, Robert Johnston; PAGE 499, courtesy of Kraft Canada Inc. and J. Walter Thompson, Toronto; PAGE 500, Bob Carroll; PAGE 502, reprinted with permission of Cantel; PAGE 503, Used with permission of Kellogg Canada Inc. © 1997; PAGE 505, reprinted with permission of TBWA; PAGE 506, reprinted with permission of CBC Television, Sales Promotion; PAGE 508 (top), © Visa U.S.A. Inc.; PAGE 508 (bottom), courtesy of B.C. Hot House and Lanyon Phillips Partners, Vancouver, B.C.; PAGE 510 (top), Videocart, Inc.; PAGE 510 (middle), Patrick Pfister; PAGE 510 (bottom), © Jodi Buren/Woodfin Camp; PAGE 514, Kellogg's Frosted Flakesr TONY THE TIGER®; PAGE 518, courtesy of Pepsi-Cola Canada Ltd.; PAGE 520, courtesy of F.I.T.T. and Publicom; PAGE 523, courtesy of Lamborghini

Chapter 16 PAGE 534, courtesy of Eastman Chemical Co., Corp. Headquarters, Kingsport, Tennessee; PAGE 538 (left), First Light; PAGE 538 (right), First Light; PAGE 542, © Ken Kauffman/DuPont; PAGE 544, Lotus Development Canada, courtesy Cohn & Wolfe; PAGE 548, First Light; PAGE 550, reprinted with permission of American Express; PAGE 555, © Lawrence Migdale/Photo Researchers

Chapter 17 PAGE 564, courtesy of Dell; PAGE 566, Fig. 17-1, Used with permission. ©1998 Dell Computer Corporation. All rights reserved.; PAGE 567, courtesy of Great Atlantic & Pacific Company of Canada Ltd.; PAGE 569, courtesy of Canadian Direct Marketing Association; PAGE 571, courtesy of Canadian Wildlife Federation; PAGE 575, courtesy of Sears Canada Inc.; PAGE 576, courtesy of Tilley Endurables Inc.; PAGE 577, photo courtesy of KING Products Inc.; PAGE 579, Robert Johnston; PAGE 580, courtesy of Sony; PAGE 580, Fig. 17 - 9, ©1998 Sony Online Entertainment Inc.; PAGE 581, courtesy of Richmond Savings Credit Union; PAGE 582, courtesy of AutoNet Canada Corporation; PAGE 582, Fig. 17-11, Thanks to Autonet.ca; PAGE 583, courtesy Canadian Tire; PAGE 585, courtesy of Pillsbury; PAGE 586, Fig. 17-12, courtesy of The Pillsbury Co.; PAGE 587, courtesy of Tripod; PAGE 587, Fig. 17-13, TRIPOD (R) is a registered trademark of Tripod, Inc. All rights reserved.; PAGE 588, Robert Johnston; PAGE 591, courtesy of American Standard Canada

Chapter 18 PAGE 602, courtesy of Intel; PAGE 606, reprinted with permission of Caterpillar; PAGE 607, reprinted with permission of CIGNA; PAGE 608, Whirlpool Corp.; PAGE 612, reprinted with permission of PaineWebber Incorporated; PAGE 615, courtesy of Loyalty Management Group; PAGE 616, courtesy of Northern Telecom; PAGE 618, courtesy of Hunter Technology Inc. and Barrie Press; PAGE 619, courtesy of Ford Motor Company; PAGE 621, courtesy of Toronto-Dominion Bank and TBWA Chait/Day; PAGE 622 (top), reprinted with permission of GE Appliances; PAGE 622 (bottom), reprinted with permission of Scott Paper Limited; PAGE 623, reprinted with permission of Vistakon, Johnson & Johnson Vision Products, Inc.; PAGE 624 (left), courtesy of Clearnet and TAXI Advertising & Design; PAGE 624 (right), courtesy of Bell Mobility and Cossette Communication - Marketing; PAGE 625, reprinted with permission of Motorola, Inc. and J. Walter Thompson; PAGE 628, courtesy of Steel Alliance; PAGE 629, reprinted with permission of Nissan Motor Company, Inc. PAGE 631, courtesy of Hewlett-Packard Company; PAGE 632, Phil Matt

Chapter 19 PAGE 642, courtesy of Air Canada; PAGE 646 (left), courtesy Feathercraft Products Ltd.; PAGE 646 (right), courtesy of Blitz Design Corp. and Graphics Garage, Langley, B.C.; PAGE 647 (top left), courtesy IBM; PAGE 647 (top right), Caroline Parsons; PAGE 647 (bottom left), Ted Morrison; PAGE 647 (bottom right), courtesy Bata Ltd.; PAGE 649, courtesy of J. Crew; PAGE 649, Fig. 19-18, courtesy of J. Crew; PAGE 651, courtesy of the Export Development Corporation; PAGE 652, Alison Wardman Photography; PAGE 654, © Barbara Aloer/Stock Boston; PAGE 660, Pepsico; PAGE 663, © The Walt Disney Company; PAGE 666 (top), courtesy of Leo Burnett; PAGE 666 (left), courtesy of Ogilvy & Mather; PAGE 666 (right), courtesy of Ogilvy & Mather

Chapter 20 PAGE 676, courtesy of Canadian Centre for Philanthropy; PAGE 680, © Laima Druskis/Stock Boston; PAGE 682, Edward Regan/The Globe and Mail; PAGE 684, © Enrico Ferorelli/Stock Boston; PAGE 686, © Tom McHugh/Photo Researchers; PAGE 689, courtesy Campbell Soup Company Ltd.; PAGE 690 (left), courtesy of Chrysler Canada and BBDO Windsor; PAGE 690 (right), courtesy of Honda Canada Inc. and Partners Imaging; PAGE 692 (left), reprinted with permission of Church & Dwight Co., Inc.; PAGE 692 (right), reprinted with permission of McDonald's Corporation; PAGE 696, courtesy of Forrec Ltd.; PAGE 697 (top), courtesy Lanyon Phillips Partners, photos: wolf © John Hyde; all other animals from Bruce Coleman Inc.: raccooon © H. Reinhard, lynx © R. Williams, fox © L. Rue III, seal © J. Foott; PAGE 697 (bottom), courtesy Loblaw Brands Limited; PAGE 700, courtesy Imperial Oil Charitable Foundation

Appendix I PAGE 718 (top and bottom), courtesy of Kraft Canada; PAGE 719, courtesy of Kraft Canada

Appendix II PAGE 759, courtesy of RCA; PAGE 764, courtesy of IBM